Y0-BEC-985

AN INTRODUCTION TO

GANGS

New Revised Edition

George W. Knox

Foreword by Malcolm W. Klein

"The most knowledgeable and up to date report on gangs in America..."
Dr. William Stacey, Chairman,
Department of Sociology, University of Texas at Arlington.

"Finally, a volume that synthesizes all we know about gangs..."
Dr. Daniel W. Okada, Criminal Justice Department, Marist College/New York.

Wyndham Hall Press

AN INTRODUCTION TO GANGS

by George W. Knox, Ph.D.

George W. Knox teaches in the Department of Corrections and Criminal Justice, Chicago State University (Ph.D., University of Chicago, M.A., University of Texas at Arlington, B.A., University of Minnesota). He is certified beyond the Ph.D. in "Law and Social Control" by the American Sociological Association and is a Certified Consultant by the American Correctional Association. Dr. Knox is Director of the National Gang Crime Research Center at Chicago State University and is Editor-in-Chief of the *Journal of Gang Crime Research*.

Library of Congress Catalog Card Number

94-061606

International Standard Book Number

1-55605-249-9 (cloth)
1-55605-248-0 (paper)

Copyright ® 1994 by George W. Knox

ALL RIGHTS RESERVED

Printed in the United States of America

Wyndham Hall Press
Bristol, IN   46507-9460

ACKNOWLEDGEMENTS

Never before has so much been owed to so many by myself. Much credit is owed to many professionals, nationwide, who helped in one way or another. I want to thank the hundreds of law enforcement officials who responded to our national surveys on gangs. I am also indebted to similar hundreds of superintendents of juvenile correctional institutions, and wardens of adult prisons, jail administrators, and others for their cooperation in various phases of similar research on gangs reported in this book. I am also thankful for the similar cooperation from a sample of probation and parole officers nationwide. Many criminal justice professionals nationwide had some input into this work, through their generous sharing of time and information in cooperation with my gang research.

I also want to thank --- again far too numerous to list here --- my students and colleagues and a variety of other persons including program service staff, members of the clergy, school teachers, offenders and ex-offenders, and others --- many of whom shared their story, their files, their information, etc, with me at some point during the production of this book and in making improvements for this third edition. I am especially grateful for the information provided to me by those directly involved in the American gang scene: particularly persons who were at some point in their career "gang leaders", and active gang members, and their loved ones who shared information about their gangs.

I must also thank the government and foundations for not providing any funding connected with this effort, because it afforded the opportunity to "let the chips fall where they may".

I am sincerely appreciative of comments and suggestions from editors of the Journal of Gang Research whose advise in many areas helped to dramatically improve this third edition. I am, of course, forever indebted to my colleagues from the National Gang Crime Research Center at Chicago State University for their ongoing support and assistance in a myriad of ways.

Mostly I owe the students in my own Department of Criminal Justice at Chicago State University for their keen insights. I am grateful as well to students from other midwestern colleges and universities (University of Minnesota at Duluth, Lewis University, College of Dupage, Loyola University, and many others) whose instructors used the first and/or second editions of the textbook and sometimes invited me to speak to the class --- as I am always eager to do. The feedback of students has been invaluable in preparing this third edition. I am also grateful for the help from the staff of the National Gang Crime Research Center at my university, and especially fellow researchers in various gang research Task Force projects organized by the Center over the years.

Finally, I share anything positive with many others who helped, but hold alone, as my own, full responsibility for any failures, oversights, inaccuracy, etc --- in short, any blame is all mine.

G.W.K., Spring, 1995

PREFACE TO THE THIRD EDITION

This book has been written primarily to serve as an introductory level college text on gangs or as a training book for those whose work is directly affected by gang members. It has the aim of being used as more than a simple "review of the literature" because of the discussion of theory, research, and policy. Also, because an effort is made here to avoid ideological bias and a defense of any particular doctrine or theory (by being interdisciplinary, and eclectic) this can also be of value to all who may be concerned about gang crime and violence in America today --- scholars, researchers, community groups, correctional institutions, law enforcement officials, social service agencies, educators, parents, and policy makers.

My own training has been quite interdisciplinary, even though my university degrees are in the discipline of sociology, and even though my current teaching is in the field of corrections and criminal justice. My commitment is to criminology. Which is the social scientific study of crime.

This third edition is most timely given the continuing interest in the gang problem today. It incorporates much significant new research and information that has been generated since the first edition appeared in 1991, and since the second edition appeard in 1993. The first edition was widely adopted as a college textbook on gangs and I benefited from the feedback provided by a large number of persons both here and abroad. True to the prediction of Dr. Malcolm Klein, many such new college courses on "gangs" did in fact appear for the first time at colleges and universities throughout the United States and in other countries.

This third edition is much stronger and even more comprehensive because of the variety of new and ongoing gang research projects I have been involved in as the director of the National Gang Crime Research Center. I have obviously benefited as well in terms of being attuned to the best scholarship on gang issues by serving as the editor-in-chief of the Journal of Gang Research. This third edition therefore includes 66 tables of relevant research data and 28 different figures. Additionally, more internal documents from some of the larger and more sophisticated American gangs are also included in this new edition, along with new developments in the gang problem and the response to the gang problem.

Some new chapters have been added to this third edition dealing with specialized subjects in the area of gang research such as female gang members and Asian gang members. Many new developments regarding gangs are also included to provide students with the most "up-to-date" account as possible.

G.W.K., Spring, 1995

TABLE OF CONTENTS

FOREWORD TO THE FIRST EDITION (1991)

Malcolm W. Klein

Having studied street gangs off and on since 1962, and having written, thought, and lectured about them all these years, I have been asked on many occasions why I don't teach a course about gangs. My answer has always been that there is not enough at issue to justify a full semester course on gangs. Several lectures in a criminology or delinquency course, yes, but not a whole course on gangs.

The advent of this text by Professor Knox raises the question again, but in a different and far more effective way. He offers a very comprehensive coverage of pertinent issues. And if there is a legitimate text, is there not also a legitimate course to be offered? Is there enough knowledge to disseminate? Are there a sufficient number of intriguing intellectual questions (of theory, definition, method, and generalizability) to engage students in conceptually directed discussions? Upon considering these questions, and upon reviewing the materials offered us by Professor Knox, I am compelled to alter my position. Yes, there is now a course to be offered --- a good, worthwhile course. Why this should be true now, but not before, reflects at least the following points.

1. <u>There has been a new explosion in gang knowledge</u>. It was in the late 1950s and 1960s that much of our knowledge about gangs was developed. This happened in large part because of the research projects attached to intensive gang intervention programs in New York, Boston, Chicago, and Los Angeles. Professor Knox summarizes much of this material. In the period from the mid-1960s to the early 1980s, very little was added to that earlier knowledge base, as both private and public funders of research turned their interests to new directions. But from the mid-1980s on, there has been a renewed interest in gangs as their prevalence spread from the few major gang cities of the earlier era to well over 100 cities currently.

The earlier research told us much about the structure and dynamic processes within gangs. The current expansion places more emphasis on gang context -- the urban underclass setting of street gangs, their connection to drug markets, and the relationship of gang violence to institutions of social control (police, courts, prisons). And as we learn more about these contexts in an increasingly wider variety of cities, we learn more as well about variations in gang structure: street gangs have changed in age distribution and violence; Asian gangs have become far more prevalent, revealing less territoriality and more sophisticated racketeering; prison gangs have become commonplace; white gang forms, such as "stoners" and "skinheads", have appeared in suburban areas and posed different control and ethical issues; drug gangs have reportedly emerged in more pure forms, complicating our understanding of gang functions. Many of these developments, too, find space in the chapters to follow.

2. <u>This proliferation of gangs and gang forms has forced scholars to turn to definitional issues to an extent not required earlier</u>. I can recall vividly a "gang city tour" I took in 1963, sharing my initial impressions of Los Angeles gangs with

established gang researchers in Chicago, New York, and Boston, and later in San Francisco, Seattle, and Philadelphia. Regardless of city, our gangs looked alike and our gang members acted alike. There was, thus, little pressure to attend carefully to issues of definition --- what is a gang, when is a group not a gang, what constitutes gang membership, or different levels of gang membership?

The luxury of such definitional innocence and ignorance is no longer affordable, for gangs in too many forms have now been described. A scientist who cannot define the phenomena being studied with sufficient clarity to allow comparison and replication by other scientists in the field is not in a position to contribute to the knowledge base of the discipline. And so Professor Knox gives considerable attention to the issue of gang definitions, and the student must come to understand that, far from being an arcane matter, this definitional problem is critical to our continuing capacity to understand, control, and prevent the negative components of the gang phenomenon.

3. <u>Old gang theories need correcting; new ones need development</u>. The gang scholars of earlier decades contributed theories that went far beyond gangs to become dominant themes of delinquency causation generally. Theories of "Differential Association", "Strain", "Delinquent Subculture" and "Opportunity Structure" owed much or most of their form to gang research. While they were important first steps, they were also misleading in their parochialism. For purposes of understanding gang etiology, each usually covered only one portion of the problem; an amalgam was badly needed, but never achieved. Worse, each became a mechanism for explaining delinquency or crime generally, and failed to meet the challenges of such an expansion. Criminological scholars overlooked the very special nature of gangs as (a) lower class, (b) male, (c) young and (d) group structures whose character could not easily be translated into middle class or female or adult or individual crime patterns.

Theoretical developments throughout the past two decades have been all but non-existent, except as critiques of prior attempts. But the application to the gang world of William Julius Wilson's notion of the urban underclass is becoming widespread. A fair prediction for the 1990s would be that the urban underclass and other contextual approaches will replace the strictly etiological theories of the '60s. The spread of street gangs across the nation would seem to require theories of political and economic sorts more than those stressing developmental and family processes, or subcultural pressures. Thus the intellectual surroundings of gang theory must broaden. The college course on gangs must include discourse on economic and industrial changes in American cities, the politics of federalism and local control, racism and racial segregation, class structures, and -- perhaps above all -- some appreciation for the way social values affect where we do and do not expend our national resources.

4. <u>Approaches to gang intervention have changed</u>. Street gangs in prior times seemed relatively innocuous. They were only episodically violent; the damage they wrought was more to themselves and the life-chances of their own members than to those around them. A gang member's life was dull, rather than the stuff of West Side Story or Colors. In such circumstances, gang intervention programs were principally concerned with helping gang members prepare for their adult futures. Programs emphasized education, work skills, social skills, and connecting

with the values of an adult world. Delinquency prevention was seen as the outcome of social development as much as a legitimate, direct target of intervention.

This story has been told elsewhere, and in part retold by Professor Knox, but these programs largely failed. Indeed, some of them contributed to increased delinquency. They underestimated the intractability of gangs, and overestimated their own capacities to affect the gang community. They completely failed to understand that they might have unintended consequences of a negative sort.

Now a new, diametrically opposed intervention philosophy has emerged, in part in response to the increased criminal involvement of street gangs and their spread to new cities. This philosophy -- retributive, punishment-oriented, suppressive -- is roughly based on deterrence theory but even more solidly grounded in political conservatism. It stresses arrests and convictions, police sweeps and crackdowns, new laws and policies to target street gangs as one might target the Cosa Nostra.

And, as with the socially oriented programs of earlier times, these gang deterrence interventions underestimate the intractability of gangs, overestimate their own capacities,, and completely fail to understand their unintended, negative consequences. It is my guess (if programs don't permit research evaluations, they yield guesses only) that the old and new approaches yield the same product -- greater gang cohesiveness and greater gang crime, including violent crime. A college course on the gang should prove a marvelous setting in which to explore these assertions.

5. <u>The street gang is basically an American product</u>. As a final element in my listing of issues deserving class coverage, this is in some ways the most important. The United States is not alone in being an industrialized nation, nor in having major urban areas with denotable inner cities, nor in having sizeable minority populations, nor in having failed social policies for the urban poor, nor in relinquishing much responsibility for social control to the criminal justice system. Yet, with very few exceptions, the United states <u>is</u> alone in its development of the urban street gang. Our gangs are like no others in the world - ours are far more prevalent, more permanent in their communities, larger and more complex, and more criminally involved by far. The American street gang is no temporary aberration; it is a permanent by-product of our inner city enclaves and many of their suburban surroundings. Its members are ruining their own lives, and endangering some others. Our societal response is to rant and rave about this, but not to undertake serious efforts to understand and change the situation.

What does all this tell us about our nation, about its structure, its values, its place in the society of nations? Were I an instructor about to launch a course on gangs with the aid of Professor Knox' text, I believe I would introduce the course with this question, and end it by asking the question again in hopes of having achieved some clarity in its answer. America is known for its entrepreneurial success, its stress on individualism, its emphasis on civil liberties and rights, its success in implementing democracy, its political and charitable contributions to other nations -- and its violence. Street gangs have lately become synonymous with violence, however unfairly.

In my own city and county of Los Angeles, we have produced over 2,400 gang-related homicides over the past five years, at a current rate of almost 40 percent of all homicides in the area. Los Angeles is the leader, but there are over 100 less Los Angeles' out there, and more are added each year. To understand street gangs, we must come to grips with what there is to a society that -- however inadvertently -- permits, fosters, and fails to remedy this situation.

If Professor Knox has offered us the first full text on gangs, the developments and issues outlined above would seem to guarantee that it will not be the last. In preparing this first, massive effort, Professor Knox has done us a considerable service. Now, I fear, I shall have to return to the office to prepare my lectures; I have a gang course in my future.

Dr. Klein currently teaches at the University of Southern California. He is an author of several gang books.

CHAPTER 1

AN OVERVIEW: The Social Science Approach To Understanding Gangs

INTRODUCTION

Some of our literature on gangs tends to describe "social gangs[a]" which are similar to unsupervised play groups. Social gangs, according to this author, are not really gangs at all. While they could become real gangs they are little more than the kind of precocious youths represented in movie characters like Spanky and Alfalfa in "The Little Rascals"[1]. We should be less worried about the mischief caused by play groups. They do not represent a national crime problem.

This book provides a study of the criminal gang. The most essential feature of the criminal gang is that its members routinely engage in law violation behavior. This is done individually, in small groups, and often in an organized continuing fashion. The nature of this involvement with crime will be seen to provide the basis for examining gangs from a social organizational perspective.

This is the kind of gang that is seen in both juvenile and adult correctional institutions. Correctional officers do not see "social gangs", those who never come to the attention of the criminal justice system.[b] They see, rather, the hardcore law-offending gangs[2]. It is mostly the criminal gang member we find in our jails.

Law enforcement faces little problem from small cliques of unsupervised kids. Thus, police do not face a very high threat from so-called social gangs. Law enforcement officers are, however, often shot and killed by members of structured criminal gangs. It is the criminal gang that is the focus of this book. Later it will be shown how these gangs are classified in terms of the level of organizational sophistication.

You, and the public, are not worried about being killed by a random shooting where the shooter was Spanky or Alfalfa. You are probably concerned more about the hardcore criminal gang. Some of these well known criminal gangs are examined in detail in this book. Some gangs are highly structured and have written constitutions,

---

[a] A "social gang" is what the author calls in later portions of this book a level zero gang. It is, at best, a "pre-gang" group. It commits few serious crimes. It is equivalent to a streetcorner play group such as Spanky and Alfalfa, et al, in the popular TV series "The Little Rascals".

[b] We cannot oversimplify the definition of gang by taking the viewpoint that any organized group containing offenders must necessarily constitute a gang. Were that kind of ambiguous definition used in gang analysis, then correctional officials would have to conclude that any "pro-social" club or organization behind the walls of correctional institutions constitutes a "social gang". That is not the perspective advanced in this book. Even though some wardens may use this definition of gangs, particularly in reference to Muslims.

some examples of these internal gang writings are provided in the appendices of this book. Some gangs are little more than small units of persons often no more complicated in their hierarchy than a burglary or armed robbery "ring".

Regarding the study of gangs there are many questions that must be answered if we are to truly attain a social scientific perspective. This book seeks to provide a social scientific view of gangs. That means being interdisciplinary.[3] That also means relying, where possible, on good criminological research about gangs.

The ambiguity of defining characteristics of and about "gangs" in the literature can often mean more confusion the more we read. But there are two empirical questions about gangs in America that command our attention. (1) When does a loosely formed street corner group become a gang? And (2) if gangs are involved in crime, then how much of crime in America is explained by gang involvement? These two questions, so essential to the social scientific study of gangs, are not fully answered in the prior literature. Much new data is provided in this book to shed light on these and other important issues.

SOME PRELIMINARY CONSIDERATIONS

Some may say that gangs can be socially engineered (i.e., artificially created) and even experimentally manipulated (e.g., gang social service intervention, gang deprogramming services, or capable of being manipulated by political parties). The bottom line here is: can anything be done about the gang crime problem? Some may say that it is possible to exert much impact on gangs, perhaps even destroy them (e.g., gang busting). Others may say that through social services we can work directly with gangs and gang members; and perhaps show them a better way of life. The most extreme form of this therapeutic intervention would be that we can "deprogram" gang members. Before addressing the significance of such an assumption about social engineering and gangs, it is necessary to review some of the issues concerning gangs generally. Still others may say that as a crime problem no one has ever come up with the magic bullet of rehabilitation or prevention. Therefore it may be impossible to turn around the gang crime problem if we were to listen to some viewpoints. The truth is probably somewhere in between the two extremes that we can do a lot or we cannot do anything about the gang crime problem.

In this chapter we will only examine some of the general characteristics of gangs. In later portions of this text, however, the definitional overlap and variation in what constitutes a gang will be examined in much greater detail. This will involve the analysis of the gang in terms of what we know about social group formations generally.

The approach of this book is therefore incremental. It will address the major issues and at appropriate points in the book provide elements of a more integrated view of gangs, including a gang typology. The final chapter will review in detail the competing definitions of gangs and suggest an integrated definition of gang levels of "threat severity" and membership stages.

Gangs apparently need not have a publicly known label or name for their group[4], although most American gangs do.[5] Indeed in the early stage of gang formation the name itself emerges as a function of identity and crystallization. Gangs often do not consider themselves "gangs", but rather as types of "organizations". Gangs like the Gangster Disciples in Chicago deserve their preference for being called an organization, because they have been able to stage protests with several thousand members marching in unison in front of City Hall.

A historical review of American gangs would suggest that they emerged along racial and ethnic lines. Bonn (1984: 333), discussing gangs in the context of organized crime, reported criminal gangs existing in America as early as 1760. In the urban context, Bonn described gangs as clearly having ethnic homogeneity in terms of their organization. "Irish gangs were the first to emerge.." followed by German, Jewish and Italian gangs (Bonn, 1984: 333-334). This factor will be examined in much greater detail later in the book.

To some extent gangs gain legitimacy through the tendency of American culture to romanticize, and often idolize, gang exploits[6]. Al Capone as a gang leader has been significantly represented in fiction, myth, and through the Hollywood movie industry. As a byproduct of this element of culture, Chicago as a city must still today labor under the image of a "rat...tat...tat...tat" town associated with hoods carrying Thompson submachine guns. The cognitive map of many Americans places Chicago as "gangster land", which is not exactly a tourist attraction![7] And how does America compete as a tourist attraction, as a "peaceful place" in a democratic milieu, when gangs dominate the public imagination both here and abroad? The image of gang killings communicates "when travelling to America, bring your bullet proof vest".

There is also an important ideological factor involved in both the study of gangs and policy responses to the gang problem. Hagan (1987: 231-232) characterized the study of gangs as a fetish of criminologists during the 1950s and 1960s. While the gang problem did not disappear, the attention to gang research apparently did in the 1970s according to some sources. Hagan cited the literature review by Bookin-Weiner and Horowitz (1983) to the effect that ideological polarization in the 1970s was associated with a shift in analytical interests. Here the emphasis on macroanalytic problems such as social structure, SES (social economic status), and the community as the unit of analysis are characterized as being perhaps liberal while the emphasis on individual traits as explanations of criminal activity hold more weight for a conservative ideological orientation. The legitimacy of this claim is open to discussion[8], but perhaps rests with the common hypothesis that in some regard academic research follows the budgetary process. That is, in academia, the tail of funding for research can wag the dog of knowledge development.

This ideological factor cannot be overemphasized and we must be alert to its influence at all stages in the knowledge production process. By ideology we mean those values and assumptions about the world which have implications for the control and allocation of limited resources. In the study of sociology, for example, one of the concepts that students quickly learn is "value free". That is, one should not bring one's own values into play in research; for otherwise we are advancing not social science, nor policy for the improvement of corrections and criminal justice, but rather we are advancing ideology. The problem however is that society cannot be easily placed in an aseptic vacuum free from normative influences. That is, how we view the world may often influence how we portray the origin, structure, function, composition and policy recommendations for problems such as gang crime.

There has always existed a linguistic problem in the study of gang crime. The term "gang banger" itself is perhaps more fitting for use by sensational journalism than by a social scientist. It is a label containing stigma and implications that should engender fear and loathing. Indeed our language has much to do with the problem. When discussing "gangs" in America, one of the first things a student of criminology will learn is that in reviewing the literature what some conceive of as "gangs" are little more than conspicuously obnoxious youths running head strong against societal norms, as well as, of course, highly organized and armed groups with syndicated functions and hierarchical roles who are prone to violence.

The loose and pejorative use of the label "gang" is a source of confusion. We shall have to clarify our language to be able to objectively assess the gang problem in America today. The most common variation involves labelling all gang members in a tradition of much enmity (e.g., gang banger). Another variation, espoused by those in combat with gangs, is that some authors have apparently experienced the "Stockholm syndrome", or an over-identification with the rhetoric of gang members; almost in a tradition of Chicago's Rev. John Fry (Fry, 1969, 1973), that all that is important is that we "offer them something" (e.g., give them a bone), and we should therefore provide services and programs to serve them.[9] Both views suffer from a lack of clarity of what levels of gang sophistication we are talking about and the degree of individual integration into the gang subculture.

Vagueness and imprecision can get us into a lot of trouble. Mostly, it backfires in terms of social policy and legislation. Kasimar (1971: 52) described how the zeal of Detroit prosecutors to fight crime created a "public enemy act", as well as New Jersey which passed a law making "it a felony, punishable by 20 years' imprisonment, to be a gangster", were found to be unconstitutional, in New Jersey's case because of vagueness and uncertainty.[10] It also confuses us in the arena of social service intervention: some gangs at some stages of membership integration are clearly more "reachable" than others, and not paying attention to the details of such distinctions can mean exacerbating the very problem being used as a platform for social service intervention. Generally, what the study of gangs implies in criminology is some difference from loner or individual crime, chiefly in terms of a difference in organizational terms. A single gunman acting alone in a robbery, simply put, differs from a crime resulting from a gang. The gang implies something that the lone criminal offender does not have: some sense of organizational capability. The gang also implies a continuing or persisting threat over time that can increase. It is this emphasis on organizational characteristics that is common to the study of gangs, but which is at the same time most underdeveloped in the sense of linking what we know about social organization generally to the more specific problem of the study of gangs.

The study of gang crime has always implied some element of organizational life, although this aspect of gang analysis has not always emerged in the literature to the extent that we may desire. Indeed, there is radical disagreement on this issue. But this book develops such an organizational viewpoint, because it is also one that allows for more effective law enforcement, greater choices in managing the problem in the field of corrections, and much more latitude in addressing the gang problem from all levels of prevention --- primary, secondary, and tertiary (e.g., aftercare services).

Clearly, gangs do exist and their members do commit crimes. It is, then, a proper area of study for the social sciences. And yet some may say that gang research and analysis has barely risen above the level of an esoteric craft. These same cynics condemn not only intellectuals but applied knowledge as well, to the effect we really do not know much about crime, when in fact we do know some things. This book simply seeks to fill the gap in limited choices available for someone who has the responsibility for educating and training on the topic of gangs. The book therefore addresses many issues and includes many sources of data.

WHEN IS A GROUP A GANG?

Does calling a group a gang make it a gang? It probably depends on who uses the language. The voice of a community resident differs in definitive power from the voice of a United States Attorney or a local prosecutor.[11] The difference is power.

Legally, there are few statutes addressing this issue, and specific laws addressing gangs have only recently come into being.[12] There is the federal RICO statute and its many mini-RICO versions at the state level of criminal law. These define organizations engaged in violation of the law and can be used for both criminal and civil prosecution. Again, however, language is no friend of social science here. For example, Illinois as does many other states, has a "mob action" criminal statute which covers crimes committed in a group including civil protest demonstrations. Literally thousands of persons have been arrested under this statute for protests associated with the "right to life" movement and in protesting abortion. Does arrest for mob action make one a "mobster"?

The answer is most probably, NO. That is, most of those arrested for protesting the operation of an abortion clinic would probably reveal a pro-social motivation of a higher social purpose and an intent to be arrested, not to avoid arrest, in their behavior as a matter of civil disobedience. Indeed, they may be very religious persons who know that mass media attention to their cause is most likely under conditions of the arrest of their members. But does that make them "mobsters"? No! It is a matter of intention to avoid arrest as well. Groups like those with internalized higher moral imperatives such as those who may engage in civil disobedience --- for example to protect the environment --- knowing they will be arrested for their behavior, and willfully continuing such behavior as a moral protest, cannot be considered "gangs" in any sense used in this book. The reasoning here rests with the fact that their intent is not to do harm through violence or to benefit economically through criminal code violation, and further that in such civil disobedience they do not seek to evade arrest.

Thus, many persons being arrested for protesting abortion in the traditional civil disobedience style of political and moral protest cannot be considered gang members. However, in recent years violent attacks have been undertaken against individual physicians. Also, the medical buildings themselves have been burglarized, vandalized, and attacked in a different style where the perpetrators definitely do seek to cause harm and do seek to evade arrest. Such persons operating as a group would come under the umbrella of gang analysis.

A new law did recently criminalize some abortion protest behavior, it is called the FACE Act: Freedom of Access to Clinic Entrances Act. It is a federal criminal misdemeanor where the first offense can result in six months in prison and a fine of up to $10,000 for blocking the access to healthcare services of patients trying to use an abortion clinic. The first federal charges against violators of this Act were made in June of 1994.[13] So what we have here is a change from the time the first edition of this book appeared: a new criminal code defining that behavior as a crime. So the fact is the benefit structure here is ideological in nature, just as in political crime and in terrorism, and while we can expect this "gang" behavior to profile differently, it must still be treated analytically as gang crime if the abortion protestors violate the FACE Act. The fact that most do not try to evade arrest do however make them a unique exception to what we mean by gang crime.

The same problem arises in considering gangs. And in this regard we choose at this point to forcibly eliminate the phrase "gangster" from any subsequent discussion, because it confuses more than it contributes to the scientific understanding of the problem. It carries a value connotation and a culturally prescribed image of evil. One fact that will emerge in the study of gangs is that not all of the 24 hour day spent by gang members is spent in a relentless search for evil as if it were the only goal gang members had. Gang members are not alien invaders from another planet, they are from and live in our communities.

The term "gang banger" is similarly not to be found in the ensuing discussion unless in the context of views from persons interviewed who do not represent a social scientific view of the world. It is a label of derision just like gangster and mobster. It connotes more in terms of values of derogation and the psychology of enmity (Keen, 1986) than it does in terms of scientific classification.

Anyone who grew up in the 1950s or who watches such re-runs may recall a "gang" that was portrayed every Saturday morning at cartoon time on television. It was the series about "The Little Rascals". Is that what we mean by a gang? It too is a misrepresentation, albeit one that gives a favorable image to "gang". But that is Hollywood, and the reader of this book must be willing to break free of those kind of stereotypes created by culture. Alfalfa and Spanky and their associates typified much of urban adolescents, but they hardly typified what is meant today by an American gang-affiliated youth.

Do gangs necessarily have to have illicit goals, functions, or engage in law violation collectively or as individuals? Or can a gang have pro-social purposes? The answer is historical. That is, historically the phrase gang has encompassed both sets of group affiliation. In doing so the study of gangs has suffered from more than a small amount of measurement error. There must be both a qualitative and quantitative difference between a voluntary association composed primarily of youths which simply seeks to have a good time as compared to one that has a high degree of criminality in its everyday life. In other words, if any clique or group of three or more youths together, unsupervised constitutes a gang, then all of America has at one time or another been gang affiliated.

How much deviance or crime must a group be responsible for before it is considered a gang? Are the Boy Scouts a gang if one of the ranking members is in fact secretly a cat burglar or a semi-professional car thief? No doubt about it, some legitimate social organizations and groups do routinely experience what is called a succession of goals. That is, these groups may be formed initially for a certain specific purpose, but may later in time change and come to take on a new and entirely different goal and purpose. So it is analytically possible for even a legitimate group to transform itself into a gang.

If the road to hell is paved with good intentions, then how do we account for the type of organizational climate change that took place when the Rev. Jim Jones began having his religious followers carry out the practice of drinking poisoned Kool-aid?[14] The tragedy that occurred in Jonestown, where hundreds of people died in 1978 bears much significance to the study of gangs in that it was collective behavior and it ultimately had what must be regarded as a criminal outcome -- mass suicide. How do gangs differ from cults? A cult engaged in crime, over time, is a gang. Many "skinhead" groups and white racist groups can be considered gangs, because they often engage in what are called bias crimes.[15] But it means having more than the "skinhead", it means the actual commission of such acts of racial/ethnic/sexual preference bigotry in a manner that tends to violate another persons civil rights; or more commonly, for such "hate groups" it means groups that routinely engage in crimes of various sorts, including violence, with the fact that the same group may also hold extreme political views. Early scholars like Puffer, Furfey, and Thrasher did not include adult gangs such as the Ku Klux Klan, or vigilante groups. Rather, early scholars focused on youth groups who tended to go against the grain of mainstream society, its culture, its values, and its norms. That is, some sense of youthful deviance. The present analysis will show why we must also consider such groups like the Aryan Brotherhood, the Aryan Nation, the KKK, Neo-nazis, etc, also qualify as "gangs" for purposes of both criminological research and prosecution[16].

To be more specific, here the definition of gangs will be restricted to not simply involvement with or committing acts of deviance, but rather to crime. Crime is a special subset of deviance. In this sense, members of the Jonestown religious community could not be considered a gang even though they engaged in deviant practices and their behavior was deviant from our perspective[17]. The problem with using deviance as the key ingredient to define gang behavior is that it is far too encompassing.[18]

A group is a gang when it exists for or benefits substantially from the continuing criminal activity of its members. Some element of crime must exist as a definitive feature of the organization for it to be classified as a gang. That need not be income-producing crime, because it could also be crimes of violence.[19] Examples would include such extremist groups like the Ku Klux Klan, the Aryan Brotherhood, young white racist group equivalents, and others who engage not necessarily in well known income-producing crimes, but who still commit crimes along a dimension of "bias". Often these crimes involve violence to property or persons, as "hate crimes" or "bias crimes".[20] This is a legitimate aspect of the gang problem because it is criminal behavior that is approved of, and often planned, as such by a group[21].

Crime involvement of a group must not therefore be a sub rosa function about which few of the members have knowledge if we are to consider the group a gang. Members of many legitimate voluntary associations and civic groups are sometimes arrested for a variety of offenses. But these are not offenses committed on behalf of their group, these are not offenses even necessarily known to their full social network, these are not offenses condoned and approved of in advance by their organization, or which enjoy their acceptance or blessing. To be considered a gang, the criminal involvement of members must be openly known and approved of as such.

Conspiracy laws have some application here. To prove a conspiracy it is generally necessary to prove one or more overt acts in furtherance of the conspiracy. The key word is "overt". It must be open and clearly regarded as law violation behavior. That is, they know it is wrong, they know it is against the law, and they do it anyway. Some element of criminal conspiracy to avoid detection for law violation must therefore be present, whether the actual/objective/material skill/knowledge/ability to avoid or limit the probability of arrest actually exists.

Thus, from the perspective of the analysis advanced in this book, a group is not a gang simply because it is labelled as being in some sense deviant. A group is a gang if and only if it meets the higher requirement of having a known involvement with crime. It can therefore include the Crips, Bloods, Folks, Peoples, Posse, Vice Lords, Latin Kings, motorcycle gangs (Pagans, Hells Angels, etc), and a host of others whose primary occupation is income-producing crime or who benefit substantially from it, and as well it can include those engaged in a mixture of traditional crime and political crime involving rightwing and leftwing extremism (e.g., Aryan Brotherhood, Supreme White Power, KKK, and others versus leftwing groups like the Symbionese Liberation Army, and others). Such crime patterns, particularly of more organized gangs who have been able to accumulate economic assets, can also include a mixture of legitimate income (small businesses, hustling, etc) and criminal pursuits.

A semantic problem that needs to be clarified here is that we can effectively use the phrase "youth gangs" in a logical and rigorous analysis of the gang problem. If there are youth gangs, then logically there are "adult gangs" as well; and any student of human development will recognize that there are many possible gradations along the life span in terms of age-categories. First, the term "youth" is not easily operational-ized in social policy. Secondly, there is no level one or higher "gang" known to this author which in its code of conduct or its charter or its written constitution or in its informal norms restricts membership to simply "youths"[c]. Groups like the Crips and the Bloods, the Vice Lords and the Disciples, etc, cannot simply be regarded as "youth gangs": it is more accurate to say these level three gangs have many youthful members. Youths are the easiest to exploit, particularly in drug-trafficking.

Analysts who continue to use the phrase "youth gangs" find their results hard to apply to the real world of criminal justice: there are no "youth laws", there are juvenile laws, and adult criminal codes. Anyone 17 or older in Illinois, for example, is an adult under law; and their behavior in violating the law is not regarded as "juvenile delinquency", it is "adult criminality". It is also a data problem: we do not have any census of all gang members in the United States, so we cannot accurately say that the

---

[c] The notable exception are engineered gangs: those created by adult hate groups (e.g., neo-nazis) such as were created by the NSPA nazi movement in southwest Chicago in the mid-1970's. These were specifically age-graded "sects" of the larger adult neo-nazi organization. These are discussed in more detail in a later chapter.

majority are "juveniles", or even "youths" --- whatever we interpret "youths" to mean operationally. Stephens, in quoting a police chief on gangs, says it is a myth that the majority of street gang members are juveniles, that is, in Los Angeles juveniles may constitute only about a fifth of the gang membership (Goldstein and Huff, 1993: p. 224)!

The problem, then, with using the term "youth gang" is that it inaccurately describes the social reality of American gangs. Further it implies that such gangs have no adult leaders whom they are accountable to. It mistakenly implies that just because they are "youths" they are therefore not culpable nor responsible for their acts: as if by compulsion to join a gang this would be any defense in committing violence against another citizen. No matter what their age, gang members young or old must be held accountable for their actions.

A level one gang is the most elementary form of a real "gang". At level four in the classification system advanced in this book, such a group is really "organized crime". A level zero gang is not really a gang at all, it is a play group, a peer group, call it anything you want: we have all been members of such groups who engage in many behaviors, but essentially not that of violating criminal laws over time in a context where the group knows and approves of such law violation behavior and in fact benefits from it.

Finally, many students of criminology today ask "what is the difference between prison gangs and street gangs?", and here some answers are now known. Previously it was thought that many prison gangs like the Aryan Brotherhood existed only in prisons and were not reported to be a problem for local law enforcement, or for other criminal justice personnel (probation or parole officers, etc). Clearly, we now know that gangs like the Aryan Brotherhood and their youth counterparts DO EXIST outside of the context of correctional institutions. And prison gang membership will be in most cases equivalent to gang membership on the outside of the correctional environment as well. Although, obviously, there are situations such as in our county jails and other institutions where confined persons "ride with" or temporarily show an allegiance to a gang simply while in custody and somehow reduce --- perhaps to its absolute minimum --- any such post-release gang affiliation. There are few if any "prison gangs" that do not represent if not by the same name then by proxy a similar gang problem on the "street".[22]

The language of this book is not limited to what some authors call "street gangs". We cannot define gangs simply in terms of those who "hang out on the streets", or "use the streets", or "claim the streets as their turf". The kind of gangs studied in this book are those who commit crime. Too often the casual reader about crime comes to think of "street crime" as a code word for crimes by minority persons. This book demonstrates that all ethnic groups, all races have gangs today; or had them in the past. If our social science vocabulary is so limited that we have to use the layman language of "street gang", then minimally and logically there must also exist "suite gangs" as well: those groups and organizations who commit their crimes from offices.

In sum, it is not _where_ the gang operates, it is how it operates and functions that distinguishes it in terms of its sophistication and its objective crime threat.

THE BURNING QUESTION: How Much Crime in America is Gang-Related?

The study of gangs is justified as a portion of all curricula in every criminal justice, delinquency, criminology, sociology, psychology, etc program: if and only if gangs and their members constitute a significant portion of the overall American crime problem. This gets directly to the issue of what is a "gang-related crime". Or, alternatively, when can we count the value of "gang-impact" in assessing the overall threat that a gang or several gangs may pose in terms of their contribution to crime statistics in the United States? Some would have us believe that just because little Johnny robs someone, even though he was a member of a gang, as long as the gang did not order him to rob or as long as the robbery did not occur along with several other confederates who were members of the same gang, that this individual crime by a gang member should not be counted as "gang crime". The position advanced here is comparable to the Los Angeles law enforcement definition discussed later: if the crime was committed by a known gang member, it was a gang-related crime.

The reason is good logic: the offender in this instance has a larger more encompassing influence, the gang. Bad behavior while alone as a gang member may bring a violent punishment to the gang member from his/her own gang. Good behavior (i.e., defending the nation) would similarly --- as a lone person --- be behavior honored and perhaps even rewarded by the gang. Either way, there is little escaping the implications of behavior from the viewpoint of a larger social entity the offender belongs to: the gang. One is a gang member in some gangs 24 hours a day. Gang life in more organized or violent gangs is not a part-time commitment. It is more comparable to being a member of a cult or a total institution. One acts as a "gang member", and one may feel as a gang member he or she has greater protection for any individual acts. Thus, it is comparable to a police officer on duty taking a bribe: it is a police-based crime, whether the officer did it alone or as a member of a corrupt group. It should not be necessary to say that in the case of gang crime that the gang had to know and approve of the crime in advance before we consider it gang-related crime; for that could be considered gang legislated crime. We are far from having the nationwide facts about gang crime. Until we do it is best to have the widest possible definition until we know what that yields. When we are at the stage of adequately coming to grips with the scope and extent of this national problem, then we might be able to partial out those crimes which were known and approved of in advance by the gang itself, or authorized, or directed by gang leaders. It is a moot point at this time in history, because no one has the data. In this situation, your author elects to accept the definition of gang-related crime as any crime committed by a gang member.

So, back to the issue: do the facts currently justify the study of gangs in the sense that gangs and gang members tend to account for a sizable portion of the American crime problem? Yes, is the answer argued here. But sadly, all parameters of the answer are not completely known. Some attempts to estimate youth crime portions of national crime statistics suggested that about half of all such crimes were gang-related. The problem here is very complex and needs some explanation.

First, it is widely known that there are generally three sources of data for crime statistics. There is the FBI's Uniform Crime Report (UCR), but it does not ask local law enforcement agencies to "double-tag" offense reports so that we could even know nationally what the scope and extent of gang crime in America is. There is also the victimization survey, but it does not ask respondents if they believe the crimes that they were the victims of were gang-related. Finally, there are self-report surveys and these come closest, at present, to giving an indication, at this stage of social science, of what role gangs play in criminal law violation in America. None of these three sources are as of yet adequate to provide all of the answers needed regarding the problem of gang crime. By way of comparison, "hate crime" is something that became officially tracked only in relative recent history. This is not to say that America only had "hate crime" in its recent history only. This means that our official policy was to simply recognize it, like child abuse, as a new social problem worthy of systematically tracking and reporting. No state and no federal government agency is required by law to monitor and report all known gang-related crimes, or crimes committed by gang members at this writing. This can be expected to change in the future, because like "hate crime" or bias crime, or like child abuse crimes, crimes committed by gang members appears to be taking on the role of the new national bogeyman in America.

There is reason to believe, however, that gang-related crime constitutes a significant portion of all crime in America. It is for that reason that this study represents both a challenge and a knowledge development need for the future. Many of the gangs studied by Thrasher would probably not be considered gangs at all in this analysis. Indeed, the gangs which exist in America today represent a much more formidable challenge to law enforcement, corrections, and public safety. The "gangs" that Thrasher studied were lucky to have pocket knifes and baseball bats. Some gangs today have at their disposal fully automatic weapons and even military ordnance.[23]

Gangs are a national problem and are now reported to be a problem to some extent in nearly all states. The Camp and Camp (1985: p. 11) study showed only a few states not reporting a gang problem in their prison system (Alabama, Alaska, Delaware, Kansas, New Hampshire, North Dakota, Oregon, Rhode Island, South Carolina, South Dakota, Vermont, Wyoming and missing data on New Jersey and Tennessee).

Recent data on correctional institutions, described in later chapters, shows the list of states with no gang problem behind bars to now be reduced to: New Hampshire, South Carolina, Vermont, and Wyoming. But from other sources we knew Alaska does have Filipino gangs (Jackson and Mc Bride, 1990: p. 50), and the Hell's Angels have been reported as far north as the North Pole. From the author's research, data is now emerging which shows that Alabama and Kansas have many gangs, Delaware, New Jersey and South Carolina have the Posse and others. Rhode Island has the Red Dragons (Cambodian) and others (Posse, Aryan Brotherhood, etc), Oregon has Crips and Bloods, Wyoming has the Mexican Mafia and more, and New Hampshire has skinheads at least. From the law enforcement surveys, we now know that the Dakotas are no longer completely without any reported active gangs. That leaves only Vermont[d] --- one state --- with no reported gangs. And if we looked much

---

[d] Research now shows (Nov., 1994) Vermont is no longer on the list of states "Having No Gang Problem". Vermont now has gangs in its Adult Correctional System.

closer, perhaps we would find some gang activity there. We are rapidly approaching the point where those who do not report gangs at the correctional or law enforcement level are the exception to the rule.

One of the most fascinating criminological research needs regarding gang crime is how much crime and violence committed by gangs is simply never recorded in our national crime statistics. Routine "drive-by" shootings and rival-gang shoot-outs in many inner city areas, while being well known to the residents, are simply never recorded as "real crimes" by the police. Kotlowitz (1992: p. 18) reports the case of a large-scale shoot-out between rival gangs at the Henry Horner Homes public housing complex on Chicago's near west side that when a reporter called the next day for a copy of a police report, the reporter was told no such police report existed! Many such crimes in Chicago are routinely "unfounded", that is: not listed as real crimes, and therefore never reported to the FBI for its national crime statistics: rather the police radio messages tell us what happens, because no "complainant" exists to sign a complaint, the police officer responding to the call (if a call is ever made) simply radios back it is a "nineteen Paul", the code for "no problem", "no complainant", "no arrest", "no report". Anyone with a police scanner can listen to these police radio frequencies to hear of anonymous calls from "citizens" and actual complainants throughout the City of Chicago about such daily gang shootings, most of which get handled the same way "19 Paul".

What we have now as valid and reliable information is not sufficient to answer several basic national questions: how much crime committed in the United States is gang related, or committed by gang members? We don't know, all we have are estimates. How many gangs exist in the United States and how many gang members exist in the United States --- again all we have are estimates. The FBI's criminal division did recently estimate that there may be 400,000 gang members in the United States.[24]

HOW EASY IT IS TO OVER-GENERALIZE ABOUT GANGS

Some authors have sought to systematically root out the "myths" about gangs in America today (Sanchez-Jankowski, 1991). This generates far too much attention, because the problem is really empirical, not theoretical. Theoretically, gangs can vary in terms of a wide number of characteristics, functions, structures, and behaviors. Some gangs sell drugs, some may not. But generally, if it is a real gang (one that engages in crime), given the opportunity it is certainly capable of the crime. The reason this is an issue is that some studies may have focused on the strong linkage to either drug use or drug sales and such studies may seek to generalize their findings to the entire American gang problem.

The term "myth" is not used here (e.g., It is a myth that all gangs sell/use drugs). It is rather and more accurately called a logical fallacy that overgeneralizes from a specific instance to the larger scene. The phrase "All gangs use/sell drugs" is therefore just that: an over-generalization. Just finding an exception does not mean we do not have strong evidence of the role of gangs in selling drugs, nor does it diminish the general behavioral profile showing that gang members abuse drugs more than other offenders, or than non-offenders.

Some of these types of discussions are "straw-man" techniques to raise issues. While they are not unimportant issues, there is no limit to the logical number of such issues: the family's role, the role of single-parent families, the role of educational failure, the role of being stigmatized/labelled, etc. What we need are statistics: numbers that will help to clarify the parameters of such issues. Variation in illegal groups is to be expected in the same way that such variation is to be found in lawful groups. The global factors that vary with gangs are clearly: who, what, when, where, why and how. The variations in factors which help us to classify gangs are potentially endless.

Another common error made frequently by some newcomers to the gang issue in criminology is to assume that anything that applies to juvenile delinquents (e.g., treatment) automatically applies to "gangs". As stated earlier, we lack information over time on what percent of all American juvenile delinquents are in fact gang members, or even what proportion of all crimes committed by juveniles arrested represent such gang members. Thus, it is criminologically naive to think that simply because a "therapy" program that had some application to juvenile delinquency years ago may be of value for intervention with gang members today. All juvenile delinquents are not gang members, and not all gang members are juvenile delinquents. It is possible for a gang member to technically never be arrested for a crime and grow up as an adult with no "rap sheet" at all; perhaps even get hired as a police officer.

In the search for a honest view of gangs, the goal of this book has been to provide a holistic, interdisciplinary, and historical analysis covering the main issues. It is not easy to provide an overall theme that integrates material that has never before been provided in such a format. Indeed, some experts in the field when they heard of this plan for a textbook on gangs said that "it could not be done". They believed that viewpoints in the gang literature are so different and the research methods are so diverse, that it is "premature" to have the basis for a textbook on gangs. Actually, there are a number of commonalities in the literature as will be shown.

It is no easy task to organize into a coherent whole all of the extensive gang literature. The reader is strongly encouraged to closely follow the footnotes provided. Other reading in areas of interest from the recommended readings and bibliography provided is also suggested.

Where the author digresses at various points in the book to discuss historical issues, or matters of research ethics, etc, these discussions are provided because the author felt the issues were important to raise. Please pardon some cliches to be found in the book as a deviation from a professional writing style. While the author has endeavored to provide a comprehensive analysis of gangs in America, this book by no means "covers everything". No single book could ever claim to "know it all".

In no sense does the amount of space or attention provided to specific gang authors imply any relationship to their overall contributions in the field. This means some prior authors who may have been only marginally connected to the field of gang studies could be discussed much more than prolific gang authors. This book does not try to establish such a "pecking order" of gang wisdom. New data is now emerging that will have much bearing on the analysis of gangs in America. It is, in short, a volatile field; partly because gangs are emerging as such a national problem.

Finally, not each and every "gang action program" in America is discussed here. Many are not known outside of their immediate area. There is no central "GANG CRIME INFORMATION AND REFERRAL SERVICE"[25]. The author therefore apologizes to the many local efforts not mentioned here, commends them, and hopes to hear from them[26]. Finally, "tone" in this book may vary at times. Some would say it could have been more dispassionate, perhaps softened, and much less sarcastic/argumentative/cynical in certain respects.

A QUICK OVERVIEW OF WHAT THIS TEXT WILL COVER

Chapter 2 will examine some of those factors that should probably be used in the classification of gangs. This is most important, since some current approaches to gang analysis see only three types of gangs: social gangs, delinquent gangs, and conflict gangs. Others add "drug" or hedonistic to the gang classification. That is not a precise scientific approach, it is rather a convenient such classification, based at the highest level of theoretical competence on attribution theory. We need a better classification system, because that is the first step of science. The author will at strategic points in the book provide the basic typology, and later add elements of the classification, and discuss its potential application. Towards the end of this book the reader will then be able to compare previous definitions of gangs and arrive at an integrated definition.

In chapter 3, the major milestones in the gang literature are reviewed. The purpose here is to provide a synopsis of these historical contributions to the understanding of gangs. Clearly, this is a selective summary. Not all contributions are described in this limited review. The keyword is "major contributions". Hopefully the reader shall find that this book is not restrictive about the admission of evidence. In fact, quite the obverse, as will be seen in subsequent chapters, where many such additional contributions are summarized where they are most appropriately brought into discussion. But some major figures in the field of gang studies such as Malcolm Klein, Walter Miller and Irving Spergel have added so much to our knowledge about gangs that books could be written about them individually.

In chapter 4, a current view among some gang authors (Moore, 1978; Hagedorn and Macon, 1988) regarding the societal conditions or the social context under which gangs emerge, more specifically, the racism and oppression hypothesis, is examined in more complete detail. Is this a political platform, not a theory? Is this based on social fact? Are there conceptual continuities in the literature and historical grounds for this view? These questions are answered in reviewing this gang thesis about racism and oppression.

In chapter 5, a related thesis about gangs is examined. It involves the underclass. As will be seen, it presents a provocative issue. It is an enduring issue, and one that suggests a changing research agenda for gang analysis.

In chapter 6, another historical continuity and organizational aspect is examined: the relationship of gangs to politics in America. It is another enduring issue. An issue not unique to Chicago, and one that is multiplied in varied ways in many political jurisdictions. It is an issue over the control over and allocation of scarce resources, and the political-economy.

In chapter 7, one of the primary qualitative research techniques for understanding gangs is described. This is the oral history method. Sometimes called "conversation analysis", conducting "case studies", and "field research interviews". It too has been used with considerable variation over the years. An effort is made to explain this technique in greater detail.

In chapter 8, we clarify the truth about two major early contributors to the understanding of gangs: Shaw and Mc Kay. And because our current literature appears to be confused about these authors, Chapter 9 as well examines Shaw and Mc Kay on the matter of gangs, along with some related historical discussion. Chapter 10 provides another interesting bit of history: a detailed examination regarding what, specifically, might have been involved in the research methodology used by Thrasher in his famous study of 1,313 gangs in Chicago.

In chapter 11, the gang is described not as a sign that America is "falling apart", or as a sign of its imminent collapse as a democracy, such as in a negativistic view of the future as might be implied in some of our Hollywood movies along the same lines (e.g., Escape from New York City, etc). In fact, we should view gangs (as group formations) as natural and normal. Their members may indeed engage in behavior that some of us may regard as unnatural and abnormal. But as a whole, gangs are normal under some conditions. Further, gangs are not new to America. And America is not the only society with gang problems. But America is alone, according to the current literature, in having such a conspicuous and violent gang presence in everyday life.

Chapter 12 provides a viewpoint on gangs from what we know about organizational life generally. It is an organizational approach to gangs that may help to clarify what types of gangs actually exist. They are, after all, more than groups. They have continuity and internal social organization.

Chapter 13 examines a historically legitimate issue: gangs, guerrilla warfare, and conflict. Here we find the interesting case of robber gangs from India and how the British military was able to suppress them. It is valuable because it shows that gangs have another possible level of violence other than drive-by shootings. Can gangs be a proxy force for terrorism in the decades ahead? Was Jeff Fort's Chicago gang, the El Rukn's, the only gang in America to seek out funding from foreign governments hostile to America? These and related issues are also examined in this book.

Chapter 14 seeks to clarify, from what we know about social group formations, the group characteristics of gangs. Here we see as well some evidence that perhaps gangs can arise naturally under certain conditions (e.g., economic deprivation, social disorganization, ethnic antagonism, racial segregation, the underclass context, etc) but might in fact be capable of being artificially created. That is, creating a gang by social engineering. The author's previous research on Neo-nazi youth gangs is described here as well.

Chapter 15 addresses the controversial matter of legalizing or decriminalizing heroin and hard drugs as a strategy recommended (Moore, 1978) for gang neutralization. Would taking the economic incentive out of drugs truly reduce gang problems? Or are there at least two other scenarios: one where there was "no effect", and one where there was an unintended "compounding" effect. It also examines drug use and drug sales by gangs.

Chapter 16 examines the question, of concern to many, regarding the differences between gangs and organized crime. Here again we see the importance of examining gangs in the framework of a social organizational approach. Clearly, many criminal justice officials believe that there are some gangs that should be considered forms of organized crime.

Chapter 17 examines recent research on female gang membership and how they differ from non-gang members when matched by race, age, and education. It also examines aspects related to female members of gangs, and the issue about the rights of children as this pertains to the gang problem in America. Chapter 18 focuses on another unique aspect of gangs: Asian gang members.

Chapter 19 looks at family life and aspects about the family in relationship to gangs. Similarly, chapter 20 examines the community's role in dealing with gangs.

Chapter 21 involves a review of those issues, problems, and new directions in law enforcement relevant to gangs. It also examines adjudication and statutory problems regarding the handling of gang crimes. Data from recent research is also summarized here.

Chapter 22 focuses entirely on the gang problem as it is experienced in adult correctional institutions. It shows some of the unique problems faced by correctional facilities and their limited choices in dealing with the gang problem. It also discusses the need for standards governing the control of gangs in custody. Data from recent research on this issue is also provided and discussed.

Chapter 23 examines the parallel problem of gangs and juvenile correctional institutions. This is based on recent national research and shows that gangs are truly a national problem. Again, much new information from national research on aspects of this problem are provided.

Chapter 24 discusses the importance of gang intervention and gang prevention initiatives. It describes some of the strategies and policies relevant for communities, educational institutions, and correctional institutions. It provides an analysis of those service components and program initiatives used in the past, and some new suggestions, for efforts involving gang intervention.

Chapter 25 provides a review and analysis of some of the gang programs around the country. It describes some of the best and some of the worst of such service programs. It critically addresses the issue of gang leaders being the administrators of government funded gang programs. Chapter 26 discusses gang theory and what exactly a gang theory should be able to explain about gang life today.

Chapter 27, in conclusion, seeks to integrate our knowledge about gangs and discusses the gang problem in terms of what the future holds. This closing chapter examines our options as a society for dealing with the gang problem.

SUMMARY

In criminological research, as in any research, the term gang must ultimately be put to test. It must be a concept that can be measured to be a meaningful concept. Clearly, there have been many loose definitions of what constitutes a gang in the literature. More precision is needed. Thus, the definitive criteria of what constitutes a gang is a central focus of this book in order to clarify more than confuse.

There is reason to be concerned about the gang crime problem in America. Minimally we need to know if gang-related crimes make up a large or small share of our national crime statistics. Unfortunately, little such hard, factual information exists. This too will be the focus on ongoing discussion in this book.

Additionally, a large number of persons who work in the criminal justice system --- in law enforcement, corrections, probation, parole, judges, private security, and others, as well as program/service/intervention staff, teachers and many others dealing with the problems of gang crime on a daily basis --- need as part of their training a comprehensive analysis of gangs in America today. This book may not answer all their questions. But it attempts to address all the major issues.

This book involves many sources of information and a variety of different research methods and research projects dealing with gangs. It uses official sources, it uses survey methods, it uses the oral history method or case studies, it uses secondary analysis; in short all known sources of information. Where the author has been selective about sources is in not including much from our newspaper accounts about gangs[27]. There is much good journalism being focused on gangs and dealing with topics that are worthy of investigation, and where ever possible some of these better media sources have been cited in the book as well.

Finally, we have not at this stage addressed the matter of what really makes a "gang" a gang. Or an effective gang, or a "threatening" versus a "non-threatening" gang for that matter. That is the focus of chapter two, and beyond. Chapter two begins to address this matter. The issue of gang classification, gang characteristics, factors on which gangs do or may be expected to vary.

DISCUSSION QUESTIONS

(1) Assume Bobby J. and Billy K. are both members of an organized criminal gang. Acting on their own to increase their joint income they rob a store. Does that robbery count as a "gang-related crime"? Or is "gang-related crime" limited to those offenses that are officially sanctioned and approved in advance in a conspiratorial manner by the official full gang? If they had to share some of the loot from the robbery with their gang leader, would it be a gang crime then?

(2) If a significant portion of crime in America becomes known to involve "gang-related crimes", then would our traditional response to crime (e.g., imprisonment) be the best solution when our correctional system has historically been based on the lone offender, or could gangs become more organized in the correctional setting and operate more efficiently than correctional staff, or even function to become the de facto administrators of their correctional facility?

(3) Why would gangs emerge or organize along ethnic lines? And would the most effective gang be one that is racially/ethnically integrated or one that is homogeneous?

FOOTNOTES

1. "The Little Rascals" was a TV series produced by Hal Roach in the 1930s. The series involves neighborhood kids, with a clubhouse at times, who are not adult supervised. Because they are not adult supervised some authors today would still consider them a gang. The present author does not consider them a real gang. Only a group involved in crime or benefiting from crime, over time, is a gang in the authors definition.

2. A criminologist should be a social scientist --- someone who does not simply take an "official" definition as the gospel. In prisons today, some religious groups are classified by correctional administrators as "threat groups", essentially treated the same way gangs are.

3. Gangs represent a group, collective behavior, organizational patterns, and other features that have historically been the turf of sociology. However, other disciplines have much to add to this area of study --- and these include the perspectives from law, psychology, social service administration/social work, human development, urban studies, anthropology, corrections and criminal justice, and other areas of specialization in the social sciences.

4. Vigil and Yun (in Huff, 1990: p. 159) describe the uniqueness of Vietnamese youth gangs in not having a name even within their group "for fear that it would invite police recognition". Thus, a secret society with criminal functions would also be a gang in this sense.

5. Malcolm Klein's definition of gang is that the members "recognize themselves as a denotable group (almost invariably with a group name)". This is generally accurate and covers most of the gang problem.

6. Gorn (1987) reports the case of massive public attendance at a gang leader's funeral, involving 250,000 people back in 1855. What all gangs and those in the funeral procession seemed to have in common was their social class.

7. The informed reader will note that the tourist industry in Chicago has adapted itself to this problem. Bus tours now routinely take tourists through the city to show them where Al Capone conducted business, where mobsters were slain, etc. An "Al Capone" museum was recently opened as a tourist attraction in Chicago as well. A bar in Peotone, Illinois is locally referred to as "Capone's place" and features a large picture of Al Capone and a sign reading "Gangsters Hall"; again a kind of reverence shown to figures like Al Capone.

8. The bibliography for this book shows over 50 such contributions during the 1970s to the study of gangs or gang members. There was in no sense, then, a "black out" on gang studies.

9. Perhaps contrary to many of such author intentions, they have also communicated by their provincial analyses that the only gang threat in America is that by "persons of color". Or that, there is no problem with Ku Klux Klan members, right wing extremists, hate groups that commit bias crimes and engage in anti-semitism, etc. In fact, our data shows groups like the Ku Klux Klan and the Aryan Brotherhood, and others prone to engage in bias crimes and illegal acts of anti-Semitism are very much a current problem facing America today.

10. It is important to note, historically, that in spite of this problem there have been significant efforts that have induced much effect in terms of using criminal justice resources to target organizations as the focus of investigation. We need only recall how in the 1950s the American Communist Party was the target of an enormous investigation.

11. The research in Hyde Park by Shireman, et al showed adolescent versions of the street corner group (Liebow, 1967; Anderson, 1978), but which were faced with fearful adults in the area who were most prone to define them as a gang or "up to no good".

12. The State of California, in its penal code, sections 186.20 through 186.27 has the "Street Terrorism Enforcement and Prevention Act" which is addressed towards gang suppression. It has become an important tool for intelligence and prosecution.

13. See: "6 Abortion Foes Are 1st Charged Under New Law", Chicago Tribune, June 7, 1994, Section 1, p. 3. These were the six arrested in Milwaukee.

14. According to some sources, we might add to this list the case of Synanon. A drug treatment organization that for years was recognized as the best in the business. Then the press and mass media uncovered how the organization had controlled vast economic enterprises, operated with the use of firearms, and was less than a organization with a "wholesome" appearance.

15. Some states do not consider groups like the Aryan Brotherhood or Ku Klux Klan "gangs"; rather they are considered "hate groups". Presumably hate groups prone to crime.

16. It would appear to be somewhat discriminatory to consider group criminal behavior as "gang crime" when it is committed by groups who consist predominantly of racial minority group members, and not applying the same standard to white groups who also engage in such continuing criminal behavior patterns. This is particularly important in terms of the legal validity of enforcing gang abatement or gang crime statutes. Allowing groups like the Aryan Brotherhood to escape the investigative and prosecutorial thrust of anti-gang legislation may make such statutes unconstitutional (see Destro, 1993: p. 235).

17. The issue is: is it illegal to prepare for suicide or simulate it under the laws of the country in which this particular tragedy occurred? If they knew it was illegal to self-destruct, or encourage others to do so, then it is a criminal code violation behavior over time, a crime of violence, not income-producing crime.

18. Obviously, social scientists are always free to use some literary license here in defining what they think should be considered to be gang behavior, just as criminologists rejecting the legalist definition of crime are free to declare what they think should be a crime. Such a list is potentially endless, particularly for youths given the tendency of adults to view with alarm any non-conformity among youths; and the historical tendency of each new adult generation to declare its youth population "gone to the dogs". The analytical focus here, to repeat, is on crime; not deviance; not "ill", "malo", or "immoral" behavior; and not even on what should be legislated as crime.

19. The Ku Klux Klan and related political extremist groups are clearly included in the definition of criminal gang. Obviously, like some of our more organized gangs to be discussed in later chapters, some may believe they are really emergent varieties of organized crime.

20. Typical examples of actual crimes committed involve: bombing business establishments and painting graffiti, such as anti-Semitic threats on synagogues. See: "Supremacist Guilty in Bombing, Vandalism", Chicago Sun-Times, Sept. 14, 1994, p. 19.

21. Some gang analysts see only three possibilities: youth gangs, hate groups, and organized crime. The problem is, this is not a classification system where logic is on our side. Youths can be members of hate groups, and of organized crime. Some groups loosely considered "youth gangs" may simply mean "youth members" of various types of gangs, indeed: gangs whose top leadership structure is not in any sense "youth controlled", but is rather driven by adults with long criminal records.

22. The chapter on gangs in the adult correctional institutions also addresses this issue: for example, two such gangs were felt to exist only inside prisons in Illinois (e.g., Northsiders, and the S.I.A.). However, recent additional research has now shown "Northsiders" to be an identification used at the jail inmate level as well.

23. Let us keep a historical perspective here on the armed offender in the gang context. Prior to 1968 anyone in America could readily acquire firearms over the counter, through the mail, etc. If Thrasher's gangs wanted them, at that time in history they could also purchase as much dynamite as they wanted in local hardware stores. Both explosives and weapons laws changed dramatically in 1968, making it somewhat more difficult for offenders to acquire these instruments of destruction.

24. See: "Feds Can Help Cities Fight Gangs, FBI Says", by Jerry Moskal, Chicago Sun-Times, Feb. 10, 1994, p. 8.

25. Shortly after the first edition of this book appeared in 1991, the National Youth Gang Information Center appeared as an information service on gangs similar to what the National Criminal Justice Reference Service does. But all it did was collect information on gang research, particularly federally funded projects on gangs. At the time of the second edition (1993), the NYGIC was under threat of closing and being absorbed by the NCJRS. It is now gone completely. A separate national clearinghouse on gangs and gang intelligence is still sorely needed. The fact that federal leadership on this has been lacking has resulted recently in correctional gang intelligence coordinators forming their own clearinghouse.

26. Actually, at this writing, such a national analysis of actual gang programs is underway; tracking all federal and foundation support to programs involving "gangs" or "gang members". The full and complete book on recent and contemporary gang programs has not yet been written. I am working on it now.

27. This is not in any sense to denigrate journalism, in fact while some authors condemn the mass media for being "alarmists" the role of the media is also very positive when it documents the role of racial conflict in the study of gangs. Much information of that nature has emerged in the printed media. We should also recall that being a newspaper reporter was one of the background skills before training in sociology that Thrasher brought to bear on the analysis of gangs (see Geis, 1965: p. 17).

CHAPTER 2

CLASSIFICATION FACTORS FOR GANG ANALYSIS

INTRODUCTION

Science begins with classification. The best form of classification would be that of the typology. A typology must meet two fundamental rules: (1) The categories must be exhaustive --- that is to say, the classification covers the entire gamut and the full spectrum of possibilities, there can be no exceptions to its categories, and (2) The categories must be mutually exclusive --- that is to say, something can fit into only one category, not two or more. This chapter describes those factors that may be useful for gang classification, threat analysis, and typology development. Classification, for example in the field of corrections, is also fundamental to effective processing and management.[1] We must examine factual data and background factors. In the correctional setting, we must also take into account adjustment factors. These are important and allow for public agencies like correctional institutions to more effectively carry out their mission. The same, it will be found, is true in the study of gangs.

Threat analysis, or applying screening for risk and profiling to gangs, must also be research based: using those factors known from research on gangs to predict and correctly assess their objective crime threat. That is, to be useful, and to hold up in court, it must be empirically demonstrated that such factors can significantly differentiate high risks of crime or violence from low risks. The rise of gang intelligence positions throughout the American criminal justice system in recent years is a response to the gang threat problem. The direction of such developments seems to be headed towards something similar to Targeted Offender Programs, where strategic purposes of intelligence prove invaluable, particularly in gang member database development, and gang member tracking systems.

This chapter will not provide a full classification system, it will only identify some of the major factors that should probably be included in it. In a later chapter this classification approach will yield four such gang classification categories in terms of their level of organizational development and crime threat. How these factors might be figured into a scheme for examining the differences in gangs along organizational dimensions will be illustrated later in the book. We will alert the reader now, however, what the author means by Level Zero, Level One, Level Two, and Level Three gangs.

A Level Zero gang, in the typology developed by author, is not a true gang at all, it is at worst a "pre-gang". It is in the language of sociology an informal group. It is the kind of clique or "Spanky and Alfalfa" group that most human beings have belonged to. Some call a youth group unsupervised by adults a gang, unfortunately if we accepted this definition of "gang", then we could easily estimate how many gang members there are in the United States: over two hundred million, because everyone at one point or another during their childhood has done this. But this would confuse more than it elucidates in the field of criminology. That is why the present author would not include such play groups or Level Zero gangs and their members in any stimate of criminal gangs and their members: because they are not a part of the ational crime picture. A Level One gang, in the typology developed by the author nd discussed in greater detail elsewhere in this book, is an emergent gang, typically onsisting of only one unit of operation. It may be less structured as an entity of uman organization. All members belong and clearly function as a small organiza-ion, but a type of informal organization, without written rules typically. It typically onsists of only one unit of operation.

A Level Two gang, in the typology developed by the author, is a crystallized gang and as a definite structure. It is comparable to what could be called the formal group. t typically consists of several units of operation that are not geographically ontiguous.

A Level Three gang, in the typology developed by the author, is sometimes called the supergang" or the "corporate" gang. It is a highly structured gang. It can be egarded in classical sociological language as a formal organization. It may include umerous "chapters", "sets", or franchises throughout an entire society. A number f such gangs are found in almost all states (i.e., Aryan Brotherhood, Bloods, Crips, Jangster Disciples, Latin Kings, Vice Lords, etc). This type of gang typically has ormalized its "code", and may have a written constitution and by-laws. Several examples of these types of written constitutions and by-laws, and other internal vritten memoranda are provided in the appendices of this book.

Thus, in the authors typology the levels zero through four for types of gangs at a igher level of abstraction, simply reflect the level of organizational development in hese gangs.

n order not to overwhelm the student, however, the full typology advanced by the uthor will be presented and discussed at points further in this book where it is ppropriate. Because the student must first understand the classification factors that night be used, the history of gangs, and a number of other empirical trends about gang members. In doing so, an incremental approach will be made. This will be ased on the literature and on previous research. The objective is to provide a omprehensive set of factors that can be used for gang classification. These factors re also important in quantifying any gang threat assessment.

n specifying the various organizational features of gangs, it is possible to therefore expect as many different variations and permutations as there are such factors on vhich to classify them. This would not, however, offer a manageable approach to leveloping a gang typology. In practice we can expect hundreds, perhaps thousands, f such unique variations when a large number of such factors exist.

The following discussion therefore encompasses those factors which are relevant to gang classification.

One of the questions that is frequently asked of gang experts in America is "which s the most dangerous gang in America today?". That question can only be answered vith reference to those factors which spell out the differential ability of gangs to exist and function in society. Thus, the factors discussed below can be used to classify gangs along dimensions of risk. These factors also help understand the myriad of ways in which a gang, as a form of social organization, develops and strives fo greater sophistication.

LEVEL OF ORGANIZATION

Obviously, gangs vary by this factor, we do have criminal gangs that are not wel organized and we have some that are very organized. This is the basis of the author typology. This helps to make sense out of the literature on gangs, because some authors will simply deny that gangs have any organization, that is they are simpl "near groups", not even real groups! Recently Spergel wrote "despite some polic and media reports, especially reports by national law enforcement agencies, stree gang organization and crime patterns are not highly organized" (1994: p. 3).[2] Thi may be an example of over-generalizing, because we do not have a complete nationa picture nor a very good empirical basis to say much about the national picture whe we do not know how much crime gang members commit or even how many gan members actually exist. It is safer to assume that natural variation exists in the leve of organizational sophistication of gangs. The fact is there are highly organize gangs, some do exist, and we cannot simply define them out of our analysis by sayin "oh, those are organized crime groups" without at least documenting when and hov the "street gang" transformed itself into a higher category of threat. Organized crim groups are, as will be illustrated in a later chapter, the epitome of gang crime. Why Because they are criminal organizations.

LEADERSHIP

A gang crime specialist in Chicago once remarked that "gang leaders have been shor in physical stature". They need not be intellectual giants either. But some level o charisma and an ability to use wits and cunning is presumably necessary. Being trained military veteran might help. Krisberg (1975, Chapter VI) sees the mos conspicuous feature of gang leadership as being "their superior verbal ability... capacity to deliver emotional speeches" (Krisberg, 1975: p. 74); that is, "verba talent...excellent language control...verbal abilities" (ibid, p. 75).

No doubt about it, there are different classifications of leadership. Our socia sciences can help here. Thrasher's (1927) analysis suggests it is simply a matter o "natural leaders", or being older than followers. But today, does gang leadership fi the "crude democracy" pattern described by Thrasher? Or, as will be explained late in this book, is this leadership attribution mostly applicable to the lower end of the gang development spectrum. That is to say, we might assume some variation i leadership style along with differences in the level of organizational developmen among gangs. It is an issue, also, of "gang tenure": how long has the gang existed a a group entity?

It is probably too late to study this feature in its natural formative stages, but prison would have been great opportunities to study the natural history of offender leaders. Today, most prisons are highly impregnated with gangs. It is too late to be able to go in and set up an opportunity for leadership emergence and to study the characteristics of those who can dominate relatively innocuous prison organization (Jaycees, A.A./N.A., Toastmasters, etc, etc). The problem with seeking to do thi kind of study today would be that gangs already exist in these prisons and would naturally want to have some influence over these groups. Or these groups do not control the kind of resources that other sub rosa groups can control within the prison population, making them of little interest to the continuing offender.

Gang leaders in larger more structured gangs may be regarded as God-like figures to younger members of the gang. Most gang leaders at the upper end of the gang income flow are older adults. Often in their 40's and 50's. Some of these gang leaders are able to effectively run their gang operations from behind prison bars[4]. A typical description of a gang leader of a level three gang, like the El Rukns, was that description of Jeff Fort as follows:

"It was Fort's charisma, and his amazing recruiting skills, that made him special. He traveled with an entourage, wearing snappy clothes that dictated neighborhood fasion, and when he walked by Woodlawn's elementary schools, kids on the playground would pile up on the fence just to get a look at him."[5]

TERRITORIALITY

Presumably a gang must lay some claim to control of a specific turf. However, there are some known exceptions and it is worth further discussion (see Hardman, 1969: p. 176).[6]   Basically, most gangs do arise and have a local network with a specific geographical pattern of activity. They even recognize the specific boundaries of gang domination. But some gangs do not. The Aryan Brotherhood would seem to be a gang group, found in many prisons nationally, that on the outside of the prison has no specific territorial control at least that has yet been reported in the literature.[7] Also, there do exist "hybrids" as gang formations. Turf defense is most conspicuous as a gang feature in the early stages of gang formation; and at the higher end of organizational development when turf also equates to market share or marketing area (e.g., drug distribution). Inside the correctional institution, turf can have its symbolic equivalent: an exercise area, etc, where turf translates to a "controlled resource" rather than "home".

Some believe the gang problem in America is easy to explain: it is nothing more than a "territorial imperative". That is, of course, an over-generalization and fails to consider the more important factors also discussed in this chapter on gang organizational features. Turf today for many criminal gangs in America means drug distribution territory.

INTERNAL ORGANIZATION

There must be a certain level of sophistication regarding internal organization. This means a hierarchy of authority, a chain of command, and the division of labor. It is difficult to imagine anything being classified as a gang without some level of internal organization.   On the other hand, gangs do differ on the factor of internal organization. We shall learn more about this in subsequent chapters.

Some of these internal functions include recruitment, discipline, inculcating the gang code of values, and other functions such as preventing defection.[8] How a gang spends its "treasury" tells us a lot about internal functions. If it is spending its money on guns and drugs, for example, its function is predisposed towards crime. Internal organization also means having at least a second layer of leadership: those who have sufficient experience or education to be on a "council", or to serve in a function of mid-management (e.g., "one star Maliks" in the Vice Lords, etc). For example, in the Brothers of the Struggle (B.O.S., aka Gangster Disciples), there is a "Board of Directors" composed of the Chairman (the top gang leader, "King" Larry Hoover) at the top of a rather complex organizational structure.

EXTERNAL ORGANIZATION

To function effectively, a gang must have alliances and outside connections, often with other gangs or subcultures. The highest level of functioning would be to have an apparatus that is capable of paying off local politicians and local law enforcement, as well as facilitating rewards for staff who work in the correctional facilities where gang members are incarcerated. External organization includes other resources such as political alliances and resources mobilization generally. In other words, a gang that has a lawyer on call 24-hours a day has a higher level of external organization than one that does not.

The important aspect about external organization is the public relations function a modern gang needs today. When a South Central Los Angeles member of the Crips uses the expression "we have only love for South Central", they use like many gangs a code word or subcultural argot. To a South Central Crip, "love" has the meaning: let our vision educate. Gang literature often provides some aspect of this propaganda function by presenting the gang image as something "positive" (e.g., fighting oppression, helping the community, etc). This dual image is very functional for a gang and some gangs go to enormous expense and effort to be able to present a positive public image. This includes providing fully catered large scale picnics such as that held at Starved Rock in 1992 to celebrate the gang leader Larry Hoover's birthday[a]. Existing community groups find gangs more than eager to cooperate with them, particularly when such groups are willing to hire their gang members as "liaison"/street workers, etc, because some gangs clamor for positive publicity. What young children hear about during gang recruitment are the external organizational features: the myth of the gang, its "front", its claim to be a protector of the community, its claim to be a defender of traditional values such as peace, loyalty, justice, you name it.

Many experts on cults offer us some additional insight into the way gangs gain new members. Cults like gangs have always existed in America.[9] In Chicago during the 1994 political season, a gang political activist defended the Gangster Disciples by saying the gang does not have to recruit members, rather than members want to join the gang. Cult experts remind us that in cults, the typical cult member is not necessarily recruited as a member; rather the person is deceptively seduced and

---

a This event sponsored by the gang was very professionally done involving lot of rented buses, their own "picnic police", special T-Shirts, and obviously represented a major cost in food alone for about 1,000 or more persons. The event was also professionally videotaped (12 hours) by law enforcement.

enticed to join the cult. The gang has a similar variation to this cultural universal cult recruitment mechanism. And it works quite effectively on young children.

The reason a criminal gang adopts the "public relations" gimmick of claiming it has prosocial aspects, or may even want to venture into politics or community action, is real simple to understand. A gang that claims it is a political or religious group can hide from law enforcement investigation behind constitutional grounds. A gang that can claim it does something for the community allows it to deflect law enforcement attention. A child whose parent discovers he is in a gang, say the Gangster Disciples, can immediately claim to the parent that "we are not gangbangers, we are about growth and development for the community".

RELIGIOUS OR POLITICAL TRAPPINGS

This issue is examined elsewhere in the book, but it basically means the gang uses a religious or political front for its public image. It also means providing a basis for organizing and attracting members. This helps in prison and on the streets where the gang can hide behind constitutional safeguards. Willie Lloyd, leader of Chicago's Unknown Vice Lords, developed an extensive written guide to what was called "The Amalgamated Order of Lordism", a religious identity that was superimposed on the gang's business: drug dealing.[10] Willie Lloyd could use his "public relations function", his identity as a "do gooder", to claim he was a contributor to a "gang peace treaty" or truce in Chicago, in fact he was granted an award in an official ceremony held by school officials at Chicago's Englewood Public High School. Lloyd just did not come and accept the award, because at the time members of his own gang were trying to assassinate him and the federal government was also investigating him.

Jeff Fort was the master of this charade and provided the blueprint for other gangs to follow. Fort used religion as a springboard for his first major foray in gang organization --- conning a minister to help him get money for the gang (i.e., Rev. Fry), and later establishing his empire as a legal religious identity, owning real estate under the same identity. The religious identity --- Moorish Science Temple of America and Islamic influences --- was just a front.

Gang members in prison know this routine: they go to chapel to act like they are a prayer group, but it is just a meeting place for the gang members to transact business. African-American gang members seem clearly represented in the religious front, just like neo-nazis who use the Identity Church variations for their front. It is an interesting twist, that according to one source a member can effectively leave one gang, the Latin Kings, if the member makes a genuine conversion to religious life; that is, the individual must be sincere for it to be effective, because if it was just a ploy and the individual is caught subsequently in a compromised situation he will be violated the same way he would as if he tried to simply quit the organization --- a three minute "head to toe", which involves the exiting member standing in front of two of the largest members of the chapters who will beat the member for three minutes, and the member cannot fight back, if he fights back he may die. The three minute "head to toes" are in some cases replaced with a bullet to the knee.

WRITTEN RULES, CONSTITUTIONS AND INTERNAL GANG LITERATURE

Surprisingly, for the level of literacy and educational under-attainment that is so often typical of many individual gang members --- at least that is an "image" we get from much of the literature, some contemporary gangs have written codes and written rules (i.e., constitution and bylaws). Some examples of these gang constitutions are provided in the appendices. Some gang researchers point to the fact that this may have arisen because once a gang leader is imprisoned he has much time to spend applying his interests to gang development. No doubt about it, many of the written codes that are widely circulating throughout the criminological community regarding gangs have been confiscated while in some form of correctional custody (prisons, jails, etc).

Not all of this type of evidence surfaces within the walls of corrections. Gang crimes officers routinely come across this material. Over ten years ago, in carrying out oral history studies of gang members, and in evaluating programs designed to rehabilitate gang offenders, I routinely had individuals willing to turn over their written gang codes to me. Later in this text, it will be shown how in the early 1800s a group existed (similar to the Aryan Brotherhood) which also had such an elaborate written constitution and by-laws. Also, some contemporary examples of written constitutions from major contemporary gangs will be analyzed. Parents sometimes discover the "homework" that new young gang recruits are studying: it is not school books, it is more often than not the gang "prayers" and constitution. These kind of documents are readily available from a variety of sources including the gang members themselves[b].

The internal gang literature also includes poems and prayers of various sorts. Figure 1 provides an example of one such poem from the Aryan Brotherhood. Some larger gangs have been around so long and are large enough (e.g., Crips, Black Gangsters) that some of their members have formed musical bands that have produced their own musical tapes and records (e.g., rap music). Such songs as much as they exemplify an art form and offer a way to perpetuate the symbols and values of the gang are also important aspects of organizational capability.

Figure 2 provides an example of such a poem for the Brothers of the Struggle (BOS), that is, their "Prayer". Inside the Illinois prisons the Black Disciples (the Freeman faction of the Disciples) and the Gangster Disciples (the Hoover faction of the Disciples) basically "ride together".[11]

---

[b] This fact that such constitutions do exist and that they have not previously been given any attention or discussion by some authors who have studied some of these gangs (whose constitutions are provided in the Appendices), may render their findings suspect. That is, if such authors were really studying "gang leaders" or had any level of serious penetration into the gang, they would have come across these documents. Even to an anthropologist such documents are a goldmine of information on the codified values and beliefs of a gang.

FIGURE 1

A Poem of the Aryan Brotherhood

An Aryan Brother is without a care,
He walks where the weak and heartless won't dare.
And if by chance he should stumble and lose control,
His brothers will be there, to help him reach his goal.
For a worthy brother, no need is too great,
He need not but ask, fulfillment's his fate.

For an Aryan Brother, death holds no fear,
Vengeance will be his, through his brothers still here.
For the Brotherhood means just what it implies,
A brother's a brother, till that brother dies.
And if he is loyal, and never lost faith,
In each brother's heart, will always be a place.

So a brother am I and always will be,
Even after my life is taken from me.
I'll lie down content, knowing I stood,
Head held high, walking proud in Brotherhood.

FIGURE 2

B.O.S. PRAYER

Looking out the window as far as I can see,
All my BOS Brothers standing around me,
GD's and BD's has combined,
As we both unite our star will shine,
King David he recruited, gave the (G)
Strength on the street,
He recruited the (D) on the history of our G
We will last forever,
As the Brothers of the Struggle,
Struggle together.

ETHNIC HOMOGENEITY

Ethnicity should encompass culture, skin color, country of origin, and language[12]. Generally, gangs are ethnically homogeneous; that is, their membership constitutes a majority of a certain ethnic group. There are no known Jewish members of the Tongs. Gangs tend to be ethnocentric. This need not be, from a strict theoretical viewpoint. In fact, perhaps the most powerful gang conceivable would be one that was thoroughly integrated. The reasoning here is obvious: domination and control relies on ability to as smoothly as possible have as much penetration of the illicit market place as possible, and the more diverse the ethnic and linguistic content of the gang membership then the higher its capability for national and even international operations.[13]

One recent development in areas outside of larger urban gang scenes, has been the situation where gangs using larger well-known names often associated with a specific race, are in fact very integrated along racial lines. That is, it is not to find white kids not only active but holding leadership roles in gangs often thought to include only African-Americans. The possibility of a rainbow gang could prove to be a formidable challenge. For as will be seen in the chapter on organized crime, there is a real limiting effect when the gang is homogeneous with respect to race or ethnicity.

SHIFTING MEMBERSHIP

While it is a common practice for gang members to have their own business cards printed up with their gang logo imprinted on it, it is not the case in gang organization that all gangs are the equivalent regarding membership patterns. In the Aryan Brotherhood, for example, one of their favorite slogans is "kill to get in, die to get out", implying specifically, that you can never "drop your flag", that if you become a member then you become a member for life.

Our gang literature is not in agreement on this matter of whether it is easy or difficult to voluntarily terminate gang membership. The reason for this lack of consensus is not theoretical or analytical. It reflects simply the fact that our literature is quite diverse on the levels of gang sophistication data being analyzed. Certainly, at the lower end of the gang organizational development spectrum, it is probably easy to say "I quit". But at the higher end of organizational sophistication that same intent could mean "termination with prejudice". Most gangs found in the prison system are of the "no quit" variety. Camp and Camp (1985: p. ix) showed that "in nearly two-thirds of the gangs, membership is perceived as a life-time commitment, "blood in, blood out".

The issue is paying dues and showing allegiance to the gang organization. A gang where a member can "float in" and "float out" as he or she chooses is less effective than one with strict guidelines regarding membership obligations.

We shall later analyze in greater detail this factor of group commitment, particularly in relationship to policy choices regarding gang dismemberment.

ROLE DEFINITIONS

One of the most interesting areas of research on prisoners has been those roles that they are allowed to take on within the correctional institution. There are many such roles that are legitimated for inmates. There are other roles that are regarded as being taboo (snitch, informant, etc). That gangs should provide the same kind of role differentiation is to be expected.

Clearly, it is known that one of the essential roles that must be filled in any gang organization is that of the disciplinarian. Someone who metes out punishment for violating gang mandates. Someone who is the "chief of violations".

Role definition is a matter of the bureaucratization of a gangs infrastructure. Ideally, the more status-enhancing roles that exist, the higher the rewardive capability of the gang; and the more it can integrate those who themselves experience a competitive social existence. America is a status-seeking society. Gangs can provide such status. The organizational infrastructure of the typical gang delineates various roles and functions which can be assigned to gang members.

LEVEL OF COHESION

Much of the literature on gangs is in agreement on the simple issue that gangs generally show some level of cohesion. However, gangs do vary on this factor, as do all types of social organizations. Clearly, anyone who studies organizational life will find that in addition to the existence of an actual formal organization, all such organizations also have an informal social organization. We would therefore expect the same for gang organizations. There is competition and there can be strife and there can be leadership battles within a gang. Cohesion shows in mobilization and in attaining group goals and in accomplishing group objectives.

LEVEL OF MORALE

Generally, as in the military analogy, the higher the morale the higher the effectiveness of organizational performance. However, we can also expect morale to vary over time because of the periodic imprisonment or interruptions in gang functioning that are brought about, often randomly, by law enforcement initiatives. In the case of Chicago's El Rukns, the high number of ranking gang members who were willing to testify in federal court tends to bring with it an unrecognized measure of fighting the gangs from a law enforcement perspective: the fact that group morale deteriorates rapidly when multiple members are found to be in complicity with government prosecutors. Also, from the viewpoint of psychological warfare, it is generally known that there are measures that can be taken to erode morale. The point here is that morale, like self-esteem, is a factor subject to much variation over time and by experience.

NORMATIVE CONSENSUS

Simply stated, do the members of a particular gang agree on what is expected of them in terms of conduct and behavior? There is a significant organizational climate difference between a gang which has explicit norms and mores in comparison with one that manifests a high degree of normlessness or anomie. This is a way of distinguishing between what some call the highly organized gang and the "loose knit" gang. Like any organization, the higher the normative consensus, the more effective it can be expected to perform. Conversely, a gang that has few such internalized guidelines for personal conduct can be expected to experience varying degrees of internal conflict between members --- simply because they do not agree on what is or is not expected of them. In some gangs "tree jumping" (a gang phrase for rape) might be approved of on a conditional basis if it is a target of opportunity or if it involves a rival gang or its turf; while in other gangs this particular type of personal conduct might be considered taboo and sanctionable. In the Black Gangster

Disciple's literature, for example, forcible rape of an another prison/jail inmate is expressly forbidden; but consensual favors in terms of homosexual sex would apparently be allowed.

Gangs today enforce their internal norms by the use of rigid discipline involving fines and physical punishment. To break the gang rules as a member may often bring about more punishment than would occur from the existing law enforcement structure. More importantly, some things that are "crimes" as defined inside the gang ideology are not really "illegal" per se. A common version is "dropping the flag", or not upholding the honor of the gang organization; there is no law that compels someone to be a hero or to be a loyal member of any civilian organization, but in the gang this kind of "violation" brings about a most violent punishment.   Gangs use such internal codes and behavioral expectations to increase the compliance structure of members. The more such internal gang rules and gang "laws" are enforced, the more the gang exerts its own formal social control over members by the use of force and punitive sanctions.

MEMBERSHIP EXPECTATIONS

What the command structure of a gang can consistently rely on from its members in terms of level of effort, resources, and time allocation has much to do with its organizational effectiveness. A gang requiring regular dues, that has meetings at which attendance is expected or a fine is levied, that charges special "franchise taxes" for drug operations/chop shop operations/extortion gambits, etc, is different from one that has a laissez faire philosophy. It is a matter of organizational centralization of the focus of personal identity as well. We would hypothesize that the higher or the clearer the membership expectations, the greater the organizational performance of the gang. Thus, the higher its potential threat as well.

Even former members of large gangs like the Black Gangster Disciples can be counted on for "aid and support" when confronted by current members of the gang. One female member of this same gang (an "intellectual sister", or S.O.S., Sister of the Struggle, the female counterpart of the B.O.S.) who is now attending college described how she was essentially forced to sign a petition demanding the parole of the B.O.S. gang leader during the summer of 1993. The gang members came to her house and asked her to sign. Could she have really said "no"? Not at some significant personal and imminent risk of harm!

LEVEL OF STABILITY

Stability has to do with both control over existing operations and the organizational membership and its hierarchy. A gang that changes chiefs frequently is one that has a low level of stability. A gang that cannot maintain its share of the illicit market is one with a low level of stability. Stability also has to do with the matter of aging membership. In other words, a gang that loses members to a rival gang because of the more lucrative or higher rewardive capability of the rival gang has a lower level of organizational stability in terms of its ability to keep and promote its recruits. A highly stable gang is one that will have its own investment portfolio, with a capability to provide a gang members family with its own form of subsidized housing in a residential building owned by the gang, or provide legitimate employment in a business owned by the gang to a "straight" family member.

LEADERSHIP QUALITY

The quality of leadership is perhaps the most vital ingredient in terms of any perspective that seeks to undermine or erode gang influence.   Many gang researchers have commented on the emotional or psychological instability of gang leaders. As if it communicated to the rank and file, "hell, what will he do next?" Generally we must be willing to assume that someone that is more emotionally stable, who is fair, who is impartial, who weighs the facts, who provides the kind of image that most Americans would prefer in a boss, would generally have an organization more effective than one with the obverse characteristics.

To my knowledge, few discussions of management style have been provided about gang organizations in America. And yet from an organizational perspective this is most essential! We can generally assume that many, such as Al Capone, have been authoritative types. But not always, because things are not always as they seem or appear to be. In fact sometimes this means in the study of crime don't believe anything you hear, and half of what you see and you will probably have an adequately scientific level of skepticism about the difficult problem of measuring and understanding crime in America. It may be that some gang leaders have a cult-like hold over their members and that the introduction of religious and ideological content into their constitutions will make some gang leaders appear to have charisma.

RECURRENT ILLEGAL ACTS

Even college and fraternity organizations periodically engage, either collectively or through individual members, in acts of deviance and/or crime. But to be considered a gang we must be willing to add the additional requirement that it be a recurring type of action.   Not a one-time act of vandalism or outrage.   Not a singular, spontaneous, event. Indeed, to be considered a gang characteristic the emphasis on illegal acts must have the quality of being recurrent, indeed ongoing.

Some legitimate groups and organizations have their own equivalent of the Mardi Gras. The Mardi Gras in our culture is a way of once a year, or in a "planned release", to let the steam valve open and "let down your hair", to "get funky".   A seasonal involvement in deviance differs clearly from a year-round capability to commit crime.

The point of this discussion is that an organizational environment that has a once a year "escape" is not generally an organization classifiable as deviant. Most voluntary associations, even professional associations, and trade groups, have what is commonly known as an annual meeting. A chance to party? Conventions!

To consider a group a gang, one of the required defining characteristics must be this factor of recurrent criminal activity. Activity committed as sub-groups of the wider organization, activity committed as members of the organization in an approved fashion, or activity committed by leaders in cooperation with lower ranking gang

members, all of this would qualify as a defining characteristic of a gang if and onl
if it was recurrent in nature. That is, if it was not an isolated incident. It mus
continue as a crime pattern over time.

AGE-GRADED   PARTICIPATION

Gangs tend to be age-graded, like many other forms of group affiliation and socia
organizations in society. This is normal social behavior. But gangs may no
necessarily be homogeneous with respect to age. That is to say, we have yet to see
a gang in America that has its own retirement home for aging gang members[1]
Then perhaps we would see the true organizational epitome in the development o
gangs in America. As extensions of a community or orientation, many gangs are
intergenerational in nature. Typically, however, the leaders of the more serious
gangs (the ones we have to worry about) are not youths, but are adults. The term
"youth gang" is therefore only a heuristic device.

Age-graded participation does not mean necessarily having the complete life span
accounted for, it means having specific roles available for special age categories, i
means status variation by age. A gang can be a young gang, a teenage group. A
gang can also be an adult-teen gang. A gang can be an adult-only group. And
theoretically, a gang can be a complete age-span organization having the capability
to integrate members regardless of age status.[15]

One characteristic of most gang research and gang literature is that it specifies the
attraction that gangs have for youths in America.[16] Particularly because of the
special problems associated with the transition from youth to adulthood in America
We need only recall that the transition from youth to adulthood in America can be
a turbulent period. A period of maladjustment. A period of chaos, of confusion.

These are conditions ripe for the recruitment of youthful members. Like a cult
group carrying out a marketing analysis, looking for ways to recruit new members,
a gang would probably rely heavily on the works of social scientists like Erik
Erickson, because the identity crisis of American youth is almost universal. A major
critique of American society today is in fact that youth has lost its innocence. There
is no longer a genuine childhood free from stigma. Kids at all ages can get in
trouble today.

Kids do kill. Kids do drugs. Kids do carry and use firearms. But these are things
they must learn to do. The socialization process itself may have been significantly
altered in recent years. And yet it seems that every adult generation in America
condemns its youth as the most rebellious and most devil-worshiping generation that
has yet hit the pages of American history.

A gang composed primarily of elementary school children does not represent as
formidable a threat to public safety as does a group that also has adult gang leaders.
The modern gang has adult leaders, who usually have extensive criminal histories as
well. Most serious gangs have "pee wee" members: those being brought up into the
gang. But while youths may constitute the most visible age-graded aspect of the gang
problem, the term "youth gang" is used only sparingly in this book because it is a
phrase that may obscure more than enlighten us about "gangs".

Because of the age differences among members of the same gang, a gang like any other group or organization in society is subject to the same social processes; thus, it is not uncommon to find gang members reporting a problem of a "generation gap"; essentially, older members complaining about the lack of respect and tradition among younger members.

GENDER-GRADED   PARTICIPATION

Similar to age-graded participation is the issue of gender-graded participation. That is, separate functions and roles implied for female members of the gang. The "intellectual sisters" memorandum from the Brothers of the Struggle (B.O.S.) gang illustrates this. This document was apparently written in prison and rapidly found its way into the hands of gang members on the outside. Local Chicago gang research has revealed that some female gang members do now in fact regard themselves as "intellectual sisters" or as "Sisters of the Struggle".   These adolescent gang girls are basically getting their marching orders from imprisoned male adult gang leaders. This memo is provided in Figure 3 below.

FIGURE   3[c]

"Creed for the Intellectual Sisters

We the Intellectual sisters of the struggle believe in the teaching of our honorable chairman and executive staff. You and I will become as one and aid an assist each other and reach our fullest potential.

I feel strongly upon the six point star utilizing, Education, Economics, Political, Social Development, Unity, and Love. I will learn to look and listen to anything that may be conductive to the eccelleration of our organization.

I will strive everyday to remain an outstanding member and never abandon the struggle; Therefore with no struggle theres no progress. We are special group of sisters with love and respect for ourselves and others.

We are endowed with a great leader, together we shall see and share in his vision, as we grow to be a powerful group of intellectual sisters.

7.4"

ADVANCEMENT   OPPORTUNITY

Ask yourself, would you rather work for a local fast food "burger joint" or a local gang? Part of the answer would probably lie in the matter of opportunity for advancement. That is, how can you personally achieve your own culturally prescribed goals through involvement and participation in the gang organization?

---

[c] Transcribed exactly as it appeared in its original typed version.

Clothing, getting a car, jewelry, items of conspicuous consumption, these are the things that a gang involved in the criminal subculture can most readily offer. At least they can offer them at a more competitive basis than can working at a fast food establishment. Because there is no wait, it is a "go for the gold" situation. It is an application of the crudest form of America's spirit of capitalism --- "go for it....grab what you want".

Here, as in all organizations, think of it as the "benefit package" of employment. Most persons want an opportunity for advancement, few want a dead-end position as a foot soldier for the duration of their life span. There must at least be the hope of achieving some important material goals through such an association.

The bottom line, in gang studies, is that there is a qualitative organizational difference between one that is "growth oriented" just as an employer would offer similar opportunities. There must be opportunities to achieve personal goals within the framework of the organizational goals. There is a significant recruitment and motivational advantage for a gang that offers opportunities for advancement. Unfortunately for American citizens, as will be discovered elsewhere in this book, our traditional criminal justice response to gangs has often meant inadvertently inducing leadership training opportunities for gangs.

In modern American gangs, one of the quickest ways to get a promotion is to go to jail. Someone who carries out a "hit" behind bars may spend a couple weeks in the "hole" and come out with an automatic promotion in rank that carries over once released from jail.

PRESTIGE

Along about payday at the university some academicians may have had occasion to find themselves in the position of saying what is often remarked about professors, "we work for the status, not necessarily the bucks". A university professor scores very high in what is called the occupational prestige scale. Gangs can also confer prestige. It is a rewardive function of the organization.

How a gang confers prestige can occur along several different dimensions. It is communicated through status and role within the gang organization. It is conferred by recognition for accomplishments. The military confers medals for almost everything, the Boy Scouts confer badges for a variety of competencies, and similarly the gang organization at least has the social capability to confer similar levels of status for social recognition to its members. Some gang analysts remark, in this respect, that going to prison is no long a fear for gang members: because they might be able to meet their top gang leader, and in this way, in a social process not dissimilar from the cult member who would do anything to personally meet or be in the presence of the cult leader, the modern gang member may see prison not as a "punishment", but may rather see our modern expensive penal sanction as an "opportunity" to hook up with the top gang leadership structure.

Status and prestige go hand in hand. However, the capability to impart these conditions varies between gangs. Obviously, the gang capable of providing for these social-psychological satisfactions is the gang that is going to be more capable of keeping its rank and file members at an optimal level of morale. And the higher the morale, the higher the organizational performance.

A first lesson about Chicago politics probably goes something like this "reward your friends and punish your enemies". Clearly, the more powerful gang will be capable of rewarding its members, particularly along the dimensions of status attainment. Youths live for status, it is something they are deprived of structurally by society. A sense of "honor" is similarly important to gang members.

GANG MIGRATION VERSUS SOCIAL IMITATION AND EMULATION

Some gangs clearly do migrate, for example Vietnamese gangs that specialize in home invasion migrate from one city to the next looking for opportunities in their specialty area: robbing other Vietnamese who may keep substantial amounts of cash in their homes rather than using a bank account for their savings. This does not mean that the same Vietnamese gang specializing in home invasion is also seeking to develop a new franchise or cultivate new members in the same target areas of its criminal operations. It is important to note as well that individual gang members routinely travel domestically and abroad, so does that constitute "gang migration"? The answer has to do with intent and behavior: if the member is on a mission, it is gang migration; if the member seeks to develop his/her own chapter, it is gang migration.

Some gangs such as those that are formal organizations have roles equivalent to an "ambassador" for members who definitely seek out new areas for cultivating additional factions of the gang. This comes close to capturing what is meant by "gang imperialism", that is the intentional conquering or "taking over" of a new geographical area. It also captures what is meant by "gang franchising", that is the intentional cultivation of new chapters or sets in other jurisdictions or geographical areas, the intent of which often centers around basically developing new drug income markets.

Several other common methods by which "gang migration" occurs are basically unintended consequences. Two examples can be provided here. One of the most common is transferring gang member inmates from one state to another, or from one location to another; in their new confines, they organize a local chapter of the gang. Another unfortunately all too common way in which gangs spread is when a parent/guardian either voluntarily (after realizing the youth is a gang member and thus wants to "protect" the best interests of the child: get them out of the "hood", send them to live with the parents in the south, or in Mexico, move to the suburbs, etc) moves the child to a new residential location, or is forced to do so because the youth has come to the attention of the criminal justice system. What happens, it appears, all too often is that once the youth is moved to a new location; the values the youth has picked up in the gang also move with the youth. That is, it is common to find the youth starting his/her own chapter of the gang of orientation in the new location to which he/she has been relocated. Such may constitute what are called "transplanted gangs".

The National Gang Crime Research Center recognized this problem and controversy several years ago and has continued to develop and monitor gang proliferation and migration. The problem, however, is attributing causality. It is relatively easy to identify the gang names that exist nationwide and where they are located. It is not easy to ascertain if in fact any national network actually exists. Nor is it easy to ascertain which gangs engage in intentional imperialism and the cultivation of new chapters or sets. This is a most important aspect of gang classification, screening for risk, and threat assessment. Some obviously do engage in this behavior. Some do, once they have established their "chapters", maintain routine contact with their "homebase" or gang of orientation. It is, after all, an efficient way to gain "rank" in the gang: simply declare yourself the local chief, and get as many members as you can to join.

Some of these gangs carrying the same names are regarded as "renegade" gangs. Sometimes, however, they are integrated into the established gang, and do function in an interstate and international capacity.

The truth is, however, we do not know how much of the gang proliferation that the United States has witnessed in recent years is due to genuine migration, or whether it is due to "emulation", transplantation, or social imitation via the "copycat" phenomenon. For example, the "Warriors" was a gang movie. It is not surprising, therefore, to find gangs existing by that name in cities such as Chicago and Boston, but they may not know each other if they actually met, they may not even know (unless they study criminological research) that another gang by the same name exists somewhere else in the United States! The word "Warriors" is simply a threatening symbol produced by Hollywood that the gang has adopted as its own name. One of the truly most needed research projects on gangs is to ascertain how much of the gang proliferation can be attributed to mass communications[17]. The fact is that little such empirical evidence currently exists, in spite of the fact that many believe it to be possible that gangs might spread or proliferate (via emulation, social imitation, etc) because of the social space created for our youths in the negative images created by Hollywood movies and the mass media coverage given to gangs. Some gangs are clearly that: copycat gangs.

PUBLIC RELATIONS FUNCTION: "We are not just Gangster Disciples, we are about Growth and Development for the Black community."

Over a period of time, a more organized gang learns the value of having a public relations function. Not unlike the appeals used by members of the Rev. Sun Yen Moon cult ("Moonies") in their long history of effectively hustling donations by claiming they are a "patriotic group...we are trying to fight communism", etc, gangs today and for many years have made similar claims. In the early history of the Chicago's El Rukn empire, the El Rukn gang formed the Grassroots Independent Voters of Illinois and had it incorporated as a not-for-profit corporation.

The idea is to maintain some "positive public image" as a "do gooder" group or association. Gangs in Chicago today still provide large scale summer picnics (all you can eat, free transportation, etc) for such a public relations function. Some gang leaders that operate drug sale rings in and around public housing complexes have organized conspicuous "litter clean-up campaigns". The novice gang researcher is quick to believe in this "other side", or they want to believe in it perhaps; but the fact remains that such public relations functions are just that: a front, a cover, a smoke screen. Anyone who really knows the gangs, like the residents that have to put up with them daily, knows the truth: it is all a scam, not unlike the soup kitchens to serve the homeless that Chicago's Al Capone maintained. One prosocial act does not neutralize a crime spree; one good deed does not translate as a "pro-social" organization. Gangs have historically, however, been able to use such "put on's" as a social-political platform to provide a counter image to that which develops when the police and others want to "crack down" on them.

Hispanic gangs in southern California (Surenos) basically have a multi-colored glossy magazine that has catered to them since 1980. White extremists like the White Aryan Resistance (WAR) have produced a cable television show about "Race and Reason" which has been viewed in 50 American cities[18]. WAR, like other white racist gangs, also publishes its own newspaper.

INTERNATIONAL INVOLVEMENT

Some U.S. gangs have, apparently, show signs of international movement. This is true in several different ways. One is there the gang member flees the U.S. to another country, for example a Latin King or Mexican Mafia member avoiding a criminal warrant for their arrest and fleeing to Mexico. This is true also where gang members are sent back to their country of origin, for a variety of reasons, such as in the case of the TAP boys (Aka: The Arab Posse) in the Chicago area, who have been seen in middle eastern countries.

Another way this international movement occurs is when the U.S. Immigration and Naturalization Service (I.N.S.) does its work effectively in facilitating the deportation of illegal alien offenders. The I.N.S. in 1992 formed the Violent Gang Task Force to address gang problems among illegal aliens. In the United States such an illegal alien might be a member of a well known gang, and when deported to another country like El Salvador, they bring their gang orientation with them. It is the issue of the internationalization of gangs. They get their feet and operations established in several different countries. The I.N.S. deported 70 Salvadoran gang members back to El Salvador in 1993.[19]

And, of course, there are those cases where gangs that exist in other countries try to come into the United States and stage operations here.

The present author therefore clearly recognizes there is an international connection with some American gangs. This was illustrated in the killing of a Catholic church official mistaken for a "hit" target inside Mexico carried out by American gang members from San Diego under contract with a Mexican drug cartel. America certainly has no monopoly on "social gangs", as this must be regarded as a cultural universal, it is just an area not of concern to the present author because it does not involve crime. Finally, there is the known connection that American gangs have to drug cartels in other countries. Just as Latino and Hispanic gangs have their connections for drug sources in Mexico, Latin American and South American countries, African-American gangs have connections for such drugs in African countries like Nigeria[20], and Asian gang members have their counterpart connections as well.

OFFENSE PATTERNS

Knowing that a gang derives some or a substantial amount of profit from certain types of offense patterns is important to gang classification. A gang is what a gang does. Some offense patterns will therefore tend to suggest a gang is closer to organized crime.[21] These offense patterns can include levying "street taxes" (extortion), narcotics trafficking, and others discussed below.

NARCOTICS TRAFFICKING

There was a period in the study of organized crime when the concept was advanced in criminology that some major figures in organized crime considered it a taboo to traffick in narcotics or illegal drugs (e.g., heroin), because of the negative attention it brought to the organization. Thus, the willingness of a gang to engage in practices with the highest level of risk necessarily sets it apart from those who prefer to limit risk.

Most of the more organized gangs today have an unmistakable involvement in the narcotics trafficking area. Still, it would seem important to know those gangs that will not touch certain kinds of drugs in the distribution and sales function. Will all gangs sell all drugs? Probably not. Profit, risk, clientele, all enter into the equation. It is an equation that must also be taken into consideration in evaluating the nature of the gang organization. Gangs and gang members as drug users is nothing new (Dumpson, et al, 1952).

Collecting "street taxes" is a gang function as well. The gang may shake down other independent drug distributors, forcing them to pay a commission (e.g., 5 percent). If they do not pay up, such independent drug dealers may receive what gangs call a "money bag" (a hit is put out on them).

GAMBLING

Gambling has been the traditional mainstay and staple of organized crime in America. To the extent that a gang involves itself with this particular aspect of vice crime means something unique about it as a corrupt organization. There are many variations and scenarios for entering into this business. Obviously, there are also differing levels of penetration of this most lucrative field. The difference tells us much about the complexity and capabilities of the gang organization.

Because it is such a uniquely income producing offense, gambling also offers a major organizational incentive to its members with little risk. Many criminologists still discuss gambling as a "victimless crime", as if it is illegal but not really bad, because so many "so-called respectable people" do it.

That is not a position that will be advanced here. Both gambling and prostitution have definite victims and our laws reflect this moral consensus.

LOAN SHARKING

Slums, ghetto, inner city, barrio, and other areas of economic under-development have traditionally been a prime environment for the operation of the juice business, or loan sharking. This crime pattern is a mainstay and prime characteristic of the income generating capability of organized crime. Thus, the extent to which a gang has generated a surplus revenue sufficient to allow the operation of loan sharking activities says much about its organizational capability.

Having this kind of crime pattern capability also speaks to the ability of a gang to replace traditional organized crime operations that may have been displaced by aggressive prosecution efforts of local and federal law enforcement authorities. We must at least consider the potential that the displacement effect in crime is also considered a benefit for indigenous organizations like street gangs, when higher visibility groups like the Mafia get prosecuted and put on ice, leaving much of their market open to penetration by independents and groups like existing street gangs. Theoretically, we should also expect some of these functions of organized crime to come to be filled by the more local and more visible street gang.

The extent to which this does occur means a gang organization with a unique income-generating capability. The higher the income in low-risk enterprise, the higher the gangs ability to reward and increase gang effectiveness.

CHOP SHOP OPERATIONS

This is simply a very lucrative field and its operations are typically interstate in nature. The extent to which a gang involves itself in this type of criminal enterprise makes it especially unique from a law enforcement perspective. The scope and extent of these kinds of operations vary considerably from custom-order car theft procedures, and custom-order parts theft[22]. This can also involve the theft, transportation, and sale of farm machinery, aviation, and heavy construction equipment --- much of which also has an international market. But the routine local car theft ring enjoys the largest crime violation impact from gangs in America[23].

COUNTERFEITING AND CREDIT CARD FRAUD

In what seemed like a routine gang arrest in Chicago during early October, 1993, the police officers discovered that a faction of the local Disciples (Brothers of the Struggle) gang had something more than the typical assortment of illegal drugs in their "spot" (i.e., their operations center). They had video equipment used by the shorties (younger gang members) to videotape the police officers working in the district. They had police scanners. The police also found sheets of recently printed five, ten, and twenty dollar counterfeit United States currency.

In a recent article published in the <u>Gang Journal: An Interdisciplinary Research Quarterly</u>[24], Jackson (1993) describes a quasi-gang group that specialized in large scale credit card fraud. With the ease of using credit cards for a variety of purchases of goods and services, gangs and gang members can be expected to increase their involvement in this area in the future.

PROSTITUTION/VICE

Many gangs have some level of involvement in commercialized vice operations. These can serve as additional opportunity crimes particularly in the area of extortion and robbery. Again, it is a crime capability factor that is important in the classification of gangs. It is also one that can be used in connection with extortion and attempts to compromise those who work in the field of law enforcement and corrections. One Illinois gang ran a prostitution ring for prisoners inside an Illinois state prison, inmates were allowed to have sex with female correctional officers who had been corrupted and compromised by drugs.

VIOLENT TAKE-OVER STYLE ROBBERIES

Gangs have also been known to specialize in, or be involved in, violent take-over style armed robberies of armored cars, banks, credit unions, and casinos. This scenario features gang members heavily armed who do use the weapons if they have to. The Aladin casino was one of seven recent such armed robberies of casinos in Las Vegas by gang members from Los Angeles during the first half of 1994. In the Aladin robbery the members came in violently with shoulder weapons, some holding citizens and security at bay while others jumped over cash counters to rapidly collect the money, and two minutes later they were out of the casino with $47,000. In some cases, as in the San Remo casino robbery, shots were fired to terrify the citizens. The robbery at Harrah's netted the gang members over $100,000 in cash. The Flamingo Hilton casino robbery netted the gang members over $125,000. The money from Harrah's and the Flamingo was not recovered in spite of arrests.[25]

FREIGHT AND WAREHOUSE THEFT

There are several variations of this type of offense pattern, but the target is any source of valuables: a freight shipment, by train or truck etc, a warehouse, or any place where such shipments or storage pass through. Sometimes this involves using the gang members to quickly unload such items, for example from a railroad car or container. Sometimes this involves gang members who work at the site and use their inside information to arrange thefts with the help of confederates from their gang who basically have a very limited risk: all they have to do is pick up the goodies. Axelson (1984: p. 3) documents where a gang will try to "rip off" trucks.[26] This type of pattern certainly extends far back in American history.

FEMALE GANG MEMBER INVOLVEMENT

The issue here is both equality and force strength. The equality issue has to do with two competing concepts in criminology regarding gender and crime. These are the chivalry hypothesis and the convergence hypothesis. The former implies that female gang members will be relegated to subservient positions, reflective of the sexist orientation of predominantly male members, such that female gang members will constitute almost an auxiliary group and will take second seat to male members[27], with no genuine hope of full advancement within the gang organization (as would be potentially the case if the member was a male). The latter (the convergence hypothesis) implies that just as wider society has now given much more power and responsibility to females in the legitimate opportunity structure, therefore gangs will follow suit and reflect these same wider normative influences by granting female members more complete rights within the gang organization. Mostly it is a matter of force strength: that is, what proportion of the gang membership is made up of females? This is simply an important parameter to measure and compare in terms of its relationship with other indicators of female representation in the criminal justice system such as that of the imprisonment function in America (where females make up only about five percent of those incarcerated).

TATTOOS

For some time in Chicago, some gangs are so completely represented within the family structure, that gang involvement is very much an intergenerational experience. This includes gang members who report their father being a member of the same gang, and who now have children who are being brought up as gang members.[28] Indeed, this can mean having the baby tattooed with the gang insignia as soon as it was out of the hospital after birth.

There have been a variety of studies of inmates and tattoos, much of this couched within the framework of self-mutilation analysis from a psychological perspective. Many authors in the study of gangs quote examples of gang members being proud of their "red badge of courage" by having visible scars, self-induced or otherwise. Clearly, it is a level of commitment that is measured by this factor of gang differentiation. Gangs that tend to require tattoos which identify the gang affiliation are going to be able to command more from their members. Sadly, we know little about this function within the gang organization: in what gangs is it required, or is it optional, does it convey any special capability for advancement in the gang organization, etc. These are questions that have simply not been answered in the literature.

Clearly, though, there is an important difference between those gangs that have many members that have taken this severe step as opposed to those that have not. As will be seen in a later chapter, simply having a permanent tattoo is a factor that significantly differentiates the variable of ever joining a gang.

ALIASES

Most genuine gangs routinely assign aliases to their members, these become "gang names". It is a basis for a new identity. An identity reinforced by gang life itself. It is obviously most useful within the law violation context as well. It is a factor of differential identity: gang members with aliases come to live up to that identity because it can be one of the few social networks that affords them what all human beings need --- praise and a sense of being a part of something larger than oneself.

TOTEMS

Totems are symbols which carry much significance for those who hold them in importance, and these are associated with various taboos. Gangs routinely have symbols for their nation or their organization. These are considered sacred symbols and are treated uniformly with much reverence. Their origins are not as mystical as Sigmund Freud would have us believe, however, because for the most part they come into existence at the onset of the emergence of the gang organization. Sometimes it is little more than a set of numbers. Sometimes it is a variation on other legitimate symbols used in society. And any functional street gang has its own hand signs for signifying gang affiliation. This is complemented with color patterns, the typical variation of which is at least one color is black.

Customized cars with unique color patterns and symbols, any potential item of clothing with special symbols or color patterns, robes, jewelry, hats, shoes, pins and buttons, window decals, and a number of objects are designed and used by gangs to carry their symbols. The sale of this gang paraphernalia is big business[29].

Gangs and gang members use a wide assortment of cultural objects and artifacts as totems. Generally, the higher the sophistication of a gang and the longer its tenure, the more it uses and accumulates such totems. Businesses (tattoo parlors, sports clothing outlets, "airbrush" design your own t-shirt shops, jewelry stores, etc) respond to this market demand by gang members and therefore tend to encourage the gang problem.

INITIATION RITES

A large amount of social imitation is endemic to gang organization today. While there is some high level of organizational functioning in the contemporary gang problem no gang has yet been reported that uses Robert's rules of order for their gang meetings[30], but most gangs have some variation of initiation rites. Often this involves an element of violence. That is to say, for the male gang member it may involve enduring some physical punishment such as having every gang member present authorized to give a full force closed-fist punch to the chest of the gang initiate. For the female member it may involve the equivalent of a "gang rape", that is, allowing every gang member present to engage in any sexual act of his or her choice with the new female gang initiate[31].

Such initiation rituals vary widely from gang to gang. Sometimes this can be little more than learning to memorize a gang prayer, and sometimes this can involve both a symbolic humiliation and then some act of violence against the opposition. When gangs seek to develop new members in more affluent suburban areas, for example, such "blood in" ceremonies are purposefully de-emphasized. It is only after joining the gang that the member may have to shed blood or endure some other form of physical violence or humiliation.

SUBCULTURAL   DIFFUSION

An interesting organizational question must be raised regarding gangs from an organizational perspective: to what extent do they tolerate other forms of deviance within their own ranks? In other words, can an openly homosexual person operate effectively as a gang member of any level of authority?[32] It is a matter of the degree to which the gang organization is an open-system in terms of its subcultural diffusion. And by no means is this discussion meant to derogate sexual preference.

Rather, the point is obvious here: some organizations that have a deviant function and purpose, such as gangs, may or may not allow such an open approach to wider societal influences. The level of variation here is between broad and narrow tolerance levels for subcultural integration outside of the gang context.

FORCE STRENGTH

Whether we conceive of only two levels of gang affiliation (periphery vs. core members) or as "regulars" versus "wannabees", or casual associates, ultimately after considering the specific crime pattern of any gang, we must come to the matter of risk assessment in terms of the actual force strength represented by any particular gang. That is simply: how many members can be mobilized for purposes of gang crime? We shall see later that because of the "franchising" of gangs, that outside of the correctional environment, gang leaders are themselves not really sure of exactly how many members they may or may not have at any given time. And at what level of involvement? This most critical aspect of an organizational approach to gang studies has only rough estimates in our literature as to what might constitute the actual parameters of the scope and extent of this problem facing America today.

ARSENAL

Some gangs, whether they are conspicuously engaged in income-producing crimes or not, tend to want to accumulate more weapons and firepower than others. Right wing extremist gangs like the Aryan Brotherhood, Ku Klux Klan, and others have historically sought to develop their own military-style arsenals. The differences in the scope and extent of the firearms acquired and used is a most important factor for assessing threat.

Any technological device that can be used in support of organizational operations should probably be included in this classification factor relating to the gang arsenal. Gangs today use "police scanners" that they can buy at their local Radio Shack and pick up a copy of the local police frequencies free of charge from the same place.

THE FUNCTIONAL AND PRO-SOCIAL ASPECTS OF GANGS

Some ethnographic researchers studying gangs have said that there is a good side to gangs[33]. Criminologists do not study the good side, they study the criminal side; a criminological researcher compares persons who violate the law with those who conform to test and develop knowledge that helps us to better understand and predict crime and criminal behavior. Much of the nature of the status-seeking behavior, the role playing, learning the language of the gang --- is not criminal in nature. In fact, gangs and gang members do engage in a host of pro-social behaviors; some of these intentional in nature, such as the public relations function where the gang that controls the drug trade in a public housing complex will enforce anti-littering norms of its own, and actually clean up the litter, most conspicuously.

At another level, quite accidental, but creating a kind of symbiotic relationship between the gang and the community of which it is a part are the functional aspects that the gang plays for the neighborhood. While living in a Chicago neighborhood with a large gang population this can be understood, but not to the casual observer. When the cop on the beat is expected to write a quota of parking tickets, the non-gang member resident of the area may be less likely to get a "citation", particularly when the members of the gang routinely leave several beat-up cars, often stolen, often inoperable, where they accumulate large numbers of tickets. The police officer on the beat has a safe "hole" to write the tickets on, satisfying the expectations of the police administration, and giving a break to the rest of the citizens parking cars in the area. Eventually the "trap car" is towed away, often with twenty or more tickets. Having lived in such neighborhoods and on occasions not having always fed the parking meters, I am grateful to this function provided to the community by gang members. They take all the heat!

But on the otherhand, most of what passes for prosocial behavior of the modern criminal gang is a smokescreen and public relations function. Simply because the members of the same gang are friendly to one another, party and enjoy each other, is not to be taken as a finding that the gang is prosocial. Rather this means there are many social aspects to a gang.

WHAT COULD FOSTER GANG DEVELOPMENT?

It is interesting to ask what policies or conditions might inadvertently foster gang development, assuming naturally that gangs are viewed as a problem that citizens do not want to see expanded. There are some organizational features of gangs that are important to consider. Gang leadership should not be cultivated nor enhanced. Any community member who thinks gangs are good because they "help defend the neighborhood" legitimizes gang turf and accentuates the gang problem. Community based social services that work with gangs should not be in the business of improving gang morale. In the absence of competitive methods of recognizing and positively reinforcing prosocial behavior among law-abiding youths, youth gangs will dominate the market on prestige.

An inverted kind of "Horatio Alger" myth, which basically says "you can be filthy rich even as a child, and perhaps have your own new Mercedes, if you join the gang and sell drugs", also contributes to the problem. Because as long as it is believed or believable, it is then always a potential motivational force for new gang recruits. In this book we shall discover many such "lessons" on what could exacerbate or erode the gang crime problem. We shall also discover many myths about gangs, aspects of misinformation that have systematically accumulated in the public imagination and perception of gangs today.

SUMMARY

Discussed here have been some of those factors that can be considered as important for the classification and assessment of gangs. Threat analysis assumes that gangs can and will vary in terms of the kind of impact they are capable of. Not all gangs are equal in crime threat. This form of inquiry is a question important to the gangs themselves. The question is: Who is the biggest? Who is the toughest? Who is the strongest? More specifically, how do we rank and evaluate gangs regarding their threat to the public in terms of crime or violence?

Gangs represent a national problem,[34] and many believe, a potentially increasing problem of violence. This discussion has advanced a basis on which to systematically evaluate gangs in terms of control and interdiction. As we know, prosecutorial resources and correctional resources are limited. The more we can focus in on the gang target for prosecution in terms of its objective threat rather than treating all gangs and gang members alike, the safer a community will be. But it is going to be difficult to translate much of our gang literature into such an applied manner, because of its tendency to focus on the personality and psychology of the individual gang member rather than the gang as an organizational unit.

Using a threat assessment or some type of objective procedure to classify gangs along a dimension of "risk" or "threat" is similar to the problem of dealing with terrorist groups. A risk assessment must be made in order to allocate investigatory resources and to expend resources in plans for intervention. The problem is there has not been agreement on what constitutes a high risk gang as opposed to a gang that represents a low level of threat to the community. Such a classification system will be advanced in later chapters.

What this chapter has hoped to accomplish is to establish the fact that theoretically gangs can vary along any variety of the types of factors used in their classification. As real or incipient organizations, like any social organization, they can go in a variety of different directions. Gangs today can take on a variety of shapes and functions, just like many of our legitimate groups and organizations function.

This chapter has pointed to a variety of factors that will emerge later as most important in the study of gang organization in America today. More is necessary to achieve a classification system, and we are not even close to having a typology yet. We have simply summarized some of these organizational features in a descriptive way.

DISCUSSION QUESTIONS

(1) Could much of gang behavior be simply a matter of "emulation", that is "social imitation", a kind of "trying out" of organizational forms and social roles to which they have been socialized along a power/authority dimension as "the controlled" or subordinates seeking a superordinate position in a kind of role-reversal? Would the gang organization therefore attract members who have a combative personality or does the gang produce members with such a combative personality?

(2) Could the role structure, that is the specifically identified layers of authority and role positions that can be filled in a gang, be predicted from socialization? That is, among gang members with an experience of being incarcerated in correctional institutions, could we anticipate that they would evolve along paramilitary lines in the same fashion as American law enforcement agencies have a paramilitary structure?

(3) The student who closely reads the gang literature will find an interesting example where in Philadelphia, to reduce gang homicides, a private group arranged for a

citywide gang meeting, bringing all gang leaders together, and the claim that this actually reduced gang-related killings "from 43 in 1973 to...one in 1977" (see Stephens, 1988: p. 41).[d] Is it a good idea, theoretically, to negotiate with gang members as "organizations"?
Would "leadership training" for youths involved in gangs be a good service to provide through a local social work program?

FOOTNOTES

1. It should also be part of any "gang awareness/gang training" curriculum. But it usually is not. Rather this type of training usually focuses on identification of gangs/gang members, and less on the social/historical context.

2. Testimony of Irving A. Spergel, Feb. 9, 1994, Subcommittee on Juvenile Justice, Committee on the Judiciary, United States Senate.

3. For example, prison riots prior to the 1970s tended to show a general consistency among the pattern of inmate leaders that emerged under such conditions. This ideal-typical profile was not dissimilar from Thrasher's "natural leader" and a pattern of "crude democracy". The pre-1970 riot leader was likely to be a "right guy", "tough" or having physical prowess. The problem is, with the advent of prison gangs, the inmate culture has changed. The 1950s inmate culture is a thing of the past.

4. It should be noted that the lack of any scientifically based national assessment of prison gangs has helped to foster confusion and denial of the gang problem in state correctional facilities. In some state prison systems, the gangs basically run the show. This is less true in the federal prison system which has adopted more of a zero-tolerance approach.

5. Tom Brune and James Ylisela, Jr, "The Making of Jeff Fort", Chicago, November, 1988, p. 202.

6. A skinhead bias crime and drug specialty street gang known as the "Bomber Boys" were active in Chicago during the 1980s on Chicago's northside and were known to be nomadic; originating in San Diego, coming to Chicago for the warmer months.

7. In our research on law enforcement, using data from a national survey sample of police chiefs, we can now report, however, that a number of sources have identified the A.B.'s (Aryan Brotherhood) as a community gang problem as well. That does

---

d This and other recent claims are often made by the gang alliance spokes persons. However, as in the Philadelphia case there were so many extraneous variables involved (including the reduction in gang effectiveness through prosecution, mortality, etc), that it is not possible to attribute any reduction in gang deaths to such a variable. In some cities, with an increased political value attached to the "law and order" issue and "quality of life" issue surrounding gang homicides, the political response is sometimes to simply "unfound" or reclassify the incidents: they become to be called "drug related killings" not "gang related killings".

not, however, mean A.B.'s are territorial, it just means we now see them operating outside of the prison context for which they have been previously known.

8. See Shukla (1981) for a discussion of these aspects of internal organizational.

9. See: "Cult Leaders' Roots Deep in U.S. History", Chicago Tribune, April 8, 1994; section 2, p. 9.

10. See: Anne Keegan, "Death of the Vice Lords", Chicago Tribune, May 15, 1994; Section 5, pp. 1,4.

11. The GD's (Gangster Disciples) are headed by Larry Hoover; and clearly outnumber the BD's (Black Disciples). On Chicago's southside alone (Gang Crimes South, CPD, 8-29-91), the BD's in police districts 2, 3, 5, 6, 7, 8, 21, and 22 were estimated at no more than 464 such members; compared to 5,755 for the GD's in the same police districts. Thus, the GD's basically constitute the B.O.S. as well. Any of the literature of the B.O.S. referring to the Chairman of the Board is therefore referring to Larry Hoover.

12. On the matter of language and gangs, language communicates social values. Our social-anthropology analyses of gangs have not taken to heart the social-linguistic analysis by Barker (1950, 1979) which analyzed how the unique language pattern or subcultural argot was used by the gang. It is obviously an important factor to analyze. But we have not seen the level of analysis conducted on this matter since the time of Barker's study of the Pachuco's in Arizona.

13. Similarly, when we address the issue of what differentiates the highest level of gang organizational development from traditional patterns of organized crime, we will see that the extent to which such a deviant organization can integrate into larger society shall certainly limit the degree to which it can dominate and control legitimate business enterprises in any society.

14. Although, Kaplan and Dubro (1986: p. 137) document how a Yakuza gang conglomerate provides "retirement pay" for its members. See also Skolnick, Blumenthal, and Correl (1993: p. 200) who report regarding drug-dealing among California gangs that "if a gang member is sent to prison, largess is expected both to keep him well-equipped there and to ease his transition back into the drug business upon his release".

15. Klein (1990) reports a major change in America's history of gang crime, the fact that modal age is now higher for gang members; while it "used to be around 16" it is currently "at 19 or 20" (p. 6).

16. In a case study of a college-educated Latin King member, case LK-29, this showed, among other things, how a three-year-old infant had already been taught by gang family members to "throw up" the Latin King gang sign and "throw down" the rival gang signs; or the case, perhaps, of a very young "wannabe" gang member, but more likely a "gonnabe" gang member, because such a child faces an almost historical imperative to follow the tutelage and older sibling gang affiliation pattern.

17. I am grateful for some ideas from Jeffery T. Walker, Ph.D., Department of Criminal Justice, University of Arkansas at Little Rock, who mentioned to me in a conversation how "mass communications" may be an important factor to examine regarding gangs.

18. See "Hate Groups in America: Part One - White Supremacists", Jeff Mc Caddon, P.B.S.P., 1993, March, p. 30.

19. Some 230 gangs are said to exist in El Salvador. These can be just as violent, use the same hip-hop dress pattern as in the U.S., but they have access to a lot of the military hardware from El Salvador's civil war. The violence of that civil was a socialization experience for children that would facilitate the combative personality syndrome and predispose youths towards violent gang behavior. See: "U.S. Gangs Hit Streets of El Salvador", by Tracy Wilkinson, Chicago Sun-Times, June 26, 1994, p. 37; "Deportees Find Willing Pupils for Violence", by Tracy Wilkinson, ibid.

20. For how an African-American gang like Chicago's Gangster Black Souls (a folks gang) use Nigerian drug connections, see: "19 Are Charged With Operating Gang Drug Ring", by Lee Bey, Chicago Sun-Times, Jan. 7, 1994, p.23.

21. Particularly if the crime pattern analysis reveals any capability of more sophisticated crimes such as might be regarded as traditional 'white collar' crimes (e.g., insurance fraud, etc) (see Johnson, 1981).

22. Some motorcycle gangs specialize in the theft of Harley-Davidson motorcycles and are said to be involved in shipping quantities of these to Europe where their value is vastly increased.

23. According to the Illinois Motor Vehicle Theft Prevention Council, "Organized street gangs have been and continue to be significantly involved in the motor vehicle theft problem". (p. 64, April, 1993, Statewide Motor Vehicle Theft Prevention Strategy, Chicago, IL).

24. The Gang Journal was published initially by Vande Vere Publishing, Ltd. (Buchanan, Michigan) as the official journal of the National Gang Crime Research Center. That publisher was fired for excessive delays and fiscal irresponsibility. The journal was reorganized during the summer of 1994 to become totally independent. It is now known as the Journal of Gang Research. Subscription information can be obtained by contacting the National Gang Crime Research Center, Chicago State University, 9501 S. King Drive, HWH 329, Chicago, IL 60628. (Tel. 312 995-2108).

25. See: "7 Heists Jeopardize Resort's Family-Fun Image", Chicago Tribune, May 19, 1994, Section 1, p. 10.

26. Roland G. Axelson, "The Psychological Influence of Street Gangs on School-Aged Youth: A Case Study in Hartford, CT", 1984, the I.N. Thut World Education Center.

27. The written constitution of the Vice Lords, for example, contains various clauses on "queen power" and "queen ladies", but essentially establishes female gang members as subservient. Up to and including their role in housework, hygiene, and

:hild rearing. Some of these written constitutions of gangs (from level three gang ormations) are discussed in a later chapter and can be examined in the Appendices.

'8. Such an "intergenerational" feature of gang involvement, or its transmission from older siblings or relatives to young family members, must certainly be regarded as a problem worthy of social service intervention and prevention efforts.

'9. Shortly after the National Gang Crime Research Center aired its one hour cable elevision program "Gangs in the Schools" and detailed the sale of imported socks containing gang logos (people and folks symbols), and other items that are routinely old in stores around and near schools, local media was quick to document and validate this issue. See particularly Robert Blau and David Jackson, 1993, "Jewelry o Die For: Teens Drop Big Bucks on Gang Totems", Chicago Tribune, June 22, Section 1, pp. 1,16.

80. That is, outside of the context of prison and jail where gang members may "take over" such a legitimate group and use its structure and methods for gang purposes.

81. A number of varieties of this kind of "sexual violence" initiation for female members occurs in gangs. Some gangs may use an element of chance, such as rolling the dice" to see how many members the new member must have sex with. More typically, it means complete sexual bondage for a time period where any member of the gang can take sexual advantage of the new gang member in any way hey want.

82. Other authors have described "homosexual tendencies" of gang members (e.g., heir preference for male contacts), but it was Leissner (1969: p. 13) who actually showed such homosexual relations among gang members in terms of a sociogram or social network form of analysis.

83. See Joan Moore, 1993, "Gangs, Drugs, and Violence", pp. 27-46, in Scott Cummings and Daniel J. Monti (Eds.), Gangs: The Origins and Impact of Contemporary Youth Gangs in the United States, Albany, NY: State University of New York Press.

84. I recall attending a so-called "gang crimes planning group" involving government agencies, private groups, and criminologists in Chicago over ten years ago. I was very frustrated because the law enforcement representation was strictly city in nature. I earned no level of positive attention when I remarked before the group "gangs travel interstate in their operations, so why do we not have the U.S. Attorney's office or the FBI represented here today?" It is not a local problem anymore. It has been a national problem for a long time. It might be an international problem.

CHAPTER 3

MAJOR MILESTONES IN GANG STUDIES

INTRODUCTION

In the field of corrections and criminal justice, as in any area of high responsibility it is important to have as broad a knowledge as possible about any given subject. In the study of gangs, corrections and criminal justice personnel need to know much more about the actual nature of previous gang studies. To read all of these studies as can be seen from the large bibliography on gangs, could be a formidable task. One solution is to provide an executive summary of the larger contributions to this literature.

The purpose of this chapter, therefore, is to provide a brief historical overview of major gang authors, their basic concepts, methods, and views regarding the study of gangs. The approach here will be chronological and a review of authors and their contributions by order of their appearance in the literature. This is not intended to be an "exhaustive" coverage. Other authors, books, articles, papers, etc, will be covered in this text. But examined here are the "major" milestones in the gang literature. There are a number of works that appeared prior to Thrasher, but these are not professional criminological contributions. These are, however, analyzed in some detail in later chapters of this book. Our real social scientific understanding of gangs begins with Thrasher.

FREDERIC M. THRASHER (1927)

The Gang, A Study of 1,313 Gangs in Chicago is worth discussing at some length not simply because it was an early study of gangs, but because of the enduring influence of Thrasher's approach to gang research. Thrasher's approach can be called the natural history approach which has been heavily associated with the "Chicago school" of sociology. But the gangs analyzed by Thrasher were at best periodically delinquent, and certainly did not reach the level of violence associated with gangs in the 1990s.

A most interesting etiological sequence is suggested by Thrasher for gang development. It is provided in graphical depiction by Thrasher - the Natural History of the Gang (Thrasher, 1968: p. 56). This developmental sequence recognizes five sources of gang input: (1) a spontaneous play group, (2) a casual crowd, (3) the family itself, (4) intimacy groups (adolescent dyads), and (5) the formal group. Importantly, Thrasher sees eight developmental outputs of the gang: (1) a mob (not implying organized crime), (2) a secret society, (3) public, (4) ring, (5) criminal gang, (6) orgiastic group, (7) political machine, and (8) a psychological crowd (both action type and orgiastic type). The three stages of gang development proposed by Thrasher were (1) diffuse (amorphous), (2) solidified (well-knit), and (3) conventionalized (formalized).

While we do not obtain a very high level of quantitative assessment in the profiles of the 1,313 gangs studied by Thrasher, what does emerge is the recognition of the variation in organization sophistication. This natural history of the gang gives a graphic illustration of gang etiology. It is this etiological sequence that makes it still of value as a primary reading today.

Thrasher's work is not statistically oriented. We never learn much about the overall picture of the 1,313 gangs, or their estimated membership, their estimated income enhancements from gang activities, etc. It is, plainly, an important historical work. The many photographs it contains are also valuable documentation of the urban context of the gang.[1]

Thrasher's gang etiology sequence recognizes a difference between the pseudo-gang, the gang itself, and separately the criminal gang (1968: 56). The gang itself can develop, incrementally, into three stages of development: (1) diffuse or amorphous, (2) solidified or well-knit, and (3) conventional or formalized. The gang in its embryonic state can first emerge from a variety of sources such as the spontaneous play group, a casual crowd, the family, a small intimate dyad, or even a formal group. As we shall see later, the kind of gangs studied by Thrasher were mostly at the lower end of the organizational sophistication spectrum. Many criminologists simply do not know the full story about Thrasher. Thrasher's first research dealing with gangs was actually reported in his 1918 Master's thesis. Many criminologists simply assume from a casual reading of Thrasher that the 1927 study represented seven years of ethnographic field research, when apparently it was some level of effort less than this. The 1927 classic was really, word for word, Thrasher's 1926 Ph.D. dissertation in the Department of Sociology at the University of Chicago. The work of Thrasher is so important that a new chapter has been added for this third edition, which seeks to solve a historical mystery about what exactly was the research methodology that Thrasher used.

WILLIAM FOOTE WHYTE (1943)

Street Corner Society is a study of one Italian community called Cornerville, circa 1937. Using the case study/oral history method, interviews with a gang member named Doc showed that gang fights were common and Whyte (1968: 5) describes one where the rival gang was armed with banana stalks and milk bottles. To fight with another gang was to "rally" on them. Doc's gang the "Nortons" was also highly capable of engaging in legitimate behavior including organized bowling tournaments. Doc matures and when he is 30, most of his fellow gang members have married and moved out of Cornerville.

But Doc wanted to run for political office. Lacking formal education, Doc received a short tenured job placement from a local community center. Doc left the gang, and withdrew from the election, even though he had mobilized some level of support. The Norton's disintegrated. The new "corner" gang was the Angelo's Boys. The latter was also highly integrated into legitimate activities such as the Cornerville Dramatic Club (Whyte, 1943: 49). Chapter 2 in Whyte (1943) covers the etiology of an Italian social club that has all the characteristics of a traditional legitimate voluntary association. Chapter 4 is a summary of more traditional Mafia-style organized crime, and its involvement in gambling and pay-offs to law enforcement officials. Chapter 5 provides an analysis of the changing informal social organization of a voluntary association called the Cornerville Social and Athletic Club. Chapter 6 is a detailed discussion of the role of this in traditional electoral politics. The conclusion chapter discusses aspects of leadership traits and correlates of this lifestyle. Social structure here meant social economic status as well and the obvious difference in life chances between a "college boy" like Whyte and the "corner boys" who hang out in the slum. A very detailed appendix describes how Whyte came to choose this particular slum area for study.

In short, little of what Whyte (1943) analyzed is comparable to the nature of the typical urban street problem which characterizes American society today. The image of the gang that emerges in Whyte is that of the famous <u>West Side Story</u>. It is, however, a very important piece of research. Indeed, there are some important parallels between Whyte's (1943) work and some of those conditions which may exist today.

For example, Whyte sees the streetcorner gang arising from "the habitual association of members over a long period of time" (1981, p. 255).[2] When some gang members left the community, a group would disintegrate, and its members merge with another group. Family life and spending time with the family at home was absent for most of these corner boys. They did acquire and use aliases through the gang. Whyte pointed out the distinction in obligations between members who were single and those who were married, and the latter were allowed extra social space for meeting this social contract. The gang is a system of mutual obligations.

We shall see in a later chapter there are ethical problems in both studying gangs and in dealing with gangs. It is not a problem that should be addressed without advance knowledge of what we are doing.

ALBERT K. COHEN (1955)

Cohen's (1955) <u>Delinquent Boys: The Culture of the Gang</u> is a theoretical discussion of delinquent subcultures. The general theory of subcultures advanced by Cohen is termed the psychogenic model. It is not a research-based analysis, but it was clearly rooted in the scholarship of its time. Cohen alternately praised or criticized the Chicago school approach, favorably recognizing the works by Thrasher and Whyte, while often criticizing cultural transmission theory (Shaw and McKay, 1942).

Cohen's focus on social class has been a matter of much discussion even though it is secondary to the more pivotal argument he advanced that psychogenic factors such as status seeking behavior, age-graded norms, group loyalty, and other aspects of a social-psychological nature account for the onset and persistence of youth gangs. Cohen devoted much attention in this early 1950's publication about "growing up in a class system" when it was probably somewhat risky to give a candid analysis. It is a comparison between working class and middle class differences.

Cohen explicitly addressed the anticipated popular question of how do gangs originate, how do they arise? He assumed all behavior including gang behavior is problem-solving behavior (Cohen, 1955: P. 50). Gangs, therefore, to quote from a much earlier contribution (Merton, 1938) "innovate", that is, they solve problems uniquely in their particular adaptation to society.[3] To the extent that Cohen was evasive about providing all explicit details of his theory for fear of criticism, many contemporary writers on the gang problem in America are quick to criticize Cohen on a variety of reasons.

Yet Cohen's (1955) work has had enduring impact on criminology today and still has much to add to the understanding of gangs. The entire subcultural theory of crime owes much to Cohen who brought to fore the elements of hedonism, negativism, and fate as differentiating persons prone to either delinquency or non-delinquency. Cohen's discussion and frame of reference may not be current, but it included aspects of enduring significance and represents like those others here an important contribution to the literature.

Basically, Cohen sees youth gangs emerging as a reaction formation to status frustration among working-class youths who are less likely to have been socialized into middle-class values. Cohen's influence on subsequent research is evident where Miller (1958) similarly considered the lower-class social status factor as a primary determinant of gang delinquency.

Cohen's value for criminal justice, then, lies in understanding the "larger picture" of societal forces at work in producing those situations favorable to gangs.

BLOCH AND NIEDERHOFFER (1958):   The Generation Gap

Herbert Bloch and Arthur Niederhoffer in their work entitled The Gang: A Study in Adolescent Behavior (1958) advanced the hypothesis that there is variation in all societies in terms of the mechanisms of status, rituals, roles, etc, made available to adolescents and that these also vary across cultures in terms of how difficult a transition it is from youth to adulthood. Basically, their position is that there is a large generation gap in American society, and that the more difficult the transition or the greater the identity-crisis, then the greater the likelihood of gangs.[4]

Bloch and Niederhoffer (1958) were quick to point out that gangs seem to provide the adolescent with those things not provided by traditional social institutions. Therefore the gang becomes a surrogate family and provides other necessary functions as well which may not be satisfied through the existing social structure. They were later roundly criticized by Cloward and Ohlin (1960: pp. 56-57) for their lack of definitional clarity in specifying what is or is not a gang. That is, Bloch and Niederhoffer (1958) tended to equate adolescent gangs with delinquent gangs.

This study is important because of the comparable problem faced everyday by offenders behind bars. They may be adults chronologically, but maturationally, and educationally, and in terms of moral development and personality they may still function at a less than optimal level of adult responsibility. The gang reinforces this commitment to deviance.

CLOWARD AND OHLIN (1960): Differential Opportunity Theory

The seminal work by Richard A. Cloward and Lloyd E. Ohlin (1960) entitled _Delinquency and Opportunity: A Theory of Delinquent Gangs_ is often cited as just a general theory of delinquency, but in fact like Cohen's is oriented to gang delinquency. That a great deal of research has been generated in support of the main propositions from differential opportunity certainly lends some credence to this theory. Basically, the theory assumes that in every community there are both legitimate and illegitimate opportunities, however when a youth experiences or perceives closure in the legitimate opportunity and simultaneously has chances to make a living in the illicit or illegal opportunity structure --- then delinquency occurs.

A factor cited by Cloward and Ohlin as well as many other contributors to the gang literature is the difficulty of being a youth in America. Social participation is age-graded, there is an identity-crisis factor, there is the gap between being young and dependent and being an adult and responsible. There is not a smooth transition from youth to adulthood.

Cloward and Ohlin were able to anticipate some developments in gang crime, particularly the hypothesis of ethnic succession. They discussed how domination of the lucrative rackets (e.g., gambling, drugs, etc) by the Italian and Jewish syndicates (1960, pp. 199-201) would eventually dissipate by control from local ethnic residents. They also correctly predicted "as a result of the disintegration of slum organization" that gang crime would become increasingly aggressive and violent in the future (1960, p. 203).

Cloward and Ohlin are especially important for correctional personnel because they suggest a solution: good training, and job placement. Develop good work habits, portable skills, and be prepared to enter the world of work. Aftercare services structured in such a manner to provide continuity with correctional industries can clearly make a significant difference in reducing recidivism.

Scholars and researchers interested in further insights into this major gang book are urged to read the recently published interview of Richard Cloward published in the _Gang Journal_ (Rush, 1993: 51-53). After publishing the book in 1960, Cloward basically abandoned criminology.

LEWIS YABLONSKY   (1962)

Yablonsky's work entitled _The Violent Gang_ (1962) is often criticized under the global concern that early youth gang analysts did not consider anything other than the large cities (New York, Chicago, Los Angeles, etc). In point of fact, however, Yablonsky explicitly recognized the emergence of the same problem in smaller communities regarding the "kill for kicks" phenomenon (Yablonsky, 1962: p. 3). In point of fact, while Hagedorn (1988) would probably not legitimate the analogy, there is even a continuity in terms of how Yablonsky felt gang infrastructure was less formal than often conceived and how Hagedorn suggests gangs are truly less formalized than they are sometimes portrayed to be./ Yablonsky's work deserves a significant amount of discussion here.

Yablonsky's classification of gangs included three types: (1) delinquent gangs, (2) violent gangs, and (3) social gangs (1962: p. 149). These are discussed not as a pure typology meeting the requirements of exhaustive and mutually exclusive categories. Rather, Yablonsky describes them in the "ideal-typical" construct. In this fashion, what dominates the gang ethos explains its gang function (e.g., delinquency, violence, social, etc). Thus, what kind of gang it is depends on the type of norms, behavior patterns, and personalities of the gang membership.

It is the violent gang organization that Yablonsky analyzes in detail. The picture that emerges of the violent gang according to Yablonsky (1962) is as follows: the gang emerges spontaneously, it provides a sense of power, joining is easy, initiation rites are pretty much a myth, it is easy to quit the gang, but leaders and core members seldom leave the gang (p. 155), the leaders are self-appointed manipulators who "manifest paranoid delusions of persecution and grandeur" (p. 156), they use the myth of vast alliances with other gang nations and affiliates, gang warfare is like a group contagion and often has no clear purpose other than trivial things that trigger conflict. The sociopathic members live in slums in urban communities facing negative forces of decay and erosion. Prejudice and discrimination aggravate the gang problem (p. 184).

From Yablonsky comes the differentiation between "core" versus "marginal" members. Also provided is a discussion of the gang infrastructure in terms of a continuum of organized-unorganized. In this scheme a mob fits the pattern of unorganized, the violent gang fits the pattern of being a near group, and social/delinquent gangs fit the pattern of being most organized. Basically, the differences in personalities mediate all causal factors and the personality types determine what kind of gang a youth joins.

Yablonsky's final chapter was on gang intervention programs and services. It provided, perhaps prematurely, a blanket and glowing endorsement of Synanon as a vehicle for rehabilitating core gang members. Still, it is important for criminal justice staff because it provides some interesting insights into the psyche of gang members.

THE MANY WORKS OF MALCOLM W. KLEIN

A quick inspection of the gang bibliography for this book shows another important trend. Some authors are obviously not new to the study of gangs. For some gang researchers, like Malcolm Klein, the study of gangs has been a continual lifelong research interest. The many works of Klein date back over 25 years ago.

If there was a single summary statement from the works of Klein it is his 1990 Edwin H. Sutherland Award address to the American Society of Criminology (Klein, 1990). It says that some of what is contained in the gang literature is myth, particularly mass media accounts. It says we should realize that there are different varieties of street gangs and so all who study gangs, particularly criminologists, must be careful not to create an artificial image of the gang crime problem.

Klein's ties to Chicago involved interacting with a number of different researchers: "Short, Suttles, Spergel, Kobrin, Feinstein, McKay, Gordon, Miller, Ohlin, Simon, and Lerman" (Klein, 1990: p. 5) as well as Hans Mattick.

What has changed in American gangs according to Klein is modal age and propensity for violence (Klein, 1990: p. 6) as well as additional ethnic group representation in the gang scene, more specifically Asians (p. 7). Modal age appears to have changed from around 16 to about 20 (p. 6). More homicides are today associated with gangs and account for nearly 40 percent "of all Los Angeles County homicides -- a truly astounding figure" (p. 6).

Klein joins other contemporary authors, this author included, in noting that the tendency to blame and stigmatize among criminal justice agencies and other "labelling" institutions is itself a problem to be overcome. The gang problem is not a simple problem, it is a complex problem. And we still do not know why some cities have gangs and others do not, or why some persons in the same area join gangs and others do not (p. 12).

Law enforcement agencies and the mass media are quick to assume "street gangs are well-structured, cohesive collectives with strong individual leaders", but Klein says this is clearly in most instances incorrect (pp. 13-14). Also, gang members do not spend their 24-hour day enmeshed and engulfed in a full schedule of violence, they also have normal lives (p. 14).[5] The evidence does not exist that gangs truly control all or even a significant share of drug sales in America (p. 15). Finally, no evidence exists that L.A. gangs like the Crips and Bloods have franchised and exported crack distribution rings to the rest of the United States (p. 15). But these are four misconceptions widely held by criminal justice officials and reinforced by the mass media.

Because he has devoted his career to the study of gangs, Klein will be referred to throughout this book. His contributions reflect an entire era, and are ongoing.

THE MANY WORKS OF IRVING SPERGEL

Two major works appeared in the mid-sixties, and ongoing contributions have come from the same author, Irving Spergel of the University of Chicago's School of Social Service Administration. The first monograph was Racketville, Slumtown, Haulburg: An Exploratory Study of Delinquent Subcultures (1964). The second was Street Gang Work: Theory and Practice (1966). Both works have had extensive and enduring positive impact on the study of gangs in America.

Spergel's (1964) Racketville, Slumtown, Haulburg is important for several reasons. First it describes three different community areas: (1) Racketville, (2) Slumtown, and (3) Haulburg. Each such community generates a unique type of delinquent subculture or gang. The organized crime syndicate or crime cartel emerges from the Racketville type of community. The conflict subculture emerges from the Slumtown type of community. And the theft subculture emerges from the Haulburg type of community.

What is exceptionally important about Spergel's work (1964) is that it anticipated perhaps the devastating impact of drugs and youth gang involvement such as is currently evident in American society. Spergel explicitly indicated that the drug-using or drug-addiction adaptation could arise in any of these three types of communities. Another important fact that distinguishes Spergel from previous researchers on gang studies is that hard data was collected on gang members. This information came from his work as a gang outreach worker in an eastern city. While the sample size was not exceptionally large (N = 125) it was given more analysis that was the case in any previous studies, such that we get a much stronger picture, quantitatively, of the differences between various gang and non-gang types of affiliation. Spergel clearly demonstrated that self-report data could be effectively collected from gang affiliated youths (1964) and used effectively to explain variations in their life chances and outlooks on life.[6]

Spergel's (1966) Street Gang Work: Theory and Practice is itself a milestone in developing a comprehensive strategy for working with the gang problem at the community level. Heavily influenced by the "Chicago school" of sociology and serving as a faculty member[7] there for a long time, he must also be regarded as an important contributor and shaping force in the Chicago criminological tradition.

Generally, it seems Spergel's work is under appreciated, even though from an overall analysis it (1964) represented the most social scientific treatment yet offered of American gangs. It recognized problems still cited today as primary causal factors: high unemployment (p. 3), low income (p. 4), the "struggle for security and decency" (p. 14), age-role integration (p. 22), social and economic deprivation (p. 27), status aspirations/expectations (p. 29), criminal code norm internalization (p. 34), role-models (p. 36), and more. Further, Spergel was the first to empirically "test" major factors as hypotheses (p. 106) with hard data.[8]

Spergel's work shows continuity and growth and it is an enduring concern rather than a passing interest. There is little new being advocated for gang intervention that had not been proposed three decades ago by Spergel (1964, 1966).

Spergel's work is important because more and more corrections personnel are involved in family counseling and in aftercare services. A gang member often provides impetus for other family members to join the gang. Such works like those from Spergel suggest methods to "reorient" or work with gang members in the community. It may also provide, if structured properly, an alternative to working with gangs inside the correctional milieu itself. Thus, Spergel's contributions reflect an entire era, and are ongoing.

THE MANY WORKS OF WALTER B. MILLER

Empirical research on gangs owes much to the pioneering and modern work of Walter Miller which covers half a century. Miller's 1982 report showed gang problem existing in slightly over one out of every ten of America's smaller cities (less than 10,000 population), and in two-fifths of medium size cities (populations 100,000 and above), and in five out of every six of our larger cities. It is from Miller that we find one of the only clues about the puzzle of how much crime in America is "gang related". Miller (1975, 1980) estimated that gangs may account for half of all juvenile crime in our largest cities. It was further hypothesized that gangs may account for as high as a third of all crimes of violence committed by juveniles (Miller, 1975: pp. 75-76).

In summary, as seen from the many contributions of Miller represented in the bibliography, Walter Miller --- like Malcolm Klein and Irving Spergel --- has had a career of gang research. Miller years ago established that gangs are a national problem and established national gang research as an essential knowledge development need. Miller's work also reflects an entire era.

SHORT AND STRODTBECK (1965): Status Threats and Aleatory Risks

In Group Process and Gang Delinquency (1965) James F. Short, Jr. and Fred L. Strodtbeck extend the Chicago school tradition of gang studies to be the first major study with a large sample size using multivariate statistical analysis. It was a unique contribution set in the context of both field research and applying general social science skills to the social reality of urban life. Generally, this represents an analysis that includes comparisons along white and African-American dimensions only, with no Latino nor Asian groups. Importantly, Short and Strodtbeck note that gangs in depressed inner city areas are not only normal they are also apparently universally expected because of their appearance in many other countries (1974, p. 1). It is the first major contribution to use multivariate probability statistics. It also recognized that since the time of Thrasher, "apparently the gang of today is not the gang of yesterday" (1974, p. 77). In providing the first comprehensive comparison along racial lines (1974, pp. 102-115) it also documents white racist bias crime through qualitative data.

The major concepts developed here involve status equilibrium in the group context. It involves the "status threat" as an immediate factor which may precipitate inter-gang violence. The authors are among the first to note the parallels between gang violence and guerilla warfare (1974, p. 200). They also note the problems of employment counseling and job placement services with the youthful offender (1974, p. 225) which was borne out in much additional research years later on the offender population generally.[9] The concept of aleatory risk is based on game theory and assumes a differing level of subjective evaluation of various decision outcomes.[10] It involves the utility-risk paradigm (1974, p. 254).

Thus, the basic position taken by Short and Strodtbeck (1964, 1974) is that status related to general society (employment aspirations, legitimate career potential, educational attainment, etc) is important but that status within the small group context is more immediately likely to have impact on outcomes like gang violence (e.g., status threats, and status enhancing functions of the gang). Both the social structure and the group process must be taken into account.

This book is important for a variety of reasons: its superior research method, its findings, and its implications that gangs cannot be dealt with as we deal with individuals. We are dealing with a group which takes on a higher level of significance, and requires "special handling".

KEISER (1969, 1979): Anthropology of the Vice Lords

This is a very short monograph and the 1979 reprinted edition with additional commentary follows the Whyte pattern and includes new personal insights from the author. The author sought to overcome racism and as a white researcher from Northwestern University "lived with" the predominantly African-American Vice Lords. The entre was telling the gang he wanted to write a book about them and share the royalties with them. It involved about four months of such fieldwork. It provides useful information on the gang infrastructure, its adaptation to the risk of arrest and loss of members to the criminal justice system, and the "franchising" of gang branches within the gang organization, including their operation of a restaurant, a recreation center, an employment service, their business office, and their status as a legally incorporated not-for-profit corporation as far back as 1968.

The importance of Keiser is in realizing that over twenty years ago we had highly organized (what we shall later call "level three") gang formations in our country. This is an important historical contribution documenting one gang in Chicago[a].

POSTON (1971): Gangs as Grant Funding Hustlers.

Richard W. Poston's (1971) book, The Gang and the Establishment: A story of conflict rising out of the federal and private financing of urban street gangs, is a detailed historical chronology of an indigenous ex-gang member managed social program originally called the "Real Great Society" or RGS located in New York City. In short, it finds this particular type of indigenous community group to be 99 percent fluff and one percent substance. Its leaders use theatrics, myth, mass media manipulation and political grandstanding to generate contributions from government, corporate, and private foundation sources. The book epitomizes what might be imagined of the worst of the 1960s programs where the highest level of program accountability in reporting service impact was a year end statement to the effect "saw client, served same".

This is not a theoretical discussion of gang formation, nor a quantitative piece of research. Rather it is a policy case study with a substantial amount of inside information. It clearly cautions against knee jerk funding allocation decisions to programs with exoffenders or ex-gang leaders in administrative capacities.

To the extent that it documents an important historical phase of social policy reaction against providing funding to gangs, it was and remains a valuable contribution, however cynical. The reader is simply alerted to a more powerful manner in which this same kind of experience reported by Poston was analyzed quite differently in the work by Krisberg (1974). What Krisberg showed is that sure, gang leaders were hustling, but society hustled them too, programs themselves are "hustles" promising to fulfill broken dreams and never delivering.[11]

---

[a]David Dawley wrote a similar book A Nation of Lords: The Autobiography of the Vice Lords (1973, 1992). This author includes a photograph of himself showing the "gang sign" and claims to be "the only white Vice Lord". The author helped the gang get grants and loans to start business enterprises.

HASKINS (1974, 1975): A Historical Perspective

Based largely on historical materials this work shows gangs have always existed in America. It includes many interesting photographs from historical archives, even some from Keiser's work. It focuses on the urban nature of gangs and the SES factors that foster gang activity. It sees the first organized gang in America as the "forty thieves" gang, circa 1826. It also traces the history of the Ku Klux Klan as a group that experienced a succession in goals towards bias crime. It makes very effective use of printed news media accounts of gangs in America. And also shows the political connection with gangs as well as the high levels of violence such that the National Guard was routinely called to quell gang disturbances.

JOAN W. MOORE (1978): Homeboys --- gangs, drugs, prisons, barrios

Moore's (1978) Homeboys: Gangs, Drugs, and Prison in the Barrios of Los Angeles brings the sensitivity and verstehen of the researcher to the deviant population not seen since the work of Sutherland. A potential criticism is that perhaps there was too much, in the sense that if "applied" persons or those working in the field of law enforcement or corrections would be required to read it, they might regard it as somewhat of an anomaly and that the writer appeared in some instances to be glamorizing the gang and accepting their definitions of the social reality, almost as a justification for gang violence. This is not a text that is easily adapted by law enforcement for the repression of gang organization.

Nevertheless, it is a remarkable and fresh contribution giving insights to the gangs having a Mexican-American ethnicity. It uses their language: pintos are convicts or ex-convicts, barrio refers to a named neighborhood and gang, tecato is a drug addict (1978, p. 4). The data comes from three "hard-core barrios of Mexican East Los Angeles" (p. 7).[12] The essence of the viewpoint presented tends to follow, to some extent, a racial oppression thesis.

Gang structure becomes defined as having the following components: territoriality based, age-graded "with a new klika, or cohort, forming every two years or so", and all Chicano gangs are fighting gangs, with high levels of drug use (35-36). The gang is regarded as a quasi-institution in the barrio and involves the adult world. The author is quick to defend gang intervention/service programs: "Chicano gang subculture is responsive to programs" (p. 41). Unlike other previous social workers that label and stigmatize the gangs, Moore assiduously avoids this and in fact allowed the gang members in her study to have much veto power and control over research functions such as instrumentation, data collection, etc.

Tremendous insights into drug trafficking and marketing in the barrio are presented which must be regarded as important contributions in their own right (pp. 78-87). A theme developed is that barrio men sent to prison made new connections and became more sophisticated in their criminal operations (p. 87). The policy implication is that prisons should do less experimenting with group therapy and start paying inmates work salaries commensurate with civilian life. Moore is an avid supporter of the prisoner and barrio self-help movement and writ writers[13] and also recommends the legalization of heroin.

Moore curiously limits the generalization of the research findings to the extent that such barrio "ethnic traditions in Los Angeles are quite different from those of blacks, and are even unlike those of Chicanos in other cities" (p. 169).

ANNE CAMPBELL (1984): The Girls in the Gang.

Campbell's study is a close-up look, using the oral history method and extensive dialogue with three female gang members. Two were from Brooklyn and one was from Manhattan. The estimate is that ten percent of gang members in New York City are female (p. 5). Gangs arise "from conditions of poverty and alienation common to those at the lowest levels of urban life" (p. 33). The researcher used the entre to the three gangs of a police officer from the local Gang Intelligence Unit. One photograph shows both the author and the policeman with a jovial relationship with several male gang members (p. 133).

This qualitative research is described as a form of participant observation. From the photographs of the author in the home and in other settings with the three female gang members highlighted in the book, much is conveyed. The gangs themselves were somewhat curious. Connie was one of the female gang members interviewed and belonged to a biker gang called the "Sandman Ladies", but it had only one operational motorcycle (a BSA 650) (p. 49). Sun Africa, one of the other two female gang members interviewed, belonged to the gang called the "Five Percent Nation" which turns out to be a quasi-religious organization emphasizing Islamic teachings.

There is no "theory testing" per se here, rather it is an elaborate descriptive account of the viewpoints of the three female gang members chosen for study.

The final chapter of the book (pp. 232-267), however, provides some interesting political commentary regarding gang life. Here we find that while these three women may have been unhappy with their economic plight, they had no aspirations to overthrow American capitalism; indeed they wanted to be in their highest aspirations members of the well-dressed, well-eating, high-consuming, happily married American middle-class.

Campbell notes that "72 percent of all juvenile homicides committed in 1974 were gang-related" (p. 232). Campbell takes the position that "youth gangs are not a universal phenomenon" (p. 233) and that it is pretty much an American social invention. Gangs become indirectly defined by their attributes of "membership initiation, demarcated roles, rules, names, "colors", territoriality, discipline, a specific philosophy, or feuds with other groups" (p. 233).

Gangs were nurtured and promoted by American politicians. The gang members have a geographical dependency that keeps them locked into a specific urban community area. They rarely venture out of these small areas, even when they are wanted by the police (p. 236). Those with the "least to gain from the status quo" are the ones who join gangs. Gang members are far from being potential revolutionaries, they often have conservative views (p. 237). Basically, "gangs do not represent a revolutionary vanguard rejecting the norms and values of a capitalist society that has exploited them" (p. 267).

JACKSON AND Mc BRIDE (1985, 1990)

Jackson and Mc Bride have provided what many believe to be the single best law enforcement view of the gang problem in America. It was one of the first works to document that some highly organized gangs have written gang constitutions and truly do function as something comparable to a military organization. Much more than simply a law enforcement view, it provides a reasoned analysis of gangs that blends the practical problem of police work with the need to understand larger social issues that are associated with gangs in America.

HAGEDORN AND MACON (1988): Gangs as part of the Underclass.

Hagedorn and Macon in their (1988) People and Folks: Gangs, Crime and the Underclass in a Rustbelt City focus on previously unexplored aspects of racial oppression in explaining predominantly minority group membership in Milwaukee's youth gangs. Joan Moore provides an insightful introduction to the book. Rather than a single theory developed per se, the authors present their tape recorded oral history data from 47 "top dogs" or gang founders, and then evaluate previous contributions in terms of what fits the Milwaukee context.

The authors denounce criminal justice research and law enforcement efforts, and certainly the use of the penal sanction against gang members, as being counterproductive. White sociologists are seen as part of the problem for "too much theory, too few facts" about gangs (pp. 26-27).[14] And criminology as a "white social science" is equally useless having "not produced any studies of note about modern gangs" (p. 28). For their own points of departure, the primary researcher (Hagedorn) describes a personal background of being a community activist and the other author (Macon) being a former Chicago street gang leader.

The introduction by Moore (pp. 3-17) provides a very cogent discussion of the definitive characteristics of gangs. Gangs are seen as: friends sharing common interests, from poor and marginal communities, in an age-graded system of gang participation, that are not hierarchical organizations (p. 5). Here underclass differs from previous uses of the phrase to mean "these are men and women permanently excluded from participation in mainstream occupations" (p. 7). That seems pessimistically tantamount to defining them as an American social caste rather than a part of the surplus population from which there might be some escape if adequate policies and service resources were available.

It seemed somewhat unbelievable, indeed contradictory, to see Moore declare "Gang members and their individual friends dealt in drugs, for example, but with very rare exceptions the gangs themselves did not become involved in crime" (p. 11).[15] It goes without saying that even the most hardened career criminal or organized crime member, if we were to conduct a time and motion study of their daily lives, would not be violating the law 100 percent of the time. Both Moore and Hagedorn seek to change the image of the gang and to challenge the stereotypical and alarmist portrayal of the gangs in the mass media.

Regarding any gang or offender research, as well as basic criminal investigation, it is a practical matter of social science to have a high level of skepticism when it comes to the matter of crime. What we need is facts. And there are many different research methodologies that have been used to acquire these facts about gangs. Perhaps the facts that Hagedorn seeks so vigorously.[16] The social reality of crime, especially gang crime, is sufficiently complex as to be least amenable to journalistic styles of investigation.[17] Unless of course we devalue the matters of validity and reliability.

The authors clearly sought to "change the public image of gangs" (p. 31). Employment data is cited to show a declining economic opportunity for inner city minority group members. Gang members are described as being uniformly school drop outs (p. 44). Gang formation occurred in Milwaukee in the context of a race relations crisis, thus racial oppression has some causal significance to gangs (p. 50). The authors reject the notion that gangs can be "exported" (p. 79), but clearly their data show that at least four gangs were imported (p. 58). The rest of the gangs arose out of dancing (N=3) and traditional street corner groups (N=10), or as female auxiliaries (N=2) (see p. 58).

Importantly, the authors document the interstate shipment of firearms (p. 74) between gang members. And that there are in fact high levels of continuing gang involvement from adolescence into adulthood for gang members (pp. 124-125). Most of the gang members they interviewed had at least one pistol, none of which had been acquired legally (p. 144). The authors describe the problem of police coverups and denial of a problem of gang crime as part of the public image for a city. The correctional sanction was not a deterrent to continued gang involvement (p. 162). They agree with Cohen that gangs have a rebellious aspect, but it is "cynical" and destructive of the communities in which they live (p. 164). The solution is jobs and education (p. 168).

VIGIL (1988): The Multi-Marginality Concept

Focusing on the barrio gangs of East Los Angeles this ethnographic study sees the gang arising and persisting because of the marginality of gang members in terms of ecological, socioeconomic, cultural and psychological factors.[18] What Vigil argues is that it is not a simple matter of alienation, but rather gangs arise and persist because of an accentuated estrangement. The psychodynamic factors of gangs are discussed in terms of Erikson's identity and related ego and self-identity formations. Family conditions, when stressful, also are seen as important ingredients in gang affiliation; and why the gang itself becomes a kind of surrogate family.

TAYLOR (1990): A Close Look at Detroit Gang Data

Taylor's (1990) analysis of gangs is a modern one. It is social scientific, it lacks any obvious ideological bias, and it involves the multi-method approach. The hard data collected on gang members is of much value because it probes into areas of much concern to gang analysis. The qualitative data involves focused interviews on subjects of much relevance (industry, drugs, family, role models, etc).

Taylor (1990) advances the concept of the quisling effect in gang analysis. This is the notion that gangs are more than simply destructive to the community, they are "sell-outs", they are functionally --- in spite of their own rhetoric to the contrary (e.g., working for "oppressed peoples", etc) --- working to destroy their own country and community. The gang member as parasite and germ collaborating for destruction is the essence of this concept.

HUFF (1990):   Prior Gang Viewpoints   in America

This is a reader containing fourteen papers on gangs in America. The forward by Albert K. Cohen is most interesting in its own right. These are selections written by persons who are well known gang authors.

There is much that is new, but not necessarily unanticipated.   For example, Hagedorn's discussion is quick to point out the need for more "field work"[19] Hagedorn also criticizes other authors in this reader (e.g., Spergel and Curry) as "courthouse criminologists", because they do not get their information directly from the mouths of gang members.

KNOX (1991):   The First Full Textbook   on Gangs.

The first edition of this book appeared in 1991 and while several "readers" (collections of various papers by different authors) existed on gangs, the first edition of An Introduction to Gangs was the first serious effort by a single author to address all of the major issues is a textbook format since the time of Thrasher. It was the very first to provide actual full length written gang constitutions showing the formal structure of some of the more notorious criminal gangs. The 1991 first edition also included a geographical listing of gangs that was dropped in the 1993 second edition[20].

SANCHEZ-JANKOWSKI   (1991):   Ten Years Hanging Out With Gangs.

This work represented a major step forward in dispelling certain myths about gangs. It is based on ten years of qualitative research: hanging out with different gangs in several states. This is much more time than Thrasher (1927) ever spent with gangs. While the methodology of the author has been criticized, the quality of the results make this a book of enduring value. The criticism that the work may over-generalize its research findings is a charge that can be put at the door of almost all gang researchers.

GOLDSTEIN (1991):   Gangs as Hyperadolescents.

One of the biggest intellectual issues in the study of gangs today is the matter of "stigma" and "labelling". That is, there is a fear that some research and scholarship will add to the public fear of gangs. The work of Goldstein (1991) summarizes much of the sociological literature on gangs including a chapter on "Gangs as Communities", and also includes a unique psychological perspective as well by viewing gangs as hyperadolescents. What this concept implies is that younger gang members face more than the normal amount of tension and "trouble" in terms of identity formation and status seeking behavior problems. Thus, while gang leaders may be in it for the money, young kids involved in gangs may be in it for the status itself.

KOTLOWITZ (1991): The Gang Stranglehold on African-American Public Housing Residents

This book details the everyday life events of several children growing up in the Henry Horner public housing projects over a two year period. Gangs and the violence and drug business the gangs control are examined from the viewpoints of youths like Pharaoh who are not gang members. This is one of the few such participant observation studies that takes the viewpoints of non-gang members into account. What we learn is that gangs like the Vice Lords who earned thousands of dollars a day in their drug business are a menace from the viewpoints of law abiding public housing residents.

Mc LEAN (1991): The Evangelical Outreach to Gang Members

The author describes his early work at the Green Hill Training School in Chehalis, Washington to his present work with juvenile and adult offenders --- many of whom are gang members. While working in a juvenile cottage he was attacked and tied up in an escape effort. From 1982 to present, the Chicago gang scene is described; and covers many of the same aspects of the gang problem discussed elsewhere. It also describes ten years of experience in a "United Nations" component of the ministry to offenders where rival gang members were brought together for peaceful meetings[21]. This is the group that issued "Officially Retired Gang Member" photo I.D.'s. in the Chicago area.

CERVANTES (1992): Drugs and Gang Violence

This short work provides a lot of traditional discussion about drugs. The only new gang research presented is small sample (N = 81 cases). It provides a mental health focus by authors who are mostly from the L.A. area. It tells us nothing about gang drive-by shootings in relationship to gang drug disputes. The small sample of gang members incarcerated in L.A. focuses on the psychological issue of post traumatic stress disorder (PTSD); not the PTSD the gang members induce in the community, but rather their own PTSD.

PADILLA (1992): The Gang as a Business Enterprise.

This study of former members of a Chicago gang focuses on an important aspect of gang life: drug selling as "work". Work that is not very rewarding, but provides a basically "hand to mouth" subsistence with the real profits going to the higher up gang leaders. Despite the rhetoric in their gang constitutions, the gangs basically mimic their capitalistic society and seek to exploit the "workforce" of gang members willing to push drugs or commit other crimes of economic profit.

KNOX, LASKE, AND TROMANHAUSER   (1992):   Gangs and Schools.

This short monograph focuses exclusively on the gang problem among school children. It includes much new research showing the strong linkage between drugs and gangs. It provides a special look at Asian students and concludes the "gang profile" is similar across all ethnic groups. It specifically tests a variety of hypotheses from the gang literature using recent data (students, parents, teachers, police, etc).

CUMMINGS AND MONTI (1993):   Another Diverse Reader on Gangs

This reader --- a collection of various articles by different authors --- contains thirteen chapters, four of which were authored by the editors. The viewpoints on gangs are very much grounded in the criminology and criminal justice literature. It contains useful new contributions not previously published: particularly on gang graffiti as an art form in the study by Ray Hutchison. Other useful contributions include new viewpoints on gang migration and on the civil rights of gang members. It also provides an excellent summary of Thrasher's enduring value to gang analysis.

GOLDSTEIN AND HUFF (1993): Psychological,   Contextual   and Criminal Justice Interventions

Containing eighteen chapters a third of which the editors contributed, this reader seeks to address the issue of gang intervention. The assumption is that both the stick (criminal justice punishment) and the carrot (psychological and community services) are needed to intervene with gangs.   Much of the literature upon which gang intervention is based as discussed by a number of the contributors was not the more specific and unique form of deviance and criminology we call "gang literature", but was the wider "delinquency intervention" literature.   Unstated assumptions for psychological intervention amount to little more than "attributions" and labels to gang members, by assuming that the literature on "conduct disorders" among youths has any proven effectiveness value in gang intervention.   It is a fairly large stretch of intervention logic to assume that any prior program intervention dealing with delinquency or psychological disorders can automatically be applied to gang intervention with the same results. They are not the same phenomena!

Some mistakes in our previous gang literature such as that by Brooks (1952) were based on the same lack of logic.   The book on "Girl Gangs" by Brooks (1952) becomes on closer inspection not a documentary of a full gang composed ONLY of females who engage in serious crime.   Such a serious criminal gang composed only of females was not fully documented in the gang literature until the recent work of Lauderback, Hansen and Waldorf (1992). Thus, the title by Brooks like some others on gang issues, was really misleading; what the Brooks book did was simply discuss some of the more vicious accounts of female delinquency that had appeared in the mass media --- not gangs of girls, but the individual behavior of females mostly acting alone.   In other words, routine delinquency and criminology literature.   The fact is that the gang literature is a specialized subset of the crime and delinquency literature.

Calling it a handbook does not make it a single source reference book on gang programs. The book describing the history of gang programs in America and their effectiveness has yet to be written.

HAMM (1993): Skinheads as Gang Members

This is a major positive contribution to the study of white racist gangs. It is a detailed and in-depth scholarly monograph based on mainstream criminology and establishes that groups such as skinheads and neo-nazis who engage in bias crimes should be included in what we mean by "gangs". Such hate groups do accumulate military weapons and ordnance and should be regarded in the domain of domestic "home grown" terrorist threats. These are not just "kids", these are more often than not problems of crime and violence created by adult-led political extremist organizations. See also Jack B. Moore's work Skinheads Shaved For Battle: A Cultural History of American Skinheads (1993) for a view and analysis that complements the Hamm study.

SANDERS (1994): Gangbangs and Drive-Bys

Sanders provides the best sociologically-grounded approach to ethnographic research on gangs. Much analysis is presented within a wider social perspective that includes such well known theorists as Goffman. This particular study deals with gang violence in San Diego. It helps to explain why some social values like loyalty have different meanings to gangs than they do to others, or rather how in the gang context the value of loyalty is "grounded" in the specific gang culture. This may help to explain how some have regarded gang members as having twisted or upsidedown value systems. Gang members are gang-centric is what Sanders shows.

GOLDSTEIN AND GLICK (1994): The Prosocial Gang?

The idea of a prosocial gang seems to some to be a contradiction in terms and therefore an oxymoron. The authors of this book appear to have conducted a small program for juveniles, a psychological treatment program called aggression replacement therapy. They claim it works on gang members, although their own data (p. 95) shows the participants did not change in terms of anger control. They do claim a reduced recidivism rate that is significant. It is fair to say that the methodology for this evaluation was not the best. Calling a comparison group a control group implies an experimental design, when it is in fact not clear that random assignment was used. It is not clear what types of gangs may have been specifically represented in the treatment group, or their comparison group. The present author is highly skeptical that such a simple program could turn around anyone but the lowest level gang member of the lowest possible threat level. Why? Because the gang problem is not simply a psychological problem. The gang problem is not something so simple that it could be chemically treated by an "anti-gangbanging" pill, or as some turn of the century writers believed that a "gang instinct" existed, that any biological or genetic manipulation will reduce the gang problem.

SUMMARY

This chapter has provided a short overview of some of the major milestones in the study of gangs. We have not provided a simplistic summary of all criminological theories as they might pertain to, or could conceivably be interpreted as apply to, gangs.[22]   Also, there are other books and monographs not cited here, which represent such distinct contributions (e.g., Klein) or such interesting accounts that these will be examined in detail in later chapters. We will also find the opportunity later in this book to examine the contributions of other authors, whose works are not always cited as gang contributions, and what they have provided for a more social scientific and historical analysis of gangs.

We have not reviewed here a number of books that serve as gang identification guides. The work by Olivero (1991) is based on newspaper accounts and includes a number of symbols and pictures[23]. One of the worst is by Fox and Amador (1993), which is little more than a local listing of some gangs, and their symbols. Probably the best privately published gang identification guide is that describing Peoples and Folks gangs, which provides a very detailed cross-reference manual for midwest gangs (Gang Prevention, Inc., 1994)[24]. A number of police departments throughout the U.S. have produced local gang identification guides. Chicago's has always been popular. Some statewide law enforcement groups have also recently began to design statewide gang identification manuals.

We have not reviewed a number of books that are basically fiction or apologia about gangs. The book by a Crip gang member, Monster, for example is not a professional contribution to knowledge, it is his autobiography portraying himself with the best of motives however stylized an account it is. Books by gang members are becoming a new genre and can be expected to increase in the future on the principle that we like to read about what generates much fear. Nor have we considered reviewing gang movies, as many of them that exist, just as we have not reviewed pure fiction works that while interesting, for example from a perspective on feminism (i.e., Foxfire: Confessions of A Girl Gang, by Joyce Carol Oates), are still more likely as non-professional contributions to reinforce stereotypes and give unfounded conclusions about the gang problem.

What this chapter demonstrates is a diversity of approaches to the understanding of gangs. And along with this comes a range of research approaches that have been used. The analysis of gangs has also represented a theoretical and social policy focus. All of these contributions must be taken into account to understand the history and evolution of gangs in society.

If it is solid and useful theory, if it is careful and replicable analysis, or if the concepts still apply, then just because their contributions are not recent ones is no reason to discount them as "dated" and therefore not of any value. Obviously, all of the gang members from Thrasher's analysis are now probably dead and buried. But we cannot at the same time reject out of hand the value of potentially useful concepts advanced in such prior analyses. It is not simply a matter of old theory and new gangs. As we shall see in later chapters there are some important historically grounded conceptual continuities in the gang literature.

DISCUSSION QUESTIONS

(1) Could a plumber, carpenter, or bus driver carry out a study of gangs as equally scientific and valid in findings as a Ph.D. trained in criminology if the method of study was that of "hanging out" with the gang?

(2) Are ethics involved in the study of gangs? What should such ethical guidelines consist of?

(3) Why should a gang researcher be knowledgeable about the prior literature and theory, generally, before studying the gang crime problem?

FOOTNOTES

1. For example, p. 11 (Thrasher, 1968) shows a picture of the "heart of Chicago's ghetto", the famous Maxwell street market. This area has been studied by a number of authors.

2. While Whyte does not indicate any references to the literature in his book, it is fascinating to find the phrase "habitual association" also used by Sleeman (1849: p. 357). Sleeman's work will be described later in reference to guerilla warfare, terrorism, and gang conflict.

3. Clearly, Cohen (1955, p. 59) seems knowledgeable of Merton's (1938) contribution of the typology of deviance by discussing "innovation" as something that should almost be avoided behaviorally. Cohen recognized the high value of Merton in accounting for adult crime, but criticized it for not being able to account for the non-utilitarian aspects of gang crime (see Cohen, 1955: 36).

4. Unfortunately for this "age-role" integration theory of gang formation, suggesting that society does not allow enough status for youths therefore they become gang affiliated to acquire their equivalent status and role functions, is the position advanced by authors such as Denisoff and McCaghy (1973, p.153-154), quite au contraire, which sees no such version of the British rebellion against the status system, rather in fact, views the selection of gang targets as rarely representing the adult world which should, according to such a "youth rebellion" theory, be directed more towards those symbols of "unjust domination" by adults.

5. Leissner (1969: p. 9-10) takes a similar position in avoiding the use of the term "gang" completely, because it implies "crime and violence" which overemphasizes the destructive factors of these groups. Thus, Leissner prefers the term 'street corner group', "because this term avoids the implications of exclusive preoccupation with violence and crime..." (1969, p. 10).

6. The appendix in Spergel (1964) clearly indicated that only in the case of the Racketville (organized crime, crime cartel) type of community was there difficulty gathering data by qualitative and quantitative methods (p. 198).

7. Dr. Spergel teaches in the Social Service Administration at the University of Chicago.

8. Spergel (1964) typically analyzed three communities each having three groups for a nine-cell table, but usually reported only ten cases per cell, for a presumable sample size of only N = 90. That may not seem like an impressive sample size today by some standards, but for the time it was a major turning point in gang studies.

9. The problem is job tenure, job retention, keeping the job, and conversely, quitting or getting fired from the job gotten through agency services. Current Chicago data shows that for one of the largest such offender job placement agencies in the country, that only about 1/3 get a job placement, and that after about 90 days only a fourth of them are still employed in the same job. This is not to deride job placement services: they are essential and based on good theory and they should be continued, indeed expanded and improved. Neither Short and Strodtbeck (1965, 1974) nor myself imply these types of services should be "cut back". Au contraire, they should be vastly refined qualitatively and quantitatively.

10. As a rational-choice model, the aleatory risk schema must face the criticism discussed by Jackson and Mc Bride (1990, p. 15) in that gang murders "are committed by emotional, violent gang members who do not think of the consequences". Horowitz (pp. 37-54 in Huff, 1990) similarly brings out the issue of whether it is a matter of "instrumental" (rational, calculating) or "expressive" (integrative, spontaneity, etc) motivation. Actually, a third problem is that of the error of organizational aggregation: the social-psychological polarity of motivation involving integrative versus instrumental is one applied historically to individual actors, not GROUPS of persons or organizations.

11. For the other side of this Poston (1971) story, that is, an equally vigorous policy discussion but one that is pro-RGS (the Real Great Society) see the work of Mottel (1973) which includes an interesting assortment of gang views in terms of conversation analysis with gang members.

12. Oddly, we never find out even in passing about their relationship to such other gangs as the Bloods and Crips, or the Aryan Brotherhood. These other gangs were perhaps less prominent at the time of the book's preparation. But there had to be other gangs in outlying neighborhoods, and we never hear about this aspect of intergang relationships that extend beyond the Mexican-American community.

13. That is, "jail house lawyers".

14. Oddly, the authors have no problem quoting such contributions to their own use when it serves their purposes.

15. To belabor the obvious: if they are selling illicit drugs, then they are committing crime; and depending on the type of drug, perhaps very serious crime. And with drug dealing go a host of other related crimes, including armed violence, retaliatory strikes, income producing crime to support drug purchases, etc.

16. Where I can certainly stand in agreement with the authors is that what facts we seek shall certainly determine, limit, and constrain what can ultimately be said about

gangs. Thus, the best mode of starting an investigation is not necessarily from an atheoretical point of departure.   Indeed, while Hagedorn often quotes from the underclass, racial oppression, and economic urban infrastructure deterioration literature, these concepts do not appear to be operationalized in their own data collection instrument (Hagedorn and Macon, 1988: pp. 171-180).

17. The case study by Olivero (1991) intentionally uses such a journalistic style and makes much reference for data to news media accounts.

18. Appearing, simultaneously, was Harris (1988) who espoused a view of Los Angeles female gang members that was not dissimilar from Vigil's marginality thesis. At least Harris is quite compatible by seeing these gang members "caught in a socially non-existent place in terms of the dominant culture" (Harris, 1988: p. 189).

19. Another lesson from the sociology of knowledge, to use an adage, is perhaps that sometimes we have to watch what we pray for, because it could come true. Which is to say, there is nothing new about getting "close up" to a crime problem to study it. Such was the essence of the early Chicago school. But getting "close up" is just as equally subject to be used from a conservative perspective (e.g., Slack and Schwitzgebel, 1959) as it might be from a leftist one. (see Slack, Charles W. and Ralph Switzgebel, 1959, "Interpersonal Research: A New Approach to Reducing Delinquency", Alabama Correctional Journal (6)(Oct): 32-40.)

20.   This reflected the "National Geographic Guide To Gangs", developed and maintained over the years by the National Gang Crime Research Center. This is now a very extensive listing of book length itself. It identifies the major gangs that are active in any capacity throughout the United States, using data from all sources: law enforcement, adult prisons, jails, juvenile correctional institutions, county sheriffs, etc.

21. This was not meant as a serious academic book, it was meant as a serious religious view of the problem. The photographs in the center of the book are somewhat interesting, but appear to be contrived. For example, one page (following p. 96) shows a black youth holding a very small revolver with the caption "O.Z., a Chicago gang member, armed on a dangerous street" (he was actually posed, looking out a window), with the same young man in the same identical clothing, hat, same sunglasses, same shirt, on the bottom photo holding a Bible with the caption "and later, with his Bible", apparently not much later.

22. Jackson's (1989) review of theories and findings about gangs is such a global assessment of the Chicago school, Miller and Cohen, plus other potentially applicable theories. It brings into discussion labelling theory and Matza's drift and bonding as potential such theories to apply to gang research.

23. J. Michael Olivero, Honor, Violence, and Upward Mobility: A Case Study of Chicago Gangs During the 1970s and 1980s. Edinburg, TX: The University of Texas-Pan American.

24. The Street Gang Identification Manual, is available from Gang Prevention, Inc, PO BOX 7400, Elgin, IL 60121.

CHAPTER 4

THE RACISM-OPPRESSION THESIS FOR GANG ANALYSIS

INTRODUCTION

The serious reader of gang studies will sense that there is more than simple disagreement between some authors who have contributed to this line of inquiry. It is comparable in some sense to the more general question of does racism account for any variation in criminal justice outcomes, such as sentencing disparity, etc. This analysis, however, finds much historical continuity with regard to the linkages between factors related to racism and oppression and gangs in general.

The most complaints about this chapter come from white students, so a few words are in order here. First, this is a theoretical concept that is being explored and in the social scientific approach to finding solutions we must have an open mind about all logical possibilities. Secondly, this is not a line of argumentation that advances racial conflict or divisions, but rather brings the issue into the open light of public discussion; it is only how some react to this potential platform that might be a source of division, such as where the discussion prompts a person towards dogmatism by stating some over-generalization such as "all police are racists", etc. Thirdly, the evidence exists for this thesis and it deserves to be understood correctly, such as the fact that similar to how the abused child without treatment reproduces this behavior by becoming a child abuser, the gang may arise and prosper during racial conflict but it also reproduces and exacerbates racial tensions.

Indeed there appears, at times, to be a striking, even ideological, difference between many authors in their basic orientations to the study of gangs. However, the astute observer will also find, upon much closer examination, that there are important conceptual continuities represented in the literature on gangs. One of these commonalities has to do with racial and ethnic conflict.[1] Racism can therefore be regarded as a factor causing the onset of gangs (Jackson and Mc Bride, 1990: pp. 8-9).

In short, there may be more consensus among gang researchers that we have previously been willing to recognize. This paper seeks to flush out one of these major commonalities in some detail. This cluster of related concepts will be called the racism-oppression thesis.

What it means for corrections personnel is that while no ACA[a] standards exist on programs for improving race relations within correctional facilities, we need to be keenly aware of the subtle nuances of race relations when gangs are organized along ethnic lines. What it means for modern law enforcement officers is that resolving

---

[a] The American Correctional Association (ACA) is the professional membership society --- the largest of its type in the world --- which sets operating standards for jails, juvenile institutions, prisons, halfway houses, etc. To use an analogy, the ACA is to corrections in America what the AMA is to healthcare.

racial and ethnic conflict must also be a goal within the context of community policing. Gang conflict often mirrors racial conflict, as is seen in violence that occurs in high schools.   Also, contrary to some reports on gangs that see them as having predominantly conservative views, the view of the gang member may take on such a "world view" as to see larger society as a force that discriminates and oppresses along racial lines.[2]   Some of the written gang constitutions typically contain such an "oppressed people" theme. Some recent research shows how racial beliefs are factors that vary significantly along the dimension of gang involvement.

OVERVIEW

The racism and oppression thesis basically holds that patterns of ethnic conflict and competition in America, the social structure and institutionalized patterns of race relations, the accommodation of poor and minority group members to an affluent society, and the individual experiences, patterns of enduring racial conflict, and perceptions of racism and oppression ---- all of these forms of social injustice, as objective and material conditions or as perceived by the individual, tend to be important causal determinants and reinforcing agents of gang delinquency and gang crime.

Indeed, there is some evidence, as shall be developed here, that the gang is a historically important and even contemporary apparatus through which racism is violently engendered, reinforced, and challenged at various levels (the community, prison, etc). The conservative reader will probably at this point conceive this to be a "no fault" conceptualization that relieves the individual gang member of social and moral responsibility. But that is not exactly correct.   In fact, gang members may today be the leading cause of continuing racial violence in America; and certainly play a large role in "bias crimes".

Rather this is a more macro-analytic approach that focuses on larger issues and social forces beyond the level of the individual actor. These may not be things that can be easily or even ever controlled completely, but we need to be alert to these viewpoints.

ETHNIC HOMOGENEITY IN AMERICAN GANGS

A central axiom of the racism-oppression thesis is that institutionalized racism manifests itself in the context of deviance, delinquency, and criminality by the gang's tendency to be ethnically homogeneous.   From a sociological viewpoint, gangs tend towards ethnocentrism --- the age-old concept of "ours is best, put down the rest".[3] However, there is an enduring and clear pattern of intellectual continuity in the identification of gangs as being ethnically homogeneous. This means that specific gangs more often than not consist of members who are predominantly of one racial or ethnic group.

That gangs are ethnically homogeneous has been cited by a number of authors over a long span of research and analysis (Thrasher, 1927; Thompson and Raymond, 1940; Bernard, 1949; MacIver, 1960; Gannon, 1967; Gordon, Short, Cartwright, and Strodtbeck, 1970; Hagedorn, 1988: p. 134; etc). As Suttles (1968) showed, African-

Americans gangs had no members from other ethnic groups, while the other gangs tended to be predominantly of one or the other ethnic identification (1971, p. 164). This includes conflict along the dimensions of race, religion, ethnicity or nationality of origin (Asbury, 1927).   It includes as Yablonsky points out, quoting from Thompson and Raymond (1940), certainly those gangs prior to the Prohibition Era being "classified by their national or racial antecedents" (1962, p. 116). It amounts to a kind of multiplicative relationship[4] between ethnicity and neighborhood ties: "The Irish controlled the West, and the East Side belonged to the Italians and the Jews" (Yablonsky, 1962: p. 116).

That gang crime involves conditions of competition and ethnic succession is also documented (Cloward and Ohlin, 1960: p. 200-202;) in the literature.

Earlier data from the Chicago Police Department on Chicago street gangs also shows this condition of ethnic homogeneity. Figure 4, below, shows this breakdown by gang and ethnicity. This excludes gangs listed as inactive. There are also various branches of the Disciples, Vice Lords, Latin Kings, and others in different areas of Chicago. Clearly, the vast majority of these major gangs operating in Chicago using official police statistics meet this criteria of being ethnically homogeneous.

FIGURE 4

Police Reports on Chicago Street Gang Membership

Gang Name	Racial Composition
Ambrose	98% Latin
Ashland Vikings	60% Puerto Rican, 35% Mexican,5% white
Assyrian Eagles	100% Assyrian
Bishops	98% Latin
Black Eagles	100% Oriental
Black Gangster Disciples	100% Black
Black P Stone	100% Black
Black Souls	100% Black
Braizers	100% Mexican
C-Notes	90% white, 10% Latin
Cobra Stone	100% Black
Cullerton Boys/Duces	99% Latin, 1% white
Dragons	97% Puerto Rican, 2% Cuban, 1% white
Dueces (Insane)	70% Latin, 15% white, 15% Black
El Rukns	100% Black
Freaks	100% white
Gaylords	99% white
Ghetto Brothers Organ.	97% Latin, 2% Black, 1% white
Ghost Shadow	100% Oriental
Harrison Gents	70% Black, 30% Latin
Imperial Gangsters	90% Latin, 8% white, 2% Black
Kenmore Boys	90% white, 10% Latin
Kents/Stone Kents	100% Latin
Kool Gang	99% Black, 1% Latin & white

Latin Brothers	95% Latin, 5% white
Latin Counts	99% Mexican, 1% white
Latin Disciples	95% Latin, 3% Black, 2% white
Latin Eagles	80% Puerto Rican, 10% Mexican, 5% white, 5% Black
Latin Jivers	95% Puerto Rican, 5% Black
Latin Kings	90% Latin, 5% Black, 5% white
Latin Lovers	98% Latin, 5% Black, 5% white
Latin Saints	90% Latin, 10% white
Latin Souls	80% Latin, 15% white, 5% Black,1% Arab
Orchestra Albany	95% Latin, 4% white, 1% Black
Paulina Barry Community	75% white, 22% Latin, 3% Black and American Indian
Popes	95% White, 5% other
P.R. Stones	90% Latin, 5% white, 5% Black
Racine Boys	100% Latin
Reapers	50% white, 30% Latin, 20% Black
Uptown Rebels	100% white
Ridgeway Lords	White and Latin
Satan's Disciples	95% Latin, 5% white
Simon City Royals	97% White, 3% Black & Latin
Sin City Boys	97% Latin, 3% White & Black
Spanish Cobras	80% Latin, 18% white, 2% Black
Spanish Cobra Disciples	95% Latin, 5% white
Spanish Lords	90% Latin, 10% white
Tokers	100% Latin
Two-Six Nation	95% Latin, 5% white
Unknowns (Insane)	95% Latin, 5% Black & white
Vice Lords	100% Black
Villa Labos (Lone Wolves)	98% Latin, 2% white
Warlords	95% Latin, 5% Black & white

Finally, we must take advantage of the rich detailed account provided by Thrasher (1927). Indeed, all of Chapter 10 in Thrasher's gang study involved this aspect of ethnic homogeneity and ethnic conflict via the gang. The historical change implied by this continuity of two such predominant factors that have appeared throughout the gang literature --- (1) the gang arising and persisting as a racially or ethnically homogeneous group, (2) in a depressed or inner city neighborhood --- is that of social organization.

What has remained somewhat intact is that of social organization in the Chinese community, where their pattern of ethnic accommodation involves preserving traditions and local organization. It is the least changed in terms of ethnicity and inner city processes of ethnic succession and displacement. Thus, there has been a continuous gang problem dating back to the role of the Tongs over a hundred years ago.

What changed in the 1960s was the civil rights movement and strengthened social organization among African-Americans. Latinos and Hispanics followed in this line of seeking ethnic parity. This backdrop provided an important historical opportunity for their representation among gang organizations as well. Along with equal opportunity to attend white schools came the equal opportunity to have your own gangs.[5] What was emancipated was social organization. Racial prejudice, discrimination, and oppression did not necessarily change drastically and certainly did not disappear.[6] When it does, however, and African-Americans and other persons of color are free to live wherever they want in America and have genuine educational opportunities, then perhaps we might see the emptying out of high rise ghetto buildings and inner city areas filled with the inter-generationally poor, and in so doing, removing one of the backbones that give rise to American street gangs.

BIAS CRIMES IN THE GANG CONTEXT

From the most formative and early writers on American gangs comes the recognition of cases of bias crimes. While bias crimes were not formally recognized until the late 1980s[7], a bias crime involves simply bigotry towards race, ethnic, religious, or other (e.g., sexual preference) group attribute as the primary precipitating and motivational factor in the commission of a crime. That is to say, a person or group of persons are singled out because they have such an attribute (e.g., skin color, etc). This is most conspicuous when it involves acts of brutality involving white racism (Schwartz and Disch, 1970; Kovel, 1984). A neo-nazi skinhead spinoff gang group called the Bomber Boys, about ten years ago in Chicago, specialized in attacking homosexuals and African-Americans on the near north side.

What has passed in our history as the recollection of "zoot suit" riots in California during W.W. II, was shown by Gonzalez (1981) to be little more than organized racist violence against any Mexican person. That is, a cultural difference of clothing or apparel (the "zoot suit" or "drapes") was a sufficient condition at the time to facilitate the social production of deviance; that is, whether they were or were not "gang" members, anyone wearing such apparel was automatically conceived to be a Mexican gang member.[8] And, often, whether they were or were not wearing such zoot suits when they met large angry mobs of military men on shore leave in California cities, they were still violently attacked if they were Mexican males.

There have been many variations on this theme, both here and abroad (Carey, 1985). Skinhead groups, neo-nazis, and other extremists (KKK) have figured prominently in this role. Suall and Lowe (1988) estimated only a couple hundred active skinheads in the USA, but that such "white power" groups may be growing. Apparently a number of criminal justice agencies do view these groups with some concern, as they are most certainly well reported in the appendix "gang listing".

RACIAL AND ETHNIC SLURS AS A CAUSAL VARIABLE IN GANG VIOLENCE

Racial tension as a provocation or precipitating factor in gang violence has been denied by Gannon's analysis involving a mail questionnaire approach with N = 80 gang outreach workers in New York City (see Gannon, 1970: p. 348). Yet the same research, curiously, showed that in 1964 among those factors cited by these gang outreach workers as "most often" being a factor related to group conflict, racial tension was the single largest factor most frequently reported as a precipitating factor of gang conflict (p. 347). This factor of racial tension was viewed as most often being a cause of, or being associated with, gang conflict by 45.3 percent of the detached workers responding to the survey. This was higher than for any other of the precipitating factors analyzed (drinking, girls, neighborhood group differences, individual reprisals, "sounding", price of liquor or drugs).

Yablonsky's (1962) ten hours of tape recordings with gang members was able to document the role of ethnic slurs and counter reaction as a prelude to gang conflict. This showed that "some boys used racial or ethnic discrimination as a reason" for inter-gang conflict (pp. 10-11).

RACE RELATIONS AND GANG PROBLEMS

Heavily influenced from the earlier research in Los Angeles showing similar conditions (Moore, 1978), the study by Hagedorn (1988) in Milwaukee was significant in contributing to the elements of analysis in the racism-oppression thesis. Denial and avoidance of the "race question" in gang research and analysis was ably demonstrated by Hagedorn (1988, p. 25). Some non-sociological or non-academic reports have simply taken the position of denying the significance of race and ethnicity.

Yet, if Hagedorn's thesis is correct regarding racial and ethnic subjugation, then confirmation comes from analyzing the differences in gang membership/structure during different periods of American history. Hagedorn's position regarding the etiology of Milwaukee's street gangs is that "gang formation took place in a context of continuing crisis in race relations" (1988, p. 50). The implication for the present would be, that those race and ethnic groups most subjected to racism and oppression (African-Americans, Latinos, American Indians[9], Asians,[10] etc) would be the most conspicuously represented in gang organization.[11] Similarly, those cities experiencing heightened levels of racial conflict would likewise be those more likely to show the stronger emergence of a gang problem.[12]

Racial and ethnic antagonisms were not born in the 1960s. Gangs have probably existed in America since the day America was first colonized. Thrasher's and Whyte's emphasis upon recent immigrants as a "feeder mechanism" for gangs can therefore be viewed not as the gang problem as originating among "aliens", but rather that these new immigrant groups represented the bottom of the social pyramid and faced harsh stigma --- because of their language, customs, cultural pattern/dress, etc.[13]

The Rodney King case provides another example of how a crisis in race relations can provide the ideal setting for the onset of serious gang violence and civil disorder. That gangs in Los Angeles were heavily involved in the rioting during 1992 is not to say they were the only ones involved. In conditions of civil disorder, the rule of law disappears and the only rule is that of force. Gangs and gang members obviously benefited after the rioting as well by the declarations, demands, and massive media coverage. Unfortunately no government agency has declared war on the race relations problem in America.

The continuing problems of race relations are to be found throughout the United States. In seeing the rise of the "cool pose" behavior typifying a crisis in manhood development which they go on to say provides the fertile ground for gang behavior as well, Majors and Mancini (1992) state:

> "We are concerned with how some black males use coolness to counter the stresses of oppression...People of all racial...groups use cool behaviors to some extent. However, because of the legacy of slavery and because black males in the United States have been subjected to systematic discrimination...we suspect cool behaviors have emerged with more frequency and intensity among low income black males than in other groups (Majors and Mancini, 1992: p. xii)".

ADULT PARTICIPATION   AS AN INDICATOR   OF MINORITY GROUP OPPRESSION

A second theme generated from Hagedorn is that adult participation in gang crime has as a fundamental cause "drastically changed economic conditions in poor minority urban neighborhoods" (1988, p. 111). Campbell (1984) came close to suggesting something compatible here, in the sense that the estrangement of the underclass, their detachment, their displacement, their disassociation, etc, ---- whatever we want to call it, has something to do with gang affiliation. In Campbell's view, those persons who join a gang are the same persons who have the least to gain from the status quo (p. 236). As will be seen in chapter 5, addressing the concepts of underclass, surplus population, and human capital, this experience need not be an objective material condition --- it can also be a perception.[14] As Short and Strodtbeck note, gang members certainly express a feeling of deprivation (1974, p. 126).

RUMORS HEIGHTEN THE ANTAGONISM

Suttles (1968) showed that racial bias and racial fears were important ideological components of the content of rumors at the community level.[15] "Every spring for example, there were several rumors which preceded the closing of school: for instance, the Negroes are going to cause a riot in the Italian section, or vice versa" (Suttles, 1968: p. 197). If the Kerner commission, studying civil disturbances in the 1960s, was any indication; then rumors play an important role in the onset of conflict.

The Kerner report (Wicker, 1968) documented the historical role that rumor has played in racial strife in America. This included the 1917 race riot in East St. Louis: as several white men worried about the threat of African-Americans to their job security and status "were leaving City Hall, they heard that a Negro had accidentally shot a white man during a holdup. In a few minutes rumor had replaced fact: the shooting was intentional --- a white woman had been insulted --- two white girls were shot. By this time 3,000 people had congregated and were crying for vengeance. Mobs roamed the streets, beating Negroes. Policemen did little more than take the injured to hospitals and disarm Negroes" (pp. 217-218).

Rumors played such a large part in civil disturbances, that some law enforcement agencies such as in Chicago established rumor control centers "where individuals who hear rumors can call to find out what is actually happening. These centers have proved to be highly effective" (Revere, 1982: p. 301). Such rumor control "hotlines" were also used during the 1993 federal trial involving the Rodney King case.

In 1992 a "memorandum" became widely circulated throughout the African-American community of Chicago. To the casual observer it was real, or you wanted to believe it at least. It as a memorandum from the Ku Klux Klan, only it was spelled "Klu Klux Klan". It thanked gang members for their good work in killing Black people and encouraged them to "keep it up". It was later revealed that this was a moral joke played by an activist minister.

In early September, 1993, in Chicago another underground communication was quickly spread by fax machine --- the infamous "Lights Out" memorandum. It was believed by so many that it was often retyped by the recipient and spread rapidly throughout the city to all races, and all sectors. The present author received four versions, each produced by a different typewriter or printer. This memo panicked the city until a local television station revealed it to be a rumor gone astray. Here is the text of the memo:

"BEWARE!! There is a New "Gang Initiation". This new gang initiation of murder is brought about by Gang Members driving around at night with their car lights off. When you flash your car lights to signal them that their lights are out, the Gang Members take it literally as "LIGHTS OUT", so they are to follow you to your destination and kill you! That's their initiation. Two families have already fallen victim to this initiation ritual. Be aware and inform your families and friends. DO NOT FLASH YOUR CAR LIGHTS FOR ANYONE!!"

It was a hoax. But it showed how the public can panic and take these rumors as genuine truth: the element of fear takes over, the ordinary person wants to believe gangs are capable of such evil. The "Lights Out" memo was posted in colleges, in government offices, in businesses, and handed out in churches throughout Chicago until it was revealed about a week later as a hoax. White racist groups are experts as trying to spread such rumors in their organizing efforts (see Ridgeway, 1990). It could have very well been such a source for the related "gang panic" rumor that spread rapidly through the sororities of the University of Illinois at Champaign in the fourth week of September, 1993. The gang rumor being spread was that a new gang initiation rite involved gangs sexually assaulting female students, and leaving a gang "brand" on the body of African-American co-eds. Computer bulletin boards are sometimes the source of such rumors.

THE RURAL-URBAN DIFFERENCE

William Kornblum's Blue Collar Community (1974) was a study of Chicago's southside steel mills. Kornblum lived in the area and worked in the steel mill during the period of study. While contributing much to the understanding of urban ethnicity, this study also documented conflict in the steel mills between African-Americans regarding gang affiliation. The basic difference was the that between the younger African-American male socialized in the urban setting, and often having a gang affiliation, and that of the rural older African-American (1974, p. 45). It was a "dimension of cleavage" (p. 45) and a source of "tension and disunity" (P. 48).

Importantly, in the "neutral turf" of the work place, "gang membership itself does not cause visible tension between members of rival gangs who work in the mill" (p. 48). Each gang would put its slogans and epithets on the bathroom walls.

Logically, however, while gangs in America have traditionally been studied as an urban phenomenon, it is equally possible to have gangs in rural areas and smaller cities.[16] That is, if the racism-oppression thesis is correct, such wider societal and social structural forces operate to impact equally strong outside of urban areas. These forces therefore could also play a part in the emergence of gangs outside of urban areas.

GANGS AS VEHICLES OF ETHNIC CONFLICT

Do white gangs function as surrogate defenders for the status quo of ensuring the continuity of racial segregation?   Is the gang in American cities the contemporary vehicle through which ethnic rivalry is concentrated?   Are white gangs the modern violent defenders of "ethnic purity"?   These are research agenda items for future criminologists. For now we must speculate only towards their affirmation.

But first, it bears repeating that many skinhead and almost all neo-nazi and white racist groups can be classified logically as gangs using our definition of gang: it is a group that benefits from the continuing criminal activity of its members. The crimes in these instances may not be drug sales income, but are rather ideological crimes, that is bias crimes, offenses that reinforce their ideology. They benefit as well because such crimes occur in a group context, more often than not, and this is a mechanism for building greater solidarity among such group members.

That American race relations shifted from conflict to competition was demonstrated in the work of Wilson (1978[b]). But was some segment of the conflict modality then shifted to a less conspicuous form such as in the gang subculture is the question raised here?   The continuing historical pattern of ethnic homogeneity among American gangs is of some import. As a struggle over power, privilege and resources, the gang is a natural combat force readily employed in this struggle to maintain or challenge the status quo. Any community has "plausible deniability": it was only the gang, it was not "us".

Terrorism was directed against African-Americans in the form of mob lynchings well up through the time of Thrasher's and Whyte's research. As Raper (1933: p. 1) documented, between the period of 1889 and 1930 at least 3,724 people were put to death by mob lynchings in the United States. We can correctly assume that much of this was directed at racial and ethnic minorities. According to Scwhartz and Disch (1970, p. 29), in fact, there were 3,811 African-Americans lynched between the period 1889 to 1940. When you can be lynched for attempting to vote, you do not develop

---

[b] The Declining Significance of Race: Blacks and Changing American Institutions, University of Chicago Press.

a community infrastructure with social organizations allowing for political control and access to scarce resources. It is hard to develop a "tong" or protective society or gang that is conspicuous under such conditions of overtly targeted violence and repression.

Returning to the work of Thrasher (1927, Chapter 10), we find that only 7.16 percent of the 880 gangs about which ethnicity was known involved African-Americans. The rest were of a wide variety of white-ethnic groups, and they were all in this sense homogeneous with respect to skin color. Antagonistic relations between various white ethnic groups were "carried over into gangs and color many of their conflicts in Chicago" (Thrasher, 1968: p. 133). Indeed, "among the most bitter of these intercultural enmities transplanted from the old world is that between Jews and the Poles" (p. 133). Pogroms in Europe had their parallel forms with American gangs in cities like Chicago.

The infamous "march on Skokie" by a neo-nazi group in the 1970s had its equivalent form involving gang members in Thrasher's account of anti-semitism (pp. 134-135) in Chicago (Knox, 1976). Random violence, conflict at the mode of consumption and in recreational areas was common. And it was reciprocal ethnic antagonism, prejudice, discrimination and bias crime. Jewish gangs found their sport in the "Polock hunt" (p. 135). What Thrasher documented beyond gang activity was the important historical process of community change involving the "process of invasion and succession" (p. 137). Dating back over a hundred years ago, one ethnic gang would inevitably dissolve by its ethnic groups displacement to the arriving newcomers to the neighborhood, and the "new kids on the block" would emulate the social organizational infrastructure they were exposed to, and develop their own ethnic gang.

Another important contribution from Thrasher that seems to have been missed throughout all subsequent discussions involving gang analysis, is that of race riots and the gangs (Thrasher, 1968: pp. 139-140). Clearly, Thrasher documents that white gangs were heavily involved throughout the 1919 race rioting in Chicago. "Gangs and their activities were an important factor throughout the riot. But for them it is doubtful if the riot would have gone beyond the first clash" (p. 140). These white gangs operated to perform bias crimes against African-Americans "without hindrance from the police" and quoting a judge Thrasher also noted "they (the gang members) seemed to think they had a sort of protection which entitled them to go out and assault anybody. When the race riots occurred it gave them something to satiate the desire to inflict their evil propensities on others" (p. 140).

Thrasher documents the rise of Chinese gangs, or "tongs" meaning protective society, in response to their victimization from white racism (pp. 144-149). Thrasher's (1927) chapter 10 should be required reading for everyone because of its richness of details about ethnic conflict, the culture complex (p. 149), the cultural frontier and oppression psychosis (pp. 152-153), and Thrasher's conclusion that the base "problem is one of reconciling these divergent heritages with each other and with America. If there has been any failure here, it can hardly be laid at the door of the immigrant" (p. 154).

IMPORTATION THEORY AND THE SPECIAL CASE OF THE ARYAN BROTHERHOOD

Importation theory relates to the correctional institution and how gangs came to have such a large and conspicuous presence in jails, correctional institutions, and prisons. It basically means the gang members were "imported" into the correctional milieu through aggressive "gang targeting" prosecution efforts. In other words, the more gang members were prosecuted, the more they were represented in the prison system.

Clearly, in the 1960s and 1970s those gangs most targeted for prosecution in American cities were not white gangs. They were minority member gangs. It came as no surprise that minority gangs were heavily represented in America's prison system. In fact, the racial composition of the American prison population has changed most dramatically since the time of Thrasher (1927). In 1927, only 21 percent of the inmates admitted to state and federal prisons were Black; this figure has steadily increased since 1927, to the point where by 1986 the proportion for Blacks had reached 44 percent[17]. Similar trends have been noted in the juvenile correctional population.

But did the Aryan Brotherhood fit the same pattern of being imported into the prison? Most suspect not. That is, AB's were not imported, at first, directly; even though, today, through transfers we find AB's in various correctional institutions. Some critical observers have taken the position that it was an invention fostered by correctional staff to "counter balance" the threat of disorder represented by minority gangs. The indigenous formation view is that the white inmates themselves entered into a gang formation that did not exist outside of the correctional institution because of the need to maintain parity in group power.[18] White inmates simply developed their own patterns of group cooperation to maintain such parity with other forces inside the correctional institution. This seems the most plausible explanation rather than believing the "conspiracy theory" that "white gangs" were artificially created. It is not easy to artificially create a gang. Even though, it can, technically, be done.

The existence of large numbers of juvenile correctional institutions reporting the existence of separate white gangs in their facilities, often skin heads, tends to suggest the possibility that such groups functioned outside of corrections and may have in fact been imported. Remember, if law enforcement is effective, or if correctional officials have to transfer gang members, then importation occurs.

What we do know about adult institutions is that "the phenomenon of racism is fierce inside prisons and gangs usually organize along racial lines" (Camp and Camp, 1985: p. viii). We also know that about half of all juvenile institutions in America report a problem with racial conflict; those who have problems of racial conflict in corrections generally are those same institutions more likely to report a gang problem as well.

An assessment of the research at this point must conclude that white extremist gangs are to be found throughout the United States. This includes skinheads and "A.B.'s" in many adult and juvenile correctional institutions. The recent work of Hamm (1993) views such bias crimes as racial terrorism and regards such groups as terrorist youth subcultures. The importance of preventing such domestic terrorism requires according to Hamm, several recommendations: "Boycotting White Power Rock...Expanded Litigation Against Publishers of Racist Literature...Conservative Gun Control Legislation...Standards for Responsible Media Coverage" and research (Hamm, 1993: 219-220). The bottom line here is that skinheads who commit bias crimes are a gang, just as the KKK is a gang: they may not be on the street corner selling drugs, but they benefit from violating laws nevertheless. It is a mistake to simply regard them as "hate groups". Hating is not a crime. Putting hate into action in the context of racial violence is a crime. The "benefit" may not be financial, it may be ideological. But it is a crime pattern all the same[c].

What will also emerge from national data is that wherever correctional institutions report a gang problem, they also tend to report a problem of racial conflict among inmates as well. This is a very consistent research finding in many contexts including schools.

VARIANCE IN CRIMINAL JUSTICE SYSTEM CONDITIONS AND OUT-COMES RELATED TO RACE AND ETHNICITY

Short and Strodtbeck (1965, pp. 224,258) estimated that for African-American gang boys their probability of an arrest for offenses related to violence are about .04 --- that is, in only 4 cases out of one hundred would the offense result in an arrest. Indeed, they argue for the more sophisticated or experienced offender this probability may be cut in half to 2%. However, does it make a difference if these are "Black on Black" crimes of violence, or if the victim is white? Such is an issue that must be resolved, empirically, regarding the racial oppression thesis.

Official data on homicides in Chicago for the year 1989 bears some relationship here. For the 480 African-American male offenders there were 353 victims, and only 21 of these victims were not cases of "Black on Black" crime (Chicago Police Department, 1989 Murder Analysis, p. 19). From the same report, among the 187 unsolved murders, there were 4 female whites and 18 male whites (p. 21), the other victims were persons of color.

MINORITY GROUP REPRESENTATION WITHIN THE RANKS OF CRIMINAL JUSTICE PERSONNEL

The 1964 Civil Rights Act gave minority group members a chance to begin working in law enforcement, corrections, probation and parole, and related criminal justice positions. This act required criminal justice agencies to have an affirmative action program to ensure that minority group members were adequately represented in these various governmental positions. It means recruiting from minority groups and

---

[c] When the first edition of this book came out, it was not uncommon at national criminology and criminal justice conventions for other gang researchers to ask me "how can you include groups like the KKK and skinheads in a gang analysis?". The first edition included a preliminary version of the national gang tracking list and such groups like skinheads, the KKK, and other white-power gangs were even shown to be widely dispersed across the United States.

having "policies and procedures protecting minorities from racial and sexual harassment" (Klofas, Stojkovic, and Kalinich, 1990: p. 20). Thus, simply hiring minority group members at the lowest echelon or entry level position is not enough. There must be a fair opportunity for advancement within the organization and there must be an atmosphere free of racism.

Regarding corrections alone, according to the 1987 Sourcebook of Criminal Justice Statistics published by the U.S. Department of Justice, Bureau of Justice Statistics, 1,118 of the 7,076 employees of the State adult correctional institutions in Illinois were African-American (p. 37). Another 316 of the 854 employees of in community-based facilities were African-American (p. 37). Yet it is difficult to say that the institutional employee capability to relate to the inmate population along racial and ethnic lines holds when 15.7 percent of the prison personnel are African-American and over 60 percent of the inmates are African-American. This is a growing gap.

A report published by the American Correctional Association in 1988 showed that while African-Americans are 12 percent of the American census population, they constitute almost 50 percent of the prison population nationwide (Petersilia and Turner, 1988: p. 92).[19] Oddly, in Illinois, while whites constitute only about a third of the prison population, whites also receive over half (55%) of the placements in the community-based facilities in Illinois (see Table 6.62, p. 635, Sourcebook of Criminal Justice Statistics, 1988).[20]

In July of 1993 a class action lawsuit was brought against the U.S. Federal Bureau of Prisons by some 4,300 of its Black employees[21]. The law suit charges the federal prison system with discrimination in terms of promotions. About 18 percent of the federal prison system employees are Blacks, but few Blacks actually hold higher management positions.

That there exists evidence of institutional racism at various levels in the criminal justice system is felt apparently by some. Because of this, clearly our society must do more to encourage and cultivate minority representation within the corrections and criminal justice field. To conclude otherwise is to deny some important truths that must be faced. The point here is that this means not simply the treatment of those adjudicated and confined in custody, it also means hiring and promotion opportunities for minorities within this field. Clearly, much progress remains to be made in this area.

THE RELATED ISSUE OF THE DUAL LABOR MARKET

The dual labor market hypothesis basically argues that in American society our legitimate occupational opportunity system can be divided into two broad, but very different, categories: the competitive sector, and the monopoly sector. In the competitive sector, these are jobs with little potential for advancement, low pay, low job security, low benefits, and low prestige (e.g., burger flopper jobs at fast food restaurants). In the monopoly sector, these are jobs with high security, high pay, many benefits, and more prestige (banking industry, etc).

Crutchfield (1989) using Seattle, Washington census tract data and annual police reports showed some support for the dual labor market hypothesis where labor instability was found to be associated with violent crime rates. This is a critical issue in criminology. It is more directly related to the issue of the underclass, the surplus population, and human capital factors that are emerging as significant factors in gang research. This issue will be addressed in much greater detail in Chapter 5. But to the extent that it becomes the vehicle through which racial differences emerge in society, then it too must be taken into account for providing such an analysis of the racism-oppression thesis.

To test the racism-oppression thesis one cannot simply go to a correctional facility and ask the inmates if they believe that the reason they have a criminal record is because this is a racist society. That is not the best manner in which to test the racism-oppression thesis. Many so affected may not simply understand the larger societal processes. This is an area best suited for macrosociological analysis, not the individual level of analysis. Provided below is an effort that uses American juvenile correctional institutions as the unit of analysis.

CRIPS: ARISING IN A CONTEXT OF CONFLICT

If we believe the public relations imagery of more educated members of the Crip gangs, as in the story Monster, then we would believe that the gang was basically formed in response to institutionalized racism. Actually there are a number of rival explanations for how the Crips began, the five most common being: (1) They adopted their title from the TV movie series "Tales From The Crypt" starring Vincent Price to be "scary" in a tinsel town; (2) Some early members were suffered injuries to the legs, rendering them handicapped, the word "cripple" then being shortened to "crips"; (3) One phonetic explanation is that the Crips sprang from an actual group called the "Cribs" who were themselves the surviving influence of the Slauson street gang which dates to the earlier 1960s; (4) Another phonetic explanation is that "Crips" became the phonetic spelling of "krypts" the personified version of "kryptonite", which kills Superman, that is, the term simply was adopted to imply a powerful image; and (5) That youths were actually politically active in a protest orientation and that the very word Crip was an acronym that meant "Common Revolution In Progress".

About all anyone agrees in the facts about the origins of the Crips is the issue of when they were first brought to the attention of the criminal justice system. It was in 1969 that the Crips first got such attention. It was fighting behavior in Washington High School that got the Crips noticed.

RACIAL DIFFERENCES NOT RACIAL OPPRESSION

The issue is whether some gangs are simply different by the type of motivating force they have. One of the classic dichotomy's in any introduction to psychology course discussing motivation is the difference between expressive versus instrumental. In the expressive version of a gang, it is motivated by social and not economic concerns. In the instrumental version of a gang, it is motivated primarily by money making concerns.

Some authors have suggested this concept applies to modern gangs including the Crips and Bloods compared with Hispanic/Latino gangs.   One in this line has interpreted differences in homicide rates among Chicago gangs to conclude that predominantly African-American gangs like the Vice Lords and Gangster Disciples were more likely to commit homicides because of money making concerns; while Hispanic/Latin gangs like the Latin Kings and the Latin Disciples were more likely to commit homicides because of expressive concerns like turf defense (Block and Block, 1993: p. 8).

This would appear to be reductionism or an over simplification of the gang reality. To extend it to its logical extreme, such a comparison between African-Americans and Hispanics would be arguing that one racial group has a monopoly on a human motivation. It would also, logically, be assuming equal variances in the extent to which gang members join a gang for chiefly economic reasons. It would also, logically, be assuming a lot more about racial differences than would appear to be justified by data.

But such overgeneralizations are easy to make about gangs as has been noted earlier in this book. We have not yet seen much empirical research on gang economic issues. What we do know from the literature is that such an expressive-instrumental classification is probably a fallacy even in Chicago. The work of Padilla shows Latin gangs are clearly concerned with making money too. But to future research, some of which is now underway, we can add these empirical questions to settle this issue: are there more ballers and high rollers in African-American gangs than in Latino/Hispanic gangs, that is those who are gang members because they are making money at it; are African-American gangs more dog city than Latino/Hispanic gangs, that is they are working for the money; are there differences by ethnic gangs in terms of making ends in the gang, that is making money in the gang; are African-Americans the only gang members trying to get their thirties on, that is making money selling drugs; are there differences by racial gangs in terms of living large, that is being able to make money and live a psuedo-wealthy lifestyle? These hypotheses have not been tested yet in the literature.

THE RACISM-GANG   PROBLEM: A PRELIMINARY   TEST

The gang problem appears to have some relationship to the problem in race relations as well. That adult prison disturbances have had racial overtones has been previously reported in the literature. Less is known about the juvenile context of this same problem.   What is known is that in recent years the percentage of Black and Hispanic youths has increased over 30 percent among children in custody (Snyder, 1990).

Our question to juvenile correctional administrators was "are racial conflicts a problem among juveniles in your facility?". Some 155 institutions are included in this sample representing 49 states. The findings show that nearly half (47.4%) indicated this was true. That some environments can foster a destructive demeanor appears to have some empirical support at least when examining this factor of racial conflict in relationship to reports of property damage, overcrowding, and recidivism.[22]

This factor of racial conflict is shown to significantly differentiate any extent of gang member damage to government property as seen in Table 1 below. This means that where a juvenile institution has a problem of racial conflict the chances are increased of having a problem of gangs damaging government property in the same institution.

TABLE 1

FREQUENCY DISTRIBUTION OF RACIAL CONFLICT BY REPORT OF GANG DAMAGE TO GOVERNMENT PROPERTY

		GANG DAMAGE TO GOVT. PROPERTY	
		NO	YES
RACIAL CONFLICT			
PROBLEM:	NO	51	26
	YES	20	52

Chi square = 22.05, p < .001

Also, overcrowding is shown to be significantly associated with racial conflict as seen in Table 2. This means those juvenile correctional institutions that are overcrowded are those more likely to report a problem of racial conflict.

TABLE 2

FREQUENCY DISTRIBUTION OF REPORTS OF OVERCROWDING IN JUVENILE INSTITUTIONS BY REPORTS OF RACIAL CONFLICT

	Reported Racial Conflict	
	NO	YES
OVERCROWDING PROBLEM:		
NO	45	25
YES	31	48

Chi square = 9.4, p = .002

The reports of racial conflict in juvenile institutions appear to be associated with the problem of high recidivism rates as well. Table 3 shows the distribution for reported racial conflict by whether the same institutions also reported a recidivism rate higher than twenty percent. This means those juvenile institutions with racial conflicts are more likely to have higher recidivism rates.

TABLE 3

DISTRIBUTION OF RACIAL CONFLICT BY REPORTS
OF HIGH RECIDIVISM RATES

		Recidivism Higher Than 20%	
		NO	YES
Reports of			
Racial Conflict	NO	47	26
	YES	34	39

Chi square = 4.6, p = .03

There is a need for standards to govern the handling of gangs within correctional settings and to address the matter of racial conflict. But these have not been forthcoming from the American Correctional Association in spite of its recognized ability to generate standards for just about every other aspect of care, treatment, process, and human behavior.

HOW PESSIMISTIC RACIAL BELIEFS VARY WITH HAVING EVER TRIED TO QUIT THE GANG AMONG A LARGE SAMPLE OF GANG MEMBERS

Gang members generally are more likely to have beliefs that exemplify a problem in relating to other races, particularly whites. Further, this appears to vary consistently along the dimensions of the gang risk continuum. The gang risk continuum represents the extent to which one is involved with gangs.

The data analyzed here come from a recent larger study of gangs and guns.[23] This data represents a large sample of criminal gang members surveyed in the midwest in the summer of 1994. The gang members are combined from four different social contexts: eight jails, a high school, a probation program, and an innercity social services program.

What this data shows is that the more hard core gang member has a significantly higher distrust of white persons. The survey question asked them to agree or disagree with the statement "It is usually a mistake to trust a white person". Among those who had tried to quit the gang, some 23.5 percent agreed. Among those who had never attempted to quit the gang, some 44.4 percent agreed. The significant difference here is shown in Table 4 below.

TABLE 4

FREQUENCY DISTRIBUTION OF BELIEFS ABOUT WHITE PEOPLE BY WHETHER THE PERSON HAS EVER ATTEMPTED TO QUIT THE GANG AMONG A SAMPLE OF MIDWEST GANG MEMBERS

		Ever Attempt to Quit The Gang?	
It is usually a mistake to trust a white person.		NO	YES
	AGREE	105	48
	DISAGREE	131	156
		Chi-square = 21.1, p < .001	
There are many white people who are not prejudiced.	AGREE	154	164
	DISAGREE	83	44
		Chi-square = 10.4, p = .001	

The findings about the more pessimistic views on race relations among the more hard core gang member (i.e., the ones who have never tried to quit the gang), shows that the stronger the commitment to the gang, the more the same person distrusts white people and views white people as prejudiced. This shows that among those who had never attempted to quit the gang some 64.9 percent agreed that there are many white people who are not prejudiced, compared to 78.8 percent among those who had tried to quit the gang. Clearly, it is the more committed the person is to the gang as measured by having never attempted to quit the gang, the more the same person has pessimistic racial beliefs about white people.

SUMMARY AND CONCLUSION

What has been so obvious, on a closer examination of the gang literature, is the undeniable fact that racism has played an important role in the onset and persistence of American gangs according to many authors.[24] This implies, also, that gangs will exist as long as ethnic or racial oppression exists. For poor whites in gangs this is less a matter of their ethnic or racial subjugation than it may be their competitive relationship with minorities in a context of mutually disagreeable economic conditions; particularly in social and human capital development terms.

In short, there is reason to believe historically that an important condition that fuels both the onset and persistence of gangs is that related to the racial-oppression hypothesis. It is remarkably predictive in the correctional setting, the educational setting, and the community setting. Research on juvenile correctional institutions shows where we have a gang problem in terms of damage to government property we also have high reports of the incidence of racial conflict.

Perhaps, then, from a larger point of view one method of dealing with gangs would be a strategy that involves improving race relations generally. Just as a sense of good will must be developed with inmates, such a network of interracial "good will" among correctional inmates could be an important factor in limiting the potentially destructive influences of gangs in our prisons today. That racial conflict among inmates in American correctional institutions is now becoming shown to be a very large problem. It simply reflects the enduring pattern of ethnic rivalry and ethnic antagonism and racial discrimination that is often at the base of much of the gang problem in America[25].

Unfortunately the strained race relations we have in our prisons and jails are only a reflection of the same problem in the outside surrounding communities. The escalation of racism and racial conflict will mean the escalation of the gang violence problem, because gangs step in to act as the power brokers in such conflict, and out of fear, others join the gangs of their particular ethnic and racial composition.

DISCUSSION QUESTIONS

(1) Can a peace treaty between gangs of only one ethnic group really be expected to solve the "gang violence problem"? Could such peace treaties, if they involved the entire "rainbow", eventually lead to the absence of a gang crime problem?

(2) Racial conflicts in high schools and other contexts can be the catalysts for deadly gang violence. What should be done to reduce racial tension?

(3) Can riots in the atmosphere of racial injustice be expected to be even more violent when a strong gang presence also exists in the same community?

RECOMMENDED READINGS

Breed, Allen F.
    1990 "America's Future: The Necessity of Investing in Children", Corrections Today (February): pp. 68-72.

Camp, George and Camille Graham Camp
    1985 Prison Gangs: Their Extent, Nature, and Impact on Prisons. Washington, D.C.: U.S. Dept. of Justice.

Crutchfield, Robert D.
    1989 "Labor Stratification and Violent Crime", Social Forces (68)(2): 489-512.

Fong, Robert S.
    1990 "The Organizational Structure of Prison Gangs: A Texas Case Study", Federal Probation (Mar): 36-43.

Knox, George W.; David Laske; and Edward D. Tromanhauser
    1992 Schools Under Siege. Dubuque, IA: Kendall-Hunt Publishing Company.

Kornblum, William
    1974 Blue Collar Community. Chicago: University of Chicago Press.

Kovel, Joel
1984 White Racism. New York: Columbia University Press.

Linster, Richard L.; Pamela K. Lattimore; and Christy A. Visher
1990 Predicting the Recidivism of Serious Juvenile Offenders National Institute of Justice Discussion Paper, Washington, D.C.

Perkins, Useni Eugene
1987 Explosion of Chicago's Black Street Gangs. Chicago: Third World Press.

Petersilia, Joan and Susan Turner
1988 "Minorities in Prison: Discrimination or Disparity?", Corrections Today (June).

Rader, Arthur F.
1933 The Tragedy of Lynching. University of North Carolina Press.

Ridgeway, James
1990 Blood in the Face: The Ku Klux Klan, Aryan Nations, Nazi Skinheads, and the Rise of a New White Culture. New York: Thunder's Mouth Press.

Schwartz, Barry N. and Robert Disch
1970 White Racism. New York: Dell Publishing Co.

Smith, Melinda
1990 "New Mexico Youths Use Mediation to Settle Their Problems Peacefully", Corrections Today (June): 112-114.

Snyder, Howard N.
1990 Growth in Minority Detentions Attributed to Drug Law Violaters. OJJDP Update on Statistics. U.S. Department of Justice, Office of Justice Programs, Office of Juvenile Justice and Delinquency Prevention. Juvenile Justice Bulletin. Washington, D.C. (March).

Suttles, Gerald D.
1968 The Social Order of the Slum Chicago: University of Chicago Press.

1971 -----.

Tromanhauser, Edward
1981 "The Problem of Street Gangs", chapter IV in Chicago Safe School Study, Board of Education, City of Chicago.

Vigil, James Diego and Steve Chong Yun
1990 "Vietnamese Youth Gangs in Southern California", pp. 146-162, Chapter 7 in C. Ronald Huff (ed.), Gangs in America, Newbury Park: Sage Publications.

Wilson, William J.
1987 The Truly Disadvantaged. Chicago: University of Chicago Press.

FOOTNOTES

1. And, of course, with institutionalized racism (see Perkins, 1987).

2. Such a view of the world as controlled by white racists was typical of the gang members interviewed by Krisberg (1975: pp. 15-17).

3. However, this is clearly implied in the work by Haskins (1975). Also, Vigil showed that prejudice and discrimination played an important role. That is, particularly in educational settings, ethnic derogation provided the impetus to the gang affiliation process; in defense of such threats to identity (Vigil, 1988).

4. That there can be a multiplicative, rather than an additive relationship between two factors causing deviance, delinquency, or crime is traced to the statistical work of Blalock. In the work of Suttles (1968) this thesis is brought to the forefront as an analysis of the two factors of ethnicity and territory in the inner city.

5. The interesting social scientific question is why did many northern cities see the proliferation of African-American street gangs, when similar inner-city conditions of racial oppression were also to be found in large southern cities (e.g., Dallas, etc)? Could this variation in gang emergence be explained to any degree by the differences in social organization?

6. In fact, even qualitative researchers such as Keiser (1979) report the need to overcome racism even to carry out such a social-anthropological research method (Keiser, 1979: p. 85).

7. It should be obvious to the reader that "bias crimes" have existed the entire history of American society, and well before that in other countries. The fact that these offenses have just recently been "discovered" is comparable to the discovery in the 1970s that there existed offenses called "child abuse". In either case, this is not to assume that these were non-existent before legislation made them sanctionable by imprisonment.

8. The social-historical analysis by Gonzalez (1981) suggests that law enforcement still produces such gangs by the labelling process or by the social creation of such expectations of deviance. Again, however, Gonzalez points out that the role of institutional racism is a powerful force explaining the onset and persistence of gangs among Mexicans.

9. While not widely known, American Indians or Native Americans either have their gangs too, or some believe it to be a substantial enough problem to warrant foundation grants. A grant from the Mc Knight Foundation (Minnesota) for $150,000 was made in 1988 for a "prevention program to reach gang prone Indian youth and their families" (source: Grants Index, DIALOG). Similarly, we have received field reports from an area in Oklahoma where a number of Cherokee youths clearly identify with the Crips, but would not tattoo Crip symbols on their

body when a Crip leader approached them about the use of other Crip symbols in their embryonic stages of emulating the Crip gang.

10. The research by Tromanhauser (1981: p. 188) based on a random sample of over 12,000 students in Chicago's public school system, is one of the few studies to compare American Indians, Asians, Hispanics, Blacks, and whites. In this data, American Indians reported the highest rate (18.2%) of any ethnic group for being solicited for gang membership when out of school, and (17.2%) for being attacked or threatened on or near the school by gangs, and (16.2%) for being solicited for gang membership while in school. This also showed that Asian students reported the highest level of fear from the presence of street gangs (14.7%).

11. In fairness to Hagedorn, who postulates gang membership being a problem mostly facing African-Americans and Hispanics (p. 25), persons of Asian or American Indian background probably represent a special case. Certainly, there have been specialized gangs from East Asia (Vietnamese, Cambodian) operating in sections of Chicago and elsewhere as well as the Chinese dominated Tongs. American Indians, facing a policy of racial extirpation in America, however, have taken a different form of adjustment. In the urban area, this is markedly, to rely on previous terminology, a "retreatist" mode of adaptation --- alcoholism, governmental dependency, becoming institutionalized into the surplus population, or as Hagedorn calls it the "underclass", and on the reservation a pattern, recently, of parallelling traditional organized gambling operations. The point is that African-Americans and Hispanics are not the only targets of racism in America, and thus from a strict theoretical accounting, we can expect gang activities wherever racism rears its ugly head. On Chicago's far southside, a recent report shows the emergence of an Arab-American gang, emerging as a problem during the period when persons of Middle-Eastern heritage were subject to considerable stigma and discrimination in American society.

12. For example, in explaining the development of Chinese gangs in New York, Chin (1988) describes how these were simply students living in fear and desiring to protect themselves in the context of ethnic antagonisms. That was in the 1960s. Later they experienced the organizational development cycle of greater sophistication and evolved into highly organized criminal groups, in relationship to organized crime (the tongs).

13. The arrival of large numbers of Haitians in the recent years has in fact coincided with their representation in gang activities (Posses). Similarly, the Mariello boat lift operations, had subsequent Cuban gang activity. As did the Vietnamese. The point is that all three groups were racially mistreated by the media and by social stigma during and upon their arrival.

14. I have found it useful to distinguish between these two forms in explaining the difference in measurement and equivalent impact. I often tell students that when it comes to oppressing someone, that is to destroy all hope of a decent future, there are actually two equivalent options: (1) let the person actually experience repeated discrimination and rejection, or (2) let the person believe that there is no hope. The latter amounts, in terms of impact, to the same thing.

15. Cohen (1955) provides a fascinating and useful footnote on the matter of rumors (see footnote 2, pp. 186-187).

16. Other research (FN# 23, this page) shows this to be the case. Just because it is a rural or suburban area is no reason to automatically assume, also, that gangs in these types of communities cannot function at the higher end of the gang organizational spectrum.

17. See Race of Prisoners Admitted to State and Federal Institutions, 1926-1986, 1991, U.S. Department of Justice, Bureau of Justice Statistics, Washington, DC.

18. The Aryan Brotherhood are said to have began as the "Blue Bird Gang...to protect white inmates from other racially-oriented non-white gangs" (Jackson and Mc Bride, 1990: p. 53).

19. Similarly, a federal survey in 1982 showed that 47.8 percent of all state inmates in America were African-American. (See p. 397, George F. Cole, The American System of Criminal Justice, Monterey, CA: Brooks/Cole Publishing Company.

20. While few Americans will probably agree with me, let me go on record with a growing number of criminologists who take the position that there are in fact limits to the use of the penal sanction, and that America overuses this formal mode of social control. So much so, that it is anti-productive. We can recall the words of one spokesperson on this issue as follows: "It is not unfair to say", remarked Hans W. Mattick, "that if men had deliberately set themselves the task of designing an institution that would systematically maladjust men, they would have invented the large, walled, maximum security prison" (see Gordon Hawkins, 1976, The Prison: Policy and Practice, Studies in Crime and Justice, Chicago: University of Chicago Press, p. 45).

21. See "Prison Workers' Complain", Nation Briefings, Chicago Sun-TImes, July 13, 1993, p. 8.

22. In Juveniles and Jail (National Coalition for Jail Reform, 1985, pp. 1-15) overcrowding is argued to be a condition that will contribute to violence and conflict.

23. Gangs and Guns: A Task Force Report, National Gang Crime Research Center, November, 1994. Co-principal investigators included: George W. Knox, James G. Houston, John A. Laskey, David L. Laske, Thomas F. McCurrie, and Edward D. Tromanhauser.

24. This includes even the law enforcement perspective of Jackson and Mc Bride (1986; 1990: p. 9).

25. Apparently this is a universal phenomenon, as illustrated in the case of Japanese gangs. In Japan, the "burakumin" are like a "untouchable caste", and are subject to much discrimination. This minority group feeds many members into the various Yakuza gangs. See Kaplan and Dubro (1986: pp. 22, 145).

CHAPTER 5

GANGS: UNDERCLASS, SURPLUS POPULATION, AND HUMAN CAPITAL

INTRODUCTION

What students of criminology as well as corrections and criminal justice personnel of the 21st Century must realize, and we are shortly there, is that social scientists over the years have examined "mega trends" that may have something to do with gangs. In fact some recent gang authors take exactly the same view: that is, factors like the "underclass"[1] figure prominently in explaining the onset and persistence of gangs. This "human capital factor" is another truth that emerges from a meta-analysis of our gang literature.

In terms of theory in accounting for the onset and persistence of gang crime there are different levels of explanation possible. Cloward and Ohlin's (1960) approach can be regarded as a "middle range" theory because its level of generality and its unit of analysis involves the individual in relationship to their community's opportunity system. Psychological theories relying simply on individual traits or characteristics that can vary from one person to the next, such as Cohen's (1955) status-frustration/reaction-formation approach, can be regarded as being in the microanalytic range. At the societal-wide level of generality there are macroanalytic approaches which tend to look at the "bigger picture".

One such macroanalytic approach is represented in the attempts to apply underclass theory and surplus population theory to the problem under investigation --- gang crime. This chapter highlights this macro-demographic view regarding gang crime.

GANGS AND THE UNDERCLASS

A variety of contributions to the gang literature assume the important analytical role that the underclass concept has for explaining gang formation and persistence. The first such contribution in the gang literature that specifically saw the underclass status as a cause of gang forming and gang joining behavior --- and the crime and violence that gangs can be responsible for --- was the work of Moore, Livermore, and Galland (1973). The lead author had seen the process from several perspectives being the former superintendent of the Cook County Jail.

Hagedorn (1988) also argues the relevance of analyzing gang crime in terms of overall differences in "life chances" as represented through the application of underclass theory. Much more needs to be done to legitimize this approach if it is to also be linked with institutionalized racism. Hagedorn (1988) is careful not to call such persons in the underclass a "permanent underclass" and not to quote Karl Marx's closely related concept of the "dangerous underclass",[2] or the Neo-Marxist American version "the surplus population". In fact, the introduction written by Joan Moore alludes to such a fixed distinction as the permanent underclass[3], yet Hagedorn clearly sees it as something other than permanent by the optimistic potential for gang crime reduction represented by national policies emphasizing education/job training and job placement programs (Hagedorn, 1988: p. 168).

Vigil (1988) advances the concept of multiple marginality. It means persons of color who face prejudice and discrimination experience an accentuated estrangement or intense alienation and it involves a cluster of interrelated socioeconomic, cultural, psychological, and ecological factors. Thus, an examination of underclass life and how it affects gangs is essential for a macroanalytic analysis. To Vigil, "the underclass phenomenon entails the longitudinal effects of poverty" (1988, p. 11).

In linking the masculinity crisis --- the problems of manhood development experienced by Black males --- to gangs, Majors and Billson (1992) in their book Cool Pose: The Dilemmas of Black Manhood in America point to the extraordinary high unemployment rate among inner city Black teenagers (as high as 70 percent in some areas) and aspects of the underclass experience itself:

> "Joining a gang is a way to organize and make sense of the marginal world of the inner city neighborhood....For black males who have been locked out of the social and economic mainstream, running with a gang can be a form of social achievement, as can engaging in fortuitous violence (Majors and Billson, 1992: p. 50)."

For the record, it is important to note that the concept of the underclass or its conceptual equivalent in relationship to crime has an important legacy predating Hagedorn, Moore, Vigil, etc. Indeed, the works of O'Connor (1973), Quinney (1977), and Young (1978) having direct bearing on this issue are not even cited by Hagedorn. As will be seen, however, there is much compatibility between these analytic approaches.

SURPLUS POPULATION THEORY vs. UNDERCLASS THEORY

Are they different? Not really. The concept of the surplus population has been brought up as a relevant theoretical concern by few scholars (O'Connor, 1973; Quinney, 1977; Young, 1978; Knox, 1980). The term "surplus population" is sometimes used in economics and demography, but some have clearly used it in the context of referring to crime (Quinney, 1977; Young, 1978; Knox, 1980).

According to O'Connor (1973, pp. 25-26) the surplus population, which is also a condition called technological unemployment, is further divided into the absolute and the relative. The relative surplus population (RSP) being the reserve army of the unemployed. Thus, the RSP includes those who have worked perhaps sporadically, seasonally, in the spot labor market, etc. So the RSP includes those with some work history who have some type of skill or labor potential, who are both willing to work and eager to work out of economic necessity. The absolute surplus population (ASP) being, apparently, a subset that traditionally has an even more difficult time entering the labor force. The ASP would therefore include youths, women, minorities, exoffenders, etc, and persons seeking employment for the first time.

The reader unfamiliar with the admittedly scant literature addressing itself to the surplus population may feel uneasy with this concept and its implications. Not being familiar with the overall concept, one might raise the humanist question of "how can there possibly be a surplus population --- are these people who are just not needed by America's legitimate opportunity structure?" This concept implies that some persons are simply "surplus" to the mode of production, while simultaneously, obviously, being highly oriented to the mode of consumption. A surplus population is that group which cannot be readily absorbed into a productive capacity in the economy through selling their labor and thereby attaining a legitimate source of economic livelihood.

In American society, the surplus population tends to be differentiated by ethnicity, language, and education.[4] Crime is expected to rise with the size of the surplus population as is the use of the criminal sanction and the number of persons placed in total control institutions. Crime and deviance are viewed as the natural outgrowth of a surplus population in a culture which constantly emphasizes material success.

The concept of the surplus population, for those persons whose educational training has instilled a repulsion towards "deterministic" philosophies such as Marxism, need not be viewed in such a mechanical fashion. This condition is felt to be somewhat amenable to policy intervention by social engineering schemes such as national level programs funded by the government. Some critics may claim this only tends to "cool out" the surplus population because it can be argued that no amount of welfare policy will truly restructure the economic system which might be viewed as the ultimate source of the problem.

Quinney (1973, pp. 131-140) cites a direct positive relationship between the use of the punitive sanction and the growth of the surplus population. The American criminal justice system is viewed in the Gramscian[5] sense as the state repressive apparatus which functions to control the unemployed --- and presumably dangerous --- surplus population. As will be seen, data on federal prison admissions and unemployment rates show a close association. This association cannot be automatically discounted as spurious and tends to be cause for much concern.

Being a part of the surplus population is an objective material condition which need not be a part of a conscious motivational force in order to produce criminality. The condition of deprivation which is implicit in this concept, as well, need not show that crime is rebellion --- although it may often be, or at least may have that appearance, ex post facto. Being a part of the surplus population is equivalent to being defined as having membership in the underclass.

Axial concepts of surplus population theory is an analysis of the nature of the opportunity (learning and performance) system itself and the role of work and occupations in society. We are not likely to find complete consensus on what the opportunity system really is (legitimate vs. illegitimate, monopoly vs. competitive sectors, etc) and how it actually works. The role of the state in all of this, however, is assumed to be prominent through social policy initiatives and governmental controls.

An understanding of the surplus population, like the concept of the underclass ala Hagedorn (1988), does lend itself to another way to interpret problems like crime and gangs. Here we shall consider the surplus population in the force it plays in both the process of initiation into crime and its systemic persistence and continuity in individual criminal careers. It will be argued that as a social condition, to be functionally defined as surplus to the legitimate opportunity system can be a necessary precondition in the chain of causal events that ultimately has as its deviant outcome criminality or gang membership.

Young (1978) advances the position that with the growth of the surplus population "we are driven to desperation to objectify and brutalize people who, in other times, would be defined as kin, friend, or kind" (Young, 1978, p. 7). Authors who even have the appearance of being apologists for gang crime are themselves quick to point out the destructive impact that gang crime has on any given community in which it operates. We need only see the parallel between gang violence in the community, for example "Black on Black crime" etc, and observations such as those from Frantz Fanon's The Wretched of the Earth regarding colonialized persons and the way they internalize violence: they do not strike back at the cause of their frustration and oppression, they strike back at themselves more conveniently.[6]

The definitions of the surplus population certainly are congruent with most definitions of the underclass when it comes to operationalizing or measuring this concept. Young (1978, p. 7) suggests that the surplus population is composed of the following segments of society: the unemployed, those over 65, those on A.D.C., welfare, aid, etc, and those confined in correctional facilities. The historical analysis sketched by Young (1978) views the surplus population as a "deadly plan" of capitalism in the same sense that the growth of the capitalist middle class was for feudalism. An important distinction made by Young is whether the population is "surplus" to the mode of production or to the mode of consumption.

A concept similar, in definitional components, to that of the surplus population and underclass is that of structural unemployment in what might be called price theory in economics. Basically, some economists have argued that a certain level of unemployment is probably necessary in the sense that too high of an employment rate[7] will negatively impact on price stability. It is in this sense that Bergmann and Kaun (1966, p. 1) clearly assume the existence of the surplus population in their definition of structural unemployment as the "amount of employment (less minimal frictional and seasonal) which cannot be removed by monetary and fiscal policy without creating substantial continuing inflation deriving from shortages of labor". Other economists assume that there is a kind of "Phillips Curve" which accounts for the relationship between unemployment and prices in a fashion similar to the standard Phillips Curve relationship assumed between wage rates and unemployment rates (Phillips, 1958; Lipsey, 1965).

According to some liberal and conservative Keynesian economists there is a "trade-off" between unemployment and inflation as well. In other words, the government cannot take policy steps to reduce unemployment without also risking a rise in prices. It is also assumed that there is a "natural" rate of unemployment which is necessary for the economy. The accelerationist school of economics, sometimes called the Freidman advocates, happen to deny this trade-off; but they still assume a natural rate of unemployment --- almost in the Weberian tradition of the Protestant Ethic and the Spirit of Capitalism that "the underclass (and surplus population) shall always be with you" ---and feel that no policy intervention should be directed at the problem of unemployment. Indeed, they argue not for education, training, and job placement ala Hagedorn (1988) and others before him (Amandes, 1979), but rather for policy initiatives that should be directed chiefly towards the goal of price stability (Ginsburg, 1975, p. 23).

In the gang crime situation, the surplus population refers to those, who for a variety of reasons, do not have a functional relationship to the means of production. This includes those considered "unemployable" as well as the unemployed. This includes the "hidden unemployed", and those kept out of the work force by legal control. This includes those who could clearly function in the world of work, but who are dissuaded from doing so by pervasive forms of racial, ethnic, and other bias-oriented discrimination felt at the individual level, as a perceived "closure of the opportunity system" (Bailey, 1969). These persons are not involved in a productive capacity involving the competitive sale of their labor.

The role which the concept of the surplus population plays in a theoretical explanation of deviance, delinquency, criminality, and gang crime may best be conceived of as a structural or institutional social condition that amounts to an antecedent variable important to the initiation process itself, and for secondary deviation (repeated criminality, gang involvement, etc) or powering its continuity, rather than as a simple kind of direct cause and effect variable.[8]

While skin color, race, ethnicity, age, sex, and other important correlational variables cannot be experimentally manipulated, one set of factors that relates to the surplus population theory can be. This involves a cluster of human development traits often called "human resources" or "human capital".[9] While there are ample references to the so-called "K factor", the cognition and intelligence factor in which it is assumed there is natural variation among human beings (not ethnic groups or races), there are growing references to the human capital or what might be called "H-Factor" variables which are inextricably involved in any analysis of surplus population theory, the underclass, etc. This "H-factor" can be conceived of as either a factor at the individual level of analysis facilitating the onset of deviance, delinquency, crime, or gang activity or a factor that compounds the ability of society to reintegrate these persons into a legitimate career trajectory.[10]

What this suggests for corrections and criminal justice personnel as well as for our communities is HOPE. Something can be done about the problem. Job training. Educational upgrading. Skill enhancement. Aftercare services involving job placement, etc, along with all of the counseling that is required in between these steps.

Throughout the criminology literature we will find consistent references to important variables that can be included in the "H-factor" (education, employment history, socialization, etc,).[11] This H-factor is not always explicitly identified, per se, in surplus population or underclass theories, but it is clearly present and important. More importantly, it is something we can do something about. The research by Berk, Lenihan and Rossi (1980) was not able to demonstrate the impact of these human capital attributes, however, their analysis did show that in looking at the number of arrests among exoffenders in Texas and Georgia (in the TARP program) that the single factor having the strongest inverse relationship from their regression analysis was that of "weeks employed" (1980, pp. 781-783).

At the level of the individual actor, these H-factor attributes tend to differentiate measures of crime, deviance, and gang affiliation. The corrections literature, dealing with the treatment of offenders and various program strategies, has focused extensively on experimentally manipulating these factors; ostensibly for purposes of rehabilitation. Some of this programmatic knowledge has been encouraging in the sense that from this body of evaluation research it can be concluded that genuine social policy alternatives do truly exist for reducing the crime problem.[12] Recall that these intervention strategies are valuable for consideration here because they occur at the most difficult level of impact: the tertiary level of prevention.

Whatever we call it --- human capital[13], human resource development, human potential optimization, etc, --- the "H" factor refers to the amount of investment in education, training, and skill development in human beings. This is relevant here for the understanding of gang crime because it includes consistent patterns of knowledge development about factors associated with deviance, delinquency, crime, and gang proliferation. Perhaps more important is the fact that the H-factor is amenable to experimental manipulation. It is a condition we can do something about.

Deviance, delinquency, criminality, and gang affiliation should not be viewed as an inevitable lifestyle for the underclass. It is probable, varying by historical conditions, and community structures. But not all persons with subordinated levels of human capital follow such a path of human development. Similarly, not all persons from an impoverished ghetto become offenders. There are other equally self-abusive or self-destructive options (alcoholism, suicide, mental illness, cults, etc). Moreover, the existential choice of the individual, to commit crimes or join a gang versus overcoming barriers to legitimate success, cannot be denied for some. Nor should we ignore the fact that if there is a net shrinkage in the sector of industrial and unskilled employment opportunity, then individual motivation reduces to little more than fierce rugged individualism in competition for these limited chances of productive affiliation. In such an economy one persons success in landing a job can often mean the displacement of another person.

The matter of what constitutes a radical political analysis in reference to these concepts centers around the attribution of intention and purpose. A radical with a hidden agenda in his or her criminological rhetoric would probably take the position that employers prefer such an industrial reserve army. That is, a vast pool of applicants for a job has always been used as a weapon against collective bargaining among workers.[14] Similarly, perhaps a large surplus population is a political benefit only to the ruling elite in that it artificially reduces wage rates and this itself generates more surplus value.

For the gang-affiliated person, who experiences a variety of rewardive power from the gang including its potential for income-producing opportunity however illegitimate, or any offender --- who may show the characteristics of the surplus population (through measured "H-Factors"), it may be difficult to convince them that entering an unskilled or semi-skilled occupation is a more rewarding alternative than a life of crime. Certainly the wages may not be satisfactory for someone used to issuing themselves an allowance or payroll advance, through drug sales or through illegally appropriating someone else's valuables. Further education and training, with some hope of advancement for a career ladder, would appear to offer the best inducement. The decision to enter the legitimate occupational opportunity structure is also a voluntaristic one; and this implies that manpower programs may have to rely entirely on motivational force alone to impact on this population.

The "H-factor" overlaps between concepts of the surplus population and the underclass. Underachievement in education and the dearth of skill training is clearly one of the most important features defining underclass status for most gang members. It is not uncommon at all to find among these youthful and adult offenders, that these are persons whom after their conviction and release from prison cannot correctly spell the crimes for which they were adjudicated. Persons who cannot spell the crimes they are committing may surely be expected to have problems integrating into the mainstream of society.

Occupational success in America is often a combination of marketable skills, perseverance, and ambition. At least in theory. At least if white skin privilege has no effect. It is amazing sometimes to find the same tenacity of dedication among gang members to pursue delinquency and crime as might be found in the competitive business world. It may be a difficult task indeed to convince some of these gang members that they can "make it" in our society --- as if, via a positive mental attitude or the like, all they have to do is think and grow rich. That they lack marketable skills for America's labor force is obvious to most observers.[15] The problem is not lack of aspirations or motivation for having a better life, the problem is our society's institutional forces that would rather keep and maintain an expensive underclass that reproduces, ala Bell (1953), as much gang crime as we seek to manage through the repressive apparatus.

DATA SUPPORTING THE UNDERCLASS THESIS

Three themes using three different modes of analysis will be used to argue that there exists some amount of empirical support for the underclass thesis.[16] How institutionalized is the impact on the underclass law offender in America --- indeed, using the human capital aspect of educational attainment, can it be said that the gap or educational lag is of such magnitude as to constitute, along with legal restrictions on employment (for those convicted of a felony offense), a "caste"? Secondly, from a cross-sectional analysis can it be demonstrated that the effects of unemployment and welfare dependency are indeed factors that differentiate the likelihood of being arrested for a crime in America? Thirdly, using census data for three countries can it be demonstrated that there is any relationship between the size of the underclass and the use of the penal sanction? These three research questions are addressed here in an effort to shed some light on the issue.

The underclass thesis is important to address. If we must take the position that there is a "permanent underclass"[17] with no hope, then that leaves us few options. It suggests that nothing works. It provides few alternative recourses to the solution of the crisis.

THE EDUCATIONAL LAG IN THE AMERICAN OFFENDER POPULATION

From a research point of view there is little doubt that educational attainment is an important variable. It plays a significant role in explaining crime, especially recidivism. The level of educational attainment is also a very important variable affecting employability and earnings potential in America. That is to say, someone with at least a high school education has a greater likelihood of getting a job and staying "clean" than someone having less than a high school education. Educational attainment also tends to vary inversely with recidivism. As Spergel stated "it used to be that as gang members got older, out of their teens, they'd leave gangs to take decent-paying jobs, now there's no jobs for people like that".[18]

The historical trend in educational attainment in the United States has shown a continual decrease in the percentage of the adult population (those 25 years of age or older) who have not completed high school. Let us summarize this trend here by referring to the U.S. Census figures in Table 5.

TABLE 5

Yearly Distributions of U.S. Census Statistics For
the Percentage of Adults Not Completing
High School Since 1940

Year	% of U.S. > = 25 Years of Age with < = 11 years of Educational Attainment
1940	74.6 percent
1950	63.8
1960	58.8
1970	44.9
1972	41.8
1973	40.2
1974	38.7
1975	37.5
1976	36.0
1977	35.1
1978	34.1
1979	32.3
1980	31.4
1981-2	30.4
1983	27.9
1984	26.8

SOURCE: Statistical Abstracts of the United States, U.S. Department of Commerce, Bureau of the Census, Social and Economic Statistics Administration. 1985, p. 134; 1982-83, p. 143; 1981, p. 142; 1980, p. 149; 1979, p. 145; 1978, p. 143; 1977, p. 136; 1976, p. 123; 1975, p. 119; 1974, p. 116; 1973, p. 115; 1971, p. 110.

Educational lag is defined here as not having a high school degree or GED or at least 12 years of education completed. Table 5 indicates that the distribution of this characteristic in mainstream America has steadily decreased from nearly three-fourths of the population in 1940 to less than one-third today. The question is, how does the offender population compare with the rest of America regarding this condition. To review this parameter for the offender population we must necessarily make reference to a number of previous, independent, research projects that are summarized in Figure 5.

FIGURE 5

Research Literature Citations for Adult Offenders,
Percentage Lacking a High School Education

Author	Sample	% < = 11 Years Educ.
********************	******************	******************
Clemmer (1940, p. 50)	N = 2,3458 adult (circa 1931-1934)	97 percent
Rumney and Murphy (1952, p. 75)	N = 1,000 New Jersey probationers (1937)	92 percent
Simpson, et al (1976, p. 100)	N = 27,390 DARP Drug Addicts	63 percent
Diamond, et al (1977, p. 3)	N = 221 Chicago probationers	59.4 percent
Knox (1978d, p. 391)	N = 24,047 State of Illinois inmates	69 percent
Lenihan (1978, p. 55)	N = 431 Baltimore Parolees	88.3 percent

As seen in Figure 5, the research literature on offenders has consistently shown that the offender population lags behind their American peers in educational attainment. Current levels of educational attainment among America's offender population are characteristic of literacy levels of the general population only by comparison to this same human capital attribute before World War II. Some correctional researchers may also point out that the correctional process itself may be a co-determinant of this problem and that correctional facilities themselves may be responsible for some of the disruption in the educational process for both delinquents and adult offenders.

The finding of interest here is that the offender population is two to three times as likely to have a non-marketable level of educational attainment (e.g., not a high school graduate, or < = 11 years of education) when compared with America generally. The validity of this educational lag is mitigated only by the fact that the offender population itself tends to be increasing homogeneous with respect to SES (i.e., Social Economic Status) and ethnicity --- both of which correlate highly with educational attainment.

Ask yourself, how are these under-educated persons going to fit into the American economy in a productive, fulfilling, and integrative capacity?

THE UNDERCLASS AND CRIMINALITY

The notion that the underclass in America contributes disproportionately to arrest, conviction, and imprisonment rates is not a new one. Myrdal (1969) has been interpreted to the effect that lower class delinquents can be viewed as part of the American underclass whose characteristics include poverty, substandard housing, limited opportunity, underemployment and under-education. Marxist authors have referred to the "dangerous underclass" in a similar vein. Some analysts have regarded the surplus population in terms of a subculture of poverty where, it is assumed incorrectly, there is little motivation for economic success and that poor people are the way they are because they have not internalized middle class success goals.

While contributions from liberal, radical, and conservative perspectives have tended to cite some relationship between crime and conditions of economic immiseration there is sharp disagreement on what the nature of this relationship really is.

Something pointed in the work of Glasgow (1981) is that to be defined as part of the African-American underclass is equivalent, functionally, to essentially lack any organized political interest or social organizational infrastructure to be recognized as an entity in the polity. It is often said that the reason prison reform movements persisted for decades, indeed longer, even as little more than a spark of an interest, with little more than technological progress in the effectiveness of physical security devices is that there is no substantive political base to support these kinds of major social policy changes and the public funding they require.

If there is anything pervasively common to the surplus population or the American underclass it is their lack of legitimate social organization. Where political clout is defined as the size of a financial contribution to an electoral campaign, and where poverty itself is stigmatized (as is unemployment), it is unrealistic to expect traditional forms of power seeking from a group that is functionally disenfranchised.

Johnson (1977) argues that the concept of the underclass may be more fruitful for testing delinquency theories than traditional measures of socio-economic status (SES) such as father's occupational status. Johnson (1977) therefore focuses on the merits of alternative operational measures of social class such as: unemployment or marginal employment, poverty level income, recipient of welfare benefits, etc. According to Johnson (1977) these should show a stronger relationship with problems such as delinquency and crime.

The NORC (National Opinion Research Center) General Social Survey (Davis, 1980) data for 1980 was used to examine the effects of unemployment and welfare dependency on self-reported arrests. The unemployment measure is a dichotomous variable reflecting whether or not the person has been unemployed and looking for work for more than a month during the last ten years. Welfare dependency is a general measure reflecting the receipt of any government welfare aid. The self-reported arrest variable reflects whether the person has been picked up, or charged, by the police for any reason other than traffic violations.

Table 6 below shows that within this nationally representative sample there is in fact support for the proposition that employment varies inversely with being arrested for crime. Those persons experiencing unemployment are shown in Table 6 to have an arrest rate of 20.8 percent. This is twice as high as the 9.3 percent arrest rate for those persons not experiencing unemployment. In summary, unemployment using this cross-sectional data significantly differentiates arrests.

TABLE   6

Unemployment and Arrests in the 1980 Sample
of the NORC General Social Surveys

Were Americans Arrested
****

		NO		YES	
		**********		**********	
		N	%	N	%
		*****	****	****	****
Were Americans Unemployed?	NO	932	90.7	96	9.3
	YES	312	79.2	82	20.8

Chi square = 33.2, probability < .001

Similarly, government dependency (welfare recipient) is shown to significantly differentiate self-reported arrests among Americans. These findings are reported in Table 7. This shows that 17 percent of those receiving aid were arrested compared to 9.9 percent for those not receiving various forms of government aid.

TABLE   7

Government Dependency and Arrests in the 1980 Sample
of the NORC General Social Survey

ARRESTED BY THE POLICE
****

		NO		YES	
		************		************	
		N	%	N	%
		****	****	****	****
Welfare/Aid Recipient?	NO	800	90.1	88	9.9
	YES	439	83.0	90	17.0

Chi square = 14.5, probability < .001

THE UNDERCLASS AND THE PRISON POPULATION

The relationship between the size of the surplus population or the underclass and the amount of crime or use of the prison sanction is also an important relationship to examine. Employment has been a variable examined that bears some relevancy to this question. While much research has been done in this area, much of it is also relegated to the "fugitive literature" and hard to find. For example, one of the most detailed analyses of unemployment and crime was that done by Kleeck, Winslow and Reid reported in 1931. It clearly showed a strong consistent relationship that the higher the unemployment the higher the property crime and this covered the period of 1893 to 1926 for the State of Massachusetts (p. 303, 312).

The research by Glaser and Rice (1959) uncovered a significant inverse relationship between employment and crime for the period 1932 - 1950 in the U.S. The ptolemic by Guttentag (1968, p. 110) sought to discount these findings without a secondary analysis or empirical approach to counter the evidence by Glaser and Rice, and others such as Fleisher (1966).

Here we examine related measures of the underclass thesis as an independent variable in determining the strength of the relationship with the volume of criminal justice processing. For the United Kingdom, covering England and Wales during the years 1859-1910 this involved the distribution of "able-bodied adult paupers" expressed as a rate per 1,000 of the population in census data. For lack of a better word we could call this the pauperization rate or simply the underclass ratio. When this is regressed against the rate per 1,000 criminals brought to trial in the same year a very strong positive correlation ($r = .90$, $p < .001$) emerges.

Data on Americans are taken from the U.S. census. Here the analysis focused on the unemployment rates and the volume of imprisonment for the years 1941 - 1978.[19] Here again we find what appears to be a moderately strong and significant correlation ($r = .62$, $p < .001$).

The Canadian experience with the Depression had a very similar skewed effect for imprisonment. The analysis reported here, therefore, dates from 1941 to 1968. The imprisonment variable reflects the total number of prisoners received during the year taken from the Annual Report to the Commissioner of Penitentiaries, and the unemployment variable taken from the Canada Year books. Again we find a significant ($r = .73$, $p < .001$) positive correlation between unemployment and imprisonment.

In summary, these aspects of the underclass experience of being defined as marginal to the economic mainstream of society, are shown to be significantly related to the rates at which the same three societies (America, Canada, England and Wales) adjudicate or imprison law offenders. The larger the underclass, the larger the prison population.

PERCEPTIONS OF HOPELESSNESS CAN HAVE THE SAME IMPACT

The perception of closure in the legitimate opportunity structure is itself significantly associated with delinquency, crime, recidivism, and gang affiliation. In other words, internalizing a defeatist belief that there is little hope for success via traditional means, regardless of objective material conditions regarding occupational opportunity, can itself be a tremendous social-psychological force operating to propel a person into deviance, delinquency, crime or gang membership.

This attitudinal measurement approach has dealt mostly with delinquency and is traced to opportunity system theory (Cloward and Ohlin, 1960). A number of independent efforts have shown basically the same finding: that perception of "blocked" legitimate opportunities is closely associated with delinquency (Elliott, 1962; Spergel, 1963; Palmore and Hammond, 1964; Blalock, 1965; Short, Rivera and Tennyson, 1965; Knox, 1978(b)). In short, the belief held by the individual that society offers little chance of legitimate success is shown to be a very significant variable differentiating delinquency.

COROLLARY RESEARCH FINDINGS

A good deal of research over the years has been undertaken on the relationship between employment and various measures of deviant outcomes (delinquency, criminality, recidivism, gang affiliation, etc). Suffice it to say, that in most of this literature, there is a significant volume of support for the proposition that employment varies inversely with crime. The more basic research by Zatz (1985) found that one of the most powerful variables differentiating gang members from non-gang members was that of their status of being currently employed.

In that much of this comes from program evaluation research, the interested reader should examine reviews such as those by Leiberg (1978) to examine aspects and details of these programs for adults, and Knox (1981) regarding delinquents.

The inverse relationship between employment and crime is documented in basic research (Glaser and Rice, 1959; Glaser, 1964; Fleisher, 1966; Holahan, 1970; Votey and Philips, 1974; Sedlak, 1975; Knox, 1978(a)) and in much evaluation research (Miller, 1972; Mills and Walter, 1974; Killinger and Archer, 1974; Easton, et al, 1974; Whitney, 1974; Bernardo, 1977; Bowker, 1977; Wadsworth, 1977; Greenberg, 1978; Knox, 1978 (d); Cook et al, 1978; Mills and Walter, 1979; Rulo and Zemel, 1979; Pirog-Good, 1979).

We need not use conjecture here or rhetoric, we need only examine more completely the extant literature. The research like that by Fleisher (1966) clearly demonstrated "that change in economic position is a core element in the social control of delinquent behavior" (Janowitz, 1966).

THE GANG AS A NATURAL COMPETITIVE DEVELOPMENT IN A GROWING UNDERGROUND ECONOMY

Where we have one gang, another will shortly follow. The author calls this the law of natural group opposition formation. When the Crips arise, the Bloods shortly follow. When the Folks appear in an area, the People also appear. The vast amount of illegal income that could be made from the underground economy, particularly drug sales, may have provided a social environment that facilitated the formation and growth of gangs.   This does not mean that the two warring or competing factions have to be necessarily equal in size or power or in terms of their market share. Because by some estimates, the Crips outnumber the Bloods three to one in actual numbers of members.   Where they are equal is in the number of different locations they are found in throughout the entire United States.   In all social contexts, where we find the Crips we will also find the Bloods.

The competition and rivalry therefore existed before and gives rise to such patterned varieties of organized conflict.   It could be as simple as the Blues (Crips), extending a color from their high school symbols; and the Reds (Bloods) adopting their color from their high school[20].   Thus, the underground economy itself is advanced as an explanation for being the engine that powers the emergence of gangs, and that the competition in this market is normal behavior, such that while one group may tend to dominate, the competition will extend to all geographical areas.

HOW A STRAIGHT JOB IS LESS APPEALING TO THE MORE HARD CORE GANG MEMBER

Employment is no panacea, but most agree or assume it would have a positive effect. Rodriguez (1993) explains how he left gang life and would expect many others to quit the gang if they could get a job paying a livable wage.   But there is some research that recently revealed that the more hard core gang member would not take a good paying job even if it were offered, one hypothesis being that perhaps the gang pays better.   The data here come from the recent research on gangs and guns cited in an earlier chapter, and uses a sample of 476 gang members in the midwestern United States.

This data shows that among those gang members who have never attempted to quit the gang, some 16.9 percent would not take a job paying $9.00 per hour.   This compares with only 6.2 percent who would not take a job paying $9.00 per hour among those gang members who have tried to quit the gang.   This shows that even providing such jobs would appear to attract the less hard core gang member.   The more hard core gang member, that is someone who has never tried to quit the gang, is less likely to want to take a job paying $9.00 per hour.

SUMMARY

The underclass thesis regarding gangs clearly involves a host of related concepts. Some of these are traditional Marxist (the dangerous underclass) concepts, others are related concepts without direct ideological classification (the permanent underclass, the truly disadvantaged, etc), but refer to comparable and historically similar such conditions. This set of concepts articulates a more societal wide "condition" favorable to the production of crime and gangs.

This thesis does enjoy both theoretical and empirical support dating back some time. It also poses some hard choices for America: what do to about the underclass? Some gang authors simply recommend legalizing heroin, and we shall see in a later chapter this might be equivalent to simply creating a true "caste" in America. That is, a group both functionally at the bottom of the social and economic pyramid, kept there by a variety of factors, and officially/legally recognized as such an entity.

One fundamental problem exists with this type of historical continuity in the literature about gangs. It is the issue of why some poor people never become criminals or gang members and do they therefore represent an ipso facto exception to the theory or does their very existence challenge the theory? Further, it is now well known that suburban gang members may be less likely to join a gang for chiefly economic reasons. It seems clear that a large percentage of members of more organized criminal gangs typically join "to make money", but this is not universal, and while characteristic of innercity gang members is not a profile factor for suburban or smaller town gang members who can float in and out of the gang, having a relatively comfortable home life and even middle class existence to return to.

Can we help them get out of this underclass? Can we instill the hope of a better life? These are the issues that must be faced and answered as America enters the 21st Century.

DISCUSSION QUESTIONS

(1) Do you think there is any merit to the concept of the "underclass", "surplus population", etc, in describing societal wide groups of persons who are excluded from a productive relationship to their society? Is this the group most at risk of joining a gang?

(2) Can a society measure its strength by the size of its underclass or surplus population? What national policies do you feel should be adopted to reduce the size of such groups in America today? Is the human capital theory fatally flawed because gangs can be found in suburban affluent communities as well?

(3) If the federal government declared a war on gangs and appointed a Gang Czar that felt there was some merit to the underclass theory, or surplus population theory, or the multiple marginality concept, how would it be possible to implement such concepts in terms of doing something about the gang problem?

FOOTNOTES

1. Most authors of the underclass approach refer to the urban African-American underclass (Wilson, 1987; Duster, 1987), but it certainly transcends color.

2. Again, for the record, let me point out that Joan Moore's use of the underclass was not the first applied to gangs. An earlier account which Moore (1978) and Hagedorn (1988) failed to acknowledge was that by Moore, Livermore and Galland (1973). In the Moore, Livermore, and Galland (1973) analysis the process of urban deterioration was analyzed and its accelerated destruction left behind "a dangerous underclass spawned by poverty, joblessness, misguided welfare policies, and ineffectual corrections and educational programs" (p. 43). Gangs in this process were described as having a terrorism function in the community.

3. Moore says in referring to Wilson's use of the concept "underclass", "These are men and women permanently excluded from participation in mainstream occupations" (Hagedorn, 1988: p. 7).

4. Short (1990) astutely applies the closely related concept of "social capital" to explain why one person may grow up in the same inner city area and go on to live a law-abiding life and be a good citizen and how another --- in the same environment --- might become a gang leader. Social capital, then, has to do with social skills, without which the more economic investments (e.g., a University of Chicago education, manpower training in business or the crafts, etc) as measures of human capital, will not be able to put to use effectively. See James F. Short, "New Wine in Old Bottles? Change and Continuity in American Gangs", pp. 223-239, Chapter 10 in C. Ronald Huff (ed.), Gangs in America, Newbury Park: Sage Publications.

5. Gramsci is an Italian political economist who was at one time a political prisoner. See Antonio Gramsci, 1971, Selections from the Prison Notebooks, New York: International Publishers.

6. This same tendency has it social equivalent in Douglas G. Glasow's The Black Underclass: Poverty, Unemployment, and Entrapment of Ghetto Youth.

7. Note that Hagedorn (1988) rallies around the traditional call for "full employment".

8. As has been amply demonstrated, however, and quite impressively, poverty has a strong relationship to crime, as measured by income and recidivism (see Berk, Lenihan and Rossi, 1980).

9. I explain this concept to my students in a straight-forward fashion: Compare yourself, a university student, with someone in the penitentiary the same age, the same ethnicity, etc. Chances are you have a lot more "dollars" invested in the cultivation of your human talents. Your training, your formal education, your instruction, your documented skills, your health, your licenses and certifications, etc, etc. That amount of capital spent on refining and cultivating your talent as a human being is your "H factor", your human capital, your human resource development expenditure, your human development investment.

10. Yablonsky is quick to point out that the goal of persons doing social work with gangs, outreach workers, detached workers, community organizations, etc, should have as their goal not simply making resources available to the gang members, but rather the "dismemberment", the disintegration of the gang itself, and thereby creating the opportunity to bring these persons back into the main stream. Clearly, such a proposition cannot be made in good conscience without first noting the discrepancy between their level of human capital development and what is expected in larger society. This includes language, social skills, even hygiene itself.

11. I wish to anticipate some criticism and divert it now: this is not a "deficit" approach to stigmatize. Any deficit that is implied is not teleological by imparting purposive lack of motivation. Indeed, quite the obverse is true: these are human

beings who have had their dreams of a good life crushed by the institutional forces at work in their way of life. They wanted good education, good training, skills and experience from a rewarding career opportunity --- but these doors were closed to them.

12. At the time of interviewing for a university position, once, a high ranking member of the university administration posed the question to me "do you really think we can do something about crime, that is make society safer?" I answered, most definitely, but how much money are you willing to spend towards that goal, or if not that, how much of your civil and constitutional rights are you willing to part with.

13. See James S. Coleman, (1988), "Social Capital in the Creation of Human Capital", American Journal of Sociology (94)(S): 95-120.

14. I speak to you, I hope calmly, and without wild-eyed fanaticism, in disclosing that while I teach at a University, the first thing I did after getting my Ph.D. was joining the American Association of University Professors. I am currently a union member, local 4100 of Illinois, AFL/CIO, University Professionals of Illinois. Yet I truly recall growing up in America, especially in high school, finding tremendous animosity and propaganda directed against anyone who was "pro union".

15. Huff (1989: p. 527) notes, in support of the underclass thesis, gangs are clearly drawn from the urban underclass, and they are often "economically and socially marginal youth who has dropped out of or been expelled from school, and/or is without job skills" (Huff, 1989: p. 527).

16. A note on meager resources with which to carry out the research reported here: This book was not written with funding of any sort. Obviously, with adequate funding a much more direct and more complete analysis of this kind of research problem could be undertaken. I am only alerting the reader that this analysis must be evaluated also in terms of the level of effort, which unfortunately in this case was a meager one.

17. John Irwin's The Jail: Managing the Underclass in American Society sees the population feeding American correctional institutions as consisting of that social group loosely labelled "the rabble" who are a permanent underclass (1985: p. 103). This permanent underclass is therefore related to "persistent ("structural") unemployment among our least integrated citizens" (Irwin, 1985: p. 104).

18. Irving Spergel quoted in: "The Gang's All Here", by Jennifer Halperin, 1994, Illinois Issues (April): p. 16.

19. The depression era (1930-1940) was problematic and masked any relationship because nearly a fourth of Americans were unemployed in 1933. Also, some crimes prosecuted vigorously under other historical periods (e.g., prostitution, gambling, drugs, etc) were less aggressively prosecuted during the early part of the 20th century because these offenses did not directly affect the affluent (see Gordon, 1972, p. 62;

Clark, 1970, pp. 55-56). The depression era, also, tended to be a "good time Charlie" period of law enforcement, a more permissive period with regard to vice.

20. The red color may have therefore represented Centenial High School in Compton, California where many of the OG's of this group are supposed to have lived. Blue was a clothing color from Washington High School in Los Angeles.

"There is one thing worse than a crook and that is a crooked man in a big political job. A man that pretends he is enforcing the law and is really taking 'dough' out of somebody breaking it, even a self-respecting hood hasn't any use for that kind of fellow. He buys them like he would any other article necessary for his trade, but he hates them in his heart".

Al Capone (See Landesco, 1929: p. 1049)

CHAPTER 6

POLITICS AND GANG CRIME: Another Continuity
In Thinking about Gangs

INTRODUCTION

As demonstrated in Chapter 4 the historical continuity in the gang literature regarding ethnic homogeneity in American gang formations was supported by a number of authors. Similarly, there is another conceptual continuity when it comes to the matter of politics. How, exactly, such linkages and political ties or involvements develop and what form they take are examined here. Gang involvement in the modern American electoral process deserves closer attention.[1]

Correctional veterans of the 1970s will recall the political activism of prison inmates and the force they represented. Could gangs provide such a similar level of organizational challenge in the years ahead? Clearly, we need to understand the linkages between politics and gangs to be adequately informed in this area.

GANGS AND POLITICS: Another Historical Continuity in the Literature.

One of the other conceptual continuities in the gang literature is the matter of politics. As will be seen, since gangs were first described in America over a hundred years ago, a continuing study of American gangs has repeatedly found a relationship between the gang and political life (Short, 1975; Short and Molland, 1976). Yet many questions remain unanswered about this relationship.[2]

The strongest continuing theme that has emerged in the literature is that gang members have been cultivated and used as repressive or corruptive functionaires in the urban political scene.[3] A second related theme, regarding direct and indirect aid from political incumbents to gang organizations, is that in urban areas the gang is used to maintain hegemony on voting patterns. Thirdly, many authors cite the covert use of gang capability for extralegal functions. A fourth theme is illicit collaboration, a pattern of "quid pro quo", existing in one form or another between gangs and public officials.

The proof of the enduring relationship between politics and gangs can be found in many cities today. In Chicago, for example, during the summer of 1993 when gang leader "King" Larry Hoover was up for a parole hearing, some major Chicago elected political officials wrote letters to the parole board and even appeared before the hearing on his behalf. The gang itself had pledged to help bring in the votes. Many other studies are showing similar efforts by gangs to ingratiate themselves to liberal politicians. The longterm effects of collaborating with gangs is yet to be felt in such contemporary examples, but historically it dramatically backfires and has proven to be a major political blunder and liability.

Each of these four themes will be reviewed here. Part I simply provides a summary of this literature in relationship to gangs and politics. Part II provides a discussion of the voting rights of ex-offenders and gang members as well as an interview related to the gang-politics theme.

PART I: What The Literature Shows on Gangs and Politics

1. POLITICIANS   CULTIVATING   GANGS

Have some corrupt high ranking political figures in America intentionally rewarded, reinforced, and strengthened gang organizations through the sharing of their power, resources, and protection?[4] Absolutely yes, is the answer from the literature. But this should be viewed in the historical context.

Asbury's (1927) account devoted considerable length to the discussion of earlier American urban politics and gang life. In fact, both Thrasher and Whyte also gave separate chapters in their analysis to this matter of politics. Many other contributors to the gang literature have subsequently cited the interface between politics and gang.[5]

Asbury's contribution was in showing this continuity in the relationship between gangs and politics to a point before the American civil war. The intense competition for scarce resources between newly arrived ethnic groups in urban areas is quoted by Campbell (1984, pp. 234-235) as a precondition that allowed gangs to be "nurtured by politicians" (p. 235). Indeed, while the gangs that were cultivated by politicians as in a sense "political machine maintenance" staff for both Tammany Hall and for other corrupt regimes in Chicago and elsewhere have all but disappeared or have taken new forms, there continues some reference in the literature to the ongoing problem of politicians cultivating gangs. However, today it works both ways: gangs cultivate politicians, and vice versa.

Perhaps the most thorough account, however, is that presented by Landesco (1929). Here much painstaking documentation is provided of the role of both neighborhood gangs and "business gangs" in relationship to political corruption. Landesco gives many details, complete with addresses of bombings, indictments, etc. It concludes with a chapter from E.W. Burgess, suggesting the need to take politics out of law enforcement, and a host of other recommendations.

A more recent citation is that by Suttles quoted in Short and Strodtbeck (1974, pp. viii-ix) who indicated this problem had not disappeared well into the 1960s. That is, politicians still "cultivated" gangs. What is also important, however, is the contribution which Suttles made regarding the valence of political ideology among gang members. Clearly, Suttles indicated that any political sentiments shared by gang members in their ties to politicians were likely to be of the anti-leftist variety.[a] As if patriotism was the last refuge of the scoundrel, gang members clearly identified with conservative, even patriotic, political images. This was also to be subsequently reported by Campbell's study.[6]

Why did politicians cultivate gangs? According to Thrasher, politicians cultivated gangs because of their potential enduring use in the social organizational infrastructure of urban life. Gang members could be used to promote a politician's own interests, and it also meant that in having such an affiliation or tie with the politician, there was an indirect positive impact that could be mobilized in terms of the voting behavior of the parents and adult family members related to the gang (Thrasher, 1968: p. 313).

Let there be no mistake about the accuracy of Thrasher's observation as a continuing rule of thumb for politicians today. The larger the household or family network unit in the ward or precinct, the more a precinct captain, alderman, etc, can "overlook" in the deviance, gang affiliation, etc, of such a social unit. Such voting clusters represent persons related by birth and marriage.

Thrasher showed how politicians encouraged the increasing formal organization of the gang structure (p. 315), by encouraging it to become a "club". Why? Because many important politicians at that time had their start in such gangs. Such that at one point the Chicago city government was, in effect, in the business of promoting the growth of predominantly white gangs. This was indicated by Thrasher's account of how a park employee had a program involving the transitioning of these groups from recurring indigenous nomadic tribes into chartered organizations with a fixed base in a building or office (or clubhouse), with the rent either paid entirely by the politician or in some way subsidized (p. 316).   An important detail about gang vitality and its ability as an organization to survive was also contributed by Thrasher in the context of the early American history regarding gangs and politics. There were two variations: "subsidized" and "self-supporting" gangs (pp. 316-317). The latter generally had a much higher rate of organizational failure and inability to continue. Without economic support --- direct aid or indirect subsidies --- these gangs simply "went under", that is they disappeared.

How were gangs used by politicians? Mostly in electoral politics. To some extent it was a seasonal function. That is, gangs were more likely to be actively mobilized by a politician during the campaign seasons (p. 317).

Thrasher quotes Robert E. Park on the feudalistic nature of gang cultivation by politicians (p. 322). In a sense, the politician was the "serf" or royalty in the feudal sense, and the gang member was a loyal "vassal" who comes to expect protection. A strong "us versus them" identification characterized this differentiation between those affiliated with the political machine and other citizens (pp. 322-323).

---

[a] This is amply documented by Sale (1971, pp. 66-67) where Jeff Fort's gang, at that time in history known as the Black Stone Ranger's, was paid to keep the Black Panthers from operating effectively on Chicago's southside. Later Jeff Fort would also be paid for African-American vote suppression in the Harold Washington election.

Variations of this continue today in many areas, where political affiliation brings with it political patronage. Entire criminal justice agencies --- police departments, correctional systems, probation departments, etc ---experience the strangle hold that newly elected politicians place on their agencies, particularly in staffing and promotion. Political clout still matters a great deal today in the criminal justice system.

What were the "pay-offs", the incentives, and the reward structure for gangs affiliating with a politician and for engaging in what in their own minds must have certainly been regarded as rather pro-social activities? Jobs with the city government or in the private sector where the politician had significant influence are cited by Thrasher as part of this reward structure that could motivate gang members. It involved the traditional "spoils system" (p. 330).

Of course, political pressure on a criminal justice agency (e.g., police department, prison, etc) on behalf of a gang member, to give a sense of immunity, was also obvious (pp. 327-329). In this sense to demonstrate historical continuity, at least in the basic structural conditions that allow for this relationship between gangs and politicians, one should assess the basic problem of political encroachment upon criminal justice agencies such as the police department. If external political pressure can be applied to such agencies to impact on their own internal policies or in special individual cases, then the basic structural problem giving rise to illegitimate influence still exists.

The largest single chapter in Whyte's (1981) Street Corner Society was that entitled "Politics and the Social Structure" (pp. 194- 252). Here we see the exchange process function between the gang and the politician with favors, and quid pro quo. They have mutual influence and mutual interests in common (p. 205). Says Whyte "the politician must take the social organization of the neighborhood into account" (p. 213). Whyte documents the role of gangs in elections as "stooges" (p. 218), their "nuisance value" (p. 219), and in general campaign work and getting out the vote, or alternatively --- suppressing or redirecting it. For a more recent example, the study of children affected by gang violence in Chicago's Henry Horner public housing complex by Kotlowitz describes how a politician used gang members in the campaign after his life was threatened and his vehicle was shot up:

> "At Henry Horner, a young local politician recruited gang members
> from playgrounds to pass out leaflets and accompany campaign
> workers in his successful 1987 bid for Democratic ward committee-
> man. He paid each gang member $20 a day (Kotlowitz, 1991: p.
> 39)".

2. AID FROM THE POLITICIAN TO THE GANG ORGANIZATION

As Whyte indicated, there is a system of reciprocal obligations or expectations in the relationship between the gang and the politician. What form that aid, direct or indirect, can take is of interest in the understanding of the etiology of a variety of contemporary problems such as political corruption, political violence, the integrity of the democratic process, and even racketeering.

Gang members tend to be predictably exploitive of any resource. Remember as well, that gang organizations and gang members are not from another planet: they are indigenous to our neighborhoods, they are someone's children. What seems incredulous is after nearly fifty years of different versions of the detached worker program, that little research has surfaced on the nature of the communications pattern between power brokers, opinion leaders, and influential community members in relationship to the gang.

White gangs seem to be able to take their cues from their respective communities along the lines of racist sentiments. White gangs have historically had a continuing function of fighting for their respective versions of "ethnic purity". It always means segregation. Further examples of this will be highlighted in a discussion of racism and gang crime in a later chapter.

Racism is political and in fact there is evidence that some gangs were able to be simply manufactured by adults, almost from blueprint specifications. Such was the case of the neo-nazi group called the National Socialist Party of America (NSPA) which operated in Marquette Park, on Chicago's southwest side, during the mid-1970s.[7] Two age-graded youth gang auxiliary groups were organized: (1) the White Youth Front, aka "The Young Wolves", ages 12 and under, and (2) the Young National Socialist Corps aka "The Exterminators", ages 13 to 17.[8] Anyone 18 or over was a regular storm trooper (see Knox, 1976). These were, by the way, neo-nazi's who were running for political office, and almost made it.

Preventing organized dissent or preventing organized attempts to undermine the political domination by a given elected official can be another circumstance in which gangs become useful to the politician. Beyond and including the American scene, there is ample historical evidence of using "thugs", or persons having predispositions similar to modern gang members, in a political context to maintain power, to reinforce power and dominance, and to have such political functions carried out, under some social contract. This process usually involves an expectation of reward from the politician. While there is likely to be much "buffering" of the communications between the politician and the gang member, making it difficult as Thrasher and Whyte showed to gather hard evidence that could be used in court, this relationship still constitutes a political reality of gang members as allies, hired hands, or in violent or criminal functions as mercenaries.

Some politicians, in areas such as Chicago, today make no effort to conceal their relationship to "street organizations" (i.e., gangs). Today politicians may in fact openly and conspicuously seek to work with gangs, for example seeking to influence the parole board to release an imprisoned gang leader. The political reality may in fact be that such politicians enter into such relationships by little choice of their own. Rather it may be simply be impossible not to recognize the power that such large gangs may represent in an urban area where a local alderman draws support from.

3. COVERT USE OF GANGS FOR EXTRALEGAL FUNCTIONS

It is in this instance that the linkage between a politician, or powerful individual who may not be a public official but who still seeks or exerts power and control, and a gang must be interpreted as something other than pro-social behavior. Here we are dealing with political crime and the gangs role in it.

Historically it has meant everything from cutting tires, breaking windows, violence to the individual or property, within election campaigns, and has extended most recently in the case of Chicago's Top El Rukn, Jeff Fort, to seeking contractual terrorist work with hostile foreign nations (see Useem and Kimball, 1989: p. 77) --- wanting to blow up American planes or installations for a price. As an organizational vehicle of conflict and violence, the gang deserves much comparative analysis and is also likely to have its parallels internationally. Campbell cites an example of a New York City police sergeant who is quoted to the effect that gangs have been actively recruited and paid for terrorist work (1984, p. 22). Tannenbaum also described the gang as a political instrument (1938, pp. 128-134) and noted their violent role played for management in labor disputes (p, 37). Cloward and Ohlin (1960, pp. 195-196) reference Asbury's account of gangs in politics, even before the civil war, and gang relationships with corrupt politicians in Tammany Hall.

Much of the gang violence that occurs in American cities today has many of the elements of urban guerilla warfare. This analogy and differentiation will be further developed later.

The literature shows gangs can provide a host of extralegal services and functions; from supplying sex and prostitutes, to providing drugs to campaign workers, etc.[9] Figure 6 below is only a suggestive list and certainly does not give an exhaustive list of these many and varied functions.

Another excellent example of the covert use of gangs for extralegal and even terrorist functions is found in recent research on Jamaican posse gangs (Mc Caddon, 1993). According to this source, two major Jamaican posse gangs now operating in the USA were used in the political infighting in Jamaica:

> "The Spangler Posse was an enforcer for Michael Manley's People's National Party, while the powerful Shower Posse worked for Edward Seaga's Jamaican Labor Party" (Mc Caddon, 1993: p. 15).

Some evidence of C.I.A. involvement with street level enforcement groups in Haiti's 1994 crisis did emerge, the goal being to control the groups to prevent anti-American leadership from emerging. In the United States, vote suppression emerged as an issue because of the remark of an aid involved in the campaign of New Jersey's republican Governor elect Christine Todd Whitman, the charge being that $500,000 was spent to suppress the African-American vote.[10] Theoretically, street gangs could be put to quite effective use in this regard.

4. GANGS AND POLITICIANS: Quid Pro Quo

"You scratch my back, I'll scratch your back", the essential meaning of quid pro quo, represents the application of the norm of reciprocity and the social exchange relationship between gangs and politicians. Figure 6 below shows this enormous potential lure represented by "what" the gang has to offer to a politician.

FIGURE 6

WHAT A GANG CAN OFFER, WHAT A GANG MAY WANT[2]

WHAT THE GANG OFFERS	WHAT THE GANG WANTS
Extra Legal Functions	Directed police discretion
Plausible Deniability	Freedom to Operate
Violence against detractors	Political Interference
Violence against property	Political Protection
Intimidation	De Facto Immunity
Help With Handbills	Tampered Court Cases
Help Tearing Down Signs	Resource priorities (e.g.,
Help Putting Up Signs	drug programs, etc)
Drugs for Campaign Workers	Laissez-Faire
Prostitution & Sexual Favors	Correctional/Service Favors
Blackmail Capabilities	Privileges
Stolen Goods	Continuity

The gang clearly has a vast potential capability for operating outside of the legal system. When adequately "buffered" by various layers of contacts to the politician, then any of these essentially criminal acts where the objective material impact is to increase the power and control of the politician, the politician can also enjoy the covert nature of these operations. "I didn't do it", the gangs did; "I didn't run no prostitution ring", somebody else did; "I didn't take any illegal payoffs", the gang did.

Yet there is a norm of reciprocity that operates here and it has to do with an exchange relationship between the politician and the gang. A gang can build up a reservoir of such "good will" with a politician that can be "cashed in" at a later date. A gang can also contribute its unique resources for specialized favors negotiated in advance on a contingency basis: "if we prevent X from winning, then you will help get Y off on probation"; or "if we keep all X's political signs out of the neighborhood by constantly ripping them down and putting yours up, then you will transfer the current Police District Commander out of this ward"; etc, etc.

POLITICS IN THE GANG RIGHTS ACTIVIST MOVEMENT

Many level three gangs today represent themselves as political and civil rights groups, and they are successful in many instances. The Gang Summit held in Kansas City in 1993 was able to convince the Mayor of Kansas City to prevent police from interfering with the event; indeed, the Mayor welcomed the gang leaders at a special breakfast for those attending the Gang Summit. Some gang representatives make no apologies for their gang membership, and like Sharif Willis from Minneapolis indicate there is nothing "former" about their leadership: they are still the top ranking member of their gang --- the Vice Lords in this instance. A number of politicians in a number of cities have therefore met with such gang leaders, typically their public remarks imply that they can coopt the gang into doing prosocial work for the community. The gangs claim that too: that is, that they are the last hope to reverse the deterioration of our urban areas. Are we to believe them is the real question here.

The political "platforms" of gangs today are easily to predict. As a gang leader turned informant for the federal government told the author, "gangs are in favor of gun control...if there is a gun around, they want to be in control of it". Gangs would tend not to be attracted to a conservative political agenda. Gangs and gang members are more attracted to very liberal and even radical political ideals. There are some notable exceptions, however, as we have yet to see a gang really endorse gun control legislation and disarm themselves in the spirit of being politically consistent. It is useful to summarize some of the political issues that arise in what now exists as the "gang advocacy" press.

Gangs, then, often have a critical or even radical political slant. Often this includes some racial conflict analysis. An example that seeks parity in social policy is provided in the Teen Angels (Issue 122) magazine in its editorializing. Teen Angels is a gang magazine[11], particularly for Cholos, it includes glossy color photos of various Hispanic gangs (e.g., SUR 13, Surenos, 18th Street Gang, etc) mostly in California; but includes other western states as well (e.g., Texas, Colorado, Arizona, etc). It is the real thing. It has existed since 1980 and gives gangs and gang members what they want, in fact what they are willing to pay for: an outlet for their messages, and their art. Their art is predictable: guns and sex are the most common themes, followed by customized car scenes, always of course with the gang logo.

In the first issue of Teen Angels many young females had their photographs published; and it was in fact a "membership" type of association: one could join the Teen Angel Fan Club and buy Teen Angel T-shirts[12]. This magazine truly has the best gang art, being the first gang magazine in the world. Its first issue also included a full-page drawing of a gangster in a 1930s black car holding a Thompson submachine gun with the advertisement for the name and telephone number of a criminal defense attorney "He's On Your Side".

By its own description (Teen Angels, Issue 118: p. 2):

> "Teen Angels Magazine is a "gang" Rights Activist News Agency
> Organization dedicated to informing the Barrio Youth of their Civil
> Rights and Liberties as defined in the U.S. Constitution, The Bill
> of Rights and the Hildalgo Treaty between the U.S. & Mexico".

One will often find gang and gun photos in the magazine, but it does not include "drug stash" photos such as might be found in the centerfold of High Times magazine. One can find religious-based anti-gang ads from California groups seeking to get Cholos to quit the gang for Jesus. Since its first issue in 1980 and continuing to present, it has included specific gang contributions (e.g., SUR 13). Because it is exclusively focused on Hispanic gangs and gang members, and recognizing that such magazines are not known to exist for African-American gangs, the casual observer might be tempted to suggest some cultural difference in the need for expressive outlets. However, it is probably much more complex that this, and the present author would hypothesize that if a similar group such as that which tried to organize a National Truce in Kansas City in 1993 were to market a similar publication geared primarily to African-American gangs, it would be equally as successful as <u>Teen Angels</u>.

The magazine rarely includes editorials, but those that are included are of some political interest. One such editorial consisted of a comment or published reply to a letter/article by an inmate. The editorial (Issue # 106) was very pro-law enforcement and encouraged its readers to believe that most cops are good cops. What it also said was the real issue was how the network television news was controlled by the Japanese (called "Japs"), and that what readers needed to worry about was "the coming war with Japan!" Another editorial in the same issue raised the "double standard" problem of how some might complain about pictures of Chicano gang members with guns (who have the right to own guns, unless they are convicted of a felony), while pictures of white persons with guns and depicted in acts of violence can be found in many comic books.

Another editorial (Issue 122) was in the form of a one page poem entitled "Indian Drugs, War Drums are Beating!" and was accompanied by commentary that Americans have overly ignored Native American Indians. It goes on to raise a similar issue on overlooking the Latinos:

> "The school system celebrates Black history week. Is there a Latino history week? HA! Latinos are now the official majority of the population of the state of California and don't even have their own week. Teen Angels Magazine demands that there be not only a Latino week, but also a Native American week!"

Articles from the ACLU are reprinted in the magazine, along with those written by prison reform/activist groups in California.

The July 15th 1993 Gang Summit held in St. Paul, Minnesota tends to epitomize what is meant by indigenous "gang politics". About 150 persons attended the meeting held at the Church, many of whom were not necessarily gang members but were long standing "community activists", and groups such as the American Indian Movement who can be counted on to attend and speak at such events that are critical of the status quo. The style and the rhetoric of the "march" held after the first day's Gang Summit meeting in St. Paul was remarkably similar to some of the 1960s and early 1970s radical political protests[13]. The main message was that of anti-racism and anti-law enforcement, particularly how cops had killed gang members. During the same time frame as the Gang Summit in the Twin Cities, sniper attacks continued on Minneapolis police (e.g., a police car was simply doing a traffic stop on the southside of Minneapolis when it was hit with five gun shots). Thus, in addition to the role of the gang in relationship to traditional politics and political corruption, there is the additional feature of gang rights and gang activist movements.

ON THE ISSUE OF ELITISM AND POLITICS

The law of the land is that you don't have to be a highly educated white home owner to vote. The voting franchise is certainly a right to be used by any gang member of age and so qualified to vote. Anyone who thinks that social status and stigmatizable qualities should restrict persons from voting in America necessarily operates under an elitist view of democracy. Modern gangs are definitely involving themselves in the electoral process. The issue is not whether they have the right to vote. The larger issue is that of responsible participation in the political process as opposed to something less prosocial.

On the other hand, we must recognize that as a typical scenario in the relationship of a gang to local politics, the gang volunteers to work for political candidates in handing out leaflets, house to house, etc. When the media hears about this, or rival candidates can use it, typically the candidate refuses such volunteered help. As a result, local newspaper editorials may attack the same candidate on the grounds that it was a chance for "steering the gangs into something pro-social". But we must simply recall from the limited data available on the subject (see Taylor, 1990) that most gang members are not normally in the habit of voting. One might ask, in light of this, is their interest in electoral politics, then, one of instrumental rather than integrative motivation? That is, does the gang want something, quid pro quo, for such volunteer work? Does the hidden agenda of the "21st Century Vote" initiative of midwestern gangs today include the release of high ranking imprisoned gang leaders or greater influence over local policing practices? In such a context, obviously, gang help could truly be a political liability and an astute candidate knowledgeable of the impact of the mass media might refuse such assistance in the same vein that constituents would expect an elected official to also refuse assistance and especially material support from organized crime.

My own position is, hopefully, clear: we cannot legally exclude gang-affiliated persons from the political process.[14] Nor can we automatically assume that if we see someone on televised videotape at a major "mass" event, open to the public, showing a gang sign, that this is in any sense "proof" that the official sponsoring or benefiting from the event is necessarily a cultivator of gangs, a benefactor of gangs, and a corrupt politician whose power is tied directly to gang crime. Finally, recall that differential access theory could predict more intense violence from gangs if they were excluded from the political process. This is true particularly where gang ideology takes on revolutionary or insurrectionist tones.

So here, guided by previous research, are the merits of doing focused oral histories with gang members. Such a case is shown below in the case of LK41. No names are used. And names of politicians, ward numbers, etc, have been edited out. Otherwise, it is an exact transcription of tape recorded interview material.[15]

CASE STUDY OF LK41:

I'm a Latin King. I figured getting involved in politics was an easier way to help other people that have created problems for themselves. For example, to help people pull a few strings here and there when it is possible. Being a Latin King member for 25 years and a former War Lord of the Boulevard, from the gang fights I have had, from the people I have destroyed in one way or another, the younger people look up to me. They respect me.

RELATIONSHIP   WITH   FORMER   ALDERMAN   E.V.:

I was a part of the ___nd ward, I was a part of the organizers. Ah, I was what they would call, in the field. My job was to try to recruit gang members into the ___nd Ward to help build an army, not in the sense of against the police or anything, but for voters. My job was to get the gangs politically involved into the neighborhood.

I didn't receive anything, but I was promised Latino Youth Centers for the Latin Kings. I myself, I really didn't want anything, I felt that at that time being a part of the problem in the ___nd ward, that I could put something back into it, such as Centers, educational programs, maybe even a boys club if possible, something to get the gangs off the street. That was my main objective.

E.V. didn't help, which was a promise that never given, because we lost to Ald. C_____ G_____. That was an issue, that if we won we would receive, if we lost we would receive nothing.   I am currently involved with the ___nd Ward with Mr. ___, and I expect the same thing I expected out of Mr. V____ at the time. I expect at least youth centers. I expect to try to help the community. Yes, there is gangs, there is Latin Kings, there is gang members involved, as in all politics.

I believe that at if Mr. ____ is elected Alderman that he will keep his promise. Which is to try to curb the gangs by opening up a few centers. Maybe a few parks. Maybe even a possibility that to try and put some of these guys into jobs.
By keeping them on the streets all you are doing is creating a problem. Not solving it.

WHAT IS THE GANG SOLUTION?

Education. I believe that low fixed income people would go with more than just a few dollars. Politicians have a habit of wanting to pay you two dollars for a hundred thousand dollars worth of work. I believe that if the politicians, aldermans, committeemen, congressmen, senators, that if they took a little more interest in their sons and daughters, who probably are gang members, would see another side of the coin.

I believe by creating jobs for them, by not just locking them up and creating problems, such as calling them animals, and dope fiends and drug dealers, these are the labels that people have put upon these people. And in return, they are reacting towards what society expects them to be. Not what they want to be.

I believe the politicians prey on the gangs, they use them to their advantage, they use them for their campaigns, they use em to bring an image into the neighborhood which they in return promise the public that they will curb once they are in office. I believe a lot of gangs are paid by politicians, to be used. I believe the police officers play the same role. The police have a job to perform but I think they only perform it due to the fact because the politicians want them to perform it. By arresting, twelve, thirteen, fourteen-year-old children for curfew doesn't resolve a problem, it creates a problem. The younger look upon the police and instead of respecting them look upon them with animosity. How can you expect a 12-year-old girl or boy to respect a police officer when he is slapping him or her upside the head with a club? Or using a term like bitches or punks in front of their friends, what if they are not a juvenile as the police makes them out to be, when they are 19 or 20 years old, how can you expect them to honestly trust and respect somebody that doesn't have no respect for them?

HOW MANY LATIN KINGS ARE THERE IN THIS _th District or _nd Ward?

I couldn't honestly say, possibly maybe a thousand. Active, maybe 5 to 6 hundred total. They range from probably 12 to, I'm 41 years old.

The Latin Kings, we started out originally, which may sound far fetched, ah, a social activity organization. Our main goal was to try to keep which all of em said, to keep the enemy out of the neighborhood. When we first formed, when I first became a gang member in 1965, my main objective was to try to clean up the neighborhood, there was drug addicts in the neighborhood, there was a lot of burglars, and a lot of killing. Our main thing was to join a coalition (pronounced "correlation") to try to keep and try to straighten out the neighborhood, not to create problems. As time went on, we were turning away from not only from the politicians but from the police officers, we were harassed because we went out on the corners and we fought against other gang members who were raping and robbing and stealing off of our own people. I don't think the Kings want to be known as the killers and rapers and drug dealers, child molesters, or whatever for the rest of their life. I would like to think they would like myself that they have done something constructive. By turning over a new leaf if given a chance. I mean how can you keep expecting somebody to try be a, try to be a citizen, when people keep putting them down. I mean even a dog has its own day. I think that the Kings, if given a chance, I think they would like to come into this neighborhood and clean it up. I think the Kings are just like anybody else. That given the right chance, I think what they are looking for actually is somebody to really sit down and talk to them. Not to disrespect them. I believe that if there was a program set up for some of the older guys to sit down with some of the younger guys I think we could at least eliminate some of the wrong doing that has been done in this neighborhood. Not total. But I believe that if we have helped one out of ten we are doing something.

WHO HAVE THE KINGS ELECTED TO POLITICAL OFFICE?

Well, I know, C___ G____ was one of them, as a matter of fact, the Kings had backed up Rudy Lozano. Rudy Lozano was one of our main image. He was somebody that was our savior for the neighborhood. He came into us, talking to us, relating what was expected of us, promising to help the neighborhood, but I am not saying that was wrong. I think he took an interest in us. But I do know that C___ G___ has used the Kings for his own benefit, by promising jobs, by working work with the kings that work with him, by knocking on doors, doing whatever is possible to get him elected. By him being elected we had the neighborhood to ourselves, which was a false promise. C___ G___ used us and there is no doubt in my mind he has probably used other gang members, not only Kings, but probably the Two-Six also which is another gang in the neighborhood.

WHO DO YOU BELIEVE KNOCKED OFF RUDY LOZANO?

I believe it was a political move. I don't believe that C___ G___, ah...I mean Rudy Lozano was killed because of drugs. I find that hard to, I knew Rudy Lozano, I sat down and talked to Rudy Lozano on several occasions. I believe because there was a struggle in the neighborhood for the, for politics. I don't think it was, so much that the, Rudy Lozano was not a drug user. And I would put my life on the line for that. Rudy was not, he didn't believe in drugs, that was not his image, he was for the people. I find it pretty hard to believe that people would even consider even thinking that he was a drug user. I mean, the man had everything to gain and a lot to lose, and he lost his life over it. And I believe it was over, what he was trying to do was form the unions in the neighborhoods, such as your tortillas, and your, ah, ah, and your restaurants, and I believe and this is to my heart that somebody put up somebody to kill him. He was much too strong for him to use drugs.

I believe it was true that what the newspapers reported, that the Two-Six gang member killed him, that he just got too strong, politically. They used it as, as, a drug issue. The individual was probably paid and probably his family got paid off also. Understand this, the man was becoming a political image in this neighborhood to a lot of people. Especially the poor people. Especially the Hispanic people. Now I am not saying it was a white or a black that killed him. We know that somebody killed him. And I had gone with Rudy Lozano on a few voyages through the neighborhood confront different store owners, and ah restaurants, and businesses. And they did not like Rudy Lozano. Due to the fact that because he was for the Hispanic people. He was trying to straighten the neighborhood out. He was trying to form a union here. A coalition for the Hispanic people, instead of the same thing, like I said for the Kings, instead of taking advantage of them, that he wanted to do something for them. And I believe that was the reason why they killed him.

Gangs and politics go hand in hand. I believe that an Alderman that has been an alderman for the last 20 years, and there aint no doubt in my mind, I would probably stake my life on it, he has probably taken a bribe along the way. Not all of them. But a good majority of them. But the record shows it for a fact. You have aldermen in the penitentiary. I believe the Kings are probably just waiting for something or somebody to come to relieve them. Of giving something. So they can start their life all over again. Put their life together. You know it is a funny part of this, the politicians ask for the Kings for the gangs help, but they refuse to help them when it is all over. And in every election you hear the same thing, you have to clean the gangs up, you have to take them off the streets, you have to build more penitentiaries, take the graffiti off, but in return it is the politicians who ask the gang members to go out and hang their signs, to destroy the other candidates as much as possible, to disgrace them if possible. And I am not going to sit here and say they would even go as far as to kill them. But I do know they will probably use them as much as possible to hurt another candidate if push comes to shove.

AN UPDATE ON THE RUDY LOZANO ASSASSINATION

In the summer of 1993 a high ranking member of the Latin King organization who had "flipped for the G" (i.e., being a confidential informant for federal law enforcement agencies) and who was now being held in a snitch farm was interviewed on the Rudy Lozano issue. Lozano was a very popular local political leader in the Chicago Hispanic community, as well as a labor organizer, who was assassinated on June 8, 1983. This was truly a "former member" or "ex" member of a gang, in this case the Latin Kings. He was really an "ex-member" of the Latin Kings because there was and still is a $250,000 "hit" out on him. Thus, he was being held in a very secure special protection unit. By special permission I was able to visit this secure facility and conduct in-depth private interviews with this person. This person had been a member of the Latin Kings for twenty years and had gained at his forced retirement the position of a Prince and carried the special tattoo that the position entailed!

Many of the details in the multiple in-depth interviews with this person proved to be corroborated. We were not paying for our information either. As the person in this instance, an inmate, explained the true story about Rudy Lozano:

"Rudy Lozano was going out with one of Baby King's sisters".

Baby King a/k/a "B.K." was then and is now the single highest top ranking member of the Latin Kings and may rise to the Sun God position in this burgeoning national organization. As our source further indicated:

"BK got with David Ayala, the chief of the Two-Sixers, because he was upset with Rudy Lozano and in the crime business, well the business part of it is you put your differences aside even if you are rival gang organizations. The dude who was arrested and convicted for the Rudy Lozano killing he's in prison now, I've met him. He was Latin Folks, being a two-sixer, which I could not get along with being Latin Peoples. Well, his name is Gregory Escobar, he was the fall guy. He knows now that it was a King hit, it bothers him now. But he didn't know it was a Latin King hit when he did it."

Many including the present author had suspected the Rudy Lozano assassination of a major local grassroots political leader was at the time a crime that could be put at the doors of the Latin King organization. Obviously, the true facts of the crime had been effectively concealed a very long time officially[16]. But the true story was known apparently to many in these two gang organizations (Two Sixer's and the Latin Kings). Gangs continue today throughout America to seek to develop and cultivate ties to elected politicians. What those politicians need to know are stories like the Rudy Lozano case[17].

As some gangs approach the point of operating in the fashion of organized crime, this problem can be expected to escalate. For after all, being able to cultivate or use political corruption is one of the defining features of what we mean by organized crime. That some gangs are operating as groups that can mobilize thousands of votes (e.g., the Disciples Annual Picnics are an example: in their summer 1992 they attracted 5,000, in 1993 some 10,000 attended their picnic, all food and transportation free[18]), and that they engage in voter registration drives as well, and particularly to the extent the gangs use a public relations strategy where they manipulate the mass media into scenes showing their involvement in "Truces" and "helping the community" (e.g., anti-litter campaigns in public housing complexes, where they may themselves "fine" a litterer), then such grey areas of political "right and wrong" and outright ethical misconduct and worse can be expected in the political arena.

THE GANG ISSUE IN LOCAL AND NATIONAL POLITICAL CAMPAIGNS

During the 1992 presidential campaign, the incumbent President George Bush did not use the gang issue as part of his political campaign. Why? In a later chapter on gangs and law enforcement we will find part of the answer, as apparently a large portion of our Nation's gang problem basically exploded during President Bush's term of office. Presidential candidate William Clinton did refer to gangs in his nomination acceptance speech at the Democratic National Convention. In that speech, one of the "covenants" referred to addressing our Nation's gang problem by means of a new kind of "national service", involving college graduates who perform public services that might be useful in preventing some of the problems associated with gangs.

Another candidate running for the president's office in 1992 was James "Bo"Gritz, the famous Green Beret activist for P.O.W.'s. In a videotape used in his presidential campaign, entitled "The Healing of America" (1992), gangs are given much more prominent attention. The kind of discussion of gangs in the Gritz (1992) political platform basically sees major gangs profiting from drugs, and political corruption having a lot to do with the importation of drugs, and the rise of a secret-style military-police force who are ever present to hold back the rising threat of violence and riots from gang members and other groups driven to desperation.

In some local municipal elections, gangs are also a campaign issue. The most popular and effective political use of the gang issue is that of the get tough approach. In short, the gang problem has become an issue that is relevant to the campaign positions of candidates seeking office in all levels of government.
Given the rising importance of the gang problem we can probably expect this trend to continue.

LEFTIST POLITICAL EXTREMIST GROUPS CULTIVATING GANGS

Some groups who regularly show up at Gang Summit Meetings, meetings of gang members and gang leaders held under the banner of working for peace sometimes directly or indirectly subsidized by the federal government held in recent years that this author monitored, are traditional and well known left wing extremist groups. They show up wearing radical T-shirts with their symbols of revolution, but stick out as some of the only white people present not representing the media. This happened in Kansas City, Minneapolis, and Chicago; three different gang summit meetings. In Minneapolis a variety of such groups appeared. In Chicago two white teenage members of the Revolutionary Communist Party, Chicago Branch distributed flyers calling for revolution. In the Chicago meeting another group using the black panther symbol superimposed over the globe called the New African-American Vanguard Movement (NAAVM) based in Los Angeles also distributed a flyer explaining its platform: peace and justice, better food and housing, reform of criminal justice, legalized drugs, sentence reductions, end of police brutality, end of military aggression, and religious tolerance. All of the political analysis was couched in traditional 1960s radical leftist language, but updated to specifically attract Crips and Bloods to their own way of thinking. There has also been a Latin and Hispanic version of this, where in Chicago some groups tending to be supportive of the terrorist group known as the F.A.L.N., have tried to cultivate gang members and have apparently succeeded in some regards as discussed elsewhere in this book. The F.A.L.N. is a leftist group that seeks independence for Puerto Rico. White gangs provide numerous examples of mostly rightwing cultivation.

GANG POLITICAL INFLUENCE ON GOVERNMENT AGENCIES

In 1993 Gangster Disciple gang leader Larry Hoover engineered a public petition drive to influence the Illinois Prisoner Review Board to grant him a parole. The petition cover was endorsed by a number of African-American politicians and activists[19]. When it was submitted to the parole board it contained the names and addresses and signatures of nearly 5,000 persons.[b] By chance we had been interviewing female members of the gang at the time, and one who had "de-activated", basically trying to "socially slip away" from the gang, responded to a knock on her door one night and was basically told by the local gang members to sign the petition, and thus she expressed the view of being compelled to sign the petition. We did feel it was very curious to subsequently discover that such an important document was destroyed by the Illinois Prisoner Review Board.

This attempt by the gang to engineer the release of their gang leader included using well-known current and former elected officials to speak or write to the parole board on behalf of such a parole, in addition to a number of business and religious leaders. The parole was not granted[20], but another parole hearing was scheduled for December, 1994 which also corresponds to a time of a build up of political action by the gang. And it would appear from closer analysis that Hoover also has a back up plan for trying to get a parole from the Illinois Department of Corrections.

Hoover's back up plan surfaced in 1993, when Illinois State Representative Coy Pugh introduced House Bill 513 and House Bill 240 to the General Assembly.[21] The thrust of these bills, had they been passed, would have converted so-called "C-numbers" to a flattime sentence for inmates currently in the system. Hoover has a c-number, meaning it is an indeterminate sentence. The state law proposed by Pugh would have converted c-number sentences to fixed sentences, allowing many in prison

---

[b] The National Gang Crime Research Center realizing the potential research value of this data, did make an official Freedom of Information Act request to the Illinois Prisoner Review Board, by registered mail to (Ill. Governor Edgar; chairman James K. Williams and Kent Stenkamp of the Prisoner Review Board) have access to this public information. However, the list "was disposed of...because it was not needed after the parole hearing" which denied inmate Hoover a parole. In his 1994 re-election campaign television ads, Gov. Edgar claimed to be the candidate to wage the best war against gang crime. As it was reconfirmed in October, 1994, the story was "we just did not need all the names, all we needed was an example of the front of the petition form used, which has been preserved in the file". Thus, one page of the overall petition was all that was kept for official files.

to automatically be released. Pugh was one of several who wrote a letter on July 15,1993 to the prisoner review board in behalf of Hoover's attempt to get released.[22] Pugh is friendly to the "21st Century V.O.T.E." group and was featured in a press kit photo standing with their main leaders at the summer 1993 picnic held at a private farm in Kankakee, Illinois which drew nearly 10,000 persons --- mostly Gangster Disciples.

POLITICAL ACTION BY GANGS

When the Gangster Disciples in Chicago formed the Young Voters of Illinois in the mid-1980s, these folks were quickly followed by the same put-on among peoples. The Unknown Conservative Vice Lords (UCVL) in 1985 formed and obtained a state chartered not-for-profit group called the United Concerned Voters of Illinois (UCVL). This type of development is more of a public relations function for the gang than a serious attempt to enter politics and unseat incumbents. Jeff Fort's El Rukn gang formed the Young Grass Roots Independent Voters, similarly, but according to 1991 testimony apparently to suppress the African-American vote against Harold Washington by backing another candidate and then mayor Jane Byrne, that is a straight-forward contractual arrangement with the gang being paid for its power to intimidate.[23]

More recently, however, the Gangster Disciples have taken a more serious turn in political action by forming "21st Century V.O.T.E."[24], and have developed a large war chest for the group to have some impact. This same group had very high access to political elites when one of its main gang activists, Wallace "Gator" Bradley, was able to meet with the President in the White House[25]. Some longtime gang analysts point to the fact that there is nothing new about gang leaders meeting with the President and cite the case of Jeff Fort and Richard Nixon in 1991. Actually, while Jeff Fort was invited to Nixon's inauguration, Jeff did not personally attend and in fact sent two of his lieutenants in his place to attend the inauguration.[26] However, some analysts of this development are less worried about the success of the GDs in electoral politics under the theory that in the light of day the group will be viewed as a deviant group and not be supported in spite of its efforts to hand out Thanksgiving and Christmas food baskets, even though they can be obviously effective in pressure politics by their simple ability to disrupt. The GDs did not need have to read up on Saul Alinsky to realize they can have an impact in Chicago just by showing up with 5,000 members in Chicago's loop with protest signs, chanting nasty slogans about Mayor Daley.

Current thinking seems to be that the recent more sophisticated approach to Chicago politics by the Gangster Disciples is no longer a put-on and that they are having a definite impact on elections. The first major battle was in the March 15th 1994 primary elections in which 21st Century V.O.T.E. supported Jerry Washington as a challenger to Rep. Daniel Burke[27]. While Burke won the election easily, gang involvement in the election was very obvious, and their preferred candidate Washington did do a lot better in terms of votes than in previous attempts in the same race.[28]

The spring 1994 election followed an earlier public relations event that drew harsh criticism when 21st Century V.O.T.E. had staged an awards ceremony at Chicago's

Englewood Public High School. This ceremony and media event happened during the Chicago Gang Summit meeting held in October, 1993. Among the recipients of awards was of course Larry Hoover, but Willie Lloyd[29] the leader of the Unknown Vice Lords was also given an award like Hoover in absentia, along with other gang leaders active in the Gang Summit Meeting.[30] Students at the school had to attend this ceremony, and one teacher reported several non-gang members told her they now wanted to join the gang.[31]   While it showed the ability of the gang to be able to use a public high school through sympathizers who worked there[32], the media generally gave it harsh reviews and it was roundly criticized as an inappropriate use of government property[33].   Still, late in 1994 it was the Gangster Disciple's front group "21st Century V.O.T.E." that was said to be responsible for an attempted takeover of the southside branch of Chicago's NAACP, when a group friendly to these same gang activists and which was also a co-sponsor of the 1993 Chicago Gang Summit (No Dope Express) walked into the NAACP office with 5,000 new and recently completed applications for membership in the NAACP --- along with nearly $50,000 in cash for the membership fees to go along with the applications, in an attempt to engineer a political takeover of this branch of the NAACP.[34]   While erring on the side of flamboyance, the political education of gangs could improve over time, and with the ability to walk in with 5,000 new memberships there are few organizations, fraternities, not-for-profit groups, membership associations, etc, that could not easily find themselves held hostage in this fashion. This is a twist on the same type of "terrorist threat" style of shake-downs used by the Yakuza, where they would simply buy shares to a corporation, show up at the stock holders meeting and disrupt the activities therein, and literally shake down the corporation systematically in elections and stockholders meetings.

SUMMARY AND CONCLUSION

Politically, most gangs are opportunistic, conservatively oriented[35] in the sense that they have as their ideal type a function as a business organization, and their attachment to the legitimate social order through politicians tends to be characterized by lower-level field functions. Gang members are not, as a group, over-achievers in the field of higher education, particularly political science. They are not likely to be used as strategy or policy makers in a political campaign, rather their function is, like their life style, a "street function". The gangs attempt to form its own political organization can only further expose the same gang to systematic investigation and will thus backfire in the long run.

Chicago has a somewhat unique political context. Currently, an appointed Alderman sits on the City Council who is an "ex-member" of a large gang organization. Some like to loosely use the phrase that Chicago "has elected a U.S. Congressman who is a gang member" --- but they are referring to someone who had only a political association with the Black Panther Party[c]. In its time, certainly the Black Panther

---

[c] For a view of the Black Panther Party which could possibly define it as a gang in terms of its leaders and controlling figures having a pattern of criminal activity or corrupt practices, see Hugh Pearson, 1994, <u>The Shadow of the Panther: Huey Newton and the Price of Black Power in America</u>, Addison-Wesley Publishers.

Party was treated as a gang[d]. Some in corrections still define Black Panthers in the same way, as they do the Fruits of Islam, as a threat group. And, of course, Chicago politics is somewhat unique in what can best be described as being an open-system capable of integrating most organized political factions, and accommodating the rest. Chicago is not any more or less corrupt than any other city in America it just has enjoyed more than its share of attention in that regard, so much so that Chicagoans themselves joke about it in the popular witticism "vote early and often".

The problem is that gangs are quick to learn the laws and the laws on financial disclosures for politicians are well known. Any cash donations below a certain threshold do not have to have a name or donor source associated with it for Ethical Disclosures in Financial Activity required by law. A gang is uniquely qualified to "wash" and "launder" very large hidden cash contributions, by having its many members hand-carry such smaller cash donations to the political function. This helps explain why in the fall of 1994 the Gangster Disciples political action committee known as "21st Century V.O.T.E." was able to file a financial disclosure report indicating over $100,000 in donations, but only $2,500 was accounted for by specifically named sources.

And yet, it is often remarked for gang leaders, like Jeff Fort that the extent of mind control over fellow gang members is extraordinary. Some also like to see the parallel qualities that some gang organizations have with cult groups in terms of the remarkable control of member behavior. This type of parallel of gangs to cults has the common elements of an authoritarian leader, a group that threatens harm to one who tries to leave it, and harsh discipline against its own members for violating internal rules. If the organizational efforts and energy of a typical modern organized gang were applied for pro-social activities, then it would be considered a heroic development from the underclass: just to get these persons on a trajectory out of a pattern of typically inner-city impoverishment. It is a political coup in its own right to be able to organize such persons to do anything positive. However, no evidence exists that anyone has ever been able to "treat" an entire gang, let alone rehabilitate it in terms of its individual members or its composite function and purpose as a group or organization. Thus, most of the conspicuously prosocial aspects of a gang are part of its public relations function designed to deflect law enforcement attention and just like in community policing where the police officer wants to have a friendlier relationship with the locals, the gang seeks more cordial relations with those locals who could potentially testify against them.

The difference between the present position from that of implied prior positions in the literature is the matter of a gang member's right to vote and participate in the electoral process. Any offender has that right, if local laws allow it. Remember, over ten percent of all Americans have an arrest record according to NORC[36] data. Any view which implies exclusion of deviants or exoffenders is necessarily an elitist view of how democracy should work.

---

[d] See also the book review by Sol Stern, "Charismatic Thugs: Exposing the Criminal Behavior of the Black Panthers", Chicago Sun-Times, Sunday Arts and Show Supplement, July 3, 1994, p. 12 (B).

The reader who accepts, to any extent, the popular "reintegration" strategy for rehabilitation or preventing criminal relapse or recidivism, cannot have the cake and eat it too --- we cannot in policy claim to want to reintegrate offenders back into our communities and put them on a legitimate career trajectory and at the same time through elitist practice prevent them from exercising constitutionally guaranteed rights, such as the right to vote. Clearly both racism and the double standard operate here when it comes to how some ultra-conservative whites have characterized Jesse Jackson's or Operation PUSH's efforts to register Cook County Jail inmates to vote. That was not cultivating gang organization, it was a lawfully entitled effort to reach out to an important segment of America's "other half" ---- that half that never votes anyhow.

In the long run, the success of a gang in spurring an increase in voting behavior may be the penultimate solution to the historical question of "how do we increase voter turnout?". The reason this is answer is theoretically forthcoming is to be found in the work of Emile Durkheim. Durkheim informs us that norms are strengthened and social solidarity may increase because of crime in some instances by the application of sanctions and response to the crime problem. The American "lazy half" that never really votes might actually get off their bar stools, register to vote and actually vote if they knew the full extent of gang involvement in local American politics.

Finally, we cannot from a strict social scientific basis rule out the possibility that powerlessness and the search for power are codeterminants of gang organization. We shall see later that another contemporary theory says essentially the same thing: multiple marginality causes gangs, that is they are not simply alienated individuals, they are multiply labelled, some persons face "double", "triple" jeopardy, and beyond, in terms of their life chances for "making it in America". Or as Vigil (1988) says, they are multiply marginal. We should not alienate offenders from our mainstream political institutions, or else they have but one recourse: subcultural politics --- and political extremism. Indeed, with advance knowledge of any gang's potential to abuse such political resources, it might be more effective to stimulate citizenship and voting behavior as a general thrust towards a more "pro social" orientation of the type of offenders we find in our correctional institutions today. The trouble comes when denying the political linkages and the tendency of gangs to gravitate towards sources of political legitimation.

DISCUSSION QUESTIONS

(1) How do you think the evolution of the mass media has impacted on the relationship between the corrupt politician and use of gang members in the political arena? Is it as easy today as it was several decades ago, just to get away with it unnoticed?

(2) Campbell (1984) felt that gangs (at least the female gang members she studied) were not revolutionary. How then do we account for the existence within highly organized gangs (level 3 gangs) that have in their written constitutions, language that identifies "their struggle" with the Third World, and oppressed persons generally?

(3) Are today's white gangs by most standards likely to be political by definition, and political extremists, if they organize along the dimensions of "white power"?

FOOTNOTES

1. Remember that in American politics, appeasement is always a factor. Is it is possible that some gangs sustain nourishment and legitimacy from such political appeasement? Through having "social programs" ostensibly created for gang prevention work, that may in actuality function au contraire in terms of actually providing the meeting grounds for gang organization development? And all with public monies or enjoying not-for-profit status? Poston (1971) described some of this problem.

2. One of these is the interface with political forces. Not all gangs have such ties to larger political forces. Most can reasonably be assumed to want to exploit such relationships. If given the chance. The maxim "through understanding comes control" has more than some significance in this analysis of politics and gangs in the correctional environment.

3. Bensinger (1984: p. 5) quotes the 1968 Senate Investigating Committee looking into the $927,341 OEO grant to the Blackstone Rangers where a gang leader named "Watusi" alleges "the federal monies were used to pay off gang members not to riot".

4. Recently in Chicago when the City Council seat for the 22nd Ward became vacant, Mayor Daley appointed Ricardo Munoz to fill the open position. Much local media attention and editorials shortly appeared; because Mr. Munoz admits to prior gang affiliation and an arrest history for drugs and weapons charges. One letter to the editor by Hector Linares in the Chicago Tribune blasting the appointment said "The message his appointment makes to the gangbangers and drug dealers is clear - -- the more you break the law, the better your qualifications for Chicago political office".

5. Haskins (1975) provides a powerful historical analysis as well. That is, most local political leaders in New York City many years ago "had at least one gang working for" them, "thus the gangs of New York play no small part in the political struggles of mid-nineteenth century, starting under the approving eye of the politicians" (Haskins, 1975: p. 32).

6. And, of course, in other studies as well, Jeff Fort's early gang development formation, in the stage of the Blackstone Rangers, prior to the stage of "Moorish Americans" and prior to the "El Rukn's" was reported by Denisoff and McCaghy (1973, p. 155) quoting the work of Mc Pherson (1966) to be anything but "militant" and totally uncooperative with the Black Panther Party, they were in a nutshell, "out for themselves". Opportunists in every sense of the word. Ultimately, Jeff Fort's group (the El Rukns) would be vigorously targeted for federal prosecution when they made the decision to enter into the political arena and seek to carry out domestic terrorism functions for foreign countries.

7. A current nationally known neo-nazi in Lincoln, Nebraska (Gerhard Lauck) began with this Chicago neo-nazi group that operated in Marquette Park. In fact, he was the chief propagandist for Chicago's NSPA headed by Frank Collin. Lauck has a history of exporting native American fascism to Germany. See: Rogers Worthington, "From A Distance, Nebraska Nazi Agitates At Will", Chicago Tribune, Section 1, pp. 21,24, Jan. 9, 1994.

8. A neo-nazi with a similar profile to Frank Collin has established a similar operation, although less organized, in St. Paul, Minnesota. See: Conrad deFiebre, "Nazis Take Root: South St. Paul Keeps Watch on Neofascists' Activities", Star Tribune, June 2, 1993.

9. Early American urban politicians quickly realized the potential extra-legal functions and roles that gangs could play and that such "arms-length" distance allowed these politicians plausible deniability for such extralegal acts. For example, "gang leaders were paid for taking care of jobs like blackjacking political opponents and voting many times over at the poles" (Haskins, 1975: p. 32).

10. See: Editorial "Probe Vote-Suppression Charges", Chicago Sun-Times, Nov. 12, 1993, p. 35.

11. Teen Angel, P.O. Box 338, Rialto, CA 92376.

12. The gang art included in Issue #1 of the magazine includes a collage with young Hispanic men and teenage Hispanic females; one of the females holds a switchblade, another holds a pistol; the message written reads "Cliques all over Aztlan are uniting with the 'Teen Angels', de Aztlan, Together we are a powerful force! Join Today ese!" No page numbers are provided in Teen Angels. The notation and referencing system to be used henceforth in referring to such materials will count the front cover as page one. The above collage is therefore on page 19.

13. See Tim Nelson, 1993, "Gang Members Launch Summit", St. Paul Pioneer Press METRO, July 16th, p. 1, 4C.

14. The data from Taylor (1990: p. 133) would have us believe that this is probably not something to worry much about, as gang members don't vote, at least in Taylor's Detroit sample.

15. This particular interview was conducted by a Hispanic leader and student of mine, Arturo Mota.

16. The version presented here is consistent with another theory of the Rudy Lozano assassination, which is that the arrested and convicted killer Escobar was himself an accomplice during the early stages of the prosecution of the case, an accomplice in the cover-up of the murder. Escobar was prosecuted by then State's Attorney Richard Daley. See: Michael Rosenfeld, "Who Killed Rudy Lozano?", Grey City Journal, October 15, 1993 for an extensive review of the facts of the Lozano murder.

17. How the Bamboo Gang was used by Taiwanese politicians to assassinate a Chinese-American journalist --- Henry Liu --- in San Francisco is described in Kaplan and Dubro (1986: p. 219). In fact, the "hit" was contracted with the Bamboo Gang through the Taiwanese Defense Ministry Intelligence Bureau.

18. See George Papajohn, "Gang Shares Peace - and Potatoe Salad", (pp. 1,3), Chicago Tribune, September 12, 1993. In the 1993 version of the B.O.S. (includes BD's, GD's, BGD's) picnic, the front for the group was the 21st Century --- a voter registration campaign and political organization. Earlier in 1993 as the above story documents, the same "political" group staged a protest in downtown Chicago with 5,000 protesters.

19. Among the politicians names that appeared printed and endorsing the front of the "Petition to Parole Larry Hoover" were: former Mayor Eugene Sawyer; Joe Gardner, Commissioner, Metropolitan Water Reclamation District; Alderman Allan Streeter, 17th Ward; Alderman Shirley Coleman, 16th Ward; and Alderman Virgil Jones, 15th Ward. Under these pre-printed endorsements the petition included the paragraph "WE HEREBY, INDIVIDUALLY AND COLLECTIVELY, do believe, as evidence of his present actions, Larry Hoover, to be rehabilitated and of sound mind and judgement, and as such, an asset to the communities-at-large in the capacity of a prime component in the institution, maintenance and subsequent longevity of the existing United in Peace Coalition Nations' Truce that currently attributes to the continuous, dramatic drop in the percentage of violent crimes and homicides in the African-American communities from Chicago to Peoria and throughout the State of Illinois". Obviously, that "truce" was a farce, it never really did work.

20. One of the major opponents against the release of Larry Hoover was Cook County State's Attorney Jack O'Malley. Jack Hynes, supervisor of the gang prosecution unit under State's Attorney O'Malley, pointed out the following in a 1994 memorandum: "Larry Hoover is the leader of the Gangster Disciple street gang in Illinois. He was sentenced to 150-200 years in the Department of Corrections in 1973 for the murder of Joshua Shaw. Due to the sentencing law in effect in 1973, Hoover now comes up for parole every year. Last year supporters of Hoover organized a letter-writing and media campaign to gain his release. The tenure of this campaign was that Hoover is reformed and would be a positive role model for the community. It is the position of the State's Attorney's Office that this is not true. Information gathered from the Illinois Department of Corrections, police gang intelligence, and official court documents in criminal trials reveals that Hoover remains the undisputed "King" of the Gangster Disciples. His release would unify thousands of Gangster Disciples, enabling them to increase the efficiency in which they inflict injury and terror in our communities".

21. See: "TO: C NUMBER PRISONERS, FRIENDS, FAMILIES AND SUPPORT- ERS OF C NUMBER LEGISLATION", by Shango, Inside Out, a publication of the Prison Action Committee, Dedicated to the memory of Fred Hampton and Mark Clark, Vol. 1, No. 5, December, 1993, p. 1.

22. The letter read: "Please accept this communique as letter of support on behalf of Mr. Larry Hoover, who will be appearing before the parole board in August. I am personally endorsing his release at this time. From all indication concerning his personal reform and evident rehabilitation I strongly urge that the Board consider this case with due diligence and in a positive frame of reference. Mr. Hoover has more than demonstrated his willingness to take a responsible place in society. His work and efforts to bring about badly needed changes are quite known to myself as well as others in the community".

23. See: Jim Merriner, "Gang Charges Set the Tone in 2nd Dist. Race", Chicago Sun-Times, Dec. 19, 1993, p. 5.

24. A tape-recorded conversation between Larry Hoover, "King" of the Gangster Disciples from his prison cell and rival gang leader Willie Lloyd, showed Larry bragging "I got a political action committee, a 21st century vote". See: "Jailed Gang Chieftan Says He Started PAC", by Lee Bey, Chicago Sun-Times, Sept. 29, 1994, p. 20.

25. Gator got his name from preferring alligator shoes when he was a Black Gangster Disciple (BGD). Of course he told President Clinton he represents a group called Better Growth and Development (BGD) for urban areas. See: "Gator Gets Say With Clinton", by Lee Bey, Chicago Sun-Times, Jan. 26, 1994, p. 3. This meeting between the president and Gator was widely criticized as an affront to countless victims of gang violence, see: "Outrage: Gator at White House", Editorial, Chicago Sun-Times, January 26, 1994, p. 31. Jesse Jackson defended the visit, noting that forgiveness is necessary, and we should not stigmatize such persons, see: "Personal View: Jackson Defends Gator Visit to White House", Chicago Sun-Times, Feb. 1, 1994, p. 24. At the time Gator met with President Clinton in the White House, Gator was out on bond for a charge of criminal trespass to a stolen vehicle and was not supposed to leave the jurisdiction without the permission of the judge, see: "Gang Activist's Trip Unlawful", by Lee Bey, Chicago Sun-Times, Jan. 31, 1994, p. 3. Columnist Richard Roeper also criticized the President for this, see: "Gadflies Gator, Ziff Hang With Bubba", Chicago Sun-Times, April 17, 1994, p. 11. The motor vehicle theft charge resulted when Gator rented a Cadillac from Avis using the offer of credit card help from a news reporter, and later the bill for the car was reported in the computer as being unpaid, where in a routine terry stop Gator was arrested because Avis reported the car as stolen, see: Lee Bey, "Chance Meeting Steers 2 Into Trouble", Chicago Sun-Times, Nov. 27, 1993, p. 6.

26. For an excellent history of Jeff Fort, see: Tom Brune and James Ylisela, Jr., "The Making of Jeff Fort", Chicago Sun-Times, November, 1988.

27. See: "Group Tied To Gangs Facing Test of Voters", by George Papajohn and Steve Rhodes, Chicago Tribune, Section 2, p. 1-2, Jan. 23, 1994.

28. See: "Losing Teaches VOTE Lessons for Next Time", by John Kass and George Papajohn, Chicago Tribune, Section 2, pp. 1-2, March 20, 1994.

29. It was Willie Lloyd who captured much media attention during and after his release from prison, leaving prison in a fur coat and a limousine, and later in Chicago being the target of an assassination attempt from his own gang in the fashion of a roaring 20s style shoot-out on the Eisenhower expressway, which was followed by another failed attempt near the criminal court building at 26th and California. See: Jim Casey and Art Golab, "Gang Leader, 3 Others Shot on the S.W. Side", Chicago Sun-Times, Oct. 20, 1993, p. 76.

30. See: Lee Bey and Fran Spielman, "Gang Awards Program Hit as Bad Message", Chicago Sun-Times, Oct. 27, 1993, p. 12.

31. See: John Kass and George Papajohn, "High School Role in Gang Summit Hit", Chicago Tribune, Section 2, pp. 1,8. October 27, 1993.

32. The assistant principal of the school had been one of those who wrote a letter on behalf of paroling Larry Hoover in 1993. The principal was seen in a press kit photo provided by 21st Century V.O.T.E. for their large picnic on a farm in rural Kankakee in 1993.

33. See: "Gang Awards Send Appalling Message", Raymond R. Coffey, Chicago Sun-Times, Oct. 28, 1993, p. 3.

34. See: Jerry Thomas, "NAACP Upstart Brings in 5,000 New Members", Chicago Tribune, Oct. 20, 1994, section 2, p. 2.

35. This analysis does recognize the existence of language and written gang constitutions that indicate affinity with "third world" causes and "oppressed people" generally. But this is often little more than double talk.

36. NORC (National Opinion Research Center) conducts the General Social Survey.

CHAPTER 7

THE ORAL HISTORY TECHNIQUE AND GANG RESEARCH

INTRODUCTION

Another continuity in gang studies has been in the application of qualitative research methods that approximate or aspire to the use of what will be described here as the oral history technique. This chapter focuses exclusively on the variations in the research methodology itself. This is of much practical importance in evaluating contributions to the gang literature that use some variation of this research method. What emerges here is that some approaches are better than others and while holding an advanced degree in the social sciences may not be required to effectively carry out this technique it may not be sufficient either, because from a human relations viewpoint this technique can be more complex than some would have us believe.

As will be seen, there are both similarities and differences between the classical oral history method and what has been done in sociology and criminology applications. There are also important ethical dilemmas of using recording technology in addition to the wealth of analytical complexities in the social encounter between the researcher and the law offender in the "oral history" interview situation. There are, simply, many strategy variations in use by researchers using this method. This needs to be clarified from a methodological viewpoint.

Field work as a research method for understanding gangs can encompass a variety of experiential factors. But ultimately it boils down to the differences in the strategy used to collect information from gangs and gang members using basically "talk therapy" or simply hanging out with them. This qualitative research strategy involves the use of narrative information and speech. It differs from quantitative approaches that may involve the use of surveys or questionnaires, where numbers become the primary data collected. As will be seen, there are different names for what may involve rather similar elements of the qualitative research method. Thus, the terms oral history, case study, field work, ethnomethodology, depth interviews, etc, all refer to "how to get it, and what to do with the verbal data" so acquired. In this sense we need to know much more about the oral history method and conducting oral interviews. The oral history technique deals with how to get "their story" for use in conversational analysis, case studies, depth studies, focused interviews, etc.

THE FIGHT FOR QUALITATIVE METHODS

The oral history or case study approach is clearly a type of qualitative methodology. In the last four decades the more quantitative research methods have been the preferred techniques for sociologists and criminologists, especially those studying the offender population. Two points must be made about this qualitative research approach: (1) it complements traditional quantitative methods and can be, and should be, used in conjunction with other research designs for the collection of data on the offender and gang population for the purpose of testing or developing theory, and (2) it makes for spicy reading in as much as it goes behind and beyond the mere numerical codification of human experiences and in this sense provides a more humanistic orientation to the study of deviants, delinquents, offenders, gang members, etc.

James Bennett, in Oral History and Delinquency, University of Chicago Press, 1981, presents a critical appraisal of the oral history tradition in the study of delinquency. It expresses skepticism about the quality of oral history studies conducted to date and discounts the worth of such a methodology for testing or illustrating theories.[1]

Bennett refers to the use of the oral history method as a humanistic tradition in criminology (1981, p. 6) and rightfully so; because most of the criminologists who have used this method have tended, it seems, to represent a liberal ideology as well. Logically, it does not necessarily follow that the oral history method is inherently humanistic. It has appeared to be this way in the American criminological literature. It is, of course, subject to abuse by scholars and intelligence agents who could very well have a conservative-reactionary ideology, although this has not surfaced in any significant fashion -- at least intentionally so -- as of this date. There is nothing to stop ultra conservative "law and order" researchers from using the same method to advance their particular analyses as well. Thus, it is a logical error to think that such a research strategy is inherently humanistic.

Scattered throughout Bennett's book are discussions of the variation in conducting oral history, but lacking is a systematic treatment of the components of the research method itself. One concludes from the book that the oral history method must be more art than science. In fact, Bennett reported trying to conduct such a method without success.

While there are fine gradients of methodological variation that will be explained later in this chapter, for now let us assume that the oral history method also encompasses much of what is also meant by the case study method in studying gang members.[2]

Importantly, this method itself is not unique to the Chicago school of sociology or criminology. Goffman (1961) used a variation of this method, focusing on the asylum as a total control institution. Thrasher and Whyte used it to observe street gangs. It has also been used to study college administration (Clark, 1960), political life (Dahl, 1961), and even casual sex contacts in cocktail bars (Roebuck and Spray, 1967). Using oral history, to record the story of the offender or gang member, is a technique that has been prominently identified with the Chicago tradition, particularly Shaw and McKay (1931) and Sutherland (1937). Obviously, however, no one has a patent on such a technique.

THE ORAL HISTORY INTERVIEW METHOD USED BY HISTORIANS

What we mean by the classical oral history method is that interview technique used by historians. It is an interview conducted under conditions of informality and in a relaxed atmosphere and it absolutely requires the use of tape recorders or high technology (e.g., video cameras). It focuses on the use of spoken words as data, transcribed fully, editing out only the "er's" and the "ah's", or pauses, and keeping intact any vulgarity.

Harris (1975, p. 3) favors tape recorders and the use of tapes as data because "the nuances, the inflections that human speech can convey have a subtlety that escapes the most accurate of transcriptions". Along with the use of the tape recorder, of course, comes the use of videotapes as well.[3]

The intellectual norms appear to differ in comparing the classical method with that used in sociology and criminology. In the former it is an accomplishment in its own right to document an important aspect of history for centralized use and secondary analysis by other researchers. In sociology, it often boils down to "what did you say from the data." And, of course, while there are quantitative data archives for criminologists, there exists no such "criminological or gang studies oral history archive" at this point in history, even though, obviously, it too could, from transcription, be stored on computer. There is not, as well, a "speech sample" data bank, for the investigation of offenders, yet.

The purpose of the classical oral history method is to collect tapes and transcripts that other scholars of history can use. That is, the method itself assumes the prominent role of secondary analysis; or the involvement of other scholars who will later use the same data. This forces a consideration of research and publishing policy. Our social science journals do not require the author to provide the dataset for each research article published, or insure its availability at a central repository, so that other social scientists can do a secondary analysis or even build upon previously published findings. The classical oral history method, then, differs from any such use ever made of this interview technique in criminology. As Bennett (1981) noted, even the hand written documents in the Shaw and McKay tradition were routinely disposed of after transcription thus making it impossible to confirm their authenticity.

ORAL HISTORY Vs. WRITTEN SELF-ACCOUNTS BY YOUNG OFFENDERS

In examining the writing samples of youthful and adult offenders one might easily conclude that their literacy level itself, their constricted vocabulary, their limited repertoire of communication symbols, prevents us from getting much in the way of systematic written "self-accounts."[4] The youthful gang member who can write lengthy, legible, detailed accounts of personal experiences is an exception to the rule. It requires a command of a language, a written language as well, but several such gang authored accounts have appeared since 1981.[5]

Having offenders write out such accounts about their life, and how they "got into trouble with the law, etc", has been used as part of the psychological diagnostic intake in some correctional facilities and programs. This type of data has not yielded much analysis that, to the author's knowledge, has been reported in the literature.

Many will probably want to cite the book Monster as an exception. The hollywood glitz and glamour is all over this book, romanticizing gang life as a cultural form and portraying the gang member/leader as a freedom fighter in an occupied land undergoing guerilla warfare. This book has had the benefit of much stylizing in the vein of Truman Capote's In Cold Blood, where the underdog never has to accept responsibility for anything. The book Monster was a commercial effort, not a social scientific effort. Still the book does tend to demonstrate what some recent authors have called the combative personality syndrome: someone who prefers violent solutions over all other recourses of action. It is a person predisposed, by choice, toward violence; but where the person does not consider the moral implications of their behavior, and further refuses to accept any responsibility for their actions. Such a person is "fighting the system", a rebel with or without a cause but with little or no hope of success.

The skinhead neo-nazi who chose to tell his story in a way to denounce his gang in Germany, in the book _The Reckoning: A Neo-Nazi Drops Out_ by Ingo Hasselbach, quickly sold 15,000 copies of this popular account.[6] There are other gang-authors who like the retrospective account by Rodriguez (1994) do not glorify gang life. Co-authoring with gang members dates back some time, Hagedorn's co-author describes himself as a Chicago gang member transplant to Milwaukee. The recent account by Padilla and Santiago (1993) takes this to the level of co-authoring with a wife of an imprisoned gang leader.

Oral history clearly differs from written self-accounts taken from gang members, either while in custody or in a community treatment/intervention program context. It means writing down notes and their comments during the course of a semi-structured interview. The use of the tape recorder, while a source of potential contamination with law offenders, has been reported by a number of gang researchers. The use of the tape recorder or higher technology could be problematic for several reasons.[7] It is reactive under some conditions and the subject may feel more inhibited, as if it were an interrogation. It could encourage "performing" for the interviewer, rather than generating natural speech patterns, because of the defensive posture induced by the presence of a tape recording device. Most importantly, for the gang member who is truly candid and discloses specific names, dates, and locations of serious crimes, this represents very sensitive information.[8]

TAPE RECORDERS AND THE PROTECTION OF HUMAN SUBJECTS

The use of the tape recorder in capturing oral history data on offenders raises some concerns and problems regarding the protection of human subjects. Criminologists who use the self-report method often come across many serious crimes that have not been officially detected or adjudicated; crimes for which the statute of limitation may not apply. While it has not been addressed in recommended policy by groups such as the American Society of Criminology, certainly the criminologist should not feel compelled under any circumstances to release this confidential information to law enforcement or any other authorities. Not using a tape recorder at least prevents the existence of any such material evidence that could be potentially subject to government interest. However, written notes have also been known to have been targeted, for example in the study of organized crime.

THE DYAD INTERVIEW AS A SOCIALLY DISTANCED ENCOUNTER

While Goffman would certainly say that interviewing the offender in a one-on-one situation consists of a social encounter, it is also one characterized by much social distance when carried out by a Ph.D, or someone who is obviously not indigenous to the community. We cannot dismiss the material differences in social class position, life chances, and other factors of social power in the context of interviewing gang members. These things do matter, and will impact on what ultimately is "heard." For many of these types of field interviews it comes to resemble, in some ways, the confessional relationship between a priest and the penitent.

The dyadic interview simply involves asking the offender or gang member to "share" experiences, amounting essentially to "giving up information." For researchers who have used this method with offenders effectively, and it may be argued that perhaps not everyone can from a personality requirement be expected to have the human capability to carry out this method, many have found the tendency in a number of these kinds of interviews for the relationship to be interpreted by the self-reporting offender as an opportunity to "snitch."[9] Hagedorn (1990) does not refer to gang members as "data sources" or "respondents", but frankly calls them "informants." We can probably be assured that Hagedorn did not approach these gang members and ask them "hey, would you be my informant for a study I am doing?"

To a certain extent we should probably expect that in an oral history interview session the offender is "performing" or "acting a role" that may be defined, by default, in terms of the status and authority of the interviewer. The oral interview is not equivalent to interrogation. And unlike the forced-choice item in the survey method the researcher must often be on a "fishing expedition" unless factors to be elicited or focused on are specified in advance, and the researcher is in fact skilled, clinically, at "probing."

STRATEGY VARIATIONS IN THE ORAL HISTORY METHOD WITH OFFENDERS

There appear to be a number of different strategy variations in the manner in which the oral history method is employed by criminologists. Described here are ten such component variations that may affect the overall interpretation of "how was this information generated?"

(1) Using Background Information Before The First Meet.

Reading the available reports, records, files, public information, etc, from official sources, and using related information readily collected on the individual's social milieu (neighbors, retail stores, bars, etc in the area where the person lives and is known) before the actual interview can play an important role in the oral history method. Can criminologists be conned? Certainly, and they are much more likely to be misled when they do not prepare for the interview by gathering as many facts as possible about the person before the first meeting. Not reading the prior offense data on an offender allows the interview session to unfold naturally without the interviewer focusing on specific offenses. From a related perspective, if the interviewer is not highly trained, perhaps it could be argued that knowledge of this official criminal history and social background information could have the potential for interviewer prejudice. Generally, the author would recommend having as much information possible prior to the interview.

Such "advance information" allows at least the calibration of the interview data for genuineness and validity. Asking the obvious questions about which confirmed answers are already known in advance allows some judgement about the extent to which the person being interviewed is really cooperating. This validity factor is most important and is one of the most avoided points of discussion in many of the examples of field research involving such qualitative methods with gang members.

(2) Type of Entre or Introduction.

The type of introduction which assures access to the individual for being interviewed in the oral history fashion importantly shapes the ensuing interview. A preferred situation is one where a host agency or individual acts as a buffer or broker for the interview; ideally it is a host who is respected indigenously.[10] A common approach is that of the quality social service provider, a private agency known to provide jobs and education, etc, to the offender population. That is, one that is well known in the area. Lacking this, there is always the snowball method of using one offender to provide the entre to another offender.

This gets somewhat complicated in gang studies by the fact that different gangs are, naturally, known to compete and exist as bitter rivals. So the snowball method works best inside one gang group. To be seen with one gang may preclude obtaining valid data from a rival gang under conditions of intense distrust as may often exist in some of our urban communities today.

(3) Mode of Interviewer Dress/Appearance.

Casual and relaxed is the order of the day in oral history studies. It may be assumed that the variation in dress mode and appearance of the interviewer could have some relationship to the consistency and quality of the information gathered through the oral history method. Generally, what will be found is that social distance can be either minimized or maximized by dressing either casually or very formally. A suit and tie approach generates the least information on first interviews.

(4) Honorarium/Fee Offered for the Interview.

Offering to pay for the interview produces the highest rate of voluntary cooperation for the oral history method when dealing with offenders. Depending on the nature of the introduction with individuals, however, this is not necessarily required in all instances. The author has seen cases where the persons refused the "fee", and agreed to the interview for less instrumental types of motivation. Shaw and McKay (1931) report no use of stipends or fees paid to their sources[11], such as in the classic case study of "Nick".

Timing can be everything in offering even the smallest types of monetary incentives. Again, however, such tokens are not likely to be appealing to anyone who has a serious commitment to criminality. Someone who the previous night robbed a yuppie trying to buy $1,000 worth of cocaine is not likely to be very responsive to a small two figure cash honorarium. Similarly, we have yet to see anyone seriously entertain offering such petty "rewards" for interviews with more seriously involved criminal offenders (e.g., organized crime, and higher level gang organizations).

Such interview fees work best with the Alfalfa and Spanky type of gangs, and with the lowest possible level of involvement with criminal gangs. Why would a gang leader, presumably controlling a significant illicit income, want to "open his guts" for $25.00 and tell the world his secrets?

(5) Consumable Amenities.

Is it "breaking bread together" that establishes a mutual basis for interaction? Well, offering "goodies" at the time of the interview start-up is little more than a lure in some cases. But it does work. Offering refreshments without any advance notification of the availability of these consumable amenities (cans of cold soda pop, donuts, coffee, etc) establishes a "respect" for the respondent. It is a welcoming ritual.

Apparently there are more than some authors in our literature who have simply invited the gang members to their homes. In the "Streetcorner Research Lab" to be discussed in a subsequent chapter, the principal investigator (Schwitzgebel) always offered sandwiches, candy --- whatever they wanted to consume. Indeed, in some of our prior gang researchers reported experience, they offered alcohol. But at the point that a researcher is providing alcohol we are out of the realm of oral history method and into the realm of covert interviews and more.

(6) Interview Site Location.

The interview site location may figure prominently in the quality of the interview results. Interviewing an offender while still in custody is often difficult (distractions, noise, the security environment, etc). It would depend on the skill of the researcher in adjusting to this kind of situation to be capable of overcoming the environmental press that mitigates against good data. Interviewing the offender in a natural setting, in the field, is often difficult. Office sites are convenient, along with universities, but also communicate an "officialdom" to the respondents.

While prisons and places of confinement have been criticized as "contaminated" zones; there is no theoretical reason to expect any difference in validity or reliability. Indeed, there is a higher motivation to want to talk. Certainly much more than exists in the field. Again, the issue may center around "what are we studying?" If we are principally focusing on the psychology of the individual gang member, then perhaps some conditions are better than others. But, again, there is no hard evidence that shows this to be true. And, of course, if we are not focusing on the self-reporting of the offender's deviance, but the deviance of "others" (e.g., the gang group/organization), it may not matter where we interview someone.

(7) Explanation of Purpose and Informed Consent.

The interviewer needs to explain the overall purpose of the interview and give some assurance of anonymity or protection of privacy, unless otherwise covered in written contract with the respondent. Informed consent is best accomplished by showing the person an example of a "case study" or "oral interview" or "oral history" and explaining in writing before the interview session and orally at the time of the first meeting, what type of content the interview may cover and what will become of the resulting "data".

A researcher whose entre to the respondent is through a community-based program who verbalizes an objective "to help out the program" may be eliciting a response shaped by the need of the respondent to present information in light of its most favorable interpretation to the program, not the research problem per se. A direct "honesty in interviewing" approach is probably best; telling the respondent "I am a sociologist/criminologist studying _____ and I want the truth about it" has a virtually neutral effect on interview response.

A gang researcher may potentially violate such a promise of anonymity to the gang member by subsequent publication. We should not assume that gang members cannot read our works. For example; assume one spent the summer interviewing gang members in Podunk, Arizona, promising them anonymity, and then published a book detailing their federal criminal law violations and providing probable cause to federal authorities to directly target such gangs in the city and state so explicitly identified in the book. Is that a violation of the promise of anonymity? It probably would be from the gang member's point of view, particularly when the feds started making arrests.

(8) Reliability.

In its most elementary sense, reliability in research means the degree to which the researcher can get the same story again and again. Would two trained Ph.D.'s conducting oral history studies of the same persons, simultaneously, get the same results? There could be much variation in results. But having the same respondent interviewed by two or more interviewers at least provides multiple observations on the same case and a basis for comparison whether the same story is coming through. That would be inter-rater reliability. Similarly, having the same person interviewed at two or more different points in time, with redundancy in the content of probes, provides more of what is meant by content reliability. The comparison of single cases by multiple interviewers, or the comparison of single interviewer responses at multiple points over time, allows for the assessment of the quality of the interview results.[12]

Again, this kind of "technical issue" has not been adequately addressed in our gang research literature.

(9) Validity Issues.

Is it really the truth or is it a crock of mumble jumble? It is a clear problem in determining whether "data" from oral history methods really measures what it purports to measure because of the obvious human tendency to misrepresent reality. However, some information is subject to verification. Also, if the researcher takes the time to use "test questions", or validity items, in the context of the interview, which correspond to items of known information relating to the respondent, known in advance, and there is not a consistent pattern of responses to these test questions, or if there is significant variation from these "base lines", then one would be well advised to assume some level of deceit emerging from the respondent.

A gang researcher may not know when a gang member is or is not under the influence of a controlled substance. Which, at least in the more controlled environment of the prison, jail, detention or treatment center, etc, we might assume at least has a somewhat lower probability; although, obviously, a matter not entirely to be dismissed. Do gang members in the community use drugs? Does the consumption of drugs or alcohol affect the validity of what might come from such field interviews? We might assume the affirmative. Again, we find no discussion of this matter in the recent qualitative research on gangs.

(10) Anonymity.

Anonymity should be assured to the respondent both verbally and in writing. Unfortunately when dealing with law violation behavior this means a slight alteration from the classical oral history approach. That is, names, addresses, etc, must often be blanked out or obscured so as to not give away, indirectly, the identity of the respondent. If we were in Podunk, Arizona for our gang "field interviews" and published the data showing that all of the gang members in that city have illegal, fully-automatic Uzi's, if government agents (ATF) used the publication as probable cause for targeting the group or as the basis for starting such an investigation, could we say that such anonymity has been violated? It may not matter if the individual researcher is even willing to go to jail for "not disclosing" who exactly said they had an Uzi submachine gun. The issue is, from a policy and research utilization viewpoint, someone reads the report; sees a major federal law being violated, en masse, and targets the group in the city so identified in the book. When the gang members begin to go to jail for such a hypothetical case, would this be an ethical violation? Many may believe so.

Any promise made in good faith must be fulfilled to a respondent or data source. We live in an information age. And law enforcement agencies are obligated to act on information about wrong doing. The issue of anonymity is no small matter. If we do not promise it, then it is similar to the Miranda warning. But if we do promise it, it is something we should most certainly live up to. At least in the sense of limiting potential harm.

ORAL HISTORY Vs. INTERROGATION

In what respects does oral history differ from, or is it similar to, criminal interrogation? Surely the element of "confession" is common to both, but also common to both is that the interviewer be patient and consistent. Bennett's work (1981) touches on this to some extent.

Bennett critiques charity/service organizations dealing with offenders when they use the oral history method to "toot their horns", that is to proclaim their accomplishments and effectiveness, but mostly to seek financial support for their mission. Bennett (1981) amply shows oral history has been capable of being corrupted for such self-serving causes.

Bennett (1981) shows some interesting parallels between oral history and "confession". Regarding the introduction of solitary confinement in corrections, specifically the solitary cells of the Preston Jail in 1839, "W.L. Clay aptly dubs this oral history site the 'cell confessional' (Bennett, 1981: 73)". Clay's success in getting such oral history "stories" was his kindness to the inmates as a prison chaplain in a situation of stark contrast to the oppressive ethos of the jail environment after the introduction of solitary cells. Thus, Rev. Clay's "kindness" in that context was not functionally different than a traditional "Mutt and Jeff routine".[13]   Actually a current book on gangs from an evangelical point of view, while not knowing it was a legitimate research technique, actually produced very comparable results --- on the importance of the underclass, the role of violence, the role of the family, jobs, etc, as impacting on the growth and persistence of gangs --- suggesting anyone can "do" qualitative research (Mc Lean, 1991).

Many criminal interrogation textbooks point out the importance of the personality requirement to the effect that "you either have it, or you don't".[14] Similarly, in classical oral history methods "some people are simply incapable of properly conducting interviews" (Harris, et al, 1975: 10). Perhaps in this sense, the "art", as opposed to the "science", is reflected. Perhaps both interrogation and oral history are arts which should be approached scientifically.

As seen in Figure 7 below, there is more in common between interrogation and oral history than exists the differences between these two forms.

FIGURE 7

COMPARISON OF ORAL HISTORY AND INTERROGATION

Oral History ************************	Rel. ****	Interrogation ************************
1. Put your respondent "at ease"	D	Increase the psychological tension to confess.
2. An informal dress mode is preferred.	D	Conservative suit should elicit respect, not fear.
3. Make interview setting comfortable for having a conversation.	D	Use stiff back chairs; face to face, 27 inches apart in a bare room.
4. Show no emotion which may communicate that you are offender by what you hear.	C	Use emotional ploys; let "S" know that nothing they say will shock you, "we've heard it all before".
5. Don't be offended by what the offender might say.	C	Minimize the moral implications.
6. Show empathy or a genuine positive regard for the "R".	C	Sympathize with the "S" (e.g., "anyone might have done the same thing")
7. Be scholarly, but ask questions in plain words.	C	Speak in simple terms; use "their" language if necessary.
8. Interview cunning is always important.	C	Interrogation is a true battle of wits.
9. Personality is important.[15]	C	A flexible personality is required.
10. Even if you are nervous, don't show this to the "R"	C	Don't show your own nervous tension; don't smoke, and

or they will "clam" up.

if you do, offer one first to the "S" as a gesture of kindness.

11. Review background information   C
before the interview.

Interview victim and witnesses first; know all facts and the "S" records before the interview.

LEGEND: "R" = respondent, "S" = subject
Rel. = nature of the relationship
D = difference   C = Commonality

As seen in Figure 7 above, there are three differences and eight commonalities in looking at oral history methods and interrogation methods. The obvious difference, though, is that of purpose: the difference between documenting for social science and the law enforcement purpose of effective prosecution.

CRIMINAL JUSTICE TRAINING FOR INTERVIEWING GANG MEMBERS

The purpose of this kind of interviewing is the development of intelligence on gangs. A number of training manuals exist for gang training that address this issue of how to best interview the gang member. Most are largely consistent with the advice given in this chapter for the purpose of plain research. One of the best ideas is to ask the gang member not about his own deviance, or his own exploits and crimes, but rather to ask about the competition. The competition can be members or sets/factions of his own gang or other gangs.

While all gangs view "snitching" as the ultimate wrongful act of a fellow member, they do this regularly by "dry snitching" --- that is informally disclosing information about their associates. Some gangs tolerate this more than others. Some gangs go to great lengths to prohibit certain types of social interaction and disclosures to the "outsiders", such as the Latin Kings who in one incident shot a member in both knees for having an interview with a television station that came to the hood for a story.

Some manuals are very specific and develop specific guidance for investigators about certain gangs like the Crips and the Bloods:

> If a particular Crip or Blood is not bragging about his very successful business, dealing, or womanizing; he will want to be known as a deadly, ruthless person. Insane-style tattoos and monikers will reflect their self-proclaimed reputation---examples being: Killer Kev, Crazy Ed, Psycho Mike, etc."

That is, gang members are egoistic, egotistic, and enjoy attention and performing their important roles. They will talk and provide information about others, but they do not consider this snitching when the others are competition. Still, some gangs train their members in how to resist interrogations by police and investigators, such as the training memo from the imprisoned Gangster Disciple leader to members on the streets, a copy of which is provided in the appendices of this book.

Some of the common tips for criminal justice personnel offered in gang training manuals today include these taken from a midwestern corrections training document on gang awareness: (1) work on their ego, (2) use their sense of individualism, (3) uses their self-proclaimed "playboy" image, (4) play on their entrepreneur self-image, (5) play on their hero/warrior/freedom fighter self-image, (6) have some background on them, (7) show interest in their politics and ideology, (8) show interest in how they able to lead an extravagant life style to get them to talk about how they make money, (9) show interest in how deadly they are and how fearsome their reputation is among their own gang members and to other rival gangs to get them to talk about weapons, monikers, violent incidents, etc., and (10) show interest in their leadership abilities to get them to talk about how the organization functions.

ORAL HISTORY AND THE "CASE STUDY"

In a classic paper on the sociological use of the case study approach, Burgess (1928) addressed the matter of rival interests between social workers and sociologists. Burgess explicitly detailed aspects of the "social case record" that should be focused on to make the data useful for research. Missing in the nearly 70 years after Burgess is a well developed approach for training in the methodology itself.

Yet there are interdisciplinary parallels in the use of this kind of qualitative method. In market research it can be called the case approach or a depth interview[15] and still bear much resemblance to what has been regarded as an oral history approach (Woodside and Fleck, 1979). The purpose is what is different, in market research the aim might be to find out why the person prefers one brand of beer over another. A similar comparison exists between oral history and "case analysis" in management or organizational change research.

Perhaps some of the current favor enjoyed by the case analysis methodology is its legitimacy established by the parallels in almost all of the behavioral and social sciences. The analytical potential of this research methodology is therefore best revealed when considering the diverse disciplines in which it has been applied. Different names for the variation in this methodology also are evident when the perspective is interdisciplinary.

In fact, case analysis is also called the case study method, the case history method, the depth interview, the case method, social casework, case research, the clinical interview, etc.

CASE ANALYSIS IN MANAGEMENT

Paine and Naumes (1982) place the matter of strategic management at the heart of using broad concepts and strategy to survive in a changing environment. Most of their book is devoted to actual cases (pp. 167-610). Here we find that:

> In the case study method, learning takes place as the
> students try to discover, refine, and answer critical

questions using real-life situations. The end goal of case analysis is suggested management actions based on the analysis (Paine and Naumes, 1982: p. 167).

Thus, case studies are used for a variety of purposes such as exploring values and their effect on decisions and to "demonstrate the methods, inputs, style, and environmental setting of such decisions" (p. 167).

Here are the basic analytical elements for a case study according to these authors. It means a current definition of the concern and the current objectives of the organizations and groups involved in it along with current strategic actions and policies (p. 168). It means taking into account the values and relative power of major constituency and policy-making groups. A "capability profile" must be developed to include: "a. key factors or mobility barriers, b. need for more information, c. competitive advantages, and d. strategic implications" (p. 168). The external environment must also be examined for such things as "competitive factors, economic factors, legal factors, regulation, and social issues" (p. 168). It should, in short, be a factual basis for decision-making based on a close relationship with reality.

Niehoff (1966) calls it not the case study method, but the case history method (p. 5). Its benefit is to be able to learn from study of past efforts. The many cases of change and development affecting peasant farmers in the Niehoff book are therefore "case histories" (p. 7) at the project level, not the planning level. Regarding the case history method itself, we are told not so much how to carry it out as to be able to recognize when we see it. The ideal case history method has these attributes according to Niehoff: "professional and complete...so the...reader can get a clear picture of what happened" (p. 7), "interestingly presented" material that is not dull, with the "most information presented in the most succinct manner" (p. 8).

The use of the case method, as White, Stamm, and Foster (1976: p. iii) call it, has been applied to health care facilities such as hospitals and other formal organizations. The case method is also used in teaching and the work by Sprague, Sheldon and McLaughlin (1973) explains its use in health care and provides more specifics on "how to" properly carry out the development of case materials (Sprague, et al, 1973: pp. 110-113). Burns and Stalker (1968) also explain in some detail this same method (pp. 12-14).

SPECIFYING THE ELEMENTS OF THE CASE STUDY

The classic treatise by Neihoff (1966) identifies seventeen major elements, the first eight of which are innovator characteristics and the rest are recipient characteristics: (1) role characteristics, (2) communication by the innovator, (3) participation obtained, (4) utilization of local culture, (5) timing, (6) flexibility, (7) continuity, (8) maintenance, (9) communication among the recipients, (10) motivation of felt need, (11) motivation of practical benefit perceived, (12) other types of motivation, (13) leadership, (14) social structure, (15) economic pattern, (16) beliefs, and (17) practices (Niehoff, 1966: p. 12).

Whatever we call it, case study, case history, case method, etc, what is generally being dealt with are actual empirical examples described in an interesting way to depict important qualitative aspects at the individual, organizational/group, or societal level.

Observation is a key component of case analysis and in the methodology of Strauss, et al, (1985) observation means daily experiences and interviews over a long period, in their case five years (see Strauss, et al, 1985: pp. 291-296). This can produce significant details which are normally not documented and yet which give more meaning to understanding the project's success.

PARTICIPANT OBSERVATION AS A SOURCE OF MISINFORMATION

Participant observation with real gangs, not wannabes, could put the researcher at more than some risk: is the researcher going to collaborate in terms of drug sales, consume drugs and get high with the gang informants, and become a party to their patterns of criminal law violation?   Non-participant observation is probably the concept that more aptly describes what some researchers have done in "hanging out with gangs". No non-offender scholarly researcher has yet to report going undercover to join a gang and report on its activities.

Many such gang researchers who employ such a "field work" research technique are often viewed by the gang as "egg heads". Hanging out with gang members in a neutral setting where an observer has a legitimate right to essentially "be there", as in drop-in centers, Boys and Girls clubs, etc, offers one way to overcome this problem. Yet there are still substantial problems in terms of validity regarding the data obtained through such types of participant observation.

The fact is offenders are prone to lie. Talk to any gang member long enough and you will hear at some point a presentation of self as a "gang leader" of some sort; even if they were only the "leader" of one housing unit of one juvenile detention center for one time in the distant past. The astute and responsible researcher who engages in participant observation as a research method would use social network analysis to ascertain who is in fact a leader, rather than relying on self-report.

A close reading of the contemporary gang literature reveals that taking such statements from gang members as the "gospel truth" also may fatally flaw ones research conclusions and analysis.   One such participant observation study of Milwaukee street gangs, for example, claimed that the El Rukn gang had never existed or penetrated the city. The fact is Jeff Fort was paroled to Milwaukee and started his first El Rukn organization there, and with success returned to Chicago to expand[16].

The issue of validity here is a cognitive one: some gang members simply may not be knowledgeable about the history, facts, and functions of gangs (especially rival gangs) that they may be more than willing to comment on. An example of how and where this would be likely to occur could be in studying a gang that identifies itself as a Latin King chapter, say somewhere in Florida, but which was started by a transplanted lower level member; and few of its members know much of anything about the original Chicago group and its two main branches (the northside branch from Humboldt Park, and the southside branch from 26th Street). Asking such an emulation/social imitation gang about Latin King gang organization could not be generalized to the Chicago or national picture. It is simple: you cannot get the truth from someone who may not know the truth or the big picture.

Another related possibility that some critical analysts of the gang literature have recently surfaced is the problem of the "Stockholm syndrome". The profile here is of someone who discovers and becomes involved in criminology only after hanging out with a gang. One should be thoroughly familiar with criminological literature well prior to trying to interpret and understand gang phenomena. This is more than accepting what the gang member says as the gospel, thus publishing essentially a public relations document for the gang (e.g., the gang is not about crime and drugs, it is about growth and development for the community), it involves overidentifying with the gang to the point where the "gang research" if we are to call it that basically amounts to an apology for the gang. Thus, the researcher affected by the Stockholm syndrome somehow converts to being some kind of an academic/professional/intellectual member of the gang[17].

SUMMARY AND CONCLUSION

This chapter must be regarded, contra Bennett, as a clear defense of the oral history or "own story" approach. The primary evidence of its enduring utility is that it has comparable approaches in other disciplines. The oral history or case study method must be regarded as being slightly more complex than a simple open-ended item in survey research where there is no time limit. Methodologically, there are subtle differences and variations, but essentially much of what is called by various names --- field approach, ethnographic studies, case studies, depth studies, etc, and at the highest level of analysis, the oral history method --- much of it entails a direct face-to-face and personal approach. To get the story right from the gang member in a qualitative way.[18]

The other obvious criticism of this qualitative approach, from a strict methodological perspective, is that it has yielded little in the way of content analysis reported in the literature. Content analysis is a rigorous method of quantifying such qualitative data as might emerge in open-ended questions or even the oral history or case study approach. No one has yet to report an inter-rater reliability coefficient for assumed findings from the oral history approach; rather, the raw data has simply been presented as ipso facto "proof" for author assertions --- sometimes along ideological dimensions. Some of the best such accounts (e.g., Taylor, 1990) have simply sought to obtain data on specified topical areas of relevance to a descriptive analysis of gangs.

Secondly, just "hanging out" with a gang, or even moving in with them to study their lifestyle (ala Keiser), presents its own ethical dilemmas. Most importantly, the more organized gangs have strict rules in their constitutions against disclosure of such privileged information about their organization. A necessary implication of this tendency of higher level gang organizations to punish their members who disclose information to outsiders is that the so-called field study approach is not really going to be likely to generate much quality research on higher level gang organizations. That is, it is considerably easier to do field research on groups like Spanky and Alfalfa than it is to do so on groups like the El Rukns, Aryan Brotherhood, etc.

Hopefully what has been established here is that there are some interesting parallels across the social science disciplines for what essentially involves the same types of research strategy. This method is sufficiently complex that it can be regarded as irresponsible to basically send out someone untrained into the field, maybe because they are not skilled in quantitative methods, and expect them to automatically be good at qualitative research methods such as oral history interviews[19].

In this sense, perhaps it is incumbent upon researchers in this area to demonstrate their efficacy in some manner where through secondary analysis with the "raw materials", independent analysis can ascertain the quality of such interview results. A basic standard may be where multiple professionals interview the same gang member.   Much gets edited out.   And the problem of over-identification during close contacts with gang members represents another potential source of invalidity of this method.   Getting "conned" into assuming the ideological accentuations preferred by the gang member, or "adding yeast" as the offender might say, would mean that some "case study methods" could potentially have the impact of disinformation as much as they could objectively inform us about the gang reality. It bears repeating here, as stated elsewhere, that the study of crime at the individual level is sufficiently complex to require a certain level of skepticism about verbal information gleaned from simply talking to gang members.   So much hinges on what motivates the gang member to disclose information in the first place.

DISCUSSION   QUESTIONS

(1) In the absence of a full disclosure of all details of a field study, does what gets "edited out" in terms of information, come to function overall as a "black box" problem where we really do not know for sure what went on?

(2) If oral history, case studies, etc, can be abused, then what would be the most likely scenario for such intellectual dishonesty?

(3) When can "hanging out with the gang" become social science and when can it become an invasion of privacy to the extent of covert undercover operations? Similarly, when does "hanging out with the gang" become complicity in gang crime? Should higher standards of ethical behavior be established for such types of "hands on" research where the researcher intends to become intimately involved with the gang and its activities?

FOOTNOTES

1. Remember this was directed at the abuse of methods in explaining delinquency. For example, Kramer and Karr (1953) would be one such example. In Kramer and Karr (1953) the authors call their method "dramatic narrative", which turns out really to be a kind of journalistic/impressionism from talking with detached workers and on this basis making fictionalized "composites" describing gang rumbles, the gang life, etc.   Yet Kramer and Karr (1953) were certainly liberal reformers, advocating preventative measures rather than prison sentences, and being a social-political lobby for expanding detached worker programs.

2. The qualitative method reported by Vigil (1988) is described as the "life history" using "case informants" or alternately, the "life history and self-reflexive history method" (Vigil, 1988: p. 174). It is clearly in the oral history tradition.

3. Video products must generally have a "signed release form" from the subject. Also, to my knowledge no one has ever applied forensic psychology to this data in the same fashion that the polygraph has been used to determine the validity of traditional survey data. That is to say, could "voice stress analysis" uncover important variations in speech patterns, again using words as data.

4. The notable exception to this is in using high ranking adult imprisoned gang members who have become confidential informers --- thereby denouncing the gang --- for the government. In visiting such persons, the present author has found that it is useful to have them call you (they will always have to call collect from the prison) and tell them what you intend to discuss in advance, they will often prepare "statements" from their recollection in their eagerness to assist.

5. For a most excellent such exception, see Dino Malcolm, 1981, "D To the Knee! Stone To the Bone!", pp. 81-91, Best of Hair Trigger: A Story Workshop Anthology, Chicago: Columbia College Writing Department. Which provides an insightful experience of the Disciples and Black Stone Rangers gangs in Chicago.

6. See: Thom Shanker, "A Skinhead Recants", Chicago Tribune, Section 5, May 11, 1994, p. 1,3.

7. Keiser found that simply whipping out his notebook and pencil when in public with the gang induced panic among the gang members present (1979). Also, some authors report the complexity implied by transcribing tape recorded material.

8. Hagedorn was able to secure a federal government agency "protection" against subpoenaed disclosure.

9. Generally, known offenders tend to under-report their own extent of deviance and law violation and over-report their degree of legitimate integration. Which means, when interviewing a known gang member, such a person is more likely to report on the deviance of friends and associates than their own acts or behaviors at variance with society values, norms, and laws. Thus, it may be a more valid focus to raise questions about the gang as an organization and focus on other actors in such an enterprise.

10. Sometimes it seems like the researcher in some previously published reports was trying to "go indigenous". That is, communicating at least an indigenous status to the offender being interviewed, perhaps with something that on its surface may seem innocuous such as "I've done things too, everyone has, I just wasn't caught like you", or something. But to what extent would such a strategy have the reverse intended effect in research? Could the respondent interpret such an admission as patronizing?

11. I want to apologize for using the word "subjects" at this point, recalling once how Morris Janowitz lectured me similarly that in sociology "we don't have subjects, only kings and queens have subjects .... in sociology we have data sources and respondents". I fondly recall, in his spirit of egalitarianism, during this encounter adding "and don't call me Doctor Janowitz, I don't deliver babies" (circa, 1978).

12. I will not address the matter of using unskilled, indigenous persons, or offenders belonging to the same network carrying out this kind of data collection as a hired hand. It is not the best idea if quality data is the goal. As will be seen, even in simple interviewing techniques, social skills and personality come into play. Training is important, but not everyone perhaps can be a good interviewer.

13. A "Mutt and Jeff" routine involves two interrogators, each playing a separate function: one to play the good guy, one to play the bad guy; so as to elicit a confession. The "bad guy" there was the situation: the harsh reality of the prison; the "good guy" was the kind Reverend willing to show kindness, and get a story.

14. The implication should be clear and is even more obvious from a critical review of former works involving "field work" with gangs (Whyte, Schwitzgebel, etc): to belittle the sophistication required for doing effective field work with groups as potentially violent as gangs is to take an equally serious ethical risk. Some authors might say it is "easy" to conduct field work. But that does not address the matter of quality of data gathered or the risk of deleterious impact through unintended negative consequences as a result of the "experimental/manipulator" overzealousness.

15. Arnold (1965) called his gang interviews "focused interviews" and used this subjective social encounter as the basis for collecting essentially quantitative data, for a remarkable analysis that is rarely cited in our gang literature.

16. A number of sources verify Jeff Fort's formation of the El Rukn gang organization while in Milwaukee after his release from federal prison, and in a continuing fashion well into the 1980's. See, for example, p. 21 of the Gang Awareness Module, #17, Corrections Training Academy, Illinois Department of Corrections, 7/1/90.

17. Paul Hoffman's (1993) review of the book by David Dawley states "This book contains many photographs including one of Dawley signifying, apparently, his gang allegiance: crossing his arms in the fashion of 'Peoples' (Dawley, 1992: p. 204)". Dawley claims to be the "only white member" of the Vice Lords, the group he hung out with in the late 1960s and early 1970s.

18. This conversational analysis approach therefore crosses over many disciplines of the social sciences. Particularly sociology, psychology, and anthropology. But obviously, potentially others. Recently some authors have restated the argument by Hogrefe and Harding (1967) that gangs can be studied only through such methods as participant observation. Such quantaphobia and "anti-number crunching" is, of course, while reminiscent of a period of the 1970s referred to by Bookin-Weiner, etc, little more than intellectual posturing. (see Hogrefe and Harding, "Research Considerations in the Study of Street Gangs", 6 Applied Anthropology (21), 1967).

19. Horowitz (1986) showed this complexity in the different types of researcher identities and how these can shape the efficacy of the data collection process.

CHAPTER 8

THE TRUE STORY ABOUT THE SHAW & McKAY TRADITION

INTRODUCTION

Too often the novice to the study of gangs is quick to denounce all prior studies as "dated". Which is to say the neophyte entering the gang social science literature may take the viewpoint "they didn't know what they were talking about", or it is simply a case of "old theory and new gangs".[1] In criminal justice and corrections, as in all of society, that is not simply the case. We cannot denounce prior research in psychology or economics on such a similar basis or we would have to basically find ourselves in the odd situation of creating new "theories" every time a new gang problem emerged.[2]

This is not to deny that society itself has not changed since the 1920s. Indeed, many major changes have occurred since then in terms of technology, demography, values, and economics. These include changes in technology (mass communications, transportation, etc), changes in demography (i.e., a shift of population to urban areas, increased educational attainment, new groups entering American society, etc), changes in values (e.g., a new recognition of the rights of children and the creation of "child abuse" laws to protect the young), economic changes (i.e., the shift from an economy characterized primarily by industrial occupations to one that consists mostly of jobs in the service sector), and many other such structural change factors. These changes also include the fact that America has now surpassed the Soviet Union and South Africa in terms of penal incarceration.

The value of studying the past lies in understanding historical continuity and more generalizable concepts that can still be applied today. Such a historical focus also increases our understanding of continuing problems that have yet to be resolved. In corrections, we still have yet to conquer the "recidivism problem" and, curiously, this emerges in the gang literature; if we are astute enough to find it. In law enforcement, we have yet to eliminate political encroachment; and this too surfaces in the gang literature; if we look closely enough.

This chapter therefore seeks to place an important historical tradition in criminology, especially as it pertains to gang crime, in closer and more accurate focus. We need to know the truth. Too many students must rely on second-hand versions of what was represented in the Shaw and McKay tradition. It will be demonstrated that this tradition is often unfairly criticized and inadequately credited regarding concepts central to the understanding of gang crime. In fact, the truth is that many of the variables used by Shaw and McKay in their early research are the same variables being used in contemporary gang research.

Just what were the contributions of this tradition for the study of gang crime? Does the criminological literature really provide the true story?

UNFAIR CRITICISM

Both Clifford R. Shaw and Henry D. McKay in fact were applied criminologists. But then, just as today, such applied competency does not mean they were any less scholarly or that what they had to say was of any less theoretical significance. Hagan (1987) implies it is "ironic" then that they are associated with the "Chicago school" of criminology, because "they never enjoyed faculty status at the University of Chicago" (p. 439).[3] Clearly, Shaw and Mc Kay attended the University of Chicago and both continued to interface with academics, many academics, not just at the University of Chicago. But as Hagan says (p. 439):[4]

> "Snodgrass (1972) indicates that neither Shaw nor McKay received their doctorates due to foreign language requirements, but worked closely with many faculty and students from the university (Carey, 1975, pp. 84-92)."

Again, however, one gets the impression from this kind of introductory text that the only contribution was their basic thesis that social disorganization implies it is not abnormal persons as offenders, but abnormally disorganized social environments that produce crime. Hagan, like many contemporary writers, gives no credit to Shaw and McKay in a contribution to the understanding of gangs (pp. 231-232).

There appears to be a very unfortunate tendency among some writers to want to "pigeon hole" and give salient caption labels to other authors. However, when we are talking about an entire life tradition of criminological research ideally a more holistic examination would be the fairest way to go. Only a lazy scholar, someone without the energy to go back and actually read the originals, could make some of the untruthful and disparaging attributions that have been made to the Shaw and Mc Kay tradition. Shaw and Mc Kay used many research techniques to come to a better understanding about crime and delinquency and gangs. They basically helped to legitimatize and establish a research tradition used by those who could seem most prone to denounce Shaw and Mc Kay today. Shaw and Mc Kay, unlike some contemporary gang researchers, did not simply conduct one little research project on gangs or crime and then move on to some other sociological problem --- they carried out many, many different research projects, focusing on much of the same thing. One research project hardly makes anyone a gang expert.

Any contemporary gang researcher who thinks they have discovered the "best way" to get "close-up" to real criminals or real gang members, or that something they did they felt they did uniquely (e.g., collaborate with the persons being studied), is probably suffering from delusions of grandeur if not a total blindness to the history of the criminological literature, particularly about the contributions from the Chicago school. But then again, intellectual politics being what it is, some are prone for whatever reason to take shots at the "Chicago school" of criminology. And there is nothing wrong with that, no one is perfect; and debate is healthy. But the fact remains, there is little that is new under the sun in terms of human relationships and human interaction --- and that is what we are talking about when we are talking about qualitative research methods, simply getting cooperation in a non-exploitive way.

Unlike most contemporary gang researchers, Shaw and Mc Kay used both qualitative and quantitative research methods.

Shaw and McKay are sometimes criticized for being naive about the use of obviously unreliable, under or misreported official statistics (see Siegal, 1983: p. 193). Siegal felt this reliance on official data "seriously damages the potential value of their work" (pp. 172-173). Hagedorn (1990) would later call this "courthouse criminology" in a criticism of modern Chicago school authors Spergel and Curry; the idea being that any information that comes from "official" sources like police or courts is unreliable and not the best source of information on gangs or gang members. First, Shaw and Mc Kay supplemented this "official data" with extensive qualitative data in the form of case studies and oral histories the quality and rigor of which have not yet been surpassed. Secondly, let's keep this in historical perspective. While the formative Shaw and Mc Kay monograph discussed and cited below is dated 1931, the Uniform Crime Report system maintained by the F.B.I. was not itself authorized for a go ahead until 11 June, 1930 (Inciardi, 1984: pp. 119-120).[5] Thirdly, as will be shown later in this chapter, it is just not true that Shaw and Mc Kay were unaware of the problems of official data, they were aware of the limitations and reported these qualifications. Fourthly, it is absurd to think that in criminology we can ignore official statistics and what happens in the criminal justice system as if any one research method (qualitative vs. quantitative) was scientifically superior.

Also it is worth noting that Shaw and Mc Kay used important data that is not analyzed in the FBI's U.C.R. statistics, or the BJS (Bureau of Justice Statistics), or even in most "self-report" surveys (because they must often be anonymous) ---- they used one thing: the home address.[6] It is doubtful that a cogent argument can be made to the effect that the courts, etc, didn't really know the correct address of the offender, which would provide some basis for a criticism of Shaw and Mc Kay on the basis of systematic measurement error.[7] Shaw and Mc Kay's ecological analysis involved marking the location of the address on a geographical map of the city of Chicago: an approach being revived today by researchers using computer mapping of crime complaints and incidents to support innovations in community policing.

At this point it is useful to specify what works by Shaw and McKay will be examined here. The issue may simply be that when we are talking about these two criminologists maybe we have not been talking about the same known works. Two works in particular never seem to be examined very closely in our recent literature when crediting or discrediting Shaw and McKay. One is the 1931 monograph that served as the blueprint for their most frequently cited 1942 text.[8]

COGNITIVE DATING OF SHAW & McKAY

Pardon the neologistic expression, but hopefully the astute reader has heard of cognitive maps.[9] Cognitive mapping is to associate a certain attribute with a certain geographic area on any city map. Cognitive dating is the only expression that seems to put this matter into perspective, but refers to the tendency for scholars to "time stamp" in history, a given authors contribution. So when should we chronologically date the major Shaw and Mc Kay contribution to American criminology?[10]

Many persons use the year 1942, but the well read criminologist will suspect this intellectual charting is due to an inadequate and superficial reading of Shaw and McKay. The 1942 publication, entitled <u>Juvenile Delinquency and Urban Areas: A Study of Rates of Delinquents in Relation to Differential Characteristics of Local Communities in American Cities,</u> should have probably earned Shaw and Mc Kay the contributory salutation in terms of theory classification as "differential social organization"[11] to append to the long list of other such "differential this and that" in the Chicago school of criminology.[12] Most such one liner definitional attributes for Shaw and Mc Kay give them the phrase "cultural transmission theory" or "social disorganization theory", or when referring incorrectly to only one of the analytical tools they used "concentric zone theory",[13] or ecological/area analysis.

The 1942 text by Shaw and Mc Kay included separate contributions from six other authors.[14] The document that clarifies the problem about dating Shaw and McKay's theoretical contribution and their gang analysis was really published in 1931. This was volume II, National Commission on Law Observance and Enforcement, Report on the Causes of Crime, United States Government Printing Office, Washington, D.C. (price 50 cents). It is formally entitled <u>Social Factors in Juvenile Delinquency: A Study of the Community, the Family, and the Gang in Relation to Delinquent Behavior,</u> (416 pages).[15]

In truth, a sizable portion of what Shaw and Mc Kay reported in the 1942 text was taken paragraph by paragraph, and map by map, from the 1931 monograph. The 1942 text simply updated some of the data. Admittedly, the 1942 text dropped the title reference to gangs, just as their 1942 index contained no such reference to the gang.

It is possible to suspect that the 1931 monograph may have been the origin of the alternative moniker applied to the Shaw and McKay theory being called "cultural transmission theory". In the 1931 monograph, gangs are treated as evolved forms of play groups.[16] They spoke of the "transmission of delinquent tradition" (pp. 223-240) and its norms and values. More of Cohen's work than is probably acknowledged as Shaw and Mc Kay influenced may be found here when it comes to the matter of delinquent norms and values, also a topic examined in elaborate detail by use of case studies and oral history materials (pp. 240-250).

Technically, the introduction to the 1942 text, which was written by Ernest Burgess (pp. ix-xiii), should have been sufficient to unquestionably cement and legitimize Shaw and Mc Kay in the hall of criminological fame referred to, so loosely at times, as the "Chicago school".[17] Shaw and McKay worked closely with Burgess. But Shaw was unquestionably the senior of the Shaw and Mc Kay team. Shaw's title in 1931 was Head of the Department of Research Sociology, Institute for Juvenile Research and Behavioral Research Fund; while Mc Kay's title was Associate Research Sociologist. A later document, dated in 1949, carries the identifier of simply "Shaw and Associates".

Much of the material in the 1942 text clearly appeared in the 1931 monograph and this is a summary of that reprinting. The 1926 police series (N=9,243) appears in both (1931, p. 67; 1942, p. 80). The 1917-1923 court series (N=8,141) appears in both (1931, p. 41; 1942, p. 59). The 1900-1906 juvenile court series (N=8,056) appears in both (1931, pp.49-50; 1942, Maps 12 and 13).

What Shaw and Mc Kay did not continue in their 1942 text was a discussion regarding gangs. One can only speculate, but perhaps because of this, and the fact that their 1942 text is what they are identified with, they are lumped with generic delinquency theories rather than with those having direct implications for gang crime. But the fact is, the 1931 monograph did focus on gangs. Oddly, Shaw's 1951 natural history study of the delinquent career continued the reference to organized gangs and criminal groups (p. 15),[18] as did the 1931 version of Shaw's "The Natural History of a Delinquent Career" (Shaw and Morre, 1931).

Chapter 6 in Shaw and Mc Kay (1931) was an effort to show that most delinquency is group activity. What else is noteworthy about this chapter is that the authors were fully aware of the limitations of "official data", as will be seen. An earlier study by Shaw and Meyer (1920) is quoted showing that among some 6,000 cases of stealing in the juvenile court, only 9.6 percent of these involved lone offenders, the rest (90.4%) were group offenders (1931, p. 196). Additional data collection on another 4,663 youths with theft charges showed in chapter 6 that 89 percent were group offenders.

In chapter 6, Shaw and Mc Kay were clearly aware of the limitations of official data and perhaps this can dispel some of the criticism leveled at them for being criminologically naive regarding this. It is well to quote Shaw and Mc Kay in their entirety here:

> "It should be borne in mind that these statistical tabulations have been restricted to offenders known to the juvenile court authorities. It is not assumed therefore that the relative frequency of lone and group offenders in the general delinquent population is identical with the percentages presented in this study. Obviously, not all of the boys engaged in delinquent activities are known to the court". (Shaw and Mc Kay, 1931: p. 198).

They actually anticipated such criticism and advanced the defense that their estimates for lone offenders were very conservative, and in fact overestimated their representation involving theft cases because of the natural tendency of gang boys to not "squeal" on each other when caught.   Further, "it is obvious that not all such group delinquencies are committed by well-organized gangs" because while "many of the delinquents may be members of such gangs, they usually commit their offenses in the company of one or two other boys" (p. 199).

Chapters 7 and 8 in Shaw and Mc Kay (1931) involve the delinquent group and their traditions.   Chapter 7 describes the case of Sidney Blotzman, who over the period from 1913 to 1928 was actually involved with three different gangs. The residential mobility of this youth meant that by moving from one neighborhood to another, within Chicago, he also found himself in a different gang (p. 201). Admittedly, at times the playgroup, the companionship group, and the gang tend to be concepts used interchangeably (p. 204). Sidney's first gang was not a highly organized gang (p. 214), but the 3rd gang was the lower age grade affiliate of an adult criminal group, the membership of which "included some of Chicago's most notorious criminals" (p. 218). In this third group, Sidney became involved in armed robbery and rape (p. 219).

Clearly, a most significant difference between the 1931 monograph and the 1942 text is the use of many case studies and oral histories. While many are provided in the former, few are given in the latter. The 1942 text contains mostly quantitative data. Many of the 1931 case studies referred directly to various aspects of gang activity.

Yet there are other analytic differences even in the focus on quantitative measures in comparing the 1931 monograph with the 1942 text. As seen in Figure 8 below, there were continuing analytical measures in common between both works. What is significant is the expansion in the 1942 text. The 1942 text included new measures of differential social organization giving rise to delinquency such as: rental values, truancy, infant mortality, tuberculosis rates, mental disorder rates, home ownership, and economic segregation. Clearly, in the 1942 text Shaw and Mc Kay see racial differences having the common origin of economic segregation. In the 1931 monograph broken homes were shown to have a negligible relationship with delinquency and perhaps because of this was excluded from analysis in the 1942 text.

FIGURE 8

Comparison of Community Measures in the Two Shaw and Mc Kay Contributions

The 1931 Monograph	(pp.)	The 1942 Text	(pp.)
**************************		*******************	
Economic dependency (AID)	74-75	Families on relief	34
Condemned Buildings	69-70	Demolished Buildings	28
Changing Population Size	71-72	Changing population	31
Race/Ethnic segregation	79-80	Black Segregation	32,37-42
Neighborhood Succession	82-94	Ethnic succession	42
CJS Ethnic Intake Change	94-98	Same	152
White Racism	117-129	Similar	149
Presence of Adult offenders		Adult offenders	100
Broken Homes	265-268	Not analyzed	
Not Used		Rental Values	35
" "		Truancy	86
" "		Infant Mortality	94
" "		Tuberculosis Rates	96
" "		Mental Health Rates	99
" "		Home ownership rate	144
" "		Economic segregation	33

ANALYTICAL PARALLELS TO CURRENT APPROACHES

It is certainly the case, from the official record, of contemporary published materials about gang crime that some authors acknowledge more familiarity with the work of Shaw and Mc Kay than do others. This review pertains only to major works, not journal articles, or presented papers at professional societies. What this may demonstrate is an enduring influence from Shaw and Mc Kay, whether it is acknowledged, whether it is unconscious, or whether it is simultaneous independent discovery of the same factors examined by Shaw and Mc Kay within some of the current approaches to gang crime. This review shows, then, that basically the same variables used by Shaw and Mc Kay are still in use today by an array of authors on the topic of gangs.

Hagedorn (1988) likes to have the cake and eat it too, but does not quote a single contribution from Shaw and Mc Kay and makes only one indirect reference to a quote of Shaw via Miller (1976, p. 120) (see Hagedorn, 1988, p, 20, fn p. 185). This is most curious considering that some of the factors examined by Hagedorn include those also previously analyzed by Shaw and Mc Kay. These factors in Hagedorn (1988) include: adult involvement (p, 110), the minority experience (p. 17), disorganization and deprivation via Bogardus (p. 43), racial economics (pp. 25-26), the gang as a launch pad for criminal careers via Tannenbaum (1938) (p. 9)[19], ethnic conflict (p. 44), gang loyalty (p. 184), the repudiation of middle class standards via Cohen, the role of AFDC and public assistance (p. 190), ethnic and nationality conflicts via Cloward and Ohlin (p. 194), not truancy but school dropouts (p. 199), the stage of immigration (p. 203), urban prejudice via Yablonsky (p. 183), social and economic discrimination via Yablonsky (p. 184). Now are we supposed to believe none of this was examined in the works of Shaw and Mc Kay?

Moore's (1978) emphasis on the relationship between the barrios and the prisons could have certainly been strengthened by reference to Shaw and Mc Kay's findings on gang affiliation and the correctional experience. How dissimilar is the structural condition between bootlegging under the prohibition described by Shaw and Mc Kay and the bootlegging in drugs described by Moore? Moore surely quotes the importance of government aid and welfare (p. 30), clique succession (p. 60), and the strong sense of nationalism (p. 107) in analyzing gangs in Los Angeles. And there are no parallels drawn by Moore with the prior work of Shaw and Mc Kay.

Campbell (1984) refers to Shaw (1929) only in terms of ecological pressures (see Campbell, 1984: fn, p. 268).[20] There are also references to issues of immigration and how New York neighborhoods are segregated along ethnic lines (p. 234). Does it seem more reasonable to conclude that many of the factors studied by Shaw and Mc Kay are more or less the same factors subsequently used by other criminological researchers?

Yablonsky (1962) seemed so heavily influenced by the work of Shaw and Mc Kay he used the phrase "differential socialization" (p. 232)[21]. Yablonsky was certainly aware of the 1931 monograph and quoted it (p. 124, 126). Also discussed in Yablonsky were themes related to the Shaw and Mc Kay work such as "the twisting threads of prejudice and discrimination" (pp. 184-185), the gang as an outlet for bias crimes (p. 186), ethnic conflict and rivalry (p. 187), and in fact five of Yablonsky's seven causal factors (p. 232) seem tied to the Shaw and Mc Kay tradition.

Suttles (1971) cites the 1942 Shaw and Mc Kay text (p. 18), the problem of white vs. African-American school tensions (p. 58), and presents a fascinating ecological analysis involving the short distance between place of gang offense and gang members closest residence (pp. 208-209). It is certainly a theoretical refinement on differential social organization, by showing that communities such as those examined prior to Suttles (1968) were not monolithic conditions of equal forms of social disorganization. Indeed, they often have more "infrastructure" than casual observers credit them with; that is, they have ordered segmentation.[22] Ordered segmentation, we assume, is a function of ethnicity and territory, and allows for the management of social relations within and between neighborhoods, which is further refined by normative patterns paralleling differences in age, sex, kinship, and residential groupings, so as to facilitate regulated assembly, a localized provincialism and pattern of movement in face to face aggregates, having standardized role capacities.

Spergel (1964, 1973) must be considered part of the Chicago school of criminology, even though if a person seeks to take course work at the University of Chicago they will find no such division called "the School of Criminology", they will find only the existing Department of Sociology, and other social sciences that work closely with it. There is no "major" in criminology, although obviously a Ph.D. special field examination can probably be taken in this topical area. Spergel is currently an associated faculty member, teaching as he does from the Social Service Administration on the other side of the "Midway". In the Chicago school tradition, he also coined the phrase "differential life styles" (1973, pp. 63-92)[23].

What Spergel proves is that one can both build directly upon a prior acknowledged tradition and advance new theoretical structures that are largely consistent with the Chicago school tradition. Spergel (1971) gives no credit or mention to Shaw and Mc Kay in the East Coast community he studied, but by means of independent discovery or simple good research basically discovers and identifies many of the same variables. For example, Spergel does include indexes of social breakdown"ization"[24] that measure public assistance and aid, infant mortality, venereal disease, and psychiatric discharges in the three communities he studied (p. 5). Spergel also discusses relationships with adult offenders (pp. 145-146) which Shaw and Mc Kay dealt with as a problem for a community, it provides the opportunity for delinquents to acquire adult tutelage in gang crime.

Spergel (1971) seems to wrestle with two conceptual themes, not one as he has been unfairly criticized (ala Hagedorn). There is both the implied community social disorganizational structural backdrop and the social-psychological aspect relating to perceptions of the opportunity system. Figure 9, below, tries to place this in graphic form.

FIGURE 9

THE SPERGEL ANALYSIS OF TWO THEMES: SOCIAL DISORGANIZATION AND OPPORTUNITY SYSTEM TYPOLOGY

The Nature of the Opportunity System
****

		Legitimate ****************	Illegitimate ****************
Community Social Disorganization Levels	LOW	Nice, low crime, middle class, ideal neighborhood	Racketville and Outfit, Inc type neighborhood
	HIGH	Working class poor, pre-deindustrialized neighborhood (Haulburg?)	The slumtown extraordinaire, Moore's Gulag neighborhood.

The only problem with such a scheme is the first quadrant, the "nice, low crime, middle class, ideal neighborhood": how do we promote and develop it? Sometimes students of criminology are told that in order to understand criminality we must first understand why persons conform to the law. Perhaps what this problem in criminology indicates is the more general problem in the search for the ideal community structure and environment.

Cohen (1955) directly quoted the 1931 monograph by Shaw and Mc Kay regarding the fusion of versatility and malice in one of their oral histories (p. 29). Once the reader of Cohen becomes acclimated to a "stream of consciousness" monologue writing style, and diction such as "niggardliness" (p. 52), Cohen could actually be quoted perhaps contra original intellectual intentions in support of a segmented labor force thesis (pp. 94-95). Cohen does call the 1931 Shaw and Mc Kay monograph "cultural transmission theory". But sees Shaw and Mc Kay's cultural transmission approach being rehashed in "criminal behavior" theory by Sutherland "couched in what are essentially cultural-transmission terms" (p. 180).

Cloward and Ohlin (1960), clearly a part of the Chicago school modern criminological tradition, call Shaw and Mc Kay "cultural transmission" theory as well (pp. 35-36). They refer to Shaw and Mc Kay's 1940 version of Delinquency Areas and Shaw's (1933) article on delinquency as a group tradition (Cloward and Ohlin, 1960: pp. 37,162).

WHAT SHAW AND MC KAY SAID ABOUT "CORRECTIONAL INSTITU-TIONS"

Getting personal, I am having the same problem explaining Shaw and Mc Kay as I did in the early 1980s explaining the social reality of "nothing works, oops, I'm sorry, maybe it does" Martinson. Martinson had been the chief ideologue for a long time that "nothing works in rehabilitating offenders". Then on November 20th, of 1978, at the Second National Workshop on Criminal Justice Evaluation, in Washington, D.C., in a panel where I was also presenting a paper[25], he stunned the standing room only audience when he announced to the effect "I know many of you may be expecting me to tell you more about how rehabilitation does not work; but I was premature in my conclusions; in fact I am here to tell you that perhaps some things do work, now that I have started using real data".

I would tell my students about this story and Martinson's self-inflicted death just shortly after the above presentation, and students in the class would make the strangest comments. Such as "I bet the CIA killed him and made it look like a suicide, didn't he get a lot of money from the feds?", etc, etc. Mostly the students began to distrust what they read. This is probably good, because the research monograph I am going to summarize here, from Shaw and Mc Kay (1949), also has incredible implications. But this is an authentic document, so I think we had better believe these previously unknown findings from Shaw and Mc Kay.

This is an unpublished study entitled Subsequent Criminal Careers of Juvenile Delinquents, School Truants, and Special School Pupils, dated 1949. On the yellowed by age copy that I inherited is marked boldly Confidential and has what may or may not be the signature of "C. Shaw" in the same ink. Penciled on the front of this sixty page monograph was the writing "Note: This study was financed by Wiebolt $49,000 and was never published because of the effect it would have on collections for work in juvenile delinquency". How I got it is a longer story that can be told somewhere else.

It is an extensive follow-up study of official efforts to rehabilitate children through sending them to institutions whose purpose had that stated goal of "the reconstruction of human lives" (Shaw and Mc Kay, 1949: p. 1). There are no case studies here. This is a straight forward quantitative study. It studied cohorts of four dispositions for these children: (1) boys who are repeatedly delinquent as children and are sent to the State Training School, (2) boys whose delinquency has brought them into the juvenile court as official delinquents, (3) boys who have been found to be repeatedly truant, and (4) boys who "are problems in the school system" (p. 3).

The data from the Illinois State Training School for boys (St. Charles) includes: (1) "a series of 327 boys committed to the State Training School from Chicago during the year 1930", (2) "a series of 435 boys paroled from (St. Charles) to Chicago during the years 1942-44", and (3) "a summary of the findings of an earlier....follow-up of 263 boys paroled (from St. Charles) for the first time during the years 1923-25" (p. 13).

The data on delinquent boys brought before the Cook County Juvenile Court includes: (1) "a series of 1,336 boys brought before the Juvenile Court during the year 1930", and (2) "a series of 1,178 boys brought before the Juvenile Court during the year 1920" (p. 13).

The data on boys adjudicated as school truants by the Cook County Juvenile Court included: (1) "a series of 408 boys committed to the Chicago Parental School by the Juvenile Court during the year 1930", and (2) "a series of 543 boys brought before the Juvenile Court on truant petition in 1930" (p. 13).

The data on boys who are behavioral problems in the Chicago Public School system included: (1) a series of 382 boys admitted to the Montefiore Special School during the years 1932-33 (p. 13).

Table 7 below summarizes the findings from this Shaw and Mc Kay study (1949). These statistics are vulgar in the extent to which they demonstrate how juvenile institutions appear to be in the business of systematically producing adult criminals. These figures are beyond being alarming, they should be indictable. And such results from the City where juvenile processing was supposed to be the best in the United States? I fear for those other jurisdictions and their own rates of mass producing adult criminals. What shame there must be in needing to reproduce crime along the lifespan to feed adult prisons!

Or can we simply discount these powerful findings from Shaw and Mc Kay?

I suspect these findings are true. We cannot assume that any major societal impetus has given us reason to believe, also, that these same parameters have changed in the direction of reduced levels of recidivism. What it implies for gangs, and correctional staff, should be clear.

We are not doing the best job in preventing recidivism.

In fact, apparently, as a society we really do not care to address this matter of the hidden industry in our criminal justice system that systematically produces adult criminals from the raw materials of errant youths.

In fact, recidivism problems among juvenile institutions are as equally problematic today as they were in the time of Shaw and Mc Kay's study (1949). The problem has never been tackled. The problem has been systematically ignored.

TABLE 7

Summary of the Shaw and Mc Kay (1949) Findings on the
Percentage of Juvenile Boys in Chicago Who
After Being "Cared For" By Institutions
Designed to Redirect Their Lives
Actually Became Adult Criminals

	FUP (yrs)	%SJ&AR	%ARA	%ARC	%ARI	MEANS ANA	ANC	ANI
ST. CHARLES:								
1930 Intake	17	82.9	76.1	68.5	60.5	5.1	3.0	2.2
1930 Intake	5	78.3	68.8	61.2	52.9	NR	NR	NR
1942-44 Parolees	5	71.0	63.9	52.2	42.1	3.0	1.9	1.7
1923-25 Parolees	5	80.2	75.7	69.6	58.2	2.9	1.8	1.6
JUVENILE COURT:								
1930 Intake	18	73.3	66.2	52.2	36.1	4.7	2.5	2.0
1920 Intake	28	67.8	59.6	42.7	22.5	5.5	2.8	2.3
TRUANCY SERIES:								
1930 CPS Intake	18	69.6	57.8	44.4	32.1	5.0	2.7	2.2
1920 Juv. Court	18	71.3	58.2	45.3	31.9	4.8	2.6	2.1
MONTEFIORE SERIES:								
1932-33 Intake	15	74.6	53.7	42.4	30.9	4.2	2.5	2.1
1932-33 Intake	9	71.2	47.9	36.6	28.5	NR	NR	NR

Legend: FUP = Follow-up Period
%SJ&AR = Percentage with Subsequent Juvenile & Adult Record
%ARA = Percentage with Adult Record of Arrests
%ARC = Percentage with Adult Record of Convictions
%ARI = Percentage with Adult Record of Imprisonment
ANA = Average Number of Arrests as in adult record
ANC = Average Number of Convictions in adult record
ANI = Average Number of Imprisonment commitments (adult)

COMBINING TWO SHAW AND MC KAY THEMES ON THE PRODUCTION OF CRIME

The theme for which Shaw and Mc Kay are known, or should be understood from their published literature, is that at the level of the community, above and beyond the control of those who are born there or who reside there, are structural forces in society having to do with what Shaw and Mc Kay called aspects of social disorganiza-tion and conditions of inequality, including racism, prejudice, discrimination, and segregation --- and these forces, while being discernible from communities without or with less delinquency, gang crime, etc, in terms of their variation or differences in social organization, basically bring about the onset of delinquency and gangs. What the 1949 study shows is that once the government becomes involved in the welfare of these youths brought to the attention of "authorities", through a series of repressive institutional life experiences, we as a society also take these young errant boys and make them into adult criminals. That's how I read Shaw and Mc Kay. And I believe them.

SUMMARY AND CONCLUSION

The Hollywood caricature of the arch conservative-bigot in the persona of Archie Bunker tends to communicate "it's not what it is, it's what it appears to be, that's important". Along these lines, I do not consider myself a defender of Shaw and Mc Kay, although obviously it may appear that way. I have to "call em' as I seem em'". But I do feel some authors have either not known the whole story or else simply discount Shaw and Mc Kay for reasons we cannot readily surmise. The whole truth needs to be told.

The truth is that Shaw and Mc Kay indeed contributed much to the gang literature, as demonstrated in their 1931 monograph. Also, whether we acknowledge them or not, there appears to be a large influence from Shaw and Mc Kay or minimally, there are research parallels with many current approaches to gang research.

Finally, perhaps what could have been their most powerful contribution to criminology was never allowed to be released to the public and remained "confiden-tial" (Shaw and Mc Kay, 1949).

So the truth is that Shaw and Mc Kay probably have been unfairly maligned in some of the literature, under-acknowledged often, and even misinterpreted in some of our literature. Perhaps this is somewhat related to what Martinson (1978) said "I was premature in my conclusions...", because it would appear that these same authors bent on criticizing Shaw and Mc Kay may not have had a grasp of the larger picture --- the other contributions from Shaw and Mc Kay.

We need a much fuller grasp of this literature before taking on any responsibility and authority to "do something about it". This should not discourage such attempts at rehabilitation, it should incite and further motivate them. But just as in tackling the gang problem, we should do so not based on intuition and "hunches" of what programs should be put in place, it should be a strategy based on social science and known research results of "what works".

DISCUSSION QUESTIONS

(1) In early radical intellectual circles during the 1960s and early 1970s, "empiricism" itself, that is, using numbers in research, was considered the supreme act of academic fascism: reducing the problem to numbers. This belief system did change when

radicals found they could use computers too. So does the denunciation of gang research because it uses "official statistics" mean that only "first hand qualitative methods" are the answer to generating knowledge about gangs in America? Or can some official statistics be used effectively? Is this a problem of political rhetoric or science? Census data are "official statistics" too, so can the same radical criticism apply? Is the ultimate radical position that any data collected by any governmental agency or governmental representative necessarily means a "big lie"?

(2) Do you feel that Shaw and Mc Kay have become "type cast" in our criminological literature?

(3) What do the recidivism statistics reported by Shaw and Mc Kay (1949) imply about America as an advanced civilization?

FOOTNOTES

1. James Short (in Huff, 1990) sees much historical continuity in his analysis of "new wine, old bottles".

2. In fact, if we are truly to have a social scientific perspective, we must at least strive for a cumulative body of knowledge. Even if a student of criminology is to deny such a cumulative body of social science, then minimally we should at least be informed about the mistakes of the past or run the risk of repeating errors.

3. My data indicates that during the Fall Quarter of 1946, that Henry D. McKay was the instructor of record for Sociology 271, a course entitled "Crime & Juvenile Delinquency". My source of information for this is the personal files of the late Don T. Blackiston, Ph.D., who took this course, and others from Mc Kay. Shaw apparently taught "Criminology" and others (Soc 377) "Community Organization and Delinquency Prevention", (Soc 397) "Criminal Careers".

4. We have a boundary maintenance problem here in defining what is meant by membership in the "Chicago school of criminology". Hagan seems to imply one must teach in the sociology department of the University of Chicago, and have completed the Ph.D. requirements.   Does this mean that many of the fine and unique contributions from many, many Master's theses completed at the University of Chicago's Department of Sociology are not genuine contributions either? Does this mean that any of the many U of C Sociology Ph.D.'s that worked in the Illinois prison system as "sociology actuaries", because it was field work, not academia, were somehow less legitimate? We shall have to come up with some working definition of what is and is not "Chicago school" tradition. I suspect, however, because of the complete variation in both methods and ideology that there is no one-dimensional tradition, but rather many different traditions focused on much the same thing.

5. Not to belabor the obvious, but at the time of Shaw and Mc Kay's early work there was not even a messed up national system of "official statistics" to worry or lament about!

6. I often ask students undergoing criminal investigation training about how to solve crimes involving the residential propinquity factor when no centralized, routinely updated, arrest/event dated address file really exists in the U.S.A. Perhaps Shaw and McKay should be read more closely by law enforcement students.

7. Shaw and Mc Kay were admittedly descriptive and bivariate in their (1931,1942) statistical analysis, using maps, bar charts, percentage distributions, rate calculations, and correlation coefficients rather than multiple regression. But they were dealing with large volumes of data as well, without the use of a computer other than that their Creator gave them!

8. I am indebted to the wife of the late Don T. Blackiston, who graciously turned over his personal files to me. Blackiston had earned his Ph.D. in sociology from the University of Chicago. He never taught, he worked his entire life as an applied criminologist. The works I shall be quoting from in this chapter came from Blackiston's collection.

9. This is similar to what Suttles (1971) refers to as a process by which any given location in a city may have a stigma associated with it, such as the housing projects being associated with persons of color (Suttles, 1971: p. 16).

10. Many persons seem to place Sutherland's theory of differential association before the contribution of Shaw and Mc Kay. Differential association theory had its first version in 1939, in the 3rd edition of Sutherland's Principles of Criminology. As I shall argue here, whatever we call Shaw and Mc Kay's theory, its first version was in the 1931 monograph, not 1942.

11. Indeed, Shaw and Mc Kay (1942) use this particular phrase, differential social organization (pp. 177-183). I have always presented the Shaw and Mc Kay tradition to my students in this terminology, only to have them find, quite to their confusion, that other criminologists do not use this phrase in reference to Shaw and Mc Kay.

12. Sutherland (1939) differential association; Cloward and Ohlin (1960) differential opportunity structure; Daniel Glaser's differential identity, etc, etc. Actually, Cloward and Ohlin also made reference to "differential integration" (1960,pp. 189-192); but seeing that no one called their framework by that, I used the phrase myself (Knox, 1978).

13. My point is this: we as human beings probably want to pigeonhole everything; and maybe one document can be so classified if it has a single thrust, but we cannot as readily pigeonhole a person's whole lifespan of productivity.

14. So let's be fair here, the 1942 text was Shaw, et al.

15. Not all gang authors were unaware of this important contribution. Morash (1983) was one who certainly cited this work.

16. Shaw and Mc Kay clearly, however, distinguished between the play group and the gang (see 1931, p. 240).

17. And, of course, Short and Strodtbeck's (1965, 1974) legitimation of Shaw and McKay as part of the old Chicago school that compiled natural histories (p. 77).

18. Cultural enrichment is a service intervention style often held out for delinquents, gang members, etc, at a primary to secondary level of prevention. Depending on your view if this works to reduce crime or not, one can alternately blame or credit, perhaps, Shaw, at least to some extent, for the later emergence of many variations of the cultural enrichment programs for delinquency treatment and prevention. Because the 1951 study by Shaw emphasized the disjunction between a delinquent boys environment and the "little access to cultural heritages of conventional society" (p. 15).

19. This cites the 1929 study by Shaw and Myers.

20.   Similarly, perhaps due to the historical "pigeon holing" of the intellectual contributions of criminological authors, Shaw and Mc Kay become "type cast", such that authors (e.g., Denisoff and Mc Caghy, 1973: p. 150) continue to refer to Shaw and Mc Kay's contribution as little more than the "ecological theory".

21. Please note, as part of the ongoing concern about boundary maintenance with WHO is really a part of the "Chicago school" of criminology, that simple use of the prefix "differential" is not necessarily an automatic means of inclusion within this intellectual tradition.   Otherwise anyone could generate frameworks such as "differential assimilation", "differential competition", "differential whatever", and lay legitimate claim to such an intellectual gang/ingroup.

22. Suttles notes that among African-Americans there may be less such spatial ordering because of lower amounts of mobilizable resources for local social organization in their community infrastructure (p. 226).

23. Many of the criminological theories from the Chicago school have this "differential" prefix: differential association (Sutherland), differential social organization (Shaw and Mc Kay), differential identity (Glaser), differential opportunity (Cloward and Ohlin), differential integration, etc.

24. Pardon my added suffix here.

25. My paper was "A Comparative Cost-Benefit Analysis of Programs for Illinois Offenders", and was certainly a defense of and an argument for expanded resources targeting aftercare and prevention services for youths and adult offenders. I was a young turk who just got his Ph.D. two months ago and was there arguing "for rehabilitation" and I did not know until I got in the room and looked at the name plates on the speakers table that Dr. Martinson was also presenting. Needless to say, I felt at the time like I was "set up" for a clashing debate between the renowned and highly funded Dr. Nothing Works and me the Dr. Young Turk Who Thinks Something Works. It didn't happen. In fact, when Martinson took the podium, he

recanted his whole "nothing works" doctrine, which generated much verbal stirring in the huge mostly governmental audience. I had the distinct impression that he almost wanted to be "let back into the fold" of such groups like the American Society of Criminology, where he was not too popular. I guess we will never know the full story.

CHAPTER 9

SHAW AND MC KAY ON GANGS: With Commentary
and Historical Analysis

INTRODUCTION

It remains somewhat of a sociological mystery why Shaw and Mc Kay gave so much emphasis to gangs in their 1931 monograph and seem to have mostly abandoned it thereafter. Clearly, few contemporary authors credit Shaw and McKay with any contribution to our understanding of gangs. That is a historical mistake. Recall that Thrasher's (1927) work was gaining acclaim as the definitive study of gangs, as was Asbury's analysis. Factually, we can only recount what Shaw and Mc Kay had to say about gangs and provide some background material. That is the purpose of this Chapter.

The implications for the field of criminology should be evident. We have missed an important segment of the knowledge development spectrum if we do not understand that Shaw and Mc Kay had more to say about gangs than contemporary authors give them credit for. This is particularly important for those readers concerned about the future of America's gang problems and what social policy initiatives or programs should be put in place. We need more than a casual understanding of the past, for otherwise we make a major risk of misinterpretation; indeed a risk that should not be taken when dealing with a problem as significant as gangs.

The same applies to the field of law enforcement. It is a mistake to ignore the past. Thus, any analysis of gangs must be able to offer an understanding of the past, present, and the future. Hopefully, the present analysis is such an account. Which is not to say that criminologists should write first of all for policy makers, but rather that social science findings bearing on such obviously important topics have an obligation, morally, to not ignore the possibility that such findings could be misinterpreted in the absence of any such policy suggestions or overall position statements.

By providing a summary of what Shaw and Mc Kay contributed to our understanding of gangs, this is more than simply giving historical documentation to their role in the study of gangs. What they have to offer is of continuing significance.

DISORGANIZED NEIGHBORHOODS, ORGANIZED GANGS

In comparing economically depressed inner city neighborhood life with a more prosperous neighborhood, what is of importance regarding the propensity for law violation are the sources of norms and values, "conceptions of right and wrong" (Shaw and Mc Kay, 1931: p. 111). In the urban poor enclave a youth has restricted access to the established social order in the sense that it may be limited to "formal contacts with the police, the courts, the school, and the various social agencies" (p. 111).   In a more prosperous community, perhaps a youth could have extensive formal relations with the established social order: through tutors, nannies, adult supervised travel and tours, and a host of other socialization functions. This might include those at the young adult collegiate level, like that of the anticipatory socialization/training grounds often found at prestigious or private universities like the University of Chicago, and their "student run" Society for Social Research.

This points to a fundamental aspect of youth socialization: a condition of normative ambiguity or normlessness, as a condition of anomie, is going to be a source of much alienation; therefore in the natural search for human meaning in a social or collective setting, when the formal mechanisms do not work, informal ones take over. It is truly a matter of the qualitative differences between having a positive and functional relationship to the adult run apparatus and being warmly welcomed into it; or conversely, of being in a "control mode" by major social institutions, where the most frequent contact with the legitimate adult authorities is in a combative relationship with the established social order. We can add, of course, to this the variations in power, privilege and racism ala Wilson to see that while everyone might in theory be "equal under the law", by the nature of their social attachment to the social order some are clearly going to be "more equal" than others.

According to Shaw and Mc Kay (1931) it is more than a material difference, it is a difference between being "excluded" or "included" from channels of normative learning (p. 111).[1] These are conditions of the social structure of society and how they impact locally at the neighborhood or community level.[2] What the social structure communicates to many of our nation's youths is therefore that "you are NOBODY". Today, in the 1990s we often have heard the call in educational policy discussions for "value added" education, that is to put values back into the curriculum. Today's students get "valued added" education anyway: they get it in the subcultures surrounding the school zone, they get it from gang members, they get it from our mass media --- but not necessarily adding the values conducive to pro-social behavior or good citizenship.

Shaw and Mc Kay were keenly aware of the societal forces that produce gangs. That is to say, if the major social institutions (family, school, church, economy, government) are not functioning for America's children, then informal or indigenous institutions will naturally arise:

> "Very often the child's access to the traditions and standards of our conventional culture are restricted to his formal contacts with the police, the school, and the various social agencies. On the other hand his most vital and intimate social contacts are often limited to the spontaneous and undirected neighborhood playgroups and gangs whose activities and standards of conduct may vary widely from those of his parents and the larger social order" (p. 111, Shaw and Mc Kay, 1931).

The family sticks out as a social institution in that it is regarded as the last line of defense. The family is expected to be the primary agency of socialization.[3] The problem is, and was demonstrated by Shaw and Mc Kay, that the inner city or poor family differs in not having or controlling resources with which to carry out this mandate. It becomes a social institution in effect with high levels of social responsibility and low levels of functional authority (e.g., use of rewardive power, incentives, etc). Most observers of social organization would say that if such a family does prevent its children from deviance, delinquency, gang affiliation, etc, in a condition of having responsibility without authority, that we have witnessed a kind of socialization miracle.   What Shaw and Mc Kay seem to imply is that a parent today should not pray for a miracle, they should pray for social justice. That is, the hope that child development in America does not translate for them as criminal development. What Shaw and McKay would later (1949) find is that the their worst fears were true: our nation does in fact systematically produce, with alarming effectiveness, adult criminals from the raw materials of school behavior problems, truants, and delinquents.

Demographic transitions and demographic changes translate into social changes in the population. Population changes and the immigrant's adjustment to American society, were factors taken into consideration by Shaw and Mc Kay[4]. The importance of these factors, overall in terms of America's social structure, to use an illustration, is that between the period 1900 and 1910 immigrants accounted for about two-thirds (about 10 million) of the total population increase in the United States (about 16 million). Between 1930 to 1940 immigrants accounted for less than ten percent of the increase in the U.S. population. Thus, expressing total immigration in relationship to the total size of the U.S. population shows an important aspect impacting on American society. Table 9 below shows this data on the United States.

TABLE 9

Comparison of U.S. Total Population and Size of Immigration Waves Over Time

Year	Total U.S. Population	Total U.S. Volume	Immigration Wave Date
1990	248,709,873	7,338,000	1981-1990
1980	221,700,000	4,493,000	1971-1980
1970	204,351,000	3,322,000	1961-1970
1960	179,245,000	2,515,000	1951-1960
1950	150,697,000	1,035,000	1941-1950
1940	131,669,000	528,000	1931-1940
1930	122,775,000	4,107,000	1921-1930
1920	105,711,000	5,736,000	1911-1920
1910	91,972,000	8,795,000	1901-1910
1900	75,995,000	3,688,000	1891-1900
1890	62,948,000	5,247,000	1881-1890
1880	50,156,000	2,812,000	1871-1880
1870	38,558,000	2,315,000	1861-1870
1860	31,443,000	2,598,000	1851-1860
1850	23,192,000	1,713,000	1841-1850
1840	17,069,000	599,000	1831-1840
1830	12,866,000	152,000	1820-1830
1820	9,638,000	38,689	1820-1824

Note: Near 1911-1912, about the time of Puffer's (1912) book on gangs, almost 1 out of every 10 Americans had immigrated to America in the last decade. This was the highest period for immigration rates.

The early works on gangs that came before Shaw and Mc Kay, like that by Puffer (1912) and Furfey (1926), reacted in response to some of these demographic changes impacting on American society in terms of its potential relationship to social conditions and gangs. Shaw and Mc Kay quote Puffer regarding, then, the ability of the family to function in capacities of normative socialization for children or for a recent immigrant parent, who may not speak English, to be able to truly exert control over a child --- because for one thing, the child will have more power: the power to buffer information and to function as the translator, when the child understands English as a second language (Shaw and Mc Kay, 1931: p. 112).

Actually, Shaw and Mc Kay (1931) had to battle intellectually against much prevailing social-Darwinist theory which was then so popular in American conceptions of how society works. Puffer (1912) was one such social Darwinist theory. Puffer like others before (Franklin Chase Hoyt, Quicksands of Youth; etc, see Thrasher, 1968, p. 34) argued from what was called "recapitulation theory" that the child is just a savage, and the gang is his tribe, such that ones ancient animal history means that all boys (girls don't have it) have a "gang forming instinct". Thrasher was quick to attack this "gang instinct" approach. Says Thrasher: "It is not instinct, but experience---the way he is conditioned---that fixes his social relations." (Thrasher, 1968: p. 35).

Recognizing that there has been a kind of resurgence of bio-sociology in recent years, perhaps we should digress shortly to comment further about Puffer's approach. Not to encourage it, but to demonstrate some of the mistakes of the past. The 1990s is a time of gene splicing and much genetic knowledge development. The 1960s saw the appearance of the XYY chromosomal anomaly as a controversial (but convenient and conservative) explanation for crime, the so-called "super man" deviant, who has an extra "Y" gene.[5] Perhaps the modern bio-sociologist should read Puffer closely and begin searching for the "gang instinct" genetic code marker.

PUFFER'S (1912) SOCIAL-DARWIN THEORY OF GANGS

We must preface this discussion with the statement now widely accepted that "genetics" does not cause "crime", it has a complex social, cultural, and economic inter-related cluster of causes. If you think boys are apes, or men are naturally savage, or if you believe in channeling and "getting in touch" with your primordial self, or if you believe in transcendental multi-generational ancient-ancestral or contemporary-New Age gobbledygook, then you are going to truly enjoy Puffer (1912) about American gangs.

First the "gang-forming instinct" is only felt by boys. Girls, then, must have, if we are to carry this to its logical extreme conclusion, a "follower or self-debasement" instinct when they are represented in the ranks of gang membership. Or maybe there is something called the "super woman" equivalent to the XYY "super male". We should doubt it all.

But the gang has a desire for "local habitation...its own special street corner, its club room, its shanty in the woods" and the gang instinct is therefore "set deep in the soul" and accounts for "their spontaneous organizations" (Puffer, 1912, p. 24).[6] Recall the imagery of Lord of the Flies as Puffer explains gang etiology:

"The typical boys' gang, then, is no mere haphazard association. Accidents of various sorts...age, propinquity, likeness of interests,..bring together a somewhat random group...One or more leaders come to fore. The gang organizes itself, finds or makes its meeting place, establishes its standards, begins to do things...in some sort, a collective mind...the gang is, in short, a little social organism...it is the earliest manifestation in man of that strange group-forming instinct, without which beehive and anthill and human society would alike be impossible" (Puffer, 1912: p. 38).

Certainly there are studies of social groups that point to the existence of the "group think" tendency (Janis, 1972), but this was analyzed in terms of how our nation's leaders made decisions. The "risky shift" phenomena is also routinely cited in social-psychology and group behavior (Stoner, 1961; Wallach, Hogan, and Bem, 1962) and can affect any age-grade of group. Risky shift means a person is more prone to commit a crime in a group than as a lone individual. The risky shift concept has much use in explaining gang behavior today. But these are social process theories, they are not concepts that argue for genetic determinism.

Puffer felt that the risk of gang formation was a problem endemic to a certain phase of the lifespan[7]. That is, the "gang age...is from ten to sixteen", a period of "organized group life" that can theoretically begin slightly earlier and therefore can probably last longer; mostly, however, it appears to be a period in which "boys prefer boys" and boys scorn girls, because we know they are exiting from this phase or stage, when the boy "cultivates individual friendships, or courts a girl" (Puffer, 1912, p. 26).   Did Puffer (1912) therefore influence, or manifest conceptual parallels with, subsequent gang authors such as Bloch and Niederhoffer (1958)[8] and Yablonsky (1962)? If we could believe Bloch and Niederhoffer (1958), then we must revise the human development life-span theories, including Erickson and identity, Kohlberg and moral development, to realize that:

> "the adolescent period in all cultures...< is a >...striving for adult status...< such that when >...society does not make adequate preparation...for the induction of its adolescents to the adult status...equivalent forms arise...< therefore >...the gang structure....appears to...(satisfy)...deep-seated needs experienced by adolescents in all cultures. Such, very briefly, is our hypothesis" (Bloch and Niederhoffer, 1958: p. 17).

Reading Yablonsky, we find a neo-Freudian observation compatible with the "boys only" approach of Puffer, to the effect that Yablonsky sees gang boys as kind of closet homosexuals[9] or latent or manifest homosexuals:

> "Fear of responsibility and emotional isolation from females generates the gang as a kind of 'homosexual' community. Consider...the projections of felt internal homosexual problems. Most gang leaders, in particular, manifest homosexual attitudes in their ridicule, exploitation of females, and their closer feelings about members of their male peer group. Along these lines there is evidence of homosexual experimentation among gang boys" (Yablonsky, 1962: p. 200).

Apparently Puffer's analysis applied only to Aryan's:

> "The normal boy between ten and sixteen is really living thru the historic period, which for the races of northern Europe, began somewhere this side of the glacial period, and came to an end with, let us say, the early middle ages. He is, therefore, essentially a savage, with the interests of a savage, the body of a savage, and to no small extent, the soul of one. He thinks and feels like a savage; he has the savage virtues and the savage vices; and the gang is his tribe" (Puffer, 1912: p. 77).

For the record, it should be pointed out that the Ku Klux Klan and Birth of a Nation were powerful social forces in their own right at the time of Puffer's writing (see Schwartz and Disch, 1970: p. 33).   Oddly, though, a Pufferism viewpoint again recently surfaced in the gang literature that sounds remarkably similar:

> "There are many similarities between the turf-marking behavior of gangs and the territory-marking behavior of certain animals...the stratification dynamics and competitive behavior of many gangs are quite similar to the dominance and deference rituals of wolves and other animals...Understanding Darwin also helps in understanding certain aspects of the gang's behavior, especially male dominance and deference rituals and the predatory victimization of 'the weak' on the streets (Huff, 1993: p. 18)."

This kind of syllogistic logical fallacy (it is similar to animals, therefore crime must have a biological/genetic cause) was certainly not to be taken seriously by the Chicago school. Thus for completeness, perhaps a few words should be added about the record of the "Chicago school" of sociology.

THE CHICAGO SCHOOL WASN'T PERFECT, BUT IT WASN'T RACIST

Shaw and Mc Kay cannot even remotely be accused of an "anti-Foreigner" or "anti-alien" ideological theme.[10] Indeed, the critical thinker will note that it was Shaw and Mc Kay who implied that American society constantly replenishes its groups that live under conditions of social disorganization, as if it were a perpetual need for a "group" at the bottom of the social pyramid; and it is from this group that comes the arrests, the convictions, and the swelling of the prisons (Eisenstadt, 1951). Indeed, as some ethnic groups have advanced up the ladder and out of the inner city "arrival zones", they were proportionately less represented as offenders in the criminal justice system and perhaps more integrated into its defense.

The Chicago school of sociology and criminology has never been accused of racist dogma or ideology.   The early sociologists included those being arrested for protesting racism and social injustice in the 1920s onward. Many had left of center or liberal views. It is useful to briefly demonstrate the point, legitimately included as a methodological concern in gang analysis, that high quality oral history material can, like quantitative data, be used for secondary analysis. Here the oral histories were done on sociologists from the "Chicago school".

The data collected by Carey (1976) in the historical archives collection at the University of Chicago contains high quality oral histories (see Carey, 1975) on major figures of the Chicago school of sociology. Carey (1975) showed that the source of legitimacy for the Chicago school was the practical use of sociological knowledge and policy input. In some ways, this supported the conception by Schwendinger and Schwendinger (1974) arguing that corporate liberalism dominated the ideological precepts of American sociologists,[11] as did that data collected in the Luther L. Bernard survey (1927).[12]

These two data sources were used for the content analysis reported here. Only three of these sociologists were intensely religious (3); eight were mildly religious, and most (26) were non-religious. Along political lines, ten were socialist oriented, four were conservative or anti-socialist, and most (23) were not active or apolitical.[13] Data on party affiliation was not available for 16; but for those who did report this information, most indicated (13) they were democrats, or liberals (3), or indepen- dents (2), with only 3 republicans.[14]

This information shows the Chicago school sociologists were more likely to be fighting racism. For example, Herbert G. Blumer said "by and large the members of the department and faculty they were what we would speak of as genuine liberals in their perspective" (Carey Collection, Box I, Folder 2, p. 12). Leonard S. Cottrell recalled "we were for radical justice....and I remember that some of us got at least as far as joining the socialist party and contributing money for Normal Thomas" (Carey Collection, Box 1, Folder 6, p. 5). E.R. Mower recollected that "there were marches at the Bug House square. Louis Wirth used to enter in these. He was arrested, I remember. He came to class, a Burgess class, after being absent for a couple of weeks, and he had been in jail or something" (Carey Collection, Box 1, Folder 16, p. 19).   In fact, some of the Chicago school was under physical attack from the ultraright. An antecedent to the political violence of May 5, 1969, when Professor Richard Flacks was attacked in his office and severely beaten by a rightwing extremist group[15] is found in the fact related by Edgar T. Thompson that once the home of professor Herbert Blumer was attacked and the Ku Klux Klan burned a cross in front of it (Carey Collection, Box 1, Folder 24, p. 8).

If the climate in the Chicago School was a politically liberal one, then it must have also been reflected in its relationship to interpersonal aspects of racism.   The Bernard sample contains an autobiography of an early African-American sociologist from the University of Chicago, George F. David who states:

> "Later I attended the University of Chicago and it was my first
> contact with whites on a basis of equality of any kind. At that time
> there was only about twenty Negroes in attendance here and we
> rarely came in contact with each other on the campus" (Bernard
> Collection, Box I, Folder 21).

Franc L. McCluer related the following anecdote about Robert Park:

> "I remember the story they used to tell about Park. He was making
> a study of race relations in the South, which you probably heard.
> He lived with 'em, according to the story, for awhile - the Blacks in
> Kentucky or Tennessee. He blackened his face, and one of them

said to him one day after they'd become friends with him, he said:
Brother Park, you dress yourself up and go up North, you can pass
yourself off as a white man." (Carey Collection, Box I, Folder 14,
p. 17).

Mc Cluer also told how the Society for Social Research, the sociology student
organization of the University of Chicago, would hold its meeting at the Hyde Park
Hotel and when they would invite guests like Black poet Kelly Miller to their
meetings that the hotel officials "wouldn't let him eat with us" (Carey Collection, Box
I, Folder 14, p. 6).

Do not jump to conclusions too fast about the Chicago school, because my data also
supported the contention by Schwendinger and Schwendinger (1974) on another
point. While the Chicago school had many liberal types among the faculty-student
body, the ideology officiated from at least one prominent member of the faculty, the
Chairman Albion Small, appears to have been a fervently anti-Marxist one. Asked
to characterize the political climate of the department of sociology, John Dollar said:

"It was firmly anti-Marxist that I knew, and I had already read to a
certain degree in Marx before I became a student there. It was
very clear that sociology was something distinct from Marxism and
it was not revolutionary---it had no revolutionary thrust" (Carey
Collection, Box I, Folder 7, p. 7).

According to Dollard students were not reading Marx because it was officially
dismissed as a monolithic error. This is more clearly explained by examining
statements made about the Albion Small seminar on Marx. For example, E.R.
Mowrer recalled:

"It's very strange, but I had a seminar with Small and I hadn't the
slightest idea of what it was all about. He had taught before a
seminar on Marx, Karl Marx. I guess his seminar had always been
on Karl Marx for several years. And the year I took it he shifted
to something else. I had hoped it would be Karl Marx. But it
turned out not to be. I've seemed to have forgotten what it was
about at all". (Carey Collection, Box I, Folder 16, p. 19).

Similarly, the following statement from Martin H. Neumeyer is also quite revealing:

"I took only a few courses (from Small). He offered one on
Marxism. He told us why there were some professors in another
department who were too much inclined to accept Marxism and he
wanted the students to know the fallacies of Marxism, so we had a
seminar. Incidentally, we had a Marxist in the class, who was
taking it and after we discovered it we went after him and argued
nearly every week, and I guess Dr. Small thought that was a good
teaching procedure, finally Dr. Small leaned forward and said "once
a Marxist, always a Marxist, and no amount of objective evidence
can convince him different"." (Carey Collection, Box 1, Folder 18,
p. 3).

TO RECAP, WHAT HAVE WE LEARNED ABOUT SHAW AND MC KAY?

The answer is, truthfully, not a hell of a lot. But it's been a slice of history that we need to understand. Therefore, onward and aggressively forward in a continuing discovery of what, if anything, Shaw and Mc Kay had to contribute to our understanding of gangs.

BACK TO SHAW AND MC KAY

Imagine Shaw as a detective, interviewing a young gang member, what would be Shaw's first question? Quite possibly it might be this "okay, what kind of values and norms do you have and where did you get them from, whose are they?" Because clearly Shaw and Mc Kay pointed to the socialization of youth under conditions of social disorganization such that two things occur:

> "The child in this situation is not only isolated from the traditions of our conventional culture but is subjected to a great diversity of behavior norms, some of which come from the family, others from the schools and courts, and still others, perhaps the most stimulating and enticing, from the undirected play groups and neighborhood gangs." (Shaw and Mc Kay, 1931: p. 115).

Exposure to the pattern of social relations in the gang therefore can make it harder then for traditional outreach to the youth through the family.

That the family has a difficult time competing with the social lure provided by the gang was indicated in Case # 1 of the many case studies provided in Shaw and Mc Kay (1931). Says the youth "We did everything in the gang, anything for a thrill and excitement. I can honestly say that we never went home unless we had done some kind of excitement, summer or winter" (p. 118). Often that excitement had the thrust of being white racist violence. The content of that excitement therefore deserves some analysis here and the case studies by Shaw and Mc Kay (1931) provide that content. Many readers will find a remarkable similarity of the basic human elements of these cases with contemporary examples.

Is baseball exciting enough? It is when you can fix the game according to Case # 2:

> "We didn't play baseball on the square, for we always had an umpire who could really cheat for us, so we would win all our games. If he would cheat for the other team he sure would get a licking...if he ever showed up again he sure would be caressing a sore jaw and head" (Shaw and Mc Kay, 1931: p. 121).

This excitement also took racist forms:

> "All the kids hated a negro and if any made an attempt to touch us we sure would give them a fight. They use to bar us from swimming at the lake and would steal and burn our clothes up. So if they came in our neighborhood, we sure would mess up them tar

babies. They sure would get slaughtered" (Shaw and Mc Kay, 1931: p. 122).

Another common scenario in the "thrill and excitement" content of gang life was when the group agreed that an income-producing crime had to be committed, and they would all agree that a designated offender to pull off the job would be chosen fairly, by chance, such as the following account in Case # 3:

> "I remember...one afternoon where we needed something to smoke but didn't have any money to buy smoking tobacco with, so the oldest of the crowd suggested shaking dice. The loser had to grab the purse of the next woman who passed along the street. The loser happened to be the bully. Well, just then an old lady came by with one of those old-fashioned purses and the bully walked over and grabbed her purse" (Shaw and Mc Kay, 1931: p. 124).

Parental complicity in delinquency takes many forms, from covertly endorsing delinquent stealing "oh, mom, look I found this new television in the alley...and I've got it working" and it continues to work and be enjoyed by the family, to obvious direction and overt manipulation and encouragement of law violation behavior. Similarly, adults who are upstream beneficiaries[16] of ill gotten gains is a factor also demonstrated in Shaw and Mc Kay's case study # 4:

> "You can just about judge for yourself how the adults in the naborhood thought about delinquency. The way they looked at it was 'let him steal if he wishes to, so long as its not from me, but for me'....It seemed to me that many of the people encouraged young boys to crime by buying stolen articles...They never asked any questions. They didn't care how, what, or when the goods were gotten, just so they were able to buy them. Some of the money would go for the mothers and fathers of these children, so nine times out of ten they will encourage the child's mind to work for easy money" (Shaw and Mc Kay, 1931: p. 125).

Case # 5 in Shaw and Mc Kay (1931: 128-132) provided much discussion, then, of adults in the "fence" role and how their existence in a neighborhood also contributes to the ongoing thefts by gang members. The existence of such adults willing to buy stolen property in a neighborhood gives it an illicit infrastructure and subeconomy that economically sustains gang organization. Just as "fences" would send out the word to gang members that a certain item was "needed" to facilitate crime on a custom order basis (e.g., "I'm in the market for new caddy tires with spoke rims"), so too apparently can this occur in the family. As case # 6 shows sometimes theft proceeds were directly profiting the parents and it became a family affair:

> "After a year of breaking into box cars and stealing from stores my stepmother realized that she could send me to the market to steal vegetables for her. My stealing had proved to be very profitable for her...I knew it was for my own good to do what she wanted me to do...anyway, I didn't mind stealing, because William (stepbrother) always went with me, and that made me feel proud of myself, and

it gave me a chance to get away from home" (Shaw and Mc Kay, 1931: p. 133).

Case # 7 in Shaw and Mc Kay shows the scenario where an unrelated adult cultivates a band of youths in a quid pro quo arrangement, where he provides them with adult legitimacy and resources, and they provide him with custom-ordered stolen property.   It can involve a creative mix of what on the surface appears to be legitimate employment, but which is substantially supplemented through illicit activities of the young gang members. As a social formation, we must ask ourselves, does this still exist today in some variation:

> "Across the alley was Mr. Smith's shanty, where he kept his coal
> and did his business...our gang, use to help Mr. Smith make his
> deliveries. He would sell coal by the bag at 35 cents a bag.
> Whenever another coal man was making his deliveries and left his
> wagon load of coal sit in the alley or street, a couple of us kids
> would steal the wagon load of coal and take it down to Smith's
> shanty and unload the wagon of coal...Smith had a junk yard, too,
> and he bought junk and sold it. He had a big bunch of us kids that
> stole all the kinds of junk for him in the neighborhood and in other
> neighborhoods....Smith let us have our clubhouse in his barn as pay
> for stealing for him" (Shaw and Mc Kay, 1931: pp. 134-135).

In a large family, sometimes the small gang formation took the variation of involving the boy siblings as the nucleus and with several other youths from the neighborhood. In Case # 8 Shaw and Mc Kay describe this kind of situation. It involves the older brothers being involved in more serious crimes (burglary, etc) and the younger brothers being involved in routine theft. Importantly, it means the tutelage down the birth order from one sibling to the next in law violation.

Part III of the Shaw and Mc Kay (1931, pp. 189-257) monograph addresses "The Companionship Factor in Juvenile Delinquency" and is the more direct contribution to understanding gangs. It includes chapters 6, 7 and 8, each of which will be examined here.

Chapter 6 in Shaw and Mc Kay (1931) addresses "Male Delinquency as Group Behavior" (pp. 191-199). While most youths form social groups, often spontaneously, and which "constitute a primary group relationship" they "differ widely in regard to cultural traditions, moral standards, and social activities" (p. 191.). That is, "in certain areas of the city the practices and social values of many of these groups are chiefly of a delinquent character" (p. 191). And clearly, at a higher stage of gang formation the group can become a kind of social institution "some of these groups are highly organized and become so powerful in their hold on members that the delinquent traditions and patterns of behavior persist and tend to dominate the social life throughout the area" (p. 192).

The primary concept developed in Chapter 6 is that much delinquency is, in fact, group behavior. Data on 1,886 juveniles was used to determine this, by going back and determining if other juveniles were involved in the offenses. For all such offenses, Shaw and Mc Kay found that 81.8 percent involved a group of offenders, mostly in groups of two (30.3%), three (27.7%), or four or more (23.8%) (Shaw and

Mc Kay, 1931: pp. 194-195). However, when the offense pattern was limited to include only offenses of stealing, then 89 percent of the cases involved this element of group behavior (p. 196). And finally, that:

> "It is obvious that not all such group delinquencies are committed by well-organized gangs. While many of the delinquents may be members of such gangs, they usually commit their offenses in the company of one or two other boys" (Shaw and Mc Kay, 1931: p. 199).

Many researchers have tried to emulate the life-span or developmental analysis presented by Shaw and Mc Kay in Chapter 7 of the 1931 monograph. It is time-series oriented to analyze one gang member, the case of Sidney Blotzman[17], and his involvement over the years 1913 to 1928, and an "active" offense pattern period within this time span including first offense at age 8 and last offense at age 20, and Sidney's complete known record of offenses, and the three different gangs he committed these offenses with over this period of time (pp. 200-201). Not unlike what can happen today, here the youth was a gang member, moved to another neighborhood, became a gang member there in a second gang, moved again and in that neighborhood became a member of a third, and different, gang (p. 201).

This delinquency career was punctuated with trips to jail and all the "child saving" agencies and institutions designed to redirect wayward youths. Sidney went through, successively, (1) a home for dependent children, (2) the police lock-up, (3) juvenile court and release to parent, (4) juvenile detention home, (5) the Chicago Parental School, (6) probation (supervision), (7) back to the Chicago Parental School, (8) escape from Chicago Parental School, (9) committed to the Chicago and Cook County School, escape from there, returned, and eventually paroled, (10) St. Charles, and then state prison for a twenty year stint.

Shaw and Mc Kay would discover in 1949 how serious this problem of recidivism and criminal relapse is. And there is no reason to believe that the pattern of "Monte-fiore...Audy Home...St. Charles...adult prison" has changed. Shaw and Mc Kay were keen to point out that the system changes little, what changes is the ethnic input to the criminal justice system. Such that today it probably reproduces mostly African-American and Latin adult offenders; or those groups, including poor whites, who are essentially, ala Gans, "trapped" in the inner city conditions of social disorganization.

Finally, chapter 8 addresses "The Activities and Traditions of Delinquent Groups" and includes 27 more case histories (pp. 222-257). It is here, perhaps, that some writers have felt that Sutherland's theory of differential association was influenced by Shaw and Mc Kay:

> "It is clear from the study of case histories that very frequently the boy's contact with the play group or gang marks the beginning of his career in delinquency. These groups, with their fund of delinquent tradition and knowledge, often become the chief source from which the boy gains familiarity with delinquent practices and acquires the techniques that are essential in delinquency. Many forms of delinquency require special skill and knowledge which are

usually acquired through contacts with older and more experienced delinquent companions" (Shaw and Mc Kay, 1931: pp. 222-223).

This chapter also demonstrates the formation of ties with other gang members inside correctional institutions and the continuity of their gang crimes after release (see Case 2, p. 227). In Chicago today, expensive gym shoes are frequent targets of gang strong-arm tactics. Consider, then, Shaw and Mc Kay's case # 4 that occurred back in the 1920's:

> "We did the same with them fancy gym shoes. Me and Sheenie bummed from school one day and went downtown, and we were both basket-ball players, and some of the other fellows had a pair of good gym shoes that cost $4 or $5 dollars; so Jack and myself decided to get ourselves some (e.g., steal them)" (Shaw and Mc Kay, 1931: p. 233).

Shaw and Mc Kay noted the gang's tendency not to pass up "crimes of opportunity" (p. 234). Again, perhaps all that has changed is the price of gym shoes and who needs to steal them.

The gang, according to Shaw and Mc Kay (1931), transmits criminal behavior "through the intimate personal contacts" and in this medium "the boys gain familiarity with the attitudes, standards, and code of the criminal group" (p. 240). Theirs is an upsidedown value system, at odds with conventional society. Stigma from courts and jail strengthens their commitment and status within the gang hierarchy (p. 241). For the gang member his behavior is normal, so that he has low levels of respect for the law, and "efforts to suppress his delinquent tendencies by formal methods...often give rise to attitudes of rebellion and hostility" (p. 242). The reason is that "like conventional social groups, the delinquent and criminal group demands conformity to its code and ideals on the part of its members" (p. 243). Gang members detest "snitches" and traitors to their in-group.

The gang member is viewed by Shaw and Mc Kay as normal and motivated by normal human factors:

> "Like the nondelinquent boy, he is apparently motivated by those common and universal desires for recognition, approbation and esteem of his fellows, for stimulation, thrill and excitement, for intimate companionship, and for security and protection" (Shaw and Mc Kay, 1931: p. 250).

It just so happens that in areas of conspicuous gang activity, these normal human desires are being fulfilled by the gang, not legitimate groups.

Finally, whatever their value in contributing to our understanding of gangs, we should point out also that Shaw and Mc Kay (1931) must take some of the blame (or credit, however you see such developments) for the fads in "group therapy", "guided group interaction", "confrontation group therapy", and the myriad of other such forceful invasions on the privacy of the confined involving mandatory group counseling techniques. Because it was Shaw and Mc Kay who felt there was a "great need for developing methods of group treatment in the field of delinquency, since it appears that delinquent behavior is in many cases a form of group activity" (p. 257).

SUMMARY AND CONCLUSION

Hopefully what this discussion has demonstrated is that Shaw and Mc Kay have probably not been adequately credited with contributing to the gang literature. Clearly, they had much to say about gang membership, gang crime patterns, motivational factors, the confinement-to-community gang linkage, and more. Apparently they said more than some have been willing to give credit for.

Gangs have always existed in America. It is important to understand previous research on gangs. Understanding the historical continuities about gangs also helps us to arrive at a more theoretically sound analysis of the gang problem. More importantly, a conceptual framework for "doing something about the gang problem" requires more than a casual grasp of the gang literature.

DISCUSSION QUESTIONS

(1) To what extent is the work of Shaw and Mc Kay compatible with the "multiple marginality" gang theory advanced by Vigil (1988)? Can this be synthesized in the hypothesis that the greater the social disorganization, generally the higher the marginality?

(2) Can Puffer's approach be reformulated to imply that gang affiliation is not only normal behavior, it may even be prosocial behavior within distressed communities? Or is Puffer's work a pre-scientific contribution to the gang literature? Is any biological determinism model of crime causation likely to be frought with controversy?

(3) Can Shaw and Mc Kay's analysis of gangs, and factors involved in gang crime (e.g., parental complicity), be just as appropriate today? Or useful as hypotheses for gang research? Can you give some examples?

FOOTNOTES

1. This theme of "exclusion", in multiple ways, would later be amplified by Vigil (1988); as an entirely independent intellectual contribution; because Vigil gives us no clue to his understanding of the literature summarized here from Shaw and McKay. Vigil's theory of gangs, called "multiple marginality", is discussed later in this book.

2. They must, we presume, operate at a more macro-analytical level as well; as for instance, in the differential patterns of human capital development nationally tending to correspond to ethnic and social class positions. If ever there was a need for strong policy statements from criminological research, then it is here: we need more educational investment. We need also to formally educate our prison populations.

3. The family seems to be expected to be everything to everyone; and, simultaneously, not be equipped with the resources to accomplish it; it cannot be deducted from taxes for those who can earn a living, and it cannot be supported from supplemental aid for those below the poverty line. The family is much discussed, and much maligned.

4. Vigil (1983) predicted that continuing Mexican immigration would feed barrio gangs.

5. See Sarbin, Theodore R. and Jeffrey E. Miller, 1970, "Demonism Revisited: The XYY Chromosomal Anomaly", Issues in Criminology (5)(2)(Sum): 195-207.

6. Redl (1945) would later suggest, well after Puffer, that such clique behavior may be due to a genetic factor, perhaps not unlike the XYY chromosomal anomaly (see Fritz Redl, 1965, "The Psychology of Gang Formation and the Treatment of Juvenile Delinquents", 1 Psychoan. Stud. Child. 367).

7. Puffer can in this context be considered a close friend of more conservative views in criminology; that is, the popular conservative doctrine often identified with the "burn out" hypothesis holds that an offender is never really rehabilitated, they simply burn out, usually in their 30's. (see Knox, 1980).

8. An interesting implication of the "status attainment" frustration approach has to do with the duration of the socialization period and when should youths take on adult responsibilities? My own research shows that many of our offenders behind bars had to take on, perhaps prematurely, such adult responsibilities as those pertaining to family roles and functions. The reader should be alerted then to not inferring that we should necessarily expedite transition to adult roles, but that this is an issue for further analysis. Should the socialization and nurturing period be shortened or lengthened? Should there be a mandatory "national service" for all youths as they approach adulthood? These are interesting questions.

9. Perhaps this comes from the prior work of Blanchard (1959) who in explaining gang rape noted the homosexual implications of boys sharing sex, or of the gang leader having a kind of brutal "constant fear" homosexual hold on gang followers.

10. But the one contribution that can be is that by Davis (1982, pp. 5,8) who offers the same conception of gang history shown by Gonzalez (1981) to be a fraudulent and scurrilous misconception advanced by law enforcement officials. Davis sees the rise of gangs in southern California (pp, 5,8) as having been importantly shaped and affected by the arriving waves of Mexican "aliens". The dissertation by Gonzalez provides a thorough analysis of the early 20th century history of California, especially in relationship to the "Zoot suits" and the rioting and racial violence directed against Mexicans.

11. See also Ort (1975, pp. 66,69). Or the notion that sociology "served primarily as a conduit through which European conservative social thought was introduced into the American academic milieu" (Nicholaus, 1973: p. 49). Or counter, that there was much ideological heterogeneity (Baker, Long, and Quensel, 1973; Baker, Ferrell, and

Quensel, 1975).   Mills (1943) contended that American sociology was rural, protestant, and pragmatic.

12. Now held in the Historical Archives section, Special Collections, Regenstein Library, University of Chicago. These have been described elsewhere (Baker, Long, and Quensel, 1973; 1975).

13. In an interview of Daniel Glaser (Carter, 1972), Glaser did say that when he arrived back at the University of Chicago in 1949 "there was an instructor in sociology at the University of Chicago named Joe Lohman, who was active in politics and close to Adlai Stevenson.   When Stevenson became Governor he made Joe chairman of the Parole and Pardon Board. Lloyd Ohlin, then a Chicago graduate student while employed as a sociologist-actuary at Joliet, became Lohman's Research Sociologist...and in 1950 they hired me to work at Pontiac, the youth prison, to revise the prediction tables there" (Carter, 1972: p. 24).

14. By the way, for the enthusiastic reader, Henry McKay is included in the Carey sample. When Mc Kay was asked about what persons had intellectually influenced him, he quoted: Park, Burgess, Farris, and Shaw.

15. See the Chicago Tribune, December 19, 1975.

16. Adults who knowingly benefit financially from acting such roles or functions as "fences", etc, for youthful gang members is itself another cross-national continuity in the study of gangs. See Patrick's (1973, pp. 28-29) discussion of the "punter" role, essentially an adult who collaborates with younger gang members, exploiting their risk-taking criminal behavior.   Also Taylor (1990, p. 102) describes how some "businesses covertly cater to gang types".

17. Who is given a complete case study in Shaw's 1931 "The Natural History of a Delinquent Career", University of Chicago Press.

CHAPTER 10

THE THRASHER CRIMINOLOGICAL RIDDLE:
What Was His Actual Research Methodology?

INTRODUCTION

An important social science issue that enjoys some salience is the matter of defining gangs in empirical research. For the historical record we have added this new information about Thrasher's gang research. It will help clarify an important issue. As a criminological classic, Frederic M. Thrasher's 1927 book entitled The Gang: A Study of 1,313 Gangs in Chicago, is certainly well known today. Many contemporary contributors to the specialized area of gang research recognize its enduring value. Even the critical extreme view, which discounts its relevance under the historical analysis which asserts "gangs are different today", recognizes the importance of how Thrasher's research had a large impact on the field. Still, all would agree that a major criminological riddle exists here: what was Thrasher's actual research methodology and could it be replicated today? This paper seeks to clarify this one aspect of American criminological history.

Few details have been previously reported about the methodology that Thrasher used[a]. This paper began out of an interest in replicating Thrasher, only to find that a much larger problem exists from a validity point of view (Knox, 1992). As the historical record is less than clear, some of the possible methods that Thrasher may have used are discussed in relationship to recently discovered historical materials. A large number of documents and sources of information on Thrasher were+ collected and examined and are discussed here. In a comparative sense it also vindicates Thrasher from the harshest contemporary criticism.

What seems, therefore, a simple question: How many gangs are there in Chicago; or the USA for that matter; is really much more complicated than it may appear and requires a much more complex social organizational analysis than has yet surfaced in our literature. Examining this issue helps to shed light on one of the many historical puzzles about American gangs.

The riddle is answered as best as historical records allow in terms of how Thrasher actually collected his data. We begin this historical analysis by examining Thrasher's "data". Then simple historical questions are analyzed in relationship to documents from the period. These questions focus on why, when, what and how the data was collected. We begin first, however, with a brief and somewhat more complete biographical sketch of Thrasher.

---

[a] James F. Short, Jr., who wrote the introduction for the latest edition, was also not aware of what exactly this Thrasher methodology entailed (personal letter).

THE LIFE AND TIMES OF FREDERIC MILTON THRASHER

Thrasher (1892-1962) was born in Shelbyville, Indiana, the son of Milton B. Thrasher and Eva Lacy Thrasher. He is most noted for writing The Gang: A Study of 1,313 Gangs in Chicago. In 1911 he worked as a newspaper reporter in Frankfort, Indiana where some of his family members still live today. He obtained his B.A. degree from DePauw University where he was also elected to Phi Beta Kappa. In 1917 he became an instructor in sociology at Ohio State University. He completed his M.A. degree from the Department of Sociology at the University of Chicago in 1918. It was his 1918 Master's thesis which represented his first known research involving gangs. The 1918 thesis dealt with the history of the Boy Scout movement. The Boy Scouts were viewed as offering the kind of socialization that could prevent young men from joining gangs. It was this early formative research on youths that would set the stage for his entire life specialty in sociology. He would later work extensively with a variety of organizations like the YMCA. This concentration on keeping kids out of trouble and especially out of gangs became a life long quest for Thrasher. Much of his theory and wisdom on gangs is still of value today even though America has a more violent gang problem and a problem that today is not necessarily limited to large urban areas.

In 1923 he became an assistant professor in sociology at Illinois Wesleyan University. His Ph.D. degree was awarded from the Department of Sociology at the University of Chicago in 1926. This period of 1923-1926 was also the period of time listed on what is known as the Thrasher gang map, a document that appeared in the first edition of his book only. It is an important historical document because it dates in print when the gang data was collected.

In 1923 Thrasher was the mover and shaker who established the Department of Sociology as a separate department at Illinois Wesleyan University. Prior to 1923, which was when Thrasher arrived, there existed only the Department of Economics and Sociology. Under Thrasher a separate department of sociology was established of which he was chair, which today is called the Department of Sociology and Anthropology.

By 1926 he was the chairman (Head) of the Department of Sociology at Illinois Wesleyan University. He had earlier in his career additional experience in teaching sociology courses at DePauw University, the University of Chicago, and Indiana University. Records at the university reveal that Dr. Thrasher taught what would be considered very heavy course schedules, teaching numerous courses on a variety of topics. In other respects this period of his life also prompts some to say he is a real enigma because important details are not readily accounted for with regard to social facts about Thrasher himself. An analysis of articles about Professor Thrasher in the Argus, the student newspaper at Illinois Wesleyan University, suggested to one source that perhaps Thrasher commuted to and from Chicago to the university located in Bloomington, IL. Regular train schedules during that time period could have allowed rather efficient travel to and from Chicago on a daily basis.

With a heavy teaching schedule, possibly travelling to and from Bloomington during the week, and doing his Ph.D. dissertation research on The Gang: A Study of 1,313 Gangs in Chicago how much time and when was he able to gather much information and geographically plot out the 1,313 gangs in the Chicagoland area[b]? Newspaper clips and book order advertisements during the period provide some of the only clues. Consider these early comments in a flyer describing "How Professor Thrasher Gathered His Data" written by Henry Justin Smith in Collier's Weekly:

> "Thrasher is a lively and ingenious fellow. A man who wore a solemn face or asked questions carelessly could never have "got in" with the wary Black Hands and Tomahawks, not to speak of the Night Riders or the Skeiks and Wailing Shebas. He would have been forced to run for his life in the North Side Jungles, the West Side Wilderness, and the South Side Bad Lands - the three empires of gangdom in Chicago.
>
> But Thrasher could sing songs; he could tell stories; he could even do 'magic tricks.' He was such an amusing and likeable fellow altogether that he was simply adopted into this tribe and that. Now he knows the rank and sobriquets of more than 1,300 gang leaders in Chicago alone, and has gathered not only data -- as they call it sociologically -- on the 50,000 or more gangsters in Chicago, but also facts of interest to other cities."

In 1927 he took the position of Assistant Professor at New York University in the field of Educational Sociology. He was involved in a number of different research projects dealing with delinquency prevention and other issues. He was the organizer of the American Friends of Turkey in 1930 and a past president of that organization. In 1931 he was promoted to Associate Professor of Education at New York University. In 1933 he was appointed the Chairman of the Council of Lower West Side Social Agencies in New York City.

Some of his other interests and activities during this time frame included being the director of the American White Cross Association on Drug Addiction, chairman of New York City's Action Committee for Delinquency Prevention, and president of the Metropolitan Motion Picture Council.[c]

In 1937 he was appointed to full professor at New York University. His contributions to the field of sociology after the Ph.D. were centered primarily in the specialty area of educational sociology. He was in fact one of the founding fathers of this special field of sociology today. By 1945 he served as an associate editor of the

---

[b] Thrasher's 1927 book was the only one to include this gang map. The map specifically indicates the 1923-1926 period for data collection and plots out all 1,313 gangs on the Chicago street grid. No subsequent edition of the book included this map.

[c] Anticipating some contemporaries, Thrasher felt the mass media needed more regulation because of its possible effect on juvenile behavior. See the recent interview of James F. Short, Jr. (Jensen, 1994) for a similar view that takes the mass media to task as a possible cause for gang emulation behavior.

Journal of Educational Sociology published by the Payne Educational Sociology Foundation in New York, NY.

Until the mid-1950s his classic enjoyed almost complete domination of the field of gang studies. His gang book went through several editions including one posthumous edition in 1963 edited by James F. Short, Jr. all by the University of Chicago Press. All the editions after the first in 1927 dropped the use of the "gang map" however. The gang map plotted the 1,313 gangs by dots on a street grid of the City of Chicago. It was historically important because the gang map contained the only data on geographical dispersion of two types of gangs (those with and without "club houses"). Many of those with club houses were also known as "Social Athletic Clubs".

On March 9, 1955 he submitted a plan for a new book on gangs to the University of Chicago Press. All copies of his classic had sold out by then and it appears the publisher wanted something fresh that would reflect the gang problem after World War II. His plan of attack for the new gang book, entitled "The Delinquent Gang in the American Community: Cause and Cure" was never to be realized however.

In 1956 he began teaching half-time in preparation for retirement. He had just achieved Professor Emeritus status in 1959 and began his retirement, when on February 5, 1959 he was in a accident as a passenger on a bus that was in a collision with a truck. He sustained a major head injury requiring hospitalization, from which he would never recuperate. On June 12, 1959 he was transferred to Bellevue Hospital for treatment and observation. On September 24, 1959 he was certified incompetent and transferred to the Central Islip State Hospital in Long Island. He died in March, 1962 at the age of 70. He is buried in the family cemetery in Frankfort, Indiana.

His estate was inherited by a 20-year-old adopted son in 1963. He had previously married and divorced after completing his Ph.D. degree.

Shortly after his death, the University of Chicago Press hired noted gang researcher and author James F. Short, Jr. to publish an abridged edition of his famous study of 1,313 gangs in Chicago. The abridged edition eliminated two chapters that were not important at the time, but which later emerged as being of enduring value: a chapter on "Wanderlust" (travel, migration), of potential value today with regard to gang migration issues, and a chapter on "Dime Novels, Crime Movies and Cinema", of enormous value from the viewpoint of how the mass media contributes to gang emulation behavior, the "copy-cat" phenomena, or as some call it the contagion effect as seen in the many gang movies that exist today.

Many of the social conditions which Thrasher analyzed in relationship to gangs remain salient today. These include the variation in the organizational sophistication of gangs, their involvement with politics or political corruption, their ethnic homogeneity, the role of racism or racial prejudice, gang warfare, gangs and organized crime --- these and other historical continuities were first analyzed in a detailed way by Thrasher. It is in this sense that while today there are important differences reflecting historical changes as well in the composition of gangs, their level of penetration into the criminal justice system, and the intensity of violence itself, some basic social phenomenon have remained the same even though the type and behavior of the social actors may have changed.

His other written works include numerous articles on delinquency published in the Journal of Educational Sociology from 1927 to 1949. But Thrasher's foremost legacy is contributing to our understanding of gangs. Unfortunately, if the Thrasher research cannot be replicated it is not research at all. How could be replicated? Well, first we must understand a lot more about what remains an enigma in our criminological history. It is the question of exactly how did Thrasher carry out and implement a research methodology, and what was it? We can begin to unravel this historical riddle by first examining Thrasher's data.

THE THRASHER DATA

Some current gang analysts assume that Thrasher was an autonomous actor whose definition of gang in his research was not defined by social control agencies, but rather reflected his own definition in close interpersonal contact with the gang:

> "Researchers from Thrasher to Keiser to Jankowski have done excellent studies with virtually no reliance on the police for defining their topic of inquiry --- gangs." (Sanders, 1994: pp. 178-179).

This is a historical interpretation of Thrasher's methodology, but it appears to be based on insufficient information. More specifically it might be an inference based on the ambiguity of Thrasher's methodology, because Thrasher did not provide many such details, thus one might assume --- perhaps incorrectly --- that because Thrasher did not say he relied very much on social control agencies like the police, that perhaps one could conclude to that same negative effect. We shall see in a later section on "how" Thrasher collected his data that recently discovered historical materials do in fact show Thrasher relied heavily on reports from police and social control groups (e.g., Chicago Crime Commission). Thus, to prevent future incorrect conclusions about the historical record of Thrasher's data, it useful here to briefly review what Thrasher's data consisted of.

Statistically, the original Thrasher (1927) work is less than complete[d]. The N = 1,313 gangs are never listed by name. In fact, there were only four data elements quantified by Thrasher: age range (1968: p. 60), race and nationality (p. 130), whether from a foreign nationality (p. 131), and number of members (p. 222) as seen in Table 10.

---

[d] The book by the University of Chicago Press released in 1927 is based on the Ph.D. sociology dissertation by Thrasher (1926).

TABLE 10

THRASHER'S DATA REPORTED IN RELATION TO THE N = 1,313 SAMPLE

Variable	N of Cases Reported	N of Cases Missing
Age range	1,213	100 (7.6%)
Race/nationality	880	443 (33.7%)
Foreign nationality	396	n/a[e] (n/a)
Number of members[f]	895	418 (31.8%)

Clearly, as seen in Table 10 the Thrasher gangs were not very well documented. Thrasher's strongest data is for the age range variable with only 7.6 percent of the cases missing. The race and nationality of a third of the gangs was not known and for 31.8 percent of the gangs the number of members was not known. This was the basis for the earlier questioning of the validity of Thrasher's information (Fletcher, 1964).

Actually, a fifth variable was available to Thrasher about these 1,313 gangs but it is never analyzed in relationship to other factors in either the dissertation (1926) or the book (1927). The fifth variable comes from the plotting of the 1,313 gangs on a grid map of the City of Chicago; with two types of gang markers: one symbol for gangs with clubrooms, and another symbol for gangs without clubrooms. A fourth of the 1,313 gangs had such clubrooms. Thrasher called these gang with clubrooms the conventionalized type of groups (Thrasher, 1968: p. 52). These were typically social athletic clubs.

WHY DID THRASHER WRITE A GANG BOOK FOR HIS DISSERTATION

The answer here seems simple enough, Thrasher's interests in youth socialization became his area of lifetime specialization in sociology. The fact is, the 1927 first edition of the gang book was actually Thrasher's 1926 Ph.D. dissertation in

---

[e] This was a dummy variable: whether the gangs represented a single foreign nationality group.

[f] Actually, some work prior to the 1927 publication was more specific that the book itself. Thrasher claimed in 1926 that these 1,313 gangs contained a total of 25,000 members (boys and men). See "Chicago's Gangs", Religion and Social Service, The Literary Digest for November 6, 1926 (pp. 28-29). A YMCA fund raising flyer for 1925 highlighting the 1,313 gangs identified by Thrasher indicated "1,313 different gangs enrolling 50,000 boys in the city have been studied".

sociology[g]. Another less known fact is that this was not Thrasher's first professional writing on the subject of gangs.

Thrasher's first formal writing on gangs was not the 1927 book based on the 1926 dissertation, but was rather his Master's thesis entitled "The Boy Scout Movement As a Socializing Agency" (1918)[h]. It is here that Thrasher first wrote about "wanderlust", which was again to appear in the gang book (1926, 1927) but which was dropped from the most recent abridged edition (1965). Thrasher also examined the "gang spirit" in his master's thesis.

This early coverage of the "gang" included such topics as the following:

> "The boy demands activity and excitement. If there is no chance to get it in a constructive way, he will take advantage of every opportunity the city offers, and there are many, to get it in ways that lead to disorganization. If he has no club, he will find a "gang" (Thrasher, 1918: 8-9).

> "A critical examination of original human nature....reveals certain tendencies...like gregariousness (the "gang spirit")....which may easily be socially useful or the contrary depending upon whether or not they are carefully directed" (Thrasher, 1918: 37).

In fact, a long section was devoted to "Scouting and the Gang Spirit" (Thrasher, 1918: 53-58). These and other materials have been analyzed here. While the 1918 master's thesis gives no clue as to his research methodology for The Gang, it does give the same conceptual blue print: the idea is that the gang is a corrupting influence on youths, and that adult supervised recreation such as that provided by professional socialization groups like the YMCA and Boy Scouts are to be preferred over allowing youths to entertain themselves.

Thus, in many ways the cognitive foundation for his famous book on gangs was actually established some time earlier in his 1918 master's thesis. There is continuity in the ideas presented in both works.

WHEN DID THRASHER COLLECT HIS DATA?

Many criminologists have suffered from only a casual reading of the classic by Thrasher (1927) and have assumed typically that Thrasher conducted seven years of fieldwork. This is apparently a false assumption.

---

[g] No copy of the original dissertation exists in the Department of Sociology at the University of Chicago, or at least that is what I was told when I tried to examine it. I was told one such copy did exist up until around the mid to late sixties, a student borrowed it and it was never returned.

[h] Department of Sociology, University of Chicago (August, 1918).

The social base map of gangs lists the location of nearly all 1,313 gangs[i]. It was a fold-out map provided in the dissertation, and an enlarged version was sold with the 1927 book by Thrasher. The dissertation itself gives few specific details on methodology. In fact, the original dissertation plan submitted by Thrasher and included in the Burgess files at the University of Chicago described this work as "The Gang: A Study of Collective Behavior". It had thirty chapters and five appendices. Other documents authored by Thrasher included a "Plan of the Investigation", "Sources of Data and Their Use" and "Specimen Questionnaires". But none of these documents which might have enlightened us as to the specific nature of Thrasher's research methodology have yet to surface in the literature[j]. The gang map created by Thrasher suggests the data was collected during the period 1923-1926.

A 1927 University of Chicago Press flyer promoting Thrasher's book stated "Professor Thrasher spent six years in his study of gangland -- the poverty belt which surrounds Chicago's loop district".

The gang map by Thrasher suggested three years of data collection (1923-1926).

A fund raising flyer used by the Y.M.C.A. of Chicago in seeking to raise money for the year 1925 quoted Thrasher as an endorsement: "The only way to overcome the present situation is to establish institutions like the Y.M.C.A. which will prevent their gang formation in many instances and in others, change them into clubs with the right leadership, having their sports and fun in a wholesome way". It also indicated Thrasher "spent two years investigating these gangs".

In a book endorsement by Smith (1927) included in the book order form (the book cost then was $3.10 postpaid), we get a different figure:

> "I take these facts - for facts they are - from the notebooks of my friend Frederic M. Thrasher....For a year he went out among groups, big and little, formed because boys flock together, hunting - - or being hunted -- in packs. A man who wore a solemn face or asked questions carelessly could never have "got in" with the wary

---

[i] The actual map itself appears from a Nov. 19, 1926 letter by the University of Chicago Press to be the work of the Local Community Area Research Committee: "Mr. Thrasher has confirmed my opinion that the Base Map which he has for his study of Chicago gangs was prepared by the Research Committee, and he has released us from royalty for any use of the Map without the gang material." Thus, Thrasher took this map (containing industrial, parks, railroad, and language group information and simply marked in symbols for the distribution of the 1,313 gangs.

[j] In 1993-94 the classic Thrasher, plus new materials discovered that were never included in the original 1927 edition, was supposed to be published as the book The Unabridged Thrasher, by George W. Knox. The publishing contract was with Vande Vere Publishing Company, Buchanan, MI. This book was to include all of the original Thrasher chapters, plus new information, and other material gathered about Thrasher. But the publisher dishonored the contract with the author. A new publisher is needed for this work.

Black Hands and Tomahawks, not to speak of the Night Riders or
the Sheiks and the Wailing Shebas....But Thrasher could sing songs;
he could tell stories; he could even do 'magic tricks.' He was such
an amusing and likeable fellow altogether that he was simply
adopted into this tribe and that. Now he knows the rank and
sobriquets of more than 1,300 gang leaders in Chicago alone, and
has gathered not only data --- as they call it sociologically --- on the
50,000 or more gangsters in Chicago, but also facts of interest to
other cities" (Smith, 1927).

Was it six years, three years, two years, or one year? Fortunately, additional
evidence exists having implications for answering this question. Clearly, the 1,313
gangs were identified on or before 1926 as indicated in the Gang Map (1923-1926),
so factually at best it was three years. In as much as the entire Ph.D. dissertation
was printed in 1926, it is more reasonable to assume that the field work or
codification of the gang data occurred sometime prior to this. The best estimate is
therefore in the range of one to two years.

In the fall of 1924, when Thrasher was teaching sociology at Illinois Wesleyan
University[k], the student newspaper carried a story (Argus Nov. 19, 1924, #3, p. 2)
explaining how Thrasher just completed his "survey" of Chicago gangs. If the gang
research began in 1923, then it was about one year until all 1,313 gangs were
identified, because the news story specifically used that figure and others. The 1,313
gangs had an estimated population of 50,000 members. Some 579 of the gangs met
in streets and alleys, 147 in vacant lots, 368 in club rooms or donated spaced, and 194
in pool rooms or shacks. Gangs in Illinois, Thrasher states in this newspaper story,
date back to 1810 "when a gang of murderous thieves operated throughout the state,
victimizing travellers...they had taverns and inns as their hang out and were
recognized murderers".

The first indication of the start of the gang study for data collection was 1923. By
November, 1924 a front page story in the Chicago Daily Tribune carried the feature
headline "Finds 1,313 'Gangs' In City: Crime Cradle, Says U. of C. Professor". Thus,
along with the detailed comments provided in the 1924 November issue of his own
school newspaper, two such extant sources show the data was in by 1924.

The use of magic would help in identifying 1,313 gangs through fieldwork alone ---
hanging out, participant observation, etc ---in that limited time frame.

WHAT WERE THE DATA SOURCES FOR THRASHER?

Here the historical record has helped us, although the book by Thrasher is certainly
less than complete on this issue. In a student newspaper interview where he taught
sociology (Illinois Wesleyan University) during the time of the gang research,

---

[k] I am grateful to David L. Laske, Ph.D., for assistance in collecting historical
records from this university. Officially, however, the most important records there
(e.g., his personnel file) are missing, or so we were told.

Thrasher did reveal some of details of what, specifically, were the data sources for his famous gang study[1].

According to the story (Argus, Nov. 19, 1924), "Mr. Thrasher obtained much of his information from the police and crime commissions...some was obtained from politicians, but in this instance, the men did not know for what use the information divulged was to be put." So, clearly it can be said that some systematic approach to data collection was evident in the Thrasher's methodology. But it also appears to have been a research methodology that used multiple sources, including actual gang members interviewed in juvenile correctional settings.

The same story goes on to state that Thrasher did some observation of youths 17 to 19 years old in their play and recreational settings. But he also apparently got much information from gang members who were interviewed in the context of juvenile corrections[m]. The part of data collection Thrasher enjoyed most was that part involving the interviewing "of the boys in the Chicago and Cook County School....some of those lads whose goodwill the researcher worker gained by entertaining them with mind reading and sleight of hand stunts, came to visit the college instructor when they had been released from the school...in many instances, the young professor was invited to parties, and played tennis with his young gang protegees...he stated that he became interested in this work after following the Boys Scouts movement for some years" (Argus, student newspaper of Illinois Wesleyan University, Nov. 19, 1924, #3, p. 2).

It seems reasonable to believe based on this historical information, therefore, that Thrasher began his research using a methodology that was designed in one sense to be the first guide to gang identification in Chicago. A kind of systematic cataloging using official sources like the police, agency reports, information obtained from political groups, and young offenders themselves. If Thrasher used a "worksheet" or note cards for each gang he ran across this way, and tried to collect as much information as he could on each gang, and included each and every gang anyone ever reported to him as ever having existed, then a simple alphabetical listing could easily account for the large "sample" (N = 1,313). The unit of analysis is, after all, the gang itself in this research methodology.

There is a potential for over-estimation of the number of such groups based on age-grading and multiple faction names. This is discussed in greater detail shortly, but

---

[1] I am grateful to Dr. Jim Sikora, chairman of the Department of Sociology, Illinois Wesleyan University for sharing transcribed copies of early news items in Argus, the school newspaper, pertaining to Thrasher.

[m] James F. Short, Jr. in a recent interview acknowledged that he first got interested in doing research on gangs because of encountering gang members in juvenile correctional facilities back in the 1950s. See "An Interview with James F. Short, Jr.", by Eric L. Jensen, Interview and Focus on History, Journal of Gang Research, Volume 2, Number 2. For subscription information about the Journal of Gang Research, contact the National Gang Crime Research Center, Chicago State University, 9501 S. King Drive, HWH 329, Chicago, IL 60628. (Tel. 312 955-2108).

basically it could mean double or triple counting what might amount to one gang. There is no evidence uncovered from this study, however, which indicates this potential criticism actually applies to Thrasher. It is an operational issue: would the "Sheiks" and the "Pee Wee Sheiks" be counted as two gangs or one? If the polish members were, as a clique within the "Sheiks", sometime referred to as the "Sheikowskis" would that be included as a third gang? Would the female auxiliary, perhaps the "Sheikettes", be a fourth gang? This is a potential problem, however, if anyone actually replicated Thrasher's today. Perhaps one important reason no one has yet to actually replicate Thrasher's study is that much remains a mystery about how, exactly, Thrasher actually collected his data.

HOW DID THRASHER COLLECT HIS DATA?

Thrasher was clearly prone to quote statistics and numbers provided by the Chicago Crime Commission and local groups such as the YMCA. The promised appendix on methodology by Thrasher never actually surfaced in print. We can only speculate, then, on how Thrasher collected his data.

HYPOTHESIS #1: Thrasher Used a Card Index File to Identify Gangs. Many documents cited by Thrasher are never specifically identified other than examples such as "see document 231, p. 231". It is fair to assume many of these came from the 26 different organizations or government agencies that Thrasher acknowledged as a source of reports, bulletins, and records (Thrasher, 1926: p. 544). We must be willing to assume that Thrasher took these reports and supplemented this data with some degree of actual field work. It is therefore reasonable to assume that Thrasher simply went on a quest to find as many gangs as he could from all sources and treated each source with equal validity.

In other words, Thrasher may have had 1,313 index cards about what he assumed were different gangs in Chicago. Some cards had ethnic identification, some did not; some had age estimates, some did not; some had membership estimates, some did not; some had age-ranges, some did not. This would explain the missing data situation faced by Thrasher's quantitative presentation. One thing he also had: the geographical location of the gang. He used either an address or a geographical coordinate in order to prepare the gang map.

HYPOTHESIS #2: Thrasher Used a Questionnaire/Census Form. Another possibility based more directly on the specific language of documents not widely known[n] is that Thrasher's methodology involved the approximation of a census. This could have involved a questionnaire form seeking basic data elements and eventually Thrasher ended up with N=1,313 of these, with previously mentioned amounts of missing data.

---

[n] One document examined here was what appeared to be a 1927 letter from Thrasher to Burgess along with a detailed program/research proposal for further research and intervention/experimentation on Chicago gangs. Never subsequently published or referenced in our literature, these materials make use of the methodological descriptors of both "census" and "survey" of gangs.

If we are willing to accept a certain historical reporting format as continuous prior to the time of Thrasher among Chicago agencies working with gangs, then this method becomes even more plausible as the manner in which Thrasher identified his 1,313 gangs.   Other information of import here was obtained from the Chicago Historical Society. For example, a reporting form used by the YMCA as recently as 1963[o] contained the same kind of statistical information used by Thrasher: age range, sex, ethnicity, location; and often included other information --- opposing gangs, agency/worker information dealing with the gang, when the gang was formed, its hang-out and area of operation.

The issue, then, is whether this 1963 YMCA format for gang data was based on Thrasher's 1927 work or Chicago school researchers working with these agencies at the time (Short and Strodtbeck, 1965), and thus the YMCA simply sought to emulate the gang tracking system of Thrasher or as recommended by Chicago school researchers; or whether the YMCA data format was in existence in substantially the same manner prior to and during the period 1923-1926 when Thrasher codified these 1,313 gangs.   One thing is not disputed by the historical record: Thrasher worked very closely with the Chicago YMCA and in fact endorsed their work in their fund raising initiatives; and generally saw them, like the Scouts, as a positive force for adolescent socialization.

Another agency reporting format would be ideally suited to such a secondary analysis using a kind of census questionnaire coding form and would provide additional gang names and identifiers because its program services targeted different groups in different areas of the city than the YMCA efforts.   Another agency reporting form used by the Welfare Council of Metropolitan Chicago in its Youth Services Division[p] shows, similarly, the name of the gang, age range, sex, ethnicity, hang-out location, area of operation, allied gangs, name or worker/agency contact.

If similar forms were in use by agencies during the 1923-1926 period, then all Thrasher would have had to do is take these regular reports, complete his own tracking/census form with their information, and perhaps on the basis of unique names or variations in the names --- and with some unknown amount of field work during a period of less than two years supplemented this agency and official information (e.g., from interviews with criminal justice officials) to generate the sample of N=1,313 gangs.

The issue of how Thrasher documented his 1,313 gangs is relevant to contemporary research and especially to the important historical issue of validity.   Our best evidence is that Thrasher spent some unknown about of time in the field "face to face" with gang members, maintained some type of data collection form on each gang, the "data" being collected in about a year from a variety of sources: but a

---

[o] Source, Chicago Historical Society; a report by Fred D. Hubbard, Director; Program for Detached Workers; March, 1963; funded by NIMH Grant 5R11 MH541-3 (1959-1963).

[p] Available: Chicago Historical Society, March 10, 1959 document from the Hard-to-Reach Youth Project.

secondary analysis of agency reports and interviews with officials appear to dominate as such sources; and finally, any "club" that was not a part of the YMCA or other "approved" social service/social control apparatus was considered a "conventionalized gang" --- constituting one-fourth of the Thrasher sample. And further, that all 1,313 gangs had been recognized as early as 1924.   Any subcultural group of three or more members might be mistaken for a gang if there are no rules of evidence in data collection. Some would regard the Black Panther Party as a "gang" of the 1960s and early 1970s[q]. Some would improperly regard the American Indian Movement (AIM) as a gang today[r]. These are both minority groups with essentially political purposes; and it is not surprising that some of their members have had contact with the criminal justice system subsequent to their politicization. However, these two groups are not themselves "criminal", nor even "deviant", but are only labelled as gangs by the criminal justice system which views any potentially disruptive group as a "gang". Criminologists as social scientists cannot allow journalists or social worker files to define "gang" if we are to ultimately have a valid and reliable national or even local analysis of gangs. A social service agency like the YMCA during the time of Thrasher (1923-1926) had a political-economic investment in labelling some groups as "gangs": in as much as these represented a growth market for the expansion of the legitimacy and service apparatus of the YMCA.   Criminologists or serious researchers cannot afford to have their research methodology compromised by allowing someone else to "define the situation". The issue is a large one for the sociology of knowledge and research ethics.

How then are criminologists to ultimately answer the simple question that many have assumed was adequately answered by Thrasher --- the estimation issue of "how many gangs and gang members are there" in a given city or jurisdiction? Collecting and codifying agency reports from government, news media reports, and social service agency reports (presumably a dominant source of Thrasher's data) represents only the first step. Collecting primary data on youths and young adults is the main and logically necessary step.

It may be necessary to collect multiple self-report samples (school population, out of school population, probation, parole, detention, jail, drug abuse treatment, etc) to adequately tap into the full subculture of any city or jurisdiction. Again, this is only a beginning step. It will then be necessary to codify the gang identifiers and actually go back to the population and determine how these groups are or are not related to each other. Ultimately, a social network analysis is going to be required to answer the question; and it would require an enormous research undertaking to provide a longitudinal assessment of some of the types of real gangs that exist in America

---

[q]   The typical law enforcement definition of gangs as any group that is threatening to the community allows a white-dominated police department to label the Black Panther Party as threatening, ergo, a "gang"; threatening not necessarily to the African-American community, but to the status quo.

[r]   To the extent that stigma and collective national guilt are also factors mediating the labelling process, we can anticipate that some may want to define groups like ACT UP as a gang.

today. While gangs are dynamic groups our research methods have to date been very static in nature.

Anyone who today thinks they can study a serious gang like the Aryan Brotherhood solely through the use of social worker files is truly delusional. Nor are most such groups readily accessed by qualitative researchers eager to "get into the field"; as their reports often reflect they made most of their contact with those most prone to respond to an educated adult (often of another racial/ethnic group): kids. Yet it is clear that the preferred analysis is one that includes all sources of information, very strong quantitative methodologies supplemented with qualitative data.

The alliances between gangs must also be taken into account. Within an institutional social control setting --- such as the public high school --- gangs with slight different names may actually function as one allied group. This gang aggregation phenomenon appears to function similarly in correctional settings where "folks" and "peoples" differentiate most of the gang population in Illinois corrections.

Some harder and more replicable research basis is needed to answer the question of "how many gangs and gang members" there are in any social context or geographical area (e.g., City of Chicago). It is certainly not sufficient to rely on reports from agencies of socialization (schools, churches, etc) nor from agencies of social control (e.g., police). For gangs, this may come only from social network analysis. It would be important to establish that a gang exists and functions as an autonomous group rather than just in name within a community. Several different variations of the "Vice Lord" gang can be obtained by simple semantic shifts in prefixes (Insane Vice Lords, Undertaker Vice Lords, Cicero Vice Lords, Conservative Vice Lords, etc[s]). If its members exist only in name --- say, hypothetically, the Cicero Insane Undertaker Vice Lords --- and function only as "Vice Lords", then gangs of similar variation cannot be counted as separate gangs. They may be instead conceived of as cliques, units, or factions of a larger gang organization.

On the other hand, if the gang functions both as an autonomous group in the community and in the institutional setting (e.g., high school) it may very well be possible to call it a separate gang; albeit a variant, chapter, or unit of a larger gang identification. But if it exists in the institutional setting by its proclamation or admitted membership, but does not exist as a group which functions specifically by that name in the larger outside community, then what we have is a gang chapter; not a separate gang.

The issue then is clear: if we include "gang chapter" as a distinct gang even if it does not function as an autonomous group by that specific identity outside of an institutional setting, then we may be in the situation of grossly overestimating the

---

[s] A more recent gang identification guide by the Chicago Police Department (1991, p. 125) recognizes ten factions of Vice Lords: (1) Conservative V.L., (2) Cicero Insane V.L., (3) Traveling V.L., (4) Unknown V.L., (5) Rockwell Garden V.L., (6) Renegade V.L., (7) Horner Home V.L., (8) Four Corner Hustlers, (9) Insane V.L., and (10) Undertaker Vice Lords.

number of different gangs existing in time and space[t]. Without documenting any form of systematic communication and cooperation between the Aryan Brotherhood that exists in California and that which exists in Texas, are we to then assume that these are two separate gangs? The logical tension confronts us: those who believe gangs are "loose knit" groups that do not function in interstate relationships must then be willing to grossly overestimate the number of gangs in any census of gang groups. The Aryan Brotherhood reported by one California prison would be counted as a separate gang from the AB's from one Texas prison. The same or roughly similar gang name in different settings or different jurisdictions would be assumed to be different distinct gang groups. In cities like Chicago where the official police estimate is that there are 42 different gangs[u], it may very well be easy to generate a listing well in excess of that by Thrasher if the same group name is found in separate jurisdictions or geographical areas. The potential multipliers would only be limited by the number of different analytical settings (schools, program service sites, police beats, community areas, neighborhoods, parks, prisons, jails, service caseloads, etc).

THE THRASHER MYSTIQUE

Beyond the simple mystery of how Thrasher collected his "data" there is a certain mystique to The Gang classic. A large part of this is the projected persona of one who dangerously enters the close-up intrigue of real gang life. Thrasher was not bounced from a bar like Whyte (1942), nor ripped off for his booze like Schweitzgebel (1965), nor shot like Jankowski (1991). At least nothing has surfaced in the official records to effect that Thrasher faced the threat of personal harm in his work, even though clearly the promotion of his book did claim such a related mystique about dealing with the underworld.

During the course of investigating Thrasher, tracing all names and figures and events, a surviving close friend of Thrasher was located. This was someone who moved to New York City about the time Thrasher did and also some who literally was his boyhood friend of several years younger. They grew up in the same home town. In a series of open-ended oral history interviews with this survivor, he revealed what I had probably wanted to relegate to unwritten history, because at the time I thought it to be totally unbelievable. But it, too, now that corroborating evidence exists, shall now become part and parcel of the Thrasher mystique. Because apparently Thrasher really did face some danger.

---

[t] During the 1923-1926 period it is unknown, because Thrasher did not report the list of gang names, how many of the 1,313 gangs in Chicago were really "unique and autonomous" functional groups; or how many were variations of a smaller such number. For example, Pee Wee Vice Lords and Anciano Vice Lords might simply count as two gangs the younger Vice Lord identification and the older Vice Lord identification.

[u] The author makes no evaluation here of the validity of Chicago police estimates of either how many gangs exist or how many gang members exist.

Thrasher's boyhood friend told me "he was run out of Chicago, that's why he went to New York". That is, basically Thrasher had made some kind of serious enemies in Chicago and that he was forced to leave town. The chronological life-event record for Thrasher does reflect that he was the chairman of the Department of Sociology that he himself founded at Illinois Wesleyan University when in 1927 he took a lower position (i.e., assistant professor) at New York University. One published story (Argus, Nov. 19, 1924, #3, p.2) quotes Thrasher in a kind of moral panic as follows:

> "The real significance of the survey is the baring of the alliance of gangs and politicians. The politicians protect them in their practices and in return, receive the support of the gangs. We have obtained enough stuff on politicians, which if published, would turn the whole government of Chicago upside down. We also have much discreditable information on state and national politicians. The whole city political situation is unspeakably corrupt --- it is impossible to exaggerate it."

It is easy to see how in the nationally covered newspaper coverage about Thrasher during the time frame of 1924-1927 that he may very well have earned the ire of some individuals.

SUMMARY AND CONCLUSION

It was not Thrasher's (1927) assertion that the $N = 1,313$ gangs he studied represented all existing in Chicago. Using the more restrictive definition of gang from Knox (1991) which does not include simple deviance or acting out behavior among streetcorner groups[v], it is not possible to ascertain how many of Thrasher's gangs were active in crime[w]. The issue is whether Thrasher can be replicated and in doing so how would it be possible to measure how many gangs exist in any city.

There are certain validity problems with self-reported deviance data from officials, students, and other such respondents. The Thrasher temptation would be to consider all sources equal in validity. The problem with this assumption is that it may be

---

[v] Indigenous organizations like Social Athletic Clubs, included as gangs in Thrasher's work, are therefore not considered genuine gangs in the Knox (1991) definition. Rather, such "conventionalized groups" as Thrasher called them, would be regarded as Level Zero groups whose social organizational formation and development pattern took them away from an ongoing involvement in or benefit from crime.

[w] Major sources of information and established ties in the historical record between Thrasher and the Chicago YMCA help explain why about a fourth of the 1,313 gangs probably were not gangs in the Knox (1991) definition; they were SAC's. These SAC's were in competition with the YMCA for leisure time legitimacy. Simply labelling these SAC's as "unwholesome influences" was not then nor is now a justification to be defined as a gang: it is patently ideological.

prone to overestimate the scope and extent of the gang problem as illustrated in the case of the single high school closely examined in the present research. It is simply a matter requiring much more definitional clarity. Students who are members of a gang but are not active while in the school setting can be counted as a separate gang that is represented in the school population. But this may not translate as equivalent to gangs presenting a problem in the school environment.

Are we to count "midget vice lords" and senior "vice lords" as two distinct gangs? Are we to count the same gang name with a unique prefix typically representing different geographical areas as separate gang (e.g., Cicero Vice Lords vs. Undertaker Vice Lords)? If we are willing to assume that a gang by the same name reported as active in any jurisdiction or facility is a separate gang because it may reflect a "unique chapter" or faction, then we must be willing to assume that literally thousands of gangs exist in the United States today[x]. And compound this by a rule of evidence clause that allows any reported gang from any social control agency as admissable into the sample.

There is a need to examine the relationship among and between gangs in any estimation of the gang problem. There is also a need for establishing whether such gang factions are in fact autonomous groups and organizations existing substantially apart from their gang "nation". So if there is one thing we can learn from Thrasher, it is that we need a systematic and empirical approach to gang assessment. We cannot treat all gangs alike. Some are clearly more of a genuine threat than others.

DISCUSSION QUESTIONS

(1) Is it possible to monitor and assess how many gangs there are in the United States?

(2) Which governmental entity should ideally be responsible for a nationwide intelligence assessment and threat analysis of all gangs that engage in crime?

(3) Is it important to look not just at how many gangs or factions of gangs exist, but is it important also to look at how much risk or threat a specific gang may represent? What factors would you include in a nationwide threat analysis system for gang assessment?

RECOMMENDED READING

Fletcher, Colin
    1964 "Value or Validity", A Review of Thrasher, New Society (21 May).

Jensen, Eric L
    1994 "An Interview With James F. Short, Jr.", The Gang Journal: An Interdisciplinary Research Quarterly, (in Press).

---

[x] The Geographical Guide to U.S. Gangs data file maintained by the author consists of 100 single-spaced pages of gang names reported from criminal justice officials in all states.

Knox, George W.; David Laske; and Edward D. Tromanhauser
    1992. Schools Under Siege. Dubuque, IA: Kendall-Hunt.

Landesco, John
    1932. "Crime and the Failure of Institutions in Chicago's Immigrant Areas",
    Journal of Criminal Law and Criminology (23): 238-248.

Rosenbaum, Dennis P. and Jane A. Grant
    1983. Gangs and Youth Problems in Evanston: Research Findings and
    Policy Options. Center for Urban Affairs and Policy Research, Northwest-
    ern University (July 22).

Sanders, William B
    1994 Gangbangs and Drive-bys: Grounded Culture and Juvenile Gang
    Violence. New York: Aldine De Gruyter.

Simandl, Robert J. and John K. Konior
    N.D. Guide for the Identification of Chicago Street Gangs. Chicago Police
    Department. LeRoy Martin, Superintendent of Police; Sherwood S.
    Williams, Deputy Chief, Special Functions Group; Sollie W. Vincent,
    Commander, Gang Crime Section. Prepared by Robert J. Simandl and John
    K. Konior, Gang Crime Specialist's, Gang Crimes Section.

Smith, Henry Justin
    1927 "How Professor Thrasher Gathered His Data", book endorsement,
    University of Chicago Press book order form. Quotations from Collier's
    Weekly.

Thrasher, Frederick Milton
    1918 The Boy Scout Movement As A Socializing Agency. M.A. Thesis,
    University of Chicago, Department of Sociology.

    1926 "The Gang as a Symptom of Community Disorganization", Journal of
    Applied Sociology (XI): 3-21.

    1926 The Gang: A Study of 1,313 Gangs in Chicago. Ph.D. Dissertation,
    University of Chicago, Department of Sociology.

    1926 "The Gang", Survey LVII: 71-75.

    1927 The Gang: A Study of 1,313 Gangs in Chicago. Chicago: University
    of Chicago Press.

    1928 "How to Study the Boys' Gang in the Open", Journal of Educational
    Sociology (I)(Jan): 244-254.

    1968 The Gang: A Study of 1,313 Gangs in Chicago. Abridged with a new
    Introduction by James F. Short, Jr. Chicago: University of Chicago Press.

CHAPTER 11

GANGS AS AN URBAN WAY OF LIFE

INTRODUCTION

If a correctional officer, or a law enforcement officer, or a probation/parole officer, or a school teacher --- someone who must deal with gangs and gang members in everyday life --- had to read some of our prior books about gangs and try to relate these concepts to their work, they would probably experience more than a little confusion or dismay in being able to do so. The scene of a police officer facing a march of 5,000 gang members protesting in Chicago's loop, or the scene of a correctional officer watching as a gang leader controls the entire inmate body, or the scene of 10,000 gang members and associates holding their own "Woodstock" style gang picnic on a farm just south of Chicago (these are all real scenes) --- one would be tempted to remark "Near-groups nothing, these are real groups alright, in fact too damn organized for my good". Those gang researchers who study less formidable gangs may find it easier to interview Spanky and Alfalfa types of kids, but they will not be able to understand more complex gang organizations such as those found in Chicago and elsewhere.

Part of this problem is "over simplifying". Some of our literature describes gangs as a cultural form that are wrongly labelled by an over-reacting public and the government both caught up in a moral panic. Some of our literature sees the urban gang member as the new urban guerilla or political messiah. Some of our literature sees the urban gang member as a quisling, that is an enemy within, someone whose very presence deteriorates the neighborhood. The biggest problem in understanding the truth about gangs is that it is not a subject that can be simplified, because it is a complex problem with equally complex explanations.

Clearly, the problem of gangs is not new[1]. Not to the United States. Not to other countries[2]. What we need to understand is the context and environment in which gangs do arise and persist.

It is a misconception to view gangs as being anything other than social organizations with varying degrees of formalization and complexity. They are more than simple social groups and they are less than bureaucracies. They can be much more destructive than they are now, and their association with killing, the use of firearms, and explosives or military weapons is not new. Every major newcoming ethnic group in America has had its role to play in gangs. The gang is an expected outgrowth of social institutional arrangements and grows as a new fabric to community infrastructure when these social institutions are inadequate to meet human needs.

While any society can theoretically generate gang formations, those with social orders of recurring inequality such as slavery and racism in the U.S., must take account of the historical character of social relations in any theory of gangs. Such societies have as much crime as they can manufacture and process through the criminal justice system, and the same applies to gang crime. Not much is truly new in gang life in America. Every ethnic group in America has had its gangs. The current gang crime crisis is one that reflects only the continuing lag between hope for a better life and its fulfillment for persons of color.

ORGANIZED GROUP AFFILIATION PATTERNS

The fact is that American society is a nation known for its multi-graded clubs, special interest groups, voluntary associations, membership associations, professional associations, and even secret societies. Gangs are but one variation on this natural tendency of organized group affiliation. America has always had gangs in one form or another and probably always will. It is also true that the failure to appreciate the organizational characteristics of gangs has to some extent been associated with reinforcing the strength of gang organization through ill conceived policies of the past.

Rival football teams from local high schools provide another historical context for competition and moderated conflict. But we must recall the Crips and Bloods arising in two separate high schools in Los Angeles and adopting their school colors as their gang colors to recall that group conflict is part and parcel of American society. One finding in this regard has the overwhelming statistical evidence to be regarded as a social law: the law of natural group opposition formation --- when one threatening group arises and makes a presence, another opposing group will shortly follow and exist in the same social context.

THE AMERICAN NIGHTMARE

American society has not yet necessarily seen the worst case scenario in terms of gang organization. We must gauge potential by the history of such related organizational forms. What the 1920's showed is that gangs can be involved in the assassination of political leaders, state's attorney's, they put out "hits" on police officers who obstruct their operations[3], etc; gangs can be the forces that both foment urban race riots as well as actors that escalate such violence. As organized forms of deviance, theoretically all such historical variations could appear.

If Rev. Jim Jones could sway several hundred followers to mass suicide, if cults can use drugs, hypnotism, sleep deprivation, "love bombs", and an ever increasing social grip on the individual to achieve nearly total compliance among its members, then could an educated, highly skilled, or very charismatic individual organize or assume leadership of a vast gang umbrella organization ---- citywide, statewide, nationwide, or even international? Organizationally, anything is possible.

The "bad news" of continuing patterns of inter-gang homicides throughout the United States is really the good news in terms of indicating that no such syndication or higher level gang organizational functioning yet exists; even though some gangs operate throughout many different states in America today. The fierce competition among and between gangs in fact has shown, in the past, that a next potential stage is that of monopoly formation. Clearly, the potential exists for such hybrid variations of the gang structure and function to emerge.

GANGS, GUNS AND KILLINGS ARE NOT NEW

Students of gang crime must be careful to avoid the direct comparison of contemporary gang organizational patterns with "play groups" and "street corner groups" described by Thrasher and Whyte. Most certainly, even during the period of Thrasher, America had an enormous problem with armed offenders --- including, of course, the use of fully automatic weapons and explosives in routine daily business. The reader should simply be cautioned that the first instinct in reading works like Thrasher and Whyte is that one is also cognizant of higher levels of gang organizational functioning and the natural tendency is therefore to assume that this is a problem of "old theory, and new gangs". One needs to examine the early historical periods, such as the 1920's, to discover that the best analogy is that between contemporary gangs and organized crime groups of an earlier era.

The analogy breaks down, of course, in terms of the factor of ongoing, conspicuous political corruption. Today that corruption pattern is likely to be much more concealed; in fact, it is likely to at least have the "plausible deniability" feature. We are, after all, dealing with other changes in society here as well; including the role of the mass media.

Regarding gang-related homicides and shootouts when comparing the 1920's period of Thrasher to present day conditions, this shows one thing that Shaw and Mc Kay predicted: the ethnic composition of gangs in America has changed.

FROM GANGS TO ORGANIZED CRIME

The prison of language is such that many who write about and carry out research on gangs, never use the adverb "gangster" in referring to one who is a functionally active gang member.[4] Clearly a "street corner play group" whose most serious impact on crime statistics involves a few burglaries over a period of several years is hard to equate as "organized crime". It therefore seems that the inadequacy of prior gang studies have been in terms of their inability to account for that circumstance in which the gang is effective and successful over time, such that it truly becomes an equivalent form of an organized crime group or cartel.

It is a matter of organizational development and maturation, and the gang must be at least conceived of as a point of origin for organized crime.[5] The gang is a manifestation of all social institutional fabrics of any given community in which it is found. In any community the social institutions include the family, employers and business (the economy), religion, schools (education), and the government, and some would have us add healthcare as a sixth social institution. But the inferior quality of life in many of America's communities means that in terms of power and being functionally viable, the gang is more dominant than all such social institutions and takes on, by neglect from without and by lack of developmental resources from within the community, its own localized status as a social institution in its own right.

Racism is the missing link between gangs and a transition to organized crime. White skin privilege allows organized crime to use illicit gains to enter traditionally legitimate business, and once inside the mainstream economy, to milk it and defraud it for everything it is worth. That is less of an option, regardless of how effective the gang is in developing a war chest (capitalization money for gang use or investment), among persons of color.

Many contributions to the gang literature are explicitly directed at whites, others have trouble analyzing the minority communities. Most certainly there is a notable exception to most gang theories and that is the matter of the historical patterns of racism in America. All things are not treated equal when it comes to race and gangs. Two variations exist: (1) Persons of color, notably African-Americans and Latinos, have experienced continued intergenerational disadvantages[6], and secondly (2) white gangs have historically tended to be more explicitly racist[7] in their function and purpose.

GANGS ARE VERY NORMAL, GROWING UP IN THE INNER CITY WITHOUT AN ARREST RECORD IS NOT

By most accounts in the gang literature, another empirical continuity has to do with the norms of the gang. Such social values internalized by the gang members as: loyalty, "follow the rules", personal sacrifice, etc, these are attributes actually in high demand by American employers and they are to be found in most active gang members. The gang ethic and the spirit of capitalism have much in common. Particularly, the aspect of rugged individualism.

But one aspect of crime tends to put the community-gang relationship in better context. It is the fact that members of minority groups face a disproportionate chance of being arrested in the first place when they live in a high crime inner city area. Gangs are normal in the sense that they rationally seek to attain power and respect. It is not "abnormal" to want a better life. The problem of gangs cannot be reduced to any simple psychological generalization, as gangs are fundamentally social in character.   For complex reasons, members of minority groups simply do face a higher chance of being arrested. The gang is the one place where an arrest or even a prison record is a "positive" resume item. When there are more African-American young adults under the correctional sanction than there are enrolled in higher education, we can see how larger processes within the American social structure also operate to limit the power of any community to "do something" about the gang problem.

BARRIO-OLOGY: THE STUDY OF THE BARRIO

A gang rights magazine called <u>Teen Angels</u> released its first issue in 1980. Few whites, and literally no Blacks, are included in the many, many photographs that the gangs send in (for a small fee) to have their group or individual message published in the magazine. It is clearly focused on the Hispanic market. As with all other gangs, a favorite type of photograph the gangs send to the magazine to be published is a small group holding guns or displaying gang hand signs. "Placas", are also common: drawings of gang symbols and a listing of the gang names.

Like the work by Moore (1978), a strong emphasis is placed on the role of the prison. Most the magazines include pictures sent in by prison inmates; and many names and addresses of inmates seeking pen pals. Another common type of material in the magazine are memorial "R.I.P." statements on recently killed members of the gang. A wealth of barrio "gang art" in these magazines could be analyzed in the fashion of Hutchison (1993).

The magazine reprints articles by the American Civil Liberties Union and strongly encourages its readers to join the ACLU. Erotic sketches of attractive partially clothed Latinas are to be found in most of the magazines. It is a magazine for Hispanic gangs, not anyone else. Of course, through the mail rival Black and white gangs could readily purchase a complete set of these magazines (some of the older back issues cost as much as $35.00 at this writing); as could, and presumably have, law enforcement agencies. A published photograph in this magazine where they are signifying the gang dress and signs could easily be used to establish gang membership for purposes of prosecution using recent laws that provide for stiffer sentences if the prosecutor can prove gang membership. Knowing this, will gang members continue to send in photographs of themselves in gang poses? A recent trend appears to be sending in just a photograph of the "arsenals": a long display of AK-47's, machine guns, sawed-off shotguns, etc, on display with no human faces, just the gang logo. Which, of course, may provide probable cause for such a gang facing an investigation by the ATF.

Clearly, the American economic market has found the gang to be a large consumer group; we may expect such magazines for other gangs as well. In many cities "air brush" clothing logo "SLANG WEAR" shops have sprung up: putting the gang logos and symbols on T-Shirts, pants, and other clothing items. Some gang paraphernalia is professionally produced abroad (e.g., Brothers[8] and Folks socks embroidered with their respective symbols), imported and sold in inner city sports stores. An enormous market exists in the sale of gang jewelry items. Gangs in Los Angeles and Chicago and perhaps elsewhere also have their own musical bands thus some of the organized gangs (e.g., Crips, Disciples) also sell their own gang records and tapes of music --- typically rap --- that portrays their own gang in a positive light.

THE PRISON SYSTEM AT THE MACRO-ANALYTIC   LEVEL

Does the prison system or the use of the criminal sanction have a natural "limit", or can a society have the capacity to truly punish everyone? And what are the trade-offs for such an over dependence on the use of such methods of formal social control? How do we as a society firmly instruct new groups and successive generations left behind in urban squalor residing in our inner cities that we "are about business"? Step out of line and they'll come and take you away. To prison. But the American prison was designed for the individual recalcitrant. Can it really function equally effectively with larger organized groups as its primary class of prisoners? The evidence suggests the gangs are winning in the prison system; that is, the gangs are becoming in some jurisdictions the de facto administrators of our nations prisons (see Lane, 1989).

GANGWEAR: Business Enterprises Adapt to the Gang Market

It is common today to find a variety of specialized "sports shops" which sell what amounts to gang clothing and gang attire. Some examples from the midwest include custom-designed socks with the gang symbol and initials of the gang. Jewelry stores have tapped into the enormous profitability of selling gold medallions and symbols used by gangs on necklaces, rings, and pendants. Custom "air brush" shops are now common to create uniquely designed slogans and multi-color symbols for gang T-shirts.

FRAME OF REFERENCE AND UNIT OF ANALYSIS IN GANG THEORY

The gang literature is quite fragmented in terms of the frame of reference and the unit of analysis. This problem for theory development deserves our attention here. Despite the existence of rich and highly detailed qualitative data collected on gangs since and including the time of Asbury and Thrasher, the more disciplined reader will search unproductively for an integrated and systematic analysis of gangs.

Figure 10 below gives a graphic depiction and overview of this problem for gang theory. Few contributions have been offered in the higher end (sectors 3,1 and 3,2) of the analytic spectrum encompassing causal forces or channels (micro vs. macro) and units of analysis (individual, community, society). Yet such an approach can help to clarify our thinking considerably and allows, hopefully, transcending the personal bias that appears to be present in reading the gang literature, over and over again.

This should not be construed as an attempt to reduce approaches to a specific area of relevance, but should rather force a consideration of what roles particular contributions have played in extending the social scientific analysis of gangs.

FIGURE 10

GANG STUDIES IN TERMS OF BOTH THEIR
LEVELS OF EXPLANATION AND
UNITS OF ANALYSIS

		Levels of Explanation in Theories	
		1. Microanalytic	2. Macroanalytic
UNIT			
of	1. Individual	(1,1) Almost all psychological theories, e.g., Yablonsky	(1,2) Social process and social exchange theories; e.g., Short and Strodtbeck
ANALYSIS			
	2. Community	(2,1) Social control theory, e.g., Thrasher	(2,2) Social disorganization theory, e.g., Shaw and Mc Kay
	3. Society	(3,1) Differential opportunity theory	(3,2) Underclass and surplus population theory.

As seen in Figure 10, virtually all psychological approaches would have as their level of analysis, the microanalytic level, and their unit of analysis as that of the individual. Such is Freudian psychology and behaviorism, and Yablonsky is appropriately classified here. Similarly, social process and social exchange theories derived from social-psychology may have a more macroanalytic level of analysis in terms of being generalizable beyond specific aspects of human behavior but are still focusing on individuals as the actors in this transaction and are therefore appropriately using the individual as the unit of analysis (that is, does the individual invoke a norm of reciprocity, is it quid pro quo for the individual, etc).

A somewhat larger unit of analysis than that of the individual actor is that of the community. As seen in Figure 10, Thrasher's emphasis on the breakdown of social control at the individual level, manifested in communities with gangs, puts Thrasher at an intermediate unit of analysis but at a microanalytic level of explanation. Compare this with Shaw and Mc Kay, whose work was macroanalytic in implying more universal processes that apply to all cities in America, albeit at the community level of analysis.

Finally, where society itself is the unit of analysis we find a much higher level of measurement. Such works as Cloward and Ohlin qualify here for the microanalytic level of analysis in terms of differential opportunity structure. Similarly, surplus population and underclass theory apply to a more macroanalytic explanation, also using society as the unit of analysis. We should probably be sufficiently convinced that because of the problem of inter-rater reliability in such global content analyzing, we are probably not going to generate much consensus with classifying all such previous gang research authors, and the present book has therefore made no attempt at such a classification.

This observation is offered only as a prelude to what is possible in theory and research on gangs. Obviously, there is a "middle range" between microanalytic and macroanalytic because these two terms are little more than heuristic devices. Already perhaps this position has confused more than it has enlightened, but the point bears repeating: we need to consider what the causal forces are in their explanation of human behavior (levels of explanation) and we need to then consider what impact these explanatory concepts have as they are measured (i.e., the unit of analysis: individual, community, organization, society, etc).

The reader who compares and closely follows various contributions to the gang literature will, it is believed, discover that our greatest gaps in the literature are not at the individual or community unit of analysis, but at the societal level for both micro and macroanalytic explanations.

WHYTE: A Critical View

William Whyte's <u>Street Corner Society</u> has been critically analyzed by Geis (1965). By his own account, Whyte was not highly experienced in dealing with lower class communities, he was rather a middle-class, ivy league graduate student who studied a community in Boston's north end via a Harvard University fellowship.[9] Louis Wirth at the University of Chicago would later criticize the merits of <u>Street Corner Society</u> as a Ph.D. dissertation. Whyte appears to be the Chicago school's version of Poston (1971).[10] On much closer reading Whyte is not simply atheoretical as was Poston, but worse may be anti-theoretical![11] And yet no one criticizes Whyte[12]? Why?

Whyte never quoted one piece of literature or social science in his book. Whyte smugly rejected all previous knowledge on the subject as "irrelevant". He obviously rejected even Chapter nine in Shaw and Mc Kay which described in detail where Whyte could have found delinquency subcultures. Chapter nine in Shaw and Mc Kay's 1942 version included an analysis of Boston. Whyte admits he was not sure for a long time what, exactly, he was studying or what he was doing in Boston other than collecting fellowship support from Harvard.

If a social scientist or applied criminologist is truly committed to developing knowledge in the field, then there is a moral obligation to not be deceitful, to not conceal, to test theory, even theories we may not personally favor.

If Louis Wirth, from whose famous essay comes the spirit of this present analysis, knew that Whyte had intentionally engaged in voting fraud in Boston's elections in order to "study gangs", then would he have been as gracious and accommodating as he was in agreeing to a compromise in allowing Whyte to obtain the Ph.D. from the University of Chicago? It's an interesting question. The informed reader cannot tell what Whyte's approach really was: was it as an economist, as a fiction writer, as a street psychologist? Or some of all three with the cloak of sociology?

The point at which a researcher must commit crime to study crime is a point of ethical no return.[13] Had Whyte committed this type of election crime in Illinois he might be subject to prosecution even today; because forgery has no statute of limitations in Illinois, prosecution can commence at any time --- the clock never "runs out". And for Whyte to sign ballots using names and signatures other than his own, just to have a window of opportunity to study the politics in relationship to the gang, amounts to just that ---- forgery. Moreover Whyte, by his own account of this self-reported deviance, would have no legitimate legal defense such as "compulsion" or acting under duress. He was simply naive, gullible, low on internal locus of control, and apparently as well unwilling to read works like that by Landesco (1929) documenting in elaborate detail the manner in which such political crimes could be researched. Stated alternatively, Whyte could have read Landesco (1929) and would have had a variety of ways to study the linkages between politics and gangs rather than being a political stooge himself. By reading Landesco he could have been alerted to the etiology of political crime in America. This is not an indictment of all participant observation research, field research, or ethnographic accounts in the study of gangs. Obviously, many such accounts exist which do not involve joining in the deviance, but rather involve joining in activities such as football, board games, and social conversation (Santamaria, et al, 1989; see also, Sanchez-Jankowski, 1991[14]).

This is not a repudiation of Whyte, nor is it an assertion that nothing he had to say was worthwhile. This has been a straightforward criticism along other dimensions. It is equally notable that one of the youths that Whyte worked with recently shared his story in the <u>Journal of Gang Research</u> in a regular feature called "Interview and Focus on History". In this story Angelo R. Orlandella credits Whyte with showing him how to deal with organizations in a prosocial way, because he went on to lead

a productive life including a military and government career.[15] This new information was developed through the recent interview of William F. Whyte by Joe
(1993).[16]

GANG STUDIES AS AN IDEOLOGICAL BATTLEGROUND: A Personal View

It shouldn't be, but life is not always fair; even to the social sciences. Is there so
much riding on the answer to "why we have gangs in the USA?" that author ideology
triumphs over scientific method itself? The present analysis has entered this fray
cognizant of the undercurrents of such ideological conflict. Let this analysis go on
record as being non-aligned to any such ideological camp.

Bookin-Weiner and Horowitz (1983) advanced the notion that seemed to say we
found less gang research because leftist scholars in a rightwing national political
climate did not want to study gangs. Recent contributions to our gang literature
should dispel that analysis. In fact, Bookin-Weiner and Horowitz should have noted
that the comparable problem of research on the Mafia gangs did not increase during
the period of fascism (see Hobsbawm, 1965: p. 44). It significantly decreased. So
one can technically argue, from a social-political rhetoric standpoint, either direction
of blame: the left wing, or the right wing.[17]

This, however, takes us no where analytically. Like anything else, the gang crime
problem certainly has its political and ideological issues. But just because a gang, as
we will see in Chapter 15, has a written constitution dedicated to working for
"oppressed peoples" should not, ipso facto, be any similar basis for assuming a new
urban insurrectionist mass movement is developing in America[18].

On the other hand, if there is one thing the present author has learned about gangs
it is this: never say gangs lack certain capabilities just because they have not yet been
documented in the literature. What is historically unique about gangs in America
today is that by taking advantage of technological advances in communications and
the ease of travel, some gangs in the United States today are in communication with
each other from shore to shore. Gang "summits" and national meetings sponsored
for the gangs under the guise of reducing their own violence have facilitated this new
national networking among and between gangs. We shall now face the future of
gangs in America with the certainty that more is being done to facilitate organizational development in gangs than is being done to prevent their growth and expansion.
If there was any place in the world to form a gang and enjoy a host of civil and
constitutional rights, then it is in the United States. Unless we are willing to allow
our constitutional rights to be systematically eroded, then without a substantial shift
in federal policy there may be little that can be done about the gang problem in
many communities.

GANGS AND THE QUEST FOR HUMAN SIGNIFICANCE

Between the two extreme conditions of absolute powerlessness and having an
inordinate amount of social power are the many gradations of human existence that
most of us probably call our own. As a way of affirmation of self it is normal to seek

out something larger and more significant than ones own self. For many this may be accomplished through religious institutions, for others perhaps the corporate world or politics, or even academia. Gang life is a natural mechanism for the fulfillment of this human need, particularly when avenues to more legitimate sources of fulfillment are either blocked or found wanting.

To belong, to be accepted, to be recognized and esteemed by like-minded persons, to have a sense however fragile that you are in some way important or needed --- you fit in --- this is what the gang offers. It is an offer that is apparently taken and accepted by those American youth who are subjected to intense forces of alienation. The result is their marginal connection to the established social order and its highly routinized manner of "getting ahead" in the world. Because whatever the tenuous tie the youth may have had to the legitimate social order prior to joining a gang, this subcultural integration tends to further erode legitimate ties.

GANGS AND SOCIAL INSTITUTIONS

Social institutions are relatively permanent forms of group affiliation that do not just persist over time, but which have legitimacy; and serve crucial functions of socialization and social control. That which externally erodes the effectiveness of a society's social institutions at the neighborhood level is, in no necessarily ranked order of negative impact, basically: poverty, prejudice, discrimination[19], political neglect, economic exploitation, and double standards. This includes the lack of needed national policies and the existence of those that are less needed or which may counterproductive at the macroanalytic level.

As an invisible societal wide process, then, the social institutional erosion becomes added to conditions of deprivation and human capital lag to present America with a sad twist on the Turner slave rebellion thesis --- because when gangs become predominantly persons of color, particularly African-Americans who are not new to America, but who have been subjected to the repeated onslaughts of prejudice and discrimination (something most youths do not need a university education to understand), with the effect of intergenerational poverty, then we truly have a new variation on gang crime in the United States. And a new variation in race relations as well.

For the law abiding and well adjusted reader it must simply be asked: conduct a self-inventory of your own social institutional experience. Did educational agencies or institutions at any time "work" for you? Did the church, Synagogue, Mosque or place of religious worship at any time work for you? Did the economic structure in terms of the transmission of wealth or the world of legitimate employment ever work for you --- do you have a work history or did you derive indirect benefits from it? Was your relationship to the government a generally positive one, Laissez faire, or a negative one? Was your family structure a viable and functional one, useful in learning mainstream social values or was it such that you hit the streets to feed yourself when you would wake up about noon and sought out nurturance elsewhere? Both the nature and quality of such institutional ties have much to say about the human condition.

If even a single social institution "worked" for you at a formative period in your life, then that may be much more than what we can expect from a great many members of our society for whom these institutional structures have never worked properly, or who have given up on them once they became gang affiliated. And when they do break down as viable and functional sources of social control and socialization, what you have is someone that no one can "reach" but the gang. Gang affiliation must be regarded not only as normal, but as expected under some of these conditions. It is normal because gang affiliation is but one possible result for those who do not "fit in" to their society. There has always been the options of self-destruction, the asylum ala Goffman, alcohol and drug dependence, and of course crime and the gang life. What should be of most concern to social scientists curious about what is "possible", is that the gang can become itself such an institution competing quite effectively with malfunctioning mainstream social institutions.

THE GANG AS A SOCIAL INSTITUTION

In a 1949 journal article, Henry Mc Kay showed that the gang was different than a play group and different from organized crime. The gang, because of its higher level of organizational formalization and persistence as a group formation, is actually an indigenous social institution (Mc Kay, 1949: p. 36).[20] Recent discussions by some authors of gangs being "institutionalized" in American society, are therefore, whether or not they read Mc Kay (1949) or acknowledged him, simply repeating what has already been specifically described in the gang literature.

Not all indigenous social institutions (as alternatives to the big five: family, education, economy, government, religion) are deviant or criminally inclined. Saul Alinksy proved such indigenous social institutions could take a political and self-help form. Mc Kay calls these "conventional" forms of indigenous social institutions because the thrust of the group activity is related to mainstream society and these could include: social athletic clubs, ethnic group organizations, and perhaps neighborhood block/watch clubs/committees. Visibility and continuity are the life blood of such indigenous social institutions.[21] The nonconventional or unconventional or deviant such indigenous social institutions include the gang, organized crime, perhaps even political extremist groups, or even cults.

What is more fragile about these indigenous social institutions is that they often disappear upon the two conditions of loss of leadership and loss of resources. The second, loss of resources, makes leadership succession or the emergence of new leadership unattractive if there is no worthwhile instrumental goal worth shooting for. Loss of leadership alone is not sufficient to neutralize an indigenous social institution, or dismember it. Hopefully we have realized at this point in history that simply sending a gang leader to prison is also not accomplishing true "loss of leadership".

In summary, that gangs are often "institutionalized" is not a new observation.[22] Mc Kay (1949) noted this long ago. The real question is one of social organization. More specifically, in what sense do gang organizations function to attract and promote gang membership? That is, by what organizational mechanisms is the gang able to persist over time and compete with the big five social institutions and even other indigenous social institutions? These are questions that must be answered by gang theory.

THE RELIGIOUS TRAPPINGS OF SOME GANGS: A Look at the Black P. Stones

Called "Brothers", the African-Americans who compose the Black P. Stone Nation, ride under the five point star (which they have now attached the letters A, L, L, A, H clockwise along the five points, as a symbol. As they operate today in Chicago, a new recruit truly does his "homework" and must literally completely and correctly memorize a number of different "prayers" and aspects of the gang constitution. The recruits are given materials to study, and are frequently quizzed on their rote memorization of the materials. The following materials come from someone who did not enjoy the rigid indoctrination methods and volunteered to cooperate with police. The "Stones" still exist, and are also called the Cold Soldier Army.

The Stones, riding under the five point star, are categorized as "People"; but over the last few years, the African-American gangs riding under the five point star call themselves "Brothers". So the major two factions are Brothers and Folks. Oddly, the largest "Folk" gang (BGD's) are to themselves known as the Brothers of the Struggle (B.O.S.). The language of gangs sometimes becomes confusing. The "Ye" language in the following document is socio-linguistically reminiscent of something out of the Bible, but is used in a context that actually denounces Christianity in favor of Islamic teachings:

BLACKSTONE FOUNDATION

"The Foundation of our Nation must not perish within the ignorance of self. For the love we have bonded has connected and linked, one to the other, with the greatest of strength. As knowledge be ye cup and wisdom be like that of water, ye shall walk those miles together. If ye fall lame ye shall be broken. If ye forsake our Bound ye shall be formed into dust. Peace and blessings are for the righteous who shall carry the message to the four corners of the world for all nations to see. Behold, Blackstone Foundation.

Allah is most great, there is no God but Allah, and Mohammed is his prophet, come to prayer, come to salvation, Allah is most great, there is no God but Allah."

Consider the following gang written document to see how the gang identity "Stones" is intermeshed with a mystical Black Stone[23]:

BLACK STONE CREED

"Out of the darkness into the light, Black Stone gave me courage. Black Stone give me sight, Black Stone give me something no man should be deprived of, a true and Divine Happiness called Stone love.

For many are called, but few are chosen, a head sees but only a few know that 9,000 miles due east across the waters likes a Black Stone which was placed there by the Holy Kaba. Many have tried to remove the Stone, but failed. For it is written that whom so ever falls upon the Stone will be broken. Whom so ever the stone falls upon shall be ground to dust. We hold to the bone, Almighty Black Stone.

ALL WELL
(Prayer for Feasting)

As Allah is my creator and I his image, I bless the fruits of the earth that I'm about to eat in knowledge and growth and of good health. Amen"

The "Cold Soldiers" army or nation appears in another highly secret oath of the Black P. Stones, as in the other internal documents above, the exact transcription is provided here and the present author suspects that some words were not correctly recalled by the informant:

COLD SOLDIER'S OATH

"My right hand to my father, God Allah and mister Emir, I hereby do declare to preserve the sacred doctrine of all Cold Soldiers silent brotherhood and keep the secret covenant of Cold Soldiers hidden from the non-believers. This I will do even to death. While I live the man and the Mecca remains safe, I will build upon and assure foundation stone and enforce law seven times both in and out. Those in relation in the sweet and honorable name of the Emmand the most high Allah, with my own hand will IL create, save, and destroy and woe unto the unbelievers. Allah speaks to man through man in a still small voice and those who hear will act as the soul dictates and the end shall always be right. But if ever I fail to perform my duties thus being a Cold Soldier or violating the universal laws of Allah and the Cold Soldiers Nation, thus at the risk of anothers life let my name be there after Judas peace and book of the dead. Let the finder of Dersvia point mental strength. Let the wrath of Allah's avenging angels strike 7 times upon the diaplate of heaven and my life span by the right hand of my brother man shortened."

The enormous social control of such religious and military language spells an enormous challenge to any urban area that contains such gang formations. In traditional "neutralization theory" in criminology, the offender minimizes the moral implications of the criminal behavior, or is able to rationalize the crime. Here we see such matters taken to a higher extreme, where the gang claims religious authority for its mission. Such ideologies are truly believed similar to the indoctrination of those who join or are recruited into cults.

A CRITIQUE OF GANG THEORY

What it is that constitutes the foundation for gang life in America seems to fundamentally revolve around three separate functions all of which must be present to some extent. First is the condition of social institutional erosion, either materially or functionally experienced as such, so that conventional social institutions are not effective sources of social control or socialization. Secondly, there is the function of either relative or absolute deprivation, either symbolic, or perceived; real or imagined; which is more specifically a test of what "hope" exists in traditional routes to success (e.g., through mainstream conventional social institutions). Thirdly, there is the more psychologically oriented state which functions as a human development or human capital lag or breakdown --- essentially a condition of underdeveloped or abused human capital, where society communicates loudly and clearly "there is no room for you in a productive capacity in America".

To the extent, therefore, that gang theory either fails to address these major and necessary components, such theory does not enjoy a firm foundation in the existing social science literature. It is very much a binary process whereby such incrementally adverse conditions virtually assure deviance or societal displacement. Those who are normal under these conditions probably gravitate towards gangs. One condition added to another compounds the problem of social adjustment. To restore even one of these conditions in conventional function, therefore, offers some hope of re-directing the lives of those who constitute the American gang population. Placing these youths in juvenile detention and state training schools serves no purpose other than to accelerate the binary process of dehumanization.

It is much as some may perceive it to be, a problem in the "value of human life" itself.

The initiation sequence to create and propel gang membership seems, from the existing literature, to require one or more of these three conditions. The higher the instability represented in these conditions, the higher the probability of gang crime. The existence of all three seems to assure a gang problem.

THE MILLER MISTAKE

Miller (1958) followed the psychological tradition of a microanalytic level of explanation for individual differences in "focal concerns of the lower class".[24] The logic offered was that Miller assumed a relationship between two macroanalytic concepts (e.g., culture and class) but used data from detached worker reports on gangs --- and some of his own participant observation and tape recordings (i.e., micro level data).[25] Miller (1958) assumed that if a household was "female-based", then it was lower class and associated with delinquency. In this fashion he estimated that about half of all the USA is "directly influenced by lower class culture" with about 15 percent being a hard core lower class group.

This is fascinating social commentary but what does it really say about the origin and persistence of gangs in America? What is the causal nexus for Miller (1958)? Is this really anything more than academic stereotyping using gang motivational compo-nents?

Was Miller blowing smoke or did he have something to say based on good research? His primary data consisted of "over eight thousand pages of direct observational data". Social worker files is more like it. And unless it was data specifically collected with the purpose of measuring the concepts Miller was researching, it is little more than an ex post facto content analysis without the methodological rigor implied by content analysis. Eight million pages of nothing will not lead to something. It was a research mistake. A mistake that is often pointed out to students in the manner "calling a person something does not make them that". If we are to believe Miller (1958), then cultural values or as Miller dubs them "focal concerns", are also by way of the causal chain in some sense "cultural imperatives". Overall what really was Miller's "motivational theory" of gangs?

First, it implied no structural problem for American society other than that of the lower class' own making. It was a convenient way to both label and stigmatize those who were poor and who were represented in gangs. The blame, if any, was the offenders. It had an aseptic analytical quality to the extent that it implied "you wouldn't be a gang member if you hadn't internalized those lower class values which have kept you out of the mainstream".

Secondly, it diverted attention from social policy initiatives. That is, little could be done to change "hillbilly cultural beliefs" of trouble, toughness, smartness, excitement, fate and autonomy. This thinking became a convenient way to avoid discussion of more systematic bases of the problem, e.g., at the macroanalytic level and the societal level which might call for some measure of social change. By which it is implied that the only blame is that on the individual hillbilly or Eurobilly for having such "lower class" motivations. It is a an individual "deficit" analysis.

If we were to extend Miller's (1958) analogy to the present, then our explanation of gangs would be little more than a variation of the "deficit" or "culturally deprived" thesis.[26] That is, the explanation of contemporary gangs ala Miller would be that the large numbers of African-Americans and Latinos represented in contemporary American gangs is explained by their version of being culturally disoriented or deprived. That is, they are hedonists, with an instinct for kicks, incapable of deferred gratification, who believe in luck rather than individual initiative. Or expressed somewhat differently, they "are not interested in what white people are interested in" or "they don't want to make it in America", which may be a convenient analysis for not doing anything about the problem other than locking them up.

The real danger here is twofold: (1) the Miller mistake deflects analysis from more critical aspects of our society wherein the option to change and re-allocate resources might imply a corresponding change in the gang problem,[27] and (2) it is a cultural or motivational variation of the demonism theme --- i.e., the tautology that "they are gang members because they are lower class persons motivated by lowerclass focal concerns".

Let us examine this mistake by Miller by using a slightly higher level of disciplined thinking. Let us analyze this in terms of an axiomatic theoretical model. Here would be such a version:

A ---+----> B   lower class people have lower class values
B----+----> C   lower class values are found in gangs

Therefore, by transitivity, the proposition that:

A---+---> C   that lower class people constitute the gang threat. An equally vicious logical fallacy could be constructed along more patently racist lines. It casts blame, it does not explain. It exploits elitist preconceptions, it does not offer genuine solutions. It is a mistake. A mistake social scientists should assiduously avoid to truly understand the gang problem in America.

"WE ARE NOT A GANG, WE ARE...."

Another universal phenomenon in the urban context about gangs is that eventually when they become the target of close criminal justice scrutiny, like the Moonie who denies he is a cult member, the gang denies it is a gang and claims to be something else entirely --- indeed, it makes a claim of being a positive force in society, a prosocial organization. In some cities, the gang name itself is used for the duality: Gangster Disciples say they are not a gang, they are a community organization about "Growth" and "Development". In some cities in the northeast and southeast, spokespersons come forward to tell the mass media that gangs like the Latin Kings are not really gangs at all --- they are cultural groups. Thus, raising a charge of racism against the police and others who may want to investigate them.

This is not a new situation in the field of criminology. Cults usually deny they are cults, they profess instead to be firm believers in their religious doctrines. Very firm, apparently. Similarly, when major organized crime figures face the mass media, they deny that a "mob" even exists. It is common for such major organized crime figures to say, typically on their way to being sentenced or in responding to an indictment, that "this garbage about a Cosa Nostra or a Mafia is all a hoax...we are only legitimate businessmen...we are being persecuted because we have Italian last names and belong to the same social athletic club".

Gangs must be expected to want to exploit any propaganda and misinformation they can put to effective use. Much of their propaganda centers around their recruitment myths: they are progressive even revolutionary organizations seeking some higher form of justice and greatness for all of humanity, then the kids join the gang to find out it was a crock! Similarly, gangs in prisons throughout the United States have used religious and ethnic group organizations as "covers" and "fronts" for their gang organizations. Jeff Fort's El Rukn gang organization claimed to be an Islamic sect of the Moorish American variety. It also happened to engage in murder and heroin trafficking, and eventually terrorism.

Gangs in places like Chicago make effective use of propaganda stunts like "litter clean up" campaigns. Maybe once in a lifetime they conspicuously do something genuinely positive, like help an elderly person across the street, and in their own minds this vastly outweighs the myriad of crimes and negative effects they have had on the community. Another common scenario is where they claim to be some contribution to law enforcement itself: they help identify or help to turn in some serial rapist, etc. Gang peace initiatives, commonly called "Gang Truces", represent another scam that gangs are prone to promote in order to claim bargaining power in restoring public order. Gang truces are discussed in greater detail later in this book. The idea is that they want to be included and recognized as a power broker in reducing gang violence. It is an issue not unrelated to that of negotiating with terrorists.

SUMMARY AND CONCLUSION

The above discussion has broken tradition somewhat by a criticism of two earlier examples of gang research (Whyte, 1943; and Miller, 1958). Only the historical record can show whether this was correct or incorrect. And the historical record is something we should be keenly concerned about. Indeed, this author believes it has been overly ignored or perhaps even misrepresented in some contemporary gang analyses. This is especially true regarding the tendency where Shaw and Mc Kay appear to have been some of the most influential and the least recognized contributors to this literature.

Any systematic and integrated theory of gangs must, as pointed out here, contain the elements for being tested by all three units of analysis: (1) the individual, (2) the community, and (3) the society. It should also speak to both the micro and macroanalytic concerns raised by social scientists.

A frequent first impression in reading the gang literature is that almost every author seems to begin with an expression of frustration to the effect that "unfortunately, we know nothing about gangs". Truly our literature is fragmented and does not answer all of our questions. But it does contain some historical truths as well.

The other problem is that some authors find it convenient to engage in a denunciation of all past scholarship, as if gangs had just landed in a spaceship. Such writers follow the mold of an Evangelical preacher who is the only one with the "true story", with the "word". Serious students of criminology should beware of such pretensions, because that is not social science, that is intuition and revelation.

Gangs today are so strong in some communities around the United States that they are the "power" to be reckoned with. Some level three gangs are intergenerational in nature: the children and the parents are members of the same gang. The homogenizing process that generates new potential gang recruits is the criminal justice system itself, by the propensity to use the criminal and penal sanction against minority group members and poor persons. The gang is the one place such "records" and deviant labels take on a reverse effect. Perhaps we should, in our communities, seek to resolve human conflicts by methods proven at the international level: dispute resolution, mediation, conflict management, etc. The alternative to peaceful means to resolve the underlying issues of the gang problem is a military style solution, and one of suppression. Do you want surveillance video cameras permanently installed on light and telephone poles on every street corner in your community, where the police monitor everything you do? Do you want --- as has been seriously discussed[28] --- sophisticated listening devices (applications of defense and munitions industry technology) also monitoring your entire community --- such technology exists that can identify the precise location of the sound of shots from firearms, and could help catch those persons shooting guns in gang dominated communities. Do you want police agencies to handle the gang threat the same way the federal government handled the David Koresh religious cult in Waco, Texas?

DISCUSSION QUESTIONS

(1) In a 1956 article entitled "Is Gang-Busting Wise?" by Shaw and Sorrentino[29], it is suggested that what this book calls level zero gang formations can be redirected into prosocial community activities. Every community probably has level zero gang types. Do you believe these groups can be prevented, through local adult involvement, from patterns of serious crime or delinquency?

(2) What limitations does the qualitative research method (oral history, field studies, etc) have in terms of unit of analysis in relationship to "levels of explanation" in terms of theory?

(3) What basic human needs would have to be satisfied in order to counteract the attractiveness of gang affiliation?

FOOTNOTES

1. Geis quotes the rather vicious account of a London gang circa 1712 known as the Mohocks who would today be regarded as a middle-upper class organized, continuing variation of "wilding" and far more brutally violent than anything surfacing in the contemporary media about such events (Geis, 1965: p. 6).

2. See Tompkins (1966) for citations by state in America, as well as citations of gang literature from localities such as Japan, Canada, Britain, Australia, Ceylon, Taiwan, and France (pp. 71-77).

3. This, too, appears to be a historical continuity in terms of gang crime threats. As recently as the Fall of 1993, a Disciples gang leader let it be known that he was putting out a hit on one or more police officers working on the southside. Other police officers did not immediately swell to their defense, because the officers so targeted or threatened with a "hit" had been accepting pay-offs from the same gang to facilitate the gang crime pattern (typically, drug sales operations). Once compromised, it is difficult for a police officer to enforce a "crack down" order; the gangs expect their protection regardless seems to be the historical trend.

4. Whyte, for example, uses extensively the verb form "ganging; not "gangbanging" as is popularized in layman's terminology today.

5. A later chapter addresses this issue in much greater detail.

6. So much so for women Latinos, in fact, that a recent census report showed their earnings declining; that is, while historically women in America have tended to make about 70 cents on each dollar that the American male makes, this figure had dropped considerably for Latino women.

7. And, of course, anti-semitic.

8. Today, in Chicago, members of what have been called "Peoples" gangs (Black P. Stones, Vice Lords, etc) now refer to themselves --- among African-Americans at least --- as "Brothers", not "peoples".

9. See appendix A of the 1981, third edition of Whyte (pp. 279-360).

10. The reader should note, for the record, that what you see is not always what you get. Hagedorn (p. 26) takes the position that apparently its not how you study gangs, but "when" that's important. Ergo, Whyte's study was the best book since Thrasher till Hagedorn, because its data dealt with the period of the depression. The serious reader should examine Rundquist and Sletto.

11. Hagedorn's criticism of Spergel, we recall, was that Spergel was a good example of theory misguiding research. A social scientist without a theory is like a soldier shooting blanks. Hypothesis testing cannot be done until there is a theory operationalized to guide data collection. The problem for many social scientists, those reviewed here included, is their dogmatic and male authoritarian bias puts them in the situation of denouncing all other theories than their own. That, at least, is their justification for testing only their own theories.

12. Geis (1965, p. 22) is one of the few to take notice of Whyte's admission of vote fraud. Geis also takes Whyte to task over the bar scene where Whyte, intent on meeting a girl as a data source over drinks, which if we are to extend Hagedorn's criticism of "courthouse criminologists" in this case means adding "cocktail criminologists", because when Whyte approached a threesome at a bar table a man promptly threatened to throw Whyte down the stairs, and needless to say Whyte immediately abandoned this particular research methodology.

13. Keiser (1979) reports some emotional distancing trouble in doing participant observation with Chicago's Vice Lords. "As a participant observer I was involved in the first stages of one actual gang fight, and was part of the preparations for another that never materialized" (Keiser, 1979: p. 88). Remember Patty Hearst? When she passively participated did that mean she was no longer a hostage, but a confederate in the crime? That's why she was convicted.

14. Some scholars obviously are more motivated than others to get the truth: Professor Martin Sanchez-Jankowski was shot in his efforts over ten years to study gangs in three states. The Sanchez-Jankowski (1991) study shows it is not always easy to carry out true participant observation research on serious gangs. Obviously, prior to Sanchez-Jankowski (1991) a variety of authors have shown us it is easy to collect data on playgroups or level zero gangs (e.g., Alfalfa and Spanky groups).

15. See Angelo R. Orlandella, "A More Effective Strategy for Dealing With Inner City Street Corner Gangs", Journal of Gang Research (in press).

16. See Karen A. Joe, 1993, "The Legacy of Street Corner Society and Gang Research in the 1990s: An Interview with William F. Whyte", The Gang Journal (now the Journal of Gang Research), Volume 1, Number 4, pp. 45-51.

17. Also, not to belabor the obvious, but to the extent that gangs were a problem in the 1970's (some say there was a "lull" in gang crime in the seventies), there were a number of gang studies --- and some current authors should be delighted to see many of these were qualitative affairs. And some of the authors published their results in critical criminology journals.

18. A gang crime unit officer in Chicago during September 1993 disclosed that he had heard rumors of gangs getting together nationally for the purpose of staging large scale "rioting" three years from now to influence national elections. I remarked, disbelievingly, "that is impressive that they could plan anything that far in advance".

19. Poor whites in Appalachia, etc, as well as those clustered on the fringe of or inside our nation's urban areas may not admit it as readily, but they too feel such prejudice and discrimination; not along the lines of race, but along the lines of social status and social worth. Indeed it is a social complexity all its own to find such persons derogated as "white trash" who themselves become the often frequent basis for actual conflict with African-Americans.

20. On the continuing theme of the importance of theory, this article by Mc Kay tends to clarify some of the problems now being rehashed in our literature regarding "what can be done" to help solve or prevent gang crimes. Mc Kay argued that even treatment must be based on a theory of crime causation (1949, p. 40).

21. The research findings on Chicago's Safe School Study reported by Tromanhauser (1981: p. 183) showed that at least half of all public school students reported some street gangs in their neighborhoods (56%) or some street gang members in their school (52.3%).

22. Hagedorn and Moore's discussion of such institutionalization (1988) uses language remarkably similar to Mc Kay's (1949), but this contribution by Mc Kay (1949) is never apparently acknowledged whether or not these authors were aware of its existence.

23. Another source provides this typed version reproduced exactly: "CORNER STONE. Man is the corner stone of all creations. Many are called but few are chosen. We are those chosen few symbolicly proclaiming our national birth rights of all creation to do so. We must measure within the bonds of moderation reason. We must practice to free our selves from one bondage matters. Man is god allah within himself. Allah is mind and mind made all creations. The corner stone represents all four branches of stone belief for the uplifting of peace and unity among all stones. In the east sites of the holy city of meca, in the holy city of mecca sites the holy kabba, in the upper left hand corner of the holy kabba sites the eternal black stone which we all represent for his everlighting our sunrise for it's the last giving love light to all peace 360 of knowledge and wisdom. (amen)."

24. Note, however, that the many continuing, lifetime, contributions well after and beyond this 1958 contribution by Miller make Miller a major and ongoing contributor, like Malcolm W. Klein, to the gang literature.

25. It is, at a minimum, a large problem of what researchers call the "rules of correspondence" between concepts and what is actually measured.

26. For an excellent critique of these "deficit-deficiency" stereotyped concepts, see Joseph L. White, 1984, The Psychology of Blacks: An Afro-American Perspective, Englewood Cliffs, New Jersey: Prentice-Hall, Inc.

27. I have always assumed that a social problem, like gangs in America, is a problem about which something can be done. That does not emerge from Miller (1958). What would Miller have us do to fight gang crime? Perhaps instill conservative values, I don't know.

28. See John Mintz, "Agencies Listen to New Crime-Fighting Idea: System Would Hear Gunfire and Inform Police", Chicago Sun-Times, p. 38, Oct. 1, 1993.

29. The little known research by Johnson (1949) showed some merit to such an approach. It is an approach that is also well-grounded in the literature: that not every waking moment of a gang member's life is spent in a ruthless pursuit of crime and wrong-doing. See also: Jereczek, 1962.

CHAPTER 12

AN ORGANIZATIONAL APPROACH TO GANG ANALYSIS

INTRODUCTION

A common fact about modern higher threat level gangs is that they mimic, imitate, or emulate sophisticated organizations by the very nature of their titles of authority and their authoritarian chain of command structure. Gangs like the Gangster Disciples (i.e., the Gangster Disciples, aka the Brothers of the Struggle, B.O.S.) use a corporate structure that includes the very top gang leader as the Chairman of the Board (also known affectionately as their "King"), and includes a large network of gang management staff, as depicted earlier in this book. Within the Latin or Hispanic "folks" gang conglomerates like the Spanish Gangster Disciples (SGD's), they have an Executive Committee, the top leader of which holds the business style title of "C.E.O."[1]. The SGD "Latin Folks" conglomerate currently includes a number of gangs such as the Two Sixers, the Imperial Gangsters, the Maniac Latin Disciples (M.L.D.'s), Ambrose, Latin Eagles, and others[2]. Gangs like the Insane Spanish Cobras include positions of national rank as well[3] and represent organizational interactions of gang leaders across state lines. In some gangs like the Imperial Gangsters the various chiefs of the "sets" or "factions" of the same gang act as major shareholders in the corporate crime decision making structure of the gang[4]. Gangs like the Maniac Latin Disciples (M.L.D.'s) include positions of authority that imitate government organizations[5]. Gangs have their own organizational language to define anyone as outsiders or non-members or as members of the opposition (e.g., "flakes"). Some early internal literature from the Crips emphasized their money making purpose in life, such as "power in this society is money, so the sword we must possess is money...we must adopt a business organization mentality". It is important, therefore, to examine the organizational factors about gangs.

The best evidence is that which comes from social science research. Anyone can hypothesize, or guess, at what causes a gang to form and what causes someone to join a gang. Anyone can conjecture about it and anyone can form an opinion. Opinions are like noses, everyone has one. But hard information, quantifiable information, data and findings from empirical research is probably going to enjoy greater merit. Particularly when the data collection has been guided by theory or the prior social science literature.

One such body of theory that needs to be applied to gang analysis is that of organizational theory and our knowledge of group affiliation and group dynamics. The value of such an approach will be developed here along with suggestions for research methodology and the application to present problems.

WHAT KNOWLEDGE DO WE WANT TO DEVELOP ABOUT GANGS?

What knowledge we want to develop will be importantly shaped by what our framework of analysis is and what data is collected. Clearly, there are different knowledge development needs regarding gang crime in America. Here are just a few of these different types of knowledge needs.

1. Law enforcement. From a law enforcement point of view a gang analysis is useful if it helps to triage in terms planning and response to gang problems. There is also the need for an analysis that can guide the use of criminal investigation strategies. More importantly, there is a need to prevent serious gang crimes like drive-by shootings.

2. Parent's and Child Development. From the point of view of the parent who learns that gangs exist in the community, the parent wants to know how to avoid having their child end up as a gang member. The parent wants to be able to know the "warning signs" of gang affiliation, so it can be confronted at an early point a child's development. Such would be gang prevention at the primary level.

3. Primary and Secondary Level Educator's. From the point of view of our primary and secondary level educational institutions, both public and private, it is a matter of "keeping the peace" --- at least during school hours and throughout the school term. Their mission to educate the youths of our society is threatened when gang violence or intimidation has a significant impact on the social climate of the educational institution. What the educator wants is better control strategies. Educators cannot revitalize the community infrastructure in which they work. Their only option is to employ better management techniques to deal with the gang problem. Perhaps much more could and should be done to also address, by prevention efforts, one of the most consistently significant background factors found among gang members --- the fact that the typical gang member has a significantly higher likelihood of having an experience where he or she assaulted a school teacher. Patterns of suspension and being expelled from school also are highly correlated with the gang member profile. Thus, a working agenda for schools would be to being to provide more prevention of events likely to label a student as violent and propel someone further into the criminal justice system, and also improve school safety by simply reducing assaults on teachers. This would in turn reduce suspensions and expulsions.

4. Community Organizations. From the viewpoint of local community organizations, they need to know what can be done to pacify and prevent the escalation of the gang problem. It is a damage control operation, the gangs may already be present, the problem is how to limit new recruits, encourage periphery members to attach themselves to more legitimate pursuits, while targeting core members and leaders for something else --- prosecution, reintegration, rehabilitation, etc. Taking the bang out of the gang would mean removing its economic incentives and preventing new recruits. Combined with pro-active law enforcement efforts this might give the community back to its citizens by taking power away from the gang. Where there exists a modest gang problem already, efforts to deal with it will be those at the secondary level of prevention and intervention. It is easier to prevent the problem than to rehabilitate those who manifest the problem.

5. Correctional Service/Treatment Programs. Whether it is in the public or private sector, as a not-for-profit organization that is citywide in its catchment area, or whether it is a service modality that becomes a part of regular "probation" or "post-release" aftercare services within a correctional agency, there is a different kind of knowledge need here. What is needed here is: how to prevent secondary deviation,

how to prevent relapse and recidivism in light of the more obvious threat posed by a return to gang crime, and the powerful resources that the gang can offer in both rewardive and coercive ways. This would constitute prevention and intervention at the tertiary level.

Add to this a host of basic questions from all avenues of life. From the business world, from academia, from architectural and community planners, etc. The point should be clear: depending on how the gang problem impacts on someone, such will tend to shape their specific knowledge needs. The homicide investigator is not going to want to know very much about the potential for rehabilitating gang offenders. Similarly, the public official charged with the responsibility to "do something about" the gang problem is not going to be particularly interested in social-anthropology dimensions of the rites, customs, and special language in the gang. That kind of material from participant observation may make interesting reading, but it is not likely to help an elected official develop a solution to the gang problem. We will need hard data for policy analysis and program development.

In fact, this is really an issue having to do with "solutions". Perhaps some scholars will take the position that there are no solutions to gang crime, just as it can be argued it is a problem about which something can clearly be done. For the gang crime victim, the solution desired more often than not is the use of the penal sanction: imprisonment. The issue is: "what is to be done" about the gang crime problem in America.

How we conceive of the gang problem is therefore going to determine what we can say about what should be done, if anything. Good research is a way to impact on or change social policy. One fear is that even if there was an unlimited research budget and the principal investigator was able to completely replicate all prior research, we would still be in the situation of having a great many unanswered questions.[6] It is a matter of being able to generalize findings beyond a specific sample or specific time period or situation. It is here that organizational theory has as much a role as research methodology to play in future knowledge development regarding the gang problem.

WHAT DO WE MEAN BY ORGANIZATIONAL   THEORY?

In the social sciences organizational theory is the study of a variety of organizational forms and processes. In business management, in sociology, in political science --- depending on what the discipline of orientation is, there are different aspects of organizational life that are examined. The advantage of organizational theory is that it has this interdisciplinary aspect: it is relevant to psychology, sociology, business administration, political science, and others.[7]

Organizational theory, no doubt about it, is often associated with the study of formal and complex organizations, and bureaucracy. The critic might say that trying to apply a social organizational theory to the gang problem is tantamount to overkill. Some might say, as well, that we need to study the gang in the social-psychological laboratory which has been the primary knowledge development approach for small group behavior. The problem is that gangs are more than small groups and less than bureaucracies.[8]   But is a mistake to believe gangs do not have some things in common with formal organizations and we should recognize from our organizational literature the gradients of formality and organizational development in groups.

Some of the larger gangs do have elaborate written codes as will be discussed later. They do issue written "memos" and "updates". Some have complex mechanisms, including the creation and operation of for-profit and not-for-profit corporations. White racist gangs even make use of computers.

So, here an effort will be made to demonstrate the value of such an organizational approach to the study of gangs. It shall set the basis for a method of gang analysis in terms of level of organizational development that is provided in Chapter 14.

THE VALUE OF RETIRED OR INACTIVE GANG MEMBERS AS DATA SOURCES

The value from an organizational approach is this: one of the best ways to study any organization is to interview its former members or employees. Indeed, from what we know about data contamination and measurement error from self-report methods with offenders, there is another justification as well. It is this: most law offenders under report their bad qualities, and over report their good qualities. Mostly, offenders are less likely to report their own deviance, and more likely to report on the deviance/crime of their confederates/associates/friends.

What we are recommending to be studied here is not the individual gang member, but the gang as a group, the gang as a social organizational unit.

OVERCOMING METHODOLOGICAL PITFALLS IN ETHNOMETHOD-OLOGY

The problem with Whyte, discussed in a previous chapter, is but one of the problems of ethnomethodology involving gangs and crime. Remember, that with some white gangs it can also be essentially the study of an extremist hate-group not dissimilar to the KKK or Nazi party. Any scholar who "hangs out" with a gang must at some time report, if the gang is really doing anything illicit or illegal, that the researcher is regarded with distrust. Not just as an outsider, but as someone who could be a government agent.

The marginality of the ethnomethodology research, the participant observer, is that if it truly involves a Ph.D. or graduate level researcher studying a deviant group, then the researcher is basically in the position of trying to get information as a "hanger on", not as truly a confederate in crime. Even Saul Alinsky's participant observation of the Chicago mob meant simply being a "groupee", not being privy to authority.

What must be challenged is the notion often made from an ethnomethodology viewpoint that the only way we can understand the gang problem is from such an "inside" story. For to understand the social organization in question one truly need not "join". The difference between Whyte's "joining" behavior, and that of traditional law enforcement infiltration techniques, is that the latter definitely can take on leadership roles and make use of experimental conditions to assess organizational functioning. Whyte did caution against such "controlling" influence. What we have here is also an enormous ethical problem for researchers.

One of the pitfalls is obviously ethical. A real sociologist is bound by the ethics of the American Sociological Association which explicitly forbids conduct such as Whyte's involvement in vote fraud. To "join" a gang or an extremist organization is to essentially be a part of the very problem which is being researched. To what extent would the confused, well-meaning, liberal researcher, by simply "hanging out" with the gang also become an important resource for them to exploit and manipulate? If gangs thrive on attention, then they will certainly prosper with the kind of sympathetic treatment they get from some authors.

While some may be reluctant to do it, it should not be viewed as objectionable for some authors to routinely invite what they portray to be "heavy hitting criminals" into their homes. But let's be honest here: there is an immense social distance between the social status of most Ph.D.'s and typical gang members or offenders. They are in different social worlds.

Indeed, while such risk-taking is often essential, and it was this willingness of the researcher to get away from the office and prison cell type of interview situation that led to some of our most important contributions to criminology (e.g., Sutherland's research).[9] Rather, the issue has to do with the quality and the nature of the data being gathered specifically on gangs as social groups and organizations, not individual offenders.

The problem is this, even for a researcher to become a "non-crime involved hanger-on", it must be recognized that the moment a researcher declares an affinity to group goals and values with the target organization/group, then the researcher necessarily accepts the definition of the situation offered by such respondents/cases/informants, etc. What gives us the assumption that gang members have such high levels of personal insight that they can explain "their own story" satisfactorily and objectively to be able to test theory? A sociologist today cannot ethically conceal his/her identity, disguise self to under represent educational attainment, or through a regression in vocabulary try to impart that deceit. Human subjects have rights. So do gang organizations.[10]

The other problem is that of group or intergang conflict. One cannot become identified with a particular gang and as easily make a transition to a rival gang group. To collaborate with one group may very well preclude the possibility of getting any cooperation from other groups. Here again the tendency in prior research to focus on the "individual" as a way to understand an essentially group and organizational problem does not lead to a logical accumulation of social science knowledge --- it gives us only a larger puzzle.

For example, Horowitz (1983, 1987) describes the importance of a sense of honor in the etiological sequence leading to gang violence. In some sense, personal autonomy, independence, or self-management equates as a cultural basis for honor. As Reid (1990: p. 84) correctly notes along this basis, then:

> "For a parent to supervise the gang member's behavior too closely
> would compromise his honor and development as a man. It also

might alienate him from the approved family and community activities in which he takes part" (Reid, 1990: p. 84).

What remains unclear is how does either the ethnomethodological researcher or a detached worker impact on or threaten this same variable? Is such a close involvement with individual gang members or their "top dogs" viewed as honor enhancing or honor threatening? On the basis of the gang classification system that will be presented in a later chapter, it would appear to me that at the lower level of gang formalization, such intrusion is status enhancing because it involves highly educated adults recognizing youths as a group power; but at the higher end of the gang development spectrum, such "hangers on" must clearly be regarded as a threat to honor, in the sense that to divulge too much information to such "hangers on" is to certainly place gang crime operations in potential jeopardy.

There is a problem when gang research that depends for its "evidence" as that of simple routine field reports from detached workers and social workers "hanging out" with gangs, such as that research methodology used by Miller (1958) and others. The difficulty is that even though such persons presumably remained on the "periphery", did not join in the deviance or crime, did not do drugs with the gang members they were studying, etc, there is still the complication of the interpersonal involvement arising from such a reporting source. Whether it is a university student doing an internship, being paid for the research/service, or as a hired hand using indigenous aids or ex-offenders, these persons are important new actors and if they are at all effective in making a surreptitious or open entry into the confidence of the gang members, then they still must face the criticism that the role structure they entered into will importantly color and shape whatever information they garnish or collect.

The research dilemma with participant observation and gangs is that you are damned if you do join in and you are damned if you don't. If you do join in their illicit activities like Whyte did, then you are producing the very deviance you are studying. If you don't join in, then you are not "privy" to the real "inside story".
Interviewing offenders is not the easiest task. In fact if someone does carry out a quality "oral history" interview, they are going to hear some shocking details of crime. And like the interrogator they cannot afford to provide editorial comment to the offender, or go off into a treatment modality providing "counseling". As much as you might like to or want to do so, particularly when an offender is describing in bloody detail his accomplishments at "tree jumping" (i.e., rape) or victimizing senior citizens, to do so is to cut off further disclosures. So in light of this, we must evaluate data sources from such detached workers and similarly employed data collection persons to the effect that if they were in the business of informal counseling and covert therapy, then what they heard is probably not the real story. The moment you attack or question the morality of a gang member, that is the moment the relationship changes and what gets disclosed to the "observer" is probably self-fulfilling ---- they hear what the gang member thinks they want to hear.

In summary, it may be less problematic for solid research to focus not on the individual offender, but on the group; and this can be accomplished, as indicated above, by alternatives to traditional "participant observation" or related ethnomethodology approaches. Indeed, perhaps these approaches if they are to prove their worth should be applied in the analytic context suggested here: for the group or gang organization as the unit of analysis, not the individual member. As an example, the case study approach used by Shaw and McKay did not simply mean a "depth interview" with the offender in question, it also meant using all other outside information --- interviews with family, neighbors, significant others, and of course, official information from secondary data sources (police records, school records, public records, etc).

ELEMENTS OF AN ORGANIZATIONAL ANALYSIS

The value of specifying the elements of an organizational analysis is to provide the agenda for future research in terms of measurable variables; factors that can be used for gang analysis and classification. One of these primary factors that distinguishes a formalized gang from that of an informal group is the existence of a formalized written or oral code. But, as we shall see later, there are many other such social organizational factors to consider. A fuller accounting of the elements of an organizational analysis will be provided in a later chapter. For now it is important to simply introduce some of these elements such as the formalized "code".

The value of specifying these measurable elements of organizational analysis was previously demonstrated by the research of Arnold (1965). Arnold was one of the few gang researchers to take earlier definitions of the gang such as those by Thrasher and to quantify these factors in order to generate a rating system for gangs. Indeed, Arnold's research is one of the few to actually measure gang membership size and to recognize some of the commonalities and differences between gangs and other forms of group affiliation.[11]

THE FORMALIZED WRITTEN OR ORAL CODE

With the publication in 1847 by J.H. Green of The Secret Band of Brothers or, The American Outlaws[12] comes the first reference to gang formations in America having a written Constitution and by-laws dating back to 1798 (Green, 1847: p. 90). It reads like a precursor to a mixture between the Aryan Brotherhood and the Ku Klux Klan. It specifies the authority differentiation between members and officers, the latter known as Grand Masters. It explicitly allowed for male or females (pp. 90-91). It had religious undercurrents, but was clearly against organized religion, speaking often of the "God of Nature". In so doing, it represented an early form of the "quasi-religious" or "religious front" gang formation such as Jeff Fort's El Rukns.

Like many contemporary urban variations it had a Robin Hood clause as well:

> "Article 13. We pledge ourselves to take from the rich and give to the poor....we agree to take from the one, and give to the other; and that the wealthy, or the enemies of this society, shall be the ones we will strive to harass, by disapprobation of their tyrannical course." (Green, 1847: p. 94).

The official name of this gang was the Holy Brotherhood also known as the Secret Band of Brothers. Its constitution and by-laws explicitly paralleled the contemporary Aryan Brotherhood gang norm of "kill to get in, die to get out" in its Article 22.

And, as will be discussed in a later chapter it had in common with more sophisticated gangs and organized crime the capability of "enforcement":

> "Article 22. Having now informed you of some of the benefits and duties falling upon you, as a Brother, I now come to an article of penalty, which you will find requires your close attention, as follows: If you betray a Brother, this Constitution allots to you but one punishment, which is ---DEATH BY VIOLENT MEANS!---and this sentence will surely be carried into effect---as sure as that there is a sun at noonday, or stars at night; and the Brother, so terminating your career, shall receive, in compensation, the sum of THREE HUNDRED DOLLARS, which shall be paid to him by a Grand Master, for this society" (Green, 1847: p. 100).

Like many contemporary gangs, language itself had explicit double meanings in terms of a cipher code.[13] The gang described by Green used a numbering code as well, with values between zero and nine. For example, the word "naugh" associated with the digit "9" meant an African-American:

> "Third: Naugh --- a flash word, signifies Size and Complexion --- and, therefore, each number has a double meaning. No. 1 signifies the person to be large and tall, 2 low and heavy, 3 tall and slender, 4 medium, 5 small, 6 sandy complexion, 7 light complexion, 8 dark complexion, 9 Coloured" (Green, 1847: p. 109).

For the record, these white gang offenders predated contemporary forms by using the word "crib" as slang or subcultural argot to refer to ones "house" (Green, 1847: p. 113).

If we can believe Green, then this group was either the first known gang with its own formalized constitution and by-laws or it was clearly an antecedent of organized crime in America. Either way it deserves our interest and tends to support the proposition that gangs are not only normal, they have always existed in one organizational form or another in America. It also shows the enduring historical commonality among gangs that they adopt special symbols and use a linguistic code that allows them --- like the 19th century Budhuk gangs in India --- to maintain the duplicity of gang affiliation when interacting with or in the presence of non-gang members: they can literally carry on a conversation using gang argot (e.g., slang) that a non-gang member would not normally be able to truly understand.

As the study of African-American psychology, and other cultures as well, has shown, this can also consist of an oral tradition. If it formalizes roles or language or sanctions for the violation of group norms, then whether it is a written or oral code it still qualifies as a formalization of gang structure. Its existence means the difference between a gang organization and that of simple recurrent aggregative social encounters (e.g., meeting persons you know by face on an ongoing basis, but with little normative consensus, for example at a bus stop on the way to work in the morning, etc).

CONSOLIDATION, ALLIANCES AND MERGERS

While many social scientists discount the work by Sale (1971) because it was clearly the work of a journalist, not a trained social scientist, such accounts are useful to the extent that we can assume they are factual. A gang as an organization if it is to survive over time must face the possibility of consolidation, alliances, and mergers. Sale's description of the etiology of Jeff Fort's gang career prior to the emergence of the El Rukns is illustrative. In describing the emergence of the Blackstone Rangers, Sale narrates that:

> "He told me then how, back in 1959, there had been a small street clique on 66th St. that had a modest ten members. Jeff Fort was the man at its head and it controlled a turf known as Jackson Park. But there had been a rival gang, small one as well...on 70th Street...the gangs clashed...They fought together many times. When they found that neither one could inflict a final, decisive defeat, they came together and talked. A short time later they combined" (Sale, 1971: pp. 63-64).

It is curious, in light of this general trend in the literature showing such varieties of conflict/alliance/new formations, that conflict theory itself has not been applied to the gang problem. Clearly, the existence of gangs that have undergone organizational development processes such as consolidation, the creation of alliances, and even mergers sets this type of gang apart from one that is in its incubational stage or its embryonic level of development. It is the role of the criminal justice system that plays an important part in the creation of such alliances, mergers, and even consolidation. Consolidation by sheer minority number strength may be a possible hypothesis for the emergence of the Aryan Nation white racist gangs in prison. Such a natural consolidation hypothesis must compete with the rival explanation of fostered development and informal cultivation from prison staff themselves, where the existence of such a white gang counterbalances the domination of minority group gangs in the correctional setting.

The bottom line here is that we do not know how exactly the Aryan Brotherhood emerged to be represented in so many different prisons throughout the United States and in many different communities outside of prison and no such news report like R.T. Sale has been able to "get the story". Nor has any sociologist, ethnographer, or activist reported such knowledge. The only explanation offered to date is that prison transfers of such gang members meant the reproduction of such gangs to all new environments to which the inmate gang members were shipped. From an organizational viewpoint, that might mean the need for a central national unit to which to ship such inmates rather than to other institutions that are not experiencing a gang problem.

In fact, we know really little about the "franchising" of gangs outside of limited data (Waldorf, 1993), some estimates on the problem of gang migration from police, and the one case reported in the present study of the franchising of the Latin Kings to the State of Indiana through Chicago's southside "bush" chapter of the Kings. It is the issue of whether gangs can be "exported" from one state to another. Klein takes the DEA and others to task for simply assuming such a direct exportation or "national conspiracy" kind of explanation, for example, of the existence of Crips and

Bloods in many different states (1990). It is an issue needing more research and less conjecture. Like other controversies in the gang arena, the truth is probably somewhere in between the extreme polar views (i.e., no gang migration occurs versus much gang migration occurs).

COMMUNITY AND SOCIAL STIGMA

Without stigma as a deviant group, the gang would not be a gang it would be a legitimate voluntary association in the pre-incorporation stage. The stigma arises, mostly, from fear of criminal victimization. Shireman, et al (1958)[14] described one such gang at its most embryonic level of organizational development called the "Clovers" who came to be regarded as a gang by the community and by the process of the self-fulfilling prophecy were, ipso facto, a gang in spite of their lack of formalization in other organizational qualities:

> "The group of Negro boys, who later became known as the "Clovers", range in age from 14 to 18. Most of them are new to the community, are of Southern background, and have lived elsewhere in Chicago before moving to Hyde Park. Although most of them live within a five block radius of the HPNC, ninety-five percent of them were not members of the agency and had no previous experience in the HPNC program. They attended the local elementary and high schools. Most of the youths would be classified as being from upper-lower class families, if we take into account the realistic and preferred values and economic status of the Hyde Park community. The boys did not identify themselves as being a group or gang, although they were identified in this manner by the adults of the community because they gathered frequently in front of the home of one of the youths, and often traveled together within the community. They were also accused, by the neighborhood people, of thefts, purse snatching, intimidations, assaults, unnecessary noise, insults and crowding sidewalks" (Shireman et al, 1958: p. iv).

Clearly, a hostile adult community towards youths appearing organized gave rise to an escalation of stigma. A group committing acts of deviance, public disorder, and crime is more severe than single individuals in such capacities. Shireman et al, who helped pioneer the detached worker approach to gang work in Chicago, demonstrated early this factor of community and social stigma associated with a particular group of such young persons.

That the media play a role in this is demonstrated by the account from Zatz (1987). It is an image, akin to the psychology of enmity (Keen, 1986), which portrays youths --- especially minority youths --- when in a group as being a priori evil. That is, "they are up to no good".

The analytical variation exists, of course, to operate outside of ones community of orientation in an illicit fashion or to function without a territorial boundary. In such cases, the gang assumes a higher level of organizational functioning by avoiding the stigma and potential recrimination from those in the most advantageous position to informally monitor their life style and thereby be sources of information for law enforcement efforts against them.   Clearly, some of the robber gangs of India reported by Sleeman (1849), to be discussed later, fit this profile.

A number of authors have cited this factor of the gang arising from an informal group given formality through their treatment from the social order.   Parents and community members, the media, criminal justice officials --- responding to an informal group as if it were more formalized may tend to add more cohesiveness and organizational capability to the gang through the expectations such images communicate. It is here that we are truly lacking in our gang literature an adequate classification system that can help guide both research and policy initiatives. We should not be in the situation of treating all groups as an equal threat to society, because we know there are some important differences. The classification system that will be developed in a later chapter therefore includes an analytical spectrum ranging from the informal group (pre-gang formation) to the formal organization (a formalized criminal gang).

FAMILY AS A VEHICLE OF GANG INSTITUTIONALIZATION

Just as the family as a social unit can be a powerful source of socialization and training for legitimate pursuits, it can also be one that takes on the more deviant function of solidifying gang organization. To the extent that a gang organization has membership of siblings and successive generations --- parent/child --- it also has a higher level of institutionalization.   What the history of India's gangs --- to be discussed in more detail in the next chapter --- seems to imply is that in the absence of social control efforts to the contrary, when the family reinforces gang values and purposes by directly benefiting financially, these gangs continue to exist from one generation to the next.

Adults, particularly family members or those with some legitimate status in society, therefore function as gang sponsors when they lend legitimacy to the gang as a group entity. Within any particular gang the existence of members from the same family of orientation must constitute, at a minimum, a collective identity heightened and accentuated by these internal bonds.   There is an important qualitative difference between a gang that has no such family-related infrastructure and one that does. By implication, then, any social institution probably carries this capability of, through its gang membership, reinforcing the gang's organizational strength: members of the same school, members of the same religion, members of the same political party, etc.

THE ORGANIZATIONAL   FEATURES OF GANGS

Useful for analysis if nothing more than the classification of gangs are a host of organizational features.   Does the gang have satellite units, is there interstate involvement, is the leadership a "cult of personality" or democratic, the internal organization -- is it age-graded, does it have a female auxiliary, is there a territorial control claim, is the level of adult participation high or low, what level of institutional permanency exists in terms of the number of years of operation for the gang, is its membership local in character, citywide, or not bound by geographical limits, are the weapons in use by the gang of low threat (clubs, rocks, knives, zip guns, etc) or high threat (automatic and shoulder weapons, ordnance, etc), what is the force strength in terms of mobilizable numbers, is there a formal initiation mechanism, how complex is the role structure, and what special language (argot) exists, is there a uniform, is there a written code, what alliances or networking exist, is there a headquarters or does the gang own its own property, is decision-making regulated by gang hierarchy or is it spontaneous, what sanctioning mechanisms exist to enforce the gang code, the process and extent of mind control over gang members, what are the rewardive powers of the gang, what is the nature of delegating responsibility and authority in the gang --- these are but some of the organizational questions that have yet to be answered systematically regarding gangs in America.

Further, these are questions for which answers are needed through a national level research initiative. Our gang research literature is too fragmented to be able to piece together an overall picture of the current state of gang organization in America. The need is great for such a research initiative.

THE NEED FOR A NATIONAL CONSORTIUM RESEARCH APPROACH

We need as a society to conduct a version of what Short and Strodtbeck (1974) were involved in, but at a national level. This should include freedom for individual researchers, if they are not comfortable with the collective research design, to control a portion of the resources for individual initiatives. All quantitative and qualitative data collected should a priori, that is by agreement prior to data collection, be available for secondary analysis and future researchers. This ideal national approach would have to be interdisciplinary in nature[15].

TYPES OF SOCIAL GROUP FORMATION AND GANG THEORY

The basic distinguishing features of present, and probably former, gang formations have to do simply with formality and the difference between groups and organizations. Figure 11 shows this basic typology for gangs, based not on individual attributes which may change over time, or on behavior which may not be culturally universal, but rather on the factors of formality and group formation.

FIGURE 11

A Gang Typology Based on Type of Social Group Formation

		Level of Social Formality	
		Informal	Formal
Type of Formation:	Group	Level 0	Level 2
	Organization	Level 1	Level 3

Perhaps many of what prior authors have focused their attention on have been these level zero informal groups. Every community, rural or urban, can be assumed to have these. A level 1 or emergent gang means having at least the implied goal of psychic or economic benefits from crime and typically means simply the emulation of an organization, not a true formal organization, it is striving to be such a social formation, and is often little more than an emerging, ad hoc gang[16]. A level 2 or crystallized gang has attained, in pursuing crime, a certain level of formality by its hierarchy and division of labor but functions like a single pseudo-family in a single-tiered but often multi-level group structure. A level 3 or formalized gang has satellite units, organizational goals, is diversified in its criminal income sources, has highly stable leadership and is comparable analytically to what law enforcement officers call the "super gang" or some authors call the corporate gang.

This typology would suggest that level zero gangs can readily be given adult supervision and perhaps redirected into prosocial functions for a community or neighborhood as Shaw and Sorrentino (1956) claimed; because it is not, truly speaking, a gang --- it lacks the pattern of law violation. A level one gang might be that most readily reached through such initiatives as detached worker or street outreach programs; again, because the level of commitment, the level of threat, the level of group cohesiveness, and illicit income sources are low or limited.

This typology, based on organizational and group theory, would also suggest that a level two gang might be the easiest to target using conventional law enforcement strategies. But, conversely, a level three gang is not going to be readily put out of business, and might even gain further strength through conventional law enforcement strategies including the traditional use of the penal sanction. All a level three gang has to do to become what many regard as an organized crime cartel is to shield itself from prosecution more effectively via political corruption and to penetrate the legitimate opportunity structure. This will be discussed later in this book.

SUMMARY AND CONCLUSION

The serious student of criminology must recognize that some gangs are easier to study than others through qualitative methods (ethnomethodology, participant observation, etc). From an organizational perspective we must also recognize that gangs do not necessarily have to originate from an urban tradition, although that has been the predominant pattern in America. In fact, later in this book we shall learn that the gang problem has certainly penetrated many smaller towns in America.

Gang organization, to parallel what we know from organizational theory generally, can therefore have different levels of organizational development: incipient, mature, formalized, and institutionalized. Thus, attempts to control gang crime must recognize this basic distinction. How prior attempts to "help society" in the name of such social control initiatives have actually functioned, objectively and materially, to strengthen gang organization also deserves our critical attention.

To the extent that interviewing itself can constitute "therapy" by its dramatic personal thrust and a re-awakening of charged emotions, then to what extent, we must ask from an organizational perspective, does inviting the gang to the university for "study purposes" also give it more legitimacy and organizational strength than it deserves if our interest for society is a reduction in gang crime? This discussion has attempted to point out some of the pitfalls of ethnomethodology regarding the production of knowledge about gang crime. It has also argued the merits of shifting attention from the individual to that of the group or organization itself.

That those who do not understand history are condemned to repeat it is a claim made throughout the ages. That our gang research literature contains some mistakes that should not be repeated should be evident. Clearly, the work by Asbury (1927) differed from Thrasher (1927) in that the former included a more historical analysis which showed gangs operating in America prior to the civil war. The work cited here by Green (1847) also reinforces the claim that America has probably always had gangs. Indeed, the important work by Sleeman (1849) appeared about the same time frame to demonstrate gangs operating in British colonized India. It is a mistake to assume that these works are not of value in understanding group forms of criminal conduct[17].

This chapter must, therefore, be interpreted as an argument for an organizational analysis or a focus on the gang organization itself. All answers, all questions, all issues have yet to be raised in this regard. It is a continuing concern for us all.

Finally, returning to the issue of "what knowledge do we want developed?", it is useful to conclude with some remarks concerning scholarship and the political-economy arena.   If we really are not concerned about the future of gang crime in America or its escalation to heights as yet unseen in terms of devastation and societal cost, then we should probably continue a national policy that provides little incentive for social science research, we should probably continue to associate "sociology research entrepreneurs" with the infamous Senator Proxmire "golden fleece awards" describing the absurd use of public funds. Gangs in America will thrive under such an atmosphere of anti-intellectualism. If the Senators want to do something about the quality of research they should insist that agencies like the National Institute of Justice and the Department of Health and Human Services establish true competitive bidding and eliminate political influence in "who gets what".

Implied here, in regards to the political economy, is that some scholars may be importantly influenced by what side their bread is buttered on. Therefore, what is studied can be that which is rewarded. For criminological interpretation, we need only recall how some such cases of intellectual prostitution regarding "nothing works in terms of rehabilitating offenders" meant millions of dollars in "do nothing, say what we say" research money in the 1960's which justified a more punitive national policy. This resulted in the official philosophical ethos being remarkedly repressive in America during the 1970's. So if we don't want to be really serious, we can continue to focus on the "how do you feel?" kind of individual gang member as the unit of analysis as a preferred research agenda. Unfortunately, those who have been the heaviest advocates of setting as a national research priority the conducting of "field work" with gangs tend also to contribute to the national image that the only gang problem in America is a problem of "color". Hopefully the national findings reported in this book will establish that whites can also constitute a gang problem.

It is, after all, a matter of what knowledge do we really want developed.   Someone, for example, in a rendition of misquoting Durkheim could say "gangs are good for America....look how they keep our prison systems expanding, and providing jobs for corrections and law enforcement.".   Or, alternatively, gangs are the "bogeyman" we all fear in our sleep and the repressive apparatus must therefore be expanded.

A true social scientist must probably be strictly eclectic in showing no allegiance to theory per se, but rather a comparable enthusiasm to "test theory". It should not be a mission of establishing support for one's own individualistic view of the world, it should rather be a mission of gang research to be more responsible to gang members and gang victims and the gang's society by a willingness to consider all views --- especially an organizational view --- as they might improve our ability to account for these developments.

Let us hope that, in the process, no one seriously entertains the function of reinforcing these gang developments.   Because it is possible to argue, from an organizational analysis, that just as gangs can be manipulated[18] gangs can in fact be artificially generated, created, propelled, given direction and resources, and yielding predictable functions. A national policy of America as the ostrich with its head in the sand surrounded by gangs having varying levels of sophistication, avoiding general research, avoiding facts, avoiding the truth ---- that is the nightmare.

DISCUSSION QUESTIONS

(1)   Do you think a focus on organizational characteristics can help classify or "triage" a response to the gang crime problem? At what level of the gang threat continuum would you classify the "Clovers" studied by Shireman?

(2)   Should all gangs be treated alike, or is it possible that some strategies and programs may be differentially effective depending on the type of gang? Is it ethical for a researcher who studies or treats lower level gang members in low threat gangs to try and generalize findings to all gangs?

(3)   In correctional settings, non-gang affiliated inmates are called "neutrals" or "neutrons" but experience an enormous pressure to affiliate with a gang. Do you think the correctional environment is a good opportunity to study what may or may not work to prevent gang affiliation or to evaluate gang deprogramming or gang dismemberment strategies?

FOOTNOTES

1. His gang name is "Shakey"; he was also chief of the Milwaukee, Wisconsin chapter of the Latin Kings; but he broke off from the Latin Kings; changed colors from Black and Gold (King colors) to Orange and Black.

2. Other members of their executive committee according to our sources include: "Maddog" (Ronnie Carrasquilo), a cop killer now imprisoned in Dixon, Illinois, who is Chief of the Imperial Gangsters; "Tuffy" (Anibel Santiago), president of the SGD's, and Chief of the Spanish Cobras; David Ayala, Vice President of the SGD's and Chief of the Two Six boys; Fernie, vice president of the SGD's and Chief of the

Maniac Latin Disciples; Paul Villa Gomez, Vice President, and Chief of the Ambrose; and "Drac" AKA Dracula, vice president and Chief of the Latin Eagles.

3. The Spanish Cobras headquarters are said to be located near Maplewood and Potomac in Chicago. The key figures in the Spanish Cobras, according to our very reliable source, include: Anabel Santiago "Tuffy", the King Cobra (i.e., chief of the Cobras); Edwin Losario (a rappy or crime partner of Tuffy's, AKA "Rabbit"), who is chief of all Spanish Cobra's inside the prisons; Slim, the National President; "Burner", the executive National Vice President (a name that in gang slang means Killer); Lil Man (Tuffy's brother), and an Advisor to Tuffy; Bradley C., an advisor; Fro (a derivative of Afro haircut), an Enforcer; Mr. Mike, a treasurer; Horse, a Lt. Governor; Polaco (means Pollock in Spanish), a Lt. Gov.; Blancito (means White Boy in Spanish), a Lt. Gov.; Alex and Pico (brothers), Lt. Gov.'s.; "Drac", a Lt. Gov.; Lurch (killed Hector Sanchez, a major gang figure), a Lt. Gov.; Rubin Santiago (Tuffy's cousin and now in a wheelchair, but still said to be active), a personal hitman who shot our informant; and Charlie C. (chief of the Milwaukee, Wisconsin chapter of the Cobras), a Lt. Governor as well.

4. According to our source the key players in the Imperial Gangsters include: Ronnie Carrasquilo, chairman of the SGD's, and Chief of all Imperial Gangsters, now imprisoned in Dixon, Illinois; Paulie Carrasquilo (brother of Ronnie), chief of the Imperial Gangsters on the streets; David Ramirez, AKA "T-Bags", treasurer and Maddog's personal enforcer (someone said to have killed twelve rivals but never caught for it, who also owned a $6 million dollar a year cash business called Dirt Busters, a car wash business, that was confiscated by the feds); Hector G., an enforcer for all chapters of the Imperial Gangsters; Jose Martir AKA "Casper G.", chief of the Grand and Division chapter of the Imperial Gangsters (the Imperial Gangsters are said to have originated at the Cammeron School nearby); "Mems", chief of the North Avenue and Central Park chapter of the I.G.'s; and "Chico", chief of the Armitage and Drake chapter of the I.G.'s in Chicago where they own several buildings.

5. The key players and roles in the Latin Disciples, according to our sources, include: Fernando Zayas, AKA "Fernie", chief of all the Maniac Latin Disciples (M.L.D.'s); Pachaco, Minister of Finance; Victor Matas, Minister of Defense (an enforcer role or title); "King Vic" (who used to be chief of the MLD's and who wrote the literature for them), Minister of Literature; "Mousie", a chapter treasurer; "Ricky D." (Ricky Garcia actually), an assistant minister of defense; Victor Nieves, a chapter treasurer; Miguel, a chapter treasurer; and Pete "The Burner", semi-retired, but still considered to be the Latin Disciple of all Latin Disciples as he helped start the gang with co-founder "Hitler" (Hitler is now deceased, killed by the C-Notes).

6. This would be particularly true if gang research continued to focus explicitly along psychological-deficit dimensions of the individual gang member, as if, in a continuing quest to find a personal trait causing gang affiliation we can in the same sense "cure" them of their gang affiliation patterns.

7. Such as "educationists" (Parsons, 1969: p. 32).

8. The view of organizations by Parsons seems to be comparable to many gang authors who deny hierarchy or complexity in gangs. According to Parsons "cliques of friends, and so on, are not in this technical sense organizations" (Parsons, 1969: p. 33). For Parsons "organization" was almost equivalent to "bureaucracy" and was a highly restricted definition (Parsons, 1969: p. 32).

9. Professor Martin Sanchez-Jankowski (1991) is such a highly trained, sociological version of this "close up" research approach. But it is anything but easy. In fact, Professor Sanchez-Jankowski was at one point shot and wounded during his research.

10. Here we see a potential liability associated with field research, participant observation, and ethnographic "get in there" kind of approaches. Hagedorn (1990: pp. 255-256) in describing his relationship with one of his "informants", (Howard) related the experience where rumors began circulating about Hagedorn being a cop and that the informant (Howard) was "informing". Howard was threatened. Hagedorn went out into the community with Howard to defuse the situation. But what if Howard had been killed? Or any of the other data sources? A prison warden that uses an "informant" to snitch or penetrate a target group faces legal liability if anything happens to the snitch. Is there not a comparable problem in such "field work" situations? I fear that should Milwaukee gang members get a copy of Hagedorn's book, and gang members do read, they would see the word "informant" and perhaps renew their threats on Howard. Police have informants, researchers have data sources and respondents.

11. See also Muehlbauer and Dodder (1983: pp. x-xi) for another view of gangs as deviant organizations, "something more tangible than a subculture" (p. x).

12. Published in Philadelphia by G.B. Zeiber and Co, No. 3 Ledger Buildings.

13. The use of codes reported by Green were far more complex than those more recently reported among prison gang members by Fong (1990, pp. 41-42). On the other hand, we might assume some of this kind of coded message behavior has gone on along time among inmates, including the use of urine to right "hidden messages" on paper that become revealed under heating the paper (because of the iron content of urine).

14. The document referenced within the selected bibliography was prepared by Willie C. Watson, Street Club Worker of the Hyde Park Neighborhood Club (HPNC) of which Charles H. Shireman was the director through the Hyde Park Youth Project (HPYP), and John M. Gandy, Director of Research (HPYP), and John Ramey, director of the HPNC. Watson and Gandy are indicated as the senior authors. See also Gandy, 1959.

15. See "Preliminary Findings from the 1992 Law Enforcement Mail Questionnaire Project", Gang Journal: An Interdisciplinary Research Quarterly (1)(3), 1993 for an example of how such projects can work.

16. The report by Dunston (1990, p. 6) on New York gangs gives an excellent example of a level one gang. New York is not seeing the highly organized "super gangs" found in Chicago and elsewhere. Rather "the typical New York State gang is a loose association of irregularly anti-social youth, often anonymous, more nomadic than territorial, and of shifting or changeable leadership" (Dunston, 1990: p. 6). In fact, "these groups are like pick-up basketball teams. They live all over the city and come together at school. They meet on a subway platform, a leader steps forward and they're off and running" (Dunston, 1990: p. 6).

17.   The recent viewpoints expressed by Covey, Menard and Franzese (1992) illustrate this kind of blatant disregard for historical works as if gangs suddenly landed in a spaceship in the 1980's; that, at least, is the implication when they say that criminologists know little about gangs and what is known in criminology is out of date with regard to gangs. Of course, the very title of their book is a misnomer: Juvenile Gangs; for as discussed elsewhere in the present analysis, no gang is known to expel members when they reach adulthood, thus no pure 100 percent "juvenile" gang exists at the higher level of the gang organizational spectrum (i.e., the more notorious gangs that present communities with the largest threats).

18. Ko-Lin Chin (Huff, 1990: p. 135) describes in Chinese gangs how gang mentors induce conflict intentionally.

"Gang conflicts have become a form of urban-guerilla warfare over drug trafficking. Informers, welchers and competitors are ruthlessly punished; many have been assassinated."

Newsweek (Jan. 28, 1988: p. 23)

CHAPTER 13

GANGS, GUERILLA WARFARE, AND SOCIAL CONFLICT[1]

INTRODUCTION

Gang violence and conflict has been previously described as guerilla warfare (Short and Strodtbeck, 1974: p. 200). The Crip gang member who gave his glamorized story of gang life in the book <u>Monster</u> similarly describes himself as a trained combat veteran and freedom fighter in an undeclared urban guerilla war. The rebellion theme has similarly been common in the gang literature (Hagedorn, p. 164;) as is the relationship of gangs to various forms of social conflict (Tannenbaum, 1938). The gang member as warrior (Pound, 1930: 178-179) is a similar theme corresponding to the book title of Keiser (1971).[2] Is it only that, a simple analogy?[3] Or do gangs represent the highest threat yet seen in terms of maintaining the security of our nation's communities and public institutions and, comparably, do gangs represent a continuing threat[4] or menace in terms of the essence of what is implied by "terrorism" (Davis, 1978)? Similarly, calling gangs "urban terrorists" as an official criminal justice council in California did (California Council on Criminal Justice, 1989: p. viii) is strong language, but again does labelling gangs terrorists make them terrorists?

This issue exemplifies one of the intellectual debates about gangs today. Some authors had concluded earlier that gangs --- whatever their rhetoric --- were simply not well organized and in no sense constituted a revolutionary group. Some contemporary gang analysts in direct contradiction of such assertions may point to groups like the Black Guerrilla Family as a clearcut example of such a revolutionary gang. As in some of the other debates about gangs, what we must realize is that there are sufficient variations in group function and organizational capability that all dimensions (apolitical to that of revolutionary, rightwing to that of leftwing, etc) can probably be found in the modern reality of American gangs. The "debate" in this and other instances is more often than not simply a problem of authors overgeneralizing from inadequate previous research. It is an error to consider all "gangs" equal --- either in terms of the threat they may represent, or in terms of the potential for intervention.

For those who have studied guerilla warfare and unconventional combat forces there is a striking commonality between the basic affinity group represented by the typical urban street gang, of whatever stage of organizational development, and guerilla combat operations. Further, the nature of the conflict --- its direction, its intensity, the means by which it is moderated and controlled --- is also of some comparable interest. At least this provides the rationale for introducing to the reader the gang "study/research/experimentation" by Lieut.-Col. W.H. Sleeman from Calcutta in 1849 and other authors and views in the analysis of social conflict.

JEFF FORT'S MISTAKE ABOUT IDEOLOGY

Jeff Fort the leader of Chicago's El Rukn gang seemed to follow a historical pattern in organizational emulation. When Louis Farakhan was able to get a five million dollar no interest loan from Libya's Moammar Gadhafi, Jeff felt he could get some too, and proceeded to seek $2.5 million to engage in domestic terrorism inside the United States on behalf of Gadhafi:

> "In five years, Federal agents taped some 3,500 hours of conversa-
> tions. Eventually they heard what sounded like an extraordinary
> transaction: Fort was trying to cut a deal with Moammar Gadhafi.
> For $2.5 million ("two dinners and half a lunch" in El Rukn code),
> the El Rukns would bomb government buildings and commit other
> terrorist acts in the United States, the Feds believed.
>
> But they needed proof. It came when an El Rukn bought a rocket
> launcher from an undercover agent. And the icing came when
> Trammel Davis, an El Rukn amir, agreed to turn state's evidence
> in return for $10,000 for his family."[5]

Had Jeff Fort's Chicago gang, the El Rukn's, not contemplated seriously the ideological exploitation value of being a terrorist for hire organization for a foreign nation hostile to America (Useem and Kimball, 1989: p. 77), do you think Jeff Fort would still be operating on the streets of Chicago, indeed perhaps throughout America today? In the late 1960s, during a time of intense ideological strife in America, much of it having to do with civil rights and the anti-war movement in reaction against the war in Viet Nam, was it not the Black Panther's who were attacked rather than Jeff Fort's gang of thugs and robbers? That gangs in America, whatever their skin color, have previously had the overall characteristic of being rightwing, and reactionary, supportive of the status quo, tends to be supported from most of the extant literature.[6] But that may have changed today with the advent of greater sophistication in the organizational structure of gangs.

Some early gang authors (e.g, Campbell) have said that gangs are anything BUT revolutionary organizations --- they are rather thugs and exploiters, mostly opportunist, often reactionary. Unthinking. Unreflective. Functionary operatives. Grand scheme of things followers. Defenders of the social order. They seek not to overthrow and revise, rather they seek their fair share. They seek the equal opportunity to exploit.[7] But let me remind you, that has been the preceding historical variation. There are, obviously, some alternative social-political variations. What we see now may not be what we get in the long term. Gangs, as armed peasants, could become a larger problem than they are now. Some of the level three gangs in America today have well articulated political beliefs, some formalized, and they are well armed as well.

Also, many of the recent researchers who have contributed to our prior literature on this issue have focused almost exclusively on African-American gangs. White gangs may be different as implied earlier. Groups like the KKK, Aryan Brotherhood, and many others can be assumed to have a clear and unmistakable rightwing ideology or philosophy. And yet even among African-American gangs there do exist at least some contemporary forms that take on what amount to essentially leftwing beliefs.

The early 1970's Krisberg (1975) study provided an excellent analysis of gang views on racism and revolution. Interviews with gang members showed, as might be expected, a projection that most white prison guards are racist (Krisberg, 1975: p. 16). That is, there was little more than enmity towards white people with the noted exception that "if some rich white man will buy guns for Black revolutionaries, then he would be spared" (Krisberg, 1975: p. 16).

Apparently, the group studied by Krisberg saw themselves ready for revolution, where revolution meant "a large rumble (gang fight)" (ibid). Said one of the gang members "we're the experts in revolution...I know how to stab, he knows about dynamite, and none of us is afraid to use a gun" (Krisberg, 1975: p. 16).

MONSTER'S MEDIA SUCCESS VIA IDEOLOGY

The author of Monster in a "60 Minutes" interview (July 31, 1994) outlined a chronology of how he gave up the life of "Crips" as "Monster Cody" and converted to a revolutionary ideology supportive of the New African Republic. Prison, he said, was just a place for studying revolutionary science. He denied he was a sociopath, "I am just an ordinary guy" he said, in response to a sound bite from the prosecuting attorney who put Monster in prison. "He is extremely intelligent" and uses his cunning and personal power to manipulate others is what the prosecuting attorney implied.

Since writing the book he has gained much attention in the mass media. He renounced any loyalty to the United States in the interview, but vowed support for revolutionary ideals. With tears dripping from his eyes during a period of questionning about his football star legend father, whom Monster said he hated for essentially "not being there", he was quick to point out how he can be regarded as a political prisoner because he was a "political organizer" in the California prison system prior to being transferred to Pelican Bay.

The book Monster is highly stylized and superbly edited to defend this Crip gang member and present him in the most embellished positive light in a way that he avoids taking any responsibility for his behavior because he was a freedom fighter in an urban war. To the extent that apologists for gangs are themselves fair in terms of a policy of equal time coverage, we should therefore expect a Blood version of the same book. And in order to give fair play to midwestern gangs this could, naturally, rest on the bookshelf next to "The Historic Rehabilitation of a Criminal Gang Into A Prosocial Gang: Changing the Gangster Disciples into The Growth Developers".

GANG INVOLVEMENT IN THE LOS ANGELES RIOTS

No one disputes the fact that gang members and gangs were actively involved in the Los Angeles riots after the "not-guilty" verdict regarding Rodney King. Gang rights activist and advocacy views tend to downplay the role of gangs in the riots and point to the widely viewed television news footage showing entire families and many diverse individuals who were looting stores. The record shows that during the riot over 800 buildings were torched resulting in property losses exceeding $750 million dollars. Among the subsequent arrests made for arson related to the riot, about a third were gang members or gang-affiliated[8].

In a riot situation, a condition of civil disorder and the breakdown of legal regulations, it is the individual "one-time" rioter or the novice (e.g., a homeless person, a mother, etc) who is most likely to be arrested. A gang member could be expected to operate with members of his/her own gang; and thus, acting as a group they are much more formidable, and therefore less likely to actually be caught. Gangs are predisposed to criminal activity, and therefore are more likely to systematically benefit from looting in a riot or civil disturbance. Gang members were not stealing Pampers or canned food goods, they were targeting businesses like the 29 gun shops that were looted of about 5,000 firearms. Gangs in L.A. were believed to have taken most of those guns including two hundred police uniforms that were also stolen[9].

POLICE POLICY AND AMERICAN GANGS

In Chicago, an ancient tradition of dealing with gangs involved simply picking up a gang member, asking for information and when not getting cooperation, driving the gang member to another part of the city, indeed an area known to be thoroughly controlled by a rival gang, and dropping the gang member off, out of the police car, right then and there. "Fend for yourself". It was a control policy reflecting the cultivation of internecine violence between rival gang members. This policy was not much more sophisticated than a "divide and conquer" approach. Without the "conquer", because these gangs were never "conquered".

Most gangs in urban America, through ill-designed social and law enforcement strategies, have been unintentionally cultivated and organizationally reinforced, if not through their imprisonment, then through their official recognition, and the legitimation accorded them. Or through the conflict that is increased which gangs thrive on. Or through ill-conceived gang programs and policies that increase rather than decrease the problem.

Chicago is instructive in this instance regarding law enforcement policy. For a period in Chicago, the gang abatement/control policy hinged on using the "disorderly conduct" statute to simply arrest and detain, for whatever short period of time, any conspicuous accumulation of persons on a "street corner" who looked like a gang formation --- most characteristically, persons of color from inner-city neighborhoods. When the federal court later ruled this unconstitutional, and ordered the Chicago Police Department to: (1) go back to their files and notify each such person so unlawfully arrested that they had the right to bring suit against the City of Chicago for false arrest, and (2) to erase 800,000 such records of unconstitutional arrests for disorderly conduct, this approach of "street gang control" was modified.[10]

VOLD: THEORETICAL CRIMINOLOGY AND GANGS

Vold (1958) reviewed the shortcomings of anomie theory and gang formations via Cloward and Ohlin as well as the work of Cohen. More importantly, however, Vold advanced the discussion of crime as minority group behavior (see Vold, 1981: pp. 288-292) as well as discussing the political nature of crime (pp. 292-296). It is here that Vold argues that the gang as a collective enterprise is by its very nature a minority group, not necessarily a racial minority group, but one that is clearly at odds with the larger society.

The nature of this structural conflict is one where the gang is the outgroup and legitimate society is the ingroup. Similar to underclass theory, the gang member becomes defined as being marginally important to his/her society, and with different values come different goals and methods to attain those goals. As Vold indicated:

> From a more general point of view, however, this prevalence of collective action in crime may reasonably be interpreted as an indication of the banding together for protection and strength of those who are in some way at odds with organized society and with the police forces maintained by that society (Vold, 1981: p. 289).

In essence, the gang is normal in wanting to exert power over resources for the benefit of its individual members. In seeking to expropriate the wealth of others, by the use of illegitimate or coercive power, the gang therefore is in a natural state of combat with the criminal justice system. States Vold further:

> The delinquent boys' gang is clearly a minority group in the sense that it cannot achieve its objectives through regular channels, making use of, and relying for protection on, the police powers of the state (Vold, 1981: p. 289).

Vold was clearly aware of how for white gang members in America the gang maturation process often meant a springboard for entering the legitimate opportunity structure, of escaping from the competitive sector of the economy, such as Chicago's famous Mayor Richard J. Daley, the "Boss" who was a member of the Hamburg street gang in Chicago's Bridgeport neighborhood which later became a powerful political organization.[11]

Thus, at the individual level this conflict with larger society can be accommodated under conditions of white skin privilege. For the individual who is a person of color, however, who faces racism in daily life as well as institutional racism, the social structure is less accommodating in the transition to adulthood legitimacy. Says Vold:

> The juvenile gang, in this sense, is nearly always a minority group, out of sympathy with and in more or less direct opposition to the rules and regulations of the dominant majority, that is, the established world of adult values and power (Vold, 1981: p. 290).

Further, the use of coercive force such as imprisonment or any such label as "treatment/intervention" by the majority group is not likely to succeed with a minority group. It is similar to the typical resistance that any prisoner-of-war experiences who holds loyalty to ones own group (see Vold, 1981: p. 291).

Gang members, then, do not accept the definition of the situation offered by the criminal justice system of their behavior, however illegal or violent, as being anything other than honorable and acceptable to their own group code. As Vold says, the gang as a microcosm of larger society manifests a larger and more general problem of conflict:

> The more basic problem, therefore, is the conflict of group interests
> and the struggle for the control of power that is always present in
> the political organization of any society (Vold, 1981: p. 202).

Herein is the problem that gangs appear to seek control of the streets, of a street corner, of an area of "turf", of exerting influence over a particular institution such as a public school, or a recreational area they seek to dominate and control for their own. According to Frantz Fanon[12], violence is power as well.

To the extent that a gang entity is highly predictable in its behavior in terms of its propensity to want to exploit any valuable resource, then the gang functions normally in a quest for such power and control. It is equally of interest to note that for those persons of color who may be objectively and materially powerless in terms of economic and social power, this is an even more escalated function. It accounts for the relative importance of something as simple as a "status threat" as the precipitating factor in serious acts of violence.[13]

Vold clearly speaks to the racism-oppression hypothesis as one of the four variations of the political nature of crime. Basically, much crime arises from attempts to induce social change in the context of institutional racism. For example, both South Africa and the United States are cases in point where the person of color is historically expected to assume a subordinate role and position in society. Attempts to rock the boat of the "caste system of racial segregation" (Vold, 1981: p. 295) therefore often result in various crime charges.

As we will see, social caste subjugation in ethnic status was also highly associated with the robber gangs of India as well.

THE EARLY GANGS OF INDIA

Here we shall rely on the wealth of information on robber gangs operating in India reported by Sleeman (1849). This is an oversized, 433+ page military government document describing the nature of the "Budhuk" gangs of India and their suppression by the military[14]. Here we find, among other things, an assortment of "confessions" or depositions taken from gang members and gang leaders about their exploits. The clear difference between these and later American "oral history" methods is not in the content, because they have been meticulously transcribed and translated into English; what differs is that these were taken by force.

The basic structural elements of these gangs had some factors in common with American gangs today and some very important differences. The commonality is that these gangs reflected a constituency of those at the very bottom of the social ladder with little hope of legitimate advancement in society. Gang membership was very much intergenerational through the family. Additionally, in and outside of the periodic episodes with prison life the gang members generally considered themselves more adept at crime than their non-gang counterparts. The commonality, to reiterate, between these early 19th century gangs in India and those in America today had much to do with the surplus population theory of crime: both were marginally tied to their society, both were surplus to having a productive role to play in the overall economy. The major difference is that these gangs were, like guerrilla forces, based in very "wild" or dense jungle type of rural areas[15]. In fact, they located their entire families in these swamp/wood regions where it was difficult for government troops to effectively pursue them. When government military troops did pursue them into these jungles, they often had high casualties (mortality losses) from fever.

Their specialty, to give it a historical update, was that of what might be comparable today to robbing "big scores", either treasuries, or Brink's trucks, and secondly, home invasion of the rich. Theft, kidnapping, murder were commonplace to these gangs. Their notoriety was for being "robbers" or "decoits". Like gangs today, they had their own subcultural argot, and could communicate in the presence of a potential victim without alerting the latter of their intent.

These were very professional and dedicated criminals: they would often travel hundreds of miles, in disguise, to "pull a job" based on their intelligence gathering capabilities, and would take over an entire section of town while the "score went down", doing so typically at night under cover of darkness, with swift and unexpected violence against all who might resist. Often, in these frays, they would never lose a single fellow gang member. They carried out highly organized attacks on specific pre-identified targets of crime opportunity.

The life style of these gang members, was therefore, one of the ideal-typical contemporary income-oriented criminal: they would make a score, and live the rest of the year in their version of luxury --- drinking, feasting, having fun with as many wives as they could support.[16] What this revealed about the effectiveness of the gang organization, and its high level of morale on such criminal expropriation "quasi-military/insurgency" maneuvers, was that the wealth from such "scores" was shared with all in the gang. The wives got a share, all children got a share, if a member was killed or in jail, he still got a share. It was the primary source of economic support for a large number of persons and their families. None of them worked legally, they condemned "hard work" with great ferocity.

That these gangs continued from one generation, in a family, to the next was clearly evident. The gang was an organization with a clear leader, no necessary written code, but an extensive oral code including subcultural language/argot that allowed them to communicate with others. The gang was rarely in conflict with other gangs. Their targets were not the street corner, their targets were often chosen within the city for example, home invasion of an important "banker", but would equally focus on the informal calculation of risk/benefit ratios designed to maximize their ability to get away with the crime --- to be able to move as rapidly as possible out of the area of the crime undetected and with the loot intact.

If there is a primer on how to be an effective gang, this military report by Sleeman (1849) is it. When your gang membership numbers fall to prison, sickness, death in action, etc --- take new children into the "family fold". These gangs were often accused of kidnapping babies and youths. The economic incentive was clearly there: the women in the clan would receive an extra portion of the share of booty if they had more children, it did not matter if they were their own children. The children would, if they survived, be raised to serve the gang. The haunting question for America is, then, have any of our Nation's many missing children "disappeared into the gang"?

Like the modern gang member counterpart, these Indian gang members were prone to engage in conspicuous consumption with the spoils of their successful income-producing crimes. They did not mind paying higher rents, when the landlord knew they were gang members, because the landlord became that way a confederate and supporter, someone whose best interest was in having the gang member stay "as long as you like". Paying in cash, such merchants then as now are upstream economic beneficiaries of gang crime.

Like similar accounts of American gangs on their way, en masse, to a foray, conflict, or event --- they never travelled so as to draw police attention, they travelled "separately, by two or three and four" (Sleeman, 1849: p. 33). These gangs also provided quasi-political control functions of a repressive nature for local property owners or officials of significance. They provided "protection" to the status quo and the local ruling elite from depredations by outsiders by their conspicuous presence.

These gangs had small arms comparable to those in use by the military and police, but lacked the artillery which the military was able to employ frequently to successfully attack their forts and demand their surrender. With the spoils of their "war on society" they simply outfitted themselves with rifles and pistols in the open market.[17] If they needed a boat to pull off a job, they would buy it and sink it later to cover their tracks.

These gangs were not about theatrics, and "representing" their colors. They were about business. The business of income-producing crime. They were unlike many contemporary gangs that conspicuously allow their identification, such as the El Rukn's who during Jeff Fort's reign were easily identified even on a name search by computer because they would in addition to wearing their colors daily add the "-el" to their last name such that "Jackson-el" was readily identified to anyone cognizant of this "put on". These Indian gangs would more frequently adopt a variety of disguises that allowed them to more effectively travel and commit their crimes. A common variation was the "religious/holy person" journey ---- to bury a persons remaining ashes, to attend a wedding, to a pilgrimage, etc., all the time enacting a role of religion to avoid critical scrutiny. They would frequently "hire" genuine such "holy men" for front-line effect in these deceptions.

To those interested in the nature of social conflict and its relationship to exchange theory, the "pay off" matrix was such that many officials would not hazard an attack on the gangs, because of the direct costs associated with it and the obvious risk to life and limb, while the same officials in taking a Laissez-Faire attitude or "hands-off" position, had benefits without risks. To attack the gangs is to risk much loss ---- personal and political, to acquiesce to the gangs (that is, to permit them relative freedom of operation or a zone of comfort for their staging area) means benefiting indirectly with no risk at all. It is here that Sleeman (1849) makes the assertion that many of "the first nations in Europe, countenanced and supported the Algerine pirates, from the same feelings and views" (Sleeman, 1849: p. 79). Gang members can spend their money too, seems to be the general drift. And today, of course, gang members and their families also represent a political vote sector as well.

The value of Sleeman is showing the continuity with gangs of modern America. Sleeman (1849) showed that in some instances the gang leader "assumed the character of the high priest, and all the rest that of his followers and disciples" (pp. 80-81). This is not dissimilar from some variations of American gang formation reported in the literature, including Jeff Fort and the El Rukns. And, of course, just as the "gang-breaking" philosophy has characterized much of the American law enforcement response to gangs (see Needle and Stapleton, 1983: p. 30) which involves targeting gang leaders, this was also essentially the mission of Sleeman.[18]

Gangs then were nomadic when they had to be, that is they would leave their encampment and establish a new one if cause necessitated it. What we know about urban gang members, urban felony offenders generally, is that they too have a high level of residential mobility. They are the counterpart in being urban nomads. Probation and parole officers often remark that they seem to move as frequently as they have to submit monthly reports. From my experience in interviewing gang members, many shared something in common with these Indian gang members: their behavior being influenced significantly by superstition. They also had in common the societal-wide social stigma: not of color, but of being "eaters of anything", e.g., pork, meat, even snake in a culture that was rather reverent towards the cow.

What the British military did was of some significance in law enforcement policy for gang control[19]. One law passed in 1836 made it an imprisonable offense to be a member of such a gang:

> ACT No. XXX of 1836. It is hereby enacted, that whoever be proved to have belonged, either before or after the passing of this Act, to any gang of Thugs, either within or without the Territories of the East India Company, shall be punished with imprisonment for life, with hard labor (Sleeman, 1849: p. 353).

The military also recognized the value of separating these gang members from their territory of operation and legislation was passed in 1843 (Act No. XVIII) to allow a more federalist approach, because local jurisdictions lacked the capability for secure detention, and this 1843 legislation allowed for the confinement of gang members in other parts of India. Another law, Act No. XXIV made it illegal for any person to receive economic benefit from the gang, in the language of "the offense of unlawfully and knowingly receiving or buying property stolen or plundered" by the gang (Sleeman, 1849: p. 354-355).

"Habitual association" with like-minded individuals was the key definitive ingredient in defining who was or was not a gang member in the 1848 law instituted for the suppression of Indian gangs (Sleeman, 1849: p. 357).[20] Here again, child stealing, was a major emphasis or concern of the established social order; there was at least the widespread fear that these gangs routinely engaged in "child stealing", using murder if necessary, in order to replenish their members lost in combat or to the criminal justice system.

Of vital significance is the effort reported by Sleeman (1849) to experiment with these organized gangs. One proved effective: it meant, offering conditional pardons to those who would become informants, called "approvers", and rather than seeking to suppress them all, asking them once in custody to submit to what was an elaborate oral history method to identify all other names of gang members operating in India, and in this way develop a very large gang data base.[21] This was effective for the military in repressing the gangs and in carrying out even assassination against key gang leaders, and mostly, of effecting their eventual capture. It amounted to a kind of informal social network analysis, where the interrogators had means to cross-check the validity of such self-reports. Again, as recommended earlier in this book, the focus was not on the individual, but rather on what the individual knew about the gang organization and their previous exploits. It proved to be a powerful mechanism of law enforcement.

Secondly, another experiment was somewhat less successful, but appeared to have some positive effect, and that involved what to do with all the gang members in custody. The military established a "school of industry" where the gang leaders' children and the "approvers" (snitches) were held in a somewhat more comfortable facility and the hard core gang members and leaders were housed in a more secure facility. The idea was to have the inmates produce goods for sale. Mostly they produced textiles; rugs, tents, clothing, etc. Like many modern prison industries in America, they made little profit, but it looked good.[22] Evaluation research and "recidivism" had not yet come into the terminology of such corrections personnel, so we have little knowledge of whether this really "worked". The idea of separating confidential informants, snitches, "approvers", from the gang they have turned on has apparently come back into vogue recently. California now uses the Pelican Bay Security Unit involving a no-human contact status to encourage gang members to "debrief". Other states have created "snitch farms", physically separate facilities for informants.

Clearly, during the "interrogation"/"plea bargaining" version of the oral history data collection phase of military intelligence gathering on gang force strength and social network analysis, another frequent question that appeared in the "depositions" was to the effect "how much money, per diem, do you think it would take to get these gang members to be happy with their life style and stop their gang crimes?". This was used to formulate the school of industry approach, and to provide a rough approximation of what was needed to contain and control the gang members once they were in custody. Curiously, there is no mention of whether these gang members, including the snitches (approvers) were allowed conjugal rights.

What must be emphasized here is that this was a national problem for India, it meant during the time frame from 1803 to 1848 some 516 persons killed, and 1,270 wounded in gang attacks (Sleeman, 1849: p. 429). And this was official data: it was clearly recognized that many such gang crimes never got recorded. What constituted "gang related crime", then, has as much relevancy in the 19th century in India as it does today in America. No one really knows. Or if they do, they are not talking.

ON GANGS, VIOLENCE, AND REVOLUTIONARY THEORY

Not to confuse those who thought up to this point they had a complete grasp of the "Chicago school of criminology" through the recognition of the recurrent prefix of "differential" this and that, let me add at this point, with some obvious risk of confusion, the introduction of a non-Chicago school use of the "differential" logo, another such "differential" theory. This use of the term comes from the political science area dealing with guerilla warfare, terrorism[23], and violent conflict. It is called "differential access", a derivative of deprivation theory. As Nieburg (1970) describes it:

> Differential access focuses on the disparities in political influence and power as the most salient and influential factors. The less access to a remedy for its grievances a group has, the more violent it tends to become in demanding such access (Nieburg, 1970: p. 40).

It is an issue of dispute resolution as well. Where can the gang member go to resolve a conflict? To the police? To the court system?

In light of this "differential access" is it not possible that much of what might appear on its surface to be utterly senseless violence, devoid of value for human life, might such, unfortunately, ongoing incidents in America actually represent another possible view of reality? Before interpreting this in best light of those who are gang members please note that this may also imply that routine offenses, from drive by shootings, adjudicated as "manslaughter" may more forcefully be conceived of as being, more seriously, premeditated "murder one" offenses.

That gangs are more prone to internecine violence rather than random violence against civilians seems to be the evidence to date on the American scene. Most accounts of gang victimization show that there are innocent victims, but other gang and former gang members seem to be the target (see Rothman, 1974: p. 10). These victims, too, are typically of the same social status of the gang member pulling the trigger. These drive-by shootings are not occurring in our most lavish and wealthy areas. They occur, indeed recur, one feeding on the other in an endless succession of retaliatory feuding, in our more impoverished inner city areas. Areas where the quality of life has and continues to be a problem for us all.

THE URBAN GUERILLA ANALOGY

A gang may use "guerilla tactics" but most gangs in America today certainly could not, in their present form, be regarded as a guerrilla army. As Janowitz said "guerrillas are a part of an organization, proceed with a plan, prepare paths of withdrawal, and develop sanctuaries (Janowitz, 1970: p. 182)." To other authors, they also seek to control a given area or territory at a successful stage of development. Oppenheimer (1969) was one of the few authors on urban guerilla warfare to at least address the unique nature of gangs and social conflict.

The early Indian gangs would seem to fit the definition of guerilla offered by Janowitz. Are gang members a part of an organization[24], even if it is an organization with varying degrees of formalization, sophistication, and permanence? Do some gangs direct planned activities including drug sales and retaliatory violence?[25]? Do gang members prepare paths of withdrawal --- in their own turf and in other jurisdictions? Do gangs develop sanctuaries, areas where they feel protected? Most certainly is the answer to all of these analogous factors that might fit the definition by Janowitz (1970).

What the reader must ask is this: is it just an analogy[26], perhaps a false one at that, or is it a potential scenario for American gang development?   Sibley recently observed that "the police and the public are facing an enemy army with its own uniforms, weapons and rules" (1989, p. 403). Some conspiracy buffs feel gangs are being fostered by home-grown communists and the domestic violence is being allowed to develop in order to implement the National Security Act and thus suspend the Constitution. There is a lot of misinformation being published by and about gangs[27]. And, of course, there are many views seeing the gang-drug connection nationwide to represent a very formidable and apparently growing problem[28].

Oppenheimer discussed gangs in several contexts, including a mention of Jeff Fort's Blackstone Rangers involved in political activities (1969: p. 38), but sees them generally, like Hobsbawm, as "bandits", with the caveat that one scenario could allow for the blurring of distinctions between criminal bandits and guerrillas, allowing for an escalation of conflict. From Oppenheimer's view:

> People with guns but without ideology are bandits; people with ideology but without guns are liberals....the analogous social formation in the urban area is the gangster, or on a less organized level, the juvenile fighting gang (1969: p. 34).

Presumably gangs need only an ideology of pro-social systematic self-help to become, then, guerrillas by most definitions. The author's appraisal would suggest that this exists already.[29]

Moore's (1978) work tends to suggest similarly a "self-help" internalized ideology in the context of a visibly obvious in-group/out-group relationship between the gang member and larger society. Oppenheimer had recognized that:

> From time to time urban gangs (mainly juveniles, not racketeers) go "social", that is, abandon fighting and adopt tasks of a "social welfare" character, such as recreation, clean-up campaigns, and so forth (1969, p. 35).

Perhaps what made the Symbionese Liberation Army different than the Crips or Bloods was their epitomizing this "social welfare" character in their role in food give-aways to the poor.

The haunting question, knowing that Jeff Fort's gang could be eager to carry out, for a price, terrorist activities in America, is this: How have other gangs have fared in this developmental direction[30]? Do gangs carry out political assassination?[31]   Are gang members terrorists by definition?[32]   Some new research on this issue is now emerging, in terms of access to military weapons by gang members, and their firearms usage patterns. This new research does show the gang member to have greater access to better firepower including fully automatic weapons, explosives, and military weapons, and a higher likelihood of wearing body armor during the commission of a crime.[33] A recent development in Chicago's gang community exemplifies this trend, several leaders of the Four Corner Hustlers gang were so angry about the effectiveness of a recent community policing initiative that was cutting into their drug operations income, that the gang members tried to acquire missiles and machineguns to blow up the local police station and wage a total war against the local police. They had turned over a large amount of cash and cocaine as their deposit on the purchase of an M72A2 LAWS anti-tank rocket. They were very serious about wanting to blow up the police station.[34]

The issues here are many. Could today's street gang be tomorrow's terrorist/urban guerilla group in armed warfare or low intensity conflict? Organizationally, the early India gangs were able to effectively function much like guerilla groups.[35] That they kept their apolitical and ethnocentric views of the world, as professional bandits, may have kept them from seizing political power. What qualitative aspects of ideology must be present before we can consider the gang as a guerilla group? In the absence of such a formalized ideology is their opposition to be interpreted as little more than mercenary behavior? Or as Taylor (1990) would call it, "quisling" behavior? Or is the typical military terminology used by higher level gang formations just a social "put on"?

For the record, several scenarios are obviously possible. The research by Hans Mattick was the basis for what we know about the "Dirty Dozen".[36] What Mattick showed was that offenders paroled to the U.S. Army fared well, and in fact, such military socialization was useful in reducing their recidivism. Again, the question seems to hinge on this: "is there a productive role for these persons to play in America?" If not, get ready for the worst case scenario.[37] Finally, some readers may find the analogy to guerilla warfare in terms of solutions, in terms of the battle against gangs. For example, the Chicago Area Project sees the struggle for community control as a "neighborhood by neighborhood" approach to provide greater community empowerment.[38] Some readers may find that not dissimilar to "house by house" military fighting often associated with urban warfare.

POLITICAL EXTREMIST GANGS: The Case of the Black Guerrilla Family

The Black Guerrilla Family (BGF) is typically found in adult prisons, but has also been reported as active by local law enforcement, in adult jails, and in juvenile correctional institutions. While it is found throughout California, the BGF has been reported in a number of other states (Arizona, Georgia, Indiana, Minnesota, Missouri, Nevada, New Jersey, Texas, Washington, and Wisconsin). The written constitution of the BGF consists of 16 pages of single spaced typed text. This is one of the few gang constitutions that clearly indicates an intent to engage in armed conflict.

The BGF in its written constitution clearly regards other gangs like the Aryan Brotherhood and the Mexican Mafia (EME) as enemies; in fact, as "tools" of the penal administration. Of all the written gang constitutions, that of the BGF is clearly the most politically sophisticated. Yet much of it seems as if it could have been copied --- in terms of phrases, "pat expressions", etc --- straight out of radical leftist newspapers or periodicals. The BGF also recognizes its beginnings in the "guiding example and teachings of George Jackson". George Jackson was a famous African-American militant who died of gunfire while imprisoned. He helped ignite the "prisoner rights/reform/protest" movement of the 1970's (Jackson, 1970).

The BGF oath like that of their arch enemy (the Aryan Brotherhood) rhymes in the form of a poem[39]:

OATH OF THE BLACK GUERRILLA FAMILY

If I should ever break my stride,
And falter at my comrades side,
This oath will kill me.
If ever my world should prove untrue,
Should I betray this chosen few,
This oath will kill me.
Should I be slow to take a stand,
Should I show fear to any man,
This oath will kill me.
Should I grow lax in discipline,
In time of strife refuse my hand.
This oath will kill me.

Under its section on Exemplary Punishment, the BGF constitution specifies a death sentence to any member who basically doesn't go along with the program. Several gang laws are listed, such as "use of heroin", "selling or giving weapons to the enemy", etc. Many gangs have the rights of trial for members, but not the BGF which includes this very efficient clause: "Time not permitting a chance of review, the Generals, for security reasons, may order and have a sentence of death carried out against a member for violation of one of the above laws".

In addition to its "do's" and "don'ts" in terms of expected behavior (basically political indoctrination), the BGF constitution includes a very elaborate "Party Platform". It specifically identifies the "Party" as the overall reference group, apparently the Communist Party from this paragraph in Part III of the BGF constitution:

"We use Marxism, which is positive in spirit, to overcome liberalism, which is negative. A communist should have largeness of mind, and he/she should be staunch and active, looking upon the interest of the revolution as his/her very life and subordinating his/her personal interests to those of the revolution. Always and everywhere he/she should adhere to principles and wage a tireless struggle against all incorrect ideas and actions, as to consolidate the collective life of the Party, and strengthen the ties between the Party and the masses. He/she should be more concerned about others than about himself/herself. Only thus can we be considered a Communist."

In its ideal and self-described form, then, this particular gang does in fact see itself by name and intention as a group that is "about revolution". Guerilla warfare and political terrorism are definitely potential interests of this gang.

It is of some interest, as well, that gangs behind bars in states like Illinois such as the Brothers of the Struggle (B.O.S.) refer in their internal literature to their development goals as a "movement". See Appendix D for examples of such internal written documents of the B.O.S. gang (it encompasses Black Disciples, and Gangster Disciples). As reported elsewhere[a], this same gang that operates inside jails and adult prisons (and juvenile correctional institutions as well) has evolved to the point where it now has it own written "Disciplinary Report Forms" that it completes on its own members when they violate one of the internal rules and regulations of the gang (see Appendix D).

A PRELIMINARY TEST ABOUT POLITICAL EXTREMISM USING CONFINED JUVENILE OFFENDERS

While some authors may claim gangs have no ideology, emerging data shows some gangs are truly formalized. Obviously, if we are to consider groups like the Ku Klux Klan and Aryan Brotherhood "gangs", as is done in the present analysis, then we must admit that some gangs do have such fairly developed ideology (Helmreich, 1973). Some gangs even have written constitutions which express this ideology. Many observers in the study of guerilla warfare and terrorism also observe that the element of ideology must be present as well. Described here are results from the survey of juvenile institutions reported more completely in a later chapter.

In the Fall of 1990 all juvenile correctional institutions (training schools and camps) were sampled using a four page survey instrument designed to be completed by the Superintendent. Some 155 institutions responded representing 49 states. Below are some of the findings relevant to the present analysis.

When asked "to what extent are gang members involved in extremist political beliefs" on a scale from zero (not at all) to a high of ten (a great deal), 61 percent indicated zero. The ideology variable was then recoded to reflect a dummy variable of the presence or absence of any such reported extremist beliefs. In this fashion, its effects on other gang problems is most significant as seen in Table 11.

---

[a] George W. Knox, Ph.D., "Gang Organization in a Large Urban Jail", American Jails (January/February), 1993: pp. 45-48.

TABLE 11

Significant Relationships Between Gang Political
Extremism And Indicators of Gang Population Size,
Reports of Gang Damage to Government Property,
and Racial Conflict

		Any Level of Political Extremism Reported Among Gang Members? ********************************	
		NO	YES
Institutions Reporting 10% or More of their Population Are Gang Members	NO	66	16
	YES	35	39

Chi square = 19.1, p < .001

Institutions Reporting a Problem of Gang Damage to Government Property	NO	67	8
	YES	32	47

Chi square = 43.1, p < .001

Institutions Reporting a Problem of Racial Conflict	NO	58	20
	YES	39	34

Chi square = 7.2, p = .01

What these findings suggest is that the extent to which gangs do have such an element of ideology as measured by the presence or absence of political extremism is itself significantly related to problems such as gang force strength, the damage they do to government property, and reported problems of racial conflict. Ongoing research dealing the same problems in adult institutions and other criminal justice settings is now underway by the author.

GANG MEMBERS SEEKING FIREARMS AND ORDNANCE FROM FRIENDS IN THE AMERICAN MILITARY

The findings reported here are based on a exploratory study of N = 91 members of a unit of the Illinois National Guard. On the morning of October 13th, 1992 a 7-year-old child named Dantrell Davis was killed by sniper fire from an AR-15 rifle in the Cabrini Green public housing complex on Chicago's near north side. The shooter who had served in the Army, was determined to be a gang member. It was a gang-related killing that occurred as the child was being walked with his mother on the way to school.

Enormous attention was given to this incident in the mass media and a public outcry ensued that gained national attention. During this aftermath several city officials were quoted as giving was serious consideration to bringing in the National Guard to help suppress the gang problem in Cabrini Green.

Outside of the official report by Sleeman (1849) documenting the role of the military in the suppression of the Budhuk gangs of India there is little in the literature that provides any linkage between the two separate issues of "gangs" and the "military"[b]. One notable exception is the analysis of the Yakuza by Kaplan and Dubro (1986, p. 200) who mention how the Yakuza operating in South Korea in their production and sales of illegal drugs, more specifically methamphetamines (i.e., "speed", a drug of choice in Japan) had spread in terms of illicit use to U.S. soldiers stationed in South Korea[c]. But little documentation and no indepth analysis of the possible impact that a gang can have on military personnel is provided anywhere in the public literature.

Most of the literature on gangs that provides any citation to the military is therefore cursory at best. The "Zoot suit" riots, which could have equally been called "military riots against Pachucos", are an example of this cursory treatment. Most analysts have had to rely on what was printed in the newspapers and on oral history recollections from the viewpoints of the Pachucos, with no known follow-up on the members of the military who were obviously very important actors in the fray. Similarly, the early role of the National Guard (19th century, New York City) in the suppression of gang street battles is mentioned in the literature only in passing, that is they were effective in dispersing the gangs fighting in the streets (Haskins, 1975: p. 29)[d].

A magazine called Teen Angels published since 1980 in California, describing itself as a gang rights activist news organization, routinely includes pictures and names of Hispanic members within the military and encourages military enlistment[e]. It is not implied that these are "gang members"; but everyone else in the magazine indicates they are...complete with the photos the gangs send in of themselves, their arms caches, and their "placas". It is a magazine for west coast Hispanic gangs.

---

[b] Lt.-Col. W.H. Sleeman, 1849, Report on Budhuk alia Bagree Decoits and other Gang Robbers by Hereditary Profession and on the measures adopted by the Government of India for their Suppression. Calcutta: J.C. Sherriff, Bengal Military Orphan Press.

[c] David E. Kaplan and Elec Dubro, 1986, Yakuza: The Explosive Account of Japan's Criminal Underworld. Reading, MA: Addison-Wesley Publishing Company, Inc.

[d] James Haskins, 1975, Street Gangs Yesterday and Today. New York: Hastings House Publishers.

[e] Such as in Issue #107, two pages were devoted to the military men and women (including full names, rank, and photos); usually the Teen Angels magazine lists this type of material as "Green Angels", and gives the P.O. Box 338, Rialto, CA 92376 - the same address as Teen Angels magazine.

The book about gangs from an evangelical view of a minister providing outreach to gang members describes the case of "Trigger", a gang member who wanted to do well in school and join the Marine Corps for the benefit of subsequent college education benefits, and the gang leader encouraged this goal (Mc Lean, 1991: p. 78)[f].

Some very limited newspaper coverage has been given to the problem of gangs near large military bases. One of the best of these journalistic efforts deserves some recognition here[g]. First, military kids were considered potential risks to gang membership because they are very transient, moving from one place to the next. A local police officer near a military base in Oceanside, California stated that he knows of military children who were heavily influence by gangs, some of whom still live on the military base. Staff running youth programs for the Defense Department acknowledge such problems, although military spokespersons are quick to say they are just "wannabe" gang members. One military base commander was quoted as saying "The general has a strong policy....if you're caught in gang-related activities, you're [moved] off base" (Jowers, 1993).

An anonymous survey questionnaire was designed to measure various aspects of the gang problem. The instrument used is a one page, double-sided questionnaire. The front page contained forced-choice items and the back page contained open-ended items. Many of these items replicate previous research on groups that deal with gang problems (e.g., law enforcement, etc).

In mid-November 1992 the data collection began using a student who is a member of the same military unit who sought informal cooperation from other members of the National Guard unit where he was stationed. The unit sampled is located on Chicago's southside and is predominantly African-American.

Because of the sensitive nature of the questions about gangs and crime no identifying variables were included in the survey. Only one background variable was used: length of service.

The sampling technique used here qualifies only as a purposive or exploratory study and is not generalizable.

Only about one third (32.2%) of the respondents expressed the belief that the National Guard should be sent to Cabrini Green (or any other gang environment) to stop gang warfare. Half (50%) rejected this utilization of National Guard troops. Some 17.8 percent indicated they were not sure.

These National Guardsmen were asked if the armed forces should try to recruit gang members just in case the military has to be used in response to a riot situation where many gang members could be involved. About a third (34.4%) accepted the validity

---

[f] Gordon McLean, 1991, Cities of Lonesome Fear: God Among the Gangs, Chicago: Moody Press.

[g] Karen Jowers, "Kids at Risk: The Spread of Gangs Has Some Military Communities Antsy, and Getting Involve", Life In the Times, 1992.

of this notion. The majority (65.6%) rejected the idea of recruiting gang members for use by the military.

The overwhelming majority (95.6%) of the respondents expressed the belief that the federal and state government has not done enough to try to prevent the gang problem.

These members of the National Guard were presented with the scenario where they should not be used to deal with gang problems and were asked "who should" be used instead. The single largest group (41.4%) indicated the local police should be used. Some 10.3 percent indicated the state police. Some 24.1 percent indicated federal troops. And 24.1 percent indicated "other".

These members of the National Guard were also asked to estimate based on their knowledge what percent of all U.S. armed forces personnel they believe are probably gang members themselves. Only 2.8 percent indicated "zero percent of the U.S. armed forces are probably gang members". In fact, the percent of estimated gang membership within the U.S. military ranged from a low of zero to a high of 75 percent. The mean, or arithmetic average, was 21.5 percent.

Table 12 presents the findings for a somewhat more general inquiry of "what would be your estimates for the percentage that are current or former gang members by branch of military service". As seen in Table 12, the Coast Guard is shown to have the lowest estimated current or former gang member population, followed by the Air Force. The Coast Guard are shown in Table 12 to have a mean estimated former or current gang membership of 6.3 percent compared with 7.8 percent for the Air Force. It is of some interest that these National Guard respondents gave their own outfit the highest mean average of former/current gang membership (mean = 25.6%).

TABLE   12

ESTIMATES OF THE % WHO
ARE CURRENT OR FORMER
GANG MEMBERS BY BRANCH

	Low *****	High ******	Mean *****
Army	0%	90%	16.3%
Navy	0%	80%	10.9%
Marines	0%	70%	14.8%
Air Force	0%	60%	7.8%
Nat'l. Guard	2%	80%	25.6%
Coast Guard	0%	50%	6.3%
Army Reserve	1%	90%	19.8%

Asked if the National Guard can truly stop the problem of gangs in places like Cabrini Green, over half (58.2%) indicated in the negative. Only 12.1 percent expressed the belief that the National Guard could truly stop the problem of gangs in places like Cabrini Green. Some 29.7 percent indicated they were "not sure".

Just over a fourth (26.7%) expressed the belief that the National Guard are adequately trained to go into a place like Cabrini Green to stop gang violence. Most (73.3%) felt the National Guard lacked adequate training for such a mission.

These members of the National Guard were also asked if they have ever, as individuals, been approached by a gang member who wanted to acquire military weapons or ordnance (e.g., grenades, etc). Most (90.8%) said no. However, some 9.2 percent indicated they had in fact been approached by such gang members seeking military weapons. It is not known, because of the brevity of this particular survey, whether any of these events were ever reported to authorities. Nor is it clear what specific reporting guidelines or policies are in place with regard to this matter.

These members of the National Guard were also asked their opinion on whether the U.S. armed forces should discharge a soldier who is determined to be a current gang member. The respondents were almost evenly divided on this issue. Some 59.1 percent felt that the military should not discharge gang members. Some 40.9 percent felt that gang members should be discharged.

These members of the National Guard were asked if they believe that gang members are depicted as an overblown "threat" by the news media, politicians, and others. Over half (59.5%) expressed the belief that gang members are not depicted as an overblown threat. However, some 40.2 percent affirmed the belief that gang members are depicted as an overblown threat.

These personnel of the National Guard in Chicago were also asked "how many of your close friends and associates are gang members". The distribution of results for this item was as follows:

	How many of your close friends or associates are gang members?					
	0	1	2	3	4	5 or more
N	62	1	7	3	2	11
Percent	72.1	1.2	8.1	3.5	2.3	12.8

Thus, over a fourth (27.9%) of these members of the National Guard had one or more close friends or associates who are gang members. It is unlikely that those social forces calling for the utilization of the National Guard in Cabrini Green were aware of the fact that the same military personnel might be in the situation of confronting gang members who could --- at some unknown level of probability --- be friends or associates of the soldiers assigned to such duty.

It is of some interest that 12.8 percent of this sample of National Guardsmen reported having five or more such close friends or associates who are gang members. This type of question is often a measure of subcultural integration and a predictor of gang membership itself. It is also of interest that one respondent chose to mark a large "Star of David" six-pointed star symbol on the back of his survey instrument;

which is the insignia/logo used by the Disciples (BDs, GDs, BGDs, B.O.S.) in the Folks gang nation.

The survey also included the question used with other populations (e.g., police, etc) to the effect "do you believe that if many of today's gang leaders had entered the military instead of joining a gang they could put their leadership skills to better use as good soldiers"? Three-fourths (77.8%) of the respondents expressed this belief that such gang leaders could have made good soldiers. Just over a fifth (22.2%) rejected the idea that gang leaders would make good soldiers.

Almost two-thirds (65.2%) of the sample felt that they knew how --- with relative certainty --- to identify a gang member by their colors, behavior, or language. Just over a third (34.8%) did not know how to identify a gang member in this fashion.

When asked how long they themselves had served in the National Guard, the distribution showed a low of one year to a high of 21 years. The mean, or average, was 6.3 years.

About one in ten (10.2%) reported that in the last year they had been a victim of a gang crime.

A bivariate analysis was made of a number of variables in the survey. This was accomplished by recoding some of these variables the details of which are explained below. Described here are some of the significant findings from this inquiry.

Table 13 shows that, among this sample of National Guardsmen, by recoding the "gang friends" variable (none versus having one or more) and the "belief pattern about what percentage of all U.S. Armed Forces personnel are probably gang members" yields a statistically significant relationship. In other words, the profile that emerges here is that the gang friendship variable is significantly differentiated by the level of perceived gang membership throughout the armed forces. Specifically, those National Guardsmen who have one or more close friends and associates who are gang members are those more likely to perceive a higher representation of gang members in the U.S. Armed Forces. Recall that overall some 27.9 percent of this group had one or more such friends who are gang members. Table 13 shows that among the low belief pattern only 19.4 percent have one or more such gang friends; but among the high belief pattern some 44.1 percent have one or more such gang friends. There is clearly a relationship between these two variables.

TABLE 13

BELIEF ABOUT GANG REPRESENTATION IN THE U.S.ARMED FORCES IN RELATIONSHIP TO HAVING ONE OR MORE GANG FRIENDS AMONG A SAMPLE OF NATIONAL GUARDSMEN (FREQUENCY DISTRIBUTION)

	Have One or More Close Friends Or Associates as Gang Members	
	NO	YES
Belief Pattern of What % Gang Members Are in all U.S. Armed Forces:		
Low ($< = 15\%$)	29	7 (19.4%)
High ($> = 20\%$)	19	15 (44.1%)

Chi-square = 4.93, p = .02

This finding is similar to that uncovered in gang studies in high schools where the gang member is more likely to project a higher estimate of the percentage of the student population who are gang members. In fact, this tendency for perceived gang representation levels becomes even more pronounced in relationship to having one or more gang friends when the more specific variable of gang members in the National Guard is examined as seen in Table 14.

Table 14 shows the same pattern profile where the gang-friend variable is significantly differentiated by low-high perceptions of the extent to which gang members are represented in their own ranks (e.g., the National Guard). Those who have the low perception of gang members in their own ranks show only 16.6 have one or more gang friends themselves. But among those with a high perception of gang members in their own ranks some fifty percent have one or more such close friends who are gang members.

Finally, these perceptions are clearly directly related to one another. That is, those who perceive low levels of gang representation among the ranks of the U.S. Armed Forces generally are pretty much those who also perceive low representation of gang members among their own ranks of National Guardsmen. This finding in shown in Table 15.

TABLE 14

BELIEF ABOUT GANG REPRESENTATION IN THE
RANKS OF THE NATIONAL GUARD IN RELATIONSHIP
TO HAVING ONE OR MORE GANG FRIENDS
AMONG A SAMPLE OF NATIONAL GUARDSMEN
(FREQUENCY DISTRIBUTION)

	Have One or More Close Friends Or Associates as Gang Members	
Belief Pattern of What % Gang Members Are in the National Guard:	NO	YES
Low ($<=15\%$)	25	5 (16.6%)
High ($>=20\%$)	16	16 (50.0%)

Chi-square = 7.68, p = .006

As seen in Table 15, not only are the perceptions of gang penetration into the military related to having gang friends, but the perceptions overall are related to the perceptions in their own ranks. This is highly significant (p < .001).

Table 15 also shows that among those who have a low level perception of the extent to which gangs are represented in the overall U.S. armed forces most of these (22 out of 28) also perceive low levels of gang representation among their own ranks. Vice versa, those with high perceptions of the gang presence within the overall U.S. armed forces mostly see their own ranks as also penetrated by gang members.

TABLE 15
FREQUENCY DISTRIBUTION OF PERCEIVED LEVELS OF GANG
MEMBERSHIP IN THE OVERALL US ARMED FORCES IN RELATIONSHIP
TO PERCEIVED LEVELS OF GANG MEMBERSHIP WITHIN THE
NATIONAL GUARD AMONG A SAMPLE OF NATIONAL GUARDSMEN

	Belief Pattern of What % Gang Members are in the National Guard ********************************	
	LOW ($<=15\%$) **********	HIGH ($>=20\%$) **********
Belief pattern of what % gang members are in the overall U.S. Military.		
LOW ($<=15\%$)	22	6 (21.4%)
HIGH ($>=20\%$)	5	26 (83.8%)

Chi-square = 23.11, p < .001

Another factor that significantly differentiates the perception of gang members within their own ranks is their belief about what the military should or should not do if a soldier is discovered to be a gang member. Table 16 provides this test.

TABLE 16

FREQUENCY DISTRIBUTION OF BELIEFS ABOUT WHETHER GANG MEMBERS SHOULD BE DISCHARGED FROM THE MILITARY IN RELATIONSHIP TO PERCEIVED LEVELS OF GANG MEMBERSHIP WITH THE NATIONAL GUARD AMONG A SAMPLE OF NATIONAL GUARDSMEN

	Belief Pattern of What % Gang Members are in the National Guard ********************************	
	LOW ($< = 15\%$) **********	HIGH ($> = 20\%$) **********
Should the U.S. Armed Forces Discharge Anyone Determined to Be a Current Gang Member?		
NO	13	23 (63.8%)
YES	16	10 (38.4%)

Chi-square = 3.92, p = .04

As seen in Table 16, those with the more tolerant position about gangs in the military who believe current gang members should not be discharged show some 63.8 percent with a high perception level of gang representation among their own ranks. Conversely, those with a less tolerant view and who do believe a soldier discovered to be a current gang member should be discharged show only 38.4 percent with a high perception level of gang representation among their own ranks. This factor of gang policy in the military significantly differentiates this perception of the extent to which gang members are present among their own ranks (p = .04).

The only genuine "background" factor within the data environment of this survey is years of service within the National Guard. Recoding this variable to reflect recent versus long term soldiers reveals a significant finding in relationship to perception levels of the gang presence among U.S. armed forces. This is shown in Table 17. Also, Table 17 shows that this factor of tenure in the national guard also significantly differentiates those who have one or more close friends who are gang members.

This background factor of years of continuous service in the National Guard was recoded to create roughly two groups: the young guard, and the old guard. The young guard are those with less than or equal to four years of service. The old guard are those with between five to twenty-one years of service. Therefore this difference between young and old guard does not reflect actual age, but is rather a surrogate measure of age, experience, and military socialization by measuring specifically the years of service within the National Guard.

TABLE 17

FREQUENCY DISTRIBUTION OF PERCEIVED LEVELS OF GANG MEMBERSHIP IN THE OVERALL U.S. ARMED FORCES IN RELATIONSHIP TO SERVICE TENURE LEVELS AMONG A SAMPLE OF NATIONAL GUARDSMEN

	Years of Service Within The National Guard **************************	
	Young Guard (< = 4 yrs) **********	Old Guard (> = 5 yrs) *********
Perceived Levels of Gang Membership Overall in the U.S. Armed Forces		
LOW (< = 15%)	10	25
HIGH (> = 20%)	20	15

Chi-square = 5.83, p = .01

Table 17 shows that the old guard are more likely to report a low perceived representation of gangs in the overall ranks of the U.S. armed forces. Duration of service appears to be inversely related to the perception of gang membership levels in the overall U.S. Armed Forces.

Similarly, Table 18 shows that it is the younger guard who have a statistically significant higher likelihood of having one or more close friends and associates who are gang members. In other words, the actual condition of these National Guardsmen having such gang friends itself is a factor that profiles quite differently by years of service.

TABLE 18

FREQUENCY DISTRIBUTION OF THE PROFILE OF HAVING ONE OR MORE CLOSE FRIENDS OR ASSOCIATES WHO ARE GANG MEMBERS IN RELATIONSHIP TO SERVICE TENURE LEVELS AMONG A SAMPLE OF NATIONAL GUARDSMEN

	Years of Service Within The National Guard	
	Young Guard ($< = 4$ yrs)	Old Guard ($> = 5$ yrs)
Have one or more close friends or associates who are gang members?		
NO	23	38
YES	16	7

Chi-square = 6.81, p = .009

It seems reasonable to believe that some gang members are present within the ranks of the U.S. armed forces. However, very little is actually known about this aspect of gangs. It would reflect what is called an adaptation of marginality: high integration into legitimate organization (e.g., the military) and high integration into an illegitimate or subcultural organization (e.g., the gang). What side is such a person really on? No one knows, this has been the first effort reported in the literature to examine the issue. So, hopefully, this study has begun to shed some light on the issue of gangs and the military.

The one respondent who did intentionally affect a gang posture by inscribing a large gang symbol on his survey may reasonably be assumed to be a gang member. However, the situation under which this data was collected did not lend itself to such self-reported gang membership research. At the time of this study these same members of the military were under consideration for being sent into a housing complex (e.g., Cabrini Green) to quell gang violence. Indeed, there is another reason this standard self-report question was not included here: if discovered, it could be cause for serious difficulty.

Therefore the present study focused only on surrogate measures of the self-report research method by asking the respondent to report on the deviance of their friends and associates not their own. This meant asking these national guardsmen how many of their close friends and associates were gang members rather than asking if the respondent was currently in a gang. Self-report research among deviants shows that they are more likely to report on the deviance of their friends and associates than their own.

A gang member in the military must be regarded as a unique condition of deviance: someone who literally marches under two sets of colors and to two different drummers, one legitimate (the military) and one illegitimate (the gang). How pervasive this situation is cannot be objectively estimated from simple perceptions or beliefs as are measured in this survey. What orders of the day would the gang member in the military actually follow if they were on a domestic mission to suppress a gang-related civil disturbance: those from the military, or if they were facing their own gang those from the gang?

While exploratory in nature, several findings from this research deserve serious attention[40].

What should be the position on gang membership among military personnel? Not all gang members have criminal records. It is real simple to understand: not all gang members who commit crimes are always caught and even if caught always convicted. The Knox (1991) textbook referred to a case where the Latin King gang member committed a possible homicide (he still to this day does not know if the person died from the gunshot wounds) as part of an initiation ceremony and later "chilled out", went to college, and is now working in the Cook County court system. He has no police record. He was never caught.

It is very similar to the situation for dealing with the marginality of some police officers. A police department cannot terminate the employment of someone who simply associates with "undesirables". It is a freedom of association and constitutional issue that has not been given much legal analysis.

No military code of conduct is known to the present author that specifically prohibits members of the U.S. armed forces from having close friends and associates who are gang members. It is an issue having enormous implications.

THE POWER OF GANGS IN SOCIAL CONFLICT

Could a criminal gang literally take over a legitimate organization? Yes, it is theoretically possible. The reasons why a gang might want to engage in this type of social conflict would have several potentially diverse explanations. One would be the monetary resources such a legitimate not-for-profit or membership or fraternal organization might own, resources that under the right leadership could be rapidly liquidated or exploited. Another reason might be the political platform base that such a group might represent as a target for a take over.

Some discussion on this issue has focused on the case of the Gangster Disciples, through their political arm the "21st Century V.O.T.E." group, in late 1994 tried to wrench control of a branch of the N.A.A.C.P. in Chicago. A surrogate force was said to be used here, a group that had for a couple years established itself as an anti-drug program or drug rehabilitation/counseling program, which while very popular in some circles (No Dope Express), was actually a co-sponsor and heavily involved in the October 1993 Gang Summit meeting held in Chicago. Some have indicated that the gang in this instance is being used to divide and fractionate the political infrastructure of the African-American community, almost to a blueprint plan.

The tension that had existed in Chicago's southside branch of the NAACP reflected an induced conflict between the older vanguard of the civil rights struggle, including noted figures like Vernon Jarrett, and the new and much younger sector. Earl King, from No Dope Express, apparently had only about a year or so membership in the chapter and ran for president. By doing so, the "split" or social conflict began. When Vernon Jarrett joined in with the opposition, within a short time later, Earl King walked into the NAACP office in Chicago and handed in 5,000 newly completed applications for membership along with the $50,000 in cash. Some read this development as an effort by the gang to take over this chapter of the NAACP.[41]

The potential exists, of a gang which can rapidly generate large numbers for a turnout, for a gang to take over a legitimate organization. The disruptive legal impact of this type of tactic carries enormous implications for social conflict. The astute observer of this scene will also be able to recall examples of some political extremist groups sympathetic to and/or existing as an above ground propaganda vehicle for a terrorist group like ALF, where such activists were able to take over legitimate groups in the animal rights arena, converting their funds and assets to a different use. While in the terrorism example of ALF and its front groups was successful, the Chicago gang strategy to take over a chapter of the NAACP was much more directly combative and designed to backfire because it was not done in a quiet, subtle, fashion --- but rather in a Rambo-style display of conspicuously threatening force. Any group that can rapidly generate 5,000 to 10,000 members or associates for a picnic, like the Gangster Disciples were able to do in recent years, is obviously a group also capable of having such persons fill out membership applications to join any association legally, and literally take it over by overwhelming numbers of voters in any election of officers.

SUMMARY AND CONCLUSION

Stinchecombe's (1964) analysis of youth rebellion is useful here in coming to a summation on the matter of gangs, guerilla warfare, and social conflict. It advances the "articulation hypothesis" which amounts to this element of hope: to those who can articulate little relationship between their current socialization and relationship to dominant social institutions (e.g., the schools, etc, which are designed to train persons for such future productive roles in American society) and their subsequent life chances in the hope for a better existence --- it is among these for whom rebellion is strongest. Whether it is perceived or objective, the net effect is equally the same: alienation. In a high school context it became, ala Stinchecombe (1964), "expressive alienation". In a subsequent gang maybe it can become "active alienation" to the extent that these same persons carry on a war against their own society.

Perhaps this is all too conjectural. The cynic could say whatever the potential for gangs becoming guerilla's, undereducated drug abusers do not make good soldiers[42]. So perhaps another variation would be a toned down variety of social protest, without the use of arms. There are certainly a lot of different scenarios for what could happen to America's gangs.[43] One thing we can probably rule out, however, was an option used by the military suppression effort against gangs in India: exiling the gang member for life "across the seas".

Clearly, there is a need for further and more indepth research on the potential for gang involvement in terrorism, civil disorder, and low-intensity conflict. We have much to do in the analysis of the gang crime problem in America.

The serious student of criminology knows that a wide variety of "wilderness" and "survival" programs have been used with delinquents throughout the years. If "boot camp" training is all we as a post-industrial society (where theoretical knowledge is supposed to be the principal basis for social change)[44] can come up with, then we are certainly headed for disaster. Not dissimilar from the well-intending social service program that makes its resources available to a gang for manipulating/abusing in the interest of "reaching out" to them and then finding out too late (e.g. Chicago's Fry) that something has truly "gone awry"; the correctional fad of "boot camps" when it comes to gang members should be viewed with some caution as a "solution".

Some hard historical facts remain undisputed about the role of gangs and higher levels of violence. Some of these facts remind us of how pitifully little we have done about the gang problem; and of how scant the answers are to major gang questions like "how many gang members are there in America?". The two top Catholic leaders of Mexico were gunned down in 1993 in Guadalajara, Mexico near the airport because their car resembled that of a rival drug lord targeted for assassination. The shooters that killed Mexico's Cardinal on May 24th, 1993 were American street gang members hired by a Mexican drug lord to hit a rival[45]. The facts show that important linkages have been made between foreign groups and American gangs: Islamic terrorist groups and the El Rukns, the Yakuza and the Latin Kings, and the above instance of a Mexican drug lord and the 30th Street Gang in San Diego. It would seem gangs may be expected to figure prominently in such future scenarios unless our society confronts this problem most forthrightly.

DISCUSSION QUESTIONS

(1) Up until 1994 patterns of gang violence at the highest level (e.g., those involving homicide as a routine outcome) tended to involve a pattern characterized by retaliatory shootings (vengeance for the death of a fellow gang member) against rival gang members, drive-by shootings in areas where the cognitive maps tend to identify the area or residential location as a gang member site, arson against residential buildings known to be occupied by gang members, street stops (attacking persons who wear colors or look like rival gang members in streets controlled by a rival gang), assassination within the correctional setting by any of a variety of violent means including planned or opportunistic attacks upon rival gang members as well as correctional staff, and "false flag" random shooting (driving through a neighborhood, displaying a false gang hand sign and shooting the person who responds with the same gang hand sign). Can you envision any other future patterns of violence based on human history?

(2) Is it possible to have true nationwide gangs, functioning in virtually every state and major city in America? Do you feel that Philadelphia's MOVE group was a gang? Was the Symbionese Liberation Army a gang?[46] What problems can arise in using a definition of the gang as not simply that it is involved in crime over time, but that it or its members come to the attention of the community which views it as

in some sense "threatening"? That is, could any political group be then defined as a gang if the local power structure felt "threatened by it"?

(3) If gang members are so hostile to legitimate authority, as is often presumed in the gang literature, then why are many rank and file gang members so highly compliant with the directives of the gang leaders, up to and including the order of carrying out a homicide or other serious assault involving great personal risk?

FOOTNOTES

1. I am indebted to Professor Thomas F. Mc Currie for help on establishing the interface between the gang literature and the terrorism literature and who helped co-author a closely related paper on the same subject.

2. And, of course, the gang member as "quisling" in Taylor (1990).

3. Chapter 15 discusses some of the written gang constitutions and by-laws and shows the important element of "oppressed peoples" ideology. In fact, in the Spanish Gangster Disciple Nation the language of greeting to fellow gang members is "comrade", indeed these higher level gang formations come to view their fellow members as comrades in arms.

4. As Sibley says "the police and the public are facing an enemy army with its own uniforms, weapons and rules" (1989: p. 403).

5. See: Tom Brune and James Ylisela, Jr., "The Making of Jeff Fort", Chicago, November, 1988.

6. Clearly, the strongest evidence yet to emerge that gangs have a left-wing ideological base is from the present study of gangs. In later chapters, in examining actual written gang constitutions, it will be noted how some major Chicago gangs have a common ideological component regarding their official declaration as being the avant guard for "oppressed peoples" generally, or at a minimum identifying with struggles of the oppressed groups.

7. See Campbell and Muncer (1989) for how American gangs have historically lack a revolutionary ideology, in fact, their values have tended to be those of the "mainstream" society, albeit somewhat distorted.

8. "Probers Hint Gangs Used L.A. Riots To Get Guns, But Not All Agree", Chicago Tribune, June 18, 1992: Section 1A, p. 41.

9. Chicago Tribune, ibid.

10. Hagedorn (1988: p. 203) was knowledgeable of this "street sweeping" tactic of gang repression.

11. See Royko's (1971) Boss.

12. See his The Wretched of the Earth.

13. It also accounts, across race, for the ability of sting operations to net large numbers of such offenders using a "double con" method. See also, the related honor threats resulting in gang homicides in Quebec (Cusson, 1989).

14. See Srivastava (1981) for a recent discussion of these "robbery gangs", which also links the conflict to caste and social class factors.

15. See Cole and Momen (1986) for a similar example of how urban gangs functioned in political violence and did control entire towns, involving a coalition of gangs (circa 1843, Iraq).

16. The contemporary, updated, drug-related version would therefore include drug consumption, and perhaps thereby, a shorter "crime free" time span of rest and relaxation.

17. Patrick (1973, p. 47) reports the case of a Glasgow gang routinely acquiring its firearms in the local "black market" (e.g., criminal subculture), and one case of the gang burglarizing a military installation to steal fully automatic shoulder weapons, hand grenades, and other military equipment.

18. Keiser (1969, 1979) should have been sufficient for law enforcement analysts to realize that this "gang-breaking" approach, while often "used by insurgent groups to weaken the effectiveness of organized governments, societies, and competing organizations" (Needle and Stapleton, 1983: p. 30), may not be effective with gangs at the higher end of the organizational development spectrum --- particularly the Vice Lords, which were studied by Keiser, which as a gang basically planned for their leaders to face such targeted prosecution programs and therefore to provide gang organizational continuity, the Vice Lords "institutionalized" leadership within roles. That allows for leadership succession in much the same way that the military command "passes" down the ranks to those eager to fill these positions.

19. For a contemporary version, see Sibley (1989, pp. 420-421) who describes California's 1988 Street Terrorism Enforcement and Prevention Act, a piece of anti-gang legislation passed making it a felony to "participate in a street-gang" or if convicted of a gang-related crime (p. 421), which carries another three years imprisonment.

20. William Whyte (1981: p. 255) used the same phrase "habitual association".

21. This allowed for an early form of a Targeted Offender Program; identifying those gang members most active, in leadership roles, and at large for law enforcement initiatives.

22. What we know did fail, as a third such experiment, was integrating the gangs into the military en masse into one unit. This did not work at all.

23. Most training materials would have us believe that terrorism usually implies the use of violence for political, religious, or ideological goals, with the noted exception of criminal terrorism which means the opportunistic use of violence for instrumental purposes (e.g., income motivated), planned or unplanned.

24. Some contemporary gang experts when talking about the goals of many action programs since the 1950's to present (e.g., New York City Youth Board, Chicago Youth Development Project, Community Youth Gang Services) use the term "to destabilize gang structures", as if they were small foreign countries, and such youth workers were CIA SOC/INT social engineering agents.

25. "Planning" was a necessary ingredient in Thrasher's definition of the gang and its behavior.

26. Most of such contemporary gangs would fail to even meet Cuba's revolutionary hero/theorist, Che Guevara's, three tenets of guerrilla warfare: constant vigilance, ok; constant distrust, ok; but constant mobility --- probably not, because to the extent they are "homies", bound to a specific turf or street corner or geographic "base", they are then vulnerable. Che's three guidelines (constant vigilance, constant distrust, constant mobility) were either not enough to be an effective guerrilla or he simply did not himself live up to them, having met a violent death at the hands of counter-insurgency forces.

27. In describing how large gangs get their guns and bombs, one recent book aimed at the layman audience (not a social scientific analysis or study of gangs) claimed "they buy these weapons from international arms dealers" (Webb, 1991: p. 75). Some gangs would probably like to have such a connection, but it is substantially less than factual to claim major American gangs have and use such connections now.

28. See for example the article quoting everyone from Malcolm Klein, Sgt. Wes Mc Bride, to the FBI on the nationwide expansion of the gang-drug-violence problem by Robert Mc Garvey, 1991, "Gangland: L.A. Super Gangs Target America", The American Legion (130)(2)(Feb): 25-27,60-61.

29. Recall that the California prison gang, the Black Guerilla Family (BGF), is very political and "is an adjunct of the Black Liberation Army (BLA) which operates as a Marxist-Leninist terrorist organization on the streets of America" (Jackson and Mc Bride, 1990: p. 53). But outside of the prison context, Jackson and Mc Bride see the BGF as apolitical, due to the waning of the political movement, such that this gang is "now almost totally a criminal group trafficking in narcotics" (ibid).

30. According to a gang informant a relationship does exist between a known terrorist organization (the F.A.L.N.) and a street gang (Spanish Lords). This is a cultural tie, both being oriented towards and composed of members descending from Puerto Rico. This has a prison connection as well. Luis Rosa, the informant indicated, was tied to the FALN; and is like a brother with Carlos Vega, who was

said to be a leader in the Spanish Lords. Further ties become established in the prison setting when, for example, in 1988 in Stateville Penitentiary a Latin Exchange Cultural Committee (an inmate organization with outside ties) was established to increase political awareness among inmates.

31. The murder of Chicago's Rudy Lozano is one such case known and documented. But, apparently, still not completely "solved".

32. The work of Davis (1982) is worth some attention here. It is a short book filled with pictures and horror stories; everything from a prison gang rape to "how to" approaches to making explosives. It does provide much discussion about terrorism generally (Davis, 1982: p. 50) and does tend to equate gang members with terrorists (Davis, 1982: p. 52).

33. See: "Gangs and Guns: A Task Force Report of the National Gang Crime Research Center", Nov. 11, 1994. For release at the Annual Meeting of the American Society of Criminology, Miami, FL. Co-principal investigators on this Task Force included: George Knox, John Laske, Jim Houston, Tom McCurrie, and Edward Tromanhauser.

34. See: "Plot To Blow Up Police Alleged Gang Sought Rocket Launcher, Feds Say", by Tom Seibel and Art Golab, Chicago Sun-Times, Oct. 21, 1994, p. 1, 12. See also: "Five in Gang Accused of Plan to Blow Up Police Station", Chicago Tribune, Oct. 21, 1994, section 2, p. 10.

35. Program literature from the BUILD, Inc program in Chicago described in a later chapter for example states "Youth gangs are like street armies, marching to a different drummer".

36. The "dirty dozen" were more like the dirty thousands. Mattick only analyzed several hundred from the Chicago area. These felony offenders were integrated into regular units during W.W. II and did well. See his Master's thesis, Department of Sociology, University of Chicago.

37. Cynicism here would mean this: for some white gangs like the Aryan Brotherhood, Ku Klux Klan, SWP, and others, these are not persons facing racial discrimination. They are often simply right-wing extremists, and not because of any condition of their own poverty.

38. Based on personal interviews with current staff and training materials used by the Chicago Area Project.

39. I am grateful to correctional gang investigator and researcher Jeff McCaddon for internal documents and indepth analysis materials on the BGF and other major gangs.

40. I am grateful for the help in data collection from a member of the same military unit; who would prefer not to be explicitly mentioned in print.

41. See: "NAACP Upstart Brings in 5,000 New Members", Chicago Tribune, October 20, 1994, section 2, p. 2.

42. But they may make good surrogate terrorists. See Rachel Ehrenfeld, Narco Terrorism: How Governments Around the WOrld Have Used the Drug Trade to Finance and Further Terrorist Activities, 1990, Basic Books.

43. Another variation is intense violent partisan conflict an example in Jamaica of which is described by Harrison (1988).

44. Or so says Daniel Bell, in The Post Industrial Society.

45. Hugh Dellios, 1993, "Mexican Drug Lords Recruit U.S. Street Gangs", Chicago Tribune, July 11, Section 1, p. 3.

46. Remember it is convenient, for example, to exclude some groups like the Posse from gang analysis by saying "they are not gangs, they are organized crime" even though they have significant numbers of juvenile members. Does that mean we are simply being convenient by expanding our "inclusionary definition" of organized crime?

CHAPTER 14

TOWARDS THE UNDERSTANDING OF GANGS:
The Group Factor

INTRODUCTION

It is the "group" aspect of the gang that challenges our modern criminal justice system. It is the unique context of the group as a crime committing apparatus that also constitutes the definitive feature of a gang. The nature of the gang as a cohesive group behind bars also poses a new and formidable management problem for adult and juvenile correctional institutions. The study of group behavior is the legitimate domain of sociology, as the field of criminology is rightfully grounded in sociology as well. In this chapter we will examine aspects of gang group behavior much more closely.

Much of the variation in definitions of what constitutes a gang seems to be explained by the conceptual differences within a variety of theoretical orientations among gang authors. Here we review in as precise detail as possible some of the previous definitions of gangs in terms of their group components. Regarding group behavior our gang literature is surprisingly aloof from our social science knowledge of groups and what can or cannot be accomplished in doing something about gangs. So by addressing some of these issues and questions regarding the "group" factor and gangs, our analysis is at least one that is more explicitly grounded in our knowledge of social group formations from the social sciences.

In sociology a group is defined as two or more persons, and thus "threat group" can then be an umbrella from which to also examine political extremist groups and gang groups. But in much of the gang literature, it is generally agreed a gang must be a group of three or more persons. The reasoning is organizational: only in a group of three is it possible to achieve the primordial act of organizational life, the delegation of duty, the delegation of tasks. The Three Stooges could therefore constitute a level zero gang of mischievous adults, because it is possible for Moe to tell Curly to have the third stooge do something. Sending orders down through the command structure, that is delegation of responsibililty or duty or even authority, is the primordial function of any organization. So the other truth that emerges here is that some gangs can become real organizations, and some function much more informally. Numbers of members and resources available to the gang are the determinants of whether the gang evolves into a greater level of organizational complexity and sophistication. And generally, the higher the organizational sophistication of the gang, the higher its crime threat.

This focus is important because when, for example in corrections, when we think we are dealing with individual inmates we may be actually dealing with groups of individuals related by gang affiliation. Therefore, to understand these group dynamics is an important leap forward in being better prepared to deal with the gang problem in any situation.

ALL DEFINITIONS AGREE GANGS ARE A GROUP

While not all contributions to the gang literature provide an operational definition of the "gang", among those who at least provide us with the elements of what they consider a "gang", all definitions of gangs agree that gangs are a group of persons.[1] What remains rather ambiguous and uncertain is the logical question: what kind of social groups are gangs? And finally, what group characteristics do they have? Are gangs primary or secondary groups, membership or reference groups[2]? Formal or informal groups? And can a group become something more sophisticated?

It does not intellectually advance our understanding of gangs to simply categorize gangs as being outside of the extensive literature on social groups such as: conflict groups, deviant groups, subcultural groups, etc. That becomes little more than a definitional tautology: they are gangs, because they are deviant groups; ergo, because they are deviant, they are gangs. It is tautological because they become defined in terms of themselves.[3] The one contribution to the gang literature which was clearly grounded in this "group" literature was that by Short and Strodtbeck (1974).[4] Strodtbeck is, of course, represented within the social-psychology literature on groups (Bales and Strodtbeck, 1951). The study of groups has been an area studied primarily by sociology, and by social-psychology. It is not an area of analysis carved out traditionally by the field of psychology which is more oriented towards the analysis of the individual mind, although obviously some such authors have advanced their analyses of gangs apparently aimed at a social-psychology or psycho-social explanation.[5]

Returning to our question: what kind of group is the gang, the analysis advanced here will take the position that the gang can be at its earliest formative stage a secondary[6] group, and at its higher stage of development is certainly somewhat more than a primary group. Most important to the linkage of this discussion of gangs to the wider social group formation and affiliation literature is the assertion that social organization is necessarily implicit to any gang analysis. Therefore, to the extent that we simply "label" the gang as having no formal organizational aspects or denying such paramilitary or "pyramidal" types of infrastructure as police are allegedly prone to believe, we are avoiding a closer analysis of this most important aspect relating to the social organization of gangs.

A social group, as differentiated from temporary collectives of human beings (as in aggregate recurrent interaction at a bus stop, etc), must by its definition have social organization. It must not only be a recurrent collectivity, it must have social organization and it must have an identity and objectives in common. Size is only one of the factors that will complicate all group analysis.[7]

Inside the gang, as a social group, is such affiliation principally integrative or is it instrumental? That is, is gang membership enjoyed and valued for its own sake as an end in itself, or is it instrumental: as a means to an end, to earn money, boost one's reputation, get protection, etc. Clearly, Thrasher had some grasp of this literature, by showing such a powerful influence from the work of Tarde.

From the gang literature, most conceptions of the gang see it as more than a social group, they generally see it as a primary group. But in addition to this, there are other characteristics of the group formation as a gang unit that have been cited in the literature. Figure 12, below, summarizes some of these group characteristics defining the gang. Clearly, these factors differentiate the gang from simple "Bowery Boy" or "drinking buddy" street corner groups that may be considerably more pro-social indigenous organizations.

Perhaps this lack of clarification on what type of social group formation being analyzed as a gang has accounted for some of the reader's sense from reviewing the American gang literature that "these authors are not talking about the same thing".[8] How many of Thrasher's 1,313 gangs were "gangs" and how many were "loose knit", "recurrent street corner adolescent gatherings", with little group behavior function qualifying as "criminal"?   By the same adult tendency to view with alarm youth culture generally, in all generations as being rebellious, is its racist equivalent that of defining any group of two or more males of color gathered together as a gang?

Can there be a gang of two persons?[9] This is the question of group characteristics and group functions that has been assiduously avoided in most prior discussions of American gang formations. Let us examine Figures 12 and 13 below to answer this Socratic inquiry.

FIGURE   12

GROUP CHARACTERISTICS IN DEFINING THE GANG

GROUP CHARACTERISTICS[a]:	AUTHOR(s)
Interstitial group	Thrasher
Recurrently associating	Klein
Gathered together on continuing basis	Wrobleski & Hess
Forming allegiance for common purpose	Jackson & McBride
Having an identifiable leadership	Miller
Having internal organization	Miller
Territorial oriented	Miller; Bobrowski
Attached to local territory	Thrasher
Adolescents	Klein
Perceived as a gang by others	Klein
Self-recognized as a distinct group	Klein; Rothman; + more
Integrated/strengthened thru conflict	Thrasher
Meeting face-to-face	Thrasher
milling,movement thru space as a unit	Thrasher
Conflict and planning: resulting in:	Thrasher
Tradition	Thrasher
Unreflective Internal structure	Thrasher
Esprit de corps	Thrasher
solidarity, morale, group awareness	Thrasher
Prone to possess and use weapons	Most authors
A system of mutual obligations	Whyte
Relatively stable composition	Whyte

---

[a] We can add to this list: boundary maintenance functions, the fact that the gang as a group is always an "open system", and that as an organization it will have both an informal social organization (e.g., cliques inside it) as well as its declared formal social organization.

FIGURE   13

FUNCTION AND BEHAVIOR OF THE GANG AS A GROUP

FUNCTION AND BEHAVIOR:	AUTHOR(s)
Organized to protect turf by violence	Rothman, p. 2
Engage in anti-social behavior	Wrobleski & Hess
Unlawful and Criminal Activity	Jackson & McBride
Involved in conflict with police	Arnold (1965)
Individual or collective violence or illegal behavior	Miller
Violent or illegal activities defined as collective actions	Horowitz
Involved in enough delinquency to get a negative response from their community or law enforcement	Klein
Today have M-16's, grenades, and C-4	Vetter & Territo (1984)
Training and propelling others into a criminal career	Early Chicago School[10]
Create an atmosphere of fear and intimidation in the community	Dunston (1990: p. 6)

CAN A DYAD GROUP BE A GANG?

A group of two persons could certainly have all of the following characteristics generally attributed to gang organizations: it could be homogeneous with respect to race or ethnicity, recurrently associating, gathered together on a continuing basis, forming an allegiance for a common purpose (legitimate or illegitimate), having an identifiable leadership, having internal organization (with two persons obviously the minimal levels of vertical and horizontal dimensions), being territorially oriented, or attached to a local territory or turf, they could be persons of any age including adolescents, could be perceived as a gang (whether they are or are not) or recognized as a distinct group, and could recognize themselves as a gang (regardless of their objectively minimal size and force), their bonds could be strengthened further by being labelled or through conflict with others (including adult authority), they meet face-to-face, mill around and have mutual movement through space as a unit, they experience or engage in conflict and planning, they develop a tradition, have an esprit de corps, a sense of solidarity, morale, group awareness, have boundary maintenance functions defining "in group" and "out group"/friend and foe, it can be an open system with mutual obligations and a relatively stable composition. That could describe any dyad, triad or larger group in America.

What differentiates gangs from conventional forms of group affiliation is "what the group does, how the group functions". That is, its group behavior. When it serves a protective or any other illicit function through violence, engages in anti-social conduct that is also unlawful and criminal activity, in either individual or collective violence or illegal behavior, when it is involved in sufficient amounts of delinquency to get a negative response from either the community or law enforcement officials, or when it trains and propels others into a criminal career ---- then we are talking about a gang.

To borrow from the psychology of Yablonsky (1962) perhaps two sociopaths together meeting the above qualifications, but otherwise functioning perhaps in governmental service, would technically meet, sans the definition of violent or law violating deviance, etc, the qualification of being defined as a gang (Yablonsky, 1962: p. 196). We really do not want to be in the intellectually limited situation of having to agree, by an insufficient definition, that two persons engaging in anal sex in Georgia --- where such behavior is illegal, even felonious --- therefore constitutes a "sex gang".[11]

The consensus of gang researchers and criminal justice practitioners alike is that there must be three or more members to be considered a "gang". A dyad simply constitutes a "team" at best. With three persons, it is possible to engage in the primordial act of any organization: delegation, actor X can instruct actor Y to have actor Z commit a crime.

CAN GANG MEMBERS BE DEPROGRAMED?

The most extreme extension of this logical inquiry must be this: can gangs be artificially created, in either a laboratory situation or in real life in their natural habitat? The answer on both accounts appears to be yes. But before elaborating further, let us add to Figure 12 some of the other definitional continuities found in the literature, one previously discussed as ethnic homogeneity. Let us consider a variation on this, that being social homogeneity.

In the "Robbers Cave" experiments by Muzafer Sherif, et al (1961) the basic pattern of adolescent group conflict was artificially created. This involved using young boys (11 and 12 year olds) in the situation of a summer camp who were randomly separated after a short period of time. In a few days, both groups of boys developed their own group names "the eagles" and "the rattlers" along with a corresponding level of group loyalty. The groups were experimentally manipulated to induce group rivalry and inter-group conflict. The enmity induced became real to the point where bringing the two groups together under any pretext of "making peace" actually accentuated and increased the level of potential violence between them. It increased aggression towards the "out-group" and increased cohesion and solidarity for the "in-group".[12] When Sherif and his experimenters created the artificial situation of a common "external" enemy, a superordinate goal, they had to act together and in so doing all inter-group conflict was eliminated.[13]

A somewhat related piece of evidence is found in the work of Schwitzgebel, who started a kind of "gang drop-in center" that sought to create a laboratory "subculture" (Schwitzgebel, 1965: p. 21). Few quote this research even though a close reading of it suggested that the author claimed some success in using professional psychological services to help youths leave the gang. Obviously, the "gang" in this instance, however, was probably a level zero or level one type of gang formation. That is, not a more highly organized gang organization.

In our correctional gang research we included "gang deprograming" as a service in a list of such services for incarcerated juveniles as a validity item. We expected no one to say they provided such "gang deprograming" services. We were more than somewhat surprised to find more than a few claimed to provide this service that we thought at the time was only a figment of our gang researcher imaginations.

THE INTERESTING WORK OF SCHWITZGEBEL   (1965)

The research by Schwitzgebel at Harvard offers a similar affirmation of the thesis that gangs can be artificially created, albeit from a somewhat different angle. Schwitzgebel as a graduate student in psychology, set up an elaborate off-campus laboratory. They rented a store front and made it appear like a scientific laboratory, with electrical equipment, and even a rat until they had to get rid of it. When Schwitzgebel went out cruising on his "hunt" for street-corner/gang-affiliated delinquents telling them he would "pay them in cash" to come near the university to his laboratory and "talk into his tape recorder", most of them thought he was a homosexual, not a cop.[14] Few contemporary scholars seem to acknowledge the self-professed contribution to gang analysis and research by Schwitzgebel (1965) entitled Street-Corner Research: An Experimental Approach to the Juvenile Delinquent so it bears some attention here.

It is unclear from reading Schwitzgebel (1965) what if anything was his guiding theory prior to engaging in such "street" research. He quotes everyone from Nietche to Freud, to the Nuremburg trials and sado-masochism in France.[15] But he was very sophisticated and effectively outfitted with resources desired by youths. His described statistical project involved 30 white males with an average age of 17.8,[16] but other cases were also described from this Research Laboratory Street Center known as the Streetcorner Research Lab (SRL).

It was a remarkable improvement on Whyte's research project, which Schwitzgebel was aware of and positively disposed towards.[17] First, according to Schwitzgebel this project "did not begin with a logical design later given to others to complete" (p, 12).[18] Rather it was --- like Whyte --- a very risk-taking and personal, psychological, approach; almost "interviewing as therapy" as Schwitzgebel coined the term (p. 26).

The language here is very clear. Schwitzgebel was always the "experimenter", and the gang member (50% were gang members) or delinquent was the "subject". He was clearly an affectively inspired experimenter:

> The participants in the therapeutic experiment, whether called doctors and patients or experimenters and subjects, may thus proceed "inspired by love and guided by knowledge" toward that excellent life so fervently advocated by Spinoza long ago (Schwitzgebel, 1965: p. 93).

His approach to obtaining research cooperation from delinquents was quite unique. It meant in one case hanging out playing pin ball for a long period and doing this so effectively at "winning free games" that he naturally attracted the attention of a nearby young male who eventually confessed to him a pattern of delinquency and agreed to come at once to the lab with him to be a "subject". In another case it meant pulling up to a street corner in a car in front of a group of boys and saying he wants to meet "Bongo" a delinquent, to make movies:

The experimenter stopped his car...several boys were standing there...the experimenter explained that he was looking for Bongo to give him a job. The job would be taking movies. "I'm on the level, and here's the camera." The gang was noticeably impressed by the new, streamlined camera. (Schwitzgebel, 1965: p. 95).

Schwitzgebel was not only in vogue, knowledgeable of research, but also anticipated "electronic monitoring" for offenders. He was aware of the difficulty of gaining public understanding:

Certainly a part of the difficulty lies in the great difference between the standards of "proper" behavior established by law and custom and the actual, covert behavior of many "proper" people (Schwitzgebel, 1965: p. 107).

The Streetcorner Research lab was so successful in penetrating the subculture that it attracted others not included in the statistical analysis of delinquents. One was a sailor with a drinking problem who was treated with syrup of ipecac (an emetic) for aversive conditioning in stopping his crime of writing bad checks (ISF, insufficient funds). Another was a homosexual college student who:

referred himself to the laboratory for treatment of "homosexual tendencies". He agreed to participate as an assistant in the designing of an experimental treatment procedure (Schwitzgebel, 1965: p. 127).

For baseline data collection, the homosexual recorded his sexual impulses in a log over a thirteen month period before the "treatment with syrup of ipecac was begun" (P. 128).

Schwitzgebel reports the convenience or appearance of success in aversively conditioning this homosexual away from "gay bars". The subject eventually got married and was "very content". Although, the man still had such impulses, but just didn't consider them a problem (Schwitzgebel, 1965: p. 128).

Schwitzgebel did not claim to have totally rehabilitated all these delinquents, perhaps because after all he and his Streetcorner Research Lab was an elaborate "black box". Who knows what, if anything, did work? Was it the priest, the philosopher, or the experimenter that brought about the desired change towards law abiding behavior? We wouldn't know.

What is interesting is the apparent eagerness of these youths to engage in deviance under the direction of the "experimenter". One situation was described where several boys came in to the lab, got a couple dollars, and:

On the way back to the amusement center, the boys asked me when the real job started --- meaning when do we roll the drunks or do the actual work (Schwitzgebel, 1965: p. 16).

That is, apparently these youths wanted to perform delinquency under experimental conditions for Schwitzgebel. Once the "lab" was underway, the written instructions asked the youths to defer to the seasoned veterans of the laboratory for any questions they might have. This method set up a natural group formation by introducing one delinquent to the next, thereby creating groups that would have never possibly formed in the absence of the Streetcorner Research Lab (SRL).

If it took an attractive young blond female with a convertible car to impress the kids, then it was used; and in so doing, imprinting significantly on their tendency to be more attracted to the SRL. Cash, bonuses, tickets to ball games, beverages, sweets, sandwiches ---- whatever lured them.

Before rushing to get a copy of Schwitzgebel (1965), please note that no theory of gangs was ever offered or developed. It is certainly made more reference to the scholarly literature and it was more quantitative than Whyte, but is not a direct contribution to gang theory. It has an indirect value through possibly being linked to the conception that gangs can be artificially created or socially engineered, as shown by the offering of resources to be exploited, or pooling together delinquents who would not have otherwise engaged in group delinquency together. So in a "prisoner's dilemma" of owning two books and being told by prison officials you would have to dispose of one of them, a good hypothesis would see Whyte's book staying, and Schwitzgebel's going to the trash --- if it was an astute prisoner. We did not need Schwitzgebel to know that desired resources can be used to attract offenders. For as much discussion as he gave to the ethics of research and getting "informed consent", he would have probably also advised these youths: "you will be meeting other delinquents and statistically you could perhaps find yourself engaged in new crime patterns with these other offenders should you develop close ties to them".

For the record, Schwitzgebel did provide in an appendix some information on client "outcomes" (after association with the laboratory). Here it gets confusing. In the first table of data (N = 30), 22 of the subjects are indicated to have been gang members before lab association, and only 3 afterwards. Were it not for the fact that at best this might have entailed a level zero to level one gang formation, such results based on psychological intervention would constitute a miracle from a gang dismemberment or gang deprograming point of view. And accomplished apparently without syrup of ipecac. But we are not given any indication of the nature of the time lapse for the follow-up period. As experiments go, this one was more than sloppy.

CAN AN ADULT OR AUTHORITY CREATE A YOUTH GANG?

The position advanced here is: affirmative[19]. But as an artificially produced social group formation, not arising naturally from conditions of conflict, deprivation, etc, this should be qualified by saying as well: with varying degrees of effectiveness and continuity.[20] Basically, it is much easier to manipulate than to create. The question is not dissimilar to this: can a powerful country like the USA help create, foster, cultivate, support and give direction to an insurgent force in a foreign hostile nation? Can it succeed is the real question, and the answer again in some situations is a historical yes. Such groups can obviously be created, even in the laboratory. This raises, analytically, the again unanswered and unaddressed question in our gang literature: how long must a gang operate to be considered a quasi-institution? Is a one-night escapade sufficient to define a group with extra-legal goals, objectives, and illegal functions as a gang?

A similar analytical difference exists between that which is legally defined as a "gang" or "mob" in terms of law violation behavior, which can be punished as such, and the need for the criminologist to have a more social scientific definition. For example, mob action statutes, such as those in Illinois:

> Chapter 38, Section 25-1 **Mob Action.** (a) Mob action consists of any of the following: (1) The use of force or violence disturbing the public peace by 2 or more persons acting together and without authority of law; or (2) The assembly of 2 or more persons to do an unlawful act; or (3) The assembly of 2 or more persons, without authority of law, for the purpose of doing violence to the person or property of any one supposed to have been guilty of a violation of the law, or for the purpose of exercising correctional powers or regulative powers over any person by violence. (b) Mob action is a Class C misdemeanor. (c) Any participant in mob action which shall by violence inflict injury to the person or property of another commits a Class 4 felony. (d) Any participant in a mob action who does not withdraw on being commanded to do so by any peace officer commits a Class A misdemeanor.

In such mob action statutes, which addresses as seen above cases involving rioting or vigilante groups, do not require the group to have previously existed as a group entity for purposes of prosecution. It is rather sufficient that they existed as a group at the time they collectively engaged in what amounted to a violation of the criminal code. Thus, analysis of "mob action" convictions will not be a good source of data for the explanation of gangs.

On the other hand, if aggression is a measure of violence or its potential, then a low threshold of frustration can apparently be induced in groups of children from laboratory experiments relating to this aspect of artificial gang formation. Such was the nature of the lab experiment by Davitz (1952). Twenty children (7 to 9 year olds) were used to create 5 groups of 4 each. These children were trained to be aggressive through physical games similar to "king of the hill", etc (Spot). Another 20 children were given constructive training on how to deal with frustration. This was a comparison of "aggressives" versus "constructives" by inducing both qualities in the child groups. Aggressives were trained to damage property and their aggressive interpersonal behavior was both praised and positively reinforced. Later comparisons of both groups (aggressives vs. constructives) showed that such training significantly differentiates reaction to frustration. Did the Davitz lab provide adult legitimacy for this aggressiveness without which it may not have surfaced? We don't know, it is a plausible rival hypothesis. Just as it is plausible to believe that natural experiments in the field occur along the same lines, such as when one high school originates a gang like the Crips and another nearby high school follows with the Bloods, as happened in Los Angeles in 1969. Two gangs rising to play their version of "king of the hill" in the underground economy of illegal drug sales income, and then spreading nationally in the late early 1990s to the point where today sets of Crips and Bloods can be found in all states, in all social contexts, in many cities large and small. Crips and Bloods gangs do not persist because they are unsupervised kids, they are supervised by adult leaders of the same gang, their "OGs" (original gangsters).

A prototype of the Davitz social training model for engineering gang violence would have to: (1) segregate by sex to allow the macho hypermasculine factor to operate as happened in the movie classic Lord of the Flies, (2) allow them to self-segregate on the basis of ethnicity to artificially create the ethnic homogeneity factor so historically associated with gang life, and (3) induce hostility towards wider society and an increase their levels of aggression[21]. Obviously, the efficiency of manufacturing gang violence/aggression could be increased or accentuated by screening out those youths who had high levels of internal locus of control, and conversely, screening in those most likely to be influenced by their group setting: those with strong scores for having an external locus of control. Such would be the social engineering model for producing gang violence based on prior research involving essentially the manufacturing process of youthful aggression. Further, this tells us much about how we might go about preventing gang violence as well by reversing or neutralizing these principles.

The question of artificially creating a gang is comparable, in group control terms, to the issue: can someone start, develop and expand, and continue over a relatively long period of time with high tenure among members and low turnover, and function as a total control "cult"? Some knowledge of cults, as groups, can perhaps help us to understand the internal group dynamics of gangs. Cults, like gangs, "exist outside of the mainstream of society" and often have "strong, flamboyant leaders" (Popenoe, 1983: p. 443). Cults, like gangs, have been described as arising in reaction to feelings of deprivation (Glock, 1964).

What social-psychological fulfillment, then, does the cult and gang provide is the question from a control or dismemberment point of view, because that will have to be known to create equivalent such "counter functions" to be able to effectively, through propaganda or other means, "weed out" gang members by attracting them to something equally fulfilling but more pro-social in nature. Such a question must be answered prior to any responsible effort to "intervene" with gang members, for otherwise we are, by the lack of social scientific guidance, unwittingly taking the risk of strengthening or reinforcing gang organization or increasing its members level of commitment to the gang through our otherwise good intention to target gangs and gang members for social services.

We shall, in a later section, address more directly the matter of social service intervention, outreach, detached worker programs, etc, for social policy purposes. Just as the lack of theory before engaging in research or experimentation is an intellectual danger, we know from the past (e.g., Fry) that program initiatives not based on social science are similarly inclined to failure --- indeed, worse, can even help foster gang development. It bears repeating here that if a program has no analytically sound direction it will have no logical basis for what to expect in terms of impact or results. The difference in probability terms of achieving desired results is one between a crap shoot and playing a million-to-one lotto. Even with good theory, it can still be a crap shoot: there is still the problem of correctly implementing the theory. But with the atheoretical program, anything could happen, there could be as many possible outcomes as there are definitions of the situation. We would be best advised to take the crap shoot any day over the atheoretical program, it is a simple matter of the probability gain in doing some good.

The other evidence that a gang can be artificially created is found in what we know about native American fascism movements (Knox, 1976). One such group, which gained national attention for its "march on Skokie" was the NSPA (National Socialist Party of America) based in Chicago's southwest side neighborhood known as Marquette Park in the mid to late 1970's. The group thrived on the ethnic antagonism in the area; Marquette Park was virtually all white, and the neighboring community to the east was predominantly African-American. It developed and "outfitted" two such neo-nazi gangs.

The NSPA created the "Young Wolves" for children ages 12 and under, and it created "the Exterminators" for youths between the ages of 13 and 17. Anyone 18 or above could be a regular storm trooper. Both of these youth groups were organized as violence-oriented gangs and were given much reinforcement by adults in the NSPA. Both youth groups were given their own "publications" to extol their commitment to the nazi cause. In so doing the youths would put their "by line" on articles and increase their commitment to the nazi group. Through this kind of publication the NSPA youths would distribute the publications at schools, etc, to attract more delinquency-prone youths and encourage racial violence. Youths were offered free "white power" t-shirts, nazi arm bands, and were offered training from the adult nazis in "how to shoot all kinds of rifles and pistols at a real range with live ammo" to draw youths into the nazi organization.

In keeping with the overall anti-intellectual tendency of NSPA ideology the nazi youths were encouraged to drop out of schools where they had to "sit behind a desk all day". The public schools were portrayed as Jewish-communist dominated institutions which forced the youths to take liberal "social studies" and which "tease your mind with algebra formulas you'll never use after you graduate".

To support the contention that youth gangs can be artificially created, at least in the context of white racist gangs, it is helpful to quote directly from some of the publications from these two youth auxiliary units of the NSPA. One such newsletter, for the "exterminators", had several photographs of youths participating with the NSPA "white power" marches and notes that:

> The Youth were the most active marchers of all. They bombed the windshields of passing Cadillacs with rocks and bottles. They even clashed with the police and went to jail for their race.

> The Youth are always in the forefront for the struggle for White Power. In 1966, it was mainly the Youth who burned the cars of Martin Luther King and his invading Black hordes. They lit the night skies of Marquette Park with the fires of total resistance. That same spirit of White resistance in the Youth will someday strike a nation-wide up-rising against Black terror and White betrayal!

Similarly, the "young wolves" in their publication noted that:

> At the first march, on August 23rd, White Youth members bombed
> cars with rocks and bottles along 71st street. Even a bus-load of
> coons was attacked by the "Young Wolves" of the White Youth
> Front! After the second march, on October 12th, the Youth
> stormed the house of a nigger who just moved into the white
> neighborhood east of Western avenue. The White Youth Front is
> at the head of the fight for White power.

It was clear that the NSPA adults offered these youths a good deal of serious recognition and provided for social interaction with adult NSPA members. The youths were given a sense of identity and purpose which enabled them to be manipulated for performing illegal acts of violence consistent with the racist goals of the NSPA leaders.

Of more than some interest to the gang student, this Chicago neo-nazi group was effectively put out of business through coordinated and effective criminal prosecution of the core members. The top leader went to state prison for deviate sexual assault on a minor, and other high ranking nazis caught federal beefs for firearms violations, etc. Had their leader gone to prison for anything other than being a homosexual pedophile he might have effectively used this to continue gang operations. But he was not, to the present author's knowledge, able to come back to Chicago from prison and effectively continue such large scale operations.

CAN A GANG BE DISMEMBERED?

If we are to view gangs with some degree of concern if not simply a recognition that they are destructive to the community, then how could a community-based program be structured to achieve the specific objective of gang dismemberment? This assumes we should not repeat the gang suppression criminal justice policy of the past, to simply "lock up" all such gang members, because at a late 1980's average cost of $75 per day for juveniles, that is an average cost of $27,375 per year and is likely to be a very expensive proposition not to mention its obvious potential for being counterproductive. America's prisons today are overcrowded to an all time high. We do not have the capacity to lock them all up. The only answer is that which is to be found in the communities of our nation. So in light of this, can the value of gang membership be undermined or used to triage in an effort to instill new values or dislocate periphery members to a more pro-social type of group affiliation? The answer, on the basis of social science research, is yes. But it could also mean inadvertently inducing a variation of "Gresham's law of conflict".[22] The research by Kelley and Volkart (1952) is instructive here.

Kelley and Volkart (1952) tested a Boy Scout troop on their valuation of group membership in the scouts. Then they gave the scouts an experimental propaganda speech by an adult outsider to the effect "camping and woodcraft are evil --- camping destroys nature and threatens our ecosystem, and its dumb too, the city is more fun, and scouts don't need a knowledge of the forrest, they need a knowledge of city life to survive". They found a definite inverse relationship between prior value placed on group membership and the strength of induced new values via propaganda. That is, those scouts who least valued their membership or group affiliation were those with the highest induced value change from the propaganda; and vice versa. Remember, this is only inducing attitudinal (values and beliefs) change, not behavioral change. Kelley and Volkart did not after their psy-war phase create another organization that could be used to float off scout members alienated from their troop. It is one thing to change attitudes, and it is an altogether different and more difficult task to change behavior; especially group affiliation.

It has not been the custom to directly refer to gangs or offenders generally and in the same context of social services to make reference to the use of psy-war or propaganda techniques. At least most of the literature seems to avoid such mentioning of psy-war or propaganda. But to be intellectually honest many programs explicitly have this function or intent. Secondly, propaganda and psy-war can work under some conditions. This is not to recommend or endorse, but rather a recognition of a larger body of social science that can inform us more precisely about our expectations for gang intervention strategies having to do with dismemberment. Mostly, it is an honest and open recognition from an interdisciplinary perspective which is taken here to best understand group dynamics relevant to gangs.

Viewing the gang as a group in which their members make public commitments sheds some light on the difficulty of swaying their hearts and minds. A gang member has much that is expected in terms of behavior and values from the group. The research by Hovland, et al (1957) showed that propaganda is only minimally effective among a group with a public commitment. That is, their research showed only 14% vulnerable to propaganda in such a "public commitment" group (students who were told their views would be published in the student paper) as compared with a much higher vulnerability (41%) to propaganda among students who were allowed to be anonymous, or for whom there was no induced "public commitment". Such rituals of public declaration, oaths, etc, become, apparently, strong reinforcing mechanisms and the higher the commitment to the gang, the less likely any propaganda initiative is going to be effective at achieving voluntary dismemberment.

Clearly, the difference is one of having to defend and "stand up" to such a groups public views and beliefs. When a person feels no such external expectation or environmental press, then propaganda is likely to be much more effective. Finally, to achieve gang dismemberment, more than value change will be required. There will have to be alternative such organizations, perhaps something like the WPA, or relocation programs providing for income-generating opportunities and residency, genuine alternatives, perhaps a national service program, who knows, but it will have to represent a genuine alternative to the gang organization before we can expect the gang members to defect.

If we want them to defect then we will have to offer something to defect to. What that might consist of entails the much larger issue of how our society decides what are or are not appropriate government expenditures. That is a political science question beyond the scope of the present analysis.

IS INDIVIDUAL CRIME COMMITTED BY GANG MEMBERS "GANG CRIME"?

Assume a motorcycle gangs rides into town for a good time. You are in the wrong place at the right time and one of the members of the motorcycle gang has a verbal altercation with you. The next thing you know, you are mortally wounded. Would you consider this a "gang crime" even though it was not approved of in advance by the entire membership of the gang on a voting referendum on whether to kick your ass or not? Or take a more typical example: you are in the park with your children, gangs are selling drugs nearby unbeknownst to you, and a rival gang approaches the area in a slow moving car and opens fire with an AK-47, spraying the area with gun shots, and your child is accidentally killed from stray gun shots meant perhaps for the gang members nearby. Would the death of your child be considered an urban accident, or would you consider it a gang-related homicide?

This is a most profound issue because it has many implications for the suppression of gang crime in America. Perhaps the way to begin this analysis is to note that group dynamics that a gang provides are different from the kind of lone-ranger criminal who acts alone as a sole actor. A crime committed by a gang member may bring status to the member. There is an incentive to commit crimes of violence that the lone-ranger or individual non-gang member criminal lacks. Further, the "risky shift" effect operates in a gang context all the time: persons commit crimes, sometimes excessively brutal, that they may not have had the guts to commit as lone individual non-gang member criminals. The group gives them some sense of a larger reference group, a strength and support group.

The gang may have the good sense not to declare in its written constitution that "we are official enemies of the USA and we commit our lives to the commission of any and all crimes that will facilitate the erosion of the American way of life; and thus, all members are encouraged to commit crimes daily with our blessings and protection." In other words, the gang need not officially approve of the crime, nor need the entire gang be involved in the crime, before the crime by a gang member can be considered "gang-related" crime. Why this is so deserves some criminological background that some commentators have failed to acknowledge in their efforts to minimize the criminal impact or threat of gangs today by claiming that most such crimes are not "gang crimes" at all, they are simply the errant behavior of individual gang members.

An ethnographer who wants to study the social linguistic behavior of gangs rather than their criminal behavior patterns would be on solid ground in speaking to such unique aspects about gangs --- further it would be a worthwhile contribution that has not yet surfaced from such "hang out with the gang" researchers. But it would not be appropriate to jump disciplines and begin asserting that "gang crime" does not exist....only individual crime exists by individuals who may or may not be members of gangs. The reason this is faulty is that to deal with crime issues one must be linked into the much larger body of cumulative knowledge called criminology. Then and only then do such assertions become defensible in relationship to the previous literature on crime and gangs. Any analysis of gang behavior or its impact on crime that is not grounded in the wider social science of criminology runs the risk of being little more than wild-eyed rhetoric or pseudo-intellectual demagoguery. Why? Because it ignores what we already know!

What we already know about juvenile delinquency, for example, is that by far the largest amount of it in America is group related. It is committed in small groups. This was one of the many contributions documented by the early work of Shaw and Mc Kay in their Chicago research on crime and delinquency. Delinquents and criminals seek out "partners", they feel safer somehow having a "rappy". Morally, the very presence of a partner in crime helps to neutralize the moral implications of normative violation: whether it is robbing an elderly person, or a run of the mill burglary. The presence of a "partner" means socially "I am not doing wrong....I am doing my necessary business".

Many crimes of gangs simply are never reported, particularly the crimes of violence against their own members. In fact, in the typical violent initiation ritual, few prosecutors are successful in prosecuting a "beating" that someone agrees to accept as part of a gang initiation ritual. But how voluntary was it? Taken to its extreme, citizens do not have the right to go to the gang and say "please end my life...I am suffering from a terribly painful disease". Gangs --- for a fee --- would probably accommodate anyone who could not be served by physicians who have become prominent in the media for their "right to die" practice of supervised suicide.

The real issue here in resolving whether any given crime committed by a gang member is or is not a "gang-related" crime is legal and social: it is the issue of accountability and motivation. In short, would the crime have been committed if the offender had not been a gang member? Using this standard, most such crimes committed by gang members would be considered "gang-related". Let us take a real case to examine this more closely.

In Chicago's Cabrini-Green public housing complex, gang shootings did decrease for a time after the public outcry over the killing of Dantrell Davis in October 1992 and the "gang truce" that followed. But in 1993 gunfire claimed another victim: two rival gang members vying for the affection of a young lady quarrelled, the result --- one of them pulled out a gun, and killed the rival. Was this simply a "crime of passion"? Or could it be considered a gang-related homicide? If they were not gang members, would they still have such easy access to firearms or actually be in the normal routine of carrying concealed firearms? It is use of the firearm, after all, that caused the death. If the gang facilitated possession of the firearm, or if the offender carried the gun in performing gang duties or "defending his nation", then it was clearly a gang-related crime: the offender used the power the gang gave him to commit the crime. Did the fact that both men were members of rival gangs accentuate the conflict and thus increase the likelihood of using lethal violence to settle a dispute? If so, then it could be considered a gang-related homicide because the enmity predisposed the two suitors in the love triangle toward a higher level of violence, the loser in any non-violent resolution to who will win the affection of the lady in question would lose much face with his own gang --- particularly knowing a rival gang member persevered. Gang members are required to attack if their gang is "put down", or else it is "dropping the flag" and can be severely punished if discovered by fellow gang members. If both combatants exchanged verbal gang put-downs as well, then the crime is clearly "gang-related" no matter what the crime was: it is not a matter of whether both gangs gave each of these two men authority in advance to use lethal violence to win a romance war, rather they acted not just as "individuals", but as members of a larger reference group to which they are accountable.

The gang exerts enormous social control over its members. It also psychologically empowers the individual gang member into possibly committing crimes that he or she would not do alone or if they were not a gang member. As gang members are prone to claim, once a gang member they have "back up". Thus, under the theory of plain accountability most crimes of violence as well as income-producing crimes committed by gang members can still be considered "gang-related". Without crime as an ongoing pattern of activity by its members it would not be a gang at all. The gang facilitates crime by its individual members by providing the group approval and support for such deviance.

Would the millions of dollars in damage to American property every year by gang graffiti in the endless series of "throw ups" (putting up the gang logo) and "throw downs" (putting down the rival gang logo) occur if the individuals who are responsible for these acts were not gang members? Not likely. Thus, gang graffiti in terms of criminal damage to property is almost always a gang-related crime. Similarly, most violence by individual gang members can be considered gang-related; the reason, similarly, is that while it may have been committed as an "individual", it was not just an individual lone actor that committed the violent crime: it was someone who is uniquely under the web of influence from a larger group that is supportive of such crime.

Beyond this issue lies the legitimate criminological inquiry into how much crime in America can be attributed to gangs and gang members. Without the sense of personal power that a gang provides to a gang member it would be possible to argue that much such "individual crime" is not gang-related. But the fact remains: the gang exists and persists because of this social-psychological empowerment and reinforcement of criminal behavior.

If we listened to and believed the gangs, then the "gangs" per se commit no crime. That is an apology for gang crime, not a social scientific analysis of gang crime. The gang provides the psychological reinforcement for crime, the motivation for crime, and the social environment that morally neutralizes the stigma of crime and violence. The gang is a group structure that therefore facilitates the crime of its members. If it is not possible to isolate the definition of the situation any gang member experiences in his or her larger society away from the gang and other gang members, then it is not possible to say that the gang has no effect on the crime the person commits as an individual. Ergo, the lone gang member in a forest who sets it afire thinking he is getting back at the "system" is acting out his own interpretation of the gang manifesto, and this would be a gang crime. Similarly, the gang member who has a "reputation" to uphold for his gang, who commits an act of domestic violence is still committing a gang crime, because it is a part of the motivational sequence and the predisposition of the offender.

SUMMARY AND CONCLUSION

We have, in opening up the discussion of the gang as a social group, only touched the surface of a wealth of social science research and literature that can help inform us more about both understanding the gang in modern society and in devising policy for "what" if anything to do about the gang problem. The inquiries made here raise questions that the astute student of criminology would want to raise: can a gang consist of two persons, how long must they so associate to have the "gang" label, etc. This focus has the goal of leading to a clarification of some of the critical issues surrounding gangs today.

Finally, this chapter has offered an initial basis for the assertion that gangs can be artificially created,[23] in the laboratory and elsewhere. Which is to say that adults can create youth gangs. The evidence is scant at this point, but is still quite suggestive.[24]   On the same basis, little direct evidence exists regarding dismemberment and therefore this chapter has tried to bring into discussion what are considered to be related conceptual difficulties.

Clearly, we have only begun to understand the gang as a group.

DISCUSSION QUESTIONS

(1)   Do you think that experiments without an Institutional Review Board (giving input on issues of ethics and the rights of human subjects in research) involving gang members could "go astray" or potentially have a reverse-intended effect?   How might this happen?

(2)   Given sufficient resources, do you think an adult could create a youth gang?   If so, what would it take for that gang to become institutionalized over time?

(3)   Raising a child to hate is no accomplishment.   How could raising a child to be a gang member or inculcating beliefs and values of racial or ethnic hatred be construed as "child abuse"?
Why do you think it is still not a crime for adults to recruit or lure children to be gang members?

FOOTNOTES

1. Yablonsky's "near group" may imply it is not a genuine group, and certainly not an institutionalized group. Again, Yablonsky's concept probably applies at the lower end of the analytical spectrum: to level zero gangs, the "Spanky and Alfalfa" playgroups. A more updated version of Yablonsky is found in Oetting and Beauvais (1987) who use the phrase "peer clusters". Takata and Zevitz (1990) also resurrect "near-group" analysis in the case of Racine's apparent lack of a gang problem. That is, apparently gangs exist in Racine only in the minds of individuals.

2. Harris (1988) provides an interesting account of female gang members using a larger sample than Campbell and found that the gang functioned as a reference group for these females in stronger fashion than did families or other social institutions.

3. The need for more analytical rigor here is evident in several gang authors who describe their three or four "social types" of gangs, and call them, if there are three, "the following three typologies", etc, abusing the very essence of what is meant,

linguistically, by the word typology. What these authors probably wanted to do was advance "a typology". This will be addressed in more detail later.

4. Leissner (1969, p. 9) takes Yablonsky to task for denying that gangs are truly "groups" at all, that is that gangs are simply "near groups". Leissner (1969: pp. 8-9) terms them "dynamic groups" ala Hubert Bonner (1959). But Leissner rejects the usage of the term "gang" or "gang clusters" and prefers to use the term "street corner groups" because the term gang connotes wrong doing. We might simply remind Leissner that ignoring their wrong doing will not make go away, no matter how sensitive our language gets.

5. From an educational perspective (of course, showing a heavy influence from mainstream sociology) Harris (1988) provides an analysis of the gang in terms of reference group theory, "the group as an important factor in the motivation of human behavior" (Harris, 1988: p. 189).

6. Sheu's (1990) presentation describing nonsyndicated organized crime groups in Taipei, Taiwan characterized gangs as secondary groups.

7. The significance of group size is this: using the formula $R = n(n-1)/2$; where R = number of potential relationships, and n = size of the group; a gang size of 35 would have 590 possible different combinations of relationships for the gang infrastructure, points of possible internal alliances, and possible internal conflicts. As Wilson (1971) showed, the arithmetic increase in number of group members has a geometrical increase in the number of possible relationships. This means the need for more "chiefs" in the internal social organization of the gang the higher the group number size is (see DiRenzo, 1984: pp 246-247).

8. Vetter and Territo (1984, p. 517), also seem to agree that today's gangs are not those of the day of Thrasher, but in fact "have a tighter, more cohesive, and more durable structure" (p. 517), with a wide variety of hierarchical roles in an almost paramilitary style of organization.

9. Arnold (1965) says no, a gang cannot consist of simply two persons. To be a gang it must be integrated (identify with itself), have a leader, have a place to meet, and engage in conflict; further gangs must have at least six members (Arnold, 1965: p. 73). Arnold's was one of the first such efforts towards an empirically-based classification system of gangs. Arnold argued the merits of examining these "structural" characteristics (group integration, leadership, mode of conflict, size, meeting place, etc) to supplement the traditional emphasis on cultural factors.

10. This is Yablonsky's (p. 127) attribution.

11. Bobrowski (1988, p. 8) reports the interesting case that came to the attention of the Chicago Police Department --- a gang of one called the Latin Devils. That is one leader who created the illusion of a gang and proceeded to compel three members to "join", all three of which testified against him. Miller apparently believes a gang must have at least three members (ibid).

12. Recall, similarly, the famous experiment by Zimbardo (1972) in the creation of the "Stanford Jail", where students were randomly assigned to be either "hacks" or "cons". The gang of hacks became overtly authoritarian, the gang of cons became disruptive. Both groups were so highly charged emotionally, in fact, that the experiment had to be prematurely cancelled.

13. The implication for gang violence here is clear. But is may amount, perhaps, to only a choice of victims of violence. Any charitable group, social worker, political activist, etc, type of person, could probably with some degree of difficulty, get feuding gangs to come together for a meeting, to "call a truce", and establish a hot line of communications between rival gang leaders. But would this then mean the guns are fired at other citizens rather than rival gang members? It is hard to envision such a superordinate goal other than one of natural disaster or world war that could provide the means to draft gang members into national service. On the other hand, it is a fascinating theoretical issue as to what would be required to re-focus, even temporarily, inter-gang conflict towards a larger and mutual external enemy, wherein society as a whole would ultimately benefit.

14. "The experimenter was nearly always seen in the role of a homosexual, cop, bigtime operator in the underworld, or a psychiatrist looking for interesting cases...The most frequent and immediate perception of the experimenter was that of a homosexual. This was not entirely unrealistic since delinquent and homosexual populations are often involved in activities of mutual exploitation" (Schwitzgebel, 1965: p. 16).

15. Including lengthy, flowery quotes from Aldous Huxley, e.g. "how can we increase the amount of love in the world?", etc, (1965, p. 103).

16. This age is apparently only for those 2/3 of the sample who had served time. The overall mean, one must calculate from the raw data (Schwitzgebel, 1965: pp. 136-137), age for the full group (N = 30) was 18.

17. Like Whyte, Schwitzgebel found on his first outing to "find a delinquent", he had to offer the delinquents a half-pint of vodka, which they promptly took from him and exited from his car.

18. Am I wrong then by inference in concluding on the basis of this assertion that Schwitzgebel's SRL was an illogical design never intended to be taken seriously?

19. For the record, on the "hot dispute" in the area of gang ideas regarding can gangs be "exported" or franchised, I must to be consistent from such a social organizational perspective say "yes they can and are". But this is not to say that the national picture is so singularly explained by only this. Obviously there is some combination of both local conditions and indigenous formation as well as intentional imperialism.

20. Throughout the United States there are "Fagin" cases involving older adults who were able to manage a "team" or group of youths or young adults, often gang

members, in various criminal activities (burglary rings, auto thefts, etc). But these are level one gangs, operating as a single unit usually in a single jurisdiction.

21. This should sound familiar to the criminology student. It is, after all, what we do in corrections (prisons, jails, juvenile detention, etc).

22. Gresham's law of conflict is this: if the harmful and dangerous elements drive out those who would keep the conflict within bounds, what results is an even more menacing level of conflict. The distinct organizational possibility exists, at least, that siphoning off all periphery members and leaving "hard core" members could result in an even higher magnitude of violence proneness.

23. The fact that such neo-nazi youth gangs could be produced by an adult has much significance when looking at the extent to which groups like the Ku Klux Klan exist throughout America.

24. This is where the issue of "franchising" and gang imperialism come into play. Can gangs be franchised like a fast food operation in any community in America? Any literature showing that some individuals can exert influence over, or manipulate gangs, would then tend to support the notion of gang social engineering. And would, of course, also have to recognize the potential for gang dismemberment or something roughly equivalent to gang deprogramming.

CHAPTER 15

GANGS AND DRUGS

INTRODUCTION

As gangs and crime are inextricably related it comes as no surprise that gangs and drugs are also tied together in a complex way. There are several issues that must be examined to understand the relationship between gangs and drugs. One is the matter of drug use among and by gang members. Another is the involvement of the gang and its members in profitable illegal drug sales activity. Gangs like the Crips and Bloods and many Folks gangs and many Peoples gangs derive most of their income from the enormous underground economy in terms of illegal drug sales. Gangs will change their internal values if the money is right, as in the case of the El Rukns who for a long time would not sell heroin because in their written constitution they felt it was too destructive to the community, but decided to go ahead and provide this commodity for the African-American community when the income margin was profitable and when there was too much competition in other drug user products (i.e., cocaine, marijuana, etc).

Drug abuse and drug sale income are two aspects along which gangs can and do vary. Thus, from a social organizational perspective it is possible that a gang may exist that prohibits any involvement with drugs, just as it is possible to find a gang that sells drugs as its primary income source. "Stoner" gangs are portrayed as consisting of members who use and abuse drugs as an ongoing and regular activity in their recreational lifestyle[1]. Some gangs like the Latin Kings have mixed policies on drugs and drug abuse: making money from drug sales of any kind is fine, using soft drugs is acceptable, but using hard drugs by means of I.V. injection is prohibited and can be severely punished as a violation of written gang laws and rules in their constitution.

It is fair to say that a great deal of crime and drug abuse goes on in America. Neither of which is always detected, and only a portion of which ever comes to the attention of the criminal justice system. It is not true that we know everything we need to know about the linkages between the two topics of "gangs" and "drugs". In this chapter we examine drug abuse among gang members, as well as the more interesting aspect of drug sales by gangs and gang members. Finally, the issue of hard drug legalization is examined in relationship to gangs.

DRUG ABUSE AMONG GANG MEMBERS

Using the individual gang member as the unit of analysis shows that gang members are more prone to drug abuse than non-gang members. This is true inside the offender population itself, this is true in the student population in public high schools, and this is also true for special groups such as Asian students. What this trend suggests is support for the hypothesis that, generally, gang members are more prone to deviant behavior including substance abuse than their non-gang member counterparts. This is little more than common sense because gangs are, after all, important aspects of the deviant subculture due to their involvement in crime.

Three different studies of this issue will be summarized here examining the relationship between drugs and gang membership among: (1) high school students, (2) juveniles in short and long term correctional facilities, and (3) Asian students.

(1) Drugs and Gang Membership Among High School Students.

A sample of 552 Chicago high school students in an anonymous survey administered in the Fall of 1991 showed that overall, some 10.3 percent of the students reported that they had ever joined a gang. For male high school students, this was significantly higher, 17.2% compared to only 4.7 percent among females. The effect of gender on self-reported gang membership is therefore statistically significant (Chi-square = 23.05, p < .001). This particular one high school was chosen as a case study because it was uniquely integrated in terms of race: almost equal proportions of the student body were African-American, Hispanic, and white.

Self-reported gang membership is also a factor that significantly differentiates whether the same high school students have seen drug sales occur in or near the school. This finding is provided in Table 19.

TABLE 19

The Frequency Distribution of Self-Reported
Gang Membership by Having Seen Drug Sales
in or Near the School Among a Fall 1991
Sample of Chicago High School Students

	Seen Drug Sales in/near the School?	
Gang Member:	No	Yes
No	323	122
Yes	26	24
	Chi-square = 9.15, p = .002	

As seen in Table 19 above, among gang members some 48 percent have seen drug sales occur in or near the school compared to 27.4 percent among the non-gang member high school students. Gang members are significantly more likely to have seen such drug sales, in part of course because they could have been selling the drugs themselves.

A variable that taps into the drug use dimension is actually a surrogate measure of self-usage. It asks the student how many of their close friends and associates use illicit drugs. This is considered by some to be the best true measure of deviance: as the natural tendency is to over-report good qualities, and underreport deviance. By focusing on the deviance of "friends", this measures both association with and integration into the deviance represented by the drug abuse subculture. The essential finding among this sample of high school students is that among gang members 57.1

percent reported having one or more such close friends and associates who use illicit drugs, compared to 29.9 percent among students who were not gang members. This is a very significant difference, suggesting clearly that the gang member is more deeply tied into the drug abuse subculture than the non-gang member in the same student population.

(2) Drugs and Gang Membership Among Confined Juveniles.

The data used here was collected in the summer of 1991 and reflects a very large sample (N = 1,801) of juveniles confined in short and long term correctional institutions in five states (New York, Massachusetts, Tennessee, Wisconsin, and Texas). The survey instrument provided for anonymity of the juvenile: no names were used. The thrust of this study was that of the health risks of confined juveniles, such as drug and substance abuse, suicide, etc. But gang membership is a factor that significantly contributes to the morbidity and mortality rates among our Nations juveniles. Thus, this factor of gang membership allows us to examine a large sample of juvenile delinquents who have had to be incarcerated. Examined here is how gang membership among the confined juvenile population is related to drug and substance abuse at the individual level of analysis.

Just under half of all the confined juveniles (46.1%) reported having ever joined a gang. Unlike the public high school population, in this confined juvenile population no significant difference by gender existed in terms of self-reported gang member-ship. Thus, the gender difference in gang joining behavior while significant in the general population seems to disappear at the point the juvenile is incarcerated.

The strong evidence from this large study is that gang members are significantly more likely as individuals to report more substance abuse than non-gang members using eleven different drug and substance abuse variables. These factors can be summarized as follows.

1. Gang members were significantly more likely (p < .001) to report smoking cigarettes.

2. Gang members were significantly more likely (p < .001) to report first drinking alcohol at an early age.

3. Gang members were significantly more likely (p < .001) to report more drinking episodes (days when they had at least one drink of alcohol during their lifetime) than non-gang members.

4. Gang members were significantly more likely (p < .001) to report more incidents of heavy drinking (during the 30 days prior to being incarcerated, how many days they had five or more rinks of alcohol in a row, that is, within a couple of hours) than their non-gang member counterparts.

5. Gang members were significantly more likely (p = .02) to report first using pot (i.e., marijuana) at an early age.

6. Gang members were significantly more likely (p < .001) to report more pot use episodes (number of different times using marijuana during their life) than non-gang members.

7. Gang members were significantly more likely (p < .001) to report first using cocaine at an early age than when compared to their non-gang member counterparts.

8. Gang members were significantly more likely (p < .001) to report a higher frequency of the number of different times using any form of cocaine (powder, crack, freebase) than compared to their non-gang member counterparts.

9. Gang members were significantly more likely (p < .001) to report a higher frequency of the number of different times using crack[2] or freebase forms of cocaine than compared to their non-gang member counterparts.

10. Gang members were significantly more likely (p = .03) to report a higher frequency of using sundry other illegal drugs (e.g., LSD, PCP, mushrooms, speed, ice, heroin, pills) than compared to their non-gang member counterparts.

11. Gang members were significantly more likely (p = .004) to report that they had ever injected (i.e., shot up) any illegal drug (including skin popping or injecting steroids) than compared to IV drug abuse among their non-gang member counterparts. This most serious drug abuse behavior in relationship to ever joining a gang is analyzed in Table 20 below[3]. This "riskier" behavior among those who have been gang members is also examined in chapter 16 where along with sexual behavior, this type of health risk behavior may lead to higher risks of contracting sexually transmitted diseases, particularly AIDS/HIV infection.

TABLE 20

Frequency Distribution of Having Ever Joined a Gang
by Having Ever Injected (Shot Up) Any Illegal Drug
Including Skin Popping or Injecting Steroids
Among Confined Juvenile Delinquents

	Ever an I.V. Drug User?	
	Yes	No
Ever Join a Gang?		
Yes	112	722
No	91	896
Chi-square = 8.08, p = .004		

The strong consistent evidence here among 1,801 youths surveyed from juvenile correctional institutions and facilities in five states suggests clearly that gang members profile differently than non-gang members in terms of greater drug and substance abuse. The gang member is significantly more likely to report such drug and substance abuse than the non-gang member among confined juveniles. Additional information from this study of confined juveniles as the unit of analysis is discussed in chapter 20.

(3) Drugs and Gang Membership Among Asian Students.

In the Spring of 1992 a national Asian educational association facilitated data collection for the present author. This meant using an anonymous questionnaire, administered by Asian teachers to Asian students in eight states (Washington, Hawaii, Colorado, Minnesota, Louisiana, Maryland, New York, and California). The sample size used here consists of over three hundred Asian students[4].

The same relationship described previously from a sample of Chicago high school students was tested for this sample of Asian students. Thus, Table 21 shows that similar to the Chicago high school sample consisting of almost equal proportions of Black, Hispanic, and white students, that among Asian students the gang member is more likely to have one or more close friends and associates who use illicit drugs than non-gang members.

TABLE 21

Frequency Distribution of Ever Joining a Gang
by Having One or More Drug Abusing Friends
Among a 1992 Sample of Asian Students

	Have 1 or More Close Friends and Associates who Use Illicit Drugs?	
Ever join a gang?	No	Yes
No	233	72
Yes	6	20

(Chi-square p < .001)

As seen here among Asian students who report never joining a gang, just under a fourth (23.6%) report having one or more close friends and associates who use illicit drugs. Over three times that proportion is shown among Asian gang members! Among the Asian students who report having ever joined a gang, some 76.9 percent had one or more such close friends and associates who use illicit drugs. In short, it appears that across the board, a universal aspect of the relationship between gangs and drugs regardless of ethnic group differences, is that gang members have a higher integration into or association with the illegal drug subculture. Again, this is only logical inasmuch as being a gang member is itself a form of subcultural integration and association. The drug subculture appears to substantially overlap with the gang subculture is what this finding suggests.

Similarly, Table 22 below shows that identical to the Chicago student sample, these Asian students show another common profile. That is, gang members are significantly more likely to report having seen drug sales in or near the school than compared to their non-gang member counterparts. In fact, as shown in Knox, Laske, and Tromanhauser (1992) the factors predicting gang membership among a school sample where the white, Black, and Hispanic racial groups were almost equal are factors that are also significant predictors of gang membership among Asian students.

TABLE 22

The Frequency Distribution of Self-Reported Gang Membership
by Having Seen Drug Sales in or Near the School
Among a 19921 Sample of Asian Students

	Seen Drug Sales in/near the School?	
Gang Member:	No	Yes
No	241	67
Yes	8	18

Chi-square = 28.4, p < .001

GANGS AND DRUG SALES

The senseless killing of Mexican Cardinal Juan Jesus Posadas Ocampo on May 24th in 1993 illustrated one shocking truth --- that at least one foreign drug lord did have a connection with at least one American street gang. A Mexican drug lord recruited an American street gang for "hits" abroad in the fierce competition of the international illegal drug trade. The gunfire that killed the Cardinal at the airport in Guadalajara, Mexico came from the Calle Treinta (30th Street) gang in San Diego, who while recruited for the hit, actually shot the wrong person --- the top Catholic cleric in all of Mexico, the Cardinal[5]. Apparently the San Diego gang members fired at the Cardinal's car because it "looked like" that which they were supposed to target, a common phenomenon of the "mistaken identity" shooting trend found throughout the United States where gangs engage in such violence.

The fact is the kind of gangs analyzed in this book as level three gangs have been shown to have international connections for their illegal drug supplies. It is not uncommon to find large drug seizures for gangs with connections in Nigeria and Columbia[6].

The issue of gangs being involved in the profitable and illegal venture of drug sales is a more common trend than gangs being cultivated as labor pools for hitmen. Drug sales are only one of a number of crimes that gangs are involved in. To illustrate this some important recent data from American law enforcement executives will be summarized here.

The 1992 Survey of Law Enforcement was a joint project between gang researchers at four universities[7]. The data was collected in late 1992 and early 1993 by means of a mail questionnaire. A total of 398 law enforcement agencies responded: 248 police chiefs, 137 sheriffs, and 13 "other" or missing this particular variable for the type of jurisdiction[8]. Also discussed in a later chapter in this book, it is important to note that 89.5 percent of the police chiefs nationally and 79.4 percent of the county sheriffs reported that youth gangs were a problem in their jurisdiction. Thus, for cities of 25,000 or more and the component counties of metropolitan areas which constituted the sampling frame for this survey, the city or county without any gang problem is truly becoming the exception to the rule.

Table 23 below provides the results from a series of questions to these police chiefs and county sheriffs about what kinds of problems youth gangs cause in their jurisdiction. One of these crimes that gangs are involved in is that of drug sales. But as will be seen, drug sales are not the most common nor the least common type of crime that gangs are involved in according to the reports from these law enforcement administrators.

TABLE 23

Percentage Distribution of the Types of Crimes
That Gangs Are Involved in
Among Jurisdictions Reporting A Gang Problem
by a National Sample of Law Enforcement Administrators

		Police Chiefs	County Sheriffs
TYPES OF CRIMES:			
	Violence	87.8%	81.5
	Drug Sales	73.8	80.6
	Graffiti	82.4	73.1
	Burglary	67.9	71.3
	Robbery	52.5	43.5
	Drive-by shootings	61.1	50.9
	Arson	12.2	11.1
	Prostitution	2.7	7.4
	Car Theft	63.8	62.0
	Other	18.1	18.5

Table 23 shows that among those police chiefs reporting that gangs are a problem in their jurisdiction, some 73.8 percent of these police administrators also report that gangs in their area are involved in drug sales. Similarly, among county sheriffs reporting that gangs are a problem in their jurisdiction, some 80.6 percent of these law enforcement administrators also report that gangs are involved in drug sales. Violence, however, tops the list as the most frequent type of crime that gangs are involved in according to both police chiefs and county sheriffs. Similarly, gangs are least involved in prostitution at this stage of their development nationally.

GANGS AND GANG-CONTROLLED DRUG IMPORTATION INTO PRISONS

The 1992 National Survey of Prison Wardens is described in greater detail in chapter 19. It includes the viewpoints of 325 prison wardens from all 50 states. Reported here is evidence of another unique aspect of the gang-drug connection: the extent to which gangs control the importation of drugs into state correctional institutions. Summarized here are some of the findings from a much larger research project. The specific findings here show how gang drug trafficking inside American prisons is significantly related to two other problems: threats of violence by gang members against correctional officers and racial conflict among inmates.

This problem of gang members threatening staff is shown to be significant in relationship to the extent to which gangs are felt to control the importation of illicit drugs into the correctional facility and to the extent which gangs are felt to dominate the illicit drug trade behind bars. These findings are shown in Table 24.

TABLE 4

DISTRIBUTION OF DRUG IMPORTATION AND DRUG DISTRIBUTION GANG-CONTROLLED ACTIVITIES INSIDE PRISONS BY REPORTS OF THREATS BY GANGS ON STAFF

	Problem of Gang Threats Against Prison Staff?	
	NO	YES
GANG CONTROL OF ILLICIT DRUG IMPORTATION INTO		
THE CORRECTIONAL FACILITY Low[a]	94	11
High[b]	60	43
	Chi-square = 26.45, p < .001	
GANG CONTROL OF ILLICIT DRUG DISTRIBUTION INSIDE		
THE CORRECTIONAL FACILITY Low[c]	98	10
High[d]	61	48
	Chi-square = 33.50, p < .001	

As seen in Table 24, where gangs have high control over the importation and distribution of drugs in these adult state correctional institutions there is a statistically higher probability of an associated report of threats by gangs members against correctional staff in the same facilities. This finding regarding gang control over drug importation and distribution and its statistically significant relationship with a factor of violence faced by staff (e.g., threats) is very consistent with the emerging national

---

[a] Low gang control of the illicit drugs brought into the correctional facility by prison gang members was measured by those respondents that indicated less than or equal to four percent of all illicit drugs brought into their facilities were attributable to gang members.

[b] High gang control of illicit drug importation (smuggling) into the correctional facility was measured by whether the respondent indicated that five percent or higher of all illicit drugs brought into the prison were the result of gang members.

[c] Low gang control of the illicit drug trade behind bars was measured by less than or equal to four percent of the illicit drug trade in their facility being dominated by prison gang members.

[d] High gang drug distribution control was measured by five percent or higher of the illicit drug trade behind bars being dominated by prison gang members.

research literature on gangs showing that the higher the gang-drug problem the higher the individual risk of violence.[e]   Similarly, Table 25 shows that gang involvement in drug importation and distribution inside adult corrections is also significant in relationship to racial conflict. That is, the more gangs are involved in drug importation and distribution, the more racial conflict is reported from the same prisons.

TABLE 25

| | | Racial Conflict? | |
		NO	YES
% of illicit drug importation into the facility controlled by prison gang members	LOW[f]	60	52
	HIGH[g]	37	77

Chi-square = 10.28, p = .001

% of the illicit drug trade in the facility that is controlled by prison gang members	LOW[h]	61	55
	HIGH[i]	35	83

Chi-square = 12.70, p < .001

THE HARD DRUG LEGALIZATION   ARGUMENT

Many different recommendations on decriminalizing drugs or legalizing drugs have been made. There is only one issue here and it has to do not with the moral or the financial implications of such arguments, but rather has to do with the relationship between drug legalization and crime --- in fact, more specifically, gang crime. The book about barrio gang members in Los Angeles by Moore (1978) specifically concludes that we need to legalize heroin and suggested that gangs would cease to be a problem in America if only we, as a society, were not so hypocritical about our drug policies.   Decriminalization is a less extreme version, it simply would recommend reducing the penalties associated with such drug problems.   But

---

[e] See Schools Under Siege: A Study of Gangs, Drugs, Crime and Violence in the Modern American School, George W. Knox, Ph.D., David Laske, Ph.D., and Edward Tromanhauser, Ph.D., Kendall-Hunt Publishing, Chicago, IL, 1992 (to be released in August, 1992: for information write: Kendall/Hunt Publishing Company, 2460 Kerper Blvd, P.O. Box 539, Dubuque, Iowa 52004-0539. TEL (319) 588-1451.

[f] Low = less than or equal to four percent (< = 4%).

[g] High = greater than or equal to five percent (> = 5%).

[h] Low = less than or equal to four percent (< = 4%).

[i] High = greater than or equal to five percent (> = 5%).

legalization implies openly tolerating, even controlling by government supervision, such hard drug distribution and use.

Moore (1978) basically argues that if we could take away the profits from hard drugs like heroin, then the resources for American gangs would "dry up". Thus, the legalization argument as presented by Moore (1978) specifically predicts a "gang-fading scenario". As will be seen, it is not the only possible scenario for what would happen if American society took this extreme measure by legalizing heroin or other hard drugs.

Some may regard this argument as an example of the economic-determinism model of gang theory: that is, that gangs exist and persist only because of the income they can generate for their leaders and members. It is not possible to simply reduce the world of gangs to either "cultural" gangs (those who function for essentially cultural reasons and motivations) and "entrepreneurial" gangs (those who function to seek profits and wealth). It is not "gang theory" we are creating when we make up images of such pure types of gangs, such as the recent conclusion by Skolnick, Blumenthal and Correl (1993) that gangs in southern California are "cultural" and those in northern California are "entrepreneurial" gangs. Such over generalizations are also overly identified concepts[9] that truly stretch the imagination and distort the reality by being so oversimplistic[10]. Illegal income is one of the many factors along which gangs can be classified in terms of the array of social organizational features.

In summary, the argument favoring drug decriminalization or legalization in the gang context basically assumes that without penalties, or when anyone could buy their drugs at the local store legally, monetary resources would no longer be so plentiful for gangs. It further assumes that gang violence would be reduced, because the fight over drug territories would be eliminated if citizens could buy their drug of choice over the counter. The logic concerns the immediate effects in terms of how street gangs would cease to shoot each other over issues of "holding down" local drug turfs, not the long term effects on society or gangs.

There is, of course, another side of this argument regarding the legalization of highly addictive drugs like heroin. Perhaps our analysis should begin with the potential of any group to dissolve, shrink into impotence, or to swell in ranks in more solidified terms. Instead of gang dismemberment it is theoretically possible that we could see gang consolidation as well under conditions of hard drug decriminalization. In any event, it is an issue that deserves to be informed by what we know about the mechanics of group structure, group goal formation, and succession of goals. We begin this analysis, therefore, with an open mind towards both potentials: while decriminalization and legalization advocates emphasize the obvious immediate direct effects (e.g., economic disincentives for gangs involved in drugs), we must of course, in an objective spirit, recognize that often policies as drastic as this can have other unintended consequences. Which is another way of saying that the gang literature demonstrates that sometimes the most liberal imaginations have had the most deleterious effects (e.g., Fry, 1969) in terms of solidifying gang organization[11].

THREE DIFFERENT HARD DRUG DECRIMINALIZATION   SCENARIOS

If we are to believe Moore (1978) and other advocates of drug decriminalization, then gangs will cease to be a major problem in American society after market forces no longer provide the economic momentum to gang organizations. This is the "gang fading" scenario and will be discussed at some length. But there are at least two other scenarios if we are willing to look at more than the simple immediate effect of such a social policy on gangs.

Another scenario of the same policy could be an unintended nightmare: gangs previously in conflict, whose members are now free to have drug habits without facing criminal sanctions, will unite along new lines of differentiation. Perhaps even ethnic lines. Ethnicity has always been a factor of gang conflict and there is little in the drug decriminalization argument that promises better race and ethnic relations in America. Unless, of course, such decriminalization advocates are willing to assume that all bigots will turn to legalized drug dependency. Such a precarious assumption should force a consideration of alternative scenarios such as the reverse intended effect that will be called the "gangs merging/consolidating" scenario, perhaps even at a national level.

Finally, there is a midway effect or impact view which could conceivably be this: that such drug decriminalization has no real effect on gang dismemberment, in fact, because of the intractable nature of gangs as an organized subculture, legal drugs would simply mean a different mode of association. Remember, unless the government is going to give away heroin and cocaine, then these addicts are still going to have to pay for it. And how? So the third scenario is a "null effect" version, with no substantial change in the size of the gang force strength in America or its involvement with income producing crimes.

1. THE GANG-FADING   CRIME-FADING   SCENARIO

"UPI - Today, the President reached an all time high in popular support by signing dramatic new legislation authorizing all physicians in America to dispense heroin, cocaine, and other previously illegal narcotics."

Such might be the newspaper headline signaling the decriminalization and/or legalization of hard drugs. But what would be the parameters of such a policy? Do we truly envision legislation allowing minors to consume in this legal drug market as well? It would probably, like alcohol, be 21 years of age, or at least the age of 18 or consent. Thus, an large lucrative juvenile market would still exist for gangs to exploit.

Adding to the social control function of the health care system in America as is reasonably assumed in the drug legalization argument there is still the issue of who pays for the drugs and the drug dispensing service? The most pragmatic projection would be that like America's current and fragmented health care system which allows for health to the degree that you can pay for it: if you can't pay for it, you don't get it. So where are the addicts going to get the income for their habits? Thus, a large population of drug dependent persons desperate for cash could create a new income-producing crime wave that gangs will certainly want to get their share of.

The other possibility would require convincing the rest of American tay-payers that in terms of a cost-benefit analysis, that rather than allowing addicts to commit street crimes and force the criminal justice system into additional high costs, it might be cheaper to provide a ready supply of hard drugs and some form of group shelter for American drug addicts. It could involve a national registration system for addicts. But with free drugs and a home, just how large would the addict population grow to? As institutionalized addicts they could be defined out of the work force, reducing unemployment in a most revolutionary way. Would some lawyers, politicians, and Wall Street businessmen drop out of the rat race to join this addict population (i.e., the "cross over" effect)? What proportion of the American society would become addicts under this scenario, and at what point would society basically collapse because of the magnitude of drug addicts?

Who would want to work when you can get "high" and have the government take care of your basic needs? Most decriminalization advocates assume a minimal or no "cross over" effect: those who have been casual users of soft drugs turning to harder drugs because of the lack of penalties attached to this kind of deviance. That would appear to be an assumption that carries significant risk.

Because drug legalization sounds almost too good to be true it is well to remember that laws change. Remember the Prohibition Amendment to the U.S. Constitution, it was repealed allowing Americans to drink legally. So assume a national program of registering addicts began, and the gang members came forward en masse leaving their homies for the good life of government grade dope. Needing their fix, the physician would be their new gang leader. It would be a great opportunity to identify all the addicts almost over night. They would be registered, fingerprinted, photographed, DNA analyzed, and HIV tested.

The one war on drugs that no one seems to quote from, one that was quite successful at its time, was that by China's Mao Tse Tung. After Mao's communist forces seized power, they discovered a large population of Chinese addicts existed among their comrades who were not in any sense eager to participate in the restructuring of Chinese society according to Marxist-Leninism or anything else that did not get them high. But Mao had a sure fire solution: firing squads and labor camps. Thousands of addicts disappeared quite literally over night.

The point here should be clear: what if such drug legalization legislation was overturned or reversed after a period of time that allowed for the identification of America's addict population? Clearly, then, law enforcement agencies would have the intelligence base for monitoring what might be expected to be a crime prone population. What is not realistic is in thinking that America has the resources to prosecute or incarcerate all or even a major part of the criminal and/or gang population.

Let us return now with more analytical rigor in looking at the after effects of drug decriminalization. Suppose our decriminalization legislation had this clause: free drugs, but no other help. And then systematically, throughout America, we find these persons leaving the "happy houses" of approved physician drug dispensing facilities, and following their own propensity toward polydrug use, taking other substances, and routinely dying of chemical reaction and overdoses, or dying of other drug-related diseases. Knowing that drug addicts will not rank high in the triage system for health care, perhaps the highest point of gang impact of such decriminalization would be the latent extirpation policy implied in the evaluation of the social worth of the drug addict. The drug addict will not score high on social worth and thus they would not receive health care treatment, and would die off. This could truly impact on the gang problem but perhaps not in the way envisioned initially by Moore (1978).

That is the most cynical scenario. A more optimistic version would be as follows. Gangs previously in conflict over turf, racial and ethnic differences, or market share of criminal enterprises, suddenly become dissuaded from conflict because of the more powerful lure of personal psychic and pleasure gratification through legalized drug abuse. Gang members from all gangs like the Crips, Bloods, Vice Lords, Latin Kings, Aryan Brotherhood, etc, all become intoxicated with the pursuit of personal gratification and hedonism --- getting high. Gang drive-by shootings in our neighborhoods come to be replaced by drug-line riots: the fighting is no longer over color or turf or gang colors, but over who is going to be first in line to get their fix. And the non-drug abusing gang members suddenly find themselves impoverished because they no longer have a steady source of drug-sale income; so they quit the gang too and take jobs somewhere, straighten up and fly right. Legalized drugs could be a great leveler indeed.

Some don't buy it. But according to Moore (1978: p. 177) heroin should be legalized, because even as a drastic measure, it would take away the economic incentives for gang strength. However, for the record, Moore was aware that such a policy change "would have a major impact, although the precise effect is still a matter of speculation" (ibid).

2. THE GANGS MERGING-CONSOLIDATING   SCENARIO

It is important to consider what effect the legalization of heroin and other hard drugs would have outside of the obvious economic destabilizing effect that it is assumed to impact on gangs. One such post-drug legalization scenario that must be considered a logical possibility is therefore an unintended nourishing of the gang problem. This negative scenario would mean that gangs could merge, consolidate, and expand rather than shrinking into impotence. How might this happen?

One variation would be the possibility that gangs with a local character --- from Los Angeles, to Chicago, to New York, etc --- might be brought together in closer non-combative association with the potential that they could form a nationwide gang structure. Hardcore criminal gangs don't like junkies anyway, they do not make reliable gang members, perhaps because it is too easy for them to compromise their gang organization: if arrested, police can "sweat" them, going "cold turkey" in lockup they might provide any information a police officer asked if they knew they could be released and thus get a chance to get their fix. Gangs like the Latin Kings deal with these issues in their written constitutions:

"Those who are known to have previously used heroin for the purpose of addiction cannot obtain a position of rank without the approval of Las Coronas." (Latin King Constitution, see Appendix).

The "gangs merging-consolidating" scenario could therefore involve a much larger national network created out of such recent efforts as "gang summit" talks. Drug crime profits are not the only income-producing offense patterns that gangs engage in. The possibility exists, therefore, that gangs could simply continue in tact and simply adapt to the lack of drug income by specializing in other and new crimes. Perhaps they would follow the lead of the Yakuza and in the context of an open and democratic society become sophisticated "shake down" artists against American corporate business enterprises. The Yakuza have refined this to an art: buying one share of stock, allowing them to attend the stockholders annual meeting, and then threatening to disrupt the entire proceedings through skullduggery; or like the Yakuza, move into lucrative sex crime, or gambling (see Kaplan and Dubro, 1986).

Recall that legalizing the consumption of alcohol did not automatically put the Mafia, La Cosa Nostra, the Outfit, the Mob, out of business! If some of today's American street gangs were actually able to collaborate on a national level, then they could truly provide a formidable form of competition to traditional organized crime. What is known about gangs is that they do of course aspire to such an ultimate level of control and power. The heroes of the ordinary gang member are not scientists, progressive American Presidents or civil rights leaders, rather their hero worship types are major organized crime figures like Al Capone. The fact that under drug legalization they would lose some income is a given, and the fact that gangs might lose some of their "weaker" members to the legalized drugs is also a given --- but this could strengthen the gang by removing those who are not zealots of the gang organization. What would remain is a more fit and more dedicated gang core structure. One would have to be using some powerful drugs to want to assume that suddenly such gangs would simply cease to exist or would make a "succession in goals" to become a prosocial and legitimate group in American society.

3. THE "NULL EFFECT" SCENARIO

Logically, a final scenario for the effects that legalizing hard drugs like heroin would have on gangs in America would be the "null effect" scenario. As alluded to above, under this potential development existing gangs could simply experience a succession in goals or a restructuring. Drugs are not the only source of illegal income. So, like many entrepreneurial organizations with a diversified income base, or like many of our social service organizations, the gangs might simply "chase the buck"[12]. If its gambling, commercial sex, pornography, chop shop operations, counterfeiting, extortion, loan sharking, etc, then these become natural alternative recourses to the solution of the gang income crisis. Further, such traditional organized crime specialties are the natural and expected progression for an effective gang.

The logical fallacy in Moore's (1978) recommendation about legalizing heroin as a way to curtail the gang problem has to do with advancing an essentially economic solution to what amounts to a socially caused problem: the social and cultural imperative for gangs. If gangs organize, spawn, and persist to any extent because of the nature of the culture represented by its members, and develop over time into the social institutional fabric of any segment of the American population, then no simple economic quick fix is going to work. If gangs arose and persisted chiefly out of the quest for drug profits, then the drug legalization argument would at least be on more consistent grounds; as pointed out above, however, it would still be untenable, for there would still exist an underage drug market. The problem is Moore (1978) provides much keen insight into the cultural and social institutional basis for Hispanic gangs in the barrios which she studied very close up in Los Angeles over a decade ago. One cannot have it both ways and recommend legalizing heroin as a solution to the gang problem. Eliminating heroin profits from the gang would not simultaneously eliminate the cultural imperative giving impetus to gang joining behavior or the persistence of the gang as a collective or group entity.

DRUG POLICY: ASSESSING THE SCENARIOS ON LEGALIZING HARD DRUGS

This moral and ethical quagmire about legalizing heroin as a way to curtail the gang problem provides an interesting basis for discussing a variety of developmental scenarios and issues about gangs in America and elsewhere. Looking at more than the obvious and immediate effect of such a drug policy helps us to understand the underlying issues about any policy that seeks to "dismember", ameliorate, neutralize, suppress, or redirect gangs in America. Depending on the type of the gang, such a drug policy could be expected to have different effects as well.

The gang classification system used in this book recognizes Level 1, Level 2, and Level 3 gangs as "real" gangs --- they are involved in and benefit from crime over time. A Level 0 gang is not involved in crime and is therefore outside the area of discussion here. A more organized gang (e.g., Level 3) is more likely to have a written and declared policy on drug use by members of its gang; usually restricting such use, if any restriction exists, to "soft" drugs. Yet all real gangs (levels 1, 2, and 3) can be involved in both drug use and drug sales; just as it is possible to conceive of some exceptions to this rule. It is the income potential from illegal drug sales that is of most attraction to the modern American gang. Thus, a level three gang might be expected to be more capable of exploiting the illegal drug sale market. The reason this is true is that it exists in several jurisdictions. A level one gang involved in drug sales might simply constitute a local "drug ring", it controls only one small area of the much larger drug trade.

WINNING GANGS AND LOSING THE WAR ON DRUGS

No American drug czar has yet won the war on drugs. The term itself is ludicrous, as drug "czar" implies not a combat role such as that of "Generalismo" might, but rather implies --- like the culture of authoritarian aristocracy from which it is social linguistically derived --- control and benefiting from the drug market. But it raises an important concern: could the war on drugs, or similarly a war on gang crime, ever be basically "won"?

The answer is --- at what cost of liberty are we willing to sacrifice rights, including basic civil liberties Americans all claim and often assume such as that of the right to privacy. All retail theft and basic street crime in a controlled area of any density can theoretically be prevented: it would require the equivalent, however, of a "state of siege" mentality in law enforcement, and could very well involve some finely tuned version of martial law itself! In the summer of 1993, a released prisoner who had formerly been the governor of a large midwestern state, declared an intent to run again as governor; some of his first words uttered in political campaigning amounted to the following: If he were elected to be the Governor, he would look at areas with high crime and high violence and if necessary declare martial law in these areas and have the National Guard stop the crime if the local police cannot!

So, without knowing it, the above recycled politician was recommending exactly what Taylor (1992)[13] was fearful about in criticizing the federal governments "Weed and Seed" approach to the war on drugs. Weeding means specifically targeting "gang activity in high-crime neighborhoods" (Gurele, 1991: 1)[14]. A recent effort to implement this in Seattle drew harsh criticisms from the local American Civil Liberties Union (Taylor, 1992). The weed and seed operation was described as "one more overblown weapon in the federal government's discriminatory and ineffective war on drugs - a war largely directed at minority Americans" (Taylor, 1992: 1). The operations involved "street sweeps" and were felt to be functionally equivalent to transforming parts of Seattle into "virtual martial law zones". That is, the Weed and Seed approach "seeks to establish a federal paramilitary operation in our inner city" (Taylor, 1992: 2).

Modern technology in electronic surveillance could itself crush the drug dealers in America and the users. National pen registry systems are but modest computer and minor storage problems. Assume that 100 million residential and cellular phones were used on any given day in the U.S.A., assume further that nationally each of these separate 100 million lines made five calls each. Recording the 10 bytes of the caller and the 10 bytes of the other party (their area codes and seven digit phone numbers) would require only 10,000 megabytes of computer storage --- more than 80 typical Personal Computer hard drives (i.e., 120 Meg. each), but not much in comparison with large main frame computers. Having such a phone line registry data base over time would allow a retrospective identification and analysis of the social networks of drug pushers. Having such data local law enforcement would know everyone a captured drug pusher dealt with and like a real war, the rest could be "rounded up" rather easily over time using the same "on-line" data. Are you personally willing to allow such a data system to be used for anything other than national security interests of which local drug dealing is not a qualified issue? Does simple association with someone who may later be determined to have sold drugs make you a "drug pusher" suspect if you had even accidentally dialed their number?

The role of electronic surveillance in combatting other crime in America has risen dramatically in the last decade, because of its effectiveness in prosecuting more complex and sometimes organized types of criminal behavior. Gangs are ideal crime problems for using modern surveillance equipment. Public gatherings of gang members can be monitored with pole cameras and aerial surveillance, versions of which are often shown in gang training. If they are at a park, and you are there too strolling by, are you someone who should have a police file even though you have never been arrested or convicted of anything? If yes, you may be saying that everyone should have a police file; and if police have the right to investigate everyone simply by association or like the typical victim of a gang drive-by shooting --- being merely an innocent bystander --- then you are actually advocating that many features of the Bill of Rights in the United States Constitution be systematically violated in a fashion that ultimately would come to be a police state.

The moral lesson here is that if you are not the kind of person who would like living in a police state, then you should be happy that as a society we have over the years of the ongoing "war on drugs" witnessed a series of competent individuals in ineffectual roles called drug "Czars", rather than having incompetent or especially competent individuals in effective roles such as may be implied --- to use a social linguistic source other than that from which "Czar" is derived --- in the stronger title of "Drug Fuehr" who might be operating under conditions where basic freedoms could be temporarily suspended.

This is the ethical dilemma of any suppression effort directed towards drugs or gangs: to do it most efficiently may mean some impact on civil liberties to the extent that effectiveness is also an issue.

SUMMARY AND DISCUSSION

We have tried to examine a variety of issues in terms of how the topic of "drugs" overlaps with and interfaces with "gangs". The policy recommendation by a contemporary gang researcher that to do something about the gang problem in America we should legalize heroin was critically examined. The three scenarios reviewed therefore included not just the most positive scenario ("gangs fading"), but also include a "gangs merging-consolidating" and a "null effect" scenario. What this issue highlights is actually the paucity of income data on gangs: we need more research on this underground economy. What we need most are not "vignettes" reflecting how one researcher hangs out with one gang, what we really need is national data giving us hard numbers on this problem. We currently lack such information in the gang literature. We have only rough estimates of how much money is involved in American illegal drug sales and it would be even harder to ascertain with any validity and reliability how much of this economic activity is controlled by gangs or gang members.

DISCUSSION   QUESTIONS

(1) Marijuana is said to be the largest cash crop in America today. Would legalizing it mean an extension of the material temptation of "free will"? Or would it imply a societal acceptance of varying degrees of drug or substance abuse resistance and the concomitant belief that "some people will always try it if it is available"? What do you think?

(2) Do you think it would be better, because it might be cheaper, to maintain a large population of addicts under a government heroin-assistance program rather than sending these same types of persons to prison for felony offenses associated with their addiction?

(3) Should police have the right to investigate a group just because it is perceived as deviant? Or should such intrusions on privacy be limited strictly to known and substantial patterns of law violation? Could a college "clique" or three or more persons who recurrently acquire and use illegal drugs in a small group be considered a gang?

FOOTNOTES

1. The gang literature typically portrays "Stoner" gangs as white groups whose worst crime threat is they routinely engage in "getting high". In communities and college campuses across America, regardless of race, a social organizational approach to gangs as advanced in this book would consider such groups "level one" gangs if there was a continuing pattern of law violation behavior by essentially the same core group. Such gangs are very horizontal: the "leader" is the one most esteemed, the one with the drug supply connections!   Thus, a gang need not have a name and identity as such to function as a gang.

2. "Crack" drug laws are more severe than the "powder form" cocaine drug laws. In 1994 federal Judge Clyde S. Cahill of St. Louis struck down the federal anti-drug laws giving harsher penalties for crack cocaine possession. The harsher "crack" penalties were seen as an unconscious form of racism against African-American offenders.

3. This analysis of the effects of joining a gang on I.V. drug abuse uses a slightly larger sample than first reported in Knox and Tromanhauser (1991). The early report included 1,801 cases; but more data came in and was used in a slightly larger sample that was used for this test.

4. For additional information on the Asian student survey, see Knox, Laske, and Tromanhauser (1992) Schools Under Siege.

5. See Hugh Dellios, 1993, "Mexican Drug Lords Recruit U.S. Street Gangs", Chicago Tribune, July 11, Section 1, P. 3.

6. For an example, see: Fran Spielman, "City Seizes Drugs; Daley Blasts Feds", Chicago Sun-Times.

7. Issued in May of 1993 to all respondents in the survey, the monograph entitled "Preliminary Findings from the 1992 Law Enforcement Mail Questionnaire Project" involved the following universities and respective researchers: Chicago State University, George W. Knox, Ph.D., and Edward D. Tromanhauser, Ph.D.; Rhode Island College, Pamela Irving Jackson, Ph.D. and Darek Niklas, Ph.D.; St. Ambrose University, James G. Houston, Ph.D., and Paul Koch, Ph.D.; and James R. Sutton, then at the University of Illinois at Chicago. A copy of the report was printed in Volume One, Number Three of the Gang Journal: An Interdisciplinary Research Quarterly, 1993.

8. The data used for this analysis reflects all data collected, including a police chief who responded after the May 1993 report was issued.

9. It appears that Skolnick, Blumenthal, and Correl (1993) were limiting this over-generalization to Black gangs.

10. The real problem with Skolnick, Blumenthal, and Correl (1993) is their rather cavalier attitude towards minority groups. Which is to say, their language is less than sensitive. For example, in describing how most of the gangs studied by Thrasher (1927) were white-ethnic gangs, they generalize "Their moral posture seems scarcely different from today's black youth" (Skolnick, Blumental, and Correl, 1993: p. 193). Not "Black gangs", but the more general and inclusive "black youth". Thus, whether they meant it or not, implying that all Black youths were gang members. Similarly, in claiming their theory of gang migration applies outside of California, they state "This theory may also be applicable to Eastern U.S. gangs, such as the Jamaicans" (Skolnick, Blumenthal, and Correl, 1993: p. 195). They probably meant Jamaican Posse groups or Jakes as some call them. Not everyone who emigrates from Jamaica is a gang. The point is our language must be much more clear when dealing with a problem as complex as gangs.

11. It was not Rev. Fry who was indicted for defrauding the U.S. government for his gang program, it was his indigenous worker, one Jeff Fort. The history of gangs in America shows numerous examples of this kind of gang intervention initiative where a local activist is provided with funding to do "his thing" with the gang. No theory, no guidelines, no standards, no evaluation --- it sounds good or it uses the right buzz words that bureaucrats in Washington want to hear, and thus it is funded. Was Fry duped? Or was this social experimentation with gangs (providing money to the gang that would eventually become the notorious El Rukn organization) irresponsible on its face?

12. To "chase the buck" is a phrase used in American social service organizations where the social work agency tends to specialize in whatever the government is willing to pay for it to perform. To wit: an agency founded initially with legislative funds that run out, or which were provided by a government agency that may be dismantled by Congress, may not simply just cease to exist and disappear. Social service organizations simply adapt by having a succession or modification in their service delivery goals. This is normal organizational behavior, and thus we should not rule out the possibility that gangs can evolve in a similar fashion.

13. Taylor, Kathleen, 1992, Letter by Kathleen Taylor (Executive director of the American Civil Liberties Union of Washington) to Mayor Norman Rice), RE: Operation "Weed and Seed".

14. Gurule, Jimmy, 1991, Operation "Weed and Seed". Reclaiming America's Neighborhoods. U.S. Department of Justice, Office of Justice Programs, National Institute of Justice, Washington, D.C.

CHAPTER 16

GANG CRIME AND ORGANIZED CRIME

INTRODUCTION

It is common for descriptions of the gang crime problem to make the analogy with organized crime when gangs appear to function in a sophisticated manner.[1] Many see "supergangs", or corporate gangs, or what the present author calls level three gangs as simply being a new form of organized crime. But lacking in our literature is any discussion that helps to distinguish what exactly these factors of sophistication are.

Also, those previous gang authors who base most of their conclusions about the gang crime in America on the sole data of their ability to penetrate the confidence of Spanky and Alfalfa type of gangs through ethnographic studies, are not in the position of being knowledgeable about higher level gang formations --- those that exist with written gang constitutions. Some of these national gang constitutions will be discussed here. For some authors gangs in America constitute little more than hostile playgroups. That is not the full truth, but does reflect the continuing problem of gang researchers who tend to overgeneralize their findings. Clearly, there do exist some very formidable and highly organized gangs in America today[2].

While many working in the field of corrections and criminal justice may take the view that some of today's gangs should be considered new forms of "organized crime", we truly need to think such a prosecution process through. Targeting them as "Mafia" groups may give them the identity they have long sought and will seek to live up to. In a "lock em' up" atmosphere, it may be convenient to label such gang members as "organized crime". But clearly there are social organizational differences. And there may be unintended risks for society associated with targeting all gangs and gang members in such a blanket manner, to "get the terrorists off the streets". The danger is that how we officially define them may constitute what they become.

If gangs can be roughly defined along a social organization continuum of complexity, where at the lowest level we find our spontaneous "play group" formations, and at the highest level we find our more complex gang nation or "super gang" having the characteristics of advanced social organization, then at this higher end of the gang spectrum the observant student of criminology must ask: what then is the difference between a highly organized criminal gang and organized crime? To answer this question is to provide a wider method of viewing gang and group crime.

The approach here will be to begin with a summary of what we know about the structure and function of organized crime. Then we shall return to the gang classification system discussed earlier to see what differences, if any, exist between a level three gang and "organized crime" as discussed in the criminological literature. Within this context we shall also discuss in some detail the written constitutions and by-laws of several Chicago gangs.

The value of this approach is that it helps to identify, as well, those aspects of contemporary gangs that we are clearly not informed about and yet should be so obvious to even the most casual observer. It helps, therefore, to set a research agenda for the future that will help advance our social scientific understanding of gangs. It will be seen that having enough capital to penetrate legitimate business and having political corruption that can be put to use are about the only two things stopping some major gang organizations from making a transition to forms of organized crime.

DEFINITIONS OF ORGANIZED CRIME

What are we talking about when we focus on "organized crime"? Is this the "Mafia", the "Camorra", the "Cosa Nostra", the "Syndicate", Chicago's "Outfit", international illegal drug cartels, the "Black Hand Society", the "Dixieland Mafia", or what? We must seek greater clarity and precision in our review of "organized crime". Some gangs use the word "mafia" in their name (e.g, Mexican Mafia, etc). Gangs like to use "strong, virile" names. What gangs do strive for in their most idyllic goal is to emulate if not surpass their cultural hero of Al Capone.

If we wanted to induce confusion here, our definitional clarity could suffer immensely by references to areas outside of the social sciences, such as the printed mass media. Newsweek, for example, offered one of the best tautologies of defining it in terms of itself, almost to the point of comic relief in making the assertion "I feel the Mafia is controlled by organized crime":

> "The Mafia is a loose confederation of gangs spread around the country" (Newsweek, 1981: p. 35).

Here apparently, organized crime "families" are "gangs". And that certainly seems to simplify everything we wanted to know about the difference between gangs and organized crime. Not really, as we shall see. Indeed, perhaps our problems with both gangs and organized crime is our tendency, in dealing with the government and the wider lay public, to do exactly that: over simplify, to the point perhaps of adding nothing to our understanding and analytical framework. So to begin with we see that there are some enormous definitional contradictions in both the "gang" and "organized crime" literatures. If organized crime is so "loose knit" organizationally and pulls in billions in profits, then how come ordinary criminals do not enter this field in competition or even unethical business persons for that matter; clearly, these are some remarkable human beings who can accomplish so much economically with such little social organization. And finally, if these organized crime "families" are so "loose knit" why is it so difficult to successfully prosecute their members? Or finally, are many of our criminological analysts so worried about making the error of reification --- treating as real or as a concrete material form something that is really just an abstraction? Another impression from reviewing the gang literature is that our abstractions have not been such very powerful theoretical generalizations that we have to worry too much about it.

Vetter and Territo (1984, p. 36) define organized crime as "a business that provides illegal, but desired, goods and services for the noncriminal public. Also known as syndicated crime".

Cole's (1983: p. 45) definition is that organized crime is "a social framework for the perpetration of criminal acts, usually in such fields as gambling, narcotics, and prostitution, where a service the public desires is illegal".

The definition by Thio surfaces the same conflicting problem found in the gang literature about whether gangs are, or are not, organized. Thio (1988) recognized that:

"organized crime has been viewed in two conflicting ways --- as a tight and as a loose organization. The reality seems to lie somewhere in between. As a highly lucrative enterprise, organized crime involves selling illegal goods and services, racketeering, large-scale thievery, infiltrating legitimate businesses, and corrupting public officials" (Thio, 1988: p. 417).

The definition of organized crime by the President's Commission on Law Enforcement and Administration of Justice tends to focus on size of both organization and profit potential. It is a definition implying "massive scale as a business enterprise" (Di Renzo: 1984, p. 409).[3] Here was the President's Commission (1968) definition of organized crime, which was not too dissimilar from President Reagan's attribution of organized crime as being "an invisible, lawless empire" (see Thio, 1988: p. 403):

> "Organized crime is a society that seeks to operate outside the control of the American people and their governments. It involves thousands of criminals, working within structures as complex as those of any large corporation, subject to laws more rigidly enforced than those of legitimate governments. Its actions are not impulsive but rather the result of intricate conspiracies, carried on over many years and aimed at gaining control over whole fields of activity in order to amass huge profits" (President's Commission, 1968: p. 437).

A slightly less "alarmist" and somewhat more analytical definition of organized crime was provided by the 1986 President's Commission on Organized Crime:

> "Organized crime is the collective result of commitment, knowledge and actions of three components: the criminal groups, each of which has at its core persons tied by racial, linguistic, ethnic or other bonds; the protectors, persons who protect the group's interests; and specialist support, persons who knowingly render services on an ad hoc basis to enhance the group's interests (President's Commission, 1986: p. 25).

Some definitions of organized crime simply include gang crime as one of the possible variations. That is, gang crime is a subset and included in a wider definition of organized crime. Wrobleski and Hess (1987: p. 104) quote the lengthy definition that views organized crime in terms of these five categories of criminal activity:

> "1. Racketeering. 2. Vice Operations (narcotics, prostitution, loansharking, gambling). 3. Theft/fence rings (fraud, bunco schemes, fraudulent document passers, burglary rings, car thieves,

truck hijackers). 4. Gangs (youth gangs, outlaw motorcycle gangs, prison gangs). 5. Terrorists." (Ibid, p. 104).

COMPONENTS OF ORGANIZED CRIME

Does a successful criminal venture mean that only when the group becomes national in scope that it is considered "organized crime"? No. But the federal government's Organized Crime and Racketeering Unit, which was formerly decentralized and operated under the direction of local U.S. Attorneys, is now centralized for a more coordinated effort. Clearly, organized crime implies a multi-jurisdictional boundary problem by the potential such a group has for expansion. Nor should it imply the need to be an "interstate" operation, even though obviously that is helpful for federal prosecution, and even though as Cole notes organized crime operations can indeed often cut "across state and national boundaries" (1983, p. 45).

A hierarchical structure is definitely a component of organized crime according to leading sources like Cressey. The collective or organizational groupings carrying out "organized crime" are often called "families". This does not mean that all such members of any given "family" are related by blood, come from the same family of orientation, or are related by name or by "family of procreation", although obviously, there is considerable "bonding" and potential for strengthening organized crime ties through such marriages. What "families" implies is that the "chief executive officer", if his name is Tony Acardo, well, then his organized crime family becomes known as the "Acardo family". The astute student will sense, perhaps at this point, some common problem in definitional clarity also to be found in our gang studies literature. Clearly, then, the value of a social organizational approach to gang studies is that it provides for the analytical linkage to a wider analysis of other forms of collective or organized crime. This, at least, is the hope of the present analysis.

ELEMENTS IN COMMON BETWEEN HIGHER LEVEL GANG FORMATIONS AND ORGANIZED CRIME

Clearly, there are a number of characteristics that the gang and organized crime have in common.[4] At least this is true of the higher level of organizationally sophisticated gangs.[5] They both have a code of conduct. At the higher end of the gang organizational spectrum this code of conduct is in fact more than an oral tradition and can take on the form of a written constitution and bylaws.[6] Both formalized gangs and organized crime also make use of "buffers".[7] These are often "middle management" roles, lieutenants, trusted henchmen, etc, who hold status and power above the rank of regular members.

Both organized crime and gang crime involves conspiracy. Both gangs and organized crime also have "enforcement power". In the more sophisticated gang, this means having a gang role equivalent to the "chief of violations", someone who dispenses punishment for errant members, someone who "puts a hit out" on a former member turned snitch, etc. In terms of conspiracy and enforcement, both gangs and organized crime are much alike.

Violence in both organized crime and gangs has an important element of honor. In organized crime, while most violence is instrumental, not expressive, it still has the element of defending honor; particularly among those who threaten the honor of the organization. Honor is associated with gang violence in several ways (Horowitz, 1983, 1987), but mostly in relationship to defense of the "hood" being controlled, or symbolic honor as in the correctional institution where there is little "turf" to defend, or even to fellow gang members who violate one of their internal laws.

THE ETHNIC SUCCESSION HYPOTHESIS

Most useful to understanding the potential of even a highly sophisticated gang making a transition to what is ordinarily implied by "organized crime" is our comprehension of the ethnic succession hypothesis. Ianni (1974) takes essentially the definition of organized crime discussed above, which differentiates gangs from organized crime in terms of expansion into legitimate income areas. That is "organized crime activities illustrate the mixture of legal, semi-legal and illegal activities that make up that segment of the American economy we call organized crime" (Ianni, 1974: pp. 246-247).

In appreciation of Ianni (1974) the one feature that distinguishes organized crime is its systematic fulfillment of demands from the culture and society which cannot be fulfilled through legitimate channels. Indeed, chapter 5 of Ianni (1974) "The Gypsy Cabs: Organized Crime or Minority Business Enterprise" is a striking example of the large "spot market" in such illicit areas. Gypsy cabs functioned illegally, had bitter competition with legitimate cab companies, often struck up creative arrangements with prostitutes and drug pushers, but fulfilled an essential need desired by a specific public. Bribery was a feature of this kind of enterprise, as was the cultivation of political influence. Ianni sees this "gypsy cab" industry being eventually legitimized.

Ethnic succession here meant that for African-Americans and for Puerto Ricans this method of "making it in America" is not dissimilar from other patterns of how ambitious, "rugged individualists" who got their piece of the American pie (e.g., economic success) also had less than saintly beginnings. We shall avoid, for the moment, analysis of the idea that many of our nations gangs could likewise make such a transition, and if they did make such a transition towards a more legitimate business enterprise, what implications that might have for our communities.

The value of Ianni should be clear and will emerge even more strongly below in the analysis of gang constitutions. As demonstrated much earlier in this text, gangs tend to be ethnically homogeneous. The hypothesis by Ianni (1974) is therefore of much potential value to gang analysis, because it provides a means of analyzing the transition from "street gang" to "organized crime".[8]

Sale (1971) describes how during the 1960's, Chicago's Mayor Daley was upset because the money flow from Washington did not go through city agencies before being distributed to programs such as the one in which the Black Stone Rangers through Rev. John Fry were able to acquire such funding. Sale also suggests that Senator McClellan's committee investigating funding abuses was spurred by Daley's animosity towards not being able to get an administrative share of these federal funds by processing them through City Departments:

Pressure from Mayor Daley helped to explain why McClellan was making such bitter charges, claiming, for instance, that federal money was financing the formation of a new "Black Mafia" (the Stones) which was supposed to be taking criminal control of the South Side (Sale, 1971: p. 87).

THE INDIVIDUAL TRANSITION AND ORGANIZATIONAL CHANGE HYPOTHESIS

A number of authors have shown cases of youth to adult transition in crime careers. It involves both the individual and organizational forms. At the individual level, it means essentially graduating in terms of membership from a street gang to the ranks of organized crime.[9] At the organizational level, the entire gang functions with stronger leadership and a greater division of labor. As Taylor states, the gang can evolve as in the case of Chicago's "Forty Two Gang" in the 1930's from a "scavenger/territorial to corporate/organized" gang (Taylor, 1990: p. 7).[10]

The organizational change hypothesis is described mostly in current literature as showing organizational evolution. That is, the evolving higher level of organizational sophistication in gangs. The term organizational change is used here to cover the other direction of development. That is, there can also be disintegration, dismemberment, and dissolution if we are to accept the notion that gangs as social groups can either be put out of business or can sometimes put themselves out of business.

DIFFERENCES BETWEEN ORGANIZED CRIME AND GANGS

The two major differences between organized crime and gangs are: corruption and capitalization represented in the extent of penetrating legitimate business. That gangs have their own small business enterprises has apparently been the case for some time in Chicago. They are said to have video stores, game rooms, and smaller such cash business enterprises. Gangs have not been too successful in corrupting public officials or law enforcement.

The Herrera Family is an interesting case here. Is it a gang or is it organized crime? Clearly, to carry out such an ongoing high level of control of the heroin importation and distribution market it must be able to bribe --- certainly, we would assume, in Mexico. But perhaps not as effectively in the U.S.A. Yet it is also well known that many business enterprises are controlled by the Herrera family through the accumulation of wealth in the heroin trade.

Similarly, Taylor (1990) argues that many such corporate style gangs have already become forms of organized crime. This would probably include as a good candidate list: Aryan Brotherhood, Bloods, Crips, Vice Lords, Disciples, El Rukns, Latin Kings, Mexican Mafia, Black Guerrilla Family, Nuestra Familia, Ku Klux Klan, various motorcycle gangs (Pagans, Hells Angels, etc) and probably more. But we cannot simply say that we do not have a gang problem by defining the gang into a different category of analysis: organized crime. Organized crime is a gang phenomenon, indeed it is the highest level of gang development, a goal aspired to by most gang members in all gangs in America. Crips and Bloods, Peoples and Folks, all admire major organized crime figures as legends of ruthlessness and conquest, as models for achieving instant wealth and fame.

We can now add some more analytically based criticism to the policy recommendation of legalizing heroin as a primary method of gang dismemberment in America. Organized crime has found pornography to be a very profitable area. It is an area, obviously, where gangs could clearly compete. Taking away drug income could simply force gangs to diversify their income base, and enter into such fields traditionally associated with organized crime (e.g., pornography, gambling, loan sharking, protection, etc).

The real key to further understanding these differences is the extent to which American gangs have associated, directly or indirectly, with organized crime figures[11]. Do organized crime figures look at gangs and gang leaders as "dope fiend renegades" or as potentially serious competitors? We don't know for sure, because most researchers know that once we reach the top of the gang organizational continuum ladder (i.e., organized crime), obviously no one talks to skilled or naive researchers. What we do know is that when Crips gang members robbed a series of Las Vegas casinos in 1994, we can probably assume they got the attention of organized crime. There is simply limited data on this key question about the extent to which gangs interact with or cooperate with or simply compete with organized crime.[12] Ko-lin Chin (1988) did, however, indicate that the Chinese gangs in New York City worked as "protectors" for the tongs who are regarded as organized crime.[13] There was some evidence that Jeff Fort, at a point in his career when he was in the transition from the Moorish Americans operating in a political context as the Martin Luther King Movement march against neo-nazis on Chicago's southwest side during 1976-77, and before he organized the El Rukns formally, he had some contact with organized crime figures. But apparently Jeff could not work very effectively with them. But he is today imprisoned in the same place with some important organized crime figures (i.e., the federal facillity in Marion, Illinois). Such federal correctional staff are the best at assessing the nature of any such relationship between gangs and organized crime. This is an important intelligence aspect that should be used in any threat assessment of gangs.

AN ORGANIZATIONAL   CONTINUUM

For the purposes of noting how modern gangs can make the transition to organized crime, a brief version of the gang typology offered by this author is provided here. In a later chapter, more details of this gang typology are provided. Basically four levels of gang sophistication are developed in terms of their differences in organizational development. It is helpful here to simply discuss this classification system to focus specifically on how a higher level gang formation differs from organized crime. Figure 14 presents this gang to organized crime organizational continuum.

FIGURE 14

A Group/Organization Crime Continuum

Operational Characteristics:	Organizational Continuum Gang Threat Levels[a]				
	Level 0	Level 1	Level 2	Level 3	Level 4
CRIME IMPACT	None	Low	Medium	High	High
BUFFERED LEADERSHIP	None	Little	Some	Much	High
MULTI-JURISDICTIONAL	No	No	Maybe	Yes	Yes
LEGIT. Bus. Control	No	No	Rarely	Often	Always
Own Property	No	No	Sometimes	Yes	Yes
BRIBERY/CORRUPTION	No	No	Sometimes	Often	Yes
CARE OF INMATES	No	Rarely	Sometimes	Often	Always
ASSETS ACCUMULATION	No	No	Low	Medium	High
KILL SNITCHES	No	No	Sometimes	Often	Always

LEGEND:
Level 0 = Not a true gang, not involved in ongoing crime.
Level 1 = A formative gang, not highly organized.
Level 2 = An intermediate gang formation.
Level 3 = A formalized gang, often with written constitution.
Level 4 = Syndicated, Organized Crime cartels or families.

As seen in Figure 14 above, where a level three gang (the most organizationally developed and the most sophisticated) differs from organized crime (a level 4 group crime phenomenon) is chiefly in the ability to permeate throughout the society.[14] To carry out bribes and to corrupt public officials. To have a widened source of income including legitimate income from business enterprises under control, and to penetrate other legitimate business enterprises, and to in this way keep the accumulation of capital "moving" in an investment strategy rather than a milking "hand to mouth existence".

The true difference, then, between organized crime and higher level gang formations is simply a matter of degree.[15] Both level three gangs and organized crime must be regarded as formal organizations. But a highly organized gang with thousands of members and different chapters in many areas must still achieve two things that distinguish most gangs from organized crime: the ability to use political corruption and the ability to penetrate legitimate business. More specifically then the difference between more organized gangs and organized crime is the degree to which the group can operate in wider society: bribing officials, getting protection, investing and diversifying its capital, and maintaining connections with many others who are obviously not in their group. In this sense, traditional organized crime groups are more "pro social" than gangs; they have the ability to maintain cooperative ventures and alliances with a wide variety of persons, in chiefly economic relationships, outside

---

[a] See legend below.

of their own limited subcultural integration. Organized crime, therefore, requires a higher level of legitimate integration. Some gangs today try to achieve political power as a step in that direction.

Where some gangs parallel this matter of legitimate ties to larger society is in the political arena. Formalized gangs in Illinois have established their own not-for-profit corporations chartered often as "voting leagues".[16] Their ability to "get out the vote" translates into quid pro quo for whatever politician that is willing to accept their assistance.

THE FEDERAL ROLE IN GANG PROSECUTION: RICO STATUTES

No correctional administrator wants gang offenders in a facility that structurally lags behind the social change in the offender population itself represented by inmate gangs. They are most problematic. Our society has few examples that are equivalent to the infamous Alcatraz. One might be the U.S. Penitentiary at Marion, Illinois; inmates there are out of their cells only one hour a day. Another more recent example might be the Pelican Bay prison in California where violent gang members are sent; inmates there are kept under the "no human contact" security status.

The literature on India's robber gangs (Sleeman, 1849) showed that local law enforcement was not able to effectively deal with this crime problem. A national approach was required to make progress on a national problem. Then again, just because the gang is armed and organized comparable to a military unit, is that sufficient justification for bringing our own military forces into this fray? We shall examine this possibility of a stronger federal role to play in addressing the gang problem in a later chapter. But in the absence of a stronger federal role, state's must probably rely on the "mini-RICO" statutes, which can be effective prosecution tools.[17]

GANG CONSTITUTIONS AND BY-LAWS

Another area of commonality between higher level gang formations and traditional forms of organized crime is in this area of declarations of official purpose.[18] It has been a recurrent pattern for some organized crime families to have their "social athletic clubs", basically "fronts" for crime. Here we shall see that level 3 gangs, or more sophisticated gangs in terms of organizational development, also have this aspect in common with organized crime. Because according to these written gang constitutions and by-laws, the cloak of "do gooderism" is common to all.

The documents discussed here consist of the following: (1) the constitution of the Almighty Latin King Nation, (2) the constitution of the Spanish Gangster Disciple Nation, (3) the constitution of the Vice Lords, and (4) Black Gangster Disciple's Nation internal memoranda. Three major commonalities, worth discussion here, are to be found in all of these lengthy gang written documents.[19] First, they declare a "pro-social" intent. Secondly, they have some element of spiritual or religious legitimation.[20] Thirdly, they all claim to be "oppressed" and part of a larger struggle for freedom and justice.[21] All quotations of these documents made here are direct and reflect any original errors in spelling, etc.[22]

(1) A Pro-Social Intent. The most fascinating, but perhaps not unexpected, aspect that these all have in common is their written and official declaration of being essentially "pro-social" organizations. The Black Gangster Disciples, for example, in a memo describing progress with getting a not-for-profit corporation started up, declaring themselves intent on stopping the commission of crimes within their communities. It is like the skeptical professor says to students in criminology, don't believe anything you hear and only half of what you see and chances are you'll have a scientific footing in the area of crime. It is absurd to conceive of the Black Gangster Disciples as a community-development organization intent on eliminating crime[b]. It is comparable only to the Ku Klux Klan suddenly claiming an official intent and purpose of improving ethnic and race relations in America. It is a very big lie, but an interesting one none the less.[23]

It is interesting because of the potential of such a definition of the situation being promulgated in the group context. It serves an important social-psychological function to have such a "cloak" of social acceptability, even moral superiority. It is more than moral neutralization. It is moral stabilization. One can commit serious crimes and acts of violence with little of shame in this kind of group ethos. In written form, any such declaration of intent as a kind of Masonic organization or association (ala Hobsbawm, 1965: p. 50) as a "mutual aid" society, is only that --- a declaration. Indeed, it is a declaration without regard to goals, functions, or overall societal impact.

(2)   The Spiritual/Religious Emphasis. Another commonality between gang constitutions is their claim to a spiritual approval for their existence. Or the use of religion as a source of legitimation, cohesion, and internal social control for the gang[24]. Clearly, one megalomaniac tendency in some gangs is to portray a particular gang leader as such a "holy person".[25] For the Black Gangster Disciples, this means "the religious faith of this organization, tribe and nation, is founded in the very nature of all things; one religious doctrine, teachings and philosophy is that of truth...the doctrine of truth embraces and reflects every religion known to man, from the beginning of recorded time, and history reveals that all religious doctrines claim their god to be the father of all creation; but none yet have given an image to their god which can be manifested from one age to another." Here, obviously, the gang leader is the Chosen One.[26] Recall, for the historical record, the same religious backdrop for legitimation represented in the elaborate written gang constitution described by Green (1847).

For the Spanish Gangster Disciple Nation we find significantly less emphasis on religion, but a potential mysticism nevertheless[c]. Referring to their insignia, "the

---

[b] Or similarly, from the written constitution of the Black Guerrilla Family (BGF), if a reader were to simply believe the BGF Code of Conduct one might believe these are inmates truly seeking to rehabilitate themselves.

[c] A gang constitution conspicuously lacking any reference to "God" or religion is that of the Black Guerrilla Family which is specifies in writing an allegiance to revolutionary Marxism. Still, however, there is some comparable idealism as is

Spanish Cross derives from our heretic ways, the first word in our Nations name, in which we find our race, our creed, our essential beliefs and our faith". There is but a glimmer of religiosity: "we as a Nation have to have morals, to teach our young in every subject, to abide by our set of laws, to carry our Nations oath in our heart, to accept our prayer for our deceased...". In fact, there is no mention of God whatsoever in the "prayer" for "our Brother's & Sister's who have lost their lives in being part of our Nation's struggle".

In the Latin Kings written constitution and by-laws we find again the difficulty that any type of ethnographic research approach is going to encounter in trying to study this type of gang. Revealing internal affairs of the gang organization to outsiders is explicitly forbidden, and takes on much significance as a potential violation. Most interesting, therefore, is the "holy prayer" of the Latin Kings which appears to be a prayer not to God, for there is no reference to God or Jesus or Allah, but rather might be interpreted as a prayer either to gang ancestry or some visionary "sun god" who rules the gang nation. It, along with the "Kings and Queens Prayer", portrays God as a fellow gang member, where God is the Almighty King; again, however, the original author fearing some moral abomination never uses the descriptor "God" or "Jesus". We do find, however, an explicit declaration that "The Almighty Latin King Nation is a religion which gives us faith in ourselves, a national self-respect, power to educate the poor and relieve the misery around us".[27]

In the Conservative Vice Lord Nation, their oath, which all members are required to know, more specifically reflects an Islamic influence. Recall that the Chicago Vice Lords and the Chicago El Rukns are allied gangs (i.e., "peoples"). The Vice Lord oath within the Illinois State Prison setting is as follows[28]:

> "In the name of almighty Allah, I lord cocaine as a representative of a C.V.L.N. will not dishonor our most sacred weapon Lord Unity nor under the threat of death will I deny those who stand beside and as a representative of the C.V.L.N. I will listen to the truthful teaching of our elites so that upon my release I may be useful to myself and my community as a whole. Let the black god Allah bear witness to this oath. Behold Vice Lord".

Similarly, the "star" in Vice Lord totems symbolizes "the eye of Allah watching over his people". This Islamic influence is also to be found in the Almighty Black P. Stone Nation.[29]

(3) The "oppressed peoples" belief system. Here we find the strongest evidence yet that many of our nation's prison inmates may in fact be "political prisoners", in the limited sense that if they were gang members, they might have subscribed to an official code that had clear elements of a revolutionary or resistance ideology. We can loosely call this the "oppressed peoples" belief system.[30] Oddly, an analysis of these organizational belief systems from written constitutions of higher level gangs,

---

evident from the following BGF passage "I fully understand, without any reservations whatever, that our revolutionary mission is never done until our will has been complete, and the light of freedom, justice, and equality sine down on all mankind like a star in the night."

shows they actually have much in common; such that it does present some interesting possibilities in terms of scenarios for the future.[31] Let us consider some of these different "oppressed peoples" themes.

In the Black Gangster Disciple's Nation, their logo, the Star of David, is described as follows: "THE DEVIL'S PITCH FORKS REPRESENTS OUR NATION'S POWER IN OUR STRUGGLE TO OVER COME THE OPPRESSION WE ARE UNDER....THE DEVIL'S TAIL REPRESENTS THE OPPRESSION BLACK'S, LATINO, AND THIRD WORLD PEOPLES LIVE UNDER AND IS NOT A WHITE ISSUE". We shall find this same explicit identification with a "third world struggle" in other gang, including rival gang, constitutions.[32]

In the Spanish Gangsters Disciple Nation, fellow gang members are greeted as "comrades in arms". Their work is the "struggle". In this written constitution we find a fascinating hodge-podge of pseudo-political ideology:

"Through our nations decades we've enjoyed providing security, a sure safety and domestic tranquility among the lives of our people...We, brother's of the S.G.D.N. must ordain and abide by the nations constitution, to eliminate poverty and inequality among our people, to provide a structure of potential developments for the individual of our nation, to maintain a liberty for our children and a more gratifying style of social living."

From gang leader Vic, however, we find this element of ideology to be more honestly a patent and clear-cut form of individual opportunism. That is to say, at least in this gang's internal written material we find the declared purpose to be "the social elevation of it's members". Presumably the social-economic elevation of its members as well. It is essentially the same doctrine found in the India robber gangs (Sleeman, 1849). These guerilla fighters want their share, but they obviously have no plans on restructuring society and its political institutions. They are decoits, brigands, and opportunists; and only by a stretch of the imagination "political prisoners", because they are by their own account "out for themselves". What this particular constitution also shows is the important tendency of social imitation; that is, gang organization mimicking legitimate organizational forms.

In the Almighty Latin King Nation, we find a constitution that is more specifically identified with the "third world struggle against oppression". Here we find the strongest written evidence of such an official dogma, but the reader should obviously view this kind of declaration with some skepticism in terms of its sincerity not its authenticity:

"The name of this association shall be the ALMIGHTY LATIN KING NATION. An organization of international brotherhood with[d] exists for the purpose of: 1. Promoting prosperity and freedom through love and understanding to all oppressed people of the world, 2. To train our People to become aware of our social and political problems and of the conditions we are subjected to

---

[d] Presumably, the gang author meant "which" rather than"with".

live under as a Third World People, 3. To provide the aid and way in our search for peace and unity, 4. To promote and encourage education and vocational learning in order to train our People in the art of survival".

It is most interesting to compare this kind of global statement of purpose to the actual written chapter meeting notes for a long time frame.

The fact is some gangs do have regular meetings, and while Hagedorn (1990: p. 245) tells us gangs do not keep membership rosters, we should be careful in studying gangs what we say they cannot do. It is a problem of over generalizing, as many prior gang authors have been very prone to do; often on the basis of lower level gang formations (e.g., level zero gangs). Because some gangs do keep rosters, obviously for paying dues. What one such chapter meeting minutes, made available to the author, showed is this: numerous "violations" against fellow gang members, where violation implies more often than not physical punishment and ridicule, the gang chapter apparently spent much of its time disciplining its own members. Secondly, the gang chapter's monetary proceeds (from dues chiefly) were certainly not spent on community improvement; they were spent on firearms, gang paraphernalia, and spray paint "to fix the hood".

What is interesting about the Latin Kings is that they specifically deny membership to rapists, at least in their constitution. Again, however, one should view this with some skepticism; which is to say, there can be a large difference between official dogma and reality. The present author recalls interviewing a gang member from the Disciples in the 1970's and seeing one of the best examples of moral neutralization, where the youth described a common practice of "tree jumping". It was rape, but in the language of this gang member is was not violent rape but simply "tree jumping".

Generally, the totems and written codes for higher level gang formations serve the purpose of allowing allied gangs, or satellite gang units separated geographically, to share in a common system of symbols and beliefs. Thus, as true Masonic organizations have their various "lodges" separated geographically, so do level three gangs have their franchises[33].

SUMMARY

What we have tried to accomplish in this chapter is two fold. First, to those gang authors whose conception of modern gangs is that they lack any sophisticated internal organization particularly those who deny "centralized, hierarchical organizations" in the spirit of disagreeing with strawman law enforcement definitions, the position taken here, based on a classification system that reflects an organizational capability/sophistication continuum, is that essentially all such views may be correct but only in the limited context to those levels of sophistication that exist in gang formations. Level 0 groups are our typical "clicks" or "cliques", or "street corner" groups, a natural and normal and essentially non-criminal operation. Levels 1 thru 3 represent the true gang organizational development patterns, with level 4 being essentially what is meant by organized crime.

For those who continue to deny the existence of highly organized, pyramidal hierarchies, or any equivalent form of organizational sophistication and development, we have offered for analysis here several such written constitutions and by-laws for several Level 3 gangs.[34] These are fairly lengthy typed documents. Your author did not, nor did law enforcement officials intent on psy-war, manufacture these written codes. They are genuine. Indeed, as anyone who comes to understand the magnitude of the problem and discovering privileged information, here it has not been possible to present all such information because of its sensitivity, which is to imply one of many sources of data, and an appraisal that to disclose this information is to place some persons in jeopardy and perhaps to obstruct justice.

Secondly, in this chapter we have sought to compare and contrast gangs with organized crime. Higher level gang formations assuredly have much in common with organized crime. Where they differ is also important.

DISCUSSION QUESTIONS

(1) All crime is organized to some degree or another. White collar crime begins and exists only because of organization. Can gang crime begin because of social disorganization and thrive thereafter as a natural social organizational form? Does defining level two and level three gangs as "organized crime" allow law enforcement to say they no longer have a "gang problem"?

(2) What in social policy should be changed to discourage gangs from evolving into organized crime? Or, what should the federal role be in combatting gang crime?

(3) Logically, do you think we should find organized crime patterns to be as equally differentiated as gang formations?

FOOTNOTES

1. See, for example, Dean Murphy "L.A. Black Gangs Likened to Organized Crime Groups", Los Angeles Times (Front Page), January 11, 1987.

2. Apparently the "community denial" syndrome has many variations, including academic denial of some highly organized gangs.

3. Di Renzo like many authors also tends to define "organized crime" in terms of its monopolistic tendency, its use of legitimate businesses as "front groups", and its high profit volume, that is, "it was estimated in 1967 that organized crime "earns" approximately $9 billion annually, a figure that could safely be doubled or tripled" today (DiRenzo, 1984: p. 410).

4. Whether it is a "put on" ala the research on deviance by Robert Stebbins, or if it is some process of linguistic emulation, one gang member interviewed in 1991 (LK27) used the phrase common to the Chicago "outfit" or organized crime of being "made"

336 AN INTRODUCTION TO GANGS

as a member. Where "made" translates in meaning as to being accepted into the gang organization.

5. Hoenig (1975, p. 159) was one of the first to discuss the gang transplant/diffusion/franchising issue in noting that there was "some official speculation that there are links between Brooklyn gangs and the Blackstone Rangers, a Chicago gang of the early sixties that eventually grew so large that it swallowed up much of Chicago's organized crime business...". Hoenig may be referring to what is now known as Jeff Fort's El Rukn gang; or to the current derivative of the "stones", the Black P. Stone Nation.

6. Jackson and Mc Bride (1990: p. 52) report that the Nuestra Familia, a California prison gang, "has a written constitution and an identified rank structure from warrior to general".

7. From the law enforcement view, when leaders are insulated against arrest, this is a feature considered typical of organized crime (Sibley, 1989: p. 406).

8. As early as 1974 one sociologist observed about gang leaders inside prison that "certain leaders speculate about the development of a grand alliance and the rise of a Black Mafia to challenge the syndicate for control of Chicago vice (Jacobs, 1974: p. 407)".

9. One might also call this the "continuity" hypothesis. That is, it is an alternative to the maturation hypothesis. The maturation hypothesis suggests persons leave the gang when they become adults, marry, or just settle down. The continuity/individual transition hypothesis would be more compatible with contexts such as the underclass, etc, because it implies no such disavowal of gang ties. It may only imply the person has been in prison before and now knows how to limit risk.

10. Taylor cites the work of Sifakis (1987) regarding how "in 1931, two University of Chicago sociologists did an in-depth study of this gang of forty-two tough juveniles who were aggressive, reckless scavengers" (Taylor, 1990: p. 7).

11. Here we mean outside of the prison context. In the prison context, organized crime figures and gang leaders might be assumed to have a "truce", or a mutual respect for their power base. But outside of the prison context is the real test of any ties between traditional organized crime and American gangs.

12. As Bensinger (1984, p. 2) reports, at least the appearance of organizational sophistication by close observers of the crime scene, led the Chicago Crime Commission to hold a conference to discuss the link between gangs and organized crime in July, 1983 (see Chicago Tribune, July 7, 1983).

13. And further, that these Chinese gangs followed the organizational development pattern suggested in this text; first arising out of ethnic conflict, then solidifying for illicit gains, and becoming professional criminal organizations. Indeed, Ko-lin (1988) predicts that with their overseas connections these same gangs will likely play a larger role in the international drug trade in the future.

14. It is a matter, perhaps due to human capital, social skills, language, culture, and racism, to be able to "integrate" into the wider society: its businesses, its organizations, and its groups. A good cross-national example of ability to integrate into such a larger social network including businesses, would be the Jakuza gang in Japan - it is organized crime.

15. Of some relevance here is the recent testimony of a Chicago gang crimes police commander who, in referring to the El Rukns, said "I don't even consider the El Rukns or the Blackstone Rangers a gang. I'll tell you why they have gotten outside the thing we are talking about. I think a lot of emphasis or the complaints that we receive based on gangs are no more than disturbances, ordinance violations. When you are talking about the El Rukns, you can't equate El Rukns with Gypsies. El Rukns are organized crime. They have buildings, they have lawyers, they have doctors, they have banks. It's completely out of the realm of what we consider street gangs" (see Nash, 1984: p. 70).

16. Chicago's Vicelords incorporated (not-for-profit, Illinois corporation) formally as the United Concerned Voters League; for the Black Gangster Disciples, they were also known as the Young Voters of Illinois. The entity "Young Voters of Illinois" traces far back into the 1980s, while the contemporary entity "21st Century V.O.T.E." is very recent (1993), just enlarged in scope. Most theorists believe this recent development is simply a gambit fostered to get their gang leader out of prison.

17. This same hope for "stronger teeth" in the criminal code was expressed by Alderman Ivan Rittenberg who testified before the Illinois Gang Crimes Study Commission: "There's no reason why the State of Illinois and this Commission could not write a state law and make this thing for member that we can show is part of an organized gang and their attorneys, if you could show that the attorney knows in fact he's working for an organization, that is, everybody is entitled to a defense, but nobody's entitled to have their attorney participate in the crime. I believe that this Commission, and I am a member of it, I'm going to urge some serious consideration of a statewide anti-racketeering statute which will be able to reach any person who seeks to profit by professional criminal activity similar to this federal one with the same requirements of the minimum 10 years on a conviction, and I think that could be a beginning of the end of gangs, these vicious street gangs organizing and becoming organized criminal entities" (see Nash, 1984: p. 70).

18. A number of authors have shown some gangs in America to have such written constitutions (Arnold, 1969: p. 177; Fong, 1990).

19. Obviously, there are other commonalities as well, such as a special cryptic language, or its own subcultural argot; and there are differences as well. We have only a limited space here for such analysis of these and other documents that cannot be shared in this text. These are single spaced typed documents typically of about 20 - 25 pages long each.

20. The Marielitos, Cuban offenders, are also said to have their own "jailhouse religion". Their impact on America was a result of the Mariel Freedom Flotilla of 1980 in which 130,000 Cuban refugees came to the United States, of which 25,000 were believed to be hardened criminals.

21. Note, for the record, this was a common theme reported by Camp and Camp (1985) particularly for prison gangs like the Black Guerilla Family.

22. Note, for the record, that Camp and Camp (1985) reported no such major themes for white prison gangs like the Aryan Brotherhood.

23. The CRIPs, which has been said to be the acronym for Common Revolution in Progress, is similar in having such a cloak of a "cause celebre". But as Camp and Camp (1985: p. 110) report, such fragmented gangs operating under the same "CRIP" banner may come together under a consolidated or confederation of CCO (Consolidated Crips Organization) and could be a dominant force in and outside of correctional institutions in a more nationwide gang problem. Current juvenile corrections research shows the Crips and Bloods in a number of different states throughout America.

24. The Vice Lords are similarly based on the front of Islamic religion. Mostly, the M.S.T.A. --- the Moorish Science Temple of America. And commit crimes hoping that a verbal acknowledgement and written constitution that places trust in the Almighty Allah will spare them of any actual guilt for the harm they cause. The M.S.T.A. was apparently founded in Newark, New Jersey in 1886 according to the Vice Lord constitution.

25. See for example, Campbell's (1984, p. 189) description of "Sun-Africa" whose involvement with a quasi-Islamic group in which leaders were regarded as "gods" (e.g., Shamar and Barsun). Similarly, in Chicago's Mickey Cobra gang (allied with El Rukn's, and other "peoples"), in the Cobra totems of symbolism "The Red represent the blood that was shed by all stones/Cobras of our family tree, and the Holy Prophet Mickey Cogwell".

26. There is, then, more than some elements in common between cults and gangs. The Vice Lords, for example, in their constitution (which shows a heavy influence from the El Rukn's) in explaining what "Vice Lord" means: "The meaning behind the name? Vice means having faults (the human being) and second in importance (Man being second only to god). God being Rule of all worlds and universe. Man was elected by him to be his Vice Lord or (Vice Ruler) of the physical world. Lord means one having dominion over others, a ruler. We see ourselves (man) as god's highest creation, his custodians of this physical world. His Vice Lords. We believe whether you address yourself as Muslim, a Christian, a Jehovah's Witness, or etc. By the definition of that which just been defined you are still Vice Lord, the only difference is one interpretation and acceptance". Which gobblygook is typical of cults.

27. Latin Kings are also "peoples", that is allied with the Nation of Gangs which includes Islamic-influenced El Rukns and Vice Lords. But as case LK27 illustrated, some Latin King gang members routinely attended their local Catholic church and had every outside appearance of being staunch Sunday Christians. Indeed, they would say "thanks God" for not being caught after various escapades.

28. The gang constitution at the community level shows an almost identical "oath".

29. Keiser (1969) describes the case of a Black gang retaliating against a white neighborhood where the gang member quotes Malcolm X to the effect that "violence sometimes serves its purpose" (Keiser, 1969: p. 8). That is, the gang member apparently believed in deterrence theory by also saying, after such a planned foray, "they'll think twice before they do it" again (ibid).

30. Such political leanings are much more clearly articulated in gangs such as the Black Guerilla Family (see Camp and Camp, 1985: p. ix).

31. Hobsbawm (1965) in his chapter on the Mafia found similarly such tendencies in the criminal associations, gilds, or fraternities, to believe in a kind of ruthless justice against an unjust political situation.

32. In the Chicago Vice Lords, this ideology appears in their totems and use of symbols. The circle means "360 degrees of knowledge that black people rule the world and will again rule the world". Fire "represents the Black Nation's true knowledge of being suppressed and their inability to reach knowledge because of the heat created by the fire". See also the Vice Lord prayer which makes reference to "all poor and oppressed people of color nationwide" (Nash, 1984: p. 55).

33. The constitution of the Vice Lords, for example, creates a special ranking membership category for "ambassadors". They act as missionaries, to "propagate and promote Lordism", to intentionally proselytize and spread the gang influence.

34. Fong's (1990) analysis of Texas prison gangs also acknowledges the existence of such constitutions for internal member regulation (Fong, 1990: p. 40) as well as the military style of gang role structure/organization.

CHAPTER 17

FEMALE GANG MEMBERS AND THE RIGHTS OF CHILDREN

INTRODUCTION
The female gang member and especially the female gang leader is often neglected in our gang literature. This new chapter has therefore been added to the third edition. In Part I of this chapter the reader will find important new research findings about the female gang member. In Part II of this chapter, larger issues about the role of females in gangs today are discussed and analyzed. Additional discussion is made in Part III regarding the rights of young children in the larger societal context of clarifying our moral values and legal codes.

PART I. FINDINGS FROM THE MATCHED PAIR DESIGN

The research reported here seeks to add to our understanding of female gang members and how they may differ in some respects from their peers who are not gang members. The findings discussed here relate specifically to African-American female high school students[1]. The analysis compares a sample (N = 100 Folks) of those who self-report gang membership with a sample (N = 100 Neutrons) who have never joined a gang[2]. Thus, the fundamental hypothesis explored here is whether or not among African-American females gang members are really different from those who have never joined a gang. Very little systematic research on female gang members has been reported in the social science literature. What literature does exist on the topic of female gang members often relies on samples as small as N = 3. This project was undertaken to specifically add to our knowledge about female gang members.

THE MATCHED-PAIR SURVEY RESEARCH DESIGN

As reported previously (Knox, Laske, and Tromanhauser, 1992), gender is a factor that significantly differentiates self-reported gang membership among high school students. Females have a lower base rate for gang membership than do males. The research problem, then, was to over-sample female students to such an extent that a sufficient group size could be obtained for female gang members. To accomplish this research goal, two versions of the same survey were created: one for males, and one for females.

Several public high schools on Chicago's southside were used for data collection. The male version of the survey is not analyzed here and was not the primary research objective, and thus served a placebo function to basically keep the boys busy in the coed classrooms. Both versions of the survey instrument were five pages long and contained 99 different questions, some of which had multiple parts, and thus well over 99 different variables. Data collection began in early 1993 and continued until May, 1993 when a sufficient number of self-reported female gang members had been reached[3].

All survey instruments were stored by the school and classroom in which they were collected. Manual checks were made to identify self-reported gang members and then the gang member was matched by race, age, and grade level often from the same classroom with a non-gang member respondent. The analysis reported here therefore reflects a matched-pair design of African-American female high school students, half (N=100) of whom self-reported that they had previously joined a gang, and half (N=100) of whom reported that they had never joined a gang.

MATCHED SAMPLE DESCRIPTION

All of the female gang members (N = 100) are members of the Folks gang nation. More specifically, they self-identify as Sisters of the Struggle (S.O.S.), Intellectual Sisters, Intellectual Sisters of the Struggle (I.S.O.S.), or simply members of the Gangster Disciples gang. The "Intellectual Sisters" identity comes from the written internal literature of the Brothers of the Struggle (B.O.S.), which is essentially the conglomerate group of the Disciples Nation. While other "Folks" gangs exist which have female members, our data allowed the identification of specific gangs to which the respondents self-reported their membership in. For all practical purposes, then, the female gang members analyzed here can be regarded as "Intellectual Sisters" or S.O.S. --- the female constituency of the clearly male dominated B.O.S. organization.

All of the African-American females (N = 100) who have never joined a gang are typically regarded as "Neutrons" in the context of the high school and community environment. A "Neutron" is a person who is not gang-affiliated, having never joined any gang and not being aligned with any gang nation (e.g., People or Folks, Brothers or Folks, Crips or Bloods, etc).

The school grade level among folks and neutrons was almost identical as seen here:

	Neutrons	Folks
9th grade	29	30
10th grade	28	27
11th grade	22	24
12th grade	21	19
TOTAL	100	100
Mean	10.3	10.3

Similarly, the age distribution among folks and neutrons is very similar as seen here:

		Neutrons	Folks
AGE:	< =14	12	9
	15	22	23
	16	33	28
	17	22	26
	18	10	10
	> =19	1	4
	TOTAL	100	100
	Mean	15.9	16.1

The family structure in terms of number of siblings (brothers and sisters) and total number of persons living in the household also show the two groups are similar, but with tendency being for somewhat larger sizes among those who self-report gang membership as seen below:

		Neutrons	Folks
Number of Brothers	Mean	1.75	2.36
Number of Sisters	Mean	1.77	1.83
Total Household Members	Mean	4.66	4.91

Family function in terms of "openness" also appeared to vary little between these two groups. Two separate questions addressed this issue, asking "how easy or hard is it for you to speak with your mother" and father, using a response mode of zero (very hard) to ten (very easy). Openness for communication with mother showed a mean of 6.60 for neutrons compared to 7.17 for folks; and with fathers a mean of 5.34 for neutrons, and 5.16 for folks.

FINDINGS COMPARING FOLKS AND NEUTRONS

It is helpful to begin this discussion with a summary of those factors for which no significant difference emerged in comparing those African-American females who had, or who had not ever, joined a gang. Figure 15 lists those factors from the survey for which no significant difference emerged using the Chi-square test (p > .05). As seen in Figure 15, some factors reported recently in the literature to be important with regard to gang membership (e.g., suicide ideation) are shown here to be factors not significantly differentiated by gang membership within this sample.

FIGURE 15
FACTORS NOT SIGNIFICANTLY DIFFERENTIATED BY
HAVING EVER JOINED A GANG AMONG AFRICAN-AMERICAN
FEMALE HIGH SCHOOL STUDENTS IN A MATCHED-PAIR DESIGN

Description of Survey Instrument Question or Variable:

Do you think some types of rap music encourages crime or violence?
Are you mother and father either divorced or separated?
Have you ever given birth to a child?
Do you plan on graduating from high school?
Have you ever joined Girl Scouts?
During the past 12 months did you ever seriously consider suicide?
Have you ever tried cocaine?
Do both of your parents live in the same household with you?
Are girls more likely to get a break from police?
I often think people are talking about me.
I am not as emotional as other people.
Do you have any regular part-time or full-time job?
What is your official Grade Point Average for high school?
Do you have a lot of resentment about the way some racial groups are treated differently than others?

Nobody tells me what to do.
I want to eventually marry and have children.
This is a sexist society that discriminates against women.
Have your parents verbally abused you one or more times in the last two months?
Has your boyfriend verbally abused you one or more times in the last two months?
Have you defied your parents' authority to their face one or more times?
Have one or more close friends and associates who have been wounded by gunfire in a gang shooting?

Table 26 provides the frequency crosstabulation of those variables that were significantly differentiated by gang membership among this sample of African-American female high school students in Chicago. These results can be summarized in terms of six profile patterns: family life, substance abuse, school discipline, dating, violence socialization, and aggressive personality characteristics.

(1) The Family Life Profile. Female gang members are significantly more likely to report that they have siblings (brothers or sisters) who are also gang members. Female gang members are significantly more likely to report prior pregnancies. Female gang members are significantly more likely to report that their family receives Public Aid. Female gang members are significantly less likely to report that they regularly attend church. Female gang members are significantly more likely to report having struck (hit) a parent one or more times. Female gang members are significantly more likely to report ever having run away from home. Female gang members are significantly less likely to report receiving an allowance from their family.

(2) The Substance Abuse Profile. Female gang members are significantly more likely to report that a lot of kids in their neighborhood use illicit drugs. Female gang members are significantly more likely to report using marijuana at least once a week. Female gang members are significantly more likely to report drinking alcohol at least once a week. Female gang members are significantly more likely to report having close friends who have shot up/injected drugs (e.g. IV drug use) and who use illicit drugs.

(3) The School Discipline Profile. The female gang member is significantly more likely to report knowing the police officers who work at the school. The female gang member is significantly more likely to report having been (a) suspended from school, (b) having an 'in school' suspension, and (c) having an 'in-school' detention. The female gang member has a lower educational aspiration by being significantly less likely to expect to graduate from a 4-year college. The female gang member is significantly more likely to report also having been previously arrested.

(4) The Dating Profile. The female gang member is significantly more likely to report having a boyfriend who has an arrest record. The female gang member is significantly more likely to report having ever been beaten or assaulted by a boyfriend. The female gang member is significantly more likely to report that she could marry someone who is an active gang member; and, reminiscent of the classic Westside Story, apparently more willing to date a rival gang member if he showed respect. The female gang member is significantly less willing to marry someone of another race.

(5) The Violence Socialization Profile. The female gang member is significantly more likely to report having been previously threatened with gang violence. The female gang member is significantly more likely to report having ever carried a weapon to school for protection. The female gang member is significantly more likely to report having been in one or more fights during the last year. The female gang member is significantly more likely to report having ever had to pull a knife on someone. The female gang member is significantly more likely to report having had experience in shooting a handgun. The female gang member is significantly more likely to report having a permanent tattoo.

(6) The Combative Personality Profile. The female gang member is significantly more likely to believe she can take a beating just like a man. The female gang member is significantly more likely to report that she would never back out of a fight. The female gang member is significantly more likely to report that she sometimes feels like smashing things for no apparent reason. The female gang member is significantly more likely to think of herself as someone who fights first and asks questions later. The female gang member is significantly more likely to report that other persons consider her a very defiant individual and to distrust other people.

TABLE 26

SUMMARY TABLE: FREQUENCY DISTRIBUTION OF VARIOUS
FACTORS IN RELATIONSHIP TO GANG MEMBERSHIP
AMONG AFRICAN-AMERICAN FEMALE HIGH SCHOOL STUDENTS

	EVER JOIN A GANG?	
	NO	YES
In your neighborhood, do a lot of kids use illicit drugs?		
NO	23	12
YES	24 (24%)	40 (40.4%)
DON'T KNOW	53	47
Chi-square = 7.81, p = .02		
Has your boyfriend ever been arrested for any crime?		
NO	71	39
YES	27 (27.5%)	60 (60.6%)
Chi-square = 21.82, p < .001		
Have any of your brothers or sisters been in a gang?		
NO	74	44
YES	25 (25.2%)	56 (56%)
Chi-square = 19.48, p < .001		

Do you know the police officers
who work at your school?
| | NO | 40 | 15 |
| | YES | 60 (60%) | 85 (85%) |

Chi-square = 15.67, p < .001

Have you ever been beaten or
assaulted by a boyfriend?
| | NO | 88 | 75 |
| | YES | 12 (12%) | 23 (23.4%) |

Chi-square = 4.47, p = .03

Do you plan on graduating
from a 4-year college?
| | NO | 15 | 29 |
| | YES | 84 (84.8) | 68 (70.1%) |

Chi-square = 6.11, p = .01

Do you have a permanent
tattoo?
| | NO | 90 | 43 |
| | YES | 10 (10%) | 53 (55.2%) |

Chi-square = 45.89, p < .001

How many times have you been
pregnant?
	0 times	75 (75%)	59 (60.8%)
	1 time	21	23
	2 or more times	4	15

Chi-square = 8.32, p = .01

Do you use marijuana at
least once a week?
| | NO | 96 | 60 |
| | YES | 4 (4%) | 40 (40%) |

Chi-square = 37.76, p < .001

Do you drink alcohol at
least once a week?
| | NO | 92 | 62 |
| | YES | 8 (8%) | 37 (37.3%) |

Chi-square = 24.52, p < .001

Have any of your close
friends ever injected
(shot up) drugs?
| | NO | 95 | 87 |
| | YES | 4 (4%) | 13 (13%) |

Chi-square = 5.11, p = .02

Have you ever been
arrested for anything?
| | NO | 88 | 37 |
| | YES | 12 (12%) | 60 (61.8%) |

Chi-square = 52.77, p < .001

Is it hard to get out of
a gang?

	NO	5	48
	YES	24	36
	% Yes	(24.4%)	(37.5%)
	DON'T KNOW	69	12

Chi-square = 77.38, p < .001

Have you been helped by
a police officer before?

	NO	66	44
	YES	33 (33.3%)	53 (54.6%)

Chi-square = 9.03, p = .003

Would you go out with a
rival gang member if he
showed respect for you?

	NO	46	21
	YES	50 (52%)	74 (77.8%)

Chi-square = 13.96, p < .001

Do you think you could marry
someone who is an active
gang member?

	NO	79	32
	YES	20 (20.2%)	64 (66.6%)

Chi-square = 42.91, p < .001

Do you receive an allowance
from your family?

	NO	29	47
	YES	69 (70.4%)	53 (53%)

Chi-square = 6.34, p = .01

Have you ever been suspended
from school?

	NO	61	25
	YES	38 (38.3%)	73 (74.4%)

Chi-square = 26.10, p < .001

Have you ever had an
'In School' Suspension?

	NO	67	49
	YES	31 (31.6%)	50 (50.5%)

Chi-square = 7.24, p = .007

Have you ever had an
'In School' (hit) detention?

	NO	57	37
	YES	42 (42.4%)	62 (62.6%)

Chi-square = 7.68, p = .006

Do other persons consider
you a very defiant individual?
| | NO | 60 | 39 |
| | YES | 34 (36.1%) | 51 (51%) |

Chi-square = 7.77, p = .005

Does your family currently
receive Public Aid?
| | NO | 69 | 49 |
| | YES | 29 (29.9%) | 46 (48.4%)|

Chi-square = 7.19, p = .007

Have you ever helped to
recruit other females into
a gang?
| | NO | 95 | 50 |
| | YES | 3 (3%) | 47 (48.4%)|

Chi-square = 52.68, p < .001

Do you regularly attend
church or religious worship?
| | NO | 49 | 61 |
| | YES | 50 (50.5%) | 30 (32.9%)|

Chi-square = 5.98, p = .01

Do you think you could marry
someone of another race?
| | NO | 38 | 55 |
| | YES | 59 (60.8%) | 37 (40.2%)|

Chi-square = 8.02, p = .005

Have you ever run away
from home?
| | NO | 76 | 56 |
| | YES | 23 (23.2%) | 37 (39.7%)|

Chi-square = 6.11, p = .01

In the last year, have you ever
been threatened with violence by
a gang member?
| | NO | 82 | 68 |
| | YES | 17 (17.1%) | 28 (29.1%)|

Chi-square = 3.95, p = .04

Have you ever carried a weapon
to school for protection?
| | NO | 78 | 42 |
| | YES | 21 (21.2%) | 53 (55.7%)|

Chi-square = 24.56, p < .001

I can take a beating just
like a man.
| | FALSE | 83 | 45 |
| | TRUE | 17 (17%) | 51 (53.1%)|

Chi-square = 28.21, p < .001

I would never back out of a
fight.   FALSE   43   28
                          TRUE   56 (56.5%)   68 (70.8%)
                          Chi-square = 4.28, p = .03

I sometimes feel like smashing
things for no apparent reason.
                          FALSE   70   48
                          TRUE   27 (27.8%)   49 (50.5%)
                          Chi-square = 10.47, p = .001

A person like me fights first and
asks questions later.   FALSE   82   46
                          TRUE   17 (17.1%)   51 (52.5%)
                          Chi-square = 27.10, p < .001

I have had experience in shooting
a real handgun.   FALSE   84   46
                          TRUE   15 (15.1%)   50 (52%)
                          Chi-square = 29.91, p < .001

At least once, I've had to pull a
knife on someone.   FALSE   78   41
                          TRUE   19 (19.8%)   56 (57.7%)
                          Chi-square = 29.75, p < .001

A person is better off by not
trusting anyone.   FALSE   64   44
                          TRUE   35 (35.3%)   53 (54.6%)
                          Chi-square = 7.36, p = .007

Have one or more close friends
and associates who use illicit drugs?
                          NO   72   47
                          YES   28 (28%)   51 (52%)
                          Chi-square = 11.92, p = .001

Been in one or more fights in
the last year?   NO   56   22
                          YES   42 (42.8%)   74 (77%)
                          Chi-square = 23.63, p < .001

Ever struck your mother or
father (hit them) one or more times?
                          NO   81   61
                          YES   19 (19%)   35 (36.4%)
                          Chi-square = 7.47, p = .006

HAS FEMINISM AFFECTED GANG LIFE?

What do these female gang members report in terms of convergence and chivalry hypotheses? Are the females in this particular gang on equal status and enjoy equal opportunity for advancement as found in the male gang member counterparts (the convergence hypothesis)? Or are females given special duties because of their gender and are still basically relegated to a subservient position in a male dominated organization (the chivalry hypothesis)? Here we can test these issues by taking a closer look at the viewpoints of our sample of female gang members.

About half of the female gang members (52.1%) report that their boyfriend is also a member of the same gang.

When asked "within the gang, are female members treated the same as males (i.e., do they have the same status and privileges as males)", some 60 percent said "yes". About a fourth (26.3%) said "no". And the rest (13.7%) were not sure.

When asked if the females in the gang are used for specific jobs or tasks because they are females, about half (53.7%) said "no". About a fourth (28.4%) said "yes". And the rest (17.9%) were not sure.

When asked if females in the gang have special duties which males do not have, some 37.8 percent said "yes". About an equal proportion (40.8%) said "no". And about a fifth (21.4%) were not sure.

When asked if female members are permitted to date males who are not members of the same gang, about two-thirds (65.6%) said "yes". Some 17.7 percent said "no", and the rest (16.7%) were not sure.

When asked if female members are allowed to be leaders within the gang nearly three-fourths (74.2%) said "yes". Some 9.7 percent said "no", and the rest (16.1%) were not sure.

When asked if female members are allowed to lead or control male gang members this story of equal opportunity tends to unravel. About half (51.6%) of the respondents said that they were not allowed to lead or control gang members in their gang. Still, some 29.5 percent said it would be possible for females to exert this power over males. And some 18.9 percent were not sure.

One of the classical ways in which male gang members exploit female gang members and female gang associates is to use them to limit their risk of apprehension and arrest. Numerous examples exist in the literature, for example, showing that female gang members are often asked to carry guns for their male members as Dawley described in his tenure with the Vice Lords that the females were used for "whatever was needed" including sex:

> "A Vice Lady was also used for carrying guns. The police couldn't search females so she could carry a shotgun up under her dress and the fellas could walk alongside" (Dawley, 1992: p. 31).

When asked if female gang members are expected to carry guns for the male gang members, some 32.3 percent said "yes". About half (50.5%) said "no". The rest (17.2%) were not sure.

Theoretically some gang organizations can be expected to display more of the chivalry pattern than others. This is true, as documented elsewhere, because some gang organizations like the Black P. Stones and the Vice Lords have a strong Islamic ideological influence in their internal beliefs and in their written gang internal literature and belief system. Historically, women have not gained the same power and status as men in Islamic groups or societies. The group studied here is not one that has a pronounced Islamic influence. The "Brothers" gang nation has the more pronounced Islamic identity. Thus, theoretically it is possible to hypothesize that greater convergence would be found in this group (S.O.S.) than among gangs composed primarily of the same racial group representing a rival or opposition gang nation (e.g., Stones, Vice Lords, etc).

No clear cut answer, thus, is forthcoming on this issue. The data suggest a mixed set of findings in a gang that held the best possibility for convergence. To a large extent, however, it would appear that females have not exactly liberated this particular gang organization. While this particular gang organization is very adept at sponsoring regular educational meetings for its members called "Awareness Sessions", not one of them in the list of subjects known to the present authors has dealt with "Feminism Today".

What is very clear from this research is that female gang members differ in significant ways from their non-gang member counterparts matched by the same race, age, and school grade level. This still does not answer the more fundamental question of whether female gang members differ significantly from the social, psychological, and behavioral or background profile found among male gang members.

PART II: THE MANY OTHER ISSUES ABOUT FEMALE GANG MEMBERS

We know so very little about the role of females involved in gangs consider the scope of the problem. In the recent research on 232 police chiefs an 25 county sheriffs in Illinois, when these law enforcement administrators were asked whether females were also involved in the gangs in their areas, some 74.2 percent of the police chiefs and 68.2 percent of the county sheriffs indicated this was true.[4] Thus, it is a problem much larger than its knowledge base.

There are many other interesting issues about female gang members that need further research. Some of these larger issues are described here, and where possible new and other additional hard data is provided. Finally, the rights of children are examined in the context of the gang problem today.

Are Female Gang Members More Violent In Some Situations Than Their Male Gang Member Counterparts?

I recall witnessing my first female gang member violence. It happened in Bridgeport, a community area in Chicago, one of the many Chicago communities I have lived in. This particular incident occurred in the mid-1980s, and it involved about ten female members of the Satans Disciples. The female gang members had lured another female into an ambush on the corner of Racine and 31st Street. I ended up taking the victim to the hospital, so both witnessing the event and debriefing the victim afterwards as a resident of the community, this gang experience is treated as nothing more than anyone who lives in an urban area may have also had in terms of life experience. It is direct observation and focused interviewing with the victim.

First this particular gang violence was exceptionally brutal. The victim was 18 years old and in a late stage of pregnancy at the time she was attacked. What I saw caused me to holler from a second floor window to down below on the street and rush to take the victim to the hospital. The female gang members felt slighted by this neutron at the high school. The victim had said something that was taken as verbal insult to one of the female members of the Satans Disciples. No chance for an apology was to ever come.

What happened was a classic physical assault ambush. A confederate of the female gang members had lured the victim out to meet at the corner "store" (a small lean-to mom-and-pop style grocery that catered mostly to kids for snacks, but also sold drug paraphernalia). Once the victim was out of her house and got to the corner where the store was located, the other female members of the Satans Disciples "swooped" from three directions, waiting in hiding nearby.

There about ten female gang members, ranging from 15 to 19 years of age, including Mexican-American and white members. The first few punches to the face and head of the victim from the first several female gang members that ran up on the victim were sufficient to knock the victim to the ground. Subsequent kicks by the about ten female gang members that surrounded her body, on and about the head, rendered the victim helpless as she laid on the sidewalk with the gang girls pummelling her. This all happened in a quick instant and lasted only a minute and then the female gang members had dispersed in different directions leaving behind a bloodied victim. Actually two victims. Because the victim in this instance was in a late stage of pregnancy.

The female gang members eagerly tried to get close to the victim on the ground and kick the victim in the stomach. It was obvious the victim was pregnant. But the female gang members focused their attention on kicking the fetus. As the attack happened I hollered to the gang members to stop, and then ran from the building to the scene. Just as I got to the scene the female gang members had retreated.

With a neighbor I took the victim directly to the hospital and notified the police.

The issue here is whether female gang members are, as some have alleged, more violent or more vicious than their male gang member counterparts? Much informal information developed by numerous interviews with gang members and others has often led to the final appraisal of this issue by responses to the scenario: if you were in alley and at one end you faced the male members of the gang, and at the other end of the alley you faced the female members of the gang, and there was no way out, which end of the alley would you prefer to taking your beating from? I have never seen someone prefer the female end of the alley. Many seem to point to a kind of over-compensation phenomenon where the female gang member will be predictably more violent.

No systematic research has yet answered this question. There is other evidence that speaks to this issue. But for the most part, the gang member problem in America is a male problem; the vast majority of the leaders of serious criminal gangs are older adult males. The traditional exploitive arrangement seems to be the norm: where the female gang members act almost as the "Womens Auxiliary" of the male dominated gang culture.

ARE THERE ALL FEMALE GANGS?

Yes, is the clear answer here. There do exist, just as among males, gangs of varying levels of sophistication in terms of their organization and in terms of their level of crime threat, which are gangs composed almost entirely if not exclusively of female members. Most examples of this type of all female gang are those at the lower level of the gang crime threat continuum. However, some recent research does show that the all female criminal gang does in fact exist.

Perhaps the strongest evidence documenting the all female criminal gang is the work entitled "Sisters Are Doin' It For Themselves: A Black Female Gang in San Francisco" by Lauderback, Hansen, and Waldorf (1992) published in what is now the Journal of Gang Research. In their work they documented the group called the Potrero Hill Posse, or PHP. Their study basically showed this all female gang to be primarily involved in drug sales operations. It also seemed to attract less attention from the police, in fact their study showed that only a half of the members had an arrest record. Is it possible that the chivalry hypothesis operates here: that is citizens are more likely to call the police when a group of boys hang on the corner, and be less likely to call the police about a complaint of suspicious girls on the corner? This would make for a fascinating actual field experiment for those interested in future research on gangs.

What happens to male dominated gangs also happens to female gangs is another finding of the Lauderback, Hansen, and Waldorf study. When one group forms, another will form to oppose it. This has been called the law of natural group opposition formation; where a blue gang starts, a red gang will shortly follow; where a folks gang starts, a peoples gang will shortly organize to counteract it. The Potrero Hill Posse had their opposing local gang in a group called the Valencia Gardens Mob, also composed primarily of African-American females.

THE CORRECTIONAL ENVIRONMENT FOR FEMALE GANG MEMBERS

Nationwide a lower gang density is always reported for females than for males. This consistently appears in research on the different types of correctional environments as well: juvenile short term detention facilities, juvenile long term correctional institutions, local jails, and adult state correctional institutions. However, this lower gang density is that reported as the official estimate only. There is reason to be somewhat skeptical about the official estimates from those who are the chief administrators of the same facilities.

The fact remains, however, that in the female component of the correctional system what we have are groups of females that interact along gang lines. One thing appears to be true and deserving of much more research: that females are in this context much less violent than their male counterparts. One can readily find numerous examples of male gang members behind bars who kill other inmates and who even assassinate correctional officers, and who routinely "riot". In a recent gang riot at Cook County Jail, a male gang member situation, the Vice Lords fought the Disciples over who would have first use of the shower. Seven inmates were stabbed, and two were killed in this frivolous fight over who showers first.

We do not seem to hear as much such gang violence in the female correctional context. Is this a problem of statistical proportions that is masked and biased by the very nature of the use of the penal sanction in America? Possibly so. For please recall that historically in America about only five percent of the prison inmates have been female, and this trend is largely consistent over a very long period of the history of American criminal justice. One possibility we can rule out for those that would claim that female gang members are less violent in custody than their male counterparts, is the idea that female inmates are treated better. The fact is most correctional programs are geared towards males, especially the rehabilitation and vocational training programs. Much fewer resources are allocated to the womens division of most state correctional systems. So one cannot effectively argue that women gang members are less violent because they are treated better than male inmates.

What we do know about inmate roles is that female inmates take on more of a quasi-family function, and do appear to have social skills to be able to avoid and mediate conflicts. What we do know about male inmates is that many, particularly gang members, have a kind of combative personality syndrome that prefers conflict over all other options for problem solving. Still the issue is a gnawing one that deserves greater research. Our correctional institutions provide a natural arena in which to ascertain the nature of the differences in gang violence and much more research needs to be done in this area.

BURNING OUT: Slowing Disengaging From Gang Life As Some Approach Adulthood.

A number qualitative interviews with female gang members have shown this type of scenario. The basic situation was that of where the female gang member of a larger male dominated gang, usually a very structured criminal gang, slowly disengages from the gangs routine activities. The end result is the ex-gang member or what could also be called the inactive gang member. Some simply "grow out of it", their affiliation with the gang was contextually centered, that is typically in a high school situation, so when they reach their early 20s, their social network changes, and they find themselves progressively avoiding the trouble that gang life provides.

Case #1: White Female Member of White Gang.

A white female gang member of the Simon City Royals, a predominantly white gang in Chicago, simply found herself hanging out with the gang less and less over time as she had to find a job, and pay her own bills. Quitting shortly after high school, relocating to a new neighborhood, and not renewing high school contacts, she established an entirely new social network of friends and associates. She still has the gang tattoo, but it is on an area of the body not normally exposed in public. And so it is easy to simply act like she knows nothing about gangs and live a law abiding existence. Which is what she does. Gang life for her was a temporary adolescent fad, it had its value in high school, but it lost its value as she faced the need to seriously address how she was going to fit into her society --- and pay the bills and the rent. She is today a highly responsible citizen, who works like anyone else for a living at ordinary jobs.

Case #2: African-American female member of the Gangster Disciples.

An African-American female member of the Gangster Disciples provides another example of this disengagement theory about severing ties to the gang. This person began to sever the ties to the gang at the time she enrolled as a student in university. By the time she had graduated she still lived in the area where she grew up, but she no longer was active in gang life on the streets. In fact, she had thought that she was completely out of the gang until one night in 1993 some Gangster Disciples came to her house.

While she still lived on the southside, she had moved and did not think her gang knew where she lived. But they appeared at her door one night and handed her a petition and basically ordered her to sign the petition. The petition was that being circulated in the Chicago area, which ultimately had over 5,000 names on it, demanding that the Illinois Prisoner Review Board (i.e., the parole board) grant Larry Hoover (their gang leader) a parole because he was now rehabilitated.

The Gangster Disciples are and always have been male dominated. We can demonstrate this by examining the infrastructure of the Gangster Disciples below. This particular chain of command was analyzed and created by someone in law enforcement. The author has not been able to verify how accurate the list is currently, as this gang as all others are open-systems, and do change, gang members particularly gang leaders are killed routinely. So it has not been completely updated nor validated. But using it as a basis for routine interviews with gang members including high ranking members, does suggest it is accurate.

George W. Knox   355

GANGSTER DISCIPLES CHAIN OF COMMAND

Larry Hoover
"King Larry"
IR # 190647
CHAIRMAN OF THE BOARD

ASSISTANT CHAIRMAN: Melvin Haywood, "Head"[a].

BOARD MEMBERS: Leon Bolton, "Bo Diddley", IR # 2692948; Duffy Clark, "Guy", IR # 257920; Ernest Wilson, "Smokey", IR # 255775; Robert Dordles, "Coal Black", IR # 385784; Vincent Galloway, "Legs Diamond", IR # 342983; Robert Lowe, "Big Lowe", IR # 181344; Michael Scott, "Speedy", IR # 362031; Henry Griffin, "Money", IR # 10010; Charles Harris, "Sundown", IR # 472523; Gregory Sharpe, "G Sharpe", IR # 289496; Jeffery Hatcher, IR # 295827; Ernest Hope, "Junior", IR # 141819; Michael Smith, "Michael G.", IR # 369474; Kirk Williams, IR # 510708; Andrew Howard, "Dee Dee", IR # 69789; Michael Johnson, "Pair a Dice", IR # 269463; Gregory Shell, "Shorty G", IR # 704666; Carey Smith Jr., "Lucky G", IR # 112018.

FINANCE AND COMMUNICATIONS: Lucy Kemper, IR # 29623; Bertha Mosby, IR # 393682; Stephanie Powe, #IR # 827544; Johnny Jackson, IR # 899836; Miranda Goodloe, IR # 132030.

GOVERNORS AND AREA COORDINATORS: Dontay Banks, "Dirk", IR # 786407; Michael Baptiste, "Bap / White Mike", IR # 343836; Dave Smith, "Heavy D", IR # 640147; William Baptiste, IR # 624366; Victor Thompson, IR # 582181; Darryl Brent, "Pee Wee", IR #350360; Willis Richardson, "Dollar Bill", IR #605286; Samuel Bryant, "Big Wayne", IR # 509590; William Edwards, "Too Short", IR # 887190; Antoine Stewart, "Magellan", IR # 597036; Alexander Faulloner, "Champagne Black", IR # 562872; Delano E. Finch, "Trouble", IR # 901570; Ricky Harris, "Slick Rick", IR # 668316; Dan Wesson, "Dan Tanna", IR # 431704; Darryl Johnson, "Pops", IR # 672416; Tommy London, IR # 739111; Lamont O. Mattick, "G Money", IR # 865244; Terry McClinton, IR #752581.

REGENTS/STREET ENFORCERS: Robert Berry, "Renegade", IR # 633222; Eddie Clark, IR # 930027; Johnny Walker, IR # 680305; Kevin Reed, IR # 952171; Arthur Jones, IR # 821482; Darnell Thames, IR # 872922; Kyle Dunqy, IR # 558602; Vincent Martin, "Peanut", IR # 404140; Michael Mason, "Midnight", IR #834077; John Williams, IR # 376872.

Clearly, there are few females in this command structure. Where the female gang members are concentrated are in the finance and communications area. The leaders, then, are primarily males. Returning now to the case study, this particular former female member reported that she basically had to sign to petition. She had no choice, the gang members knew who she was and simply told her to sign the petition. When she explained this situation to me, she was obviously somewhat frightened and now alarmed that the gang had discovered her again. She had effectively avoided the

---

[a] Incarcerated

gang for several years and was on the verge of graduating from the university and going on the establish a normal American career.

She did decide at this point, however, to move far from the community she grew up in. She did not want to be surprised again by a knock on the door and find herself facing the same gang associates she had grown up with. As a post script to this case study, I had realized that the petition would represent a legitimate source for gang research, therefore on May 9th, 1994 I did make a Freedom of Information Act request for the full petition contain all names and pages[b]. A month later, no results, so I made the same request again by registered mail to several officials[c]. Then I was told that because the petition was not needed any longer, now that the parole hearing was over, that the petition and all its contents had been destroyed, that is discarded. The full truth here may never be known. Was it really destroyed? And if so why? We could not afford an attorney to challenge the agency in court to comply with the Freedom of Information Act, so it must remain a mystery until someone else examines the issue. We did view it as a goldmine for gang research because it might be one case where gang members actually gave their true and correct names and addresses --- for if they did not, and they belonged to the gang, they could certainly count on stiff sanctions from their own gang, that is a "violation". But the fact remains, the agency through its staff reported to us verbally that they had disposed of the petition and thus could not comply the FOIA[d].

Case #3: Female Associate of Latin Gang.

This case shows the classic situation of being dually integrated at a high level into conventional society and into the subculture, a kind of marginal adaptation. She prefers the Barrio life even now as she is capable of moving out and starting a professional career. Why? Because that is where she grew up and has many friends there. She was able to basically leave the gang alone, and to this day remains friendly with them, because they are part of the very fabric of the Hispanic Chicago community she lives in. She still knows the gang members, and the gang leaders, and has family members in the gang. She is not, however, likely to be active in any gang criminal operation nor involved in its street life. She is, however, cordial to the homies. And has simply been able to disengage over a period of years while working and attending college, a period of time that corresponded to her own maturation and entry into young adulthood. Not uncommon, she has no arrest record and plans to

---

[b] The FOIA request was made to James Williams, chairman of the Illinois Prisoner Review Board.

[c] This time the FOIA went to James Williams and Kent Stenkamp at the Illinois Prisoner Review Board, as well as to Gov. Edgar.

[d] Up until a national investigative television report in late September, 1994, Larry Hoover was running his gang from behind bars, living in a minimum security facility in Vienna, Illinois. Not exactly hard time for someone serving time for a murder sentence. However, on October 3, 1994 after the expose, Hoover was transferred to a more secure facility in Dixon, Illinois.

work in the criminal justice system. She would like to work, in fact, for the FBI now that she is a college graduate and considering going to law school.

She was not sure what she would do when I posed the moral dilemma to her as follows: she graduates from law school, still lives in the same area, and because of her language and cultural skills she is assigned as a new FBI agent to investigate and develop indictments on her own brother who is a local leader of this particular chapter of the Latin Kings. It was not possible for her to tell me precisely what she would do. She was in a quandary over this moral dilemma situation. Being a part of both worlds, the non-gang and the gang life, this situation describes a number of persons who are able to do a fine balancing act: having close ties with the gang world, and the "straight" world.   But not unlike the undercover vice detective immersed in a deep cover investigation, they take on language and habits that expose them systematically to personal risks. It is the marginal adaptation: and the lure of the subculture is addictive, and sometimes deadly. In the Hispanic and Latino gang structure, the culture is one of male domination. Female "members", or associates, are basically a supportive function, with some noted exceptions.   The notable exceptions do capture front page newspaper headlines: such as the case in Chicago where two female gang members lured members of an opposing gang into a park late at night, under the pretense of romance, and then summarily executed the two rival male gang members with shots to the back of the head.

Female gang members do take the initiative in some situations.   Female gang members are able to hold positions of rank in traditionally male-dominated gangs. Female gang members are able to at least feel as if they are treated equally, and "part of the family" by gangs that have mostly male leaders. Female gang members are able to get in a gang through means other than offering themselves as sexual objects, and to be "blessed" into the gang by having family members or others in high position who give them special status, or who simply decide to take their licks like the male counterparts in a "jumping in" type of ceremony. That is, the violence can be physical punishment or sexual in nature as a part of the initiation.   Being the sexual object as a part of the initiation process can mean total humiliation by a variety of measures: including shaking the dice to see how many members they will have to have sex with, or more usually having to submit to any and all sexual acts desired by anyone present at the initiation ceremony. It is less status-enhancing to a career in gang life for a female member to opt for the sexual object version of gang initiation. It is more status-enhancing to a career in gang life for a female member to want to be jumped in or who is willing to make her bones in a retaliatory attack on an opposition gang (i.e., a gang drive-by shooting, etc).

Female gang members do congregate and create a critical mass in public conflicts just as do their male gang member counterparts. Still there is something very unique about the female gang member that deserves further analysis --- motherhood.

A GANG MOTHER RAISING HER KIDS AS PROPER GANG MEMBERS

It happens more often than many would suspect. Young mothers active in the gang and having children, raising them from infancy on how to properly show their gang signs and the like. The fact is our current laws do not define raising a child to be a gang member as a crime or even as constituting child abuse. The fact is that white extremist gangs routinely raise their children in the same doctrine of hate and this is also not defined anywhere in America as a crime or as a prima facie case of child abuse. The sadder fact remains that in spite of the many agencies designed to protect the rights of children and the public of children throughout our federal and state government bureaucracies, we have no idea of how pervasive this problem may be, nor what it may portend for the future.

The astute reader must recall the history of this issue of the moral awakening of American society. Up until the 1970s in some parts of America child abuse as a crime was limited to unique situations where the child was admitted to the emergency room with multiple bone fractures. Today, obviously, a lower standard of "proof" of child abuse exists. It was not until the 1980s that we saw actual criminal laws appear defining "hate crimes" or "bias crimes" in America. Obviously, this does not mean that it America only had criminal child abuse until after the 1970s, or that we only had bias crimes until after the 1980s; what this means is that it took us this long to get laws passed reflecting the moral consensus of Americans. We still have a very long way to go to get our policy makers and our law makers serving the best interests of the American child today.

Should mothers who raise their kids to be gang members lose their rights of being responsible parents? That is, should there be a law enabling the public guardian of any community to take custody of such a child and put the child up for adoption or in foster or group homes until it an adult? Or is it an inalienable right of any parent to raise their child to be a racist or klansman? And what of the rights of the children involved here? Do they have any rights? And how do we weigh these against the rights of the parents and the public?

ABUSE OF FEMALE GANG MEMBERS BY MALE MEMBERS

This scenario has many variations, and is well documented, painting the picture of the traditional exploitative relationships that male gang leaders have over female members. Many were shocked to hear the case in Texas where two adolescent females were required to have sex with what they were told was an HIV positive gang member as a mandatory part of their initiation ceremony into the gang, for which they did comply. Other cases of violence against female members emerge when the female member is suspected of "knowing too much" about the gang, particularly its criminal operations, at which point the female member becomes a liability to the male gang leaders and she is executed. The case of Yummy is similar to this scenario, he knew too much too, and was executed by his own gang before he could talk.

One particularly brutal case of violence was in the case of 20-year-old Kristin Ponquinette, a high school graduate, and the daughter of the school superintendent in Aurora, Illinois. In this case, Ponquinette had simply been a wannabe, hanging out with lower level gang members. She witnessed the gang business operations, became sexually involved with some of the male gang members, and after a confrontation with jealous female members of the gang, she was targeted for execution[5]. This execution was described thusly:

"On April 17, 1992, according to testimony in the trials, Mobley's gang tied and gagged Kristin Ponquinette in a basement garage, threatened her with a chain saw, chopped off her hair, beat her and locked her in a closet.

Then they led her to a railroad bridge at 127th Street and Eggleston Avenue, where they smashed her over the head with a chunk of cement, wired a manhole cover to her feet and threw her into the Cal-Sag Channel.

The body eventually broke loose from the manhole cover and was found floating miles downstream in Alsip nine days later by a Coast Guard boat".[6]

VIOLENCE AGAINST THE FAMILIES OF GANG MEMBERS

This is another common scenario, particularly with level three gangs that recruit children. The youths find out that once in the gang, it is very hard to get out, in fact they simply try to slip away. But the gang knows where they live, and shows up looking for the kid. In one recent case, the kid was not at home, so when the gang members broke in, they simply shot his parents instead.

For female gang members who like in the case above, try to avoid taking their "outing" or violation for leaving the gang, that is a physical beating in a ritual ceremony, the same result happens to them as happens to male members. They will be targeted for worse violence. This happened in the case of 15-year-old Connie Ayala in Elgin, Illinois, where the gang put out an S.O.S. (Slaughter On Sight) order on her for not taking her beating to get out of the gang. Then one day on the street with her aunt, Connie was again attacked by female members of the gang, who ended up stabbing the aunt.[7]

Gang members present a collateral risk to anyone who associates with them; this includes everyone, police officers simply standing by gang members on the street, kids who just hang with gang members, and in cases involving dating with gang members. In June, 1992 Victor Garcia, age 17, was convinced that he could join the gang if the gang could have sex with his girlfriend. Garcia agreed with this unique arrangement for his gang initiation ceremony in Chicago. The girl was subsequently lured to a party where the gang members lay in wait. She was then physically assaulted and repeatedly raped by four gang members until the following day when she was let go.[8]

PART III: THE RIGHTS OF AMERICAN CHILDREN AND GANGS WHO WANT THEM

The incontrovertible and historically documented argument that exists across all cultures is that a society is civilized to the extent to which it protects and provides for the nurturing of its young. How then do we reconcile this cultural universal with the fact that no where in American society today will we find that it is against the law for adult gang leaders to systematically corrupt innocent children by attracting them and allowing them to join the gang? Our lack of any such laws stand in stark contrast to many other criminal codes that provide stiff sanctions for crimes against children --- harsher penalties for violence against, and the sexual exploitation of, children are now common place in all fifty states and the federal criminal code as well. Simple possession of child pornography can result in an automatic prison sentence. This type of law reflects the moral awakening of a society and its attempts to overcome the sexual exploitation of children.

But what laws do we have to prevent, even monitor, the gang exploitation of children? We have none. We have had laws dating back over twenty years making it a crime to "conscript" a person into the gang. This is also known as compelling gang membership. It means the person must join because they were intimidated to do so. But we do not have a single law, to the knowledge of the present author, which holds any adult gang leader accountable for systematically corrupting the values of the underage members, the children not of legal age, who become the new cannon fodder of almost every criminal gang in America today.

The highly trained gang expert knows that there is only one way to effectively suppress gangs in a society like our own: viewing the gang as an open-system, and counteracting on its ability to attract new members. The new members are always children. Underage teens and pre-teens. Adolescents. Even infants. A gang that cannot attract new members is a gang that will not survive, because as an open-system it will lose members by defection, death, and imprisonment.

American society makes it easy for a gang to flourish today. How? By enabling the gang to freely recruit new gang members from the ranks of American children at no legal risk --- civil or criminal. Some of the only statutes on the books in many jurisdictions are traditional "contributing to the delinquency of a child" laws. These are not easy to prove, and often have weak punishments (i.e., misdemeanor offenses typically). In this regard American gangs are proliferating and evil is triumphing because good citizens did nothing: nothing to protect the rights of children.

A child like "Yummy" is a case in point. This Chicago case gained instant international attention in 1994, when "Yummy" a member of the Black Disciples, a full eleven years old, was executed by his own gang for fear that he may testify against others in a gang-related killing. Yummy typifies how American society really looks after the rights of children. Those government agencies that are chartered "in the best interests of the child" allowed this eleven year old, and many more just like him of all ethnic groups in many places in America today, to basically fall through the cracks of public interests.

YUMMY: Executed At Age 11 By His Own Gang.

Robert Sandifer's gang name was "Yummy", because he loved to eat cookies. As a member of the Black Disciples gang, the BDs', he was "folks". But the BD's often fight with the GD's on the streets. In jail and behind bars they will routinely "group up" in a mutual assistance pact, to discourage attacks from their mutual enemies the "peoples" or "brothers" among African-American members of the Peoples gangs (Black P. Stones, Vice Lords, etc).   Yummy hand a long criminal record at the time of his death, even though he died violently at the age of 11. A lot of newspapers and television news programs in the USA and abroad described the story of Yummy. A lot of versions of this story exist. It was the cover story in <u>Time</u> magazine for September 19, 1994. It was front page news in many areas of the country, and it was also international news.

Yummy had his own extensive record of arrests and convictions, including robbery and arson, but he was also a victim of child neglect and child abuse. Yummy got his name from the gang he joined, the Black Disciples, for his love of cookies and other sweets. On August 28, 1994, perhaps seeking an elevation in rank or other rewards from his gang, Yummy opened fire with a weapon supplied by the gang to shoot at a gang rival, he wounded his target but not fatally, but a stray bullet fired by Yummy killed an innocent bystander, and a child named Shavon Dean became added to the mounting toll of innocent bystanders killed by gang warfare in Chicago. The police manhunt ensued, the heat was on the gang, and the gang did what was expedient: they executed Yummy in a dark underpass.[9] This is not uncommon for a gang to protect itself, for if Yummy talked, older adult leaders would be implicated. The gang had been hiding Yummy during the manhunt, so when it came time to execute him, they simply conned him into thinking that a car was waiting at the other end of the tunnel to take him out of state. Yummy entered the tunnel and was carried out by the coroner. Another expendable child used as cannon fodder by American gangs is the statistic Yummy represents, lured into the gang with candy money from gang business, manipulated as a young gang member, and then simply eliminated when by accidentally shooting an innocent victim he changed from an asset to a liability.

SUMMARY AND CONCLUSION

The gang attracts female gang members who have a history of abuse and abuses them further is what our data suggests. There are exceptions, but generally gang life for female members continues to pattern itself after an exploitive pattern of male chauvinism rather than providing genuine equal opportunity across gender lines. There are few female members in high command in level three gangs today, this remains a male business, open for female customers. At the high school level it is easy to find a significant difference by gender in the general population in terms of who has or who has not joined a gang: males predominate. However, our evidence from juvenile correctional populations using the confined juvenile as the unit of analysis, that is surveying these confined children themselves, revealed in a 1991 study of nearly two thousand detained juveniles that no significant difference existed in terms of the proportion who were gang members by gender. That is, inside juvenile institutions, when we ask the youths confined there if they have ever joined a gang, we will not find the difference we find in high schools out in larger society. What we will find in juvenile institutions when we ask the children themselves if they have ever joined a gang is convergence: about half of all males and females admit to such gang membership.

There are a number of factors that significantly differentiate the non-gang member from the gang member among female students surveyed in Chicago is also a major finding from this chapter. The female gang member profile is consistent with the hardening effect found among gang members generally: having been exposed to trauma, the person produces more trauma, and the cycle continues to play itself out. It is rare to have a happy ending to such a cycle, it is more likely one preprogrammed for a casualty in the making. So it is not uncommon that the cycle ends in the death of the player, or a long prison sentence.

Much more research is needed on female gang members and on very young gang members as what we have here appears to be the crime within a crime: the systematic exploitation of persons by criminal gangs. Crimes that never get reported because there is no one to report them too without great immediate danger. Your author has used some rather harsh language in this chapter, particularly calling the body of laws we call our own legal statutes as a fallacy when it comes to the protection of the rights of children. I shall not apologize for this slight against our policy makers until there are no more Yummy's and no more incentives for the adult gang leaders to use our Nation's children to do their bidding. We cannot continue with our head in the sand like an ostrich in this matter. Gangs are using children. We need to wise up.

Imagine, for a moment, that you were in the following scenario. You are a young student in a public school. Your principal and teachers routinely escort you and all the other students to the auditorium for another lecture on good citizenship. This time you hear a group of well dressed men addressing you in the audience of other school children and all the teachers, these men are surrounded by cameras and therefore obviously very important persons as well. The men tell you they represent a group called Truth Heals Urban Groups, they make speeches, everyone applauds. They hand out awards, and everyone is attentive. They do not hand out membership applications for their group, but would you consider joining too given that these men were so important that they commanded the respect and admiration of the principal and all other school staff, plus government elected officials, and others who appeared to be dignitaries? You might, just as some kids might be swayed and influenced by such messages.

How then to we interpret what happened in a Chicago Public High school? Gangs grandstanding, showing they control school infrastructures, showing they have their contacts in vital places, and that they are an acceptable lifestyle for children? Or do we take the most logically extreme redemptive explanation: these were not gang members at all, sure some awards were given out to what the government calls gang members (King Larry Hoover, leader of the Gangster Disciples, and Willie Lloyd, leader of the Unknown Vice Lords), but you cannot believe the media and certainly not what the government says about them, for these leaders claim to be doing something good for their communities, and if they say they have had a change of heart, well then we should have an open heart and listen to them, right? Wrong. You forgot about the children.

You might have that right to extend any amount of forgiveness you want to a gang leader, you might have that right to forgive by the book, the Great Book, 70 times 7, and then realize that the gang leader only has committed and been convicted of 489 crimes....so he should still be forgiven even if you were the victim of all of these offenses; you have that individual right to act upon whatever moral beliefs you want to believe in. But you do not have the right to communicate to children that gang members run the school, and that gang activists are such important people that the children begin to believe that what their parents may have said about gangs is all a lie, that joining a gang could be a good thing, they are not thugs, they are a group committed to the idea that Truth Heals Urban Groups or any other such non-sense that a cult or a gang might come up with.

The awards ceremony held in a Chicago public high school in October of 1993 was exactly as given in the scenario above. The students heard about a group called Growth and Development, and teachers reported that afterwards some students who had not been gang members now wanted to join that gang[10]. Some 2,500 persons were in the assembly at the school auditorium, a lot of gang activists and all the school children, when two well known top gang leaders each received an award.[11] If you were attending that school and shortly after joined the honored gang, then would your parents have a right to school the Chicago Public School system for facilitating not your educational growth and development but your membership in the Gangster Disciple gang?

Some gangs still continue today to conscript young children with the simple message: "join or die".[12] The more common pattern is covert recruitment: the child is systematically cultivated, or "courted" as the gangs say, allowing the youth to come with on trips, and to parties, eventually growing closer and closer to a new group of "friends", until one day sometime early after gaining complete membership by an often violent ritual ceremony, the youth learns these are not friends at all, and it is very hard to actually quit. The enormous fear that gangs have instilled in children across our country has children now thinking about and planning their own funerals, kids fantasizing about what color patterns they want on their caskets.[13] And few if any legal penalties await the adult gang leaders who benefit from the young new recruits who systematically replenish the membership base of gangs throughout the United States today. How many kids do we have bury, killed from gang violence, until we consider the rights of these children? What will it take to wake up complacent adults and have them recognize that their children have the right to live free from gang recruitment, indeed gang recruitment so systematic in some cases that it can include proselytizing the entire school assembly? The rights of children to live free from the fear of gang violence remains one of the most important and most neglected issues in the current debate about the gang problem in America today.

DISCUSSION QUESTIONS

(1) In English literature, the older cunning criminal Fagin who used young hungry street children to steal and pickpocket on his behalf is actually a cultural universal. With the ability of adult gang members to manipulate children, should much stiffer legal provisions be enacted, "Fagin laws" or "Yummy protection" laws, whatever we want to call them? What language would you use in such a proposed amendment to your state criminal code? Write it and send it to your elected officials.

(2) Do you think that gangs attract alienated female members who may have a history of neglect and high risk behaviors, or do you think that the gang reinforces these traits?

(3) Is the violence that female gang members experience symptomatic of how women in general in our society are the targets of male violence? Does the gang simply provide a new vehicle by which to accomplish the exploitation of and violence against women?

FOOTNOTES

1. The findings presented here are a part of a larger study of female gang member-ship. Currently, data collection on Hispanic, Caucasian, and Asian females has not been of appreciable size to warrant serious analysis. Such research will continue to examine the same issues with other ethnic groups. The present analysis, however, is limited to African-American females.

2. The analysis reported here, again, is restricted to one "folks" gangs. The Black Gangster Disciples, B.O.S., is the largest such gang in Chicago in terms of actual gang membership. In the summer of 1993, some 10,000 persons attended a "picnic" sponsored by the political arm of this group (21st Century Vote). Other and similar data on various other factions of "folks" and "Brothers" gangs (Black P. Stone Nation, Vice Lords, etc), or what has traditionally been regarded as "Peoples" gangs (Peoples and Brothers are used interchangeably, with the latter being the current and politically correct referent for African-American gangs), like the Latin Kings. The sample sizes for "Brothers" or "Peoples" gangs were not large enough at the time of this writing to warrant in-depth analysis; nor of comparisons between such gang nation affiliations.

3. I am grateful to a large number of research assistants who helped at various stages of this project. Usually, this meant having at least one university student assist by being trained in the administration of the anonymous survey, and standing by in each of the classrooms to maintain the conditions of the research (no talking or sharing of responses, collecting the completed surveys, etc).

4. See: Results of the 1994 Illinois Law Enforcement Survey: A Preliminary Report on Gang Migration and Other Gang Problems in Illinois Today. A Task Force Report of the National Gang Crime Research Center. Co-Principle Investigators: George W. Knox; Thomas F. McCurrie; James G. Houston; Edward D. Tromanhaus-er; John A. Laskey. March 31, 1994.

5. See: Cameron McWhirter, "Gang Member Convicted of Drowning Aurora Woman", Chicago Tribune, Jan. 11, 1994, section 2, p. 2.

6. See: Tom Pelton, "Gang Leader Guilty in Woman's Murder", Chicago Tribune, June 17, 1994, Section 2, p. 6.

7. See: "For Ex-Gang Members, Violence Hasn't Stopped", Chicago Sun-Times, Aug. 22, 1994, p. 17.

8. See the commentary on how this overlaps with the gang true issue by: Richard Roeper, "Here's Your Chance, Gang Peacemakers", Chicago Sun-Times, Nov. 10, 1993, p. 11.

9. The underpass was marked with gang graffiti and the lights in the tunnel did not work. After the killing of Yummy there, the lights were immediately fixed and the walls were immediately painted.

10. See: John Kass and George Papajohn, "High School Role in Gang Summit Hit", Chicago Tribune, Section 2, pp.1-2, Oct. 27, 1993.

11. See: Lee Bey, "Principal: I Don't Favor Gang Honors", Chicago Sun-Times, Oct. 28, 1993, p. 3.

12. See: Tamara Kerrill, "Pilsen Teenagers March to Reclaim Turf From Gangs", Chicago Sun-Times, May 2, 1994, p. 16.

13. See: "Black Youths Tell How Gangs And Guns Have Them Planning Their Own Funerals", Jet, Jan. 31, 1994, pp. 26-28.

CHAPTER 18

ASIAN GANG MEMBERS:
A Risk Profile Common to Students
of Other Ethnic and Racial Groups

INTRODUCTION

A number of previous gang studies have involved surveys of school students
(Tromanhauser, 1981; Morash, 1983; Rosenbaum and Grant, 1983; Spergel and
Curry, 1990; Fagan, 1990; Thompson and Jason, 1988; Schwartz, 1989; Sherer, 1990;
Takata and Zevitz, 1990; Bastian and Taylor, 1991). Missing from this prior
literature, however, is research that specifically focuses on the Asian student
population. The research reported here seeks to examine some contemporary gang
concepts using data from a national sample of Asian students.

DERIVING HYPOTHESES FROM THE LITERATURE

While Asian gangs are portrayed in the mass media as a major threat and new
menace to American society[a], Ko-Lin Chin (1990: p. 130) estimates no more than
2,000 Chinese members nationwide; further, that Chinese gangs recruit "vulnerable
youths...those who are not doing well in school or who have already dropped out (p.
134)." Most importantly, Chin describes how Chinese gangs are portrayed as
significantly different than other ethnic gangs (p. 136) and portrays unique aspects
of the Chinese gang organization, its income, investment in legitimate business, and
extortion. All the present research can do is speak to whether Asian students as
gang members show a different trend than that of their white, Black, and Hispanic
counterparts.

Both the works of Chin (1990) and that by Vigil and Yun (1990) assert that students
with high academic achievement have a lower risk of gang affiliation. The
proposition that Asian youths who experience low achievement in terms of grades in
school and who come to be labelled through the school disciplinary system are those
who are more likely to join and be involved with gangs has, however, not been
empirically tested. The present research addresses this and other issues.

Much of the research literature about gangs can be reduced to three dependent
variables for which explanations are sought: (1) why gangs arise, (2) why persons join
gangs, and (3) why gang members behave the way they do. Why gangs arise, or the
etiology of gangs, is exemplified in the early work of Thrasher (1927), the social
disorganization theory of Shaw and McKay (1942), and perhaps even the racism-
oppression thesis (Knox, 1991). Other theories are best at explaining why persons
join gangs as in the subcultural approach of Cohen (1955), Yablonsky's (1962)

---

[a] See "Asian Street Gangs Emerging as New Underworld," The New York Times
Metro, Wednesday, April 1, 1992, by James Dao.

sociopathy approach, Stinchcombe's (1964) articulation hypothesis and the Cloward and Ohlin (1960) opportunity approach. Finally, some theories specifically focus on explaining specific gang behavior such as violence, fighting, and drug abuse (Short and Strodtbeck, 1965; Sanchez-Jankowski, 1991; Fagan, 1990).

The research reported here sought to test the hypotheses in Figure 16. The issue is whether these hypotheses, most of which are based on traditional gang concepts, still hold value for explaining aspects of the gang problem among Asian students.

FIGURE 16

AUTHOR(S), CONCEPTS, AND HYPOTHESES ABOUT GANGS

Author(s)	Concept	Hypothesis
Cohen (1955)	Subculture: Belief in "good luck".	The higher the belief in good luck, the more likely the gang affiliation.
Stinchecomb (1964)	Articulation Hypothesis	The higher the articulation of present education for future value, the less likely the gang affiliation.
Vigil and Yun (1990)	Asian Pragmatism	Asian gangs (e.g., Vietnamese) are less likely to engage in "persistent fighting that characterizes African-American and Chicano gangs" (Huff, 1990: p. 158).
Chin (1990)	Vulnerability Factor	The higher the academic failure, the higher the gang affiliation.
Sanchez-Jankowski (1991)	Defiant-Individualist Character	As gang members have this defiant individualist character, they are more likely than their non-gang member counterparts to report a higher level of fighting and involvement in violence.
Cloward and Ohlin (1960)	Legitimate Opportunity	The higher the legitimate employment and income, the lower the gang affiliation.
Knox (1991)	Self-esteem[b]	The higher the self-esteem, the lower the gang affiliation.
	Internal-locus of control	The higher the internal locus of control, the lower the gang affiliation.
Yablonsky (1962)	Paranoia	The higher the paranoia, the higher the gang affiliation.

[b] A variety of authors have cited the importance of self-esteem in relationship to gang involvement (Berland, et al, 1989; Mok, 1990).

METHODOLOGY

The Asian student survey used here was the result of a probono research project conducted by the National Gang Crime Research Center for the National Association for Asian and Pacific American Education (NAAPAE). Asian teachers were identified who were teaching classes to predominantly Asian students. The selection of geographical sites was designed to stratify by size of the Asian population cluster and therefore the eight cities used reflect both large and small Asian communities. An officer in NAAPAE then called the selected Asian teachers (also members of the association) to secure their cooperation for data collection in the following sites: Aurora, Colorado; Minneapolis, Minnesota; Harvey, Louisiana; Tacoma, Washington; Kahului, Hawaii; New York City; Alhambra, California; and Rockville, Maryland[c].

In March of 1992 each of the target sites was sent several letters explaining the Asian student study and giving explicit written directions on how to collect the data. The sample size generated from this survey was 361 Asian students. The instrument used was an anonymous five page survey that was pretested earlier on Chicago students. For further analysis based on this national assessment of Asian gang members see Knox, Laske, and Tromanhauser's (1992) Schools Under Siege.

DEFINITION OF GANG

As described elsewhere (Knox, 1991) gangs vary by the nature of their social organization and the level of affiliation. The present author defines a gang as a group of persons who individually or collectively commit crime, or who as a group knowingly benefit from the crimes committed by its members, and where law violations persist over time. The present analysis does not use the gang as a social organization as its unit of analysis. It uses self-reported gang membership. Figure 17 shows a listing of the types of gangs that these Asian students self-reported joining. This is traditional self-report survey research. Some 15.7 percent of the Asian sample reported that they knew the names of the gangs active in their school[d]. It was not possible to control for the level of organizational sophistication or the level of membership involvement with the various gangs identified in this research.

INDEPENDENT VARIABLES: MEASURES USED FOR THE HYPOTHESIS TESTING

Three demographic measures were used to determine if variations existed with regard to the gang problem among Asian students: grade level, age, and sex.

---

[c] I am indebted to Dr. Kay Tokanaga (Chicago Board of Education) for this assistance.

[d] The survey by Takata and Zevitz (1990) showed students perceived the gang as less formalized than did adults.

To test implications from the work of Chin (1990) three dichotomous variables were used: (1) ever suspended from school, (2) ever had an in-school suspension, and (3) ever had an in-school detention. In addition to these measures of academic failure and labelling, another measure is also used: (4) high grades. High grades is recoded from the self-reported grade point average (GPA) to reflect a dichotomous variable: those with "A" or "B" grade point averages, versus those with lower GPA's.

The Stinchecombe (1964) articulation factor was operationalized here in terms of its career or employment prospects. The articulation hypothesis argues that if students do not know what they will be doing after completing educational requirements they will be more likely to be gang active or at risk of joining a gang[e]. This work articulation factor is a dichotomous variable reflecting whether the students know what career or profession they will enter after completing their education.

The Cloward and Ohlin (1960) hypothesis includes two measures of legitimate opportunity. These are dichotomous variables reflecting: (1) whether the student has any full or part-time job, and (2) whether the student receives a regular allowance from the family.

The self-esteem measure is based on the full ten item scale by Rosenberg (1965). The internal-locus of control scale consists of five items taken from James (1957). The median score on these scales was used to group the sample into a dichotomous measure reflecting high or low values.

The Cohen (1955) subculture variable of "belief in good luck" is an item taken the internal-locus of control scale (James, 1957). The item asks the student to agree or disagree with the statement "when things are going well for me I consider it due only to a run of good luck."

Fighting behavior was used to test an implication of the Sanchez-Jankowski (1991) concept of the defiant character. This is a dichotomous variable reflecting whether the student has been in one or more physical fights during the last calendar year[f].

DEPENDENT VARIABLES: MEASURES USED FOR THE HYPOTHESIS TESTING

In some concept frameworks, due to temporal ordering differences, what some treat as an independent variable, others treat as a dependent variable. Some of these independent variables that can also be examined as dependent variables include: high grades (academic success), fighting behavior, knowledge of drug sales, having gang friends, and having drug abusing friends.

---

[e] This is true, according to Stinchcombe Rebellion in a High School, because from this poor articulation of the present status in relationship to the future the student will be more prone to rebellion.

[f] See Loeber, et al (1989) for a related psychiatric concept called "high oppositional behavior" shown to be highly related to fighting in school.

Ever joining a gang is a dichotomous variable (yes/no) and simply measures prior gang membership[g].

Ever being asked to join a gang (yes/no) is a related dichotomous measure of gang recruitment attempts.

Knowing the names of the gangs active at the school is a dichotomous variable (yes/no) that measures cognition of gang activity in the school.

DEMOGRAPHIC CHARACTERISTICS OF THE SAMPLE

The student sample included grades six through twelve and ages eleven through twenty-one. About a fifth (21.6%) were in grades six, seven and eight, with the rest distributed as follows: 15.2 percent in grade nine, 24.7 percent in grade ten, 18 percent in grade eleven, and 20.5 percent in grade twelve. Just under half (45.2%) were 15 years of age or less. The students are equivalent with regard to gender: 50 percent males, and 50 percent females.   Ethnicity and national origin showed the following distribution: 19.9 percent Chinese, 8 percent Japanese, 9.1 percent Pacific Islander, 0.3 percent Native Alaskan, 11.1 percent Vietnamese, 8.6 percent Cambodian, 0.6 percent Laotian, 6 percent Hmong, 19.9 percent Filipino, 0.9 percent Thai, 6.5 percent Korean, 0.3 percent India, 0.3 percent Indonesia, 0.6 percent Asian/Hispanic, 0.9 percent Tongan, 6.8 percent Hawaiian, 0.3 percent Marshalese, and 0.3 percent Micronesia.

The distribution by state was as follows: 50.3 percent of the Asians student in the present analysis were surveyed in Hawaii[h]; 11.5 percent from Washington; 5.1 percent from Colorado; 4.2 percent from Maryland; 8.1 percent from Minnesota; 2.5 percent from Louisiana; 12.6 percent from California; and 5.6 percent from New York.

OVERALL FINDINGS AND THE EFFECTS OF AGE AND GENDER

Age significantly differentiates fighting behavior, observing drug sales in or near the school, joining a gang, being asked to join a gang, and number of close friends who abuse drugs. Here the age variable has been recoded to compare two age groups: ≤ 15 versus ≥ 16. Table 27 provides the frequency distributions for those variables significantly differentiated by age.

---

[g] Current gang membership was also measured in the survey. About half of those who admitted joining a gang were willing to admit that they were still considered a gang member. Current gang membership (self-reported) therefore has a very small base rate (3.8%).

[h] Gardner, et al (1989) showed that by the 1980 Census about half of Asian Americans resided in California or Hawaii. Thus, the sampling here does tend to roughly mirror the geographical cluster desired.

As seen in Table 27, it is the younger age group that appears to report a larger gang problem. The younger Asian student group was significantly more likely to report one or more fights during the recent year (36.2%), to have seen drug sales in or near the school (31.5%), to have ever joined a gang (11.3%), having ever been asked to join a gang (19.4%), and having one or more close friends who use illicit drugs (34.2%).

Gender significantly differentiates the following variables: fighting behavior, ever joining a gang, ever being asked to join a gang, number of drug using friends, and knowledge of gang names. Table 28 provides the frequency distributions for these variables. As seen in Table 28, as in other high school studies, males predominate in the area of gang activity. Female Asian students are were less likely to report one or more fights during the last year (22%), to have ever joined a gang (4.5%), to have been asked to join a gang (9.2%), to have one or more friends who are gang members (19%), to have one or more friends who abuse illicit drugs (20.7%), and were less cognizant of the names of the gangs at their school (9.4%).

THE EFFECTS OF SCHOOL DISCIPLINE AND HIGH GRADES

The measures of academic failure and labelling are shown to be among the strongest variables from this analysis. For example, ever being suspended from school is shown to significantly differentiate all the dependent variables except for the knowledge of gangs variable. The measure for ever having an in-school suspension significantly differentiates all of the dependent variables. The variable for in-school detention significantly differentiates all but joining a gang and knowledge of gang names. The high grades measure significantly differentiates fighting behavior, joining a gang, being asked to join a gang, number of gang and drug abusing friends.

It would appear from these findings that schools are either good at picking out 'gang prone youths' among Asian students and meting out deserved discipline to them for their deviance in the school environment, or that these social ceremonies of stigma and labelling become clearly associated with higher gang problems (Peiar, 1985).

TABLE 27

FREQUENCY DISTRIBUTIONS OF VARIABLES SIGNIFICANTLY
DIFFERENTIATED BY AGE AMONG ASIAN STUDENTS

		>= 1 Fights in Last Year	
		NO	YES
AGE GROUPS:	< = 15	95	54 (36.2%)
	> = 16	125	31 (19.8%)

Chi-square = 10.1, p = .001

		Seen Drug Sales At School	
		NO	YES
	< = 15	102	47 (31.5%)
	> = 16	150	37 (19.7%)

Chi-square = 6.11, p = .01

		Ever Join a Gang	
		NO	YES
	< = 15	141	18 (11.3%)
	> = 16	182	8 (4.2%)

Chi-square = 6.34, p = .01

		Ever Asked to Join a Gang	
		NO	YES
	< = 15	120	29 (19.4%)
	> = 16	167	20 (10.6%)

Chi-square = 5.11, p = .02

		>= 1 Friends Who Use Drugs	
		NO	YES
	< = 15	100	52 (34.2%)
	> = 16	140	41 (22.6%)

Chi-square = 5.48, p = .01

TABLE 28

FREQUENCY DISTRIBUTION OF VARIABLES SIGNIFICANTLY
DIFFERENTIATED BY GENDER AMONG ASIAN STUDENTS

		>=1 Fights in Last Year	
		NO	YES
GENDER:	Male	101	53 (34.4%)
	Female	120	34 (22.0%)

Chi-square = 5.78, p = .01

	Ever Join a Gang	
	NO	YES
Male	159	18 (10.1%)
Female	166	8 (4.5%)

Chi-square = 3.97, p = .04

	Ever Asked to Join a Gang	
	NO	YES
Male	131	33 (20.1%)
Female	157	16 (9.2%)

Chi-square = 8.01, p = .005

	>= 1 Gang Member Friends	
	NO	YES
Male	119	47 (28.3%)
Female	140	33 (19.0%)

Chi-square = 4.01, p = .04

	>= 1 Drug Abusing Friends	
	NO	YES
Male	108	58 (34.9%)
Female	134	35 (20.7%)

Chi-square = 8.45, p = .004

	Know Names of the Gangs	
	NO	YES
Male	131	36 (21.5%)
Female	153	16 (9.4%)

Chi-square = 9.38, p = .002

Increased marginality via such labelling is clearly associated with higher deviance (Graham, 1986). While this profile is not unique to Asians, it clearly supports the academic vulnerability hypothesis derived from Chin (1990): the higher the school adjustment problems, the higher the gang involvement; and, vice versa, the higher the academic achievement, the lower the gang involvement.

TABLE 29

FREQUENCY DISTRIBUTION OF VARIABLES SIGNIFICANTLY DIFFERENTIATED BY BEING SUSPENDED FROM SCHOOL AMONG ASIAN STUDENTS

		High Grades (Overall GPA)	
		C or Less	A or B
EVER SUSPENDED FROM SCHOOL:	No	78	199 (71.8%)
	Yes	24	18 (42.8%)

Chi-square = 14.08, p < .001

	>= 1 Fights During Last Year	
	NO	YES
No	200	56 (21.8%)
Yes	14	26 (65%)

Chi-square = 32.12, p < .001

	Seen Drug Sales Near School	
	NO	YES
No	222	62 (21.8%)
Yes	20	22 (52.3%)

Chi-square = 17.85, p < .001

	Ever Join a Gang	
	NO	YES
No	275	17 (5.8%)
Yes	37	8 (17.7%)

Chi-square = 8.11, p = .004

	Ever Asked to Join a Gang	
	NO	YES
No	255	27 (9.5%)
Yes	24	21 (46.6%)

Chi-square = 42.63, p < .001

	Have >= 1 Gang Friends	
	NO	YES
No	228	56 (19.7%)
Yes	20	23 (53.4%)

Chi-square = 23.24, p < .001

	Have >= 1 Drug Friends	
	NO	YES
No	220	65 (22.8%)
Yes	17	25 (59.5%)

Chi-square = 24.73, p < .001

Table 29 provides the frequency distribution for variables significantly differentiated by whether these Asian students report ever having been suspended from school. Clearly, this condition of ever having been suspended from school shows: significantly lower grades, higher fighting, higher observation of drug sales in or near the school, and a greater likelihood of joining a gang, being asked to join a gang, and having one or more friends who are gang members and drug abusers.

Having an in-school suspension, as seen in Table 30, significantly differentiates all of the dependent variables examined here. Again, as in the research on white, Black, and Hispanic students in Chicago, this factor of problematic school adjustment is highly associated with the gang problem among Asians. Similarly, having a "hit" or an in-school suspension, as seen in Table 31, is a factor that significantly differentiates all but two variables: gang joining and knowledge of gang names variables.

THE ARTICULATION FACTOR, SELF-ESTEEM AND LOCUS OF CONTROL

The work articulation factor is shown to significantly differentiate observation of drug sales in or near the school and ever joining a gang. Table 32 shows the frequency distributions for these two variables. Prior theory predicts that the higher the articulation, the lower the rebellion (Stinchecombe, 1964). Unfortunately, while significant in relationship to two variables, the direction of the effect is in reverse of that expected. As seen in Table 32, those Asian students who do articulate future benefit from present schooling (as reflected in they know what occupation or profession they will enter after completing their education) are more likely to have seen drug sales near the school, and they are more (not less) likely to have ever joined a gang.

The self-esteem variable appears less predictive than the literature suggests regarding gangs, at least among the Asian students studied here. Table 33 shows the frequency distributions for the three variables that high self-esteem should impact on. The first two are not unexpected: the higher the self-esteem, the higher the grades; and the higher the self-esteem, the lower the fighting. Those with higher self-esteem were also more likely to know the names of the gangs in their school.

The internal locus of control scale scores yield no significant effects on any of the gang variables, and are only able to differentiate the high grades variable. This shows that those with higher internal locus of control scale scores are more likely (76.4%) to report high grades than those who do not (60.9%).

TABLE 30

FREQUENCY DISTRIBUTION OF VARIABLES SIGNIFICANTLY
DIFFERENTIATED BY HAVING AN IN-SCHOOL SUSPENSION
AMONG ASIAN STUDENTS

		High Grades (Overall GPA)	
		C or Less	A or B
EVER HAVE AN IN-SCHOOL			
SUSPENSION:	No	76	189 (71.3%)
	Yes	27	25 (48%)

Chi-square = 10.7, p = .001

		>= 1 Fights in Last Year	
		NO	YES
	No	186	57 (23.4%)
	Yes	25	26 (50.9%)

Chi-square = 15.76, p < .001

		Seen Drug Sales Near School	
		NO	YES
	No	214	57 (21%)
	Yes	25	28 (52.8%)

Chi-square = 23.16, p < .001

		Ever Join A Gang	
		NO	YES
	No	264	17 (6%)
	Yes	45	9 (16.6%)

Chi-square = 7.13, p = .008

		Ever Asked to Join a Gang	
		NO	YES
	No	242	29 (10.7%)
	Yes	34	20 (37%)

Chi-square = 24.39, p < .001

		>= 1 Gang Member Friends	
		NO	YES
	No	217	54 (19.9%)
	Yes	28	26 (48.1%)

Chi-square = 19.32, p < .001

		>= 1 Drug Abuser Friends	
		NO	YES
	No	212	60 (22%)
	Yes	22	31 (58.4%)

Chi-square = 29.2, p < .001

		Know Names of Gangs at School	
		NO	YES
	No	230	35 (13.2%)
	Yes	38	15 (28.3%)

Chi-square = 7.59, p = .006

TABLE 31

FREQUENCY DISTRIBUTION OF VARIABLES SIGNIFICANTLY
DIFFERENTIATED BY HAVING HAD AN IN-SCHOOL SUSPENSION
AMONG ASIAN STUDENTS

		High Grades (Overall GPA) C or Less	A or B
EVER HAD AN IN-SCHOOL DETENTION:	No	76	187 (71.1%)
	Yes	26	28 (51.8%)

Chi-square = 7.6, p = .006

		>= 1 Fights in the Last Year NO	YES
	No	186	53 (22.1%)
	Yes	29	28 (49.1%)

Chi-square = 16.81, p < .001

		Seen Drug Sales Near School NO	YES
	No	214	56 (20.7%)
	Yes	28	29 (50.8%)

Chi-square = 22.2, p < .001

		Ever Asked to Join A Gang NO	YES
	No	245	26 (9.5%)
	Yes	35	22 (38.5%)

Chi-square = 31.7, p < .001

		>= 1 Gang Member Friends NO	YES
	No	216	56 (20.5%)
	Yes	34	23 (40.3%)

Chi-square = 10.08, p = .001

		>= 1 Drug Abusing Friends NO	YES
	No	207	62 (23%)
	Yes	30	29 (49.1%)

Chi-square = 16.44, p < .001

TABLE 32

FREQUENCY DISTRIBUTION OF VARIABLES SIGNIFICANTLY
DIFFERENTIATED BY THE WORK ARTICULATION FACTOR
AMONG ASIAN STUDENTS

| | | Seen Drug Sales Near School | |
		NO	YES
Know what occupation or profession will enter when finished with education:	No	82	20 (19.6%)
	Yes	147	64 (30.3%)

Chi-square = 4.01, p = .04

| | | Ever Join A Gang | |
		NO	YES
	No	105	3 (2.7%)
	Yes	194	22 (10.1%)

Chi-square = 5.54, p = .01

TABLE 33

FREQUENCY DISTRIBUTION OF VARIABLES SIGNIFICANTLY
DIFFERENTIATED BY HIGH SELF-ESTEEM SCORES
AMONG ASIAN STUDENTS

| | | High Grades (Overall GPA) | |
		C or less	A or B
High Self-Esteem Score:	No	66	83 (55.7%)
	Yes	27	106 (79.6%)

Chi-square = 18.3, p < .001

| | | >= 1 Fights in Last Year | |
		NO	YES
	No	91	43 (32%)
	Yes	105	27 (20.4%)

Chi-square = 4.64, p = .03

| | | Know Names of the Gangs | |
		NO	YES
	No	138	15 (9.8%)
	Yes	102	32 (23.8%)

Chi-square = 10.33, p = .001

BELIEF IN GOOD LUCK AND PARANOIA

It is fair to say that most gang concepts in the literature have not been vigorously
tested. A subcultural belief in good luck could be expected to be associated with

higher gang affiliation according to Cohen (1955). A higher level of paranoia would be expected to be associated with gang affiliation according to Yablonsky (1962).

Table 34 provides the frequency distributions for those three variables significantly differentiated by belief in good luck. Consistent with the hypothesis, those who agree with the good luck question from the internal-external locus of control scale: are less likely to have high grades[i], more likely to have had one or more fights in the last year, and more likely to have one or more close friends and associates who are gang members.

Table 35 provides the results for the paranoia question.   Consistent with the hypothesis, those who express this measure of paranoia: have lower grades, more fights, are more likely to see drug sales near school, more likely to be asked to join a gang, and are more likely to have one or more gang friends.

TABLE 34

FREQUENCY DISTRIBUTION OF VARIABLES SIGNIFICANTLY DIFFERENTIATED BY BELIEF IN GOOD LUCK AMONG ASIAN STUDENTS

	High Grades (Overall GPA)	
	C or Less	A or B
"When things are going well for me I consider it due only to a run of good luck." Disagree	32	114 (78%)
Agree	64	85 (57%)

Chi-square = 14.86, p < .001

	> = 1 Fights in Last Year	
	NO	YES
Disagree	110	29 (20.8%)
Agree	97	45 (31.6%)

Chi-square = 4.24, p = .03

	> = 1 Gang Member Friends	
	NO	YES
Disagree	122	27 (18.1%)
Agree	113	47 (29.3%)

Chi-square = 5.36, p = .02

---

[i] This finding is consistent with that by Yan (1991) who found that academic success among Asians was attributed more to effort than to good luck.

TABLE 35

FREQUENCY DISTRIBUTION OF VARIABLES SIGNIFICANTLY DIFFERENTIATED BY THE PARANOIA QUESTION AMONG ASIAN STUDENTS

		High Grades (Overall GPA)	
		C or Less	A or B
"I often think people are talking about me."	False	50	131 (72.3%)
	True	52	75 (59%)
		Chi-square = 5.97, p = .01	

		>= 1 Fights in the Last Year	
		NO	YES
	False	129	36 (21.8%)
	True	79	42 (34.7%)
		Chi-square = 5.85, p = .01	

		Seen Drug Sales Near School	
		NO	YES
	False	147	37 (20.1%)
	True	88	45 (33.8%)
		Chi-square = 7.58, p = .006	

		Ever Asked to Join a Gang	
		NO	YES
	False	163	21 (11.4%)
	True	109	26 (19.2%)
		Chi-square = 3.81, p = .051	

		>= 1 Gang Member Friends	
		NO	YES
	False	153	31 (16.8%)
	True	89	47 (34.5%)
		Chi-square = 13.3, p < .001	

EMPLOYMENT AND INCOME

Some recent research has challenged long-held views about the value of employment for youths with regard to its ability to prevent deviance. The present findings must be added to this exception to opportunity theory. In this analysis knowing whether a youth has a full or part-time job has no effect on any of the gang variables. In fact, those respondents with full or part-time jobs appear more likely to have one or more drug abusing friends, and to know the names of the gangs. Thus, the nature of the relationship is obverse to that which might be expected from Cloward and Ohlin (1960). This is shown in Table 36 and is consistent with similar findings among non-Asians (Knox, Laske, Tromanhauser, 1992).

TABLE 36

FREQUENCY DISTRIBUTION OF VARIABLES SIGNIFICANTLY
DIFFERENTIATED BY HAVING FULL OR PART-TIME EMPLOYMENT
AMONG ASIAN STUDENTS

Have any regular part-time
or full-time job?

		>= 1 Drug Abusing Friends	
		NO	YES
	No	180	55 (23.4%)
	Yes	54	38 (41.3%)

Chi-square = 10.4, p = .001

		Know the Names of the Gangs	
		NO	YES
	No	206	31 (13%)
	Yes	72	20 (21.7%)

Chi-square = 3.79, p = .051

The Chicago high school research found that youths with jobs were in fact more likely to be asked to join a gang, not less likely. Perhaps because of the disposable income which such employment provides, it may provide a youth with greater access to the drug subculture.

Finally, the income variable (whether the student receives a regular allowance from the family) is significant in relationship to all variables except that of high grades as seen in Table 37.

TABLE 37

FREQUENCY DISTRIBUTION OF VARIABLES SIGNIFICANTLY DIFFERENTIATED BY HAVING AN INCOME ALLOWANCE AMONG ASIAN STUDENTS

		>= 1 Fights in Last Year	
		NO	YES
Receive an allowance from your family:	No	114	29 (20.2%)
	Yes	99	51 (34%)
		Chi-square = 6.94, p = .008	

	Seen Drug Sales Near School	
	NO	YES
No	135	28 (17.1%)
Yes	102	54 (34.6%)
	Chi-square = 12.69, p < .001	

	Ever Join A Gang	
	NO	YES
No	160	8 (4.7%)
Yes	145	18 (11%)
	Chi-square = 4.50, p = .03	

	Ever Asked to Join a Gang	
	NO	YES
No	147	13 (8.1%)
Yes	122	35 (22.2%)
	Chi-square = 12.37, p < .001	

	>= 1 Gang Member Friends	
	NO	YES
No	130	29 (18.2%)
Yes	115	45 (28.1%)
	Chi-square = 4.37, p = .03	

	>= 1 Drug Abuser Friends	
	NO	YES
No	125	35 (21.8%)
Yes	103	54 (34.3%)
	Chi-square = 6.15, p = .01	

	Know Names of the Gangs	
	NO	YES
No	149	16 (9.6%)
Yes	123	34 (21.6%)
	Chi-square = 8.77, p = .003	

The problem, however, is that the nature of the observed relationship is not that which might be predicted from opportunity theory. The youths with family allowances appear to have higher gang problems than those youths who do not receive an allowance. Apparently not receiving an allowance from the family may be a blessing in disguise according to the findings in Table 37. Students who receive a family allowance are more likely to have been in one or more fights during the last year (34%) than students who do not receive an allowance (20.2%), they are more likely to have seen drug sales occur in or near the school (34.6%) than those who do not receive an allowance (17.1%), they are more likely to report having joined a gang (11%) than those who do not receive an allowance (4.7%), they are more likely to have been asked to join a gang (22.2%) than those who do not receive an allowance (8.1%), they are more likely to have one or more close friends and associates who are gang members (28.1%) than those who do not receive an allowance (18.2%), they are more likely to have one or more close friends and associates who use illicit drugs (34.3%) than those who do not receive an allowance (21.8%), and they are more likely to know the names of the gangs in their school (21.6%) than those who do not receive an allowance (9.6%).

These findings run directly against the grain of conventional thinking and opportunity theory. It may be that gangs find youths with allowances more attractive to recruit because they can pay their regular dues. It may be that youths with allowances and disposable income are more likely to be exposed to the drug subculture. It may also reflect some aspect of change in traditional family function among Asians[j].

FIGHTING BEHAVIOR

Prior research shows that gang members report a higher level of fighting behavior than non-gang member youths. It may be tied to some aspect of the defiant individualist character described by Sanchez-Jankowski (1991). But does this same finding documented for whites, Blacks, and Hispanics also apply to Asian students?

The frequency distribution for the effects of fighting behavior are shown in Table 38. This shows that fighting behavior is clearly associated with lower grades and with a higher likelihood of observing drug sales, joining a gang, being asked to join a gang, having one or more gang member friends, having one or more drug abusing friends, and knowing the names of the gangs. Fighting shows a consistent significant effect for all gang variables and is consistent with the finding by Knox, Laske and Tromanhauser (1992) that gang members face a higher likelihood of fighting and assault than their non-gang member student counterparts.

---

[j] Betty Lee Sung, in The Adjustment Experience of Chinese Immigrant Children in New York City, suggests such major family changes combined with the increased role played by the school, create the context where peer groups such as gangs play a more prominent role. The present research did have one variable about family function: Whether parents helped or encouraged the student with homework, but it was not significant in relation to gang membership, being asked to join a gang, or having one or more gang member friends.

TABLE 38

FREQUENCY DISTRIBUTION OF VARIABLES SIGNIFICANTLY DIFFERENTIATED BY THE FIGHTING VARIABLE AMONG ASIAN STUDENTS

		High Grades (Overall GPA)	
		C or Less	A or B
One or more fights in the last 12 months:	No	51	150 (74.6%)
	Yes	35	44 (55.6%)

Chi-square = 9.55, p = .002

		Seen Drug Sales Near School	
		NO	YES
	No	171	45 (20.8%)
	Yes	43	37 (46.2%)

Chi-square = 18.83, p < .001

		Ever Join a Gang	
		NO	YES
	No	215	7 (3.1%)
	Yes	70	16 (18.6%)

Chi-square = 21.41, p < .001

		Ever Asked to Join a Gang	
		NO	YES
	No	190	20 (9.5%)
	Yes	56	27 (32.5%)

Chi-square = 23.37, p < .001

		> = 1 Gang Member Friends	
		NO	YES
	No	181	31 (14.6%)
	Yes	48	37 (43.5%)

Chi-square = 28.71, p < .001

		> = 1 Drug Abuser Friends	
		NO	YES
	No	170	41 (19.4%)
	Yes	39	44 (53%)

Chi-square = 32.68, p < .001

		Know the Names of the Gangs	
		NO	YES
	No	185	30 (13.9%)
	Yes	63	19 (23.1%)

Chi-square = 3.66, p = .056

Suggesting that the gang recruitment lure of "protection" (Hochhaus and Sousa, 1987) is more rhetoric than reality.

PREDICTING GANG MEMBERSHIP

Prior efforts to predict aspects of the gang problem involved variables similar to those examined in the present research and in one case was able to correctly classify 74 percent of the cases (Truckenmiller, 1983).   More recently another research project was able to correctly classify 8 in 10 youths (Winfree, Vigil, and Mays, 1991: 14).   Taking some of the factors shown to strongly be associated with gang membership it is possible to compute a discriminant function using these predictor variables. This linear model is basically a "one-way multivariate analysis of variance" (SYSTAT, 1986: 107). The F-values for the predictor variables used are shown in Table 39.

TABLE 39
UNIVARIATE F STATISTICS IN PREDICTING GANG MEMBERSHIP

Variable	F-Value	Prob.
> = 1 Gang Member Friends	37.99	< .001
> = 1 Drug Abuser Friends	22.16	< .001
> = 1 Fights in Last Year	20.08	< .001
Age: (0=LE15; 1=GE16)	7.38	.007
High Grades (1=A,B;0=LE C)	6.61	.01

The actual group membership (gang/nongang) compared to the predicted group membership (gang/nongang) is provided in Table 40. This shows that 83 percent of the cases were correctly classified as either gang or nongang members. The largest error in predicting gang membership here is among those who are not gang members who are predicted to be gang members (N = 42).

TABLE 40

ACTUAL VERSUS PREDICTED GANG MEMBERSHIP

		Prediction	
		Gang	Nongang
ACTUAL	Gang	19	3
	Nongang	42	201

SUMMARY AND CONCLUSION

The basic finding of interest from this research is that in many respects Asian students face the identical "gang problem" or "gang risk" that is documented among white, Black, and Hispanic school students (Knox, Laske, and Tromanhauser, 1992).

The sample of Asian students used is a purposive rather than true national random sample and the findings reported here are at this point only suggestive.

High self-esteem while clearly related to high grades, fighting, and the cognitive variable (know gang names), but was not significant in relation to joining a gang, being asked to join a gang, or having gang friends. Similarly, the measure for high internal locus of control was significant only in differentiating high grades; and not any of the gang involvement variables.

Whether the student had a full or part-time job was shown to be significant only in relationship to having drug abusing friends and knowledge of gang names. Yet the allowance variable showed significance in relationship to all variables other than having high grades. Unfortunately both of these legitimate opportunity variables were shown to have the reverse effect than that which would have been logically expected. They are not associated with a lower, but rather a higher gang problem.

The belief in good luck variable is shown to be significantly related to high grades, fights, and having gang friends. Similarly, the paranoia variable was shown to be significant in relation to high grades, fights, seeing drug sales, being asked to join a gang, and having gang friends. The fighting variable was shown to be significant in relation to all variables. The academic vulnerability hypothesis tested from Chin (1990) yielded the strongest consistent support in the analysis undertaken here. Fighting behavior, examined in terms of Jankowski's (1991) defiance hypothesis also yielded consistent results.

The variables most predictive of gang membership were: having one or more close friends who were gang members, having one or more close friends who use illicit drugs, and having one or more fights in the last year. Age and grades were also significant in predicting gang membership.

In summary, this survey research sought to test various hypotheses from the literature on gangs using an Asian student sample. In fairness to the opportunity model, future research should examine perceived closure in educational and occupational structures, as well as illicit income sources. An urgent need exists for more comparative national research using ethnicity as a control variable.

DISCUSSION QUESTIONS

(1) Among some Vietnamese gang members in America it is not uncommon to find them using the phrase "Toi o gica", meaning "my crazy life", or "I do not care about anything". Is this commonality with other ethnic groups, for example in the barrio, a possible cultural universal or do you think this is simply a part of the personality syndrome adopted or shaped among gang members?

(2) Some Vietnamese gang members have a rather violent way of targeting Vietnamese businessmen, where it typically involves a home invasion, and the use of violence even torture, to force the victim to turn over their money. Is this another possible cultural universal about gangs, that is that they do their most damage to their own ethnic and racial groups, or is this a function of opportunity itself?

(3) How do we explain the rather common "profile" that emerges for Asian gang members that is also found for the most part among gang members of most other racial and ethnic groups? Is this the homogenizing influence of gang life, the common desensitization about violence?

REFERENCES

Bastian, Lisa D. and Bruce M. Taylor
1991 School Crime: A National Crime Victimization Survey Report. U.S. Department of Justice, Office of Justice Programs, Bureau of Justice Statistics (Sept).

Bergman, Brian
1991 "Terror in the Streets: Young Asian Gangs Are Spreading Fear, Violence, and Death in Canadian Cities", MACLEAN'S, Canada's Weekly Newsmagazine, March 25, pp. 18-26.

Berland, David I; et al
1989 "Adolescent Gangs in the Hospital", Bulletin of the Menniger Clinic (53)(1): 31-43.

Chin, Ko-lin
1990 "Chinese Gangs and Extortion", pp. 129-145 in C. Ronald Huff (Ed.), Gangs in America, Newbury Park, CA: Sage Publications.

Cloward, Richard A. and Lloyd E. Ohlin
1960 Delinquency and Opportunity. New York: Free Press.

Cohen, Albert K
1955 Delinquent Boys: The Culture of the Gang. Glencoe, IL: The Free Press.

Fagan, Jeffrey
1990 "Social Processes of Delinquency and Drug Use Among Urban Gangs", pp. 183-222 in C. Ronald Huff (Ed.), Gangs in America, Newbury Park, CA: Sage Publications.

Gardner, Robert W., et al
1989 "Asian Americans: Growth, Change, and Diversity", Population Bulletin (40)(4)(Feb).

Goldstein, H.S
1986 "Conduct Problems, Parental Supervision, and Cognitive Development of 12- to 17-year Olds", Psychological Reports (59)(2-I): 651-658.

Graham, J
1986 "Schools and Delinquency", Home Office Research and Planning Unit Research Bulletin (21): 21-25.

Hochhaus, Craig and Frank Sousa
    1987 "Why Children Belong to Gangs: A Comparsion of Expectations and
    Reality", High School Journal (71)(2)(Dec): 74-77.

IAACI News
    1992 Newsletter for Law Enforcement on Asian Gangs, International
    Association of Asian Crime Investigators, P.O. Box 7221, Falls Church, VA
    22046.

James, W.H
    1957 Internal Versus External Control of Reinforcement as a Basic
    Variable in Learning Theory. Ohio State University, Ph.D. dissertation.

Knox, George W.; David Laske; and Edward Tromanhauser
    1992 Schools Under Siege: An Interdisciplinary Study of Drugs, Crime, and
    Violence in the Modern American School. Dubuque, IA: Kendall-Hunt.

Loeber, R., et al
    1989 "Continuity and Desistance in Disruptive Boys' Early Fighting at
    School", Development and Psychopathology (1)(1): 39-50.

Mok, Bong Ho
    1990 "Community Care for Delinquent Youth: The Chinese Approach of
    Rehabilitating the Young Offenders", Journal of Offender Counseling,
    Services & Rehabilitation (15)(2): 5-20.

Morash, Merry
    1983 "Gangs, Groups and Delinquency", British Journal of Criminology
    (23)(4)(Oct): 309-335.

Peiar, J
    1985 "School as a Mechanism of Social Control", Revija za Kriminalistiko
    in Kriminologijo (36)(4): 318-329.

Rosenbaum, Dennis P. and Jane A. Grant
    1983 Gangs and Youth Problems in Evanston: Research Findings and
    Policy Options. Center for Urban Affairs and Policy Research, Northwest-
    ern University (July 22).

Rosenberg, M
    1965 Society and the Adolescent Self-Image. Princeton, N.J.: Princeton
    University Press.

Sanchez-Jankowski, Martin
    1991 Islands in the Street. Berkeley, CA: University of California Press.

Schwartz, Audrey J
    1989 "Middle-Class Educational Values Among Latino Gang Members in
    East Los Angeles County High Schools", Urban Education (24)(3)(Oct):
    323-342.

Shaw, Clifford R. and Henry D. Mc Kay
1942 Juvenile Delinquency and Urban Areas. Chicago: University of Chicago Press.

Sherer, Moshe
1990 "Criminal Activity Among Jewish and Arab Youth in Israel", International Journal of Intercultural Relations (14)(4): 529-548.

Short, James F. and Fred L. Strodtbeck
1965 Group Process and Gang Delinquency. Chicago: University of Chicago Press.

Spergel, Irving A. and G. David Curry
1990 Differential Patterns of Gang Involvement Among Hispanic and Black Adolescent Males: Promise For Prevention. School of Social Service Administration, University of Chicago.

Stinchecombe, Arthur L
1964 Rebellion in a High School. Chicago: Quadrangle Books.

Takata, Susan R. and Richard G. Zevitz
1990 "Divergent Perceptions of Group Delinquency in a Midwestern Community: Racine's Gang Problem", Youth and Society (21)(3)(Mar): 282-305.

Thompson, David W. and Leonard A. Jason
1988 "Street Gangs and Preventive Interventions", Criminal Justice and Behavior (15)(3)(Sept): 323-333.

Thrasher, Frederick M
1927 The Gang. Chicago: University of Chicago Press.

Tromanhauser, Edward
1981 The Chicago Safe School Study. Chicago, IL: Chicago Board of Education. August.

Truckenmiller, James L
1983 Predicting Gang Fight Participation in a General Youth Sample Via the HEW Youth Development Model's Community Program Impact Scales, Age, and Sex.

Vigil, James Diego and Steve Chong Yun
1990 "Vietnamese Youth Gangs in Southern California", pp. 146-162 in C. Ronald Huff (Ed.), Gangs in America, Newbury Park, CA: Sage Publications.

Winfree, L. Thomas; Teresa Vigil; and G. Larry Mays
1991 "Social Learning Theory and Youth Gangs: A Comparison of High School Students and Adjudicated Delinquents", paper presented at the Annual Meeting of the American Society of Criminology, San Francisco, CA.

Yablonsky, Lewis
    1962 The Violent Gang. New York: MacMillan.

Yan, Wenfan and Eugene L. Gaier
    1991 "Causal Attributions for College Success and Failure: An American-
    Asian Comparison", paper presented at the Annual Meeting of the American
    Educational Research Association, Chicago, IL (Apr).

FIGURE 17

RANK ORDERED LISTING OF MOST FREQUENTLY LISTED
GANG NAMES ACTIVE IN SCHOOLS ATTENDED BY ASIAN STUDENTS

Hawaii Gang Names:
Bloods
Crips
Tongan Crip Gang (T.C.G.)[k]
No Guts, No Glory
H.H.B.
Delta
Tao-Gama
Gamol
Baung Gang
Akuat (Akyat) Bahau (Bahay) Gang
Scorpios; Scorpians
Central Bloods
Upcountry Boys
Cross Sons
P.S.I.
Crazy Samoan Warriors (AKA Warriors)
Sons of Samoans
Peace Makers
Hawaiian Boys
Baja Gang
F.O.B. (Fresh Off the Boat)
C.I.A. (Criminals in Action)
Lahaina Mob Squad
Hydros
Homeboys
Boys from the Darkside
Jkalihi Valley Home Girls
The Posse
B.G.C.
Lahaina Boys

---

[k] The Tongan Crips were documented in 1990, 1991 in Utah's juvenile
correctional system (see Knox, 1991 An Introduction to Gangs). The Kingdom of
Tonga population is estimated to be approximately 8 percent Morman which may be
related to the migration pattern to Utah.

H.W.A.
The S.I.
L.M.S.

Washington Gang Names:
Crips
H.T.C.G. (Hill Top Crip Gang)
O.L.B. (Original Local Boys)
O.L.G. (Original Local Gang)

Colorado Gang Names:
Born To Kill
K.P.
L.L.K.
Dojoyby
Hojing
White Dragon
Korean Dragon
Blue Dragon
C.P.
J.K.P.
C.C.K.

Maryland Gang Names:
Flying Dragons
Pythons
Wolfpack

Minnesota Gang Names:
White Tigers (W.T.'s)
Cobras
Lost Boys
Laos Boys
R.C.B.
O.C.S.

Louisiana Gang Names:
Dragons

CHAPTER 19

THE FAMILY AND THE GANG

INTRODUCTION

When a member of a Crip gang greets a fellow member he calls him "Cuz", meaning cousin. Just as Blood gang members call each other Blood, as in family blood. Is it just a put-on, a thin veneer of friendly language that disguises a pattern of ruthless competition among and between gangs and gang members, or do some gangs actually function like a surrogate family? As a primary agency of socialization, the family as a social institution has a crucial role to play in understanding gangs. Reid (1990: p. 84) suggests that males and females join gangs for essentially the same reason, that is "to find a sense of belonging that they have not otherwise found". This would suggest that the family and other institutions are not functioning at such an optimal level to provide an attractive form of belonging for America's young gang members. Therefore, it is important to focus on the family in relationship to the gang for this and other reasons.

Emerging national data, to quote from preliminary results of the author's law enforcement survey discussed in a later chapter, shows that among police chiefs nationwide 73.2 percent agree that parents are to blame for the gang membership of their children. Nearly all agree that the family is an important agency that can be used to prevent gang affiliation. And when asked to choose who has the primary responsibility for dealing with gangs among five options (family, religious institutions, businesses, schools, local law enforcement), about half of the police chiefs designate the family. We clearly need to know more about the family factor.

As gang affiliation is high among prison and jail inmates, and as felons in state and local custody tend to reflect the same socio-economic and community background as gang members, our knowledge of this inmate population has some bearing on gang members as well. Interviewing family members is also a way to better understand the social world of the individual gang member[1]. It is relevant to consider any family factors that are related to crime. This also represents a knowledge development need in terms of gang research. Some findings like Jeffrey Fagan's (in Huff, 1990) show measures of family integration having less impact than the role played by substance abuse. But the effect is as theoretically expected: the higher the family integration, the lower the gang problem. But not everyone agrees that the family matters regarding gangs, for example Sanchez-Jankowski[2] (1991) observed in his fieldwork with gang members that their family situations were like anyone else's: they did not all come from bad or dysfunctional families. Obviously a great need exists for more hard data on the relationship if any of family factors to gang problems. Some new research findings are therefore presented in this chapter.

FAMILY AS THE FIRST LINE OF DEFENSE

When the family provides for all the basic human needs of American youths, then we can safely say that the influence on youthful behavior from other sources such as the community will be negligible. But when the family does not provide for all of the needs of its children, as Wrobleski and Hess (1987: p. 75) point out, this weight of responsibility will have to be carried elsewhere to produce good citizenship, and if this burden of citizenship training is not taken up, then what we can look forward to is a greater probability of gang problems.

GANG DISATTACHMENT THROUGH MARRIAGE

Several authors in the gang literature have referred to the transition from youth to adulthood represented by entering into marriage as a common means by which a gang member severs his ties to the gang organization (Denisoff and McCaghy, 1973: p. 153). According to this argument marriage can be looked upon as a legitimate social commitment and as a means of avoiding gang life. But again, there is little hard data on this topic.[3] Secondly, this would seem to apply mostly to those gangs at the lower end of the organizational development spectrum. Thirdly, if a gang member marries someone from within the gang social network, then we are not at all necessarily in the context of disjoining the gang, but could, like the data from India's gangs (Sleeman, 1849), be in the position of producing gang members from the family institution itself.

Marriage, then, is seen as the epitome of the transition from youth to adulthood; and somehow signals the end of gang affiliation. This has been, admittedly, a common theme of earlier works on gangs; but may not adequately represent contemporary standards of gang affiliation. But if it did, then we have at least the element of a viable gang intervention strategy: help these offenders "settle down" and raise a family, to drop their flag and give up gang life.

But again, before anyone interprets this as advocating a marriage matchmaking program for gang members, let it be pointed out that absolutely no experimental data has been yet reported on this matter supportive of such a position.

One thing is known: the more a gang member marries into the same social network that constitutes the gang social organization, the stronger the commitment is to be expected to the gang; and it can often mean raising offspring as gang members (see Sleeman, 1849). In the more sophisticated gang organizations it is not possible to simply say "I quit", or "hey homes, I'm married now...I don't have time to gangbang". Only in lower level gang organizations is marrying out of the gang ever going to be a feasible option.

PARENTAL HELP WITH HOMEWORK

Knowing whether or not parents or extended family adults (grandmother, etc) help a student at home or encourage a student to do their school homework appears to be an important factor that significantly differentiates gang membership. The dimension of family life this measures is one of family function and family structure. It is an aspect of family structure in as much as we are presuming such parental figures are present. It is an aspect of family function because helping a child with homework is a common element of socialization and support provided by the family unit.

A sample of 552 Chicago high school students in an anonymous survey administered in the Fall of 1991 provided a way to directly test whether this family variable had any effect on gang membership. Table 41 shows the results of this test.

TABLE 41

Frequency Distribution of Whether
Parents/Grandparents Help or Encourage With School
Homework by Having Ever Joined a Gang Among A Fall
1991 Sample of Chicago High School Students

| | Ever Join A Gang? | |
	No	Yes
Does your mother, father, grandmother, etc, help you or encourage you with homework? NO	59	13
YES	411	41

Chi-square = 5.42, p = .02

Table 41 shows that the chances of ever joining a gang appear to double where the family does not provide such help or encouragement with school homework. Thus, among those students reporting that their family does provide such help with homework only 9 percent reported they had joined a gang. Yet among those students who report that their family does not provide such help with homework some 18 percent report having joined a gang. This factor of family function therefore significantly differentiates gang membership among this sample of high school students.

DO ALLOWANCES KEEP KIDS OUT OF THE GANG?

One aspect of family function for youths, particularly high school age youths, is whether or not the family provides any regular financial "allowance". In the spring of 1992 a national Asian educational association collaborated with the present author to conduct an anonymous survey of Asian students in eight states. Some of these findings about gangs are also discussed in chapter 14. Greater details on the findings from this study are described in Knox, Laske, and Tromanhauser (1992).

There are as many possible hypotheses to test in the relationship between "family" and "gang" joining behavior as there are different aspects and functions of the family. Normally, the higher the functional level of family life it is presumed that the lower will be the probability of a youth from such a family joining a gang. Thus, a family that provides an allowance for its school age children is generally assumed to be more structured or perhaps more economically advantaged. The curious finding here, at least among this sample of Asian students, is that gang membership as measured by ever joining a gang was actually higher among those students who were provided with a regular allowance from their family. This somewhat counterintuitive finding is provided in Table 42

TABLE 42

FREQUENCY DISTRIBUTION OF WHETHER FAMILY
PROVIDES A REGULAR ALLOWANCE
BY EVER JOINING A GANG
AMONG A 1992 SAMPLE OF ASIAN STUDENTS

		Ever Join a Gang?	
		No	Yes
Do you receive an allowance from your family?	No	160	8
	Yes	145	18

Chi-square = 4.50 p = .03

Table 42 shows that among those Asian students who did not receive a family allowance, some 4.7 percent also reported ever joining a gang. Yet among those receiving an allowance, some 11 percent report joining a gang. Thus, a student with an allowance appears to have a higher risk of joining a gang.

One possible explanation for this curious finding is that gangs may seek out members who can pay dues, who have expendable income on a regular basis. Because no "causality" can be proven with snapshot survey research like this, another possibility is that the "allowances" began after the youth became a gang member: as if the family could "buy back" the loyalty of their family member from the gang. Either way, this finding suggests the need for greater national quantitative research on this important issue.

WERE GANG MEMBERS EVER SEXUALLY ABUSED?

Sexual abuse is an important variable to examine in relationship to gang membership. This is not to say that in all or even most instances the perpetrator of sexual abuse of a minor is a family member, although that is a common scenario of such sex crimes. The issue here is examining sex crime victimization among juveniles to ascertain if differences exist by comparing gang members with their non-gang member counterparts.

The data source used here is described in greater detail in a later chapter. It represents an anonymous survey of confined juveniles in five states during 1991[4]. The survey did measure whether the juvenile had ever joined a gang; further males and females did not differ significantly on this variable as they often do in research on high school samples. These juveniles were confined in both short term and long term correctional institutions.

The variable measuring sexual abuse among these juveniles asked if they had ever been forced to have sex through abuse or assault. Here we can directly answer an important question not previously addressed in the literature: are gang members more likely to be sexually abused during their childhood?

Table 43 shows the effects of gang membership on having ever been sexually abused among a large sample of confined juveniles. As seen here, gang membership is not a factor that differentiates self-reports of sex abuse among confined male juveniles. That is, among confined male juvenile delinquents gang members and non-gang members report about the same levels of sexual abuse. However, among female juvenile delinquents a much different pattern emerges.

TABLE 43

Frequency Distribution of Having Ever Joined a Gang
by Having Ever Been Sexually Abused
Among Male and Female Confined Juveniles

		EVER BEEN SEXUALLY ABUSED?			
		Males		Females	
		Yes	No	Yes	No
Ever Join a Gang?	Yes	86	632	48	41
	No	87	751	46	72
		Chi-square = .99		Chi-square = 4.57	
		(p = .31, n.s.)		(p = .03)	

The sad story that begins to emerge here is the high rate of sexual abuse among those juveniles who are found in our nation's juvenile correctional system. As seen in Table 43, overall some 11.1 percent of the confined boys and an amazing 45.4 percent of the confined females report that at some time in their past they have been forced to have sex through abuse or assault! Obviously, females are significantly more likely to be sexual abuse victims.

Among the males in Table 43, no significant difference emerges in sexual abuse victimization by the factor of prior gang membership. As seen in Table 43, 11.9 percent of the confined juveniles who had ever joined a gang report such sexual abuse. This differs little from the rate of 10.3 percent among confined juveniles who never joined a gang.

The significant relationship in Table 43 is not among males, but it is among females where the sexual abuse history is shown to be significantly differentiated by gang membership. As seen in Table 43, among the confined females who have joined a gang some 53.9 percent report being previously sexually abused. Similarly, among confined females who had never joined a gang, they show a significantly lower rate of such sexual abuse (38.9%). It is the female gang member who appears in this instance to be significantly more likely to also report being sexually abused.

An important matter that cannot be solved in Table 43 is causality: which came first, the sexual abuse, or the gang membership? While age at joining a gang is a variable available in the survey data, and age at time of completing the survey is available in the survey data, the age at time of first sexual victimization would be needed to test the two rival hypotheses about sexual abuse and gang membership among females. Unfortunately this question about age at time of first sexual abuse is not a question that was included in the survey. The two rival hypotheses about sexual abuse and gang membership are as follows:

(1) Females who have been sexually abused are more likely to subsequently join a gang out of a social-psychological breakdown. The logic being that the trauma, personal outrage and anger that can be expected in the aftermath of the life of a young child abuse victim may propel or predispose such a juvenile to join a gang subculture.

(2) Females who join gangs are more likely to subsequently be sexually abused --- as is often the case in the initiation ritual that among females may involve sexual violence and sexual humiliation. The logic here is that gangs are basically composed of males in control whose sexist views of the world and other interpersonal qualities tend to ensure that females are invited and even enticed into joining a gang --- the payoff being the right to sexually conquer the female juvenile. We need only recall the infamous case from San Antonio in 1993 where female juveniles were required as a part of their gang initiation ceremony to have sex with an AIDS/HIV infected gang member.

Analytically, however, with the two variables that are available (age at time of the survey, age at time of first joining a gang) it is possible to investigate this phenomenon of sexual abuse among confined juveniles more closely in a way that has implications for the two rival hypotheses. But to begin this analysis we will need to first test whether there is any difference between males and females in terms of the age at which they joined a gang. Table 44 below provides this test.

TABLE 44

Frequency Distribution of Gender by the Age
at Time of First Joining a Gang
Among Confined Juveniles

	Age at time of first joining a gang					
	< =8	9-10	11-12	13-14	15-16	> = 17
Gender:						
Males	40	107	215	254	125	15
Females	6	12	24	36	13	1

As seen above, 47.8 percent of the males joined a gang when they were twelve years of age or less. This differs very little from the females, where 45.6 percent joined the gang at the age of twelve or under. In other words, there is no significant difference among confined juveniles in terms of the effect of gender on age at joining a gang.

This is useful to know in further investigating gang membership among the unique subpopulation of sexually abused confined juveniles.

Table 45 shows the effect of ever joining a gang on current age at time of the survey among the select population of confined female delinquents who also are sexual abuse victims. This shows an important finding: among confined juvenile sexual abuse victims, the younger the age the more likely the female is to also report having joined a gang. Among those confined juvenile sexual abuse victims who have joined a gang, 54.1 percent were less than or equal to fifteen years of age at the time of the survey. This compares to 34.7 percent among those who had never joined a gang. This is a substantial difference suggesting that gang membership among females does carry an added risk of earlier sexual abuse.

TABLE 45

Frequency Distribution of Ever Joining a Gang
By Current Age Group
Among Confined Female Sexual Abuse Victims

		Current Age	
		< = 15	> = 16
Ever Join a Gang?			
	Yes	26	22
	No	16	30

The above findings show that the younger confined juvenile sexual abuse victim is more likely to be have joined a gang. While this does shed some light on the issue, a complete testing of the rival hypotheses is not directly possible here.

FERTILITY IN RELATIONSHIP TO GANG MEMBERSHIP AMONG CONFINED JUVENILES

There is nothing that more directly gets at an important aspect of whether the complex factor we call "family" has any effect on gang membership than that of fertility itself. The fertility variable used here from the same study described above measures how many times the females have previously been pregnant and among the males how many times they have gotten someone pregnant. The important finding that emerges here is that both male and female gang members are apparently more likely to engage in sexual behavior that results in pregnancy than their non-gang member counterparts.

The other issue of fertility in relationship to gang membership as in all underage pregnancies, is the matter of children having children, and thus by physiological capability alone being prematurely catapulted into the adult role of a parent. This gets at one of the most fascinating aspects of gangs and family: how gang members raise their own children. Our data on confined juveniles, however, allows us only to test the null hypothesis that there are no differences in fertility by whether or not a juvenile has ever joined a gang.

Table 46 below shows the results of this test for confined juvenile males.

TABLE 46

Frequency Distribution of Ever Joining a Gang
by Number of Times the Male Has Gotten Someone Pregnant
Among Confined Juveniles

Ever Join a Gang?	How many times have you gotten Someone Pregnant?		
	None	Once	Twice or more
Yes	276	221	128
No	455	203	91

Chi-square = 39.9, p < .001

As seen in Table 46 above we can reject the null hypothesis that no significant difference exists with regard to this aspect of fertility in comparing male juveniles who have and who have not joined a gang. In fact, as seen in Table 46, among the non-gang joining youths, 60.7 percent have never gotten someone pregnant. For youths who have joined gangs, however, some 44.7 percent have never gotten someone pregnant. Youths reporting prior gang membership clearly have a higher likelihood of reporting that they have gotten someone pregnant.

Finally, we can examine the same issue of fertility among female confined juveniles and this test is provided in Table 47 below.

TABLE 47

Frequency Distribution of Ever Joining a Gang
by Number of Times Ever Being Pregnant
Among Confined Female Juveniles

Ever Join a Gang?	How many times have you Been Pregnant?		
	None	Once	Twice or More
Yes	48	17	23
No	72	34	14

Chi-square = 7.92, p = .01

Table 47 above shows the interesting finding that among confined females juveniles who have joined a gang, some 26.1 percent of them have been pregnant twice or more, compared to only 11.6 percent among their non-gang joining counterparts. The factor of ever joining a gang is shown to significantly differentiate the number of times these female juvenile delinquents have ever been pregnant. The trend in the data shows higher pregnancy rates among the females who have joined a gang.

SEXUAL BEHAVIOR AND GANG MEMBERSHIP AMONG CONFINED JUVENILES

The simple question about whether gang members are more promiscuous has never been quantitatively researched in the previous literature. Yet the sexual behavior of gang members represents an important domain of human behavior itself and as shown above, at least the sexual experiences of some gang members, particularly females as discussed previously, may play a prominent role in explaining some aspects of their behavior. Here we provide the first known national data on this crucial topic of sexual behavior in relationship to having ever joined a gang among confined juvenile delinquents.

The variable used here to measure sexual behavior in the 1991 survey of confined juvenile delinquents actually measures age at the time of first consensual sex. It asks how old were you the first time you willingly had sex. Let us begin this inquiry by examining Table 48 below. This shows the separate distributions for males and females on age at time of first consensual sex.

TABLE 48

Frequency and Percentage Distribution of Age At Time
of First Willingly Having Sex
Among Male and Female Confined Juveniles

	Males		Females	
	N	%	N	%
How old were you the first time you willingly had sex?				
I Never willingly had sex	65	4.1	24	11.1
Less than 12 years old	647	40.5	37	17.1
12 years old	396	24.8	50	23.1
13 years old	252	15.8	45	20.8
14 years old	145	9.1	40	18.5
15 years old	60	3.8	12	5.6
16 years old	27	1.7	6	2.8
17 or more years old	6	.4	2	.9

As seen in Table 48 above, there are some juveniles in this sample who report that they have never in their life willingly had sex with anyone. Some 4.1 percent of the males and some 11.1 percent of the females indicated that they have never willingly had sex. Thus, in order to truly evaluate the issue of consensual sex among these confined juveniles, it is useful to eliminate these persons who have never had sex or who have never willingly had sex. Table 49 below shows the adjusted distribution among males and females for age at time of first consensual sex where we have eliminated from the sample those who claim to never willingly have had sex.

TABLE 49

Frequency and Percentage Distribution of Age At Time
of First Willingly Having Sex
Among Male and Female Confined Juveniles
(Minus Those Who Claim to Never Willingly Have Had Sex)

How old were you the first time you willingly had sex?	Males N	Males %	Females N	Females %
Less than 12 years old	647	42.2	37	19.3
12 years old	396	25.8	50	26.0
13 years old	252	16.4	45	23.4
14 years old	145	9.5	40	20.8
15 years old	60	3.9	12	6.3
16 years old	27	1.8	6	3.1
17 or more years old	6	.4	2	1.0

As seen in Table 49 above, males are twice as likely as their confined juvenile female counterparts to report that they first willingly had sex before the age of twelve. Some 42.2 percent of the males and some 19.3 percent of the confined females report that they first willingly had sex before the age of twelve. What this shows is a substantial gender difference in human sexual behavior in terms of those first reporting consensual sex before the age of twelve among confined juvenile delinquents. Thus, we enter the gang membership question in relation to sexual behavior knowing this important difference does exist.

Whether gang members have sex at an earlier age than their non-gang counterparts among confined juveniles can now be directly tested. Table 50 below provides the breakdown of ever joining a gang by age at time of first willingly having sex among males, Table 51 provides the same results for females.

TABLE 50

Frequency Distribution of Ever Joining a Gang By Age of First Willingly Having Sex (Eliminating Those who Never Willingly Had Sex) Among Confined Male Juveniles

Ever Join a Gang?

	< 12	12	13	14	15	16	>=17
Yes	343	178	107	60	24	9	5
No	302	216	144	85	36	18	1

Chi-square = 20.3, p = .002

As seen in Table 50 above for males, the significant difference here is the factor of first having consensual sex before the age of twelve. Among males who have joined a gang some 47.2 percent report first willingly having sex before the age of twelve, compared to 37.6 percent among confined males who have not ever joined a gang. If we are willing to arbitrarily use the age of twelve as the point distinguishing when someone enters the period of adolescence, then gang members clearly seem to engage in more pre-adolescent consensual sexual behavior than their non-gang member counterparts in this sample of confined juvenile delinquents.

Table 51 below provides the same test what effect the variable of ever joining a gang has on the factor of human sexuality involving the age of first consensually having sex among confined female delinquents. Again, a substantial difference emerges here, but to see it we have to go one year in advance of the males and examine the percentage of females who first had sex not before the age of twelve, but on or before the age of 12.

TABLE 51

Frequency Distribution of Ever Joining a Gang By Age of First Willingly Having Sex (Eliminating Those who Never Willingly Had Sex) Among Confined Female Juveniles

Ever Join a Gang?

	< 12	12	13	14	15	16	>=17
Yes	21	28	12	14	6	1	1
No	16	22	33	26	6	4	1

As seen in Table 51 above, among females who have joined a gang some 59 percent report first having consensual sex on or before the age of twelve; compared to 35.1 percent for their counterparts who have never joined a gang. This says that female gang members are more likely than those who never joined a gang to have consensual sex at an earlier age (i.e., twelve or under). It is fair to assume that the gang as a subculture of deviance appears to accelerate deviance and risky behavior at an earlier age; it is the gang socialization and the effects this has on the individual that can be expected to propel such a person into greater difficulty and trouble.

PARENT AND OTHER ADULT GUIDANCE ABOUT AIDS AND HIV INFECTION

Generally, most would be willing to assume that the more functional family structure is one that has the capability where the parents or other adults can and do talk to the child about the risks of AIDS or HIV infection. It is not just a sex education issue. Minimally, the lines of communication as a family function, would be higher in the family that is able to have such a dialogue with a child on the dangers of AIDS and HIV infection. Here we can directly test one very limited aspect of whether kids who join gangs come from less functional or dysfunctional families than those who do not join gangs. For here we will examine the effects of ever joining a gang on the variable of whether youths from the confined juvenile sample have ever talked about AIDS or HIV infection with a parent or other adult outside of school[5].

Table 52 below shows the effects of joining a gang on this factor of family/other adult guidance about AIDS/HIV infection. The null hypothesis that there is no difference in this factor that relates to parent and other adults providing such guidance between youths who join gangs and youths who do not join gangs cannot be rejected. No significant difference emerges here for confined juvenile males.

TABLE 52
Frequency Distribution of Ever Joining a Gang By Whether
Parent or Other Adult (Outside of School) Has Ever Talked
to the Confined Male Juvenile About AIDS or HIV Infection

	Parent/Adult Talk About AIDS?		
	Yes	No	Not Sure
Ever Join a Gang?			
Yes	448	257	38
No	542	288	31

Chi-square = 2.73, p = .25 (n.s.)

Similarly, no significant difference in this factor emerged among confined female juveniles as shown in Table 53 below.

TABLE 53

Frequency Distribution of Ever Joining a Gang
By Whether Parent or Other Adult (Outside of School)
Has Ever Talked to the Confined Female Juvenile
About AIDS or HIV Infection

	Parent/Adult Talk About AIDS?		
	Yes	No	Not Sure
Ever Join a Gang?			
Yes	68	20	3
No	83	33	7

Chi-square = 1.52, p = .46 (n.s.)

In summary, virtually no difference exists among confined males with regard to this possible family function of parents or other adults talking to the youth about AIDS or HIV infection. Males who had joined a gang (60.2%) were almost identical to those who had never joined a gang (62.9%) in terms of reporting that they had in fact talked to a parent or other adult outside of school about AIDS/HIV infection. Among females a slightly higher percentage (74.7%) of the females who had joined a gang had received such talks from parents or other adults outside of school, than had their non-gang joining counterparts (67.4%); but again this is not a significant difference.

In summary, the fact that this factor of ever joining a gang fails to significantly differentiate this aspect related to family life would tend to support the contention by Sanchez-Jankowski (1991) that gang members like non-gang members are equally likely to come from good or bad, functional or dysfunctional families. This is not, however, the strongest empirical evidence for such a claim, as has been pointed out, because the other findings in this chapter would tend to vastly outweigh such an overgeneralization. The fact seems to be, yes, the family does matter. It simply depends on what we are looking at, where we are looking, and how we are looking (i.e., doing research)[6].

Another way of looking at this finding of no significant difference regarding gang joining behavior and reports of parents/adults talking about AIDS/HIV infection to them emerges when we examine more specifically the rates of sexually transmitted diseases (STD's)among juveniles who join gangs and those who do not. If those who join gangs are significantly more likely to report having been diagnosed with an STD, which would be logically consistent with the fact that early sexual activity and I.V. drug use being more prevalent among youths who join gangs, then perhaps what we have here regarding "talking about AIDS" is a greater failure among parents of gang members to monitor their behavior and to therefore adequately protect them through such counseling and guidance.

GANG MEMBERSHIP IN RELATIONSHIP TO SEXUALLY TRANSMITTED DISEASES

Do juveniles who join gangs differ from their non-gang joining counterparts in terms of whether they have ever been diagnosed as having a sexually transmitted disease? Here we can directly test this relationship using the confined juvenile sample.
The variable about STD's asked the youth whether they have ever been told by a doctor or nurse that they had a sexually transmitted disease such as genital herpes, genital warts, chlamydia, syphilis, gonorrhea, AIDs or HIV infection, including common slang terms such as "clap" and "drip".

Table 54 below provides the results of this test. As can be seen here, joining a gang significantly differentiates contracting an STD only among males. And it is the male juvenile who reports ever joining a gang who is more likely to report acquiring an STD than the juvenile who does not join a gang. However, among females no such significant difference exists with regard to gang joining behavior.

TABLE 54

Frequency Distribution of Ever Joining a Gang
By Being Diagnosed with a Sexually Transmitted Disease
Among Male and Female Confined Juveniles

	Ever Diagnoses With an S.T.D.?			
	Males		Females	
Ever Join a Gang?	Yes	No	Yes	No
Yes	123	597	32	58
No	99	739	34	86
	Chi-square = 8.80		Chi-square = 1.24	
	(p = .002)		(p = .26, n.s.)	

A closer inspection of Table 54 above shows what appears to be a much higher prevalence of sexually transmitted diseases among confined females. It is worthwhile, therefore, to examine without regard to gang membership, but more generally, whether gender is a factor that significantly differentiates STD's among these confined juveniles. For if it is, the much higher rate among females may obscure any effects of gang membership.

Table 55 below provides this test of gender by contracting STD's among confined juveniles.

TABLE 55

Frequency Distribution of Gender by Ever Being Diagnosed
With a Sexually Transmitted Disease Among Confined Juveniles

	Ever Told You Had an STD?	
GENDER:	Yes	No
Male	222 (14.1%)	1342
Female	66 (31.2%)	145
Chi-square = 39.9, p < .001		

As seen in Table 55 above, gender is very significant in differentiating the health factor of ever being diagnosed with an STD among this sample of confined juveniles. In fact, confined female juveniles are twice as likely to report having been diagnosed with an STD than their male counterparts (14.1% male vs. 31.2% female). We can probably assume --- given the gynopeia[a] of male dominated social policy making bodies like those who make the recommendations and who control the budgets --- that our national social policy on STD awareness is not proportionately balanced in

---

[a] Gynopeia in sociology means the "BLINDNESS TO FEMALE ISSUES" among males.

terms of prevention efforts in line with the vastly higher objective health care risks that apparently serious female juvenile delinquents face in comparison to their male counterparts.

It is useful, in light of this issue, to examine another variable about individual behavior and responsibility regarding sex: the use of condoms. Table 56 below shows the effects of ever joining a gang on use of condoms during the last sexual encounter among male and female confined juveniles. No significant difference emerges here[7].

TABLE 56

Frequency Distribution of Ever Joining a Gang
By Condom Use the Last Time They Willingly Had Sex
Among Male and Female Confined Juveniles
(Eliminating Those Who Never Willingly Had Sex)

	The last time you willingly had sex, did you or your partner use a condom?			
	MALES		FEMALES	
Ever join a gang?	Yes	No	Yes	No
Yes	226	497	29	54
No	273	530	28	80
	Chi-square = 1.29		Chi-square = 1.82	
	(p = .25, n.s.)		(p = .17, n.s.)	

A test was made of the gender difference, if any, on this variable of using a condom during the last time having sex; but no significant difference emerged in comparing male and female confined juveniles. Some 32.6 percent of the males and 29.6 percent of the females indicated they made use of a condom during the last time they had sex.

DO CHILDREN OF ADULT INMATES BECOME THE NEW GANG MEMBERS?

It is a tragic possibility that the large numbers of children left behind by our American prison inmates may themselves be the most likely candidates to feed gang membership.[8] All we can hope to do here is develop such a hypothesis based on the magnitude of the problem represented by incarcerating mothers and fathers and leaving behind, in our cities, large numbers of children.[9] These are children in unknown conditions of care and supervision, and presumably from the same environment as that which placed their parents in prison.[10]

The "baby boom" that fed our prisons in the 1960's and 1970's might be artificially created in terms of large numbers of children without adequate care and supervision if in fact our nation's inmates are leaving behind children whose career trajectory places them directly in line for deviance, crime, and gang affiliation. Just how serious is this problem?

The 1991 first edition of this book described statistics on the offspring of adults incarcerated in Illinois state prisons.
More than half of these Illinois prison inmates had one or more children regardless of their marital status.   Now comes the interesting work of estimating how many children in our nation have parents in prison. Any way we go, we are talking about substantial numbers of children who have parents in correctional custody.

Estimate # 1: Using as a parameter the 55 percent of IDOC inmates who report having children, under the assumption that Illinois inmates are not significantly different than others in the USA, then for the prison population alone which at this writing is approaching a million in state and federal prisons[11], we are talking about at least 550,000 inmates with children left behind in our communities.

Estimate # 2: When we adjust for the mean number of children left behind, and the additional numbers of persons in local jails, and for those incarcerated in juvenile correctional institutions, our estimate of children left behind rises to somewhere between one and one and a half million.[12]

FAMILY "MORAL PANIC" IN RELATIONSHIP TO GANG IDENTIFIERS

Just because the public is not in panic does not mean there is nothing to be panicky about. But all too often some element of hysteria regarding gang affiliation is to be found among parents in relationship to their perceptions of their own and other youths. What it also boils down to, usually, is a moral panic. The fear that our best children in the best of families have fallen into the clutches of gang organization.

The "evidence" to some parents is anything unusual, certainly earrings, different color shoe laces, language, hand signs of greetings or solidarity made to other youths, etc. Parents will know when their child is a gang member by a variety of factors other than so-called "tell tale" signs of clothing and demeanor. Arrest, carrying a weapon, tattoos, ongoing illegal income --- these are the real signs of gang involvement for youths.

In a school environment an effective gang/delinquency management specialist assigned to the school will certainly know through the grape vine who is and who is not gang affiliated. A parent need only consult their school officials and local law enforcement to ascertain the truth if they are too socially blind to determine it themselves.   Along these same lines, it may be useful to present some findings on behavioral correlates of gang affiliation.

THE GANG IS SOMETHING THE FAMILY CANNOT MOVE AWAY FROM

The idea of the contagion effect in the study of how the mass media may encourage some crimes is an idea that has also been extended to the situation of where a parent discovers a child to be a gang member and tries to relocate thinking just moving will squash the gang problem. They move, and nothing changes, but the child starts a new chapter of the gang in the new area. As explained by Laskey (1994)[13], one of the ways in which the gang problem spreads or proliferates may be unintentional in nature, resulting from the otherwise good intentions of parents. It means the parent relocates to a new area knowing their child was involved in a gang, and basically the gang gets "transplanted" to the new area. This would account for one of the many sources of what now constitutes the proliferation of gangs throughout all areas of the United States. Laskey's (1994) survey of 232 police chiefs and 25 county sheriffs in Illinois showed that 62.4 percent of the police chiefs and 60 percent of the county sheriffs reporting having seen cases of this familial transplanting of the gang problem. Thus, the old witticism may apply here having some moral implications: you can take the boy out of the country, but you can't take the country out of the boy; that is, simply moving without any change in values or orientation will not likely stop a child's gang involvement unless the child really and seriously wants "out" of the gang. When the child does not want out of the gang, moving will not change things is what this research would suggest. On the other hand, most observers would suggest that if a child does want "out", that moving would be very appropriate.

FAMILY, SELF-ESTEEM AND OTHER THEORETICAL FACTORS: Findings From A Study of a Gang Program.

Apparently there are some important attitudinal and behavioral differences when we compare gang offenders versus their non-gang affiliated offender counterparts. A common attribution to gang members is that they have low self-esteem or that self-esteem is a factor that may impact on gang behavior. Prior to adulthood, it is the family that is most responsible in terms of socialization to instill self-esteem. But among those collecting lists of "gang myths", another might be asserting that it is a myth that the self-esteem of gang members differs from that of their non-gang member counterparts[14]. If self-esteem is only important after the criminal justice process sets in, then self-esteem like other factors (e.g., family) may have sufficient variability and conditions and contexts under which it sets in, particularly in relationship to recognizing differences in the level of social organizational functioning in modern gangs, that the lower self-esteem may have no impact in some areas but much impact in others. Summarized here are some such relevant findings that were reported previously (Knox, Mc Clendon, and Garcia, 1983).

Using a community-based program for ex-offenders that provided educational services to youthful offenders below the age of 21 located in a predominantly Latino area on Chicago's westside, in a project of collaborative empiricism involving the program staff and clients, anonymous surveys were completed by N = 97 youthful offenders (16 - 21 years of age). These youths were adjudicated offenders, whose mean age of first arrest was 14.8 years of age. Two-thirds of this group are Latino and it is predominantly male.

More than half (52.6%) of these youths reported that someone in their immediate family was economically dependent on welfare benefits. Some 38 percent indicated that at least one of their siblings had also been in trouble with the law.[15] Mostly, for purposes of analysis here, it is important that 53.6 percent of these ex-offenders reported being a gang member at some time in the past. These were youths who were clearly on their way to more trouble unless they could turn their lives around. The mean number of self-reported prior arrests for this group is 14.3!

Relying on previous research which has shown the value of trying to overcome the natural reporting bias introduced when a researcher tries to obtain data on deviance from a known offender population --- that is their tendency to over report their "good" qualities and to underreport their deviance --- a number of the questions focused on not their own deviance, but the deviance of their friends. Offenders are much more likely to report the deviance of their associates than their own. Therefore, following the findings of Hardt and Peterson (1968), "friends" deviance may be a better indicator of true deviance than that which these offenders report for their "self".

Table 57 below provides some of these findings about the deviance of their associates. These four items all asked "how many of your current friends" had previously been in prison, belonged to a gang, were hustling and stealing to make a living, and who had been in trouble with the law. What all of these questions tend to measure is the extent of subcultural integration among these youths. That is, the extent to which their own social and friendship networks consist of those persons who have either an ongoing deviant lifestyle or have been labelled as deviant.

TABLE 57

PERCENTAGE DISTRIBUTION FOR SUBCULTURAL INTEGRATION FACTORS

| | Number of Current Friends | | | | | |
Type of Friend	None	One	Two	Three	Four	Five or more
Previously been in prison	19.6%	4.1%	9.3%	9.3%	4.1%	53.7%
Who belong to a gang	46.4%	1.0%	6.2%	2.1%	4.1%	40.2%
Who are hustling or stealing to make a living	31.9%	10.6%	10.6%	3.2%	2.1%	41.5%
Been in trouble with the law	11.5%	1.0%	11.5%	9.4%	4.2%	62.5%

An interesting picture emerges here from focusing on the social relationships these offenders have as seen above in Table 57. By asking these youthful offenders about their friends, not themselves, we do get a better picture of just how subculturally integrated they are. Over eighty percent reported having one or more current friends who have served time in prison. Over half (53.6%) report having one or more current friends who are gang members. Over two-thirds report having one or more current friends who are hustling or stealing to make a living. And only 11.5 percent indicated their current friends had not previously been in trouble with the law.

The severity level is the more serious finding in Table 57 above. By examining the percentage distribution for type of friend where the youthful offender responding to this survey reports having five or more such friends, gives us a higher level of subcultural integration in terms of severity. Over fifty percent report having five or more such friends who are ex-cons. About forty percent report having five or more friends who belong to a gang, as is also the case for friends who are currently hustling or stealing to make a living.

We did ask them about their own deviance, but as stated above that is not the most reliable approach given the tendency of known offenders to under report their own deviance. Some 14.7 percent said they smoke marijuana every day, 11.6 percent "a couple times a week", 29.5 percent "now and then", and 44.2 percent "little or none". Only 12.4 percent reported getting high off of any drugs other than marijuana. We also asked them about what crimes they either "committed or were involved with" during the last two month period. Obviously, these respondents generally expressed an unfavorable reaction to this item, but it still uncovered some levels of self-reported crime: armed robber - 3.2 percent; burglary - 5.3 percent; assault - 6.3 percent; theft valued over $50 - 11.6 percent; drug sales - 11.6 percent; car theft - 3.1 percent.

These youths had already completed the educational program at the time they were invited back to participate in this survey research, and 32.3 percent reported having been arrested for some offense since completing the program (less than a year). Generally, when youths such as these who have had such a history of academic and school failure are able to complete their GED's, this is known to give them a better prognosis in terms of the risk of recidivism (see Knox, 1980).

What is valuable about this research is not the recidivism, for which we have only self-report information, but rather the fact other theoretically relevant data was collected on these same youthful offenders. This data actually replicates previous research and involves attitudinal scales that can be used to analyze the strength of association with the known pattern of gang affiliation. Let me briefly describe the scales and their value.

The perceived closure in the legitimate opportunity structure scale (Short, Rivera, and Tennyson, 1965; Knox, 1978) measures the extent to which a person perceives the legitimate world (education and occupation) closed to them. That is, someone with high levels of perceived closure sees no hope for a legitimate life; they see obstacles, not opportunities. It is an attitudinal approach to the testing of differential opportunity theory (Cloward and Ohlin, 1960). Generally, previous research shows that the higher the perceived closure in legitimate opportunity the greater the likelihood of being an offender. Here we are concerned about whether this is also related to gang affiliation.

Self-concept and self-esteem are two widely known social-psychological factors that have been researched extensively among offenders. Here two such self-esteem attitudinal scales were used. This included the Rosenberg (1965) self-esteem scale and the Tennessee Self-Concept Scale. Generally, from prior research a youth with higher levels of self-esteem and a better self-concept is less likely to become an offender. Again, however, here we are not using a dependent variable of initial criminality or recidivism; instead we are examining gang affiliation patterns.

Finally, another scale called the Rundquist-Sletto Respect for the Law Scale (1936) was also used. This measure can be loosely conceived of as capturing some element of the legitimation crisis; that is, the extent to which anyone has respect for our legal institutions, police, etc.; or conversely, the extent to which they feel our legal system is corrupt and unfair at all levels. That is, under the racism-oppression thesis we would expect persons to have a very low level of respect for constituted authority, or "the system" as it were. It measures a social-political dimension; that is, one's attitude toward the status quo.

Figure 18 below summarizes the statistical results from examining these attitudinal scales in relationship to measures of gang affiliation. The statistic used here is the Pearson zero-order correlation coefficient. Its meaning can be summarized readily. The correlation value ranges from a complete low (no association whatsoever) of zero to a complete high (perfect correlation, e.g., between life and death the Pearson correlation coefficient is 1.0) of one. The higher the value, the stronger the association.

FIGURE 18

SIGNIFICANT CORRELATIONS[b] BETWEEN SELECTED ATTITUDINAL SCALES AND MEASURES OF GANG AFFILIATION

SCALES: ****************	Pearson Correlation ***********	Measure of Gang Affiliation ******************
Perceived Closure in the legitimate opportunity structure	.19	Ever been a gang member
Rosenberg Self-esteem scale	-.12	
Tennessee Self-Concept Scale	-.19	
Tennessee Self-Concept Scale	-.19	Currently a Gang member
Perceived Closure in the legitimate opportunity structure	.41	
Rundquist and Sletto's Respect for the Law scale	-.15	Number of Current friends
Tennessee Self-Concept Scale	-.19	who are gang members
Rosenberg Self-Esteem Scale	-.21	

---

[b] Pearson zero-order correlation coefficients.

What the findings in Figure 18 above show is largely consistent. This data shows a decidedly inverse relationship between self-esteem and gang affiliation. That is, the higher the self-esteem level, the lower the likelihood of gang affiliation. Or conversely, the lower one's self-esteem or self-concept, the higher the association with gang life. Also, respect for the law varies inversely with the number of current friends who are gang members.

The magnitude of the correlation coefficient is what is also important here. While all of these relationships in Figure 18 were significant ($p < .05$), that is we expect them in terms probability to occur by chance in less than five times out of 100, we also see some large differences emerging here in what kind of gang affiliation measure we are analyzing.

When examining the gang affiliation variables of (1) have you ever been a gang member previously, and (2) are you currently a gang member, there is virtually no difference in the magnitude of the strength of the association between the three scales --- perceived closure, self-esteem, and self-concept. Only the valence or the direction of the relationship varies. Perceived closure has a positive relationship, the higher it is then the higher the gang affiliation. Both self-esteem and self-concept have consistent inverse relationships with gang affiliation.

Indeed the Rundquist and Sletto (1936) respect for the law scale is only significant in terms of its correlation with the third measure of gang affiliation --- number of current friends who are gang members. And it too, like self-esteem and self-concept shows an inverse relationship. That is, it has a negative correlation coefficient value.

Therefore, in using as our measure of gang affiliation the simple direct question to known offenders --- have you ever been or are you currently a gang member --- we see that virtually no difference emerges in terms of a higher explanatory power between the theories thought to have some relationship to gangs (opportunity theory, self-concept/self-esteem, and legitimation). In fact, it is only when we examine the more indirect measure of asking the offender about friends who are gang members, where we probably get a more accurate measure of gang affiliation as discussed earlier, that we see some important differences emerge.

In fact, looking at the last measure of gang affiliation in Figure 18 (number of current friends who are gang members) we see that the sociological theory (differential opportunity) yields a relationship that is twice as strong as any of the others. In fact, all such correlations in Figure 18 are low except for the moderately strong relationship between perceived closure and number of friends who are gang members ($r = .41$).

While the Cloward and Ohlin (1960) theory has been found to be useful for explaining generalized delinquency, just as the measure of perceived closure has been able to significantly differentiate delinquents and non-delinquents in past research, recall that their theory was explicitly directed at gang delinquency.

THE EFFECTS OF PRIOR GANG MEMBERSHIP

Recall that nearly half of these offenders self-reported that they were at some time in the past a gang member. Therefore this one variable of prior gang membership is useful in examining some other dependent variables. What this shows, with alarming consistency, is that prior gang membership for this Chicago sample of youthful offenders significantly differentiates a variety of adjustment outcomes. These results are presented in Table 58 below.

The statistic used here is the Chi-square which is a measure of independence. If it is significant, then it suggests there is some relationship between the variables. Generally, such a chi-square value is considered significant if the probability is less than .05. Meaning it would occur, by chance, in less than one time out of twenty.

TABLE 58

THE EFFECTS OF PRIOR GANG
MEMBERSHIP ON DEVIANCE MEASURES

Arrested After the Program
****

		No		Yes	
		N	%	N	%
Prior Gang Member:	NO	35	77.8	10	22.2
	YES	30	58.8	21	41.2

Chi square = 3.92, p = .04

Use of Drugs Other than
Marijuana or Alcohol
****

		No		Yes	
		N	%	N	%
Prior Gang Member:	NO	41	95.3	2	4.7
	YES	37	80.4	9	19.6

Chi square = 4.56 p = .03

Currently "Tied in" To a Gang
****

		No		Yes	
		N	%	N	%
Prior Gang Member:	NO	44	97.8	1	2.2
	YES	39	75.0	13	25.0

Chi square = 10.13 p = .001

One or More Friends Who Are
Hustling/Stealing for a Living
****

		No		Yes	
		N	%	N	%
Prior Gang Member:	NO	21	47.7	23	52.3
	YES	9	18.0	41	82.0

Chi square = 9.51 p = .002

As seen in Table 58 above, this single factor of prior gang membership significantly differentiates four different measures of deviance among youthful offenders. This includes whether they report being arrested after completing a community-based literacy program, whether they report getting high off of drugs other than marijuana or alcohol, whether they have a current "tie in" with any gang, and whether they report one or more friends who are currently hustling or stealing to make a living.

As also revealed in Table 58, there appears to be a minimum risk of bringing such gang and nongang offenders together in a collective treatment setting. Only one person is shown to have reported no prior gang membership but has some current "tie in" to a gang.

In the interest of ethically disclosing all known findings some other results should also be summarized here. Data was also collected on the number of program hours each such offender spent in the program. Apparently, the program was reimbursed on such an hourly treatment basis as is customary in aftercare performance contracts for such counseling and assistance. This yielded the intriguing result that those who were prior gang members had an average of 20 more hours enrolled in the program than non-gang members. This amounted to a mean of 138 hours for prior gang members compared to 118 for those without prior gang membership.

There was also a significant difference found for age of first arrest. Prior gang members showed a mean age at first arrest of 13.9 years compared to 15.9 for those who were not prior gang members. Clearly, two full years difference!

SUMMARY

In the best of all worlds, the family as an agency of socialization and informal social control would be the best "first line of defense" against the gang problem. But dysfunctional families do exist, even more families experience enormous economic stress or feel the effects of residential segregation and failing relationships to other mainstream social institutions --- and these families might theoretically be expected to be less effectively instill in their youths an internal "buffer" against joining a gang. Fatalism is not an attitude we can simply change and expect the problem to go away. But fatalistic outlooks on life could reasonable be expected among families of some gang members, particularly those who lost loved ones to gang violence.

There is a need for more hard and quantifiable data on gangs in relationship to the family and the many factors involved with what we regard as "family". More often than not it is the family of the gang member that comes to suffer the effects of gang violence.[16] The family of orientation is usually what most of the gang literature issues have dealt with to date: the issue being that maybe some family conditions may be associated with a higher likelihood of ever joining a gang. But the family of procreation for anyone who has joined a gang is also a highly relevant area of much needed research, as basically very little is currently known based on any systematic national objective approach. It is a matter of civil rights: children have rights to live free from ongoing physical or mental abuse from their parents or the risks to personal harm that they may pose; and thus some civil libertarian could theoretically argue that raising a child to be a gang member by parents who are members of the same gang could be construed legally as child abuse: thus, such parents could forfeit their parental rights, and the state could take custody of their children as wards of the court, or put them up for adoption. No one knows how many children have ever been raised to be gang members. That and many other "unknowns" tends to describe the rather elementary stage of development yet attained by gang research in criminology today.

What we do know is that it would be comparable to dogmatism to say that the family does not matter in terms of gangs, gang members, or gang problems, because the family means so much: all its relationships, its functions, its structure and the variations in between. So this chapter has shown that some family variables do matter in relation to gang membership. It is therefore useful to enlist parents in the goal of gang prevention initiatives[17].

One of the haunting questions in the gang literature is whether we, as a society, tend to systematically reproduce new gang members when their parents are placed in prison.[18] Very large numbers of children are simply left behind.

We have examined several different research projects dealing with gangs that involved family issues and factors. Most of the research shows that having ever joined a gang was a significant variable in relationship to a variety of family variables. However, from a social science point of view, the causality issue is one that is not likely to be resolved easily.

DISCUSSION QUESTIONS

(1) From a position of economic comfort it is easy to say the family should be primarily responsible for preventing gang affiliation. But what of those families living in poverty? And under economic distress? Can such families really be expected to exercise social control over members whose activities or behavior results in economic benefit to other family members and parents?

(2) Should there be a modernized "Fagin" law, to make it a felony to encourage or cultivate law violation among ones own children or for whom one is a legal guardian, where benefiting economically from their known or assumed illicit activity would be sufficient grounds for conviction?

416 AN INTRODUCTION TO GANGS

(3)   Why would marriage be more likely to be a route out of the gang for lower level gang formations (level zero and level one) as opposed to higher level gang formations (level two and level three)? Should teacher and parent "gang awareness" training be provided by the federal government nationally?

RECOMMENDED READINGS

Adams, Paul L. and Jeffrey H. Horovitz
    1980 "Psychopathology and Fatherlessness in Poor Boys", Child Psychiatry and Human Development (Spr)(10)(3): 135-143.

Allen, Walter R
    1979 "Class, Culture and Family Organization: The Effects of Class and Race on Family Structure in Urban America", Journal of Comparative Family Studies (10)(3): 301-313.

Alston, Doris N. and Nannette Williams
    1982 "Relationship Between Father Absence and Self-Concept of Black Adolescent Boys", Journal of Negro Education (Spr)(51)(2): 134-138.

Ansari, Anwar and Bharati Ghose
    1957 "A Study of Family Attitudes of Children with Contrasting Socio-Economic Background", Educ. Psychol. Delhi. (4)(2): 90-102.

Aronus, Sidney
    1970 The Black Middle Class. Columbus, OH: Charles E. Merrill Co.

Ball, Richard E
    1983 "Family and Friends: A Supportive Network for Low-Income American Black Families", Journal of Comparative Family Studies (Spr)(14)-(1): 51-65.

Billingsley, Andrew
    1974 Black Families and the Struggle for Survival. New York: Friendship Press.

Brodsky, S.L
    1975 Families and Friends of Men in Prison: The Uncertain Relationship. Toronto: Lexington Books.

Brodsky, Stanley L. and H. O'Neal Smitherman
    1983 Handbook of Scales for Research in Crime and Delinquency. New York: Plenum Press.

Brown, Waln K
    1978 "Black Gangs as Family Extensions", International Journal of Offender Therapy and Comparative Criminology (22)(1): 39-48.

Brooks, William Allan
    1952 Girl Gangs. New York: Padell Book Company.

Bullard, Robert D
1984 "The Black Family Housing Alternatives in the 1980's", Journal of Black Studies (14)(3)(Mar): 341-351.

Burgess, Ernest
1928 The Prediction of Marriage. University of Chicago Press.

Campbell, Anne C
1980 "Friendship as a Factor in Male and Female Delinquency", in Hugh C. Foot, Anthony J. Chapman, and Jean R. Smith (Eds.), Friendship and Social Relations in Children, New York: Wiley.

Chapman, J.R
1980 Economic Realities and Female Crime. Lexington Books.

Cherlin, Andrew and Shiro Horiuchi
1980 "Retrospective Reports of Family Structure: A Methodological Assessment", Sociological Methods and Research (May)(8)(4): 454-469.

Coleman, Marilyn, et al
1985 "Family Structure and Dating Behavior of Adolescents", Adolescence (Fall)(20)(79): 537-543.

Cosby, Bill
1986 Fatherhood. Garden City, NY: Doubleday.

Curtis, R., W.J. Crow, L.A. Zurcher, and A.V. Connett
1973 Paroled But Not Free: Ex-Offenders Look at What They Need to Make it Outside. New York: Human Sciences Press.

Daly, Martin and Margo Wilson
1985 "Child Abuse and Other Risks of Not Living With Both Parents", Ethology and Sociobiology (6)(4): 197-210.

Daniel, Jessica H., et al
1983 "Child Abuse and Accidents in Black Families: A Controlled Comparative Study", Journal of Orthopsychiatry (Oct)(53)(4): 645-653.

de Anda, Diane
1984 "Bicultural Socialization: Factors Affecting the Minority Experience", Social Work (Mar)(29)(2): 101-107.

Dobash, Russell P.; R. Emerson Dobash, and Sue Gutteridge
1986 The Imprisonment of Women. New York: Basil Blackwell, Inc.

Dornbusch, Sanford M., et al
1985 "Single Parents, Extended Households, and the Control of Adolescents", Child Development (Apr)(56)(2): 326-41.

Drake, St. Claire and Horace R. Cayton
    1945 Black Metropolis: A Study of Negro Life in a Northern City. New
    York: Harcourt, Brace, Inc.

Dressler, William W
    1985 "Extended Family Relationships, Social Support, and Mental Health
    in a Southern Black Community", Journal of Health and Social Behavior
    (Mar)(26)(1): 39-48.

Duguid, S
    1981 "Prison Education and Criminal Choice: The Context of Decision-
    Making", Canadian Journal of Criminology (23)(4): 421-438.

Dunbar, Ellen A
    1963 "How to Help the Gang Member Through His Family", Special Service
    For Groups, Los Angeles: Unpublished.

Duncan, Otis Dudley and Beverly Duncan
    1957 The Negro Population of Chicago: A Study of Residential Succession.
    Chicago: University of Chicago Press.

Edelman, Marian Wright
    1987 Families in Peril. An Agenda for Social Change. Harvard University
    Press.

Edwards, Ozzie L
    1982 "Family Formation Among Black Youth", Journal of Negro Education
    (Spr)(51)(2): 111-122.

Ekland-Olson, Sheldon, et al
    1983 "Postrelease Depression and the Importance of Familial Support",
    Criminology (May)(21)(2): 253-275.

Fishman, S. and A.S. Alissi
    1979 "Strengthening Families as Natural Support Systems for Offenders",
    Federal Probation (43): 16-21.

Fogel, Robert William and Stanley L. Engerman
    1974 Time on the Cross: The Economics of American Negro Slavery.
    Boston: Little, Brown and Co.

Gibbs, C
    1971 "The Effect of the Imprisonment of Women Upon Their Children",
    British Journal of Criminology (11).

Gray, Susan W. and Kristi Ruttle
    1980 "The Family-Oriented Home Visiting Program: A Longitudinal Study",
    Genetic Psychology Monographs (Nov)(102)(2): 299-316.

Griffith, Ezra, et al
1984 "An Analysis of the Therapeutic Elements in a Black Church Service", Hospital and Community Psychiatry (May)(35)(5): 464-469.

Harrison-Ross, Phillis and Barbara Wyden
1973 The Black Child -- A Parent's Guide. New York: Peter H. Wyden, Inc. Publisher.

Heiss, Jerold
1975 The Case of the Black Family: A Sociological Inquiry. New York: Columbia University Press.

Hill, Robert B
1972 The Strengths of Black Families. New York: Emerson Hall Publishers, Inc.

1975. Black Families in the 1974-75 Depression: Special Policy Report. New York: National Urban League.

Hindelang, Michael J
1973 "Causes of Delinquency: A Partial Replication and Extension", Social Problems (Spr)(20): 471-487.

Hirschi, Travis
1969 Causes of Delinquency. Berkeley: University of California Press.

Holt, N. and D. Miller
1972 "Explorations in Inmate-Family Relationships", California Department of Corrections, Report No. 46.

Homer, E.L
1969 "Inmate-Family Ties: Desirable But Difficult", Federal Probation (43): 47-52.

Jensen, Gary F. and David Brownfield
1983 "Parents and Drugs", Criminology (Nov)(21)(4): 543-54.

Klaus, Patsy A. and Michael R. Rand
1984 Family Violence. Bureau of Justice Statistics. Special Report.

Kriesberg, Louis
1970 Mothers in Poverty. Chicago: Aldine Publishing Co.

Lee, Laura J
1983 "Reducing Black Adolescent's Drug Use: Family Revisited", Child and Youth Services (Spr)(6)(1-2): 57-69.

Leslie, Gerald R
1973 The Family in Social Context. New York: Oxford University Press.

Liebow, Elliot
1970 "Attitudes Toward Marriage and Family Among Black Males in Tally's Corner", Milbank Memorial Fund Quarterly (Apr)(48)(2): 151-167.

Liker, J.K
1980 "Nobody Knows the Troubles I've Seen: Post-Release Burdens on the Families of the Transitional Aid Research Project", pp. 299-317 in P.H. Rossi, et al (eds.), Money, Work and Crime. New York: Academic Press.

Lindblad-Goldberg, Marion and Joyce Lynn Dukes
1985 "Social Support in Black, Low-Income, Single-Parent, Families: Normative and Dysfunctional Patterns", American OrthoPsychiatric Association: 42-56.

Linden, Eric and James C. Hackler
1973 "Affective Ties and Delinquency", Pacific Sociological Review (16): 27-46.

Linden, R.; L. Perry; D. Ayers; and T.A. Parlett
1984 "An Evaluation of a Prison Education Program", Canadian Journal of Criminology (26)(1): 65-73.

Lyman, Stanford M
1972 The Black American in Sociological Thought. New York: G.P. Putnam and Sons.

Malson, Michelene Ridley
1983 "Black Families and Childrearing Support Networks", Research in the Interweave of Social Roles (Jan)(44): 76-85.

Mannino, F.V. and M.F. Shore
1974 "Family Structure, Aftercare and Post-Hospital Adjustment", American Journal of Orthopsychiatry (Jan)(44): 76-85.

McAdoo, Harriette
1977 "A Review of the Literature Related to Family Therapy in the Black Community", Journal of Contemporary Psychotherapy (Sum)(9)(1): 15-19.

McCullum, S.G
1977 "What Works. A Look at Effective Correctional Education and Training Experiences", Federal Probation (41)92): 32-35.

McCord, J.; W. McCord; and P. Verden
1962 "Familial and Behavioral Correlates of Dependency in Male Children", Child Development (33): 313-326.

McCord, J.; W. McCord; and E. Thurber
1962 "Some Effects of Parental Absence on Male Children", Journal of Abnormal and Social Psychology (64): 361-69.

McCord, J
1979 "Consideration of the Impact of Parental Behavior on Subsequent Criminality", paper presented at the American Sociological Association, annual meeting.

McCord, W. and J. McCord
1959 Origins of Crime: A New Evaluation of the Cambridge-Somerville Study. New York: Columbia University Press.

McCord, William, et al
1969 Life Styles in the Black Ghetto. New York: W.W. Norton and Company, Inc.

McCubbin, H.I.; B.D. Dahl; G.R. Lester; and B.D. Ross
1975 "The Returned Prisoner of War: Factors in Family Reintegration", Journal of Marriage and the Family (Aug)(37): 471-478.

McLanahan, Sara S
1983 "Family Structure and Stress: A Longitudinal Comparison of Two-Parent and Female-Headed Families", Journal of Marriage and the Family (May)(45)(2): 347-357.

Minor, W.W. and M. Courlander
1969 "The Post-Release Trauma Thesis: A Reconsideration of the Rise of Early Parole Failure", Journal of Research in Crime and Delinquency (16)(July): 273-293.

Moore, Helen B
1982 "Motivating Black Learners to Excel", Journal of Negro Education (Spr)(51)(2): 139-146.

Morris, P
1965 Prisoners and Their Families. London: Allen and Unwin.

Mullin, James B
1973 "Birth Order as a Variable of Probation Performance", Journal of Research in Crime and Delinquency (Jan)(10)(1): 29-34.

Norman-Jackson, Jacquelyn
1982 "Family Interactions, Language Development, and Primary Reading Achievement of Black Children in Families of Low Income", Child Development (Apr)(53)(2): 349-58.

Patalano, Frank
1977 "Height on the Draw-A-Person: Comparison of Figure Drawings of Black and White Male Drug Abusers", Perceptual and Motor Skills (Jun)(44)(3,2): 1187-1190.

Pederson, Frank A., et al
1979 "Infant Development in Father-Absent Families", Journal of Genetic Psychology (Sept)(135)(1): 51-61.

Petty, Douglas and George A. Robinson
    1982 "Common Philosophical Themes in the Oral History and TCB Content of Four Black Octogenarians", Journal of Non-White Concerns in Personnel and Guidance (Jan)(10)(2): 57-63.

Poussaint, Alvin F
    1972 Why Blacks Kill Blacks. New York: Emerson Hall Publishers, Inc.

Queen, Stuart A. and Robert W. Haberstein
    1974 The Family in Various Cultures. New York: J.B. Lippincott Co.

Rainwater, Lee
    1970 Behind the Ghetto Walls: Black Families in a Federal Slum. Chicago: Aldine Publishing Co.

Robins, Lee; Patricia A. West; and Barbara L. Herjanic
    1975 "Arrests and Delinquency in Two Generations: A Study of Black Urban Families and Their Children", Journal of Child Psychology and Psychiatry (16): 125-140.

Robinson, Ira E., et al
    1985 "Self-Perception of the Husband/Father in the Lower Class Black Family", Phylon (Jun)(46)(2): 136-147.

Ross, Arthur M. and Herbert Hill (eds.)
    1967 Employment, Race, and Poverty. New York: Harcourt, Brace and World, Inc.

Sager, Clifford J., et al
    1970 Black Ghetto Family in Therapy: A Laboratory Experience. New York: Grove Press, Inc.

Scanzoni, John H
    1971 The Black Family in Modern Society. Boston: Allyn and Bacon, Inc.

Schaefer, Earl S
    1965 "Childrens Reports of Parental Behaviors: An Inventory", Child Development (36): 413-424.

Schneller, D.P
    1975 "Prisoner's Families: A Study of Some Social and Psychological Effects of Incarceration on the Families of Negro Prisoners", Criminology (12)-(Nov): 402-412.

    1975 "Some Social and Psychological Effects of Incarceration on Families of Negro Inmates", American Journal of Corrections 29-33.

Silvers, Steven B., et al
    1984 "The Role of Racial Identity Constancy on Children's Perceptions", Journal of Social Psychology (Apr)(122)(2): 223-226.

Schultz, David A
1969 Coming Up Black: Patterns of Ghetto Socialization. Englewood Cliffs, NJ: Prentice-Hall, Inc.

Spain, Johnny
1972 "The Black Family and the Prisons", The Black Scholar (4)(Oct): 2-

Staples, Robert
1971 The Black Family: Essays and Studies. Belmont, CA: Wadsworth Publishing Co.

1971 "Towards a Sociology of the Black Family: A Theoretical and Methodological Assessment", Journal of Marriage and the Family (Feb)(33)(1): 119-138. 1973. The Black Woman in America: Sex, Marriage, and the Family. Chicago: Nelson-Hall Publishers.

Stack, Carol B
1974 All Our Kin: Strategies for Survival in a Black Community. New York: Harper and Row.

Steelman, Lala C. and John T. Doby
1983 "Family Size and Birth Order as Factors on the IQ Performance of Black and White Children", Sociology of Education (Apr)(56)(2): 101-109.

Studt, E
1967 The Re-Entry of the Offender Into the Community. Washington, D.C.: Government Printing Office.

TenHouten, Warren
1970 "The Black Family: Myth and Reality", Psychiatry (33)(2)(May): 145-173.

Willie, Charles V. and Susan L. Greenblatt
1978 "Four 'Classic' Studies of Power Relationships in Black Families: A Review and Look to the Future", Journal of Marriage and the Family (Nov)(40)(4): 691-694.

Wilson, James Q. and Richard J. Herrnstein
1985 Crime and Human Nature. Chapter on the Family. New York: Simon and Schuster.

West, Donald J
1982 Delinquency: Its Roots, Careers and Prospects. Cambridge: Harvard University Press.

Wilson, Melvin N
1986. "The Black Extended Family: An Analytical Consideration", Developmental Psychology (Mar)(22)(2): 246-258.

FOOTNOTES

1. One exception to this is the brief, but directly focused, oral history data reported by Taylor (1990: pp. 62-65). This data by Taylor involved an approach similar to the original work by Shaw and Mc Kay's case study method involving interviews with family members and what they had to say about a family member who was involved with the gang.

2. Sanchez-Jankowski runs the risk of overgeneralizing from very limited data, but the iconoclastic viewpoint expressed is sure to have an overall positive effect by stimulating further research. Basically, Sanchez-Jankowski says it is a myth that gang members come from "bad families", because he found numerous cases where the family was a very functional and very nurturing one. For the record, it is not hard to find such cases.

3. In the written constitution and by-laws of the Latin Kings we find the fascinating application of what appears to be a human development life span "stage theory" authored by a well placed gang member. Here we find in the second stage, the Latin King constitution explicitly recognizing and warning against the maturation hypothesis, that is the tendency to "marry and settle down" avoiding fellow gang boys and a lowering of commitment to the gang.

4. The analysis reported here was beyond the scope of the initial project undertaken by Knox and Tromanhauser (1991) and which is reported elsewhere (Knox, Laske, and Tromanhauser, 1992). Thus, the analysis of sexual abuse and fertility in relationship to gang membership by gender is new and additional analysis. Because this occurred well after the project completion, which had a data submission deadline, and because additional data did in fact "come in", the sample size used here reflects N = 1,844 confined juveniles.

5. The important methodological limitation that must be pointed out here is that many juvenile correctional institutions now routinely provide AIDS and HIV "awareness" information to the youths entering these facilities. Thus, in the analysis that follows, the validity of the findings must take account of this potential confounding influence from "other adults outside of school" who could potentially include correctional staff!

6. The technique used by Sanchez-Jankowski (1991) relied apparently only on the reports of gang members themselves, and did not involve a validity check by actually assessing the family situation of said gang members. The more recent research by Scott Decker and his colleagues in St. Louis, Missouri provides a more rigorous research method: where both the gang member and his/her family members and parents are interviewed.

7. The results may have been different if the question specifically ruled out all sexual activity that might occur inside the juvenile correctional institution (i.e., homosexuality). The fact is, we cannot rule this out. The question did not specifically say: prior to coming to this institution, the last time you willingly had sex did you or your

partner use a condom. The last time, for some unknown number of them, may have been inside the institution in which they resided at the time of the survey.

8. Spergel states that "male offspring may also follow in their father's or uncle's footsteps as gang fighters" (Spergel, 1984: p. 220).

9. Jackson and McBride (1990: p. 11) discussed families with gang lineage and stated that "in these cases the parents are usually graduates from gangs themselves and see little wrong with their children belonging to gangs. In fact, such parents often encourage their children to belong".

10. Johnstone (1981) in describing suburban gangs points to this factor of absent parents or single-parent families as being important.

11. See Jackson, et al, (1989, p. 120). Ronald W. Jackson, Edward E. Rhine, And William R. Smith, 1989 "Prison Overcrowding: A Police Challenge for Parole", Corrections Today (Aug.): 118,120, 122-123.

12. In a recent nationwide sample of inmates in American prisons Wright and Rossi (1985) reported that 62 percent of the male inmates had fathered a child.

13. "The Familial Gang Transplant Phenomenon", paper presented by John A. Laskey, Morton College, at the Annual Meeting of the Academy of Criminal Justice Sciences, Chicago, IL, 1994. See also: The 1994 Survey of Illinois Police Chiefs and County Sheriffs by the National Gang Crime Research Center.

14. See Knox, Laske, and Tromanhauser (1992) for where self-esteem as a variable was not really different in comparing gang members with non-gang members among high school students.

15. Percent of siblings with juvenile court records was also a very significant variable that differentiated gang and non-gang members in the research reported by Zatz (1985).

16. The case of the young Korean student, Jeanin Earl Ghim (age 17), is a case in point. He joins a Chicago-area gang, tries to quit without his violation, and the gang busted into his parents house one night looking for him, and not finding him, they killed his mother and shot his father and sister. See: Philip J. O'Connor and Lee Bey, "Gang Member's Family Shot In Surburban Home Invasion", Chicago Sun-Times, Apr. 7, 1994, p. 1, 26.

17. The McGruff headquarters has recently offered a kit for $24.95 on "Tools To Involve Parents in Gang Prevention". This is not a product endorsement, but simply an acknowledgement that such materials are now being produced under the assumption --- a good assumption from the present review --- that the family CAN do something about the gang problem.

18. Campbell (1990: p. 182) quoting Hagedorn and Moore states that among gang girls "94% will go on to have children, and 84% will raise them without spouses"

CHAPTER 20

THE COMMUNITY'S ROLE IN DEALING WITH GANGS

INTRODUCTION

The last defense against gang crime is the community itself if we cannot rely on the family as an effective agency of socialization. It may also be the best defense. This chapter will examine those practical measures such as program initiatives that can be undertaken by community groups as well as community-development strategies. Further and more detailed issues about gang programs --- particularly what not to do --- are also reviewed in a later chapter.

The experience with gangs and the community has often led to a recurring and common situation found in many of our communities. It is the complaint about gang crime as if it were a problem of "outsiders". More often than not it is not outsiders. They are not monsters from another galaxy. We do not intentionally import gang members into the United States from abroad. These gang members are our neighbors, perhaps our relatives. They are members of our own community or local neighborhood.[1] In fact, from at least one empirical study on the issue the younger the gang member the more likely the same gang member is to live in the immediate neighborhood (Suttles, 1968: p. 168).

Since the time gangs have first been recorded they have been described as having a territorial function. Most urban gangs still do have a sense of territoriality. Or at least a cognitive map of where they are or are not "safe". This has explicit meaning for a community that wants to do something about the gang problem.[2]

THE TERRITORIAL FUNCTION OF GANGS

Since Thrasher's early work on gangs, and including gangs today at all levels, the territorial function continues in one way or another. A major difference between the gang territorial claim of today and that during the time of Thrasher is probably that today's territorial claim also has the hallmark of being a market territory (e.g., drug sales) as well in many instances. What this means is that the base of operations for gangs will continue to be in our own American communities.

A typical gang meeting in Chicago today can be of two varieties: a regularly scheduled weekly meeting, or a special emergency meeting. In either case, the meeting is usually held in someone's home and in the same community area of its territorial claim. It will include the use of at least one fellow gang member who will be posted in a "security or sentry" role function to alert gang members inside of any potential outside threat (other gangs, police, etc).

Sadly, in some of our American neighborhoods the gang seems to function much more effectively and meet more regularly than do the local community organizations. To the extent that information is power, the gang meetings which facilitate the dissemination of local information to other gang members, means that from a social structural point of view we as community members are basically giving the gang more power than they deserve. Comparatively, that is. The local community organization at the neighborhood or block level that meets only infrequently if at all, and on a unpredictable basis, is one that functions as a group at a very low level of effectiveness.

Finally, there is another problem here in dealing with gangs at the very local level. Even if the neighborhood "crime watch" or related "improvement association" does meet regularly, and if it is open to all who live in the area; then what do you do when the identity of local gang members are known, along with their errant behavior patterns, and their "families" are so integrated into the same neighborhood that among many persons, any suggestion that "Johnny XXX" is a gang member engaged in crime or other destructive influences in the community brings the critical reaction "I have known the XXX family for twenty years or more, and they are good people".

Someone who has even a tenuous social tie to the XXX family will find themselves sharing in the guilt of any accusation that a member of the XXX family is a gang member. That "someone" may be the first to stand up and deny any such gang involvement with the XXX family. They may use their voice to further suggest "it is an outside problem", that is "it is not the XXX family". Which shows another variation of the "denial syndrome": it is not "our people", it is a problem of "outsiders".

In fact, often at the early stages of such anti-gang crime groups, many of the local members who join in the initiative are of the impression that these gang crimes "must have been committed by persons from outside our neighborhood",[3] when in fact, the obverse is true. That is, these offense patterns are explained often by the existence of local gang members who sense that to commit these offenses in their own "turf" gives them a higher level of protection and a reduced level of detection from law enforcement. Or, the very existence of such a gang means a rival gang may intentionally chose such an area for more serious property crimes (car theft, burglary, etc).[4]

VIDEOTAPED GANG AFFILIATION PREVENTION/AWARENESS EDUCATION

Videos such as that produced by the Ontario Police Department ("Gangs, Move 'Em Out of Your Life", 1989) can be useful educational tools for heightening community awareness of the signs of gang activity. Most community members know if they have a gang problem through the existence of pockets of "gang graffiti", and periodic gang-related crimes, most typically criminal damage to property, and thefts associated with motor vehicles (stolen radios, tires, batteries, parts, etc) or damage to vehicles in a systematic fashion (serial puncturing of tires, breaking car windows, etc).

Perhaps the best such videos are those that are locally produced. Because just as gangs are each unique as social organizational forms varying in terms of a number of such factors previously described, every neighborhood in this sense has unique gang problems. That is, some gangs are a greater threat than others. Those gangs that are represented in various jurisdictions, that cross state lines and in some instances traverse the entire country, (e.g.,Bloods, Crips, Disciples, Latin Kings,

Posse, Aryan Brotherhood, some Asian gangs, etc), and those gangs which are represented in many state correctional system, are also higher level gang formations (e.g., level three) and naturally have the capacity to be a larger crime threat. But, truly, much less is known of this more national picture. Clearly we need comparative research on gangs in America and this is one of the practical reasons for such a knowledge development strategy.

BLOCK/NEIGHBORHOOD   WATCH PROGRAMS WITH AN EMPHASIS ON GANGS

There is a axiom that takes on the status of a social law regarding the role of community members and effective law enforcement and it is this: snitches alone, paid informants, and thorough detective work are not sufficient to adequately lay the basis for effective criminal prosecution --- it rests, ultimately, with the willingness of citizens to come forward, to share information, and to testify if necessary. That is, producing more eyes and ears for gang abatement.[5]   Today, it is routine for correctional officers, law enforcement officers, and school teachers to have, as part of their required pre-service and in-service training, some degree of exposure to the gang problem; typically, "gang recognition/gang awareness" training.   Citizens involved in cooperative alliances with local law enforcement also need this training, as do larger segments of our society (media, business, education, religious institutions, health care, etc). Gang awareness training most commonly involves a summary of local gang names, colors, hand signs, etc. It rarely involves more in-depth training on what is known from the literature about gangs that might help in making decisions or implementing policy correctly.

Here, again, is a prominent role that the federal government can play. In providing more generalized training materials that can be adapted to local conditions and variations in the gang crime problem. No one argues that the basic social-psychology of gang members in New York City differs from that of their gang equivalents in any other jurisdiction in the United States. While there are obvious differences in community areas and neighborhood composition, there is a remarkable similarity in some of the patterns of gang behavior nationwide. This is, therefore, an area of emphasis that federal initiatives should come to grips with in research, knowledge development, and training materials designed for state and local impact.

Some initiatives that a community group can start are low or no cost options. One good first step would be a simple photographic inventory of what gang graffiti exists in the neighborhood. How it changes, what keeps getting "put back up", and what is "crossed out" by rival gangs, is of more than some interest in determining which gangs are active in the area.

PROTECTING THE NEIGHBORHOOD

One of the profound contradictions of a community organizing against the threat of gang crime is to be found in this motivation to want to "protect the neighborhood".[6] From what we know about neighborhood watch groups, those most likely to get involved are those with the most invested: typically an employed middle-class male homeowner. It is less easy to get unemployed, lower-income, renters involved in such an initiative.

But oddly, at least one piece of research (Fagan, 1989: p. 658) suggests that gang members themselves, when asked "why did you join the gang", answer "to protect the neighborhood". That almost sounds prosocial, until we analyze it more closely. Protect it from what? From all "outsiders"? From persons of different ethnic, racial, or cultural groups? From what, indeed! Apparently, as a dominant theme, gangs as vigilantes defending ethnic homogeneity or the provincialism[7] of their neighborhood.

And to what extent is this mission informally communicated to our youths from the social structure of their community? This appears to be another unfortunate by-product of racism and discrimination. One cannot buy into racist conceptions and simultaneously desire to eliminate the gang problem. They are one and the same. And this may explain differential effectiveness of community efforts "to do something about the gang problem".[8]

The irony of all of this is or should be clear: indeed, we need to "protect the neighborhood", but like Pogo said "I have met the enemy and the enemy is us". We also need to protect the neighborhood from the destructive forces within. Psychologically we need to take away any such self-conception of the gang member as "protecting the neighborhood". Because any conception they have of their behavior as being prosocial shall certainly serve to reinforce their commitment to gang organization, not community organization.

I CAN'T BECOME INVOLVED, I'M A BUSINESS PERSON

Small business operators and proprietors need to be approached and involved in a community's response to the problem. Often, it is my experience, they will tell you "I can't become involved, I'm a business person". They need to be reminded of how they will have to pay now or later on the gang problem. It will cost them more if they let the problem get out of control, as some Englewood neighborhood stores and businesses can attest today in Chicago. The Gangster Disciples used their political wing, 21st Century V.O.T.E., as the vehicle to seek hefty donations from store owners; those who did not donate were picketed by the GDs. The Black Disciples in the same area did not honor the GD picket line however. Extortion and "protection payments" are what some business persons can look forward to in a neighborhood where the gang is allowed to thrive.[9]

CHURCH INITIATIVES

Asserting moral superiority is the essence of effective guerilla warfare and is also closely tied to the effectiveness of organized religion's role in combating local crime. Where to begin may not be with the obvious direct target of local gang members, it may rest with conditions, structures, or policies that symbolize such an internal moral decay. In Chicago, one Catholic priest has been, many believe, wrongfully accused and arrested for being the sole agent of an "anti-billboard campaign" involving painting over local billboards advertising alcohol and tobacco to inner city residents. The fact is, historically, this one member of the clergy started a campaign of civil disobedience and protest against stores that sold drug paraphernalia; a movement that was successful by its impact --- state laws were eventually passed making the sale of such drug pipes, and paraphernalia illegal.

The symbol in the billboard painting incidents are more important than the real or alleged act of criminal damage to property. The symbol of the local billboard glamorizing alcohol and tobacco dependency to the youth of an inner city neighborhood is the manifestation of a larger economic structure dependent upon consumer patterns and bold enough to make such propaganda lures in economically depressed neighborhoods which are the least able to cope in larger society. Attacking such billboards, with paint rollers or paint-filled balloons has in the years 1989-1990 in Chicago generated much mass media coverage.

Some feel that Chicago's Father Michael Pfleger has been wrongfully accused of being the "ring leader" of this moral campaign[10]. It is equivalent in one sense to any citizen wanting to paint over gang graffiti such as in the case of an abandoned building or an absentee landlord who does not take care of the building. What must be evaluated here, from a perspective of what the church can do to combat gang crime, is the larger issue of asserting effective moral leadership. It may simply not be possible to begin with an anti-gang member crusade. It may be necessary to begin with a more generalized "crime prevention" agenda. It is not easy to advocate the arrest or detention of one's fellow community members. Although, ultimately a more developed moral consensus may demand that.

Using a more conspicuous external enemy is going to be more effective in generating moral support than simply pointing the finger at errant members of one's own community. If we were to apply Kohlberg's moral development stage theory to a community level of analysis we should conclude almost equally the same thing. That is, we cannot begin at a higher stage of moral analysis, we must begin at the basic level of moral evaluation. We cannot skip to higher levels of moral functioning through a simple, single sermon or pronouncement. It is a matter of religious and moral education. We must walk before we run.

So, to the extent that some religious leaders at least acknowledge this problem of the necessity of their communities to take moral charge of their environments, they are most certainly exerting a powerful and positive influence. An influence that should undoubtedly be duplicated in many other areas of our country if the commitment to moral development is to be taken seriously.
It is a strategy that can work in the long run.

It is a strategy of taking moral responsibility for one's own individual environment, one's neighborhood, one's block, one's home. It is a strategy of peace. And of overcoming racism and discrimination.

Direct confrontation with symbols of moral threats are equally effective. In Harlem, an Islamic group that takes upon itself the responsibility to confront those persons generally regarded as selling narcotics, is a force of direct pressure to inform gang members that they are not existing in the area without moral opposition. Indeed, it is not as a vigilante action, but as a moral confrontation action, that brings to bear community awareness and greater solidarity in opposition to such collective enterprises as drug dealing. It can be an exceptionally effective tool in re-asserting the community's legitimacy, and its control.

But like the Chicago Area Project today, which has a fundamental goal of community empowerment, more specifically neighborhood empowerment, does our political apparatus really want to replicate such a project that trains local leaders to take civic responsibility, to assume responsibility, to "take charge"?

A number of churches and religious groups are now becoming involved in outreach to the gangs. Some of these are very new, others have as a part of their outreach to the confined adults and juveniles dealt with gang members for a very long time. One of these evangelical groups is described in the book <u>Cities of Lonesome Fear: God Among the Gangs</u>[11]. It is called the Juvenile Justice Ministry, which has had a long history of bringing rival gang members together in a "peace making" session that is called the "United Nations"[12]. This same group issued photo i.d. cards with the logo "Officially Retired Gang Member" to the youths[13].

USING WHAT GANGS UNDERSTAND

One of the more aggressive methods used by some community groups to combat the gang problem is that of direct confrontation. Some members of Chicago's Northwest Neighborhood Federation took advantage of the national statistic that non-gang members do outnumber gang members. They sought the goal of residential displacement for gang members living in their community. They wanted the gang members and their family to move out. So they would hand the gang members a brick with a kind of Hallmark card attached to it saying "We Heard You Were Moving".[14]

THE DISPLACEMENT EFFECT IN COMMUNITY POLICING

Prior to the rising interest in what is now known as community policing we called the displacement effect "dumping your problem on someone else". Presenting a paper on how one gang program was able to claim success by relocating some more hard core gang members to the suburbs brought one suburbanite to the point of intellectual combat, claiming this is criminal to have someone push or relocate gang members out of their community to someone else's community, and that it certainly should not be claimed as a success, it should be claimed as a damage.[15]

But today, when a community can displace its gang members out of its area, or its operations out of its area, then it is definitely considered a successful milestone in community policing. We need to understand that the problem has become so pervasive that this new technique for gang abatement is now a legitimate option. Some, obviously, have strong views on this issue[16].

SCREENING TENANTS FOR GANG CRIME PROFILES

The issue here hinges on the rights of a landlord to screen potential tenants in a process that would systematically discourage gang members from living in any given area, community, or city. There are actually a number of ways this can actually be done. But it boils down to identifying potential problem makers before then can move into a building as tenants. Rental and lease agreements can theoretically contain a number of restrictive clauses, and require security deposits for a wide variety of risk factors (i.e., water beds, pets, etc), and born out of necessity has been some new innovations in this regard that have the net effect of screening out gang members as tenants. And it appears to be completely legal, where discrimination against gang members is treated as an objective risk factor, much in the same way that a bad driving record is legitimated considered in automobile insurance rates.

What landlords in Aurora, Illinois are doing is doing criminal background checks on applicants for leasing or renting apartments and properties. With the cooperation of local police, the tenant simply completes an "Authority for Release of Information Form", and pay the police department $5.00 for a record check. Clauses in the rental or lease agreement may also include a provision for eviction for a subsequent offenses (i.e., drug sales, etc).[17] This type of policy would tend to discourage hard core active gang members from moving into the area.

THE NEW BLACK PANTHERS

Recently the group called the New Black Panthers, tracing its beliefs to the original Black Panther Party of a previous era, has emerged in a number of cities nationally. In the present book we have not regarded the original Black Panthers as a gang, primarily because a close study of their internal structure reveals numerous "internal rules" about crime; it was a group that realized it could be jeopardized by the crime of its members. This is not to say that some of its members did not commit well known crimes. But still others who were members went on to become well known elected officials. Supreme Court Judge Clarence Thomas is said to have admired the Black Panthers when he was a college student. Recently, the New Black Panthers have taken to patrolling Dallas neighborhoods, outfitted for combat, apparently to send a message to the gangs and drug dealers.[18]

CITIZEN PATROLS AROUND SCHOOLS

This type of community program initiative goes by a number of names, but it basically means enlisting parents and community adults to form a "citizen security patrol" to protect students on the way to and from schools in the area. Such a program at Austin High School on Chicago's west side was formed when residents felt that police could not effectively protect students from violence and gangs. Such a program can be easily established by working with area churches and other community activists.[19]

THE SOCIAL POWER OF A CONSPICUOUS ANTI-GANG PRESENCE

While the program names differ nationally, a number of different cities give the obvious example of one such effective use of a social power against on-going flagrant organized threats to community life. It is the role of indigenous leaders. Men and women who take to the streets in a moral crusade to communicate "they are not going to tolerate drug dealers" or gang activity.[20] Recall that Thrasher's formulation of gang development scenarios implied that a gang could become a secret society. So push the gang toward even greater levels of subcultural buffering from larger society. Make the gang drug dealers take the utmost steps to hide from our streets, from our corners, from our areas of legitimate social activity. Force them deeper underground.

Such can be an effective strategic ploy in showing that the gang has no legitimacy in the areas in which they operate. Forcing them underground takes away the related element of social power of hegemony over the streets after sunset. It can emasculate the gang structure.   And in so doing, undermine one of the primary social-psychological ingredients of gang affiliation: the sense of power and identity with an organized enterprise.   There is no "hyper masculinity" associated with living underground, with a fear of showing your colors under penalty of neighborhood and law enforcement sanctions.

THE CHICAGO AREA PROJECT

According to a recent Annual Report of the Chicago Area Project (CAP), "unlike other agencies, CAP has always worked with Chicago's gangs - identifying and meeting with gang leaders, discussing community and individual needs, and turning negative behavior into a positive force to create change for all members of a neighborhood"[21]. Also, CAP is unlike the Saul Alinksy or overt political approach to community organizing.   In fact, training materials show local neighborhood committees are supposed to be non-partisan in ideology. The Saul Alinksy approach was "issue" oriented. CAP is development oriented.

The issues change, and when other political organizers leave the community behind, CAP is still there. CAP has been in many Chicago neighborhoods for decades. A fifty-year evaluation of CAP by the Rand Corporation concluded CAP was a promising program (Schlossman, et al, 1984).   But CAP was not selected as an exemplary program during the LEAA years, and has not been replicated in its present form in any other city in America. In spite of this, according to CAP staff, representatives from other countries have come to examine the CAP process of developing neighborhood solidarity and local leadership.[22]

CAP literature quotes Irving Spergel and staff explain that a possible reason why CAP has not been replicated in other American cities is that Chicago is unique in having ethnic neighborhoods and enclaves.   But if it truly works to build local neighborhood organization, then theoretically it can work in any city, in any part of the world.   No federally supported or privately supported national project has yet been established to test whether CAP can work in other cities in America in spite of the strong support for CAP initiatives and the obviously strong theoretical underpinnings from the Shaw and McKay tradition which gave birth to CAP.

CAP literature can be interpreted as being compatible with the "multiple marginality" hypothesis of Vigil (1988). This program literature can also be interpreted as being compatible with much of the underclass theory:

"It's a simple fact. If young people can get out of the ghetto..get a job...and get some schooling...they leave the gang. But while individual gang members or ethnic groups may move beyond the gang experience, for others, gangs remain a way of life".[23]

It employs techniques similar to the detached worker program or street worker method, but it is called "curbstone counseling". This curbstone counseling is described as being most effective for what might best be described as level zero gang problems: "petty larceny, vandalism, and lewdness".[24] Curbstone counseling is most effective when it is carried out by adults or leaders indigenous to the neighborhood, rather than by outside university trained social workers who do not live in the neighborhood. It is doubtful that curbstone counseling would work very well with a deeply entrenched highly organized gang. For such a curbstone counselor would find the gang members saying "get out of my video" --- that is, stop interfering with gang business on the curbstone.

A PROGRAM THAT CLEARLY DIDN'T WORK

The Midcity Project described by Miller (1962) involved targeting seven gangs in disadvantaged Boston Communities. This "total community" method differed from the Chicago Area Project in several ways. It meant using not paraprofessionals or indigenous leaders for detached workers to provide outreach to the gang, rather it meant employing degreed social workers. For whatever reason, perhaps hoping to "integrate" the gangs into the main stream of American life, these detached workers sought to serve the gang members almost as "organizational consultants":

> "The detached gang workers changed the gangs from loosely organized near-groups to formal clubs, served as intermediaries between gang members and adult institutions, such as employers, schools, police, and other professional agencies...(Lundman, 1984: p. 69)."

Was it possible that the individual gang members viewed this "special positive attention" from the straight adult world as "manna from heaven"? There appeared to be no behavioral contracts with the individual gang members to the effect "you do this, and we'll do X for you"; thus, it was an unconditional offering of special services. That included a heightened level of organizational capability: the transformation from informal to formal organization. Did organizing the gangs, along with trying to improve local citizen groups, even providing psychiatric family counseling to gang families, work? That is, work in the sense of reducing delinquency among those known to be involved in this Midcity Project? Absolutely not was Miller's answer.

It illustrates an important problem for the community's role in gang prevention, intervention, and crime reduction efforts. It is this: if the "theory" behind the program or project, in terms of answering "why we should expect good results" is not sound, then we should not be too alarmed to find less than good results. Worse still is the situation of having "no theory" to guide the design of efforts "to do something about it". Lacking as we are in hard evidence of what works in gang abatement (Miller, 1990), then perhaps our only option is to take a theory with some degree of more generalized support in the field of criminology and apply these to the more specific area of gang crime abatement.

What was found in the Midcity Project is the same problem of affording gangs a sense of "legitimation" through recognition that has plagued correctional institutions as well. A social worker's or psychologist's training is, normally, in working with the individual unit of analysis. We are in a different ball game when working with the gang as an organized group in an unorganized community. Just how "detached" are detached workers like these? Are they detached from the goals of larger society? Does "detached" imply they will serve the gang in any capacity but not as a member?

Our knowledge about gang formation and intervention strategies is beginning to become codified. It suggests we should definitely have a plan of action, one based on a more specific theory of "what to expect" from such initiatives. In a later chapter, for example, we will see how "well intentioned" efforts to "experiment" in the prison environment with gangs meant recognizing such gang leaders and allowing them some privileges. That backfired dramatically. It contributed to the eventual rise of "supergangs" in the late 1970's.

It is frankly beyond being irresponsible to take such risks without good process and product evaluation research in addition to having a theory of what to expect.

Why should detached workers assume it is their job to help gang members by intervening as an ombudsman when they have trouble with the police? Recall Vold's theory of gangs: the gang members are a "minority power group in the sense that they are out of sympathy with and in more or less direct opposition to the rules and regulations of the dominant majority, that is, the established world of adult values....police ordinarily represent the power and values of the adult world" (Vold and Bernard, 1986: p. 274). Thus, for a detached worker to ask the police for leniency on behalf of the gang is to reinforce this conflict between the gang and law enforcement agencies. Psychological theories stressing the need for individual responsibility for one's behavior also apply here (Glasser's reality therapy, etc). Don't be a chump, get a good theory of human behavior before offering any resources to a gang that can be exploited, unless the offering is intended to simply identify the gang infrastructure and then withdrawing the resource after accomplishing the identification mission.

SHORT AND STRODTBECK (1974) AND THE YMCA's DETACHED WORKERS

Oddly, the research described by Short and Strodtbeck (1974) was based on the Chicago YMCA's Detached Workers Program. Which we shall see below, in describing the Chicago's BUILD Program apparently basically "went out of business" by the time Short and Strodtbeck's (1974) book came off the press.

But the concept of working with youths at risk of becoming gang members is an enduring one that is still supported and recommended policy today and the community is the preferred place in which to carry out such programing (see Dunston, 1990: p. 43).

B.U.I.L.D.:   A CHICAGO   PROGRAM

The Broader Urban Involvement and Leadership Development (BUILD) not-for-profit corporation began in 1969. It works with "gang prone" and "gang involved" youths. Its 1983 level of service involved 3,500 youths in six contiguous areas of Chicago through a $400,000 yearly budget. Its fiscal 1989 report shows it served 2,378 young people. Currently, it has three components: (1) the prevention program, (2) the remediation program, and (3) the community resource program.

According to Hank Bach, the founder, BUILD filled the void when the YMCA Detached Workers program stopped in 1969.[25] The YMCA was moving out of the gang field. Several left the YMCA project and started the BUILD program. When it was first started it focused on remediation, similar to the detached or street worker approach. The prevention component was added later. Then the community resource component was added.

BUILD is explicitly based on a theory about human behavior. Its program literature calls it social development theory and is the basis for implementing program services. It appears, actually, to be what is more commonly known in criminology as social control theory. BUILD literature describes social development theory as follows:

> This theory suggests that delinquency results from weak or absent social control, and that it happens because it has not been prevented. Social development suggests that there are factors which help provide social controls for youth. They are the family, the school, and the law. The greater the degree of bonding between each youth and these social institutions, the less is the probability of delinquent behavior.[26]

Obviously, all social institutions can provide for social control, and we can add the church and the employment/business community to the above list on this basis, even if the BUILD program does not explicitly identify these other agencies of social control. Also, there are both formal and informal social controls. And informal social control is probably going to have greater merit in preventing gang crime. The "law", or the government, comes to represent the agency of last resort and involves the application of formal social control.

An evaluation of the prevention component of BUILD is reported by Thompson and Jason (1988). The prevention service involves going to local schools and providing youths a specialized "classroom training" essentially in how to resist joining a gang, and can also involve an after-school services. What Thompson and Jason did was to compare a sample of those receiving the prevention services (N = 74) with those not receiving the prevention services (N = 43). Towards the end of the school year, the dependent variable for evaluation was "determined by comparing targeted youths' names with gang rosters provided by gang members involved with BUILD's remediation program" (Thompson and Jason, 1988: p. 329). This showed four of the non-serviced youths joined a gang compared to only one of the serviced group. The authors were aware of the problems of such an analysis, but the results approached statistical significance and tended to support the notion that something can be done about curtailing or preventing gang joining behavior.

BUILD's third and newest program service component parallels the leadership development strategy used by CAP. It is, at least, compatible with the CAP model, or complements it.   Both CAP and BUILD are based on a theory of crime/delinquency. In fact, both programs made presentations in a well attended session at the 1993 Annual Meeting of the Academy of Criminal Justice Sciences.

THE YOUTH SERVICE PROJECT: A CHICAGO PROGRAM

Also called the "Second Chance" program, the Youth Service Project in Humboldt Park, a westside Chicago neighborhood, was founded by Nancy Abbate in 1975, and it works with gang involved or gang prone youths who come to the attention of the criminal justice system. It is a secondary-prevention program with a rehabilitation thrust. It works with mostly juveniles; males and females. It has been very successful at working with these youths, with education and job placement services, etc,[27] and involving the youths in graffiti removal projects. In-house statistics compiled on these juvenile clients are very promising: showing the youths do sever ties to the gang, and do not get re-arrested or committed to corrections at a very high rate.

GETTING THE EDGE ON EARLY GANG PREVENTION

This program initiative was designed in the field by a gang crime specialist police officer assigned to work in schools, Tom Fleming of the Park Forest Police Department in Illinois. EDGE is the acronym for Education for Gang Evasion. It is designed to reach students in the sixth grade, and like some other similar models, is stretched out over a six to seven week period for the full curriculum. It has been particularly effective in the suburban context of gang prevention.[28]

PARENTS AGAINST GANGS (PAG)

PAG was formed by gang crime victims James and Betty Major-Rose after their daughter died as a result of being a gang crime victim.[29] Goals of PAG include establishing on-site programs in housing developments, drug and substance rehabilitation programs, witness/victim assistance, individual and family counseling, community outreach and referral, promoting educational opportunities, providing supportive services, gang and drug awareness programs in schools and communities, a legislative clearinghouse for information and public education, and a Ginneria Major Scholarship Program. Program services already in place include: grief support groups to families who are crime victims, victim/witness crisis intervention, court advocacy, sibling support groups, youth at risk placement in alternative school and job programs, substance abuse counseling, parents and youth support groups, and Students Against Gangs and Drugs. The Parents Against Gangs staff also made a presentation at a well attended session of the 1993 Annual Meeting of the Academy of Criminal Justice Sciences.

COMMUNITIES DARE TO CARE

This group grew out of an enlarged application of the Parents Against Gangs mission statement. Some of the key figures in the Parents Against Gangs group while still supporting that mission, went on to start their own larger inter-community mission of building the ability of community groups to respond to the gang problem. This is accomplished by training community leaders, educating parents and children, and general gang awareness. It is a model that was particularly designed to be adaptable to areas where "community policing" initiatives are undertaken. For it provides structure and direction to citizen initiatives which involves strengthening ties not only to law enforcement, but to other social institutions and influences in the community.

This organization, Communities Dare to Care, established the first Illinois statewide "Gang Awareness Week". It was also effective in bringing together representatives from across all ethnic and racial groups, and all political dimensions, into a common forum for attacking the gang crime problem. It goes beyond simply working with victims, even though staff are obviously still very much concerned about this, but rather it extends the model for public education to include potential new victims such as school children and their parents in a stronger prevention orientation.[30]

MOTHERS AGAINST GANGS IN COMMUNITIES (MAGIC)

MAGIC works with the Urban League of San Diego. It did receive some meager support from the Gannett Foundation for its program to get youth off the streets and away from drugs, gangs, crime and violence. This amounted to a $5,000 grant from the Gannett Foundation in 1989. But as will be addressed later in this book, clearly our foundations have not provided much in the way of funding to gang services or gang research. That will have to dramatically change if we are to provide any national climate that encourages individual initiative in dealing with the gang problem in our American communities.

MOTHERS AGAINST GANGS: Chicago

Founded in 1986 by Frances Sandoval after her son was killed by gang members, this group has earned much positive media attention, but equally --- at least in Cicero --- has earned the retaliatory attacks from gang members against the homes and residences of MAG members. It serves a public education function and advocates for family support, prevention, and lobbying for anti-gang policy reform, as well as neighborhood organizing. It also provides an important "court watch" service, monitoring judges who handle gang crime cases.

CHILDREN OF WAR

This program was founded by Judith Thompson and works with the modern version of "shell shock", gang violence trauma for innercity kids, and it also works with those children exposed to wartime brutality from Third World countries. They conduct workshops for junior high school students.[31] Such program services should probably be established in larger cities where the loss of life is routine for children, because this type of service may help to ease the shock to children when one of their school mates is killed.

THE CHICAGO INITIATIVE

This was a privately funded strategy to make sure Chicago did not have the kind of riots that plagued Los Angeles. It apparently worked. It was based on good theoretical ground: attacking racism, poverty, and gangs. Providing jobs, extending services, increasing recreation and teen programs, and creating a very large "safety net" seems to be a strategy that can work.[32]

LOCAL MEDIA

In the Soviet Union under its previous years of more totalitarian tendencies (i.e., before the period of openness), what got reported in the media (print and electronic) was what the government wanted reported. The author is aware of no opinion poll conducted in America regarding news media coverage for the printed press regarding the item: "Generally, do you favor knowing the names of persons arrested and/or convicted in your area and their charges?"

Chicago not too long ago used to at least publish sentencing outcomes. Perhaps with the influx of large numbers of such persons routinely processed through the criminal courts it is as difficult as preparing the accuracy of the classified section of any newspaper. Most smaller towns still routinely publish detailed "police blotter" sections to at least give the reader an idea of who was arrested and for what charge.

Clearly, in a city as large as Chicago, the nightly arrest report would take up a lot of space; and a weekly report, perhaps an entire page or more. But would citizens at least have more information on how law enforcement operates? Many believe so.[33]

Indeed, if gangs are not going to be abated, perhaps someone will recognize that this arrest and conviction information can be put to income-producing use; by publishing such "crime caper" materials where the larger newspapers simply avoid such coverage. One thing anyone who deals with offenders will tell you: the first thing they do when they read newspapers is look for the crime news, then they tend to also read the horoscope section, because many are said to be superstitious as well.

A true sign of the times in gang institutionalization in America within our inner cities will be when such a "crime newspaper" emerges and publishes specific sections pertinent to all existing rival gangs[a]. Who knows, perhaps a gang will fill this void.[34]   Gangs have in the correctional setting tested the limits of the freedom of religion, what remains in the community is the freedom of the press.

---

[a] Teen Angels magazine first published issue #1 in 1980 and is now in issue #124. The target audience for this magazine are "those who live and grew up in those areas where gangs have evolved for many years" (personal communication, May, 1993). It services the California area primarily. TEEN ANGELS, P.O. Box 338, Rialto, CA 92376.

In the years ahead, we will see what progress can be made in gang abatement/prevention or whether the federal governments role will continue to be a doctrine of laissez-fair and handing all this responsibility back to the state and local governments. Without substantial national level efforts, expect to see a gang with its own newsletters or publications.

What many authors agree, regarding the media's role, is to at all costs avoid sensationalism (Kramer and Karr, 1953: p, 194; Bell and Sullivan, 1987). Also, giving attention to any one particular gang, and its specific identity being given such coverage, may not be the most responsible way to cover gang crime stories, if it can be construed as a "recognition" for a gang.[35] Sometimes publishing the address of a gang member does result in providing a rival gang the opportunity for retaliation. The fact is we have both sensationalism[36] and responsible journalism. And it is a market issue: what the public wants is what the public pays for.

The study by Kramer and Karr (1953) took a definite position on this matter of providing recognition to gang members in much the same way that it can be assumed recognizing gang leaders in the correctional setting tends to be counter-productive by legitimizing them. That is, Kramer and Karr (1953) purposely avoided use of any gang member names because:

> Gang members are apt to be proud of seeing their names in print, and further inflation of sick egos is hardly desirable. In many cases the individuals mentioned are trying to reform, and more notoriety might interfere with their rehabilitation (Kramer and Karr, 1953: p. 194).

The impact of mass communications is a macro-analytic question regarding gangs; and it is not easily answered. Often the mass media is "damned if they do, and damned if they don't". But another historical continuity in the gang literature, indeed a cross-national one, is that in spite of the attribution of widespread illiteracy among gang members, they do read the papers and the first thing they look for is the recent crime news. As Patrick (1973: p. 66) stated "the papers were...scrutinized every morning for the slightest reference to gangs or gang warfare". Patrick also documents the effect of mass media and movies in terms of the emulation or "copy cat" phenomenon (p. 85).

OVERCOMING COMMUNITY DENIAL

"We don't have a gang problem" is the response of many adults and community residents, when in fact the graffiti, the local crime patterns, and repeated gang incidents point to nothing other than a gang problem. It is the classic reaction by the casting of blame externally which relieves the person of any sense of responsibility: "it must be outsiders." One of the conclusions from the national conference reported by Bryant (1989) was this very need to overcome community denial.

As in a treatment situation, help is not possible until there is an admission of a problem. Law enforcement cannot be effective on the basis of good detective work alone. Indeed, without the help of citizens, the civilian counterpart to sworn police officers, we would have few such criminal convictions. We need witnesses, we need testimony, we need leads and information. Community's must come to recognize they have a gang problem. It cannot be "outsiders" for everyone.[37] Some, many of us in fact, live in such neighborhoods with a gang crime problem.

Evidence suggests the way we learn about it may have something to do with such an appraisal. Adults may learn about gangs primarily through the mass media, while school age youths may learn about gangs through educational institutions and their peers.[38]

REBUILDING COMMUNITY FABRIC

Gang crime does not occur in a cultural-social-political-economic vacuum. It occurs in the community. If social disorganization can be said to have some positive role to play in the onset of gang crime, then we can assume as an equally strong force that gang crime also has a most deleterious impact on the very institutional fabric of any given community. The damage to these institutional linkages shall have to be repaired if a community is to successfully overcome the gang crime problem or even play its expected role in larger policies regarding gang abatement.

Here again is where federal resources are needed. Because when gang crime flourishes, those first to leave the community are those most likely to be the more upwardly mobile portion of the tax base. What gets left behind are those least able to contribute in an economic sense. Cities like Chicago are experiencing "crime flight", citizens leave because they do not feel safe; they fear having their children in public schools where only half the incoming freshmen ever finish high school, they fear the spread of drugs and the gangs with which they are associated. It will not be easy to reverse this process but it can be done.

One of the most under researched aspects about gang crime in our literature is the social impact of gang crime and how it shatters and tears asunder relationships within the community and between the community and other social institutions. Durkheim was right in the limited historical context with which he said crime can have a positive impact, but if any only if the perpetrator is caught and punished and in so doing this tends to reinforce and strengthen the norms of the group. But in the context of gang crime this may be less sound; because even if a gang offender is incarcerated, the gang structure remains intact within the community and the criminal justice system simply plays a latent role by facilitating leadership training. That is, the pattern has been to target gang leaders for prosecution, inducing status promotional opportunities for other gang members who are not on their way to the penitentiary.

Citizens of our inner city community's become polarized and progressively isolated from mainstream America. We need to reverse that process. We need to allow the "system" to work for them. That means taking seriously some of the recommendations by Bell and Sullivan (1987), such as establishing conflict/dispute resolution centers perhaps in the structure of a multiservice community program that enhances the institutional linkages of these citizens to their larger society --- through healthcare, through education, through employment opportunities, family counseling, community-based corrections, through a more positive relationship with their government and the services it offers. The local religious institutions would have a prominent role to play here, if they wanted to.

In essence, the best way to arm the citizens who face our nation's gangs on a daily basis is to re-build and strengthen this community infrastructure; its institutional linkages, its very fabric and identity as a "community". This is, after all, the essence of what Shaw and Mc Kay intended through the Chicago Area Project as a general delinquency prevention strategy. Summaries of the overall effectiveness of the Chicago Area Project such as those by Kobrin (1959) are not able to point to direct conclusive evidence that the initiatives produced significant reductions in delinquency, but then again no one to your authors knowledge has ever taken the position that this was a counterproductive effort as a variety of other intervention/control projects have tended to be.

THE ROLE OF LOCAL COLLEGES AND UNIVERSITIES

Here is where we can get some good advice, and a theory or two. Professors in the social sciences, in criminal justice, etc, are often expected to provide some level of "community service". It is good for them to have this contact with the community on behalf of their university. And they are not supposed to charge for it. It should be pro bono. Otherwise it is not community service, it is proprietary hustling. A community organization should take definite steps, in writing, to contact local colleges and universities: the various departments of Sociology, Psychology, Criminal Justice, etc., and express an interest in working with any faculty members who are willing to help. Or agree to accept student interns.

Many faculty members would be pleased to assist local community organizations. But like anything, you don't the get the help unless you ask for it. This can be a "win/win" situation. Greater involvement by university faculty in the real world means research opportunities for them, it means they get credit for community service, and the community gets knowledge and hopefully good advice. It can be a creative partnership and it should definitely be expanded throughout American society. It too could help "rebuild the fabric" of our communities.

The recent work by Takata and Tyler (1994)[39] illustrates how nicely the skills and capabilities of individuals from a local university can dovetail with the pragmatic needs of a local community in terms of "doing something constructive" about the gang problem. Creating a Task Force as in their case is usually a good first step. Using university experts in criminological research is then a next good step to determine how serious the problem is and what if anything might be feasible in terms of "doing something about the problem".

Colleges and universities need to be concerned about the gang problem because more and more they are now feeling the effects of gang violence. Numerous instances of gang violence targeting campus areas and university students have appeared recently. Gang graffiti and drive-bys on campus appear on the rise.[40]

THE FEDERAL GOVERNMENT's (OJJDP) "I.D.E.N.T.I.F.Y" STRATEGY

The federal government includes many different agencies so it is not really accurate to say that any single coherent and coordinated federal response to the national problem of gangs really even exists. Almost all federal agencies have someone who interfaces in someway with gang issues. But as mentioned earlier, no "Gang Czar" exists. But a variety of "concepts" have been offered by federal agencies, one deserving mention here, the IDENTIFY strategy.

Bryant (1989) reports a recommended strategy for dealing with gangs at the community level based on what the Office of Juvenile Justice and Delinquency Prevention was able to compile. It recommends prevention, intervention, and supervision. IDENTIFY is the acronym for:

Identify the problem. Define the system components. Enumerate polices, procedures, etc. Needs clarification. Target strategies. Implementation plan. Focus agency responsibilities. Yell.

It suggests what criminologists have been saying for centuries: "schools, law enforcement, recreation, mental health, housing, community agencies and churches --- all part of the prevention component --- must work together" (Bryant, 1989: p. 4). The trick is: how to do it. It is good advice. But for many of our nation's neighborhoods where this strategy is needed, these same neighborhoods are also going to need some federal resources to really carry it out.

The educated reader who examines gang issues will eventually find that if any blame is to be cast on anyone regarding the proliferation of the gang problem, then it is not the family, it is not the local police, and it is not the local community that should be blamed. Rather, the federal leadership in Washington deserves much more blame for seeing the gang problem begin to rise and fester all across the United States and virtually adopting an ostrich with its head in the sand type of response. It seemed like throughout the Reagan and Bush administrations about all they did regarding the gang problem was develop acronyms for what could be done about the problem. It is interesting, of course, to note that even the IDENTIFY acronym ends with "yell": perhaps "yelling" at our elected officials might help. Because not much has changed as we enter 1995.

THE CLINTON COVENANT TO COMBAT GANGS: AN UNFULFILLED PROMISE

President Bill Clinton advanced a novel idea in his nomination acceptance speech at the 1992 Democratic National Convention. But is it a good idea? His concept for combatting gangs was couched within a larger social policy idea of allowing recent college graduates to repay their college loans by community service. A kind of highly educated Urban Community Corps perhaps. A closer examination of this idea shows some historical mistakes that deserve special consideration.

Efforts to combat gangs are not new just as gangs are not new. Our social science literature contains numerous examples of gang service programs and projects at the street level. Some worked. Some worked significantly in the reverse intended direction. We need only recall how in Chicago during the 1970's when Reverend Fry helped the El Rukn gang leader Jeff Fort gain federal grants. Some volunteers of the past have helped gangs become stronger.

Not every volunteer, whether possessing a college degree or not, is capable of combatting gangs in our communities. They would need direction, supervision and training before entering the field. Two well-known programs that use volunteers and do have a positive impact on combatting gangs are Chicago's BUILD program and Parents Against Gangs. There are still costs associated with using volunteers and especially training them properly.

There are genuine anti-gang programs, and there are anti-gang programs. The genuine ones, like BUILD and Parents Against Gangs, have experts with considerable experience in the area and they operate with both a theory of achieving a positive effect and a well defined plan of action.

Other programs sound good, but are upon closer scrutiny bad ideas. One genuine bad idea is providing gang members with leadership training skills. Another bad idea is providing gangs with organizational development skills. Both of these bad ideas are still being promoted today in less educated circles. Helping gang members to be better organized under some guise of coopting them is not a well founded concept. Hopefully Bill Clinton did not have either of these two ideas in mind in recommending the use of volunteers to combat gangs in our urban areas.

There does exist considerable expert opinion that youths can be prevented from joining gangs. What it would take, however, to prevent this gang joining behavior would be providing something equal to or greater in attraction than the lure of the gang itself. Excitement, kicks, status, a sense of protection, a tight-knit group that provides a sense of identity, and more often than not income itself --- these are the things that the gang offers. The Clinton covenant would not work unless it could effectively compete with the current attractions that the gang affords. To prevent youths from joining gangs is slightly more complicated than simply providing a bunch of English major volunteers with recent bachelor's degrees.

To combat the gang problem through the use of college graduate volunteers will require specialized training in our social sciences, particularly sociology and criminal justice. These are the disciplines where full gang courses are taught in our nations universities. If we expect any volunteer to do good, then they must be trained. We cannot assume all college graduates have completed courses dealing with urban gangs. Institutions such as Chicago State University, Loyola University of Chicago, Lewis University, and many others throughout the U.S. --- they regularly teach courses on gangs. To use most of our recent college graduates to combat the gang problem the Clinton covenant would require additional college work in this specific area of expertise.

There is growing support among gang researchers for the value of a WPA-style, depression-era mass public employment or public service program to be able to offer poor and minority youths an alternative to drugs and the gang. Perhaps it is here, in the context of providing adult supervision for recreation, educational upgrading, vocational training, etc, that recent college graduates could best be put to use in working with the several million underclass youths who could benefit from such a program. Still the potential for major mistakes in dealing with gangs must be taken into account in any implementation of the Clinton covenant to combat gangs. Such a program initiative would require a national advisory commission staffed by professional gang researchers. Gangs have benefited in the past from political corruption and attempts to pay them to "chill out". If the Clinton covenant seeks to provide recognition to the gang as an organization and basically give it legitimacy, it would be equivalent to negotiating with terrorists.

To effectively combat gangs in America will truly require enormous new federal resources. It will take more than a bunch of volunteers. It will cost a great deal. But it will be worth it. It could save many lives, it could prevent the burgeoning costs associated with imprisonment, and it could truly help to restore a sense of community in some of our nation's troubled urban areas. The Clinton covenant, then, is not a bad idea. However, it will require considerably more thinking and planning and therefore must be regarded as a pie in the sky plan at this point.

Years of neglect by the Federal government with regard to the gang problem began to change only recently in 1991-92 when federal agencies received the command to get concerned about gangs. Research funding and prevention programs are still extremely meager in relationship to the scope of the gang problem. Agencies like the National Institute of Justice that have recently gotten interested in funding gang research are not required to have true competitive bidding. So the 'good ole boy' network of political favoritism in providing such funding still exists in our federal agencies. No one has promised to clean up this problem.

What the federal government should be doing is not experimenting with gang problems, rather it should use what current knowledge exists and apply this in a single, standardized, national model of gang prevention and suppression. As discussed in a subsequent chapter in this book, some very recent federally funded "gang programs" may have resulted in situations remarkably similar and equivalent in impact to the notorious mistakes of providing federal funding to gang leaders like Jeff Fort via Rev. Fry in Chicago, where the money was not really spent on trying to put the gang out of business, it was spent in a fashion to increase the strength of the gang. That kind of federal government blunder has not entirely disappeared is what a subsequent chapter will reveal.

BUILDING CONSENSUS TO COMBAT CRIME

Most of the ethnomethodological, participant observation, "hang out in the hood" qualitative studies about gangs do not take into account the viewpoints of the vast majority of the citizens. The viewpoints of adults and juveniles alike who are not tied into gangs have not been heard from systematically. Yet many appear to be willing to speak on their behalf, usually without any objective assessment of citizen views. A way to build consensus to combat the gang crime problem is to start with a systematic social survey of the viewpoints of those who live in the community: particularly those who are registered voters, and of course those who invest in and work in the community.

CREATING A CITYWIDE GANG-FREE TASK FORCE

Using official agencies, churches, political groups, citizen volunteers, schools, business people --- the entire gamut of social institutions, one of the best things a city can do is create a citywide Gang-Free Task Force or a Violence Free Task Force[41]. Such a committee needs to be as broad-based as the gang problem is itself, and include all segments and levels of society.[42] Examples of such initiatives exist in many parts of the country.[43] It can help target aspects of the gang problem that can be easily remedied: such as removing gang graffiti. Having the Governor or Mayor declare a certain week as "Gang Awareness Week" can then allow some groups like this to hold numerous functions across the city working with all segments of the problem: recreation, school, etc.

WHERE TO BEGIN?

A community anti-gang organization can begin with one interested citizen. We can even assume that such a person knew absolutely nothing about criminology or how to fight crime. But what they should do is immediately contact the National Crime Prevention Council.[44] This is the "Mc Gruff" headquarters. They have an assortment of helpful materials that can be put to use at the community level for "taking a bite out of crime". Or they could be adapted in the spirit of "taking the bang out of the gang". These are the type of very elementary materials for persons who have no knowledge about crime or gangs. It is recommended, however, that any local effort invite local police and criminal justice personnel to their Task Force for the most effective way to apply concepts to local problems.

SUMMARY AND CONCLUSION

A high ranking police official who grew up on Chicago's southside once remarked to the present author, about his own adolescence, that one of the things that has changed through the years in Chicago that may have some bearing on the gang problem is the role of parks and public recreation. "There were a lot of adult supervised park programs that kept us busy", he remarked. Today in Chicago these socialization resources are unevenly distributed and probably at a premium. But such park programs as a community resource probably have been under represented in our gang literature in terms of their capability to "do something" (positive) about the gang problem.

It is unrealistic to expect the gang problem to be solved independently throughout America at the city and state levels. Federal assistance is going to be necessary (Huff, 1989). While much can be done at the local and state levels, it cannot be done effectively alone. First, local initiatives that are successful must be able to be replicated in other jurisdictions, and such a clearinghouse function can only be effective at the national level. Secondly, coordination is also vital at the state or regional level, because gangs are not simply a problem to our communities, they are also a problem for state correctional institutions and their boundaries of influence extend to different and often non-contiguous geographical areas.

Local schools are going to be required to play a much more prominent role than they have historically played in dealing with the gang problem (Ackley, 1984). Stephens (1988) shows a variety of ways in which this can be done.[45]

By most accounts the community itself can play a formidable role in both prevention and in gang suppression. It is a question only of organization, effort, support, and resources. If our nation's gangs are so "loosely organized"[46], then why are we so ineffective at all levels of society in gang dismemberment? The answer appears to be this: we have been doing the wrong thing. And typically these failed efforts have also been those with no theory as to what to expect from any given experiment, program or initiative.

Two Chicago programs that are based on good theory were described here (CAP and BUILD). They appear to work, or have great merit in terms of design. And, of course, there is much more to be done. Neither of these programs have been replicated elsewhere in America. They truly deserve to be.

DISCUSSION QUESTIONS

(1) Should local community groups and programs try to work with level zero and level one gangs and their members, seeking to reintegrate these youths and young adults in more prosocial activities, and leave more sophisticated gangs (level two and three gangs) to law enforcement?

(2) Could a program be designed for a community other than Chicago that reflects the best of both the BUILD and CAP programs? What would it involve as a solution to the gang problem? Could it be established as part of a strategic plan for community gang-violence reduction using a local Gang Violence Reduction Advisory Task Force? What would your ideal program for gang abatement be like?

(3) Poston (1971) was highly critical of direct funding to gangs and gang members because of their propensity to exploit the "establishment" as Jeff Fort did with Rev. Fry's assistance in Chicago. But if the government knew it was going to get ripped off, could this also function as a Trojan Horse strategy (recall Jeff Fort received a felony conviction out of such funds misappropriation) to make gangs more amenable to intervention?

FOOTNOTES

1. Suttles (1968, p. 168) showed a direct inverse relationship between age of gang members and local residence patterns. That is, the younger the gang member the more likely such a youth is to live in the same neighborhood. In age categories and residence, Suttles found those in the 11-14 age group showed 100% lived in the same neighborhood area, in the 14-16 age group some 88% lived in the same area, and in the 16-18 age group 80 percent lived in the same neighborhood area (Suttles, 1968: p. 168).

2. Some legislative efforts directed against youth gangs have sought to declare "safe zones" where the commission of a gang related crime in these areas constitutes grounds for more severe criminal penalties (e.g., schools, etc). Including section 8 housing and "projects" extends this institutional protection to the law abiding poor and is a worthwhile protection.

3. The research by Suttles (1964: p. 207) showed that 94% of the malicious mischief or property damage was committed inside the same neighborhood area, as well as 55 percent of all theft cases (Suttles, 1964: p. 208). However, Suttles also hypothesized that gang offenders would be reluctant to victimize those persons who live in close proximity to them. What matters is the type of offense. Some offenses are more likely to occur in the local area than others.

4. If local gang members are not the source of local property crimes, which I am reluctant to accept as a hypothesis even with some of the empirical support advanced by Suttles; then obviously, from the same hypothesis, gang rivalry can be extended to include intentional choice of a neighborhood for serious offenses because of this potential for "insulting" the local gang. Here, most obviously, is an area of much needed research that has significant practical implications. Such findings do emerge from more recent studies such as Moore, Hagedorn, etc.

5. Sometimes all it takes is a "tip" from a citizen. A routine tip on Chicago's southside led to the arrest of 61 gang members. Tips do pay off for law enforcement. See: Phillip J. O'Connor, "Tip Leads to 61 Gang Arrests", Chicago Sun-Times, Oct. 20, 1993, p. 22.

6. That is, one of the other historical continuities in the gang literature is the tendency of the gang members to express the view that they are "just defending the hood", and in some fashion therefore performing a valuable function, sanctioned by their social structure, or at least such a desired role function is communicated to such gang members, often along the lines of ethnic and racial conflict.

7. Is provincialism a good thing or a bad thing? Or is it everything, but in moderation? In an increasingly inseparable world community, and even within nations and cities with an increasingly more mobile population, is provincialism the denunciation of a more cosmopolitan view of the world? Provincialism implies territoriality. It can also be the refuge of residential segregation patterns (e.g., ethnic purity, etc).

8. The excellent summary about the lack of previous program effectiveness in gang crime intervention programs described by Walter Miller (1990) points to the problems of lack of theory, lack of hard evaluation research, and service organizations that continue "business as usual" even when they know their services don't work or may in fact be counterproductive.

9. See: George Papajohn, "Korean Store Boycott Splits South Siders; ties to gangs, politics seen", Chicago Tribune, Dec. 28, 1993, section 2, p. 1,4.

10. See Tom Siebel, "Surprise Defense Delays Priest's Vandalism Trial", Chicago Sun-Times Thursday, March 21, 1991, p. 22.

11. See Gordon McLean, 1991, Cities of Lonesome Fear: God Among the Gangs, Chicago: Moody Press.

12. According to Mc Lean (1991: p. 92) "More than forty representatives from twentysome Chicago street gangs and organizations have attended the sessions, currently being held at Calvary Memorial Church in Oak Park".

13. As McLean (1991: p. 94) indicates "It often causes a stir when used as identification on the street".

14. See: Art Golab, "Group Gangs Up on Crime", Chicago Sun-Times, Mar. 21, 1994, p. 1,14.

15. This was a presentation at the Annual Meeting of the American Society of Criminology.

16. Should the government do this? Actually, some in government are the least supportive of it, for a very selfish reason: for example, one of the larger obstacles to emptying out highrise public housing projects and dispersing the tenants to suburban areas where they might prefer to live, and where they could be assured of much greater job opportunities resulting in a substantial decrease in public expenditures on welfare, is that the politicians who get elected from such high rises are the least supportive of any such dispersal plan --- and for good reason, they might lose their voting base.

17. See: Philip Franchine, "Arrest Records Weed Out Bad Aurora Tenants", Chicago Sun-Times, July 11, 1994, p. 15.

18. See: Pamela Burdman, "Black Panther Philosophy Coming Back in Vogue", San Francisco Chronicle, Aug. 29, 1994, pp. 1,6.

19. See: The Austin Voice, March 1-8, 1994, Vol. 9, No. 12, pp. 1,4.

20. Often this is sexually divided, as a men only group, or as a group that emphasizes predominantly mothers (MAG and MAGIC), but also parents (PAG) together.

21. Chicago Area Project, The Nation's First Community-Based Delinquency Prevention Program, Chicago Area Project, 407 S. Dearborn Street, Suite 1300, Chicago, IL 60605 (312) 663-3574, p. 12.

22. Personal interview with CAP staff on 12-7-90.

23. Page 12, Chicago Area Project, The Nation's First Community-Based Delinquency Prevention Program, no date, late 1980s. Chicago Area Project, 407 S. Dearborn St., Suite 1300, Chicago, IL 60605.

24. Material quoted from staff training documents supplied by CAP.

25. Personal interview, October 26, 1990.

26. Page 3 of BUILD, Inc document entitled "Program Profile".

27. Counseling (individual and group), sports/cultural/recreational outings, home visits, teen parenting skills, and the like.

28. See: Barbara Dargis, "Park Forest Police Officer Trying To Help Area Youth", The Star, Feb. 13, 1994, A-4 CUP.

29. PAG is located at: Lower North Center, 1000 N. Sedgwick, Chicago, IL 60610 (tel. 312 - 787 - 2490).

30. Contact information: Communities Dare To Care, Dorothy Papachristos, Co-Founder, 7059 N. Greenview, Chicago, IL 60626. Telephone: (312) 338-CARE.

31. See: Chicago Sun-Times, May 4, 1994, p. 12.

32. See: Leslie Baldacci, "Show More Initiative For City, Daley Urges", Chicago Sun-Times, May 4, 1993, p.4.

33. The issue here is adequate information. If gangs do engage in drive-by shootings based on their knowledge of where rival gang members live, then do you think that the families that may also live in such a building or next door have the right to know whether such a building contains known gang members?

34. Recall the fondness of gang members keeping scrapbooks "describing their gang exploits" discussed by Jackson and Mc Bride (1990: p. 24).

35. At a public hearing, before the Illinois Gang Crimes Study Commission someone in the audience asked for more detailed "hand outs" from the police department, in responding to this a police commander said "That's a danger because what happens, the competition --- did you read the article in the Chicago Tribune about a month ago about gangs? The Tribune Magazine had about a nine-page article where they interviewed me and two of my people rode with them. It covered all gangs. We had some shootings as a result of that article because they involved one gang symbol and the other then in competition started up" (see Nash, 1984: p. 72).

36. See: Ken Parish Perkins, "60 Minutes in Little Rock's War Zone", Chicago Tribune, Section 5, pp. 1,3, August 1, 1994.

37. Horowitz's (1987) article "Community Tolerance of Gang Violence" is most useful here. Horowitz says "Parents often can maintain the fiction of their son's conventional conduct outside the home if he behaves properly when at home (Horowitz, 1987: p. 443)". We want to believe little Johnny is a good boy. But are we willing to join a recent Chicago campaign reported extensively in the mass media to "turn in a family member" who sells or uses drugs?

38. The biggest sample of hard data relating to this question so far was reported by Tromanhauser (1981). Regarding youths in school it showed: males know more about gangs than females, the older the student the more they are likely to report gang members in their school, the younger the age the greater the fear of gangs and percentage of youths reporting they are solicited for gang membership in school varies inversely with age (p. 187).

39. Susan R. Takata and Charles Tyler, "A Community-University Based Approach to Gang Intervention and Delinquency Prevention: Racine's Innovative Model for Small Cities", Journal of Gang Research (in press, 1994).

40. See: Roger Flaherty, "Security Beefed Up at NIU As Crime Shakes Campus", Chicago Sun-Times, Sept. 17, 1994, p. 12.

41. Several examples of these exist, one with some apparent success is that in Duluth, Minnesota "Violence Free Duluth", founded in response to a growing number of homicides in that northern Minnesota town. It does much direct outreach to teens.

42. For example, prosecuting gang leaders can often mean discovering everyone around the gang member was liable. The gang leader has an enormous "web of influence" that may also be tainted. This was the case in the leader of the Four Corner Hustlers, Rufus "Weasel" Sims featured on "AMERICAS MOST WANTED" television series. Pretty much everyone who worked with Sims was a co-conspirator. Convictions in the Sims case included: "his lawyer, Richard Goldstein, his 63-year-old mother, his wife, and a girlfriend". See: Tim Gerber, "Fugitive Sims Caught by L.A. Cops", Chicago Sun-Times, July 8, 1994, p. 20.

43. See the story for the one in Springfield, Illinois: Stephen Beaven, "Gang Presence Paints Hazy Picture", The State Journal-Register, July 10, 1994, pp. 1, 4.

44. National Crime Prevention Council, 733 15th Street, N.W., Suite 540, Washington, D.C 20005, telephone (202) 393-7141.

45. This document by the National School Safety Center also includes a listing of projects, and programs, nationally involved with gang intervention. One problem, however, appears that it advocates a program component of what amounts to the same mistake made by correctional institutions in terms of acknowledging and even negotiating with gang leaders (Stephens, 1988: p. 28). By suggesting that any strategy should be discussed "with student gang leaders and solicit their support", this is not too different than what correctional administrators did in earlier years.

46. Spergel (1989) summarizes some of the gang literature and concludes, generally, that gangs are "loosely organized". That is, consisting of core, regular, peripheral and recruit members. But apparently not as organized as we would think. Which were sentiments expressed similarly by Short to wit: that "gangs are characteristically unstable as a form of association and organization" (Short, 1974: p. 16). We must keep in mind, that when authors like Horowitz and Schwartz (1974) involving only one gang in one area of one large city is hardly enough data to be able to quote, as a generalization, when they say "the gang's organization is rudimentary (Horowitz and Schwartz, 1974: p. 239". It was rudimentary to their gang studied in a park in Chicago's lower west side because it was a level zero to level one gang formation. But we cannot generalize to all gangs from such limited findings.

CHAPTER 21

LAW ENFORCEMENT AND GANGS

INTRODUCTION

A police officer cannot arrest someone for simply belonging to a gang, as much as citizens might want to give them that power. Recalling the military-based legislation from India (Sleeman, 1849) there is no law that makes it a punishable offense to simply belong to such a group or to be associated with such a group. Further, not everyone who is a gang member is necessarily criminally active. What then can police do? That is the focus of this chapter. As will be seen, there are a variety of policies, programs, and initiatives that can be undertaken. Many of which could be beneficial in reducing gang crime. It requires planning, coordination, strategy, good information, and the necessary resources and support. This assumes that the fundamental responsibility for gang abatement and suppression is in the hands of law enforcement alone.[1]

GANGS ARE INTERESTED IN LAW ENFORCEMENT TOO!

Shortly after the L.A. riots when a "truce" existed between the Crips and the Bloods, these two gangs are credited with devising a plan for reconstructing their city[2]. They demanded $3.7 billion dollars for their budget to rebuild L.A. with the threat "Meet these demands and the targeting of police officers will stop: you have 72 hours for a response and commitment, in writing, to support these demands. Additionally you have 30 days to begin implementation" (p. 66).

Was it real or was it a fraud? No one knows, as no names of the authors appeared. But in addition to other ideas, they had a full law enforcement proposal which was as follows:

> "The Los Angeles communities are demanding that they are policed and patrolled by individuals who live in the community and the commanding officers be ten-year residents of the community in which they serve. Former gang members shall be given a chance to be patrol buddies in assisting in the protection of the neighborhoods. These former gang members will be required to go through police training and must comply with all of the laws instituted by our established authorities. Uniforms will be issued to each and every member of the "buddy system", however, no weapons will be issued. All patrol units must have a buddy patrol notified and present in the event of a police matter. Each buddy patrol will be supplied with a video camera and will tape each event and the officers handling the police matter. The buddy patrol will not interfere with any police matter unless instructed by a commanding officer. Each buddy patrol will also be supplied with a vehicle. $6 million shall be appropriated for this program over and above existing appropriations" (p. 66).

Whoever wrote this surely does not understand modern American law enforcement. Whoever wrote it does not know that most "police matters" do not involve subduing resistant arrestees, they involve order control: responding to domestic situations, etc -- where the last thing you need is a civilian "buddy" with a video camera. Gang members clearly are interested in law enforcement. Some without arrest records, or only minor juvenile records, actually become police officers. They are certainly eligible!

The close examination of the gang literature will show numerous examples of persons who report to being such "former gang members" as juveniles who later became responsible police officers. But were they "killers" and "drug dealers" in their youth? No. They were more typically level zero gangs, involved in local turf and periodic or seasonal very low intensity fights with rivals. Should police applicants be screened about prior gang membership? It is an interesting issue.

RICO PROSECUTIONS

As discussed elsewhere in this book, the federal RICO and state "mini-RICO" statutes are very effective tools against gangs. This 1970 federal law called the Racketeer Influenced and Corrupt Organizations Act was originally designed for use against traditional organized crime. It includes both provisions for criminal and civil prosecution. Anyone may initiate a civil prosecution under RICO, even against an employer. But the criminal sanctions and provisions in this law are effective against gangs because of the stiffer penalties against those charged, indicted, or convicted under the RICO act.

A number of effective prosecutions of gang members where almost total gang suppression, of that particular gang, occurred has been reported. This does not mean that a new gang will not come along and try to fill the void. But it does take out the gang in an effective way.[3]

CHICAGO'S EDGE AND SNAG INITIATIVES

Two recent police programs in Chicago include EDGE and SNAG. EDGE stands for Enhanced Drug and Gang Enforcement and is a proactive unit of "six sergeants and 60 officers in a unit to harass gang members and drug dealers in crime-ridden areas".[4] SNAG stands for Stop Narcotics And Gangs and involves using surveillance and sting operations against the gang, for example identifying a large scale drive-up drug retail operation, arresting the operators, and quickly setting up shop using undercover officers to arrest all the suburbanites who drive into the area asking to buy narcotics, selling them the drugs, arresting them, and impounding their vehicles. The Chicago public seemed happy to have these new programs. Unfortunately, some programs have to basically stay one step ahead of the American Civil Liberties Union which has taken upon itself to challenge a number of new laws and efforts directed against gangs.

WITNESS PROTECTION

At a cost of $19 million per year the federal government's witness protection program has provided "new identities, houses in different locations, and new jobs to over 4,889 informers since 1970" (Thio, 1988: p. 403). This has been primarily to support federal prosecution of traditional organized crime figures or racketeers. Any successful prosecution of gang leaders, using other gang members, is going to necessarily entail the same kind of witness protection program. What it means is having law enforcement agencies and prosecutors working together to offer genuine protection to gang informants.

Simply creating the propaganda illusion that those who are high-ranking gang members and who defect for purposes of prosecution to law enforcement are provided with "great comfort" can itself be a powerful mechanism for inducing defection. Sometimes it is useful to simply allow such a gang member to accept conditions of controlled witness protection and relocation, not because the offender may in fact be useful for prosecution, but rather because it may instill the legitimacy of such a choice among other gang offenders. And, of course, it has a demoralizing influence on the gang organization itself. No one is certain exactly what such an offender can or cannot testify to.

Such defection creates a powerful negotiating ploy for inducing other gang members to accept such immunity and protection. Witness protection is a key ingredient to spurring key gang informants to "roll over" and should be made available for strategic use by law enforcement personnel responsible for gang crime investigation[5]. It is an expensive proposition. But used effectively and strategically it can have optimal effects on successful gang prosecution.

Some current research is underway by the National Gang Crime Research Center to ascertain the extent to which expanding this kind of service might result in more effective prosecution of gang crime. It is not uncommon to find well placed gang members who area willing to testify against their gang leaders, and basically cripple the gang, for a small price; such as $10,000 for their family to relocate when the testimony is needed.

VICTIM ASSISTANCE

Generally, only twenty percent of all reported crimes in American society result in an arrest (Senna and Siegal, 1984: p. 24). For even serious felony crimes among those actually arrested only a fourth of these offenders do time (Senna and Siegal, 1984: p. 102). Here the math means only five percent of those offenders arrested among reported crimes, for serious offenses, actually serve a correctional sentence. Recall, that not all such serious crimes are even reported to the police. Thus, the actual probability of doing time in America for serious crime is most likely less than this five percent figure.

This is not to recommend more prison sentences. But rather to suggest in dramatic terms the fact that perhaps something could be done, through victim assistance programs, to at least increase the effective adjudication of many of the serious offenses that occur in our society. The fact is: victims of crime need more help, and their immediate sense or perception that they are alone or "left hanging" translates into their non-appearance at court and that means offenders go free.

Experienced police officers know how to handle victims to ensure their appearance at court. They make sure the victim has a number they can call for any problem that arises regarding the case. They make sure they call the victim the night before court and arrange, if necessary, for transportation to and from the location of the court appearance. They also try to give some sense of reassurance and confidence in the psychologically vulnerable period during the first stages of trial. They make sure victims are not intimidated by the offender in or out of the courtroom.

In too many our of cities, when victims appear at criminal court, they are left to their own devices to manage somehow to appear as state's evidence. What happens is all too common. In spite of the existence of such "victim assistance programs" within the State's Attorney's offices, victims still must find their own place to park, must still go through metal detectors in the same fashion as offenders out on bail, must wait in the hallways often side-by-side with the offender they must testify against when they have the eagerness to arrive for a court appearance early, and are often placed in the less than friendly environment of a cold and hard atmosphere that communicates little support from wider society for the victim or witness who must appear in court: that is, they often must sit side-by-side on the same bench, often ending up sitting next to the person they must testify against. Clearly, even minor accommodations could be made to have a more dramatic improvement of the environment that facilitates a stronger and more effective judicial handling of criminal cases for the purpose of reinforcing pro-social behavior on the part of victims and witnesses. This is even more important in the context of gang crimes.

To the victim and crime witness, such a "bureaucratic" treatment, forcing a levelling effect, where they are treated just like the offender, means ultimately they may never come back after such a first appearance. We lose testimony and witnesses systematically, because of the callous disregard for the social-psychological state of such potential witnesses for the prosecution.

Which brings up the organizational effectiveness hypothesis that perhaps we need not necessarily increase law enforcement strength in the gang crime specialty area, rather we need to ensure that we do not lose our witnesses "through the cracks" of bureaucratic justice! Higher conviction rates would occur if more could be done to reinforce cooperation with the judicial level of the criminal justice system. This should not be left to simply the law enforcement officials, nor to local community organizations, indeed it ultimately has its responsibility with the local state's attorney or U.S. Attorney. When a gang crime victim has never met the prosecutor before the time of court appearance, we are dealing with an environment that communicates only one thing to the potential witness "you are not important" or "we don't really care about you".

Gang crime victims and witnesses are those who especially need such assistance. Many of these crimes occur in their own neighborhoods and the offenders are also likely to be on the same streets. Victims and witnesses need "orders of protection" to ensure that as a matter of official record, such offenders, once convicted, cannot if let loose on probation, harass by their presence such citizens who have the courage to come forward and make the judicial system work.

SCREENING FOR RISK (SFR)

Gangs can be classified in terms of their level of organizational sophistication. Similarly, in an earlier chapter dealing with organized crime, it was seen that the scope and extent of criminal violations and the magnitude of illegal income or numbers of persons involved in such crime, are also important. Here both should be tied together in a screening for risk (SFR) application. This is the type of quantitative research methodology that is also called threat analysis when it focuses on the measureable danger represented by a gang.

The primary justification for SFR rests with the limited resources any society has for "control". We do not have an unlimited supply of criminal investigators. We do not have a unlimited supply of prison cells. By targeting offenders who are "high risk", "high volume", or "high impact" an SFR application applied to gangs would mean focusing law enforcement efforts on those gangs representing the largest threat to law and order. That is, those gangs involved in the highest levels of crime and violence.

Here, for the sake of simplicity, we shall revise the classification system from a range of "level zero thru level three" to that of including level "four" where level four corresponds to organized crime groups. Then we shall be able to add a numerical "crime potential severity code rating" to each such gang formation. This numerical assessment of a gang's real or potential capability to represent a threat of crime or violence to the public shall vary between zero (the lowest) and nine (the highest) in terms of threat analysis.[6] In this configuration, the lowest gang threat problem in America is the "Spanky and our gang" variation of Level zero-zero (0-0), corresponding to the pre-gang (streetcorner, playgroup, neighborhood clique) with no major potential for crime and violence; to the worst case gang scenario of a Level 3-9, corresponding to the "super gang" armed with fully automatic shoulder weapons and controlling a vast empire of illicit income-producing crimes. This leaves level 4 crime threats for organized crime groups. Figure 19 below summarizes this screening for risk (SFR) application to law enforcement.

FIGURE 19

A Screening For Risk (SFR) System for Gangs In
Relation To Their Organizational Sophistication
and Crime/Violence Potential in Law
Enforcement Applications

LEVEL OF ORGANIZATIONAL SOPHISTICATION:	LEVEL OF THREAT FROM CRIME AND VIOLENCE[7]
	0 1 2 3 4 5 6 7 8 9
	**
LEVEL 0	(not a true gang, a pre-gang)
LEVEL 1	(emergent gang)
LEVEL 2	(crystallized gang)
LEVEL 3	(the supergang, the corporate gang)
LEVEL 4	(organized crime groups)

Targeted Offender Programs (TOPS) operate under similar guidelines. Intelligence gathering is conducted to show which offenders are "highly active", typically as repeat offenders. A case file is prepared and a review process is conducted to make a decision as to whether a police department should, through its targeted offender program, "accept" such a case. Once accepted, the offender is targeted for prosecution.

It can involve the use of all techniques of criminal investigation, covert operations, and undercover techniques. The purpose is to "get that offender" off the streets, because the offender is highly active in local crime functions.

The same successful strategy can be adopted for gang crimes. But it will mean more than a subjective appraisal of any such gang offender's individual "threat". A more quantitative appraisal is needed to supplement the investigative strategy suggested for gang prosecutions by Burns and Deakin (1989). As they admit, the major problem is finding those gang members willing to roll over.[8] Otherwise, their method is not too dissimilar from the ancient "vice ladder"; that is, giving up small fish to catch bigger fish.   Obviously, such SFR values may change and fluctuate over time and would need constant updating. As an example, assume a local Posse group is used in this SFR rating system. It would minimally be a level three gang, being interstate in character. Assume that prior arrests in the area are high, that it is believed from intelligence sources to be highly armed, and that it has many fiscal resources to draw upon from its ongoing criminal activity. It might rate an SFR score value of 3.75 compared to 3.25 for a local group of the Miami Boys who met only one of the same three factors. It is never as simple as this and screening for risk methods require much more statistical analysis than is implied here. But basically, it would mean wanting to allocate investigatory resources in a manner that focuses on the higher risk gangs. And then, of course, adjusting the strategy to the results of prior efforts; through a continuous appraisal of the problem.

THE CHALLENGE OF GROUP DISRESPECT FOR THE LAW

The "risky shift" phenomena means basically that persons will act more severely in a group than they would perhaps behave as individuals. The challenge for law enforcement, then, is dealing with gangs as a group phenomenon and one flavored with more than a little disrespect for the law. According to some authors, gangs simply do not fear law enforcement:

> "Gang members are getting so bold that not only do they show total disregard for their fellow man, but they have no fear of police or any formal consequences for their actions" (Trojanowicz, 1978: p. 402).

It is a serious crisis of legitimation for law enforcement that is represented by the contemporary criminal gang. If not dealt with effectively, then it shall surely manifest erosion of confidence in law enforcement among other civilians.

MULTI-JURISDICTIONAL   EFFORTS

A simple truism is that gangs, while often having a territorial claim or a historical beginning that may be dependent on a specific "turf", do not limit all their crime activities to any specific political jurisdiction.[9] The problem in any given state is going to be, depending on the level of gang formation, multi-jurisdictional in nature. Task Forces and programs designed to address the gang problem must also, therefore, be able to cross traditional lines of political jurisdiction.[10]

This must include information sharing and subpoena power. Here both the state and federal courts have an important role to play. The one genuine organizational feature reflecting a change from earlier gang formations in the criminological literature is this matter of operational mobility. And the creation of satellite gang crime operations, often involving drug distribution, in other geographic areas. The California Council on Criminal Justice and its State Task Force on Gangs (1989) recently concluded, similarly, that gang drug trafficking is no local matter --- it is a statewide problem.[11]

State's today need enabling legislation to both create Metropolitan Enforcement Groups, or MEG units, and to allow these units to purse gangs and gun crimes just as they are traditionally enabled to investigate drug crimes. The simple fact is drugs, gangs, and violence are very inextricably related. More federal Gang Task Force groups that can work with local law enforcement can achieve the same effective results.

LOCAL AND STATEWIDE GANG INTELLIGENCE FILES

Most gang members, as part of the social-psychology of individual identity that reinforces gang affiliation, have gang names or monikers. The San Diego Police Department reported the value of maintaining a moniker file. It cross-indexes such nicknames, monikers, and aliases with true names and other identifying information (e.g., date of birth, gang of affiliation, etc) (see Kolender, 1982: p. 20). Alpha files are used for making name checks, and vehicle files are used to keep track of what vehicles and license numbers are known to be used by gang members.

The state-of-the-art in this area, however, is having a statewide gang and gang membership database maintained for intelligence purposes. The Illinois "SWORD" is one such example. The Statewide Organized Gang Database (SWORD) Act became effective in Illinois on January 1, 1993. It provides model legislation for other states in seeking to coordinate and monitor the scope and extent of the gang problem. The SWORD computer system is maintained by the State Police. The details of this model legislation are provided in their entirety here:

> "Illinois Criminal Code and Procedure. (1993). Chapter 20. Executive Branch. Act 2640. STATEWIDE ORGANIZED GANG DATABASE ACT.
>
> Section
>
> 2640/1. Short title.

2640/5. Definitions.

2640/10. Duties of the Department.

2640/15. Duties of local law enforcement agencies.

2640/1. Short title. This Article may be cited as the Statewide Organized Gang Database Act.

Title of Act: An Act to create the Statewide Organized Gang Database Act and the Illinois Streetgang Terrorism Omnibus Prevention Act.

2640/5. Definitions. "Department" means the Department of State Police. "Director" means the Director of State Police. A "SWORD terminal" is an interactive computerized communication and processing unit that permits a direct on-line communication with the Department of State Police's central data depository, the Statewide Organized Gang Database (SWORD).

2640/10. Duties of the Department. The department may:

(a) provide a uniform reporting format for the entry of pertinent information regarding the report of an arrested organized gang member or organized gang affiliate into SWORD;

(b) notify all law enforcement agencies that reports of arrested organized gang members or organized gang affiliates shall be entered into the database as soon as the minimum level of data specified by the Department is available to the reporting agency, and that no waiting period for the entry of that data exists;

(c) develop and implement a policy for notifying law enforcement agencies of the emergence of new organized gangs, or the change of a name or other identifying sign by an existing organized gang;

(d) compile and retain a historic data repository relating to organized gangs and their members and affiliates, in a manner that allows the information to be used by law enforcement and other agencies, deemed appropriate by the Director, for investigative purposes;

(e) compile and maintain a historic data repository relating to organized gangs and their members and affiliates in order to develop and improve techniques utilized by law enforcement agencies and prosecutors in the investigation, apprehension, and prosecution of members and affiliates of organized gangs;

(f) create a quality control program regarding confirmation of organized gang membership and organized gang affiliation data, timeliness and accuracy of information entered into SWORD, and performance audits of all entering agencies;

(g) locate all law enforcement agencies that could, in the opinion of the Director, benefit from access to SWORD, and notify them of its existence; and

(h) cooperate with all law enforcement agencies wishing to gain access to the SWORD system, and facilitate their entry into the system and their continued maintenance of access to it.

2640.15. Duties of local law enforcement agencies. Local law enforcement agencies who are members of the SWORD system may:

(a) after carrying out any arrest of any individual whom they believe to be a member or affiliate of an organized gang, create or update that individual's electronic file within the SWORD system; and

(b) notify the prosecutor of the accused of the accused individual's gang membership or gang affiliate status.

There is only one good feature missing from this Act, and that is the provision for logging in known gang members previously arrested in a given period, for example within the last five years; and all of those currently in confinement at the local and state level. It will take awhile to "feed in" the data, but eventually it will be a very powerful tool. It would be even more powerful if it had a provision for "priming the pump", and thus requiring local law enforcement agencies to report all such gang members or gang affiliates arrested in the last five years. Then, once the data was processed into the system, it would be operational in a very short period of time.

Citizens who live in states where this kind of law does not exist, and who want to do something to help empower their law enforcement agencies to "win the war" against gangs, should endeavor to have such legislation passed in their own states. Gang researchers will someday discover this kind of systematic data is the real way to answer many of the questions in our literature about gangs in America.

CHANGING POLICE PATROL STRATEGIES

Wilson and Kelling (1989) describe the value of changing police patrol functions from the traditional "incident oriented response" to a "problem oriented response". The incident oriented or traditional patrol technique is to simply respond to radio dispatches from citizen complainants. The problem oriented response means allowing the police officer more flexibility and having the police work more closely with the "good guys" rather than seeing their fundamental mission as being only to "lock up the bad guys". It also means, essentially, being more pro-active with regard to the gang problem.

It is, by the way, a recommended solution that can be very compatible with gang neighborhood programs such as CAP and BUILD described earlier. The idea is to put police into guarding and maintaining the local social infrastructure through their conspicuous presence. It is an idea whose time has truly come, and seems to genuinely offer a way to reduce fear of crime as well.

But it would mean, according to James F. Short, also changing what police are trained in and capable of doing. It would mean giving our police more skills in mediation, in conflict resolution, in consensus building, true "peace making", such that "police might become community advocates...rather than community adversaries".[12]

CHANGING THE CRIMINAL LAWS

Gang crime cannot be effectively prosecuted or investigated unless state criminal codes are consistent with regard to such organized threats against law and order. State criminal codes should not have "holes" or "prosecutorial gaps" such as those in Illinois. For example, Illinois criminal law technically allows an adult gang offender between the ages of 17 to 20 to direct a younger gang member in facilitating a felony crime by a juvenile, and cannot, if detected, be prosecuted under the more serious statutes for contributing to the delinquency of a minor. Let us review this Illinois "Fagin" law in some greater detail, for the large "hole" it contains favorable to gang crime operations:

> "Chapter 38. Illinois Criminal Code. Section 33D.1. Contributing to the Criminal Delinquency of a Juvenile. 33D-1. (a) Contributing to the criminal delinquency of a juvenile. Any person of the age 21 years and upwards, who with the intent to promote or facilitate the commission of a felony, solicits, compels or directs any person under the age of 17 years in the commission of such felony commits the offense of contributing to the criminal delinquency of a juvenile. (b) Sentence. Contributing to the criminal delinquency of a juvenile is a felony one grade higher than the offense committed, except when the offense committed is first degree murder or a Class X felony. When the offense committed is first degree murder or a Class X felony, the penalty for contributing to the criminal delinquency of a juvenile is the same as the penalty for first degree murder or a Class X felony, respectively (see Illinois Criminal Code, St. Paul: West Publishing, 1989 edition, p. 168).

Certainly, anyone 17 years of age or older charged with a felony is going to be prosecuted as an adult; but, oddly, this particular statute leaves a "gap" between the ages of 17 through 20, and can allow for such stiffer prosecution only at ages 21 and above. This kind of gap must be eliminated. The first segment of any society to come to understand the criminal code is the offender portion. They should not be able to "slip through the cracks" so easily. It is a good law, but one that was poorly constructed in terms of its scope. It allowed for a gap. Thus, technically, a fellow gang member 17 to 20 years of age can direct a juvenile to commit a serious crime and escape the prosecutorial impact of this criminal code.

State laws should also bolster local enforcement powers through the ability to confiscate vehicles and real estate property used in the commission of gang crimes, and explicitly authorize intelligence gathering activities related to crime to overcome restrictions such as those faced by Chicago police.

In the urgency to "do something" about the gang problem at the local city level, some municipal governments like Chicago have passed ordinances that were aimed at the gang problem. One law made it illegal to sell spray paint to persons under 18 years of age. The idea was to reduce access to the spray paint and maybe reduce gang graffiti. Passed in 1992, it was challenged, and in the fall of 1993 a federal judge ruled that the ordinance was unconstitutional under due process grounds. Similarly, a Chicago ordinance making it unlawful for known gang members to conspicuously loiter on street corners was ruled unconstitutional by a Cook County judge --- it was too vague, and thus subject to abuse[13].

DO POLICE HAVE THEIR "HANDS TIED" IN GANG CRIME INVESTIGATION?

"Our hands are tied", rang the sentiments of many police officers after the famous Miranda decision. But the Miranda decision did not, in the long run, have any deleterious impact on criminal investigation. In fact, it might have induced an element of professionalism that may have otherwise never been adopted in policy.

It is, however, a legitimate issue for discussion. But not about the Miranda warning. Rather it involves intelligence gathering activities, data processing capabilities, use of fingerprints and photographs of juveniles, and related issues that can be critical to solving any crime, including gang crime which often involves underage youths.

To illustrate these limitations of power and authority that law enforcement must work with, let us use a scenario. Assume someone, while you are away, breaks into your home and takes everything of value. A neighbor sees the youths leave your home with the "goods" and could identify them. So you insist that the neighbor be able to look at "mug shot files". You are also knowledgeable about forensics and insist on an evidence technician, one in facts arrives on the scene and collects some good fingerprint sets on the crime suspects. Now you must feel your case is solved, right? Wrong.

In Illinois the Juvenile Court Act does not allow police officers to show photographic "mug shots" of known gang members previously arrested to victims of crimes. These youths have the right of privacy under the law. So there goes the neighbor as witness, unless you can somehow catch the offender yourself.

In many jurisdictions, the Automated Fingerprint Identification System (AFIS) involves only a database for adult offenders. Juveniles, again for the protection of their privacy, are excluded from such computerized data sources. If you were really smart you might want to check about two and a half years later (that is, in Illinois most felony offenses including residential burglary have a three year statute of limitations, so you hope maybe that the offender is arrested again later as an adult and gets into the AFIS system), but then you may find that few police departments with the AFIS technology keep separate "unsolved crime" physical evidence files for "aging/follow-up" purposes.

In fact, let's assume you get really lucky. You and your neighbor spot one of the burglars and you are able to effect an arrest. Theoretically, in Illinois anyway, the offender could be taken into custody and could conceivably have four or five other outstanding felony warrants, but the fact that no centralized computer index exists for juveniles for purposes of a "name check" means the offender could be let free even with a series of outstanding felony warrants. And if the arresting police officer wants to do a "station adjustment" (a verbal reprimand, "don't do it again", and lets the offender go) you really have little recourse other than to grin and bear it..

But let's assume you were indeed very lucky, the offender was arrested and placed in custody and now it is court time. In Illinois, you do not have the right to be privy to all the matters before the juvenile court. In fact, you as the actual victim may be the only one allowed into the juvenile courtroom. In Illinois juveniles have more rights than adult offenders; what juveniles cannot have that adult offenders themselves do not take much advantage of anyhow is the jury trial.

In late 1993 an appeals court took away an effective tool for law enforcement: the use of mug shot books for gang suspects was ruled to intrude on individual liberties (Police, 1994: p. 15).[14] Police in many smaller jurisdictions have new recent ordinances about curfew and graffiti, some of these efforts are more effective than others. In some towns there have been backlashes against such efforts. But most seem to believe there is some value in hardening the target of smaller jurisdictions to make it harder for gangs to move in.

USE OF THE GRAND JURY

During the 1960s and early 1970s the grand jury was often used as a device to investigate groups. Largely those groups, often student leftist groups, who opposed the war in Vietnam or who espoused a radical philosophy (SDS, Black Panthers, etc). Fishing expeditions were common. It is curious, then, to see that the same relentless use of the grand jury has not been as prominently used in the prosecution of genuine law violation behavior on the part of organized criminal gangs.[15]

The value of the grand jury is that it can develop much more information than lone investigators. In fact, the fundamental investigative advantage of the grand jury, over individual efforts of local law enforcement investigators is that the grand jury is more suited to "unravel a complex criminal structure" (see Kasimar, La Fave, and Israel, 1990: p. 636). It can grant immunity from prosecution, apply psychological pressure, and operate in secrecy to essentially force a known gang member to testify.
Simply issuing large numbers of such subpoenas to members of the same gang can induce an enormous amount of infrastructure damage to morale and cohesiveness. It is a legal way to make an effective arrest as well among those who are most prone to resist legitimate authority. Arresting such offenders routinely for "disorderly conduct" charges has been shown to be less than effective. But not responding to a grand jury subpoena means contempt of court and an opportunity for strategic arrests.

States that in their criminal code of procedure authorize the investigative subpoena power function through mechanisms other than the grand jury, the so-called "one-man grand juries", typically a judge and a special prosector (see Kasimar, La Fave, and Israel, 1990: p. 641), can eliminate the high cost and complexity of grand jury criminal investigations of gangs. Thus, the "special prosecutor" approach represents a genuine low-cost alternative to a grand jury investigation. The advantage of the "special prosecutor" approach is its county wide jurisdiction, and through the intelligence gathering function, to be able to share information with other jurisdictions in the same state. Because few states have "state-wide grand jury" mechanisms. Even though, these will come to be more politically attractive as the gang problem posed for states increases beyond city and county jurisdictional lines.

THE CONTRADICTION OF COMMUNITY RELATIONS

What is the best policy for dealing with a community that is experiencing high rates of gang-related crime? To disclose the full severity of the problem to such residents and induce a panic that has obvious political implications to the effect that the status quo is not geared up to provide for adequate police protection and thereby possibly eroding respect for law enforcement? Or is it best to "triage" and through such law enforcement functions as Chicago's "beat representative" program to alert those more responsible and pro-law enforcement citizens to the "bigger picture"? That is, a balanced approach to disclosing the severity of the local crime threat.

In 1990, opinion polls showed that large numbers of persons living in New York City would move elsewhere if they could. Because of street violence. Presumably much of it owing to a gang origin. Cities like Chicago continue to experience a declining population; a "flight to the suburbs", a flight to greater security, a flight away from gang crime.

The contradiction, then, is that to be brutally honest with all citizens of the extent to which they face gang crime in the urban area is to risk both political and economic impact of a deleterious nature. Those most capable of moving out are those who have the higher incomes, leaving behind those who are more economically dependent.

Ultimately, it is a political issue. And local law enforcement agencies should be free from outside political pressure or influence regarding their decisions about responding to citizen pressures to brief them on the scope and extent of the problem. They have just as much right to know exactly how serious the gang crime threat is as they do to know whether their home is constructed on top of a toxic or radioactive waste site.

Universities and their police departments are by now totally familiar with the so-called "third party law suits". If they do not provide adequate protection, and a serious crime occurs, or if they are knowledgeable of such a clear and present crime threat and do not alert students and staff to its existence, and such a crime subsequently occurs, the "third party" law suit means not suing the actual offender, but suing the university or the facility in which the crime occurred, including employers. The issue is negligence. Failure to inform of real dangers, and thereby exposing innocent persons to undue risk of life or limb.

Finally, there are absolute limits on the scope and extent of social service functions that a police department can provide to its community. If they wanted social workers, then why train them to be crime fighters? Is it really that easy to wear both hats? Also, remember that the gang problem is not simply a law enforcement problem. In fact, as Muehlbauer and Dodder have stated "a community has failed its youth when its police force becomes the principal vehicle for the expression of community interest in young people outside the school" (1983: p. 129).

TRACKING, MONITORING, AND REPORTING "GANG-RELATED CRIME"

The police study by Needle and Stapleton (1983, p. 35) showed that "only four of the 27 departments reporting youth gang problems have written policies and procedures" dealing with gangs. That means chaos for police organization and management. Without adequate on-going training, without standards, without even a common definition of what is or is not a "gang-related crime", a law enforcement agency cannot ever hope to get a handle on the problem.

The definition of "gang-related crime" cannot be left up to the discretion of each and every police officer on the force. There must be clear guidelines for this, for otherwise any information reporting system faces the "garbage-in, garbage-out" (GIGO) problem of having no reliability.

JACKSON AND MC BRIDE: A LAW ENFORCEMENT VIEW OF GANGS

Jackson and Mc Bride provide a detailed, non-technical discussion of the gang crime problem in the Los Angeles area. All of Part II of their book (1989, pp. 87-136) is devoted to law enforcement. Chapter 5 describes the difficulty of measuring gang violence and how some police departments have very conservative definitions of gang crime such that if there are not at least five more gang members who attack five or more rival gang members, it is not gang crime (p. 91). Which is, of course, a very convenient way to "define out" any local gang crime problem.

Chapter 6 in Jackson and Mc Bride describes the gang unit of police organization and management. It provides one of the most complete discussions to date on management information systems applied to the gang problem, and what information needs to be collected. Chapter 7 in Jackson and Mc Bride discusses police patrol issues. This advises a positive, fair relationship with street gang members, because the police officer "whether he realizes it or not, is a de facto role model" (Jackson and McBride, 1990: p. 110).

Chapter 8 in Jackson and Mc Bride covers techniques of gang investigations. It suggests that the gang related crime scene should be considered a more expanded one than non-gang crime scenes. It provides helpful suggestions for investigating gang crime, including the cultivation of informants[16]. It also advocates witness protection not just for "violent cases, but in many others as well" (1990: p. 134).

These authors have also played a very positive role in setting law enforcement policy regarding gangs in America. Their book remains the single best law enforcement perspective on gangs today.

BURNS AND DEAKIN (1989): CHANGING INVESTIGATIVE APPROACHES

Traditional investigation techniques may not work as effectively with gangs is what Burns and Deakin (1989) argue. The gang crime problem reflects a pattern of such crimes and the traditional police response has been to look at these crimes in isolation, not as a recurrent pattern. Many of these individual crimes, alone, may therefore appear on the surface "senseless"; however in terms of a crime pattern may tell a different story.

These authors argue that there are varying levels of loyalty to the leaders among gang members and this can be exploited. One such method is the use of the grand jury investigation to heighten the psychological tension among gang members to provide information. The assumed prosecution policy here being to target leadership alone. Allowing some discretion for cooperative lower level gang members. Two other methods included: controlled arrest situations, and routine interviews of any arrestee who is a gang member. Again, the goal being that of getting greater amounts of information.

No difference is implied here between strategic or tactical intelligence on gangs. The authors express the belief that it is next to impossible to find out the exact force strength of any particular gang, only the top gang leader would know that if anyone.

SUCCESSFUL PROSECUTION METHODS: Sibley (1989)

The discussion by Sibley (1989) ties together successful criminal prosecution methods against gang offenders. It notes the difficulty of prosecuting gang leaders and takes the position that standard criminal prosecution techniques are ineffective (Sibley, 1989: p. 406). Importantly, it shows a growing body of criminal case law that allows as admissable evidence the factor of gang membership itself (p. 407). Gang membership or affiliation has probative value and can often establish a key element of motive (p. 408), and, of course, as a factor relating to witness credibility (p. 410).[17]

Bringing gang membership into play will mean using expert witness testimony on gang crime.[18] Typically police gang specialists (p. 412). Going up the gang organizational ladder to prosecute mid-management and leaders will mean the use of conspiracy charges (pp. 413-416). New criminal statutes are also emerging such as California's Street Terrorism Enforcement and Prevention (STEP) Act regarding violent gang activities.

In Illinois, the "Streetgang Terrorism Omnibus Prevention Act" was put into law at the same time as the SWORD gang computer information system discussed earlier. The Streetgang Terrorism act is a mini-rico statute that allows for additional criminal and civil penalties for crimes committed by gangs or gang members. States that do not have such statutes need to adopt them. A complete copy of this statute is provided in Appendix F. Citizens and policy makers who want to do something to strengthen the laws, to be able to more effectively confront the gang problem, should ask their state legislature to pass a similar Act. The concerns about the constitutionality of new laws aimed against gangs --- typically raised by the gangs or gang apologists themselves --- are moot issues when considering the right of any legislative body to seek to protect its citizens against known crime threats. Such laws are not directed against Spanky and Alfalfa, they are directed against groups whose members routinely commit crimes on behalf of or with the aid of the group, organization, or other members. That is, they commit crime, over time. That is what makes a gang. Put more simply: a gang is a more formidable crime threat than any sole, single, individual acting criminal offender.

THE G.R.E.A.T. PROGRAM

First known for its popularity in Phoenix, this has become a program nationwide through the Bureau of Alcohol Tobacco and Firearms (ATF). However, only in the fall of 1994 was a systematic effort unleashed to provide for program evaluation, so we shall have to wait for results on this federal research. It is a program similar to the DARE training for students, but applied to gangs it is Gang Resistance Education And Training (GREAT). An early evaluation of GREAT and two other gang prevention programs did not yield enthusiastic results (Palumbo, Eskay, and Hallet, 1993)[19] however.

NEW RESEARCH ON GANGS AND GUNS SHOWS POLICE ARE TARGETS OF GANGS

A Task Force Report on Gangs and Guns released at the Annual Meeting of the American Society of Criminology in 1994 by the National Gang Crime Research Center showed new important findings about how gangs get their guns and how they use them. This was a study of over 500 gang members in the midwest. Gang members have many sources in the underground economy for firearms and explosives. It is not uncommon for gang members to wear body armor during a crime. Another alarming trend is the tendency for gang members to be more likely to be involved in a police shoot out. Some gangs like the Insane Popes of Chicago make it a game in their initiation ritual to have the new member break into the home of a police officer and steal the firearms.

THE FBI SPY CHASERS ENTER THE HOOD

With the collapse of the Cold War, the FBI in 1992 reassigned 300 agents from its counterintelligence division to the violent crime divisions. These FBI agents work very closely with local law enforcement, and are having a stunning effect in the short time they have been on this mission. Federal convictions against gang leaders have soared in recent years, and much more work remains to be done in this regard.[20]

AN EXPERIMENTAL APPROACH: THE WESTMINISTER POLICE DEPARTMENT'S PROGRAM

One of the most professional law enforcement programs implemented and a successful one is the TARGET program in the City of Westminister, California: Tri Agency Resource Gang Enforcement Team (TARGET). This program was necessary in order to adapt police work to new laws such as the STEP Act. The STEP Act provides for increased prison sentences, where gang membership is viewed as a factor in aggravation, and carries an increase in penalty. In order to obtain a conviction under the STEP Act, however, certain intelligence needs must be met. Proving the gang membership of the offender, that the gang has three or more members, etc.

A very useful feature of the TARGET program is that it interfaces with other criminal justice personnel. An interface is established, for example, between probation officers and the police, and of course the district attorney. Probation and parole officers have an important role to play in gang crime suppression. The TARGET program has been viewed as a successful effort because of the increased arrests, gun seizures, and incarceration of gang leaders (Cook, 1993).

ESTABLISHING A LIAISON/PARTNERSHIP PROGRAM WITH LOCAL SCHOOLS

In the midwest many gang analysts know of the program started by one concerned juvenile police officer specializing in gangs. The Police-School Liaison Program was basically started in 1985 and continues today under the impetus of police officer Thomas Flemming from the Park Forest Police Department in Illinois. As the program literature describes it, this kind of interactive program is beneficial to both police departments and students: "Positive personal contacts with young people by police officers is therapeutic for both parties...students and police officers need to see each other as real people."[a] It certainly fits nicely into any community policing initiative, because it essentially means establishing linkages and rapport where it did not previously exist. Such an initiative is low-capital intensive, it requires very little "start up" funding.

THE 1990 NATIONAL POLICE CHIEF SURVEY

Based on the prior literature and relevant issues, survey items were designed and used in a national survey of police chiefs. This mail questionnaire approach was based on the 1990 Directory of Law Enforcement Agencies. This involved a ten percent random sample of all municipal police departments in the United States. The sample size of N = 236 used here therefore reflects those police chiefs responding to the survey.[21]

Of the police chiefs responding to this survey some 160 indicated that gangs have existed as a law enforcement problem in their jurisdiction for some period of time.

---

[a] From the Park Forest Safe School Consortium brochure.

Among this group (N = 160) when asked how long have gangs existed as a law enforcement problem in their jurisdiction, most (81.3%) indicated for under five years; 11.3 percent stated gangs have been a problem for between five and ten years, and another 7.5 percent indicated the gang problem had existed for over a decade.

Nationwide, among all responding to the survey, only 36.8 percent of these police departments receive pre-service training in handling gangs or "gang awareness". However, about half (50.7%) receive such in-service training.

When asked to estimate the total core and periphery gang membership in their jurisdictions, about a third indicated "zero" such members. The remaining police departments reported numbers ranging from 2 (small rural town) to 45,000 members (L.A.). Overall, among the police chiefs responding to the survey reported a total of 17,786 sworn law enforcement personnel on their force at the present time, compared to a total of 72,657 core and periphery gang members in their jurisdictions. It would appear worse than assumed: that gang members not only outnumber municipal police officers in America, it may be a situation of being substantially outnumbered by a factor of 4 to 1 or higher.

Here we sought to get directly to the issue of how much crime in America can be attributed to being "gang-related". When all police chiefs regardless if they reported they had a gang problem responded in percentage terms to the question "what is your estimate of gang involvement (gang as a group and as individual gang members) in all reported crimes" in their city, 46.5 percent indicated "zero", .4 percent indicated "one percent", .4 percent "two percent", 2.2 percent indicated "five percent", 30.4 percent indicated "ten percent", and 7.8 percent indicated 20 percent, 6.1 percent indicated "thirty percent", and the remainder indicated levels of up to 70 percent. This indicates an overall mean or average of 9.6 percent of all crimes among all police chiefs in America, regardless if they report a gang problem, being viewed as "gang related crimes".

When asked the same question, framed "how about gang involvement as a percentage of all crimes committed by youths in your city", 44.7 percent indicated "zero", .9 percent indicated "one percent", 1.8 percent indicated "five percent", 25.4 percent indicated "10 percent", and the remainder indicated levels of up to 80 percent of the youth crime problem being explained as a function of the gang. For an overall average, 13.5 percent of the crimes committed by youths in their city were considered to be gang related; whether or not the same police chiefs reported that they had a gang problem.

Here then are the most conservative estimates of what gangs contribute to the overall crime problem in the United States. It would range from 9.6 percent for all crimes, to 13.5 percent for all crimes committed by youths. But obviously, some cities contribute to more of the overall national crime picture than others. So it is useful to select as a subsample those police chiefs who report a definite gang problem, and within this set of cities to report the same "GRC" (Gang Related Crime) statistics.

Among those police chiefs responding who indicated that gangs have existed as a law enforcement problem in their jurisdiction for at least some period of time we find somewhat higher estimates of what gangs contribute to the overall crime problem and the youth crime problem. This "partials out" those police chiefs who report that gangs have not yet existed in their jurisdiction as a crime problem. Among this group (N = 160) who do acknowledge a gang problem existing for some period of time we find these police chiefs reporting a mean or average of 13.6 percent of all crimes in their city were gang related and 19.1 percent of all crimes committed by youths were gang related. At a higher level of gang crime problem seriousness, in terms of whether gangs are reported to currently be a crime problem in their district, which is a smaller sub-sample (N=74), we find figures of 21.6% and 29.4% respectively for gang percentage of all crimes and all youth crimes.

Most (64.2%) believe that federal agencies should play a greater role in the investigation and prosecution of gang crimes. Also, only 26.1 percent felt that the mass media and newspapers tend to over estimate the extent of the gang problem. And, most (73.2%) felt that parents are to blame for the gang membership of their children.

Nearly all (93.5%) believed gangs in their city were loose knit groups as opposed to (6.5%) highly organized groups. This actual belief reported by police obviously varies significantly from the belief in "military pyramid" style gangs attributed to them by Hagedorn (1988: p. 86). Klein (1990: pp. 13-14) stated that law enforcement agencies are quick to assume "street gangs are well-structured, cohesive collectives with strong individual leaders". Even when we examine the same data among only those police chiefs reporting a gang problem has existed for "any period of time" we find that 91.7 percent say the gangs are loose knit groups rather than higher organized groups (8.3%).

Seeking to compare the implications of the Short and Strodtbeck (1974) probability estimation with police chief estimates, they were asked "if a gang member committed a crime of violence in your city (other than homicide), what do you estimate the chances are that the gang member would be arrested?". Table 59 below shows this perceived probability of arrest distribution for gang assaults. Obviously, police chiefs see themselves as much more efficient than Short and Strodtbeck do in terms of making an arrest for a gang-related assault.

TABLE 59

DISTRIBUTION OF POLICE CHIEF ESTIMATES OF THEIR
PROBABILITY OF MAKING AN ARREST FOR A
GANG RELATED ASSAULT

Probability of an Arrest	Percentage
************	**********
0%	7.4
10%	6.4
20%	4.9
30%	2.0
40%	4.4
50%	14.8
60%	5.4
70%	11.8
80%	15.3
90%	13.8
100%	13.8

Most police chiefs responding (66.8%) rejected the idea that male police officers are better able than female police officers to handle the gang crime problem.

Regarding the efficacy of federal research dissemination we find police chiefs are equally likely to report a knowledge of the actual research of Needle and Stapleton (1983) as they are to report a knowledge of a non-existent study.   Most (90.2%) were not familiar with the Needle and Stapleton (1983) report.   And an almost identical percentage (90.3%) were not familiar with a totally non-existing report included as a separate question in the survey as a validity factor.[22]

Nationally, about half of the police chiefs (54.9) felt that gang members were not at all involved in extremist political beliefs.   But then, again, only 32.7 percent (N = 74) felt there was a current problem with gangs in their district.   But 57.7 (N=123) percent felt it is a growing problem.

Most (84.5%) believed that there are some street gangs that should be considered forms of organized crime.   Nearly all (96.4%) believed that the family is an important agency that can be used to prevent gang affiliation.   About a third (30.9%) indicated that correctional institutions cooperated to address the gang problem.   And nearly all (99.5%) would like to see more systematic interfacing between corrections and law enforcement in terms of information sharing.

Similar data will be reported in a subsequent chapter regarding the survey results from juvenile corrections superintendents, but among these police chiefs 43.3 percent felt we could more effectively deal with the gang problem if convicted gang members could be transferred to a central-national federal unit.

Most police chiefs (77.6%) believed that the "occult" or "satanism" (worshipers or dabblers) are also involved with gangs, although obviously no major research has surfaced on this issue yet in the literature. But increasingly, such material is also included in law enforcement and corrections "gang awareness" training.

When asked "do you feel that motorcycle gangs are a crime problem", 81.7 percent indicated yes.

When asked, do you feel that "detached workers" (social workers assigned to work with gang members on the streets) is an effective way to reduce gang violence, some 47.6 percent indicated "yes", and 52.4 percent "no".

It is interesting to note, in comparison however, that 46.5 percent believed that the military should be permitted to play a role in addressing the gang crime problem.[23] And 81.1 percent believed that expanding witness protection services would be helpful in addressing the gang crime problem.

Overall, when asked if they believed the gang crime problem is primarily a local problem or a multi-jurisdictional one, nearly all (91.5%) indicated it was a multi-jurisdictional problem, not a local problem (8.5). And most (88.9%) felt that we need tougher laws specifically dealing with the gang problem.

When asked, do you feel that local law enforcement should have the same options regarding juvenile offenders as adult offenders in terms of computer name checks on both, AFIS file checks on both, and authority to release names on both, nearly all (97.8%) indicated they wanted the option for computer name checks, 89.7 percent indicated they wanted AFIS for both juveniles and adults, and 68 percent indicated they wanted the authority to release names on both juveniles and adults.

About two-thirds (71%) felt that the grand jury should be used more to deal with the gang problem.

When asked, who has the primary responsibility for dealing with gangs (family, churches, business, school, police), a majority indicated (53.8%) the family, .5 percent the local churches, zero percent for business, 1.0 percent for the school system, and 44.8 percent indicated local law enforcement.[24]

All believed that the formation of regional gang intelligence meetings to brief each other and share information between different criminal justice agencies would be useful in addressing the gang crime problem.

A significant finding that warrants attention here is that while only about half (53.7%) of the police chiefs responding to the survey stated "yes" that the gangs in their jurisdiction were primarily of one ethnic or racial group, that the factor of in-service training significantly differentiates this belief. That is, among those police chiefs reporting that their departments provide in-service training on gangs, they were much more likely to report that in fact the gangs in their areas were of course primarily ethnically and racially homogeneous. Similarly, those police chiefs reporting that gangs were a problem in their district were also significantly more likely to report that gangs are ethnically homogeneous. What this cognitive factor means is that among those who are most truly likely to know about the gang crime problem, they are indeed more likely than not to affirm the historical continuity of gangs being ethnically and/or racially homogeneous.

THE 1992 LAW ENFORCEMENT SURVEY

As described in Chapter 14, this survey project was a collaborative effort among editors of _The Gang Journal_[b] representing researchers from four universities[25]. The analysis here simply summarizes some of the major descriptive findings about gangs from this large national sample of police chiefs and county sheriffs[26]. This study includes 248 police chiefs and 137 county sheriffs, and their assessments and views of the gang problem. The data was collected in late 1992 and early 1993.

Asked if youth gangs are a problem in their jurisdiction, 89.5 percent of the police chiefs and 79.4 percent of the sheriffs answered affirmatively. The percentage ratings of how serious a problem gangs represented were as follows:

	Police Chiefs	County Sheriffs
Major problem	18.4%	11.9%
Moderate problem	53.8	46.8
Minor problem	27.8	41.3

The higher percentage among police chiefs rating the gang problem as a major problem may reflect the urban-rural difference between these two types of law enforcement agencies.

The survey also asked the law enforcement administrators to provide two estimates: one for the percentage of the total crime in their jurisdiction that is caused by gang activity, and one for the percentage of total juvenile crime caused by gang activity. The results are as follows:

		Police Chiefs	County Sheriffs
% of Total crime caused by gangs:			
	Range	0-67%	0-60%
	Mean value	14.4%	11.1%
% of Juvenile Crime caused by gangs:			
	Range	0-90%	0-100%
	Mean value	26.7%	19.2%

This suggests, again, a somewhat larger overall average of what proportion of the total crime statistics can be attributed to gangs among police chiefs. Police chiefs on the average attribute just over a fourth of all juvenile crime (26.7%) to gangs. To date, these are the best estimates for what percentage of the overall crime problem

---

[b] _The Gang Journal: An Interdisciplinary Research Quarterly_ was formed in early 1992 and released its first issue in November, 1992, it is the official journal of the National Gang Crime Research Center at Chicago State University. The journal reorganized in 1994 as a totally independent journal, and is now known as the Journal of Gang Research.

in the U.S. is "gang related". Obviously, as well, it varies immensely from one jurisdiction to another.

It is further interesting to compare these figures with the degree to which these law enforcement agency budgets are specifically focused on the gang problem. Only 1.8 percent of the police chief budget and .5 percent of the county sheriff budget was directed toward the youth gang problem. In that gangs represent for many of these departments a relatively new phenomenon, perhaps these organizations have not yet adapted to accelerated social changes represented by gangs. Only 35.2 percent of the police chiefs and only 22.1 percent of the county sheriffs indicated that their department has a strategic plan for dealing with youth gangs.

Has gang activity become more violent in recent years? Most definitely, is the answer from this survey. Some 80.4 percent of the police chiefs and 66.7 percent of the sheriffs felt that gang activity has become more violent in recent years. Few felt it had become less violent (3% for Chiefs, .8 percent for Sheriffs), suggesting gang political activists have a long way to go before they can convince these respondents of any success in reducing gang violence through "gang truces".

These law enforcement professionals were also asked to rate the extent to which social programs are available in their jurisdiction that are designed to reduce/prevent the gang problem. On a scale of 0 (few programs) to 10 (many programs), the mean rating for police chiefs was 3.36 compared to 2.68 among county sheriffs. In their view, then, little is being done about the gang problem in America in terms of social programs. About half of the respondents (54.8% police chiefs, 45% county sheriffs) agreed that "detached workers," defined as social workers assigned to work with gang members on the streets, represent an effective way to reduce gang violence. Some 41.6 percent of the police chiefs and 21.3 percent of the county sheriffs reported that their departments have programs or services specifically aimed at youth gangs or youth gang members.

One of the most interesting findings has to do with the specific year the gang problem first came to be recognized in the communities represented in this survey. While cities like Chicago, Los Angeles, and some others have always had gangs, the present data suggests recent proliferation of the problem. The mean for police chiefs was 1985.2, compared to 1987.2 for county sheriffs; thus, on the average nationwide police chiefs first recognized the gang problem in 1987, county sheriffs in 1987. In fact, 95.6 percent of all gang problems by county sheriffs were first recognized in their jurisdictions on or after 1980! Further, some 85.6 percent of police chiefs first recognized the gang problem in their jurisdiction in the time frame of 1980 to present.

It is useful to examine this regarding in what year did gangs first become recognized as a problem in the jurisdictions of the respondents to this survey. In terms of recent presidential time periods, the findings are as follows:

	Police Chiefs	County Sheriffs
In what year did gangs first become recognized as a problem in your jurisdiction?		
On or before 1980	14.9%	6.1%
1981 - 1984	10.0	7.1
1985 - 1988	35.6	36.8
1989 - 1992	39.5	50.0

As seen here, about three-fourths of the city and county jurisdictions in America first recognized their gang problem during the time period between 1985 and 1992. During this eight year period --- the last term of President Ronald Reagan and the one term of President George Bush --- the gang problem quietly exploded in American cities and counties. Whatever the claims of these two presidents to being "crime fighters" the historical record reflected here shows that the gang problem vastly proliferated and expanded across America on their watch.

When asked, specifically, to rate the degree to which sworn police officers in their departments are provided with adequate ongoing training to successfully confront the modern gang problem, on a scale of zero (poor) to ten (excellent), both police chiefs and county sheriffs offered somewhat less an average answers. The mean or average value for police chiefs was 4.3 compared to 3.3 for county sheriffs on a scale from 0 to 10. Among police chiefs, about half (49.6%) report that their officers receive pre-service training in gang awareness or handling gang problems; compared to 43.8 percent among county sheriffs. Similarly, 70.2 percent of the police chiefs and 64.7 percent of the county sheriffs indicated that their officers receive such in-service training.

These law enforcement administrators were also asked to rate the extent to which the lack of a coordinated national policy has increased the youth gang problem in American cities. Again, a scale from a low of zero (no effect) to a high of ten (large effect) was used. The mean value for police chiefs was 5.7, and 5.4 for county sheriffs for the sample overall.

About four-fifths of police chiefs (83.3%) and county sheriffs (82.2%) agreed that tougher juvenile laws would aid the law enforcement response to the youth-oriented gang culture. Most similarly felt that the increased use of computer systems which store information on gangs will be an effective device in aiding investigative action against gangs (98.8% for police chiefs, 96.3% for county sheriffs).

The respondents were also asked to rate the extent to which language and cultural barriers may be a problem affecting their own law enforcement efforts at curbing the increase of Asian gang activity. On a scale of 0 (not a problem) to 10 (a large problem), the average value for police chiefs and county sheriffs was identical - a mean of 5.1 on the scale.

Overwhelmingly the respondents expressed the belief that the observed expansion of city gangs to suburban areas will continue through the mid-1990s (99.2% police chiefs, 99.3% county sheriffs).

The survey also asked the respondents whether their department can identify the leaders of the gangs within their jurisdiction. Some 82.1 percent of the police chiefs and 65.9 percent of the county sheriffs said they could identify the gang leaders in their area.

About three-fourths of the respondents believed that parents are to blame for the gang membership of their children (77.5% police chiefs, 74.4% county sheriffs).

When asked if the gangs in their area are loose knit or highly organized, most of these police administrators also do not believe the gangs in their areas are highly organized. In fact, 89.4% of the police chiefs and 91.6 percent of the county sheriffs thought the gangs in their areas were loose knit groups. Thus, only 10.6 percent of the police chiefs and 8.4 percent of the county sheriffs felt their gangs were highly organized.

The respondents were also asked to estimate the total gang membership in their jurisdiction. For police chiefs providing this data (N=214), this ranged from a low of zero to a high of 58,300; an overall sum for all police chiefs of 231,574 and a mean of 1,083. For county sheriffs providing this data (N=103), this ranged from a low of zero to a high of 13,000; an overall sum for all sheriffs of 75,151 and a mean of 749.

Most of the respondents (73.5% police chiefs, 66.4% county sheriffs) expressed the belief that federal agencies should play a greater role in the investigation and prosecution of gang crimes. This is easier to understand in light of figures on how many sworn officers are assigned full-time to work on the gang problem: an average of 5.3 officers among police chiefs, and an average of 1.3 among police chiefs. Almost half (47.7%) of all police chiefs and nearly a fourth (24.8%) of all county sheriffs indicated that their department does have a special unit to handle gang problems. Most of these law enforcement professionals also felt that the gang unit should be centralized rather than decentralized (65.4% police chiefs, 75.6% county sheriffs) where centralized was defined as city/county wide gang unit. Those supporting a decentralized gang unit, meaning each area commander responsible for a specific community area has his/her own gang crime officers for deploying locally, were in the minority (34.6% police chiefs, 24.4% county sheriffs).

Motorcycle gangs were felt to be more of a crime problem among county sheriffs (34.1%) than among police chiefs (22.7%). Further, some 29.7 percent of the police chiefs and a larger 43.7 percent of the county sheriffs felt that "hate groups" (KKK, neo-nazis, skinheads, etc) are a crime problem in their area.

The vast majority of the respondents (93% police chiefs, 94.7% county sheriffs) felt that the gang problem was multi-jurisdictional problem rather than simply a local crime problem. Nearly all of these law enforcement officials (98.4% police chiefs, 98.5% county sheriffs) expressed the belief that some gangs can migrate to jurisdictions like their own[27]. In fact, nearly four-fifths (80% police chiefs, 78.8% county sheriffs) expressed the more specific belief that at least some of the gang problem that existed in their jurisdictions was due to gang migration.

As a cross-check on this migration issue, the respondents were also asked additionally to rate the extent to which the gang problem in their area arose because of gang migration defined as outside gangs coming into their area to develop their own local franchises or local chapters; a scale of zero (not a factor) to ten (major factor) was used. For police chiefs the mean was 4.97 compared to 4.61 for county sheriffs.

Another question asked the respondents to estimate to what extent the gang problem in their area arose because of the "copy cat" phenomenon defined as youths who use the names of national groups without really having ties to the same groups in other areas; the scale varied from a low of zero (not a factor) to a high of ten (major factor). For police chiefs the mean was 5.4 compared to a mean of 5.2 among county sheriffs. Clearly, when put in this comparative context, the officials in this sample give greater credence to the "copy cat" syndrome than they do to intentional gang imperialism (i.e., developing franchises) in terms of the higher mean scores.

Over two-thirds of the respondents (71.2% police chiefs, 72.1% county sheriffs) also agreed that the grand jury should be used more to deal with the gang problem.
It is interesting to note that when asked if they believe the public recognizes that there is a problem with gangs in their area, 30.3 percent of the police chiefs and 55 percent of the county sheriffs said "no". What this means, clearly, is that more law enforcement agencies recognize the problem than the public does. Only 27.5 percent of the police chiefs and 24.2 percent of the county sheriffs felt that elected officials have worked to sufficiently educate the public about youth gangs. About a fourth of the police chiefs (25.2%) and about an eighth (12.8%) of the county sheriffs believed that their local governmental bodies (city councils, county boards, etc) have allocated sufficient resources to combat the gangs in their area.

SUMMARY AND CONCLUSION

There are many issues in law enforcement related to gang crime. These are issues of policy, of structure and organization, and of resource allocation. Obviously, as well, there are many other issues in the overlap between law enforcement and gangs that have not been discussed here[28].

What this shows is that some things can and do work and deserve being expanded significantly, such as witness protection and victim assistance. Changing police patrol methods and using more innovative investigation techniques have also been recommended ways of addressing the gang problem.

Greater use of the grand jury and the increased belief that gang crime represents a multi-jurisdictional problem also have major implications for change in law enforcement. While the data collected and reported here represent some of the largest studies of their kind since the earlier work of Needle and Stapleton (1983), clearly more research is needed. Most smaller police departments do not have their officers trained on gang issues, and do not have a strategic plan for dealing with gangs.

Finally, there is one thing that can be done at little cost to help American law enforcement address the crime threat represented by gangs. Many smaller police departments are isolated and do not routinely interface with other law enforcement agencies to receive updated information on the gang problem. In some areas of the USA, "Gang Investigator" associations have formed. The two largest being the California Gang Investigators Association and the Midwestern Gang Investigators

Association. Some other states like Arkansas have started their own statewide Gang Investigators Association. What is needed is a National Gang Investigators Association! Many criminal justice personnel other than police have vital roles to play in these types of training and education associations, including those who work in prisons, in juvenile institutions, in probation and parole, etc. Here again, the federal government has not been a leader in stimulating what could really pay off immediately for those who are responsible for protecting citizens from the threat of gang crime.

DISCUSSION QUESTIONS

(1) Why would a decision support system be useful to law enforcement in managing the investigation of gang crime? Indeed, what planning issues should be dealt with in a "strategic plan" to deal with local criminal gangs?

(2) What special problems might arise in a gang crime unit where different policies and laws apply to the handling of juvenile versus adult offenders? How should a gang unit operate under the terms of what is known as "community policing"?

(3) How would you explain the discrepancy reflected in the data reported in this chapter in terms of the proportion that gangs contribute to the overall crime pattern and the much smaller organizational readiness of these law enforcement agencies to "tackle the problem"?

RECOMMENDED READINGS

California Attorney General's Youth Gang Task Force
    1981 Report on Youth Gang Violence in California. California: Department of Justice.

California Council on Criminal Justice
    1986 Final Report: State Task Force on Youth Gang Violence. Sacramento, CA. 1989. State Task Force on Gangs and Drugs. Sacramento, CA.

Collins, H. Craig
    1977 "Street Gangs of New York: A Prototype of Organized Youth Gangs", Law and Order (25)(1)(Jan): 6-16.

Crime Control Digest
    (Various works, consult the bibliography).

Dahmann, J
    1981 "Operation Hardcore: A Prosecutorial Response to Violent Gang Criminality", interim report, MITRE Corporation, McLean, VA.

David, J.J. and M.H. Shaffer
    1988 Intelligence Gathering in the Investigation of Motorcycle Gangs, National Institute of Justice, NCJRS, Rockville, MD.

Day, D
1987 "Outlaw Motorcycle Gangs", Royal Canadian Mounted Police Gazette (49)(5): 1-42.

De Leon, Aleister
1977 "Averting Violence in the Gang Community", The Police Chief (44)(7)(July): 52-53.

Duran, M
1975 "What Makes a Difference in Working with Youth Gangs?", Crime Prevention Review (2): 25-30.

Florida House of Representatives
1987 Issue Paper: Youth Gangs in Florida. Committee on Youth. Tallahassee, FL.

Gott, Raymond
1991 (Audio training tape) "Juvenile Gangs and Drug Trafficking", available through the National Juvenile Detention Association, 217 Perkins Bldg, Richmond, KY 40475-3127.

Haire, Thomas D
1979 "Street Gangs: Some Suggested Remedies for Violence and Vandalism", The Police Chief (46)(7)(July): 54-55.

International Association of Chiefs of Police
1986 Organized Motorcycle Gangs. Gaithersburg, MO 20878.

Jameson, S.H
1956 "Policeman's Non-Official Role in Combatting Gangs and Vandalism", Association for Professional Law Enforcement, Quarterly Journal (3)(June): 1-3.

Johnson, W.C
1981 "Motorcycle Gangs and White Collar Crime", The Police Chief (47)(6)(June): 32-33.

Juvenile Justice Digest
1980 "Police Community Relations: Crime Prevention of Gangs", (Feb. 22): 7-8.

Kasimer, Yale
1971 "When the Cops Were Not 'Handcuffed'", pp. 46-57 in Donald R. Cressey (ed.), Crime & Criminal Justice, Chicago: Quadrangle Books.

Klein, Malcolm W
1965 "Juvenile Gangs, Police, and Detached Workers: Controversies About Intervention", Social Service Review (39): 183-190.

Klein, Malcolm W.; Cheryl Maxson; and Margaret A. Gordon
    1986 "The Impact of Police Investigations on Police-Reported Rates of
    Gang and Nongang Homicides", Criminology (24): 489-512.

Kobrin, Solomon
    1964 "Legal and Ethical Problems of Street Gang Work", Crime and
    Delinquency (10)(2): 152-156.

Lyman, M.D
    1989   "Street Youth Gangs", (From Gangland: Drug Trafficking by
    Organized Criminals, pp. 95-111), Newbury Park, CA: Sage Publications.

Mc Guire, P
    1986 "Outlaw Motorcycle Gangs - Organized Crime on Wheels", National
    Sheriff (37)(2)(Apr-May): 68-75.

Mc Kinney, K.C
    1988 Juvenile Gangs: Crime and Drug Trafficking. U.S. Dept. of Justice,
    Office of Juvenile Justice and Delinquency Prevention, Washington, D.C.

Miller, Walter B
    1982 Crime by Youth Gangs and Youth Groups in the United States, report
    prepared for the National Youth Gang Survey, Washington, D.C.: Office of
    Juvenile Justice and Delinquency Prevention.

    1989   "Recommendations for Terms to Be Used for Designating Law
    Violating Youth Groups", paper presented at the Conference of the National
    Youth Gang Suppression and Intervention Project, Chicago.

Moore, Mark and Mark A.R. Kleiman
    1989 The Police and Drugs. Washington, D.C.: National Institute of Justice.

Morash, Merry
    1990   "Gangs and Violence", in A.J. Reiss, Jr., N. Weiner, and J. Roth
    (eds.), Violent Criminal Behavior, Report of the Panel on the Understand-
    ing and Control of Violent Behavior, National Academy of Sciences,
    Washington, D.C.: National Academy Press.

Ontario Police Department
    1989 "Gangs, Move 'Em Out of Your Life", (video), Ontario, CA 91761.

Pennell, Susan and Christine Curtis
    1982 Juvenile Violence and Gang-Related Crime. San Diego: San Diego
    Association of Governments.

Philobosian, R.H
    1986   State Task Force on Youth Gang Violence. Sacramento, CA:
    California Council in Criminal Justice.

Reuter, P
    1989 Youth Gangs and Drug Distribution: A Preliminary Enquiry. RAND
    Corporation, Washington, D.C.

Sipchen, Bob
    1993 Baby Insane and the Buddha. New York: Doubleday.

Spergel, Irving
    1989 Report of the Law Enforcement Youth Symposium. National Youth
    Gang Suppression and Intervention Program. University of Chicago, School
    of Social Service Administration.
    1990 Law Enforcement Definitional Conference -Transcript.

Stapleton, W. Vaughn and Jerome Needle
    1982 Police Handling of Youth Gangs. Washington, D.C.: Office of
    Juvenile Justice and Delinquency Prevention.

Weiner, Arthur K
    1965 "C-R-A-C-K-I-N-G The Hard Core Area", Police Chief (32)(Jan): 27-
    31.

Werthman, Carl and Irving Piliavin
    1967 "Gang Members and the Police", in David Bordua (ed), The Police:
    Six Sociological Essays, New York: Wiley.

FOOTNOTES

1. Huff (1989, p. 525) reports research that most school principals view police as having the primary responsibility for dealing with gangs. Presumably, we are talking about criminal gangs. A level zero gang formation, a "pre-gang", is not within the legitimate purview of law enforcement until it comes to the attention of local police through law violation.

2. The Bloods and the Crips, 1992, "L.A. Vision: Program to Rebuild Los Angeles", Z Magazine (5)(7/8)(July/Aug): 63-66.

3. See: "U.S. Drives Out Bronx Drug Gang", by Matthew Purdy, Chicago Tribune, Oct. 20, 1994, Section 1A, p. 33.

4. P. 9, Chicago Tribune, June 9, 1994, Section 2, p. 9.

5. Lacking any federal support in terms of facilitating the linkages and information sharing across law enforcement jurisdictions, in recent years "gang investigator associations" have formed. California has one. There is also the Midwest Gang Investigators Association covering Minnesota, Wisconsin, Iowa, Illinois, Michigan, Indiana, Ohio and other states. What is needed is a national version. Many southern states (Florida, Texas, etc) lack this information sharing network.

6. Daniels (1987, p. 126) recommends in addition to regional gang intelligence sharing the same opportunity to conduct, among gang crime investigators and those charged with dealing with the gang offender in the correctional areas (prison, parole, probation, etc) the use of such regional meetings to update "threat analysis" of various gangs.

7. There are numerous ways to derive "threat level". One of the simplest is a percentile of all known gang members who have a history of serious felony convictions. It could focus on the "violence proneness" in a similar format. Recognizing that such "force threats" would have to be re-calibrated and revised periodically.

8. We might suggest that opportunity is everything. Gang infrastructure requires periodic internal discipline. It is invariably of the nature of a violent assault upon the gang member, with the ending admonition, "be a better gang member" and "all is well". Like a fatherly spanking. But psychologically, these routine internal "violation" events have not been adequately researched. We do not know if there are lasting effects of such "violations" from a social-psychological account. The idea, here, is that those "expecting" a "gang trial" soon, or expecting a serious violation, or who have recently suffered from such a beating, may be those more susceptible to law enforcement cooperation --- assuming that law enforcement could genuinely provide some alternatives (e.g., witness protection, relocation, etc, or rely on the myth of the effectiveness of such methods used strategically).

9. Contemporary gang authors are not in agreement on the matter of whether gangs can be "franchised" or exported from one state to the next. But the evidence that emerged from the present study in the case of LK29 is that at least in the case of the Chicago Latin Kings, there was an intentional development effort to create such a franchise in Indiana. The gang member, in this case a former gang member, is in fact college educated (lacking 22 hours for a Bachelors degree) and currently works in the court system. He is considered very reliable and admits to his own violence for purposes of being "made" into the Latin Kings.

10. This was also a recommendation by the Committee on Youth to the Florida House of Representatives (1987), where the recommendation for dealing with the increasingly severe gang problem involved a more comprehensive approach, one that was multicounty in nature.

11. Vigil (1988: p. 175) reports that the California Gang Investigators Association meets to discuss and share information along the lines suggested here.

12. See James F. Short, "New Wine in Old Bottle? Change and Continuity in American Gangs", p. 232, in C. Ronald Huff, 1990, Gangs in America, Newbury Park: Sage Publications.

13. See "Laws Struck Down on Gangs, Graffiti", p. 1,4, Chicago Sun-Times, Thursday, Sept. 30, 1993. However, Mayor Daley instructed the police department to continue to enforce the ordinance on gang members loitering, saying the people

needed the law and that judges don't live in the real world. See Fran Spielman, "Police to Ignore Gang Law Ruling", p. 12, Chicago Sun-Times, Oct. 1, 1993.

14. "Police 'Gang Book' Photos Ruled Illegal", Police, January, 1994, p. 15.

15. Recently (Burns and Deakin, 1989) the grand jury has been used to induce psychological pressure and as part of a new strategy in gang prosecutions Baltimore.

16. For an excellent case study in the development of a very useful gang informant see Sipchen (1993), which describes how a member of a San Diego Crip gang was cultivated and put to effective use.

17. From the defense attorney viewpoint, however, there is another side of the story. Professor Pamela Hill, Department of Corrections and Criminal Justice, indicated "the first thing a prosecutor wants to bring out is that the defendant is a member of a gang...but from my perspective as a defense attorney, if it is an individual crime, then gang membership is irrelevant...some gang members get accused of crimes just because they are gang members" (1991, personal interview).

18. Again, Professor Pamela Hill reminds us that in this process many "have failed to take into consideration why young people join gangs, it may not be initially for a purpose of crime; crime is secondary, crime was not in most instances the primary purpose for joining a gang...and all members do not necessarily partake in criminal activities....those are often individual acts more than group decisions (personal interview, 1991).

19. Dennis J. Palumbo, Robert Eskay, and Michael Hallett, 1993 "Do Gang Prevention Strategies Actually Reduce Crime?", The Gang Journal, (1)(4): 1-10. The Gang Journal is now known as the Journal of Gang Research.

20. For an excellent summary of this FBI initiative, see: Thomas Ferraro, "The FBI Takes Aim At Gangs", Insight on the News, October 5, 1992.

21. This is a preliminary analysis of this data, and the sample size will most surely increase, but has been analyzed here up to the point in time when this book had to go to press (March, 1991).

22. There were two separate questions, "Are you familiar with the 1983 Needle and Stapleton report on the Police Handling of Youth Gangs?" and "Are you familiar with the 1985 Springer and Detwyler report on Police Response to Gang Problems?" Springer and Detwyler were two students of mine involved in phases of this research, and they never wrote such a report, and the report simply does not exist.

23. Recall from Haskins (1975, p. 29) that in early American history when local law enforcement was not sufficient to deal with gang urban disorders, the military was called in. The military generally "had no trouble dispersing the gangs" that were in group conflict (p. 29). So there is a historical context under which the military has been brought into play regarding gang violence.

24. Obviously, to compare with the findings from Huff (1989, p. 525) what we seem to see here is a general tendency of "passing the blame". Educators say the police are primarily responsible, the police say it is mostly the family, etc.

25. Chicago State University: George W. Knox and Edward D. Tromanhauser; Rhode Island College: Pamela Irving Jackson and Darek Niklas; St. Ambrose University: James G. Houston and Paul Koch; and the University of Illinois at Chicago: James R. Sutton.

26. All data was used, which means the present analysis was able to use one or more additional "cases" that came in by mail after the release of the Preliminary Report on this research.

27. The prior evidence on gang migration has been, prior to this survey, been primarily anecdotal. Bartollas (1993: p. 20) describes interviews with gang leaders and reported the gang intentionally sought to develop a national organization, more specifically the gang member made the claim "it won't be long before we are coast to coast", and accomplishing this goal by means of sending out gang ambassadors to develop "sets" or factions of the parent gang organization. As Bartollas notes, gang migration also occurs by means of shipping prisoners from one prison to the next, and when gang members are involved in interstate travel and are caught and prosecuted in another state, they often set up their own local chapters of the gang.

28. One issue not discussed is the power of the gang to corrupt police officers. Knowing what history shows us as "possible" can help predict what is probable to occur. Kaplan and Dubro (1986: p. 159) describe the crisis in law enforcement in Japan when a closer investigation revealed hundreds of Japanese police officers were accepting bribes from Jakuza gangs.

CHAPTER 22

GANGS AND ADULT CORRECTIONAL INSTITUTIONS

INTRODUCTION

The correctional institutions of any society are open systems. As crime patterns change and as criminal prosecution patterns change, such societal output is the new input to corrections. That is, as their incoming prisoner population changes, the jails and prisons also change. As society changes, so does the prison. But maybe not as fast as it needs to. Here we examine a major problem facing all aspects of adult correctional institutions today: the gang problem.[1]

The gang problem, as will be seen, is tied into a number of other larger issues and problems associated with adult correctional institutions. Ultimately it is not the prison walls, the barbed wire, the machine gun turrets and rifle towers, and the threat of legitimate force that keep prisoners from escaping. It is the sense of control by legitimate authority. It is not an easy task. In fact, it is considerably more complex given the magnitude of the gang problem in American corrections as implied by the organizational nature of gangs in the correctional setting. As will be seen, the changing nature of the threat represented by gangs behind bars has meant that the correctional system itself has had to adapt as well: one response has been to seek to develop more secure "super maximum security" facilities for violent gang members who continued to be violent behind bars, such as that at Pelican Bay State Prison in California. Other states like Illinois are also seeking to implement such initiatives, with a super maximum prison in Tamms, Illinois scheduled to open in 1996.[2]

This chapter therefore examines a number of issues about gangs behind bars. Recent research on the problem in adult prisons and jails is also summarized.

WHAT GANGS ARE IN PRISON?

All gangs in prison are not simply "prison gangs". The fact is, most gangs are imported into the prison when their members and leaders are successfully prosecuted for major crimes. Most of the gangs that exist in prisons are also gangs that exist outside of the prison, what some simply call "street gangs". There are, however, some unique variations here; particularly where a threat group exists and may function as a gang inside the prison but is not known to exist as such an entity outside of prison. For a long time, many thought the Aryan Brotherhood were simply "prison gang" chapters. In fact, the Aryan Brotherhood does function as a criminal gang outside of the prison context.

In Illinois there are two such examples of gangs that originated in prison and appear only to function in the correctional setting: the Southern Illinois Association (SIA), and the "Northsiders". Both formed as a white extremist reaction against conspicuously organized minority inmates who had their gangs. The SIA was less successful in recruitment and is not considered a major threat today. The "Northsiders", on the other hand, still continues to function by that name in Illinois prisons, but not on the northside streets of Chicago. The "Northsiders" are white extremist inmates, said to be first organized by an inmate named Joseph Ganci in Menard. The "Northsiders" gang appears, then, to fit the profile of the "self-protection" group formation process: it arises in reaction to the perceived threat or fear of other inmates who are organized into such a gang. The correctional setting is an ideal breeding ground for such gang formations.

The answer to the question "what gangs are in prison" is therefore all gangs that commit crimes in the free world whose members are sent to prison; in addition to those that form inside prison as a threat group to counter-act what the members may perceive as a threat from other gangs or gang members that exist inside prison society. That is, gangs can be "imported" into a prison; and they can naturally arise, typically in reaction to the existence of other threat groups or gangs.

IMPORTATION VERSUS INDIGENOUS FORMATION: Gangs Behind Bars

The magnitude of the gang problem was not as bad as it is today, apparently, in the same institutions when Jacobs conducted his famous study of Stateville in the 1970s (Jacobs, 1974; 1977). Did society change, thereby reflecting the same problem in our prison system? Or were gangs targeted for prosecution above the priority of lone "non-gang affiliated" offenders? Importation theory sees subcultures such as gangs arising in the prison system because they have essentially been "imported" into the prison system via their targeted prosecution on the streets. Jacobs (1974, 1977) observed the empirical trend correctly in Illinois: most of the gangs that functioned behind bars were imported into the prison system.

Indigenous formation theory sees the gang arising naturally in response to threat, conflict, or victimization from an existing gang. Most gangs operating in adult correctional institutions would seem to fit the explanation offered by importation theory. Still there are examples known where gangs form in reaction to the obviously organized presence of other threat groups in the prison environment.[3]

The strongest evidence for the indigenous formation theory is that from Fong and his colleagues in research on gangs inside the Texas Department of Corrections (Buentello, Fong, and Vogel, 1991). Eight such gangs which represent most of the problem in the Texas correctional system are said to have basically grown and developed inside the prison. Fong and his colleagues see prison gangs arising in the following indigenous sequence: fearful inmates enter into a "clique", which can become a "protection group", which can become a "predator group", which ultimately can become a "prison gang".

One gang begets another gang in opposition is the way some gangs form, both inside correctional settings and at the community level outside of the context of confinement. The clique or friendship patterns of group association found in prison life are comparable to those found in any institutional culture, such as the military, where the most common bond is the proximity of ones geographical origin (e.g., "where do you come from?", "where did you live?"). The social factor superceding this "homie factor" is that of racial differentiation in patterns of human interaction, which is of racism and patterns of racial enmity.

There is one major unique situation that must be taken into account in any theory that addresses the etiology of Texas prison gangs: the fact that until the federal courts said to stop it, Texas prisons were basically run by inmates called "Building Tenders" also known unaffectionately as "B.T.'s" by the inmates who they would often beat, and kill if necessary, to maintain order. The B.T.'s were trustees with the authority to administer discipline; and as inmates themselves, the amount of cotton picked by Texas prisoners was directly proportional to the amount of fear that the B.T.'s could induce among the prisoners.

Texas correctional officials using "B.T.'s" was not an isolated instance in American corrections as institutions were being administered similarly in other states. Was it cruel and unusual punishment because it denied due process to inmates? It depends on your perspective. The Texas public probably wanted it that way, the BT system was in effect from the late 1800s to 1982.[4] So the Texas Department of Corrections was not doing anything that was not pretty much an accepted practice in its own state and existed in similar forms elsewhere in the United States. The "B.T. system" is known by other names in other states: the barn boss system, the trustee system, etc, its just that Texas did it in a big way. Did the Texas Department of Corrections stop using B.T.'s when the legislature ordered it to? Yes, of course.

But therein lies the problem. Prison culture --- the prison environment, the prison ethos, the prison organization, the inmate value system --- is hard to change over night. In the Texas prison inmate society the "B.T. system" had existed for a very long time. The essential feature of the B.T. system was cooptation; coopting some of the biggest and meanest inmates to control the other inmates. This process of informally granting disciplinary power to inmates was clearly violating the United Nations standards (1955) on the treatment of prisoners[5], it had just not been brought to the attention in a formal complaint until inmate law suits began to be filed and prison reform activists became involved. The Texas legislature in 1973 revised prison law to the effect of prohibiting the use of B.T.'s[6]. But apparently BT's continued well up until 1982. In 1983 many new correctional officers were hired to take the place of BT's. In 1984 the intelligence unit started to create gang files. In fact, the first few years after the actual end of the BT system is when a gang analysis begins. Before 1983 inmates controlled inmates officially, in roles as building tenders (BT's).

The problem then is that the Texas Department of Corrections was uniquely predisposed to the formation of such power groups, threat groups, or gangs forming indigenously once the B.T. system was abolished. The prisonization process Texas inmates went through was getting used to another inmate called a B.T. who would always get his way, and could have many amenities through the use of force or the threat of force. And what did the B.T.'s do when they were told "sorry guys, thanks for the help, but the feds say we can't use you any more". It is unlikely that all B.T.'s were suddenly paroled or released. The real research question then for any theory of the etiology of gangs in Texas was what role the B.T.'s played in such indigenous gang formation.

Prior to being abolished, the B.T.'s clearly functioned as a "goon squad" for the Texas Department of Corrections. The B.T.'s were, in a real sense, a gang with government approval. The B.T.'s functioned like vigilantes for correctional management; they made things run real smooth, very similar to the way Nazi concentration camps used prisoners to control other prisoners. As Fong and his colleagues report, no official records of "non-fatal stabbings" were kept in the Texas Department of Corrections before 1984 (1991: p. 4). So what we have here is a failure to communicate the scope and extent of violence in everyday life in the Texas correctional environment including such routine stabbings and other life-threatening injuries sustained from assaults. The modern correctional manager knows these kinds of injuries received by inmates are sources of legal liability to the correctional system itself.

THE SCOPE OF THE PROBLEM

Shortly before the Director of the Illinois Department of Corrections transferred to another state agency outside of the field of corrections, he published an interesting account of gangs in the Illinois prison system (Lane, 1989). This article in Corrections Today estimated that "between 80-90 percent of the inmates in the Illinois system have some affiliation with street gangs" (Lane, 1989: p. 99). Implied in this article is that if prison administration is lax or incompetent, then the prison will be de facto "gang administered".[7] That is, the gangs will literally exert such power and influence that they will control the prison, not the warden. Recent reports tend to suggest this is close to being the reality now inside IDOC:

> "According to one highly placed source, the gangs control the Stateville tiers and the correctional officers are cowed and intimidated by them. "If the officers refuse to allow friends and relatives to bring contraband into the prison for the inmates the correctional officers are shown that the prisoners possess photographs of their homes, their wives, and children".[8]

Multiple sources same to say the same thing adding greater validity to this story. Correctional officer Lawrence Kush was one of 30 on a gang's hit list at Stateville, these were prison employees who did their job, not taking any crap from the gangs, and not being compromised.[9] Kush was assassinated by the same gang on July 1, 1989, by the same gang that warned in a letter this would happen unless the employees "eased up" on gang operations.[10] A level three gang operates as a formidable terrorist group behind bars is what the evidence suggests. The official record indicates correctional officers are being undermined in their work when administrators negotiate with gang leaders under the pretext of avoiding prison riots.

In early June 1994 correctional officers at Pontiac prison in Illinois complained through their union that the prison administrators were making deals with the gangs and demanded more of a zero tolerance approach to gangs. The authority of line correctional officers is systematically undermined when wardens grant special privileges and "discretion" to gang leaders. This 1994 problem is possibly a holdover from a previous administration, as once the gang has been "negotiated with" it is difficult to go back to a zero tolerance approach without inducing much change and population restructuring and staff reassignment. Gang violence is not limited to the maximum security units, but has also spread to the medium and minimum security facilities in Illinois.[11]

The single national survey of corrections regarding gangs reported in our literature is that by Camp and Camp (1985) conducted in 1983[12]. It focused on prison systems (i.e., one prison system per state), the adult component of corrections.[13] It found prison gangs existed in 33 states. State leaders in prison gang membership were Pennsylvania, Illinois and California. Some 29 states reported a combined gang membership of 12,624.[14] There has been no reported update of these statistics since then.[15] And from the prior literature we have no knowledge about the state of juvenile correctional populations.[16] What we do know is that nearly 96 percent of all prison inmates eventually return to society.

The Camp and Camp (1985) study was basically replicated by the American Correctional Association (ACA) with a federal grant from the National Institute of Corrections to conduct a national assessment of gangs in corrections. The ACA report (1993) estimated that only six percent of the American prison inmate population were gang members. This definition of gang members included security threat groups (STG's) like Muslims, or groups of two or more with a bad attitude. This gang density estimate is believed to be notoriously unreliable and more fictional than factual. Simple math helps us here: if only 6 percent of the one million inmates in America are gang members, that means we have a small problem nationwide, only 60,000 gang members behind bars to worry about. California is said to have more than that number alone in its adult system. The California gang density rate is estimated to be comparable to that in its juvenile division (CYA), about 75 percent.

What we also lack is an analysis of the differences, if any, in post-release behavior of such gang-affiliated prison releasees. Do they have higher rates of recidivism? In Illinois, current statistics tend to suggest that two out of every three such released state prisoners will be arrested and/or convicted of a new crime within a two year period. Even conservative criminological doctrines have been less than productive in this area of research, for we do not know if the "burnout hypothesis"[17] is applicable to such gang-affiliated felons.

One of the few quantitative researchers adding to our understanding of the prison gang problem is Fong (1990) who provides a very a detailed analysis of the gangs in the Texas prison system. Fong shows that the largest Texas prison gangs are organized in a military style hierarchy (1990, p. 39). Equally important Fong documents the existence of written gang constitutions in the Texas prison situation (p. 40). Finally, Fong shows that prison gangs do not simply disband when their gang members are released. In fact, quite the contrary there is much continued communication and involvement with the gang in a way that allows the gang to expand its criminal activities (p. 42). In this way, Fong[18] establishes that the gang problem is in fact "exported" to our communities outside of the prison.[19]

THE ROLE OF STANDARDS GOVERNING CORRECTIONAL SETTINGS

The existence of policy standards guiding the function and operation of correctional institutions is the essence of the role that the American Correctional Association (ACA) plays in accrediting correctional facilities of all types. Such standards are good. They provide for uniformity, fairness, continuity, and better structure.

Standards promulgated by ACA cover virtually every aspect of correctional facilities from the physical plant and security to medical care and inmate grievances.

While gangs are such a critical aspect of correctional life, representing tremendous potential for violence, disruption, and security problems, the American Correctional Association at this point in time requires no standards for dealing with prison gangs. Particularly when it is shown that racial conflict among inmates tends to be a significant co-variate or surrogate measure of the inmate gang problem[20]. Perhaps some topics are taboo. Or perhaps here we see the "community denial" syndrome affecting American corrections as well. Recall that correctional institutions must be "safe and secure" facilities. Definitions of what constitutes cruel and unusual punishment evolve constitutionally as does society. So perhaps litigation could induce some change in corrections.[21]

In the absence of policy standards, correctional administrators are essentially in the awkward managerial position of "flying by the seat of their pants" regarding gangs. One might ask, logically, is it okay to group all gang members of one particular gang in one particular section of the institution; or reserve an entire correctional facility for one gang if its membership is large enough? Certainly, that would be the simple way to manage inter-gang violence. But is it really a good idea to segregate gangs? Or should gang members be mainstreamed, mixed in with the rest of the correctional population strictly on the basis of their security level classification?

Should correctional administrators officially recognize their inmate gang leaders and meet with them regularly, even hold "multi-gang conferences", allow them to have "group picnics" in the prison for their own gang members,[22] to work out more amicable relationships between the various gangs in the facility? Or does this official recognition[23] translate as legitimizing the gang as an organization? Could it even be tantamount to a condition of de facto gang administration of the correctional facility?[24]

It is a violation of the United Nations guidelines on the treatment of prisoners to place any inmate in a position of having "disciplinary power" over other inmates[25]. Therefore a correctional administrator cannot in good conscience urge a gang leader to do anything to control other prisoners. It is equal in force to a delegation of power.

Our prison systems have changed with the advent of extensive litigation dating from the 1960s which has created much case law establishing, in effect, prisoner rights. Inmate trustees can no longer be handed a 12 gauge shotgun, a whip, or a billyclub and be told to "restore order" or "keep them convicts in line".[26]

Effective management today means well designed policies and procedures, ongoing staff training, and effective security, all balanced by inmate rights. Therefore, in light of the management problem posed by inmate gangs, there appears only one logical choice. This involves using the law and disciplinary codes to suppress gang crime, gang violence, and gang disturbances within the correctional setting. It should mean no delegation of informal authority to gang leaders and it should mean no official recognition or deference to such influential gang figures.

For to officially recognize the gang leader is equivalent in function to recognizing all other gang members as "prisoners of war", feeding whatever existential notion they may have as being "political prisoners" because of racism, oppression, what have you. This is not to deny that such political prisoners exist, or prisoners of conscience as Amnesty International considers them.   But our typical prison gang member is anything other than a educated intellectual or leader who came to the attention of law enforcement through political protest. Perhaps we should distinguish between prisoners with a developed political consciousness and political prisoners. In any case, recognition of gangs can only mean, ultimately, a larger problem of correctional management. And further problems, for society as a whole, when they return to our communities more organized than they were when they entered prison.

Prison should not be an opportunity to expand gang membership and to solidify gang operations outside of the prison context. Poor management is at the heart of any such condition of "de facto" gang control of the correctional facility. As a general rule of thumb, all correctional officers develop a reservoir of "good will" with their inmate charges, but this is done most effectively on an individual basis. Not in a group fashion.

The prison administrator who fosters such a "participatory management" alliance with gang leaders creates only a more difficult problem for correctional line staff. And remember, it is the line staff, the correctional officers, who do most of the most difficult work in corrections. The development of policy, procedures, an overall strategy, and effective staff training is an absolutely first step in even "getting a grip" on the gang problem in corrections today.[27]

FIRST AMENDMENT RIGHTS AND PRISON GANGS

Does the first amendment's clause about "freedom of association" guarantee an inmate's right to hold gang meetings?[28] Or to congregate en masse in what could be viewed as an intimidating crowd? Or when a particular gang virtually "takes over" what was established as a legitimate inmate organization (e.g., Toastmasters, Jaycees, etc, etc,), and begins to operate in such a fashion as to use this, or even a religious occasion, for its gang meetings, is the correctional administrator at risk of violating first amendment rights by shutting down such groups from further activity? These are but some of the issues that need to be examined here. Generally, the need for security and to maintain order tend to override such concerns when there is the genuine threat to correctional discipline and good order.

That is, running a "safe" correctional institution will tend to justify a number of restrictions.   The difference between jails from one county to the next, both contiguous, may be enormous regarding visitation procedures.   One may allow contact visits, the other (citing security grounds) may not. In the latter case, if the government agency can show a compelling interest in preserving order and security, it can clearly prohibit such contact visits. The same principle seems to apply to the gang organization situation.

Remember, the Constitution is a living document. Even notions of what constitutes "cruel and unusual" punishment may change as society and its moral standards change. As society changes, so does the prison. Or, more appropriately, so should the prison. But the fundamental policy question facing American corrections today is: what is the best policy for dealing with inmate gangs?

Also, this must be balanced with another constitutional right of prisoners: their right not to live in fear of physical harm. Gangs clearly represent a pervasive threat of physical harm. And those states that have the death penalty routinely have inmates sitting on death row for homicides committed against other inmates in gang conflicts within the prison setting.

This right to live free from fear of physical harm also has implications for the implemented policies in many of our nation's prisons and jails which is called among other things, the "off set" approach to managing the gang problem. It means screening inmates as they come into the facility for their gang membership. Then inmates are assigned to units where a "balance of power" is established numerically in terms of inmates in the cell-house, unit, etc. Such an approach must be constantly monitored for frequent gang conflict flare ups, and therefore always needs daily "fine tuning" as a gang management method. But essentially, it means keeping two often warring groups in the same living unit.

The major problem with this approach is that it generates new gang members. Someone entering such a unit will have to join one side or the other. Neutrals or "neutrons" as they are called do not fare well. But again, this illustrates the kind of problems that can arise when local administrators are able to make their own decisions on how to handle the gang problem. In a situation where there are no written guidelines or standards promulgated by groups like the American Correctional Association, what happens is the informal process takes over. Then we get such policies as the "off set" method. An enormous variety of such methods that clearly recognize the gang and allow it to claim authority as a group exist.

OUTSIDE GANG RESOURCES SUPPLIED TO INMATE GANG MEMBERS

If Chicago's Latin Kings are representative of how gangs are capable of providing resources for their fellow gang members who are incarcerated, then we must recognize that gangs provide something unique to prison life generally. Gangs provide outside desirable resources, particularly cash, or commissary money. Historically, inmates have been in the situation of having nothing other than their family members to periodically send them "commissary" money to supplement the meager legitimate income they can make in prison. The same applies, in a stronger sense, to those locked up in our local jails; where there is no legitimate source of income that can be earned in the jail, you either have someone on the outside who can provide you with "cigarette" money, or you don't smoke.

Because the information here comes from what should be considered privileged sources, that is a well placed gang member holding office, who was able to provide the weekly minutes from each gang meeting, the specific identity of this particular Latin King gang chapter cannot be revealed.[29] The minutes, however, are hand written, often punctuated with gang insignia, and are considered authentic. They detail dues collection, gang unit accumulation of funds, expenditure of funds for the purchase of handguns, the specific instances of "violation" or giving disciplinary attention to other gang members, and also in some instances reveal a pattern of the local gang unit sending money to some of its members who are in custody. It also details minor expenditures such as "$6.00 was spent on spray paint to fix the hood". Mostly, it detailed a pattern of using dues money in amounts such as $30 to $40 to send to fellow gang inmates who are incarcerated.[30] By the way, after firearms being the major source of gang expenditures, gang apparel (shirts, etc) and gang totems (e.g, emblems for the meeting place, etc) constituted the next highest single item area for expenditures from gang income.

More organized gangs such as the Yakuza also use their dues to pay for basically "gate money" (i.e., post-release spending money) for their members who are released from prison (Kaplan and Dubro, 1986: p. 132).

CORRECTIONAL PROGRAMING FOR THE SOCIAL PSYCHOLOGY OF GANGS

If it is the gang that provides so many inmates under confinement with a sense of identity and a social role, then perhaps correctional programing should focus on inducing role distance. That is, role distance means having a sense of "self" apart from that of one's functional role. To manage a correctional facility with high levels of gang affiliation must necessarily mean struggling against the enormous power of the gang to reinforce individual identity. To provide identity alternatives to the gang is to provide an additional source of social control.

Role distance is not estrangement or alienation in the typical sense. Clearly, at the heart of gang affiliation is the deeper cluster of motives and experiences generally spelling out alienation. Alienation, anger and conflict tend to feed and reinforce gang membership. Therefore, to reduce alienation, anger, and conflict is potentially a logical method of countering the hegemony of the gang in a correctional setting. Conflict resolution is becoming increasingly popular in early childhood education as a primary prevention method for reducing violence.

The problem with the use of inmate organizations such as the Jaycees, Toastmasters, Dale Carnegie courses, and especially ethnic identity and religious "clubs", etc, inside correctional institutions, is that these are typically structured in a voluntaristic fashion. That is, anyone can join. Recognizing that the inmate population represents various gangs that may seek to control or influence these legitimate organizations, often correctional administrators have had no choice, once these officially sponsored meetings turned out to be dominated by specific groups, other than to eliminate them entirely or allow them to continue to operate knowing they are little more than "fronts" for specific gangs, and that realistically such inmate organizations "serve" only members of a specific gang rather than the entire inmate population.

The prison inmate culture portrayed in the 1950s as having the primary orientation of "do you own time" can be expected to disappear with the increased density of gang members in the same inmate population. Looking at this problem by interviewing released prisoners one study (Hunt, Riegel, Morales, and Waldorf, 1993) highlights this problem. It noted that the older "cons" view with some apprehension the arrival of a new "Pepsi generation" of aggressive younger inmate gang members who are basically out to make a reputation for themselves[31]. As the prison system is an open system this changing ethos of the inmate culture should come as no surprise. What it signals is a clear and major problem for correctional management: we are no longer dealing with the "lone offender" who believes in "doing you own time", what we are dealing with when we are facing a critical density of gang members in the inmate population is an entirely different management problem: such gangs represent sub rosa organizations.

THE QUEST FOR DOMINATION AND GANGS

Prison violence provides a unique look at race relations in America. The prison gangs tend to be clearly differentiated along racial and ethnic lines. The conflict pattern is both inter-gang and gang versus non-gang inmates. Regarding racism, prisons are more like steaming cauldrons than peaceful melting pots; it is an enmity that is deep-seated and rests along with a less than pro-social urge for the conquest and domination of others. And here lies one of the biggest challenges to correctional management today: how to reduce or control this enormous potential for violence.

For the social scientist, interested in race relations, this challenge is a natural for a field experiment in changing values and improving race relations.[32] But that has not been a pattern of much correctional research in America. If it is true that in all adversities there is a seed of equal or greater benefit, then the benefit of such controlled racial conflict environments is that they present an enormous opportunity for scholarly research and experimentation on improving the nature of race relations. If it can be effective in a prison, then it can replicated anywhere.

Unfortunately this is not a "hot research area" receiving much in the way of knowledge development reinforcement via government or foundation funding. The critical reader may ask "why"? For example, the American Correctional Association does not require programs regarding the encouragement of better race and ethnic relations within the correctional atmosphere. The Camp and Camp (1985, p. viii) report was quite direct in stating "the phenomenon of racism is fierce inside prisons and gangs usually organize along racial lines".[33] ACA mandates a variety of services and functions for inmates, such as education programs, hygiene, counseling, legal protections, and a host of factors making for a "safer correctional climate", but ACA requires nothing in the area of improving race relations among inmates. In spite of the historical evidence suggesting this pattern of conflict is one of recurring significance for all correctional institutions in America. It is a stunning and most curious situation. Let us hope it changes in the direction of becoming a more rational approach.

LAW ENFORCEMENT/CORRECTIONS   INTERFACE

With so much in common, dealing with the same offenders, we would expect a higher level of cooperation and interface than currently exists between corrections and law enforcement. In addition to having an "institutional parole officer" what current gang problems suggest is also having an "institutional law enforcement officer". This more systematic interface is justified for several reasons.

First, much crime does occur inside the correctional institution, some of it very serious. Illinois criminal law is no friend here to prosecuting crimes that occur inside the prison. In Illinois, the State's Attorney Office in the county in which the prison is located may be used for criminal prosecution --- but the cost of prosecution must be paid for by the prison system itself.[34] Which is no incentive for criminal prosecution and may mean, ultimately, prosecuting only those more serious offenses such as homicide. Here again is an area of needed federal aid.

Secondly, from a social intelligence point of view correctional institutions are in a unique position to add to our knowledge about gang networks nationwide. As Daniels (1987) recommended, simply sharing information about known gang members could be used in a national computer-based analysis to more effectively manage the problem. Most such gang members do return to our communities. Therefore, is the only legal responsibility of state correctional institutions to notify the local law enforcement agency that a prisoner has been recently released, or should corrections also be required to alert local law enforcement to whether or not this person is still active in the gang?

Thirdly, the Camp and Camp (1985: pp. xiii-xiv) report indicated that about half of the correctional institutions reporting a gang problem had some basis for believing (e.g., informants, law enforcement contacts, etc) that the prison was the site for gang crime planning of major or serious crimes occurring in the outside community. Including, obviously, first degree murder. The prison as a base for criminal activity should be a major concern to law enforcement and a clear justification for providing a more systematic and effective interface with corrections. It is also bi-directional[35], gangs outside of the prison can apparently order "hits" on inmates or institutional staff inside a prison.[36]

Finally, the law enforcement needs cited above are for state and local purposes. As a fourth reason, more developed gangs now have a significant interstate web of influence. States like Iowa have not only gangs hailing from Chicago, Illinois (Vice Lords, Disciples, etc), but also members of the Crips, Bloods, Mexican Mafia, and Aryan Brotherhood.[37] Therefore, there should also be federal law enforcement representation in this interface.

CORRECTIONAL STAFF TRAINING

Not enough is being done to adequately train correctional staff in a competent manner to understand the vital role they play in dealing with the gang problem. Considering the magnitude of the problem there is embarrassingly little being done in terms of training academies for correctional officers. There are, however, some such gang materials that are being used by correctional institutions to train staff. Much of it is locally produced and reflects a clear lack of comprehension of the literature and often has a definite political bias.

THE LIMITS OF BUS THERAPY

Bus therapy, also known as "diesel treatment", is essentially the punitive transfer of a prison inmate from one facility to another.[38] Either in the same correctional system, or to another jurisdiction or state.[39] It was effective in the 1970s with the breakup of a protest/religious group of federal inmates, who under the impetus of a national prisoner's rights movement sought radical prison reform under the guise of a "religious" front. But "bus therapy" may not be as effective with some gangs.

One reason is that more than one source suggests, even in official correctional staff training materials, that for such gangs as the Aryan Brotherhood, giving them "bus therapy" meant not the dissolution of its gang influence, indeed it spread and inflamed the problem: "due to transfers of gang members to federal institutions, the Aryan Brotherhood has spread throughout the country" (Illinois Department of Corrections Training Academy, Gang Activity, July, 1985: p. 11). It could, then, contribute to the so-called contagion effect.

Unless we are prepared to bus them to a truly remote region (upper Alaska, Yukan, Guam, etc), apparently many of these gangs will still be able to operate and flourish. No matter where they go they will still have communications rights (mail, telephone, visitors, etc) that cannot be lawfully taken away. And there exists no such central federal correctional unit to send hardcore gang leaders and members to.

TRADITIONAL STRATEGIES FOR DEALING WITH PRISON GANGS

In the absence of standards and written policies for dealing with gangs in the correctional environment, gang administration amounts to little more than a local judgement call. That is, taking the best shot on an ad hoc basis. The research by Camp and Camp (1985) showed a variety of techniques were being practiced by those thirty three states reporting a gang problem in correctional institutions. These techniques, included, in the rank order of their frequency used: (1) move or transfer (bus therapy) (N=27), (2) use of informers[40] and prevent events (N=21), (3) segregation of gang members (N=20), (4) lock up leaders (N=20), (5) lockdown (N=18), (6) prosecute (N=16), (7) intercept communications (N=16), (8) ID and track (N=14), (9) deal with situations case by case (N=13), (10) refuse to acknowledge (N=9), (11) put different gangs in particular institutions (N=5), (12) infiltration (N=5), (13) co-opt inmates to control (N=3).

Unfortunately, what this suggests especially with regard to strategy option number ten reported by Camp and Camp (1985, p. xvi) is that most of these states having a gang problem apparently "DO RECOGNIZE OR ACKNOWLEDGE" the gangs. What else are we to infer if only 9 of the 33 states indicate they "refuse to acknowledge" the gangs in their custody?

Of course, there has been absolutely no evaluation research whatsoever reported on the efficacy of any of these techniques or strategies for dealing with gangs in the correctional environment. This is doubly unfortunate. Because not only are we therefore in the situation of not knowing "what works" in controlling gangs in corrections, but as correctional institutions are highly controlled environments ideal for social experimentation we also are not generating any useful information for gang abatement, control, or dismemberment generally that could be applied outside of the correctional environment. We are wasting an enormous research potential here. A potential to develop knowledge on "what works" with gangs that could conceivably be applied for gang prevention and intervention methods throughout American society.

TARGETING GANG RESOURCES

If it is true that one of the primary dynamics of gang organization is the accumulation of money and power, then some states like Illinois have unique statutory options for targeting gang resources. Under Illinois state law it is possible to enact such an economic emasculation policy:

> Illinois Criminal Code and Procedure. Reimbursement for expenses. The Director may require convicted persons committed to Department correctional institutions or facilities to reimburse the Department for the expenses incurred by their incarceration to the extent of their ability to pay for such expenses. The Attorney General, upon authorization of the Director, may institute actions in the name of the people of the State of Illinois to recover from convicted persons committed to Department correctional institutions or facilities the expenses incurred by their confinement.

To the author's knowledge this statute has never been used in Illinois[41].

But the question remains: are there really such economic assets controlled or owned by gang members that can be readily discovered by means other than self-report? Real estate, bank accounts, motor vehicles, etc, in their name? If it takes a higher level of security to care for an inmate gang member, then would it not be possible to employ such a strategy? Remember, a prison term for adults is going to amount to a figure of around $20,000 per year; and can go well over $40,000 a year for juveniles.

It might be expected that certain prison inmates would regard this suggestion as cruel and unusual punishment to expect them to pay for their own incarceration. But as stated early in this text, we must be willing to consider all possibilities. This is a legal possibility. In fact, the situation is so severe in American corrections today that all legal recourses to the solution of crisis should be explored.

ANOTHER POSSIBILITY IS CONJUGAL VISITING

The value of Columbus B. Hopper's (1969) classic study of conjugal visits in the Mississippi prison system is that it demonstrated a powerful mechanism of social control.[42] Prisons today need all the social control they can get. If gang activities and gang conflicts were disciplinary infractions that a prison considered so severe that such behavior would mean forfeiting conjugal visitation privileges, then would there be a theoretical basis for expecting a safer correctional climate? It is certainly worth trying.

Recognizing, from discussion earlier in this text, that few prison inmates are legally married will mean extending such a conjugal visitation policy beyond legal marriage in order to have any appreciable effect. Objections relating to sexually transmitted diseases could easily be overcome by required testing. If there were child births as a result of conjugal visiting, then that would seem to have an additional potential positive effect instead of the arch-conservative objection that this would mean the systematic reproduction of criminals. It could mean, rather, strengthening family ties and instilling hope and perhaps even a higher level of responsibility. All of which translate into potential societal forces that could be enlisted in the war on gangs.

Generally, as will be seen from findings of the National Gang Crime Research Center, few in the criminal justice system are actually supportive of allowing conjugal visiting. There is some evidence, however, that "informal conjugal visiting" occurs in many different contexts of the adult correctional system. But no one talks about it, except in those rare cases such as happened in Chicago, where the El Rukn gang members who became informants and helped in the federal prosecution of other El Rukn leaders were allowed such "informal conjugal visiting", and other inmates heard about it and it became reported in that fashion --- in an effort to overturn the federal criminal convictions of El Rukn gang leaders.

Apparently, however, the gangs themselves (if we can believe what one El Rukn informant has recently claimed) have recognized the economic income potential of sponsoring such sexual favors from females for inmates. According to a story in the Chicago Tribune (May 25, 1993: section 2, p. 7) entitled "Prostitution Ring in Prison Detailed" a gang informant claims that before "flipping" as a mid-level leader of the El Rukn gang, he operated a prostitution ring from 1983 to 1987 inside the Stateville penitentiary. This informant claims to have been able to hire at least four female correctional officers in addition to six other women who provided, for a fee, sexual favors to Stateville inmates who could afford it. At this writing, none of these allegations have been proven. The same inmate turned informant also claimed that correctional staff were bribed to bring in illegal drugs and allowed the El Rukn gang to operate underground "restaurants" inside the prison as another income source.

GANG RECOGNITION AS OFFICIAL LEGITIMATION

Should a correctional administrator hold periodic chats with designated gang leaders? Or allow the gangs to meet regularly in the hope that this will appease them or reduce existing levels of intergang conflict in the correctional institution? Such a policy "experiment" in Illinois in the early 1970s, to essentially the above effect, backfired dramatically.

What appears to have happened is that in 1971 at the Pontiac prison in Illinois "special times were scheduled by the administrator for meetings of the respective gangs. This special class developed the power to create violence, pressure inmates and staff, and usurp authority from institutional officials. Gang jealousies and intra-gang strife were also by-products of gang recognition" (Illinois Training Academy, July 1988: pp. 6-7). Recognition became equivalent in function to legitimating the gangs and giving them de jure justification to operate within and without of the correctional institution. It clearly exacerbated the problem.

It is a situation that is truly comparable to the matter of negotiating with terrorists. To negotiate is to recognize such a force as legitimate actors. Simple recognition provides political legitimation, which can be a larger gain than a military victory. In political science, similarly, an incumbent who enjoys name recognition or is widely known to the public is always advised to never debate with an opponent who is not so well known. What happens in such debates is the opponent automatically gains greater recognition and legitimacy, and the cognitive hegemony of the incumbent is systematically eroded. It is an attention/authority transfer phenomenon.

The same thing appears to happen in our dealings with the gang organization. In both law enforcement and in corrections, we can sometimes inadvertently reinforce gang strength. Recall that many authors in the gang literature assert that gangs emerge from, grow, or are reinforced in terms of identity and cohesiveness out of a pattern of conflict. Historically, this means the community labels them, other social institutions come to regard them as a gang, the police respond to them as a gang, and they become a gang. Almost in a self-fulfilling prophecy.

Recall from the study of Jacobs (1977, pp. 82-83) that Warden Twomey ceased the practice of physically dragging a recalcitrant inmate gang member to the isolation unit. Rather, the policy became "cell lock in" until the inmate was ready to go peacefully. For otherwise, the witnessing gang members themselves had an opportunity to "rally" around such "brutality". They had a visible "enemy" (e.g., correctional officers using physical force) to protest. It meant higher solidarity for gang inmates. So taking away this opportunity to protest was a wise policy. The same implication also holds for local law enforcement. That is, perhaps it is much better to effect an arrest outside of the purview of other gang member witnesses.[43]

A HIDDEN PRISON INDUSTRY: THE MAKING OF "SUPERGANG" NATIONS

The prison or correctional setting as an arena of conflict provides, unfortunately, the organizational enhancement opportunity for establishing inter-gang alliances. Bobrowski (1988) posits that in the 1970s such an alliance was formed between the Black Disciple gang and the predominantly white Simon City Royals gang; where the latter agreed to be a connection for narcotics, and the former agreed to provide protection. In response to this alliance, the rival gangs (Latin Kings, Vice Lords, El Rukns) also established a pact. Thus was born the "Folks" and the "Peoples" and two large nations of gangs separated geographically (Bobrowski, 1988: pp. 30-31).[44]

Today in Illinois, to be in the Folks nation is to ride under the six-pointed star; to be "People" is to be about the five-pointed star. The "cause" of supergangs, then, is a finger pointed at the door of correctional agencies and their mishandling of the gang problem situation. Can prisons provide the setting in which we systematically provide a true training ground for new gang leaders? Yes is the general answer. For example, the Camp and Camp (1985: p. 152) report showed that a recurrent prison strategy for dealing with gangs was to "as a last resort, select leaders from the second layer of the organization and ship them out". Does that mean, afterwards, that within the shipping organization new middle-management are inducted into the gang hierarchy with an even higher level of commitment to the gang now that they have gained leadership or position status? And, similarly, does it mean that for the institutions receiving the shipped gang members these middle management gang leaders now have the charter to head up gang branches of their own at the new institutions? Again, the answer in both instances is probably yes.

The question then should be clear for the many other correctional systems outside of Illinois: could the conflict in the prison be such that gangs must establish such general alliances of almost equal proportion and in this manner facilitate the natural growth of groups of gangs?   Whether intentional or not, this is the strongest argument yet that correctional institutions may in fact be "adding fuel to the fire" of the gang problem.[45] As society comes to understand the potential developments in this area we might expect more in the way of standards and guidelines for the handling of gang conflict in the correctional setting. It is no small problem.

LATINO GANGS AND THE TEEN ANGEL MAGAZINE: A FREEDOM OF THE PRESS ISSUE?

Organized deviant groups, extremists, and ideological fanatics can be expected to test the limits of constitutional protections. The Teen Angel magazine is a gang rights activist news organization. Its first magazine was published in 1980. Virtually every issue has photos of inmate gang members (always Hispanic/Latino/Chicano only) or their drawings, where they are seeking pen pals (e.g., females). Rapists and drug dealers are not allowed such pen pals according to magazine policy (Issue #107)[46].

While most such gang member inmates are in California prisons, other states are also represented. Sometimes a list of inmates and their numbers and addresses are provided where anyone interested can write directly to the inmate. More recently, such persons interested in being "pen pals" are instructed to simply write to the person "in care of" the magazine (enclosing $3.00 and stamps for the fee), where the letter is forwarded directly to the inmate.

This magazine is more than an outlet for Latino gang art. It is a self-described gang rights activist news organization. It does publish articles by jailhouse lawyers (pp. 12-13, Issue # 117) giving advice to gang members on the street on how to neutralize police interrogation and investigation techniques. It does reprint articles previously published by the ACLU. It also publishes agit-prop "information" handouts on prison reform/activist groups in California, such as the Pelican Bay Information Project[47].

It is useful to summarize some of the viewpoints from the Pelican Bay Information Project (PBIP)[48]. What the PBIP is all about is "prisoners rights", more specifically those confined in the Security Housing Unit (SHU) within the Pelican Bay State Prison which is a maxi-maximum facility for gang leaders and others who have committed violent crimes within the correctional system (e.g., assaulting correctional officers).

The SHU at Pelican Bay holds about one thousand inmates in lockdown status equivalent to that in the Marion Federal Penitentiary. What makes SHU unique and a security improvement on Marion is the architecture: inmates cannot successfully talk to each other through bars, there are no bars. The inmates are in solid rooms that are all monitored with audio-video equipment. It is similar to the "no human contact" status described in The Hot House (Earley, 1992). The inmates eat in their cells and do not get together in groups (e.g., for church, etc).

The SHU inmates are reported in the PBIP literature to experience a psychological pressure to "snitch": their choices are "debrief, parole, or die". To "debrief" is to explain the nature of ones gang affiliation, how one fits into the hierarchy, who else is involved, etc, and most gangs would regard such behavior as high treason and punishable accordingly. The PBIP report goes on to say that predominantly white correctional officers have made racist remarks to inmates, and that Pelican Bay may be increasing violence rather than reducing it, and that such treatment constitutes "torture". What the public does not know is that there is a very good reason for such super maximum security facilities. The reason has to do with the enormous amount of serious crime and violence that occurs inside prisons, or that is directed from behind prison walls by imprisoned gang leaders, and which never gets included in our national crime statistics!

THE SNITCH FARM: PROSECUTING GANGS THAT ASSAULT AND KILL CORRECTIONAL OFFICERS

Someone who is willing to become an informant by providing testimony in court that can help convict gang members may in fact be a gang member, so what does a correctional system do with such persons who may automatically face a sentence of execution (e.g., a "hit") from their own gang? A recent idea that appears to be an effective solution and is consistent with the earlier work of Sleeman (1849). This recent idea is to create a separate and secure facility for such persons willing to cooperate with law enforcement agencies.

The snitch farm visited by the author was created in 1991 with a capacity of 60 inmates. It had 27 inmates on my visit. All of the inmates are known only by their initials (e.g., "G.D.C."), not their full and correct names. Correctional officers are not supposed to know their real names and also refer to them in routine interaction by their initials (usually a two letter combination, e.g. "D.C."). Obviously, though, that is to prevent casual use of the names in ordinary business. It is a security precaution taken to protect the identity and location of said inmates.

The units typically have their own separate budget. They are isolated physically and visually. No strangers can visit: one of the security precautions is that all visitors into the actual snitch farm complex itself are required to have a polaroid photograph taken of them, which is then shown to the inmate; the inmate then checks this photograph to make sure it is not an assassin sent by the gang that is trying to visit him.

Providing certain amenities and privileges that inmates outside of the snitch farm may not receive is not in any sense "pampering". For after all, without these inmates violent crimes including the assassination of correctional officers may have never been solved, nor the gang culprits convicted. By putting their life on the line for legitimate authority, we must come to recognize that such informants have earned some increased favorable treatment.

RECENT RESEARCH FINDINGS ON GANGS IN ADULT CORRECTIONS

The author as the director of the National Gang Crime Research Center initiated an ongoing series of national surveys dealing with literally all aspects of the criminal justice system and gangs. Here it is useful to summarize the findings from some of these various research projects that involve the adult corrections component of the criminal justice system.

Three different aspects of the adult correctional system are examined here. The first is a close look at gang problems in adult state prisons in America. The second is a close look at gang problems in adult local and county jails in America.

GANG PROBLEMS IN ADULT STATE PRISONS.

The first U.S. national gang research survey of adult state prison wardens was carried out and completed in 1991 and represents a national random sample of N = 184 state prisons[49]. The second U.S. national gang research survey of adult state prisons was carried out and completed in 1992 and represents a national random sample of N = 325 state prisons[50]. The unit of analysis in the adult state prison surveys of gang problems reported here is that of the individual state prison warden. This is therefore more detailed than any prior analysis such as that by Camp and Camp (1985) where the unit of analysis was the whole state, and it therefore faced the validity problem of over-aggregation: as if someone in each state in 1983 when their research was conducted knew everything there was to know about their gangs.

As seen in Table 60, for the 1991[51] survey some 40.5 percent indicated they believe that corrections would function better if gang members could be transferred to a central-national federal unit, compared to 33.9 percent in 1992. Less than half (40.8%) in 1991 indicated that their staff receive formalized training in dealing with the gang problem, compared to 45.5 percent in 1992. In 1991 some 11.9 percent indicated gang members have been a problem in terms of assaults on staff, compared to 10.4 percent in 1992.

Perhaps one of the most important findings has to do with the parameters for what percentage of the adult prison inmate population are estimated to be gang members. Two such estimates were obtained: one for male inmates, and one for female inmates.

For the 1991 survey regarding what proportion of the male inmates are gang members, this estimate ranged from a low of zero percent to a high of 65 percent; compared to a low of zero percent and a high of 95 percent in the 1992 survey. The mean or average estimate, as seen in Table 60, of what percentage gang members are of the total male inmate population was 9.41 percent for 1991 and 10.29 percent for 1992.

For the 1991 survey regarding what proportion of the female inmates are gang members, this estimate ranged from a low of zero percent to a high of 20 percent; compared to a low of zero percent and a high of 50 percent in the 1992 survey. The mean or average estimate, as seen in Table 60, of what percentage gang members are of the total female inmate population was 3.53 percent for 1991 and 2.75 percent for 1992.

Table 60 also shows that in about one out of every ten adult prisons in the USA, for both the 1991 and the 1992 surveys, gang members have been a problem in terms of assaults on correctional staff. In the 1992 survey a question also asked whether gang members have been a problem in terms of threats against staff, and 24.2 percent of the adult prisons indicated affirmatively.

The only substantial difference between the 1991 and 1992 surveys is to be found in the existence of separate gangs for white inmates. The question was, "Do white inmates have a separate gang?". What this really measures is whether these adult prisons have such groups as the Aryan Brotherhood, etc. Thus, in the 1991 survey some 27.3 percent of the adult prisons indicated such separate white gangs existed; compared to 41.1 percent in the 1992 survey.

TABLE 60

COMPARISON OF THE 1991 AND 1992
SURVEYS OF PRISON WARDENS

Question About Gangs	% Yes in 1991	% Yes in 1992
Do you believe corrections would function better if gang members could be transferred to a central-national federal unit?	40.5	33.9
Among staff who know about gang members, what is the current estimate of what percentage gang members are of the total inmate population? (Males, mean)	9.41	10.29
(Females, mean)	3.53	2.75
Do your staff receive formalized training in dealing with the gang problem?	40.8	45.4
Have gang members been a problem in terms of assaults on your staff?	11.9	10.4
Do white inmates have a separate gang?	27.3	41.1
How long have gangs existed as a problem in your facility? Under 5 years:	66.7	70.9
5 to 10 years:	7.6	18.0
Over 10 years:	25.7	11.1
Do you believe federal agencies should play a greater role in the investigation and prosecution of gang crimes?	73.3	76.8

THE 1991 WARDEN SURVEY: Additional Findings

Some 56.4 percent indicated that racial conflicts are a problem among the inmates confined in their facilities. Some 26.4 percent indicated that white inmates have separate gangs. Among the ninety-seven institutions reporting that gangs have existed as a problem in their facility, most (64.9%) indicated this problem has existed for under five years; while 7.2 percent indicated it has existed between five and ten years, and 27.8 percent indicated the problem has existed over a decade.

Similarly, most (94.9%) felt that there were some street gangs that should be considered forms of organized crime. Most also (93.7%) felt that the family is an important agency that can be used to prevent gang affiliation.

Nearly all (98.8%) felt that the community should assume more responsibility for dealing with the gang problem. Some 80.1 percent believe that the "occult" or "satanism" (worshipers or dabblers) are also involved with gangs. About three-fourths (78.2%) felt we need tougher laws specifically dealing with the gang problem.

When asked who has the primary responsibility for dealing with gangs, a majority (59.7%) indicated the family of the gang member, zero percent indicated local churches, .7 percent indicated business, another .7 percent indicated the school system, and 38.9 percent indicated local law enforcement.

Generally, about half of these institutions reported they were overcrowded (54.2%). Some 38 percent indicated they were ACA accredited which significantly differentiated whether their correctional officers were provided with tuition support for college classes[52]. About half of the institutions reported such tuition support for correctional officers.

Finally, when asked what is the current estimate of what percentage gang members are of the total inmate population, the estimates ranged from zero to a high of 65 percent.[53] Based on these estimates and total inmate counts reported, this sample shows some 17,191 male inmate gang members and 65 female inmate gang members for a total of 17,256. The total inmate population from this sample across all institutions was 148,117. That means that gang members appear now to constitute over ten percent of the inmate population nationwide, not three percent as estimated by Camp and Camp (1985).

The "community denial" syndrome has its equivalent function in correctional institutions. That factor was felt by the author to bias the reporting of gang members downward.

THE 1992 WARDEN SURVEY: ADDITIONAL FINDINGS

With the responses of 316 state prison wardens from all 50 states and Puerto Rico this study represents the largest of its kind to date. Some of the additional findings about gangs are worth summarizing here.

Nearly one out of ten (9.5%) adult correctional state institutions in the sample reported that gang members have been a problem in terms of assaults on their staff.

In nearly a fourth of the facilities (24%) gang members have also been a problem in terms of threats on staff. About half of the respondents (54%) agreed that giving staff recognition to prison gang leaders is similar to negotiating with terrorists.

Very few (8.7%) believed that conjugal visiting could be used as a reward to control gang problems in prison. More believed (48.4%) that better training programs could be used as a reward to control the gang problem among inmates. Over a third (37.2%) expressed the opinion that prison gangs have tended to result in more improvised weapons production (e.g., "shanks", homemade knives, etc). among the inmates in their facilities.

Some 41.9 percent indicated that their institution does not have enough resources and programs to control the gang problem.

Just over half (52.8%) felt that the American Correctional Association should establish standards for controlling prison gangs.

Under half (41.6%) of the wardens felt that the "set off" method, defined as balancing the number of rival gang members in any given living unit or cellhouse, was an effective way to control prison gangs. Using a check-off list where the warden was asked if their institution uses any of these strategies to control gangs, the rank ordering by the most popularly used methods was as follows: transfers (65.5%), displacing members to different facilities (54.2%), segregation (48.1%), use of informers (46.8%), case-by-case dealings (45.5%), isolating leaders (42.3%), interrupting communications (28.7%), prosecution (26.1%), lockdown (24.5%), balance the number of rival gang members living in the same unit (16.5%), meeting with gang leaders on "as needed" basis (5.8%), ignoring their existence (5.5%), coopting of prisoners to control gangs (2.6%), infiltration (1.6%), joint meetings between various gang leaders (1.3%). These, then, are the most popular methods actually being used to deal with prison gang problems.

Nearly three-fourths (74.8%) expressed the opinion that gang members tend to have higher recidivism rates.

GANG PROBLEMS IN LOCAL AND COUNTY JAILS

The first U.S. national gang research survey of local and county jails was carried out by the National Gang Crime Research Center and reported in the spring of 1993 representing a national sample of N = 140 jails[54]. Again, to our knowledge, this is the first effort to assess the scope and extent of the gang problem nationally in local and county jails[55].

The jail administrators were asked what percentage gang members constitute of the overall inmate population. For male inmates, the estimates ranged from a low of zero for 36.2 percent of all jails responding to the survey, to a high of 60 percent. For female inmates, again the estimates ranged from a low of zero for over two thirds (72.7%) of the jails, to a high of 85 percent. The mean or average estimate for all jails for male inmates was 5.05 percent, and 2.18 percent for female inmates.

Only about a fourth (26.6%) of the jails indicated that their staff receive formalized training in dealing with gang problems. Among those jails that did provide such gang training to its officers, in over four-fifths (83.8%) of these jails providing such training, the amount of training was eight hours or less. In fact, the average or mean hours of gang training was 6.6 hours. Two-thirds (67.9%) of the jail administrators responding to the survey expressed the opinion that their staff could benefit from professional outside training dealing with gangs.

Only 2.9 percent of the jails report that gang members have been a problem in terms of assaults on their staff. Yet a fourth (26%) of the jails in the survey reported that gang members have been a problem in terms of threats against jail staff.

Very comparable to their adult state prison and juvenile correctional counterparts, some 43.2 percent of the jails in the survey reported that racial conflicts are a problem among the inmates in their facilities. In fact, some 19.8 percent of the jails report that whites have a separate gang.

About half of the jail administrators (52.9%) agreed that giving staff recognition to inmate gang leaders is similar to negotiating with terrorists.

Supporting the validity of the claim that gangs have vastly proliferated in a relatively recent period of American history, the jail administrators report almost identically to the views of law enforcement administrators reviewed in the previous chapter, that when asked in what year did gang problems among inmates first become recognized in your facility ---- 91.5 percent of the jails report that the gang problem first arose on or after 1981! The breakdown over yearly periods was as follows:

In what year did gang problems among inmates first become recognized?

	% of Jails
On or before 1980	8.5%
1981 - 1984	6.8
1985 - 1988	22.0
1989 - 1992	57.6
1993	5.1

Only ten percent of the jail administrators believed that conjugal visiting could be used as a reward to control gang problems in jails. When asked if providing college tuition support for staff could help control the inmate gang problem, some 38.5 percent of the jail administrators agreed. Some 18.6 percent of the jails expressed the opinion that inmate gangs have tended to result in more improvised weapons production among their inmates. Three fourths (76.9%) of the jail administrators felt we need tougher laws to control the gang problem among inmates.

Only about half (51.8%) of the jail administrators felt that their facility had enough resources and programs to control the gang problem. Stronger support exists among in jails than in prisons for establishing national and professional standards to deal with the gang problem. When asked if the American Correctional Association should establish standards for controlling inmate gangs, some 72.3 percent agreed. When asked if the American Jail Association should establish such standards, some 74.6 percent agreed.

Using the checklist approach, the respondents were asked to report what strategies were used in their jail facilities to control gangs. The following reflect the rank-ordered results from the most used to the least used of the gang control techniques among the jails in this sample: segregation (39.6%), case by case dealings (33.1%), transfers (30.9%), isolating leaders (30.2%), lockdown (26.6%), use of informers (19.4%), interrupting communications (18%), prosecution (17.3%), displacing members to different facilities (15.1%), balance the number of rival gang members living in the same unit (14.4%), ignoring their existence (3.6%), meeting with gang leaders on "as needed" basis (3.6%), coopting of prisoners to control gangs (2.9%), infiltration (2.2%), joint meetings between various gang leaders (1.4%).

Still, only 11.6 percent of the jail administrators report that inmate gangs have significantly affected their correctional environment. The jail administrators were also asked a couple technical questions that yielded interesting results. When asked if they were familiar with the Camp and Camp (1985) report, only 5.9 percent indicated they were familiar with it. When asked if their jail facility has been able to make use of any of the research reports available from the National Institute of Justice, 55 percent said "no".

Gangs inside major urban jails operate very similarly to their counterparts in state adult correctional institutions. The larger gangs issue memos to their members, these gangs even maintain their own "disciplinary system" to control their members. So the modern gang member inmate has several codes of conduct to obey: that of the prison system itself and the "official rules and regulations", and the rules imposed by the gang --- the latter probably being the rules that get obeyed more often. Consider the following handwritten memo from the Brothers of the Struggle (BOS), an actual example:

"DATE: 9-01-92
SUBJ: Violations
FROM: 4ou C.O.S.
TO: Decks C.O.S.

Greetings my 7/4 brothers, this memo is to inform you that there will be no head to toe violations given out unless you are given word from 2ft C.O.S. or BLD. C.O.S.. Anyone who goes against this will be bogus and violated on spot. Also all C.O.S. are to attend church on Sundays if not they are subject to disciplinary Actions. Pass word to your decks that all B.O.S. are to lace their right shoe by missing the bottom 2 holes. Example (||:) This is so that we can identify each other. Brother security is to be on the entire yard; rec. when ever called. I leave as I came with plenty much love.

Important - all reports are to be in code, all minor and major incidents must be in report.

In the vision of our great leader and through his vision, we can become a more reckoning power of people beyond boundaries without measures.

2-15-19
(19-3-15-14-5-25) (7-4)".

As seen in the above B.O.S. memo, an elementary code is used: 1=a,2=b,3=c, etc. Thus the expression 7/4 means "G.D.". The expression "2-15-19" means "B.O.S.". The B.O.S. includes G.D.'s (Gangster Disciples), and B.D.'s (Black Disciples), and naturally, Black Gangster Disciples. It's Honorable Chairman of the Board is "King" Larry Hoover.

SUMMARY AND CONCLUSION

The gang problem for corrections is growing, not declining, and is expanding throughout the United States. As a problem that may be responsible for assaults and threats on correctional officers the problem appears to be significant enough to establish written standards governing gang control strategies and techniques. These are necessary in order to cope with the changing character of prison populations. Programing for the social psychology of gangs should involve a closer examination of group capability to dominate legitimate prison organizations (Jaycees, etc).

Certainly, a stronger interface between law enforcement and corrections is essential for any effective strategy of gang control. As "fiefdoms" some prisons and state systems simply are not routinely interacting with law enforcement agencies in the sharing of gang intelligence. This may change now, however, as a recent issue of Corrections Today indicated that an intelligence clearinghouse is being created, allowing correctional officials in various states to share reports and information that might be helpful in gang control policies and procedures. Providing more effective gang training for correctional staff is equally important.[56] There are simply limits to the age-old technique of "bus therapy". No one wants gangs bussed in. Traditional strategies and techniques for dealing with prison gangs appear to represent a "shoot from the hip" approach to ad hoc correctional management and decision making rather than enjoying the benefits of a decision support system or any evaluation research on their efficacy. Some such techniques still in use are believed to be counterproductive and detrimental in the long term.

Targeting gang resources in some state statutes is permitted. Perhaps, as well, it is time to develop more "carrots" of social control and the time may be ripe for allowing conjugal visiting programs in more of our prisons. Not as an appeasement, but for the value of compliance and social control that such a program implies when offered as a "honor" for good behavior.

Gang recognition in the correctional setting is a common technique, but is a stop gap measure and an unsound gambit in the long run. It is equivalent to affording the gang organizational legitimation. In Illinois, a Chicago Police officer in a paper prepared for the American Society of Criminology argues that "super gangs" were made in prison (Bobrowski, 1988). Gangs can be expected to expand in the combat and racial strife that is endemic to some of our larger institutions. This suggests the merits of programing and services centered around the goal of improving race and ethnic relations among inmates. Alternatively, the absence of such policies and procedures to reinforce better race relations in a context of racial violence and racial enmity can only mean when trouble does erupt, and it can be anticipated, here we go again with another potential area of legal liability --- from both correctional staff and inmates.

DISCUSSION   QUESTIONS

(1)   Do you think that prison holds as much fear as a deterrent today for gang offenders as it is assumed to have had historically for lone criminal offenders, when going to prison is like a "homecoming" for gang members, indeed a chance to earn higher rank and get to know their gang leaders better?

(2)   If being a "neutral" or "neutron" (non-gang affiliated inmate) is next to impossible inside a correctional facility, do you feel that this poses some liability for correctional officials under the "cruel and unusual punishment" doctrine where inmates are assumed to have the right to live free from harm or violence?

(3)   If our prisons are dominated by gangs, then our halfway houses or work release centers can also be assumed to enjoy the same notoriety. Should "safe houses", designed as secondary alternatives for community-based corrections and reintegration, be provided to released prisoners to allow them to get away from gangs and live outside of the influence of gang organization after their release? How could such initiatives be made effective?

RECOMMENDED   READING

Baird, L.H
    1986 "Prison Gangs: Texas", Corrections Today (18)(July): 22.

Bartollas, Clemens
    1990 "The Prison: Disorder Personified", Chapter 1 (pp. 11-22) in Are Prisons Any Better: Twenty Years of Correctional Reform, John W. Murphy and Jack E. Dison (Eds.), Sage Criminal Justice System Annuals, Newbury Park, CA: Sage Publications.

Buentello, Salvador; Robert S. Fong; and Ronald E. Vogel
    1991 "Prison Gang Development: A Theoretical Model", The Prison Journal (LXXI)(2)(Fall-Winter): 3-14.

Caltabiano, Michael L
    1981 "National Prison Gang Study", Unpublished report prepared for the Federal Bureau of Prisons (August).

Conrad, J.P
    1979 "Who's in Charge? The Control of Gang Violence in California Prisons", in Correctional Facility Planning edited by Robert Montilla and Nora Marlow, pp. 135-147, Lexington, Mass: D.C. Heath.

Cox, V
    1986 "Prison Gangs - Inmates Battle for Control", Corrections Compendium
    (10)(9)(Apr): 1,6-9.

Earley, Pete
    1992 The Hot House: Life Inside Leavenworth Prison. New York: Bantam.

Fong, Robert S
    1990 "The Organizational Structure of Prison Gangs: A Texas Case Study",
    Federal Probation (54)(1)(Mar): 36-43.

Harland, Alan T
    1991 "Prison Gangs: Introductory Overview", The Prison Journal (LXXI)-
    (2)(Fall-Winter): 1-2.[a]

Hunt, G.; S. Riegel; T. Morales; and D. Waldorf
    1992 "Keep the Peace Out of Prisons: Prison Gangs, An Alternative
    Perspective". San Francisco, CA: Institute for Scientific Analysis, Home
    Boy Study.

    1993 "Changes in Prison Culture: Prison Gangs and the Case of the Pepsi
    Generation". San Francisco, CA: Institute for Scientific Analysis, Home
    Boy Study. Social Problems (forthcoming).

Knox, George W
    1991 "Gangs and Social Justice Issues", Chapter 1 (pp. 1-19), in Sloan T.
    Letman (Ed.), Prison Conditions and Prison Overcrowding, Dubuque, IA:
    Kendall/Hunt Publishing Co.

    1992 "Gang Organization in a Large Urban Jail", American Jails.

Knox, George W. and Edward D. Tromanhauser
    1991 "Gangs and Their Control in Adult Correctional Institutions", The
    Prison Journal (LXXI)(2): 15-22.

    1991 "Gang Members as a Distinct Health Risk Group in Juvenile
    Correctional Facilities", The Prison Journal (LXXI)(2): 61-66.

    1993 "Gang Training in Adult Correctional Institutions: A Function of
    Intensity, Duration and Impact of the Gang Problem", Journal of Correc-
    tional Training.

Krajick, K
    1990 "The Menace of Supergangs", Corrections Magazine, (June): 11-14.

Lane, Michael
    1989 "Inmate Gangs", Corrections Today (51)(4)(July): 98-99, 126-128.

---

[a] Published semi-annually by The Pennsylvania Prison Society, Three North
Second Street, Philadelphia, PA 19106-2208 (215 352-2300).

Lotter, J.M
    1988   "Prison Gangs in South Africa: A Description", The South African Journal of Sociology (19)(2)(May): 67-75.

Padilla, Felix and Lourdes Santiago
    1993   Outside the Wall: A Puerto Rican Woman's Struggle. New Brunswick, NJ: Rutgers University Press.

Pelz, Mary E. (Beth); James W. Marquart; and C. Terry Pelz
    1991   "Right Wing Extremism in the Texas Prisons: The Rise and Fall of the Aryan Brotherhood of Texas", The Prison Journal (LXXI)(Fall-Winter)(2): 23-37.

Ralph, Paige H.; James W. Marquart; and Ben M. Crouch
    1990   "Prisoner Gangs in Texas", paper presented at the 1990 Annual Meeting of the American Society of Criminology, Baltimore, MD.

Ralph, Paige H.; and James W. Marquart
    1991   "Gang Violence In Texas Prisons", The Prison Journal (LXXI)(Fall-Winter)(2): 38-49.

Scallan, J.H
    1987   Prison Codes and Communications. Texas Department of Corrections, unpublished.

Shelden, Randall G
    1991   "A Comparison of Gang Members and Non-Gang Members in a Prison Setting", The Prison Journal (LXXI)(Fall-Winter)(2): 50-60.

FOOTNOTES

1. Gangs in the correctional setting date back to the 19th century as illustrated by Hobsbawm (1965: p. 34) involving Mafia gangs in the Milazzo jail.

2. See: "Prisons Boss Seeks Funds Hike", Chicago Sun-Times, March 30, 1994, p.22. Tamms is in southern Illinois. The same article indicates IDOC has 35,049 inmates in a system designed to hold 22,007.

3. Here for those who are skeptical of the racism-oppression thesis we actually find motivation relating to racism playing a very large part in decisions to join a gang. Recall that Jackson and Mc Bride (1990) report the early formation of the Aryan Brotherhood (as the Bluebirds), not unlike Chinese gangs in New York, forming to protect against perceived threats. But also like the New York Chinese gangs, once established the Aryan Brotherhood and its equivalent youth gang counterparts, often take on a life of their own.

4. For an excellent history of the BT system see: Aric Press, "Inside America's Brutal and Overcrowded, The Texas Prison System Was Told to Reform or Else", Newsweek, October 6, 1986.

5. The United Nations Standard Minimum Rules for the Treatment of Prisoners and Related Recommendations, is U.N. resolution adopted 30 August 1955. Its provision # 28 says "No prisoner shall be employed, in the service of the institution, in any disciplinary capacity". (See John W. Palmer, 1977, Constitutional Rights of Prisoners, Anderson Publishing Company, p. 953).

6. Steve J. Martin and Sheldon Ekland-Olson, 1987, Texas Prisons: The Walls Came Tumbling Down, Austin, TX: Texas Monthly Press, Inc; Ben M. Crouch and James W. Marquart, 1989, An Appeal to Justice: Litigated Reform of Texas Prisons, Austin, TX: University of Texas Press.

7. Says Lane "if prison administrators are not in control of their facilities, the gangs will attempt to exert their influences" (Lane, 1989: p. 99). Another author (Bartollas, 1990) also explicitly asserts that some prisons are really "run" by gangs.

8. See: p. 13, "High Noon at the D.O.C.: How Dick English Made It Work", Illinois Police and Sheriffs News, Spring, 1994.

9. The killer in this instance, David Starks, 32, was sentenced to natural life; avoiding the death penalty by claiming he was ordered by his gang to commit the "hit". See: Jerry Shnay, "Inmate is Spared Death Penalty", Chicago Tribune, Section 2, March 15, 1994, p. 2. This law needs to be changed immediately, making it an automatic death penalty case for murdering a correctional officer, police officer, or public official.

10. See: Jerry Thomas, "Gangs A Rising Threat to Prison Guards", Chicago Tribune, Nov. 28, 1993.

11. See: Gary Marx, "Medium-Security Prisons No Longer Medium Secure", Chicago Tribune, Section 2, pp. 1, 4.

12. Hunt, Riegel, Morales and Waldorf (1993) note that the first national study of prison gangs was that by Caltabiano (1981) involving 45 state prisons. Caltabiano's (1981) findings were not made known to the public as it is an unpublished report for the Federal Bureau of Prisons.

13. The Camp and Camp data was collected in 1983 and reported in 1985. Just a few years would lapse until Lane (1989) would report that 80 to 90 percent of Illinois prison inmates are gang affiliated. What that means is either two things: (1) either there was an enormous rapid reproduction of gang membership in American prisons during this period, or (2) the Camp and Camp data seriously underestimated gang force strength. Camp and Camp (1985) estimated 12,624 prison gang members, nationwide. But Lane (1989) reports much more than that in Illinois alone!

14. In the next chapter results will be shown for juvenile correctional institutions and the gang problem. As a comparison to Camp and Camp (1985), these juvenile institutions in the Fall of 1990 reported a combined total of 4561 male gang members and another 212 female gang members. Recall, however, that juveniles have always constituted but a fraction of the overall adult prison system population. But has always been a feeder or filtering mechanism to the adult system. This and other research suggests that today's prison gang force strength is many times the figure of 12,624 suggested by Camp and Camp (1985). A test of this is now in progress. Obviously, the Illinois prison system alone has more gang members than the total figure reported by Camp and Camp (1985).

15. Such research is now underway by the author and is expected to be reported later.

16. In the next chapter, such information will be provided based on results from 155 juvenile institutions in 49 states. This is the juvenile correctional institutions survey.

17. The "burnout" hypothesis asserts, basically, that rehabilitation does nothing; what changes a felon to live a law-abiding life is a simple process of maturation and a sudden realization, around the age of the late thirties, that "this is a crumby life"; or some variation of "I fought the law, and the law won". This is not dissimilar from the point of view in Vigil (1988) "Gang members who secure a good job often refocus and redirect their lives into more conventional routes; such a change in orientation is referred to as "maturing out" (Matza, 1964: 22-26)" (Vigil, 1988: p. 31).

18. See also, Robert S. Fong, 1987, A Comparative Study of the Organizational Aspects of Two Texas Prison Gangs: Texas Syndicate and Mexican Mafia. Ph.D. Dissertation, Sam Houston State University, Huntsville, Texas.

19. See also the recent and emerging work of Fong and his colleagues: Fong and Buentello (1991), Fong, Vogel and Little (1991).

20. This was demonstrated earlier for juvenile institutions and re-emerged in the present analysis. For space limitations we shall summarize this finding here. Any report of racial conflict in the prison significantly differentiated whether these same prisons reported having five percent or higher of their inmates as gang members (Chi square = 7.54, p = .006). Racial conflict is more likely to be found where a higher density of gang members exist in the inmate population is what this finding suggests.

21. This is cryptic comment is particularly directed against county jails in larger gang-oriented cities where the incoming inmate is asked at intake "WHO DO YOU RIDE WITH?", meaning what gang are you a member of? And no one can answer "I don't belong". They go in one or another designated categories, such as "neutrons", or neutrals. But they are rarely functionally neutral in such a facility that uses an "off-set" gang management policy of filling cell-houses with roughly "half and half" of the rival gangs. Once inside, anyone not a gang member (e.g., a "neutron") may find themselves having to affiliate just to eat.

22. Livingston County Circuit Court Judge Charles Glennon is quoted to the effect that Illinois gang members in Joliet were allowed such picnics and that prison officials tried to work with the gang leaders up until the time of the 1978 riot, but that this "philosophy" still persists among prison administrators in Illinois. See Wes Smith, "Pontiac Prison Gangs' Ultimate Weapon is Fear", Chicago (Illinois) Tribune, September 20, 1987.

23. Jacobs (1974) describes, almost like a scene out of Hogan's Heroes, how prison administrators would routinely call in a gang leader when they had problems with one of "their" members: "in numerous cases the chief guard has called the leaders to his office to discuss problems with one of their soldiers (Jacobs, 1974: p. 407)". It became status enhancing for the gang leader to then "cool out" the situation.

24. Remember that the United Nations code for dealing with prisoners says it is forbidden to delegate any kind of disciplinary function to prisoners. It is a human rights violation. It is unconstitutional, as in the Texas prison system where "Building Tenders" were used, and the equivalent role functions in a variety of other state prison system.

25. John W. Palmer, 1985, Constitutional Rights of Prisoners, Anderson Publishing Company, p. 953.

26. Some authors like Moore (1978) have, however, gone on record as stating something almost equivalent in contemporary corrections: "custodial staff often manipulates racial and ethnic differences, both for public relations purposes (to distract public attention from institutional malfunctioning), and for inmate control (the divide and conquer principle) (Moore, 1978: p. 136)". Which, if anything, is another reason to have ACA standards and policies enacted to promote better race and ethnic relations among inmates and staff and for handling the more specific problem of gangs in corrections.

27. Camp and Camp (1985, p. xix) recommend, similarly, that "agencies should develop a general position (policy) and strategy concerning gangs".

28. Regarding the freedom of religion, similarly, the question arises: given the tendency of prison gangs to self-segregate by race, is such a "religious front" group that really functions as a gang organization constitutional when it excludes persons of other races? No one has yet sued on this matter.

29. Obviously, in no sense has the author felt confident about sharing all his information known about gangs in this text. There are risks of public disclosure.

30. Incarcerated was spelled "incarserated" in the chapter notes, again showing a continued pattern of organizational sophistication without the highest level of literacy attainment.

31. This "generation gap" problem simply says that gangs are subject to the same type of internal conflicts that other groups, organizations, and voluntary associations

experience. For an example of how the "generation gap" also affects higher level gangs, like the Yakuza, see Kaplan and Kubro (1986: p. 128).

32. And, of course, the obverse is also true: if little can be done to reduce gang violence in prison, where gangs are the surrogate force of ethnic and racial strife, by mode of attitudinal and value change; then a leap beyond social-psychology and into the arena of the political-economy is warranted.

33. For an account of institutional racism and how inmate racism can fuel gang formations perhaps even in the other direction see Al Salvato, "Prison 'Ready to Blow' Racial Hatred Plagues Lucasville", Cincinnati (Ohio) Post February 19, 1990.

34. Illinois Criminal Code and Procedure, Chapter 38, Section 1003-6-5, covers crimes committed by persons confined by the state department of corrections reads as follows: "When any person is charged with committing an offense while confined by the Department, cognizance thereof shall be taken by the circuit court of the county wherein such crime was committed. Such court shall adjudicate and sentence the person charged with such crime in the same manner and subject to the same rules and limitations as are now established by law in relation to other persons charged with crime. The expense of prosecution shall be paid by the Department".

35. Similarly, as Jacobs (1974: p. 398) observed at Stateville "gang fights on the streets are immediately felt behind the walls".

36. See Wes Smith, "Gangs' Power Tied to Pontiac Policies", Chicago (Illinois) Tribune, September 6, 1987. This describes how the assassination style killing of an Illinois correctional officer was apparently "ordered" by gang members outside of the prison.

37. See William Petroski, "Prisons See Surge in Gang Membership", Des Moines (Iowa) Register, February 14, 1990.

38. Related approaches involve rotating gang leaders from one institution to the next.

39. The idea for much of this policy option is to segregate gang leaders and hard core members from the general inmate population.

40. Professor Carol Davis, Department of Corrections and Criminal Justice, Chicago State University, who has worked in a number of adult correctional institutions suggests that there are additional hidden problems associated with the cultivation of informants (1991, personal interview). That is, most informants want quid pro quo and it is a liability issue: if the informer is discovered and has to be placed in protective custody or faces danger, then the institution has essentially entrapped them. One solution, to be discussed shortly, is to create a special physically separate correctional unit for informants: a snitch farm.

41. Apparently, then, those who say that members join gangs out of chiefly economic motivation must be saying as well that this is more "lure" than "reality". Because little such forfeitures on gang members have been reported in the literature through this statute or through RICO criminal and civil statutes. Shortly before going to press, in early October, 1993, the statute was used by the Illinois State Attorney General to sue John Wayne Gacey shortly before Gacey was executed.

42. See Columbus B. Hopper, 1969, Sex in Prison, Baton Rouge, Louisiana: Louisiana State University Press.

43. This could be a formidable law enforcement strategy. Police officers can defer an arrest until a time that is more convenient in routine seizures of small amounts of drugs or other criminal code violations. Arresting in the presence of other gang members can, we hypothesize, therefore heighten gang cohesiveness and solidarity. It would be better to issue a warrant and randomly arrest the gang members in their homes when they least expect it and when there are no other gang members present to witness the event. Then arrests could be demoralizing, instead of a "cause celebre".

44. But as early as 1967 the Vice Lords were a "level three" gang organization with its own not-for-profit corporation. Bobrowski is not saying that prisons trained gang members in higher levels of organizational training, management, strategic planning, etc, to convert level two gangs to level three gang formations. In fact, another view is that by Short (1974) that macro external processes (civil rights consciousness of the 1960s etc) created "supergangs". See also Sherman's (1970) account of the rise of "supergangs" as existing before Bobrowski's claim. Note, also, the lack of definitional clarity here: "supergang" can mean anything, and perhaps something different to, respectively, Sherman (1970), Short (1974) and Bobrowski.

45. Daniels (1987: p. 66) agreed that prisons currently seem to function as an incubator for gangs --- that is, gangs "recruit, expand, and solidify in a prison setting". Similarly, Moore (1978: p. 191) indicates that Mexican super gangs exist in California prisons (Mafia and La Familia) and "were being used by correctional authorities as the rationalization for a newly repressive policy toward Chicano convicts". As in other discussions of "supergangs", this is little more than a colorful adjective; with little definitive power beyond implying these are "bigger and badder" kinds of gangs. I hope some authors that use this "supergang" concept can see the merits of perhaps instead considering these "level three" gang formations in the organizational development classification system advanced in the present work.

46. "PEN PALS IN PRISON. Inmates in federal or state institutions may submit their art or photos and pen pal ads only if they first order Teen Angels. No more free-loaders! Also, we want no drug dealers or rapists. Do not send in anything! We don't want you! Also, no inmates in city or county jails, or people with less than one year to serve. Because pen pals get the letters because you are no longer at that address" (Teen Angels, Issue 107, p. 44).

47. PBIP, 2489 Mission Street, #28, San Francisco, CA 94110; Tel. (415) 821-6545.

48. The material printed in Teen Angels was the exact script from the Pelican Bay Information Project, but carried the by-line "White Guards Gang Up on Chicano Prisoners and Beat Them!"

49. The monograph "Findings From The 1991 Adult Corrections Survey: A Preliminary Report" was mailed in May, 1991 free of charge to all wardens requesting a copy who were respondents to the survey. The author was the principal investigator. Research Associates on this project of the National Gang Crime Research Center included: Michael Adekale, B.A.; Mary Castaneda, B.S.; Harold Dade, B.S.; Renee Del Vecchio, B.S.; Haven P. Fisher, M.S.; Joanne M. Geraghty, B.A., M.S.; Henry Glees, B.S.; Keith J. Griffin, B.S.; John E. Hemingway, B.S., M.S.; Sunsaray Hodges, B.S., M.S.; Paul F. Hoffman, B.A., M.S.W.; Carlton Jackson, Jr., B.S.; Gloria Jones, B.S.; Cynthia D. Lewis; Irving Miller, Jr., M.S.; Elvis Slaughter, B.S.; and Research Assistants included: Rodney Alexander, Carlton Jackson, Sr.; and Stephanie Williams.

50. The monograph "Preliminary Results of the 1992 Adult Corrections Survey" was provided free of charge on May 11, 1992 to all wardens requesting a copy of the report who were respondents to the survey. The author was the principal investigator. Research Associates of this project of the National Gang Crime Research Center included: Christopher Anaele, B.A., M.S.; Elizabeth S. Boaz, B.A.; Kenneth G. Brown, B.A.; Raimondo Brown, B.S.; Raymond I. Carrell, B.A.; Robert J. Edwards, B.A.; Sunsaray G. Hodges, B.S., M.S.; Paul F. Hoffman, M.S.W.; Carlton Jackson, Jr., B.S.; Clara Massey, B.S.; Maryann Riley, B.S.; Romelio Rogel, B.S.; Willie J. Simmons, B.A.; Clifton L. Thomas; and David R. Williams, B.A., M.A..

51. The sample size is larger here than reported in the first edition due to the nature of mail surveys: more data "straggles" in over time. The increase in the number of respondents for the 1991 survey over the time it was first reported in the first edition therefore accounts for slight differences in results.

52. Those who were ACA accredited were more likely to offer tuition support to their correctional officers.

53. Some of the institutions known to have a very significant gang problem did not respond to the survey.

54. The monograph "Findings From the 1993 Jail Survey: A Preliminary Report" was released on May 5, 1993 by the National Gang Crime Research Center. The author was the principal investigator. Research Associates included: Kenneth G. Brown, B.A., M.S.; Bettie Durrani, B.S., M.S.; Robert J. Edwards, B.A.; Janice Y. Evans, B.S.; Joseph F. Garrett, B.A.; Paul F. Hoffman, M.S.W.; Carlton Jackson, Jr., B.S.; William M. Misczak, B.A.; John E. Morris; Michael Walton, M.S.; and Steven E. Wright, B.S.

55. A random sample of N = 613 jails were asked to participate in the study; mail questionnaires were completed by 140.

56. According to Professor Carol Davis (personal interview, 1991) gang awareness and gang recognition training should be more, not less, refined than training outside of the institutional gang context: because it is more subtle in prison. Gang leaders do fear separation. Gang members will deny they are gang members. The gang problem may be less visible in terms of graffiti and territoriality in the community context. Who inmates hang around with may provide a better clue to whether or not they embrace gang membership.

CHAPTER 23

GANGS AND JUVENILE CORRECTIONAL INSTITUTIONS

INTRODUCTION

Juvenile correctional institutions represent one of the most crucial components of the American criminal justice system. If they fail, much else fails. This assertion is true because these are institutions that are intended to re-direct the lives of serious law-violating youths into a more pro-social pattern. There has never been a war on youthful recidivism. But recidivism from such juvenile correctional facilities is very high and it is definitely a social problem about which something can and should be done.

Unfortunately, until rather recently, there has been little known about the youth gang problem nationally as it impacts on juvenile institutions. More has been known about gangs and adult state prisons. A series of research projects undertaken by the National Gang Crime Research Center focusing on the gang problem are described in this chapter.

PROSECUTING JUVENILES AS ADULTS

WIth an upsurge in violent crime committed by juveniles, in the late 1970s and in the early 1980s, many states began to pass new aggressive laws that allowed for juveniles to be prosecuted as adults under special circumstances. This is sometimes called "being bound over", or the "binding over" process (also called a "Transfer hearing" or proceeding, meaning to transfer the minor from the juvenile into the adult criminal justice system), because a special hearing is held in juvenile court where the prosecutor must convince the juvenile court judge that the case is serious enough that the juvenile should be tried as an adult. In the late 1980s and the early 1990s, gang crime involvement by juveniles was added in some states as a new reason for trying juveniles as adults.

This is a "get tough" law for juveniles, the idea behind it is that will give such juveniles much stiffer adult sentences. Illinois is typical of such "get tough" states in terms of its laws in this respect. Any youth who is at least 15 years of age can be tried as an adult if the crime involves a forcible felony, and the youth had previously been adjudicated for an offense that if tried as an adult would have constituted an adult felony, and with regard to the instant offense "the act that constitutes the offense was committed in furtherance of criminal activity by an organized gang" [Illinois Criminal Code and Procedure, 1993, p. 98: 705, 405/5-4.(3.1)]. For purposes of that law, an "organized gang" was defined as "an association of 5 or more persons, with an established hierarchy, that encourages members of the association to perpetrate crimes or provides support to members of the association who do commit crimes" [Illinois Criminal Code and Procedure, 1993, p. 98: 705, 405/5-4.(3.2)].

Needless to say, prosecutors have been using such laws. Gang membership is a factor that prosecutors often use to convince a judge that a juvenile is "not rehabilitatable", and thus suitable for transfer to the adult system. The youths tried as adults often must continue to serve their time in juvenile correctional facilities until they become "of age"; at which time, if they can be transferred to an adult prison. Often the juvenile correctional system has the discretion as to when exactly, typically after the age of 17, the youth is transferred to an adult correctional facility. Such cases, however, are becoming more common to longterm juvenile correctional institutions.

THE 1990 SURVEY OF STATE JUVENILE INSTITUTIONS

On October 1, 1990 the questionnaire was mailed to approximately 300 state juvenile institutions[1]. These were sent to the superintendents or wardens identified through the 1990 American Correctional Association (ACA) Directory. Some 155 responded representing 49 states which constitutes the sample size used here[2].

Several check-off questions about service programs were similarly included in the questionnaire. The responding juvenile institutions were to indicate whether their facility did or did not have these types of service programs. The results indicate some 88.6 percent (N=132) indicated that they provided sex education. Some 94.1 percent (N=144) indicated that they provided drug rehabilitation/counseling. Some 85.7 percent (N=126) indicated that they provided job readiness skills training. Some 75.7 percent (N=109) indicated that they provided treatment for depression. And some 16.6 percent (N=24) indicated that they provided "gang deprograming" even though we intentionally designed this item as a validity check, believing as we did from a review of the literature that no such program service actually existed anywhere other than "cult deprograming" services in the private sector.[3]

A report from adult prisons in Illinois suggested that between 80 and 90 percent of all inmates were gang members (Lane, 1989). No comparable statistics have ever yet been reported nationally on juvenile institutions.[4] We sought to fill this gap in our knowledge by asking the reporting institutions to indicate "among staff who know about gang members, what is the current estimate of what percentage gang members are of the total population of your facility?" The percentages for males and females were sought.

Among male juveniles, our findings show this ranges from a low of zero percent for about one fifth of American juvenile institutions (21.7%), to a high of 97 percent. About half (52.2%) of these juvenile institutions report a rate of ten percent or higher of such male juvenile inmates as gang members. In fact, 30.4 percent of the institutions report a rate of one out of every four juveniles as gang members. In more than one of every ten American juvenile institutions (12.3%) this rate is fifty percent or higher.

Reported gang membership among females in juveniles institutions is substantially lower than for their male counterparts. Among female juveniles confined, the estimates of percentage of gang members of the total population ranges from a low of zero for over half of the institutions (60%), to a high of 40 percent. But in nearly one out of every five such female juvenile institutions we find a rate of 10 percent or higher for those who are gang members.

From our total sample, at least one of every five juvenile institutions (21.7%) reported that whites have a separate gang. These are called a variety of names, often simply "skin heads". Other names included, however, the following: Bootboys, Honky Love, Simon City Royals, White Knights, Supreme White Power, Supreme White Pride, Suicide White Power, White Gangster Disciples, Folkz, and others including skinheads and neo-nazis.

Clearly some gangs are more organizationally sophisticated, with written constitutions, and have definite political leanings that can be roughly characterized as an "oppressed peoples" ideology. Further, white gangs have traditionally shown a clear propensity towards white racism. Our findings here are in response to the question "to what extent are gang members involved in extremist political beliefs"? Recall that Camp and Camp (1985: pp. 59-61) reported 17 states with African-American activist prison gangs and 16 with white supremacist prison gangs.

What our findings show is that on a scale between zero (for not at all) to a high of 10 (for a great deal) most juvenile institutions (61 percent) indicated their gang members were not involved in political extremism. Over a third (39%) indicated at some level that this factor was evident in their juvenile institutions among gang members. Again, however, this is an under researched area about political ideology and gangs.

Several questions dealt with the matter of gang-related violence inside of the juvenile correctional institutions. This focused on both the correctional staff member as victim and on assaults generally. Thus, the findings have only indirect significance for estimating the potential impact of gang violence inside juvenile correctional institutions against other juvenile inmates.

When asked "have gang members been a problem in terms of assaults on the correctional staff", some 14 percent of the juvenile institutions reported yes.

When asked to "estimate the number within the last one year period, how many assaults or attacks on correctional personnel by gang members", more than one fourth of these juvenile institutions reported one or more such incidents (N = 39, 28.3%). Further, when asked "did any of these assaults by gang members on correction staff require hospitalization?", some eleven institutions indicated yes. Which suggests that in about a third of these institutions reporting gang assaults on correctional officers it was serious enough of an attack to require hospitalization.

For comparison purposes, Camp and Camp (1985: p. 50) reported eighteen such confrontations with staff in six adult correctional systems during 1983; of which only four states reported staff injuries. Here we find, among juvenile institutions during 1989-1990, that 150 different assaults or attacks by gang members on correctional staff were reported, which were serious enough to require hospitalization in eleven such institutions.

At a more global level, with no specification of victim status as either staff or inmate, when asked to estimate "within the last one year period, how many serious injuries occurred from attacks/fights/assaults involving gang members", some 33.1 percent indicated one or more such incidents. A total of 209 such incidents were reported in the sample. Clearly, this rate of violence is higher than all reported cases involving attacks or assaults on correctional staff, suggesting at least that some of the other victims had to be fellow juveniles confined in these institutions.

When asked "does the fear of violence represented by gangs, in your view, contribute to staff turnover in your facility?" thirteen (9.3%) of the juvenile institutions, nationwide, indicated this was true. Recall that four killings of correctional staff were attributed to gang members during 1983 by the Camp and Camp (1985) study.

Apparently, juvenile gang members inside the correctional institutions are also responsible for a considerable amount of damage to government property.[5] A question directed towards this line of inquiry asked "to what extent are gang members responsible for damage to government property in your facility?". The response modes included a low of zero for "none" to a high of 10 for "chiefly responsible". Our findings show that about half of the juvenile institutions (53.2%) report some level of gang member responsibility for such damage to government property while in juvenile correctional custody.

The gang problem in America has no panacea. And correctional institutions can do little about the conditions that give rise to gangs in our nations' communities. In fact, correctional institutions are the true "last resort" of our continuum of legal sanctions against gang offending. But no required standards currently exist from the American Correctional Association on the appropriate techniques for handling gang problems. At least one source has recommended such "strict standards to prevent gang activity or membership in custodial institutions where gang members are detained" (Stephens, 1988: p. 33). As Camp and Camp (1985: p. xix) recommended that correctional agencies should develop policy positions and strategies for the gang problem.

Our survey replicated previous research conducted on adult institutions and what techniques were used by corrections staff to deal with gangs (Camp and Camp, 1985: p. xvi). We also added some new dimensions to our investigation.

One question asked "would your facility function better if gang members could be transferred to a central/national federal unit?" Some 31.9 percent indicated yes.

A question about gang awareness training asked "do your staff receive formalized training in dealing with the gang problem?" About one third (33.1%) indicated this training was now in effect. But if training should be required to help "maintain order and prevent trouble" (Shannon, 1987: p. 173), then clearly the emerging gang problem will require more standardized and specialized training in dealing with gangs.

Finally, we sought to ascertain the extent to which previously documented techniques for dealing with gangs inside correctional institutions were also being used in juvenile corrections. Our findings show that, nationwide, the following techniques were used: transfers (33.6%), use of informers (17.8%), segregation (27.1%), isolating leaders (38.3%), lockdown (22.4%), prosecution (17.8%), interrupting communications (32.7%), case by case dealings (72%), ignoring their (gangs) existence (6.5%)[6], infiltration (0.9%), displacing members to different institutions (29%), coopting of prisoners to control gangs (2.8%), meeting with gang leaders on "as needed" basis (15.9%)[7], joint meetings between various gang leaders (9.3%), and other (19.8%).

Figure 20 below summarizes the differences between the rank ordering of techniques for dealing with gangs from the Camp and Camp (1985) study of adult prisons with this study of juvenile institutions. As seen in Figure 20, the present study has a larger sample but shows clear differences between the way adult prisons handle gangs in comparison with the way juvenile institutions handle gangs.

FIGURE   20

RANK ORDERING OF MOST FREQUENTLY USED METHODS
IN DEALING WITH GANGS COMPARING THE CAMP AND
CAMP (1985) ADULT FINDINGS WITH THE
1990 STUDY OF JUVENILE INSTITUTIONS

ADULT PRISONS Camp and Camp (1985) Study	JUVENILE INSTITUTIONS The 1990 Survey
**************************	***************************
Move or transfer (N=27)	Case by case basis (N=77)
Use Informers (N = 21)	Isolate leaders (N=41)
Segregation (N = 20)	Intercept communications (N=35)
Lock up leaders (N = 20)	Move or transfer (N=36)
Lockdown (N = 18)	Segregate (N=29)
Prosecute (N = 16)	Lockdown (N=24)
Intercept Communications (N=16)	Use informers (N=19)
Case by Case (N = 13)	Prosecute (N=19)
Refuse to Acknowledge (N=9)	Meet with leaders (N=17)
Infiltration (N=5)	Ignore (N=7)
Co-opt Inmates to control (N=3)[8]	Coopt (N=3) Infiltrate (N=1)

Another question to juvenile correctional administrators was "are racial conflicts a problem among juveniles in your facility?". Our findings show that nearly half (48.3%) indicated this was true. That some environments can foster a destructive demeanor appears to have some empirical support at least when examining this factor of racial conflict in relationship to reports of property damage, overcrowding, and even recidivism.[9] Recall from Chapter 4 in presenting some of these same juvenile institution findings in the context of the racism oppression thesis that the problem of racial conflict significantly differentiates those same juvenile institutions reporting a problem of gang damage to government property and high recidivism rates (e.g., over 20 percent). Also, overcrowding is significantly associated with reports of racial conflict.

Some 70 juvenile institutions provided written responses to an open-ended question about "what to do". Here is what juvenile correctional administrators recommend doing about the gang problem to make their facilities a safer place. It is clearly a staffing and training problem. Only a third of the institutions indicated that their staff receive formalized training in dealing with the gang problem.   Many administrators see the need to hire more staff. This is justified because as one respondent indicated "the gang problem is 95% African-American, so hire an African-American with good group skills who can work directly with these youth".

Having more staff would mean more people to deal with youth problems, with social issues, and increasing the staffing ratios to reflect more counselors, not security guards.

Many also saw the need for increased training of staff. This would mean training staff in gang awareness and recognition of gang members, or generally to deal more effectively with gang problems. It can also mean setting up an educational curriculum along with intensive staff training. And the need to define gang behavior, to identify gang members and to increase staff understanding of the gang problem.

Providing more counseling is another major recommendation of the institutions surveyed here. This would mean increasing self-esteem because it varies inversely with gang affiliation. Or developing a speakers bureau using ex-gang members with reformed outlooks who are willing to discourage offenders from future gang activity. Providing an alternative to the gang life style. Perhaps even a program for parents of gang members. Or combined with an isolation policy, using staff with appropriate gang counseling skills.

Separation of the gang members in the institution was a policy recommended by some. It would mean designing facilities that separated youths into smaller, more manageable groups to decrease the contamination and contagion factor.[10] It can also mean a separate area of detention just for gang members. Or isolating gang members until they are ready to return to the general population and display appropriate behavior. Or transporting gang members to separate facilities, keeping them as separate as possible. Perhaps through new construction to provide a section to segregate disruptive residents, or placing them in a "special" program away from the facility. The idea being to divide and keep the gangs separate within the institution; secondly to isolate gang leaders from other youths.

But a few indicated this policy "does not work". They recommended keeping them together and providing therapeutic counseling. One simply indicated that isolation and separation do not work, perhaps joining some adult correctional agencies in the alternative method of "set-off" approaches, or balancing the gang problem by controlled gang affiliation assignments.

The largest single recommendation was a "get tough" policy. This view would make it a statutory offense to engage in gang activity in the institution, and prosecuting them for criminal activity inside the institution. Providing stiffer penalties. Increasing the use of restraints and tougher punishment to fit the crime. Such that those who refuse to dissociate from gangs would understand there are serious consequences. Or providing greater security measures (TV monitors, etc). Or transferring documented gang members to adult systems, prosecuting or "certifying" the violent or disruptive youths as unamenable to the juvenile system. Overall, this approach meant a "zero tolerance" for gang behavior. Prosecuting and extending their time in confinement if necessary, placing the gang members in a more secure setting (e.g., maximum security), providing more severe consequences for inappropriate behavior.

THE 1991 JUVENILE CORRECTIONS SURVEY

The findings reported here are from a national random sample of N = 274 state juvenile correctional facilities. This represents a 42.7 percent return rate for the sample frame of N = 641 facilities and includes responses from 44 states and the District of Columbia. Conducted in October, 1991 this survey sought to replicate some of the variables analyzed a year earlier (Knox, 1990). The findings relevant to gangs in juvenile corrections are summarized here from a much larger and more in-depth report on juvenile corrections generally[11]. The unit of analysis here is therefore the individual juvenile correctional facility or the views of its administrator.

Using a checklist approach, these juvenile correctional facility administrators were also asked to indicate if their facility had any of a list of specific service programs. Unfortunately, the term "program" can often be construed as any informal effort, as is likely here. That is, ideally we need to know if these are formalized, funded programs with full-time staff and resources allocated to these types of service programs. Such an analysis will have to wait for the 1992 survey. What we can present here is a comparison of the 1990 and the present 1991 surveys as shown in Table 61 below.

TABLE 61

DISTRIBUTION OF SERVICE PROGRAMS

| | "yes" have the Program | | | |
| | 1990 Survey | | 1991 survey | |
Type of Program:	N	%	N	%
Sex education	132	88.6	237	89.8
Drug rehab./counseling	144	94.1	237	90.5
Job readiness skills training	126	85.7	221	86.3
Treatment for depression	109	75.7	169	68.7
To enhance self-esteem	135	91.2	249	94.7
To increase life coping skills	143	94.1	249	94.0
To decrease propensity to commit self-destructive acts	109	74.7	204	80.3
Gang deprograming	24	16.6	57	23.8

In the 1990 survey the "gang deprograming" service program was included, initially, as a validity factor. That is, as the principal investigator had recently published the first full text book on gangs (Knox, 1991) the research associates felt that one way to determine whether the survey was properly completed or not was to include a type of program that was not indicated anywhere in the literature (e.g., "gang deprograming"). Thus, when the 1990 survey revealed some 16.6 percent reported having such a "gang deprograming" service program in their juvenile correctional institution calls were made to these facilities to inquire about these unique initiatives. Generally, what this revealed was the belief that is empirically consistent with the drug-gang research literature, that secondary and tertiary prevention/intervention initiatives can be undertaken to erode "gang ties", to "dismember" gangs, to "coopt" those who are not hard core gang members, and to basically "siphon off" gang members whose commitment level is not very high. But these are informal, not formal, initiatives.

Another set of variables measured in both the 1990 and the 1991 juvenile corrections surveys dealt with the matter of gang force strength. The reader is simply cautioned that these are estimates of what percentage of the juveniles in their correctional facilities are gang members which were provided by agency administrators. We might reasonably expect some differences, for example, in comparing the estimates of administrators with line staff regarding what percentage of their juvenile charges are gang members. One dramatic research finding that cannot be reported here[a] (Knox and Tromanhauser, 1991) in specific detail is this: there is a much higher rate of gang membership when we directly ask the confined juveniles themselves through survey research than appears through agency administrator surveys.

The 1991 survey shows that for male juveniles the estimate of gang affiliation ranges between a low of zero percent (15.9%) to a high of 100 percent. And, similarly, the estimate for confined females ranges from a low of zero percent (58.3%) to a high of 100 percent. The 1991 means for the current estimate of what percentage gang members are of the total population of these juvenile facilities was 20.8 percent for males and 4.9 percent for females[b]. This compares with 17.7 percent for males and 4.4 percent for females from the 1990 survey. Obviously, from this kind of survey research methodology we cannot speak to whether there are objective increases in gang membership, per se, within American juvenile correctional institutions; because the increase in the 1991 survey may simply reflect a more open admission of the problem, overcoming agency denial, or a host of plausible rival hypotheses.

A similar gang finding trend is found in comparing the 1990 and the 1991 surveys with regard to the question "do whites have a separate gang in your facility?". From the present 1991 survey, about a fourth (25.4%, N = 57) indicated yes, that among whites who are confined in juvenile correctional facilities, there exist separate basically "white gangs". In the 1990 survey some 21.7 percent of the institutions reported the existence of such separate white gangs.

As in the 1990 survey, the 1991 survey included the question "to what extent are gang members involved in extremist political beliefs?". The response mode included the range between zero (not at all) and 10 (a great deal). Findings from the 1991 survey show that 44.5 percent indicated zero; or no such gang involvement with political extremism. But some 14.4 percent rated this factor at "five" or higher.

---

[a] This research was undertaken using the juveniles themselves as the unit of analysis in an anonymous "self-report" survey for 45 short and long term juvenile facilities in five states. The research agreement does not allow dissemination of the research report until the final version has been approved by the funding source. Thus, we can only relate a general trend here, rather than specific data.

[b] By multiplying the population count by these percentages of gang affiliation, a total of N = 4,736 male gang members and N = 514 female gang members would be facility administrator estimate for total gang force strength in this sample.

Another series of questions on the 1991 Survey dealt with gang violence inside juvenile facilities, again replicating the 1990 research[c]. When asked to "estimate the number, within the last one year period, how many serious injuries occurred in your facility from attacks/fights/assaults involving gang members", nearly three-fourths (74.6%, N = 194) indicated none. But the range was between zero such gang violence incidents and a high of 22.

When asked, "have gang members been a problem in terms of assaults on your staff?", some 92 percent (N = 242) indicated no for the current 1991 survey. And only 8 percent (N = 21) of these responding juvenile facilities indicated "yes" for such problems of gang assaults upon staff.

While 83.7 percent of the responding facilities indicated that no such assaults or attacks had been made on staff by gang members during the last one year period, some 16.3 percent indicated such attacks had in fact taken place. Among fourteen of the responding institutions these attacks on staff by gang members were serious enough to require hospitalization of the staff members involved. Further, some 8.2 percent of the responding juvenile facilities indicated that the fear of violence represented by gangs, in their view, contributes to staff turnover.

When asked "to what extent are gang members responsible for damage to property in your facility", using a response mode that ranged from zero (none) to 10 (chiefly responsible), the present 1991 findings are similar to the previous year (see Knox, 1991). Some 53.9 percent indicated zero, that is, gang members are not at all responsible for damage to such government property. Clearly, then, somewhat less than half indicated that this was to some extent true.

Another question was designed regarding the gang problem and corrections, and it was this "Would your facility function better if gang members could be transferred to a central-national federal unit?". Obviously, no such "gang Alcatraz" exists, nor has anyone proposed such a measure. What this really tends to measure, then, is the frustration with the gang problem and the tendency to want to "dump the problem" on someone else in the same way that gave rise to the gang presence within juvenile correctional institutions generally. Nearly a fifth, some 19.9 percent indicated "yes" they would like to transfer their youthful gang members to a central national unit.

As in law enforcement and adult corrections the term "gang training" can mean a lot of things. Some consider this equivalent to "group disturbance" training. As if all the gang problem implied was some factor of "potential disruptiveness" during correctional confinement. Like racial conflict, it is a problem found in many adult and juvenile correctional institutions, but it is not a factor that carries any guidelines from national groups like the American Correctional Association.

---

[c] Earlier work used the phrase "socialized delinquent" as being ideal candidates for long-term secure care facilities and made specific reference to gang members: "the ideal candidate is the older socialized delinquent: an extroverted gang member who is at least 16 years of age" (Grissom and Dubnov, 1989: p. 60). To speak of the over 16 year old gang member as a preferred correctional client is an anomaly in the literature.

The present 1991 survey showed that nearly a third (33.8%, N = 88) indicated their staff do receive such formalized training in dealing with the gang problem. Which means, of course, that about two-thirds of these same juvenile correctional facilities do not provide such staff training. One recent report (Knox, Mc Currie, and Tromanhauser, 1991) shows how juvenile institutions from the 1990 survey would prefer to deal with the gang problem. Analysis of this gang training factor for the present 1991 survey reveals that several factors account for significant differences. Table 62 shows that long term facilities are much more likely to report such formal gang training. Similarly, those that are community-based are the least likely to provide such formal gang training as seen in Table 63.

TABLE 62

FREQUENCY DISTRIBUTION FOR
TYPE OF JUVENILE CORRECTIONAL FACILITY
(SHORT TERM, LONG TERM, OTHER)
BY FORMAL GANG TRAINING

	Do Their Staff Receive Formal Gang Training?	
Type of Facility:	NO	YES
Short Term	95	28
Long Term	68	53
Other	7	5

Chi square = 12.4, p = .002

TABLE 63

FREQUENCY DISTRIBUTION OF WHETHER THE JUVENILE
FACILITY IS COMMUNITY BASED
BY FORMAL GANG TRAINING

	Do Their Staff Receive Formal Gang Training?	
Whether Community-Based:	NO	YES
Not Community-based	71	54
Community-based	98	34

Chi square = 8.67, p = .003

As in the 1990 Survey, the 1991 Survey again examined the techniques that correctional administrators used to control gangs in their juvenile facilities. As shown below in Table 64, the "case by case" method is the most frequently cited strategy for dealing with gangs in juvenile correctional facilities. Genuinely, this "case by case" method simply means a catch all category of something approximating deal with it "as it arises", or on an individual basis.

As seen in Table 64 below, transferring gang members is the second most frequently cited method for dealing with the gang problem.   Intercepting communications presumably relates to a variety of internal and external informational processes affecting the facility.   It was interesting to see that "balancing the number of rival gang members living in the same unit" enjoyed such a prominent position in the rank ordering of methods for dealing with gangs in juvenile correctional facilities.

TABLE   64

FREQUENCY DISTRIBUTION OF METHODS FOR DEALING WITH
THE GANG PROBLEM IN JUVENILE
CORRECTIONAL AGENCIES

Method of Gang Control:	N
Case by case	130
Transfer	59
Intercept Communications	54
Balance the number of rival gang members living in the same unit	37
Isolate Leaders	34
Lockdown	25
Displacing members to different facilities	28
Ignoring their existence	16
Segregation	19
Use of informers	19
Meeting with gang leaders on "as needed" basis	23
Prosecution	19
Joint meetings between various gang leaders	13
Coopting others to control gangs	9
Infiltration	3

What this "balancing" option is often called is the "set off" principle, meaning in a particular ward, cell house, or living unit, provide a "balance of power" by basically putting in just as many "crips" as "bloods", essentially a "balance the opposition" under some conception of the famous divide and conquer thinking. As a way of dealing with the gang problem, however, this may not be very well thought out at all. In fact, such a strategy could conceivably increase the gang problem and induce conflict, including violence, within a juvenile correctional setting.

Let the record reflect the social scientific truth here: there has been absolutely no evaluation research reported anywhere regarding which, if any, of these gang control methods is effective, counter-productive, or having "null effect". Those working in juvenile corrections, as elsewhere, who have to face the gang problem, are simply advised to "get the best facts". And the best facts are not necessarily from other practitioner points of view. The best facts are those that are based on hard research and an appraisal of the social science literature. Unfortunately for juvenile and adult correctional administrators today, the current federal gang research funding initiative gives no attention to evaluating these problems.

But the literature is suggestive to correctional administrators. The study by Brobrowski (1988) concluded that the rise of "gang nations" (confederations of previously oppositional gangs, e.g., "folks" versus "peoples" in Illinois prisons) was due entirely to a misdirected and misguided prison policy of allowing gang members to meet as groups, recognizing them as groups, and official negotiation with their gang leaders. It is fair to alert the reader that there is more than some level of legal liability implied by the use of some of these methods of gang control from a prisoners rights viewpoint. Mostly, if taken to its extreme logical conclusion the tendency to want to "do what others are doing about the problem" runs the serious risk that if the others truly are doing the wrong thing there is more than some social policy jeopardy represented by simply imitating or adopting procedures with unknown possible long term effects. They are unknown effects because none of these strategies have been evaluated.

The cost factor of juvenile corrections was also measured here in terms of the daily cost for one youth. This ranged from a low of $16 to a high of $300 in terms of daily costs[d]. The mean was $102.24 for the N = 238 respondents who provided this information. It is fair to assume that some significant variation exists with regard to the cost of care factor when controlling for type of facility. For example, an analysis of variance test showed a significant difference (F = 6.04, p = .01) in comparing the costs in terms of whether these were community-based facilities. The average cost for community based facilities was $94 compared to $110 for those facilities that were not community based. Community based juvenile facilities therefore reported significantly lower daily costs. No significance emerged in contrasting short term and long term facilities or whether the facility was located in rural or urban areas.

THE 1992 JUVENILE DETENTION SURVEY

Reported here are the findings of a survey of local juvenile detention centers with special attention on the gang problem[12]. A saturation sampling technique of all 576 juvenile detention facilities was used for this survey. The facility directors were asked to participate in a mail survey in February 1992. Some N = 228 facilities responded to the survey providing the sample used here, representing a 39.5 percent response rate. Stated alternatively, the data reported here represents 39.5 percent of all juvenile detention facilities (other than holdovers and group homes) as listed in the first edition of the National Juvenile Detention Directory (ACA, 1992).

---

[d] Mardon (1991: p. 33) reports a correctional program, a "marine/outward bound" type of program, that averaged $36 per day per client. Clearly, some of those at the lower end of the cost spectrum were of this type of correctional program variety: e.g., day centers, etc.

Using a check list of nine different program services, the facility administrators were asked to indicate yes or no regarding whether their facility had any of these types of service programs. Often, in answering yes, the respondent would write in the margin of the survey a remark typically to the effect "not a formal program per se...but accomplished informally". Table 65 presents these results.

TABLE 65

The Availability of Various Service Programs
Reported as Existing in Juvenile Detention Centers

| | Does It Exist? | | | |
| | No | | Yes | |
Type of Service Program:	N	%	N	%
Sex Education	57	26.1	161	73.9
Drug Rehab./Counseling	54	24.4	167	75.6
Job Readiness Skills Trng.	111	51.6	104	48.4
Treatment for Depression	106	49.1	110	50.9
To enhance self-esteem	63	28.4	159	71.6
Increase life-coping skills	63	28.8	156	71.2
To decrease propensity to commit self-destructive acts	89	41.0	128	59.0
Gang Deprograming	193	90.2	21	9.8
AIDS/HIV awareness	45	20.3	177	79.7

Estimates of Gang Membership Among Confined Juveniles. This question to facility administrators asked "Among staff who know about gang members, what is the current estimate of what percentage gang members are of the total population of your facility?" and separate estimates were sought for both males and females. Among males the estimate of gang membership ranged from a low of zero to a high of 100 percent. Among females the estimate ranged from a low of zero to a high of 90 percent. The mean or average for males was 14.6 percent. The mean or average for females was 4.17 percent.

Another way of looking at this problem is in relationship to the actual population counts for males and females. Because both of these variables are on computer, it was possible to use simple arithmetic to multiply the "percentage" gang member by the respective gender population of confined juveniles. This yields 2062 male gang members and 62 female gang members represented in the facilities included in this study.

White Gangs. As illustrated elsewhere (Knox, 1991; Knox, Tromanhauser, and Laske, 1992) the correctional climate regarding gangs is very consistent: where minority gangs exist, separate white gangs are also commonly found. The reason for this has to do with the role that racial and ethnic conflict holds as a factor that fuels the gang problem. The data shows that 41 percent of the juvenile detention centers in the present study report that in fact whites do have a separate gang.

Gang Member Assaults on Staff. The data show that 10.3 percent of the juvenile detention centers report that gang members have, in fact, been a problem in terms of assaults on their staff. The estimate of the number of such assaults on staff by gang members ranged from a low of zero to a high of ten during the last one year period. However, only 5.3 percent of the administrators reported that the fear of violence represented by gangs has contributed to staff turnover in their facilities.

Gang Members Responsible for Damage to Property. The administrators were asked to rate the extent to which gang members have been responsible for damage to property in their facility along a scale of zero to ten, where zero represented "not responsible" and ten represented "chiefly responsible". Just over half of the facilities (52.4%) indicated the very lowest possible estimate in this range of estimates, suggesting that gangs or gang members were therefore not responsible to any extent for damage to property within these facilities. Yet some 13.7% indicated a rating of five or higher on this zero to ten point scale. The mean value was 1.57.

Formalized Gang Training for Staff. The data show that in 35 percent of the facilities the staff receive formalized training in dealing with the gang problem. The majority of these juvenile detention facilities (65%) report that their staff do not receive formal training in dealing with gangs.

Racial Conflicts Among Confined Juveniles. Racial conflicts are a problem among the confined juveniles in nearly half of the facilities studied here (49.6%).

Strategies Used to Control/Manage Gangs in Juvenile Detention Centers. The juvenile detention center administrators were asked about what strategies their facility uses to deal with gangs. A check list of known techniques was provided and the respondent was able to simply check off all those that apply. Presented in Table 66 are the results of the analysis that first controls for the density of the gang problem itself in these same facilities. That is to say, what strategies a facility uses to deal with gangs becomes important only to the extent of their gang problem. The extent of their gang problem was measured here by the percentage of the male youths who are gang members.

As seen in Table 66 the techniques used to control or manage gangs and disruptive groups do in fact vary with the density of the actual problem (e.g., percentage of males who are gang members). Three different density levels are used for analysis here. This basically partials out of the analysis any facility that claims none of its confined juvenile males are gang members. This shows that the higher the density of the gang problem, the more likely these juvenile correctional facilities are to use certain control strategies (use of informers, segregation, isolating leaders, lockdown, prosecution, interrupting communications, coopting of inmates to control gangs, joint meetings between various gang leaders, balancing the number of rival gang members in the same living unit --- also known as the "set off" technique).

Table 66 also shows that with increases in the density of the problem certain techniques do not show a consistent upward rate of utilization. Ignoring their existence, for example, is shown to be a decreased option when 25 percent or more of the youths in the facility are gang members. Similarly, the lower the density of the problem the more likely these facilities are to report using the option of infiltration. Displacing gang members to different facilities (also known as "bus therapy" or "diesel treatment") is also shown to not be an option that varies directly with the density of the gang problem. Meeting with gang leaders on an "as needed" basis is also shown to not be an option that consistently increases with the density of the problem.

TABLE 66

Percentage Distribution for Strategies Used in Juvenile Detention Centers To Deal With Gangs By Three Levels of Gang Density

Gang Control Methods:	Density Level of the Gang Problem (percentage of males: gang members)		
	>= .02%	>= 5%	>= 25%
Transfers	20.9	22.3	22.7
Use of informers	11.1	12.5	15.9
Segregation	37.3	42.0	52.3
Isolating leaders	41.8	47.3	54.5
Lockdown	32.0	39.3	59.1
Prosecution	23.5	25.9	27.3
Interrupting Communications	35.9	41.1	56.8
Case by case dealings	56.9	59.8	59.1
Ignoring their existence	5.2	5.4	4.5
Infiltration	2.6	1.8	0.0
Displacing members to different facilities	11.1	9.8	11.4
Coopting of inmates to control gangs	2.6	3.6	4.5
Meeting with gang leaders on "as needed" basis	8.5	9.8	9.1
Joint meetings between various gang leaders	3.3	3.6	6.8
Balance the number of rival gang members in the same living unit	22.9	29.5	43.2
Other	8.5	10.7	18.2

Average Daily Costs for One Confined Youth. Overall, the average daily cost for one youth ranged from a low of $11.50 for a non-residential day detention facility to a high of $307 dollars for a secure detention setting. The overall mean was $100.40 per day for all such facilities represented in the sample. It is more meaningful, however, to look at costs in relationship to the security levels of the facilities and whether they are residential or non-residential facilities.

In short, the local juvenile detention centers which are designed to securely hold the juvenile awaiting trial or for very short term periods have much in common with the state juvenile correctional facilities that are designed to hold youths who have been sentenced and adjudicated for acts of juvenile delinquency.

THE 1991 SURVEY OF CONFINED JUVENILES ON HEALTH RISKS

The study described here was a first large scale effort that examined gang membership at the level of the individual juvenile delinquent locked up in short and long term juvenile correctional institutions. Only a small section of the larger report dealt with gang membership[13].

This national survey data was collected during the period May-June, 1991. The survey itself contains forty five forced choice questions designed to be completed by respondents inside short and long term juvenile correctional institutions. In March-April, 1991 this survey instrument was pre-tested using juvenile correctional facilities in two states with over N = 100 respondents. The pretest indicated very little item difficulty for the lowest range of reading ability.

The sample of forty four (N = 44) juvenile correctional facilities was provided by NCCHC and these facilities represented a potential sample frame of N = 2533 respondents[e]. The superintendents of these facilities and their governing agencies were contacted by mail in April, 1991. The purpose of the NCCHC Health Risk Survey was explained, a copy of the survey instrument was provided, and their participation in the national research project was sought.

By July 10, 1991 a total of N = 1,801 completed surveys had been returned and processed for data analysis. This represents a slightly higher than 70 percent return rate of questionnaires for the complete sample frame of 44 institutions[f]. Summarized here are the findings about how gang membership among confined juveniles is significantly related to a number of other factors.

Outside of the Camp and Camp (1985) study where the unit of analysis was adult state prison systems (not individual correctional institutions) and which had much missing data on states reluctant to report on this problem, the only other research on gangs in corrections is that by Robert Fong and his associates (Fong, 1987, 1990; Fong and Buentello, 1991; Fong, Vogel and Little, 1991; Fong, Vogel and Buentello, 1991) focusing exclusively on gangs in adult Texas prisons and that by Knox (1991) focusing on juvenile and adult correctional institutions nationwide.[g] There has been little prior research reported in the literature involving a survey of actual juveniles detained in correctional facilities nationwide regarding the gang problem. The present effort, therefore, has much knowledge to offer regarding this most important social policy issue.

---

[e] The original NCCHC list included 46 such institutions; however, one had been changed to a non-correctional facility and the other (a private program) had closed down. Thus, only 44 actual juvenile correctional institutions were able to be contacted.

[f] Partialing out those five institutions that refused to participate in the survey obviously increases the response rate to a somewhat higher level.

[g] See also the correctional training policy analysis on dealing with gangs inside juvenile institutions by Knox, Tromanhauser and Mc Currie (1991).

The most significant finding, not from a statistical viewpoint but from a knowledge development viewpoint, from the present analysis is that such a large proportion of these confined juveniles report ever having joined a gang. Recall that 46.1 percent of the juveniles from the present national survey reported such gang membership. The Camp and Camp (1985) research estimated that only three percent of our nation's adult prison population was gang affiliated; and while the national assessment of gangs in corrections by ACA (1993) estimated six percent, using a similarly flawed methodology to generate results that border on fantasy, it neglected entirely the field of juvenile corrections. The recent research by Knox (1991) using a more rigorous unit of analysis[h] showed that this figure was over ten percent for adult institutions, and even higher for juvenile correctional institutions[i].

The methodological improvement of the present study is that its unit of analysis is the individual confined juvenile and represents data from short and long term facilities in five different states. The findings below suggest that gang membership is associated with other health risk behaviors as well.

While age[j] and sex are independent of gang membership, race of these confined juveniles significantly differentiates gang membership. While our sample included few Native Americans or Alaskan Natives (N=31), 11 of them reported gang membership. Similarly, there were few Asian or Pacific Islander respondents (N = 32), but 21 of them reported gang membership. Overall, the largest proportion of gang membership was found among Hispanics (59.4%), followed by Blacks (46.3%) and whites (34.8%).

Time served showed that gang members had been incarcerated longer than their non-gang member counterparts (p = .03). Some 70.5 percent of the gang members had gone to the nurse or doctor for health problems since being incarcerated compared to 64.2 percent of non-gang member juveniles (p = .004). As might be expected from the hypothesis that gang members would be more aggressive or prone to conflict, the number of physical fights during the twelve month period before incarceration also significantly differentiated gang membership. Some 63.1 percent of the gang members reported two or more such physical fights compared to 50.5 percent of their non-gang counterparts (p < .001). Similarly, gang members were significantly more likely to report one or more injuries sustained from these fights (p < .001). The potential deadly nature of some of these conflicts shows gang members face a significantly higher likelihood of being injured as well when comparing the number of fights in which deadly weapons were used (p < .001). As

---

[h] Surveys of the wardens and superintendents of the individual correctional institutions, nationwide.

[i] The advantage to the anonymous survey approach such as that used in the present NCCHC Health Risk Survey is that self-reporting in this instance is likely to produce less of a reporting bias. Most correctional estimates of gang affiliation are based on self-reporting as well, but at time of intake, a time when detained persons are more likely to underreport their deviance.

[j] Age as an independent variable nears significance (p = .06).

an illustration, some 67.9 percent of the gang members had 4 or more such fights involving deadly weapons during their lifetime compared to 35.3 percent of youths who were not gang members.

Gang members are significantly more likely to report cigarette smoking when compared to non-gang members (p < .001). While 23.1 percent of the gang members reported suicide ideation compared to 20.7 percent of their non-gang counterparts this was not a significant difference. Where the significant difference emerges is in making a plan for suicide within the last twelve months. Gang members showed a significantly higher tendency to make a suicide plan (22.2%) than did non-gang members (17.2%) (p = .008). Also, gang members reported making more such actual suicide attempts than did their non-gang counterparts (p = .001). Also, gang members were more likely to have to be treated by a doctor or nurse for such attempts (p = .001). For example, 10.3 percent of the gang members reported requiring such medical treatment for suicide attempt injuries compared to 6.3 percent of their non-gang counterparts.

With the longstanding linkage between drugs and street gangs it comes as no surprise to find strong consistent relationships between drug and substance abuse variables and gang membership among these confined juveniles. Gang membership significantly differentiates all measures of drug and substance abuse as seen below.

DRUG AND SUBSTANCE ABUSE VARIABLES
SIGNIFICANTLY DIFFERENTIATING
GANG MEMBERSHIP AMONG
CONFINED JUVENILES

Variable	Relationship/Direction	Probability
Item 17 (age 1st drink)	Gang drink earlier	< .001
Item 18 (days drinking)	Gang members drink more	< .001
Item 19 (heavy drinking)	Gang members drink more	< .001
Item 20 (age pot use)	Gang members use pot earlier	.02
Item 21 (# pot uses)	Gang members use more pot	< .001
Item 22 (cocaine use)	Cocaine use higher for gangs	< .001
Item 23 (# cocaine uses)	Gangs use more cocaine	< .001
Item 24 (crack use)	Crack use higher for gangs	< .001
Item 25 (other drugs)	Gangs use more other drugs	.03
Item 26 (IV drug use)	Gang members shoot up more	.006

In a recent survey providing a partial replication of the famous Chicago Safe School study (Tromanhauser, 1981) data collected in June, 1991 among over 500 Chicago high school students showed 32.5 percent of the gang members had permanent tattoos compared to only 9 percent of non-gang affiliated Chicago public high school students. In some of the more organized gangs in America, children at a very early age whose parents are gang members have their offspring tattooed with their gang sign, and for gang members the permanent tattoo is another form of gang expression and representation.

Among these confined juveniles having permanent tattoos significantly differentiated gang membership (p < .001). Some 45.7 percent of the gang members had permanent tattoos compared to 29.6 percent of non-gang juveniles. Gang members also reported getting these tattoos at an earlier age than their non-gang counterparts (p < .001).

While there was little variation among these confined juveniles in reporting whether or not they have ever willingly had sex, gang members showed a higher rate of reporting that they had willingly had sex (p = .02). Gang members were significantly more likely to report willingly having sex at age twelve or earlier than non-gang juveniles (p < .001) and to report having sex with more persons (p = .008). Consistent with the earlier tendency for gang members to have a higher drug and substance abuse history, they were also more likely to report using drugs and alcohol during the last time they had sex before their incarceration (p < .001).

During the last time these confined youths had sex before being incarcerated, gang membership also differentiated those who did not use any method to prevent pregnancy (p = .02). Gang members were more likely not to use birth control options. Of course, gang members were significantly more likely to report being pregnant or getting someone pregnant (p < .001). Finally, consistent with the findings just discussed, gang membership significantly differentiates reports of being diagnosed with an STD among these confined juveniles. Gang members are more likely to report an STD (19.3% for gang members, 14.1% for non-gang members) (p = .004).

SUMMARY AND CONCLUSION

The research projects on gangs and juvenile corrections reviewed in this chapter show that these facilities, like their adult prison and jail counterparts, face a large and apparently growing problem with gangs. There is a need for national standards to govern the handling of gangs within correctional settings and to address the matter of racial conflict. Racial conflict among confined juveniles significantly differentiates gang damage to government property; those with racial conflict were more likely to report a problem with damage to property. Juvenile correctional institutions could clearly benefit from more mediation programs (Smith, 1990).

There is a very large need for professional training for the correctional personnel who work in these institutions that specifically helps them to better understand gangs: not simply gang awareness, but more in-depth and advanced training. The reason this is true is the growing incidence of gang assaults upon these correctional officers and the violence that the institutionalized younger gang member is capable of. The study of the 1,801 confined juveniles, where the actual confined youth was the unit of analysis, not the superintendent of the correctional facilities, provides dramatic reason enough for this urgent training need. Beginning with the 1990 survey of juvenile correctional institutions where the respondent was the administrator of the facility, the estimates of the percentage of the confined juveniles that were gang members has been and continues to be very low. Their estimates differ greatly from the self-reported gang membership of the juveniles themselves. From the 1991 survey where the juveniles themselves where the unit of analysis, the estimate would be more likely that about half of all of these youths in short and long term juvenile correctional facilities in America are gang members.

These findings also have enormous implications for adult corrections as well; for after all, it is the juvenile institutions of America that feed our adult institutions through the recidivism process. Further, the research funded by the National Institute of Corrections in their award of the national assessment of gangs in corrections to the American Correctional Association, we find an inappropriate agency responsible for this kind of knowledge development and we should not be surprised that their results are far from reality. The present author did bid on that same research, but our proposal was rejected for being too scientific. Part of the problem is that federal agencies like the National Institute of Justice are politically-minded, and are not required to have true competitive bidding as they should be required when expending public monies. We still lack any valid national assessment of the gang problem in corrections generally, after two NIJ funded projects (1985, 1993), and we still have no information whatsoever about the scope and extent of gang problems in juvenile corrections nationally --- at least from federal agencies like NIJ. It is possible to contact a Washington consulting firm that would be used as a reviewer for NIJ, have them write your proposal and review it too, and it is still not a violation of the law under current procurement regulations --- something that would be called bid rigging and a felony crime in many other state and local government agencies.

RECOMMENDED READING

Adams, Stuart
1967   "A Cost Approach to the Assessment of Gang Rehabilitation Techniques", Journal of Researchin Crime and Delinquency (Jan).

Bartollas, Clemens and Christopher M. Sieverdes
1982   "Juvenile Correctional Institutions: A Policy Statement", Federal Probation (46): 22-26.

Bessette, Joseph M
1989 Children in Custody, 1975-1985. Census of Public and Private Juvenile Detention, Correctional, and Shelter Facilities. May, 1989. U.S. Department of Justice. Bureau of Justice Statistics. Washington, D.C.

Blomberg, Thomas G. and Sherry L. Caraballo
1979   "Accelerated Family Intervention in Juvenile Justice", Crime and Delinquency (25)(4): 497-502.

Breed, Allen F
1990 "America's Future: The Necessity of Investing in Children", Corrections Today (February): pp. 68-72.

Camp, George M. and Camille Graham Camp
1985 Prison Gangs: Their Extent, Nature and Impact on Prisons. Washington, DC: U.S. Government Printing Office.

Crowner, James M
1963 "Utilizing Certain Positive Aspects of Gang Phenomena in Training School Group Work", American Journal of Correction (25)(July-August): 24-27.

Feld, Barry C
1977 Neutralizing Inmate Violence: Juvenile Offenders in Institutions. Cambridge, Mass: Ballinger Publishing Co.

Jacobs, James
1974 "Street Gangs Behind Bars", Social Problems (21)(8): 395-408. 1977. Stateville. Chicago: University of Chicago Press.

Knox, George W
1989 "Family Services in Corrections", The State of Corrections, Proceedings of the Annual Conferences of The American Correctional Association, pp. 179-182.

Knox, George W. and Edward D. Tromanhauser
1991 "Gang Members as a Distinct Health Risk Group in Juvenile Correctional Facilities", The Prison Journal (LXXI)(Fall-Winter)(2): 61-66. 1992. "Comparing Juvenile Correctional Facilities: A Brief Overview", Journal of Juvenile Justice and Detention Services (7)(1)(Spr): 7-13.

Knox, George W.; Edward Tromanhauser; and Thomas F. McCurrie
1991 "Gangs in Juvenile Corrections: Training Issues", Journal of Correctional Training.

Knox, George W.; Edward D. Tromanhauser; and David Laske
1992 "Students Who Really Failed: The Institutionalized Juvenile Population in Relationship to Gangs", chapter 8 (pp. 119-132), in Schools Under Siege, Dubuque, IA: Kendall/Hunt Publishing Company.

Lane, Michael
1989 "Inmate Gangs", Corrections Today (51)(4)(July): 98, 99, 126-128.

Linster, Richard L.; Pamela K. Lattimore; and Christy A. Visher
1990 Predicting the Recidivism of Serious Juvenile Offenders National Institute of Justice Discussion Paper, Washington, D.C.

Mc Lean, Gordon
1991 Cities of Lonesome Fear: God Among the Gangs. Chicago: Moody Press.

Miller, Stuart J
1971 Post-Institutional Adjustments of 443 Consecutive TICO Releases, Ohio State University, Ph.D. dissertation.

Milner, John G
1959 "Working With Juvenile Gang Members", California Youth Authority, Quarterly (12)(Spr): 3-7.

Morici, J.; and D. Flanders
        1979 "Chinatown Youth Gangs - Past, Present and Future", California
        Youth Authority Quarterly (32): 19-24.

National Council of Juvenile and Family Court Judges
        1988 "Youth Gangs - A Special Problem", Juvenile & Family Court Journal
        (39)(4): 47-51.

Nidorf, Barry J
        1989 "Community Corrections: Turning the Crowding Crisis Into Opportu-
        nities", Corrections Today (Oct): 82-88.

Oberst, Margaret
        1988 Inmate Literacy Programs: Virginia's 'No Read, No Release' Program.
        Lexington, KY: Council of State Governments.

Palmer, T. and Wedge, R
        1989 "California's Juvenile Probation Camps: Findings and Implications",
        Crime and Delinquency (35): 234-253.

Propper, Leonard M
        1957 "Juvenile Delinquency and the Gang Problem", Juvenile Court Judges
        Journal (8)(Mar): 24-28.

Rakis, John
        1984 "Suicide Prevention Measures in Urban Detention Facilities Through-
        out the United States", Journal of Prison & Jail Health (4)(2)(Fall): 91-95.

Rowan, Joseph R
        1989 "Suicide Detection and Prevention: A Must for Juvenile Facilities",
        Corrections Today (August): Pp. 218, 220, 226.

Shannon, Michael J
        1987   "Officer Training: Is Enough Being Done?", Corrections Today
        (April): pp. 172-175.

Smith, Melinda
        1990   "New Mexico Youths Use Mediation to Settle Their Problems
        Peacefully", Corrections Today (June): 112-114.

Snyder, Howard N
        1990 Growth in Minority Detentions Attributed to Drug Law Violaters.
        OJJDP Update on Statistics. U.S. Department of Justice, Office of Justice
        Programs, Office of Juvenile Justice and Delinquency Prevention. Juvenile
        Justice Bulletin. Washington, D.C. (March).

Stephens, Ronald D
        1988 Gangs in Schools: Breaking Up is Hard to Do. National School Safety
        Center, Pepperdine University: Malibu, CA. Torres, Dorothy M.

1979 "Chicano Gangs in the East Los Angeles Barrio", <u>California Youth Authority Quarterly</u> (32)(3): 5-13. 1980. <u>Gang Violence Reduction Project 3rd Evaluation Report</u>. Sacramento, CA: California Department of the Youth Authority.

1981 <u>Gang Violence Reduction Project: Fourth Evaluation Report</u>, July 1979-June 1980. Department of the Youth Authority, Sacramento, CA.

van Wormer, Katherine
1990 "Norway's Juvenile Justice System: A Journey Back in Time", <u>Corrections Today</u> (August): pp. 106-113.

Wooden, Wayne
1989 "Profile of Stone Gang Members in the California Youth Authority", paper presented at the American Society of Criminology, Annual Meeting, Reno, Nevada.

1990 "Contemporary Youth Identities: Problems and Issues", paper presented at the Western Society of Criminology, Annual Meeting, Las Vegas, Nevada (February).

DISCUSSION QUESTIONS

(1) From the research reported here, does it seem like much has changed since the Shaw and Mc Kay (1949) study showing how our juvenile correctional institutions appear to be in the inadvertent business of producing adult criminals?

(2) Along with the gang problem for juvenile corrections, comes other problems: overcrowding, illiteracy, and more. Do you think those incarcerated in state training schools are probably already too far down the road of criminality and gang affiliation, or do you believe that secondary and tertiary prevention efforts can still work with them?

(3) This research is the first to demonstrate a strong link between racial conflict and the problem of gang damage to government property inside correctional institutions. Do you think anything can be done to reduce racial conflict through programs, services, education, training, etc?

(4) At a cost of about $50,000 per year to incarcerate one juvenile in a juvenile correctional facility, and knowing that these same facilities have notoriously high recidivism rates, can you envision a better solution; particularly knowing that the same system of juvenile corrections now faces a very large gang problem as well?

(5) The Illinois Youth Correctional Center at Joliet provides an olympic size swimming pool and premium cable television channels for the youths serving time there. Most of these youths are gang members. Should privileges and scarce resources be allocated on the basis of the degree to which the confined juvenile does not continue to present a gang problem for the facility? Or do such convicted persons in your view automatically deserve the same type of services they would be entitled to if they were not locked up?

FOOTNOTES

1. No federal facilities were included in this sample.

2. Graduate students that assisted with this research undertaken by the National Gang Crime Research Center were as follows: Mary Castaneda, Dorenda K. Dixon, Glenn Evans, Sonya Hines, Bruce Jackson, Gloria W. Jones, Monice Lillie, Jordanette Matthews, Walter Mc Cullough, and Jamere Price. All helped in the instrumentation and mailing in a much larger study of juvenile institutions per se.

3. This is one of the problems of researching the "gang frontier". In consulting with a noted Chicago gang expert about this finding, he indicated this was not unusual; there are such "gang deprogramming programs", perhaps patterned after "cult deprogramming", etc. I remarked that "cult deprogramming generally doesn't work", and he said "that doesn't matter". Which is to say, anyone with a Ph.D. in psychology can take a government report on gangs and summarize it, adding their own comments here and there, and put their name on the front and begin offering themselves as experts in "gang training" for criminal justice personnel.

4. Our sample of juvenile institutions, nationwide, reflecting 49 states, suggests that about 17 percent of the males in these institutions are identified as gang members, and about five percent of the female juveniles confined.

5. This was a revised item focusing on what Camp and Camp (1985: pp. 46-47) reported about administrative problems reported by confined gang members. The Camp and Camp (1985) item measured "what percent of the problems are attributable to gangs?" The item as analyzed here reports any level of reported problems.

6. Camp and Camp (1985: p. 14) showed that from adult prisons, submitting and ignoring are the two worst approaches administrators report taking towards gangs.

7. Such a participatory management approach that essentially seeks out the gangs advice has also been recommended for dealing with gangs in our school system. For example, Stephens (1988: p. 28) recommends that to prevent conflict school officials should "discuss the solution strategy with student gang leaders and solicit their support". Obviously, these would not be recommended from the author's analysis presented in this book.

8. Coopting inmates, juvenile or adult, as even through such "peer pressure" implied in required group counseling/confrontation sessions, might be interpreted as simply a more subtle but systematic version of Feld's (1977) finding, contra United Nations guidelines, of using inmates for the repression of other inmates in a disciplinary role. Obviously, some case law is now developing to suggest de facto gang control amounts to the same thing in some of our correctional institutions.

9. In Juveniles and Jail (National Coalition for Jail Reform, 1985, pp. 1-15) overcrowding is argued to be a condition that will contribute to violence and conflict.

10. The "subtle process of contamination" was mentioned in the foreign gang literature (see Robert and Lascoumes, 1974: p. 436). But presumably, here, as used by a warden, means essentially the same thing: one gang member "contaminates" another inmate. Therefore the policy should be to segregate gang members from non-gang members. Which is workable when there are only small proportions of gang members. Not when 97 percent of the entire institutional residents are gang members as in some states.

11. The monograph provided to respondents to the survey was released in December, 1991 and is entitled "Findings from the 1991 National Survey of Juvenile Corrections". The present author was the principal investigator. Research associates included: Bridgette Adams; Michael Adekale, B.S.; Bernard Akpan, B.S., M.S.; Robert Bonner; Raimondo Brown, B.S.; Ne'Cole Bryson; Nora Bush, B.S.; Rochelle Carey; Lashoney Carter; Cecelia Crenshaw, A.A., B.S.; Willie D. Cross, B.S., M.S.; Rolando Currington, B.S., M.S.; Harold Dade; Renee Delvecchio, B.S.; Mike Dooley; Linda Dozier; Yvette Gilmore-Hayes; Trenton Fedrick; Keith Griffin, B.S., M.S.; Abubakr Hamad, LL.B., LL.M., M.S.; Denise M. Hardin, B.S.; Paul Hoffman, M.S.W.; Carlton Jackson; Levelle Kimble, A.A., B.A.; Sam Lacey; David Laske, Ph.D.; Clara Massey, B.S.; Arturo Mota; Fitzgerald Mullins, B.S.; Willie Nance; Benita Parker, B.S.; Odessa Randle; Romelio Rogel, B.S.; Elvis Slaughter; Emile Spearman; Barbara Vasquez; David R. Williams, B.S., B.A.; Yolande Williams, B.S.; Deborach Y. Yackery, A.A.; and Carolyn Zook, A.A..

12. The full report is 46 pages long and is entitled "Gangs in Corrections: Findings from the 1992 Juvenile Detention Survey", available through the National Gang Crime Research Center.

13. The formal title of the monograph is "The 1991 NCCHC Health Risk Survey: An Analysis of N = 1,801 Respondents from Juvenile Correctional Institutions", by George W. Knox and Edward D. Tromanhauser, December, 1991.

CHAPTER 24

GANG PREVENTION AND INTERVENTION

INTRODUCTION

Can gangs be prevented?[1] Can we effectively socialize our children so as to "insulate" them from joining a gang? Can anything be done after they do join a gang? These are but some of the complex, but interesting, issues examined here. From an organizational viewpoint to prevent gang crime or violence at the primary level means to stop the flow of new members into the ranks of gangs. Here again, the open systems approach is helpful. Because a gang cannot continue indefinitely, especially when it is prone to lose it members through violent death or to the correctional system, without replenishing its membership through the induction of new members.

The issue from a primary level of prevention is therefore: how to prevent new gang recruits? And, from an organizational perspective, how to effectively compete with the social-psychological rewards afforded by the typical gang. This is the focus of the present discussion. A subsequent chapter will also critically examine some recent and specific "gang programs".

THE SOCIAL-PSYCHOLOGICAL   BENEFIT STRUCTURE   OF GANGS

In a nutshell, what psychic rewards can the gang offer? Is it just a matter of identity/recognition, protection/intimidation, and fellowship/brotherhood?   To answer this question is to provide the agenda for counter-gang programs designed for American youths. Here, again, we shall review our gang literature to ascertain what these psychic benefits of gang affiliation entail. In so doing, we will also codify important aspects of the gang infrastructure and its function in the community.

According to Vigil (1988) what the gang does, social-psychologically, is fill the vacuum left by traditional sources. The gang provides, by the peer group's sense of belonging and group protection, a facility for the cultivation of self-identity. What is unique about the gang is that its emphasis, for males, is that on hypermasculine behavior. It is not easy to create a counter-hegemonic organization that can compete with the gang in this sense.   Traditional youth groups (Scouts, 4-H, Junior Achievement and its religious variations such as National Foundation for Teaching Entrepreneurship, etc) cannot, easily, under law as not-for-profit organizations function with a sexist bias. Some volunteer groups, such as the Guardian Angels, may provide the kind of equivalent "macho" roles; as would Junior ROTC programs. The need, organizationally, however is for a "full time" group counterpart as a viable alternative for the gang. Here, perhaps, we as a social service society have been less than creative in responding to the needs of modern urban youths.

What gangs emphasize, in the prison context at least, in terms of social-psychological rewards for gang affiliation or membership is the dual combination of power and prestige (Camp and Camp, 1985).

One must ask, hypothetically, what would Saul Alinsky do in trying to organize an economically depressed urban neighborhood that was dominated by gangs? Would he mimic their own organizational styles, seek alliances with the gangs (e.g., if you can't beat em', join em'), declare a holy war against these traitor "quislings" in the community, or any combination of these? Some authors recommend more programs and assistance for community development. That is, a kind of "trickle down" approach, where with sufficient resources provided, presumably with federal aid comparable to CETA programs with a twist of being designed to attract the underclass, gangs would simply cease to be a problem. The problem here is that the gang exists and functions over time not simply as a problem of economic determinism.[2] It clearly provides social and psychic rewards in the way of roles, status, recognition, and identity. It provides social relationships. Those needs will not necessarily go away simply through the provision of programs for education, training, and employment. One can read Kornblum's Blue Collar Community to realize that even with union scale jobs, some employees continue their gang allegiance and in fact it carries over into the work place.

It is the same problem with providing job placement and employment opportunities for ex-offenders generally. The skeptic tends to take the position that simply affording such legitimate opportunities is no guarantee of the offender's instant conversion to a legitimate life style. Indeed, the skeptic worries about how the employed offender will continue crime, slightly altered, combining a pattern of crime and legitimate employment.

From Klein (1967), youthful gang members are the "fallout" from the social-identity and emotional turmoil found in the transition from youth to adulthood. That is, we need to provide more suitable, more responsible, more attractive roles for youths to play in society. Bloch and Neiderhoffer add the element of a gangs ability to confer status to youths under a powerful social structure that makes them, as many of us, motivated by the "search for status".

PREVENTION AT ALL LEVELS

As in the medical "prevention" analogy, someone who has not yet caught the "disease" is at the primary level of prevention, someone who has been exposed to the "disease" is at the secondary level of prevention, and someone who is suffering from the disease is at the tertiary level of prevention. Here we examine what choices our society faces in dealing with all levels of prevention. This necessarily means those persons who have been exposed to gangs or who are already members of gangs, who have been gang members, who are associated with gangs, and whom we want to prevent from returning to the gang, or whom we want to dissociate from the gang.

GRAFFITI REMOVAL: Community Service Sentencing

Sending gang youths to our already overcrowded detention centers is itself becoming less of an option regardless of the severity of their offense. But community service sentences have proven effective for adults and are now a routine part of the adult criminal adjudication process. What is needed in many jurisdictions is the same sentencing sanction for use with juvenile offenders. At least one study has shown it to work (Agopian, 1989). Obviously, this kind of program needs to be supervised either by juvenile probation officers or a private-based program capable of such projects and working with communities that want their gang graffiti removed. In some cities, just keeping the gang graffiti off street signs and public places in the downtown business center is a recurring problem.

CONFRONTING THE GANG IDEOLOGY

While there are a number of commonalities in gang ideology, there are also likely to be some important differences. It is not as simple as Campbell and Muncer (1989) would have us believe. Their study compared American gangs with British subcultures. American gang members, from Campbell's earlier work, are not apparently interested in overthrowing capitalistic society as serious rebels; while British subcultures are more clearly antagonistic to the status quo. American gang members according to Campbell and Muncer (1989) simply use distorted versions of more main stream American values such as consumerism, patriotism, elitism, and competitive success.

More simply put, there exist two different strategies for dealing with gangs in terms of anticipating and using their ideology: (1) at the group or gang level, and (2) at the individual level. Recall, however, that no one has ever claimed to have "rehabilitated" an organization of offenders. At the best, individuals have been "reformed" or "rehabilitated" when the existential choice of the individual takes over and they basically want to "change their life".

GANG DISINTEGRATION SCENARIOS

According to Arnold (1965, p. 61) the gang disintegration process should proceed in this fashion: (1) first there is an erosion of normative consensus and solidarity, (2) secondly gang leadership becomes ineffective or lost, (3) thirdly, the gang ceases to meet, and (4) finally, the gang loses the value of its group name. The problem with this linear model of gang disintegration is that gangs are open systems. They can recruit new members and terminate old members.

Step one in Arnold's conception, if this disintegration scenario were to be taken as a blueprint for intervention at the secondary and tertiary levels, would be through a combination of community-based social services (education[3], training, subsidized work, or job placement, etc) to provide viable lifestyles for allowing gang members to enter into a productive role in their society.[4] Simultaneously, using the power of community-organizations at the neighborhood level, including religious institutions, to blanket current gang members with direct outreach including detached workers --- with the goal of preventing the escalation of gang attachment for marginal members and to sway their belief systems away from gang allegiance, and failing that counter with the natural threat to any organization: the internal competition for power and rank. Younger members of any organization are always eager to seize the power of older members. The question is can this internal competition be induced? Add a communications component that portrays local gangs as "anti-American", "racist", "latent homosexual" (ala Yablonsky), "quisling" (ala Taylor), etc, in a clear propaganda strategy to attack directly the primary social psychological values of gang membership (prestige, etc).

Gang leadership would then have to be targeted on multiple levels.[5]   One is obviously prosecution and confinement; another is focused and calculated individual programing, which will require higher levels of resources.   It could include intensive family services, housing/relocation assistance, special desired educational placements, etc.   The idea being to fill up the leader's time as much as possible away from the gang formation by whatever means.   Technically, it would be cheaper to send a gang leader on a long ocean cruise than to send them to prison.   But the leadership vacuum from any such initiative must be calculated and dealt with strategically.

We must join Arnold in assuming that theoretically gangs can be disintegrated through social engineering.   Indeed, it is a logical extension of the assumption that gangs can be artificially created.   The informed reader will recall the infamous COINTELPRO counter-intelligence operations in the 1960s and early 1970s, the record reflects clearly that our government was able to establish "sham organizations for disruptive purposes" (see The Iron Fist and the Velvet Glove, 1975: p. 128). However, it would represent a most fascinating challenge involving a powerful mixture of social service administration and criminological sophistication. And, again, there are political trade-offs here; that is gang disintegration at what cost to the invasion of privacy and freedom.[6]

The hope for such a scenario is to be found in the very nature of gang organization and gang behavior: they have a natural tendency to exploit resources.[7] Therefore the "trojan horse" method could conceivably involve a planned strategy to intentionally allow a local gang to "take over" a resource designed in advance to be attractive to gang members.   This could be a drop-in center with free video-games, pinball machines, pool tables, etc.   It would be a strategy of cooptation and planned disintegration conditioned on advance knowledge of the structure and function of such a local gang organization.

The model suggested here is not too dissimilar from sting operations designed to prosecute large numbers of offenders in one large net.   Some very successful efforts in law enforcement have been made in this fashion.   A typical variation being that of the "phony fence set-up" where active offenders bring in their stolen goods for sale, and meanwhile they are on camera, and fully identified.   They wake up one morning and find themselves, along with many others, indicted on criminal charges. Even bringing in fugitives en masse, such stings involving the "double con" clearly work: a hard to arrest offender is notified by mail that he has recently won a "grand prize" (superbowl tickets, etc) and can claim it by coming to the local hotel for the awards ceremony on a given date.   The offenders show up eager to get their "free" booty, and much to their surprise find themselves under arrest.

History shows that gangs can be organizationally disintegrated and even experimentally manipulated.   The implication this has for policy intervention is that within lawful means some measures should be used in the direction of gang abatement. This implies, of course, that a strategic plan for gang suppression exists in any geographical area considering this type of objective.

JOB PLACEMENT SERVICES

Everyone seems to point to the value of integrating potential gang members or gang members who want to "go straight" into the legitimate world of work. The biggest problem with this strategy is that in today's work place few employers want an illiterate, and unfortunately illiteracy, and other social handicaps, go hand in hand with the rank and file of today's gangs.[8]

The hope of job placement services for ex-offenders and gang members, at the secondary and tertiary level of intervention, rests with the large amount of theory and research pointing to an inverse relationship between employment and crime generally.[9] What is somewhat unique about most of these job placement services, nationwide, is that when operated in the private sector it is a kind of service that can truly have an important positive impact. But a few observations are necessary here regarding the special case of the gang affiliated ex-offender.

Few of these job placement service programs ever have their ex-offender clients sign a "vow of good citizenship". That is, we simply hope they will straighten out after giving them a job. Contract programming could be useful here. Particularly regarding the gang affiliated ex-offender. Contract programming means give and take, between the service provider and the ex-offender client. What if, theoretically, such a job placement agency had the policy of obtaining such signed behavioral contracts where the offender declared, among other things, "I am not a gang member, and I will support no gang, nor will I affiliate with any gang, nor will I come to the assistance of any gang"?

If a moral wedge can be placed between the gang-affiliated ex-offender and the gang leadership, and such declarations as above might have that effect, as most gangs require a pervasive kind of allegiance, then perhaps there is at least the possibility of taking the offender outside the web of gang influence.

In some states, like Illinois, those persons released from state prisons have the statutory right to employment counseling and job placement services.[10] Job placement agencies become popular among offenders and are not as likely as correctional institutions to face offender-initiated court suits. The question, then, is can a private program establish administrative guidelines to protect the employers it works with by demanding, as a necessary condition for providing job placements, that the offender make such a declaration of non-gang allegiance? Where these kinds of private programs do end up in court is by being sued via "third party" law suits, typically, an offender is placed in a job, another employee at the work place is not aware of the offender status of the fellow employee, and the offender commits a serious crime (e.g., rape, etc), and the employee victim sues both the employer and the job placement agency for recklessness.

THE DECLINING DETERRENT VALUE OF IMPRISONMENT

The organizational and group aspects of gang life translate into a very unique situation for gang members and the threat of sending them to prison. It is not, in all instances, a very powerful threat. Because for the highly integrated gang member, that is one with a fervent and high level of commitment to the gang enterprise, and whose identity is shaped and molded around gang life, then the threat of sending such an individual to prison carries little of the traditional value of deterrence. The reason for this is simple: a prison term will not necessarily interrupt their gang career and status seeking behavior within the gang. Indeed, imprisonment for gang members can be a "homecoming".[11]

If imprisoned, they might be lucky enough to finally meet one of their esteemed gang leaders; and in this process, gain title and prestige that later transfer back to the outside community. From a social-psychological perspective, gangs also emphasize a "macho-man" value orientation. Prisons are some of the few "male-only" organizations that exist today. If Yablonsky was right, and there is an important latent homosexual component to gang affiliation --- speaking here only in terms of its theoretical value --- then, clearly, there is little "threat value" in sending such a person to an all-male prison where they get the chance to "hook up" with buddies.[12] Our prisons today are little more than gladiator training schools.

ACTORS IN THE GANG RESPONSE STRATEGY

A lot of finger pointing goes on today in regard to the gang problem. What we must realize is that the problem is here, and here to stay unless some major initiatives are undertaken. Who should be involved in any strategy for dealing with America's gang problem? A number of different sets of actors need to be involved.[13] They are described here not necessarily in order of their importance[14].

(1) The government. At the federal, state and local levels. Some of the problems that give rise to gang membership need to be confronted directly through new national policies. These include the problems of illiteracy and drug abuse. Drug rehabilitation services, programs, and shelters are urgently needed. Much more in the way of training and educational resources are also needed before it becomes realistic to assist these same youths to enter the into legitimate employment. For the higher level gang formations, perhaps new laws will be required for effective prosecution. But mostly, our government must be willing to invest in our nation's social infrastructure to combat gangs where they arise.

(2) Businesses and Employers. One need only talk to sales persons who have sold large ticket items (cars, furniture, jewelry, etc) to gang members or other offenders to find out that these businesses do not feel it is a moral problem to accept large amounts of cash, having a very reasonable suspicion that the money may be tainted in terms of its source. Transactions over $10,000 now require an IRS notification. Drug dealers and other "high roller" offenders obviously know about this and readily circumvent it by making installments under that level.

It is ultimately a choice for society. Should successful drug dealers and other offenders be able to readily enjoy the fruits of their crimes or should the IRS, state and local revenue agencies have greater latitude in being able to track such large scale cash expenditures according to the social security number of the purchaser? A sixteen year old illiterate youth buying a new Mercedes in three cash installments (each under $10,000) can now easily escape IRS detection. The question is should that escape be easy. A voluntary notification program with businesses would at least begin to provide some moral and ethical guidance to this problem. It is an another issue to tackle this problem with more regulatory structure.

Also, if government in cooperation with the social service industry and local community organizations begins to take seriously the problem of integrating our nation's youths into the legitimate opportunity system, then employers will also need to do their share. That will mean higher levels of involvement in such programs like JETPA.

Finally, employers will probably have to develop new and creative approaches to really providing a drug free work place. Perhaps it should rely less on coercive methods such as drug testing, and should provide incentives for those who are "drug free". Businesses need to be more concerned about the gang problem than simply trying to exploit it commercially by offering inner-city dwellers bullet-proof aluminum siding for their homes.[15]

The Special Matter of Advertising and Gang Symbols.

Professional business and commercial advertising has come to realize the importance of gang awareness, especially when mass media is involved with the unintentional use of gang symbols in targeting minority demographic markets. In the rush to develop hip advertising copy for the hip hop generation in particular, a softdrink (cola) bottling company advertising poster in the spring of 1994 showed the importance of using certain types of symbols. The poster featured about five different dress styles of minority youths around the boarder of the poster, one looking like a preppie, one looking collegiate, etc, and the one at the bottom of the poster was clearly decked out in hip-hop clothing and had his hand down with the pinky and index fingers extended, with thumb out. This poster was routinely put up one day as part of regular commercial advertising in the cafeteria at a Chicago Public High School where a substantial density of Latin Kings happened to attend school.[16]

The hand sign in the poster was basically "throwing down the crown", that is the upside down version of what the Latin Kings use as a hand sign. Any sign that a gang uses, the insult to them is to do the same sign upside down. It is a gesture that a truly suicidal person would find quite effective in a variety of communities throughout the United States. Anyhow, when the students entered the school cafeteria at lunch time, they immediately saw the posters showing what appeared to them as someone throwing down their sign. This caused a substantial school riot with violence and damage to property. The poster was immediately pulled off the market, but we kept one for our Gang Cultural Artifact Exhibit used in providing training by the National Gang Crime Research Center.

Another example of an exploitational approach to advertising in Chicago happened when a major beer company put up billboards with a picture of the beer product with a message to the consumer to the effect that Al Capone would prefer them to drink this type of beer while in Chicago. Mayor Daley protested the billboards, the media attacked them as tasteless, and the billboards about Al Capone were immediately removed.[17]

Language in advertising is also unfortunately subject to the same "double meaning" or "hidden meaning" trouble. Much more cultural awareness is needed on this particular issue. Language and symbols communicate social values, and sometimes even the best of intentions can generate controversy.

(3) Educational institutions. Both private, and public; both secondary schools, as well as colleges and universities --- all have an important role to play in addressing the gang problem. Unfortunately, as recent research indicates (Knox, Laske, and Tromanhauser, 1992), many schools today are experiencing the gang problem. It is a problem that can reach well into higher education as well, as the recent policy discussion about allowing students to wear gang colors in college (Martin, 1993). Because gang behavior in the school setting tends to be regarded as threatening, if not an outright guarantee of violence and other disturbances among the student body, some schools have worked with the local police departments to implement a "zero tolerance" policy regarding gangs[a].

Rather than "giving up" our schools should accept gang members unless the federal and other governmental units along with the private sector programs are sufficiently capable of absorbing these youths.[18] Because otherwise, expulsion means the right to roam the streets; expulsion means no social control, expulsion means they have the right to be illiterate. Our nation's school buildings have many useful resources that can be put to effective use for after school programs in serving youths and in serving the community which subsidizes these physical plants. A school that is open only from the hours of 9:00 am till 3:00 pm is not one that is adequately serving its community.

Our colleges and universities need to become more directly involved in all communities having a gang problem. They can do this in the name of community service, but ultimately they will probably find it is in the name of self-help: they really need to get out into the community and into our secondary schools and mentor and attract minority students if they want to be effective institutions themselves. Also, there is a more fundamentally practical reason: colleges and universities are increasingly coming to experience the gang problem as a vulnerable target for gang crime.[19] They can also help by assisting with more GED programs and providing more college level instructional programs in our nations correctional institutions. Education works. There is very strong evidence that educational attainment level varies inversely with crime and recidivism. We also urge that this be done responsibly. An irresponsible version of this outreach would be where a college asks the permission of the gang to work in the community and tries to hire the gang or work with the gang in some financial relationship.[20]

(4) Community groups and associations. Addressing the gang problem means addressing a host of related problems and it is ultimately a question of democracy itself, a question of getting involved, a question of community empowerment. This should be the first step: get organized, get incorporated as a not-for-profit group. Many of the gangs are in places like Chicago. A community that is less organized than its own gangs is a community that needs to wake up. Should such community

---

[a]   Gang Specialist Thomas Fleming from the Park Forest, Illinois Police Department has pioneered a pragmatic approach by developing partnerships with the schools and the community --- called the School Liaison Program which has been operating since 1985.

organizations suddenly arise throughout our Nation's neighborhoods, then perhaps that would bring greater resources than are currently available to fight the gang problem where it is most deadly and most visible: at the community and neighborhood level.

(5) Religious institutions. We should continue to pray for a solution, but in the mean time we should get off our duffs and really try to do something tangible about the gang problem. There are many possibilities for greater involvement of our nation's religious institutions. In Chicago's First Unitarian church an alternative to street gangs called the "Chicago Childrens Choir" brings about a "win/win" situation. It includes every racial and ethnic group and has successfully operated for decades. If nothing more, then even the buildings themselves should be open to greater participation in the community: making the space available for meetings, programs, etc, on a non-denominational and non-proselytizing basis. A large number of examples exist of cases like Rev. Greg Boyle --- persons who can "connect" with those at risk of gang violence, and this type outreach is about as genuine as we can get, and in this regard must be argued as equal to or superior to any "detached worker" style of gang intervention.[21] Some churches have taken to marching, to show a unity against gang violence. Some have established "anti-gang oaths" that kids can take with their parents in a pledge against the temptations of gang life. Some religious groups have simply created their business extension-training-employment programs, like in Chicago, and established their unarmed security guard firms that receive funding to regularly patrol public housing projects.[22]

(6) Healthcare institutions. Like businesses, our healthcare institutions that profit from the community also have some ethical obligation to put something back into the community which they benefit from. Most certainly there are many mental health and other services that can and should be provided on a true sliding scale basis: if they cannot pay, they should not have to pay. Some of our nation's neighborhoods have infant mortality rates that are not higher in many places of the less developed world. More drug detox centers are needed. Laser technology can now be more effectively used for tattoo removal than previous abrasion and surgical methods. Youths and young adults should be able to benefit from this kind of tattoo removal service when they want to get out of the gang life.[23] There are also many health related issues surrounding both juvenile and adult correctional institutions holding gang members.[24]

One this is for sure, the gang problem is now well known to the medical field and to health service agencies. In a youth mental health facility in Chicago, for example, a psychiatrist basically had to negotiate his own "gang truce" inside the facility between warring rival gang members who were patients.[25]

(7) The family. Everyone blames the family, everyone seems to want to say it is the family's responsibility to tackle our nation's gang problem and drug problem. Unfortunately, this has become a kind of national past time of kicking the dog. The family structure, its functions and roles, today is not the image that many have from 1950s Hollywood television shows. We should not expect more out of the family unless we put more resources into the family.

Perhaps the family itself, however, should at least receive its own "report card". What kind of grade does it earn for extra involvement at the school? What kind of grade does it earn for involvement in community and neighborhood organizations and affairs? What kind of grade does it earn for volunteer functions? What kind of grade does it earn for impressing neighbors that they are truly capable of adequately supervising their own children?

Those with good report cards might be enlisted in the war on gangs. The rest have many troubles of their own and might better be envisioned as being the recipients of strategic services.

(8) Social service industry. Social service programs have historically "followed the buck". When government funding dries out for one service, they drop that service. When new government funding for a new service is available, they suddenly provide that service. Like the Marine Corps, they improvise and survive. So, that is good news. It means some flexibility exists, and that if federal government resources were available for targeting our nation's gang problem, that there would be many bidders.

What we know about gangs is that they do respond to programs and services, as criminal offenders do generally. Social service providers have gotten a "bad rap" from incidents like Jeff Fort's involvement with Rev. Fry (which still today, in the minds of many, is interpreted falsely to the effect that it was the University of Chicago that was at fault, when in fact the University of Chicago had nothing to do with it --- Fry was simply operating in the ecological fringe of the university community, in Hyde Park) or like that scathing review of wasted federal money provided by Poston (1971).

The research reported in this book on social workers in juvenile corrections shows they do make a positive difference. We need more professional social service providers to have any positive impact on our nation's gang problem.

(9) Unions and voluntary associations. A significant problem that must be overcome is the view from many existing groups capable of doing something about it, but who take essentially the policy position "it is not our problem". These groups, particularly trade unions, professional and voluntary associations, need to be more directly involved. Crime is everyone's problem. A nation that lives in fear cannot itself survive as a democracy very long. Every such group should adopt a "neighborhood in need" and work with it in a coordinated strategy for doing something about the gang crime problem in America today.

(10) The military. Only exploratory research has been conducted to the present authors knowledge about how gang members actually represent a problem within the American military. There are some problems apparently, enough to justify a policy position. This is not the analogy of the war on drugs, to get the military more involved[26]. But historically this book has shown that when the gang problem does get out of hand and beyond local control, that the military is viewed as the choice of last resort[b]. With our nation's gang membership at this point in history outnumbering our nation's sworn police officers, it is a matter of some concern to prevent an

---

[b] After the October 1992 sniper killing of a child in Cabrini Green, the Director of the Chicago Housing Authority was frequently cited in the local media to the effect that the Illinois National Guard was needed to restore peace to the area.

escalation of violence. Our nation's gangs often have better firearms than their local police.

But this is not to advocate direct military action or involvement, although obviously as our American history demonstrates, the military has had a record of being called in when local police cannot handle the situation. Let us hope and pray it does not come to that stage of societal deterioration. The kind of low intensity conflict that an armed organization is capable of may be a real problem: it could be more violent than local law enforcement can control, and less violent than to justify a traditional military response.

Rather, this is to advocate the military in an outreach and training role as a primary level prevention alternative to gang life. The same youth who obediently follows a gang leader in neighborhood warfare, could equally serve his country to better effect. Military socialization is a good thing. The military is an option for many. Perhaps, as well, more Junior ROTC programs should be operated in areas that might otherwise feed youths into a gang organization.

Some programs have been established on a voluntary basis involving military personnel. These include mentoring programs that outreach to inner-city kids at risk of gang membership.

(11) The Mass Media and Hollywood Gang Movies. The mass media and movie producers are often criticized over the gang issue. It is true that there are some gang movies that truly glorify gang life, and that their very existence as videos that can be rented at any local store are types of socialization and education that can in the hands of alienated youths generate a "copycat" phenomenon, where youths will try to emulate such behavior. It is equally true that artists have purposes that are not always our own. It is also true that simple gang exploitation movies are produced aimed at the gang-viewing audience. Just as it is also true that given the predictable nature of a bigot, that skinheads are easy to get on a television talk show, but should we still give them air time when the net effect is the vulgarization of the air waves?[27] Gangster movies romanticize criminal exploits. There is no hard evidence that watching gangster movies produces gangsters, but it is easy to show that criminals love gangster movies. We need to be concerned about this, then, in a wider sense of responsibility of how such products are consumed: as idols or as simply fictional messages.

There are those who want to take the mass media to task on the gang issue, no doubt. There is also the positive side of the effects of mass media: good investigative journalism, whether it be in print or electronic media form. Objectively educating the public without sensationalizing an issue is something that can only help in the long run. What most media critics object to is the amount of attention that gang apologists and gang members or gang spokespersons get, but again this is a very predictable behavior for some types of gangs. Some types of gang members love media coverage. It increases their "rep" much better than graffiti.

WHAT WORKS TO PREVENT CRIME, DELINQUENCY AND RECIDIVISM MAY WORK TO REDUCE THE GANG PROBLEM

The logic here is that of pragmatism. If evidence exists that it works, use it. That is, if any theoretical or research basis exists for expecting positive impact on the gang crime problem, then it deserves our expeditious, positive, consideration. Forget ideology and purist points of view. We need to apply the knowledge we have accumulated. We recognize, as well, the legitimate criticism that "general delinquency literature" is not the same as "gang literature". Gang members are a special subset of the wider field dealing with delinquents and criminal offenders. But to the extent that such theories offer constructive advice, it is worth pursuing how perhaps such theories could be extended to apply to gangs, or at least test these hypotheses in the spirit of scientific discovery where they are merited and hold promise.

The informed reader in the social sciences knows that a lot of things work in preventing crime, delinquency and recidivism. The astute reader in criminology knows that the dogma of "nothing works" is a political hoax created in part by Martinson, and revealed as such by Martinson before he took his own life. The truth is that some conditions are more easily manipulated than others, and some solutions may cost more than others.

But America is rapidly reaching a crisis point with regard to the gang crime problem.[28] It means examining all alternatives to the solution of the crisis. The evolving definition of citizenship may therefore mean doing what we can in terms of what is humanely possible to address this national problem. It may not be easy, it may not be cheap, but it is a social problem about which something can and should be done. Perhaps, further, about which something will have to be done if we want to insure any minimal level of the quality of life in America.

Clearly, there exist many current programs throughout America that have a direct involvement in addressing the gang crime problem. It is also a volatile period. Clearly not all of these programs have been described in this book. New programs and services can be expected to arise in response to this growing problem. And to the extent that they are informed about gang problems and cooperate with other criminal justice agencies we should welcome these services as new vehicles to provide a better way of life for many Americans.

The message here is obvious: we may best be advised not necessarily by surveys of what programs exist and what they are doing now, but rather we should be alerted in advance as to what SHOULD be done based on our social science knowledge of the problem.

TARGETING GANG RECRUITS: A PRIORITY POLICY ISSUE

To put any group or organization "out of business", whether we call it "gang busting" or just plain good social defense, will mean strangling it by preventing further growth in membership. That is, stopping new recruits. Historically local law enforcement has targeted gang leaders for prosecution under the common expectation that a leader's removal will mean maximum organizational disruption. As we have seen in the case of Chicago's Vice Lords, or in higher level gang formations, that strategy will not be as successful as it hopes to be. Such "shoot from the hip" gang-busting can, in fact, via conflict and induced opportunity for gang leadership training, be counterproductive.

Perhaps "gang busting" must also target new recruits.[29] But arrests, labels, and the shame brought upon the family unit will probably not be enough. Indeed it could be counterproductive. And sending such persons to correctional institutions will only guarantee they "make rank" in the gang organization. As a society, we need more options to effectively prevent new members from joining the ranks of our nation's gang organizations.

DIFFERENTIAL RESPONSES TO DIFFERENT GANG FORMATIONS

A prevalent error of policy is in assuming all gangs are equal and that one policy will work for all. That is a big mistake. Many authors believe that level zero gangs, and perhaps even level one gangs, can be coopted (Shaw and Sorrentino, 1956). That is, they can be redirected, channelled into potentially prosocial functions and activities that would be a blessing rather than a curse for the neighborhood or community in which they exist. The research on this matter is lacking, but we cannot equally reject such a hypothesis.

One thing is certain here: there exist differences in sophistication and capability between gangs today, and this must necessarily mean a differential response to them. We cannot treat a level zero gang in the same fashion that we respond to a level three gang. They cannot be treated alike, because they are not alike. A level zero gang is not really a true criminal gang at all, it is a pre-gang if anything. They are not gangs of equal public threat.

The gang classification system advanced in this book would therefore require differences in responding to gangs from all perspectives including law enforcement and corrections, not just community-based services. A level zero gang should be directly coopted and channeled into community organization functions. A level one gang should have its members coopted and its leaders dislocated. A level two gang and above should be prevented from expansion to dry up new recruits. And a level three gang should be treated as an emerging organized crime problem.

WHAT THE LITERATURE SAYS TO DO ABOUT GANG CRIME

This is for the skeptics, for those with nothing more than the "lock em up" mentality, and this is to show we are not as ignorant as we think we are. We are not in the situation of knowing nothing about what can work. We are not in the situation of having no guidelines or ideas useful towards a solution of the gang crime problem. We have many promising ways, from social science and specifically from the field of criminology, to tackle the gang crime problem in America today.

Following, we will show twenty-five ways to combat the gang crime problem in America today. These prescriptions are based on the existing literature showing theories with empirical support for these potential ways to crime, delinquency, and recidivism generally and as such can be equally effective in addressing the gang crime problem.   These are factors that gang intervention programs should probably have incorporated as part of their stated goals.

(1) Social control theory has several variations, and is also choice theory, and social development theory. It tells us we would increase informal social controls and make formal social controls more effective.

(2) Differential social organization theory characterizes much of the Shaw and Mc Kay tradition and it tells us that we should increase local community organizational capability and improve our neighborhood social infrastructure.

(3) Differential opportunity theory (Cloward and Ohlin, 1960) advises us to increase legitimate opportunities in education, training, and employment, and decrease perceived closure or the view from potential gang members that "they will not fit in American society in a productive capacity".

(4) Differential opportunity theory also says we should decrease the attractiveness, the profitability, the viability as a career, of criminal opportunity systems.   An affluent, conspicuously high spending, protected criminal offender sends the message to American youths that they too can be predators. It also says we should increase the feasibility of youths internalizing legitimate career goals, helping them to find a place in America's legitimate world of work.

(5) Differential association theory (ala Sutherland) says we should increase social ties with our youths to persons in their social network who have a more law-abiding and pro-social orientation. In doing so, their definition of reality is more likely to become one that says "conform". There is little that competes with the gang. We need to be creative in this regard.

(6) Differential association theory also says we should decrease the probability that our youths have as their primary group those who are criminal offenders and define the world as a "dog eat dog world", a Silver Rule world of "do unto others before they do unto you". It is not going to be easy to convince some of the potential for making it in America through education. But it is worth doing.

(7) Differential identity theory (ala Daniel Glaser) suggests we should increase more viable role models and in so doing communicate less from our culture that the way to make it in America is through the barrel of a gun. Hard work is the answer.

(8) Differential identity theory also suggests we should communicate less from the social structure that our culture accepts as legitimate heroes those who were nothing more than menaces (Al Capone, etc). That is, we must decrease the attractiveness of role models such as gang leaders and successful criminal offenders. Cultural awareness programs can help here to instill ethnic and racial pride.

(9) Differential integration theory (Knox, 1978) suggests we need to increase involvement with legitimate groups and mainstream society for our youths. And (10) decrease their participation and involvement with criminal or illicit subcultures.

(11) Self-concept theory says loud and clear, with support from the research reported in this book, that we should increase the self-esteem of our youths. Those

with low self-esteem are most at risk of joining a gang. And (12) that among youths who have already affiliated with gangs, we need to re-mold their self-concept as being an offender, as being irresponsible, as being a predator. And show an alternative "pro-social", "productive" self-identity.

(13) Containment theory has several variations, but basically says we should seek to increase the internal locus of control among youths; their ability to "say no". And (14) we should decrease the external locus of control, or the tendency to follow gang leaders for whatever reason.

(15) Multiple marginality theory (Vigil, 1988) says we should increase the ability of those with multiple "marks" against them (e.g., minority status plus run in with the law) to still function in wider society in a positive, productive way. And (16) that we should as a society practice more of what we preach, e.g., forgiveness, salvation, equal opportunity, etc., and therefore decrease the impact of prior stigmas our society seems so highly capable of manufacturing. Or (17) as Dr. Martin Luther King said, we should judge persons on the nature of their character rather than on the color of their skin, or to update it slightly, by the size of their juvenile record. That is, (18) we should never throw away the welcome mat, anyone, any offender, hopefully at least our nation's youth, should be "welcome back to society", or else we create our own permanent class of enemies.

(19) Identity crisis theory (Erik Erickson) for youths generally tells us we should increase the ease of transition from youth to adulthood, it should not be as turbulent and as uncertain as to what the future holds. And (20) age-role integration (Suttles, etc) suggests we should have stronger, closer, more effective channels of interaction between youths and adults, our youths should not see their world as one of required rebellion. And (21) as Bloch and Niederhoffer showed, we should increase the role space for responsible, rewarded, desired, and prestige-filled positions available to youths, when they express a willingness to accept responsibility citizenship should mean to them the right to participate fully.

(22) Some psychological approaches (e.g., Yablonsky) have suggested that gang members are by their nature sociopaths, so perhaps we as a society should be doing more to increase prosocial beliefs and values, and the cultivation of citizenship, human and social capital generally.

(23) Labelling theory, in its many varieties, means we should increase personal achievement and human capital development among those at risk of joining gangs, and for those who have already found themselves involved in gangs, and in so doing opening up the possibility at least of another direction in life, that is, the development of attributional "off sets". (24) As a society we need to "cool out" on the need to have "someone at the bottom", we need to decrease the sticking power of prior stigmatizable labels if a person can show through good graces their value to society. It is well to remember that our history includes the granting of a presidential pardon for all crimes to a person that was technically never even convicted of a crime --- former President Nixon.

(25) And from surplus population and underclass theory, we need to give the poor and minority groups of our country a path to full participation in society --- we need to open up our social structure for allowing their productive involvement, and that

will probably take major national initiatives to first focus on developing their human capital.

FOUNDATION FUNDING PATTERNS AND THE GANG PROBLEM

Figure 21 shows the distribution of all private foundation grants that involved the keyword "gang" for the past several years.[30] The first edition of this book pointed out what appeared to be a neglect by foundations in supporting gang programs. In pointing out the discrepancy the first edition noted:

> "Clearly, foundation funding patterns do not match up equitably with known reported national trends in gang crime severity. Some cities have clearly been ignored. This is an important social policy problem that will have to change. And foundation giving patterns will also have to change to reflect a more equitable commitment to the obvious problem of gang crime in America."

Someone got the message. Gangs are hot again for foundation grants. If that is the good news, then the bad news what the foundations have been funding. The best money spent is in pure prevention, not secondary prevention, not tertiary prevention. Once involved with a gang, the road back is very difficult. Most of the money is being spent on high risk populations, and they need help, no doubt about it. The thousands of gang members behind bars need help too. But to best spend foundation and public monies to most effectively do something about the gang problem requires a closer and more logical focus. The reason is that some Foundations have clearly been hustled again, reminiscent of the Jeff Fort and Rev. Fry period.

If the money is spent on a direct service program, the Foundation should require an independent evaluation research component: for otherwise we have no idea of any positive impact. If the money is spent on policy or programs, the theory behind the initiative should be clearly laid out, and special attention must be focused on "prove to the best of your ability that this initiative will not have a reverse-intended impact on the gang problem". Some of the best investment of public and foundation funds would be in the evaluation of such gang service programs at all levels of intervention/prevention. The same program should not be "evaluating itself"! The funding for a service program should be matched with a grant to an independent researcher, who holds credentials in the field of criminology (i.e., the field of study that deals with gangs directly), to carry out basic and evaluation research on the program. In this way we may be able to generate some useful information on "what works" and "what is needed" to put a dent in the gang problem.

Government funding, foundation funding, and private fund raising initiatives will all be required to seriously come to grips with the gang crime problem in American cities today. The worthy recipient of funding are those programs and initiatives based on a good theory of human behavior explaining why what is done will can be expected to have a positive impact on the "gang problem" rather than exacerbating the problem. Programs that the gangs directly benefit are the least worthy of funding, because we should not be in a position of advancing the organizational strength of any gang. We should not be assisting a gang in its public relations campaign, or the cloak of legitimacy the gang may masquerade behind. We should not be increasing the "influence" that any gang leader may have. We should not be rewarding the threat of violence against society, and unless someone has "dropped their flag", we should not be paying active gang leaders or active gang members to be the public liaison for the gang; as such a policy only helps the gang to persist over time, and gives the gang more legitimacy than it should have.

FIGURE 21

FOUNDATION GRANTS RELATED TO GANGS 1985-1989

Foundation	Amount $	Recipient Agency/Year
The Boston Foundation	35,000	Gang Peace, Boston/1993
Weingart Foundation	30,000	Cal. Sch. of Prof'l..Psych./1993
Meyer Memorial Trust	154,000	Min. Youth Concerns Action, Portland/1993
Meyer Memorial Trust	184,000	Boys & Girls Club of Salem/1993
Chicago Community Trust	16,000	Network for Youth Svcs.,Chgo/1993
Greater Santa Cruz CCF	10,000	Barrios Unidos, Santa Cruz/1992
Chicago Community T.	1,000,000	United Way of Chgo./1992
Vira I. Heinz Endow.	750,000	YMCA, Metro Pittsburgh/1992
The McKnight Foundation	54,943	The City, Inc, Mpls,MN/1992
Cal. Community Found.	44,000	Soledad Enrich.Action, L.A./1992
Cal. Community Found.	25,000	Inland Co. Interfaith, San Bern./1992
James Irvine Foundation	40,000	Family Service Agency,Sacramento/1992
The McKnight Found.	30,000	Lao Youth Assn.of MN,Mpls/1992
The Boston Foundation	20,000	Gang Peace, Boston, MA/1991
The Frost Foundation	15,000	Open Door Youth Gang Alt., Denver/1991
Woods Charitable Trust	15,000	Northwest Neigh. Fed./1991
The Denver Foundation	15,000	Open Door Youth Gang Alts,Denver/1991
Anne Burnette/Tandy Fnd.	10,000	Citizens Crime Comm.,Fort Worth/1991
The Bodman Foundation	25,000	United Neigh. Houses of NY/1991
The Minneapols Found.	10,000	The City, Inc, Mpls,MN/1991
Stuart Foundations	25,000	Sheriffs Youth Found, L.A./1991
M. & G. Cafritz Found.	25,000	Ctr.for Child Protect., DC/1991
W.K. Kellogg Foundation	100,000	F.I.R.S.T., Dorchester, MA/1991
The Hearst Foundation	20,000	Sisters of St. Joseph, L.A./1991
Woods Charitable Trust	15,000	N.W. Neighborhood Fed., Chicago/1991
Mc Inerny Foundation	10,000	Adult Friends for Youth, Honolulu/1990
The Freedom Forum	10,000	Adult Friends for Youth, Honolulu/1990
James Irvine Foundation	25,000	Sisters of St. Joseph, L.A./1990
The Freedom Forum	10,000	United Univ. Church, L.A./1990
New York Foundation	25,000	Hot Spots Program, Sunnyside,NY/1990
Calif. Community Foun.	12,480	Boys & Girls Club, Santa Clarita/1990
Greater Santa Cruz CCF	30,000	Pajaro Valley Gang Vio.Pre.Proj./1990
Island Foundation, Inc.	20,000	Dorchester Youth Collaborative/1990
The San Francisco Foun.	25,000	Ella Hill Hutch Com.Ctr./1990
Dr. Scholl Foundation	13,000	BUILD, Inc, Chicago/1990
General Mills Found.	25,000	The City, Inc, Mpls., MN/1990
J.M. Kaplan Fund, Inc.	25,000	Found. for Study of I.S.I, NYC/1990
The McKnight Foundation	60,000	St. Paul Amer. Indian Center/1990
Woods Charitable Trust	15,000	Lincoln Interfaith Council, Nebraska/1990
Adolph Coors Foundation	10,000	Open Door Youth Gang Alts, Denver/1990
Peter Kiewit Foundation	100,000	Chamber Foun. of Greater Omaha/1989
Ralph M. Parsons Foun.	51,200	Sisters of St. Joseph, L.A./1989
James Irvine Foundation	25,000	Sisters of St. Joseph, L.A./1989
Denver Foundation	10,000	Doctors of the World/1989
McBeath Foundation	25,000	Milwaukee Police Dept./1989

Figure 21 Continued:

Foundation	Amount $	Recipient Agency/Year
Woods Charitable Trust	14,000	Malone Com. Ctr., Lincoln/1989
Atlanta Community Found.	14,000	Urban Trng. Org. of Atlanta/1989
Cooper Foundation	7,332	Malone Com. Ctr., Lincoln/1989
The Bodman Foundation	20,000	United Neigh. Houses of NY/1989
California Community F.	50,000	Boys & Girls Clubs,Los Angeles/1989
Faye McBeath Foundation	30,000	N.W. Side Comm.Dev. Corp.,Milwaukee/1989
Gannett Foundation	10,000	Adult Friends for Youth, Honolulu/1989
San Francisco Foundation	25,000	Ella Hill Hutch Com. Ctr., San Fran./1989
Gannett Foundation	10,000	Urban League of San Diego, MAGIC/1989
Clark Foundation (NY)	25,000	Boys/Girls Club,Madison Sq.,NYC/1989
George Gund Foundation	35,000	Luth. Metro.Min. Assn. of Gtr. Cleveland/1988
Public Welfare Found.	21,000	Youth Service Project, Chicago/1989
Public Welfare Found.	74,900	Com. Youth Gang Srvs.Project,Los Angeles/1989
The Freedom Forum	5,000	M.A.G.I.C., Urban League, San Diego/1989
The Freedom Forum	10,000	Adult Friends for Youth, Honolulu/1989
Gannett Foundation	10,000	Com. Youth Sports&Arts Found.,Los Angeles/1988
Minneapolis Foundation	15,000	The City, Inc., Mpls, MN/1988
Mc Knight Foundation	150,000	Migizi Communications, MPLS/1988
The Freedom Forum	10,000	Commun. Youth Sports&Arts Found, L.A./1988
Columbus Foundation	55,000	United Way/Youth Outreach Project/1988
Public Welfare Found.	21,000	Youth Service Project, Chicago/1988
Gannett Foundation	6,000	City of Rochester, NY/1988
Mc Knight Foundation	112,922	The City, Inc, Mpls, MN/1988
The George Gund Found.	35,000	Luth. Metro. Ministry Assn,Cleveland/1988
Johnson's Wax Fund, Inc.	20,000	U. of Wisc-Racine/1987
JD + CT MacArthur Found.	15,000	United Block Club Council, Chgo/1987
Clark Foundation	20,000	Boys&Girls Club,Madison SQ,NYC/1987
Woods Charitable Trust	20,000	Logan SQ. Neighborhood Assn.,Chicago/1987
Public Welfare Found.	21,000	Youth Service Project, Chicago/1987
Milwaukee Foundation	50,000	Family Service of Milwaukee/1987
Com. Trust.Metro Texas	5,000	Fort Worth Boys Club/1986
Field Found. of Illinois	40,000	United Way/Marcy-Newberry Assn[31]/1986
Primerica Foundation	10,000	United Stoner Youth Found.,Santa Monica/1986
Arco Foundation	10,000	Los Angeles "Say Yes" Program/1986
Clark Foundation	20,000	Boys&Girls Club,Madison SQ,NYC/1986
Milwaukee Foundation	5,000	North Cott Neighborhood House, Milwaukee/1986
Gannett Foundation	15,000	Com.Youth Sports&Arts Foundation, L.A./1986
Ford Foundation	60,099	Boston-Fenway Project, Boston/1986
Chicago Comm. Trust	20,000	Youth Service Project, Chicago/1986
Bodman Foundation	40,000	United Neighborhood Assn of NY,NYC/1985
Achelis Foundation	15,000	United Neighborhood Assn of NY,NYC/1985
Primerica Foundation	10,000	United Stoner Youth Found.,Santa Monica/1985
Weingart Foundation	32,035	Com. Youth Gang Services Project, L.A./1985
Milwaukee Foundation	15,000	U. of Wisc.Milwaukee/1985
Mc Knight Foundation	26,000	Park Ave.United Meth. Church, Minneapolis/1985

SUMMARY AND CONCLUSION

As the gang crime problem in America is increasing, the programs, services, and intervention strategies are also currently changing to meet this challenge. A number of prior works have summarized the existing programs.[32] These include those in New York (Dunston, 1990), which were mostly delinquency prevention programs or prosocial groups such as Boy and Girl Scouts. No single program has been tested in multiple jurisdictions nationwide.

Stephens (1988) listed 22 school and community programs, giving a short profile and contact information. Eight were operated by police or correctional agencies, such as the "program" of the Gang Crime Section of the Chicago Police Department --- that is not a program, it is a police unit, it is not a social service program seeking to prevent gang crime at the primary, secondary, or tertiary level through services. Many of the others listed by Stephens were city agencies.

For a problem as large as the gang crime problem in America we are doing remarkably little about it. It has been an interstate problem for some time now. But the federal government as of this date has not responded to this problem with any major initiative other than fund "same old stuff" projects and research, which even when published and reported are never really known by those who need the information.

Something will have to be done. The major actors in the solution have been identified here. Some of the things that can and should be done have also be discussed. It is possible, in other words, to seek creative solutions, even solutions for funding the solution. In DuPage County, Illinois one such creative solution for funding not-for-profit groups like Mothers Against Drunk Driving comes in the form of a state law permitting fines to drunk drivers as "contributions" to such not-for-profit service groups.[33] Just as those going to traffic school know about "traffic school", getting off the ticket by a short educational/video/lecture type of service, a "gang school" existed in Chicago for sometime until recently, where adults arrested for mob action and other gang crimes being referred to one court room were able to attend "Gang Free" sessions (similar to traffic school) and have their charges dropped.

The gang crime problem is a complex one. There will be no easy or simple solutions. The problem will not go away over night. And may never go away completely. There have always been gangs in America, and there may always be gangs in America. But they do not need to be as deadly and as destructive as they are today, or as much worse as they promise to be without the implementation of prevention and intervention services and strategies. Something will have to be done.

DISCUSSION QUESTIONS

(1) Do you think a community organization can, by the provision of services and opportunities and adult prosocial supervision, redirect a local neighborhood gang out of the path of delinquency and crime and into the path of better citizenship?

(2) If you controlled a budget to spend on gang crime prevention and intervention, what percentage would you allocate to primary, secondary, and tertiary efforts? And why?

(3) Is it realistic to expect the major actors who should become involved in the solution to actually "get together" and work together towards a common goal of reducing the destructive impact of the gang crime problem? How could it work?

RECOMMENDED READING

Ackerley, Ethel G. and Beverly R. Fliegel
1960 "A Social Work Approach to Street-Corner Girls", Social Work (5)(4): 27-36.

Austin, David M.
1957 "Goals for Gang Workers", Social Work (2)(4): 43-50.

Brueckner, Willilam H.
1960 "Corner Group Work with Teen-Age Gangs", Federal Probation (24)(Dec): 84.

Caplan, Nathan S.; Dennis J. Deshaies; Gerald D. Suttles; and Hans W. Mattick
1964 "Factors Affecting the Process and Outcome of Street Club Work", Sociology and Social Research (48)(Jan): 207-219.

Clark, J.H.
1981 A Report of the Gang Activities Task Force. Chicago Board of Education, Chicago, Illinois.

Crawford, Paul I.; Daniel I. Malamud; James R. Dumpson
1950 Working With Teenage Gangs. A Report on the Central Harlem Street Clubs Project. New York: Welfare Council of New York City.

Delaney, Lloyd T.
1954 "Establishing Relationships with Antisocial Groups and an Analysis of Their Structure", British Journal of Delinquency (5)(1): 34-42.

Donohue, John K.
1966 My Brother's Boy: A Treatise on Criminology. St. Paul, MN: Bruce Publishing Company.

Dumpson, J.R.
1949 "An Approach to Antisocial Street Gangs", Federal Probation 22-29.

Friedman, C.J.; F. Mann; and A.S. Friedman
1975 "A Profile of Juvenile Street Gang Members", Adolescence (10): 563-607.

Furman, Sylvan S.
1952 Reaching the Unreached. New York. New York City Youth Board.

Hunsaker, A.
1981 "The Behavioral-Ecological Model of Intervention With Chicano Gang Delinquents", Hispanic Journal of Behavioral Sciences (3): 225-239.

Kantor, David and William Ira Bennett
1968 "Orientation of Street-Corner Workers and Their Effect on Gangs", in Stanton Wheeler (ed.), Controlling Delinquents, New York: Wiley.

Klein, Malcolm W.
    1967 Juvenile Gangs in Context. New Jersey: Prentice-Hall.

    1969 "Gang Cohesiveness, Delinquency, and a Street-Work Program", Journal of Research in Crime and Delinquency (July).

    1971 Street Gangs and Street Workers. Englewood, Cliffs, NJ: Prentice-Hall.

Klein, Malcolm W. and Barbara G. Meyerhoff (eds).
    1964 Juvenile Gangs in Context: Theory, Research, and Action. Conference Report, August 25-26, 1963, Youth Studies Center, Los Angeles: University of Southern California.

Klein, Malcolm W. and Nel Snyder
    1965 "The Detached Worker: Uniformities and Variances in Style", Social Work (10)(Oct): 60-68.

Kobrin, Solomon and Malcolm W. Klein
    1983 Community Treatment of Juvenile Offenders: The DSO Experiments. Beverly Hills, CA: Sage Publications.

Krisberg, Barry
    1974 "Gang Youth and Hustling: The Psychology of Survival", Issues in Criminology (9)(1)(Spr): 115-131.

Mattick, Hans W. and Nathan C. Caplan
    1964 The Chicago Youth Development Project, February, University of Michigan Institute for Social Research, Ann Arbor, Michigan.

Maxson, Cheryl L. and Malcolm W. Klein
    1983 "Agency Versus Agency: Disputes in the Gang Deterence Model", in James R. Kluegel (ed.), Evaluating Contemporary Juvenile Justice, Beverly Hills: Sage.

Mc Connell, Elizabeth H.
    1990 "Assessing Youth Gangs in an Urban High School", paper presented at the Annual Meeting of the American Society of Criminology, Baltimore, Maryland.

Miller, Walter B.
    1957 "The Impact of Community Group Work Program on Delinquent Corner Groups", Social Service Review (31): 396-406.

    1985 "Historical Review of Programs and Theories of Work With Youth Gangs: 1920-1985", in D. Ingemunsen and G. Johnson, Report on the Illinois Symposium on Gangs, Springfield, IL: Illinois Department of Children and Family Services.

Morales, Armando
1989 "A Clinical Model for the Prevention of Gang Violence and Homicide", in A. Morales and B.W. Sheafor, Social Work: A Profession of Many Faces, Boston: Allyn and Bacon.

National School Safety Center
1988 Gangs in Schools: Breaking Up is Hard to Do. Malibu, CA: Pepperdine University Press.

Neisser, Edith G. and Nina Ridenour
1960 Your Children and Their Gangs. U.S. Children's Bureau. Publication No. 384. Washington, D.C.

New York City Youth Board
1960 Reaching the Fighting Gang. New York.

Oleson, Jim
1988 Treating Street Youth: Some Observations. Community Research Associates, 115 N. Neil Street, Suite 302, Champaign, IL 61820.

Paramount Plan
1988 The Paramount Plan: Alternatives to Gang Membership. City of Paramount, California.

Quicker, John C.
1983 Seven Decades of Gangs: What has been done, and what Should be done. Sacramento, CA: State of California Commission on Crime Control and Violence Prevention.

Spergel, Irving
1966 Street Gang Work: Theory and Practice. Reading, MA: Addison-Wesley Publishing Company, Inc.

Spergel, Irving and Ron L. Chance
1990 Community and Institutional Responses to the Youth Gang Problem: Case Studies Based on Field Visits and Other Materials. National Youth Gang Suppression and Intervention Project, School of Social Service Administration, University of Chicago (Jan.).

Stover, D.
1986 "A New Breed of Youth Gang is on the Prowl and a Bigger Threat Than Ever", American School Board Journal (173)(8): 19-24, 35.

Swans, Bennie J., Jr.
1985 "Gangbusters! Crisis Intervention Network", School Safety (Winter): 12-15, National School Safety Center.

West, Pat and Tony Ostos
1988 Pilot Study: City of Paramount Alternatives to Gang Membership Program. City of Paramount, 16400 Colorado Ave., Paramount, CA 90723.

Williams, Hampton; Rex Leonard; and Phillip Terrel
  1991 "Students' Perceptions of Some Selected Conditions That Might Lead
  to Gang Membership: An Exploratory Investigation", paper presented at the
  Annual Meeting of the Academy of Criminal Justice Sciences, Nashville,
  Tennessee.

FOOTNOTES

1. "Yes", says your author: in any community, in any situation --- it is, however, a
matter of how much effort we are willing to put into it. And how much in terms of
resources.

2. The astute reader will sense at this point that there is actually more in common
between conservative police points of view and Hagedorn's analysis than might at
glance be obvious. That is, some police may in a rejection of the "racism/oppression"
thesis, point to a stronger role of economic incentives for joining gangs. Similarly,
Hagedorn assumes this economic incentive as the primordial role for reducing the
deleterious impact of gangs on a community.

3. In one case study (LK29), this shows a perfect example of how gang members can
be dismembered from their gang, even those like LK29 who were known as "loonies"
who shoot rival gang members. LK29 was in a special program that involved
relocation and college: it worked. He now is very much opposed to all gangs. And,
thus, a great source of information on the Latin Kings; but equally, he was never
arrested, and the statute of limitations has passed on his crimes, and he is currently
working in a very responsible court role in Cook County.

4. Apparently placement in the military for those who might qualify, while shown by
Hans Mattick in his Master's thesis "Parole to the U.S. Army" to be likely to reduce
recidivism, is not necessarily consistent with gang dismemberment. That is, Horowitz
(1982, p. 7) states that gang members "in the Army were still considered gang
members and likely to rejoin the group upon release".

5. Examine Keiser (1979) on this point. Gangs like the Vice Lords simply "adapted"
to the expectation that their gang leaders would be arrested. Therefore they
"institutionalized" leadership positions in the gang-role structure. It provides for
continuity of function even after an arrest and conviction (see Keiser, 1979: p. 6). It
is not enough, therefore, in any gang dismemberment plan to simply assume that
arresting an individual leader of any significance will actually in itself be sufficient to
undermine the effectiveness of the gang organization. Indeed, as discussed elsewhere
in this text, it can mean the inducement of "leadership training" for other gang
members eager to "make rank".

6. In a frustrated reply to a citizen demanding greater police surveillance of gangs
in Chicago, a gang crimes police commander testifying at the Illinois Gang Crimes
Study Commission stated "The city has gone into a consent decree with certain
organizations, the Alliance to End Repression and the American Civil Liberties
Union. Under that we are very, very limited to what we can do on their First

Amendment rights" (see Nash, 1984: p. 75). He is referring to the law suits brought against the Chicago Police Department over its "red squad" spying on leftist groups, which was successfully battled in federal court, resulting now in restrictions even on gangs. Apparently, such surveillance and infiltration on groups also included Alinsky-style community anti-crime groups (see Candice M. Kane, 1976, Factors Related to Teacher Openmindedness as Measured by the Rokeach Dogmatism Scale and the Modified Kelly Exploration Questionnaire in a Neighborhood Undergoing Racial Change, Ph.D. dissertation, Northwestern University, pp. 23,25).

7. From the case of LK29, apparently gang leaders are equally capable of this in the sense of taking off the "cream" of home invasions, burglaries, etc, and holding out on equitable income distribution to subordinate gang members involved in such crimes. It is a source of much potential friction between leaders and core members.

8. One other problem has recently surfaced in the research reported by Taylor (1990: p. 131) whose findings showed that most gang members don't want a job, and are not looking for one; also, none would take a job paying the minimum wage.

9. Vigil (1988: p. 31) joins this support for job placement services as a method of luring offenders away from the gang, in stating "gang members who secure a good job often refocus and redirect their lives into more conventional routes; such a change in orientation is referred to as "maturing out" (Matza, 1964: 22-26)".

10. Illinois Criminal Code and Procedure, Chapter 38, Section 1003-14-3 Parole Services, "To assist parolees or releasees, the Department shall provide employment counseling and job placement services, and may in addition to other services provide the following: (1) assistance in residential placement, (2) family and individual counseling and treatment placement, (3) financial counseling, (4) vocational and educational counseling and placement, and (5) referral services to any other State or local agencies. The Department may purchase necessary services for a parolee or releasee if they are otherwise unavailable and the parolee or releasee is unable to pay for them. It may assess all or part of the costs of such services to a parolee or releasee in accordance with his ability to pay for them".

11. In the case study of LK29, he remarked "just to get back in the gang, a loonie member or former member will to go excessive lengths in violence, to get back in the gang", like a conversion reaction, a compulsive kind of compliance to show affinity where "killing someone means automatic rank". Often, as well, means automatic prison terms. But not really a prison term as it means for most Americans, it means for these gang members a chance for status elevation.

12. All we find on the topic of homosexuality from most of our so-called in-depth, richly detailed qualitative analyses are periodic reports of young gang members "jackrolling" gays. One of the few reports, actually, of gang interviews where the gang member admitted their homosexuality was that by Murphy (1978) in the case of Sandra --- a female member.

13. Dr. Irving Spergel of the University of Chicago, has developed prototype/models for gang intervention on the following topical areas: general community design, community mobilization, police, prosecution, judges, probation, corrections, parole, schools, youth employment, community based youth agency, and grassroots organization.

14. These are actors other than law enforcement. Obviously law enforcement has its hands full, or should have. Law enforcement policy should not be one that passively allows juveniles to roam the streets during the day when they are under law expected to be in school, or after curfew at night. Unfortunately, in some jurisdictions police have other more serious problems to contend with such that this aspect of youth welfare is often neglected.

15. Such a product to protect from routine drive-bys has been developed and is being marketed by a firm in San Antonio, Texas. It is not so much exploiting the gang problem as it is a sign of the times that ordinary citizens do in fact have to consider this added level of physical protection to even feel safe in their own homes. See: Kelley Shannon, "Drive-By Protection: New Siding Also Shields", Chicago Sun-Times, May 30, 1994, p. 9.

16. This was "Brite and Lymon registered trademark" ad entitled "Keys To The Future", with bubbles on the top. On March 22, 1994 these posters were put up at Farragut High School in Chicago and the Latin Kings demonstrated, a couple Latin Queens were arrested subsequently, and students and gang members alike ended up marching on the police station in a disturbance.

17. See: Editorial "Don't Include Gangs In Youth Programs", Chicago Sun-Times, June 12, 1994, p. 47. At the time, a gang activist organization in Chicago was trying to pressure Mayor Daley into granting funding for "youth programs" that would be able to be administered by gangs. Mayor Daley fervently rejected such requests that then became protest demands, the gangs demanding a part of the pot of money allocated. Marion Stamps and Wallace "Gator" Bradley were on hand at a press event to protest against Mayor Daley's decision not to fund gang-run programs. See: "Fran Spielman and Mary A. Johnson, "Youth Jobs Event Turns Into Fiasco: Daley Avoids Clash With Gang Group", Chicago Sun-Times, June 10, 1994, pp. 1, 20. Marion Nzinga-Stamps was featured in the story "Run, Mural Help Promote Peace in Gang-Plagued Neighborhoods", by Sonya C. Vann, Chicago Tribune, Sept. 13, 1993, section 2, p. 3. Stamps had been involved in a "peace walk" and media event for a mural on the organization she is an officer in, "Tranquility-Marksman Memorial Organization", 440 West Division Street, Chicago, Illinois, they claim the gang peace treaty they helped organize was responsible for the relative calm at Cabrini-Green after the sniper killing of 7-year-old Dantrell Davis there in 1992, not the sudden infusion of law enforcement and security improvements.

18. In some jurisdictions, like Elgin, Illinois, recent moves have been made to expel students who commit gang crimes regardless if this had anything to do with their school. The thinking in that regard is to prevent contagion: stop gang members from recruiting others into the gang. There is some merit to this idea, however legally we must presume that the school district would have to establish an "alternative school" program for such members.

19. Numerous examples of shootings and drive-bys near the "ivory towers" can be found. See: "Police Seeking 2 Men in Shootings at ISU", Chicago Tribune, Section 2, p. 3, Jan. 23, 1994.

20. Unfortunately, here again, we can find in Chicago how some gangs have been negotiated with. In the late 1960s one of the Chicago city colleges rented property from the Conservative Vice Lords and had gang members supervising functions of a college outpost program (see: Roger Flaherty, "College Name Outlives Controversy", Chicago Sun-Times, Apr. 26, 1994, p. 14). This is equivalent to the kind of foolishness that Rev. Fry engaged in: and ultimately gives the gang more power. One can easily develop a kind of personality profile from this literature, though, on who is the kind of person most likely to try and "buy" the good graces of the gang.

21. Rev. Boyle worked in the Dolores Mission in Los Angeles and saw 26 gang members buried during a six year period. He did have their respect, enough so to earn him the street name of "G-dog". See: Hugh Dellios, "Barrio Misses Priest Who Tried To Stop Gang Wars", Chicago Tribune, Section 1, p. 21, March 21, 1993.

22. See: "Maudlyne Ihejirika, "Muslims on Patrol at Rockwell", Chicago Sun-Times, May 5, 1994, p. 5.

23. FCH17, a member of Chicago's "four corner hustlers" gang, who joined when he was 12 "because the money got good to me", felt that dropping out of the gang was not an option for him "because I have too many tattoos". Obviously, something that could be corrected with new modern methods of tattoo removal.

24. One group, the National Commission on Correctional Health Care (NCCHC), has been most active in providing quality training and technical assistance in areas dealing with known areas of risk to health (fighting, gang confrontations, drug/substance abuse, AIDS/HIV/STD infection, etc). Clearly, gang membership in a correctional institution can be considered a factor contributing to morbidity and mortality.

25. See: Rob Karwath, "Youth Mental Facility Sought Gang Truce", Chicago Tribune, Section 2, P. 1.

26. As in the politically popular "war on drugs", the traditional federal response is to simply put someone in charge (give them responsibility, with no authority), as "drug czars". One might predict, therefore, that "gang czars" could emerge in a conservative political climate favoring a "war on gangs". We lost the war on poverty, poverty won. We lost the war on drugs, drugs won. Any war on gangs, without taking into consideration some of the issues discussed by Miller (1990) will almost insure that gangs will win that war too.

27. Five skinheads appeared on a "Jerry Springer Show" in Chicago and left the set "ready for action, pumped up". They made the mistake of picking a target for their bias crimes after the show when they came over by Chicago State University (CSU). They tried to take over a fried chicken store across from CSU, had assaulted an employee, put up some racist graffiti, and as they tried to leave they were all

captured and arrested by CSU police. See: Phillip J. O'Connor and Art Golab, "5 Skinheads Charged in Post-Show Vandalism", Chicago Sun-Times, April 29, 1994, p. 5.

28. Case study LK29 stated that the gang problem, like AIDS, is an epidemic and getting worse; nothing can be done to eliminate it entirely, all we can do at this juncture is cope, adapt, prevent, etc, essentially "damage control".

29. Targeting leaders means much work, and law enforcement are more prone to let "small fish" off the hook. Which can mean overlooking a significant portion of the problem. Especially in the case of female gang members, who as case studies indicated, may be those most likely to have the function to store weapons, firearms, and even money for other gang members. These are typically naive teenage girl gang members.

30. This is based on an analysis of Foundation Grants Index information nationwide.

31. The Marcy-Newberry Association in Chicago also received $25,000 in 1982 from the Chicago Community Trust in support of its youth gang outreach community service program.

32. Spergel and Chance (1990) provided case studies in six cities that show the need for more pro-active gang program initiatives.

33. See: Art Golab, "Price of Crime Rises in DuPage County", Chicago Sun-Times, May 20, 1994. This "fine" or "contribution" is simply enabled by state law, and could be easily modified to include the gang crime situation, and the gang prevention/intervention funding opportunity.

CHAPTER 25

GANG PROGRAMS: AN OVERVIEW, ANALYSIS AND CRITIQUE

INTRODUCTION

Many persons want to do something about the gang problem, and more often than not the response involves establishing some type of gang program. There are many, many different gang programs; some are simply better known than others. Most knowledgeable citizens want gang prevention programs, they are just confused at what level of prevention should be targeted with strategic policy intervention or planning resources. Prevention can mean: (1) primary prevention, (2) secondary prevention, and (3) tertiary prevention. Primary prevention means getting to the person before they have been exposed to gangs, attempting with a good theory of human behavior to prevent the person from ever having any involvement with gangs. Secondary prevention means getting to the person who has already been exposed to gangs, and with a good theory of human behavior and based on what we know from criminology and delinquency prevention, and attempting to extract them from gang influence and prevent them from further gang involvement. Tertiary prevention means basically an intent to "rehabilitate", and means getting to the person who is a self-reported gang member and attempting with professional guidance based on theory, research, and sound policy to reduce the future crime impact of such persons.

Prevention carries a somewhat different meaning than intervention. Intervention implies working with gang youths. Tertiary prevention therefore comes closest to the full meaning of intervention in that it implies that some type or combination of services need to be provided to "those in the gang". Given a limited number of resources, the preference assumed by the social polity here is that of primary prevention rather than intervention. Intervention implies some ability to "rehabilitate" and the literature on the success of such efforts is truly mixed. A somewhat less ambitious goal in terms of impacting on human behavior is implied in primary prevention where the emphasis is on "insulating" someone from becoming involved in the problem behavior. Tertiary intervention with gang members is basically gang member rehabilitation programming, and enjoys little evidence of blanket effectiveness.[a]

As explained elsewhere in this book, there are different levels of gang involvement. This is not simply the difference between "hard core" and "fringe" members. There are leaders. There exists in most formal organizational gangs a middle management as well. There exist those who are "honorary" members or "ancianos" (i.e., older less active, almost retired, or honorary members) from whom less is expected. There

---

[a] The most effective strategy is gang debriefing, converting the active gang member and even gang leader into a cooperative source of information for government prosecution (i.e., flipping). The gang member who becomes a government witness can be considered at the point of providing effective prosecution testimony to be a true "ex-gang member", a meaningful measure of program effectiveness from the point of view articulated in this book.

always exists the regular "foot soldiers". But there also exists those who are simply "associates", or wannabes. Knowing what level of social integration the person has into any gang will vary proportionately to the difficulty of prevention efforts. The higher the gang integration, the higher the difficulty of inducing individual behavior change.[b]

The purpose of this chapter is to take a much closer look at gang programs; their ingredients (what they do), their structure (how they do it), their goals (what they hope to accomplish), their target groups (who they provide services to), and their assumptions if any (when and under what conditions do they logically expect to achieve a positive result based on the social sciences about human behavior).

GANGS RUNNING GANG PROGRAMS

A good deal of our psychological literature and common sense would tell us that professional help is needed when it comes to restoring someone to good mental health. That is to say, an active criminal cannot rehabilitate another criminal nor rehabilitate himself. The idea behind professional trained expertise is that it is unrealistic to lock someone up and basically say "go rehabilitate yourself or someone else". On the other hand, the indigenous approach works well in some contexts, for some persons, at some times, for some specific purposes. Alcoholics Anonymous (AA) and its many related forms (NA, etc) is viewed as an important and positive part of an overall solution throughout most of the literature and in common beliefs.

There are many examples of gang leaders and gangs being the primary administrators of "gang prevention/intervention" programs. These gang programs fit a definite profile. Once the government or foundation funding disappears, they disappear. Once the government or foundations discover they have misappropriated the funds, they disappear. They will resist to the bitter end any efforts to hold them "account-able" by the means of formal program evaluation research that involves a complete statistical accounting. They see "program evaluators" as the "G-men", the "funding five-oh". They want to be able to spend their money any way they want to. They do not want to have someone tell them they need a good theory of human behavior before attempting to intervene in the life of an individual regarding the protection of human subjects (e.g., what could happen afterwards if it really was not a good theoretically sound idea to do what they did to an individual in their field-service experiment).

How do gangs whose main goal is illegal income from criminal activity end up running gang programs? The fieldwork of Kotlowitz describes this process as it worked for Jeff Fort on Chicago's southside:

> "By the late 1960s, the gangs had won some standing among the establishment, particularly with liberals who felt that these young hoodlums, given proper guidance, might turn their energies and

---

[b] The one exception to this general rule of thumb is when a gang member, including the very top gang leaders, basically "defect" (e.g., "flip") and agree to testify against other fellow gang members.

enviable organizing and leadership abilities to bettering their neighborhoods" (Kotlowitz, 1992: p. 37).

Thus, Jeff Fort in 1964 got his real start and it was not from the from the University of Chicago as some are prone to believe in Chicago. Jeff got his help from Rev. John Fry in 1964, when Rev. Fry as the minister of First Presbyterian Church of Chicago at 64th and Kimbark, felt he could use his church to create a peace treaty between warring gangs, and it was Rev. Fry who helped Jeff get his Blackstone Rangers funding from Kettering Foundation, the Community Renewal Society, and the W. Clement Stone Foundation. It was in 1967 that Jeff had the opportunity to run a complete government job training program for gang members at The Woodlawn Organization (TWO), some $927,341 that was quickly mispent.[1] Similarly, for the Vice Lords on Chicago's westside:

> "At Henry Horner, the Vice Lords gained a similar standing when a local hospital bequeathed a former Catholic boys' school it owned, coupled with a grant of over $20,000, to local gang leaders in the hope that they would open a neighborhood center" (Kotlo-witz, 1992: p. 37).

Just like Jeff Fort, the Vice Lords used those assets for something other than community improvement.

The Federal government has not been a leader in clarifying "what works" in terms of gang prevention/intervention. It has been a leader in funding a wide number of 1960s style programs that were specifically targeting gang members or potential gang members. The Federal government has, over the last three decades, supported a wide number of gang experiments seeking to intervene in the gang crime problem. Some have clearly and most certainly achieved dramatic results, but in the opposite direction! That is, some programs have inadvertently increased the wealth and power, and thereby the persistence, continuity and expansion, of certain specific gangs. It seems reasonable to conclude that this has also meant, in its limited context, increasing rather than decreasing the gang crime problem.

The well-intended work of a member of the clergy known as Reverend Fry is one such example. Whether he said it or not in his applications for federal funding, Rev. Fry assumed the theory that gang members could be easily "coopted" into leading a law abiding existence. Rev. Fry hired Jeff Fort, the leader of the Black P. Stones and the Main 21, to help "solve the gang problem". Jeff Fort quickly manipulated the situation, ciphering off funds, hiring "ghost workers", demanding "kickbacks" from fellow gang members whom he hired under the authority of the program, and outright misappropriation (e.g., program fraud).

This sudden influx of hard money into the treasury of Jeff Fort's gang, meant it accumulated more weapons and more capital with which to eventually enter large scale narcotic trafficking. Overall, it meant never asking Jeff Fort, nor any other gang member, to ever sign a "pledge" that they had dropped their gang allegiance, that they would "give up on crime". Rev. Fry was concerned about gang violence and convinced the Federal government he could "do something about it". Rev. Fry assumed that offering a context for a "peace treaty" and a helping hand to these troubled youths would have a positive result. The result was not positive, the result was the El Rukns: a formidable, highly organized, tight knit, highly selective, extremely violent, criminal gang that still operates today in spite of the incarceration of its top leadership.

Jeff Fort wrote the book on how to run an outside gang from behind prison walls. He used his "prisoner rights", the right to use the telephone. Today in prisons such as those in Illinois, gang leaders continue to "issue marching orders" to their gang members on the streets. A common technique used to maintain communications even while incarcerated amounts to the use of a "safe house" telephone that the inmate gang leader calls collect. The "safe house" contains a sophisticated "call forwarding" fast dialing machine where all he needs to do is enter another digit from the keypad of the telephone he is using and he gets automatically connected to one of his henchmen who may have a cellular phone anywhere in the world. Conference calls are also routinely handled in this fashion.

While the Federal government has cracked down on the telephone activities of gang leaders like Jeff Fort (who is incarcerated presently at the Marion Penitentiary), gang leaders incarcerated in state and local correctional systems clearly have an edge. Many still continue, as in the case of gang leaders in Illinois prisons and elsewhere today, basically "running" their gang from the inside.

A genuine "bad idea" is to basically turn over assets to a hostile group like a highly organized criminal gang. Such an example is detailed in the case of the program started in 1976 known as "GET GOING, INC" (Madden, 1993: 7). It was an aftercare program for "Pintos" (released prisoners) located in East Los Angeles. It was run by the Mexican Mafia (EME). It was clearly, then, aimed at "tertiary prevention": the hardest to accomplish[c]. According to the report this program was "actually a front for the Mexican Mafia" (ibid). Thus, "Federal grants were used to purchase heroin in Mexico" and they used their access to the prisons to increase the gang presence throughout California. When someone was about to "spill the beans" in 1977 about this federal fraud, she was killed by an EME member (ibid).

The cases of Jeff Fort and the Get Going Inc program illustrate what not to do. Providing assets that can be readily converted to the use of the gang (a criminal enterprise) is not the best idea if the goal is to reduce the gang crime threat problem. Similarly, a Boot Camp or "Leadership Training" program for some gangs might fit right into the agenda of a gang leader. A physically stronger and better disciplined gang member is the ideal soldier of any gang leader. Thus, program intervention cannot be predicated on the "terms" of the gang, but must rather be based on the "terms" and expectations of the community that must eventually face the gang problem if it gets much worse. The goals of the law-abiding community and the goals of the gang may be antithetical outside of the generalized context of "we all want a better world". In the context of specific issues, community members do

---

[c] It is the hardest to accomplish because in the extensive literature on "criminal rehabilitation", no one has yet been acknowledged as having discovered the "silver bullet", the true "cure". Some times, in some ways (typically job placements), their recidivism or relapse or return to prison seems to be reduced. It is a sufficient probability of potential impact to work on, however it is a voluntary process that leads someone to want to accept a job in the first place.

not want armed gangs shooting up the neighborhood.   No gang truce or "peace treaty" has yet to surface where gang members truly turned in their weapons. Someone who thinks the "gang truces" in Los Angeles, Chicago, Minneapolis[2], and elsewhere have resulted in a sudden permanent decrease in gang violence should get a police scanner and start listening to their local police calls like the organized gang-controlled drug-distribution rings do themselves to avoid serious arrests.

Gangs do aspire to control government funding for gang programs and sometimes appear to be able to reach to the very top of the local politicians for such support. More often than not, however, it backfires. Such was the case in October, 1985 when the mayor of St. Paul, Minnesota met with John Scruggs, the local leader of the Disciples gang who was seeking $58,000 in seed money to start a youth center. The very next day, this same gang leader executed a 16-year-old female member --- Christine Kreitz --- because he feared she could link him to a crime that if discovered would jeopardize the government grant.   Scruggs was convicted of first-degree murder and received a life sentence in prison[3].

PROGRAMS WITHOUT THEORIES ARE RISKS NOT WORTH TAKING

As used here a theory means a model of etiological logic that is consistent with prior research support and/or common sense application of validated explanations of human behavior; in this instance, human behavior involving deviance, more specifically, crime and delinquency, as well as substance abuse and violence. Intervention or prevention implies an effort to "interrupt" a sequence of human behavior, at an appropriate point in time, to motivate behavioral change. This also presumes we are talking about individual behavior; not the treatment of group behavior.   It is not assumed here that an entire group (i.e., gang in this case) is subject to such change[d].

The idea that no theory is used to guide program intervention efforts means it is an atheoretical model. In an atheoretical model, basically anything could happen as a result of the intervention because there is no logical sequence or justification for "what might happen". It is a "flip of the coin" situation. It could just as easily go "wrong" as go "right". If it goes wrong we produce criminals rather than preventing crime.   The idea of having a theoretically justified model of intervention is that the program can logically expect positive impact at a higher level of probability than a flip of the coin (50/50 chance). A good theory of human behavior increases the odds of having a positive impact, which is why it is needed.

That any program of intervention or prevention dealing with crime or delinquency --- in this instance gang crime --- needs a theory justifying what it proposes to do is

---

[d] Think about it, coopting a gang leader would not even work: how could a gang leader "order" his underlings to go straight in the same fashion any similar order comes down to violate the law? It is illogical and incomprehensible that any such genuine change could be affected in a level three gang. Certainly, much earlier work shows that non-gangs or 'pre-gangs', the level zero type of Alfalfa and Spanky groups, are certainly subject to redirection --- they are easily provided with positive direction, because overall they do not have a criminal direction as of yet.

now one of the areas of consensus not just among gang researchers, but among almost all criminologists and social scientists[4].

It is important to have rigorous evaluation research conducted on all gang intervention/prevention programs. This should include both process (what happens during the program) and product evaluations (what happens afterwards, the "outcomes"). An atheoretical evaluation is also not a good idea. The "measures" used in the evaluation (reduction in recidivism, increased self-esteem, reduced interaction with gang members, etc) need to be as closely as possible related to the specific theory of intervention being used by the program.

PRIMARY PREVENTION IN THE SCHOOL SETTING

A number of program approaches have been described in the gang literature that are useful in the school setting (Knox, Laske, and Tromanhauser, 1992). The idea is to combine anti-gang education with anti-drug education, because so often in the school setting these two problems go hand in hand. Actually, a third problem --- conflict and violence --- can also be highly correlated with gang and drug problems. Thus, in the Cleveland Public Schools a special Youth Gang Unit was created in its Division of Safety & Security[e]. The concept behind this type of added expertise is that by training teachers on gang recognition issues, on conflict resolution, etc, and working with parents and community groups, that the school has a fighting chance to curb these inter-related problems[5]. Most teachers do not get training about gangs in college, however they need it to effectively carry out their mission.

PRIMARY PREVENTION IN THE NEIGHBORHOOD CONTEXT

Recreational activities structured and supervised in such a fashion as to provide a viable alternative to what the gangs offer in terms of fellowship and "excitement" are a common ingredient for the primary prevention of gang problems. Boys and Girls Clubs offer such activities in their drop-in centers as do many others (e.g., the YMCA/YWCA). Special initiatives such as the "Take Our Daughters to Work Club" work with large corporate sponsors such as Ameritech and in addition to providing a daily safe haven for kids also provide some social skills upgrading[6]. The goal is to prevent such "good kids" from ever joining a gang, and to keep them "off the streets" where the gangs are ever present.

A program that specifically incorporated such recreational activities as well as arts and crafts for youths, and which operated continuously for 52 years and is therefore regarded by some as the oldest anti-gang program in Chicago, is that started by the late Daniel "Moose" Brindisi who was the executive director of the Near Northwest Civic Committee[7]. This neighborhood based program also acquired its own summer camp, Camp Pompeii, which is located in Park Forest, Illinois. This program also used the recommendation of Thrasher (1918) that Boy Scout and Cub Scout groups

---

[e] For additional information about this program contact: Kenneth S. Trump, Unit Coordinator, Youth Gang Unit, Division of Safety and Security, Cleveland Public Schools, 1380 East Sixth Street, Rm. 106-A, Cleveland, OH 44114.

could provide valuable socialization experiences as a way of gang prevention at the primary level. Groups like Boys Nation and Girls Nation also provide such general positive socialization experiences in an adult supervised context of legitimate social control.

There is a potentially endless list of positive, pro-social, skill-building, adult-supervised projects, programs and experiences that can be provided to children in an overall strategy to prevent gang affiliation at the primary level of prevention. At an elementary school near Chicago's Cabrini-Green, a drum and bugle corp was formed; while the staff volunteers could handle 80 children ages 5 through 9, some 300 actually applied to use the 36 drums available[8]. There are basically some very worthwhile programs that need to be funded that are not being funded. If we really want to do something for youths, then clearly there are a lot of ways to steer them away from gang involvement.

SECONDARY PREVENTION: WORKING WITH "AT RISK" YOUTHS

A common theme in secondary prevention is to target geographical areas that represent a "high risk". This has often meant targeting youths from 8 to 16 in public housing complexes. In such settings, the gang/drug/violence/crime problem is an ever present problem. Project FLOW (Future Leaders Of the World) in Philadelphia, for example, with $875,602 in funding for the first 17 months seeks to serve 490 such at-risk youths. As described in its literature, this program includes a number of traditional and unique service components:

> "The program activities developed to benefit these youth will include an education component involving tutoring, homework assistance, study groups, etc; comprehensive drug related services such as drug and alcohol education, prevention education, refusal skills building (Drugs/Violence/Alcohol) and counseling. The comprehensive gang prevention services will provide mentoring, individual and family counseling, conflict resolution and anger control workshops. Other activities will include summer programs, sports and recreation and other related cultural activities including trips to museums, parks etc. Parent support groups will also be formed to support and stabilize the family structures.
>
> All Project FLOW youth will receive basic Health Care through the Philadelphia Department of Public Health. Another major component...will be the 'Rites of Passage' module which is designed to increase awareness and develop skills associated with positive culture and ethnic identities of the youth served"[f].

As should be expected, the FLOW program is evaluated by a University in its area. All programs with direct contact with youths should be subject to such thorough independent evaluation.

---

[f] Project FLOW, Mayor's Office of Community Services, 101 N. Broad Street, 3rd Floor, Philadelphia, PA 19107.

Some consulting firms have arisen rapidly to the potential market for such services to local government. It is not unusual for such consultants to be paid $100 an hour for their services in helping establish such programs[9].

THE COMMUNITY-BASED CONSORTIA APPROACH

In recent years, the federal funding for gang programs has emphasized a community-based consortia approach. What it means is bringing together a number of different programs and services under a larger umbrella-style program; all of the actors targeting a specific population for intensive prevention services. An example of such a program that bases its expectations for impact on the prior research and on sound theory is that of the "Mujeres Y Hombres Nobles" (Noble Men and Women) program of the Los Angeles County Office of Education. Funded with a $3 million grant that will last five years the consortium will serve 30,000 residents and 350 school age children in East Los Angeles. Its program components include: "gang risk reduction, drug prevention and treatment, HIV/AIDS prevention, vocational training, cultural pride and esteem, spiritual and moral rencounterment, mentoring by Madrinas and Padrinos, intergenerational gang family systems intervention, conflict resolution and mediation, education and community awareness, and linkages to services".

This program is unique in being capable of dealing with the intergenerational gang family situation. Unfortunately, it is a not infrequent problem apparently, and one of the least researched aspects of the gang/family area. The Mujeres y Hombres Nobles program summary gives an example:

> Teen Angel Magazine published exclusively for California gang members, regularly publishes pictures submitted by teen mothers of their children and babies dressed in gang clothing and giving gang hand signs; these teen mothers are unknowingly enculturating a new generation of gang members.

CONFUSED GANG PREVENTION: AN EXAMPLE OF A PROGRAM WITHOUT A THEORY

The Gang Project described here was funded by the Administration on Children, Youth and Families of the U.S. Department of Health and Human Services (DHHS). It had as its first broad purpose to "develop an action plan in the city which identified the community's vision for a gang-free city, the obstacles blocking that vision, new directions to take to overcome the obstacles, and implementation plans for each new direction". The strange idea here was that the gang problem could be solved with an administrative solution: some master plan that would take a couple years to develop. As the program "unfolded", it changed its goal away from "gang-free" to that of having gangs be less violent in their city. To quote their final report to DHHS:

> "A shift occurred in the original language of the goals from 'gang free' to one that focussed on creating a climate in which gangs did not act in violent ways. It was felt that some hypocrisy would be in

place if our goal was gang free but we said nothing about 'gangs' such as Rotary or Kiwanis or Lions."

The project offered "training" of an unspecified nature to community groups and nonprofit staff, which along with "community meetings" were not well attended[g]. At some point, the project engaged in direct service to youths in schools and juvenile corrections; using former addicts and ex-gang members to speak to them on --- presumably --- the evil of gangs and drugs.

So what happened at the end of the project funding period? No such coherent strategic plan was ever actually written. The final report included a lot of vague generalities about the need for community empowerment. It evaluated itself, and felt it did a good job.

That is the danger of an atheoretical program: it can literally change its goals, which must be viewed with some criticism. The Project was probably not the best use of public monies. It probably sounded good to Washington (holding community forums, interfacing various agencies, etc), but the Project lacked any coherent theory and then changed its goals and began doing direct service work. This same program not only changed its goals and language after receiving federal money, it may have used the money to help sponsor a "Gang Summit Meeting".

A GANG OUTREACH PROGRAM THAT DOES NOT GET ALONG VERY WELL WITH GANG COPS

This is another federally funded program, but which as an "advocacy organization", receives funding from a variety of other sources especially foundations. A highly educated police officer who is also a gang researcher first told me about this program in his city. The word among police was that the program served as a site for gangs to hold their meetings and conduct their gang business. This program bills itself as a "gang outreach program". There is no theory of just how, exactly, it would prevent anything. The idea itself was peculiar: not a traditional "detached worker outreach program" to individual gang members, for which there are a lot of materials that can be used for training such detached workers; but rather it sought outreach to the "gang" itself. Such on-line program service personnel would clearly have to be organizational and group psychology experts; which of course they were not, they were indigenous staff, paraprofessionals at best. What is the single most important criteria of program success in such detached worker programs is the ability to increase a more law abiding and prosocial lifestyle, and to reduce a delinquency and criminality lifestyle. Most prior evaluation research on such detached worker programs has not shown the ability to actually accomplish this goal (Mattick and Caplan, 1962; Klein, 1968; Miller, 1974; Quicker, 1983).

In the program being described here, what it did do is basically turn the program over to the gang. To quote from its final report: "Access to Gang Leadership: staff know the gang leadership in the city; some of the program staff have been recruited from this leadership". The program provides its staff with beepers and car radios,

---

[g] This may have been due to a program lacking a "needs assessment".

and thus claims it is a "round the clock" operation. The program employs active gang members, and "has hired most of its junior staff from the ranks of gangs in" the city. Without any indication of training for such staff, the report goes on to claim how it provides gang outreach, case management, crisis intervention, family services, school services, some type of "ministry to gang members"[h], security work at public events, and prison work. Hiring gang leaders and active gang members under the guise of working with the local gang scene somehow gets translated into establishing a Gang Council and sponsoring a gang conference.

Here we see the real danger of an atheoretical program evaluating itself: of course, it claims to literally have walked on water. It provides a number of statistics which on their face would appear to be "doing something": during 1991, 235 meetings with gangs or gang leaders to prevent conflicts (does that include meetings the gang members themselves who work in the program have between each other, we don't know), 156 mediations of gang-related conflicts at schools (does that include the conflicts in its own school program that it runs, we don't know), 195 mediations between gangs in conflicts on the streets.

What we have here are paraprofessionals at best who while indigenous to the city, are employed in a social service and a crime prevention and public safety function, who might potentially be part of the problem itself. The media coverage gained by some of the gang leaders has certainly helped them to promote their gang as an organization "about Growth and Development" --- a code word for Gangster Disciple --- so it provides a public relations function for the local gangs. There is nothing in the program report documentation about success in reducing drug use or drug sales, of actual reductions in gang violence, or actual reductions in gang membership involvement. In fact, one would have to postulate from the declarations in this report back to the federal government that gang membership probably increased --- at least for those gangs whose leaders were put on the payroll. It is comparable to the early Jeff Fort and Rev. Fry phenomenon[10].

Needless to say this program did not have, as is apparently required of many programs receiving federal funding, any external quantitative process and product program evaluation. But it continues today. Is it possible that the beepers and car phones given to these gang members were used in anything other than "making peace"? Is it really a good idea to have gang members provide "security work" for concerts as this program does, is that not similar to hiring the Hell's Angels at Woodstock? What is the theory here for such a program that it is going to reduce the gang problem? It is certainly not well articulated.

THE FEDERAL GOVERNMENT FUNDING FOR GANG PROGRAMS

The federal Youth Gang Drug Prevention Program was authorized by legislation in 1988 (section 3501 of the Anti-Drug Abuse Act of 1988). The federal Youth Gang

---

[h] This should have been a "red flag" to the federal agency providing funding in the first place: the government has no business subsidizing "street versions" of religious prosyletizing. What religious doctrine was being "pushed" to these gangs?

Drug Prevention Program awards funding to actual gang programs "to prevent and to reduce the participation of youth in the activities of gangs that engage in illicit drug-relate activities and to promote the involvement of youth in lawful activities". The federal agency having the responsibility to administer this funding is the Administration on Children, Youth and Families (ACYF) and is managed by the Family and Youth Services Bureau, both within the Department of Health and Human Services. Since it first began in 1989, this federal initiative has provided over $50 million dollars in funding to over 100 different gang prevention programs.

The FYSB Youth Gang Prevention Program has issued a number of printed newsletters. The Connections newsletter provides updates on various programs funded by FYSB and other features such as its National Conferences. At any particular time there are a sufficient number of such federally funded programs to hold a National Youth Gang Conference. The First National Conference was held June 5-7, 1991 in Alexandria, Virginia; the Third such conference was held in 1993. A number of other conferences have been funded by the FYSB as well.

Many of the programs funded by this federal initiative publish short guidelines in the Connections newsletter. Much very useful and important information is published in the newsletters[i]. It promotes practitioner/researcher interaction; gives advice on hiring gang outreach workers, provides highlights of gang programs in the news; and contact information.

PROGRAMS TO ESTABLISH "GANG TRUCES"

A number of efforts have been made historically to establish "gang truces". Typically these are ad hoc arrangements and do not reflect a formal program per se. Some programs seek "mini-truces" on an individual level, for example in the context of a single school, where this kind of gang program service is sometimes called "gang mediation". The Youth For Christ evangelical group in Chicago has been holding its "United Nations" meetings for a decade: bringing rival gang members together in groups representing over twenty different gangs over time (Mc Lean, 1991) - the goal being to allow the individuals to appreciate the Christian faith[11]. Such counseling and prosocial advice where the unit of service delivery being targeted is the individual does not seek to work with the gang as a collective enterprise, but rather simply seeks to apply conflict resolution skills at the level of the individual. Such work at the level of the individual is certainly worthwhile.   But what "gang truces" involve typically are not services, nor are they formal programs accountable for their actions, and the unit of service delivery target is the entire gang as a collective identity. A common theme of such truce efforts is to bring together warring or rival gangs and unite them under a larger umbrella organization. The position taken in the present book is that such endeavors are rarely successful and are indeed risky. Supporting the present position that negotiating with gang leaders basically means that through such official recognition the gang becomes stronger are a number of other analyses (Haskel and Yablonsky, 1982) and more recently Kodluboy and Evenrud:

---

[i]   The Connections newsletter is published and distributed by the Cosmos Corporation, 1735 Eye Street, NW, Suite 613, Washington, DC 20006.

"It is probable that mediation with gang members or gang leaders may sometimes be necessary to forestall immediate violence or prevent loss of life. It is also probable that such mediation increases the risk of validating the gang as a legitimate social entity, thus buying short-term peace at the price of long-term persistence of the gang (Goldstein and Huff, 1993: p. 285)."

Still, it is not hard at all to find those who felt the "truce" between the Crips and the Bloods in Los Angeles was a major positive development[12]; just as it is not hard to find the skeptics either.

It is helpful, however, to briefly outline some of the recent "gang truce" efforts. Four such efforts are critically examined here: (1) the Chicago Cabrini-Green case, (2) the Minneapolis case, (3) the Kansas City summit, and (4) the Chicago Gang Summit Meeting.

1. The Chicago Gang Truce.

In October-November, 1992 the Chicago official "gang truce" button began appearing and was worn by many of the gang members whose gangs were signed parties to this truce. The "gang truce" button has the slogan "UNITED IN PEACE" with two hands (a left hand and a right hand) clasping, along with ten gang "logos" or symbols --- all in black on a white round background. The logo symbols for the following gangs appear on this "gang truce" button: Vice Lords, New El Rukns (seven in circle), Black P Stone Nation, Cobras, El Rukns, Four Corner Hustlers (+ sign, 440), Black Disciples, Black Gangster Disciples, and Black Gangsters.

White gangs, Arab gangs, and Hispanic gangs were not a party to this "truce". Recall that such racial enmity is a part of the fuel that fires the engine of the gang problem. Any such genuine "truce" would have to include all ethnic gangs across the board. This alliance of Black gangs arose in the aftermath of the sniper killing of a child in Cabrini-Green and the public uproar it caused. The pressure was put on the gangs. Political activists took advantage of the situation to "bring the gangs together". In this fashion, a tentative alliance was formed between rival gangs; giving them greater legitimacy and recognition in the mass media. Gang leaders and gang activists claimed credit for the "calm" at Cabrini Green after the sniper killing of the 7-year-old child there, killed by a gang member shooting at someone else with an AR-15 assault rifle. No one should seriously believe any gang involvement caused any peace at Cabrini Green, rather this Chicago Housing Authority complex was flooded with international attention and was swarmed with new services and resources, including a vast number of intensive and proactive law enforcement initiatives by such agencies as the Secret Service.[13]

Gang killings, gang shootings, and gang violence continue in Chicago today in spite of any 1992 "gang truce". While the violence committed by gangs has not stopped in Chicago, this did give certain gang leaders who were a party to the "truce" a great deal of positive attention in the mass media. Some elected local Chicago politicians almost a year later believed the truce was successful enough to support a bid for parole by a major gang leader. The fact that the Chicago Police Department decentralized its gang unit during the same time frame has led others to believe that this simply unfounded much gang violence.

But the facts suggest the Chicago truce was little more than a public relations gimmick by the gangs. In July 1993, during the "truce", Chicago had the deadliest month in its entire history in terms of homicides. According to the "truce", anyone who engaged in such gang killings was supposed to be treated as a "renegade"; a term for a very errant gang member --- thus, they would be turned in by their peers to the police for prosecution. According to the Cook County State's Attorney, no gang ever turned in anyone during the time period up to and including August of 1993.

2. One gang truce in Minneapolis was paid for with federal funding, but just like the Chicago and Los Angeles version there is little evidence to show it was effective. The Minneapolis gang truce came out of a "gang intervention" program called The City, Inc which received grants from the U.S. Department of Health and Human Services --- through the FYSB federal initiative described above --- and additional funding from foundations and corporate donors.

"United For Peace" was the Minneapolis gang truce slogan and began in the spring of 1992. Did gang violence drop in Minneapolis? No is the answer, in fact gang-related violence may have increased according to one report[14]. In fact, a gang-war between two factions of the Vice Lords arose during the so-called gang truce[15]. So the factual evidence is that at a minimum, the gang shootings and killings continued.

For some time, the program that sponsored the gang truce also claimed as part of its success the fact that it had strong positive ties with the local police. Police had been meeting with the United For Peace leaders, but that ceased when on September 25, 1992 a Minneapolis police officer --- Jerome Haaf --- was slain execution style by gang members.   One of the four members of the Vice Lords arrested for the murder was a relative of Sharif Willis[16] --- the Minneapolis leader of the Conservative Vice Lords and the president of United for Peace[17]. With federal funding The City, Inc --- the not-for-profit program that provided the financing for the Minneapolis gang truce --- was supposed to hold a Gang Conference to show social workers from around the country how effective it was in working with police. The conference was supposed to square off Spike Moss, the gang leader founder of the truce, and Minneapolis Police chief John Laux. The police chief did not attend the conference[18].

The facts of this "gang truce" are quite fascinating. Did the leader of the "gang truce" turn fellow Vice Lords who were charged with the murder of police officer Haaf? No! But the suspects were in fact arrested in the home of the leader of the "gang truce". Police learned that the plot to kill Officer Haaf to send a message about "police brutality" was in fact hatched in the same dwelling. In fact, A.C. Ford one of the persons charged with the assassination of Officer Haaf was a major Vice Lord leader and also a member of the United for Peace coalition[19]. In November, 1992, Jerome Copeland the Gangster Disciples gang leader who was the Vice President or second in command in the leadership of the United for Peace "gang truce" was himself arrested for firearms and narcotics charges![20]   Copeland was a "gang outreach worker" employed by The City, Inc in Minneapolis. Some media attention to The City, Inc has likened it to the funding fiasco with Jeff Fort and his misuse of federal funding in Chicago[21]. It certainly seems to have the same elements in such a profile.

3. The Kansas City "Gang Summit"

During the period April 28 through May 2, 1993 at the St. Stephen Baptist Church in Kansas City, Missouri, the first National Urban Peace and Justice Summit was held. It was informally known as the "national gang truce summit". The Kansas City gang summit was truly historically unique. The Mayor, a minister, welcomed those attending at a special breakfast for them. The concept for this summit was originated by the political activist Carl Upchurch in Granville, Ohio. Although many others were obviously involved, including all those from the Chicago "truce" movement, the Minneapolis version, and those in Los Angeles. The single "inside story" indicated "one hundred and sixty four current and former gang leaders and members from 26 cities, and 53 observers" attended the event[22]. The organizer was Carl Upchurch whose group is called Council for Urban Peace and Justice in Columbus, Ohio.[23]

In the press release, gangs were given a Chicago-based public relations title "grassroot street youth organizations and nations". Calling it a "peace movement", the intent in the future is to hold such "summits" in every city and to have a yearly summit.

Much of the material reads similar to gang constitutions: it gives a "positive" side of gang life, it does not talk about how much death, destruction, and violence the gangs themselves have created. If we were to believe it at face value, some of it would lead us to believe these were a group of young republicans. Consider this excerpt[24]:

> "Women's Issues: Sisters of the Summit.
>
> We the mothers, the sisters, the girlfriends, women in organizations and the street gangs stand in unity to stop the violence!
>
> As women we have always known violence. This violence is beyond street violence and police brutality; it includes domestic violence, rape, child abuse, and poverty. We insist that women be justly represented on any advisory group or board of directors at any future events.
>
> Honoring our ancestors and elders is important to teach respect, family values, and cultural traditions to our youth.
>
> We are committed to work with our brothers in teaching our children how to replace self-destruction with a commitment to life, family, education, and community empowerment."

It sounds good, but how many guns were turned in? How many signed pledges not to distribute illegal drugs? How many agreed to compensate innocent bystander victims of gang violence or the families of those who died from gang violence? A peace movement led by highly organized gangs for whom violence is a way of life is comparable only to a group of pyromaniacs who have been convicted of arson seeking to replace Smokey Bear as the spokespersons for a National Forest Fire Prevention Campaign.

Anyone who can get gangs to turn in their guns, give up on crime, violence, and drug distribution does however truly deserve not only a Nobel Peace Prize, but something much higher in recognition --- for they would have discovered the "magic bullet" of rehabilitation on a massive scale. Unfortunately, it is not realistic. Waiting for such a large scale of genuine change in deviant behavior is comparable only to someone leaving the porch light on in the hope that Jimmy Hoffa will return.

The Summit had a number of recommendations: reducing police brutality gained much discussion. Another recommendation was to repeal all laws against gangs: "Repeal of all anti-gang legislation, and ordinances, both state and federal, around the country, including existing statutes in California, Minnesota, and the City of Chicago, Oregon, and the federal program Weed and Seed." There were no recommendations in the Summit literature denouncing the use of automatic firearms, MAC's, AK-47's etc. There were no recommendations in the Summit literature demanding that drug trafficking cease and desist.

According to an ex-gang member from a Chicago program who attended, this Summit was a motivational seminar. "I heard a lot of feel good stuff", he reported. But he came back to Chicago believing that the program he works in must cooperate with this new peace movement. He also described a power-brokering incident that apparently resulted in the cessation of a rift between two factions of "Folks"; and in the process gave new meaning to the potential powers that could be held by an "ex-gang". The ex-gang member from the Chicago program was a Latino who was a former member of a Disciples gang faction that consisted primarily of Latinos. Another ex-gang leader from the Disciples, an African-American, also from Chicago, was also attending the summit. The Latino ex-gang member mentioned to the African-American ex-gang member how a rift now existed in a west side neighborhood in Chicago. Very quickly the African-American ex-gang member made a call to an Illinois prison[j]; almost immediately the African-American faction of the Disciples received a call from prison and were basically ordered to "chill out". The "rift" (a kind of discernible tension that could get out of hand) between the two different ethnic factions of the Disciples was immediately eliminated.

Is that an example of peace making or just good gang nation maintenance and management? These were two factions of the same gang nation. They were not traditional rival gangs, they were as ethnic gang factions gradually developing apart however.

What is most interesting here is just how "ex" the ex-gang member was who called the prison where the Disciples chief was serving time. Apparently this is some kind of social drift. The person has a marginal integration: highly integrated into gang life (enough to be able to call the gang leader), and simultaneously highly integrated into conventional society (representing himself as an "ex" gang member who wants peace and goodwill for humanity). Such a person moves in and out of both legitimate

---

[j] I had been familiar with how gang members inside the Illinois Department of Corrections were able to effectively "run" their gangs using their access to the telephone, but it meant the inmate had to call collect to someone on the outside. I had not heard, prior to this account, of ex-gang members calling the gang chief inside the prison.

society and the deviant subcultures; gravitating to one or the other sectors of society as the need arises, drifting in and out at ease. It would seem reasonable to hypothesize that in the presentation of self to the imprisoned gang leader in the above instance would not be that of an "ex-member" of the gang. This is the kind of issue that needs to benefit from close-up research such as that of ethnomethodoly (i.e., hanging out with the gang). Does someone ever become an "ex-member" of a level three gang (e.g., the Aryan Brotherhood, the Latin Kings, etc) other than entering a witness protection program? Or can some persons, depending on personality and skills, actually penetrate the confidence and have influence over a gang?

4. The October, 1993 Chicago Gang Summit Meeting.

The Chicago Gang Summit Meeting drew enormous media attention and while it had its main events in a downtown hotel also held "field events" at various locations, including the Englewood Public High School for an awards ceremony honoring "community service for peace" leaders like Larry Hoover and Willie Lloyd and other gang leaders. When those attending the summit meeting went to hear Louis Farrakhan, what they heard was the message others also had for the gang members: "Peace cannot be a slogan...you have got to make it real...Put down the guns...You mean peace? You don't need a weapon".[25] Others also demanded that the gangs show a sign of good faith in making their rhetoric reality by turning in guns, but no guns were ever turned in. Actually the gang leaders attending the event got a mixed message in that regard, as one of their main speakers at the downtown main event challenged them "so you think you are bad and you can go and bum rush somebody huh, well if you think you're so tough you just go on up into the C.I.A. headquarters and you bust them up". The audience had heard of how the C.I.A. in Los Angeles was spying on gang members following them around and who also were said to use guns with tracer bullets[26].

Such gang truces appear to have some common etiological sequences. First, such gang truces are not limited to the United States, and have been reported among Asian gang crime groups in Hong Kong (Kaplan and Dubro, 1986: p. 219). What precedes such gang truces are periods of intermittent conflict with relatively equal losses and casualties or the onset of a sudden major surge in public opinion. The greater the intensity of police repression in response to such a public outcry, the greater the incentive for the combatant gangs to establish an alliance. The "heat" is on in otherwords, and public opinion may be developing rapidly as supporting even more intensive police repression. The more disruption in the income-producing functions of a gang from such developments, the more it is likely to agree to enter into an alliance with a rival gang. No one knows the long term effect of working with the gang as an organization and giving it a public platform, it is possible to at least hypothesize that the increased mass media role legitimating gang leaders as "keepers of the peace" may in fact further erode the willingness of potential crime witnesses to ever cooperate with law enforcement or testify if they had to --- as the fear of the gang will increase, it will make the gang appear to be "ever present".

Activist style leaders emerge in the context of such "gang truces" and "gang summit meetings" who represent themselves as being part of both worlds: the gang world, and the "straight" world. Others tend to act as spokespersons for the gang itself. None of these persons has ever really agreed to sign a statement accepting responsibility for the crime and violence of the gang it represents. They want the authority, esteemed status, and public recognition of a kind of Henry Kissinger to the gangs without the responsibility for their behavior and actions. They should not be taken serious until they are willing to accept civil legal responsibility --- and that means the many court suits that could potentially be brought against a gang, for its graffiti, for its theft crimes, for its robbery crimes, for its violence particularly, and such financial damages would be very enormous indeed in any city of 100,000 or more in the United States --- for the gang(s) they claim to represent in "peace" or "truce" negotiations.

Negotiating with gang leaders truly does set a bad precedent however. The logical extreme of such a criminal justice policy is that who knows, perhaps next burglars and rapists will want to negotiate --- "give us what we want....or else". Terrorists always want to negotiate, but anyone who knows anything about terrorism will advise that it is the worst of all decisions in practice and in policy to actually do so. Why? Because negotiating with terrorists provides the behavioral incentive for other terrorists to use extreme violence to achieve their ends as well. That is, negotiating with terrorists encourages more terrorism in the long run. Much gang violence can be considered "street" or "urban" terrorism.

SUMMARY

The full and complete book the history of gang programs has yet to be written. It cannot be accomplished in the limited space here. Some of the programs that had the best theoretical basis for prevention were those making use of the social control that comes from involving the family of the youth in the process[27]. Such programs like the FOCUS Project in Washington, D.C. provided support group activities, family counseling, home visits, working with other social service agencies and police, and sought to prevent gang involvement and drug-abuse and with some promising results. It enlisted the parent in the effort to impact on the children in a systems approach. The good news is that there are a number of such positive impact programs throughout the United States. The bad news is that after the federal funding runs out after one or two years, the program services stop, and the problem returns. We cannot rely on band-aid approaches, the best strategy is the one that prevents new gang recruits from joining the gangs. The federal approach has been piecemeal and segmented. It may not even involve true competitive bidding, that is: politics still seems a factor in who gets funding. We never hear of how knowledge development is improved by these programs. We already know some such program models and services can truly have a positive impact. And yet, still today, such specific services are not standardized nor does the funding agency provide an overall summary of "what works". And it certainly does not do a very good job at disseminating this needed information to the communities that could benefit from it: just in case they wanted to do something without federal funding.

Examining a number of such current federally funded gang prevention programs the typical program that operates at the primary level of prevention has the service components shown in Figure 22. By and large, the vast majority of these service components are indeed traditional social service approaches and can be found in many correctional aftercare programs with similar program goals (e.g., to reduce recidivism). Thus, they can be assumed to be useful as well in secondary and tertiary prevention programs.

A couple of the services in Figure 22 stand out as being uniquely related to the gang-drug problem. The "court advocacy" is not a new service, it was tried throughout the 1960s and 1970s and before. It simply motivates the client to participate in the program. But on a large scale, it basically means supplementing the resources of the juvenile public defenders office. Logically, it works against "Weed and Seed" and the strict accountability concept. Because through this service component, some juvenile offenders will get off the hook via the advocate from the program. It is a cheap way to generate clients: they may have to participate in the program as part of their probation agreement. But clearly, if the youth is at the level of being involved in the juvenile court system for delinquency, the program is operating for that youth at a secondary or tertiary level of prevention --- not a primary level of prevention. We cannot design our social structure to send mixed messages to the gang and expect the gang problem to cease operations. We need a logically consistent national strategy.

In none of the programs reviewed as funded by the recent federal initiative was there any breakdown by goals in terms of numbers of youths to be served at these various levels of prevention/intervention. This is truly remarkable in light of the vast accumulation of program knowledge and information in federal agencies. What this may imply is that the federal initiative should be dramatically changed. It should provide a model service intervention/prevention program and in its Requests For Proposals solicit who wants to run this specific type of Model Program (with no deviation, no changing of goals, etc). The evaluation research component would then be meaningful from a comparison and regional point of view. The federal initiative might then take on more structure and consistency. Currently, the initiative could be summarized as Requests for Proposals that solicit "do what you want to do....and if it sounds interesting we'll give you the federal money for it".

There are, however, important conceptual and policy issues in gang programs, especially the current federal initiative that need to be resolved. The foremost is comparable to the credo that physicians use: above all, do no harm. That is, whatever is done, make sure the program does not in fact increase the gang problem or the drug problem or the violence problem. The fact that very rigorous outcome evaluation research is sorely lacking in the current federal initiative unfortunately does not allow us to rule out such a hypothesis. Where that "reverse intended effect" hypothesis needs to be tested first are in those controversial programs that are substantially more than gang outreach, they may be subsidies for the gang (e.g., giving beepers and cellular phones to active gang members and leaders hired by the program).

Thus, any program that hires gang members as the staff who are involved in the prevention/intervention service delivery should probably have an intense process evaluation as well. It is not just Chicago or Minneapolis who have some history about hiring gang members, recently Fort Worth took six gang leaders on the payroll to provide dispute mediation for schools and agencies in Forth Worth.[28] History shows, however, such accommodationist efforts are more likely to backfire than to have positive results.[29] Evaluators familiar with offender programs know some of the dangers here. And clearly, some specific guidelines are needed at the secondary and tertiary levels of prevention. While it is rarely used as a sanction, probation and parole guidelines for adults and juveniles often allow for revocation because of associating with a gang. In summation, to the extent that some government and private sources tend to reinforce the gang identity and its "public relations" function, allowing the gang to persist over time, allowing it to grow and expand and attract more youths, then to the same extent our intended policies and programs that seek to reduce the gang problem are actually designed for perpetuating the gang problem.

FIGURE 22

TYPICAL PROGRAM SERVICE COMPONENTS IN GANG PROGRAMS

Program Service Component	What it hopes to accomplish.
Referrals	Send the youth to a traditional service agency for specific type of assistance (e.g., health, addiction, housing, etc).
Individual counseling	Motivate youth to change beliefs and behavior.
Group counseling	Apply positive peer culture to facilitate individual change in beliefs and behavior.
Family counseling	Apply the social control of family members to facilitate individual change in beliefs and behavior.
Peer/adult mentoring	Through one-on-one volunteers or staff, match with youth to motivate or reinforce change in beliefs/behavior.
Educational Upgrading	Increase the academic skills of the youth. TECHNIQUES: tutoring, independent study, homework assistance, computer instruction, etc.
Cultural enrichment	Increase youth awareness of the larger social order to motivate respect for conformity. TECHNIQUES: visits to museums, higher culture events, outings, etc.
Job placement	Motivate youth to seek legitimate opportunities for achievement. TECHNIQUES: subsidized employment, guaranteed summer job, meaningful work experience, etc.
Court Liaison Advocacy	Seek leniency in juvenile court for clients in return for their program involvement.

Figure 22 cont.

Parenting skills	Increase the knowledge and skills to nurture children.
AIDS/HIV prevention	Increase the knowledge of health risk behavior and motivate youth to avoid such risks.
Rites of passage awareness	Increase the awareness of youth about human development, the increased responsibilities over the lifespan, and to celebrate their own manhood and womanhood development.
Adult supervised recreation	Drop-in centers, day camp, etc. AKA: Social Recreation. Many such examples: Health & Physical education.
Parent Empowerment	Motivate parents affected by gangs and drugs to take back control of their homes, children, and neighborhoods. (E.G., Operation Parent Sweep).

DISCUSSION QUESTIONS

(1) Would hiring active gang leaders to help administer a gang prevention program be similar to having the fox guard the hens? What guidelines should be used in hiring persons known to be previously involved as gang members if they are to be used in a gang prevention program? What ideal role should such ex-gang members have in a prevention program?

(2) Do you believe that an overall strategy is needed first before implementing programs at the secondary and tertiary levels? What should be the focus of such an overall national strategy?

(3) Should public funds for gang programs be allocated on the basis of the level of prevention impact and their probability of positive results? If you were in charge of the federal initiative what percentages of the overall program funding budget would you allocate for primary prevention, secondary prevention, and tertiary prevention?

FOOTNOTES

1. For an excellent factual history of the rise of Jeff Fort in his experience up to 1988, see: Tom Brune and James Ylisela, Jr., "The Making of Jeff Fort", Chicago, November, 1988.

2. Actually, it was a "Twin Cities" gang summit, scheduled for July 14-18, 1993 at the Mount Olivet Baptist Church in St. Paul, Minnesota. Louis Farrakhan who commands a speaking fee $25,000 (a rate quoted by a New York agency in 1991 for a speech fee to a Chicago university --- which could not afford the fee) is listed as one of the speakers at the gang summit entitled "All Nations Under God". The Vice Lords who are heavily involved in the Minneapolis gang summit swear allegiance to Islam in their gang constitution. The Twin Cities gang summit founders (e.g., of the United For and In Peace gang alliance) make no claims of being "ex-" gang members...they readily admit their gang membership. (See "Sharif Willis Shocked By Testimonies in A.C. Ford Trial", by Jae Bryson, Insight: The Journal for Business & The Arts, (20)(23): Monday, June 7, 1993, p. 1).

3. See: Mark Brunswick, 1992, "A Tale of Two Cities and the Gangs that Couldn't Stay Straight", Star Tribune, Metro Edition, Nov. 19, 1992.

4. Most recently Ribisl and Davidson (1993) also argue the need for such a theory at the base of any program; they also cite the work of Lipsey (1988). Well before this Daniel Glaser also showed that one of the biggest mistakes in program evaluation was not having a theoretical approach to work with.

5. One of the most interesting spinoffs of the American gang problem is the emergence of corporate consulting firms that specialize in "gang intervention" and training. The city of Joliet, Illinois hired Urban Dynamics, Incorporated for such consulting services to the Joliet Gang Task Force; but then terminated the contract by a vote of 7-1 from the City Council --- apparently because gang violence did not subside, and rather increased. (See, Jerry Shnay, 1993, "Joliet Cuts Ties With 3rd Firm Hired to Help Fight Gangs", Chicago Tribune (Southwest), section 2, p. 1, Aug. 5, 1993).

6. Founded by LueElla Edwards after her 15-year-old daughter was killed by stray gang gunfire at Chicago's Cabrini Green housing complex, the "Take Our Daughters To Work Club" works on identity and self-esteem issues for young females at a critical age when they may gravitate towards the gang or towards early motherhood. See K.T. Le, 1993, "After Child's Death, Mom Puts Grief to Good Work", Chicago Sun-Times, July 13, 1993, p. 17.

7. Located at 1329 W. Grand in Chicago. Mr. Brandisi passed away in the summer of 1993.

8. See "Cabrini Drummers Are Hard To Beat", Raymond R. Coffey, Chicago Sun-Times, Friday, June 25, 1993, p. 3.

9. See "Jim Brown Joins Anti-Gang Team", Chicago Sun-Times, July 21, 1993, p. 20. The Chicago Housing Authority agreed to pay Jim Brown, from the Amer-I-Can Foundation, $100 an hour plus expenses up to $25,000 for establishing a program for kids at risk.

10. In fact, David Dawley was also involved indirectly with this program and was quoted in the newspapers about the program. Dawley acts today as a consultant on gangs. Dawley was the one who helped the Vice Lords get federal and foundation funding in earlier Chicago gang history. Recall that Dawley claims to be the "only white member of the Vice Lords". See also: Mark Brunswick, 1992, "A Tale of Two Cities and the Gangs That Couldn't Stay Straight", Star Tribune, 1A, Nov. 19.

11. The program is privately, not government, funded and the director prefers it that way (private communication). Of course, like many of the government funded programs too, no evaluation research is ever reported on program success (e.g., number of sinners reached, number of souls converted, followup: commitment to a Christian lifestyle Lord one year later, etc).

12. Fred Williams, an ex-member of the Harlem Crips "who works at the Cross Colours Common Ground Foundation, which helps to rehabilitate gang members", was quoted as one L.A. source who felt the gang truce was for real and the gangs need to be congratulated ("Probers Hint Gangs Used L.A. Riots To Get Guns, But Not All Agree", Chicago Tribune, June 18, 1992: section 1A, p. 41.).

13. See: Ray Long, "Secret Service Plan Targets Cabrini-Green Gangs, Crime", Chicago Sun-Times, Oct. 4, 1993, p. 5.

14. See quote of gang unit police officer in Randy Furst, 1992, "Can Gang Members Turn the Tide Toward Peace?: Praise and Skepticism Follow Effort to Cut Violence, Create Opportunity", Star Tribune, August 31, 1992, p. 1A.

15. This reflects the tie between Chicago gang leader Willie Lloyd who has strong ties to Minneapolis, the leader of the Unknown Vice Lords. According to one report, "members of United for Peace acknowledge they have few answers to account for the increase in gang shootings, but say there is no war". See: Mark Brunswick, 1992, "As Deadly Vice Lords Feud Continues, Officials Point to Imprisoned Leader", Star Tribune, Metro Edition, p. 1A, Oct. 22, 1992.

16. Four persons were arrested in the home of Willis after the assassination of police officer Haaf. See: Mark Brunswick, 1992, "As Deadly Vice Lords Feud Continues, Officials Point to Imprisoned Gang Leader", Star Tribune, Metro Edition, Oct. 22, 1992.

17. See: Laura Baenen, 1992, "Officer's Slaying Ends Anti-Crime Alliance Between Police, Gangs", Associated Press, Oct. 1, 1992. (I am grateful for these and other Lexis-Nexis articles on the Minneapolis gang truce to Doug Longhini, Producer, Prime Time Live, ABC News.)

18. See: Patrick Howe, 1992, "Gang-crisis Success in Minneapolis Forum Indicates Otherwise", Star Tribune, Metro Edition, Oct. 8, 1992. However, the Police Chief for Minneapolis did write a letter of support and endorsement for The City, Inc in its initial application for federal funding (DHHS) which probably led enormous credibility to the proposal as the letter was included in an appendix. The present author made a Freedom of Information Act request to examine the full records of

this and other programs in 1993. Anthony V. Bouza, Chief of Police, on August 2, 1988 wrote the letter addressed to The City, Inc in which he said "I am pleased to be able to enthusiastically support your impressive At Risk Youth Services proposal...I am a tough law and order advocate and practitioner....Yes there are risks, and there will be failures, but you'll be hard-put to match the existing system's impressive capacity for disaster. We've go (sic) to understand that even a 90% success rate connotes ten failures".

19. See: Patricia Lopez Baden, 1992, "Councilman Cramer Says Backing Gang Coalition Was Naive: Mayoral Candidate Calls for End to Support for United for Peace", Star Tribune, Metro Edition, p. 1B, Nov. 24, 1992.

20. See: Kevin Diaz and Mark Brunswick, 1992, "No. 2 Man at United for Peace charged: Firearms, Drug Crimes Alleged", Star Tribune, Metro Edition, p. 1A, Nov. 21, 1992.

21. See Rogers Worthington, "Plan To Rehab Vice Lords Remake of 1970s Chicago: Gang Leader Claims to Bridge Both Worlds", (pp.1,4), Chicago Tribune, August 28, 1993.

22. See Jim Wallis, "Special Report on the Gang Summit", Sojourner, August, 1993, p. 12.

23. See: James Harney, "Gang Leaders Holding Peace Summit in K.C.", Chicago Sun-Times, April 30, 1993, p. 34.

24. Marion Stamps from Chicago was active in "The Sister's Statement". According to Jim Wallis the females were virtually ignored the first day of the conference (p. 15), 1993, August, Sojourner's, "Special Report on the Gang Summit".

25. Scott Fornek and Frank Burgos, "Peace Means No Guns, Farrakhan Tells Leaders", Chicago Sun-Times, October 25, 1993, p. 3.

26. The National Gang Crime Research Center did cover this event and have prepared a short instructional video suitable for law enforcement use and qualified criminal justice professionals. Instructors should contact the Center for use of this video in connection with a course using this book.

27. For a "kit" by the Mc Gruff people (National Crime Prevention Council), see their Tools to Involve Parents in Gang Prevention that came out in 1993, created in consultation with the Boys and Girls Clubs and the Police Executive Research Forum. NCPC, 1700 K Street, NW, 2nd Fl., Washington, DC 20006-3817.

28. The gang leaders were paid $204 a week, but without government benefits being temporary workers. See: "Town Battles Youth Gangs By Putting Them on Payroll", Daily Southtown, May 12, 1994, A13.

29. See: Raymond R. Coffey, "City Shouldn't Be Fooled By Gangs Again", <u>Chicago Sun-Times</u>, June 12, 1994, p. 5.

CHAPTER 26

GANG THEORY

INTRODUCTION

A theory of gangs must be a theory that distinguishes between simple "errant" behavior, perhaps even deviance, and that of actual criminal behavior by the gang as a group, or by the gang as an organization, or by the individual members of the gang. A useful theory of gangs must be able to logically account for the many variations in gang formations. To be comprehensive, a theory of gangs must explain how gangs "arise", why gangs behave the way they do, how gangs have developed, and what future scenarios may unfold with regard to gangs. Mostly, a good theory must be able to be put to use: particularly in suppressing the gang-crime/violence problem, and in preventing an escalation of the gang problem.

This is a tall order for a theory. And it does not stop there. To be useful to the social sciences it must be a theory that can be tested. That is, it must be capable of generating hypotheses that can be evaluated empirically in actual research.
In the language of social theory, it must be falsifiable. A theory that says Great Scott created the Heaven and Earth is not falsifiable: because we cannot interview Mr. or Ms. G. Scott. Such non-falsifiable theories are subject to great abuse. One need only recall the "theory" of deviance held during the early American colonial period, the so-called "witch trials". In that rendition of "the devil made me do it" theory, women whose worst crime may have been that of some suspicion of deviant conduct, were brought to trial and accused of basically "being possessed". How can you prove that you are not possessed?

There are many complex and peculiar aspects about gangs that beg for a theoretical explanation. Why, for example, would five teenage girls in San Antonio, Texas agree to have sex with an AIDS infected gang member as a part of their initiation ceremony into the gang[1]? Unfortunately, a full and complete theory is not provided here. What is provided is a classification system and a set of propositions that begin to account for a portion of the analytical problem.

GANG THEORY PARAMETERS

Gang theory is needed to explain a variety of aspects about the origin, function, and persistence of gangs and aspects of their form of social organization. Figure 23 summarizes the five most important and essential theoretical specifications. The acronym FESPO therefore symbolizes that an integrated and complete gang theory must address itself to Function, Etiology, Structure, Process, and Outcome issues.

Many research interests today have to do with the functions of gangs. Obviously, a myriad of such possible functions exist. Another way to conceive of this is in terms of the capabilities and effects of gangs. In short, what do they do? What are gangs responsible for? One of the most controversial such current research areas concerns whether gangs "migrate" (i.e., set up shop in another non-contiguous geographical area, in another city, state, etc). Another has to do with the type of crime specialization, for example illegal drug distribution. These are issues of the function of the gang. The myopic focus on function alone leads some analysts to conceive of gangs as "drug gangs", "violent gangs", "entrepreneurial/corporate gangs", etc in a potentially endless list of such over-simplistic labels. In reality, any given gang has a variety of functions.

As in most "social problems", a theory should be able to explain the etiology of gangs: that is, how do gangs arise? Etiology implies a causal nexus, a series of conditions or experiences that may show a common pattern in explaining why, how, and when gangs form. Etiology accounts for the rise and fall of gangs, over time.

Another most important theoretical issue has to do with what variation exists in gang structure. Our literature now recognizes that such differences in organizational structure and sophistication do in fact exist. It may seem like a simple issue to assume that all gangs are not equal, either in sheer membership size, or in terms of how these social organizations are managed. But some gang researchers still do not specify these most important variables with the net effect of making comparisons problematic: for example, someone who studies a "Spanky and Alfalfa" gang cannot generalize their findings to gangs like the Gangster Disciples. Gangs do vary in the nature of their type of social organizational structures. A gang theory must account for such variations.

The process by which gangs achieve their objectives occupies a large and interdisciplinary theoretical area. How gangs function as they do is also a process issue. The logical basis for such process concerns is that gangs are open systems. Some gangs are more restrictive than others (i.e., a Black person would not be expected to join the Aryan Brotherhood, just as a caucasian would not be expected to easily join the Black Guerilla Family, but they are still "open" for the right candidates). The idea of open-systems theoretical issues has to do with the fact that to be successful gangs must have members, and some members leave the system (killed, jailed, flipped, etc), thus new members are needed to perpetuate the gang as an entity. What happens to the individual gang member is a major concern of the process question about gang theory. This is also the issue of being socialized into the gang, its values, its way or life.

The outcomes of initiatives undertaken by gangs or against gangs are of substantial theoretical interest. Programs to abate or prevent the gang problem have as their justification such an assumption that "something can be done about the gang problem". The theoretical issue is how successful such initiatives are. The debate about "gang truces" and "gang peace summits" similarly hinge around outcome assessments. For both the gang and society the issue of outcome assessment is that of effectiveness (i.e., the question "what works?").

FIGURE 23

F.E.S.P.O: ISSUES TO BE EXPLAINED BY GANG THEORY

The Larger Theoretical Issues About Gangs	Specific Issues About Gangs That Can Be Empirically Investigated
Function	Why do some gangs migrate?
Etiology	How do gangs arise?
Structure	What variation exists in gang structure?
Process	Why do persons join gangs?
Outcome	What is effective in gang prevention or suppression?

Collectively these more generalized concerns about etiology, structure, function, process, and outcome regarding gangs, if they are integrated logically, provide the elements necessary for a genuine theory of gangs. This is not to deny that other major theoretical issues exist regarding gangs. There is no logical limit to such esoterica. But these five areas specified here provide the essence of what is needed to provide a beginning criminological explanation for the gang problem. Thus, a theory that deals with only one such global area is a mini-theory: it attempts to answer part of the overall puzzle. A full theory would have to address itself to all five of these theoretical concerns.

WHY DO WE NEED A VALID THEORY?

A theory helps us "make sense" of what may appear to be a complex situation. For example a detective, in order to solve a crime, seeks out a theory for a crime, and then systematically "tests hypotheses": ruling out suspects (rejecting null hypotheses). A theory helps to account for differences, variations, and what some may regard as contradictions in the social reality.

There is no single theory that has been professionally adopted, approved of as such, and therefore completely validated with regard to gangs. Not historically, and not today. Not in America, and not anywhere else. There exists no official "government version" of gangs that works. There exists no genuine comprehensive theory of gangs today. What we have in our gang literature are a number of fragmented perspectives on various facets of the gang problem.

There are, however, a number of what might be regarded as "single-factor" theories which look at specific aspects of the gang problem. Some of the good ones will be integrated into the framework generated in this chapter.

A major reason why we need to have a good theory about gangs is that --- as explained elsewhere in this book --- at some point we are responsible for "doing something about the problem". For example, to devise and implement an effective gang prevention program, a good theory will be needed or the results of the program in terms of actual impact on human behavior could be contrary to our good intentions.

Another major reason to have a good theory about gangs is that a valid theory can more effectively guide social policy. This is best illustrated in the negation. Let us assume someone wanted to adopt a biological theory of gangs which rooted its explanation of Los Angeles gang behavior in the work of Darwin:

> "Although humans are much more complex, ethological research often suggests important similarities between the behavior of humans and that of animals lower in the phylogenetic system of classification. Understanding Darwin also helps in understanding certain aspects of the gang's behavior, especially male dominance and deference rituals and the predatory victimization of 'the weak' on the streets" (Goldstein and Huff, 1993: p. 18).

Such a theoretical explanation viewing the gang member as the "wolf" of the community would naturally bring the policy recommendation to citizens to "act like lions": get bigger teeth, or a louder bark, perhaps some Wild West solution: arm everyone, let kids carry their rifles to school, check them in at the gate as in the gang movie The Class of 1999. That is preposterous!

There is no better source for preposterous social policies and actions to "do something about the problem" than are found in the profoundly untenable theories of the problem itself (e.g., Darwinian genetics). Darwin's theory was good for what it was intended to explain: physiological facts. It does not explain social facts like gangs in America. Even if you accepted the notion that Darwin's theory applied to social problems, you could not implement such a theoretically-based prescription in America: and you would be forced to recall when such a Master Plan was attempted --- during Nazi Germany when six million Jews were viewed by Hitler to be "lower in the genetic system" and were therefore killed in concentration camps!

WHAT IS A THEORY?

The good news is that across the social sciences, there is a good deal of agreement on what we mean by "theory". And, after all, the study of the gang problem is one isolated primarily in the social sciences because of its human behavior and social context. Thus, it is useful here to provide a brief "primer" on what a theory is.

A "grand theory" covers everything about a problem. In terms of the gang problem, there are so many aspects of the problem where we truly do not know enough to be able to knowledgeably generalize about, that a "grand theory" covering all aspects of the gang problem is historically premature at this point. The theory advanced here certainly lays no claim to such a grandiose level of generalization; rather it seeks to capture the most important contemporary and salient issues about the gang problem. The theory advanced here is therefore more of what might be called a "middle-range" theory.

A theory is basically an abstract set of generalizations about a given problem (e.g., gangs). It explains the causality, the etiology, or the functioning of a given problem

--- in this case, the gang and its behavior, its impact, its origin and persistence. Theories, typically because of the specialized nature of the training and disciplinary orientation (i.e., sociologists, psychologists, social workers, etc) of the theorists themselves, are often based solely on one social science discipline; and the remaining are bi-disciplinary theories (e.g., sociology and psychology = social psychology). Few theories are intentionally interdisciplinary theories, typically because few intellectuals are truly interdisciplinary in their training or their focus.   If there is one specialty field in the social sciences that is most specifically linked to the gang problem, it is not psychology, it is not general sociology; it is criminology. Criminology is a longstanding area of specialization within the field of sociology; and obviously many other disciplines have contributed to criminology as well.   There is no discipline called "criminal justice", as it is an applied, eclectic, operations concept.

ASSUMPTIONS BASED ON THE LITERATURE AND PRIOR RESEARCH

A number of assumptions from reviewing the literature and the prior research on gangs appear to be justified generalizations.

(1) The greater the fear a gang can induce in a community, the higher the tenure will be for that same gang in the same community.

This assumption has to do with the impact of the gang on the community of which it is a part. Programs that have sought to organize citizens, to galvanize them into action against the proliferation of gang crime and violence at the community and neighborhood level, often report that success in such organizing depends on the level of fear that the gangs have successfully engendered in the populace. The ideal point in time to organize, of course, is when the gang problem is not a monumental one. For when the gang problem has existed over a long period of time, what happens is the flight of law-abiding citizens --- at least those who have the economic means to leave. Obviously, many of the urban trapped are just as law-abiding, but they cannot lift up their roots and move out. Who gets left behind are those who may be least able to resist the continuing influence of the gang.

Anyone who has tried to organize a "Crime Watch" program knows of the problem where because of the intense fear that some residents have, when they are asked to help out in such a crime watch program they are the hardest to get any cooperation from. The reasons are usually clearly articulated: they fear reprisals from the gang members, they just don't want to "get involved". They become "free riders". At the point in any community where the gangs have existed for such a long period that the gang members and the "free riders" outnumber the law-abiding citizens, that community is going to have a very hard time recovering.

In testing this proposition it would be necessary to look at the power of the gang. The gang persists because of fear that is not confronted. Incidents such as that of the Dantrell Davis killing in the Cabrini Green housing complex sparked an enormous public hue and cry to confront the fear that the gang induces in the community. Thus, it is possible that at some point a critical reaction can set in as a response to such ever present fears about safety. In such situations, sudden increased police and other attention can reduce the level of the gang problem the same way that community policing can effectively reduce the problem via the crime displacement effect.

A logical hypothesis to be tested from this assumption is that gangs in "new hot spots" (i.e., rural areas, suburban areas, smaller cities, etc) will be easier to suppress than those in major urban areas where the social recognition afforded the gang is comparable only to that of a social institution itself --- a group or organization that persists over time, after the businesses leave, after the housing deteriorates, after the social class flight occurs (i.e., those who can afford to leave do in fact leave), and can be found on the same battlefield many years later.

(2) The greater the economic competition in illicit commodities and services as income sources for local gangs, the more violent the rivalry between such gangs.

Illegal drug profits are at the heart of some significant share of the gang violence in America today. Some gangs at the lower level of the organizational sophistication spectrum may certainly be less involved in drug trafficking, but for many of the larger and more organized gangs what to other gangs is viewed as "turf" is viewed instead as an illicit drug distribution market share or retail territory. Some areas within large cities may therefore be "contested areas" and subject to bitter competition including routine drive-by shootings. In other instances, market share takeover attempts are initiated at the neighborhood level; that is, a gang may intentionally initiate a series of violent attacks against a gang that competes for drug income in a contiguous area, the goal being to displace said gang and assume their share of the market. Such a common scenario is described in the Henry Horner public housing complex by Kotlowitz (1992).

A logical hypothesis to test from this assumption would be that economic parity between gangs would stabilize not just market share, but also the intensity of the conflict between opposition forces.

(3) The higher the sense of ethnic and racial provincialism in an area claimed as gang turf, the greater the likelihood of inter-ethnic and inter-racial gang conflicts; the higher the racial and ethnic tensions, the greater the ability of a gang to form and/or recruit members. There exists a wealth of anecdotal or qualitative evidence and much empirical data showing a strong relationship between "racial conflict" and various aspects of the gang problem. New immigrant youths are particularly subject to form their own gangs in response to gang threats from outside their own ethnic/racial group.   In the prison, jail, and juvenile correctional contexts --- similarly --- the importation of gangs that are homogeneous with respect to race and ethnicity via effective prosecution, often provides the impetus for inmates of other racial and ethnic groups to form their own such threat groups. In schools, a similar phenomenon appears: when racial tension increases, we can expect an increase in the intensity of violence between rival gangs. In riot and civil disturbance contexts, from the 1919 Chicago race riot to the 1992 riot in Los Angeles, gangs are predisposed to exploit such social tensions and it is in their best interest (materially and objectively) to have such tensions continue: because in the absence of legitimate authority, they often become the most powerful functional group being an armed group, experienced in the use of violence, and benefiting from the financial gains (looting) and the opportunistic political leverage (they are looked upon as a "force" to be reckoned with) such disorders provide. Certain recurrent patterns of "hate

crimes" that occur in the context of a group or organized effort also fit a similar pattern, where the law violating behavior of the offenders can be regarded in many instances as a functional gang.

(4) The higher the organizational capability of a gang, the higher its potential crime threat.

This assumption enjoys construct validity in the most obvious sense that the greater the resources and capabilities of any group or organization, the greater its potential threat, if it is an organization that finds itself at odds with wider society. Cults fit the same pattern. Terrorist groups fit the same pattern. A threat assessment for gangs, similarly, takes into account the objective and mobilizable resources at their disposal. In fact, there exists a multiplicative effect here when the gang organizational resources are assessed in relationship to its arsenal and mobilizable forces.

(5) The lower the organizational sophistication of a gang, the more likely it and its members are capable of being "redirected" into prosocial activities.

The issue here is commitment to the group or organization. Gang members frequently express the fear that they cannot simply quit the gang because their particular gang may be represented in one "faction" or another throughout the United States. Obviously, such a gang with a national penetration is able to instill higher fear among its members that "we can get you anywhere".

(6) The greater the communications network ability that an incarcerated gang leader has, the more likely it is that the same gang will continue unabated, essentially being managed in an absentee fashion from behind prison walls.

The leadership ability of a gang leader depends on communications. Unfortunately, today major gang leaders of very large gangs are still able to effectively administer their gangs remotely from behind bars. In Illinois, one major gang leader took out a full page ad in a Chicago newspaper describing how his gang was not about gangbanging and destruction, but was rather about "growth" and "development" for the community. Individuals involved in the Chicago gang truce were able to basically call the same imprisoned gang leader and quickly relay his orders to allied gangs on the streets. Such gang leaders could probably still carry out their administrative duties even if they did not enjoy the "prisoners rights" benefit of having daily access to a telephone. They could still maintain communications by interpersonal methods of visits and letters; or of using other inmates or corrupting criminal justice personnel to "smuggle out" such important messages and communiques.

(7) The higher the cooperation with agencies of social control (e.g., law enforcement), the more it can be assumed that an individual gang member has truly disavowed his/her gang identity.

The issue here is measuring when someone is truly an "ex" gang member. Those who are willing to testify against their former gang leaders must be recognized as having made a more fervent commitment to disavowing gang influence than someone who simply says in courtroom testimony "Oh, I was a gang member, but I am not involved in that kind of thing any more". It is a measurement of behavior actually. And, thus, judging someone by their deeds more than by their words.

(8)   The lower the value of human life communicated to individuals by their perception of the social structure of their orientation[2], the higher the individual propensity for gang violence.

Here we are dealing with a very basic issue of human rights and the treatment of our citizens. Obviously some very serious discrepancies exist in the ideal notion of the chances of every American having a "piece of the American pie" and their likelihood of having to eat the crumbs of the pie intergenerationally. This is an issue of human capital, the surplus population, and the whole concept of the "underclass" in America. With such diminished objective and material chances of having a "good life" in America comes the many concomitant values of living in poverty and experiencing persisting conditions of economic deprivation.

Unfortunately, with the intensity of violence associated with such same conditions comes the message communicated from the larger social structure that: "human life is not precious....it is cheap". The messages we send our citizens who live at or below the poverty level are not messages that communicate the importance of human life. For a democracy to survive, this must change.

THE SOCIAL SPACE CONCEPT: EXPLAINING GANG EMULATION/REPRODUCTION

How do gangs form and originate? Is it possible that in the exposure to deviance during early and formative socialization that the social trajectory becomes, for many whose integration into deviant sectors develops over time in excess of their integration into legitimate sectors of society, a criminal career trajectory as well? This is the notion of the social production of gangs.

Gang suppression taken to its logical extreme means giving no harbor to gang values which perpetuate gang organizations and sustain the gang membership base. It can be seen that law enforcement alone is totally incapable of such complete suppression; police officers can enforce laws, but not values, not mores, not norms, not even folkways. Police can use their powers only to enforce laws, statutes passed by legislative bodies at various levels of government.

Gangs use all forms of power to perpetuate their values and the continuity of their social formation. Coercive power, the threat or actual use of force and violence, is at the base of gang values. Coercive power is used to generate income or resources for use by the gang leadership; and it is also used to sustain membership compliance. Once a gang has income or resources it has rewardive power: the power to pay, the power to buy, the power to impress; it confers titles, and status, rank and recognition to its members. With either coercive power or rewardive power a gang in the youth or deviant subcultures exerts social power: they are a force to be reckoned with, they have a "reputation", on the street corners they "run it", they gain prestige and come to be recognized as a "power", and deference patterns emerge. Ultimately, if the gang is able to acquire property or a business, or gain use or control of an established exploitable social-economic resource (e.g., a program site, a housing complex, etc), or simply gain tolerance by authority, it may gain legitimate power as well: the power to represent through public relations that they are not a "gang" per se, but rather are a civic organization, a religious group, a political group, etc.

GANG ADAPTATION TO THE SUPER STRUCTURE

The term "social structure" is inadequate to encompass the totality of all forms of power and social organization. The term super structure is used instead to encompass the historical and existing forms of power and social organization in any society. It therefore includes political parties, economic organizations, government agencies, organized subcultures, religious institutions --- in short, the aggregate of previous and existing forms of social organization. The universal phenomenon at work in explaining the emergence, the function, and the continuity/growth of gangs is that gangs adapt predictably to the types of organizational structures that exist in their society to which they have been exposed in their socialization.

In many respects criminal gangs emerge and develop as an infrastructure that is functional for the superstructure of any society. This does not mean, as some have misinterpreted Durkheim in terms of crime being functional for society, that "gangs are good for society". The functions of gangs certainly deserve more hard analysis, but certainly include a variety of effects and perceptions at all levels of the super structure. Some critics of federal law enforcement, for example, point to gangs as serving a "bogeyman" function that justifies their continued existence and expansion. Some community residents look upon their local turf oriented gangs as serving a kind of "junkyard dog" function[3]: they bark a lot when rival outside gang members come into the neighborhood, and in this sense provide a kind of local order enforcement function[4]. In the underground economy, gangs serve a most important function by processing large amounts of capital, little of which income is actually taxed.

Gangs therefore serve both latent and manifest functions. Gangs involved in illegal drug production and/or distribution in cities where tourism is a large part of the local economy are never going to be "eliminated", because like the prostitution trade this vice may be desired by the tourists themselves, thus the gang provides a latent function that is supportive of the tourist economy. Gangs that help politicians --- in providing protection, in carrying out "dirty tricks" in heated electoral campaigns, etc, provide a manifest function that both the gang members and the politicians recognize as valuable and deserving of the norm of reciprocity (i.e., the gang will want and get something in exchange for such services rendered).

Understanding how gangs adapt to the superstructure helps to explain some peculiarities and differences between gangs. Certain Asian gangs, for example the Vietnamese, engage in continuing patterns of crime that reflect a unique modus operandi: they case out the local Asian community they have travelled to from perhaps another city they may use as their home base, they gather intelligence and profile a target - typically a small businessman doing well - they then carry out a home invasion that may involve the use of torture and extreme violence to force the victim to reveal and turn over their "stash" of liquid assets (gold, cash, etc) knowing that such persons may have been themselves adapting to the superstructure by not trusting banks to hold their life earnings. The socialization pattern, then, impacts on gang organization and function. Youths who grew up around military violence and who at an early age were desensitized to the use of violence such as occurs in combat zones, are therefore predisposed toward similar solutions to their life problems. The continuity in the intensity of violence reflects not just socialization, but the organizational adaptation to the superstructure.

An understanding of how gangs adapt to the superstructure helps to predict the direction of future conflicts and developments. In a third world society that has a history of warlords and gunmen and rival tribes, the dimensions of the cleavage in terms of what the conflicts are really all about will constitute comparable structures that gangs can emerge as. In the United States, shortly after World War I the largest gang in terms of its membership was the Ku Klux Klan. In the period 1921-1922 there were literally several million KKK members in the USA[5]. The KKK was not the first hate group of its type in America; many others preceded it. The KKK peaked in its membership at a time of strained race relations. The Chicago riot of 1919 was one such example of how strained the relationship between whites and Black Americans was. The crime severity level of the KKK was no small issue: as many "lynchings" occurred during the first forty years of the 20th century as did legal executions in the subsequent forty year period! There was no Civil Rights Division of the United States Attorney's office in the heyday of the KKK: they got away with literally thousands of killings, and made lots of money from dues of KKK members. Like contemporary gangs, the KKK in the 1920s had its assortment of gang totems, symbols, clothing, and artifacts that were commercially produced for use by members[6].

Gangs therefore emerge, continue, and expand in the cracks and crevices of societal conflict. As some of the most intensive dimensions of such social conflict in America have centered around racial enmity and racial discrimination (e.g., racism, individual and institutional forms), some of the most predictable rises in gang patterns have followed similar superstructural forms. The intractable nature of racism in America is reflected in the proliferation of groups like the Aryan Brotherhood and skinheads. As much writing as the topic of race relations in America has generated, even in the academic circles on gang issues there appear to be some ongoing taboos. One of these taboos is equating the intensity of the accumulated experience of racial discrimination felt by African-Americans as a kind of American "caste" or "untouchable" social class --- and it has many academic names, the urban underclass, the permanent underclass, the dangerous underclass, the surplus population, etc[7], all of which mean pretty much the same thing: the systematic pattern of certain minority groups being held in a state of institutionalized poverty over several generations. As in legal issues regarding civil damages, it is not a matter of whether it is intentional or unintentional, in social policy as in civil law if the damage was done then compensation is owed. It is perhaps this aspect of the underclass concept that has the most dramatic implications for social policy[8]. The fact is, however, these are very legitimate issues and continue to be tied to unresolved conflicts in the American superstructure. Farthinking and truly patriotic American citizens who take serious their pledge to democracy will recognize that this issue cannot be put off very much longer. The strength of America is its racial and cultural diversity. Some small minded persons[9] would have us believe that such heterogeneity is a weakness, their preferred social policy does not include equity, they prefer the status quo.   In short, an understanding of the history and contemporary forms of social organization in a given society helps to identify the pattern that gangs may seek to fill. Thus, it is possible to induce such conflict experimentally given sufficient knowledge of a given society using gangs as surrogate forces to disrupt a target society[10].

A GANG CLASSIFICATION SYSTEM

That gangs can vary in terms of the sophistication of their organization should now be widely known. A primary fact seems to be that "gangs" in our gang literature have varied in terms of their organizational development and sophistication.[11] The classification system advanced here is used to examine some of the many dimensions along which gangs vary.

Recall that a gang is a gang if and only if it engages in law violation behavior, either individually or collectively, and that deviance itself is not grounds for classifying a group as a gang. There is an enormous variety of deviance and deviant behaviors in any society, but many of these deviant behaviors are just that: they violate norms, customs, even mores, but they do not break the law. In America our law enforcement community has no right to investigate a group just because it is deviant. If it goes beyond deviance and into the realm of crime, then we are in a different situation and one where investigation is warranted.[12] To believe otherwise is to be analytically in the situation of believing that if even a civil rights group that seeks a reduction in racism or seeks greater equality, in a situation where minority status and a change-oriented purpose implies deviance, therefore justifies law enforcement initiatives (spying, etc) such as Nixon's COINTELPRO operation. We cannot legally spy on, infiltrate, and monitor groups just because their beliefs are different than ours.[13] We cannot maintain "street files" just because a group is regarded as different or deviant from the mainstream of society.

What we need most in gang analysis is a classification system devoid of such bias. The one offered here is a step in that direction.

Figure 24 suggests from a social organizational perspective that gangs can be classified in terms of their level of formality, development, and sophistication.[14] Level "zero" is not a gang at all.[15] It could be become a gang. This encompasses much of "street-corner society" and loose knit groups with little such actual ongoing criminal code violation. It also includes much of Puffer's assumed tendency for all young males to "form groups".[16] Level "zero", therefore, is pre-gang or what some have called social gangs. It is comparable, certainly, to the so-called middle-class "gang" described by Meyerhoff and Meyerhoff (1964)[17], or that of Greeley and Casey (1963). It commits little, if any, real crime. It is a "Spanky and Alfalfa" kind of group (level zero) that can be assumed to be easy to study using field research, because they have little to hide, they are not involved in "drive-by" shootings.

Level "one" represents an emerging gang formation; it differs from the "pre-gang" level zero by having made a transition from an informal group to an informal organization. Horowitz (1982) description of the Lions gang in Chicago's lower west side seems to fit this description.[18] It functions as a primary group, with small size, no large arsenal, it does become recognized at early levels of "labelling" as a gang and regards itself as a unique entity. But they are typically "squatters", they do not rent or own their own "gang headquarters". They do represent a crime problem, but it is not the highest level threat in terms of crime and violence.[19] Often this kind of gang has a horizontal structure, such as the MOVE group in Philadelphia[20]. A typical burglary ring operates in much the same fashion as a level one gang.[21]

Level "two" represents a crystallized gang; one that functions as slightly more than a primary group. It has a stronger level of group commitment, it is also a reference group. Most importantly it represents two or more independent units of gang operation. It becomes a formal group because of the differentiation of roles and status positions within the gang members and it has a clear hierarchy. It may also function in two or more jurisdictions.

Level "three" represents the highest level of gang formation, aside from organized international crime cartels, and takes on the characteristics of a formal organization.[22] It is the formalized gang.[23] It typically owns its own real estate and therefore does not have to "meet on the street corner" or in a "shack". It is the highest level of threat for crime and violence as well. The threat comes from its larger size, its multi-jurisdictional boundaries, its age integration, pooled resources and higher levels of group commitment. When a gang author from the past talks about how it is "easy" to quit the gang, they were not talking about some of the gangs that exist today or, for that matter, that have truly existed throughout history.[24] In gangs like the Aryan Brotherhood (whites), El Rukns (Blacks), and Eme (Hispanics), one cannot simply say "I quit". Rather, membership becomes irreversible.[25] This kind of gang always has a vertical structure, reflecting different layers of authority inside the organization.

The need for such a system of classification is still great. At a minimum we must recognize there is certainly both a qualitative difference between a gang where one's parents are gang members[26], where the moment one was out of the hospital from child birth, one was "tattooed" with a gang sign.[27] Being born into the gang. And reinforcing gang identity through successive generations, such as in the famous early robber gangs of India. This IS going on in America.[28]

To take the position that gangs are not "Wall Street, Robert's Rules of Order, rational/calculating/goal achieving" organizations may be popular in some of our gang literature, but only as a political contrast to the portrayed assumptions from a law enforcement point of view or from "horror stories" created by the mass media. The careful reader will note that the previous discussions have not quoted much from "newspaper accounts". But they should not be denounced as a source of information. The true social scientific point of view should be open to all sources of information. Even though, obviously, in the university context some professors may encourage students to "steer clear" of journalistic impressionism, and encourage students rather to seek out "the best evidence", which is typically from our social science sources.

The classification system suggested in Figure 24 generalizes beyond the specific case of any one particular gang. Yet most gangs must necessarily follow a developmental sequence and have a particular level of maturation and function that will allow them to fall into one or the other of these categories. The advantage of this social organizational approach is that it allows for the conceptual continuity with prior gang authors, including everything from the work of Puffer to Thrasher (1927) to the present day. And perhaps the future. It allows for the integration of much prior knowledge about gangs. It looks at the gang as a unit of social organization rather than focusing solely on the social-psychological state of the individual gang member.

Most of Puffer's (1912), Furfey's (1926), and Thrasher's (1927) gangs were therefore, in all probability, level zero and level one gang formations. Level three corresponds to much of what is regarded as the "super gang" structure: Chicago's Disciples, Latin Kings, El Rukns, Vice Lords.[29] It is also possible for any specific gang to calculate its "severity of history or potential" ratings.   By having this "severity of risk" assessment it is therefore possible to classify gangs by the scope and extent of the crime and violence problem they pose to society.   Briefly, this corresponds to a typology of both organizational capability and level of threat as seen in Figure 24 below.

FIGURE 24

A Gang Classification Typology By Organizational Capability and Level of Crime Threat

```
Level of
Organizational                    Level of Crime/Violence Threat
Development:                  Low            Medium           High
                              0  1  2  3  4  5  6  7  8    9
                              ********************************
Informal Group                *                              *
(level 0)                     *                              *
                              ********************************
Informal Organization         *                              *
(Level 1)                     *                              *
                              ********************************
Formal Group                  *                              *
(Level 2)                     *                              *
                              ********************************
Formal Organization           *                              *
(Level 3)                     *                              *
                              ********************************
```

Obviously, much remains to be done to establish the rules of correspondence and the objective methods of comparative assessment prior to assigning such a "level of threat" rating for any particular gang.   This must be left to a later analysis.   For now it is sufficient simply alert the reader to this potential practical usage.   Figure 25 suggests some of these features that might be included in helping to distinguish between various gangs by the nature of their organizational development features in terms of the typology advanced here.

Figure 25 helps to quickly distinguish between a non-gang (level zero) group and the three types of criminal gangs.   To apply a complete threat analysis system to any specific jurisdiction, however, would require looking at all of the classification variables.   Figure 25 simply covers a few of the larger number of such classification variables that can be used.   No effort is made here to apply this application to all gangs known America for the obvious reason that such data is not available for analysis here.

FIGURE 25

Level of Organizational Development in Gangs

INCIPIENT ——> higher formality, sophistication ——> COMPLEX

Level 0	Level 1	Level 2	Level 3
PRE-GANG	EMERGENT GANG	CRYSTALLIZED GANG	FORMALIZED GANG
GROUP FUNCTION			
Playgroup and recreation; a malleable near-group; the gang functions as an amorphous, at times solidary secondary group	A primary group emerging as a membership group; has a developing oral code or tradition.	Gang functions as a pseudo-family; usually with some adult participation. May not know all other members.	Gang functions as a total control institution; the level of group commitment is in many respects irreversible.
GROUP SIZE			
Very small size. (local only)	Size is "pack".	Multiple Groups.	Large Size. (interstate)
WEAPONS USE			
Fists, Clubs, Rocks, etc.	Knifes, and improvised weapons.	Stolen small arms; typically handguns, used.	Military arms, shoulder and fully automatic weapons.
CRIMINAL JUSTICE IMPACT			
Not yet labelled as a gang; and virtually unknown as an entity.	Recognized as a gang or group by police or their community.	Various social institutions and the mass media label as a gang threat.	Members are often found in the correctional system and on probation/parole.
MEETING RESOURCES			
Typically can meet only as a group on a public place or a street corner.	Typically meets as a group as gang site "squatters", or in host site.	Group may have pooled its resources to rent a gang meet site.	The gang or a member may own the real estate property for meetings.
LEADERSHIP FORMS			
Leadership is unstable. (Shifting)	Leadership is developing or controlled. (Charismatic)	Leadership is tiered and shared to some degree. (Authoritarian)	Leadership is highly stable; usually an older experienced adult (Royalty)
CODE OF CONDUCT			
Norms are those of situational loyalty.	Norms develop by an oral tradition.	Norms usually enforced by disciplinarian.	May have a written constitution and by-laws.
INCOME SOURCES			
Personal only.	Limited.	Specialized.	Diversified.
CRIME INVOLVEMENT			
None.	Passive.	Proactive.	Organized.

Figure 25 cont.

		LEADERSHIP INSULATION	
Does not apply.	Leader is usually visible.	Leaders are somewhat shielded.	Leaders are very insulated. Buffered.

		INTERNAL ORGANIZATION	
Ad hoc, no role structure. Loose knit.	Usually a two-level hierarchy: leader and followers.	Usually has multiple levels including a mid-management structure.	Very centralized hierarchy which may extend across jurisdictions.

		MEMBERSHIP COMMITMENT	
Adjustable	Low (can still "quit" the gang easily)	Medium	High (cannot simply say "I QUIT" the gang)

SUMMARY

On closer examination some of the mysteries of gangs and the theoretical issues that gang life may pose are not as complex as they may originally appear. Some of what may appear to be "random" and "senseless" and "irrational" violence, may not be as lacking in motive and purpose as it may appear to be by the many stray bullets that hit and kill innocent non-gang member victims throughout the United States. Some of the ways that gangs continue to be able to operate even after their leaders have been imprisoned may not be any more complex than the theatrics of the Wizard of Oz who is finally revealed to be using little more than common technology to embellish his "presence".

No grandiose theory of gangs has been advanced here. Rather some of the common problems of gangs have been addressed and some of the best common sense has been applied to these gang problems. Throughout this book there is substantial evidence that something can and should be done about the gang problem in America. However, there is equally great evidence that we should approach this problem informed by the best evidence on the problem itself. That means having some conception of the origin and persistence of gangs as groups and as organizations.

The only caveat here is that the gang problem is so dramatically avoided as a priority in federally funded national policy making that the problem is most likely to expand and increase in its severity in the near future. Thus, the gang problem is a dynamic one: it changes everyday. And literally a number of very frightening future scenarios are possible given the absence of any such coordinated and sensible national policy on the gang problem. Thus, the observations made here are relevant for the time frame of the present only; if the gang problem increases, then we are in a different and more severe stage of the gang crime problem and the present analysis would have to be substantially revised.

DISCUSSION   QUESTIONS

(1)   What do you believe are the three primary and least disputed causal factors in explaining the existence and/or persistence of gangs?

(2)   What do you believe are the three primary and most important factors about a community that may make it vulnerable to the onset and persistence of gangs?

(3)   What do you believe are the three most important changes our society must make to address the gang problem today?

FOOTNOTES

1. This story was given national coverage; for a summary see Law Enforcement News, a publication of John Jay College of Criminal Justice/CUNY, April 30, 1993: p. 3.

2. I am grateful to James Sutton for this concept that is rooted in a socialization explanation for gang violence. The idea helps to explain how some Asian gangs (e.g., Vietnamese, Cambodian, etc), may be more prone to vicious torture in the kind of violence they use as a gang. The notion is that if someone grew up in a country that was "war torn", where death by violence was an everyday event; that one becomes "de-sensitized" to such violence. One comes to accept, as legitimate options, similarly high levels of violence to achieve goals related to seeking income, power, etc.

3. This is why, for example, many citizens who live around gangs have mixed feelings about gang members. They do not necessarily approve of their crimes and drug pushing for example, but on occasions do see the gang as a kind of local militia. Gangs make their most favorable impressions on local citizens when rival gangs establish gang truces and suddenly the shooting and open violence ends abruptly --- for a time at least --- in what was formerly a hot war zone (e.g., Cabrini Green in Chicago).

4. This sense of ambivalence in the attitudes towards gangs and gang members are the neighborhood level --- combined with genuine fear of retribution and retaliation --- also accounts for why many citizens are less than cooperative about helping law enforcement to prosecute and suppress gang members. They might call anonymously to a police 911 number if the gang members get really excessive, but they will not sign a complaint.

5. See Max Madden, 1993, "Hate Groups in America: Part I - White Supremacists", P.B.S.P.

6. See Max Madden, op cit, p. 16. Madden (1993: p. 16) notes how the Gate City Manufacturing Company in Atlanta, Georgia sold a large variety of KKK items from the KKK mail order catalog including "a variety of robes, hoods, horse robes, carrying cases, pocket knives, and miscellaneous Klan related trinkets".

7. Cummings and Monti (1993: p. 307) assert that "Despite its popularity, however, many social scientists are not enthused about the policy applications of underclass theory, and question its theoretical utility in the study of gangs". There is nothing wrong with the theory, what some may find objectionable is actually changing such a continuing pattern of social injustice. Such change would require major changes in the superstructure, particularly economic resources. Read "policy applications" (i.e., social policy) in Cummings and Monti (1993) as "American politics".

8. The existence of the underclass is an ever present reality. The existence of the underclass is therefore not a "theory". What is theoretical about the underclass is how this situation came to be as it is. Members of the underclass are not theoretical entities, they exist in large numbers.

9. Bigots and those who score high on dogmatism never get the "big picture"; they read books like the present one, and as soon as they see a chapter on the underclass or see "racism" presented as a legitimate issue involved in the gang problem, immediately label the author as a "gang apologist". They suffer from a factual deficit disorder in as much as they learn only what they are predisposed ideologically to want to learn.

10. There has been some discussion about the possible role of the Central Intelligence Agency, for example, in fomenting conflict in Haiti using this type of controlled low-intensity conflict strategy. This is not to imply that the USA has been the only nation state to be involved in this type of gang social engineering.

11. Jansyn (1966: p. 600) showed well before the appearance of "super gangs" that some gangs "have a relatively high degree of organization". Jansyn distinguished between "core" and "fringe" gang members.

12. A gang is what a gang does. A gang is supportive of some forms of individual deviance (see Moore and Vigil, 1987). But deviance alone does not make a gang. Crime is the behavior or function that matters here. Still examples exist in our literature of "playful deviant" groups being analyzed as gangs (Sato, 1982) and it is not unusual that some of these reports therefore conclude "gangs lack formal organization" (see Lowney, 1984), because obviously these are probably level zero (pre-gang) formations.

13. The Chicago Police Department's gang crimes unit, for example, is itself limited in what intelligence gathering techniques its can use because the Chicago Police Department has entered into a consent decree with the Alliance to End Repression and the American Civil Liberties Union. Here gang organizations benefit from protection of their First Amendment rights in an outgrowth of challenges to police spying that involved "red squads", that is surveillance of left groups (see Nash, 1984: p. 75).

14. Your author simply believes that other contributors to the gang literature, while having good intentions, when they for whatever reason deny that "organizational sophistication" (see Best and Luckenbill, 1982: 25), they are taking the posture of a static rather than a dynamic analysis. And perhaps even an element of close-

mindedness or dogmatism. Clearly, there exists much variation in organizational sophistication and in group capability functions.

15. Arnold (1965: p. 67) takes essentially the same position regarding youth social clubs; they may have names, they may be integrated, but if they do not engage in conflict (typically with the police), then according to Arnold they are not gangs, per se. Here I would reserve level zero to encompass deviance, but no crime or delinquency.

16. Perhaps as easy as some gang authors assert (who espouse a non-structured, non-organizationally sophisticated view of gangs only based on their own local data) "like forming a pick-up basketball game", they meet randomly, they start, and they are off and running as a functional gang. Or as Rahm and Weber (1958) said it is a very casual process (see Rahm and Weber, 1958, Office in the Alley). The truth is, joining a gang can be informal and it can be formal. It simply depends on what type of gang we are talking about. For lower level gang formations (level zero and level one) it probably is informal or casual; but initiation rites can also be very formal and can even include the prerequisite of carrying out a homicide among higher level gang formations. "Drafting", or coercive varieties of "compelling membership in a gang organization" does occur (Salisbury, 1958) and is today routine in our nation's correctional institutions.

17. As indicated by Meyerhoff and Meyerhoff (1964) this "gang" was not exactly a professional crime group, it simply engaged in deviance. Indeed, its most serious "gang" offense history involved status offenses such as curfew violations, underage drinking, drag racing, and "much sexual activity". On this basis, such an analysis could be readily extended throughout the American middle class today to include, obviously, a large number of middle-class adult such "gangs". These are not true gangs in the classification system proposed here.

18. Horowitz was unique in gang research traditions by returning to the study area and in this way obtaining "time series" data on the gang's status. The last time observation, however, was 1977. It would be interesting to know if this gang called the Lions was swallowed up by the Latin Kings or the Two-Sixers.

19. This would include many of the so-called "Fagin" varieties of gangs which are very active in crime and do have a substantial local impact (burglaries, car thefts, etc) and perhaps even many of the local "skinhead" groups who venture out on criminal escapades only on an occasional basis (e.g., weekend gang members).

20. Before the MOVE group became a crime problem (very similar to the Waco, Texas group led by David Korash, MOVE stockpiled weapons), it was a "disruptive group" problem in the prison system of Pennsylvania. In Africa v. Commonwealth of Pennsylvania (662 F.2d 1025, 1981), Frank Africa the "leader", a minister who took on the title "coordinator", described MOVE as a revolutionary organization where the organization was described as a "family" that has "only one member, one family, one body". Regardless of stated gibberish by the MOVE group, it DID have a leader in its founder Frank Africa.

21. A group called the "Yugo" gang, got their name from police, they were simply all members of a well organized burglary ring that also specialized in opening safes. See "Tempo Update", <u>Chicago Tribune</u>, April 3, 1994, Tempo Section, p. 1.

22. This formalization process is supported by the key observations within correctional facilities with major gang problems. An Illinois Correctional Training Academy document (1985, July) states "gangs are becoming more and more sophisticated, often moving toward a political power base. As was mentioned above, a number of larger gangs have applied and obtained charters, most for non-profit organization. By claiming to be religious organizations, voters leagues, etc., they are obtaining federal grands and influencing the political arena by getting out the vote" (p. 12).

23. And highly structured, organizationally. It does not have to function as effectively as a military machine; please recall many of our own highly complex governmental organizations, as bureaucracies, do not necessarily function as effectively as we would like. Recall, too, Bernstein (1964) took the view that these "large highly structured" gangs had essentially faded away, but not altogether and are more common to the urban underclass.

24. The national survey by Camp and Camp (1985) indicated that two-thirds of the gangs in our nation's prison system regard gang membership as a lifetime commitment. This is most certainly the case for all members of the Aryan Brotherhood; for as an Illinois Corrections Training Academy document expressed this "there is no known constitution for the Aryan Brotherhood. It has been learned through experience that it is for life. If you try to voluntarily drop out, they will kill you...The Aryan Brotherhood opted for the terms "hooked up" or "connected" in place of the term "member". They do not use the word "member" in order to avoid future conspiracy charges that may arise (<u>Gang Activity</u>, Illinois Dept. of Corrections Training Academy, July, 1985: p. 12)".

25. In the Latin Kings for example we will find "the first and most Law of the Almighty Latin King Nation is "Once a King, always a King", unless he is expelled from the Nation for violation of its Laws". Here presumably "expelled" is equivalent to termination with prejudice. As will be seen from the three stage "theory" in their constitution, as well, this gang leader/writer was apparently aware of the maturation hypothesis (see Tice, 1967, p. 48).

26. Moore and Devitt (1989) describe the context where females who were gang members during their adolescence go into adulthood to be mothers, but with a high rate of heroin addiction, and drug use during pregnancy.

27. Lane (1989) states similarly "sadly, gang allegiance is often passed from one generation to another. Entire families become gang members in some cases" (p. 99).

28. In dramatic terms, a photograph seized via search warrant of the Spanish Cobras shows a young child holding an automatic pistol, it is entitled "indoctrination of gang being a 'family affair'" (see Nash, 1984: p. 56).

29. A new phrase for the "supergang" is the "corporate gang" which is contrasted with the less developed scavenger gang (see Taylor, 1988). The corporate gang being, I believe, equivalent to a level three gang; and the scavenger gang a less developed organizational pattern, typical of the level one gang.

CHAPTER 27

GANGS AND THE FUTURE: Towards Theoretical
Integration and Policy Options for
Reducing the Gang Problem.

INTRODUCTION

This book has reviewed a large number of concepts and ideas from a variety of authors who have contributed to the gang literature. Gangs have been examined historically, in terms of their organizational development patterns, in terms of their "threat" to the public, in terms of "what can be done" from the family, education, the community, law enforcement, correctional institution, and prevention perspectives. Now we must face the harsh reality of ill-informed and misguided efforts, segmented and partisan-politically shaped, disjointed and often having reverse-intended effects as we examine the hope of the future.

The author's hope is that the gang problem, like any social problem, is one about which something can and should be done. The question is always: at what cost, and who is going to pay for it? It can currently cost $50 to $100 thousand per youth to incarcerate that youth for a year in a juvenile detention facility. As Americans we are already spending large amounts of public monies to administer public facilities that have no track record of effectiveness whatsoever! All Americans know that the poor exist, but rich and wealthy Americans and the corporations owned by Americans and by foreigners are not all willing enough to extend assistance to help the American poor to "pull themselves up by the bootstraps". It is also a fundamental question of racial justice; another issue that many Americans simply pray that it will "go away". It will not go away. And like any primordial matter in the psyche of the collective thinking of Americans today, it is the most healthy response to finally face this issue and make some genuine changes.

And what of the future of America and other countries in our ever-increasing sense of living in a "world community"? Will effective American gangs become transnational gangs?[1] In what sense do gangs represent a threat to freedom itself? Will some larger more organized gangs develop such effective "public relations" images as do-gooders that they can run their own candidates in local elections? These are but some of the issues that remain on the agenda described as "gangs and the future".

WHAT NOT TO DO

What has always amazed this author is that so much of our gang literature seems to be so radically estranged from our social sciences dealing with the core related problem of what we know about social groups, patterns of group affiliation, and organization development. If there can be no other single contribution to our gang literature that will have a generally positive historical impact, then it is in knowing "what not to do" in terms of gang intervention/interdiction/prosecution/etc policy. As mentioned early in this book the problem of gang studies is really one of finding solutions.

Something as admittedly complex as gang formations and being as rampant throughout our society as gangs are, is not likely to have any easy quick-fix solution. We have previously addressed the policy recommendation of Moore (1978) regarding the legalization of heroin for gang dismemberment via choked drug income. Not everyone is fully convinced of such a positive "gang fading" scenario from hard drug legalization. And there is the "slippery slope" ethical problem here as well: by providing legal heroin, do we simply find a more oppressive method of containing and controlling the surplus population? And after such a systematic devaluation of human potential itself, is there any return from this moral decline? How much moral difference is there between America in the 21st Century having a huge population of official addicts and Nazi Germany's en masse extirpation policies or the Nazi T-4 program? It seems only a difference between de facto and de jure racism, when those who may be expected to gravitate towards this "life option" are predominantly from the ranks of minority groups.

What not to do is to repeat some of the mistakes of the past. A primary consideration should be not to facilitate further organizational development, wittingly or unwittingly, through public and private sector initiatives. Inducing an organizational succession in goals in a gang, getting it to lay down its arms and give up lucrative areas of income-producing crime (e.g., narcotics trafficking), is not realistic. Making it hard for such organizations to function and preventing further new recruits is at least one way to organizationally choke some American gangs. Unfortunately, in some public and privately funded initiatives under the banner of being "anti-gang" have actually encouraged youths to join the gang by giving the gang leaders status, power, and resources --- the examples of this are legion, and stretch from New York to California, from Minnesota to Texas; and these lessons from gang history stretch back far in time, and include contemporary examples as well.

"If you can't beat em, join em" in the sense of vigilantism is another non-option. Organized vigilante groups would give gangs what they thrive on: conflict[2]. A gang or "street organization" as some may prefer to be called is weakened only by the loss of useful resources. Thus providing any exploitable resources to gangs, under whatever well-intended pretext, may very well exacerbate the very same problem --- a problem that truly does require intervention services, and prevention services, and public funding. But not necessarily in the tradition of trying to "coopt" gang leaders. Such intervention programs should be strictly monitored and evaluated in both process and outcome, much in the manner shown by the Agopian (1991) research on such a program in the Los Angeles probation department, and Spergel's (1990) evaluation of a Chicago program.

It is an issue of accountability. Recall from Taylor (1990), the "quisling effect". And some of the early warnings about the advisability of using former gang leaders to convince non-gang aligned youths not to join a gang, not dissimilar from the issues about using well dressed articulate ex-heroin addicts lecturing children on the evils of drug or substance abuse. What message really gets communicated: don't do drugs, or you can in fact do them, get addicted to them, but still be prosperous, well-dressed, and get a job with the government? Some examples discussed in this book, like the case where a public high school in Chicago was used for a gang awards ceremony, would appear to illustrate an important concept: some Americans are really confused about gangs, or use this naivete effectively as an excuse. Should the parent of a child that joins the gang after such an event rightfully sue the school system?

This is not an exclusionary viewpoint or one that says close down all such programs that use gang members. We need to balance the dominant reintegration philosophy in the case of gang services with what the research literature shows. And gang programs more than any program, because we are talking also about the rights of human subjects, should probably live up to a much higher level of program accountability in terms of quantitative program evaluation research. We don't need any "black boxes" in gang intervention services. We truly need to know exactly what is being done and if it really works.

What should also not be done is to send mixed messages to our children which imply that gangs active in crime are in any sense "legitimate groups". Inviting a gang member or leader to speak to teachers and students at a local school is a bad idea unless the speaker is prepared --- as such "ex-gang member" street-outreach workers should do to qualify for the job --- to denounce the gang, or testify against it in court. Such events and conditions may really communicate a tacit approval of gangs, particularly when the message communicated is an apology for the existence of the gang.

What not to do is to fall victim to the psychological warfare that some larger and more sophisticated gangs are capable of today. A gang leader that portrays himself as a leader of poor kids, who claims to be doing "good" for society, who claims to be the new political messiah for the underclass --- this is the contemporary rhetoric that is being replayed on television, in the newspapers, at parole boards, etc --- because gang leaders are successful in manipulating the media on occasions. It is, of course, little more than twisted rhetoric; and all too often, beneath the thin veneer of pro-social intent is a deep pattern of crime and violence.

What not to do is to negotiate with gang leaders. What not to do is to tacitly allow gang leaders to continue to effectively administer their organizations from behind bars. What not to do is to continue to deny the problem when everyone knows it exists. Some states like California, Illinois, and Virginia --- to name a few --- will not allow their prison wardens to fill out surveys about their correctional institutions for fear of the political repercussions of "gang news". The political image maintenance strategy seems to assume that if the public realizes it happened on "their shift", they will get the blame. This is counterproductive to everyone, especially those who must work in corrections, because the public will never know the resources they deserve and need to deal with the problem.

What not to do is to continue to have the U.S. Department of Justice agencies like the National Institute of Justice to continue their historical pattern of granting research contracts to the bidder with the highest political clout, not the most capable bidder. True competitive bidding has not yet become the norm among our federal agencies for crime research. The public should not be paying for misinformation passing as criminological research.

What not to do is to allow gangs to freely attract and recruit juveniles into the gang without sanctions and without penalties. Gang membership translates into objective material health risks: the morbidity and mortality that comes from gang violence.

Children must be legally protected. Children are not legally protected in America today from the gang that like a hungry vampire feeds constantly on the unending supply of young blood. Adult gang leaders must be held accountable. Our laws should discourage, not encourage, children from joining a gang.

TOWARDS THEORETICAL INTEGRATION

The foregoing discussion has urged the value of a social organizational approach to gang analysis. We must recognize, logically, the limited variation in a crosstabulation of "unit of analysis" and "frame of reference" in gang analysis. As discussed earlier, our units of analysis have typically been the individual, the community, organizations or institutions, major political jurisdictions (cities, states, etc) and entire societies.

Obviously, at the individual unit of analysis we may also want to include an examination of non-gang affiliated youths with the same eagerness that some contemporary authors fervently advocate focusing on the individual gang member via field studies or ethnographic accounts. Our logic here is that to understand criminality or deviance, generally we should want to understand what makes someone conform first. Similarly, in areas with gang problems the analysis of non-gang affiliated youths may present some stronger basis for programming and services.

A legitimate criticism of prior research was given by Jackson and Mc Bride (1990: p. 5) to the effect that "for every sociologist who has studied gangs there seems to be a different theory". Such is the nature of much of the social sciences, as social scientists seek to position themselves, not necessarily integrating theory or testing multiple theories, but advancing their own unique perspective. As if what drives knowledge development is the need to be different.

The time has come for a more interdisciplinary and empirical approach. A period of theory testing. Hopefully this book has demonstrated that many of these views are not necessarily inconsistent ideas. These competing theoretical concepts should rather be viewed as rival hypotheses to be tested. What explains the onset and persistence of gangs may, obviously, be some combination of several such theoretical orientations.

The value of an organizational approach to the study of gangs is that we begin by recognizing that natural variation is to be expected in the complexity and sophistication of styles of gang organization. The value of an organizational approach is that we can therefore subsume much undeveloped psychological approaches, by looking at the type of personality profiles and behavioral profiles that emerge from empirical gang research, and use this research in policy. We can systematically identify the type of gang that needs to be the focus of law enforcement investigation, by applying threat analysis to these gangs. We can systematically identify persons who are gang members without asking them what gang they belong to, gang membership can be predicted. We can systematically identify those in the gang who are most likely to defect or provide testimony against gang leaders, all we have to do is apply good criminological research to the problem. This has not been the agenda of most federal and foundation knowledge development research agendas.

WHAT KIND OF GANGS ARE THERE?

The truth that we have tried to impart here is that there exist many variations in the organizational complexity and sophistication of gangs today. Some are obviously more of a threat than others. The truth also is that even within a gang there exists a continuum of risk in terms of violence and crime among individual gang members --- that is, their level of commitment to the gang.

Throughout this book we have seen that a variety of concepts have been used to account for the diverse nature of gang behavior and gang organizations. In the prior gang literature we have seen a variety of such "gangs" each having a salient caption:[3] social gangs, conflict gangs, fighting gangs, violent gangs, defensive gangs, delinquent gangs, criminal gangs, retreatist gangs, hedonistic gangs, instrumental gangs, predatory gangs, scavenger gangs, corporate gangs, party gangs, etc. In the interests of trying to "tie together" much of this previous work, an organizational continuum approach has been advanced as a more objective basis for gang classification.

What this analysis has shown is that unpopular or potentially stigmatizable groups of youths or otherwise should probably not enjoy the definition of being a gang. A "gang" should probably be reserved for various forms of group crime pursuits. And the answer to "what kind of gangs are there?" is simply different levels of organizational capability and sophistication. From the informal group to the formal organization. Ultimately, if they succeed where we fail, then organized crime.

The approach recommended here does not use such salient caption labels (e.g., conflict gang, party gang, etc), nor does it reduce a social group problem to a simple dichotomy of motivational choices (e.g., instrumental vs. integrative/expressive). It is a social organizational approach that examines the varying levels of organizational complexity and sophistication in terms of group behavior. As seen in Figure 26 below, historically gangs have been classified by impressionistic attributions and salient captions. Obviously, these do not meet the rigorous requirements of a true typology.[4]

FIGURE 26

TYPES OF GANGS BY AUTHOR(s)

AUTHOR(s)	GANG CLASSIFICATION SYSTEM
Taylor 1990	Scavenger, Territorial, Organized/Corporate
Huff, 1989	Hedonistic, instrumental, predatory
Rosenbaum 1983	Fighting, moneymaking
Yablonsky 1962	Delinquent, violent, social
Cloward and Ohlin 1960	Criminal, conflict, retreatist
Stephens, 1988	Hispanic, Black, Asian, Punk Rockers, etc,
Fagan 1989	Social, Party, Serious Delinquents, Incipient Organizations

Similarly, in Figure 27, it is shown that types of gang membership also vary enormously, by author(s). Using these various categories of gang membership may help establish here a continuum reflecting level of integration into or involvement with a gang. It is, therefore, possible to conceive of gang membership as reflecting varying levels or stages of attachment and involvement.

FIGURE 27

TYPES OF GANG MEMBERSHIP BY AUTHOR(s)

AUTHOR	GANG MEMBERSHIP CATEGORIES
Vigil, 1988	regular, peripheral, temporary, situational
Camp and Camp, 1985	Full-fledged, associates, affiliates
Quicker 1974	Auxiliary (females)
Jacobs 1974	Chiefs, Indians (prison inmates)
Davis 1982	Hardcore, affiliates, peripheral, cliques
Short and Strodtbeck 1974	Core, fringe.
Klein 1965	Core, fringe
Leissner 1969	Core, regulars, fringe
Patrick 1973	Core, Marginal
Hagedorn 1988	Topdogs, maingroup, wanna bes.
Taylor 1990	Corporate, scavenger, emulator, auxiliary, adjunct member
Fong 1990	Leaders, soldiers (members) vs. associates, sympathizers (non-members).

We can add to Figure 27 gang membership categories a number of others that have surfaced in the literature. These include: leaders, regulars, sleepers, emeritus, veteran members, defacto members, neutrals or neutrons, and of course if we have "core" (Gerrard, 1964) then we have "hardcore". Hardman (1969) notes the category of "peripheral adults", as "hangers-on" or as dabblers, who were not members but who did benefit in some way from the gang activities. Similarly, from the gang members themselves we find additional "salient caption" categories: loonies, druggies, hangarounds, renegades, and dropouts.

There is no easy solution to what constitutes membership. But we can try to integrate this literature. We can try to "pull together" much of what is implied by these very different types of terminology.

This would suggest a gang membership classification system in terms of five ascending stages of gang integration as follows:

1. Top Leadership
2. Mid-Management or Second Level of Leadership
3. Core/Regular members/soldiers
4. Auxiliary/Associate/Adjunct/Emeritus members
5. Fringe/Peripheral members/sympathizers/marginal

From this codification, categories one through three are essentially the "full time" gang members who can be readily mobilized. Categories four and five provide a more supportive function and are less mobilizable. Ideally, gang prevention must be aimed at preventing entry to, and advancement in, membership integration. Clearly gang intervention must seek to move members down the ladder of gang integration, and ultimately out of it. Theoretically, it can be done.

Therefore, the gang typology developed in this text uses four categories. This can be used in a tabular form for purposes of eventually determining the actual level of severity of the gang crime problem in America today. Figure 28 shows such a needed "blank table" that represents the primary knowledge development need for future research. We clearly need to know how serious the problem is nationwide.

FIGURE 28

TYPE OF GANGS BY TYPE OF GANG MEMBERS:
Needed National Data

	Stages of Gang Membership Integration				
	Stage 1	Stage 2	Stage 3	Stage 4	Stage 5
	*******	********	*******	*******	*******

Levels of
Gang Formations:

Level 0 (We have no idea, no clue, no guesstimate,
no suggestion whatsoever, of what the

Level 1 figures would be for these various levels
of gangs in terms of the numbers of actual

Level 2 members by their member level of gang
integration; indeed, law enforcement agencies

Level 3 do not themselves know what these figures are.)

GUESSTIMATES OF THE IMPACT OF GANG CRIME

At least a hundred reporters have asked me "how many gang members and gangs exist in America?" Even more have asked "how much crime do they commit?". I always tell them the truth as I know it: no one is in charge of that. No one has the legal responsibility for that public issue. Yes, we have some guestimates, a lot of ongoing research on the issue, but we are a small group of unfunded criminological researchers. It is time for federal law to change: to mandate that the Uniform Crime Reports and other crime statistical surveys now include gang members in the unit of analysis, and gang crime in the national reporting system. The citizens have a right to know, and the government has the obligation to inform us of the scope and extent of this problem. The time is long overdue for this change in federal policy.

A sure sign of the brutal neglect by the federal government in protecting its citizens from criminal gangs is the inability of any federal agency to say with any level confidence how much crime in America is explained by the gang problem. Crude estimates are all that can be currently made of the scope and extent of the impact of gangs on crime in America. By most accounts, this is a very large problem.

One of the most curious features of this issue is the undocumented crime that is committed everyday in America. The assertion here is that the Uniform Crime

Reports compiled by the Federal Bureau of Investigation are substantially in error in underestimating the scope and severity of the American crime problem. The most dramatic proof of this assertion is that the crimes that prison inmates commit on each other every day are virtually never reported unless these incidents hit the front pages of our newspapers in a riot or similar disturbance.

Vetter and Territo (1984: p. 517) asserted a decade ago that "today, urban gangs are responsible for roughly one quarter of all juvenile crimes committed each year". And along with the changes in society and our urban communities has also come the changes in technology used by gangs. They no longer use "zip guns", they are more likely to use "sophisticated weaponry --- AR-15s, M-16s, grenades, and plastic explosives --- that would do credit to a military assault troop" (Vetter and Territo, 1984: p. 517).

Police estimates are somewhat different. Huff (1989) reports that police chiefs tend to minimize the scope and extent of the problem. In fact, minimized to a level of either fantasy or intentional misrepresentation. That is, several police chiefs in Ohio felt gang crime constituted less than one percent of all total crime, and less than 2 percent of all juvenile crime (Huff, 1989). Perhaps the real issue is this: to what extent is gang crime reporting also a political issue? Does reporting seriously high levels of gang crime tend to convey the impression that a police department is ineffectual in controlling crime in the community?   One problem here is the reporting bias. Generally, we must assume that at the community level the fear of gang retaliation, or the perception by the citizen complainant that "nothing will be done", or that the knowledge that prison and jail overcrowding means at the most a few hours or days off the street for a serious offense, must have some deflationary effect on gang crime reporting. The bias is likely to underreport gang crime. We would probably feel more comfortable, as a victim, reporting on crimes involving lone offenders than a group or gang of offenders.

Recall Short and Strodtbeck's estimate on the probability of arrest for gang violence. It is a low risk. A probability of .04 or .02 for the very skillful (Short and Strodtbeck, 1974: p. 258). Our police view this probability of an arrest as obviously being much higher.

In Illinois, the Director of the state prison system estimated that between 80 to 90 percent of all inmates were gang affiliated. Campbell (1984, p. 20) quotes findings from the Los Angeles juvenile hall to the effect that 40 percent of the youths detained there are gang members. The research reported on juvenile institutions by the present author revealed a total of 212 female gang members and a total of 4,457 male gang members in the sample of juvenile correctional institutions. Overall, this meant an average of 17.7 percent of the males confined were gang members compared to 4.4 percent of the females. Adult state prisons appear to have a national average of at least ten percent of their inmates being gang members. Again, recall that these figures come from administrators of social control facilities. When we actually ask those who are confined in the facilities, as occurred in the survey of youths in correctional institutions, a much more dramatic and higher figure emerges: nearly half of both males and females readily admit to having ever joined a gang. And as these juvenile institutions effectively do one thing --- they feed the steady stream of adult criminals to adult correctional institutions --- we might realistically assume that the actual percentage of prison inmates in America who are gang members is substantially higher than their principal keepers are prone to admit.

Tannenbaum (1938, p. 21) cited the previous research by Shaw and Myers (1929) in the specific crime offense category of theft, and of 6,000 such cases, some 90.4 percent were committed in a group context of two or more boys.

Astute criminologists know that official crime data is always problematic. But homicide data is always the most reliable; simply because a dead body must be processed, and it involves not just the police, it involves the coroner's office. While we can assume some such homicides are never detected, and may perhaps even be passed into our statistics as simply "drug overdose" deaths, etc, if the corpus delicti has a bullet hole in it, then it is more likely to be reported as a homicide, but not always. The point is this: perhaps in the absence of required and standardized reporting systems which are obviously not in place in our communities today, one reason being the lack of standardized definitions of what constitutes a gang, then perhaps our best estimate of the parameter of "gang related crime" comes from homicide data.[5]

In a nutshell, nationwide we simply lack accurate data from the law enforcement end of the problem (Bensinger, 1984: p. 1). In fact, the survey on law enforcement agencies by Needle and Stapleton (1983) had to conclude it lacked adequate information:

"Unfortunately, this preliminary survey's attempts to use these measures were inhibited by responding police agencies' inability to supply the requisite statistical data. With the exception of a few departments, reliable gang-related statistics are not compiled, and while many estimates were provided, these could not be cross-checked for reliability" (Needle and Stapleton, 1983: p. 13).

Additional research to replicate and extend the Needle and Stapleton study is now underway by the present author as part of a larger study to ascertain the scope and extent of the gang crime problem nationally.[6]

Correctional institutions seem to have information relevant to this analysis. Many correctional institutions, adult and juvenile, have a fairly good idea of the extent of gang membership among inmates. In many of the states indicated by the Camp and Camp (1985) study to not have a gang problem in adult institutions, more current research shows their juvenile and adult institutions to now report a definite gang presence.

In summary, outside of a capture/recapture analysis supplementing official statistics with self-report information, which is a research project likely to pose some difficulty, we really have no idea factually how much crime in America gangs are responsible for. It can be assumed to be quite significant. Nor does anyone know exactly how many gangs and gang members exist in the United States. We have some rough ideas, but little systematic and comprehensive data exists. Without information, no new knowledge will be developed that can tackle this problem. So in this sense America still has its blinders on regarding gang crime. While many continue to die daily in gang violence, no one is taking responsibility for tracking and monitoring and most importantly reporting on the scope and extent of this problem. A problem that is escalating, not fading away.

One hopeful sign is that the Los Angeles definition of what constitutes a "gang related crime" is being adopted more readily than Chicago's overly restrictive definition (see Klein and Maxson in Huff, 1990). Much of this has to do with the dedication of one police professional: Sgt. Wesley D. Mc Bride and his career long work in developing an appraisal of the scope of the gang crime problem (see Jackson and Mc Bride, 1990). Cities that want to honestly confront the gang crime problem will use the Los Angeles definition, those that want to politicize the problem and obscure it, hoping it will "just go away," will use the Chicago definition.   Finally, some data is emerging here. Again, however, these are estimates provided by a national survey of police chiefs. What this data shows is that among those police chiefs who report a gang problem existing under five years (N=130) when asked to estimate the percentage of gang-related crime within all crimes a mean of 11.9% emerges, and a mean of 16.3 percent for all youth crime. Among those police chiefs who report a gang problem existing for over five years (N = 30) these estimates rise to 20.6 percent for all crime, and 32.0 percent for all youth crime.

Clearly, from this less than herculean effort of trying to assess the problem, the problem still appears to be a very large one.[7] Some recent federal estimates suggest there are about half a million gang members in America, but again these are estimates. We need to stop guessing and get serious about this issue. We need new federal legislation to require the tracking and monitoring of offense patterns by gang members arrested in the United States and have this information published routinely in the FBI's Uniform Crime Reports.

WHY DO GANGS ARISE?

Our literature and research suggests that several factors are important in explaining the onset and persistence of gangs. Obviously, a great many such hypotheses have been reviewed in this book. But summarized here are those that appear to have some theoretical and empirical support.

The theoretical factors are these: (1) being economically disadvantaged, (2) racism/oppression, and (3) political corruption. These are contexts of recurring inequality that engender a sense of hopelessness for the individual. These are not problems existing only in the minds of individuals, these are real problems: objective, material conditions. They are social structural problems that require our serious attention. These are, furthermore, theoretical explanations. We are not at a stage in the development and accumulation of gang research that we can extrapolate much in terms of generalizations to the entire American society. When you ask gang members why they join, we find a wide variety of explanations: to make money, to be with friends, a family member was involved, etc. We can take no pride in the lack of systematic national research assessing the scope and extent of this problem. We have a very long way to go in terms of developing useful knowledge about the gang problem in America.

Obviously, these theoretical factors for why gangs arise can operate just as easily in rural as in urban areas, and can be assumed to figure prominently in the emergence of small-town gangs as well as in large cities. And they know no jurisdictional or national boundaries. Any community, any society can have gangs if it has these political-economic factors operating to its overall detriment. Although, obviously, our history shows gangs have been traditionally urban problems; today rural areas also have gang problems.

Differences in the motivation for joining a gang can help to explain the level of commitment to the gang, and may therefore be useful in gang intervention. The more serious hard core gang member in some recent research has simply joined the gang for income purposes "to make money".[8] The reasons for joining do vary significantly by attempts to quit the gang. Those who join for "protection" or because they were "pushed into it" are more likely to later try to quit the gang, while those who joined for income purposes apparently adjust to the gang life as if it were an alternative career and are much less likely to later attempt to quit the gang.

WHAT IS BEING DONE ABOUT GANGS IN AMERICA TODAY?

Not enough. Clearly, much more is claiming to being done about gangs than is actually being done about the gang problem. Further, it cannot be assumed from the literature reviewed in this book that all such efforts are going to be productive. Our history shows that a number of "experiments" have clearly gone awry and have generated reverse-intended effects. They have added fuel to the fire in some instances. These reverse-intended effects did not stop in the 1960s. They continue today, with government funding, by confused policy makers, whose federal files contain numerous examples of such federally funded programs that actually helped to strengthen the gang, not destabilize it.

In a nutshell, not much is being done about gangs other than improving intelligence gathering capabilities and locking up the gang members. A number of programs exist in the United States that I believe do have the necessary theoretical grounding from which we can expect positive impact and have some evidence of positive impact. Many of these programs have never been replicated in areas outside of their own jurisdiction. Most certainly much more must be done about this problem.

But programs must change too. We must adopt a more scientific and a more responsible attitude about program evaluation. Any applicant for federal or state funding should agree in writing to make all agency files and provide cooperation with a totally independent evaluation researcher who is trained in criminology. The program should not be able to pick its local friend to write a fluffy report that has no grounding in criminology, and where legally the evaluation requirement becomes satisfied, but no real knowledge ever results from the public investment. A national pool of qualified and certified evaluation research professionals should be established from which to draw upon for mandatory independent evaluations of any program dealing with gang members or persons at risk of joining a gang. Using groups like the Academy of Criminal Justice Sciences and the American Society of Criminology as a recruiting pool for this initiative would be a good first step in the right direction. There is too much riding on this issue to make mistakes. This is not a problem that can simply be used for traditional pork barrel politics and 1960s style programs. True accountability must be established for programs dealing with gang issues.

CAN GANGS BE "PUT OUT OF BUSINESS?"

Not easily is the answer. Using penal sanctions could be very expensive and would only transfer the problem from our communities to our correctional institutions. Seizing assets, effective use of immunity and pardons/amnesty, etc, could be useful in demoralizing gangs. But as social organizational forms of group affiliation something will have to take its place. Our communities will have to have something to offer the future gang members of America unless we want to reproduce the problem again and again in a cyclical historical fashion.

National Service could be an answer.[9] If it targeted economic disadvantage, if it was systematic in overcoming problems of intergenerational poverty, if it could significantly enhance human and social capital, and if it could reduce our society's overall problem with regard to race relations and social stigmatization. To be a truly "homogenizing" influence, it might have to be mandatory for all youthful citizens: a common requirement of service to their country. No one gets excluded. No one. It would be a viable way to attack the drug problem which is also so closely tied into the gang problem as well.

But it could be done. Either way it is going to cost America a great deal. But at least there is some hope attacking it frontally, with substantial preventative and intervention efforts.

CAN WE TAKE THE FUEL OUT OF THE GANG ENGINE?

The fuel of the gang engine in America is the constant supply of new children who become the new input and the new recruits into gang life. Yes, this may be the most effective strategy from a systems point of view. Because once the gang is unable to replenish its members, all that will exist are the hardcore, those at the top who with long prison sentences, and no one to do their bidding, and it is theoretically possible that nationally we could do much to rapidly suppress the gang problem in this fashion.

However, it would require legislation that defines allowing an underage child in a gang to be a sanctionable offense. It would require holding adult gang members accountable for the prima facie evidence that any child is a member of the gang. Allowing a child to freely join a gang is to allow the child to be morally corrupted systematically. We must creatively explore how gang membership translates into a new form of child abuse. We must have laws that will make it harder for adult gang leaders to take advantage of our many alienated youths. We cannot allow such criminal organizations to continue to systematically recruit and indoctrinate children and turn our children into young killers.

CAN "DETACHED WORKERS" HAVE A POSITIVE EFFECT?

Yes. But they could also have a negative effect. It depends on how the program is organized and administered. Such workers should obviously be subject to drug testing because illicit drug abuse is one of the primary corrupting influences of gangs today. It may matter less if the detached worker is a professional social worker than it matters what exactly the overall program impact is on the gang organization. Simply providing the gang another resource to exploit is not going to result in aborting new recruits to the gang organization. Ex-offenders and former gang members, with some record of successful reintegration, can be just as effective, perhaps more so, than degreed social workers in making outreach to gang members. The question for theory and program development is not what to do when that outreach has been made,[10] rather the question is what can we as a society offer them?

No simple small local project is going to solve the problem, because the gang problem extends across all jurisdictions. The gang problem is not a local problem, it is a national problem, and it requires a national solution. Some recent federally funded studies that would like to pass as professional research would have us believe no such national problem exists. I claim differently.
I claim the gang problem not only exists in virtually all states, but also that there is interaction among and between gangs nationally.   We can thank the federal government for that too: for knowingly or unknowingly funding some gang summit meetings in the guise of "anti-gang programs"[11], thus solidifying the relationships between gang leaders nationally.

So it is not totally incorrect to be able to conclude that we what we have in current federal policy regarding gangs is some agencies (i.e., DHHS) helping gangs to become stronger, others denying the problem exists (i.e., NIJ), and others (FBI, ATF, DEA, etc) who take the heat and have to clean up the mess. We need a nationally coordinated strategy, not one that both facilitates gang development and gang prosecution simultaneously.

The reader with a good ear will recall the current presidential incumbent in his 1992 nominating speech did promise to do something about the gang problem, making specific reference to gangs. The American voter must decide in 1996 whether this promise was fulfilled, forgotten, or flipped. Some gang analysts point to the case of El Rukn gang leader Jeff Fort at one point earlier in his career benefitting from a visit to the White House for the inauguration of President Nixon; this actually did not happen that way specifically, Jeff Fort was invited, but he sent two underlings in his place, and it did not mean they met with the president. However, during the last year a well-known gang activist in Chicago did in fact meet with the President.

GANGS AND AMERICA'S FUTURE

We all live in a world community, we are inseparable by a large number of factors. Whether or not a society that imprisons significant proportions of its members can continue as a democratic society very long may be the question. Clearly many prisons could probably be abolished (adult and juvenile) and replaced with more effective forms of community-based correctional services --- especially community-service --- and programs without any risk of increase in recidivism and at a significantly lower cost.

Gang crime in America is an issue of citizenship. It is an issue of "who really belongs?", of who is really accepted and capable of being integrated into wider society. It is an issue of the apparently enduring need that many Americans have for stigmatizing and labelling; to derogate and subjugate with status degradation, as if manufacturing such a social sub-strata actually meant any elevation for anyone else. It doesn't.

Gangs today clearly constitute a major national problem. Gangs hold much power locally in their communities, in their purchasing power, in their capability for extortion and violence, in outnumbering municipal police officers, and in their continuing domination of our correctional institutions --- and even more recently in their political influence. What most Americans seem to forget is that even among adult prison inmates, 96 percent of them are eventually released. And guess where they are coming? You've got it. Back to your community.

The Archie Bunkers among us will advise: "well, don't let them out of prison then". But as any informed reader of criminal justice knows, that is not a viable solution. Long term prisoners represent long term fiscal commitments of the government. The new national debt would be that of projected imprisonment costs if we took the advice of those reacting without thinking.

The ethical contradiction of our time is that we as a society are willing to spend so much for non-investment options such as prisons and jails and so little for the actual quality of life (education, healthcare, etc) and human capital development to make our nation stronger and more competitive. We have gotten into the habit of relying on formal social control for handling our concerns about order and security. The absurdity of it all is very apparent in some instances, such as the two year prison sentence given in June 1993 to a 21-year-old Illinois man for stealing a cheese snack valued at three dollars from a grocery store. The judge wanted to send this thief a "wake up call". A pretty expensive wake-up call. About fifty thousand dollars worth of criminal justice resources over a three dollar piece of cheese![12]

This is not to say we do not have serious violent criminals for which no other appropriate option exists other than secure modern prisons. The emphasis is on modern. Traditional ways of dealing with prison inmates will have to be replaced by styles of management that focus on dealing with groups of affiliated inmates. Affiliated by gang membership that is.

WILL WE ALWAYS HAVE GANGS?

Yes, in one form or another. But we do have choices here. One choice is whether we want to facilitate the organizational development of our nation's gangs or do we want to "bring their members back into the fold"? Gangs today have an enormous capacity for violence, much more than they have actually used. Gangs, as organizational forms of criminal endeavors, have for the most part always existed in America and in other countries[13] in one way or another, and probably always will. Another choice is whether we want to continue to allow gangs to freely grow and expand using American children as their new members, their shooters, and their killers, knowing juveniles will receive less severe penal sanctions. We should not allow American gangs to continue to systematically recruit our young children. We must rise to the defense of our children. We must by legislation enable the enhancement of the rights of children to include the right to not be freely captured by adult gang leaders whose overall corrupting influence is no less than that of a total control institution-style "cult". We get upset when religious cults try to attract our young, but not when the gangs attract our young is the apparent conclusion here. The other choice we have for the future of our society is that gangs need not be so large, so growing, so powerful, so potentially violent and destructive. There are some things we can do about this problem. The first step is to get educated about the problem. That is why I tried to write the first full text book on gangs.

Gangs are normal and expected in any society with problems of racial enmity, institutionalized poverty, and the mathematical jeopardy of social stigma (e.g., multiple marginality, ala Vigil). There is nothing abnormal about wanting to join a gang when you are a child, particularly an alienated unloved child: look what the gang offers --- adults who do care for you, they care how much money you can make for them, but they care; guns, drugs, sex, violence, togetherness, an entire gamut of cultural, economic, and psychic benefits. Remember, gangs are a national problem. Most states now report gangs as a problem in either adult or juvenile correctional institutions. One urgent and present research need is to track the status of these other "non-gang problem" communities and truly assess them. Because of their dwindling numbers, they represent the last chance to ascertain, as it happens, whether gangs are franchised interstate from higher level gang formations; or whether they grow indigenously, ala social imitation, perhaps emulating mass media or Hollywood "social space" or the "psychology of enmity" imaging given to gang roles; or if it is some kind of "seed spreading" contagion; etc.

IT IS NOT JUST A LAW ENFORCEMENT ISSUE

The gang problem is a crime problem that is a part of a national social problem.[14] It is inconceivable that law enforcement alone could solve the gang crime problem in America. So federal resources should go to the communities first before going to direct law enforcement aid. Such policy initiatives as LEAA were good for police. But federal policy should not be to systematically encourage use of the criminal sanction, it should encourage peace. Domestic peace. And a reduction of conflict levels. This is best accomplished by systematically enhancing the human capital of our Nation. We do know how to identify potential "informants" or gang defectors from their social, psychological, and behavioral profile; we can siphon off a lot of core gang members into legitimate pursuits; we can certainly prevent new gang recruits (our own children) from entering the fray; and we can isolate and effectively sanction those hard core persisting gang members who want to continue to disrupt and threaten our society. We have always had the choice. We have not always been educated enough to make the right choice. And we have not had the political leaders with sufficient law enforcement experience to be able to guide us along a safer path.

No doubt about it, the private security field of the future will continue to burgeon and expand, as a market phenomenon in response to our nation's perceived fear of crime. Much of it will be related to the gang problem. Some businesses will get their protection either way[15]. What needs protecting are the communities and civil rights. Because, after all is said and done, the gang crime problem in America is a problem of social justice[16]. And the solution must start with realizing that children have the right not to be targeted for gang membership. Foreign journalists seemed amazed when I would tell them that absolutely no criminal sanction existed

whatsoever for adult gang leaders who systematically corrupted young children ---
having them as loyal young soldiers of their gang, without the parents permission,
without any American governmental or private group whatsoever even objecting to
this chain of human circumstances. It is totally legal to corrupt and guide young
children into being killers is the message our society is now sending to adult criminal
gang leaders. We arrest a child killer who is a gang member and we never hold the
adult gang leaders involved responsible, how long will we be suckered by this device?
We need to change the message our society sends to adult gang leaders, and it is my
personal prayer that the reader acts on this problem.

PRISONS ALONE ARE NO GENUINE ANSWER EITHER

Those who advocate building more prisons, perhaps even centralized federal "gang
security centers" to warehouse gang members only, are not advocating genuine
solutions to the problem. They are advocating their self-interest in expanding the
penal apparatus. They are advocating expanding and exacerbating the gang crime
problem when our focus should be on prevention, but I am saying nothing different
here than what has been said for a terribly long time, it is simply my moral duty to
repeat it. Our conceptions of prisons and correctional institutions have historically
been predicated on the notion that who goes there are lone, individual offenders.
That has changed.

Today's correctional systems may have less deterrent value for gang members.[17]
Going to prison may not seem like the punishment many "hang em' high" citizens
might think it to be.[18] For many gang members, a short prison stint is much like
a homecoming affair; and, indeed, a chance to improve leadership skills and to
develop and advance organizationally.[19] For seven years the leader of the Gangster
Disciples was able to run his gang on a day to day basis from within the prison
system in Illinois --- and from the relative comfort of a minimum security facility,
even though he was serving time for murder. We must cease allowing our politicians
to make concessions to gang leaders. The coopted gang leader may not bite the
hand that feeds from correctional administrators, but the gang leader will go for the
neck of the society that allows it to freely administer gangs on the streets from
behind bars. No one should question this finding other than the gang member or
those who would apologize for the gang member.   What correctional institutions
need to do is to divert large numbers of their inmates to community-based
corrections; including the heavy use of supervised community-service in a fashion as
to increase the informal social controls in our nation's communities. Use this
enormous manpower potential to rebuild our nation's burned out, dilapidated inner-
city areas or for repairing the infrastructure of our cities. What correctional
institutions need to consider is contract programming: giving up the gang in favor of
valued training, education, and treatment. What correctional institutions need to
consider is isolating the gang leaders who continue to manipulate and control other
inmates in an overall course of action designed to increase the threat or use of
violence in any fashion. For it is by violence that the gang survives and persists. We
must take that power away from the gang. Yes, even if it means having no-human
contact status for such persons.

COMMUNITIES RESTORED WITH HOPE VERSUS THE PRODUCTION OF ZOMBIES[220]

At what cost to freedom can anyone take the position that nothing can be done about gang crime in America? Such a distrustful and negativistic psychological orientation is that which is most often projected onto our most hardened criminals. If hate breeds crime, then hope can slow it down. If cynicism breeds low expectations of performance, then a more fervent commitment to accountability can increase it. If racism fuels gang crime, then equity and social justice can put that fire out. But something will have to be done, unless we want to manufacture our gang problem into something more serious than it already is.

The hope is that what can grow is a sense of local power to address and solve problems; what can grow is a tolerance of other points of view and plurality generally; what can grow is a true and genuine defense of the meaning of liberty and freedom for all and an elimination of racial enmity and hatred; and in so doing all Americans will be allowed to grow morally and spiritually as human beings. That our nation's communities need more resources should be apparent to all. Perhaps this change can come from freeing up scarce resources: particularly those spent most unproductively in the area of imprisonment, and unnecessary expenditures in military defense.

The default option ---- that is, what will happen in the wake of not seeing a rebirth and revitalization of local community spirit and citizenship which encompasses local responsibility for social control ---- is "business as usual" in corrections: the production of zombies who return to our communities angry at the way society has treated them, becoming ever-committed enemies of society, fulfilling the labels thrust upon them. Monsters[21], stamped and numbered "MADE IN AMERICA". Dependably effective monsters. Truly reliable monsters. Because we made them.

American society made little monsters like Robert "Yummy" Sandifer and many other young, underage killers. What we may have that is unique in American history is the first generation of adults that pays tribute by symbolization alone to the rights of children, but by deeds avoids the fulfillment of the rights of American children today. This kind of benign neglect correlates highly with conservative ideology that resists government spending for youth services to produce better human beings, but encourages spending to put them in gladiator training schools where they can learn to become adult criminals. We are a very confused society. More than some Americans learn most of what they know about the gang problem from those who are least capable of educating us about anything: television talks shows and Hollywood images of the gang.

LONGTERM VERSUS SHORTTERM GOALS FOR GANG CRIME ABATEMENT

In the absence of a miracle we must assume it is not going to be easy to eliminate racism and racial enmity in America overnight. America is a cultural melting pot, but one that often steams with antagonism and intolerance. Both short and long term goals should include addressing this enduring issue shown to be so historically associated with gang crime in America. Gangs thrive on conflict of any kind, especially racial and ethnic conflict, even cultural conflict in dress styles. We must not allow gangs to exploit conflicts, but establish instead environments that defuse conflict and increase recognition for the value of diversity.

The highest level of demonstrating moral superiority as a nation state in the years to come shall certainly rest not with military power, but with domestic peace; and the ability to function in the world community not from a position of shame, but from a position of strength on the home front. Prisons filled to the walls are not a source of strength, they are a weakness. Criminal gangs dominating our neighborhoods are not a source of strength: if foreign invaders with superior firepower arrived, then gang members as quislings ala Taylor (1990) might be the first to collaborate with them, not fight them.

A sure fire formula for the debasement of the very essence of democracy and the progressive deterioration of America as a leading world nation is to continue current policies in the spirit of "business as usual". It will guarantee for every child from every home an equal opportunity to be a gang member. Why? Because we looked the other way as the adult gang leaders continue to produce future examples of young children like Robert "Yummy" Sandifer. In fact, we encouraged adult criminal gang leaders to exploit our children by providing no specific sanctions for this kind of organizational crime.

Gang members are not foreigners or aliens with no right to be here operating as they do, they are our neighbors and more often than not persons we have failed to responsibly integrate into a productive capacity in our society. They are our brothers and sisters in the larger sense of the meaning of citizenship. They are our fellow citizens and we cannot ship them abroad as "unwanted offenders" in the same manner that gave rise to our own country. It is possible to get out of the gang. It is possible to become inactive in a gang. There is no limit on the dimension of human possibilities.

It is well to recall America rising as a colony of offenders and miscreants escaping from oppression and persecution. It is well to imagine, at least, the possibility that we have reproduced a comparable form of oppression and persecution in our own society; of our own making. The shame is in not admitting it will be a costly and expensive proposition to be committed to a policy of such enormous and forceful debasement. As Houston (1994) has shown there appears to be more symbolism than substance to recent National legislation about the gang problem. It is truly a time for taking a collective moral inventory. And, after sermonizing, putting our money where our mouth is.

ON INTELLECTUALIZING   THE GANG CRIME PROBLEM

Obviously, criminologists are those in the most advantageous position to be able to speak to the gang crime problem in America. But they are not the only educational or intellectual discipline with a vested interest in the outcome of solving this problem. In fact, criminologists are best served objectively and materially by allowing the gang crime problem to escalate, and in so doing increasing the legitimacy of their "focal concerns".

And what are the "focal concerns" of criminologists? Teaching and reproducing other criminologists to serve them; getting funding grants to advice policy makers that they are on the right track, "just keep the research funding coming in"; and there are no structural defects of any significance, only minor adjustments, fine tuning, and alterations from a change perspective that need be considered. No dramatic changes are required. Such are the focal concerns of not only criminologists, but many who are a part of the status quo in a society bent on a pattern of institutional non-productivity and counter-productivity. A business of managing problems that reproduces at an alarmingly efficient rate its own problems that the rest of us must pay for. Unfortunately these are the problems affecting all citizens. It would be fortunate indeed for Ph.D.'s to finally stop arguing about "what is a gang" and recognize the facts. The facts are some gangs are greater threats than others. If some scholars want to consider Spanky and Alfalfa a gang, fine, let them do so. Their research will certainly help us better understand adolescents generally. But we need to focus our criminological expertise on what are genuinely formal gangs, gangs that some would want to call organized crime, but which are not really classical versions of organized crime; we cannot define criminal gangs out of our vocabulary of scholarly research by simply declaring them by policy or definition to be organized crime.

With the rapidly growing interest in "gang" issues, the public demands more gang books. We have seen a virtual explosion of gang books in recent years. Gang courses at the university level are now being offered across the United States, in many disciplines. Why? Because it is practical and useful for survival? Not primarily. Rather because the gang problem overlaps with so many other human functions: social services, education, the family, the community, and obviously all of course criminal justice. Some books are better than others is the advice offered here.

WHO IS REALLY "FREE"?

In a national atmosphere of intense fear and loathing, when ordinary citizens "lock themselves up" in their impregnable homes at sundown, or in their condos with armed guards, and would not hazard to walk the streets of their city or community any more than they would walk through a poison gas mine field, who is really free? Who is free is the person who has nothing to lose.

The typical American gang member is such a person. The gang member does not fear prison. Prison means friends. The gang member does not fear violence, violence was probably always a part of everyday solutions to their life problems in America. The gang member does not fear loss, for there is little to lose materially that cannot be regained through cunning or stealth; the clothes on ones back, immediate possessions, a car, money in the pocket. Yours could be theirs. The gang member has a good reason not to place much value on human life, for little has been invested in his own human capital. The typical gang member takes on a combative personality and adapts to this situation quite nicely, surviving one day at a time.

To rebuild America is to rethink our assumptions about what can or cannot work regarding problems that face us daily. The gang problem will not go away even if we send every gang member to prison. For they will come back, perhaps stronger; and if they vote, perhaps citizens who are not gang members may be the ones in custody ultimately, in one way or another; because only half of our citizens vote anyway. If they cannot vote, then we can look to more violent scenarios. Because as official "outcasts", gang members are probably more prone than the rest of us to political extremism.

THE NARROWING OF SOCIAL CHOICES IN THE 21st CENTURY

Predictability is a weakness, organizationally and militarily. America is currently committed to a narrow set of choices for dealing with the gang problem. Unless of course it is willing to take perhaps a brand new perspective, a "no holds barred", a "let the chips fall where they may" kind of analysis. The author has endeavored to provide such an analysis of the gang crime problem in America here.

While this book has sought to be comprehensive, there are certainly many contributions that may have deserved closer scrutiny. The author has endeavored to maintain ongoing consistent research in the area of gangs: as they affect our community, our schools, our police departments, our jails, our prisons, our juvenile institutions, and other aspects of modern society. The author currently serves as the editor-in-chief of the Journal of Gang Research which disseminates the best gang research our world has to offer. The author is not a simple "dabbler" in gang issues, but is committed enough to the issue to have established a think tank that continues to produce ongoing useful gang research. The gang problem is a dynamic problem, not a static problem. The direction of change, however, is very predictable in light of the lack of any coherent national federal policy regarding the gang problem. It will get worse. The rising evidence of gang members shooting police officers is consistent with this prediction. The recent case in Chicago where the Four Corner Hustlers felt so much in control of their community that they could conceive of simply blowing up the police station as a way to stop the police from interfering with their drug sales operations is another case in point.

The true power of a democracy is in the last analysis probably a power of offering choices to the solution of a crisis. The gang crime problem in America is, if not now, then soon reaching such a "crisis" point. We shall certainly need more choices than are currently available. Hopefully a scholar of crime contributes, what we mean in our more positive moments of what a criminologist should have as a job description, to more choices rather than restricting them.

Unfortunately America as a nation seems under the gun of an ideological imperative, of a progressively decreasing number of choices for dealing with its problems such as gang crime. As if it were neurotically compulsive in having only the option of imprisonment in responding to American gang members. It is truly not a solution, it is simply an expensive option. We will most certainly need more choices as we enter the 21st century.

Because without choices we shall not be free. We will be as imprisoned by our lack of creative imaginations as we would be if we were locked up with the gang members themselves. Recall, that gang members have successfully adapted to limited choices. We shall also have to adapt. By generating new choices. Choices of responsible social justice. Choices that can work.

WHAT WILL IT TAKE TO DO ANYTHING ABOUT THE GANG CRIME PROBLEM?

Resources. Plenty of them. More sophisticated training and education for our nation's police officers and criminal justice personnel. Recall that gang members in America outnumber the ranks of all our Nation's municipal sworn police officers. Social defense is a quality of life issue. If a city cannot aggressively confront its crime problem, then fear intensifies and the tax base flees the city leaving behind those least able to solve the problem --- almost in the fashion of Gresham's law of conflict.

Gang crime is a national, even international problem. It will require that scope of attention as well. Which clearly means much more from the federal budget earmarked for the suppression of gang crime, along with more logically allocated funding for prevention service initiatives. Which is to imply, yes --- some federal funded initiatives from the 1970s to the present have been substantially less than logical. Many such recently funded programs lacked any theoretically consistent basis for having a positive impact. It comes as no surprise then that we find examples of federally funded programs providing "beepers" and cellular phones to active gang members, under the guise of "staying in touch with the program"[22].

SUMMARY AND CONCLUSION

The development and accumulation of useful knowledge in the social sciences is different from that in the physical sciences (e.g., biology, chemistry, physics, etc). In the latter, "major moves forward" can occur with experimental discovery. There is much less opportunity to experiment on human beings, social groups, communities, or societies. So, in the field of criminology we can categorically say that we really do not have all the answers yet in terms of addressing the gang crime problem in America. Some profoundly simple questions have no answers from our federal leaders, such as "What proportion of the crime in America is committed by gang members?", or even "How many gangs and gang members are there in America?".

Further, no single contribution is likely to change national thinking. What this book has endeavored to provide, therefore, is an eclectic and comprehensive view of the gang crime problem. What it has also sought is to provide a discussion of the major issues today. And some of those we may face in the years to come.

Our best bet is not on intuition, our best approach is not a "belly button" method, our best solution is not a "let's vote on either punishment or rehabilitation" method; in fact, our best friend in finding solutions is that of the social sciences and what we know about human behavior and social groups generally. This has been the view articulated here. It is the view of what social science can offer in terms of understanding and solving the gang problem today.

Ideology is less important than proof of effectiveness when it comes to the gang crime problem. We need, at least, to aspire to a social scientific solution. That means leaving our prejudices and stereotypes out of the analysis. Unfortunately, politics has always been a factor in what gets researched and what knowledge gets produced and who gets funded and who does not. The fact that the gang problem in America quietly spread like a virulent plague during the second term of the Reagan administration and the term of office held by President Bush implies that some government agencies are would rather simply ignore this problem and let it fester like a local sore. Sadly, the new Clinton administration has also not done much of anything as of this date to address or even recognize this problem. The current "business as usual" policy of the federal government on gangs is that law enforcement agencies will continue to stay busy and attract media attention in arresting gang members, but that little will actually be done about the underlying causes of the problem. We are literally headed for a criminal justice disaster until some officials recognize that administering the penal sanction is not a guaranteed solution to this problem.

The gang classification system advanced here is a preliminary effort towards getting a handle on what really is going on in American gangs today. We obviously, as a society, lack the information we really need to evaluate how serious this problem truly is. But advances are occurring rapidly in the area of gang research because more and more criminologists are entering this area of study.

Many authors have had an enduring impact on our knowledge of what kind of gangs exist in American society, and how they came to exist. Not all of these can be considered true criminologists. Gang studies for some was just a "passing fancy". For others, it was their life focus. The most important point here is that all of the social sciences have something to offer to the gang crime problem when it comes to "solutions".

Some truths have emerged here. They are commonalities and historical continuities found in many different contributions to the gang literature. One of these is the racism/oppression thesis. It appears to have considerable support from a number of different authors. It means, basically, that in American society race relations is such that gangs act out the violent conflict that is often just below the surface in daily life.

Another continuity in thinking about gangs is the problem of politics and crime. That is still a problem today. Not all politicians will refuse a cash donation or "volunteer muscle". And clearly, in some urban areas, gangs are making a political statement if not in fact organizing full-scale political action committees. The PAC for the Gangster Disciples in Chicago quickly had over $100,000 in its coffers to run their own candidates for election to local offices and to support others.

Another continuity is the method of researching gangs. While many research methods have been used in the present book to describe the problem and address the issues of gangs in America, an enduring form of research has been the "conversation analysis" form of qualitative analysis. Call it oral history, case study, field study, whatever, it means getting the story from the mouths of gang members. We need only remind our fellow criminologists that we need the same attention provided to gang crime victims and neighbors of gang members. And those who work with gang members in correctional settings and in community service agencies.

But there are some quirks in our history of studying gangs as well. One of these is the apparent misrepresentation of what if anything Shaw and Mc Kay had to offer about the understanding of gangs. Hopefully this book has clarified their important historical role in the study of American gangs.

There have been a lot of "mistakes" in the study of American gangs. Some of these would be hard to commit again with currently existing standards for professional ethics and the need for the protection of human subjects. This is another justification for truly understanding gangs in a historical context. We are not in a situation of truly having "zero knowledge" on gangs. We know some things. We know absolutely nothing about other aspects of American gangs --- particularly, how much variation they explain in the overall American crime problem and how much potential mobilization they represent in terms of gang organization levels and stages of gang membership.

By the historical patterns of neglect and the decay of our neighborhood social infrastructures, gangs have become an urban way of life. The challenge of the coming decade is whether they also become a rural and suburban way of life. And whether the quality of life, in terms of security, can be preserved sufficiently to prevent en masse migration from our central cities, thereby further eroding the income base and escalating the problem.

What this book has demonstrated is that what knowledge we want to develop in the years to come regarding the gang crime problem in America is often dependent on the frame of "user" reference. Our society is organized like any other society. Each segment has a different function and need. Many, unfortunately, would like to pass on the gang problem (like the federal deficit) to someone else. We are rapidly approaching the point where we can pass on the gang crime problem to no one. It comes back to haunt us nightly. We must begin to take responsibility for this problem, recognize for what it is, take proper measures, and be prepared to pay for the costs of a massive national effort.

Violence, hate, and destruction are part and parcel of the gang crime problem. It shows no sign of anything but escalation. Historically, gangs have but a small jump to make to become urban guerrilla organizations. If ever there was a time to take seriously the prospect of intervention and prevention it is now. For to wait much longer may mean it could be too late. Conflict should be mediated and diffused. It should not be systematically manufactured as seems to be the current de facto national policy.

Gangs are groups of human beings. They speak our language, albeit, often, somewhat differently. The gang members are our neighbors, our students, our employees, and our constituents. They do have the right to vote. It is a mistake to treat them as anything other than as a human social group. They are not simply a bunch of haphazardly associating sociopaths as some gang authors would have use believe.[23]

Drugs and gang crime, today, are intertwined. They exploit the contradiction in American society that drugs are illegal, but large numbers of people want these drugs. Legalizing heroin may not be the complete answer. But we should approach such decriminalization and legalization issues from a social science point of view. We clearly need more research on this. The scenarios presented in this book, regarding heroin, include not just a "sunny tomorrow", they include a "turbulent tomorrow". We need to keep an open mind about everything.

This book has examined gang crime and organized crime. It suggests that most criminal gangs do in fact aspire to become a new type of organized crime. Gangs can and have displaced the rackets in a number of ways. It has been shown that a level three gang has but to make some prosocial adjustments to "front" a social legitimacy to impact on society as has traditional organized crime groups (Mafia, etc). Some federal wiretap conversations between gang leaders like King Larry Hoover (leader of the Gangster Disciples) and Willie Lloyd (leader of the Insane Vice Lords) show how such gang leaders talk about using politics to carve up a large city like Chicago, in the same vein that traditional organized crime groups divide up territories.

Everyone blames the family. Beware of those who do little more than blame. They often have few answers. Clearly, the family and other social correlates of gang affiliation need further analysis. We need to understand what causes someone to join and sustain their membership in a gang, just as we need to know why similar persons avoid and never join gangs. The only blame the author has been willing to engage in is the blame that must be placed at the door of our elected officials for systematically ignoring this ever increasing problem.

The community, like the family, has a much larger role to play than it is apparently willing or able to play. Like the family, it cannot do it alone, without resources, on a "boot strap" total-volunteer basis. Our families, like our communities, are going to need some national help to deal with the American gang crime problem.

What the police should do and what they actually do are two separate analytical entities. In the best of all worlds, politics would not enter into law enforcement agencies. Rather law enforcement would be driven by career professionalism alone. But that is not necessarily the situation today nationwide, and is not likely to change anytime soon. Politicians always want to control their police forces. Hopefully the present analysis has suggested some proscriptive and prescriptive issues.

If any basis for rampant fear existed about the American gang crime problem today, then it is in the statistics compiled on gangs within our adult and juvenile correctional institutions. We seem, as a society, to have dumped this problem into the field of corrections. What few citizens seem informed about is that correctional officials are mandated to ultimately dump the problem back into our communities. Few prisoners in America are really "in for their natural life". What is also clear is that the gang density problem in American corrections today is not as low as some recent federally funded research would suggest.

Prevention and intervention in the gang crime problem are both feasible, and indeed desirable. We have not tried everything. We have in fact only begun to understand the scope and extent of the problem itself. We have focused, as a society, on repression. Repression has turned out to be the sticking of the harsh finger into the Chinese finger trap. It has a reverse-intended effect. Gangs can thrive on conflict. We need new answers. We need genuine solutions. We need non-ideological advice.

We need, in short, to begin using our social sciences. The fields of sociology, criminology, corrections and criminal justice, psychology, anthropology, political science, economics, and more. Social groups are not new. Gangs are not new. Gangs are social groups we fear. Conflict, violence, and crime are not new. We have accumulated some knowledge on these issues.

The primary lesson of this book then is abundantly clear: we simply need to begin using this knowledge.

DISCUSSION QUESTIONS

(1) Do you think gangs could have an important latent function for American society in spite of their manifest function? Or, lacking any appreciation for Durkheim, do you think that gangs and gang members should command our highest priority in terms of investigation and prosecution?

(2) Why do some societies like America have a more pronounced problem with gangs than other societies? What might distinguish high gang-problem societies from low-gang problem societies?

(3) What is your solution to the gang crime problem in America today?

FOOTNOTES

1. Obviously, some of our outlaw motorcycle gangs already meet this criteria.

2. There have been numerous incidents throughout the USA, such as in the recent case in Joliet, Illinois (Chicago Tribune, 1993, Section 2, p. 7) where a family "fought back" a gang that was pressuring a child into joining a gang by assaulting the youth. The family members fired their guns back at the gang and hit their target: two gang members were wounded. Guess who was arrested? You got it, the family members trying to fight the gang.

3. The predatory and social forms seem to have been first described by Henry D. Sheldon in "The Institutional Activity of American Children", American Journal of Psychology (1898): pp. 425-428.

4. In fact, most of the gang types listed in Figure 1 appear to be based on the attribution of goal orientations or motives to these gangs. Gangs, simply, do more than get high (hedonists) and drink wine. They do more than fighting and violence. They adapt to their environment and the opportunities it provides. Thus, the categories in Figure 1 are, in essence, little more than what Schwendinger and Schwendinger call social type names: greasers, skinheads, jocks, etc.

5. With the obvious qualification: because of the political nature of defining what is or is not crime, particularly gang crime (see Klein and Maxson, in Huff, 1990), a jurisdiction like Chicago can use "very conservative" definitions of what constitutes

gang crime, while another (e.g., Los Angeles) may use a rather straight-forward method. Chicago's Police Department reported, for example, only 74 homicides, 31 armed robbery victims, 26 strong arm robbery victims, 979 aggravated battery victims, 269 aggravated assault victims, 4 burglary victims, 2 theft victims, and 2 arson victims as constituting all of what is "official gang victimization" from the period January 1, 1990 through September 30, 1990 for an overall of 1,347 such gang related crime victims. Obviously, that barely touches the surface of the larger impact that gangs have when their members commit such offenses alone, in small groups, or where they do not leave their calling card to the effect "Hey, Chicago Police: We the _____ gang did this job".

6. This is an agency/systems study examining police chiefs, probation/parole agencies, correctional institutions, community organizations, etc, in an effort to gauge the actual force strength of gangs in America. It also includes an analysis of N = 3,000 youths held in confinement nationwide in terms of the actual extent of prior gang membership, age at joining, and the relationship of these two factors to other problems: fighting, drug/substance abuse, etc. Unfortunately this information could not be included in this here. We shall have to wait.

7. How many gang members are there in America? Assume ten percent of the prison population, ADD 100,000. Assume 15 percent of the juvenile confined population, ADD ANOTHER 15,000. Assume 5 percent of the local and county jail population, ADD ANOTHER 15,000. Assume 5 percent of the population on probation ADD ANOTHER 75,000. Here our most conservative estimate would show at least 200,000 gang members who are under some form of criminal justice control. And, if we can assume there are at least as many gang members in the community who escape the penal sanction, we are probably looking at about half a million gang members as a bare minimum.

8. See: Gangs and Guns: A Task Force Report, National Gang Crime Research Center, Nov. 11, 1994. George Knox, Tom McCurrie, Ed Tromanhauser, Jim Houston, and John Laskey.

9. Muehlbauer and Dodder (1983: pp. 127-129) recommend this very thing --- "a compulsory, two-year program of service for the common good" (p. 128). They also provide some other programmatic aspects, such as a flexible enlistment option (e.g., right to enter at age 16).

10. Fossett (1974) described service results for one such program called the North Central Youth Academy, operated by the Philadelphia Committee for Services to Youth. All we learn is that the NCYA staff had made contacts on 15 different gang corners, enrolled 149 applicants, 58 of which were counseled on education, and 42 were provided with job referrals; 71 were enrolled in vocational training, and 21 were enrolled in a GED program. Such programs can therefore clearly establish ability to "reach out", and often attract some youths "at risk" of gang affiliation.

11. Clearly, the Gang Summit meeting held in Minneapolis, Minnesota enjoyed the benefits of federal funding, because it was a federal grantee in a DHHS anti-gang program that sponsored the gang summit meeting. Other examples also exist.

12. The man actually received a four-year sentence for violating a previous probation involving retail theft; plus the two years for the cheese crime. Chicago Sun-Times, Friday, June 25, 1999, p. 4, "Metro Briefings: Cheese Thief Get Prison".

13. Clearly, the literature shows gangs existing in France (Faz, 1962; Legree and Fai, 1989), Canada (Rogers, 1945), London (Scott, 1956), Israel (Leissner, 1969), and as reviewed by Tompkins (1966) in Japan, Australia, Ceylon, Taiwan, and others. Gangs are not unique to America. Much new evidence is emerging on gangs in many other countries, as well as gangs with international movement and/or international connections.

14. See Dolan and Finney, 1984 for a similar position that it is a national problem.

15. Some private security and loss prevention companies now provide gang training, gang awareness, and gang identification, to staff. The National Gang Crime Research Center has conducted a number of such contractual training seminars, but mostly for the more elite and expensive security companies.

16. As Davis (1988) indicates, context is everything, and the context that must be addressed involves such policy issues as unemployment and racial inequality.

17. Gang members are simply more predisposed to get a prison sentence for a variety of reasons, including the fact that as law offenders gang members are more likely to commit homicide than are non-gang members (see Klein, Gordon and Maxson, 1985).

18. The case study of LK29 showed he felt "some loonies kill just to get back in the gang, they don't care if they go to prison, prison don't worry them, they just want back in, back in the gang".

19. Arnold (1969, p. 177) showed that for gang members a prison record is status enhancing.

20. I am indebted to the paper by Harris, Abdullah and Rowe (1990) presented in the scheduled session of student papers at the American Society of Criminology (held at the Maryland State Penitentiary), for the concept of "zombies." See Guy Harris, Tarif Abdullah, and Joe Rowe, 1990, "Penal Philosophy and Public Policy: Cohesion Requires Some Fundamental Change", pp. 26-37, in Raymond L. Ellis, Ph.D., Student Panel Papers, Theme: Behind Bars: Perspectives on the Administration of Justice On Location at Maryland State Penitentiary., Baltimore, Maryland: Coppin State College.

21. The reader must note for the historical record that my 1991 book used this same language. I did not try to emulate anything in the gang authored book Monster, in fact my use of the term appears before that of the Crip gang member who tells his heroic tale of being a new type of urban freedom fighter. This is standard inmate language I gained from my visit with prison inmates. The book bearing the same title of this expression appears to be an orchestrated and stylized account from do-gooders working with such a gang member in a predictable direction of logic: the

gang member is never responsible for the violence and mayhem he or she creates. It is a commercial exploitation of the gang problem. It is not social science.

22. Actually, such an initiative would be a great idea if the person using the equipment acknowledged in writing by their signature that they forfeited any expectation of privacy: to wit, monitoring these communications to see what they were actually doing for the "program".

23. We cannot oversimplify the problem by labelling gangs as psychotic (Bolitho, 1930), or assume they all have such mental health problems just because some authors have taken a psychiatric approach (Baittle, 1961) or like Schwitzgebel, have sought to use experimental therapy on gang members (Brotman, 1949; Beier, 1951).

SELECTED BIBLIOGRAPHY ON GANGS

Ackley, N.
1984 Gangs in Schools: Breaking Up Is Hard To Do, U.S. Dept. of Justice, Office of Juvenile Justice and Delinquency Prevention, Washington, D.C.
Ackerley, Ethel G. and Beverly R. Fliegel

1960 "A Social Work Approach to Street-Corner Girls", Social Work (5)(4): 27-36.

Adams, Stuart
1967 "A Cost Approach to the Assessment of Gang Rehabilitation Techniques", Journal of Research in Crime and Delinquency (Jan.).

Adler, P.A.
1985 Wheeling and Dealing: An Ethnography of an Upper-Level Drug Dealing and Smuggling Community. New York: Columbia University Press.

Agopian, Michael
1991 "Evaluation of G.A.P.P. - Gang Alternative Prevention Project in the Los Angeles Probation Department", paper presented at the Annual Meeting of the Academy of Criminal Justice Sciences, Nashville, Tennessee.

Aiken, Carol; Jeffrey P. Rush; and Jerry Wycoff
1993 "A Preliminary Inquiry Into Alabama Youth Gang Membership", The Gang Journal: An Interdisciplinary Research Quarterly (1)(2): 37-47.

Amandes, Richard B.
1979 "Hire a Gang Leader: A Delinquency Prevention Program", Juvenile and Family Court Journal (30)(1)(Feb): 37-40.

Anderson, Elijah
1978 A Place on the Corner. Chicago: University of Chicago Press.

Anderson, James F.
1993 "Review Essay: A Methodological Critique of Islands in the Streets", The Gang Journal: An Interdisciplinary Research Quarterly (1)(2): 49-57.

Arnold, William R.
1965 "The Concept of Gang", The Sociological Quarterly (7)(1): 59-75.

Asbury, Herbert
1927 Gangs of New York. New York: Garden City Publishing Co.

1939 The Gangs of New York. New York: Alfred A. Knopf.

Austin, David M.
1957 "Goals for Gang Workers", Social Work (2)(4): 43-50

Axelson, Roland G.
1984 "The Psychological Influence of Street Gangs on School-Aged Youth: A Case Study in Hartford, CT". The I.N. Thut World Education Center, Hartford, CT.

Bailey, William C.
1969 "Educational and Occupational Experience, Perception, and Future Expectations of Lower Class Negro Gang Delinquents", Master's thesis, Washington State University.

Baird, L.H.
1986 "Prison Gangs: Texas", Corrections Today (18)(July): 22.

Baittle, Brahm
1961 "Psychiatric Aspects of the Development of a Street Corner Group: An Exploratory Study", American Journal of Orthopsychiatry (31)(Oct): 703-712.

Barker, George C.
1950 Pachuco: An American-Spanish Argot and Its Social Function in Tucson, Arizona. Social Science Bulletin No. 18 (Vol. XXI)(No. 1)(Jan), Tucson, Arizona: University of Arizona Press.

1979 -----

Barrett, Leonard E.
1988 The Rastafarians. Boston: Beacon Press.

Bartollas, Clemens
1990 "The Prison: Disorder Personified", chapter 1 (pp. 11-22) in John W. Murphy and Jack E. Dison (Eds.) Are Prisons Any Better? Twenty Years of Correctional Reform, Sage Criminal Justice System Annuals, Newbury Park, CA: Sage Publications.

Beck, L.M.
1962 Three Groups of Delinquents of the Family Court of East Baton Rouge Parish, Ph.D. dissertation, Louisiana State University.

Beier, Ernest G.
1951 "Experimental Therapy With a Gang", Focus (30)(July): 97-102.

Bell, J. and D. Sullivan
1987 Jackson, Mississippi Mayor's Task Force on Gangs: Final Report, Jackson, MS.

Bennett, James
1981 Oral History and Delinquency: The Rhetoric of Criminology. Chicago: University of Chicago Press.

Bensinger, Gad J.
1984 "Chicago Youth Gangs: A New Old Problem", Journal of Crime & Justice (VII): 1-16.

Bernstein, Saul
1964 Youth on the Streets -- Work with Alienated Youth Groups. New York: Associated Press.

Bessant, Judith and Rob Watts
1992 "Being Bag is Good: Explorations of the Bodgie Gang Culture in South East Australia, 1948-1956", The Gang Journal: An Interdisciplinary Research Quarterly (1)(1): 31-55.

1994 "The American Juvenile Underclass and the Cultural Colonisation of Young Australians Under Conditions of Modernity", Journal of Gang Research (2)(1)(Fall): 15-33.

Bing, Leon
1991 Do or Die. New York: Harper-Collins.

Blanchard, W.H.
1959 "The Group Process in Gang Rape", Journal of Social Psychology : 259-266.

Bloch, Herbert
1963 "The Juvenile Gang: A Cultural Reflex", Annals of the American Academy of Political and Social Science (347)(May): 20-29.

Bloch, Herbert and Arthur Niederhoffer
1957 "Adolescent Behavior and the Gang: A Cross-Cultural Analysis", Journal of Social Therapy (3): 174-179.

1958 The Gang: A Study in Adolescent Behavior. New York: Philosophical Press.

Block, Carolyn Rebecca and Richard Block
1993 Street Gang Crime In Chicago. National Institute of Justice, Research in Brief. December.

Blumberg, Leonard
1964 "A Possible Application of the Epidemiological-Public Health Model to Civic Action-Research", Social Problems (12)(Fall): 178-185.

Bobrowski, Lawrence J.
1988 "Collecting, Organizing and Reporting Street Gang Crime", 82 pp., Chicago Police Department, Prepared for the 40th Annual Meeting of the American Society of Criminology, CPD: Special Functions Group.

Bogardus, Emory
1943 "Gangs of Mexican-American Youth", Sociology and Social Research (28): 55-66.

Bolitho, W.
1930 "The Psychosis of the Gang", Survey: 501-506.

Bookin, H.
1980 "The Gangs That Didn't Go Straight", paper presented at the Society for the Study of Social Problems, New York.

Bookin-Weiner, Hedy and Ruth Horowitz
1983 "The End of the Youth Gang: Fad or Fact?", Criminology (21)(4)-(Nov): 585-601.

Bordua, David J.
1961   "Delinquent Subcultures: Sociological Interpretations of Gang Delinquency", Annals of the American Academy of Social Science (338): 119-36.

Born, Peter
1971 Street Gangs and Youth Unrest. Chicago: Chicago Tribune Educational Service Department.

Bowker, L.H. and Malcolm W. Klein
1983 "The Etiology of Female Juvenile Delinquency and Gang Membership: A Test of Psychological and Social Structural Explanations", Adolescence (18)(72)(Win): 739-751.

Brooks, William Allan
1952 Girl Gangs. A Survey of Teen-Age Drug Addicts, Sex Crimes, Rape, Kleptomania, Prostitution, Truancy, and Other Deviations. New York: Padell Book Company.

Brotman, Richard
1949   A Group Approach to the Treatment of the Aggressive Gang, Master's Thesis, City College of New York.

Brown, Waln K.
1977   "Black Female Gangs in Philadelphia", International Journal of Offender Therapy and Comparative Criminology (21): 221-228.

1978 "Black Gangs as Family Extensions" & "Graffiti, Identity, and the Delinquent Gang", International Journal of Offender Therapy and Comparative Criminology (22)(1): 39-48.

Brueckner, William H.
1960 "Corner Group Work with Teen-Age Gangs", Federal Probation (24)(Dec): 84.

Bryant, D.
1989 Community Responses Crucial for Dealing With Youth Gangs, U.S. Dept. of Justice, Office of Juvenile Justice and Delinquency Prevention, Washington, D.C.

Brymmer, R.A.
1967 "Toward a Definition and Theory of Conflict Gangs", (mimeo) paper presented at the annual meeting of the Society for the Study of Social Problems (August 26).

Buentello, S.
1986 Texas Syndicate: A Review of Its Inception, Growth in Violence and Continued Threat to the TDC, Texas Department of Corrections, unpublished.

Burns, E. and T.J. Deakin
1989 "New Investigative Approach to Youth Gangs", FBI Law Enforcement Bulletin (58)(10)(Oct): 20-24.

California Attorney General's Youth Gang Task Force
1981 Report on Youth Gang Violence in California. California: Department of Justice.

California Council on Criminal Justice
1986 Final Report: State Task Force on Youth Gang Violence. Sacramento, CA.

1989 State Task Force on Gangs and Drugs. Sacramento, CA: 95823.

Camp, George and Camille Graham Camp
1985 Prison Gangs: Their Extent, Nature, and Impact on Prisons. Washington, D.C.: U.S. Dept. of Justice.

Campbell, Anne
1984 The Girls in the Gang: A Report from New York City. New York: Basil Blackwell Ltd.

1984 "Girls' Talk: The Social Representation of Aggression by Female Gang Members", Criminal Justice Behavior (11): 139-156.

1987 "Self Definitions by Rejection: The Case of Gang Girls", Social Problems (34)(5)(Dec): 451-466.

Campbell, Anne and Steven Muncer
1989 "Them and Us: A Comparison of the Cultural Context of American Gangs and British Subcultures", Deviant Behavior (10)(3): 271-288.

Caplan, Nathan S.; Dennis J. Deshaies, Gerald D. Suttles, and Hans W. Mattick
1963 "The Nature, Variety, and Patterning of Street Club Work in an Urban Setting", pp. 135-169 in Malcolm W. Klein and Barbara G. Meyerhoff (eds), Juvenile Gangs in Context: Theory,Research, and Action, Confererence Report, August 25-26, 1963, Youth Studies Center, Los Angeles: University of Southern California.

1964 "Factors Affecting the Process and Outcome of Street Club Work", Sociology and Social Research (48)(Jan): 207-219.

Carey, Sean
    1985 "I just Hate 'em, That's All", New Society (73)(1178)(July): 123-125.

Cartwright, Desmond S. and Kenneth I. Howard
    1966 "Multivariate Analysis of Gang Delinquency: I. Ecologic Influences",
    Multivariate Behavioral Research (1)(July): 321-71.

Cartwright, Desmond S.; Kenneth I. Howard; and Nicholas A. Reuterman
    1970 "Multivariate Analysis of Gang Delinquency: II. Structural and
    Dynamic Properties of Gangs", Multivariate Behavioral Research (5)(July):
    303-24.

    ----- 1971 "Multivariate Analysis of Gang Delinquency: III. Age and
    Physique of Gangs and Clubs", Multivariate Behavioral Research(6)(Jan):
    75-90.

    ----- 1980 "Multivariate Analysis of Gang Delinquency: IV. Personality
    Factors in Gangs and Clubs", Multivariate Behavioral Research (15): 3-22.

Cartwright, Desmond S.; B. Tomson; and H. Schwartz
    1975 Gang Delinquency. Monterey, CA: Brooks/Cole.

Cavanagh, Suzanne and David Teasley
    1992 Youth Gangs: An Overview. Washington, DC: Congressional
    Research Service.

Cellini, Henry D.
    1991 Youth Gang Prevention and Intervention Strategies. Albuquerque,
    NM: Training and Research Institute, Inc.

Chazal, J.
    1964 "A Current Criminological Problem: Juvenile Delinquency in Gangs",
    Quebec Society of Criminology Bulletin (3)(2): 5-11.

Chicago Area Project
    n.d. "Shaw's Thoughts".

    1939 "Chicago Area Project", March, 1939.

    n.d. Chicago Area Project: The Nation's First Community-Based Delin-
    quency Prevention Program.

Chicago Police Department
    1989 Murder Analysis. Richard M. Daley, Mayor. Leroy Martin, Supertin-
    dendent of Police. Chicago, IL.

Chin, Ko-Lin
    1986 Chinese Triad Societies, Tongs, Organized Crime, and Street Gangs
    in Asia and the United States. Ph.D. dissertation, University of Pennsylvania.

1988 Chinese Gangs in New York City: 1965-1988. Baltimore, MD and Taipeh, Taiwan: Loyola College and National Taiwan University.

1990 Chinese Subculture and Criminality: Non-traditional Crime Groups in America. Westport, Conn: Greenwood Press.

1993 "Methodological Issues in Studying Chinese Gang Extortion", The Gang Journal: An Interdisciplinary Research Quarterly (1)(2): 25-36.

Clark, J.H.
1981   A Report of the Gang Activities Task Force. Chicago Board of Education, Chicago, Illinois.

Cloward, R.A. and L.E. Ohlin
1960 Delinquency and Opportunity. New York: Free Press.

Cohen, Albert K.
1955 Delinquent Boys: The Culture of the Gang. Glencoe, IL: The Free Press.

Cohen, Bernard
1970 "The Delinquency of Gangs and Spontaneous Groups", Chapter 4 in Delinquency: Selected Studies, Thorsten Sellin and Marvin E. Wolfgang (eds.), New York: John Wiley and Sons.

Cole, Juan R.I. and Moojan Momen
1986 "Mafia, Mob and Shiism in Iraq: The Rebellion of Ottoman Karbala 1824-1843", Past and Present (112)(Aug): 112-143.

Collins, H. Craig
1977 "Street Gangs of New York: A Prototype of Organized Youth Crime", Law and Order (25)(1)(Jan): 6-16.

Collins, Jessie
1993 "Joe: The Story of an Ex-Gang Member", Gang Journal: An Interdisciplinary Research Quarterly (1)(3): 45-50.

Conrad, J.P.
1979   "Who's in Charge? The Control of Gang Violence in California Prisons", in Correctional Facility Planning edited by Robert Montilla and Nora Marlow, pp. 135-147, Lexington, Mass: D.C. Heath.

Cook, James I.
1993 "Targetting Gang Violence in the City of Westminister", Westminister Police Department, Westminister, CA.

Covey, Herbert C.; Scott Menard; and Robert J. Franzese
1992 Juvenile Gangs. Charles C. Thomas Publisher: Springfield, IL.

Cox, V.
1986 "Prison Gangs - Inmates Battle for Control", Corrections Compendium (10)(9)(Apr): 1,6-9.

Crane, A.R.
1951 "A Note on Pre-Adolescent Gangs", Australian Psychology (3): 43-45.

1958 "The Development of Moral Values in Children: IV; Pre-Adolescent Gangs and the Moral Development of Children", British Journal of Educational Psychology (28)(Nov): 201-208.

Crawford, Paul I.; Daniel I. Malamud; and James R. Dumpson
1950 Working With Teenage Gangs. A Report on the Central Harlem Street Clubs Project. New York: Welfare Council of New York City.

Crime Control Digest
1976 "Detroit Mayor Against City's Growing Youth Gangs: Citizen Involvement in Crime Prevention", Aug. 30, 1976, p. 5, (10)(35).

1980 "Gangs - Police, Community Relations", Mar. 30, 1980, pp. 7-8, (14)(9).

1984 "Police Community Relations: Gangs - Chicago Police Department: Citizen Involvement in Crime Prevention", Mar. 26, 1984, pp. 5-6, (18)(12).

1987 "Detroit Mayor Unveils Plan to Fight Youth Crime: Gangs and Crime Prevention", Jan 26, 1987, p. 6, (21)(4).

1987 "California's Vietnam Refugees Work on Their Own to Divert Teens from Street Gangs", June 8, 1987, pp. 9-10,(21)(23).

Crowner, James M.
1963 "Utilizing Certain Positive Aspects of Gang Phenomena in Training School Group Work", American Journal of Correction (25)(July-August): 24-27.

Cummings, Scott and Daniel Monti (eds.)
1993 Gangs: The Origins and Impact of Contemporary Youth Gangs in the United States. Albany, NY: State University New York Press.

Curry, G. David and Irving A. Spergel
1988 "Gang Homicide, Delinquency, and Community", Criminology (26)(Aug): 381-405.

Cusson, Maurice
1989 "Disputes over Honor and Gregarious Aggressions", Revue Internationale de Criminologie et de Police Technique (Geneva, SWITZ) (42)(3): 290-297.

Dahmann, J.
1981 "Operation Hardcore: A Prosecutorial Response to Violent Gang Criminality", interim report, MITRE Corporation, McLean, VA.

Daniels, S.
1987 "Prison Gangs: Confronting the Threat", Corrections Today (29)(2)-(Apr): 66,126,162.

Dart, Robert W.
1992 "The Future is Here Today: Street Gang Trends", The Gang Journal: An Interdisciplinary Research Quarterly (1)(1): 87-90.

David, J.J. and M.H. Shaffer
1988 Intelligence Gathering in the Investigation of Motorcycle Gangs, National Institute of Justice, NCJRS, Rockville, MD.

David, J.J.
1988 "Outlaw Motorcycle Gangs: A Transnational Problem", paper presented at the Conference on International Terrorism and Transnational Crime, University of Illinois at Chicago, August, 1988.

Davis, James R.
1978 The Terrorists: Youth, Biker and Prison Violence. San Diego, CA: Grossmont Press.

1982 Street Gangs: Youth, Biker and Prison Groups. Dubuque, Iowa: Kendall/Hunt Publishing.

Davis, Mike
1988 "War in the Streets", New Statesman & Society (1)(23)(Nov): 27-30.

Davis, R.H.
1982 Selected Bibliography on Publications Related to Outlaw Motorcycle Gangs, U.S. Dept. of Justice, FBI Academy, Quantico, VA 22134.

Day, D.
1987 "Outlaw Motorcycle Gangs", Royal Canadian Mounted Police Gazette (49)(5): 1-42.

Dawley, David
1973 A Nation of Lords: The Autobiography of the Vice Lords. Garden City, NY: Anchor Press.

1992 A Nation of Lords. Prospect Heights, IL: Waveland Press.

Delaney, J.L. and Walter B. Miller
1977 Intercity Variation in the Seriousness of Crime by Youth Gangs and Youth Groups, Report to the Office of Juvenile Justice and Delinquency Prevention.

Delaney, Lloyd T.
1954 "Establishing Relationships with Antisocial Groups and an Analysis of Their Structure", British Journal of Delinquency (5)(1): 34-42.

De Leon, Aleister
1977 "Averting Violence in the Gang Community", The Police Chief (44)(7)(July): 52-53.

Denisoff, R. Serge and Charles H. McCaghy
1973 Deviance, Conflict, and Criminality. Chicago: Rand McNally & Company.

Destro, Robert A.
1993 "Gangs and Civil Rights", pp. 227-304 in Scott Cummings and Daniel J. Monti (Eds.), Gangs: The Origin and Impact of Contemporary Youth Gangs in the United States. Albany, NY: State University of New York Press.

Dolan, Edward F. and Shan Finney
1984 Youth Gangs. New York: Simon & Schuster, Julian Messner.

Donohue, John K.
1966 My Brother's Boy: A Treatise on Criminology. St. Paul, MN: Bruce Publishing Co.

Douglas, Jack D.
1970 Youth in Turmoil: America's Changing Youth Cultures and Student Protest Movements. Center for Studies of Crime and Delinquency, National Institute of Mental Health, Washington, DC: Government Printing Office.

Dumpson, J.R.
1949 "An Approach to Antisocial Street Gangs", Federal Probation: 22-29.

Dumpson, James R., et al
1952 "Gang and Narcotic Problems of Teen-Age Youth", American Journal of Psychotherapy (6)(Apr): 312-46.

Dunbar, Ellen A.
1963 "How to Help the Gang Member Through His Family", Special Service for Groups, Los Angeles: unpublished.

Dunston, Leonard G.
1990 Report of the Task Force on Juvenile Gangs. New York State Division for Youth. Albany, New York.

Dunston, Mark S.
1992 Street Signs - An Identification Guide of Symbols of Crime and Violence. Powers Lake, WI: Performance Dimensions Publishing.

Duran, M.
   1975 "What Makes a Difference in Working with Youth Gangs?", Crime Prevention Review (2): 25-30.

Earley, Pete
   1992 The Hot House: Life Inside Leavenworth Prison. New York: Bantam.

Eisenstadt, S. N.
   1951 "Delinquency Group Formation Among Immigrant Youth", British Journal of Delinquency (2)(1).

Elliott, D.S.
   1962 "Delinquency and Perceived Opportunity", Sociological Inquiry (32)(Spr): 216-27.

English, T.J.
   1990 The Westies: The Irish Mob. New York: St. Martins Press.

Erlanger, Howard S.
   1979 "Estrangement, Machismo and Gang Violence", Social Science Quarterly (60)(2): 235-49.

Fagan, Jeffrey
   1989 "The Social Organization of Drug Use and Drug Dealing Among Urban Gangs", Criminology (27)(4): 633-664.

Fagan, Jeffrey and Ko-lin Chin
   1989 "Violence as Regulation and Social Control in the Distribution of Crack", in M. De la Rosa; B. Gropper; and E. Lambert (eds.), Drugs and Violence, National Institute of Drug Abuse Research Monograph, Rockville, MD: U.S. Dept. of Health and Human Services.

Ferrell, Jeff
   1992 Crimes of Style: Urban Graffiti and the Politics of Urban Criminality. New York: Garland.

Fishman, L.
   1988 "The Vice Queens: An Ethnographic Study of Black Female Gang Behavior", paper presented at the Annual Meeting of the American Society of Criminology.

Florida House of Representatives
   1987 Issue Paper: Youth Gangs in Florida. Committee on Youth. Tallahassee, FL.

Fong, Robert S.
   1987 A Comparative Study of the Organizational Aspects of Two Texas Prison Gangs: Texas Syndicate and Mexican Mafia. Ph.D. dissertation, Sam Houston State University, Huntsville, Texas.

1990 "The Organizational Structure of Prison Gangs: A Texas Case Study",
Federal Probation (54)(1)(Mar): 36-43.

Fong, Robert S. and Salvador Buentello
1991 "The Management of Prison Gangs: An Empirical Assessment", paper
presented at the Annual Meeting of the Academy of Criminal Justice
Sciences, Nashville, Tennessee.

Fong, Robert S.; Ron Vogel; and Robert Little
1991 "Behind Prison Walls: Racially Based Gangs and Their Level of
Violence", paper presented at the Annual Meeting of the Academy of
Criminal Justice Sciences, Nashville, Tennessee.

Fossett, Christine A.
1974 Evaluation Report: North Central Youth Academy. Educational
Management Associates, Consultants, Facilitators, Applied Behavioral and
Management Sciences, Design, Development and Audit of Urban Programs,
Philadelphia, PA (NCJRS# 09900.00.027469).

Fox, Robert W. and Mark E. Amador
1993 Gangs on the Move: A Descriptive Cataloging of Over 1500 Most
Active Gangs in America. Placerville, CA: Copperhouse Publishing
Company.

Frias, Gus
1982 Barrio Warriors: Homeboys of Peace. Los Angeles: Diaz Publishing.

Friedman, C.J.; F. Mann; and A.S. Friedman
1975 "A Profile of Juvenile Street Gang Members", Adolescence (10): 563-
607.

1976 "Juvenile Street Group: The Victimization of Youth", Adolescence,
(44)(Winter): 527-533.

Fry, John
1969 Fire and Blackstone. Philadelphia: J.B. Lippincott.

1973 Locked Out Americans. New York: Harper and Row.

Furfey, Paul Hanley
1926 The Gang Age: A Study of the Pre-Adolescent Boy and His Recreational Needs. New York: The Macmillan Company.

Furman, Sylvan S. (ed).
1952 Reaching the Unreached. "Working with a Street Gang" (pp. 112-121)
New York: New York City Youth Board.

Gandy, John M.
1959 "Preventive Work with Street-Corner Groups: Hyde Park Project,
Chicago", Annals of American Academy of Political and Social Science
(323)(Mar): 107-116.

Gannon, Thomas M.
    1967 "Dimension of Current Gang Delinquency", Journal of Research in Crime and Delinquency (Jan)(4)(2): 119-131.

    1970 -----. Chapter 34 in Marvin E. Wolfgang, Leonard Savitz, and Norman Johnston (eds.), The Sociology of Crime and Delinquency, New York: John Wiley & Sons, Inc.

Geis, Gilbert
    1965 "Juvenile Gangs", President's Committee on Juvenile Delinquency and Youth Crime, Washington, D.C.

Gerrard, Nathan L.
    1964 "The Core Member of the Gang", British Journal of Criminology (4)(Apr): 361-371.

Giles, H. Harry
    1957 "Case Analysis of Social Conflict", Journal of Educational Sociology (30)(Mar): 289-333.

Giordano, P.C.
    1978 "Girls, Guys and Gangs: The Changing Social Context of Female Delinquency", Journal of Criminal Law and Criminology (69): 126-132.

Glane, Sam
    1950 "Juvenile Gangs in East Side Los Angeles", Focus (29)(Sept): 136-141.

Goldstein, Arnold P.
    1991 Delinquent Gangs: A Psychological Perspective. Champaign, IL: Research Press.

Goldstein, Arnold P. and Barry Glick, et al
    1994 The Prosocial Gang: Implementing Aggression Replacement Training. Thousand Oaks, CA: Sage Publications.

Gonzalez, Alfredo
    1981 Mexican/Chicano Gangs in Los Angeles. D.S.W. dissertation, University of California at Berkeley, School of Social Welfare.

Gordon, Robert A.
    1963 Values and Gang Delinquency, Ph.D. dissertation, University of Chicago.

    1967 "Social Level, Disability, and Gang Interaction", American Journal of Sociology (73)(July): 42-62.

Gordon, Robert A.; James Short, Jr.; Desmond S. Cartwright; and Fred L. Strodtbeck
    1963 "Values and Gang Delinquency: A Study of Street-Corner Groups", American Journal of Sociology (69)(2): 109-128.

1970 "Values and Gang Delinquency: A Study of Street-Corner Groups", Chapter 33 in Wolfgang, et al (eds.), The Sociology of Crime and Delinquency, New York: John Wiley & Sons, Inc, pp. 319-339.

Gorn, Elliott J.
1987 "Good-Bye Boys, I Die a True American": Homicide, Nativism, and Working-Class Culture in Antebellum New York City", Journal of American History (74)(2)(Sept): 388-410.

Gott, Raymond
1991 (Audio Training Tape) "Juvenile Gangs and Drug Trafficking", available through the National Juvenile Detention Association, 217 Perkins Bldg, Richmond, KY 40475-3127.

Greeley, Andrew and James Casey
1963 "An Upper Middle Class Deviant Gang", American Catholic Sociological Review (24)(Spr): 33-41.

Hagedorn, John M.
1987 Final Report: Milwaukee Gang Research Project, Milwaukee: University of Wisconsin-Milwaukee.

Hagedorn, John M. and Perry Macon
1988 People and Folks: Gangs, Crime and the Underclass in a Rustbelt City, Chicago: Lakeview Press.

Hagedorn, John M. and Joan W. Moore
1987 "Milwaukee and Los Angeles Gangs Compared", paper presented at the Annual Meeting of the American Anthropological Association, Oaxaca, Mexico.

Haire, Thomas D.
1979 "Street Gangs: Some Suggested Remedies for Violence and Vandalism", The Police Chief (46)(7)(July): 54-55.

Hamm, Mark S.
1990 "Dealing with Skinheads, the Ku Klux Klan and other Idiots with Ideology: Toward a Correctional Education to Reduce Racial Hatred in Prison", paper presented at the International Conference of the Correctional Educational Education Association, July 8-11, 1990, Burnaby, British Columbia.

1993 American Skinheads: The Criminology and Control of Hate Crime. Westport, Conn.: Praeger Series in Criminology and Crime Control Policy.

Hanson, Kitty
1964 Rebels in the Streets: The Story of New York's Gang Girls.Englewood Cliffs, NJ: Prentice-Hall.

Harding, J.
1952   "A Street Corner Gang and its Implications for Sociological and Psychological Theory", In J.E. Hulett and K.R. Stagner (eds.), Problems in Social Psychology, Urbana: University of Illinois Press.

Hardman, Dale G.
1963 Small Town Gangs, Ph.D. dissertation, University of Illinois, College of Education.

1967 "Historical Perspectives of Gang Research", Journal of Research in Crime and Delinquency (4)(1): 5-27.

1969 "Small Town Gangs", Journal of Criminal Law, Criminology and Police Studies (60)(2): 173-81.

Harris, Mary G.
1988 Cholas: Latino Girls and Gangs. New York: AMS Press.

Harrison, F.V.
1988 "The Politics of Outlawry in Urban Jamaica", Urban Anthropology (17)(2,3)(Sum/Fall): 259-277.

Haskins, James
1974 Street Gangs: Yesterday and Today. New York: Hastings House.

Helmreich, W.B.
1973 "Black Crusaders: The Rise and Fall of Political Gangs", Society (11)(1)(Nov/Dec): 44-50.

Hendry, Charles E., et al
1947 "Gangs", John Dewey Society, Ninth Yearbook: 151-175, New York: Harper.

Hobsbawm, Eric J.
1965 Primitive Rebels. New York: W.W. Norton & Co., Inc.

1969 Bandits. Delacorte Press.

Hodge, Patricia
1964 Self-Descriptions of Gang and Nongang Teen-Aged Boys, Master's thesis, Department of Sociology, University of Chicago.

Hoenig, Gary
1975 Reaper: The Story of a Gang Leader. Indianapolis: The Bobbs-Merrill Company, Inc.

Hoffman, Paul
1993 "A Nation of Lords: Book Review", The Gang Journal: An Interdisciplinary Research Quarterly (1)(2): 71-72.

Hogrefe, Russell and John Harding
    1947 "Research Considerations in the Study of Street Gangs", Applied
    Anthropology (6)(Fall): 21-24.

Horowitz, Ruth
    1982 "Masked Intimacy and Marginality: Adult Delinquent Gangs in a
    Chicano Community", Urban Life (11): 3-26.

    1983 "The End of the Youth Gang", Criminology (21)(4): 585-600.

    1983 Honor and the American Dream. New Brunswick, NJ: Rutgers
    University Press.

    1986 "Remaining an Outsider: Membership as a Threat to Research
    Rapport", Urban Life (14)(4)(Jan): 409-430.

    1987 "Community Tolerance of Gang Violence", Social Problems (34)(Dec):
    449.

Horowitz, Ruth and Gary Schwartz
    1974 "Honor, Normative Ambiguity and Gang Violence", American
    Sociological Review (39): 238-51.

Houston, James G.
    1993 "An Interview with Lewis Yablonsky: The Violent Gang and Beyond",
    The Gang Journal: An Interdisciplinary Research Quarterly (1)(2): 59-67.

    1994 "National Policy Neglect and Its Impact on Gang Suppression", Journal
    of Gang Research (2)(1)(Fall): 35-62.

Howson, Gerald
    1970 Thief-Taker General: Jonathan Wild and the Emergence of Crime and
    Corruption as a Way of Life in Eighteenth Century England. New Bruns-
    wick: Transaction Books.

Huff, C. Ronald
    1988 "Youth Gangs and Public Policy in Ohio: Findings and Recommen-
    dations", paper presented at the Ohio Conference on Youth Gangs and the
    Urban Underclass, Columbus: Ohio State University.

    ---- "Youth Gangs and Police Organizations: Rethinking Structure and
    Functions", paper presented at the Annual Meeting of the Academy of
    Criminal Justice Sciences, San Francisco.

    1989 "Youth Gangs and Public Policy", Crime & Delinquency (35)(4)(Oct.):
    524-37.

    ---- "Gangs, Organized Crime, and Drug-Related Violence in Ohio", In
    Understanding the Enemy: An Informational Overview of Substance Abuse
    in Ohio, Columbus, OH: Governor's Office of Criminal Justice Services.

1990 Gangs in America: Diffusion, Diversity, and Public Policy. Newbury Park, CA: Sage Publications.

Hunsaker, A.
1981 "The Behavioral-Ecological Model of Intervention With Chicano Gang Delinquents", Hispanic Journal of Behavioral Sciences (3): 225-239.

Hunt, G.; S. Riegel; T. Morales; and D. Waldorf
1992 "Keep The Peace Out of Prisons: Prison Gangs, an Alternative Perspective". San Francisco, CA: Institute for Scientific Analysis, Home Boy Study.

1993 "Changes in Prison Culture: Prison Gangs and the Case of the Pepsi Generation". San Francisco, CA: Institute for Scientific Analysis, Home Boy Study.

Ianni, Francis A.J.
1974 Black Mafia: Ethnic Succession in Organized Crime. New York: Simon and Schuster.

Illinois Department of Corrections
1984 Gangs and Gang Awareness. Training Academy.

1988 Gangs and Gang Awareness. Training Academy.

Inciardi, James A.
1984 Criminal Justice. Orlando: Academic Press, Inc.

Intl. Assoc. of Chiefs of Police
1986 Organized Motorcycle Gangs, Gaithersburg, MO 20878.

Jackson, George
1970 Soledad Brother: The Prison Letters of George Jackson. New York: Bantam Books.

Jackson, Pamela Irving
1991 "Crime, Youth Gangs, and Urban Transition: The Social Dislocations of Postindustrial Economic Development", Justice Quarterly (8)(3): 379-397.

Jackson, Patrick G.
1989 "Theories and Findings About Youth Gangs", Criminal Justice Abstracts (21)(2)(June): 313-329.

Jackson, R.K. and W.D. McBride
1985 Understanding Street Gangs. Sacramento, CA: Custom Publishing.

Jacobs, James
1974 "Street Gangs Behind Bars", Social Problems (21)(3): 395-408.

1977 Stateville. Chicago: University of Chicago Press.

James, Don
   1963 Girls and Gangs. Derby, Conn: Monarch.

Jameson, S.H.
   1956 "Policeman's Non-Official Role in Combatting Gangs and Vandalism", Association for Professional Law Enforcement, Quartly Journal (3)(June): 1-3.

Jankowski, Martin Sanchez
   1991 Islands in the Street: Gangs American Urban Society. Berkeley: University of California Press.

Janowitz, Morris
   1970 Political Conflict. Chicago: Quadrangle Books.

Jansyn, Leon
   1960 Solidarity and Delinquency in a Street Corner Group: A Study of the Relationship between Changes in Specified Aspects of Group Structure and Variations in the Frequency of Delinquent Activity, Master's thesis, University of Chicago.

   1967 "Solidarity and Delinquency in a Street Corner Group", American Sociological Review (31): 600-14.

Jayasuriya, J.E. and Sundari Kariyawasam
   1958 "Juvenile Delinquency as a Gang Activity in the City of Colombo", Ceylon Journal of Historical and Social Studies (1)(2)(July): 202-215.

Jereczek, Gordon E.
   1962 "Gangs Need Not Be Delinquent", Federal Probation (26)(Mar): 49-52.

Joe, D. and N. Robinson
   1980 "Chinatown's Immigrant Gangs: The New Young Warrior Class", Criminology (18)(3)(Nov): 337-345.

Joe, Karen
   1980 "Kai-Doi's: Gang Violence in Chinatown". Paper presented at the Annual Conference of the Rho Chapter of the California Alpha Kappa Delta association. Los Angeles, CA: University of California at Los Angeles.

   1993 "Issues in Accessing and Studying Ethnic Youth Gangs", The Gang Journal: An Interdisciplinary Research Quarterly (1)(2): 9-23.

Johnson, Gwendolyn
   1949 The Transformation of Juvenile Gangs into Accommodated Groups: A Study of Eight Boys' Gangs in Washington. Master's Thesis, Howard University.

Johnson, Patrick
1989   "Theories and Findings about Youth Gangs", Criminal Justice Abstracts (June): 313-327.

Johnson, W.C.
1981   "Motorcycle Gangs and White Collar Crime", The Police Chief (47)(6)(June): 32-33.

Johnstone, John W.C.
1981   "Youth Gangs and Black Suburbs", Pacific Sociological Review (24)(3)(July): 355-375.

Joselit, Jenna Weissman
1983   Our Gang: Jewish Crime and the New York Jewish Community 1900-1940. Bloomington: Indiana University Press.

Juvenile Justice Digest
1980   "Police Community Relations: Crime Prevention of Gangs", Feb. 22, 1980, pp. 7-8 (8)(4).

Kantor, David and William Ira Bennett
1968   "Orientation of Street-Corner Workers and Their Effect on Gangs", In Stanton Wheeler (ed.), Controlling Delinquents, New York: Wiley.

Karacki, Larry and Jackson Toby
1962   "The Uncommitted Adolescent: Candidate for Gang Socialization", Sociological Quarterly (32)(Spr): 203-215.

Kasimar, Yale
1971   "When the Cops Were Not 'Handcuffed'", pp. 46-57 in Donald R. Cressey (ed.), Crime & Criminal Justice, Chicago: Quadrangle Books.

Keiser, R. Lincoln
1969   The Vice Lords: Warriors of the Streets. New York: Holt, Rinehart and Winston.

Kleeck, Mary van; Emma A. Winslow; and Ira De A. Reid
1931   Work and Law Observance. An Experimental Inquiry into the Influence of Unemployment and Occupational Conditions Upon Crime for the National Commission on Law Observance and Enforcement, No. 13, June 26, 1931, pp. 163-333.

Klein, Lloyd
1990   "Running on the 'Wild Side': The Central Park Jogger Case and Adolescent Criminal Activity", paper presented at the Annual Meeting of the American Society of Criminology, Baltimore, MD.

Klein, Malcolm W.
1964   "Internal Structures and Age Distribution in Four Delinquent Negro Gangs", Youth Studies Center (Dec.), Los Angeles: University of Southern California.

1965 "Juvenile Gangs, Police, and Detached Workers: Controversies About Intervention", Social Service Review (39): 183-190.

1966 "Factors Related to Juvenile Gang Membership Patterns", Sociology and Social Research (51): 49-62.

1967 Juvenile Gangs in Context. New Jersey: Prentice-Hall.

1968a "Impressions of Juvenile Gang Members", Adolescence (3)(59): 53-78.

1968b From Association to Guilt: The Group Guidance Project in Juvenile Gang Intervention. Los Angeles: Youth Studies Center.

1968c The Ladino Hill Project. Los Angeles: Youth Studies Center.

1969a "Violence in American Juvenile Gangs", in D. Mulvihill and M. Tumin (eds.), Crimes of Violence, National Commission on the Causes and Prevention of Violence, Vol. 13: 1427-1460.

1969b "On the Group Context of Delinquency", Sociology and Social Research (54): 63-71.

1969c "Gang Cohesiveness, Delinquency, and a Street-Work Program", Journal of Research in Crime and Delinquency (July).

1971 Street Gangs and Street Workers. Englewood Cliffs, NJ: Prentice-all.

1990 "Having an Investment in Violence: Some Thoughts About the American Street Gang", The Edwin H. Sutherland Award Address to the American Society of Criminology, Annual Meeting, November 9, 1990.

Klein, Malcolm W. and Lois Y. Crawford
1967 "Groups, Gangs, and Cohesiveness", Journal of Research in Crime and Delinquency (4): 63-75.

Klein, Malcolm W.; Cheryl Maxson, and Margaret A. Gordon
1985 "Differences Between Gang and Non-Gang Homicides", Criminology (23)(2): 209-20.

1986 "The Impact of Police Investigations on Police-Reported Rates of Gang and Nongang Homicides", Criminology (24): 489-512.

Klein, Malcolm W.; and Cheryl L. Maxson
1985 "Rock' Sales in South L.A.", Social Science Research (69): 561-565.

1989 "Street Gang Violence", In Marvin E. Wolfgang and Neil A. Weiner (eds.), Violent Crime, Violent Criminals, Newbury Park, CA: Sage Publications.

Klein, Malcolm W.; Cheryl Maxson; and Lea Cunningham
1990 "'Crack,' Street Gangs, and Violence", Center For Research on Crime and Social Control, University of Southern California.

Klein, Malcolm W. and Barbara G. Meyerhoff (eds)
1964 Juvenile Gangs in Context: Theory, Research, and Action, Conference Report, August 25-26, 1963, Youth Studies Center, Los Angeles: University of Southern California.

Klein, Malcolm W. and Neal Snyder
1965 "The Detached Worker: Uniformities and Variances in Style", Social Work (10)(Oct): 60-68.

Klofas, John; Stan Stojkovic and David Kalinich
1990 Criminal Justice Organizations: Administration and Management. Belmont, CA: Brooks/Cole Publishing Company.

Knox, George W.
1976 The Urban Crisis in Southwest Chicago: A Research-Based Discussion of Racial Conflict, (Dec., 1976), unpublished monograph.

1978 "Perceived Closure and Respect for the Law Among Delinquent and Non-Delinquent Youths", Youth and Society (9)(4)(June): 385-406.

1978 "Determinants of Employment Success Among Exoffenders", Offender Rehabiliation (2)(3)(Spr): 204-214.

1980 "Educational Upgrading for Youthful Offenders", Chidren and Youth Services Review (2)(3): 291-313.

1981 "Differential Integration and Job Retention Among Exoffenders", Criminology (18)(4)(Feb): 481-499.

1981 "A Comparative Cost-Benefit Analysis of Offender Placement Programs", LAE Journal of the American Criminal Justice Association (43)(1,2): 39-49.

1984 "How Criminologists View Rehabilitation", Indian Journal of Criminology (12)(1)(Jan): 26-32.

1989 "Family Services in Corrections", The State of Corrections, Proceedings of the Annual Conferences of The American Correctional Association, pp. 179-182.

1991 An Introduction to Gangs. Berrien Springs, MI: Vande Vere Publishing, Ltd.

1991 "Gangs and Social Justice Issues", chapter 1 (pp. 1-19), in Sloan T. Letman (Ed.), Prison Conditions and Prison Overcrowding, Dubuque, IA: Kendall/Hunt Publishing Company.

1992 "Gang Organization in a Large Urban Jail", <u>American Jails</u>.

1994 <u>The Unabridged Thrasher</u> (Ed.). Berrien Springs, MI: Vande Vere Publishing, Ltd. (in press).

Knox, George W.; Benito Garcia; and Pat Mc Clendon
1983   "Social and Behavioral Correlates of Gang Affiliation", paper presented at the Annual Meeting of the American Society of Criminology, Nov. 10, 1983, Denver, CO.

Knox, George W.; Edward D. Tromanhauser; and David Laske
1992   <u>Schools Under Siege</u>.   Dubuque, IA: Kendall/Hunt Publishing Company.

Knox, George W.; Edward Tromanhauser; and Thomas F. Mc Currie
1991   "Gangs in Juvenile Corrections: Training Issues", <u>Journal of Correctional Training</u> (forthcoming).

Knox, George W.; and Edward Tromanhauser
1991   "Gangs and Their Control in Adult Correctional Institutions", <u>The Prison Journal</u> (LXXI)(2)(Fall-Winter): 15-22.

1991   "Gang Members as a Distinct Health Risk Group in Juvenile Correctional Facilities", <u>The Prison Journal</u> (LXXI)(2)(Fall-Winter): 61-66.

1992   "Comparing Juvenile Correctional Facilities: A Brief Overview", <u>Journal of Juvenile Justice and Detention Services</u> (7)(1)(Spr): 7-13.

1993   "Gang Training in Adult Correctional Institutions: A Function of Intensity, Duration and Impact of the Gang Problem", <u>Journal of Correctional Training</u>.

Knox, George W.; Edward D. Tromanhauser; Pamela Irving Jackson; Darek Niklas; James G. Houston; Paul Koch; and James R. Sutton
1993 "Preliminary Findings from the 1992 Law Enforcement Mail Questionnaire Project", <u>Gang Journal: An Interdisciplinary Research Quarterly</u> (1)(3): 11-27.

Kobrin, Solomon
1959 "The Chicago Area Project - a Twenty-five Year Assessment", <u>Annals of the American Academy of Political and Social Science</u> (322): 19-29.

1961 "Sociological Aspects of the Development of a Street Corner Group: An Exploratory Study", <u>Amerian Journal of Orthopsychiatry</u> (31)(4): 685-702.

1964   "Legal and Ethical Problems of Street Gang Work", <u>Crime and Delinquency</u> (10)(2): 152-156.

Kobrin, Solomon and Malcolm W. Klein
1983 <u>Community Treatment of Juvenile Offenders: The DSO Experiments</u>. Beverly Hills, CA: Sage Publications.

Kobrin, S.; J. Puntil; and E. Peluso
1967 "Criteria of Status Among Street Groups", Journal of Research in Crime and Delinquency (4)(Jan): 98-119.

Kolender, W.B.
1982 Street Gangs (Revised). In-service Training. San Diego Police Department, Training Section.

Kornblum, William
1974 Blue Collar Community. Chicago: University of Chicago Press.

1987 "Ganging Together: Helping Gangs Go Straight", Social Issues and Health Review (2): 99-104.

Kornhauser, Ruth R.
1978 Social Sources of Delinquency. Chicago: University of Chicago Press.

Kotlowitz, Alex
1991 There Are No Children Here. New York: Doubleday.

1992 There Are No Children Here. New York: Anchor Books.

Krajick, K.
1990 "The Menace of Supergangs", Corrections Magazine (June): 11-14.

Kramer, Dale and Madeline Karr
1953 Teenage Gangs. Henry Holt and Co., Inc.

Krech, David; Richard S. Crutchfield; and Egerton L. Ballachey
1962 Individual in Society: A Textbook of Social Psychology New York: McGraw-Hill Book Company, Inc.

Krisberg, Barry
1971 Urban Leadership Training: An Ethnographic Study of 22 Gang Leaders. Ph.D. dissertation, University of Pennsylvania, Philadelphia.

1974 "Gang Youth and Hustling: The Psychology of Survival", Issues in Criminology (9)(1)(Spr): 115-131.

1975 The Gang and the Community. School of Criminology, University of California, Berkeley. San Franciso, CA: R and E Research Associates.

Lagree, J. and P.L. Fai
1989 "Girls in Street Gangs in the Suburbs of Paris" (from Growing up Good: Policing the Behavior of Girls in Europe, pp. 80-95, Maureen Cain, editor), Newbury Park, CA: Sage Publications.

Landesco, John
1929 Organized Crime in Chicago. Part III of the Illinois Crime Survey. Illinois Association for Criminal Justice, 300 West Adams Street, Chicago, IL. In Cooperation with the Chicago Crime Commission.

Lane, Michael
1989 "Inmate Gangs", Corrections Today (51)(4)(July): 98-99, 126-128.

Lauderback, David; Joy Hansen; and Dan Waldorf
1992 "Sisters are Doin' It For Themselves: A Black Female Gang in San Francisco", The Gang Journal: An Interdisciplinary Research Quarterly (1)(1): 57-72.

Law and Order
1977 "Gangs: Police Community Relations", (25)(12): 20-23.

Leissner, Aryeh
1969 Street Club Work in Tel Aviv and New York. London: Longmans, Green and Co., Ltd.

Lerman, P.
1967 "Gangs, Networks, and Subcultural Delinquency", American Journal of Sociology (73): 63-72.

Liebow, Elliot
1967 Tally's Corner: Study of Negro Street Corner Men. Boston: Little, Brown and Co.

Loo, C.K.
1976 The Emergence of San Francisco Chinese Juvenile Gangs from the 1950s to the Present, unpublished Master's thesis, San Jose State University.

Los Angeles County Probation Department and Youth Studies Center
1962 Progress Report, Study of Delinquent Gangs, July 1, 1961 - June 30, 1962. Los Angles and University of Southern California.

1963 Second Annual Progress Report: Study of Delinquent Gangs, July 1, 1962 - June 30, 1963. Los Angeles and University of Southern California.

1964 Third Annual Progress Report: Study of Delinquent Gangs, July 1, 1963 - June 30, 1964. Los Angeles and University of Southern California.

Lotter, J.M.
1988 "Prison Gangs in South Africa: A Description", The South African Journal of Sociology (19)(2)(May): 67-75.

Lowney, Jeremiah
1984 "The Wall Gang: A Study of Interpersonal Process and Deviance Among Twenty-Three Middle-Class Youths", Adolescence (19)(75)(Fall): 527-538.

Lyman, M.D.
1989 "Street Youth Gangs", (From Gangland: Drug Trafficking by Organized Criminals, pp. 95-111), Newbury Park, CA: Sage Publications.

Madden, Max
    1993 The NACGI Journal. Various Copyrighted Materials in the Institution
    Gang Investigator Series.

Majors, Richard and Janet Mancini Billson
    1992 Cool Pose: The Dilemmas of Black Manhood in America. New York:
    Lexington Books.

Malcolm, Dino.
    1981 "D To the Knee! Stone To the Bone!", Best of Hair Trigger: A Story
    Workshop Anthology, pp. 81-91, Chicago: Columbia College Writing
    Department.

Martin, Richard H.
    1993 "Gang Colors: Should Students Be Allowed to Wear Them in
    College?", The Gang Journal: An Interdisciplinary Research Quarterly
    (1)(2): 69. 69.

Mattick, Hans W. and Nathan S. Caplan
    1962 Chicago Youth Development Project: Street Work, Community
    Organization and Research, April, University of Michigan Institute for Social
    Research, Ann Arbor, Michigan.

    1964 The Chicago Youth Development Project, February, University of
    Michigan Institute for Social Research, Ann Arbor, Michigan.

Maxson, C.L.; M.A. Gordon; and Malcolm W. Klein
    1985 "Differences Between Gang and Nongang Homicides", Criminology
    (23): 209-222.

Maxson, Cheryl L. and Malcolm W. Klein
    1983 "Agency versus Agency: Disputes in the Gang Deterence Model", in
    James R. Kluegel (ed.), Evaluating Contemporary Juvenile Justice, Beverly
    Hills: Sage.

    1986 "Street Gangs Selling Cocaine "rock": The Confluence of Two Social
    Problems", Social Science Research Center, University of Southern
    California.

    1989 "Street Gang Violence: Twice as Great, or Half as Great?", paper
    presented at the annual meeting of the American Society of Criminology,
    Reno, Nevada, November.

Maxson, Cheryl L.
    1983 "Gangs: Why We Couldn't Stay Away", in James R. Kluegel (ed.),
    Evaluating Contemporary Juvenile Justice, Beverly Hills: Sage.

    1993 "Investigating Gang Migration: Contextual Issues for Intervention",
    The Gang Journal: An Interdisciplinary Research Quarterly (1)(2): 1-8.

Mazon, M.
      1985 The Zoot-suit Riots: The Psychology of Symbolic Annihilation, Austin:
      University of Texas Press.

McCaddon, Jeff
      1993 "Jakes: Jamaican Posses, The Most Violent Crime Groups Operating
      in North America!", P.B.S.P, February.

Mc Carthy, J.E. and J.S. Barbaro
      1952 "Redirecting Teenage Gangs", in S.S. Furman (ed.), New York City
      Youth Board.

Mc Connell, Elizabeth H.
      1990 "Assessing Youth Gangs in an Urban High School", paper presented
      at the Annual Meeting of the American Society of Criminology, Baltimore,
      MD.

      1994 "Youth Gang Intervention and Prevention in Texas: Evaluating
      Community Mobilization Training", Journal of Gang Research (2)(1)(Fall):
      63-71.

Mc Guire, P.
      1986 "Outlaw Motorcycle Gangs - Organized Crime on Wheels", National
      Sheriff (37)(2)(Apr-May): 68-75.

Mc Kay, Henry D.
      1949 "The Neighborhood and Child Conduct", Annals of the American
      Academy of Political and Social Science (Jan): 32-41.

Mc Kinney, K.C.
      1988 Juvenile Gangs: Crime and Drug Trafficking, U.S. Dept. of Justice,
      Office of Juvenile Justice and Delinquency Prevention, Washington, D.C.

      1988 "Juvenile Gangs: Crime and Drug Trafficking", Juvenile Justice
      Bulletin, 2-7.

Mc Lean, Gordon
      1991 Cities of Lonesome Fear: God Among the Gangs. Chicago: Moody
      Press.

Mc Pherson, James Alan
      1966 "The Blackstone Rangers", The Atlantic (223)(5)(May).

Meyerhoff, Howard L. and Barbara G. Meyerhoff
      1964 "Field Observations of Middle Class Gangs", Social Forces (42): 328-
      336.

Mieczkowski, Thomas
      1986 "Geeking Up and Throwing Down: Heroin Street Life in Detroit",
      Criminology (24): 645-666.

Miller, Walter B.
1957 "The Impact of a Community Group Work Program on Delinquent Corner Groups", Social Service Review (31): 396-406.

1958 "Lower Class Culture as a Generating Milieu of Gang Delinquency", Journal of Social Issues (14)(3): 9.

1962 "The Impact of a 'Total Community' Delinquency Control Project", Social Problems (10)(Fall): 168-91.

1963 "The Corner Gang Boys Get Married", Transaction (1): 10-12.

1966 "Violent Crimes by City Gangs", Annals of the American Academy of Political and Social Sciences (364): 219-230.

1969 "White Gangs", Transaction (6)(1).

1976 Violence by Youth Gangs and Youth Groups as a Crime Problem in Major American Cities. Washington, D.C.: U.S. Government Printing Office.

1980 "Gangs, Groups and Serious Youth Crime", In D. Schichor and D. Kelly (eds.), Critical Issues in Juvenile Delinquency, Lexington, MA: Lexington.

1981 "American Youth Gangs: Past and Present", Current Perspectives on Criminal Behavior: Original Essays on Criminology, 2nd edition, edited by Abraham S. Blumberg, New York: Knopf (also 1974).

1982 Crime by Youth Gangs and Youth Groups in the United States, report prepared for the National Youth Gang Survey, Washington, DC: Office of Juvenile Justice and Delinquency Prevention.

1983 "Youth Gangs and Groups", In Sanford H. Kadish (ed.), Encyclopedia of Crime and Justice. New York: Free Press.

1985 "Historical Review of Programs and Theories of Work With Youth Gangs: 1920-1985", in D. Ingemunsen and G. Johnson, Report on the Illinois Symposium on Gangs, Springfield, IL: Illinois Department of Children and Family Services.

1989 "Recommendations for Terms to Be Used for Designating Law Violating Youth Groups", paper presented at the Conference of the National Youth Gang Suppression and Intervention Project, Chicago.

Miller, Walter B.; Hildred Geertz; and Henry S.G. Cutter
1961 "Aggression in a Boys' Street-Corner Group", Psychiatry (24)(4): 283-298.

Milner, John G.
1959 "Working With Juvenile Gang Members", California Youth Authority, Quarterly (12)(Spr): 3-7.

Mitchell, R.
1951 "Capturing Boys Gangs", Human Organization (Summer).

Molland, John, Jr.
1967 Cross Pressures: A Study of the Reconciliation by the Gang Boys of Perceived Expectations of Others, Ph.D. dissertation, University of Chicago.

Moore, Jack B.
1993 Skinheads Shaved For Battle: A Cultural History of American Skinheads. Bowling Green, OH: Bowling Green State University Popular Press.

Moore, Joan W.
1977 "The Chicano Pinto Research Project: A Case Study in Collaboration", Journal of Social Issues (33)(4): 144-158.

1978 Homeboys: Gangs, Drugs, and Prison in the Barrios of Los Angeles, Philadelphia: Temple University Press.

1983 "Residence and Territoriality in Chicano Gangs", Social Problems (31): 182-194.

1985 "Isolation and Stigmatization in the Development of the Underclass: The Case of the Chicano Gangs in East Los Angeles", Social Problems (33)(1)(Oct): 1-12.

1988 "Changing Chicano Gangs: Acculturation, Generational Change, Evolution of Deviance or Emerging Underclass?", In J.H. Johnson, Jr. and M.L. Oliver (eds.), Proceedings of the Conference on Comparative Ethnicity, Los Angeles: Institute for Social Science Research, UCLA.

1989 "Is There a Hispanic Underclass?", Social Science Quarterly (70)(2): 265-285.

1989 "Gangs, Drugs, and Violence", in M. de la Rosea, B. Gropper, and E. Lambert (eds.), Drugs and Violence National Institute of Drug Abuse Research Monograph, Rockville, MD: U.S. Department of Health and Human Services.

1989 "Gangs and Gang Violence: What we Know and What We Don't Know", paper presented at the California State University, Los Angeles, CA.

1991 Going Down to the Barrio: Homeboys and Homegirls in Change. Philadelpha, PA: Temple University Press.

Moore, Joan and Mary Devitt
1989 "The Paradox of Deviance in Addicted Mexican American Mothers",
Gender & Society (3)(1)(Mar): 53-70.

Moore, Joan; J. Diego Vigil; and Robert Garcia
1983 "Residence and Territoriality in Chicano Gangs", Social Problems (31):
182-194.

Moore, Joan W. and J.D. Vigil
1987 "Chicano Gangs: Group Norms and Individual Factors Related to
Adult Criminality", Aztlan (18)(2)(Fall): 27-44.

Moore, Mark and Mark A. R. Kleiman
1989 The Police and Drugs. Washington, D.C.: National Institute of Justice.

Moore, Winston; Charles P. Livermore, and George F. Galland, Jr.
1973 "Woodlawn: The Zone of Destruction", The Public Interest (30)(Winter): 41-59.

Morales, Armando
1963 "A Study of Recidivism of Mexican-American Junior Forestry Camp
Graduates", Master's Thesis, Social Work, University of Southern California.

1982 "The Mexican American Gang Member: Evaluation and Treatment",
in Mental Health and Hispanic Americans by Rosina M. Becerra, Marvin
Karno, and Javier I. Escobar (eds.), New York: Grune and Stratton.

1989 "A Clinical Model for the Prevention of Gang Violence and Homicide", In A. Morales and B.W. Sheafor, Social Work: A Profession of Many
Faces, Boston: Allyn and Bacon.

Morash, Merry
1983 "Gangs, Groups and Delinquency", British Journal of Criminology
(23): 309-331.

1990 "Gangs and Violence", in A.J. Reiss, Jr..; N. Weiner; and J. Roth
(eds.), Violent Criminal Behavior, Report of the Panel on the Understanding and Control of Violent Behavior, National Academy of Sciences,
Washington, DC: National Academy Press.

Morici, J. and D. Flanders
1979 "Chinatown Youth Gangs - Past, Present and Future."   California
Youth Authority Quarterly (32): 19-24.

Mottel, Syeus
1973   CHARAS: The Improbable Dome Builders. New York: Drake
Publlishers, Inc.

Muehlbauer, Gene and Laura Dodder
1983 The Losers: Gang Delinquency in an American Suburb. New York:
Praeger Publishers.

Mundel, Jerome J.
1962 Differential Perception of Gangs. Master's Thesis, Social Work, University of Southern California.

Murphy, Suzanne
1978 "A Year with the gangs of East Los Angeles", Ms. (July): 55-64.

Nash, Steven G.
1984 Gang Crimes Study Commission. State of Illinois. Legislative Council Service Unit Order 841246 (May).

National Council of Juvenile and Family Court Judges
1988 "Youth Gangs - A Special Problem", Juvenile & Family Court Journal (39)(4): 47-51.

National School Safety Center
1988 Gangs in Schools: Breaking Up is Hard to Do. Malibu, CA: Pepperdine University Press.

National Youth Gang Suppression and Intervention Program
1989 Report of the Law Enforcement Youth Symposium.

1990 Literature Review: Youth Gangs: Problem and Response. University of Chicago, School of Social Service Administration, Chicago, IL.

1990 Survey of Youth Gang Problems and Programs in 45 Cities and 6 Sites.

1990 Community and Institutional Reponses to the Youth Gang Problem.

1990 Law Enforcement Definitional Conference - Transcript.

1990 The Youth Gang Problem: Perceptions of Former Youth Gang Influentials. Transcripts of Two Symposia.

n.d. Preventing Involvement in Youth Gang Crime.

Needle, Jerome A. and William Vaughan Stapleton
1983 Police Handling of Youth Gangs. Washington, D.C.: American Justice Institute.

Neisser, Edith G. and Nina Ridenour
1960 Your Children and Their Gangs. U.S. Children's Bureau. Publication No. 384. Washington, D.C.

New York City Youth Board
1960 Reaching the Fighting Gang. New York.

Nieburg, H.L.
1970 Political Violence: The Behavioral Process. New York: St. Martin's Press.

Oetting, E.R. and Fred Beauvais
1987 "Common Elements in Youth Drug Abuse: Peer Clusters and Other Psychosocial Factors", Journal of Drug Issues (17)(1-2)(Win-Spr): 133-151.

O'Hagan, F.J.
976 "Gang Characteristics: An Empirical Survey", Journal of Child Psychology and Psychiatry (17): 305-314.

Oleson, Jim
1988 Treating Street Youth: Some Observations. Community Research Associates, 115 N. Neil Street, Suite 302, Champaign, IL 61820.

Olivero, J. Michael
1991 Honor, Gangs, Violence, Religion and Upward Mobility: A Case Study of Chicago Street Gangs During the 1970s and 1980s. Edinburg, TX: The UT-Pan American Presss.

Ontario Police Department
1989 "Gangs, Move 'Em Out of Your Life", (video). Ontario, CA 91761.

Oppenheimer, Martin
1969 The Urban Guerrilla. Chicago: Quadrangle Books.

Padilla, Felix
1992 The Gang as an American Enterprise. New Brunswick, NJ: Rutgers University Press.

Padilla, Felix and Lourdes Santiago
1993 Outside the Wall: A Puerto Rican Woman's Struggle. New Brunswick, NJ: Rutgers University Press.

Paramount Plan
1988 The Paramount Plan: Alternatives to Gang Membership. City of Paramount, California.

Parrot, Philippe and Monique Gueneau
1961 "Gangs of Adolescents: The History of Such a Gang", Excerpta Criminologica (1): 397-399.

Patrick, James
1973 A Glasgow Gang Observed. Trowbridge, Wiltshire: Redwood Press Ltd., Great Britain.

Pennell, Susan and Christine Curtis
1982 Juvenile Violence and Gang-Related Crime. San Diego: San Diego Association of Governments.

Perkins, Useni Eugene
1987 Explosion of Chicago's Black Street Gangs. Chicago: Third World Press.

Pfautz, Harold W.
1961 "Near-Group Theory and Collective Behavior: A Critical Reformulation", Social Problems (9)(2): 167-174.

Phelps, Roy David
1988 The History of the Eastside Dudes, a Black Social Club in Central Harlem, New York City, 1933-1985: An Exploration of Background Factors Related to Adult Criminality. Ph.D. dissertation, Fordham University, Bronx, New York.

Philobosian, R.H.
1986 State Task Force on Youth Gang Violence. Sacramento, CA: California Council in Criminal Justice.

Pleister, Margaret A.
1963 An Exploratory Study of Factors Influencing Nine Adolescent Girls in their Movement To and From Both School and the Gang, Master's thesis, Social Work, University of Southern California.

Poirier, Mike
1982 Street Gangs of Los Angeles County. Los Angeles: Self-published, P.O. Box 60481, Los Angeles, CA 90060.

Police Chief, The
1979 "Gangs, Violence, Vandalism: Citizen Involvement in Crime Prevention", (46)(7): 54-55.

Pope, Whitney
1962 Detached Workers, Delinquent Boys and the Theory of Exchange, Master's Thesis, University of Chicago.

Poston, Richard W.
1971 The Gang and the Establishment. New York: Harper & Row Publishers.

President's Commission on Organized Crime
1986 The Impact: Organized Crime Today.

Propper, Leonard M.
1957 "Juvenile Delinquency and the Gang Problem", Juvenile Court Judges Journal (8)(Mar): 24-28.

Puffer, J. Adams
1912 The Boy and His Gang. Boston: Houghton, Mifflin Co.

Quicker, John C.
1974 "The Chicana Gang: A Preliminary Description", paper presented at the Pacific Sociological Association meeting.

1983 Homegirls: Characterizing Chicana Gangs. San Pedro, California: International Universities Press.

1983 _Seven Decades of Gangs: What has been done, and what should be done_. Sacramento, CA: State of California Commission on Crime Control and Violence Prevention.

Quinn, James F. and Bill Downs
1993 "Predictors of the Severity of the Gang Problem at the Local Level: An Analysis of Police Perceptions", _Gang Journal: An Interdisciplinary Research Quarterly_, (1)(3): 1-10.

1993 "Non-Criminal Predictors of Gang Violence: An Analysis of Police Perceptions", _Gang Journal: An Interdisciplinary Research Quarterly_ (1)(3): 29-38.

Rafferty, Frank T. and Harvey Bertcher
1962 "Gang Formation in Vitro", _American Journal of Orthopsychiatry_ (32)(Mar): 329-330.

Ralph, Paige H; James W. Marquart; and Ben M. Crouch
1990 "Prisoner Gangs in Texas", paper presented at the 1990 Annual Meeting of the American Society of Criminology, Baltimore, MD.

Ranker, Jess E., Jr.
1958 _A Study of Juvenile Gangs in the Hollenbeck Area of Los Angeles_, Master's thesis, University of Southern California, Dept. of Sociology.

Redl, Fritz
1954 "The Psychology of Gang Formation and the Treatment of Juvenile Delinquency", pp. 367-377 in _The Psycho-Analytic Study of the Child_, Vol. 1, New York: International Universities Press.

Regulus, Thomas A.
1994 "The Effects of Gangs on Student Performance and Delinquency in Public Schools", _Journal of Gang Research_ (2)(1)(Fall): 1-13.

Reuter, P.
1989 _Youth Gangs and Drug Distribution: A Preliminary Enquiry_. RAND Corporation, Paper prepared for the U.S. Office of Juvenile Justice and Delinquency Prevention, Washington, DC.

Ribisl, Kurt M. and William S. Davidson, II
1993 "Community Change Interventions", Chapter 11 (pp. 333-355) in Arnold P. Goldstein and C. Ronald Huff (Eds.), _The Gang Intervention Handbook_, Champaign, IL: Research Press.

Riccio, Vincent and Bill Slocum
1962 _All The Way Down: The Violent Underworld of Street Gangs_. New York: Simon and Schuster.

Richards, C.
1958 "Can We Get a Focus For Our Working With Hostile or Hard To Reach Youth Gangs," _Welfare Council of Metropolitan Chicago_.

Ridgeway, James
1990 Blood in the Face: The Ku Klux Klan, Aryan Nations, Nazi Skinheads, and the Rise of a New White Culture. New York: Thunder's Mouth Press.

Riley, William E.
1988 "Prison Gangs: An Introduction, Crips and Bloods", Washington State Penitentiary.

Rivera, Ramon J.
1964 Occupational Goals: A Comparative Analysis, Master's Thesis, University of Chicago.

Robert, Phillipe and Pierre Lascoumes
1974 Les Bands D'Adolescents: Une Theorie de la Segregation. Paris, France: Les Editions Ouvieres.

Robins, Gerald
1964 "Gang Membership Delinquency: Its Extent, Sequence, and Pattern", Journal of Criminal Law, Criminology, and Police Science (55): 59-69.

Robinson, N. and D. Joe
1980 "Gangs in Chinatown", McGill Journal of Education (15): 149-162.

Rodeheffer, I.A.
1949 "Gangdom: Fists to Reasoning", Journal of Educational Sociology (22)(Feb): 406-15.

Rodriguez, Luis J.
1994 Always Running: La Vida Loca, Gang Days in L.A.. Curbstone Press.

Rogers, Kenneth H.
1945 Street Gangs in Toronto. Toronto: The Ryerson Press.

Rosenbaum, Dennis P. and Jane A. Grant
1983 "Gangs and Youth Problems in Evanston: Research Findings and Policy Options", Center for Urban Affairs and Policy Research, Northwestern University, July 22, 1983.

Rothman, Edwin, et al
1974 The Gang Problem in Philadelphia: Proposals for Improving the Programs of Gang-Control Agencies. Pennsylvania Economy League (Eastern Division) in association with the Bureau of Municipal Research Liberty Trust Building, Philadelphia, Pa. 19107, Report No. 375; supported by a grant from the William Penn Foundation.

Rush, Jeffrey Paul
1993 "An Interview With Richard Cloward", The Gang Journal: An Interdisciplinary Research Quarterly (1)(3): 51-53.

Sale, R.T.
1971   The Blackstone Rangers. A Reporter's Account of Time Spent with
the Street Gang on Chicago's South Side. New York: Random House.

Salisbury, Harrison E.
1958   The Shook-up Generation. New York: Harper.

Sanchez-Jankowski, Martin
1991   Islands in the Street: Gangs in American Urban Society.   Berkeley:
University of California Press.

Sanders, Willliam B.
1994   Gangbangs and Drivebys: Grounded Culture and Juvenile Gang
Violence. New York: Aldline De Gruyter.

Santamaria, C; et al
1989   "Study of a Juvenile Gang in a High Risk Community", Salud Mental
(12)(3)(Sept): 26-36.

Sato, Ikuya
1982   "Crime as Play and Excitement: A Conceptual Analysis of Japanese
Bosozoku (Motorcyele Gangs)", Tohoku Psychologica Folia (41): 1-4,64-84.

Savitz, Leonard D.; Michael Lalli; and Lawrence Rosen
1977   City Life and Delinquency --- Victimization, Fear of Crime and Gang
Membership. National Institute for Juvenile Justice and Delinquency
Prevention. U.S. Department of Justice, Government Printing Office,
Washington, D.C.

Scallan, J.H.
1987   Prison Gang Codes and Communications. Texas Department of
Corrections, unpublished.

Scharr, John H.
1963   "Violence in Juvenile Gangs: Some Notes and a Few Analogies",
American Journal of Orthopsychiatry (33)(1)(Jan): 29-37.

Schrag, C.
1962   "Delinquency and Opportunity: Analysis of a Theory", Sociology and
Social Research (46)(Jan): 167-75.

Schwendinger, Herman and Julia
1967   "Delinquent Stereotypes of Probable Victims", in Malcolm W. Klein
(ed.), Juvenile Gangs in Context, New Jersey: Prentice-Hall, pp. 91-105.

1985   Adolescent Subcultures and Delinquency. New York: Praeger.

Schwitzgebel, Ralph
1965   Street-Corner Research: An Experimental Approach to the Juvenile
Delinquent. Cambridge, MA: Harvard University Press.

Schlossman, Steven and Michael Sedlak
    1983 The Chicago Area Project Revisted. A Rand Note. Prepared for the
    National Institute of Justice. Santa Monica, CA: The Rand Corporation.

Scott, Peter
    1956   "Gangs and Delinquent Groups in London", British Journal of
    Delinquency (7)(1): 4-26.

Shaw, Clifford R.
    1929 Delinquency Areas. Chicago: University of Chicago Press.

    1931 The Natural History of a Delinquent Career. Chicago: University of
    Chicago Press.

    1939 "Group Factors in Delinquency Among Boys", Society for Research in
    Child Development, Proceedings of the Third Biennial Meeting: 14-26.

    1951 The Natural History of a Delinquent Career. Philadelphia: Albert
    Saifer.

Shaw, Clifford R. and Jesse A. Jacobs
    1939 Chicago Area Project, March, 1939. Chicago Area Project, Chicago,
    Illinois.

Shaw, Clifford R. and Henry D. McKay
    1931 Social Factors in Juvenile Delinquency: A Study of Community, the
    Family, and the Gang in Relation to Delinquent Behavior. Volume II in the
    National Commission on Law Observance and Enforcement.   U.S.
    Government Printing Office.

    1942 Juvenile Delinquency and Urban Areas. Chicago: University of
    Chicago Press.

    1956 Juvenile Delinquency and Urban Areas. Chicago: University of
    Chicago Press.

Shaw, Clifford R. and Earl D. Meyer
    1920 "The Juvenile Delinquent", Chicago: The Illinois Crime Survey.

Shaw, Clifford R. and Maurice E. Morre
    1931 The Natural History of a Delinquent Career. Chicago: University
    of Chicago Press.

Shaw, Clifford R. and Anthony Sorrentino
    1956   "Is 'Gang-Busting' Wise?", National Parent-Teacher Magazine
    (50)(Jan): 18-20+.

Shelden, Randall G.; Ted Snodgrass; and Pam Snodgrass
    1992   "Comparing Gang and Non-Gang Offenders: Some Tentative
    Findings", The Gang Journal: An Interdisciplinary Research Quarterly
    (1)(1): 73-85.

Sherif, Muzafer; O.J. Harvey; Jack White; William R. Hood; and Carolyn W. Sherif
1961 Intergroup Conflict and Cooperation: The Robbers Cave Experiment, Norman, OK: University of Oklahoma Institute of Group Relations.

Sherman, Lawrence W.
1970 Youth Workers, Police and the Gangs: Chicago 1956-1970, Master's thesis, University of Chicago.

1973 "Street Work History Includes Three Stages", The Forum (May): 17-24.

Sheu, Chuen-Jim
1990 "Nonsyndicated Organized Crime in Taipei, Taiwan", paper presented at the 1990 Annual Meeting of the American Society of Criminology, Baltimore, Maryland: Nov. 7-10, 1990.

Shimota, Helen E.
1964 "Delinquent Acts as Perceived by Gang and Nongang Negro Adolescents", Youth Studies Center, presented Dec. 12, 1964 before the California State Psychological Association; Los Angeles: University of Southern California.

Shireman, Charles H., et al
1957 An Examination and Analysis of Technique Used by a Street Worker. Chicago: Hyde Park Youth Project.

1958 An Analysis of the Dynamics of the Interrelationship of Agency, Group and Community in Providing Staff Service To A "Street Club". Hyde Park Youth Project. Welfare Council of Metropolitan Chicago.

Short, James F.
1963 "Street Corner Groups and Patterns of Delinquency: A Progress Report", American Catholic Sociological Review (28): 13-32.

1964 "Gand Delinquency and Anomie", pp. 98-127 in Marshall B. Clinard (ed.), Anomie and Deviant Behavior, New York: Free Press of Glencoe.

1964 "Aleatory Risks Versus Short-run Hedonism in Explanation of Gang Action", Social Problems (12): 127-140.

1965 "Social Structure and Group Processes in Explanations of Gang Delinquency", in M. and C. Sherif (eds.), Problems of Youth. Chicago: Aldine.

1968 Gang Delinquency and Delinquent Subcultures. New York: Harper and Row.

1968 "Comment on Lerman's 'Gangs, Networks, and Subcultural Delinquen-cy'", American Journal of Sociology (73)(4)(Jan): 513-515.

1974 "Youth, Gangs and Society: Micro and Macrosociological Processes", Sociological Quarterly (15): 3-19.

1975 "Gangs, Violence and Politics", In Duncan Chappell and John Monahan (eds.), Violence and Criminal Justice Lexington, Mass: Lexington Books.

1976 "Gangs, Politics, and the Social Order", in J.F. Short (ed.), Delinquency, Crime and Society, Chicago: University of Chicago Press.

1989 "Exploring Integration of Theoretical Levels of Explanation: Notes on Gang Delinquency", in S.F. Messner, M.D. Krohn, and A.E. Liska (eds.), Theoretical Integration in the Study of Deviance and Crime: Problems and Prospects (pp. 243-259), Albany: State University of New York Press.

Short, James F., and John Molland
1976 "Politics and Youth Gangs: A Follow-up Study", Sociological Quarterly (17): 162-179.

Short, J.F.; R. Rivera; and R.A. Tennyson
1965 "Perceived Opportunties, Gang Membership and Delinquency", American Sociological Review (30)(Feb):

Short, James F., Jr. and Fred L. Strodtbeck
1965 Group Process and Gang Delinquency. Chicago: The University of Chicago Press.

1974. _____ .

Shukla, K.S.
1981 "Adolescent Criminal Gangs: Structure and Functions", The International Journal of Critical Sociology (5): 35-49.

Sibley, James Blake
1989 "Gang Violence: Response of the Criminal Justice System to the Growing Threat", Criminal Justice Journal (11)(2)(Spr): 403-422.

Sifakis, Carl
1987 The Mafia Encyclopedia. New York: Facts on File Publications, Inc.

Sipchen, Bob
1993 Baby Insane and the Buddha. New York: Doubleday.

Skolnick, J.H.
1990 "Gangs and Crime Old as Time: But Drugs Change Gang Culture", Commentary, Crime and Delinquency.

Skolnick, Jerome H.; Blumenthal, Ricky and Theodore Correl
1990 "Gang Organization and Migration", Berkeley, CA: University of California at Berkeley, Center for the Study of Law and Society (2-18-90).

1993 "Gang Organization and Migration", pp. 193-217 in Scott Cummings and Daniel J. Monti (Eds.), Gangs: The Orgins and Impact of Contempoary Youth Gangs in the United States, Albany, NY: State University of New York.

Skolnick, J.H. Correl, T.; Navarro, E.; and R. Rabb
1989 "The Social Structure of Street Drug Dealing". Sacramento, CA: Office of the Attorney General, State of California.

Slack, Charles W.
1963 "SCORE -- A Description", in Experiment in Culture Expansion, Report of Proceedings, U.S. National Institute of Mental Health, Bethesda, MD.

Sleeman, Lieut.-Col. W.H.
1849 Report on Budhuk alia Bagree Decoits and other Gang Robbers by Hereditary Profession and on the measures adopted by the Government of India for their Suppression. Calcutta: J.C.Sherriff, Bengal Military Orphan Press.

Snyder, P.Z.
1977 "An Anthropological Description of Street Gangs in the Los Angeles Area", prepared for the Department of Justice, Santa Monica, CA: Rand Corporation.

Song, John
1991 "Lost in the Melting Pot? The Causes of Asian Gangs in the United States", paper presented at the Annual Meeting of the Academy of Criminal Justice Sciences, Nashville, Tennessee.

Song, John Huey-Long and John Dombrink
1990 "Gangs, Groups and Organized Crime: Defining Asian Racketeering", paper presented at the Annual Meeting of the American Society of Criminology, Baltimore, MD.

Song, John Huey-Long; John Dombrink; and Gilbert Geis
1992 "Lost in the Melting Pot: Asian Youth Gangs in the United States", The Gang Journal: An Interdisciplinary Research Quarterly (1)(1): 1-12.

Spaulding, Charles B.
1948 "Cliques, Gangs and Networks", Sociology and Social Research (32)(July-August): 928-937.

Spergel, Irving
1960 Types of Delinquent Groups, D.S.W. dissertation, Columbia University. Dissertation Abstracts (21)(Jan): 2034-35 (1961).

1964 Racketville, Slumtown, Haulburg: An Exploratory Study of Delinquent Subcultures, Chicago: University of Chicago Press.[1]

1966 Street Gang Work: Theory and Practice. Reading, MA: Addison-Wesley Publishing Company, Inc.

1984 "Violent Gangs in Chicago: In Search of Social Policy", Social Service Review (58): 199-226.

1985 The Violent Gang Problem in Chicago. Chicago: Social Services Administration, University of Chicago.

1985 Youth Gang Activity and the Chicago Public Schools. Chicago: Social Services Administration, University of Chicago.

1986 "The Violent Gang Problem in Chicago: A Local Community Approach", Social Service Review (60)(1)(Mar): 94-131.

1988 "The Youth Gang Problem: A Preliminary Policy Pespective", draft, Prepared for the Juvenile Gang Suppression and Intervention Research and Development Program, Office of Juvenile Justice and Delinquency Prevention, U.S. Dept. of Justice.

1989 Youth Gangs: Problem and Response: A Review of the Literature, Executive Summary. U.S. Dept. of Justice, Office of Juvenile Justice and Delinquency Prevention, Washington, D.C.

1989 Survey of Youth Gang Problems and Programs in 45 Cities and 6 States. Washington, DC: Office of Juvenile Justice and Delinquency Prevention.

1989 "Youth Gangs: Continuity and Change", In N. Morris and M. Tonry (eds.), Crime and Justice: An Annual Review of Research (12): Chicago, University of Chicago Press.

1990 "Youth Gangs: Continuity and Change", in Norval Morris (ed), Crime and Justice: Annual Review of Research, 267-371.

1990 "The Violent Gang Problem in Chicago: A Local Community Approach", Social Service Review (60)(1)(Mar): 94-131.

Spergel, Irving A. and Ron L. Chance
1990 Community and Institutional Responses to the Youth Gang Problem: Case Studies Based on Field Visits and Other Materials. National Youth Gang Suppression and Intervention Project, School of Social Service Administration, University of Chicago (Jan.).

Spergel, Irving A.; Glen David Curry; R.A. Ross; and R. Chance
1989 Survey of Youth Gang Problems and Programs in 45 Cities and 6 Sites (Technical Report, No. 2, National Youth Gang Suppression and Intervention Project), Chicago: School of Social Service Administration, University of Chicago.

Srivastava, S.S.
1981   "Problem of Dacoity in India - A Sociological Perspective" The International Journal of Critical Sociology (5): 23-34.

Stapleton, W. Vaughn and Jerome Needle
1982   Police Handling of Youth Gangs. Washington, D.C. Office of Juvenile Justice and Delinquency Prevention.

Steward, Samuel M.
1990   Bad Boys and Tough Tattoos. New York: Harrington Park.

Stinchcombe, Arthur L.
1964   Rebellion in a High School. Chicago: Quadrangle Books.

Strodtbeck, Fred L.; James F. Short, Jr.; and Ellen Kolegar
1962   "The Analysis of Self-Descriptions by Members of Different Gangs", Sociological Quarterly (24): 331-356.

Stover, Del
1986   "A New Breed of Youth Gang is on the Prowl and a Bigger Threat Than Ever", American School Board Journal (173)(8)(Aug): 19-24,35.

Stumphauzer, Jerome S; Esteban V. Veloz; and Thomas W. Aiken
1981   "Violence by Street Gangs: East Side Story?", in Robert B. Stuart (ed.), Violent Behavior. New York: Brunner- Mazel.

Suall, Irwin and David Lowe
1988   "Shaved for Battle - Skinheads Target America's Youth", Political Communication and Persuasion (5)(2): 139-144.

Sun, Key
1993   "The Implications of Social Psychological Theories of Group Dynamics for Gang Research", Gang Journal: An Interdisciplinary Research Quarterly (1)(3): 39-44.

Sung, B.L.
1977   Gangs in New York's Chinatown (Monograph No. 6), New York: City College of New York, Department of Asian Studies.

Suttles, Gerald D.
1959   Territoriality, Identity, and Conduct: A Study of an Inner-City Slum with Special Reference to Street Corner Groups, Ph.D. dissertation, University of Illinois at Champaign.

1968   The Social Order of the Slum Chicago: University of Chicago Press.

Swans, Bennie J., Jr.
1985   "Gangbusters! Crisis Intervention Network.", School Safety, Winter, 1985, pp. 12-15, National School Safety Center.

686   AN INTRODUCTION TO GANGS

Sweeney, T.
    1980 Streets of Anger, Streets of Hope: Youth Gangs in East Los Angeles.
    Glendale, CA: Great Western Publishing.

Takata, Susan and Richard Zevitz
    1987 "Youth Gangs in Racine: An Examination of Community Perceptions",
    Wisconsin Sociologist (24)(4)(Fall): 132-141.

    1990 "Divergent Perceptions of Group Delinquency in a Midwestern
    Community: Racine's Gang Problem", Youth and Society (21)(3)(Mar): 282-
    305.

Taylor, Carl S.
    1988 "Youth Gangs Organize Quest for Power, Money", School Safety
    (Spr): 26-27.

    1990 Dangerous Society. East Lansing, Michigan: Michigan State University
    Press.

Tennyson, Ray A.
    1966 Family Structure and Gang Delinquency.   Ph.D. dissertation,
    Washington State University.

Thompson, Craig and Allen Raymond
    1940 Gang Rule in New York. New York: Dial Press.

Thompson, D.W.
    1986 Preventing Youth Membership in Urban Street Gangs: The
    Evaluation of a Behavioral Community Intervention. Dissertation Abstracts
    International, 47, 3987B.

Thompson, David W. and Leonard A. Jason
    1988 "Street Gangs and Preventive Interventions", Criminal Justice and
    Behavior (15)(3)(Sept): 323-333.

Thrasher, Frederic M.
    1927 The Gang. A Study of 1,313 Gangs in Chicago. Chicago: University
    of Chicago Press.

    1936 _____. 2nd revised eidition. Chicago: University of Chicago Press.

    1968 _____. Third Impression, Abridged and with a Introduction by James
    F. Short, Jr. Chicago: University of Chicago Press.

Tice, Lawrence Clinton
    1967 "The National Avenue 'Rebels': A Study of a Puerto Rican Gang in
    Milwaukee", M.A. thesis, Department of Social Welfare, University of
    Wisconsin-Milwaukee.

Toby, Jackson
    1957 "Social Disorganization and Stake in Conformity", Journal of Criminal
    Law and Criminology (48)(May-June): 12-17.

Todorovic, Aleksander
    1978 "Special Conditions and Causes That Influence the Forming of
    Juvenile Gangs", Socioloski Pregled (7): 27-38.

Toll, Joseph F.
    1944 "Converting the Gang into a Club", Probation (23)(Dec): 49-55.

Tompkins, Dorothy Campbell
    1966 Juvenile Gangs and Street Groups - A Bibliography. Institute of
    Governmental Studies, University of California, Berkeley.

Torres, Dorothy M.
    1979 "Chicano Gangs in the East Los Angeles Barrio", California Youth
    Authority Quarterly (32)(3): 5-13.

    1980 Gang Violence Reduction Project 3rd Evaluation Report. Sacramento,
    CA: California Department of the Youth Authority.

    1981 Gang Violence Reduction Project: Fourth Evaluation Report, July
    1979-June 1980. Department of the Youth Authority, Sacramento, CA.

Toy, Calvin
    1992 "Coming Out to Play: Reasons to Join and Participate in Asian
    Gangs", The Gang Journal: An Interdisciplinary Research Quarterly (1)(1):
    13-29.

Tracy, Paul E.
    1984 "Subcultural Delinquency: A Comparison of the Incidence and
    Seriousness of Gang and Nongang Offensivity", University of Pennsylvania:
    Center for Studies in Criminology and Criminal Law.

Tracy, Paul E. and E.S. Piper
    1984 "Gang Membership and Violent Offending: Preliminary Results from
    the 1958 Cohort Study". Paper presented at the Annual Meeting of the
    American Society of Criminology, Cincinnati, OH.

Tracy, Paul E. and M. Epstein
    1979 Subcultural Delinquency: A Comparision of the Incidence and
    Seriousness of Gang and Nongang Member Offensivity. Center for Studies
    in Criminology and Criminal Law, Philadelphia: University of Pennsylvania.

Tracy, Paul E. and Elizabeth S. Piper
    1982 "Gang Membership and Violent Offending: Preliminary Results from
    the 1958 Cohort Study", paper presented at the annual meeting of the
    American Society of Criminology, Cincinnati.

Tromanhauser, Edward
    1981 "The Problem of Street Gangs", chapter IV in Chicago Safe School
    Study, Board of Education, City of Chicago.

Trostle, Lawrence Charles
    1987 The Stoners: Drugs, Demons and Delinquency: A Descriptive and
    Empirical Analysis of Delinquent Behavior, Ph.D. dissertation, Claremont
    Graduate School, California.

Turner, Ralph H and Samuel J. Surace
    1956 "Zoot-Suiters and Mexicans: Symbols in Crowd Behavior", American
    Journal of Sociology (62)(July): 14-20.

Useem, Bert and Peter Kimball
    1989 "A Gang in Rebellion - Joliet (1975)", Chapter 4 (pp. 59-77) in States
    of Siege: U.S. Prison Riots, 1971-1986 New York: Oxford University Press.

Vaz, Edmund W.
    1962 "Juvenile Gang Delinquency in Paris", Social Problems (10)(Sum): 23-
    31.

Vetter, Harold J. and Leonard Territo
    1984 Crime & Justice In America: A Human Perspective.   St. Paul, MN:
    West Publishing Co.

Vigil, J. Diego
    1983 "Chicano Gangs: One Response to Mexican Urban Adaptation in the
    Los Angeles Area", Urban Anthropology (12)(1)(Spr): 45-75.

    1987 "Street Socialization, Locura Behavior and Violence Among Chicano
    Gang Members", in J. Kraus et al (eds.), Violence and Homicide in Hispanic
    Communities, Washington, DC: National Institute of Mental Health, Office
    of Minority Health.

    1988 "Group Processes and Street Identity: Adolescent Chicano Gang
    Members", Ethos (16)(4)(Dec): 421-445.

    1988 Barrio Gangs: Street Life and Identity in Southern California. Austin,
    TX: University of Texas Press.

Vold, George B.
    1958. Theoretical Criminology. Oxford University Press.

    1981. Theoretical Criminology. New York: Oxford University Press.

    1986. With Thomas J. Bernard. Third edition.

Wattenberg, William M. and James Balistrieri
    1950 "Gang Membership and Juvenile Misconduct", American Sociological
    Review (15)(Dec): 744-752.

1959 "Gang Membership and Juvenile Misconduct", pp. 169-177 in Sheldon Glueck (ed), The Problem of Delinquency Boston: Houghton.

Watts, T.J.
1988 New Gangs: Young, Armed and Dangerous. Monticello, IL: Vance Bibliographies (P.O. Box 229, Monticello, IL 61856).

Webb, Margot
1991 Coping With Street Gangs. New York: Free Press.

Weiner, Arthur K.
1965 "C-r-a-c-k-i-n-g The Hard Core Area", Police Chief (32)(Jan): 27-31.

Weisfeld, Glenn and Roger Feldman
1982 "A Former Street Gang Leader Re-Interviewed Eight Years Later", Crime and Delinquency (28): 567-581.

Weissman, Harold (ed.)
1969 Community Development in the Mobilization for Youth. New York: Association Press.

Werthman, Carl
1964 Delinquency and Authority, Master's Thesis, University of California, Berkeley.

1966 "Police Action and Gang Delinquency", in D. Bordua (ed.), The Police, New York: Wiley.

Werthman, Carl and Irving Piliavin
1967 "Gang Members and the Police", in David Bordua (ed), The Police: Six Sociological Essays, New York: Wiley.

West, Pat and Tony Ostos
1988 Pilot Study: City of Paramount Alternatives to Gang Membership Program. City of Paramount, 16400 Colorado Ave., Paramount, CA 90723.

Whyte, William Foote
1943 Street Corner Society: The Social Structure of an Italian Slum. Ph.D. dissertation, University of Chicago.

1943 Street Corner Society. Chicago: University of Chicago Press.

1981 Street Corner Society. Chicago: University of Chicago Press, third edition.

Williams, Hampton; Rex Leonard; and Phillip Terrell
1991 "Students' Perceptions of Some Selected Conditions that Might Lead to Gang Membership: An Exploratory Investigation", paper presented at the Annual Meeting of the Academy of Criminal Justice Sciences, Nashville, Tennessee.

Wilner, Daniel M.; Eva Rosenfeld; Robert S. Lee; Donald L. Gerard; and Isidor Chein
1957 "Heroin Use and Street Gangs", Journal of Criminal Law, Criminology, and Police Science (48)(4): 399-409.

Wilson, Everett
1971 Sociology: Rules, Roles, and Relationships. The Dorsey Press.

Wilson, James Q. and George L. Kelling
1989 "Making Neighborhoods Safe", The Atlantic Monthly (Feb): 46-52.

Wilson, William J.
1987 The Truly Disadvantaged. Chicago: University of Chicago Press.

Wise, John M.
1962 A Comparison of Sources of Data as Indices of Delinquent Behavior, Master's thesis, Department of Sociology, University of Chicago.

Wolfe, Tom
1968 The Pump House Gang. New York: Farrar, Straus and Giroux.

Wooden, Wayne
1989 "Profile of Stone Gang Members in the California Youth Authority", paper presented at the American Society of Criminology, Annual Meeting, Reno, Nevada, November.

1990 "Contemporary Youth Identities: Problems and Issues", paper presented at the Western Society of Criminology, Annual Meeting, Las Vegas, Nevada (February).

Xu, J.
1986 "Brief Discussion of New Trends in the Development of Juvenile Delinquent Gangs", Chinese Education (19)(2)(Sum): 92-102.

Yablonsky, Lewis
1958 A Field Study of Delinquent Gang Organization and Behavior With Special Emphasis on Gang Warfare. Ph.D. dissertation, New York University.

1959 "The Delinquent Gang as a Near-Group", Social Problems (7): 108-117.

1962 The Violent Gang. New York: MacMillan.

Youth Gang Task Force (California)
1981 Report on Youth Gang Violence in California. State of California Department of Justice. Sacramento.

Zatz, Marjorie S.
1985 "Los Cholos: Legal Processing of Chicano Gang Members", Social Problems (33): 13-30.

1987 "Chicano Youth Gangs and Crime: The Creation of a Moral Panic",
Contemporary Crises (11)(2): 129-158.

Zinn, Elizabeth
1959   "He Begged that Gang Violence End With His Life", Federal
Probation (23)(Sept): 24-30.

SELECTED BIBLIOGRAPHY HAVING SECONDARY RELEVANCE TO GANGS[11]

Auletta, Ken
  1983 The Underclass. New York: Vintage.

Bales, Robert F. and Fred L. Strodtbeck
  1951 "Phases in Group Problem Solving", Journal of Abnormal and Social Psychology (46): 485-495.

Bell, Daniel
  1953 "Crime as an American Way of Life", Antioch Review (XIII)(June): 131-54.

Bennett, James
  1981 Oral History and Delinquency: The Rhetoric of Criminology. Chicago: University of Chicago Press.

Bennis, W.G.; K. Benne; and R. Chin.
  1969. The Planning of Change. New York: Holt, Rinehart and Winston.

Benton, J. David
  1975 Denver - Southwest Youth Employment Service - Annual Report, Jan. 15, 1975. National Criminal Justice Reference Service # 09900.00.029808.

Bergmann, Barbara R. and David E. kaun
  1966 Structural Unemployment in the United States. The Brookings Institute, Washington, D.C.

Berk, Richard A.; Kenneth J. Lenihan; and Peter H. Rossi
  1980 "Crime and Poverty: Some Experimental Evidence from Exoffenders", American Sociological Review (45)(5)(Oct): 766-86.

Berkowitz, Leonard (ed.)
  1978 Group Processes. New York: Academic Press.

Bernardo, A.J.
  1977 Supported Employment for Adolescents - An Evaluation. NCJRS # 0990.00.061938.

Best, Joel and David F. Luckenbill
  1982 Organizing Deviance. Englewood Cliffs, NJ: Prentice-Hall.

Blalock, H.M.
  1965 "Theory Building and the Statistical Concept of Interaction", American Sociological Review (30): 374-80.

---

[1] These are citations made throughout the text which are not directly "gang studies" per se.

Bogen, David
    1944 "Juvenile Delinquency and Economic Trends", American Sociological
    Review (9): 178-84.

Bonn, Robert L.
    1984 Criminology. New York: McGraw-Hill Book Company.

Bowker, L.H.
    1977 "Helping Delinquent Dropouts to Cope - An Evaluation of An
    Innovative Project", paper presented at the National Conference on Criminal
    Justice Evaluation, Washington, D.C. (Feb.).

Burby, Raymond J. and William M. Rohe
    1989 "Deconcentration of Public Housing: Effects on Residents' Satisfaction
    With Their Living Environments and Their Fear of Crime", Urban Affairs
    Quarterly (25)(1): 117-141.

Burgess, Ernest W.
    1928   "What Social Case Records Should Contain to be Useful for
    Sociological Interpretation", Social Forces (6): 524-32.

Burns, Tom and G.M. Stalker.
    1968. The Management of Innovation.   London: Tavistock Publications
    Limited.

Callahan, Daniel
    1987 Setting Limits: Medical Goals in an Aging Society. New York: Simon
    and Schuster.

Carey, James T.
    1975 Sociology and Public Affairs: The Chicago School.   Beverly Hills:
    Sage.

Carter, Robert M.
    1972 "Dialogue With Daniel Glaser", Issues in Criminology (7)(2)(Fall): 21-
    33.

Chin, Robert and Kenneth D. Benne
    1972. "General Strategies for Effecting Changes in Human Systems", chapter
    18, pp. 233-254 in Zaltman, Gerald, et al (eds.), Creating Social Change,
    New York: Holt, Rinehart and Winston, Inc.

Clark, Ramsey
    1970 Crime in America. New York: Simon and Schuster.

Clemmer, Donald
    1940 The Prison Community. Boston: The Christopher Publishing House.

Cole, George F.
    1983 The American System of Criminal Justice. Third edition.   Monterey,
    CA: Brooks/Cole Publishing Company.

Coleman, James
    1954 Community Conflict. Twentieth Century Fund.

Cook, Thomas J.; L. Douglas Dobson; and Eva Lantos Rezmovic
    1979 Experimental Evaluation of the Challenge Program: Final Report.
    The Safer Foundation, Chicago, Illinois.

Cottingham, Clement (ed.)
    1982 Race, Poverty, and the Urban Underclass. Lexington, Mass: Lexington
    Books.

Crutchfield, Robert D.
    1989 "Labor Stratification and Violent Crime", Social Forces (68)(2): 489-
    512.

Curry, G. David
    1985 Sunshine Patriots: Punishment and the Vietnam Offender.   Notre
    Dame: University of Notre Dame Press.

Davis, James A.
    1980 General Social Surveys, 1972-1980 Cumulative Codebook.   National
    Data Program for the Social Sciences. National Opinion Research Center,
    University of Chicago.

Diamond, Shari, et al
    1977 Community Rehabilitation Programs. Second Deliverable Product:
    Evaluation Designs. Chicago, IL: University of Illinois at Chicago.

DiRenzo, Gordon J.
    1984 Sociological Perspectives. Lexington, MA: Ginn Custom Publishing.

Duster, Troy
    1987 "Crime, Youth Unemployment, and the Black Urban Underclass",
    Crime and Delinquency (33): 300-16.

Dyer, William G.
    1984. Strategies for Managing Change. Reading, MA: Addison-Wesley
    Publishing Company, Inc.

Eisenstadt, S.N. (ed.)
    1968. Comparative Perspectives on Social Change. Boston: Little, Brown
    and Company.

Elliott, D.S.
    1962   "Delinquency and Perceived Opportunity", Sociological Inquiry
    (32)(Spr): 216-27.

Etzioni, Amitai
    1964 Modern Organizations. Englewood Cliffs, NJ: Prentice-Hall.

Etzioni-Halevy, Eva and Amitai Etzioni
1973. Social Change. New York: Basic Books, Inc.

Etzioni-Halevy, Eva
1981. Social Change: The Advent and Maturation of Modern Society. London: Routledge & Kegan Paul.

Farrington, David, et al
1986 Understanding and Controlling Crime, Toward a New Research Strategy. New York: Springer-Verlag.

Fleisher, Belton M.
1966 The Economics of Delinquency. Chicago: Quadrangle Books.

Ginsburg, Helen
1975 Unemployment, Subemployment, and Public Policy. New York University, School of Social Work, Center for Studies in Income Maintenance Policy.

Glaser, Daniel
1964 The Effectiveness of a Prison and Parole System. New York: Bobbs-Merrill Co., Inc.

Glaser, Daniel and Kent Rice
1959 "Crime, Age and Employment", American Sociological Review (24): 679-686.

Glasgow, Douglas G.
1981 The Black Underclass: Poverty, Unemployment, and Entrapment of Ghetto Youth. New York: Vintage Books.

Glueck, Sheldon and Eleanor
1952 Delinquents in the Making. New York: Harper and Brothers.

Gordon, David M.
1972 "Class and Economics of Crime", in Allen and Bacon (eds.), Political Economy: Radical and Orthodox Approaches; see also David M. Gordon, (ed), Problems in Political Economy: An Urban Perspective, D.C.: Heath, 1971.

Greenberg, David F.
1978 "The Dynamics of Oscillatory Punishment Processes", Journal of Criminal Law and Criminology, no. 69.

Guttentag, Marcia
1968 "The Relationship of Unemployment to Crime and Delinquency", Journal of Social Issues (24)(1): 105-114.

Hagan, Frank E.
1987 Introduction to Criminology. Chicago: Nelson-Hall.

Hardt, R.H. and S.J. Peterson
1968 "Arrests of Self and Friends as Indicators of Delinquency Involvement", Journal of Research in Crime and Delinquency (5)(Jan): 44-51.

Harris, Ramon I.; et al
1975 The Practice of Oral History: A Handbook. Glen Rock, NJ: Microfilming Corporation of America.

Inbau, Fred E. and John E. Reid
1962 Criminal Interrogation and Confessions. Baltimore: The Williams & Wilknis Company.

Indik, Bernard P. and F. Kenneth Berrien (eds.)
1968 People, Groups, and Organizations. New York: Teachers College Press.

Irwin, John
1985 The Jail: Managing the Underclass in American Society. Berkeley: University of California Press.

Janis, Irving L.
1972. Victims of Groupthink: A Psychological Study of Foreign-Policy Decisions and Fiascos. Boston: Houghton Mifflin.

Janowitz, Morris
1970 Political Conflict. Chicago: Quadrangle Books.

Johnson, Richard E.
1977 "The Relevance of Social Class to Delinquent Behavior: A New Test", paper presented at the 72nd Annual Meeting of the American Sociological Association, Sept. 5-9, Chicago, IL.

Kahn, Alfred J.
1963 Planning Community Services for Children in Trouble. New York: Columbia University Press.

Kasimar, Yale; Wayne R. LaFave; and Jerold H. Israel
1990 Basic Criminal Procedure: Cases, Comments, and Questions. Seventh Edition. St. Paul: West Publishing Co.

Keen, Sam
1986 Faces of the Enemy. San Francisco: Harper and Row.

Killinger, George and Glen A. Kercher
1974 Employment Assistance and Support for the Ex-Offender, Project E.A.S.E., Office of Youth Opportunities, Dept. of Community Affairs, State of Texas. Institute of Contemporary Corrections and Behavioral Sciences, Sam Houston State University, Huntsville, TX.

Kleeck, Mary van; Emma A. Winslow; and Ira De A. Reid
    1931   Work and Law OBservance. An Experimental Inquiry into the
    Influence of Unemployment and Occupational Conditions Upon Crime for
    the National Commission on Law Observance and Enforcement, No. 13,
    June 26, 1931, pp. 163-333.

Klofas, John; Stan Stojkovic and David Kalinich
    1990   Criminal Justice Organizations: Administration and Management.
    Belmont, CA: Brooks/Cole Publishing Company.

Knox, George W.
    1975   "A Critique of the Mertonian Typology of Deviant Behavior With
    Implications for a Post-Industrial Society", paper presented at the Annual
    Meeting of the Southwestern Sociological Association, March 27, San
    Antonio, TX.

    1977   "The Rise of the NSPA Nazi Movement and the Urban Crisis in
    Southwest Chicago", paper persented at the Spring Institute, Society for
    Social Research, Department of Sociology, University of Chicago, April 30,
    Chicago, IL.

    1977   "The Use of Cost-Benefit Analysis in the Evaluation of Manpower
    Service Programs", paper presented at the Criminal Justice Statistics
    Association, meeting August 11, Oklahoma City, OK.

    1978 (a) "Offender Prediction Methodology: Suggestions For Improvement",
    paper presented, National Institute of Corrections, Screening for Risk
    Hearings, May 26, Denver, CO.

    1978 (a)   The Determinants of Employment Success Among Exoffenders,
    Ph.D. dissertation, Department of Sociology, University of Chicago, Sept.,
    1978.

    1978 (b)   The Impact of Manpower Services on Illinois Offenders,
    unpublished manuscript, June 30, 1978.

    1978 (?) "Cultural and Structural Disjunction: The Concept of Differential
    Integration", paper presented at the Annual Meeting of the Midsouth
    Sociological Association, November 3, Jackson, MS.

    1978 (?) "Differential Integration and Job Retention Among Exoffenders",
    paper presented at the Annual Meeting of the American Society of
    Criminology, November 10, Dallas, TX.

    1978 (?) "A Comparative Cost-Benefit Analysis of Programs for Illinois
    Offenders", paper presented at the Second National Workshop on Criminal
    Justice Evaluation, Nov. 20, Washington, DC.

    1980 "Employment and Exoffender Recidivism", paper presented at the Fall
    Conference of the Illinois Correctional Association, March 28, Chicago, IL.

1980 "Social Disorganization Models of Deviance", paper presented at the Annual Meeting of the American Society of Criminology, Nov. 5, San Francisco, CA.

1981 "Surplus Population Theory and Criminality", paper presented at the Annual Meeting of the American Society of Criminology, Nov. 14, Washington, DC.

1981 Educational and Vocational Upgrading for Juvenile Delinquents: The State of the Art in Community Based Programs. Center for the Study in Delinquency Prevention, School of Social Services Administration, University of Chicago.

1982 "How Criminologists View Rehabilitation", paper presented at the Annual Meeting of the American Society of Criminology, Nov. 5, Toronto, Canada.

1983 "Social and Behavioral Correlates of Gang Affiliation", paper presented at the Annual Meeting of the American Society of Criminology, Nov. 10, Denver, CO.

1984 "How Criminologists View Rehabilitation", Indian Journal of Criminology (12)(1)(Jan): 26-32.

1984 "Capital Punishment: Where's The Logic?", paper presented at the Annual Meeting of the Midwestern Criminal Justice Association, Oct. 4, Chicago, IL.

1985 "The Human Relations Factor in Field Research on Serious Offenders", paper presented at the Society for the Study of Phenomenology, Chicago, IL.

1985 "Oral History and Offenders: More on Method", paper presented at the Annual Meeting of the American Society of Criminology, San Diego, CA.

1985 "Recidivism Prediction: A Duel Between the Bellybutton and the Computer", paper presented at the Annual Meeting of the American Society of Criminology, San Diego, CA.

1987 "Nominal Measures of Rehabilitation in Relationship to Subsequent Arrests", paper accepted but not presented the Annual Meeting of the American Society of Criminology, Montreal, Canada (Not presented because none of the attributes by ASC members, See Knox 1984, were significant in differentiating subsequent arrests.

1988 "The Family Services Program: Findings from the Cook County Jail PACE Institute", paper presented at the First National Conference on Family and Corrections, April 26, Sacramento, CA.

1988   "Family and Crime: Theory and Findings", paper presented at the Annual Meeting of the American Sociological Association, Session 57, August 24, Atlanta, GA.

1988   "An Oral History Study of Felons: The Post-Release Religion Identity", co-author Tyrone Staggers, paper presented at the Annual Meeting of the Midwestern Criminal Justice Association, Oct. 17, Chicago, IL.

1988   "Changing Attitudes Toward the Death Penalty: A Mass Communications Experiment", co-authored with Leonel Campos and Chris Anaele, paper at the Annual Meeting of the American Society of Criminology, Chicago, IL.

1991   "The U.S. Gang Problem: An Analysis", paper presented at the meeting of the Illinois Academy of Criminology, Jan. 22, Loyola University of Chicago, Chicago, IL.

1991   "The Racism-Oppression Thesis in Gang Analysis", paper presented at the Annual Meeting of the Academy of Criminal Justice Sciences, Nashville, TN.

1991   "Gangs, Guerilla Warfare, and Social Conflict", paper presented at the Annual Meeting of the Academy of Criminal Justice Sciences, Nashville, TN.

1991   "Social Justice Issues and the American Gang Problem", paper presented at Purdue University, West Lafayette, IN, Criminal Justice at the Crossroads: Crisis in the Black Community Conference, March 15.

1991   "Gangs: A Chicago High School Revisited", paper presented at the Illinois Academy of Criminology, Loyola University of Chicago, Chicago, IL.

1991   "U.S. Gangs: An Analysis of Recent Data", paper presented at the Annual Meeting of the American Society of Criminology, Nov. 20, San Franciso, CA.

1991   "Beliefs About Police Brutality: A Study of African-Americans", paper presented at the Annual Meeting of the American Society of Criminology, Nov. 23, San Francisco, CA.

1992   "Gangs in Juvenile Institutions: Fighting, Drugs, and Other Health Risks", with co-author Edward D. Tromanhauser, paper presented at the Annual Meeting of the Academy of Criminal Justice Sciences, March 10, Pittsburgh, PA.

1992   "Teaching About Gangs: A Research and Policy View", paper presented at the Annual Meeting of the Academy of Criminal Justice Sciences, Pittsburgh, PA.

1992   "Gangs and Related Problems Among Asian Students: Preliminary National Findings", paper presented at the Annual Meeting of the National Association of Asian and Pacific Island Educators, May 15, Chicago, IL.

1992 "Translating Community Policing Theory into Practice: The Gang Problem", paper presented to the graduating class of the Executive Officer Corp Program, Oct. 9, University of Illinois at Chicago, Chicago, IL.

1992 "Gang Identification and Gang Interviewing", co-authored with Thomas F. Mc Currie, paper presented at the National Defense Investigators Association, Chicago, IL.

1992 "The Gang Problem Among Asian Students", paper presented at the Annual Meeting of the American Society of Criminology, Nov. 8, New Orleans, LA.

1992 "The Thrasher Temptation: Over Estimating the High School Gang Problem", paper presented at the Annual Meeting of the American Society of Criminology, Nov. 8, New Orleans, LA.

1993 "From Banana Stalks to M-60 Machine Guns: Weapons Acquisition and Usage Patterns Among Contemporary American Gangs", paper presented at the Feb. 7, COPEX - Contingency & Operational Procurement Exhibition, "New World Disorder - Operational & Tactical Responses to Transnational Crime and Urban Violence", Miami, FL.

1993 "Gang Issues for Illinois Juvenile Police Officers", paper presented at the Annual Meeting of the Illinois Juvenile Officers Association Training Conference, May 6, Matteson, IL.

Kraus, J.
1979 "Juvenile Unemployment and Delinquency", Aust. and New Z. Journal of Criminology (June)(12): 37-42.

Lamm, Richard D.
1984 "When Miracle Cures Don't Cure: Long Time Dying", The New Republic (Aug. 17): 20-23.

1989. "Public Policy in An Aging Society", 9 pp. unpublished MS for presentation at the Fourth Annual National Conference - April 14 & 15, 1989, De Paul University College of Law - Health Law Institute, Chicago, Illinois.

LaPiere, Richard T.
1965. Social Change. New York: McGraw-Hill.

Leiberg, Leon G.
1978 "Crime and Employment Issues", A Collection of Policy Relevant Monographs. The American University Law School, Institute for Advanced Studies in Justice.

Lerner, Daniel
1968. "Toward a Communication Theory of Modernization: A Set of Considerations", Chapter 9, pp. 133-155 in S.N. Eisenstadt (ed.), Comparative Perspectives on Social Change, Boston: Little, Brown and Company.

Lipsey, M.W.
    1988   "Juvenile Delinquency Intervention", New Directions for Program Evaluation (37): 63-84.

Lipsey, Richard G.
    1965   "Structure and Deficit-Demand Reconsidered", in Arthur M. Ross (ed), Employment and the Labor Market, University of California Press, pp. 210-55.

Lundman, Richard J.
    1984   Prevention and Control of Juvenile Delinquency.   New York: Oxford University Press.

Luthans, Fred and Robert Kreitner
    1975. Organizational Behavior Modification. Glenview, IL: Scott, Foresman and Company.

Miller, M.J.
    1972   "Future Employment Prospects and Vocational Training in Prisons", Georgia Journal of Corrections (1)(3): 103-111.

Mills, C.M. and T.L. Walter
    1979   "Reducing Juvenile Delinquency - A Behavioral-Employment Intervention Program".   In Jerome S. Stumphauser (ed), Progress in Behavior Therapy with Delinquents, Springfield, IL: Charles C. Thomas Publisher.

Moore, Wilbert E.
    1963. Social Change. Englewood Cliffs, NJ: Prentice-Hall, Inc.

Newsweek
    1981   "How The Mob Really Works", Jan. 5, 1981.

Niehoff, Arthur H. (ed.)
    1966. A Casebook of Social Change. Chicago: Aldine Publishing Company.

O'Connor, James
    1973   The Fiscal Crisis of the State. New York: St. Martin's Press.

Olmsted, Michael S.
    1959   The Small Group. New York: Random House.

Oppenheimer, Martin
    1969   The Urban Guerrilla. Chicago: Quadrangle Books.

Paine, Frank T. and William Naumes
    1982. Organizational Strategy and Policy. Third edition. New York: CBS College Publishing.

Palmore, E.B. and P.E. Hammond
1964 "Interacting Factors in Juvenile Delinquency", American Sociological Review (29): 848-54.

Parsons, Talcott
1969 "Suggestions for A Sociological Approach to Theory of Organizations", pp. 32-46 in Amitai Etzioni (Ed.), A Sociological Reader on Complex Organizations, New York: Holt, Rinehart and Winston, Inc.

Payne, Roy and Cary L. Cooper (eds.)
1981 Groups at Work. New York: John Wiley & Sons.

Petersilia, Joan and Susan Turner
1988 "Minorities in Prison: Discrimination or Disparity", Corrections Today, Official Publication of the American Correctional Association, June.

Phillips, A.W.
1958 "The Relationship Between Unemployment and the Rate of Change of Money Wage Rates in the United Kingdom, 1862-1957", Economica (25)(Nov): 283-99.

Pirog-Good, Maureen A.
1979 "The Relationship Between Youth Employment and Juvenile Delinquency: Some Preliminary Findings", Philadelphia, PA: Wharton Management and Behavioral Science Center.

Pollard, Beatrice E.
1962. Social Casework for the State. London: The Pall Mall Press.

Popenoe, David
1983 Sociology. Englewood Cliffs, NJ: Prentice-Hall, Inc.

Pownall, G.A.
1969 "Employment Problems of Released Prisoners". Manpower Administration, U.S. Department of Labor, Contract 81-19-37 with the University of Maryland.

President's Commission on Law Enforcement and Administration of Justice
1968 The Challenge of Crime in a Free Society. New York: Avon.

Quinney, Richard
1977 Class State and Crime. New York: David McKay Company.

Radzinowicz, Leon and Marvin E. Wolfgang (eds.)
1971 Crime and Justice. Volume I. The Criminal in Society. New York: Basic Books, Inc.

Raper, Arthur F.
1933 The Tragedy of Lynching. University of North Carolina Press.

Reid, Sue Titus
    1990 Criminal Justice. New York: MacMillan Publishing Co.

Revere, Virginia L.
    1982 Applied Psychology for Criminal Justice Professionals.   Chicago:
    Nelson-Hall.

Reid, William J. and Ann W. Shyne
    1969. Brief and Extended Casework. New York: Columbia University Press.

Richmond, Mary E.
    1922. What is Social Case Work? New York: Russell Sage Foundation.

Robison, Sophia M.; H. Cohen; M. Sachs
    1946 "Autonomous Groups: An Unsolved Problem in Group Loyalties and
    Conflicts", Journal of Educational Sociology: 154-62.

Robison, Sophia M.
    1960 Juvenile Delinquency: Its Nature and Control. New York: Holt,
    Rinehart and Winston.

Rosenberg, M.
    1965 Society and the Adolescent Self-Image. Princeton, NJ: University
    Press.

Rulo, J.H. and D.M. Zemel
    1979 "I Am the Proud Mother of a Yesterday Kid", Juvenile and Family
    Court Journal (30)(2)(May): 3-9.

Rumney, Jay and Joseph P. Murphy
    1952 Probation and Social Adjustment. New Brunswick, NJ: Rutgers
    University Press.

Schneider, Louis
    1976. Classical Theories of Social Change.   Morristown, NJ: General
    Learning Press.

Schrag, C.
    1962 "Delinquency and Opportunity: Analysis of a Theory", Sociology and
    Social Research (46)(Jan): 167-75.

Schwartz, Barry N. and Robert Disch
    1970 White Racism: Its History, Pathology and Practice. An anthology of
    historical and contemporary writings on a crucial social problem: the white
    American's bigotry and his deeply prejudiced view of the black man. New
    York: Dell Publishing Co., Inc.

Schwendinger, Herman and Julia
    1974 Sociologists of the Chair. New York: Basic Books.

Sedlak, K.M.
1975 Employment Opportunities for the Released Prisoner in Relation to His Work History and Vocational Training and Work Experience in Prison. Master's thesis.

Sheffield, Ada E.
1920. Social Case History. New York: Russell Sage Foundation.

Simpson, D. Dwayne, et al
1976 DARP Data Book, Statistics on Characteristics of Drug Users in Treatment During 1969 - 1974. Institute of Behavioral Research, Texas Christian University, Fort Worth, TX.

Snodgrass, Jon D.
1972 The American Criminological Tradition: Portraits of the Men and Ideology in a Discipline. Ph.D. dissertation, University of Pennsylvania.

Spear, Allan H.
1967 Black Chicago: The Making of a Negro Ghetto, 1890-1920. Chicago: The University of Chicago Press.

Spergel, Irving
1963 "Male Young Adult Criminality, Deviant Values, and Differential Opportunities in Two Lower Class Negro Neighborhoods", Social Problems (Winter)(10)(3): 237-50.

Stoner, J.A.F.
1961 "A Comparison of Individual and Group Decisions Including Risk", Cited in Stephen Wilson, 1978. Informal Groups: An Introduction, Englewood Cliffs, NJ: Prentice-Hall.

Strasser, Hermann, and Susan C. Randall
1981. An Introduction to Theories of Social Change. London: Routledge & Kegan Paul.

Swanson, Charles R.; Neil C. Chamelin; Leonard Territo
1984 Criminal Investigation. New York: Random House.

Swift, Linton B.
1928 "Can the Sociologist and Social Worker Agree on the Content of Case Records", Social Forces (6): 535.

Tannenbaum, Frank
1938 Crime and the Community. Boston: Ginn and Company.

The Iron Fist and The Velvet Glove
1975 The Iron Fist and the Velvet Glove: An Analysis of the U.S. Police. Center for Research on Criminal Justice, Berkeley, California: San Francisco: Garrett Press.

Thio, Alex
   1988 Deviant Behavior. Third edition. New York: Harper & Row Publishers.

Vetter, Harold J. and Leonard Territo
   1984 Crime & Justice In America: A Human Perspective.   St. Paul, MN: West Publishing Co.

Votey, Harold Jr. and L. Phillips
   1974 "The Control of Criminal Activity: An Economic Analyis", in Daniel Glaser (ed), Handbook of Criminology, Chicago: Rand McNally.

Wadsworth, M.
   1977 Colorado - Southwest Youth Employment Services - Final Report, 1974-1977, Colorado Division of Criminal Justice, Denver, CO. NCJRS # 09900.00.045993

Wallach, Michael A; N. Hogan; and D.J. Bem.
   1962. "Diffusion of Responsibility and Level of Risk Taking in Groups", Journal of Abnormal and Social Psychology, 68: 263-74.

White, Bernard J.; John H. Stamm; and Lawrence W. Foster
   1976 Cases in Organizations: Behavior, Structure, Processes.   Dallas, TX: Business Publications, Inc.

Whitney, Wilbur Montgomery, Jr.
   1974 An Evaluation of a Community Based Delinquency Program on the Basis of Group and Individual Employment. Ph.D. dissertation, Michigan State University.

Wilson, Everett
   1971 Sociology: Rules, Roles, and Relationships. The Dorsey Press.

Wilson, William Julius
   1987 The Truly Disadvantaged. Chicago: University of Chicago Press.

Wolf, Kurt H.
   1964 The Sociology of Georg Simmel. New York: The Free Press.

Woodside, Arch G. and Robert Fleck, Jr.
   1979 "The Case Approach to Understanding Brand Choice", Journal of Advertising Research (19)(2): 23-30.

Wrobleski, Henry M. and Karen M. Hess
   1987 Introduction to Law Enforcement and Criminal Justice.   St. Paul: West Publishing Company.

Young, T.R.
   1978   "Crime and Capitalism", prepared for the 1978 meetings of the Western Social Science Association, Denver.

Zaltman, Gerald; Philip Kotler; and Ira Kaufman (eds.)
    1972 Creating Social Change. New York: Holt, Rinehart and Winston, Inc.

Zimbardo, Philip G.
    1972 "Pathology of Imprisonment", Society (9)(Apr).

WRITTEN CONSTITUTION AND BY-LAWS OF THE
ALMIGHTY LATIN KING NATION

CHAPTER CONSTITUTION
OF THE
ALMIGHTY LATIN KING NATION

IN THE SIXTH DECADE OF THE TWENTIETH CENTURY THE A.L.K.N. WAS FORMED. GENERATION AFTER GENERATION OF KINGS HAVE LIVED BY A CONSTITUTION OF PRINCIPLES BASED UPON THE IDEAS OF KINGISM. THOSE IDEAS, OUR LAWS AND PRINCIPLES WE NOW IMPACT TO ALL KINGS WITH THIS CONSTITUTION.

FROM THIS DAY FORWARD WE SHALL ORGANIZE OURSELVES UNDER CONSTITUTIONAL LAW TO INSURE THAT WE AS A NATION SHALL LEAD THE WAY TO PROGRESS AND NO LONGER STAND IN THE SHADOW OF IT: WE AS A NATION SHALL LEAD THE WAY FOR TRUE KINGISM.

DEVOTING YOUR LIFE TO THESE PRINCIPLES IMPLIES A LIFE OF SERVICE TO EACH OTHER AND TO THE ALMIGHTY LATIN KING NATION.

LOVE - HONOR - OBEDIENCE
SACRIFICE - RIGHTEOUSNESS

INCA

The Inca is the highest ranking officer in every chapter of the Nation. The Inca is elected by majority vote of his Chapter's membership. His term of office is indefinite. However, he must run in an election for a "vote of confidence" every two years in order to retain as position as Commander-In-Chief.

The Inca is responsible for the actions of his Chapter, its security, the treasury and the general well-fare of the membership. He is responsible for promoting academic and vocational skills and for providing the aid and way in our search for peace, unity and freedom.

The Inca must file a State of the Nation report every three months with Los Coronas concerning the affairs of his Chapter. Any action taken by the Inca shall be enforced through the Cacique.

CACIQUE

The Cacique shall be second in command of his chapter. He, like the Inca, is elected by majority vote of the membership of his Chapter and his term of office is indefinite. However, he too must run in a vote of confidence election every two years.

The Cacique is to work hand-in-hand with the Inca and assume the responsibilities of the Inca in case of the Inca's absence.

The Cacique is responsible for keeping the Inca informed on all actions taken by the Officers of his Chapter.

Any action taken by the Cacique shall be enforced through Chapter Enforzador.

ELECTIONS

The elections will be conducted by the Chairman of the Chapter Crown Council for both Inca and Cacique. Elections for these officer must be held within thirty days of their departure from office. However, if the Council Chairman has prior knowledge of an immediate or forthcoming departure of either the Inca or Cacique then he has the option of proceeding with an election thirty days prior to such departure.

The Crown Council members will each select five members as candidates of whom in their opinion are the most qualified to run for Office. The two candidates that receive the highest number of votes from the Chapter Crown Council members will automatically run for Office. The candidate that receives the highest number of votes from that Chapter's membership will be elected as Inca and the other candidate as Cacique.

In order to run for office a Brother must be a member of the Nation for a minimum of three years. This is the basic requirement. Other requirements include but are not limited to the following:

1. He must be a member in good standing and have some type of prior experiences an Officer of the Nation with the rank of Chairman of the Crown Council, Chapter Enforzador and/or previous Inca and Cacique.

2. He must also have been in the chapter for a period of six months so that he has gained experience and knowledge in understanding the policies and principles of the Almighty Latin King Nation.

Every two years the Inca and Cacique must run for re-election. This is called a Vote of Confidence and is to assure that the membership is satisfied with the leadership. A vote of confidence is not an election of new officers but a vote by the Chapter's membership to determine if the Inca and Cacique have fulfilled the responsibilities of their Office.

If the majority of the Chapter's membership is dissatisfied with their elected Officers, the People's will shall be manifested by a vote of NAY - one who votes no. If the majority of the Chapter's membership is satisfied with the rule of their Inca and Cacique they shall cast a vote of YEA - one who votes yes.

LAS CORONAS

Las Coronas are the highest ranking Officers of the Nation. Their term of office is indefinite. Las Coronas are responsible for seeing that all Officers of the Nation abide by the Constitution and respect the rights of our membership.

Las Coronas have the power to bring justice where the abuse of power or corruption has occurs by the Inca and Cacique in any Chapter. In the event the Inca and Cacique violate the Laws of this Constitution, Las Coronas have the power to place all rank on hold pending investigation and appoint temporary positions of rank until a new Inca and Cacique have been elected.

Las Coronas have the power to give Crowns to new members of the nation without them being required to be voted in by the Chapters' Crown Councils.

Any member seeking re-entry into the Nation must be approved by Las Coronas.

Once a proposal has been put to a vote and approved by the Chapter and Council, the Inca and Cacique, final approval must be given by las Coronas before it is added to the Constitution and Law.

EL CONSEJADOR

The Inca's advisor shall serve as an consejador and Cacique. This position is usually reserved for members who have served as past Inca and have been in the nation for a long period of time with a record of having served wisely.

All members reaching the age of fifty (50) years, who are members in good standing and have during their years in the Nation held the rank of Inca, Cacique, Chapter Crown Council Chairman and Chapter Enforzador shall, with the approval of Las Coronas, hold the title of National Consejador and are to be treated with the respect of an Officer.

The name of this association shall be the ALMIGHTY LATIN KING NATION.

An organization of international brotherhood with exists for the purpose of:

1. Promoting prosperity and freedom through love and understanding to all oppressed people of the world.

2. To train our People to become aware of our social and political problems and of the conditions we are subjected to live under as a Third World People.

3. To provide the aid and way in our search for peace and unity.

4. To promote and encourage education and vocational learning in order to train our People in the art of survival.

MEMBERSHIP

Membership shall be available to anyone who is willing to change their life-style for the doctrine of Kingism.

Membership shall be denied to anyone who has willfully taken the life of a Latin King or a relative of a member of the Nation.

Membership is forbidden to anyone addicted to heroin and denied to rapists.

Membership is forbidden to anyone who is expelled from Nation unless his re-entry is approved by Las Coronas. Anyone seeking re-entry into the Nation must find an Officer with the rank of Chapter Enforcer, Chapter Crown Council Chairman, Inca or Cacique, to sponsor him before las Coronas will even consider him for re-entry.

CHAPTER ENFORZADOR

The Enforzador will be in charge and responsible for the security of every member Chapter. He shall be appointed by the Inca and Cacique and report to them directly. The Enforzador shall see that the Laws are enforced and the orders of the Inca and Cacique are obeyed.

CHAPTER TESORERO

The Tesorero will be appointed by the Inca and Cacique. It shall be his responsibility to collect and invest Chapter funds. However, members of each Chapter shall determine by majority vote, the amount of dues they pay monthly and how their Chapter funds are to be spent.

The Tesorero shall file a report with the Inca and Cacique at the first of every month on his Chapter's financial status. Brothers who are delinquent in payment of dues are not members in good standing and are not allowed to vote in how Chapter funds are to be spent.

CHAPTER SECRETARIO

The Secretario will be appointed by the Inca and Cacique. His duties shall consist of the following:

1. Collection and distribution of Nation literature.

2. Keeping records of all business conducted by the Chapter Crown Council. Although the Secretario sits in all matters of business conducted

by the Crown Council, he may not interfere with the proceedings and must abide by the Rules of the Council.

3. Keep Communications open to all Chapters through the Secretario of every Chapter.

CHAPTER INVESTIGATOR

The Chapter Investigator shall be appointed by the Inca and Cacique. He shall conduct an investigation of all new members. All prospective new members shall be placed on hold until the investigation is completed.

The Investigator shall also conduct all investigations requested by the Inca, Cacique, Chapter Crown Council, Enforzador, Tesorero and Secretario. A report of all investigations, no matter what Officer makes the request, must be filed at the completion with the Inca and Cacique.

CHAPTER CROWN COUNCIL

The Chapter Crown Council shall have its powers delegated to it under this Constitution. Council members do not maintain any power outside the Council. However, Council members shall be recognized as Officers of the Nation. Council members shall be responsible to the Council Chairman, the Inca and Cacique.

The Chapter Crown Council shall be the Law making body of the Chapter and guardian of the Constitution. The Council shall the authority to make their own Rules and Regulations concerning the procedures they are to follow in order to function effectively as a Council.

The Council shall be composed of not more or less than seven of most qualified members of the Chapter.

The Chapter Crown Council shall have the absolute power of holding trials for everyone in the ALMIGHTY LATIN KING NATION regardless of who they are or their position of rank, this includes the Inca and Cacique.

Thee Chapter Crown Council has the prerogative of asking for the resignation of the Inca and Cacique but only a majority of the entire Chapter can remove either of them from Office.

The Council, under the leadership of the Chairman, shall automatically take control of the Chapter in the absence of the Inca and Cacique.

The Council shall have the power, by majority vote, to dismiss a member of the nation under the recommendation of the Inca and Cacique or Las Coronas.

Once the seven members of the Council have been selected and approved it will then become the Council's responsibility; to choose any new members whenever a seat has been vacated. A new member of the Council can be selected by majority vote from the remaining members of the Council.

Whenever the Chairman's seat is vacant, the Inca, Cacique and remaining Council members shall, by majority vote, select a new Chairman.

A council member can be removed from office by the Inca or Cacique's vote along with the majority vote of the remaining Council members.

ALTERNATE COUNCIL MEMBERS

Members of the Chapter Crown Council, by majority vote and with the approval of the Inca or Cacique, shall select members of the Chapter to serve as alternate Council members. Alternate Council members may be selected for the following purposes:

1. In order to form a full quorum.

2. In the event a member appearing before the Council requests that a Crown Council member be excused for possible prejudice.

3. In order to train new members as prospective permanent Council members.

The Chapter Crown Council shall have the power, by majority vote, to accept an individual as an Almighty Latin King or reject him from membership. All individuals seeking membership shall be screened by the Council. The Council shall also interview any member that wishes to make any comments in support of or against any person seeking membership.

The Chapter Crown Council shall try all cases that involve Constitutional violations. The Council may also try cases where an infraction has been committed outside the Constitution but only under the recommendation of the Inca, Cacique or Las Coronas.

Council members are not allowed to discuss any issues or business before it with any members outside the Council until the procedures are completed. This or course does not include their investigative work.

The Chapter Crown Council Chairman shall have no vote in the proceedings but may vote in case of a tie vote among Council members. It is the Chairman's duty to conduct the proceedings and make recommendations on all actions taken by the Council. The Chairman must also keep records of all proceedings conducted by the Council.

If the Inca and Cacique issue an order or implement a Rule that the Chapter Crown Council feels is detrimental to the Chapter, the Council by majority vote, has the authority to null and void such rule or order. However, Las Coronas must be informed in the event of such action is taken by the Council.

CHAPTER CROWN COUNCIL MEMBERS

The first Council member will be appointed by the Inca and Cacique and he shall be the Chapter Crown Council Chairman. The Chairman will then select six other members to complete the quorum of the Council. The members chosen by the Chairman must be approved by the Inca and Cacique.

Council members will be referred to ass Council members and never as "Crown" member. Only Nation Crowns of this rank will be recognized by this title.

Every member of the nation shall honor, respect and protect with his life the lives and reputations of all members of the Almighty Latin King Nation.

When a member gives another member the Nation Salute it should always be returned.

There shall be no stealing inside the Nation and proliferation of the community by acts of vandalism, destruction of property and graffiti is strongly discouraged.

No member shall use his membership or position in the Nation to exploit anyone inside or outside the Nation.

No member shall incur debts with other members that he cannot afford to repay.

Nation affairs are to be kept within the Nation and are not be discussed in the presence of anyone outside the Nation.

No King shall strike or disrespect another King unless it is in self-defense. And any Officer that strikes another member (with the exception of the Inca and Cacique) will automatically lose his rank and may be subjected to further disciplinary action pending an investigation and hearing before the Chapter Crown Council.

Any member found guilty of being a traitor or police collaborator shall automatically lose his position (if he has one) and be expelled from the Nation.

No member shall take the Law into their own hands especially when he knows that what he does will reflect upon the Nation and jeopardize the health and well-being of every member of the Chapter.

No member shall take a lie detector test without the approval of the Inca and Cacique.

No member shall conduct an interview with any person from the news media concerning Nation affairs without the approval of the Las Coronas.

Any member accused of rape shall be put on hold pending investigation by the Chapter Crown Council and subject to approval by the Inca and Cacique.

No member shall bring false charges or statements against another member of the Nation.

Any member or group of members caught disrespecting the Inca and Cacique in public, or conspiring against them or any other member of the Nation shall be brought before the Council on a charge of conspiracy and treason.

No King shall stand idle while another King is in need of assistance.

The use of what is commonly known as angel dust (tick, tack or animal tranquilizer), glue, L.S.D. (acid), heroin, downers and free-basing is unlawful, and cannot be sold in our communities.

Those who are known to have previously used heroin for the purpose of addiction cannot obtain a position of rank without the approval of Las Coronas.

Nothing which can be construed as an emblem of another organization can be worn by a member of the Almighty Latin King Nation.

In recognition of our culture, each January the 6th will be recognized as Kings Holy Day - a day dedicated to the memory of our departed Brothers and Sisters; a day of sacrifice in which each and every member of the nation will observe by fasting.

The first week in the month of March of each and every year is a Nation holiday. This holiday is known as King's Week or Week of the Sun. This holiday is the nation's anniversary and is week of celebration.

TRIAL PROCEDURES

Any member that violates a Law shall be brought before the Chapter Crown Council within a reasonable time to stand trial for his offense. If he is unable to appear he may present a written defense.

Any member that violates a Law must be presented with a copy of the charges as soon as possible so that he may be allowed adequate opportunity to prepare his defense.

Every member of the Nation has the right to have another member of the Nation represent and assist him at his trial. They shall also be allowed the privilege of one continuance for the purpose of presenting witnesses on their behalf and to give them an opportunity to gather information to prove their innocence. If the Chapter Crown Council feels that further investigation is necessary in order to assist them in their work, then they may order a continuation for such purpose. The Chapter Crown Council also maintains the right to call witnesses.

When an Officer of the Nation must stand trial, the Inca or the Cacique must be present. However, the Inca nor the Cacique has the right to vote in such matters as their responsibility is to review the decision of the Chapter Crown Council.

If a member if found guilty of an offense by the Council, the Council will determine the punishment, subject to the approval of the Inca or Cacique. If the member is an officer, the Inca and Cacique, with the recommendation of the Chapter Crown Council, will determine the punishment.

In order to try the Inca or Cacique, any charges brought against either one of them must be brought before the Chapter Crown Council. Any member has the right to bring charges.

If the Council feels the charges are valid, the Council must immediately inform Las Coronas before proceeding with a hearing. If the charges are serious enough to warrant a public trial, the Inca and/or Cacique has the option of abdicating their throne or submitting to the trial.

If the Inca and Cacique do not receive approval of their performance by a majority of their Chapter's membership, a new election of Officers shall be held according to Constitutional law.

HOW LAWS ARE MADE

Any member of the Almighty Latin King Nation has the right to make a proposal, requesting that said proposal be made a part of our Law. A proposal is introduced first to the Chapter Crown Council by any member of the Chapter.

Once the proposal has been submitted, reviewed and debated by the Council, the majority vote will then decide whether or not the submitted proposal has been approved or denied. Once the proposal has been approved by the Chapter Crown Council it will be presented to the Inca and Cacique for their approval.

If the proposal is approved by the Inca and Cacique it will be submitted to Las Coronas. The proposal cannot be Chapter Law without the approval of Las Coronas.

LAWS

Rules and regulations may vary from Chapter to Chapter but the laws of all Chapters are the same. Rules and regulations implemented by the Inca and Cacique falls under their jurisdiction and they will handle all such infractions. The violation of a Law falls under the jurisdiction of the Chapter Crown Council and they will handle all such violations.

The first and most Law of the Almighty Latin King Nation is "Once a King, always a King", unless he is expelled from the Nation for violation of its Laws.

AMENDMENTS

As of this date,_____,
passage of the following proposal has been enacted into the Constitutional Law as
the First Amendment to the Constitution of the Almighty Latin King Nation.

AMENDMENT I.

AMENDMENTS

An amendment is an amelioration of the Constitution without involving the idea of
any change in substance or essence.

For the purposes of continued growth, the modification or alteration proposed under
an amendment is, as of this date, given its force and effect in the following manner:

> Once the passage of a proposal to amend is given by a Chapter
> Inca and Cacique and approved by Las Coronas it shall be added
> hereunder as Constitutional Law. Amor!

APPROVED:

_____

DATED: _____

MANIFESTO
OF THE
ALMIGHTY   LATIN   KING   NATION

THE KING MANIFESTO

ALMIGHTY LATIN KING NATION

He who knows, and knows that he knows, is a wise man,
Listen to him!

He who knows, and does not know that he knows, is asleep,
Wake him up!

He who does not know, and knows that he does not know,
Wants to learn... Teach him!

He who does not know, and does not know that he does
Not know, is a fool... Avoid him!

Confucian

ALMIGHTY	LATIN	KINGS	NATION
OENRAOA	AMRLA	NNOLT	ALONNU
VA ERWH	TEILT	ODBOR	TLG EC
ES AMAV	IRBUU	WEIWE	UIE L
U TORE	NIEMR	LSLIN	RET E
R ND	C IA	ETING	ASH U
E YS	A NL	DRTGT	L E S
D	N A	GUY H	R
	T	EC	
	I	T	
	N	I	
	G	B	
		L	
		E	

A LOVE MEASURED IN GREAT HARMONY TOWARDS YAHVE
LATIN AMERICAN TRIBE ILLUMINATING NATURAL
KNOWLEDGE, INDESTRUCTIBLE NOBILITY and GLOWING STRENGTH
NATURAL ALLIES TOGETHER IN ONE NUCLEUS

HOLY PRAYER

Almighty Father, King of Kings, Maker of the Universe and Foundation of Life, bring peace to our souls, to the here present, to those not present, to the young and to the old.

As an Almighty Nation under one Sun protected by thine love and guidance we bring our right fist upon our heart for sincerity, love, wisdom, strength, knowledge and understanding. Three hundred-sixty degrees of Strong King Wisdom.

Illuminate our minds and our hearts. Guide our thoughts with thine righteousness. Guide and protect the thoughts of our Coronas and all those holy and righteous lovers and followers of our beloved family and tribe - the Almighty Latin King Nation.

Let the manifestation of our departed Brothers be the path to thee and let it be as it was in the beginning - Strong King Wisdom on both continents, Peace in Black and Gold.

King love! Yesterday, Today, Tomorrow, Always and Forever.

KINGS AND QUEENS PRAYER

Oh King of the Universe, Supreme maker of all things, We the Almighty Latin King and Queen Nation ask you, Almighty King, to bring peace our cause. As an Almighty Nation under the Sun, protected by your love and guidance, we bring our right fist upon our hearts for love, honor, obedience, sacrifice and righteousness.

We ask you Almighty King to bless our departed Brothers and sisters, members of our beloved and mighty Nation, who on this very day rest in the bosom of your sanctuary. May they rest in your care and may they have found the peace and freedom they sought. In our critical moments bring us comfort and guide us through those days of confusion and oppression. May the blessings of the ancients and the wisdom of the ages guide us and keep our Nation strong as we battle the forces that seek to deny us.

We, the Almighty Latin King and Queen Nation, are entrusted with a divine mission, one that transcends personal gains and recognition. As Kings and Queens we pledge ourselves ever faithful to that mission. Make us all aware that others look to us for guidance, and let us always prove ourselves worthy of providing it. For, though we are of different Nationalities, we all share the same cultures of our ancient ancestors whose every word is law throughout the world. It is our destiny to lead rather than to be led.

We, the Almighty Latin King and Queen Nation, have the blood of royalty in our veins. We are the guiding light of our People. Place wisdom in our minds love in our hearts, and fortitude to withstand the trials of time. Guide and protect our Coronas so that they may lead us to our ultimate goal - the awakening of our People to their oppressed state that they may lift our heritage to its rightful place among the thrones of Kings and Queens,

LET THE MANIFESTATION OF OUR SACRIFICED BROTHERS AND SISTERS

BE THE PATH SO THEE, AND LET IT BE AS IT WAS IN THE BEGINNING:

STRONG KING AND QUEEN WISDOM - PEACE IN BLACK AND GOLD....

ALMIGHTY LATIN KING NATION

The Almighty Latin King Nation is a religion which gives us faith in ourselves, a national self-respect, power to educate the poor and relieve the misery around us.

It is the Brotherhood of man, blending like the waves of one ocean, shinning as the Sun, one soul in many bodies bearing fruit of the same tree.

It creates in us a thirst like the heat of earth on fire, a thirst for knowledge, wisdom, strength, unity and freedom.

It is the Sun glowing in the essence of our being, the brightness in our eyes that cast reflections of its rays spitting fire in all directions.

It is the unshakable spirit and the nobleness of our hearts, the limitless power of the mind, the unrelentless will to be free.

It is pride, ambition, love, sacrifice, honor, obedience and righteousness, all our powers and all our desires thrown into the mission of human service and united into one Single Gold Sun.

If you want to find Yahve serve the Almighty Latin King Nation. Put on the Gold Sun - Black and Gold colors, place your right fist upon your heart and pledge devotion to the Almighty Latin King Nation, to Yahve and all oppressed people. This is the Nation of Kingism....

BEHOLD KING LOVE!

ICONA

The history of all hitherto existing gang feuds is the History of label struggles for the sake of "click" recognition. It is thin egotistical force for recognition which leads to rivalry and senseless disputes which often cost the high price of human life. The life of our People, the oppressed Third World People.

With the intentions of changing this social and oppressive phenomena the King Manifesto is written; to serve as a guide and enlighten our deplorable conditions under the existing order of things. With this thought in mind we proceed to create the New King, the Moral King, the King of Others, the lover of men and the Turning Wheel of Change.

Devoting your life to the principles of Kingism implies a life of service to your fellow man. We can be of service in no other way. If you turn your back on your Brother simply because of a label you are turning your back on the Almighty Latin King Nation.

One who does not know the Almighty Latin King Nation and its Laws is like a plant growing in the shade. Although it knows not the Sun, it is nevertheless absolutely dependent upon it.

The Nation is in your hands. If you turn your back on the Nation you are denying yourself the sole purpose of your existence - the right to be free!

BEHOLD LATIN KING

KINGISM

Kingism is the doctrine of the Almighty Latin King Nation. There are three stages or cycles of Nation life that constitutes Kingism. They are:

> PRIMITIVE STAGE
> CONSERVATIVE STAGE
> THE NEW KING STAGE

In order for one to grasp a good understanding of each stage and its development, one must understand and consider the social factors surrounding each stage.

THE PRIMITIVE STAGE is that stage in life where the King Warrior acts on impulse, executing his actions without giving them the serious thought that they demand. A stage of immaturity where the King Warrior's time is spent "gang-banging", getting high and being recognized as big and bad.

This can also be classified as the wasteful stage to a certain extent; to the extent that what is being done is being done unconsciously. Yet it is not wasteful in the sense that the environment conditions this type of behavior in order for one to survive the hardships of ghetto life - that undesirable level at the lowest plane of social existence. It is wasteful in that energy is being misused. There are no objectives for one's actions except for the factual phenomena that the entire affair is centered around recognition, label recognition and personal recognition. This egotistical tendency often leads to a blind alley.

Regardless of how senseless one's nations may seem at this level, this is the original stage of Kingism and from the roots of the Primitive Stage emerges the second stage. It is at this level where one either breaks or becomes strong. True lovers of the Nation develop at this stage.

THE CONSERVATIVE STAGE (also known as the Mummy Stage) is the stage of so-called maturity. At this level the King Warrior becomes tired of the Primitive Stage. He no longer wishes to participate in the senseless routine of gang fighting, hanging on the corner or being recognized as big and bad. Most often at this level the King Warrior gets married and retires, alienating himself from the boys and the

Nation, concentrating his energies and devotion to his Queen, his children and his responsibility to them; ignoring the fact that he has unconsciously been neglecting his main responsibility to them and himself i.e., to make himself and his loved ones free!

It is inappropriate to call this stage the maturity Stage due to the fact that the King Warrior at this time does not really become mature in the true sense of maturity. Instead he becomes mummified or reaches a level of mummified maturity. He, in his conservative role, lives with no future, accepting life as it has been taught to him by the existing system that exploits all People of color - dehumanizes them and maintains them under the economic and social yoke of slavery.

True members of the Nation do not quit at this level, they do not cease to identify themselves with the Kings, instead they alienate themselves from them. They do not cease to be who they are, they conserve what they are; they become conservative. There are more Kings at this level than at any other level. And, although this stage has all the characteristics of a regressive stage, it is really the stepping stone into the third stage of Kingism - the New King Stage.

THE NEW KING is the stage of awareness and decision. The Primitive and Conservative stages are a compliment to the third. They go hand-in-hand with this stage of maturity, it does not keep the King Warrior in the limbo state of being i.e., the mummy like stage. At this level there is a stage of awareness, an awareness of one's self as a subject of decision.

Under the New King stage the world takes a completely new form. One no longer continues to visualize the street corner as his turf or being tough as a man of survival as in the Primitive stage nor does he remain in the mummy stage. Instead he learns to appreciate the values of organizational work, the values of life and Brotherhood. One no longer views the rival warrior as the cause of one's ills, instead his vision broadens to the extent of recognizing himself as a subject of decision. He learns that his ills lie at the roots of a system completely alien to his train of thought and his natural development due to the components of dehumanization that exist therein.

This stage is what determines righteousness, for it is at this stage where awareness leads to the point of decision, that point where one must decide one's future. This is where he either becomes an accomplice to that anti-King system or a subject of decision - A New King!

The New King recognizes that the time for revolution is at hand. Yes, revolution - a revolution of the mind! The revolution of knowledge! A revolution that will bring freedom to the enslaved, to all Third World People as we together sing and praise with joy what time it is - it's Nation time! Time for all oppressed People of the world to unite. The young warriors and future leaders look at the New King with the hope of someday being free. We shall not destroy the faith they have in us, for in doing so we destroy ourselves.

The New King is the end product of complete awareness, presieving three hundred-sixty degrees of enlightenment. He strives for world unity. For him there are no horizons between races, sexes and senseless labels. For him everything has meaning, human life is placed above materialistic values. He throws himself completely into the battlefield ready to sacrifice his life for the ones he loves, for the sake of humanization.

The New King is endowed with the supreme natural powers that surpass the human scope of comprehension. This highly complexed energical entities separate him from the abstract world and all those who surrender themselves to vanity and idleness and place materialistic values above and beyond human principle.

The New King sees himself as a subject of decision, a Sun that must glow forever to enlighten those not so fortunate as he. He feels the rays of the Sun glowing in the essence of his being, giving him life, energy and strength - the strength of his unshakable spirit and the nobleness of his heart. The hypnotizing profundity of his gaze reflects the limitless power of his mind and the unshakable will to be FREE.

THE CODE OF KINGISM

Every member of the Nation shall honor, respect and protect with his life the lives and reputation of all members of the Almighty Latin King Nation.

Stand up for those who stand up for themselves in their quest for peace, justice, freedom, progress and prosperity.

Never exploit or bring harm to any member of the most righteous Tribe - The Lion Tribe - the Almighty Latin King Nation or any other oppressed person or nation.

Respect and protect with your life Brown Women for they are the mothers of our beautiful color the life of the future Suns of the Universe.

Love and respect children of all races, sexes, cults and religions. Protect them with your life for they are the leaders of tomorrow's Nations.

Honor and respect the Nation Salute for it means. "I DIE FOR YOU; the Sacred Colors for they represent the People we love and live for - the memory of those who rest in peace in the sanctuary of the Almighty Father, King of Kings.

Educate yourself, for an illiterate King is a weak King and a weak King has no place in a Strong Nation.

Learn your King Manifesto and live by it for it shall lead to Peace - Freedom - and Justice.

BEHOLD LATIN KING

NATIONAL EMBLEM

The Crown is the National Emblem of the Almighty Latin King Nation. It displays our royalty among men; our sovereignty and our Kingdom among Nations. The Crown is a symbol that is recognized all over the world and although there are many different types, the two that the Almighty Latin King Nation identify with the most are the Imperial and the Coronet.

The Imperial is the one most generally used to represent our beloved Nation because of its very meaning and magnificence.

Each of the Coronet's five points has a special meaning. They represent Love, Honor, Obedience, Sacrifice and Righteousness. The Crown enthrones our idealism, our belief and attitudes towards a better way of life in the universe....

SACRED COLORS

BLACK represents the solid dominant color of the universe, the brave and the bold, the darkness of the immense night. It represents People of one idea, one body, mind and soul, the Alpha and the Omega.

GOLD represents the fabulous brilliant Sun at its highest peak; the splendoring glow of hope in oppressed People, the brilliance of the mind and the solid unity in strength, love and sacrifice.

Two colors of natural creations existing since the beginning of time and enduring forever.

NATIONAL SALUTE

A fist upon our heart.... it means, "I DIE FOR YOU" for you are flesh of my flesh, blood of my blood, son of my mother who is the Universal Nature and follower of Yahve who is the Almighty King of Kings; it also means Love - Strength - Sacrifice.

BEHOLD LATIN KING

Glory to the Queens and Power to the Kings
Almighty Latin King Love, Yesterday, Today, Tomorrow, Always and Forever!

FEARLESSNESS

To the Almighty Latin King Nation, fearlessness implies absence of all kinds of fears. It is the freedom from such fears as hunger, humiliation, wrath and criticism of others. It is also the freedom from the fear of resistance, the freedom from the fear of loss of courage and the freedom from the fear of physical death. It is a necessity for a true Latin King because cowards can never be moral. Fearlessness is indispensable for the growth of other noble qualities.

How can one seek liberation, truth, or cherish love without fearlessness? Moral Bravery is, for the Nation, the highest heroism. And it consists in the readiness to sacrifice patiently and fearlessly, everything, including life for the good of other members of the Tribe of Righteousness out of love for them....

BEHOLD LATIN KING

NATION FLAG

The Flag shall consist of either two stripes - one Black and one Gold - running horizontally with a circle in the upper left corner of the top color with a Crown in the center of the circle or the Flag may consist of three stripes running vertically with a circle in the center stripe and a Crown in the circle.

The Flag shall never touch the floor or be placed where dishonor may fall upon it.

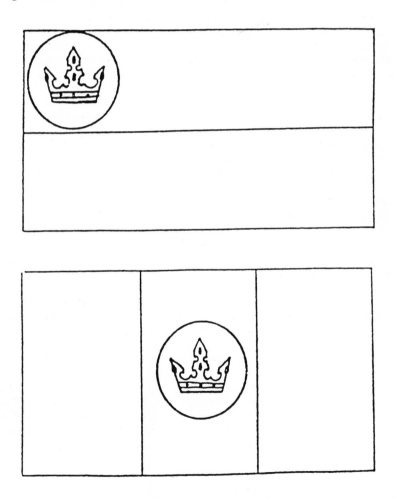

BEHOLD LATIN KING

The New King is the turning wheel of change, he recognizes what time it is - It's Nation time! He sees the rulers of our present system lavishing their treasures freely on the means of destruction, then towards that which would promote the happiness of mankind. These strifes and this bloodshed and this discord must cease and all oppressed People unite as one Nation, as one kindred, as one family.

The New King is aware of the fact that in the Almighty Latin King Nation all are servants, Brothers and Sisters - natural allies together in one nucleus. As soon as one feels a little better than the other, a little superior to the rest, he is in a dangerous position and unless he casts away the seed of such evil thought, he is not an instrument for the service of the Nation. Just as calamity is due for disobedience, so deliverance form calamity can be obtained by obedience. Turning from the Nation brings inevitable disaster and turning to the Nation brings blessings.

In order to establish the Kingdom of freedom in the world, it must first be established in the hearts of men. The King that lives the life according to the teachings of this Nation is the True King. A King who loves his Nation, his People and freedom; one who works for universal peace, universal freedom and universal Brotherhood. A man may call himself a King just as an ugly man may call himself handsome, yet if he does not live the life of a True King, he is not a King, and a ugly man deceives no one.

He who would be a New King needs to be a fearless seeker and lover of freedom. If his heart is pure and his mind is free from prejudice he shall not fail to recognize freedom from slavery. The call of the New King to mankind is that men should open their eyes and use their reason, not suppress it. It is seeing and free thinking, no servile credulity that will enable the True King to penetrate the clouds of prejudice, to shake the fetters of blind imitation and attain from the realization of truth a new revelation.

The New King will not only believe in the teachings of his Nation but will find in them the guide and inspiration for his life and joyfully impart to others the knowledge that is the well-spring of his own being. Only then will he receive the full measure of power of the Almighty Latin King Nation.

When a man becomes a New King the will of the nation becomes his will, for to be at variance with the Nation is one thing that cannot endure. The Almighty latin King Nation requires while-hearted and compete devotion.

How can divine King Love be demonstrated to an unbelieving world its capacity to endure to the utmost blows of calamity and the treachery of seeming friends; to rise above all t his undismayed and unembittered, still to forgive, bless and unite? The light of King Love irradiates his foggiest days, transmutes his suffering into hope and martyrdom itself into an ecstatical bliss. The New King longs to see believers of freedom shouldering the responsibilities of the cause. Now is the time to proclaim the Kingdom that is rightfully ours. Now is the time for union and concord. Now is the day of unity because it's Nation time!

The New King recognizes that the day of resurrection is here. A time for the appearance of a new manifestation of truth. The rising of the dead means the spiritual awakening of those who have been sleeping in the graveyard of ignorance. The day of the oppressor must now be judged by the oppressed.

BEHOLD LATIN KING

THE ALMIGHTY EYE

When a King Warrior accepts Kingism as described in the King Manifesto, his life takes a complete turn. For him everything changes. His vision is no longer limited to narrow horizons, instead he is gifted with the power of the Almighty Eye - a Sun that glows to enlighten, through the sense of sight, the New King and the Nation.

The eyes of the Nation are everywhere there is a Nation man, a True King. His perceptions, viewed in the concept of universal human progress, is the reflections of his soul, his ideology, his quest for freedom and his desire for unity among his People. His observations are free and independent; his thoughts are not clouded by any form of prejudice and his actions are based on common sense and knowledge.

Seeing, perceiving and observation by all Kings is the network of the Nation - the eyes of the Almighty Latin King Nation are everywhere.

BEHOLD LATIN KING

KING AM I

Whether in front or profile I stand
On that finished form let glory bestow
Black its midnight shadow, Gold its morning glow
In precision clear, a vision ever so bright
That over the rest the domineering light
Spreads the extensive vigor of its rays
Any yields to me the power they praise
That majesty, that grace, rarely given
To remove the restraints with which they confine
To pass before the turning wheel of change
With supreme perfection my aim
Love, truth and knowledge my claim.
Below the thunderous lofty arch of light
The whole in loveliest harmony unites
For a True King the brightest glories soar
The King of Kings applauds him and the world adores
Let then each be firm allied
And let no one separate or divide
United in strict decorum, time and place
An emulous love and genuine faith
Be Grace, Be Majesty thy constant strive
That majesty, that grace - King Am I.

Be it always remembered that the original Manifesto was written and dedicated to all oppressed people of the world, to the People and the Nation and to all our beautiful Sisters by the Brown Prince of Darkness. Amor!

BEHOLD LATIN KING

BROWN FORCE

The Latino can draw additional strength from another force too if he has the will and the faith.

Anonymous millions of Brown Men and Women have given their life in the fight for liberation. They have fought against colonialism, hunger and ignorance and for the human dignity of our People. They have drawn from one another, through unity, a force of fortitude - Brown Force - the force which provides the splendoring glow of hope in oppressed people. The seed they cast into the founding of a Nation - the Almighty Latin King Nation - has withstood the trials of time.

Drawing upon the endurance and fortitude of Brown Force, we continue our quest to unify and insure free political and culture expression among the Third World People and among the commonwealth of individuals. We are the People's liberating force - Brown Force - the foundation of the Nation.

BEHOLD LATIN KING

NATION MEN

Who is a Nation man and who is not? The difference lies in what they do, how they carry themselves and how they talk. But in order for one to really understand the contrast one must know and understand the principles of the King Manifesto and Modern Kingism.

One of the clearest contrastive examples is when the so-called Nation Man claims to be a Latin King, a member of the Almighty Latin King Nation, and by the same token says, "I am a Little; A Coulter King; A Pee Wee; I'm from such and such a branch or chapter, etc." He might be a Latin King, that is true, but he definitely is not a Nation Man.

This clearly testifies that this so-called Nation Man is really a demagogue, a preacher of a false philosophy, an agent of confusion and disunity. His mind is broad only to the scope of where his particular "click" is concerned. Outside of that click mentality his mind meets with the brick-wall of prejudice and individualism.

Nation Men on the other hand are devoted followers and believers of unity, supporters of the harmonious whole. For Nation Men there are no horizons between clicks and branches for they identify only with the Nation, not with a particular click, branch or section - natural allies together in one nucleus, one Nation, the Almighty Latin King Nation.

BEHOLD LATIN KING

APPENDIX B

WRITTEN CONSTITUTION AND BY-LAWS OF THE SPANISH GANGSTER DISCIPLE NATION

CONCEPT'S
OF THEE
20th CENTURY

TABLE OF CONTENTS

(1)

GREETING'S TO OUR COMRADES

Greeting's Comrades

Before I proceed any futher into this letter, I would like to extend our nation's love to all our family members who in their time of incarceration have served our distinguished organization faithfully and effectively.

My sole purpose is to speak to our comrades in arms through these unspoken words, in order that I may convey the basic information that you may need to function effectively in our dignified organization. It also gives me great pleasure to acquaint you with our new ideology and some of the needed changes that have taken place within our nation. To begin with, changes in our nation will continue, it's through these changes that our nation will grow to it's height. Changes come through the new ideas proposed by any family member. Each individual who is an active member of this supreme nation, is given the opportunity to grow and develop along with it.

To further the growth of our nation, I have proposed an idea that will advance the unification of all our allies. My presentation to our allies is for us to go under one name, not only in these penal institutions, but also in the free world.

I discussed my proposal over with Mad-Dog, in respect that he is looked upon as a leader among his peoples organization, and with some of our other allies, and they all endorsed my proposal. So our strength of minds were mutual.

We will assume the name of - Spanish Gangster Disciple nation, those of you who oppose our proposal will just have to step to the side and let our nation lunge forward and gain ground.

Mad-Dog and I, have dispatched word to the free world informing our comrades of the S.G.D.N. movement. All of us as a whole are obligated to spread the word to our comrades who are in different penal institutions, and to those who are in the free world.
Through full and total participation we shall achieve the development and growth of our nation, and thereby stimulate the personal development of each of our members. Those members who show leadership potentials should be prepared to assume leadership roles in our organization.

Asymbol had to be thought up, one which would characterize and represent our newly founded nation, and we came up with the idea to devise a cross that will symbolize the Spanish Gangster Disciple Nation. So Sach-Mo and I designed it. The cross bares five(5) stones, with the colors of each of the original organizations that came together to form the S.G.D.N., the cross is a process by which the "whole nation" can offer it's member's, a total experience, personal development, and not to forget, effective service to the S.G.D.N. These functions are absolutely essential for the "total S.G.D.N." to be a reality.

We must all be aware that in the history of anyone of our organizations, we have shown failure in many ways, and we have also accomplished some achievements, as for instance, the 60's for us was not a decade of many accomplishments, and the same applies for the 70's, but the 80's will be a new day for us, and not to mention a more successful decade. "No other success can compensate for failure in our Nation".

Here is something we must all acknowledge! The S.G.D.N. makeup is a composite of all the organizations that came together to form it. If we all play active roles, the S.G.D.N. will become a strong nation. And if we don't all agree to participate, our nation will become weak. "It's that simple". We can all make a difference.

Your position of leadership requires that you become totally knowledgeble in planning projects and conducting our nations business, we can make being members of the S.G.D.N. a beneficial and meaningful experience. Remember that our objective is to give our family members tools through which they can personally benifit and apply to their lives.

I urge you brothers to put in all your heart and mind, and participate in helping our nation have years of pride and accompishments. I bid you peace love an loyalty and deep respect for our fallen comrades.

>Our deeds will travel
>with us from afar, and
>what we have been,
>makes us what we are'"

VICTOR

(2)

INSIGNIA

The Spanish Cross derives from our heretic ways, the first word in our Nations name, in which we find our race, our creed, our essential belifs and our faith.

These guiding principals unite us closer together and bound us as one. The circular disc behind the cross represents the highest degree of unity, unity being the reason for which we have constructed the S.G.D.N.

To unionize and coordinate the structure of all our branches under one foundation of S.G.D.N.

The disc behind the cross is to be carved on edge with "WREATH" type circles, for our loving memories of our dead.

Each stone on the cross will represent the color of our branches, the middle stone is to be the color of your original branch, all colors on the insignia are there to show respect and tribute to each of our affiliate organizations, which secure peace, praise, and credit to the foundation of our Nation.

This "Insignia" is to be worn proud, with a constant loyalty shown to the people of thee:

S.G.D.N.

(3)

(4)

PREAMBLE

We, of thee: S.G.D.N. grateful to all our brothers for thier participation in our years of struggle, for our brothers with thier years of loyalty to our nations life. Through our nations decades we've enjoyed providing security, a sure safety and domestic tranquillity amoung the lives of our people.

We, brother's of the S.G.D.N. must ordain and abide by the nations constitution, to eliminate poverty and inequality amoung our people, to provide a structure of potential developments for the individual of our nation, to maintain a liberty for our children and a more gratifying style of social living. We bless all our people along with our families and we will constantly obtain a future for the descendants of our nation.

(5)

CODE OF S.G.D.N.

"All code word's must be in a set of quotation's."

Stateville	"Vic's Crib"
Pontiac	"Imoky's Crib:
Manard	"Slim's Crib"
Administration	"Neek's"
Police	"Pig"
S.G.D.N.	"Folk's"
Familia Disciple's	"Gente"
Cobra's	"c"s"
Gangster's	"Division"
Disciple's	"Rockwell"
Satan Disciple's	"Taylor's"
B.G.D.N.	"Allies"
B.D.N. Negro's"	"Discipulo

King's	"Corona"
S.C.R.	"Peaches"
Joliet	"Angel's Crib"
Mail	"Carta"
Nation	"Nasióa"
Segragation	"Pit"
Parole Board	"Tabla de Violar"
Law's	"Leyes"
Constitution	"foundation"
Literature	"Fact's"
Organization	"La Unión"
Incarcerated	"Pared"
Penal Institution's	"Cháteau"
Figa	"Old Spice"

Add words as needed -

(6)

A BROTHER'S   OATH   TO   THE   NATION

A sworn oath to the nación in sound form from each of our hearts, a oath to the people, for the people and accepted by the people. As a brother of the Spanish Gangster Disciple nación, I, in belief of the nación's ideology and teachings of the constitution, swear to uphold the honor and protect the nación, to show love and endure 100% loyalty toward the people of our nación.

To maintain silence in our nación, in respect to abiding by the law's of our constitution, giving my life to my brother's; never to betray a brother in code of *Death*Before*Dishonor*, securing our rights to love, to carry life, and to pursue the loyalty we share.

As this statement to be truth I, swear to our beloved insignia to carry the name Spanish-Gangster-Disciple-Nación-, and to serve as a prophet to the faith of our Nación until my death...

(7)

ADMINISTRATOR'S   OF OUR NACIÓN

Governor:

Our Governor is the chief executive of our Nación. Our Governor's responsibility is to maintain and oversee his administrator's functions toward the people of the Nación.

****

Lt. Governor:

There is one Lt. Governor in our Nación while incarcerated, his function is to exercise and perform duties handed down to him by the Governor.

****

Ambassador's:

Ambassador's are officials appointed by the Lt. Gov.- an ambassador's functions are to carry out duties handed down to them by the Lt. Gov.; an appointed ambassador must carry himself in form as follows:

    1. A) Our ambassador's must carry a positive and firm attitude, this be mentally as well as physically. He has to maintain a strick discipline upon himself in which those of our Nación can see and recognize: "A Explicit Character".

    1. B) Our ambassador is an official appointed in position of commands, but the ambassador is not to constantly impose his position upon our brother's of the Nación.

    2. A) Ambassador must have a wide understanding along with patience to relate to any situation that may arise. To be able to comprehend all information before making the decision to make a move, the ambassador must consult with the Lt. Governor before he makes the move in question.

    2. B) An ambassador has to approach and speak to all brother's of our Nación in a manner in which all the brother's understand what has been said, and to make sure all brother's comprehend the idea at hand.

    3. A) A ambassadors mental attitude must be to maintain peace at all times, this is amoungst our Nación; we are to bare arms after all avenues have been exhausted.

    3. B) A ambassador must realize for faulty decisions he is to expect the same penalty as any brother in transgression.

****

VICEROY- Appointed by the ambassador to maintain a cell-house!

(8)

ORGANIZATIONAL   STRUCTURE

There is no ideal organizational structure that fit's the needs of every single S.G.D.-member, but there is one that is right for your's, which is, "The Board Of Directors", the board of directors merely figures out all the job functions and activities that are needed. The board sensibly and fairly distributes them to certain officers on the board.

Fortunately we have been in existence long enough to assist you with the assignment. As you design your structure there are a few guidelines that will assist you, they are:

****

1.)   No one person should be required to manage more than six (6) to ten (10) member's.

2.)   The workload should be balanced between the Board Member's.

3.)   The system must be flexible so that additional people and programs can be added during the coming years. It must also be flexible enough to handle a reduction in the number of people and programs.

4.)   Each Ambassador must know what is expected of him, the importance of his role in achieving the overall objectives, and the standards by which his performance will be judged.

****

SAMPLE OF OUR ORGANIZATIONAL   STRUCTURE

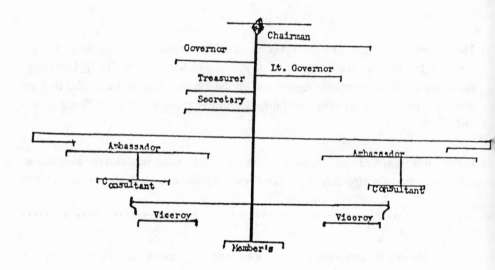

These are examples of how you can shift workloads to a new officer when it is necessary.   Whatever structure you finally choose, let it be flexible enough to accommodate the growth of your section. As you grow, al the management functions of your section increase. It's far better to add new positions to alleviatae some of the new burdens than to let the present Board members become overworked. Don't be afraid to change your structure when it is necessary.

****

(9)

COMMUNICATION   AND   MEETING'S

If you don't communicate effectively, you won't lead effectively. Leadership involves getting things done through people. How well you do this, this will be determined by your ability to communicate. You have to look upon communication as your most valuable asset, other than your own personal communication methods there is one primary way that a section can comunicate with it's member's. Thee primary way is through:

Meeting's!

****

MEETING'S

Board meetings are the single most important time where all aspects of the management of your section should be reviewed and discussed. Items that should be discussed are such items as follows:

1.) The status of all projects.

2.) Attitude of older and younger member's.

3.) Whose dues are due next month.

4.) Budget review and your sections plan of action.

5.) Review of last membership meeting's, the good point's and the bad point's.

6.) Plan for next Board meeting!

You should be an active participant at all Board meeting's, it is your elected responsibility. Regular membership meeting's are equally important. It is during these meeting's that several things are accomplished. Direction for your section is decided, the member's are informed, motivated, and the opportunities available in your section are on display.

Even though it is the direct responsibility of your Governor, Lt. Governor, or Ambassador to insure that you have effective and productive meeting's, it is your responsibility to assist them in several areas. Areas such as:

1.) You should actively participate in the planning of the next membership meeting at each Board meeting.

2.) You should insure that your reports, and reports of your Directors and committee chairman are always short, clear, and _concise_. (To the Point)- Nothing turns off members more than long and unprepared committee reports.

3.) If the meeting or an individual becomes unruly you should assist the Governor in getting the meeting back to order as soon ass possible. Or Chairman -

****

NOTE:

Always arrive at Board meetings one half hour before starting time of the meeting. You can help with any last minute set ups. Be sure that you also review the basics with all members so that they can more effectively participate in meeting's.

Speaking of Board meeting procedures, you should have a basic idea of how it works and it's importance in conducting the affairs of our organization. You don't have to be a lawyer to understand the Board's procedure. All you must do is realize that it is merely a tool to shorten meeting's, conduct business and ensure fairness to all our member's.

(10)

AMENDMENTS OF S.G.D.N.

1.) All members must respect and participate in maintaining a code of silence within our family, and at all times conduct themselves in accordance with our family's laws. All members must display faithful allegience to the family's organization and to thier appointed superiors.

2.) Discourtesy, rude, or impolite remarks will not be tolerated, absolutley no fighting amoung family members.

3.) No family members shall at anytime consume any addictive drugs, or encourage the use of drugs to any family member.

4.) All family members will acknowledge authorative commands handed down to them by thier appointed superiours. Insubordination, will not be tolerated from any member towards thier superiours.

5.) "At No Time" - will any member put up with, or tolerate any offensive critisizm towards this organization - by those non-affiliated with our family, nor shall we see any members outrage the moral feelings of any righteous family member.

6.) All members of this family are expected to sacrifice and devote thier lives for this family's cause.

7.) All members will be at any aid to the members of thee B.G.D.N. - and to this family, in any difficulty or problem that they may have, be it mentally or physically.

8.) Misrepresentation of this family, or of any appraisales, flags, embloms, or colors will not be tolerated.

9.) All members- regardless of rank or position must strive to assist each other, not to compete with one another.

10.)   All members must make a solemn declaration to uphold all commands handed down to them, and to make a oath from thier heart and soul to this family- that all members will be a part, even if there are times of depression.

11.)   All members will experience and undergo the same penalties imposed on any member of this organization who breaks or goes beyond the limits of our set laws. "No exceptions will be made!" Regardless of rank or position.

12.)   The penalty for any transgression made against this organizations laws- will be left up to the discreation of your superiors, considering the nature of the law that was broken, then the member in the wrong will be dealt with according to the law broken.

13.)   Ignorance of our laws are of no excuse, all members shall make it thier initiative to come and know each and every law, and percieve to understand the full meaning to our laws, and also apply yourselfs to them.

(11)

AMENDMENTS OF THEE INCARCERATED

1.) In each place of where you are confined, there is a box... All family members who are able must contribute to help others in the family who are not as fortunate as other members. (This includes for the people of orientation).

2.) At no time shall we disrespect any member of another nation - all grudges from the street are to be held until you return to the streets. We as a nación, are in no position to participate in meaningless struggles which will only prolong our stay in these confinements.   If any problems occur, a decision will be made by high authority.

3.) We shall not play with any officer of the jail, they have a job to do. It is to keep us here. Unless you can gain off the situation, leave it alone. Our struggle is to show love to each other, and one day be set free. The administration holds us. So consider them off limits, unless it benifits you, or any other member of this family.

4.) We are allies of the B.G.D.N., but we are an independant nación, we are our own ruler, we take orders from our own organization only... Give the members of the B.G.D.N., all due respect at all times.

5.) Attend to your personal needs, ask one another for what you lack, we shall not hold back on anything that will make one of our people be without...

6.) All members shall take orders from thier appointed superiours of any cellhouse. Disrespect in any form is an immediate violation of King Vic's laws.

7.) We shall represent with (2) fists across the chest. We all have an original way of representing. Either way will be proper. We all understand the love and meaning behind representing.

8.) We all know who we are, and what we stand for. If in any place or situation you cannot represent, well, we know one doesn't have to hit his chest to be 100% loyal to this almighty family.

9.) We are Gangsters, Disciples, Cobras, Eagles, all united into one familia de amor, We are Disciples of each other-we are King Vic's Disciples. We be about the latino organization, so spread out the laws and the teachings of our supreme Nación.

(12)

EDUCATION   + EMPLOYMENT

This section is specifically for all our fellow familia members to gain as much knowledge in these two areas as possible. Education and Employment are two essential needs throughout your confinement and also in todays society.

During ones confinement, if an individual has not yet obtained his diploma, he should take advantage of the educational system. We find in our confinement areas that there are two types of educational programs. 1.) One is the school for individuals to obtain a G.E.D. The other educational program is the vocational school, a place where a individual can learn a trade. Actual learning experiences in trades such as: welding skills, electrical training, small engines, computer programing, and a print shop trade. Of these mentioned vocational skills an individual can obtain a verified certificate of his achievement.   An individual can further the achievement into becoming a "Journey Man" in one of these specific field's.

Members of our organization with these achievements are important assets to our daily progress, but also as an individual with these skills you can become financially stable.   Employment is most important to our people's needs, whether it is employment while incarceration, or in society. But a structure of development must be set to raise our peoples standards and classification.

While in confinement there are jobs where a individual can learn a specific skill, such as; tailoring, cooking, barbering, electrician skill, plumbing or even legal aid's. Our ideas toward our people are; not letting thim sit around to let time pass by, each of our people must take a day in life to make the decision of what he or she wants out of life, and to set the structure of obtaining the set goal, whether it be through Education or Employment.

(13)

SECURITY

In maintaining security of the lifestyle we live, one must have eyes that memorize and see at the same time. The importance of memory can be vital to you and any brother around you. Communication amoung our brothers is our greatest virtue, for what one brother misses in his sight, another brother can carry the blind to see the light of a situation; as in understanding, teach our brothers understanding until they are capable of being the prophet.

In maintaining security of a organization; all information that is kept within one brothers mind can be vital to other brothers who are left in the dark of a situation. Our guard is to be up at all times and we are to strike first if need be, because for our people to be struck at first is a sure sign of being lax.

It is always best to be in the pressance of another brother at all times, if not, for best results let another bother know of your whereabouts, in case of any occurrance that may come about. When the question is asked about a brothers whereabouts, someone should know at all times. In case of any unusual happening it is a brothers first obligation to notify others, a brother is always to handle the situation at hand, any revengious act of a brother is not tolerated, especially a act alone- consult other brothers in the surrounding's to make the wisest decision as a whole, never leaving any brother in the dark.

As a individual in a organization, to maintain personal security it is wise to be properly clothed at all times, and also to have showes on instead of "Thongs", or slippers. When returning from a shower it is best to put on shoes, never lounge around - especially in jail where a incident may occur at any given time.

In maintaining personal security it is wise to sleep with the door locked, never sleep with the door open. Then again in parable form, "Never Sleep"...

(14)

WORDS OF HISTORY

The history and concepts of thee: Maniac Latin Disciples. The current slogan "You've come a long way baby" certainly applies to the "Maniac Latin Disciples".

We have evolved from the dream of a small group of youths in the late part of the sixties into a vital, effective organization.

When the scope of the Spanish Gangster Disciple Nation, of today is considered, it is difficult to concieve it's beginning as the Latin Scorpions of Rockwell and Hirsch.

The Maniac Latin Disciples, are not of recent vintage, of course. The organization had been built exactly a decade and a half ago, and it's purpose, the social elevation of it's members, a goal the organization rapidly attained. By the mid-seventies it was the most outstanding organization in the vicinity and it prepared to merge with several other similar groups to form the federation of the Maniac Latin Disciples.

During the early years of our emergence, followed a series of clashes with our rivals, a wawr that to this day is still in existence. Where upon we lost a great number of our comrades, our members pride themselves on dealing with the enemy in thier terms, I could describe hundreds of episodes that relate to the wars we've had, but it would take me forever. Also, during the early years of our existence the Maniac Latin Disciples gained support from many of it's members, but none was greater and more valuable than the support gained from our allies.

This history culminates today into what we now term "The Spanish Gangster Disciple Nation Concept". It, then, can be understood as a convenient label pinned to a whole way of life, a living system that develops and changes in the course of time.

(15)

WORDS OF HISTORY

The life of a common street gang, a historical document manufested for future purposes of: Our descendants having questions of how we as a people came about, and how we as a people still progress in todays era, as well as the yesterdays.

Speaking vividly as a original member of the Imperial Spanish Gangster's, I can only try to put over 15 years of events on paper in a brief menner, many events here with will remain known only to those of the Imperial Spanish Gangsters who lived through the history of the Nation.

To bring out the reason why we as a people became a Nation; our first lable was not Gangsters, we were just a bunch of young kids attending school, but being that the school was dominated by the white, as Latino's, we fought against the white almost every day- never having intentions of being any specific group, so as time went by more Latino's attended the school, thus giving the Latino's more power and making survival easier.

In the year 1969 a section of Imperial Gangsters had became known in the area of Armitage and Drake, by people like; Pito a said leader as well as Jabar, Lil Mexico, Lil Bug's, Goyo, and Killer, not having any real goal in mind but to be as a defense to the white street gangs.

At the end of the same year another section of people came about which added another name to the already - Imperial Gangsters, being that most members were of latin origin the second section became -- Imperial Spanish Gangster's, the section was labled the dividion and grand people, or Cameron Gangster's. In that same year a sweater was brought about by one- Jesse Rodreguez, or known as "Lil Bug's" R.I.P., the sweater being black with baby pink cuts and trim. The first sweater thought of by the people of Cameron was to be black and white, but this unballanced the two sections so to unite the two sections Cameron people accepted the pink and black, for a emblom which was a Imperial crown- it is always to be a rounded crown at the top, with 5 head band diamonds to distinguish the crown from the three point crown of the latin kings, a later enemy to the Nation.

As Imperial Spanish Gangsters, the two sections decided to have thier leader's, which was a president, a vice president and a war chief. The first leaders started to live thier personal lives with wives and from that the people of armitage and drake had to take a step of advancement, the section of armitage and drake had to move the section to a different place and vote on we leadership.

The Imperial Gangsters of armitage and drake had the business on armitage tied up in thier favor, resturants, a theator, a cleaners, and parshally a liquor lounge. These businesses were important because of the donated money handed to the people of armitage and drake. As a street gang many shootings took place, shootings against the white gangs who just didn't like the latino, and the shootings against a street gang of latinos who wanted all latins to became latin kings. But the two sections of Imperial.

Gangsters held thier ground and kept what was thier's.

A meeting took place in 1972 for the section of Armitage people to move because they were to open for target and to open for the enemy of the law. The meeting was held in the Armitage theator which was a known place of the Gangster people. During the meeting it was known that the leaders of the new section was to be Lil Mexico as president, Goyo as vice president, and the move was to be on Palmer and Drake.

Lil Bug's was considered for position, but because of his military involvment, he "Lil Bug's" didn't want position.

For positions of the Cameron people, the first leader was Spanky as president, Tito as vice president-the people of Cameron had a change in leadership after a year or two, and the leadership was in one man known as; Godfather, he was the president and instead of a vice president, or war chief, the people of Cameron had thier "main" people. People like; Tiny, Casanova, Jauquin, Mr. Doc, M.D.Ron, Cisco, "secret squarral James", Caveman R.I.P., Lil man, Alberto, Tomo, Modesto, Fingers, Lil Joe, and Miguel "Chulito", White Boy.

The Cameron people had a section of future's who were; Sinbad, Cat, Milton Juni, Speedy, Armondo "Chico", and moreno, Moreno with his aggressive style and attitude became one of the main people and participated in the Gangster Nation with his life. A credit to the future's for being young and having the heart of survival.

With Cameron being the back bone to the Nation of Gangster's and with Armitage people having thier money businesses, more sections were formed, as Palmer and Drake became larger, a section of people came about, being the Sawyer and Armitage people, stemming from the help of people like- Lil Bug's and Lil Mexico, as for other factions of Gangster's, there were- Continental Gangsters- originated by the minister, Ghetto Gangsters originated by Mijo and the newest section of Imperial Spanish Gangster's on North & Hamlin.

Two brother's by the name of Smokey and Ellio are the ones who came up with the name Gangster's. The Supreme Gangster's, turned into the Imperial Gangster's.

There were always the lady Gangster's to each section, ladies being mostly latin and dedicated in our ways; ladies like; Morena R.I.P., Miss Lee R.I.P., Flac, Goofie, Bozo, Jeanie, Liz, Luz, Anita, Chiqueta, Happy, Smiley, Troubles, Peanut, Tita Maria, Elsa, Patty, Cateyes, Mary, GiGi, Herliena and Gym shoes. These ladies being a important part in our life, being mother to our peoples children and mostly by getting bonds together for thos who found themselves in jail.

As jail became part of the Nations life it brang about different ideas and made the members of the Nation smarter with sophisticated acts instead of openly-where jail was the next step.

Jumping to the year of 1976, this was the year the Imperial Spanish Gangsters had thier share of dealing with the law, until 1976 members were going in jail and finding it hard to get out, so the next thing to do was deal with the jail system because there were more Gangster's coming in jail then leaving the jail. In the jails the people of the Imperial Spanish Gangster's found other allies that they've dealt with on the street, by allies I speak of; Maniac Latin Disciple's, Satans Disciple's, Latin Eagle's, Spanish Cobra's, O-A;S, Milwalkee Kings and the Y.L.O. DISCIPLE'S.

In the jail wa've found the enemy still existed so a merge was constructed and these Nations became silently united in the struggles of the jail, we found ourselves fighting just to go to court in peace, to be able to get the proper share of food, or because of what you belonged too and to survive in jail as a whole was a duty you had to plan, there were only a hand full of people; Vic, M.D.R., Sach-Mo, Pito, Moreno, Bad-Boy, Aggie, Slim-D, Beaver, Mustang, Killer and Lucky plus Chino. We were never able to put our guard down against the whole system and the only people who could be trusted was these members of the silently put together Nation.

After years of seperation from these people because of convictions and seperated joints the silent Nation was at a stand still, but during the past year steps have been taken to unite and foundate all the Nations under one main title, neverto forget your originating people, and instead of all the different titles and beliefs, a structure was set up by leaders of these Nations for all the people to understand one way in one belief as a whole. In this one way we all have to follow a pattern to survive, to prosper in our growth, and to set forth a accomplishing goal.

We as a Nation have to have morals, to teach our young in every subject, to abide by our set of laws, to carry our Nations oath in our heart, to accept our prayer for our desceased and accept our constitution to keep our "Families" and "Nation" in a state of peace and well being.

-- Constantly in Thought --

Always a special tribute to our ladies,
and to our families for putting up with
our chaotic ways, to all the people who
have suffered in making our Nation possible, all the goods and bads we've dealt
with and we still live. My special love
too two aggressive brothers of the Nation.

Moreno-- and TopCat.

(16)

MOTTO OF S.G.D.N.

Motto being a structure of words to express ones beliefs, ones conduct; a phrase suitable to it's character;

"Our deeds will travel with us from afar, and what we have been, makes us what we are".

****

IDEOLOGY OF S.G.D.N.

: INGREDIENTS :

1. <u>LOYALTY</u>

2. <u>SECURITY</u>

3. <u>PROGRESS</u>

****

GOALS

1. Freedom for our confined brother's

2. Enbetterment of our people, and our children.

3. Unity-North and South - Harmony within the Latino Barrios.

(17)

LOVING MEMORIES OF OUR BROTHER'S & SISTER'S

:   Please, with a powerful unseen faith, with a meaningful trust and for the sake of loving memory, let us combine our hearts in a true moment of silence for our Brother's & Sister's who have lost thier lives in being part of our Nation's struggle...

:   A mere moment is vaguely enough to show tribute for the feelings we have. With this dedicated thought to you of our desceased, we will carry you in our hearts for the peace we have had in our daily lives...

:   We feel you through music we hear, we feel you through things we see, we feel you through our conversations, and most of all we have a hold on each other's heart...

:   At times we have a picture in our hand, at times we have a vision in our mind, and at this time we praise what you be rested in your peace...

                                            : In Loving Memory
                                              of our's who --:
                                              <u>REST IN PEACE</u>

(18)

GLOSSARY

A's

1.)   Accomodate - To make fit or suitable, adapt.

2.)   Accordance - Agreement, conformity.

3.)   Affiliate - To connect closely often as a member, branch, or associate.

4.)   Allegience - Devotion or loyalty to a person, group, or cause.

5.)   Alleviate - To remove or correct in part.

6.)   Ambassador - An authorized representative of the government.

7.)   Appraisals - The value so determined.

8.)   Aspects - A particular status or phrase in which something appears of may be regarded.

9.)   Asset - Advantage, recourse.
****

C's

1.)   Compensate - To be equivalent to in return to.

2.)   Composite - Made up of distinct parts or elements.

3.)   Comrade - An intimate friend or associate.

4.)   Concise - Marked by compactness of expression or statement.

5.)   Convey - To impart or communicate or serve as a means of poparting or communicating.

6.)   Coordinate - To bring into a common action, movement, or condition.

7.)   Creed - A set of guiding principals or beliefs. Of a certain racial background.

****

D's

1.)   Descendants - Proceeding from an ancestor or source.

2.)   Disciples - A pupil or follower who accepts and helps to spread his master's teachings.

3.)   Distinguished - To recognize one thing from other things.

4.)   Domestic Tranquillity - Of or relating to the family, having no agitation free from problem.

****

E's

1.)   Endorsed - To give one's support. Express approval of.

2.)   Essential - Important in the highest degree.

3.)   Explicit - So clear in statement that there is no doubt about the meaning.
****

G's

1.)   Goals - The end toward which effort is directed.

2.)   Govenor - An official elected or appointed to act as ruler. Chief executive.

3.)   Lt. Govenor - An officer empowered to act for a higher official.
****

H's

1.)   Heritic - Ways of the forfather.

2.)   Honor - A keen sense of ethical conduct. Integrity, "respectful reputation".
****

I's

1.)   Ideology - A manner or the conduct of thinking characteristic of an individual, group, or culture.

2.)   Impose - Exploiting a relationship.

3.)   Initiative - An introductory step or movement.

4.)   Insignia - Something distinguishing, mark - emblem-badge - etc. "In our cause the Spanish cross".

5.)   Insubordination - Un willing to submit to authority, disobedient.
****

L's

1.)   Lax - Slack, loose - to open. Not being strict or stringent. (Rigid)

2.)   Loyalty - Faithful to a cause or ideal.

****

M's

1.)   Member - One of the individuals or units belonging to or forming part of a group or organization.

2.)   Moral - Expressing or teaching a conception of right behavior. Moral conduct. Teaching's or beliefs.

3.)   Motto - A sentence, phrase, or words to express one's beliefs.

****

O's

1.)   Oath - A solmen appeal to some revered person or cause to bear witness to the truth of one's word or having sacredness in one's promise.

2.)   Obtain - To gain or attain by planning or offer's.

****

P's

1.)   Parable - Ashort simple story illustrating a moral or truth.

2.)   Potential - Something that can develop or become actual. Possible -

3.)   Poverty - The state of being poor.

4.)   Preamble - An introductory statement.

5.)   Prophet - An effective or leading spokesmen for a cause, doctring, or group. Teacher-

****

R's

1.)   Righteous - Acting rightly: upright.
****

S's

1.)   Solemn - Done or made seriously and thoughtfuly. Sacred -

2.)   Status - Condition, situation.

3.)   Structure - Something constructed, a definite pattern of organization.
****

T's

1.)   Transgression - Violation of a law, command, or duty.
****

U's

1.)   Unification - The state of being unified.
****

V's

1.)   Vaguely - Not felt, grasped, or not enough.

2.)   Viceroy - An official in government who rules as the representative of the chief executive. "In our cause - an underBoss of the executive".
****

W's

1.)   Wreath - ('R_th) - Something intertwined into a circular shape: Garland, chaplet.

APPENDIX C

CONSTITUTION OF THE VICE LORDS

Amalgamated Order Of Lordism
Lah Via Va Va Illilaha Halaliil, Allah Akbun
Supreme Chief, Al-Ugdah

Salutations my brothers I greet you in the name of V/L, With dedications to V/L, And sincerity of V/L. My brothers I greet you under the master sign.

This literature is a revelation of the nature of V/L, It's principals and its superiority.

It is manifested at this time to steer this nation to its proper course and to unify V/L the world over into and Amalgamated Order Of V/L dedicated to V/L's and Lordism.

There also is another reason for the manifestation of this revelation. there is a demonstration in our midst that has confused, misled and divided V/L's. This demonstration is called the (L.O.I. Lords Of Islam Nation. V/L's have been led to believe that this is the literature and or law of the V/L's. IT IS NOT! The Supreme Chief Of V/L's is Al-Ugdag, And he has not order or give consent to V/L's being govern by the dictate of L.O.I. Every true V/L is a V/L by choice. The V/L Nation is comprised of various branches of V/L's, This has always been and will be. Every V/L has personalize roots in any particular branch and those will not be uprooted. So awaken brothers and remember from whence you came that loi is not V/L. It is a chartered motorcycle club with bylaws and laws of already set stipulations. Law governs all events. Justice is Supreme.

We leave you as we came, In Peace, In Love, and in Lordism. As the wind shall blow the whole world shall know we come as we are, We are as we come, In the name of Almighty most glorious V/L.

Behold the truth and the Law Nov, 17, 1989 Chief Al-Ugdah.....

Why we chose the name Amalgamated Order Of Lordism because we as V/L's are a diverse people, Meaning we are people with a choice, And are autonomous in our same representations of Lordism. We have different precinct preference, And yet the same principals, And Concept. These precincts, And autonomous in nature, And in essence for us the core of versatility, Such fundamentals sameness, And different are the ingredients necessary for the continuity, development, And prosperity of the Amalgamated Order Of Lordism. Question; Is that a contradiction?

Answer;NO!

Explanation; That sameness that we experience together that we are all expressing and practicing, And living Lordism as true V/L'.

The difference is that we all belong to different precincts, Our Unifying, Common Denominator is summed up in one word, Amalgamated; Draw Brothers, Amag means that we are a conglomeration of people, A family. For clarification. (And elaboration see key 14 of keys to the throne of power).

Lah Via Va Va Illilaha Halaiil, Allah Akur.....

Amalgamated   Order   Of   Lordism.....
Supreme Chief,   Al Ugdah.....
Chair of Command.....

Supreme Chief King Of Kings.....

The Supreme Chief holds the reigns of the nation in his hands. He has the power, And the authority to delegate responsibility and make law to and for all representatives of V/L. His decree shall keep the nation moving in an organize and constructive manor down the golden path of Lordism. He was, Is, And will be the choice of the consensus of the kings of V/L's, And in effect is the king of kings of V/L's, And the precepts, Of V/L's, And in effect is the king of kings is V/L. The precepts, Policies, And laws set down by his administration are absolute. The Supreme Chief does not indulge in precinct policies, He allows all precinct to be autonomous, Thus self govern. (Note: The price to appeasing certain people is total subjugation). I'm determine not to setup to any level that will compromise my manhood, Or principals in any shape fashion Or form. I will never become subservient to the wills, And expectations of others especially when such projections conflict with my own.

Prince Of The Nation.....

This brother is second only to Supreme Chief, He is to be held in high regards. In the event of Unforeseen absence of the Supreme Chief, The Prince is responsible for keeping the nation on the golden path, And is to keep a line of communications open with the Supreme Chief, And other Kings. In the event of death of this Supreme Chief (may Allah forbid) the Kings of V/L will convene to reestablish a King of Kings, And a Prince from the Amalgamated Order from their own ranks, The selections of the Nation Prince is manifested in the same fashion as the Supreme Chief (King Of Kings), Is selected, By the panel of Kings.

Minister Of Justice.....

He is to be both respected, And honored by all representatives of V/L. His functions is to make sure orders and laws directed by Supreme Chief are put into manifestation in an orderly, Prompt, Effectively fashion, He is also to advise the Supreme Chief as to the need of modification, Amending of any existence of oppose laws. He is also responsible for balancing justice within our nation, And making sure that the law and principal are adhered to.

Kings Of Nation.....

These individuals are few. They are the distinct leaders of precinct. Kings of each precincts have universal appeal, And influences, And are to be respected and honored by all precincts, And all V/L's period. In the history of V/L every branch (Precinct) head has been traditionally recognized and respected as kings. This tradition will continue to be in effect.

Universal Elites.....

In the not to distant pass, Without the express consent or authorization of the Supreme Chief, Universal Elite were appointed. That practice as is of now terminated! The Supreme Chief alone has this authority. Recommendation for brothers to be appointed will be accepted from any king, Universal status, And some circumstances from representative. All existing Universal Elites will continue to be honored, And carried in highest regard by the Supreme Chief, And all representatives of the Amalgamated Order Of Lordism, That status, Contributions, And sincerity to V/L is reviewed by the Supreme Chief, And or whomever he may appoint to an elite review committee, Which such committee will be establish in the near future, And will consist of representatives from each precinct.

Ambassador.....

The brothers, Or sisters that are blessed with the position of Ambassador have a great responsibility to undertake. They act as missionary. They are to propagate, And promote Lordism in any area designed which lack organizational structure. They will spread. And correctly expound on the way of life as V/L. And Ambassador is appointed by the Supreme Chief, And is to inform him weekly of the progress, Problem, Needs, Ect., Of the designated area which he/she has been sent. And Ambassador has Universal appeal, And require a Universal star upon his/her appointment. (Note: Kings of precincts can appoint precinct ambassadors at there own discretion., However, They will not be a Universal nature but are to be respected by all representatives.

Minister Of Command.....

These brothers will be chosen by the kings of there respected branches. There function are to insure that Laws, Orders, And directed issue by the Supreme Chief, By way of the minister Of Justice, Or issued by there respected Kings, Are being adhere to in there respected precincts. It is there responsibility to communicate with the Minister Of Justice to insure that they have the proper understanding of the letter spirit of any Laws, Orders, or directives of the Supreme Chief. They also serve as sounding post for there administration as to any difficulty do to circumstances, Or environment surrounding any particular precincts regarding effective manifestation of Laws, Orders, Or directives. (Note: In the past there has been manifestation, And demonstration of abusiveness).

(Due to display of ignorance from one Lordself to another who apparently lacks the knowledge that one branch part, Or precinct constitute in nature one nation whole. The continuity, And self reliance dictate that we adopt this new measure of identity once referred to as branches, And now precincts. This has a two fold affect. One, being the inextricable ties of precinct, And to All precincts inherently, An intrinsic relationship with the Amalgamated Order Of Lordism, So in this literature from here out branches are referred to, And indeed are precincts.

Precincts Elite.....

These brothers are to be respected, Honored, And carried high by all representatives, As it there due, And our nature. A Precinct Elite authority is to be restricted to his particular precinct, And his appointment is left to the discretion of the king of his precinct. Precinct Elite may require stars based on having a particular number of representatives in his following, And or, Meritoriously. His functions include assuring the overall effectiveness of his particular precinct, And can be viewed as a trouble shooter for his precinct.

Lieutenant.....

Appointment of Lieutenant is left to the discretion of the respective administration of each precinct. Its function is also left to the same discretion.

Minister of Literature.....

This position is a very essential position in our nation. The brother holding this position in any precinct must be respectful as well as respected at all times. His functions include teaching of the Amalgamated Order Of Lordism literature As well as any precinct literature, To his brothers, And making sure that they know the meaning behind the words. He would also help representatives to acknowledge and understand there spiritual selves.

(Note: In the past their has been disrespect from one precinct to another under the Amalgamated Order Of Lordism, Such display, Reflection, Or infractions will no longer be intolerated justice is the call today, And in this event justice will be swift).

(Note: All Universals appointed will move under the sign of the Amalgamated Order Of Lordism. Although they still have there precinct roots in there heart, As they should be, But there promotions of Lordism will encompass the totality Of Lordism. Such expression must be express thru the Amalgamated Order Of Lordism to insure proper adherence, Unity, And Respect.

Summation.....

This Chair Of Command is a structure that is in the tradition of V/L. Time, As circumstances as time dictate change. As we move into the 90's we have the opportunity to realize past mistakes, That we now put them behind us as we travel on the golden path. Gone are the days of many chief, And few indians, Gone are the days of fractured Unity, Gone of the days of selfish motives. With the strength of lions and wills of ants we will move forward for a better tomorrow for every V/L present, And future. Every V/L has a moral, And Lordly obligations to work both within, And outside of this nation to bring about a nation of V/L truth. Every position of leadership whether of a Universal Nature, Or a precinct Nature is to be honored, And Respected. We must, And will work together for the common good of all, For only together are we a nation, Lord to Lord, Precinct, And all into the Amalgamated Order Of Lordism.

Lah Via Va Va Illilaha.....
Amalgamated   Order Of Lordism.......

Code Of Conduct.....

(A) Respect: This is a very essential ingredient of a V/L character. Every V/L will at all times give proper respect to every representative in our organization, And to representatives of other organizations. We will demand by conduct, Character, Demeanor, Actions, Deeds, Respect in return. We will always give respect to persons who are not representatives of any organization also. Disrespect is a very serious violation of the principals of law of our Amalgamated Order, And will be judge according. Therefore it will not be tolerated.

(B) Discipline: Discipline has a multiple faceted character. It must, And will be maintain in all it aspects for the successful function of the nation. Discipline does not only entail efficiency in following orders. Representatives must also be discipline mentally as well as spiritually. Lack of discipline in any area could very easily be detrimentally to a representative, "Other Representatives" Or the whole nation as a whole. For those reasons one understands discipline is of the utmost importance. Every order you receive pertaining to nation business has a specific reason, And will not question unless a representative does not understand the specific order being given, failure to be a discipline representative will result in discipline actions that will be taken.

(C) Meetings: General meetings of the Amalgamated Order Of Lordism are held for the purpose of the nation business, And will be conducted accordingly. During all meetings the highest ranking representative will be first to start business of the meeting, (Unless someone else has been designed for that purpose).   That representative will be followed by administration representative if they have input at that time. Then each representative will be given the opportunity to speak about matters in relation to those being discussed at that time. When any representative is speaking at meetings all other representatives will be quite, And Attentive, Failure to do so constitute disrespect and will result in immediate disciplinary action. Any problem relating to any particular precinct will be discussed once the business of the nation as a whole is resolved every one will uphold the character, And demeanor of V/L while meetings are in progress.

(D) Fighting: While it is the unspoken obligation of every V/L to defend himself and every other V/L to the extent of giving his life if necessary, No representative of the Amalgamated Order Of Lordism will place his or herself or other representative in any situation where he is needlessly involve in fights over trivia matters. If any V/L is attacked it is the sworn duty of every V/L to overcome his or her attacker by whatever means is necessary. If any representative regardless to his or her authority within the nation, take it upon themselves to fight with another representative it is a violation of all our laws of the Amalgamated Order of Lordism, And will be addressed immediately. Therefore no representative of the Amalgamated order Of Lordism will ever fight with another representative unless authorized by someone with the authority to do so.

Amalgamated   Order Of Lordism
Lah Via Va Va Illilaha Halaliil, Allah Akbun
Supreme Chief, Al-Ugdah

Dues.....

It is understood that every organization in existence needs a financial foundation in order to sustain itself, Our organization is no exception.   There is an economic program establish for the Amalgamated Order Of Lordism, However it will not be manifested at this time. Interim representation of the order are to continue with the existing program relating to dues that are establish in there respected precinct.

Lah Via Va Va Illilaha Halaliil.....
Amalgamated   Order of Lordism.....

Rules and Laws.....

(1)   Each and every representative of the Amalgamated Order Of Lordism will be aware of, An Knowledge of these precise Chain Of Command. (Supreme Chief, Prince Of The Nation, Minister Justice, Kings, Universal Elites, Ambassador, Minister Of Command, Precinct Elite, Lieutenant, And Minister of Literature.)

(2)   Every member of the Amalgamated Order Of Lordism will at all times maintain him or herself within the Code Of Conduct Chain Of Command, And the Principals of law in the highest manor. In the past representatives have failed to honor parts of the code, The change, And the laws due both to ignorance, And lack of enforcement. These laws and bylaws of the Amalgamated Order Of Lordism Will be enforce, And adhered to.

(3)   It is the responsibility of the kings of each precinct to revise a plan within there precinct to keep and accurate account, And are census of the representatives and elites in his precinct.

(4)(5) The king of each precinct must have a way of communication with each other, As well as with the Supreme Chief and the Minister Of Justice. This is to assure readiness, And the alertness in the event that assistance is needed in another precinct. If not directed by the Supreme Chief, Prince, Or the Minister Justice, The Kings of the Precinct involve are the only ones that have the authority to call on another precinct and its representatives for assistance. No representatives can take it upon him or herself to deal with a problem that arises. He or she shall always use the proper chain with in his of her precinct. Taking things in your hands is taking the chance of making a bigger problem, And is out of accord with the chain.

(6) All precinct problems and altercations will stay within the precinct. No representative will ever take a from one precinct to another. Pertaining to the Amalgamated Order Of Lordism, Unless the problem in that particular precinct cannot be handle in that precinct due to extenuating circumstances.

(7) Representatives of the Amalgamated Order of Lordism will be nobly respected because as V/L's we demand respect by our actions, And deeds and give respect in the same matter as we demand it. Representatives disrespecting each other will not be tolerated.

(8) Every representative upon given the laws, And Principals of the Amalgamated Order Of Lordism will never stray from this principals that we stand by, And die for. The guidelines established thru out our Laws, Principals will be strictly adhered to by all representatives.

(9) All representatives are expected, And encouraged to strive for self development this include but it is not limited to acquiring high school diploma or its equivalence, College Course, Vocational training, And especially the study of Laws, And Principals of Lordism.

(10) Upon attending Religious services or nation meetings all drugs, And alcoholic beverages will be left outside the particular place. Everyone will carry themselves respectfully, And orderly at these function. Because we need not promote anything but the higherself, And to be in the right frame of mind.

(11) No V/L should ever overlook our main purpose, Which is to be a organization thru out these times, Our objective is to be sincere about what we believe in, And what we will die for. We aim to show the world what we stand on, And that is Lordism.

(12) If a representative fail to realize to meet the high standard of V/L by continuing expression of the lowerself thru continuing misuse of our divine principals, And concept, It will be incumbent on the kings of the particular precinct (Or his representative) to make the decisions as to whether that representative should be placed on hold, Or worse. We have no time for individuals who threatening to stunt our growth.

(13) As a representative of the Amalgamated Order Of Lordism we will continually seek solutions for the betterment of all our people.

(14) As a representative of the Amalgamated Order Of Lordism we must learn to live with and respect other representatives, Including those before us who paved the way for us to walk the golden path of righteous. We must also learn to with, And respect other representatives life principals, And Religious denomination, Even if they defer from our own.

(15) We the representatives of the Amalgamated Order Of Lordism should not worry about possing threat to each other person prestige, But should concentrate our

united effort, And thoughts upon solving the hurt, And injustice done daily to our representatives, And our Nation as a whole.

(16) We as representatives must understand, And highly respect that instead of arrogance that will be humility among each other, As oppose to being drunk with power, There will be stronger realization to serve our nation in the spirit of Lordism.

(17) Representatives of the Amalgamated Order Of Lordism will be guided by tenants of morality, And the divine principals of love that governs Lordism, And will show the world that we are Lords of the world.

(18) All representatives of the Amalgamated Order Of Lordism will be fair, Straight Forward, And Honest in his dealings. He or she at all times uphold the truth, And justice, Even at the cost of his or her life.

(19) We of the Amalgamated Order Of Lordism will accent our youth. The young seeds essential. They can, And should provide New Ideas, New Methods, And New approaches. Your representative following the truthful teaching of Lordism that have potentials to be in any position to benefit the nation will not be overlook because of there youth.

(20) Every representative of the order will be conscious of there appearance at all times, And will always appear neat and clean.

(21) Every representative should make it his her sworn duty to uphold the Laws, And Principals of Lordism wherever they may be where other representatives are present.

(22) If at anytime a representative of the Amalgamated Order Of Lordism wishes to remove his or herself from the nation it will be upon the king of that particular precinct or (His Representatives) to grant the request of the representatives.

Note: We are not making anyone by force be a part of the Amalgamated Order Of Lordism. We became V/L's by choice, And the choice is ours.

Principals Of Laws.....

(1) I as a representative of the A/V/L/N swear with my life never to dishonor our most high Chief, All appointed of the A/V/L/N.

(2) I as a representative of the A/V/L/N will teach our people, Protect our people, Love our people, And if is the will of Allah die for our people, So that one day they will walk the golden path of V/L as free people, As productive people progressing in the love of V/L, The knowledge of V/L, Wisdom of V/L, Understanding of V/L, And the future of V/L.

(3) I as a representative of the A/V/L/N will never go astray from the truthful teachings of our most wise, And beloved high Chief.

(4) I as a representative of the A/V/L/N will help my people with any problem that they may have, Be it mentally, Or Physically, For there problems are my problems and my problems are there problems.

(5) I as a representative of the A/V/L/N will never take word of another before that of any representative of the V/L Nation without placing the burden of proof on there accusers.

(6) I as a representative of the A/V/L/N swear with my life never to put anything or anyone before most high and beloved Chief, Any appointed Chief, Or any representative of the V/L nation.

(7) I as a representative of the A/V/L/N swear that I will never deny any V/L Materially, Apiritualy, Mentally, Financially or Physically, My help under any circumstances at all or be denied.

(8) I as a representative of the A/V/L/N swear with my life that I will never lie on any representative of the A/V/L/N or V/L from another precinct or take anything from any representative of the A/V/L/N. I swear by my life to live by these laws under any circumstances.

Flag: The flag is the national identification for any nation of people. It is what the people represent and live for. This flag is a symbol of the entire order of the Amalgamated Order Of Lordism and consist of the following:

(1) Circle: The circle means 360 degrees of knowledge and what was will always will be, That Black people once ruled the world and will once again rule.

(2) Fire: The circle is surrounded by fire. The fire means and represent our nation true knowledge of themselves as being suppressed. The flame prevent our reaching 360 degree of knowledge because of the heat (Rome or Europeans).

(3) Darkness: Inside the circle is darkness (Jet Black) and represents that universaly Black people are a majority of people, Not a minority.

Note: If we were not brainwashed into thinking that we are different from other Blacks around the world, We would have a population of over 700 Million! There are 400 Million Blacks in mother land (Africa) alone, The darkness that we have been kept in so long.

(4) Moons: Inside the darkness are (Two) crescent moons. They represents the splitting of one nation into two. One in the east (Asia And Africa) and the other in west our nation. They also represents entity of the male and female factor.

The Flag: When these two moons come together they represent the marriage between the Lord and his Lady a union which is mandatory if we are to acquire 360 degrees of pure Knowledge, Wisdom, And Understanding.

(5) Star: Also in this darkness is a golden star. This is the eye of Allah keeping watch over his people, A just and justice seeking people.

(6)   Pyramid and Triangle; The darkness also engulfed the Pyramid Triangle which is our strength. It is the phenomena that puzzle the white world today. There is still no knowledge of Pyramids building today, Even with all this technology of the white man's world, This society cannot even begin to build or understand how to build the Pyramid., Yet the pyramid was build by Black people many centuries ago. We V/L's are sheltered by this pyramid of strength, Until we are able to cleanse our minds. There are three aspects to the formation of the might puzzling pyramid. The are Physical, Mental, And Spirit. He must decide now how we want to live. Are we going to let our physical cravings take control of our minds? Or are we going to control our bodies as it is suppose to be? As V/L's, We have one choice.

(7)   Sun: Inside the pyramid is the sun. This represents the raising truth in our nation. Once our minds have gained control over our physical body, We will then think as men and be able to understand and to respect one another life position. Then we can move men (One in a righteousness direction_ We, Like all Black people who are living within the shelter of the pyramid and under the watchful eye of Allah, Are guided down the proper path.

(8)   Hat: The Hat represents the shelter of our heads until we can get them together.

(9)   Cane: The Cane is our staff of strength. As we need the cane to help us walk when we are old, The cane represents the need for us to support one another in these trying times.

(10) Glove: The glove represent purity., That we keep our hands clean of any acts that cause division among our people. This is also the reason for representing the way we do now. Our palms out and upward, showing each other that our hand are clean and that we mean no harm.

Lah Via Va Va Illilaha Halaliil

Supreme Chief, Al-Ugdah

A Message To My Muslim Brother.....

To my brother in Islam, I greet thy with the high sign of Love, In **Peace I come,** In tune I am. For what is Islam but Lordism, And Lordism but Islam? Each when served properly will give the people a different flavor of the same thing. "Almighty" is Allah, "Allah is Almighty."

Chocolate, Strawberry, and Vanilla is purposely design to meet the critera of the people taste, Yet the flavor doesn't subtract from the substance, Or change the ingredients that make up the ice cream. That which is righteous under any other name will turn out right.

I am as you are a true believer of Allah traveling the same pass you are own, But in a different vehicle adhering to the same law of caution.

I am the true V/L self and you are the true Muslim, But by virtue of our seeded part we are brother's under Allah's influence. We represent two establishments, Yet stand upon one stone, Our house built on the same foundations, "Brother," Islam, Or Lordism is just the umbrella we walk under, That Allah is the rainmaker, And sense we both acknowledge him we can walk in warmth, And confidence without the fear of getting drench, For our intentions are good, And our steps are righteous inclined.

Lah Via Va Va Illilaha Halaliil

The Keys Of V/L.....

(Key1) What is Lordism?

It is a Philosophy. Ideology, And Guidelines of a chosen way of life. A lodestone made manifest through the primitive teaching of it first teacher, The Honorable "Pep Pillow," And chiseled by devoted believers from various schools of thought into a structure of today.

(Key2) What is the philosophy of Lordism?

We believe in its authenticity in the sight of God, But we don't believe that any one person can have a monopoly on God, Or any one religion can claim Him exclusively. We believe all men are equal in the sight of God and that righteous V/L will be recipients of God's grace, The same as any other religious person regardless of their religion persuasion. The Quran says that man was put here as Vicegerents. We take that as man was put here to be V/L's in this physical world.

(Key3) The meaning behind the name:

Vice means one having faults. (The Human Being) and being of second importance, Second only to God, God being the ruler of all the worlds and the universe and man was elected by him to his "Vice Lord" Or Vice Ruler, We see ourselves as God's highest creation, His custodians of the physical world. So whether you address yourself as a Baptist, Christian, ect., By the definition of that which just been defined, You are still "Vice Lord" the only difference is interpretation and acceptance.

(Key4) What is the religion of V/L?

Lordism is the religion, Yet we are not religious fanatics. The Quran and all religion books tell men to "Take the bounties of the earth" We interpret this as a sign that man should always strive to improve his life's condition. The A/V/L should strive to balance himself Physical, Mentally, Spiritual, and materially. Man seeks to promote himself in the sight of God, But also has concerns and needs here in the physical world.

(Key5) About Religion:

A Lord is a seeker of truth and Lordism encompasses every facet of life. It acknowledge the existence of God in people and it acknowledge every person's right to communicate with him. It is a complete way of life, A life of involvement with both God and state and the belief in one true God whose proper name is (Allah) and associate no partners with him.

(Key6)   What is the Religion book of V/L?

A Lord will study any Religious book and use them selectively as reference points and guidelines as long as it will contribute to his development, But always in the frame of mind that man and not God is the author of such books. Everything in print deals with relative truth and not absolute. Absolute truth are the things that only the mind of God knows, While the relative truth are the things that the highest reason man understands them to be, But still, Of all the religious people tend to favor the Quran.

(Key7)   Why does the Lord tend to favor the Quran?

We believe that there is knowledge to be gained even from the Bible, But only after tedious process of shifting through its maze. On the other hand, Regardless of the fixation of relative truth that we automatically apply, We still find The Holy Quran the best book for our people, It corresponds with our way of thinking and supportive to our way of life, But still, we are Vice Lords and not Muslims, There exist that degree and that difference.

(Key8)   What's the difference between a Vice Lord and a Muslim since both acknowledge the Quran?

The difference is our guidelines, names, application and interpretation of faith.

(Key9)   Explain the difference a Lord and a Muslim:

Our names and Prayers, And the belief that all religious books deal with the relative and not the absolute truth. And that the righteous "Lord" will be made manifest in this physical realm of creation and we see ourselves as Allah's temple and that God exists in that temple.

(Key10)   A Lord do not pray in the conventional style of a Muslim. A Lord making prayer bring his fingers to fingers, Making a pyramid over his head (A symbolic Gesture) and says, "O Allah, I seek shelter from the forces of evil and schemes and threatening plans of my enemies," And then brings his hands down to the palms up position and recites the "Al-Fatiha" The Universal Prayer.

(Key11)   Greetings!

It would not subtract any degree from you if you would greet your Muslim brother as he would greet you, But when greeting one of our brothers, Greet him under the master sign of Lah Via Va Va, Illilaha Halaliil With your palms up and he should return that greeting with "Via Va Va Lah, Halaliil Illilaha.

(Key12)   The meaning behind the greeting:

Lah (Love), Via (vice), Va Va (Lord), Illilaha (My Sword), Halaliil (My Shield).

(Key13) What are the master signs?

Palms up and all greets of V/L's, The flag Of V/L, The Emblem Of V/L, The Meaning of V/L, And the righteous representation, These are the master signs of V/L.

(Key14) Why the various schools of thought?

Because the A/V/L/N is symbolic to the real blood line family, It represents the highest principals of the real blood line family: Love, Truth, Peace, Freedom, Justice, Harmony, and Understanding. As every family the Lord (Father) and the Queen (Mother) upon producing life have bestow a name of their favor upon that life, For every life they produce they honor that life with a first name for distinguishing proposes, And the child automatically inherit the last which will affirm his identity. Such is the composition of the various precincts or fractions that make up the A/V/L/N that have been granted autonomy and have form the various schools of thought according to their father, The brother of our father who share the family name. No matter what the first name the child or parents call that child, As long as that adheres to the dictated of his parents ads accept the family name, One must remember the root of its existence is in the family.

The teachings as administered by Chief Al-Ugdah, From the unknown school of thought.

Statement Of Love...

To you my Brother, Sister, My love for you began at birth, has manifested through out our Heritage. Because of my Black skin, which is yours, My Blood and Flesh, Which is us I am you, And you are me. Our minds are for the same goal, Our effort is for the same cause, Our souls are bound by the same determination. To this nation I give my unity, And all my vitality. To you my Brother, And Sister, I give my love.

Oath.....

In the name of the almighty, I do solemnly swear, That I as a representative of the Amalgamated Order Of Lordism will not dishonor my most sacred weapon meaning Lord unity, Nor under the threat of death will I deny those that stand beside me. I as a representative of the Amalgamated Order Of Lordism will listen well to the truthful teachings of our king, And Elites. I will use my time constructively, I will become, And remain useful to my Nation, My community, And Myself as a whole. Let the Almighty God (Allah) bear witness to this oath by birth in the Spirit, And to, And thru the heart core. I come as I am, I am as I come, Almighty Vice Lord. Lord love means I have a undying love for this Nation, And I'll die for it. Lah Via Va Va, Illilaha Halaliil.

The Warning On Treason.....

Treason is a act by no less than a life of misery. The nature of such punishment constitute by its very nature one of two extremes. The above prescription is in order when circumstances, And events dictates (So as not to jeopardize the life, Or freedom of the righteous) That we spare the most serious extreme out of consideration. And preservation for our most truest, And righteous representative. Under no circumstances will treason Or disrespect be tolerated against the crown. The crown represents the embodies of V/L world wide. This is true regardless to which king sit on the crown. The crown is the glorious representation of the V/L. Speak on it with unrighteous intent, And you speak against the nation whole. Pain will come to you as a consequence of speaking on the crown with indignation. Scheme clandestinely against it, And such scheme will be made manifest at your own expense.

The crown has the resiliency of the people support. Those who will be in grievous error head this warning. There is a boomerang around the crown. Test it at your own risk. Lah Via Va Va Illilaha Halaliil.

Knowledge Of V/L Existence.....

Let our enemies take heed to these words, we shall pay any price for V/L, Bear any burden for V/L, Meet any hardship for V/L, And support and friend for V/L, Condemn any person that tries to upset the tranquility of V/L, To assure the survival, And success of this Nation.

Faith Of V/L.....

I am a V/L, In my possession I take pride, But without vain glory. To it I owe solemn obligations that I am eager to fulfill. As a V/L I will participate in none but honest enterprise. To him that has engage my service as soldier or warrior, I will give the utter most of perfection and fidelity. When needed my skills and knowledge they will be given without reservations for the (Nation) good. From special capacity springs obligations to use it well in the service of humanity, And I accept the challenge that this implies jealousy of the high repute of my callings, I will strive to protect the entrance and good name of any V/L that I know to be deserving, But I will not shrink should duty dictate from disclosing the truth regardless anyone that unscrupulous act has shown himself unworthy of the profession. Since the age of stone human progress has never been condition by the genius of my professional forebearers by them have been rendered usable to mankind nature resources of the material and energy. By them have been vitalize, And turn to practical account of principals, Science, And Revelations of technology. Accept this heritage of accumulate experience, My Efforts will feeble, I dedicate myself to dissemination of Lordism knowledge, And especially to the instructions of younger members of my profession in all is art and tradition. To my Lord brother I pledge in the same full measure I acts of them, And interpreted, Dignify of our profession. With the consciousness always that our special expertise carries with it the obligation to serve humanity with Lords. I am proud to live, This place, And love V/L with the highest Devotion, Loyalty, And Honor.

Lordism In Focus.....

The Amalgamated Order Of Lordism is built on the laws and principals that govern everyday activities, And life of V/L. If followed properly these laws, And principals will guide our people on a path which is straight, And progressive. These codes of law is based on external principals of righteousness, And Fair Dealings, Sobriety, Cleanliness, Helpfulness, And Honesty to one another, Yet shaped into concrete form suites, And circumstances. Our goals are to abolish blood feuds, Help the weak, And the need, And harness wrong doing. Lordism is design to appeal our intellect so that we'll be able to make the best of our lives. We must not waste, Nor misuse our life for individually and indeed together we have a lot to offer. Lordism is more than just a religion of faith. It is the sewing together of knowledge, And logic, This a cooperative expression, A fraternal order which allows men as Lords of various religions the nominations to come together and the common denomination of Lordism, Thus enjoy true meaning of Lords.

Putting It In Perspective.....

We the members of the Amalgamated Order Of Lordism will continue to represent our beloved nation with Sincerity, Love, Commitment. Those who are pure in heart will no doubt be overcome by the common enemy which is rome. We as members of the Amalgamated Order Of Lordism will devote our time, Energy, And resources to advance, And uplift not only our nation, But all poor, And oppressed people with in our reach. We of the Amalgamated Order Of Lordism will greet, And honor each representative with greetings of the master sign, Not with the sign of our precinct. This is to identify with the fraternity of which we belong, And the cause that we all share. This greeting signify the meaning of poor nature, And is automatically a sign of our love, One together will cause nor show division among the m embers of the Amalgamated Order Of Lordism. We take not our oath to practice deceptions among ourselves, Nor should we attempt to promote discord. Time thru the ages bear's witness that nothing remains but faith, Good Deeds, And the teachings of Truth, Patience, And continuity. Do not slip off the golden path of Lordism my beloved brother, And for sure do not cause another brother foot to slip, You surely will experience the consequences of having rendered men from the path of God, And a mighty wraith will descend on you.

The Movement Mandates.....

We are under obligation to our nation, Our Supreme Chief, Our Elites and all the righteous representative, Of the master sign. We encourage our Elites, For its through their support for our Supreme Chief that our Supreme Chief is able to reach out, And grow it into us, And we into him, And together into the movement. But most of all we encourage ourselves, For we are the soldiers of growing nation, We are the architect for a better tommorrow. For we through our dedication, And total commitment shall build out of nothing, Something of great apprizal. We shall take an old nation and make a new movement dedicated to upliftment of our people. We shall take the name of the Amalgamated Order Of Lordism and like the world take seasons, And nature leaves her mark on man, We shall leave ours on the world.

Steps To Live By.....

In the name of the Almighty. I greet thy, All of you with the honorable thump of the thumping V across my chest. And with palms.

Greetings Righteous Seed.....

I want to spend some time on a paramount importance "What do we, You and I do as members of A/V/L/N? First, Or more directly, You must at one time or another ask yourself this question. What do I do now that I am V/L? As Ruler, Protector, And Teacher of the people, We have a really profound test ahead of us. One that cannot be viewed as being easy. How do you let other people know the beauty of your dreams of a new nation? How do you teach people, Reeducate the people to the philosophy of Lordism? Simple "By your example, By your reflective character. You my brothers and sisters are manifestations of V/L. If you profess to be about all its sublime beauties and grace, Then live it," There should never be any defamation of the V/L character. There will be acceptance and forgiveness for your fault and error. These can be corrected and improved upon. However willful Injury. Insults, Stealth, Deception, and Defamation of the V/L character shall not be condoned or tolerated. It will result in Fines, Restrictions, Or Expulsion. Your image should always be one of Love, Dedication, And Sincerity. The golden beam of Lordism should always Radiate, And Reflect from the glow of your presence. That will be the true indication of your sincere and pronounce devotion and dedications to the reconstruction of t his V/L Nation. Your conduct should be one that is full of confidence but yet not arrogance, "Respectful and yet not ostracizing. We should be on top of our knowledge, Sounding our knowledge, But not to the point that we talk to people. We are rulers, Protectors and Teachers of the people. Thus, We must be able to reach those that we need to tach and raise up to a level of awareness. We can b certain that we will have a very difficult time if we take on the air of better that thou. How many people at all times and among all nations close there heart to any distinction of knowledge or spiritual influence because of some little fragment which they have got and which they think is the whole of God's truth? Such an attitude shows really want of faith and a blasphemous limitations of Gods unlimited spiritual gift to his creatures. (Commentary 92 H.Q.).j

The times are over where we don't have to prove anything to anyone. The great fact that the longevity of our existence is a sign that we are here to stay. We have survived the necessary physical aspect of our formation. We have involve into the mental stages. This development dictated the focus on Revising, And Reconstruction from point one. We have to be professional. We are talking about a securing a future for our children. About a place in the future where the proper recognition will be giving to V/L. This will never come into existence without expertise and know how. It will never materialize without mind, And the proper effort motoring it. Obviously the present system is not *at all concerned about realistic educating our children. They are still systematically destroying them. "Force Busing". That is a illusion, Why are we so short on qualified teachers? Black Teachers? Why not upgrade the school facilities? We as a people are responsible for the teaching of our children. That and itself is the answer to this illusion.

If we qualify ourselves there will be no need to bus our children anywhere. We can teach them ourselves. But first we must feel our own heads with the necessary knowledge. Or groom and cultivate our own people so that they may fill the void. Yet that they shall never reach the thresh hole of reality unless we qualify ourselves first. We're gonna have to make a few adjustments in order to qualify ourselves from a mental perspective. We must cease being old fashioned, And modernize our ideas, And way of thinking to better serve us, All of us older Lords have or are down for game. We can do that very good. Let us put as much emphasis into seriously tightening up our knowledge and applying that knowledge to our everyday life. Lets do this so that our mere presence can demand it's respect. Its time we raise from the dark and ignorance, Into the light and knowledge of who we truly are. Its time we exhaust our energy and exploit our ability by building, Not to do so will surely reflect a cripple image of V/L's? May Allah bless and protect us in our infancy, And grant us the Strength, Desire, Dedication, And Preseverance that is needed in order to build our character and thus our nation.

Trichinosis.....

All products made of pork are forbidded to representatives of the Amalgamated Order Of Lordism. The pig was put here for medicinal, And is unfit for human consumption. There is a worm know to medical science, As the trichinosis worm. Its a parasite that attacks, And infests the organ structure of pigs. Our bodies became contaminated by these poisonous parasites whenever we eat pork. Ironically, The deterioring effect it has on us is intricately masked by the staking of times, In essence creating genetics disease. People tend to under estimate the actual danger that exist in our health. Pork is synonymous to dope. Its a gun pointed in the direction of the Black community. Every time we eat pork, The trichinosis worm penetrate our intestine and muscle tissue. Once this process begin our health slowly begin to deteriorate. The affect of pork on our health is devastating. It will inedibility induce a cycle of illness, And forgetfulness. No not immediately, Nevertheless no one really escape this parasite. Hypertension is the number one killer amongst Blacks. Why? Trichinosis! Its a killer that takes its dwelling in pork. No matter what you read about curing pork, The only solution to trichinosis is abstinence. You can smoke it, Burn tar baby black, Freeze it, Ect., But trichinosis will remain in its poignant, And deadly state. The pig have no veins, If bitten by a poison snake it will just turn around, And gobble the snake up. The pig is the world filthiest animal. Its a combination of the Cat, Rat, and Dog. Examine it microscopically if you like. It has the tail of a rat, The eyes of a cat, And the snout of a dog.

Yet most people love it. Biblical scripture has Jesus casting demons into pigs, And then driving them over a cliff.

The same scripture tells us not to eat the meat of the hoofed animal. Most religious leaders fail to mention this. Jews, Muslems, Buddist, ect., All obey Gods law when it comes to abstinence from swine, That is all about the Christian World. Most Black people state out of ignorance that their Mother, Father, Grandparents, Ect., Ate swine, and lived to be Sixty, Seventy, Or even 100, But none ever ask themselves how much older they have been if they had not consumed swine. Think about that. How can you love someone on one hand, And then turn around, And feed them that metamorphic swine?

Destiny From The V/L Point Of View.....

Being V/L mean we are in control of own destiny. If we who represent the true Lordism because victims at all or conquers, We have done it in our minds and wills, Or without faulty judgement and or illusion. If a Lord permit others to exploit him in private life, Or government he chooses it, Or he has made the fatal error of acquiescence and he should be condemned. The world forgives everything except weakness and submission. Universally men have been known to take advantage of these two traits. A V/L have no fear of battle, Even if it means a Lords death. In any event death come's to all men. How you die is your own choice. The Lord know that life is full of battles, On various levels and stages, In various forms, Which by law dictate battles that take shape by various means. Fighting or Submitting out of options, There is no halfway station in between offering supplementary premium, Lordism demands that we chose the warrior choice. Some men are born free even under the adversity of unfavorable times. Even under persecution. Even in slavery. It is strictly a matter of man's spirit on whether not man is free. V/L's are free at birth, In the spirit, And thru the heart core. If not at the birth of his mother, So at the birth of his chosen nation, For is not the master teachings of Love, Truth, Peace, Freedom, And Justice? The choice is ours that we wish to be.... No one impels us or compel us.... We may delude ourselves that is so but it is not! (Quote) "The same wind which blow a ship on the rock can blow it into a safe harbor just as well.... In short it is not the wind it is the set of the sail. (Unquote) A man who denies, That is a weakling who wishes to blame others for his life. V/L you are what you are by choice, And you have given some deliberation to the parts you have played and play in life. Move with the conscious that you can affect the outcome of many things, And cause many things to happen, Realize the two degrees of involvement, The direct and the indirect shoot of it, And set yourself up to take charge of every situation possible, For you posses the keys to do so. There are consequences involve with actions, Be man enough to accept the consequences of yours. Never say you are completely blameless without chewing on the two degrees of involvement. A V/L should strive to master total control over his life. A Lord knows he must pass away from this world some day and you have no control over this. In this sense his destiny is set. But in his dealings with the world what becomes of him will depend on his own efforts and state of mind. Allah gifted man with ability.

Thus place his destiny on earth outside of pasting away from this plan of being into his own lap.

A/V/L/N "Misrepresentation".....

In advocating the principals of this organization we find that we have been very much misunderstood, And very much misrepresented by men from within our organization, As well as others from without. Any reform movement that we seeks to bring about changes for the benefit of humanity is bound to be misrepresented by those who always taking it upon themselves to administer to and lead the unfortunate, And to direct those who may be place under temporary disadvantages. It has been so in all other movements whether social or political. Hence those of us in the "A/V/L/N" who lead, Do not feel embarrassed about this MISREPRESENTATION. About this misunderstanding as far as the aims and objectives of the "A/V/L/N" is concerned. But those who has taken timely notice of this great movement seeks not to develop the good nation within the nation, But to give expression to that which is most destructive and most harmful to society and the government. We desire to remove the misunderstanding that has been created in the minds of millions of people thru out the world in there relationship to the organization. The A/V/L/N stands for the bigger brotherhood. The A/V/L/N stands for human rights, Not only for the nation of V/L's, But all Black people world wide. We ask for nothing but the rights of all V/L's. We are not seeking to destroy or disrupt the society or the government. We of the "A/V/L/N" are determined to unite all V/L's for there own Industrial. Political, Social, And Religious Emancipation. Some have said that this organization seeks to create discord and discontent among the races. Some say we are organize for the purpose of hating other people. The A/V/L/N has no such intentions. We are organize for the absolute purpose for bettering our conditions, Industrially, Economically, Religiously, And Politically.

What Are The Master Teaching?.....

The master teachings are the master teachings of Lordism. The teachings of man as V/L second only to Allah in his relationship with the world. They are the teaching that places man in charge of his/selves and the world he live in.

"On The Selves Of (Mind) Man".....

Truth and falsehood are two absolutes, Personified they represents the develop man (Minds) and the deform man (Mind) which signify the virtuous and unvirtuous state of man (Mind). Or the higher self in coexistence with the pigmy self. The self that control will depend on the feed of the man. There entire composition of the human being rotates from the axis of these two absolute. The selves of man are inextricable. Man can only subdue his lower self not separate himself from it entirely. Destractions or temptation can open the valves and allow the lower self to seep thru. The Lord Man, Lord Father, The V/L every action, Every Reflection, Every deed spring from the balcony of the mind (His Virtuous Self) Or the basement of it. (His Virtuous Self). All the selves of man (Mind) are tied to these absolutes. This axiom is universal, Each of the three dimension of V/L spin from this fundamental truth.

The Spin Off From The Selves Of Man (Mind).....

Lord Man: The Lord man is V/L in his infancy not yet developed into the maturity of the true Lord self. His is the physical manifestation of the character of keys. He have been impress by the physical aspects of the nation, But is not yet cemented in the faith do to his lack of spiritual and mental reinforcements. He is either a new representative that the teachings have not had a chance to take firm of, Or a old unrighteous deceptor that will never graduate from the caterpillar state and in fact whole appearance and representation is false. The Lord Man is in his most vulnerable stage, He will either fall to external influences and pressures and forfeit his V/L self, Allow himself to be suspended in the stagnant caterpillar state, Or open his mind and heart to the teachings and love of V/L Thus growing into a true crowning glory.

Lord Father: The Lord Father signifies a harmonious balance of the physical and mental aspect of V/L, And a growing awareness and acceptance of the spiritual nature of it. He is one mindful of his responsibilities to his family and nation, And goes about interrupted, He knows the nation is not here to infringe upon the privacy or disrupt the order of the family but enhance the quality of the family life thru its teachings. His is the image of a righteous supporter and provider. Of love, And undying determination. He is not a stranger to trials and tribulations of life, Or the external and internal pressure and influences, Still his strength and constancy is unfaltering. His strong Lord father self bears witness to the splendor of V/L.

The V/L Developed: The fully formed V/L is in the ethereal state of the selves of man. Here the character keys are all balance and being a V/L is a state of euphoria. Lordism is a unconflicting way of life for him. A natural expression and thought form. He is V/L in his weakest moment as well as his strongest, And will die a pure state of Lordism. He have elected out of faith to carry the nation high and not to let the golden light be extinguish by the dark deeds and deception clock work by those of the caterpillar persuasion, Or the other debilitating and evenly subversive forces of men. He is loyal to his brothers and sisters and will cut his own heart out before he would betray a righteous believer. He upholds and enforces the principals of laws and articles of faith. None of the selves of man can pass hie righteous manifestation of his true Lord self because he superiorly demonstrate all the selves of man. He is the true crown and glory.....He forever V/L....., Shining!!!!!

Who Are The True Believers.....

The true Lord self is the true believers. The Lord that is not self servant or pertinacious in his representation so as to gain advantages. A true believer is one that do not falsify our love. One who has unshakable Faith, Confidence, And Trust in the nation. A true Crown And Glory.

Crown And Glory.....

A believer that exemplifies good Personal Hygiene, Good Habits, Self Discipline, Strength Of Character, Pursues Knowledge, Upholds The Principals Of Laws, And the Articles Of Faith, And truly has committed the nation to heart, Is indeed a Crown And Glory to V/L.

The Glory Of The Sisterhood And Brotherhood Of V/L.....

The sisterhood to V/L's are our biggest inspiration. Every dedicated and righteous sister is available and precious gem to us. As a jewel throws forth a light that is magnified by the light of the sun, So does the V/Lady throw forth life, And sustain life, Thus light up the sole and life of V/L. The Lord is a sun unto her, Magnifying the spirit of her soul, And given warmth to her as the sun give warmth to everything under its scope. Like the sun aid the vegetation in its growth, The Lord and Lady aid the vegetation in its growth, The Lord and Lady aid each other in there needs development. For whatever struggle or endeavor they undertake, Its done with each other in mind. Thus is the glory of the sisterhood and brotherhood of V/L.

What do A/V/Lady Represents.....

She represent the diversified transition of queen woman, to queen mother, To V/Lady. A cherish his woman and think of her and refer to her as his queen, To him every V/Lady is majestic and occupy a seat on his heart throne. This three dimensional view of our vision of beautiful also symbolizes the three character keys in the human being that every believer should be striving to develop. They are Spiritual, Physical, And Mental composition of the believer. (Referral to what a righteous represent).

Different Selves Of The Vision Beautiful.....

Queer Woman..... And The First Level of Development.....

Queen Woman is V/Lady unpredictable. Her primary entrance is in a specific V/L and not necessary the master teachings. Its the first level of development that is really responsible for her coming under the master sign, Her physical attractions to a particular Lord. If by chance things don't work out for her Lord Man she may decide to fall out of tune with the master teachings. She may develop a certain amount of spiritual and mental strength but not nearly enough to maintain fer faith. However (All praise to Allah) there are those that due come into the nation under the physical and enticement of a Lord Man and gained the spiritual and mental prowess necessary to embrace the master teachings and if there relationship with there Lord Man fail they will still exalt the master teachings, For they to are the vision beautiful.

Queen Mother..... And The Second Level Of Development.....

Queen Mother symbolizes the mental aspect of the Lord Child and also there responsibilities of being a good homemaker. Although she is dutiful in the her contributions to the life and the nation transcend beyond. Queen Mother is V/L as exemplifying the highest qualities of motherhood. Her image is Love, Concern, And Devotion to the family. Here is a true portrait of strength and a good balance of the three character keys that enhance the beauty of the human being. No mistakenly her for anyone else when you see her for she to is the vision beautify.

Different Selves Of The Vision Beautiful   Cont.....

Queen Lady.....And   The Third Level Of Development.....

Queen Lady is V/Lady in her highest manifestation of the teaching of Lordism. Because of the high esteem V/L holds for V/Lady the noble title of queen is granted, However whether the principal is called queen or V/Lady the substance remain, Either one is still the highest tribute a Lord can pay to the vision beautiful. The spiritual level of development is attached to her because as a true V/Lady her faith is unshakable, Given her a deeper spiritual sense of God in relationship to the master teachings and how it realistically comes together. She is dedicated to the principals of laws and the articles of faith. She honestly believes in V/L and will never forsake the faith. She respects all V/L's and is jealous of none for she know they are truly her brothers. She is well adjusted Spiritual, Physical, And Mentally. She is one concerned with the development of the nation and will sacrifice the best of her efforts for it. She is the true vision beautiful!!!!!

Oh Righteous Believers Never Forget.....

The V/Lady is a confinement and good manors. She is a pillar of strength to V/L. She is most ardent advocate and supporter, A buffer making him shine. She is second only to Allah in importance but most important after Allah to V/L. She is always the lady of the house, Always second in command to V/L. She is the vision beautiful!!!!!

The Collected Forces Of The Character Keys Made Manifest.

The V/L and Lady should always strive to enhance their Spiritual, Physical, And Mental state of being to draw the maximum benefits such conditioning has to offer. The proper collective force of these once balanced can open up the doors and secrets of life and help shape the believer into that righteous and harmonious self. These keys are essential to our development for they will allow for a smooth transition into this beautiful way of life. These are the keys that offer Security, Truth, Prosperity, And True Love.

The Queen Power.....

Article 1: Queenship is the highest status a V/Lady can achieve. A number of factors must determine this course of action. Sometimes emotions dictate under the guise of rational, Often times group appeal without the full season, In Essence, Dedication, Preseverance, Cultivation, Refinement, Commitment, And a Diligent application of Faith, And efforts towards the way of V/L. Because the autonomous set of order (Precinct) there can be several queens. However only one Supreme Queen. Know one can grant such a royal title, Or suspend, revoke or rescind, Other than the crown king. It is not only a expectation of the crown, But law! And law governs all events. Alternatives or Altercations: If due to circumstances beyond the crown king control dictates so, Appointment of queenship can be decreed by his prince, Or special elected committee consisting of all his elites. Under the existence circumstances the decree will be at most temporary, And subject to the capriciousness, Whims, And judgement of the crown king. Only he can pronounce with certainty, and surety (Which translate into law) the true crowning of his queen.

Article 2: The queen may appoint who ever she pleases to office, Including, But not limited it to princess. Her system of ranking, And organization take own the same structure of her kingship. Only the crown can dictate measure of law to her. She must always be studious and loyal to the (His kingship) crown. The queen can call meetings of the sisterhood at random, Or schedule fashion. All V/Ladies are to honor, And protect there queen. They must adhere to all the Precepts, Principals, And Articles of law in the same fashion, and fortitude exhibited by there brothers. V/Ladies, You have a obligation to yourself, And your nation to be morally conscious of your Hygiene, Appearance, Grooming, Conduct, Living Conducts, And Food Consumption, As well as your vocal output. ; You should always strive to exhibit these traits, And attributes that are distinguished by Refinery, Cleanliness, Sobriety, And Dedication

Article 3: The queen power is such in scope that it encompass the whole, Or part of the Amalgamated Order. Influence: If a precinct queen, Her influence will be categorize by, And limited to her precinct. On the other hand the supreme queen influence will be pervasive, Acknowledge and respected thru out our entire order. She will be carried highly and honored always, Whether precinct, Or not, by the entire order of V/L. Conduct in her presence must be one of Protectiveness, Sobriety, And Discipline. To dishonor or disrespect her image is a descration of our faith, Its a insult, And fragment disrespect to both crowns. Honor, Respect, And Protect her always! For such is law and law governs all events!

The V/L Manifesto.....

In The Name of Allah, We the righteous people of the Amalgamated Order give honor to our king Al-Ugdah, And all pioneers, Lords Of The Amalgamated Order Of Lordism. There has been tears, Bloodshed, Trials, Tribulations, And Trauma, By the pioneers of our most beloved order, We have witness the continue surfacing, And resurgence of a dedicated Ideology, And pedigree that refuses to die. We honor Prince Dank, And all the other countless Lord pioneers. For the dedicated pioneers with there Love, Knowledge, Wisdom, And Understanding, Have given Strength, Beauty, And a sense of direction, And purpose to our people. We honor our pioneers, And may Allah blessing forever be upon them for there sacrifices have been our gain. There dedication, Understanding And Tenacity has given birth to a new breed of V/Ladies, And Lords, The engineer. The engineers who strive to make a past ideology a present reality. The engineers who strive to be righteous, And productive in accordance to the vision that the pioneer held dearly. The pioneer have given the engineers a seed to nourish. And with a Love knowledge, Wisdom, And understanding even comparable to that of the pioneers, These engineers will design and perpetuate a flourishing nation second to none!!! May Allah forever bless, And Strengthen the sisterhood, And brotherhood, And inspire them to uphold the laws, And principals of the master sign, For we realize the difficult task ahead for all.

Foremost, We give the highest praise to Allah for blessing the Amalgamated Order Of Lordism with our most beloved, And dedicated pioneers, For it is thru perseveration that we are here today representing V/L..... We give the highest to Allah from blessing the Amalgamated Order Of Lordism with support, And love of our beautiful sisterhood, For they are the Delight, Love, And glory of the V/L nation.... They, And the lord child are our most precious treasures. We give high praise to Allah for blessing the V/L nation with you. The people of the most persecuted of faith, For it is thru dedication that we prevail Vice Omnipotent, For you are the engineers! Some of the pioneers are gone, Maybe some of the engineers will stray, But we rest assured with the knowledge That V/L is here to stay!!!!!

A/V/L/N "Righteous Sons".....

Almighty Righteous Sons, Of the most High, Reflecting true Lordism is not easy, Nor is it a righteous reflection displaying unrighteous acts. V/L is not sometimes, But always. Every moment, Every hour, Every week, Every month, Every year, Every breathe we take is V/L, Every step we take is V/L, Every thought we have is V/L, And know, V/L is not easy!!!!!

But each moment of our lives we righteous lords strive toward a deeper conscience of ourselves and what we are about. Knowing who and what we are give courage to stand temptation and reflect who and what we are in our weakest moment! The righteous for those who die fighting for the cause of V/L and every fallen lord spirit in the heart of us all!

We the righteous sons of the "Almighty" will never retrogress from our righteous principals and concepts. We the righteous sons of the most highest, Will defend these "Principals and Concepts" With our lives and discipline anyone found in violation of them!

In The Name of Allah, In The Name of our most High Chief, In the name of all appointed Chiefs, In The Name of all the righteous representatives of V.L's, We vow to uphold these truth's!

Lah Via Va Va Illilaha

Creed of the V/L.....

We the younger generation especially must feel a scared call to that which is before us. I go out to do my little part in helping my untutored brother. We of this less favorite race realize that our future lies chiefly in our hands, And we are struggling on attempting to show knowledge can be obtain under difficulties, That neither the old time slavery, Nor continued prejudice need extinguish self respect, Crush manly ambitions, Or paralyze effort. We know that neither institution, Nor friends can make a race stand unless it has strength in its own foundation, And that racist like individuals must stand, Or fall by there own merit, And for that to fully exceed they must practice the virtues of self reliance, Self respect, Industry, Perseverance, And Economy.

The Classifying of the young seeds.....

A young seed is a new member, Or young V/L. They are referred to as young seeds because the message (seed) of faith is being planted with in the rich soil of there fertile mind.

(A) The Way.....

Young seeds you are caterpillars not yet transformed into a butterfly (The True Believer). The possibility for such a transformation, But You must put your heart, And honest efforts into this nation.

(B) The Warning.....

There are older seeds around older seeds around that have been confined to being caterpillars, They are cripples missing the righteous attributes that are necessary in order to reach the butterfly state. They will l never become a CROWN AND GLORY, They are simply Teaches just hanging on to bleed us But one day they will be examine.

(C) Treachery of the old caterpillar seed.....

The old seed that have been confined to the caterpillar stage are like stagnant water, They collect bacteria, And its unfit to drink. They will poison your mind. If you wade in there water, Weak in your faith in the first place.

(D) The personification of V/L's at its. beset.....

Study, Be for real when you fly the love. Learn to discipline yourself, Learn patience, And Understanding.   Fight against the negative influences of the unrighteous pretender, They will inevitably let there own action trip them up. They stand before a mirror, And lack the sense to know it. Don't just settle for being a caterpillar, Be a butterfly. There are degrees to everything in life even to being a V/L.....

In The Search Of The Golden Path Or Righteous.....

In the silent of the night bountiful spoke to hunger, His voice was very vibrant, And his message touched his spirit, His soul, His heart core, There was no introduction necessary for bountiful, For the golden light of knowledge was a trademark to his degree of pureness. As hunger stared intently into the eye's of bountiful, The golden rays of compassion betook bountiful. Bountiful said I am here as a sign of what can be. I have witness your affliction. Behold hunger, For I can be of great comfort to you. I bring with me a mirror of your inner most desire's, Look into me, Now what do you perceive? Hunger answered said, "I see all the things I ever wanted out of life, I see an altruistic concern for your brother man, The flying of two great flags in the iris of your eye's. I see the coming of a new nation, A new way of life. I see a strong masculinity tide and a similar femininity one, They symbolizes the coming together of a King and Queen, They also symbolizes one purpose in life. I see little children who take pride in what they are as they adjust their golden sun's upon their heads. I see a multitude of happiness, A lack of poverty. I see a very proud people, A real display of unity, Vitality, And love, Oh bountiful, How can I be as you are? Surely all of this is merely a state of mind? Bountiful Replied.

Hunger I came you in the form of inspiration you had little hope, Little direction in life, And as you are now, Little meaning, Now I'll represent myself as truly am, So open your minds eye, Look around you, For I am a Vice Lord, A new way of life, And hunger replied "You deceived me, For I knew of you," And bountiful replied "No hunger, You only deceive yourself, As in the beginning, So shall it be in the ending, Vice Lord."

Introspection.....

Yesterday I was alone in the world, A flower growing in the shadows whos existence, Life was not aware of, And who was not aware of life. But today my soul has awakened, And I beheld V/L. I rose to my feet, And rejoice in the love of V/L, The knowledge of V/L, The wisdom of V/L And the understanding of V/L. All praise unto Allah, Today I am A V/L, And may Allah the Lord And master continue to lead me in the righteous path of V/L. Yesterday the touch of the frolicsome breeze seen breeze harsh, And the sunbeams seem weak. A mist hid the face of the earth, And the waves of the ocean roared like a tempest. All praise unto Allah, I am V/L. Yesterday I look all about me, But saw nothing but my own suffering self standing by myself, Wild pandoms of darkness rose, And fail around like ravenous vultures. All praise unto ALLAH, The Lord, And master, Today I am V/L. Whenever I look I see life's secrets lying open before me. Yesterday I was soundless word in the heart of the night. Today I am a song on the lips of time. All praise unto ALLAH, The Lord, And Master, I am V/L.....

All Praise.....

All praise to the kings and Elites, Sons of the Almighty and righteous warriors and prophet of the Amalgamated Order Of Lordism. All praise to the kings and Elites, Lord of Lords, Lord the World. All praise to the kings and Elites who have died in the name of V/L. All praise to the kings and Elites who suffered thru all the enemy had and will now lead there people to victory thru the truthful teaching of Lordism. All praise to the kings and Elites, The Way, The truth, The light. And thru them comes knowledge, Wisdom, and understanding of Lordism. All praise to the kings and Elites, who teach us to love one another, To become strong in one another, And to become one in Body, And Souls, In the true meaning of V/L. All praise to the kings And Elites, Nation builders, Builders of Nation, Mighty Nations under the golden banor that lets all righteous people walk in he golden light of 360 degrees of Lordism.....All praise to the Kings and Elites of V/L.....

Allah Akbur!!!!!

Deeper Revelations.....

Allah is the ominpotent, The Almighty, Second to none first to all. He is the face of sublimity in the appearance of the creation that exhales the holy breath of life, And hale that life by recall at the point of his readiness. He is uninfluence by the plans men have for he knows the rotation of everything that move from square to circumference, That is seen, And Unseen, of jiins, And of men for all that moves does so by his consent. His body extends, And overlaps all in creations, for his is the realm of all worlds, And nothing exist beyond him in any state, The ethereal, or material, For all that exist is thru him. He is the circle engulfing all spheres, The key that unlock all doors. His thought is beyond minds compactsity For the mind itself only còputes by his decree. He is the mind in man and far beyond the portion he receives as a result of his grace. Even if we could unite all our minds into one it would still retain its shadowness in comparison to Allah, For his depth unmeasureable. Almighty is Allah, Master of the world both seen, And unseen Thought, And behold Thought did manifest. Man he did create in his own image, And made him subservient to his will. Allah did give to ability, And capability, And it is unmatched. For by Allah design man as V/L, second to him, Lord of all fears of matter. Yet do they know? No! Indeed a sad affair. It was not Allah that reduce men to negro, Or caucasian, A Chinaman, A Mexican, Or A Romanian, Or Hulgarian, A Jew, Or even Native American. All never reduce man into a slave, Or referred to him by color simply because of the geographical conditioning of his skin. No he created men, And made him his servant, His custodian, His Vicegerent, His V/L, Second only to himself. Man took being in Allah's favor for granted and was punished, And made to scatter. Because of their shame they cloaked themselves in the garment of funny names, And cloaked every people in every direction with a differentiate between themselves in hope of vanishing blame for there Holy infractions committed in the garden of eve.

Allah did create man, And made him V/L. Man distort it, And disfigured himself. It was man that gave names to the multitude of religion, Each claiming there's to be the one true religion. But Allah put his presence in every man unchristian, And all man has to do to communicate with him is to mediate. And call within himself. Allah created man, And gave him the rank of V/L. Man created confusion, And his subself, And every atrocious act against his bother, And they tell a notorious lie by saying Allah sanction such extremities ALLAH is the ALMIGHTY, ALMIGHTY IS ALLAH, And we that are subservient to him hurl his honorable attributes before us his people A/V/L/N. Vice which signifies that we are a people weak in the flesh who submit themselves only to a higher authority of ALLAH, And lord to affirm our position as his Vicegerent, And rulers of the physical world. ALLAH sign is the master sign, Although not exclusively, For no people have monopoly on ALLAH, And wherever truth, And righteous dwells so does he.

LAH VIA VA VA ILLILAHA HALALIIL, ALLAH AKBUR

Almighty Vice Lord Prayer.....

In the name of Allah, The Beneficient, The Merciful..... We the righteous people of the Vice Lord Nation seek thy understanding and thy blessing, As we commit ourselves to our chosen way of life.

We pray that you strengthen us Allah, And bestow upon us your favor. And that you help us in our strive to turn from wrong into right. We seek thy guidance and assistance in every phase of our development. And thy patience with us as a striving people.

We pray here in convenient form. YOUR SERVANTS AND VICE AGENTS, VICE LORDS OF THIS PHYSICAL WORLD. We pray for the good of our nation, And our people. And that you help us overcome our faults. We ask that you grant us the strength to carry this burden, For being V/L is not easy!

We thank you for the gift of life, And the glory of your love. And offer our gratitude for the potential and ability you have granted us as a people.

We pray that you will help us better utilize these keys, So that we may unlock the secrets and doors of both this life and the mystery after. We ask that you bless those who have died and lived in the name of V/L. And that you help us make this work if for none, Than for the Believers..............................Amen..............................Amen

Almighty Vice Lord Prayer.....

In The Name of Allah, We the righteous of the Almighty Vice Lord Nation give praise to our Supreme Chief, righteous son of the Almighty and a divine prophet of V/L.

Behold, Here our prayers O'Lord of lords, And give us your people of the A/V/L/N the continuous courage to represent our nation, So that the world will know that we are V/L, And as such will never stray from our divine principals and concepts, The laws by which we the most righteous of your people live by.

By your divine grace and generosity, You have instilled with us thy divine seed of love, Knowledge, Wisdom, And Understanding. And as a representative of this Almighty Vice Lord Nation, It is our responsibility to apply these precious gifts to the interest of our beloved nation And all poor and oppressed people of color world wide.

It is known that if we retrogress from our divine principals and laws the wrath of this A/V/L/N will surely fall upon us. For we pledge our life, Love And Loyalty to this Nation.

.........This Almighty Vice Lord Nation..........

Let our conduct O'Lord of Lords be judged by you according to our deeds.....By Birth .....In The Spirit.....And Through the heart core.....Behold, Behold, We come as we are.....V/L.....Ar

Quranic Justice.....

The man of faith holds fast to his faith, Because he knows it is true! The man of the world rejecting faith, Clings hard to worldly interests, But let him not force his interest on men/women, Sincere, And true by Favor, Force, Or fraud. Let not men/women be intoxicated with power, Or material resources. To each is a goal to which Allah turns him/her, Then strives together as in a race towards all that is good where ever ye are. Allah will bring you together, For Allah has power over all things. Mankind was one single nation, And God sent messages with Glad Tidings, And with them he sent the book and the truth to judge between people where they differed, But the people of the book, After the clear signs came to them they did not differ among themselves, Except through selfish contumely. God by his grace guided the believer to the truth concerning that where in they differed, For God guides whom he will to a path that is straight Draw Brothers!

Ingredient of 360% Of Lordism.....

In order to obtain 360 degree's of Lordism, We as striving Lords must give fully of ourselves from ourselves.....We must apply the supreme degree of determination in all our endeavors, For through this all shall be accomplished..... Our level of conscience must be most high or life will pass..... We must incorporate all the essentials of a blood line family and from the hardcore give our support, And our Love, And if a situation dictates so. Our life..Thurst, Respect, Discipline, And Loyalty must be our appetizer, As for the main course, We through in our commitment, Our Queen should be taught of the Lords, For it is through them that our growth is finalized. With proper guidance and understanding a sister can reach 120% of pure Lordism...When a person lives it, Love it, Dream it, Eat it, Speak it, And Die in it, Then and only Then can they be called a righteous Lord to and through Hard Core. This and only this is the essence 360% of pure Lordism.

A/V/L/N Economic Program.....

1.   It will be incumbent on every representative of the A/V/L/N to pay membership dues on a regular and basis.

2.   The initial dues shall be fifty dollars per year each year there after shall be thirty dollars.

3.   A workable timetable shall be set up to accommodate each individual to alleviate and eliminate the crush of a financial strain.

4.   All monies will be placed in the subnations account in the following manner fifty percent goes to general account, forty percent subnation account.

5.   All monies will be under the authority of treasure(s): National Headquarters treasure in Chicago will be the paramount treasure and must be afforded a monthly treasure report from all Subofficers. These reports shall be submitted to the Chief or his appointed representative.

6.   No monies will be drawn from accounts without approval of Chief and representing office of SubNation. (1) NOTE, Other necessary funds for upkeeping and daily functioning of nation, In essence Rent, Salaries, Expenses.

7.   Each SubNation acting in accordance with this economic program shall be recipients of all the benefits and advantages that this entails.

One of our economic goals: Set a work program based on commitment and a work pledge. With a two hundred minimum given for the building and buying of a Lords center. Our goal will be to raise a million settling for no less than five hundred thousand dollars. Each Elite must donate five hundred dollars. Our Center/House of Lords, will be constructed from the ground once we gain the necessary funds for such a project, But initially we will settle for a building of comfort and conviency.

The National Athem.....

Throw your palms to the sky, Fly your Love most high, Be forever proud, forever real, And dedicated to the cause. Whether you be man, woman, Or Child it make no difference which one are thou. All that believe are the same. A fruit from (a) tree from which the nation sprang. Be V/L, And forever real. Oh precious people always strive to excell, Build upon your dreams, our faith, But don't let that stand in your way. We too are a living people of life with every right to be. Oh fruit from the tree which the Nation sprang, Beautiful, sweet bearing the V/L name, Throw your palms to the sky, Fly your love most high, be forever proud..........

(Note): THE CONSTITUTION OF THE UNITED STATES OF AMERICA GRANTS US THE RIGHTS TO ASSERT OUR RIGHT TO AN IDEALIZED WAY OF LIFE. LORDISM IS OUR CHOICE, AND ANY BELIEVER HAVE A RIGHT TO GIVE EXPRESSION TO IT..........

Conclusion.....

This Code Of Conduct, Chain Of Command, Principals Of Law, And all the other material containing this revelation has been designed, And arranged with great care, And consideration of every representative of the Amalgamated Order Of Lordism. It is the Law, Philosophy, And Structure of a great nation. It is established so that every V/L will know who he/she is, And who his/her Brother and Sisters are. This literature also serves to maintain a Security, Discipline, Safety, And Integrity of the order. This literature contains some of the truthful teaching of Lordism, But as Lordism literature a way of life, And the righteous truth seeking V/L cannot help but learn more truth as he/she travels the golden path of Lordism. You as V/L & V/Lady are expected to know, Respect, And Honor the Code, The Chain, And the principals of laws of this Almighty Amalgamated Order Of Lordism, And also know what Lordism is about, For in no other way can we sincerely represent V/L. Behold V/L, The Truth has now been revealed, Hold fast to it, And you will surely walk the golden path of Lordism as a true V/L.

Via Va Va Lah Halaliil Illilaha

INTERNAL DOCUMENTS AND OFFICIAL MEMORANDA
OF THE BROTHERS OF THE STRUGGLE (B.O.S.)

(typed Memo dated July 14, 1982: From an Illinois Prison;
reproduced here "as is" in the original style, spelling, and syntax)

Date: July 14, 1982

From: The Chairman and Board of Directors

To: All Brothers of the Struggle

Subj: Awareness Session

The Movement

It is a fact, without contradiction that the success of any movement depends largely upon the participation of the mass of people involved in that particular struggle. Leadership without active support, is as useless as spitting in the winds to aid in putting out a major fire. (The fire in this case is the burning effects of poverty, lost direction, and progressive states of self-destruction.) The same is true with the lack of Leadership for the people. The two must combine to coordinate the movement, and each part must do it's share in reaching the goals of the group. What is more important is that the directions of the Organization be set forth, and that each concerned member adher to those directions, making the necessary sacrifices required to accomplish the objectives.

The Objectives

A group of people organized around the idea of reaching common objectives is called an Organization. Without that Unity that comes from having a common purpose, the same group of people qualifies as a Mob, Gang, etc., Therefore it is essential that each member realize the objectives of the group. Know what it is that inspire the need for Unity, and what it is that binds them One to the Other. Otherwise, their membership becomes questionable.

One of the basic objectives of the Black Gangster Disciple Nation is: "To obtain the means to Self-Determination for our People." We can not possibly determine anything without being AWARE of our situation, as well as our alternatives.

This AWARENESS does not come from acting foolish, nor from beng lax in your efforts to learn. Therefore the Leadership has opened up avenues for you to gain a perspective on life, our situation, and all aspects of progressive AWARENESS. One such avenue is the AWARENESS SESSIONS, conducted by the Legal Arm of the Organization.

Awareness Session

The interest of our members are many, therefore the subjects of the Awareness Sessions are many. Listed below are the objectives of the Awareness Session.

1. Bring a vast range of Intelligence to the availability of the   people.

2. Promote an environment of creativity among the people.

3. Practice the art of debate.

4. Inspire dignity in our people, by introducing them to a Black   History, as well as a Black Heritage.

5. To in general, uplift the mental, emotional, and spiritual   growth of our people.

All sessions shall be in accordance with the six points of the Star of David, signifying the six principles upon which our Organization is founded. These principles are: Love, Life, Loyality, Knowledge, Wisdom & Understanding.

The goals we have set to reach in these AWARENESS SESSIONS are valid goals. We expect to range from Politics to Stock Markets. We shall speak of wars and cultures, as well as the law.

Rules of the BGDN

1. **Silence and Secrecy**.   No member shall give any information or discuss any matters that concerns any member or the function of the organization to any individual that is not a standing member.

2. **Drugs**.   No member shall consume or inject any drug that is addictive.

3. **Stealing**.   No member shall steal from any convict, inmate, or resident.

4. **Respect**.   No member shall be disrespectful to any member or non member. Being disrespectful to others only entices others to become hostile and disrespectful to you which leads to unnecessary and stilly confrontations. Always be respectful, dignified, honorable, loyal and thoughtful.

5. **Breaking and Entering**.   No member shall break in or enter any building that will cause unde heat and pressure to others making moves that cause institutional lock-ups and shake-downs is prohibited.

6. **Gambling**.   No member shall gamble in any games unles all parties have their money up front.

7. **Guards**.   No member shall engage in any unnecessary confrontations with any officer's or administrative personnel.

8. **Sportmanship**.   No member shall engage in any heated arguments or fights while participating in any sport or games. Use good sportmanship at all times.

9. **Personal Hygiene**. All members must look presentable at all times and all living quarters should be kept clean.

13. **Exercising**. All members are required to jog three times around the yard and do fifty jumping jacks together at the beginning of each yard period except on Saturday, Sunday and night yard.

14. **Exploiting**. No member shall use his membership, staff or office to exploit funds or favors from any member.

15. **A.R. 804**. All members are required to read and become familiar with the D.O.C. A.R. 804 administration discipline.

16. **Rape**. No member shall use threat or force to make any one engage in homosexual acts.

July 23, 1983

TO   : ALL BROTHERS OF THE STRUGGLE

FROM   : THE CHAIRMAN AND THE BOARD OF DIRECTORS

  RE   : MIRANDA WARNINGS

FELLOW BROTHERS OF THE STRUGGLE

"Nothing hurts a duck, but its Bill (MOUTH)." The leadership is sure that you all are familiar with this old and truthful saying, because if any one of you have ever had the opportunity to go on a hunting trip (in the free world) before being locked up, then you know full well that if the duck had kept his mouth shut, instead of quacking, he wouldn't have given his position away, and naturally, would'nt have been our dinner.

This comparison with the duck, our Brothers, is used to stress home to everyone the value and importance of keeping your mouths shut, especially when you are confronted by investigators of the D.O.C., police, Counselors, med techs, even the ministers and others.

As you are all aware, situations occur where it may be necessary to take care of organizational business. Naturally it should be understood that there will be steps taken by D.O.C. messengers to find out who, and how the business was taken care of.

Not all business can be taken care of in a smooth way without a large mass of people actually seeing what has taken place, but they are in the immediate area., naturally, you should know that there will be a general round up of everyone in the vicinity. Lets recount these steps very briefly, because they are very important. First some business is taken care of., Second, some one saw what occurred, but due to the amount of people in the vicinity at the time of discovery, everyone is detained and checked out.

Third, Whether your name was given by a notorious messenger, or you are being checked out by a group of investigators, state police, state's attorney, etc., due to the fact that the group you're in at the time (recreation period etc)., is being questioned, etc. The main question is "How do you handle yourslef at this time? What will be your reaction while you and maybe two, three, four, or more (B.O.S.) are being singled out as the persons to allegedly took care of the business, what would you say to these investigators who you know are tying to pin something on you with hopes of getting you the electric chair?

If, for whatever reason, you said you would talk to them in any way, (regardless of the exchange of words) you have just made the biggest mistake of your life, why? because, you are not, or were not to say anything at all to them. Let us explain further, here is the situation, the police, investigators etc, don't have enough information to go on that would give them a better than average chance to obtain a conviction., The only hoe they have is that they can make you convict yourself by breaking, thus implicating others, and making confessions etc. Say for instance that those of you being charged or investigated, were separated from one another and placed in different rooms, or different joints so you could'nt communicate with each other to find out what the other is saying or has said so far.

While you are in separate rooms, by yourselves for awhile, in comes two, three, or more investigators with a pen, pad or tape recorder. One of them offers a cigarette, coffee, food, or whatever, you accept it, or you Don't, its up to you. If, however, you take their offerings, then, you have implicated by your acceptance that the possibility of you breaking is very great, because, not everyone has the strong will to accept their offerings and turn around and say, "Go to hell", or "I have nothing to say".

Before any questions have been asked, you were supposed to have been given or read your rights, formerly known as the Miranda Warnings.

These warnings come from a 1966 case, (Miranda vs. Arizona), Under these wardings yu must be informed of the following:

1. You have the right to remain silent under the due process of law, 5th and 14th amendments, and that anything you say can and will be held against you in a Court of law.

2. You have the right to have a lawyer present and to consult with a lawyer during questioning., If you cannot afford one, a lawyer will be supplied by the government.

3. You are entitled to make one free telephone call so don't waste it, contact a lawyer or somebody who can obtain one for you.

While this is going on and afterwards, it is extremely important that you don't sign anything, papers, etc., without the advice of your lawyer.

Our Brothers, all of the above must be remembered, as well as, all that you say, if you made a statement or statements to the investigators in the presence of others, but did not sign it, it may still be used against you, so it is best to just remain silent, its as simple as that.

The investigators, police, state's attorney, etc., use a number of techniques to get a person to tell on himself and implicate others.

That which seems natural our brothers, is often times unatural, let us explain. Say for instance you were on your way to take care of some business and the cop stopped you, asking you for your pass but you don't have one and he tell you to return to your cellhouse, then somebody, member, non-member, etc, came passing by you and the cop, but the cop said nothing to them as he had you, and you blurt out to the cop "you let them go by why did you stop kme, and he call them back and ask for a pass, but they don't have one, this may appear to be a natural quesiton, but, what yu have done is told on someone and kept them from taking care of their business because of your big MOUTH.

This is called dry snitching and will not be tolerated from anyone, what one do reflects on the whole which you all know., To say that you let so and so do this or that, or they are doing this why can't we do it seems a natural question to ask the authorities but it clearly is not and cannot be justified, and most certainly will not be tolerated.

SINCERELY

YOUR CHAIRMAN AND BOARD OF DIRECTORS

(undated typed document)

Preface

Our governing body has decided to take on a New Concept of Organization. A concept that will bring us into the 80's and prepare us for the political and economical realities of Black America. Our Leadership feels that we must take advantage of our imprisonment; we must learn what's necessary to be a productive and disciplined organization while we're confined. If we are successful here in this inferior situation, there's no limitations on our potential in the outside world.

The Leadership doesn't expect miracles from the people in our new undertakings. We are aware of the fact that it took us eighteen (18) years to get into this shape. The Leadership also realizes without the full support of the people, it will take another (18) years or more to make this New Concept of Organization a reality. Unfortunately we don't have that kind of time to waste. Therefore, the Leadership is requesting that all qualified members help us make this transition in to the New Concept. We have wasted enough time dwelling on insignificant matters. Let's prepare ourselves for the World.

In the process of going from the Old to the New, we will have a few complications. It must be understood from the outset that we are not forgetting our past, (as some of you know, we have had good moments as well as bad moments in the past) we're putting our past where it belongs, behind us. Our past will serve as a motivating force that will enable us to have a glorious future. It's a necessity that we go through changes. You're either growing or dieing. To stand still is to Die, our Leadership has decided that we will live and flourish into something great.

All Organizations have Discipline. Discipline is a necessity in all things pertaining to development. Our organization is in transtion. Discipline is essential and must be enforced. All members will adhere to all laws governing the organization. The governing body has updated the laws. We want our laws to reflect our intelligence as well as our strength. These will be absolutely No!!!! exception or exemption from the laws.

Our governing body will be invested with the power to make policies and laws. Our Chairman will have final say on all policies and laws. Our governing body will be called board of directors. All board members will be appointed by the Chairman.

Organizational Structure

1. When it comes to the organization; the individual is subordinate to the organization.
2. The minority is subordinate to the majority.
3. The entire membership is subordinate to the Chairman and the governing body. Whoever violates these articles of organizational structure will be charged with disrupting organizational unity and dealt with in that fashion as an enemy   of the people.

We have witnessed what comes from a lack of Unity and Discipline. Now, observe what comes from Unity and Discipline.

If we are to become a power to reckon with, We must take on the concept of organization. Everyone must do their share. Everybody has a responsibility. For we make up the organization as individuals who have come together as a collective.

THE COMMON SENSE APPROACH

Notations: To be rememberd at all atimes:

Because of inadequate prevention against organization, organizing exist, a new engineering solution must be introduced for the present and future goals of this nation. In composing these solutions to the problems that deeply stagnates the body of this organization, the solutions to eradicate these problems will be given in a self-explanatory and compehensive dialogue, so that everyone may better understand the goals and concepts of our nation:

(Dialogue)

There seems to be a syndrome orientation of negativism, meaning an attitude or system or thoughts characterized by doubt and question, rather than approval and acceptance. An attitude characterized by ignorning, resisting, or opposing suggestions and orders coming from people that are in a position of authority......

(Findings)

A majority of our people are guility of this negativism, reasons are, "most people are unaware of the definition of organization, "therefore it will be spelled out as followed: (Organization is a unified & consolidated group of people, with an executive structure that deals with the well-being of all it's people. It's an executive structure of business & enterprise for individual growth and collective excelleration of the body as a whole. It does not mean a bunch of disorganized, wild radicals who have trouble in distinguishing the 80's from the 60's. Or feel they must hate and fight other organizations because their concepts are different from their own.

THere is also this attitude that some members think they have to be around the executive staff that governs the nation to be recognized. "All members will be judged on their character, loyality and ability to think; and above all, your ability to function as part of the organizations structure we have built, and is continuing to build." If we are to ascertain our success, security and endurance in this world, or the free world:

It has been noted that quite a few of our members have this attitude that they will rebel against decisions or judgement that has been made by the executive staff of this nation:

(Understanding)

It will be written here, and it will be UNDERSTOOD, "That the actions above will in no-way be tolderated by anyone, nor will we accept any group of people to disrupt the laws, the goals, and concept of progress of thils Nation:"

(Dialogue)

For effective functioning of this and other solutions, all persons with governing authority must be sincere about his responsibility, and sincere to the people the executive staff gave him authority to govern. Sincere means being sincere enough to step down from a spot if you feel that you are not capable of fulfilling it to its full capacity. Don't forsake the nation for your own personal faults, because only you can correct you, and as your people we are behind you in all that's positive and for the betterment of all. One must radiate a vibe that will let the people know that you are for the whole of our nation. With this attitude, you will generate a vibe that will let the young people of this nation know that we are for each other and about helping each other excell. Our cause is to have a successful "COSMOLOGY", which means - "the world for which we will make and live in, will be organized".

(Ignorant Outburst)

It has long been recognized that some of our people seem to have a problem in controlling the things they say out of their mouths. It should be first stipulated that the word "IGNORANT" does not mean that a person is stupid, it means a person having little knowledge, or education and experience in a particular area, subject, or matter. When a person makes a statement without first weighing it's value or logic, his out-burst in most cases become harmful to the management of this nation. When someone does this, he is being ignorant without having knowledge of it. THis kind of attitude should be eradicated to ensure that there will be no stupid rumors formulating out of our organization. This stupidity has in the past, and will in the future get people hurt unnecessarily. It also causes confusion and sometimes spookism among people that are not involved. This should be acknowledged by all the people. It is extremely necessary and important to check and evaluate all information before you spread something you only got a part of, or heard somebody else say;. If a person in authority is not around during a period in which some vital information has been passed to you, then you must begin to think about the best decision or judgement to render the situation. THis is done by simply weighing the value of the information, and the credibility of the source from which it came. 8 out of 10 times, a person in authority will be around.

(Hand written, printed, document)

We the Brothers of the Stuggle pledging whole heartedly our live, life, loyalty have embraced the teaching of our "Chairman", are covenet until fully chance, teaching laws and policy set forth by our Chairman, and Executive staff. The Doctrine of New Concept, will be a guiding light that will for ever burn in our heart and mind. This light will serve as a constant reminder and motivating force with each of us. Also it will instill in us dedication and discipline. We standing firmly in our six point stance. Concepts of Organization, Politic, Economics, Serenity, Eduction, Unity.

1) Head - life
2) Right shoulder - love
3) Left shoulder - loyalty
4) Right elbow - knowledge
5) Left elbow - understanding
6) Heel of feet - wisdom

I agree to as long as I stand proudly under the blue sky to serve this glorious organization and its every cause aid and assist my fellow Brothers of the Struggle in our righteous endeavors. I will do that I can can to help us both to reach our fullest potential as the organization grows. I know that I will for our goals are inter-related. Positive organization produces poxitive productive people. That which we are, my every action and behavior, and attitude will vividly reflect the positive, dignified principle that the organization is built upon I will never do anything that would cause embarrassment or disrespect to the integrity of our organization. Standing strongly upon our six point stand I shall utilize knowledge wisdom & understanding as I strive in our Struggle for education, economical, political, social development, I will learn, look, and listen to anything that may be conductive towards the excelleration and never abandon our struggle, as in all struggles I realize that sacrifices must be made. I will not be selfish but for the sake of the preservation of our organization; I am willing to endure my share, I believe in the goal of the organization and its honor, to aid and assist in our struggle for success. We are with a great leader. Together we shall see the vision. May His visions become our vision. For his visions are for us to grow into a productive successful people with the consolidation and diligent efforts of everyone, our visions will be manifested into a reality.

(Undated typewritten document)

KEEP-UP NOT CATCH-UP

The affairs of these modern times are designed for the thinking man, the rational logical man, the man that contemplates beyond a 24 hour span of time. We as a organization are not thinkers that only realize their existence of today, but we are men of vision with foresight with future objectives of growth and development. My brothers this is a fast-pace competitive world where the pace isn't won by those that are just trying to catch-up, but is wond by those that keep up. The term (catch-up) signifies not up to a general or expected level of development. The key word is behind and behind is a place or time and here again I state, this is a different era of time now, the modern age of existence, an age in which races arent won by the behinders, and we all know what a behind is dont we? And we dont want to be a continuous ass, a Beast of Burden. My brothers, the Preface of our Organization is a clear sign of the timesk our Preface is a Beckoning Light of Knowledge, Wisdom, and Understanding of the Concept of Unity.

This concept has....anization can win this race, its not an easy race, the strenght to endure the trials and tribulations of this world. Whats to be gained by winning this race? The realization of the Growth and Development of a nation.
Remember a wise man changes his mind often, but a fool never does...

Keep Up With The Times My Brother

BOS PRAYER

Looking out the window as far as I can see,
All my BOS brothers standing around me,
GD's and BD's has combined,
As we both unite our star will shine,
King David he recuted gave the (G)
Strength on the street,
He recuted the (D) on the history of our G
will last forever,
As the Brothers of the Struggle
Struggle together.

GD PRAYER

All GDs must use the knowledge on the six point star, 360 base on the life we belive and the love we have for one another. Wisdom is what we use to grow knowledge on the six point star in our nation flag in order to be real you must be willing to appear in front of Larry Hoover.

G.D. Creed

We believe in the teaching of our Honorable Chairman; in all laws and polices set forth by our Chairman and Executive Staff.

In the concept of ideology of the organization in aid and assisting our fellow brother of the struggle in all righteous Endeavors.

And standing strongly upon our six points utilizing Knowledge, Wisdom, and Understanding as we strive in our struggle for Education, Economical, and Political and Social Development that we are a special group of people with Integraty and Dignity.

In the vision of our great leader and throuh his vision we can be come a reckoning power of people beyond Boundaries without measures.

INTERNAL RULES OF THE B.O.S.

1. SILENCE AND SECRECY. No member should give any Information or discuss any matter that concerns any member or function of the organization to any individual that is not an outstanding member.
2. DRUGS. No member shall consume or inject any drugs that are addictive.
3. STEALING. No member shall steal from any convict inmate or resident.
4. RESPECT. No member shall be disrespectful to any member or non-member being disrespectful only intices other to become hot-stely and be disrespectful to you which leads to unnecersery silly confrontation. always be respectful, dignified, honorable; loyal and thoughtful.
5. BRAKEING AND ENTERING: No member shall breake in or enter any building that cause un-due heat and presure to other. Making institutional move that leads to lock-up and shake down is prohibited.

6. GAMBLING. No member shall gamble in any game unless all parties have there money up front.

7. GUARD. No member shell engage in any unnissery confrontation with any officers or administrative personnel.

8. SPORTMANSHIP. No member shell engage in heated arguments or fights while participating in any sports or games. Use good sportmenship at all time.

9. PERSONAL-HYGENE. All member must look presenable at all times and livin quarters should be kept clean.

10. INCIDENTS. All incidents minor or major concerning the health and well being of any member or members should be reported to the coordinatorors.

11. AID AND ASSISTING. All member shell Aid and assisting one another in all righteous endeavors.

12. DUES. All member are required to give 2 pack a month if able.

13. EXERCISING. All member are required to job three times around the yard and do fifty jumping jacks together at the beginning of each yard period except Saturday, Sunday and night yard.

14. EXPLOITING. No member shall use his membership, staff, or office to exploit or favor for any member.

15. A.R. 504. All member shall read and become familiar with the D.O.C. A.R. 504 Administrative disaplene.

16. RAPE. No one should use threat or force to make anyone engage in any homosexual act.

Disciplinary Report Form Used by The B.O.S.

MINOR:____

MAJOR:____

TIME:_____
DATE:_____
INCIDENT:_____

WE BELIEVE IN THE TEACHING OF OUR HONORABLE
CHAIRMAN; IN ALL LAWS AND POLICIES SET FORTH BY OUR
CHAIRMAN AND EXECUTIVE STAFF.

INCIDENT:_____

_____

_____

_____

_____

GD:_____   _____

BD:_____   _____

NAME:_____   _____

_____

IN THE CONCEPT OF IDEOLOGY OF THE ORGANIZATION IN
AID AND ASSISTING OUR FELLOW BROTHERS OF THE
STRUGGLE IN ALL RIGHTEOUS ENDEAVORS. IN THE
VISION OF OUR GREAT LEADER AND THROUGH HIS VISION
WE CAN BECOME A RECKONING POWER OF PEOPLE BEYOND
BOUNDARIES WITHOUT MEASURE.

WITNESS:

_____

_____

_____

ACT 147. STREETGANG TERRORISM OMNIBUS PREVENTION ACT

147/1.   Short title

§ 1. Short title. This Article may be cited as the Illinois Streetgang Terrorism Omnibus Prevention Act.
P.A. 87-932, Art. II, § 1, eff. Jan. 1, 1993.
Formerly Ill.Rev.Stat., ch. 38, 1751.

Title of Act:

An Act to create the Statewide Organized Gang Database Act and the Illinois Streetgang Terrorism Omnibus Prevention Act. P.A. 87-932, Art. II, approved Aug. 27, 1992, eff. Jan. 1, 1993.

147/5. Legislative findings.

§ 5. Legislative findings.

(a) The General Assembly hereby finds and declares that it is the right of every person, regardless of race, color, creed, religion, national origin, sex, age, or disability, to be secure and protected from fear, intimidation, and physical harm caused by the activities of violent groups and individuals. It is not the intent of this Act to interfere with the exercise of the constitutionally protected rights of freedom of expression and association. The General Assembly hereby recognizes the constitutional right of every citizen to harbor and express beliefs on any lawful subject whatsoever, to lawfully associate with others who share similar beliefs, to petition lawfully constituted authority for a redress of perceived grievances, and to participate in the electoral process.

(b) The General Assembly finds, however, that urban, suburban, and rural communities, neighborhoods and schools throughout the State are being terrorized and plundered by streetgangs. The General Assembly dins that there are now several hundred streetgangs operating in Illinois, and that while their terrorism is most widespread in urban areas, streetgangs are spreading into suburban and rural areas of Illinois.

(c) The General Assembly further finds that streetgangs are often controlled by criminally sophisticated adults who take advantage of our youth by intimidating and coercing them into membership by employing them as drug couriers and runners, and by using them to commit brutal crimes against persons and property to further the financial benefit to and dominance of the streetgang.

(d) These streetgangs' activities present a clear and present danger to public order and safety and are not constitutionally protected. No society is or should be required to endure such activities without redress. Accordingly, it is the intent of the General Assembly in enacting this Act to create a civil remedy against streetgangs and their members that focuses upon patterns of criminal gang activity and upon the organized nature of streetgangs, which together have been the chief source of their success.
P.A. 87-932, Art. II, § 5, eff. Jan. 1, 1993.
Formerly Ill.Rev.Stat., ch. 38, 1755.

147/10. Definitions

§ 10. Definitions.

"Course or pattern of criminal activity" means 2 or more gang-related criminal offenses committed in whole or in part within this State when:

(1) at least one such offense was committed after the effective date of this Act;

(2) both offenses were committed within 5 years of each other; and

(3) at least one offense involved the solicitation to commit, conspiracy to commit, attempt to commit, or commission of any offense defined as a felony or forcible felony under the Criminal Code of 1961.1

"Designee of State's Attorney" or "designee" means any attorney for a public authority who has received written permission from the State's Attorney to file or join in a civil action authorized by this Act.

"Public authority" means any unit of local government or school district created or established under the Constitution or laws of this State.

"State's Attorney" means the State's Attorney of any county where an offense constituting a part of a course or pattern of gang-related criminal activity has occurred or has been committed.

"Streetgang' or "gang" means any combination, confederation, alliance, network, conspiracy, understanding, or other similar conjoining, in law or in fact, or 3 or more persons:

(1)(I) that, through its membership or through the agency of any member and at the direction, order, solicitation, or request of any conspirator who is a leader, officer, director, organizer, or other governing or policy making person or authority in the conspiracy, or by any agent, representative, or deputy of any such person or authority engages in a course or pattern of criminal activity; or (ii) that, through its membership or through the agency of any member engages in a course or pattern of criminal activity.

(2) For purposes of this Act, it shall not be necessary to show that a particular conspiracy, combination, or conjoining of persons possesses, acknowledges, or is known by any common name, insignias, flag, means of recognition, secret signal or code, creed, belief, structure, leadership or command structure, method of operation, or criminal enterprise, concentration or specialty, membership, age, or other qualifications, initiation rites, geographical or territorial situs or boundary or location, or other unifying mark, manner, protocol or method of expressing or indicating membership when the conspiracy's existence, in law or in fact, can be demonstrated by a preponderance of other competent evidence. However, any evidence reasonably tending to show or demonstrate, in law or in fact, the existence of or membership in any conspiracy, confederation, or other association described herein, or probative of the existence of or membership in any such association, shall be admissible in any action or proceeding brought under this Act.

"Streetgang member" or "gang member" means any person who actually and in fact belongs to a gang, and any person who knowingly acts in the capacity of an agent for or accessory to, or is legally accountable for, or voluntarily associates himself with a course or pattern o f gang-related criminal activity, whether in a preparatory, executory, or cover-up phase of any activity, or who knowingly performs, aids, or abets any such activity.

"Streetgang related" or "gang-related" means any criminal activity, enterprise, pursuit, or undertaking directed by, ordered by, authorized by, consented to, agreed to, requested by, acquiesced in, or ratified by any gang leader, officer, or governing or policy-making person or authority, or by any agent, representative, or deputy of any such officer, person, or authority:

(1) with the intent to increase the gang's size, membership, prestige, dominance, or control in any geographical area; or

(2) with the intent to provide the gang with any advantage in, or any control or dominance over any criminal market sector, including but not limited to, the manufacture, delivery, or sale of controlled substances or cannabis; arson or arson-for-hire; traffic in stolen property or stolen credit cards; traffic in prostitution, obscenity, or pornography; or that involves robbery, burglary, or theft; or

(3) with the intent to exact revenge or retribution for the gang or any member of the gang; or

(4) with the intent to obstruct justice, or intimidate or eliminate any witness against the gang or any member of the gang; or

(5) with the intent to otherwise directly or indirectly cause any benefit, aggrandizement, gain, profit or other advantage whatsoever to or for the gang, its reputation, influence, or membership.

P.A. 87-932, Art. II § 10, eff. Jan. 1, 1993.

Formerly Ill.Rev.Stat., ch. 38, 1760.
1 720 ILCS 5/1-1 et seq.

147/15. Creation of civil cause of action

§ 15. Creation of civil cause of action.

(a) A civil cause of action is hereby created in favor of any public authority expending money, allocating or reallocating police, firefighting, emergency or other personnel or resources, or otherwise incurring any loss, deprivation, or injury, or sustaining any damage, impairment, or harm whatsoever, proximately caused by any course or pattern of criminal activity.

(b) The cause of action created by this Act shall lie against:

(1) any streetgang in whose name, for whose benefit, on whose behalf, or under whose direction the act was committed; and

(2) any gang officer or director who causes, orders, suggests, authorizes, consents to, agrees to, requests, acquiesces in, or ratifies any such act; and

(3) any gang member who, in the furtherance of or in connection with, any gang-related activity, commits any such act; and

(4) any gang officer, director, leader, or member.

(c) The cause of action authorized by this Act shall be brought by the State's Attorney or attorneys, or by his or their designees. This cause of action shall be in addition to any other civil or criminal proceeding authorized by the laws of this State or by federal law, and shall not be construed as requiring the State's Attorney or his designee to elect a civil, rather than criminal remedy, or as its officers, directors, leaders, and members shall be joint and severable subject only to the apportionment and allocation of punitive damage authorized under Section 35 of this Act.1

P.A. 87-932, Art. II, § 15, eff. Jan. 1, 1993.

Formerly Ill.Rev.Stat., ch. 38, §1765.
1 740 ILCS 147/35.

147/20. Commencement of action.

§ 20. Commencement of action.

(a) An action may be commenced under this Act by the filing of a verified complaint as in civil cases.

(b) A complaint filed under this Act, and all other ancillary or collateral matters arising therefrom, including matter relating to discovery, motions, trial, and the perfection or execution of judgments shall be subject to the Code of Civil Procedure,1 except as may be otherwise provided in this Act, or except as the court may otherwise order upon motion of the State's Attorney or his designee in matters relating to immunity or the physical safety of witnesses.

(c) The complaint shall name each complaining State's Attorney or his designee, and the public authority represented by him or by them.

(d) The complaint shall also name as defendants the gang, all known gang officers, and any gang members specifically identified or alleged in the complaint as having participated in a course or pattern of gang-related criminal activity. The complaint may also name, as a class of defendants, all unknown gang members.

(e) When, at any point prior to trial, other specific gang officers or members become known, the complaint may be amended to include any such person as a named defendant.
P.A. 87-932, Art. II, § 20, eff. Jan. 1, 1993.
Formerly Ill.Rev.Stat., ch. 38, 1770
1 735 ILCS 5/1-101 et seq.

147/25. Venue

§ 25. Venue.
(a) In an action brought under this Act, venue shall lie in any county where an act charged in the complaint as part of a course or pattern of gang-related criminal activity was committed.

(b) It shall not be necessary for all offenses necessary to establishing a course or pattern of criminal activity to have occurred in any one county where the State's Attorneys of several counties, or their designees, each complaining of any offense, elected to join in a complaint. In such instance, it shall be sufficient that the complaint, taken as a whole, alleges a course or pattern of gang-related criminal activity, and each count of any such joint complaint shall be considered as cumulative to other counts for purposes of alleging or demonstrating such a course or pattern of activity.

(c) Where a course or pattern of activity is alleged to have been committed or to have occurred in more than one county, the State's Attorney of each such county, or their designees, may join their several causes of action in a single complaint, which may be filed in any such county agreed to by or among them, but no such joinder shall be had without the consent of the State's Attorney having jurisdiction over each offense alleged as part of the course or pattern of activity.
P.A. 87-932, Art. II, § 25, eff. Jan. 1, 1993.
Formerly Ill.Rev.Stat., ch. 38, 1775.

147/30. Service of process

§ 30. service of process.
(a) All streetgangs and streetgang members engaged in a course or pattern of gang-related criminal activity within this State impliedly consent to service of process upon them as set forth in this Section, or as may be otherwise authorized by the Code of Civil Procedure.1

(b) Service of process upon a streetgang may be had by leaving a copy of the complaint and summons directed to any officer of such gang, commanding the gang to appear and answer the complaint or otherwise plead at a time and place certain:
(1) with any gang officer; or
(2) with any individual member of the gang simultaneously named therein; or

(3) in the manner provided for service upon a voluntary unincorporated association in a civil action; or

(4) in the manner provided for service by publication in a civil action; or

(5) with any parent, legal guardian, or legal custodian of any persons charged with a gang-related offense when any person sued civilly under this Act is under 18 years of age and is also charged criminally or as a delinquent minor; or

(6) with the director of any agency or department of this State who is the legal guardian, guardianship administrator, or custodian of any person sued under this Act; or

(7) with the probation or parole officer of any person sued under this Act; or

(8) with such other person or agent as the court may, upon petition of the State's Attorney or his designee authorize as appropriate and reasonable under all of the circumstances.

(c) If after being summoned a streetgang does not appear, the court shall enter an answer for the streetgang neither affirming nor denying the allegations of the complaint but demanding strict proof thereof, and proceed to trial and judgment without further process.

(d) When any person is named as a defendant streetgang member in any complaint, or subsequently becomes known and is added or joined as a named defendant, service of process may be had as authorized or provided for in the Code of Civil Procedure for service of process in a civil case.

(e) Unknown gang members may be sued as a class and designated as such in the caption of any complaint filed under this Act. Service of process upon unknown members may be made in the manner prescribed for provision of notice to members of a class in a class action, or as the court may direct for providing the best service and notice practicable under the circumstances which shall include individual, personal, or other service upon all members who can be identified and located through reasonable effort.

P.A. 87-932, Art. II, § 30, eff. Jan. 1, 1993.

Formerly Ill.Rev.Stat., ch. 38, 1780. 1 735 ILCS 5/1-101 et seq.

147/35. Injunctive relief, damages, costs, and fees

§ 35. Injunctive relief, damages, costs, and fees.

(a) In any action brought under this Act, and upon the verified application of the State's Attorney or his designee, the circuit court may at any time enter such restraining orders, injunctions, or other prohibitions, or order such other relief as it deems proper, including but not limited to ordering any person to divest himself of any involvement or interest, direct or indirect, in any illegal streetgang activity and imposing other reasonable restrictions on the future illegal activities of any defendant.

(b) A final judgement in favor of a public authority under this Act shall entitle it to recover compensatory damages for all damages, losses, impairments, or other harm proximately caused, together with the costs of the suit and reasonable attorney's fees. Punitive damages may be assessed against any streetgang, against any streetgang officer or member found guilty of actual participation in or to be legally accountable for a course or pattern of criminal activity under this Act.

P.A. 87-932, Art. II, §35, eff. Jan. 1, 1993.

Formerly Ill.Rev.Stat., ch. 38, 1785.

AUTHOR INDEX

SUBJECT INDEX